Lecture Notes in Computer Science 2619

Edited by G. Goos, J. Hartmanis, and J. van Leeuwen

Springer
Berlin
Heidelberg
New York
Barcelona
Hong Kong
London
Milan
Paris
Tokyo

Hubert Garavel John Hatcliff (Eds.)

Tools and Algorithms for the Construction and Analysis of Systems

9th International Conference, TACAS 2003
Held as Part of the Joint European Conferences on Theory and Practice of Software, ETAPS 2003
Warsaw, Poland, April 7-11, 2003
Proceedings

Series Editors

Gerhard Goos, Karlsruhe University, Germany
Juris Hartmanis, Cornell University, NY, USA
Jan van Leeuwen, Utrecht University, The Netherlands

Volume Editors

Hubert Garavel
INRIA Rhône-Alpes
655, avenue de l'Europe, 38330 Montbonnot Saint Martin, France
E-mail: Hubert.Garavel@inrialpes.fr

John Hatcliff
Kansas State University
Department of Computing and Information Sciences
234 Nichols Hall, Manhattan, KS, 66506-2302, USA
E-mail: hatcliff@cis.ksu.edu

Cataloging-in-Publication Data applied for

A catalog record for this book is available from the Library of Congress.

Bibliographic information published by Die Deutsche Bibliothek
Die Deutsche Bibliothek lists this publication in the Deutsche Nationalbibliografie; detailed bibliographic data is available in the Internet at <http://dnb.ddb.de>.

CR Subject Classification (1998): F.3, D.2.4, D.2.2, C.2.4, F.2.2

ISSN 0302-9743
ISBN 3-540-00898-5 Springer-Verlag Berlin Heidelberg New York

Springer-Verlag Berlin Heidelberg New York
a member of BertelsmannSpringer Science+Business Media GmbH

http://www.springer.de

Printed in Germany

Typesetting: Camera-ready by author, data conversion by PTP-Berlin GmbH
Printed on acid-free paper SPIN: 10872946 06/3142 5 4 3 2 1 0

Foreword

ETAPS 2003 was the sixth instance of the European Joint Conferences on Theory and Practice of Software. ETAPS is an annual federated conference that was established in 1998 by combining a number of existing and new conferences. This year it comprised five conferences (FOSSACS, FASE, ESOP, CC, TACAS), 14 satellite workshops (AVIS, CMCS, COCV, FAMAS, Feyerabend, FICS, LDTA, RSKD, SC, TACoS, UniGra, USE, WITS and WOOD), eight invited lectures (not including those that are specific to the satellite events), and several tutorials. We received a record number of submissions to the five conferences this year: over 500, making acceptance rates fall below 30% for every one of them. Congratulations to all the authors who made it to the final program! I hope that all the other authors still found a way of participating in this exciting event and I hope you will continue submitting.

A special event was held to honour the 65th birthday of Prof. Wlad Turski, one of the pioneers of our young science. The deaths of some of our "fathers" in the summer of 2002 — Dahl, Dijkstra and Nygaard — reminded us that Software Science and Technology is, perhaps, no longer that young. Against this sobering background, it is a treat to celebrate one of our most prominent scientists and his lifetime of achievements. It gives me particular personal pleasure that we are able to do this for Wlad during my term as chairman of ETAPS.

The events that comprise ETAPS address various aspects of the system development process, including specification, design, implementation, analysis and improvement. The languages, methodologies and tools which support these activities are all well within its scope. Different blends of theory and practice are represented, with an inclination towards theory with a practical motivation on the one hand and soundly based practice on the other. Many of the issues involved in software design apply to systems in general, including hardware systems, and the emphasis on software is not intended to be exclusive.

ETAPS is a loose confederation in which each event retains its own identity, with a separate program committee and independent proceedings. Its format is open-ended, allowing it to grow and evolve as time goes by. Contributed talks and system demonstrations are in synchronized parallel sessions, with invited lectures in plenary sessions. Two of the invited lectures are reserved for "unifying" talks on topics of interest to the whole range of ETAPS attendees. The aim of cramming all this activity into a single one-week meeting is to create a strong magnet for academic and industrial researchers working on topics within its scope, giving them the opportunity to learn about research in related areas, and thereby to foster new and existing links between work in areas that were formerly addressed in separate meetings.

ETAPS 2003 was organized by Warsaw University, Institute of Informatics, in cooperation with the Foundation for Information Technology Development, as well as:

- European Association for Theoretical Computer Science (EATCS);
- European Association for Programming Languages and Systems (EAPLS);
- European Association of Software Science and Technology (EASST); and

- ACM SIGACT, SIGSOFT and SIGPLAN.

The organizing team comprised:

Mikołaj Bojańczyk, Jacek Chrzaszcz, Piotr Chrzastowski-Wachtel, Grzegorz Grudziński, Kazimierz Grygiel, Piotr Hoffman, Janusz Jabłonowski, Mirosław Kowaluk, Marcin Kubica (publicity), Sławomir Leszczyński (www), Wojciech Moczydłowski, Damian Niwiński (satellite events), Aleksy Schubert, Hanna Sokołowska, Piotr Stańczyk, Krzysztof Szafran, Marcin Szczuka, Łukasz Sznuk, Andrzej Tarlecki (co-chair), Jerzy Tiuryn, Jerzy Tyszkiewicz (book exhibition), Paweł Urzyczyn (co-chair), Daria Walukiewicz-Chrzaszcz, Artur Zawłocki.

ETAPS 2003 received support from:[1]

- Warsaw University
- European Commission, High-Level Scientific Conferences and Information Society Technologies
- US Navy Office of Naval Research International Field Office,
- European Office of Aerospace Research and Development, US Air Force
- Microsoft Research

Overall planning for ETAPS conferences is the responsibility of its Steering Committee, whose current membership is:

Egidio Astesiano (Genoa), Pierpaolo Degano (Pisa), Hartmut Ehrig (Berlin), José Fiadeiro (Leicester), Marie-Claude Gaudel (Paris), Evelyn Duesterwald (IBM), Hubert Garavel (Grenoble), Andy Gordon (Microsoft Research, Cambridge), Roberto Gorrieri (Bologna), Susanne Graf (Grenoble), Görel Hedin (Lund), Nigel Horspool (Victoria), Kurt Jensen (Aarhus), Paul Klint (Amsterdam), Tiziana Margaria (Dortmund), Ugo Montanari (Pisa), Mogens Nielsen (Aarhus), Hanne Riis Nielson (Copenhagen), Fernando Orejas (Barcelona), Mauro Pezzè (Milano), Andreas Podelski (Saarbrücken), Don Sannella (Edinburgh), David Schmidt (Kansas), Bernhard Steffen (Dortmund), Andrzej Tarlecki (Warsaw), Igor Walukiewicz (Bordeaux), Herbert Weber (Berlin).

I would like to express my sincere gratitude to all of these people and organizations, the program committee chairs and PC members of the ETAPS conferences, the organizers of the satellite events, the speakers themselves, and Springer-Verlag for agreeing to publish the ETAPS proceedings. The final votes of thanks must go, however, to Andrzej Tarlecki and Paweł Urzyczyn. They accepted the risk of organizing what is the first edition of ETAPS in Eastern Europe, at a time of economic uncertainty, but with great courage and determination. They deserve our greatest applause.

Leicester, January 2003

José Luiz Fiadeiro
ETAPS Steering Committee Chair

[1] The contents of this volume do not necessarily reflect the positions or the policies of these organizations and no official endorsement should be inferred.

Preface

This volume contains the proceedings of the Ninth International Conference on Tools and Algorithms for the Construction and Analysis of Systems (TACAS 2003). TACAS 2003 took place in Warsaw, Poland, from April 7th to April 11th, as part of the Sixth European Joint Conferences on Theory and Practice of Software (ETAPS 2003), whose aims, organization, and history are detailed in a foreword by the ETAPS Steering Committee Chair, Jose Luiz Fiadeiro.

TACAS is a forum for researchers, developers, and users interested in rigorously based tools for the construction and analysis of systems. The conference serves to bridge the gaps between different communities – including, but not limited to, those devoted to formal methods, software and hardware verification, static analysis, programming languages, software engineering, real-time systems, and communications protocols – that have traditionally had little interaction but share common interests in, and techniques for, tool development. In particular, by providing a venue for the discussion of common problems, heuristics, algorithms, data structures, and methodologies, TACAS aims to support researchers in their quest to improve the utility, reliability, flexibility, and efficiency of tools for building systems.

TACAS seeks theoretical papers with a clear link to tool construction, papers describing relevant algorithms and practical aspects of their implementation, papers giving descriptions of tools and associated methodologies, and case studies with a conceptual message.

The specific topics covered by the conference include, but are not limited to, the following:

- specification and verification techniques,
- theorem-proving and model-checking,
- system construction and transformation techniques,
- static and run-time analysis,
- compositional and refinement-based methodologies,
- testing and test-case generation,
- analytical techniques for real-time, hybrid, and safety-critical systems,
- tool environments and tool architectures, and
- applications and case studies.

TACAS accepts two types of contributions: research papers and tool demonstration papers. Research papers are full-length papers covering one or more of the topics above, including tool development and case studies from the perspective of scientific research. Research papers are evaluated by the TACAS Program Committee. Tool demonstration papers are shorter papers that give an overview of a particular tool and its application. To stress the importance of tool demonstrations for TACAS, these papers are evaluated and selected by a specific member of the TACAS Program Committee who holds the title of Tool Chair.

In the years since it joined the ETAPS conference federation, TACAS has been the largest of the ETAPS member conferences in terms of number of submissions and papers accepted. This year, the scale of TACAS increased in several important ways. To handle the trend of a growing number of TACAS submissions, the ETAPS Steering Committee agreed to enlarge the TACAS Program Committee from 16 to 25 members. This proved to be a wise decision — TACAS 2003 received a record number of submissions: 140 research papers and 20 tool demonstration papers were submitted. From the submitted papers, 35 research papers were accepted (acceptance ratio of 25%), 6 tool demo papers were accepted (acceptance ratio of 30%), and two of the research paper submissions were invited as tool demonstration papers. Combining the paper categories, this yields an overall acceptance rate of 27%. This represents the most competitive acceptance rate to date for TACAS (the acceptance rate has never exceeded 36% since TACAS joined ETAPS in 1999).

To carry out the difficult task of selecting a program from an unusually large number of submissions in a fair and competent manner, we were fortunate to have highly qualified program committee members from diverse geographic and research areas. Each submission was evaluated by at least three reviewers. Moreover, papers submitted by program committee members were assigned an additional reviewer and were "anonymized" by removing author names and affiliations. After a five-week reviewing process, the program selection was carried out in a two-week online program committee meeting.

We believe the result of the committee deliberations is a very strong scientific program. Also, for the first time in TACAS, tool demonstrations are not grouped together in stand-alone sessions, but instead are integrated into sessions containing research papers on related topics.

Although the scope of TACAS is quite broad in that its stated aim is to provide a forum for work about rigorously justified tools based on formal methods, theorem-proving and model-checking related methods are the ones most often found in work published at TACAS. In an effort to emphasize a broader view of formal methods at TACAS, Peter Lee was invited to give a talk presenting his perspective on tools using lighter-weight formal methods such as type-theoretic methods used in proof-carrying code.

In conclusion, successfully organizing and implementing TACAS 2003 as represented by the proceedings recorded in this volume required significant effort by many different people during the past two years (indeed, the organization of TACAS 2003 started in 2001!). Although, it is impossible to mention everyone who contributed to TACAS 2003 by name, we would like to extend our sincere thanks to the following people:

- Kurt Jensen, who served as the Tool Chair,
- the program committee members and additional referees, who performed admirably in spite of the unexpectedly high workload assigned to them,

- Martin Karusseit and Tiziana Margaria (MetaFRAME, Germany), for their constant and prompt support in dealing with the online conference management system,
- Damien Bergamini (INRIA Rhône-Alpes, France), who carried out the hard work of preparing the LNCS proceedings,
- Frédéric Lang and Bruno Ondet, for their help in preparing the TACAS 2003 website (http://www.inrialpes.fr/vasy/tacas03),
- William Deng, Shufeng Li, and Robby (Kansas State University, USA), for their help in administering the online conference system, reviewing assignments, and program committee meeting,
- the TACAS Steering Committee, for inviting us to chair TACAS 2003 and for advising us in numerous matters along the way,
- the ETAPS 2003 Organizing Committee including the committee co-chairs Andrzej Tarlecki and Pawel Urzyczyn, and the ETAPS Steering Committee Chair José Fiadeiro for his patient guidance and prompting over the course of many months.

January 2003 Hubert Garavel & John Hatcliff

Steering Committee

Ed Brinksma	University of Twente, The Netherlands
Rance Cleaveland	SUNY at Stony Brook, USA
Kim G. Larsen	BRICS Aalborg, Denmark
Bernhard Steffen	University of Dortmund, Germany

Program Committee

Rajeev Alur	University of Pennsylvania, USA
Albert Benveniste	IRISA Rennes, France
Ahmed Bouajjani	Liafa, University of Paris 7, France
Rance Cleaveland	SUNY at Stony Brook, USA
Werner Damm	University of Oldenburg, Germany
Luca de Alfaro	University of California, Santa Cruz, USA
Alessandro Fantechi	University of Florence and IEI-CNR Pisa, Italy
Alain Finkel	LSV-ENS de Cachan, France
Hubert Garavel (co-chair)	INRIA Rhône-Alpes, France
Patrice Godefroid	Bell Laboratories, Lucent Technologies, USA
Susanne Graf	Verimag Grenoble, France
Jan Friso Groote	Techn. Univ. Eindhoven, The Netherlands
Orna Grumberg	Technion Haifa, Israel
John Hatcliff (co-chair)	Kansas State University, USA
Kurt Jensen (tool chair)	University of Aarhus, Denmark
Bengt Jonsson	Uppsala University, Sweden
Joost-Pieter Katoen	University of Twente, The Netherlands
Kim Larsen	Aalborg University, Denmark
Doron Peled	University of Warwick, UK
Sriram K. Rajamani	Microsoft Research, USA
John Rushby	SRI, USA
Steve Schneider	Royal Holloway, University of London, UK
Gregor Snelting	University of Passau, Germany
Bernhard Steffen	University of Dortmund, Germany
Willem Visser	RIACS, NASA Ames Research Center, USA

Referees

Parosh Abdulla
Suzana Andova
Christel Baier
Tom Ball
Anindya Banerjee
Sébastien Bardin
Sharon Barner
Gerd Behrmann
Saddek Bensalem
Cinzia Bernardeschi
Gérard Berry
Antonia Bertolino
Machiel van der Bijl
Benjamin Blanc

Stefan Blom
Frank de Boer
Henrik Bohnenkamp
Alexandre Boisseau
Patricia Bouyer
Marius Bozga
Guillaume Brat
Volker Braun
Ed Brinksma
Glenn Bruns
Doron Bustan
Benôıt Caillaud
Sagar Chaki
Swarat Chaudhuri
Yannick Chevalier
Gianfranco Ciardo
Hubert Comon
Byron Cook
Jean-Michel Couvreur
Dennis Dams
Satyaki Das
Alexandre David
Giorgio Delzanno
Stéphane Demri
William Deng
Dino Distefano
Cindy Eisner
E. Allen Emerson
Lars-Henrik Eriksson
Javier Esparza
Kousha Etessami
Marco Faella
Manuel Fahndrich
Dana Fisman
Emmanuel Fleury
Ranan Fraer
Jaco Geldenhuys
Stefania Gnesi
Gregor Gößler
Alain Griffault
Olga Grinchtein
Claudia Gsottberger
Elsa L. Gunter
Stefan Haar
Nicolas Halbwachs
Frank van Ham
Ulrich Hannemann
Klaus Havelund
Holger Hermanns
Jens Peter Holmegaard
Geert-Jan Houben
Hardi Hungar
Michael Huth
Radha Jagadeesan
David N. Jansen
Bertrand Jeannet
Thierry Jéron
Jens B. Jørgensen
Bernhard Josko
Yan Jurski
Sara Kalvala
Gila Kamhi
Daniel Kästner
Shmuel Katz
Sarfraz Khurshid
Josva Kleist
Jochen Klose
Christos Kloukinas
Jens Knoop
Lars M. Kristensen
Kåre J. Kristoffersen
Salvatore La Torre
Yassine Lakhnech
Frédéric Lang
Rom Langerak
Diego Latella
Ranko Lazik
Jérôme Leroux
Martin Leucker
Vladimir Levin
Jakob Lichtenberg
Bert Lisser
Yoad Lustig
Bas Luttik
Parthasarathy Madhusudan
Thomas Mailund
Rupak Majumdar
Oded Maler
Tiziana Margaria
Peter Marwedel

Mieke Massink
Radu Mateescu
Franco Mazzanti
Michael McDougall
Ken McMillan
Virgile Mogbil
Arjan Mooij
Laurent Mounier
Markus Müller-Olm
Anca Muscholl
Madanlal Musuvathi
Ziv Nevo
Brian Nielsen
Mogens Nielsen
Oliver Niese
David Nowak
Sven-Olof Nyström
Ileana Ober
Martijn Oostdijk
Joël Ouaknine
Corina Păsăreanu
Charles Pecheur
Wojciech Penczek
Laure Petrucci
Paul Pettersson
Nir Piterman
Jaco van de Pol
Alban Ponse
Marie-Laure Potet
Solofo Ramangalahy
Anders P. Ravn
Arend Rensink
Laurent Romary
Judi Romijn
Harald Ruess
Oliver Ruething
Theo C. Ruys
Konstantinos Sagonas
Hassen Saïdi
Philippe Schnoebelen
Roberto Segala
Natarajan Shankar
Sharon Shoham
Mihaela Sighireanu
Jane Sinclair
Oleg Sokolsky
Emilio Spinicci
Marielle Stoelinga
Scott D. Stoller
Ofer Strichman
Zhendong Su
Grégoire Sutre
Gia Tagviashvili
Jean-Pierre Talpin
Ashish Tiwari
Stavros Tripakis
Tomas Uribe
Yaroslav Usenko
Enrico Vicario
Björn Victor
Mahesh Viswanathan
Tomas Vojnar
Marc Voorhoeve
Bow-Yaw Wang
Manfred Warmuth
Westley Weimer
Lisa Wells
Wieger Wesselink
Jim Whitehead
Freek Wiedijk
Tim Willemse
Zijiang Yang
Heiseung Yoo
Karen Yorav
Sergio Yovine

Table of Contents

Invited Contributions

Bounded Model Checking and SAT-Based Methods

Mu-Calculus and Temporal Logics

Verification of Parameterized Systems

Abstractions and Counter-Examples

Real-Time and Scheduling

Security and Cryptography

Modules and Compositional Verification

Symbolic State Spaces and Decision Diagrams

Performance and Mobility

State Space Reductions

Constraint-Solving and Decision Procedures

Testing and Verification

What Are We Trying to Prove? Reflections on Experiences with Proof-Carrying Code

Peter Lee

School of Computer Science
Carnegie Mellon University
5000 Forbes Avenue, Pittsburgh, PA 15213-3891

Abstract. Since 1996 there has been tremendous progress in developing the idea of *certified code*, including both proof-carrying code (PCC) and typed assembly language (TAL). In a certified code framework, each program (which is usually in machine-code binary form) comes equipped with a certificate that "explains", both rigorously and in a manner that is easily validated, why it possesses a formally specified security property. A substantial amount of the research work in this area has been directed towards the problem of how to make certified code a practical technology—what one might call "proof engineering". Thus, many of the advances have been in methods for representing the certificates in the most compact and efficiently checkable way. For example, early on George Necula and I used LF encodings of loop invariants and safety proofs, which were then validated by a process of verification-condition generation and LF type checking. Later, we adopted the so-called "oracle-based" representation, resulting in certificates that imposed a much smaller overhead on the size of the object files, usually much less than 20%. This made us optimistic enough about the prospects for a practical realization of certified code that we devoted considerable effort in developing the SpecialJ system for certified Java. And very recently, many researchers (led initially by Andrew Appel and Amy Felty) have been developing various "foundational" approaches to certified code. These hold out the promise of making PCC and TAL even more trustworthy and easier to administer in practical settings, and in some instances may also open PCC to verification of temporal properties.

In this talk, I will start with an overview of these and other current state-of-the-art concepts in certified code. Then, I will consider a very different but equally practical question: Just what is it that we are trying to prove? In contrast to the concept of translation validation, a certified code system does not prove the semantic equivalence between source and target programs. It only proves a specified safety property for the target program, independent of any source program. So then what is the right safety property to use? Is it necessary to prove that the target programs preserve all of the typing abstractions of a particular source program, or is simple "memory safety" enough? While I have yet to claim an answer to this question, I am able to relate specific situations from practical applications that may help to shed some light on the situation.

H. Garavel and J. Hatcliff (Eds.): TACAS 2003, LNCS 2619, p. 1, 2003.

Automatic Abstraction without Counterexamples

Kenneth L. McMillan and Nina Amla

Cadence Design Systems

Abstract. A method of automatic abstraction is presented that uses proofs of unsatisfiability derived from SAT-based bounded model checking as a guide to choosing an abstraction for unbounded model checking. Unlike earlier methods, this approach is not based on analysis of abstract counterexamples. The performance of this approach on benchmarks derived from microprocessor verification indicates that SAT solvers are quite effective in eliminating logic that is not relevant to a given property. Moreover, benchmark results suggest that when bounded model checking successfully terminates, and the problem is unsatisfiable, the number of state variables in the proof of unsatisfiability tends to be small. In almost all cases tested, when bounded model checking succeeded, unbounded model checking of the resulting abstraction also succeeded.

1 Introduction

Abstraction is commonly viewed as the key to applying model checking to large scale systems. Abstraction means, in effect, removing information about a system which is not relevant to a property we wish to verify. In the simplest case, we can view the system as a large collection of constraints, and abstraction as removing constraints that are deemed irrelevant. The goal in this case is not so much to eliminate constraints *per se*, as to eliminate state variables that occur only in the irrelevant constraints, and thereby to reduce the size of the state space. A reduction of the state space in turn increases the efficiency of model checking, which is based on exhaustive state space exploration.

The first attempt to automate this simple kind of abstraction is due to Kurshan [12], and is known as *iterative abstraction refinement*. This method begins with an empty set of constraints (or a seed set provided by the user), and applies model checking to attempt to verify the property. If a counterexample is found, it is analyzed to find a set of constraints whose addition to the system will rule out the counterexample. The process is then repeated until the property is found to be true, or until a concrete counterexample is produced. To produce a concrete counterexample, we must find a valuation for the unconstrained variables, such that all the original constraints are satisfied.

A number of variations on this basic technique have appeared [1,5,9,22]. Some of the recent methods pose the construction of a concrete counterexample as a Boolean satisfiability (SAT) problem (or equivalently, an ATPG problem) and

H. Garavel and J. Hatcliff (Eds.): TACAS 2003, LNCS 2619, pp. 2–17, 2003.

apply modern SAT methods [14] to this problem. A recent approach [6] also applies ILP and machine learning techniques to the problem of choosing which constraints to add to rule out an abstract counterexample in the case when a concrete counterexample is not found.

Another recent and related development is that of *bounded model checking* [3]. In this method, the question of the existence of a counterexample of *no more than k steps*, for fixed k, is posed as a SAT problem. In various studies [7,4], SAT solvers have been found to be quite efficient at producing counterexamples for systems that are too large to allow standard model checking. The disadvantage of this approach is that, if a counterexample is not found, there is no guarantee that there do not exist counterexamples of greater than k steps. Thus, the method can falsify, but cannot verify properties (unless an upper bound is known on the depth of the state space, which is not generally the case).

In this paper, a method is presented for automated abstraction which exploits an under-appreciated fact about SAT solvers: in the unsatisfiable case, they can produce a proof of unsatisfiability. In bounded model checking, this corresponds to a proof that there is no counterexample to the property of k steps or fewer. Even though this implies nothing about the truth of the property in general, we can use this proof to tell us which constraints are relevant to the property (at least in the first k steps) and thus provide a guess at an abstraction that may be used to fully verify the property using standard model checking methods. The method differs from the earlier, counterexample-based iterative abstraction approaches, in that counterexamples produced by the standard model checker are ignored. The abstraction is based not on refuting these counterexamples, but rather on proofs provided by the SAT solver. Thus, we will refer to it as *proof-based abstraction*. This approach has the advantage that it rules out all counterexamples up to a given length, rather than the single counterexample that the model checker happened to produce.

1.1 Related Work

The notion of proof-based abstraction has already appeared in the context of infinite state verification. Here, a finite state abstraction of an infinite state system is generated using as the abstract states the valuations of a finite set of first order predicates over the concrete state. The key to this method, known as predicate abstraction [18], is to choose the right predicates. An iterative abstraction method proposed by Henzinger *et al.* [20] uses a theorem prover to refute counterexamples generated by predicate abstraction. In the case when the counterexample is proved false, the proof is "mined" for new state predicates to use in predicate abstraction.

The technique presented here is similar to this method in spirit, but differs in some significant aspects. First, it applies only to finite state systems, and uses a SAT solver rather than a first order prover. Second, instead of choosing predicates to define the abstract state space, it merely chooses among the existing constraints to form the abstraction – the encoding of the state remains the same.

Another related technique [16] uses a SAT solver to derive an abstraction sufficient to refute a given abstract counterexample. The abstraction is generated by tracing the execution of the SAT solver in a way that is similar to the method presented here. However, that method, like the earlier methods, still refutes one counterexample at a time, accumulating an abstraction.

The key difference between the methods of [20,16] and the present one is that the present method does not use abstract counterexamples as a basis for refining the abstraction. Rather, it generates an abstraction sufficient to refute all counterexamples within a given length bound. Intuitively, the motivation for refuting all counterexamples at once is that a given abstract counterexample may be invalid for many reasons that are not relevant to the truth of the property being proved. In the present method, the abstraction is directed toward the property itself and not a single execution trace that violates it.

Another important difference is that the generated abstraction is not cumulative. That is, a constraint that is present in abstraction in one iteration of the algorithm may be absent in a later iteration. Thus, strictly speaking, the method cannot be viewed as "iterative abstraction refinement". In the counterexample-based methods, an irrelevant constraint, once added to the abstraction, cannot be removed.

1.2 Outline

We begin in the next section by considering how a Boolean satisfiability solver can be extended to produce proofs of unsatisfiability. Then, in section 3, we introduce the proof-based abstraction method. Finally, in section 4, we test the method in practice, applying it to the verification of some properties of commercial microprocessor designs.

Benchmark results provide evidence for two significant conclusions: first, that SAT solvers are quite effective at isolating the parts of a large design that are relevant to a given property, and second, that if a property is true and bounded model checking succeeds, then in most cases unbounded model checking can be applied to an abstraction to prove the property in general.

2 Extracting Proofs from SAT Solvers

A DPLL-style SAT solver, such as CHAFF [14], is easily instrumented to produce proofs of unsatisfiability using resolution. This is based on the observation that "conflict clause" generation can be viewed as a sequence of resolution steps, following the so-called "implication graph". Readers familiar with SAT methods may find this observation quite trivial, and therefore may wish to skip this section. Otherwise, we will now define what is meant by a "proof of unsatisfiability", and show how one can be extracted from a run of a typical SAT solver.

To begin at the beginning, a *clause* is a disjunction of a set of zero or more *literals*, each of which is either a Boolean variable or its negation. We assume that clauses are *non-tautological*, that is, no clause contains both a variable and its negation. A set of clauses is said to be *satisfiable* when there exists a truth assignment to all the Boolean variables that makes every clause in the set true.

Given two clauses of the form $c_1 = v \vee A$ and $c_2 = \neg v \vee B$, we say that the *resolvent* of c_1 and c_2 is the clause $A \vee B$, provided $A \vee B$ is non-tautological. For example, the resolvent of $a \vee b$ and $\neg a \vee \neg c$ is $b \vee \neg c$, while $a \vee b$ and $\neg a \vee \neg b$ have no resolvent, since $b \vee \neg b$ is tautological. It is easy to see that any two clauses have at most one resolvent. The resolvent of c_1 and c_2 (if it exists) is a clause that is implied by $c_1 \wedge c_2$ (in fact, it is exactly $(\exists v)(c_1 \wedge c_2)$).

Definition 1. A proof of unsatisfiability P for a set of clauses C is a directed acyclic graph (V_P, E_P), where V_P is a set of clauses, such that

- for every vertex $c \in V_P$, either
  - $c \in C$, and c is a root, or
  - c has exactly two predecessors, c_1 and c_2, such that c is the resolvent of c_1 and c_2, and
- the empty clause is the unique leaf.

Theorem 1. If there is a proof of unsatisfiability for clause set C, then C is unsatisfiable.

Proof. By induction over the depth of the DAG, and transitivity of implication, every clause is implied by the conjunction of C, hence C implies the empty clause (i.e., false), and is thus unsatisfiable. □

Now we consider how a standard SAT solver might be modified to produce proofs of unsatisfiability. While searching for a satisfying assignment, a DPLL solver makes *decisions*, or arbitrary truth assignments to variables, and generates from these an *implication graph*. This is a directed acyclic graph whose vertices are truth assignments to variables, where each node is implied by its predecessors in the graph together with single clause.

As an example, suppose that our clause set is $\{(\neg a \vee b), (\neg b \vee c \vee d)\}$ and we have already decided the literals $\{a, \neg c\}$. A possible implication graph is shown below:

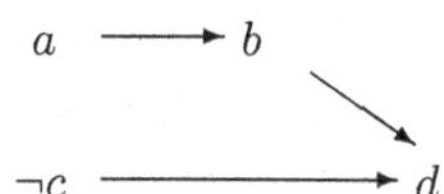

The literal b is implied by node a and the clause $(\neg a \vee b)$, while d is implied by the nodes b, $\neg c$, and clause $(\neg b \vee c \vee d)$.

A clause is said to be in *conflict* when the negations of all its literals appear in the implication graph. When a conflict occurs, the SAT solver generates a *conflict clause* – a new clause that is implied by the existing clauses in the set. This is usually explained in terms of finding a cut in the implication graph, but from our point of view it is better understood as a process of resolving the "clause in conflict" with clauses in the implication graph to generate a new clause (that is also in conflict). We can also think of each resolution step as applying an implication from the implication graph in the contrapositive.

As an example, suppose that we add the clause $(\neg b \vee \neg d)$ to the example above. This clause is in conflict, since the implication graph contains both b and d. Note that d was implied by the clause $(\neg b \vee c \vee d)$. Taking the resolvent of this clause with the conflicting clause $(\neg b \vee \neg d)$, we obtain a new implied clause $(\neg b \vee c)$, which is also in conflict. Now, the literal b in the implication graph was implied by the clause $(\neg a \vee b)$. Resolving this with our new clause produces another implied clause $(\neg a \vee c)$, also in conflict. Either of these implied clauses might be taken as the conflict clause, and added to the clause set.

In order to generate a proof in the unsatisfiable case, we have only to record, for each generated conflict clause, the sequence of clauses that were resolved to produce that clause. The SAT solver produces an "unsatisfiable" answer when it generates the empty clause as a conflict clause (actually, most solvers do not explicitly produce this clause, but can be made to do so). At this point, we can easily produce a proof of unsatisfiability by, for example, a depth-first search starting from the empty clause, recursively deducing each clause in terms of the sequence of clauses that originally produced it. Note that, in general, not all conflict clauses generated during the SAT procedure will actually be needed to derive the empty clause.

3 Proof-Based Abstraction

Now we will show how such proofs of unsatisfiability can be used to generate abstractions for model checking. What follows does not rely on the fact that we are using a DPLL-style SAT solver. Any solver which can produce a proof of unsatisfiability will suffice, although the quality of the abstraction depends on the quality of the proof.

Bounded model checking [3] is a technique for proving that a transition system admits no counterexample to a given temporal formula of k or fewer transitions, where k is a fixed bound. This can be accomplished by posing the existence of a counterexample of k steps or fewer as a SAT problem. Note that with a proof-generating SAT solver, in the unsatisfiable case we can in effect extract a proof of the non-existence of a counterexample of length k. This proof can in turn be used to generate an abstraction of the transition system in a very straightforward way.

We first observe that a bounded model checking problem consists of a set of constraints – initial constraints, transition constraints, final constraints (in the case of safety properties) and fairness constraints (conditions that must occur on a cycle, in the case of a liveness property). These constraints are translated into conjunctive normal form, and, if appropriate, instantiated for each time step $1 \ldots k$. If no clause derived from a given constraint is used in the proof of unsatisfiability, then we can remove that constraint from the problem, without invalidating the proof. Thus, the resulting abstract system (with unused constraints removed) is also guaranteed to admit no counterexample of k steps or fewer.

We can now apply ordinary (unbounded) model checking to the abstracted system. This process will have two possible outcomes. The first is that the property is true in the abstracted system. In this case, since removing constraints preserves all properties of our logic (linear temporal logic) we can conclude that the property is true in the original system and we are done. The second possibility is that the unbounded model checker will find a counterexample of greater than k transitions (say, k' transitions). Note that a counterexample of fewer transitions is ruled out, since we have a proof that no such counterexample exists (in both the original or the abstracted system). In this case, we can simply return to bounded model checking using k' as the new length bound.

This procedure, which alternates bounded and unbounded model checking, is guaranteed to terminate for finite models, since k is always increasing. At some point, k must be greater than the depth of the abstract state space (i.e., the depth of a breadth-first search starting from the initial states). At this point, if there is no counterexample of length k, there can be no counterexample of length greater than k, thus the unbounded model checking step must yield "true". In practice, we usually find that when the procedure terminates, k is roughly half the depth of the abstract state space.

In this procedure, "false" results (i.e., counterexamples) are only found by bounded model checking – counterexamples produced by the unbounded model checker are discarded, and only their length is taken into account in the next iteration. This is in contrast to counterexample-based methods such as [12,1,5, 9,22,16] in which the counterexample produced by model checking the abstract system is used as a guide in refining the abstraction.

Also note that the set of constraints in the abstraction is not strictly growing with each iteration, as it is the above cited methods. That is, at each iteration, the old abstraction is discarded and a new one is generated based on the proof extracted from the SAT solver. This new abstraction may not contain all of the constraints present in the previous abstractions, and may even have fewer constraints.

In the remainder of this section, we will endeavor to make the above informal discussion more precise. Our goal is to determine whether a given LTL formula is true in a given finite model. However, this problem will be posed in terms of finding an accepting run of a finite automaton. The translation of LTL model checking into this framework has been extensively studied [15,21,10], and will not be described here. We will treat only safety properties here, due to space considerations. Liveness properties are covered in [13].

3.1 Safety Checking Algorithm

For safety properties, we wish to determine the existence of a bad finite prefix – a finite sequence which cannot be extended to an infinite sequence satisfying the property. We assume that the problem is given in terms of an automaton on finite words, such that a bad prefix exists exactly when the automaton has an accepting run. Such a construction can be found, for example, in [11].

As in symbolic model checking, the automaton itself will be represented implicitly by Boolean formulas. The state space of the automaton is defined by an indexed set of Boolean variables $V = \{v_1, \ldots, v_n\}$. A *state* S is a corresponding vector $(s_1, \ldots, s_n)$ of Boolean values. A *state predicate* P is a Boolean formula over V. We will write $P(W)$ to denote $P\langle w_i/v_i\rangle$ (that is, p with w_i substituted for each v_i). We also assume an indexed set of "next state" variables $V' = \{v'_1, \ldots, v'_n\}$, disjoint from V. A *state relation* R is a Boolean formula over V and V'. We will write $R(W, W')$ to denote $R\langle w_i/v_i, w'_i/v'_i\rangle$.

The runs of the automaton are defined by a triple $M = (I, T, F)$, where the initial constraint I and final constraint F are state predicates, and the transition constraint T is a state relation. A *run* of M, of length k, is a sequence of states $s_0 \ldots s_k$ such that $I(s_0)$ is true, and for all $0 \leq i < k$, $T(s_i, s_{i+1})$ is true, and $F(s_k)$ is true. We can translate the existence of a run into a Boolean satisfiability problem by introducing a new indexed set of variables $W_i = \{w_{i1}, \ldots, w_{in}\}$, for $0 \leq i \leq k$. A run of length up to k exists exactly when the following formula is satisfiable:[1]

$$I(W_0) \wedge \left(\bigwedge_{0 \leq i < k} T(W_i, W_{i+1}) \right) \wedge \left(\bigvee_{0 \leq i \leq k} F(W_i) \right)$$

In order to use a standard SAT solver, we must translate this formula into conjunctive normal form. For this purpose, we will assume that I and T are each a conjunction of a collection of terms. That is, $I = \bigwedge_j I_j$ and $T = \bigwedge_j T_j$. This decomposition will allow us to abstract the problem by removing irrelevant terms. Further, to simplify matters, we can assume without loss of generality that the final condition F consists of a single literal. To ensure this we can, for example, create a new state variable corresponding to the formula F and fold the definition of this new variable into T.

We also assume the existence of some function Γ that translates each Boolean formula into a logically equivalent set of clauses. Thus satisfiability of the above formula is equivalent to satisfiability of the following set of clauses:

$$\text{BMC}_k(M) = \left(\bigcup_j \Gamma(I_j(W_0)) \right) \cup \left(\bigcup_{0 \leq i < k, j} \Gamma(T_j(W_i, W_{i+1})) \right) \cup \{ \bigvee_{0 \leq i \leq k} F(W_i) \} \tag{1}$$

Also note that in general the translation of an arbitrary Boolean formula f into CNF is exponential. In practice, the problem can be solved by adding a fresh variable for the value of each subformula of f, as in [17]. This construction does not affect the satisfiability of the result formula, and produces a CNF formula which is linear size in the size of f. The theory that follows, however, does not depend on the manner in which translation to CNF is performed.

At this point, if $\text{BMC}_k(M)$ is found to be satisfiable, then we have a finite counterexample, and we are done. If, on the other hand, a proof of unsatisfiability

[1] Actually, this is correct only when the transition relation is total. The generalization to partial transition relations is straightforward.

P is found for $\mathrm{BMC}_k(M)$, then we know only that there is no counterexample of k or fewer transitions. In this case, we build an abstraction M' of M, such that P is also a proof of unsatisfiability of $\mathrm{BMC}_k(M')$. We want $\mathrm{BMC}_k(M')$ to retain all of the clauses used in P. Thus, we let I' be the conjunction of all the components I_j such that some clause in $\Gamma(I_j(W_0))$ occurs in P. Similarly, we let T' be the conjunction of all the components T_j such that for some $0 \leq i < k$, some clause in $\Gamma(T_j(W_i))$ occurs in P. We need not abstract F itself, since we assume that F is a single literal. This gives us the following result:

Lemma 1. Let $M = (I, T, F)$, let P be a proof of unsatisfiability of $\mathrm{BMC}_k(M)$ and let $M' = (I', T', F')$ where

- $I' = \bigwedge\{I_j \mid \Gamma(I_j(W_0)) \cap V_P \neq \emptyset\}$,
- $T' = \bigwedge\{T_j \mid (\bigcup_{0 \leq i < k} \Gamma(T_j(W_i))) \cap V_P \neq \emptyset\}$, and
- $F' = F$.

M' has no runs of length k or less, and further, if M' has no runs, then M has no runs.

Proof. By definition, every clause in P that occurs in $\mathrm{BMC}_k(M)$ also occurs in $\mathrm{BMC}_k(M')$. Thus, since P is a proof of unsatisfiability of $\mathrm{BMC}_k(M)$, it is also a proof of unsatisfiability of $\mathrm{BMC}_k(M')$, so the abstraction M' also has no run of length k or less. Further, since I', T' and F' are weaker than I, T and F, respectively, it follows that every run of M is also a run of M'. □

We can now attempt to perform unbounded symbolic model checking on M', to determine whether it has a run of any length. This is preferable to applying model checking directly to M in the case when the number of variables referenced in M' is significantly smaller than the number referenced in M, yielding a reduction in the effective size of the state space. If model checking of M' determines that M' has no runs, then M has no runs, and we are done. On the other hand, if M' does have a run, we know that its length k' is greater than k. In this case, we restart the procedure with k' for k (or in general, any value larger than k' for k). The overall procedure is shown in figure 1.

Theorem 2. If M has a run, then FINITERUN(M) terminates and returns a run of M, else it terminates and returns "No Run".

Proof. Suppose, toward a contradiction, that the procedure does not terminate. Then, by lemma 1, k increases without bound. Thus, if a run of M does exist, eventually $BMC_k(M)$ will be satisfiable, and the procedure will terminate, returning a run. On the other hand, if M has no run, then eventually k will exceed 2^n, where n is the number of state variables. At this point, since M' has no runs of length up to 2^n (an upper bound on the depth of its state space) it has no runs. Hence the procedure terminates, returning "No Run". □

A number of optimizations can be applied to this basic method in order to produce smaller abstract models. These include a "cone of influence" reduction on the abstract model, as well as methods to reduce the number of free combinational variables and to improve the proofs generated by the SAT solver. These are omitted here due to space considerations, but are described in [13].

```
procedure FiniteRun(M = (I, T, F))
    choose k >= 0
    while true
        let C = Bmc_k(M)
        if C satisfiable
            let A be a satisfying assignment of C
            return the run s_0, ..., s_k, where s_ij = A(W_ij)
        else
            let P be a proof of unsatisfiability of C
            let M' = Abstract(M, P, k)
            model check M'
            if M' has a run s of length k'
                let k be some value ≥ k'
            else return "No Run"
end

procedure Abstract(M = (I, T, F), P = (V_P, E_P), k)
    let I' = ⋀{I_j | Γ(I_j(W_0)) ∩ V_P ≠ ∅}
    let T' = ⋀{T_j | (⋃_{0≤i<k} Γ(T_j(W_i))) ∩ V_P ≠ ∅}
    return (I', T', F)
end
```

Fig. 1. Procedure for existence of a finite run

4 Practical Experience

A direct comparison of the proof-based abstraction method against counter-example based methods such as [22,6,16] is unfortunately not possible, since the performance data presented in these works is based on proprietary benchmark problems (also, the most closely related work [16] appeared after this paper was submitted).

To guage the effectivenss of the proof-based abstraction procedure in generating abstractions, it was tested on a set of benchmark model checking problems derived from a sampling of properties used in the compositional verification of a unit of the PicoJava II microprocessor, available in open source from Sun Microsystems, Inc.[2] The unit in question is the ICU, which manages the instruction cache, prefetches instructions, and does some preliminary instruction decoding. Originally, the properties were verified by standard symbolic model checking, using some manual directives to remove parts of the logic not relevant to each property. To make interesting benchmark examples for automatic abstraction, these directives were removed, and a neighboring unit, the instruction folding unit (IFU) was added. The intention of this is to simulate the actions of a naïve user who is unable to localize the verification problem manually (the ultimate

[2] The tools needed to construct the benchmark examples from the Pico-Java II source code can be found at `http://www-cad.eecs.berkeley.edu/~kenmcmil`.

naïve user being an automated tool). The function of the IFU is to read instruction bytes from the instruction queue, parse the byte stream into separate instructions and divide the instructions into groups that can be fed into the execution unit in a single cycle. Inclusion of the IFU increases the number of state variables in the "cone of influence" substantially, largely by introducing dependencies on registers within the ICU itself. It also introduces a large amount of irrelevant combinational logic.

Twenty representative properties were chosen as benchmarks. All of these properties are safety properties, of the form Gp, where p is a formula involving only the current time and the next time (usually only the current time). All the properties are true. Tests were performed on a Linux workstation with a 930MHz Pentium III processor and 512MB of available memory. Unbounded symbolic model checking was performed using the Cadence SMV system. SAT solving was performed using an implementation of the CHAFF algorithm [14], modified to produce proofs of unsatisfiability (verification using a modification of the actual Princeton zChaff implementation produced substantially similar results).

None of the benchmarks could be successfully verified by standard symbolic model checking methods, within a limit of 1800 seconds.[3]

On the other hand, of the 20 benchmarks, all but two were successfully verified by the proof-based abstraction technique. In the two failed cases, the failure was caused by memory exhaustion by the SAT solver during the bounded model checking phase (at k values of 15 and 20 transitions, respectively). Notably, in all cases where the bounded model checking phase completed successfully, the unbounded symbolic model checker was able to successfully check the resulting abstraction M'.

Figure 2 shows, for each benchmark, the original number of state holding variables (solid bars), the number obtained by manual abstraction (gray bars) and the number of state variables remaining in the abstraction at the final iteration of the proof-based abstraction algorithm, without manual abstraction (open bars). Here, by state variables, we mean any variable v such that v' occurs in T. We will refer to other variables, including inputs and intermediate variables as "combinational variables". A $\otimes$ below the bars indicates that the algorithm did not complete. The number of variables obtained by manual abstraction does not necessarily reflect what could be obtained by concerted effort, but rather reflects only a sufficient effort to make the properties checkable by standard methods. Nonetheless, it is interesting to note that in 11 out of 20 cases a better result is obtained by automatic abstraction.

Figure 3 shows total run time of the proof-based abstraction procedure for each of the benchmarks, on a log scale. Comparison data are not available for standard symbolic model checking, since no problem could be completed within

[3] The primary cause of this failure appears to be inability to construct BDD's for parts of the combinational logic in the IFU. It is possible that some of the benchmarks could be completed by using more advanced transition relation decomposition techniques than are implemented in Cadence SMV.

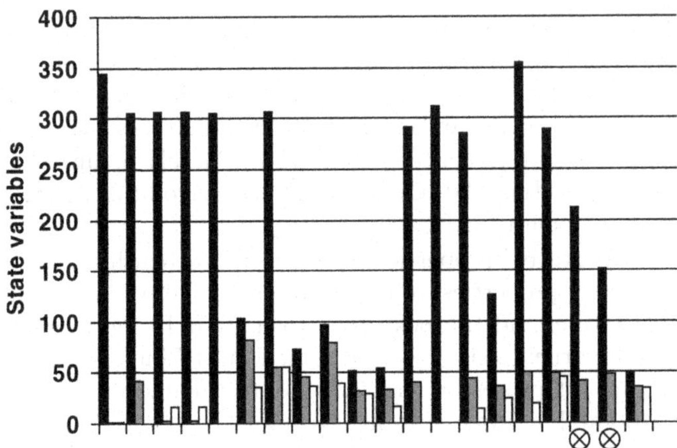

Fig. 2. State variables: (solid) original, (gray) after manual abstraction, (open) after automatic abstraction.

the allotted time. Figure 4 shows the fraction of total run time spent in the two phases of the algorithm. The solid part of the bars represent the total time spent in the bounded model checking phase, while the open part represents the total time spent in the unbounded model checking phase. Note that in most cases, the bottleneck is bounded model checking.

What these data clearly show is that the SAT solver is effective at isolating the part of the logic that is relevant to the given property, at least in the case when this part of the logic is relatively small. We have also found the technique to be very effective at falsification, since the unbounded model checking phase quickly guides the bounded model checker to the appropriate depth.

As an additional point of comparison, figure 5 compares the performance of the proof-based abstraction approach with results previously obtained by Baumgartner et al. [2] on a set of benchmark model checking problems derived from the IBM Gigahertz Processor. Their method involved a combination of SAT-based bounded model checking, structural methods for bounding the depth of the state space, and target enlargement using BDD's. Each point on the graph represents the average verification or falsification time for a collection of properties of the same circuit model. The average time in seconds for proof-based abstraction is represented on the X axis, while the average time in seconds obtained by Baumgartner et al. is represented on the Y axis.[4] Thus, a point above the diagonal line represents a lower average time for proof-based abstraction for one benchmark. Note that in several cases proof-based abstraction has an advantage of two orders of magnitude. A time of 1000 seconds indicates that

[4] The processor speeds for the two sets of experiments are slightly different. Baumgartner *et al.* used an 800MHz Pentium III, as compared to a 930 MHz Pentium III used here. The results presented here have not been adjusted to reflect CPU speed.

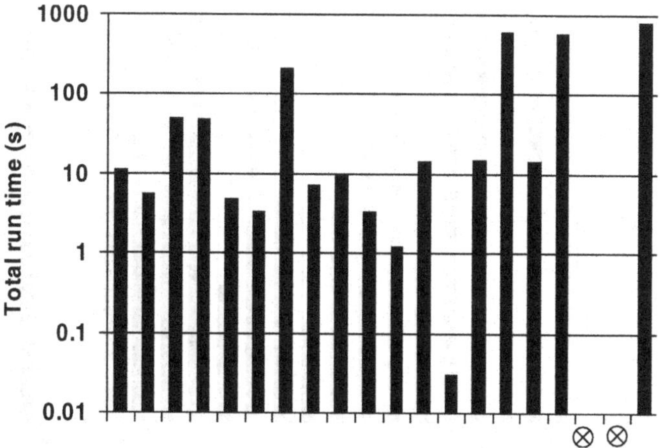

Fig. 3. Total verification time for proof-based abstraction algorithm.

the truth of one or more properties in the benchmark could not be determined. Of the 28 individual properties that could not be resolved by Baumgartner et al, all but one are successfully resolved by the proof-based abstraction method. Excluding this failed benchmark, the largest average time for the proof-based method is 2.89 seconds. The clear conclusion is that proof-based abstraction is a more effective method of exploiting a SAT solver for model checking.

4.1 A Hypothesis

The fact that the unbounded model checker is able to check the abstraction in most cases when the bounded model checking succeeds suggests an interesting (if somewhat informal) hypothesis: that is, that bounded model checking using SAT solvers tends to succeed when the number of relevant variables is small, and to fail when the number of relevant variables is large. Thus far we have tested only the case when the number of relevant variables is small. To test the other end of the spectrum, one possible approach is to use a set of scalable benchmarks, in which all or most of the state variables are known to be relevant. Such examples tend to occur, for example, in protocol verification. Here, absent any fault tolerance mechanism, a dropped bit anywhere in the system tends to cause the protocol to fail.

We will consider first a simple model of a cache coherence protocol due to Steven German [8]. This model is parameterized by N, number of processors. The property to be proved is that, if there is an "exclusive" copy of a cache line in the system, then there is no other copy. Empirically, the the depth of the state space of this model is found to be $8N+2$ transitions. Applying bounded model checking to the model at this depth, we find that the largest instance of this problem we can solve within 1800 seconds is $N = 4$, which has only 42 state variables (of which 37 are found to be relevant). This is quite surprising considering the

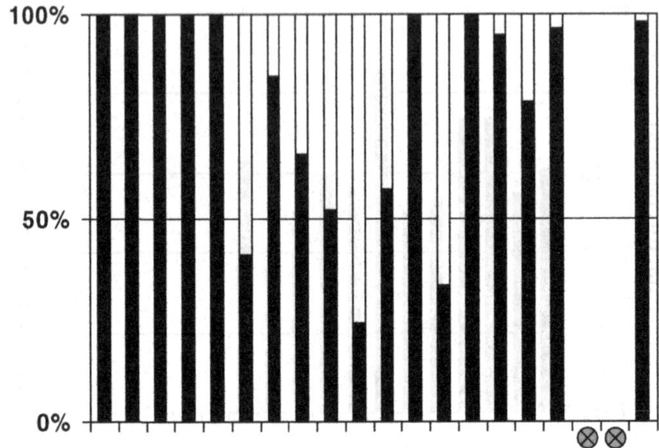

Fig. 4. Fraction of total run time: (solid) bounded model checking (open) unbounded model checking

extreme simplicity of this model relative to the PicoJava II benchmarks. In that case, the SAT solver managed to solve CNF SAT problems with on the order of 1 million variables, while in this case it fails with only about 40,000 variables. On the other hand, the number of relevant state holding variables is roughly similar to what was handled in the PicoJava II benchmarks.

As another test case, let us consider a simple circuit we will call `swap`. This circuit has n j-bit registers. At each clock cycle, it inputs a number i, and swaps the values of register i and its neighbor $i+1 \bmod j$. We set the number of bits j to $\lceil \log_2 n \rceil$ so that we can initialize all of the registers to different values. The property to prove is that registers 0 and 1 always differ. Clearly, if we unconstrain the value of any one register, the property will be false, since by a series of swaps, we can transfer the value of any register to register 0. Interestingly, we find that the largest instance of `swap` that we can successfully apply bounded model checking to is $n = 7$, corresponding to 21 state bits. At $n = 8$, and $k = 8$, the zChaff solver failed to solve a SAT problem with only 1396 variables in over 40 hours!

Testing SAT solvers on other hardware designs tends to confirm the following trend: when proofs are successfully produced by the SAT solver, they tend to involve only a small number of variables in an absolute sense. Figure 6 shows results on the set of problems in a collection of hardware verification benchmarks used at Cadence Design Systems. Each point represents a single benchmark problem, with the X axis giving the original number of state variables, and the Y axis the number of state values in the abstraction resulting from the longest successful bounded model checking run in the proof-based abstraction procedure. The trend is clear: successful bounded model checking runs tend to produce proofs of unsatisfiability using a small number of state variables,

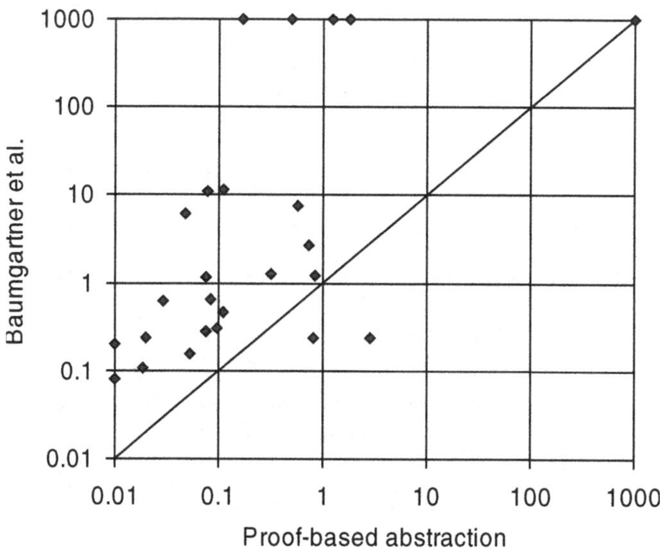

Fig. 5. Fraction of total run time: (solid) bounded model checking (open) unbounded model checking

independent of the number of original state variables. In 18 out of 20 cases, the BDD-based model checker is able to check the abstraction. On the other hand, a very large example provided by IBM produced a proof-based abstraction with over 1000 state bits. We conjecture that this was possible because a large number of these registers do not leave their initial states within the first k steps, and that the SAT solver did not in fact reach the state space depth. This has not been confirmed, however.

On the whole, while the case studies presented here are certainly too small to draw general conclusions about the performance of bounded model checking, they are consistent with the hypothesis that successful bounded model checking (defined as checking up to the state space depth) depends on having small number of relevant state variables. This suggests that a larger scale study of the question might be in order.

5 Conclusion

We have observed that information generated by bounded model checking can be used to improve the efficiency of unbounded model checking, by suggesting abstractions. Perhaps more interestingly, we have seen some empirical evidence for the hypothesis that bounded model checking succeeds when the number of relevant state variables is small, which implies that unbounded model checking is also likely to succeed when applied to the relevant parts of the system. If this hypothesis holds true generally, then it may prove unnecessary in practice to

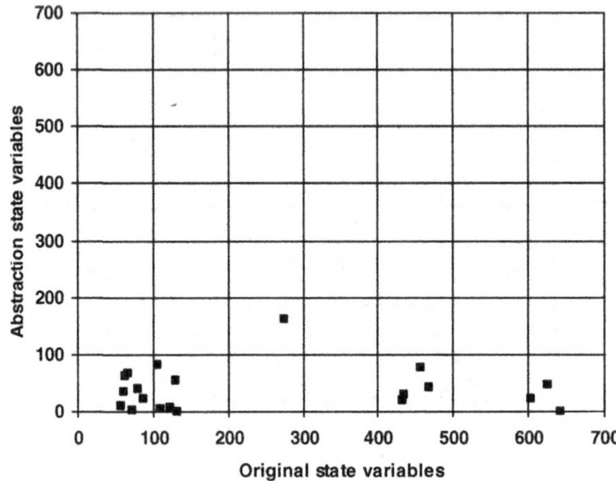

Fig. 6. Results of proof-based abstraction on hardware benchmarks.

find techniques for bounding the search depth in bounded model checking – if bounded model checking succeeds at roughly the state space depth, then the result can likely be confirmed by standard model checking.

Of course, the negative side of this observation is that it seems unlikely that bounded model checking (and hence proof-based abstraction) can be applied to global properties of systems (those that depend on most or all of the state variables). Techniques are still required to reduce the verification problem to "local" properties that can be proved using only a small set of state variables. However, SAT solvers appear to have significant potential for identifying that set of variables once a suitable property is given.

For future work, it is interesting to consider what other information can be extracted from proofs of unsatisfiability that might be useful in model checking. In addition, since SAT solvers seem to be so effective at isolating relevant facts, it might be that a similar technique could also be applied to infinite state methods such as predicate abstraction, by means of various translations from first order to Boolean satisfiability problems. A final interesting avenue of research might be to consider how the basic SAT algorithms might be modified to improve their performance in terms of producing compact proofs, which would lead in turn to better abstractions.

References

1. F. Balarin and A. Sangiovanni-Vincentelli. An iterative approach to language containment. In *Computer Aided Verification (CAV'93)*, pages 29–40, 1993.
2. J. Baumgratner, A. Kuehlmann, and J. Abraham. Property checking via structural analysis. In *Computer-Aided Verification (CAV 2002)*, pages 151–165, 2002.
3. A. Biere, A. Cimatti, E. Clarke, and Y. Zhu. Symbolic model checking without BDDs. In *TACAS'99*, volume 1579 of *LNCS*, pages 193–207, 1999.

4. P. Bjesse, T. Leonard, and A. Mokkedem. Finding bugs in an alpha microprocessor using satisfiability solvers. In *Computer Aided Verification (CAV 2001)*, 2001.
5. E. M. Clarke, O. Grumberg, S. Jha, Y. Lu, and H. Veith. Counterexample-guided abstraction refinement. In *Computer Aided Verification*, pages 154–169, 2000.
6. E. M. Clarke, A. Gupta, J. Kukula, and O. Strichman. SAT based abstraction-refinement using ILP and machine learning techniques. In *Computer-Aided Verification (CAV 2002)*, pages 265–279, 2002.
7. F. Copty, L. Fix, F. R, E. Giunchiglia, G. Kamhi, A. Tacchella, and M. Y. Vardi. Benefits of bounded model checking in an industrial setting. In *Computer Aided Verification (CAV 2001)*, pages 436–453, 2001.
8. S. German. Personal communication.
9. S. G. Govindaraju and D. L. Dill. Counterexample-Guided choice of projections in approximate symbolic model checking. In *IEEE International Conference on Computer Aided Design (ICCAD 2000)*, pages 115–119, 2000.
10. J.R. Burch, E.M. Clarke, K.L. McMillan, D.L. Dill, and L.J. Hwang. Symbolic Model Checking: 10^{20} States and Beyond. In *Proceedings of the Fifth Annual IEEE Symposium on Logic in Computer Science*, pages 1–33, Washington, D.C., 1990. IEEE Computer Society Press.
11. O. Kupferman and M. Y. Vardi. Model checking of safety properties. *Formal Methods in System Design*, 19(3):291–314, 2001.
12. R. P. Kurshan. *Computer-Aided-Verification of Coordinating Processes.* Princeton University Press, 1994.
13. K. L. McMillan and N. Amla. Automatic abstraction without counterexamples. http://www-cad.eecs.berkeley.edu/~kenmcmil/papers, 2002.
14. M. W. Moskewicz, C. F. Madigan, Y. Z., L. Z., and S. Malik. Chaff: Engineering an efficient SAT solver. In *Design Automation Conference*, pages 530–535, 2001.
15. A. P. O. Lichtenstein. Checking that finite state concurrent programs satisfy their linear specification. In *POPL '85*, pages 97–107, 1985.
16. J. K. S. S. H. V. Pankaj Chauhan, Ed Clarke and D. Wang. Automated abstraction refinement for model checking large state spaces using sat based conflict analysis. In *Formal Methods in Computer Aided Design (FMCAD'02)*, November 2002.
17. D. Plaisted and S. Greenbaum. A structure preserving clause form translation. *Journal of Symbolic Computation*, 2:293–304, 1986.
18. H. Saïdi and S. Graf. Construction of abstract state graphs with PVS. In O. Grumberg, editor, *Computer-Aided Verification, CAV '97*, volume 1254, pages 72–83, Haifa, Israel, 1997. Springer-Verlag.
19. J. P. M. Silva and K. A. Sakallah. GRASP–a new search algorithm for satisfiability. In *Proceedings of the International Conference on Computer-Aided Design, November 1996*, 1996.
20. R. M. T. A. Henzinger, R. Jhala and G. Sutre. Lazy abstraction. In *Principles of Programming Languages (POPL 2002)*, 2002.
21. M. Vardi and P. Wolper. An automata-theoretic approach to automatic program verification. In *Logic in Computer Science (LICS '86)*, pages 322–331, 1986.
22. D. Wang, P.-H. Ho, J. Long, J. H. Kukula, Y. Zhu, H.-K. T. Ma, and R. Damiano. Formal property verification by abstraction refinement with formal, simulation and hybrid engines. In *Design Automation Conference*, pages 35–40, 2001.

Bounded Model Checking for Past LTL

Marco Benedetti and Alessandro Cimatti

Istituto per la Ricerca Scientifica e Tecnologica (IRST)
Via Sommarive 18, 38055 Povo, Trento, Italy
{benedetti,cimatti}@irst.itc.it

Abstract. The introduction of Past Operators enables to produce more natural formulation of a wide class of properties of reactive systems, compared to traditional pure future temporal logics. For this reason, past temporal logics are gaining increasing interest in several application areas, ranging from Requirement Engineering to Formal Verification and Model Checking. We show how SAT-based Bounded Model Checking techniques can be extended to deal with Linear Temporal Logics with Past Operators (PLTL). Though apparently simple, this task turns out to be absolutely non-trivial when tackled in its full generality. We discuss a bounded semantics for PLTL, we show that it is correct (and complete), and propose an encoding scheme able to cope with PLTL formulas. Finally, we implement the encoding in NuSMV, and present a first experimental evaluation of the approach.

1 Introduction

Temporal logics [14] are traditionally used in formal verification to predicate about the future evolutions of dynamic systems, both with a linear model or a branching model of time. The most typical application is the representation of the properties of dynamic systems within model checking tools. However, many interesting properties of dynamic systems are naturally formulated in a way that is not limited to the future evolution, but may refer to events in the past. For instance, properties such as "if a problem is diagnosed, then a failure must have occurred in the past" or "a grant is always issued as a consequence of a previous request" are not straightforward to express with future temporal operators. For this reason, temporal logics with operators that allow for direct reference of *past* events are being devoted increasing interest in formal verification for requirement engineering [8,15,18,23], and planning [2].

We are interested in extending state-of-the-art verification techniques developed for (future) temporal logics, to encompass the case of past operators. In particular, we are interested in extending to SAT-based Bounded Model Checking (BMC) techniques, originally introduced in [5], that are being widely accepted as an effective alternative to BDD-based symbolic methods [3,13,21,22]. In BMC, an existential model checking problem for Linear Temporal Logic is reduced to a problem of propositional satisfiability, and efficient SAT solvers are then used to tackle this problem. The idea behind BMC is to look for finitely represented paths. Two cases arise: Counterexamples are either finite prefixes of paths (in the case of safety properties), or exhibit an infinite lasso-shaped structure (in the case of liveness properties) based on the existence of a loopback.

H. Garavel and J. Hatcliff (Eds.): TACAS 2003, LNCS 2619, pp. 18–33, 2003.

We tackle the BMC problem for Linear Temporal Logic with Past Operators (PLTL). From a theoretical point of view, it is well known that past operators do not add expressive power w.r.t. pure-future LTL (as opposite to other temporal logics [19]). In fact, a result from [16] states that any PLTL formula can be re-written by only using future-time operators, even though a non-elementary blow-up (w.r.t. the size of the formula) stems from every known translation procedure. Even if the expressive power of the underlying logic is left unchanged, past operators are still very useful in practice, in that they bring additional expressivity from the perspective of end users. In fact, it is of paramount importance to provide formalisms that allow for an easy-to-understand and compact characterization of the desired behaviours of the system. Past operators help keeping specifications short and simple.

The problem of BMC for PLTL is rather simple in the case of finite prefixes, since the extent of the past is clear from any point. The construction becomes non-trivial when loops are taken into account, because infinite paths are presented by means of a loopback, and there is potentially more than one past for each point in the loop (at the loopback point we have to chose whether a "back to the future" step is to be taken).

Here we provide a full characterization of the problem of BMC for PLTL, define a bounded semantics, and show how to encode PLTL problems into propositional satisfiability instances. We implement the encoding into the NuSMV model checker, and provide some experimental evidence on the advantages of the approach.

This paper is structured as follows. Section 2 introduces the syntax and semantics of PLTL. In Section 3 we recall the basics ideas underlying Bounded Model Checking. Section 4 discusses the encoding of PLTL for bounded paths. In Section 5 we highlight the problems with loop paths, and present our solution. In Section 6 we discuss the implementation of these ideas within NuSMV and present a preliminary experimental comparison. Section 7 closes the paper with a few concluding remarks.

2 Linear Temporal Logic with Past Operators

In this paper we consider PLTL, i.e. the Linear Temporal Logic (LTL) augmented with past operators. The starting point is standard LTL, the formulas of which are constructed from propositional symbols by applying the future temporal operators $\mathbf{X}$ (next), $\mathbf{F}$ (future), $\mathbf{G}$ (globally), $\mathbf{U}$ (until), and $\mathbf{R}$ (releases), in addition to the usual boolean connectives. PLTL extends LTL by introducing the past operators $\mathbf{Y}$, $\mathbf{Z}$, $\mathbf{O}$, $\mathbf{H}$, and $\mathbf{S}$, which are the temporal duals of the future operators and allow us to express statements on the past time instants. The $\mathbf{Y}$ (for "$\mathbf{Y}esterday$") operator is the dual of $\mathbf{X}$ and refers to the *previous* time instant. At any non-initial time, $\mathbf{Y}f$ is true if and only f holds at the previous time instant. The $\mathbf{Z}$ (the name is just a mnemonic choice) operator is very similar to the $\mathbf{Y}$ operator, and it differs in the way the initial time instant is dealt with. At time zero, $\mathbf{Y}f$ is false, while $\mathbf{Z}f$ is true. The $\mathbf{O}$ (for "$\mathbf{O}nce$") operator is the dual of $\mathbf{F}$ (sometimes in the future), so that $\mathbf{O}f$ is true iff f is true at some past time instant (including the present time[1]). Likewise, $\mathbf{H}$ (for "$\mathbf{H}istorically$") is the past-time version of $\mathbf{G}$ (always in the future), so that $\mathbf{H}f$ is true iff f is always true in the past. The $\mathbf{S}$ (for "$\mathbf{S}ince$")

[1] We adopt a non-strict semantics for time operators, so that all temporal operators other than $\mathbf{X}$, $\mathbf{Y}$ and $\mathbf{Z}$ take into account the present time instant.

operator is the dual of $\mathbf{U}$ (until), so that $f\mathbf{S}g$ is true iff g holds somewhere in the past and f is true from then up to now. Finally, we have $f\mathbf{T}g = \neg(\neg f\mathbf{S}\neg g)$ ($\mathbf{T}$ is called the "$Trigger$" operator), exactly as in the future case we have $f\mathbf{R}g = \neg(\neg f\mathbf{U}\neg g)$. The syntax of PLTL is formally defined as follows.

Definition 1 (Syntax of PLTL). *The grammar for PLTL formulas is*

$$PLTL \ni f, g \doteq q \mid \neg f \mid f \circ^{\mathbf{B}} g \mid \circ^{\mathbf{F}}_{\mathbf{1}} f \mid f \circ^{\mathbf{F}}_{\mathbf{2}} g \mid \circ^{\mathbf{P}}_{\mathbf{1}} f \mid f \circ^{\mathbf{P}}_{\mathbf{2}} g$$

where $q \in \mathcal{A}$ and $\mathcal{A}$ is a set of atomic propositions, $\circ^{\mathbf{B}} \in \{\wedge, \vee\}$ stands for a boolean connective, $\circ^{\mathbf{F}}_{\mathbf{1}} \in \{\mathbf{X}, \mathbf{F}, \mathbf{G}\}$ and $\circ^{\mathbf{F}}_{\mathbf{2}} \in \{\mathbf{R}, \mathbf{U}\}$ are future temporal operators (unary and binary, respectively), and $\circ^{\mathbf{P}}_{\mathbf{1}} \in \{\mathbf{Y}, \mathbf{Z}, \mathbf{O}, \mathbf{H}\}$ and $\circ^{\mathbf{P}}_{\mathbf{2}} \in \{\mathbf{T}, \mathbf{S}\}$ are past temporal operators (unary and binary).

We write $f \rightarrow g$ for $\neg f \vee g$, and $f \leftrightarrow g$ for $(f \rightarrow g) \wedge (g \rightarrow f)$. As usual, Kripke structures are used to give the semantics of PLTL formulas.

Definition 2. *A* Kripke structure *is a tuple $M = \langle S, I, T, \ell \rangle$, where S is a finite set of states, $I \subseteq S$ is the set of initial states, $T \subseteq S \times S$ is a transition relation between states and $\ell : S \rightarrow 2^{\mathcal{A}}$ is a function which labels each state with a subset of the set $\mathcal{A}$ of atomic propositions.*

For an infinite sequence of states $\pi = (s_0, s_1, ...)$, we define $\pi(i) = s_i$, $\pi^i = (s_i, s_{i+1}, ...)$ and $\pi_{|i} = (0, 1, ..., s_i)$ for $i \in \mathbb{N}$, and we say that π is a *path* in M if $\pi(i) \rightarrow \pi(i+1)$ for all $i \in \mathbb{N}$, where $s \rightarrow t$ means that $\langle s, t \rangle \in T$. We also assume, without loss of generality, that the transition relation is *total*, i.e. that for every state $s \in S$, there exists at least one state $t \in S$ such that $\langle s, t \rangle \in T$. Infinite paths which are made up of a finite prefix u followed by a portion v repeated infinitely many times are called *loop paths*.

Definition 3. *A path π is a (k, l)-*loop*, with $l < k$, if $\pi(l) = \pi(k)$ and $\pi = u \cdot v^{\omega}$, where $u = (\pi(0), \ldots, \pi(l-1))$ and $v = (\pi(l), \ldots, \pi(k-1))$. We define the* period *of a (k, l)-loop as $k - l$. The successor of the i instant in a (k, l)-loop, $succ(i)$, is defined as $k + 1$ if $i < k - 1$, and l otherwise.*

In the following, unless specified otherwise, we assume that a given Kripke structure $M = \langle S, I, T, \ell \rangle$ is given. We also assume that different states in S have different labelings, i.e. for all $s, s' \in S$, $\ell(s) \neq \ell(s')$ iff $s \neq s'$. We use π to denote a (k, l)-loop (with $l < k$), p to denote the period $k - l$ of the loop, f and g to denote PLTL formulae, and q to denote propositions in $\mathcal{A}$. We write $[a, b)$ and $(a, b]$ to denote right-open and left-open intervals of integers, and (ab)use this notation by writing $[a, \infty)$ to denote the infinite set $\{i \in \mathbb{N}, i \geq a\}$.

Definition 4 (Semantics of PLTL). *Let M be a boolean Kripke structure, π be a path in M and f be a PLTL formula. Then $(\pi, i) \models f$ (f holds in π at time i) is inductively defined as follows.*

$$
\begin{array}{lll}
(\pi,i) \models q & \textit{iff} & q \in \ell(\pi(i)) \\
(\pi,i) \models \neg f & \textit{iff} & (\pi,i) \not\models f \\
(\pi,i) \models f \vee g & \textit{iff} & (\pi,i) \models f \textit{ or } (\pi,i) \models g \\
(\pi,i) \models f \wedge g & \textit{iff} & (\pi,i) \models f \textit{ and } (\pi,i) \models g
\end{array}
$$

$$
\begin{array}{lll}
(\pi,i) \models \mathbf{X}f & \textit{iff} & (\pi,i+1) \models f \\
(\pi,i) \models \mathbf{F}f & \textit{iff} & \exists j \in [i,\infty) \,.\, (\pi,j) \models f \\
(\pi,i) \models \mathbf{G}f & \textit{iff} & \forall j \in [i,\infty) \,.\, (\pi,j) \models f \\
(\pi,i) \models f\mathbf{U}g & \textit{iff} & \exists j \in [i,\infty) \,.\, ((\pi,j) \models g \textit{ and } \forall k \in [i,j) \,.\, (\pi,k) \models f) \\
(\pi,i) \models f\mathbf{R}g & \textit{iff} & \forall j \in [i,\infty) \,.\, ((\pi,j) \models g \textit{ or } \exists k \in [i,j) \,.\, (\pi,k) \models f)
\end{array}
$$

$$
\begin{array}{lll}
(\pi,i) \models \mathbf{Y}f & \textit{iff} & i > 0 \textit{ and } (\pi,i-1) \models f \\
(\pi,i) \models \mathbf{Z}f & \textit{iff} & i = 0 \textit{ or } (\pi,i-1) \models f \\
(\pi,i) \models \mathbf{O}f & \textit{iff} & \exists j \in [0,i] \,.\, (\pi,j) \models f \\
(\pi,i) \models \mathbf{H}f & \textit{iff} & \forall j \in [0,i] \,.\, (\pi,j) \models f \\
(\pi,i) \models f\mathbf{S}g & \textit{iff} & \exists j \in [0,i] \,.\, ((\pi,j) \models g \textit{ and } \forall k \in (j,i] \,.\, (\pi,k) \models f) \\
(\pi,i) \models f\mathbf{T}g & \textit{iff} & \forall j \in [0,i] \,.\, ((\pi,j) \models g \textit{ or } \exists k \in (j,i] \,.\, (\pi,k) \models f)\,.
\end{array}
$$

A formula f is valid on a path π in M (written $\pi \models f$) iff $(\pi,0) \models f$. A formula f is existentially *valid in M ($M \models \mathbf{E}f$) iff $\pi \models f$ for some path π in M. Conversely, f is* universally *valid in M ($M \models \mathbf{A}f$) iff $\pi \models f$ for every path π in M.*

Although the use of past operators in LTL does not introduce expressive power, it allows us to formalize properties more naturally. For instance, "*if a problem is diagnosed, then a failure must have previously occurred*" can be represented in PLTL as

$$\mathbf{G}(problem \rightarrow \mathbf{O}\ failure) \tag{1}$$

that is more natural than its pure-future counterpart $\neg(\neg failure \mathbf{U} problem)$. Similarly, the property "*grants are issued only upon requests*" can be easily specified as

$$\mathbf{G}(grant \rightarrow \mathbf{Y}(\neg grant\ \mathbf{S}\ request)) \tag{2}$$

compared to the corresponding pure-future translation

$$(request\,\mathbf{R}\,\neg grant)\ \wedge\ \mathbf{G}(grant \rightarrow (request \vee (\mathbf{X}(request\,\mathbf{R}\,\neg grant)))).$$

As for the pure future case, any formula in PLTL can be reduced to *Negation Normal Form* (NNF), where negation only occurs in front of atomic propositions. This linear time transformation is obtained by pushing the negation towards the leaves of the syntactic tree of the formula and exploiting the dualities between $\mathbf{F}$ and $\mathbf{G}$, $\mathbf{U}$ and $\mathbf{R}$, $\mathbf{O}$ and $\mathbf{H}$, and $\mathbf{S}$ and $\mathbf{T}$. The case of previous time is a bit tricky, since we have to rely on the two properties $\neg\mathbf{Y}f \equiv \mathbf{Z}\neg f$ and $\neg\mathbf{Z}f \equiv \mathbf{Y}\neg f$ which extend the single future-case rule $\neg\mathbf{X}f \equiv \mathbf{X}\neg f$ (we have both $\neg\mathbf{Y}f \not\equiv \mathbf{Y}\neg f$ and $\neg\mathbf{Z}f \not\equiv \mathbf{Z}\neg f$, because of their semantics at the initial time point). Notice that whenever we limit our attention to NNF formulas, the semantic rule $(\pi,i) \models \neg q$ iff $q \notin \ell(\pi(i))$ can be substituted for $(\pi,i) \models \neg f$ iff $(\pi,i) \not\models f$ in Definition 4, with no loss of completeness.

3 Bounded Model Checking

LTL Model Checking is interpreted universally, as the problem of checking whether a certain ϕ holds on all the paths of a Kripke structure M. The problem can be tackled by refutation, by checking the existential problem $M \models \mathbf{E}\neg\phi$. BMC tackles the *bounded* version of the existential problem $M \models_k \mathbf{E}\neg\phi$, by looking for witnesses of the violation within a certain bound k. When the k-bounded version of the problem is considered, only paths with at most k distinct transitions are taken into account. Such limited paths can be either finite (in which case they are finite prefixes of a path) or infinite (in which case paths exhibit a looping behaviour). Whichever the case, if a witness is found with bound k, then the property ϕ is violated in the general sense ($M \models \mathbf{E}\neg\phi$, so $M \not\models \mathbf{A}\phi$). Otherwise, if no violation is found, the bound can be increased until either a witness with a higher bound is found, or a limit bound is reached that enables to conclude that no violation exists, and thus $M \models \mathbf{A}\phi$. In the following, we focus on the existential model checking problem $M \models \mathbf{E}\neg\phi$, in particular on its bounded version $M \models_k \mathbf{E}\neg\phi$. This problem can be effectively reduced to a propositional formula [5] that is satisfiable if and only if there exists a violation of ϕ within bound k. The satisfiability of the propositional formula can then be effectively tackled by exploiting the impressive power of state-of-the-art propositional solvers (e.g. Chaff [20]). Since the seminal work in [5], the approach has been thoroughly investigated and extended [6,7,25,22,1], and its practical applicability has been widely recognized [13,3]. Given the finiteness of M, it is possible to define a k beyond which it is impossible to find a violation. The simple limits given in [6] are too large to be reached in practice, and therefore, BMC was initially proposed as a technique oriented to debugging. Improvements are proposed in [21] and in [3], where inductive reasoning and structural techniques allow the overapproximation of the bound for safety properties.

The encoding into propositional logic is based on the standard representation of Kripke structures used in symbolic model checking, where two sets of state variables — the current set V and the next set V' — are used to represent sets of states and transitions. In the following, we write $I(V)$ for a formula in the V variables representing the set of initial states of M, and $T(V, V')$ for the formula representing the transition relation of M. Given a bound k, the vector of state variables V is replicated $k+1$ times, thus obtaining the vectors $V^0, \ldots, V^k$. Intuitively, an assignment to V_i represents a value of the state vector after i transitions. We write q^i for the variable representing proposition q at time i. The propositional encoding $[\![M \models_k \mathbf{E}\neg\phi]\!]$ of the problem $M \models_k \mathbf{E}\neg\phi$, is a formula in the variables $V^0, \ldots, V^k$, structured as a binary conjunction. The first conjunct is the formula $[\![M]\!]_k \doteq I(V^0) \wedge T(V^0, V^1) \wedge \ldots \wedge T(V^{k-1}, V^k)$, where $T(V^i, V^{i+1})$ stands for the formula obtained by substituting the variables in V with the (corresponding) variables in V^i, and the variables in V' with the (corresponding) variables in V^{i+1}. A similar argument holds for $I(V^0)$. The formula $[\![M]\!]_k$ constrains the values of the state vectors at the different time instants in such a way that a satisfying assignment represents a path in the Kripke structure.

The second conjunct, in the following referred to as encoding of the formula with bound k, constrains the $k+1$ state vectors in such a way that their assignments characterize a path satisfying $\neg\phi$, so that a satisfying assignment to $[\![M \models_k \mathbf{E}\neg\phi]\!]$ represents a path in the Kripke structure that violates ϕ. The encoding of $\neg\phi$ with bound k has the form

$$[\![\neg\phi]\!]_k \vee \bigvee_{0\leq l<k} ({}_lL_k \wedge {}_l[\![\neg\phi]\!]_k).$$

The formula $[\![\neg\phi]\!]_k$ represents a violation of ϕ on a finite prefix of a path with k transitions, without assuming the existence of a loop. So, every finite sequence of states satisfying the conjunction of this formula with $[\![M]\!]_k$ can be extended to at least one infinite behaviour violating ϕ, thanks to the totality of the transition relation.

The formula ${}_l[\![\neg\phi]\!]_k$ relates to the construction of a particular counterexample of infinite length. In fact — depending on the structure of the formula being analyzed — there are cases where the production of a particular infinite behaviour is required to show that a property is violated. Although only a finite number of transitions and states are available in the encoding, this representation is possibly enough to represent an infinite path as well. In fact, the formula ${}_l[\![\neg\phi]\!]_k$ encodes — for each value of l — the existence of a counterexample for ϕ on a path structured as a (k,l)-loop. We produce such encoding with bound k assuming that there exists a loopback at a certain previous time instant $l<k$ and enforcing this loop condition by constraining the variable of the state vectors at l and k to be pairwise equivalent, by means of the condition ${}_lL_k \doteq \bigwedge_{q\in\mathcal{A}}(q^l \leftrightarrow q^k)$. (This definition of the loop condition slightly differs from the one given in [5], in the way the loopback point is identified. The new definition also allows us to interpret the bound k as the number of transitions uniformly for the cases with and without loop.)

4 Bounded Model Checking for PLTL without Loopbacks

We now consider the encoding for PLTL formulae in NNF. We first build $[\![\neg\phi]\!]_k$, under the hypothesis that the existence of a loopback is not enforced.

Definition 5 (Translation of a PLTL formula on a bounded path). *The translation of a PLTL formula on a path π with bound k at time point i (with $k,l,i\in\mathbb{N}$ and $l<k$, $i\leq k$) is a propositional formula inductively defined as follows.*

$$[\![q]\!]_k^i \doteq q^i \qquad [\![f\wedge g]\!]_k^i \doteq [\![f]\!]_k^i \wedge [\![g]\!]_k^i$$

$$[\![\neg q]\!]_k^i \doteq \neg q^i \qquad [\![f\vee g]\!]_k^i \doteq [\![f]\!]_k^i \vee [\![g]\!]_k^i$$

$$[\![\mathbf{X}f]\!]_k^i \doteq \begin{cases} \bot & i=k \\ [\![f]\!]_k^{i+1} & i<k \end{cases}$$

$$[\![\mathbf{F}f]\!]_k^i \doteq \bigvee_{j\in[i,k]} [\![f]\!]_k^j \qquad [\![f\mathbf{U}g]\!]_k^i \doteq \bigvee_{j\in[i,k]} \left([\![g]\!]_k^j \wedge \bigwedge_{h\in[i,j)} [\![f]\!]_k^h\right)$$

$$[\![\mathbf{G}f]\!]_k^i \doteq \bot \qquad [\![f\mathbf{R}g]\!]_k^i \doteq \bigwedge_{j\in[i,k]} \left([\![g]\!]_k^j \vee \bigvee_{h\in[i,j)} [\![f]\!]_k^h\right)$$

$$[\![\mathbf{Y}f]\!]_k^i \doteq \begin{cases} \bot & i=0 \\ [\![f]\!]_k^{i-1} & i>0 \end{cases} \qquad [\![\mathbf{Z}f]\!]_k^i \doteq \begin{cases} \top & i=0 \\ [\![f]\!]_k^{i-1} & i>0 \end{cases}$$

$$[\![\mathbf{O}f]\!]_k^i \doteq \bigvee_{j\in[0,i]} [\![f]\!]_k^j \qquad [\![f\mathbf{S}g]\!]_k^i \doteq \bigvee_{j\in[0,i]} \left([\![g]\!]_k^j \wedge \bigwedge_{h\in(j,i]} [\![f]\!]_k^h\right)$$

$$[\![\mathbf{H}f]\!]_k^i \doteq \bigwedge_{j\in[0,i]} [\![f]\!]_k^j \qquad [\![f\mathbf{T}g]\!]_k^i \doteq \bigwedge_{j\in[0,i]} \left([\![g]\!]_k^j \vee \bigvee_{h\in(j,i]} [\![f]\!]_k^h\right)$$

The translation $[\![f]\!]_k$ of a PLTL formula f on a path π with bound k is defined as $[\![f]\!]_k^0$.

The index i in $[\![f]\!]_k^i$ represent the time instant at which the formula is being evaluated. The structural rules reflect quite closely the compositional semantics presented in Definition 4. At each time point – recursively traversing the structure of the formula – the quantifications over time points can be unwound into boolean connectives, over the finite set of time points of interest. For instance, in the case of the $\mathbf{F}f$, the encoding at point i results in a disjunction over the time points from i to k of the encoding of f: in fact, $\mathbf{F}f$ holds at i iff we can produce a point in the (bounded) future such that f can be shown to hold in it. Likewise, we can show that $\mathbf{X}f$ holds at i if we can produce a future point where f holds. For this reason, $\mathbf{X}f$ is always false at k, since there is no "visible" future. The case of $\mathbf{G}f$ always reduces to $\bot$, because the above encoding can not show an infinite sequence of f. The cases for $\mathbf{U}$ and $\mathbf{R}$ follow Definition 4 as well.

Let us consider the case of past temporal operators. The formula $\mathbf{Y}f$ is encoded at i as the encoding of f at the previous time step $i-1$, if i is not initial, otherwise it reduces to $\bot$. The encoding for $\mathbf{Z}f$ only differs at the initial time point. The case of $\mathbf{O}f$ behaves similarly to $\mathbf{F}f$: we need to show that there is a point between 0 and i where f holds. The case for $\mathbf{H}f$ differs from the future case $\mathbf{G}f$ in that the past is finite. Therefore, it is enough to show that f holds in all the time points from i down to 0 to conclude that $\mathbf{H}f$ holds at time point i. Similar arguments apply to the case of $\mathbf{S}$ and $\mathbf{T}$.

5 Bounded Model Checking for PLTL with Loopbacks

We now tackle the problem of BMC for PLTL in its generality, by widening the scope of the encoding presented in the previous section to the case when the existence of a loopback at time l is assumed. We aim at finitely encoding into a formula ${}_l[\![f]\!]_k$ the semantics of a PLTL formula f on an infinite path with a cyclic structure.

5.1 The Problem

Consider the following simple example, depicted in Figure 1 (above), where a deterministic counter starts at 0, then increases its value until 5, and then restarts over from 2. The path $01 \cdot (2345)^\omega$ can be seen as a (6,2)-loop. In the future case, the encoding of a specification is based on the idea that, for every time in the encoding, exactly one successor time exists. To reach the successor of the time instant 5, we loop back to time 2. The encoding is formed structurally by analyzing the subformulae of the specification in the loop between k and l. The future LTL formulae enjoy the following properties: first, the evaluation of every pure-future LTL formula f at time i *only depends on time instants not preceding* i, i.e. only depends on the suffix π^i; second, $\pi^i = \pi^j$ for any two indexes i, j at the same position in the loop (i.e., in the same set $T_m \doteq \{m + np, n \in \mathbb{N}\}$, with $m \in [l, k)$). This is the reason the pure-future encoding works fine: the evaluation of a formula f on a (k, l)-loop π at each time point $i \geq k$ can be traced back to the evaluation of the same formula at a particular time point $i' < k$. In particular, the infinitely many time points in each set T_m on a (k, l)-loop are *equivalent*, in the sense that for every $m \in [l, k)$ and every $i, j \in T_m$, it is $(\pi, i) \models f$ iff $(\pi, j) \models f$.

Unfortunately, the idea of a simple lifting of the pure future construction of [5] to the past case breaks down immediately, as past formulas do not enjoy the above properties.

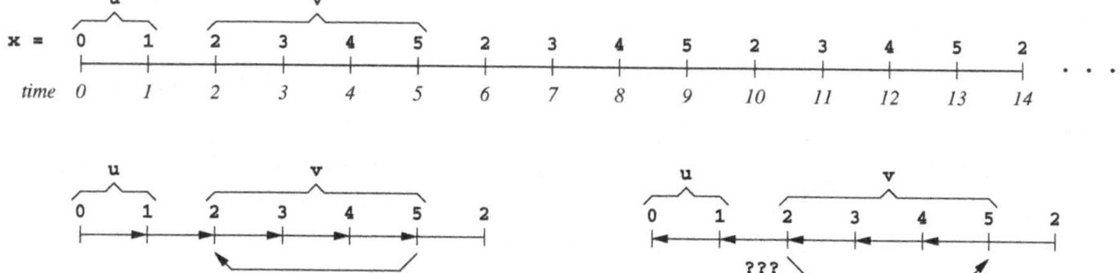

Fig. 1. An example of (6,2)-loop

First, when we progress backward in the past, at the point of loop back we have two possible predecessor points. In the case of the example, in order to encode $\mathbf{Y}(q)$ at point 2, we have to choose between progressing back through the loopback from point 2 to point 5 or moving to time 1 (see figure 1). Furthermore, we notice that this choice comes into play since the evaluation of a formula may depend on the past sequence $\pi_{|i}$, and $\pi_{|i} \neq \pi_{|j}$ whenever $i \neq j$. Consider for instance the formula

$$\mathbf{F}(x = 2 \wedge \mathbf{O}(x = 3 \wedge \mathbf{O}(x = 4 \wedge \mathbf{O}(x = 5))))$$

expressing that it is possible to reach a point where the values $\{2, 3, 4, 5\}$ of the counter occur in increasing order *in the past*. In the unbounded case, we need to get to the fourth occurrence of 2 in the path, i.e. at time 14, in order to show that $(x = 2 \wedge \mathbf{O}(x = 3 \wedge \mathbf{O}(x = 4 \wedge \mathbf{O}(x = 5))))$ holds. If we only look at the third occurrence (time 10), we can find previous points where the counter has values 3 and 4, but not 5. These issues are clearly relevant, since we are working on a bounded path representation. In order for the argument of $\mathbf{F}$ to evaluate to true, we will have to assume that we are far enough from the initial state, in order to progress in the past through the loop back a sufficient number of times. On the other hand, always choosing to progress in the past to the k-th step is not a viable option, since otherwise the encoding procedure might not terminate.

5.2 The Solution: Intuition

In order to propose a solution to this problem, we note that the evaluation of the formula $(x = 2 \wedge \mathbf{O}(x = 3 \wedge \mathbf{O}(x = 4 \wedge \mathbf{O}(x = 5))))$ is true in all the occurrences of $x = 2$ after the fourth, i.e. all the time points of the form $14 + 4i$. This is an example of the fact that a formula with past operators is able to discriminate its past, (i.e. among the number of times a loop has been traversed forwards), but only to a limited extent. Therefore, from a certain point on, it is useless to take into account more unrolls of the loop (i.e. to progress in the past by jumping from l to $k - 1$). The idea underlying our solution is to identify sets of points in which the evaluation stabilizes, and to deal with them at once. This is viable since the ability to refer to the past of a PLTL formula f is somehow predictable, once its syntactic structure is known. The key idea here is that every formula has a finite discriminating power for events in the past. So, when evaluated sufficiently far from the origin of time, a formula becomes unable to distinguish its past sequence from infinitely many other past sequences with a "similar" behaviour. The idea is then to collapse the undistinguishable versions of the past together into the same equivalence class. As we will see, only a finite number of such equivalence classes exists.

5.3 The Solution: Formalization

The intuition is captured by the notion of Past Temporal Horizon (PTH). Given a specific path, the PTH of a formula is the *minimal* number of loop unrolls after which the behaviour of the formula with respect to its truth value on π *stabilizes*, i.e. starts repeating in a cyclic way, according to the loop in the path. The PTH of a formula also provides a measure of the *maximal* amount of past a formula is able to take into account in a significant way along cyclic paths.

Definition 6. *The* past temporal horizon *(PTH)* $\tau_{{}_l\pi_k}(f)$ *of a PLTL formula* f *with respect to a* (k,l)*-loop* π *(with period* $p = k - l$*) is the smallest value* $n \in \mathbb{N}$ *such that*

$$\forall i \in [l,k) \quad ((\pi, i+np) \models f \text{ iff } (\forall n' > n\, (\pi, i+n'p) \models f)).$$

We can abstract away the dependence of the PTH on a specific path, and give a notion of PTH which is *inherent* to the behaviour of a PLTL formula on a cyclic path, no matter which particular path is considered, nor even the structure of the loop.

Definition 7 (Past temporal horizon of a PLTL formula). *The* past temporal horizon $\tau(f)$ *of a PLTL formula* f *is defined as* $\tau(f) \doteq \max_{\pi \in \Pi} \tau_{{}_l\pi_k}(f)$ *where* Π *is the set of all the paths which are (k,l)-loops for some* $k > l \geq 0$.

The following theorem shows that a PLTL formula is guaranteed to have a finite PTH, and that an upper bound can be found based on its syntactic structure.

Theorem 1. *Let* f *and* g *be PLTL formulas. Then, it holds that:*

- $\tau(q) = 0$, *when* $q \in \mathcal{A}$ *and* $\tau(f) = \tau(\neg f)$;
- $\tau(\circ f) \leq \tau(f)$, *when* $\circ \in \{\mathbf{X}, \mathbf{F}, \mathbf{G}\}$
- $\tau(\circ f) \leq \tau(f) + 1$, *when* $\circ \in \{\mathbf{Z}, \mathbf{Y}, \mathbf{O}, \mathbf{H}\}$;
- $\tau(f \circ g) \leq \max(\tau(f), \tau(g))$, *when* $\circ \in \{\wedge, \vee, \mathbf{U}, \mathbf{R}\}$;
- $\tau(f \circ g) \leq \max(\tau(f), \tau(g)) + 1$, *when* $\circ \in \{\mathbf{S}, \mathbf{T}\}$;

This result (proved in [4] together with all the others) makes precise an unsurprising property of PLTL formulas: regardless of the particular path π, the ability of a formula in referring to the past along looping paths is bounded by its structural complexity. Put another way: when a formula is evaluated along a cyclic path, its truth value eventually starts looping as well. A delay in general exists between the starting points of these looping behaviours (the formula starts looping later than the path). An upper bound to this delay can be computed as a function of the syntactic structure of the formula itself.

The intuition behind the PTH is that it specifies the least number of times it is necessary to traverse the loop backwards before safely progressing towards the origin of time. In the following we provide the formal notions to deal with the idea of repeated unrolling of the (k,l)-loop. The intuition underlying the concept of *projection* is that each formula can be "safely" encoded on a finite representation (such as a (k,l)-loop) by suitably projecting the possibly infinite time interval the formula refers to onto its finite counterpart. The key difference with respect to the pure-future case, is that the projection also depends on the formula, not only on the shape of the path.

Definition 8. *We call* $\text{LB}(n) \doteq l + np$ *the n-th left border of* π, $\text{RB}(n) \doteq k + np$ *the n-th right border of* π, *and the interval* $\mathcal{M}(n) \doteq [0, \text{RB}(n))$ *the* n-th main domain *of a* (k,l)*-loop. Let* $i \in \mathbb{N}$. *The projection of the point* i *in the n-th main domain of a* (k,l)*-loop is* $\rho_n(i)$, *defined as*

$$\rho_n(i) \doteq \begin{cases} i & i < \text{RB}(n) \\ \rho_n(i-p) & otherwise \end{cases}$$

Let $a, b \in \mathbb{N}$, *with* $a < b$. *The projection of the interval* $[a,b)$ *on the n-th main domain of a* (k,l)*-loop is*

$$\rho_n([a,b)) \doteq \{\rho_n(i) : i \in [a,b)\}.$$

We call $\text{LB}(f) \doteq \text{LB}(\tau(f))$ *and* $\text{RB}(f) \doteq \text{RB}(\tau(f))$ *the left and right borders of* f, *respectively, and* $\mathcal{M}(f) \doteq \mathcal{M}(\tau(f))$ *the main domain of* f. *The projections of the point* i *and of the interval* $[a,b)$ *onto the main domain of* f *are defined as* $\rho_f(i) \doteq \rho_{\tau(f)}(i)$ *and* $\rho_f([a,b)) \doteq \rho_{\tau(f)}([a,b))$ *respectively.*

While it is clear that the projection of a point onto the main domain of a function is still a point, it is not immediately evident what an interval is projected onto, as the projection of intervals is implicitly defined in terms of the projection function for time points. It is possible to explicitly characterize the resulting set of points as follows.

Lemma 1. *For an open interval* $[a,b)$, *it is*

$$\rho_n([a,b)) \doteq \begin{cases} \emptyset & \text{if } a = b, \text{ else} \\ [a,b) & \text{if } b < \text{RB}(n), \text{ else} \\ [\min(a, \text{LB}(n)), \text{RB}(n)) & \text{if } b - a \geq p, \text{ else} \\ [\rho_n(a), \rho_n(b)) & \text{if } \rho_n(a) < \rho_n(b), \text{ else} \\ [\rho_n(a), \text{RB}(n)) \cup [\text{LB}(n), \rho_n(b)) \end{cases}$$

This lemma shows that the projection of an interval is an interval in all but one case. It could seem that the conjunction of intervals in the last row of this lemma gives rise to a fragmentation of the interval-based representation. However, this apparent fragmentation disappears if we admit *extended intervals* of the form $[a,b)$ where b is possibly less than a (or even it is equal to ∞). With this position, we can re-write the last two rows of Lemma 1 in a single rule $[\rho_n(a), \rho_n(b))$ and generalize the notion of projection in such a way that the projection of an extended interval is always an extended interval.

Definition 9 (Extended projection). *Let* $[a,b)$ *be an extended interval. We define the* extended projection *of* $[a,b)$ *onto the n-th main domain of a* (k,l)*-loop as follows*

$$\rho^*_n([a,b)) \doteq \begin{cases} \rho^*_n([a, \max(a, \text{RB}(n)) + p)) & b = \infty \\ \rho^*_n([a, b+p)) & b < a \\ \rho_n([a,b)) & \text{otherwise} \end{cases}$$

As before, we pose $\rho^*_f([a,b)) \doteq \rho^*_{\tau(f)}([a,b))$. The intuitive meaning of the projection $\rho^*_f([a,b))$ of the interval $[a,b)$ w.r.t. f, is that the finite set of time instants $\rho^*_f([a,b)) \subseteq \mathcal{M}(f)$ is the equivalent counterpart along cyclic paths of the (possibly infinite) interval $[a,b)$ for f. For example, one might wonder whether f is true at some time point in the (possibly infinite) interval $[a,b)$ of a loop path π. This happens if and only if f is true at some time point in the (always finite) interval $\rho^*_f([a,b))$.

Theorem 2. *For any PLTL formula f, any (k,l)-loop π, and any extended interval $[a,b)$, a point $i \in [a,b)$ such that $(\pi,i) \models f$ exists iff a point $i' \in \rho^*_f([a,b))$ exists such that $(\pi,i') \models f$.*

This argument can be specialized to the case when the interval contains only one point, by saying that on every (k,l)-loop path π and for every $i \geq 0$, $(\pi,i) \models f$ iff $(\pi,\rho_f(i)) \models f$. We now define the translation of a PLTL formula on a (k,l)-loop.

Definition 10 (Translation of a PLTL formula on a (k,l)-loop). *The translation of a PLTL formula on a (k,l)-loop π at time point i (with $k,l,i \in \mathbb{N}$ and $0 \leq l < k$) is a propositional formula inductively defined as follows.*

$$
\begin{aligned}
{}_l[\![q]\!]^i_k &\doteq q^{\rho_0(i)} & {}_l[\![f \wedge g]\!]^i_k &\doteq {}_l[\![f]\!]^{\rho_f(i)}_k \wedge {}_l[\![g]\!]^{\rho_g(i)}_k \\
{}_l[\![\neg q]\!]^i_k &\doteq \neg q^{\rho_0(i)} & {}_l[\![f \vee g]\!]^i_k &\doteq {}_l[\![f]\!]^{\rho_f(i)}_k \vee {}_l[\![g]\!]^{\rho_g(i)}_k \\
{}_l[\![\mathbf{X}f]\!]^i_k &\doteq {}_l[\![f]\!]^{\rho_f(i+1)}_k
\end{aligned}
$$

$$
\begin{aligned}
{}_l[\![\mathbf{F}f]\!]^i_k &\doteq \textstyle\bigvee_{j\in\rho^*_f([i,\infty))} {}_l[\![f]\!]^j_k \qquad {}_l[\![\mathbf{G}f]\!]^i_k \doteq \textstyle\bigwedge_{j\in\rho^*_f([i,\infty))} {}_l[\![f]\!]^j_k \\
{}_l[\![f\mathbf{U}g]\!]^i_k &\doteq \textstyle\bigvee_{j\in\rho^*_g([i,\infty))} \left({}_l[\![g]\!]^j_k \wedge \bigwedge_{h\in\rho^*_f([i,j))} {}_l[\![f]\!]^h_k \right) \\
{}_l[\![f\mathbf{R}g]\!]^i_k &\doteq \textstyle\bigwedge_{j\in\rho^*_g([i,\infty))} \left({}_l[\![g]\!]^j_k \vee \bigvee_{h\in\rho^*_f([i,j))} {}_l[\![f]\!]^h_k \right) \\
{}_l[\![\mathbf{Y}f]\!]^i_k &\doteq \begin{cases} \bot & i=0 \\ {}_l[\![f]\!]^{\rho_f(i-1)}_k & i>0 \end{cases} \qquad {}_l[\![\mathbf{Z}f]\!]^i_k \doteq \begin{cases} \top & i=0 \\ {}_l[\![f]\!]^{\rho_f(i-1)}_k & i>0 \end{cases}
\end{aligned}
$$

$$
\begin{aligned}
{}_l[\![\mathbf{O}f]\!]^i_k &\doteq \textstyle\bigvee_{j\in\rho^*_f([0,i])} {}_l[\![f]\!]^j_k \qquad {}_l[\![\mathbf{H}f]\!]^i_k \doteq \textstyle\bigwedge_{j\in\rho^*_f([0,i])} {}_l[\![f]\!]^j_k \\
{}_l[\![f\mathbf{S}g]\!]^i_k &\doteq \textstyle\bigvee_{j\in\rho^*_g([0,i])} \left({}_l[\![g]\!]^j_k \wedge \bigwedge_{h\in\rho^*_f((j,i])} {}_l[\![f]\!]^h_k \right) \\
{}_l[\![f\mathbf{T}g]\!]^i_k &\doteq \textstyle\bigwedge_{j\in\rho^*_g([0,i])} \left({}_l[\![g]\!]^j_k \vee \bigvee_{h\in\rho^*_f((j,i])} {}_l[\![f]\!]^h_k \right)
\end{aligned}
$$

The translation of a PLTL formula f on a (k,l)-loop is defined as ${}_l[\![f]\!]_k \doteq {}_l[\![f]\!]^0_k$.

Notice how the encoding of each operator closely resembles the semantics of that operator (Definition 4). For example, the encoding rule ${}_l[\![\mathbf{F}f]\!]^i_k \doteq \bigvee_{j\in\rho^*_f([i,\infty))} {}_l[\![f]\!]^j_k$ is a quite straightforward interpretation of the semantic rule $(\pi,i) \models \mathbf{F}f$ iff $\exists j \in [i,\infty)\,.\,(\pi,j) \models f$, thanks to the introduction of the projection operator, which maps infinite sets of time points into equivalent but finite ones and shrinks finite intervals as much as possible, according to the upper bound given in Lemma 2.

Differently from the encoding for pure-future LTL given in [5], the above construction allows to evaluate the encoding of subformulas at time points greater than k. However, it is easy to see that no sub-formula f is encoded outside its main domain $\mathcal{M}(f)$. Furthermore, the encoding of any PLTL formula always results in a propositional formula with variables in $\{q^i\,.\,q \in \mathcal{A}, i \in [0,k)\}$, like in the pure-future case. While the encoding goes on from the root of the syntactic tree of the formula towards its leaves, the main domain of subformulas encountered along the way shrinks (the nesting depth of past operators cannot increase moving from a formula to its subformulas). When pure-future subformulas are reached the main domain is just $[0,k)$, and this is guaranteed to happen, since propositional leaves are pure-future formulas.

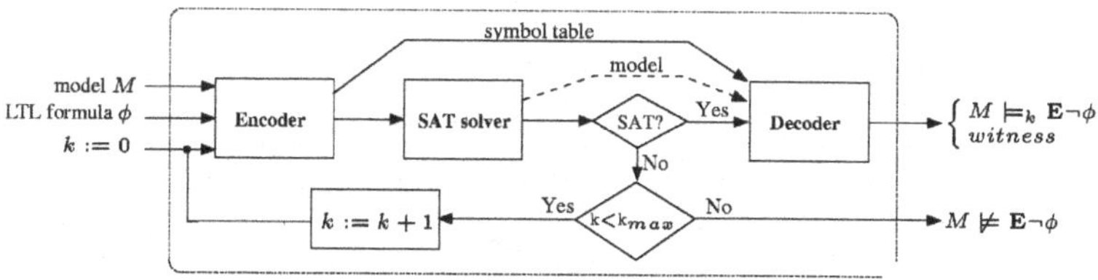

Fig. 2. An high-level view of the Bounded Model Checker module in NuSMV

For example, in the case of the formula $\mathbf{F}(x = 2 \wedge \mathbf{O}(x = 3 \wedge \mathbf{O}(x = 4 \wedge \mathbf{O}(x = 5))))$ presented in Section 5.1, the encoding is able to perform a "virtual" unrolling of the (6,2)-path up to time 14 with no necessity of introducing more than 7 different states in the propositional encoding. The loop is virtually unrolled three times w.r.t. the subformula $x = 2 \wedge \mathbf{O}(x = 3 \wedge \mathbf{O}(x = 4 \wedge \mathbf{O}(x = 5))$, because this subformula has PTH equal to 3. The example confirms that this sufficies (and is necessary) to reach time 14 where the formula first evaluates to true. Inner subformulas have smaller and smaller virtual unrolling, as the PTH decreases. For example, though the sub-formula $(x = 4 \wedge \mathbf{O}(x = 5))$ needs to be evaluated up to time 13, it is explicitly evaluated only up to time 9 (PTH=1), and this suffices to catch all the variety of its behaviour, also comprising time 8 when the formula is true for the first of infinitely many subsequent times. The encoding is guaranteed to be correct by the following result.

Theorem 3. *For any PLTL formula f, a (k,l)-loop path π in M such that $\pi \models f$ exists iff $[\![M]\!]_k \wedge {}_lL_k \wedge {}_l[\![f]\!]_k$ is satisfiable.*

The computation of the PTH of a formula is not trivial in general. Therefore, we over-approximate it by means of the nesting depth of past operators in the formula.

Definition 11 (Past operator depth). *The* past operator depth $\delta(f)$ *of a PLTL formula f is defined as follows*

- $\delta(q) = 0$*, when* $q \in \mathcal{A}$*, and* $\delta(\circ f) = \delta(f)$*, when* $\circ \in \{\neg, \mathbf{X}, \mathbf{F}, \mathbf{G}\}$
- $\delta(f \circ g) = \max(\delta(f), \delta(g))$*, when* $\circ \in \{\wedge, \vee, \mathbf{U}, \mathbf{R}\}$*;*
- $\delta(\circ f) = \delta(f) + 1$*, when* $\circ \in \{\mathbf{Z}, \mathbf{Y}, \mathbf{O}, \mathbf{H}\}$*;*
- $\delta(f \circ g) = \max(\tau(f), \tau(g)) + 1$*, when* $\circ \in \{\mathbf{S}, \mathbf{T}\}$*;*

By comparing Theorem 1 and Definition 11, we obtain the following result, that guarantees the correctness of the resulting construction.

Lemma 2. *For any PLTL formula f, it is $\tau(f) \leq \delta(f)$.*

6 Implementation and Evaluation

We implemented our PLTL bounded model checking algorithms within NuSMV [10,11, 9], a state-of-the-art symbolic model checker designed as an open architecture integrating BDD-based and SAT-based model checking on the whole input language, and such that as many functionalities as possible are independent of the particular model checking engine.

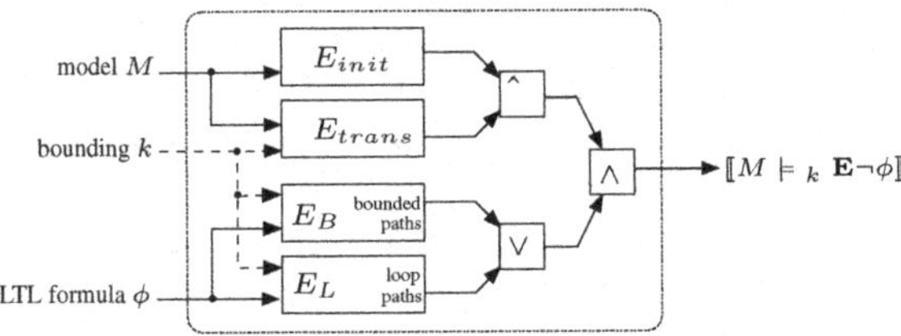

Fig. 3. The Encoder block, expanded from Figure 2

NuSMV has been used for the verification of industrial designs, as a core for custom verification tools, and as a testbed for formal verification techniques. We benefit from its pre-processing abilities, that include parsing, flattening, boolean encoding, predicate encoding and cone of influence reduction (see [11] for details).

The BMC module was extended (see Figure 2) by enlarging its input language and implementing the new encoding. Only the encoder needs changes (see Figure 3), in particular within the sub-encoders E_B (for bounded paths, see Section 4) and E_L (for loop paths, see Section 5). Formulas represented as RBCs are produced, then converted into CNF and passed to the SAT solver. The optimizing techniques used within the RBC package, the CNF-ization procedure, the interface to the solver, the trace reconstruction sub-system, and the control system are inherited from the existing architecture.

We cannot take into account other systems to evaluate the effectiveness of our approach with an experimental comparison, as NuSMV appears to be the first system featuring past LTL operators: None of the available generic model checkers encompasses past operators[2], neither in a direct way (e.g.: like we do) nor in an indirect way (e.g.: by somehow pre-processing PLTL specifications). So, we push our analysis of past operators beyond the presented results, by preliminary investigating two alternative strategies for handling LTL and past operators within a BMC framework.

LTL model checking can be implemented via reduction to CTL model checking with fairness constraints, along the lines suggested in [12] for a BDD-based framework. The approach composes the model with the observer automaton [24] $M_{\neg\phi}$ corresponding to the negation of the specification, thus looking for unwanted behaviours of the model. If a fair path in the model-automaton composition is found, then the property is violated, and diagnostic information can be returned. This construction was recently extended to allow full-fledged BDD-based PLTL reasoning within NuSMV. We modified this construction by exploiting a SAT solver to look for fair paths. Two resulting scenarios can then be compared: in one case, the encoding block in Figure 3 is presented with the original model M and PLTL specification ϕ (encoded as explained in the previous sections). In the other case, the encoding block is presented with the composition of $M_{\neg\phi}$ with M, and the BMC machinery just searches for a fair path.

We experimented with these two alternatives. Figure 4 shows a sample comparison on the models "queue" and "syncarb5", taken from the standard NuSMV distribution. Safety properties of the form $\mathbf{G}\phi$ (known to be true) are considered. None of the two approaches is dominant, even in case of pure-future specifications only: A tradeoff seems to exist

[2] It is worth mentioning that past operators are sometimes used by specialized model checkers (such as BRUTUS[17], which only works in the verification of security protocols).

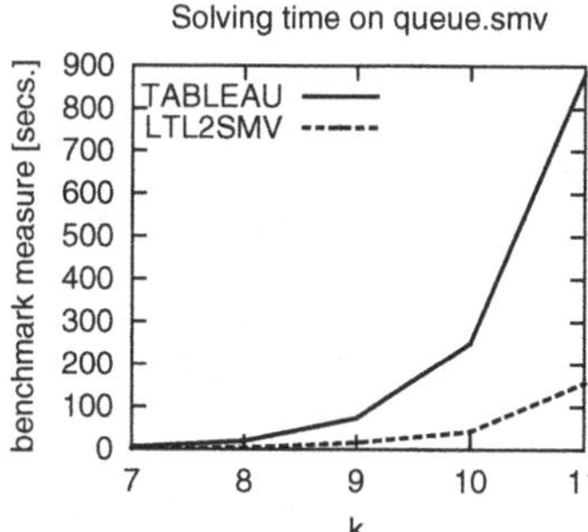

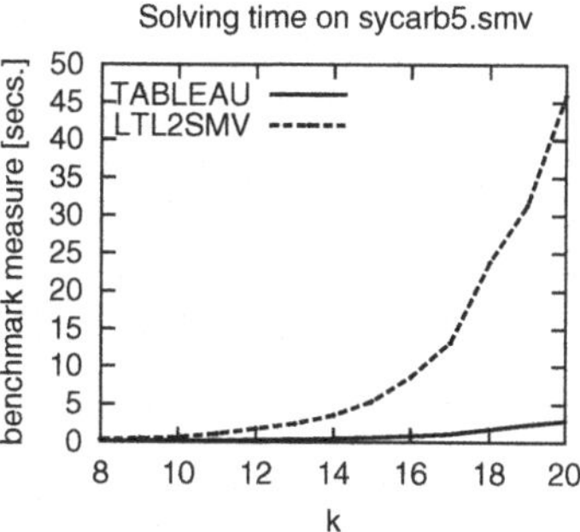

Fig. 4. Two instances showing that none of the approaches is dominating

between the additional variables introduced with the model-automaton based approach to take into account the status of the observer, and the additional number of clauses produced by the implicit unwinding of loops in the other case. However, preliminary results suggest that the tableau-based construction often outperforms the automaton-based one, despite some cases where the opposite happens. Even though such tradeoff deserves further investigation, interesting features of the encoding for past operators can still be significantly evaluated. At least two advantages come from our approach w.r.t. the automaton-based one: first, the search for a fair path can lead to a needlessly long counterexample. Second, the virtual unrolling of loop paths is potentially able to discover counterexample (far) before the actual time the property fails to be true. In both cases, the time spent solving unnecessary instances is saved. As a very simple example of this advantage, we present the sender/receiver model "abp4"from the NuSMV distribution, checked against the false property:

$\mathbf{G}$(`sender.state=waitForAck` $\rightarrow$ $\mathbf{YH}$ `sender.state`$\neq$`waitForAck`).

Our encoding is able to produce a counterexample as soon as a wait state appears in the middle of the cyclic portion of a loop path, by unrolling in a virtual manner such a cyclic portion. Conversely, the observer automaton is forced to explicitly reach the second occurrence of the wait state. Figure 5 shows how this difference can be very significant also for not so shorter counterexamples: The automaton based approach finds a counterexample at length 19, while 16 is sufficient for the tableau. This leads to a clear advantage in terms of time, as the growth of the solving time is usually dominant.

The number of virtual unrolls necessary to exhibit a counterexample increase as the PLTL formula gets more complex, and the automaton-based approach is forced to reach further and further length to find a solution. Our encoding always "foresees" the consequences of a looping behaviour up the necessary point and never needs to explicitly produce and solve additional instances. The duty paid for this advantage is that more time is spent both on producing and on solving an instance of size k w.r.t. the analogous k-sized instance of the model-based approach. The additional solving time is usually very small (see Figure 5). The additional time for generation is eventually overcome by the solving time, even if for very small models it may be sensitive. Figure 5 shows that the additional generation time is completely negligible in our example.

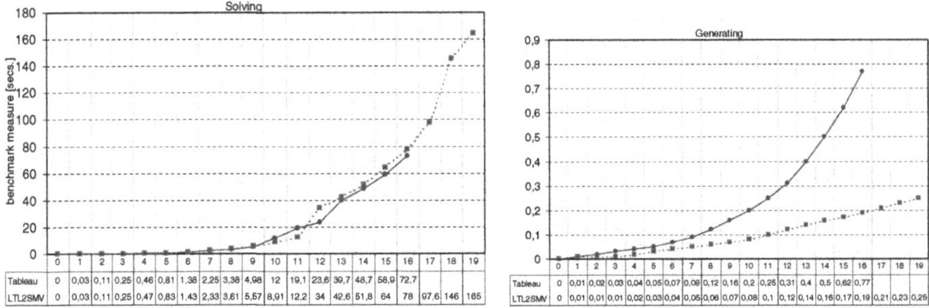

	0	1	2	3	4	5	6	7	8	9	10	11	12	13	14	15	16	17	18	19
Tableau	0	0,03	0,11	0,25	0,46	0,81	1,38	2,25	3,38	4,98	12	19,1	23,6	39,7	48,7	58,9	72,7			
LTL2SMV	0	0,03	0,11	0,25	0,47	0,83	1.43	2,33	3,61	5,57	8,91	12,2	34	42,6	51,8	64	78	97,6	146	165

	0	1	2	3	4	5	6	7	8	9	10	11	12	13	14	15	16	17	18	19
Tableau	0	0,01	0,02	0,03	0,04	0,05	0,07	0,09	0,12	0,16	0,2	0,25	0,31	0,4	0,5	0,62	0,77			
LTL2SMV	0	0,01	0,01	0,01	0,02	0,03	0,04	0,05	0,06	0,07	0,08	0,1	0,12	0,14	0,16	0,17	0,19	0,21	0,23	0,25

Fig. 5. The same instance dealt with in two ways

Though very preliminary, this experimental evaluation suggests that in addition to the increased complexity of the model, the unbounded approach may also require longer counterexamples, which in turn makes it necessary to solve harder SAT problems.

7 Conclusions

We tackle the problem of extending BMC to the case of LTL with Past Operators. We have shown that the task is not trivial in the case of loops: when traversing a path backward, we have to choose whether to proceed towards the origin or to jump "back to the future". We have provided a formal account that allows us to solve the problem by projecting infinite sets of points into equivalent finite ones. Then, we have provided an effective tableau construction that encodes full PLTL into propositional formulae, and we showed that it is correct and complete. The formal treatment is the basis for the implementation of the technique in the NuSMV symbolic model checker. A preliminary experimental evaluation was discussed. In the future, we plan to extend and optimize the construction, and encompass verification problems in Requirement Engineering.

Acknowledgements. We thank Marco Pistore for his invaluable help in the definition of the framework and in the integration with NuSMV, and Dan Sheridan for reading early versions of the paper.

References

1. P. A. Abdullah, P. Bjesse, and N. Een. Symbolic Reachability Analysis based on SAT-Solvers. In *Sixth Int.nl Conf. on Tools and Algorithms for the Construction and Analysis of Systems (TACAS'00)*, 2000.
2. F. Bacchus and F. Kabanza. Control Strategies in Planning. In *Proc. of the AAAI Spring Symposium Series on Extending Theories of Action: Formal Theory and Practical Applications*, pages 5–10, Stanford University, CA, USA, March 1995.
3. J. Baumgartner, A. Kuehlmann, and J. Abraham. Property Checking via Structural Analysis. In *Proc. CAV'02*, volume 2404, pages 151–165, 2002.

4. M. Benedetti and A. Cimatti. Bounded Model Checking for Past LTL. Technical Report 0301-05, ITC-Irst, Trento, Italy, 2003.
5. A. Biere, A. Cimatti, E. Clarke, and Y. Zhu. Symbolic Model Checking without BDDs. *LNCS*, 1579:193–207, 1999.
6. A. Biere, A. Cimatti, E. M. Clarke, M. Fujita, and Y. Zhu. Symbolic Model Checking Using SAT Procedures instead of BDDs. In *Proc. DAC'99*, pages 317–320, 1999.
7. A. Biere, E. Clarke, R. Raimi, and Y. Zhu. Verifying Safety Properties of a Power PC Microprocessor Using Symbolic Model Checking without BDDs. In *Proc CAV99*, volume 1633 of *LNCS*. Springer, 1999.
8. J. Castro, M. Kolp, and J. Mylopoulos. A Requirements-Driven Development Methodology. In *Proc. of the 13th Int.nl Conf. on Advanced Information Systems Engineering*, 2001.
9. A. Cimatti, E. M. Clarke, E. Giunchiglia, F. Giunchiglia, M. Pistore, M. Roveri, R. Sebastiani, and A. Tacchella. NuSMV 2: An OpenSource Tool for Symbolic Model Checking. In *Proc. of Int.nl Conf. on Computer-Aided Verification (CAV 2002)*, 2002.
10. A. Cimatti, E.M. Clarke, F. Giunchiglia, and M. Roveri. NuSMV: a new Symbolic Model Verifier. In N. Halbwachs and D. Peled, editors, *Proceedings Eleventh Conference on Computer-Aided Verification (CAV'99)*, number 1633 in LNCS, pages 495–499, 1999.
11. A. Cimatti, E. Giunchiglia, M. Roveri, M. Pistore, R. Sebastiani, and A. Tacchella. Integrating BDD-based and SAT-based Symbolic Model Checking. In *Proceeding of 4th International Workshop on Frontiers of Combining Systems (FroCoS'2002)*, 2002.
12. E. Clarke, O. Grumberg, and K. Hamaguchi. Another Look at LTL Model Checking. *Formal Methods in System Design*, 10:47–71, 1997.
13. F. Copty, L. Fix, E. Giunchiglia, G. Kamhi, A. Tacchella, and M. Vardi. Benefits of Bounded Model Checking at an Industrial Setting. In *Proceedings of CAV 2001*, pages 436–453, 2001.
14. E.A. Emerson. Temporal and Modal Logic. In J. van Leeuwen, editor, *Handbook of Theoretical Computer Science*, volume B, pages 995–1072. Elsevier Science Publisher B.V., 1990.
15. A. Fuxman. *Formal Analysis of Early Requirements Specifications*. PhD thesis, University of Toronto, Toronto, Canada, 2001.
16. Dov Gabbay. The Declarative Past and Imperative Future. In *Proccedings of the Colloquium on Temporal Logic and Specifications*, volume 398, pages 409–448. Springer-Verlag, 1987.
17. S. Gnesi, D. Latella, and G. Lenzini. Formal Verification of Cryptographic Protocols using History Dependent Automata. In *Proc. of the 4th Workshop on Sistemi Distribuiti: Algoritmi, Architetture e Linguaggi*, 1999.
18. O. Kupferman, N. Piterman, and M. Vardi. Extended Temporal Logic Revisited. In *Proc. 12th Int.nl Conf. on Concurrency Theory*, number 2154 in LNCS, pages 519–534, 2001.
19. F. Laroussinie and Ph. Schnoebelen. A Hierarchy of Temporal Logics with Past. *Theoretical Computer Science*, 148:303–324, 1995.
20. M. W. Moskewicz, C. F. Madigan, Y. Zhao, L. Zhang, and S. Malik. Chaff: Engineering an Efficient SAT Solver. In *Proc. of the 38th Design Automation Conference*, 2001.
21. M. Sheeran, S. Singh, and G. Stalmarck. Checking safety properties using induction and a SAT-solver. In *Proc. Int.nl Conf. on Formal Methods in Computer-Aided Design*, 2000.
22. O. Shtrichmann. Tuning SAT Checkers for Bounded Model Checking. In *Proc. CAV'2000*, volume 1855 of *LNCS*. Springer, 2000.
23. A. van Lamsweerde. Goal-Oriented Requirements Engineering: A Guided Tour. In *Proc. 5th IEEE International Symposium on Requirements Engineering*, pages 249–263, 2001.
24. M. Vardi and P. Wolper. An automata-theoretic approach to automatic program verification. In *Proceedings of the First Annual Symposium on Logic in Computer Science*, 1986.
25. P. F. Williams, A. Biere, E. M. Clarke, and A. Gupta. Combining Decision Diagrams and SAT Procedures for Efficient Symbolic Model Checking. In *Proc. CAV'2000*, volume 1855 of *LNCS*, pages 124–138. Springer, 2000.

Experimental Analysis of Different Techniques for Bounded Model Checking

Nina Amla[1], Robert Kurshan[1], Kenneth L. McMillan[1], and Ricardo Medel[2]

[1] Cadence Design Systems
[2] Stevens Institute of Technology

Abstract. *Bounded model checking* (BMC) is a procedure that searches for counterexamples to a given property through bounded executions of a non-terminating system. This paper compares the performance of SAT-based, BDD-based and explicit state based BMC on benchmarks drawn from commercial designs. Our experimental framework provides a uniform and comprehensive basis to evaluate each of these approaches. The experimental results in this paper suggest that for designs with *deep* counterexamples, BDD-based BMC is much faster. For designs with *shallow* counterexamples, we observe that indeed SAT-based BMC is more effective than BDD-based BMC, but we also observe that explicit state based BMC is comparably effective, a new observation.

1 Introduction

Model checking [CE81,QS82] is a formal technique for automatically verifying that a finite state model satisfies a temporal property. The states in the system may be represented explicitly as in [CE81]. Alternatively, Binary Decision Diagrams (BDDs) [Bry86] may be used to encode the transition relation. This approach is known as *symbolic model checking* [BCM+90,McM93] and has been successfully applied in practice. However, it is computationally infeasible to apply this technique automatically to all systems since the problem is PSPACE-complete. *Bounded Model Checking* (BMC) [BCRZ99,BCCZ99] is a restricted form of model checking, where one searches for counterexamples in executions bounded by some length k. Recent advances [BCRZ99,BCCZ99] have encoded the bounded model checking problem as a propositional satisfiability problem that can then be solved by a SAT-solver. Initial results appear to be promising and show that the new generation of SAT-solvers (cf. [MSS99,MMZ+01,GN02]) can handle large designs quite efficiently. SAT-based BMC can not provide any guarantees on the correctness of a property but it can be useful in finding counterexamples. It is possible to prove that a property holds with SAT-based BMC by computing the *completeness threshold* [KS02] and showing the absence of any errors at this bound. As observed in [KS02], since this threshold may be very large, it may not be possible to perform BMC at this bound.

This paper explores the performance of BMC with three reachability algorithms: SAT, BDDs and explicit state. We used the commercial model checking

H. Garavel and J. Hatcliff (Eds.): TACAS 2003, LNCS 2619, pp. 34–48, 2003.

tool COSPAN/FormalCheck, in which all three algorithms have been implemented. We implemented SAT-based BMC into COSPAN by using, as a post-processor, the Cadence SMV tool in conjunction with two SAT-solvers, BerkMin [GN02] and zChaff [MMZ+01]. This setup guarantees that the three types of BMC are applied uniformly to the same statically reduced model. We present experimental results on 62 benchmarks that were carefully chosen from a set of Cadence customer benchmarks based on a number of different criteria. We included benchmarks where BDDs performed well and others where BDDs performed poorly. Some of the benchmarks were beyond the scope of BDD-based model checking. Most of the benchmarks were customer hardware designs but we did include three software designs. The benchmarks are categorized according to the result and depth of the counterexample, and we include many examples with depth greater than 40. The properties were safety and liveness properties.

Several recent papers have compared BDD-based (bounded and unbounded) model checking to SAT-based bounded model checking. A recent comprehensive analysis, with respect to both the performance and capacity of BMC is presented in [CFF+01]. They compare a BDD-based tool (called Forecast) with a SAT-based tool (called Thunder) on 17 of Intel's internal benchmarks. Their results show an interesting tie between a tuned BDD-based Forecast and a default SAT-based Thunder, which suggest that, although the running times were similar, the time taken by experts to tune the BDD tool could be saved when the SAT-solver is used. However, since these were fundamentally distinct tools, there was no way to account for differences in front-end static reductions.

Our study differs from theirs in a number of key ways. First, we extended the analysis to include the explicit state representation. We found that a random search with the explicit state engine does about as well as SAT-based BMC in finding shallow counterexamples, that is, counterexamples at a depth of at most 50. Second, we focussed our study on larger depth limits. We observed that BDD-based BMC outperforms SAT-based BMC at larger depths. Last, our experimental framework uses the same static optimizations with all three engines. We believe this yields a more accurate comparison and diminishes the role that tuning the various tools played in the above work. For each of the three algorithms default settings were used, and there was no fine tuning for respective models. Thus, our results correspond better to what a commercial user might see.

Another interesting study [CCQ02] compares an optimized BDD-based BMC tool, called FBV, to SAT-based BMC with the NuSMV tool. Their results are similar to ours, in that, they find that the BDD approach scales better with increasing bounds. The key differences are that their analysis did not include the explicit state approach and they only considered safety properties. Moreover, we conducted our experiments with a larger and more varied set of benchmarks.

Over the last several years there has been considerable intent to compare the performance of unbounded BDD-based model checking versus SAT-based BMC. In [BCRZ99] they report that BMC with SAT-solvers, SATO [Zha97] and GRASP [MSS99], significantly outperformed the BDD-based CMU SMV on 5 control circuits from a PowerPC microprocessor. Similar results were observed in [BCCZ99], where they found that SAT-based BMC with SATO and PROVE [Bor97] outperformed two versions of CMU SMV on benchmarks that were known to perform poorly with BDDs. SAT-based BMC, using SAT-solvers GRASP and CAPTAIN PROVE [SS98], was found to be better in [BLM01] than unbounded model checking with CMU SMV in the verification of the Alpha chip. The results reported in [Str00] showed that a tuned GRASP was able to outperform IBM's BDD-based model checker RuleBase in 10 out of 13 benchmarks. A new SAT-based method proposed in [BC00] was compared with unbounded BDD-based model checking with VIS [BHSV+96] on two benchmarks: an industrial telecommunications benchmark and an arbiter. They found that VIS did better on the arbiter while the SAT-based approach did better on the other benchmark. In [VB01], twenty-eight different SAT-solvers and one BDD-based tool were compared on a number of faulty versions of two microprocessor designs. The results show that zChaff outperforms the BDD-based tool and all the others SAT-solvers.

Our work differs from those mentioned above in a number of important ways. In addition to the differences already mentioned with regard to [CFF+01] above, a key difference is these authors' comparison of SAT-based BMC with unbounded BDD-based model checking, which we believe is not a good basis for comparing the two representations. In this paper, we show that BDD-based BMC has several advantages over SAT-based BMC. Our implementation of BDD-based BMC, unlike its SAT counterpart, can produce a positive answer if all the reachable states have been encountered at the depth checked. In addition, our experiments indicate that BDD-based BMC appears to be more successful at deeper depths. Our study includes both safety and liveness properties. The previous work either did not consider liveness properties or did not distinguish between safety and liveness properties.

The goal of this work was to provide a uniform and comprehensive basis for comparing BMC with three different representation: SAT, BDDs and explicit state. The trends observed in our study can be summarized as follows:

- SAT-based BMC is better than BDD-based BMC for finding shallow counterexamples.
- Random explicit state is as effective as SAT-based BMC in finding short counterexamples for safety properties but SAT-based BMC is better at finding the liveness counterexamples.
- Neither technique is better than BDDs in finding deep counterexamples.
- SAT-based BMC seems to be a consistent performer and completed in most cases.
- All three approaches seem fairly effective in proving the absence of counterexamples of length k. However, the BDD-based approach has two clear advantages. First, determining that a property holds is possible with BDDs, but not with SAT or random explicit state. Next, the BDD-based approach seems to scale better at larger depths than the two approaches. Both the explicit state and SAT engines perform rather well at the smaller depths but do not fare as well as the depth increases.

- The SAT-solver BerkMin appears to be better suited for BMC and outperforms zChaff quite significantly.

The paper is organized as follows. Section 2 describes our experimental framework, Section 3 presents our results and Section 4 summarizes our findings.

2 Experimental Framework

For our experiments we used the commercial model checking tool FormalCheck [HK90]. COSPAN, the verification engine of FormalCheck, was used for BMC with BDDs and with the explicit state approach. For SAT-based BMC, COSPAN was used to perform static reductions on the model and Cadence SMV [McM99], used as a post-processor, was used to do the SAT BMC. Cadence SMV has an interface to both BerkMin and zChaff. In this way the static reductions were applied in an uniform manner, for all three engines. These reductions include localization reduction [Kur94], constant propagation, equivalent code elimination, predicate simplification, resizing and macroization of combinational variables.

2.1 BDD-Based BMC

COSPAN's BDD-based BMC, for safety properties, is done by doing Reachability analysis for k steps. In the case of liveness properties, the bounded reachability analysis is done first and then a bad cycle detection check is done on the reachable states. Therefore, BDD-based BMC with a depth k terminates when one of the following conditions holds:

- all paths of length k have been explored,
- an error state (i.e. a counterexample) is reached, or
- all the reachable states have been explored (i.e. a fix-point has been reached).

The implementation uses a sifting-based dynamic re-ordering scheme. This BDD-based BMC implementation has two advantages over SAT-based BMC. First, it is possible to verify that a property holds if the fix-point is reached within the specified depth. Second, the length of the counterexample produced is independent of the depth checked and is guaranteed to be the shortest one. In SAT-based BMC, the counterexample produced will be of the same length as the depth checked.

2.2 Explicit State BMC

We used COSPAN for BMC with the explicit state engine. BMC was implemented through a command that "kills" all transitions after the depth limit k is reached. COSPAN allows a user to set the value of k through the command line. In order to deal with the large number of input values per state that are possible in commercial models, we used a random search of the state space for counterexamples, as supported by COSPAN's explicit state search engine. Thus, we attempt to find counterexamples in some randomly chosen executions of length k. However, this process may miss executions and thus counterexamples.

We feel justified in comparing this random explicit state approach to the other two approaches since BMC is generally used to find counterexamples in contrast to proving that a property holds. The ability to use a random search is an advantage of the explicit state engine that we have exploited rather successfully.

2.3 SAT-Based BMC

For SAT-based BMC, we used Cadence SMV, as a post-processor to COSPAN, in conjunction with two state-of-the-art SAT-solvers: zChaff [MMZ+01] and BerkMin [GN02]. Cadence SMV implements many of the standard optimizations like bounded cone of influence and "BDD sweeping" [KK97] for tuning the performance of SAT-based BMC. We used a translator to convert the statically optimized programs (and properties) written in the input language of COSPAN (S/R) into the input format of SMV. The translator also translates counterexamples found by SMV back into the COSPAN format, and hence into the original HDL format via the FormalCheck interface. We found that the time to do the translations was not significant (usually a few seconds).

2.4 Benchmarks

The designs used are FormalCheck customer benchmarks that had some/all of the following characteristics.

- We chose benchmarks with deep counterexamples. The length of the counterexamples in the benchmarks varied from 3 up to 1152.
- We chose examples where BDDs performed poorly and others where BDDs performed well.
- The number of state variables in the designs varied from 11 up to 1273.
- We included software designs.
- We used both safety and liveness properties.

Informally, a *safety* property specifies that something "bad" never happens during an execution. The safety properties were of the following form: `Always x`, `Never x`, `After x Never y`, `After x Always y`, and `After x Always y Unless z`. *Liveness* properties state that something "good" eventually happens; the liveness properties we checked were of the following form: `Eventually x`, `After x Eventually y` and `After x Eventually y Unless z`. Most of the benchmarks contained only a single property to check but some were conjunctions of multiple properties.

We organized the 62 benchmarks into three groups. The first group (Group1) consisted of benchmarks where the property failed in at most 30 steps. The second group (Group2) had benchmarks that failed in more than 30 steps. The final group (Group3) had benchmarks where the property passed. The length of the counterexamples in the first two groups were already known (in most of the cases they were found using unbounded BDD-based model checking). All the experiments were run on Sun SPARC machines with 2 Gigabytes of memory.

3 Experimental Results

We ran each benchmark with FormalCheck default options with the BDD, SAT and random explicit state engines. Furthermore, we ran both the SAT-solvers, BerkMin and zChaff, on all the benchmarks.

In this Section, we analyze the results obtained. In the random explicit state approach, we ran a maximum of three random runs, increasing the number of inputs checked on each run from 50/state to 100/state and finally 500/state. If a counterexample was found we reported the time taken up to that point; otherwise we reported the cumulative time taken for all three runs.

Table 1. Results for benchmarks with counterexamples of length at most 30.

Benchmark				BDD	SAT		Exp. State	
name	type	depth	stvars	time	zChaff	Berkmin	time	result
A1	S	3	152	122.4	128.9	17.4	**0**	F
A2*	S	4	111	29.6	13.5	**13.3**	-	
A3	S	4	172	-	155.9	152.8	**4.8**	F
A4	L	5	92	61.8	**3.6**	**3.6**	-	
A5	S	7	1109	-	54.5	**46.4**	695.4	F
A6	L	7	171	-	**311.4**	736.1	-	
A7	S	7	62	4.5	4.1	1.6	**0.1**	F
A8	S	13	83	-	17.5	15.5	**4**	F
A9*	S	15	78	187.2	13909.7	807.4	**114.4**	F
A10	L	15	80	25.5	1.7	**1.4**	-	
A11	S	16	125	41.8	34.3	21.7	**2**	F
A12	S	16	58	1856.5	492.5	**259.7**	0.3	NC
A13	S	16	455	35.3	20.2	12.3	**1.2**	F
A14	S	20	132	16.1	29.4	15.1	**0.6**	F
A15	S	20	92	99.3	106.9	**7**	0.1	NC
A16*	S	21	23	79.7	1.5	**0.8**	-	
A17	S	21	115	-	3.5	**3**	97.7	F
A18	S	22	73	3477.5	3.5	**2.4**	-	
A19	L	23	93	197.4	**2.7**	3.5	-	
A20	S	23	102	34.5	34.4	**22.4**	1492.9	F

3.1 Benchmarks with Shallow Counterexamples

Group1 contained benchmarks that had properties that failed in at most 30 steps. Table 1 summarizes our results. The first column specifies the name of the benchmark, the second column is the type of property, the third is length of the counterexample and the fourth column is the number of state variables in the design. The next three columns give the time taken in seconds with BDDs and the SAT-solvers zChaff and BerkMin respectively. The last two columns give the time taken for explicit state and the final result returned by the explicit state engine, “F” indicates a counterexample was found and “NC” indicates that a counterexample was not found in any of the three runs. We used a timeout of 30,000 seconds and is depicted as a “-” in the tables. Memory exhaustion is shown as “m/o”. The symbol “*” next to the benchmark name indicates that it is a software design.

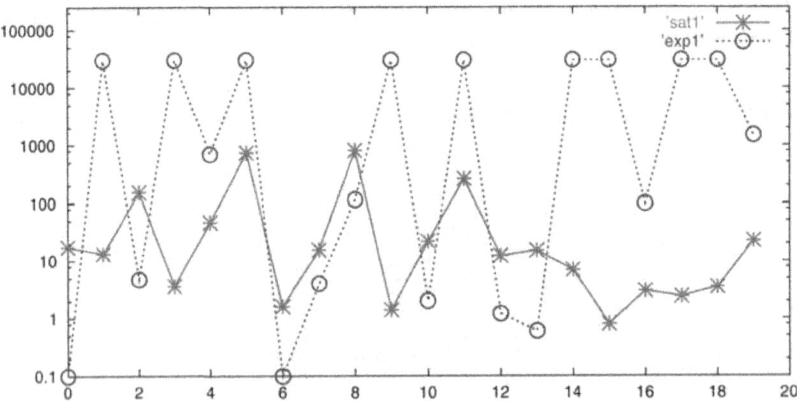

Fig. 1. Time taken for SAT BMC versus Random Explicit State on Group1 benchmarks. X-axis: benchmarks ordered by increasing depth, Y-axis: run time in seconds.

The most interesting observation in Group1 was that random explicit state, when it did finish, did extremely well, outperforming both the BDD and SAT engines on 8 out of the 16 safety benchmarks. The explicit state engine, however, did not find any counterexamples for the liveness properties. The SAT engine did better on 12 of the 20 benchmarks and did better than the BDD engine on all but one (`A9`). It also did better than the other two engines on all 4 liveness properties. The plot in Figure 1 shows that, while explicit state and SAT BMC are comparable, SAT-based BMC is more consistent.

3.2 Benchmarks with Deep Counterexamples

In Group2, where the length of the counterexamples varied from 34 up to 1152, we found the results to be quite different. Table 2 summarizes our results. The explicit state engine only completed successfully on 3 of the 17 benchmarks. The SAT engine did quite well up to a depth of 60 and outperformed the other engines on all 7 benchmarks. The BDD engine significantly outperformed the other two engines on the deeper counterexamples. This can be seen rather clearly in Figure 2 which shows that BDD-based BMC does better on all of the benchmarks that had counterexamples of length greater than 60, namely those numbered 8 and

Table 2. Results for benchmarks with counterexamples of length greater than 30.

Benchmark				BDD	SAT		Exp. State	
name	type	depth	stvars	time	zChaff	Berkmin	time	result
B1	S	34	184	1843.2	6.7	**3.6**	-	
B2	S	41	457	-	2418	**1760.4**	-	
B3*	S	41	43	-	13.3	**3.2**	-	
B4	L	52	1273	122.3	10.9	**8.2**	43.1	NC
B5	S	54	366	3699.4	422.5	**89.3**	-	
B6	S	54	195	44.1	4206.7	**37.7**	-	
B7	L	60	44	3026	58.5	**14.7**	-	
B8	S	66	11	0.1	0.1	0.1	**0.04**	F
B9	S	72	53	**12.7**	1973.4	45.5	-	
B10	S	82	46	**2.3**	1036.7	81.5	-	
B11	L	89	124	**34**	362.6	371.6	-	
B12	S	92	429	**337.9**	2988.9	27889.6	12473.8	F
B13	L	113	51	**84.1**	5946.6	1049.5	-	
B14	L	127	45	**1.4**	36	34.4	0.1	NC
B15	S	316	74	**15.6**	14159.2	229.9	150.7	F
B16	L	801	132	**75.4**	m/o	m/o	-	
B17	S	1152	153	**48.5**	2541.6	1035.9	-	

above. Overall, the BDD-based approach did better on 9 of the 17 benchmarks, the SAT approach did better on 7 and the explicit state approach did better on only 1 benchmark. Unlike BDD and explicit state BMC, SAT-based BMC did not complete on only one of the benchmarks (B16) in these two groups. We also found that BerkMin outperformed zChaff on most of the benchmarks and by a significant margin on the models with counterexamples of larger depths.

3.3 Benchmarks with Properties That Passed

Group3 contained benchmarks that had properties that passed. We ran each benchmark with a limit depth of 10, 25, 50 and 100 with all three engines. The time reported for the random explicit state engine is the cumulative time taken for three runs, systematically increasing the number of inputs considered in each successive run. Table 4 in the Appendix reports the results for BDDs, explicit state and SAT-based BMC with BerkMin. A comparison of the two SAT-solvers on these benchmarks that demonstrates that BerkMin does better, can be found in Table 3 in the Appendix. In Table 4, the first three columns correspond to the name of the benchmark, type of property and the number of state variables. The next three columns correspond to the time taken for BMC at a depth of 10 with explicit state, BDDs and SAT (using BerkMin) respectively. Similarly, the remaining columns report the results of BMC at depths 25, 50 and 100. As mentioned earlier, BDD-based BMC can assert that a property holds when it

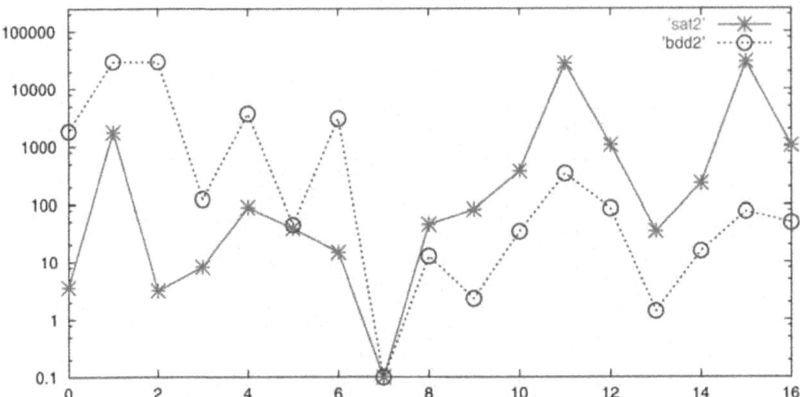

Fig. 2. Time taken for SAT BMC versus BDD BMC on Group2 benchmarks X-axis: benchmarks ordered by increasing depth. Y-axis: run time in seconds.

reaches a fix-point. This is depicted in the table by reporting the time taken at the depth where the fix-point was reached along with the suffix "P". We used a timeout of 36,000 seconds and this is shown in the table as "-".

We found that random explicit state BMC did fairly well at depth 10 and did better than the other two engines on 11 of the 25 benchmarks. However, the performance went down as the depth was increased. At a depth of 100, the explicit state engine timed out on all but 6 of the benchmarks but did better than the others on 5 of them. The BDD engine started out by doing better on only 3 of the 25 benchmarks at depth 10 but improved to do better on 13 benchmarks at final depth checked. Five of benchmarks (C13, C17, C18, C22 and C24) in this group were known to do poorly with BDDs. In these cases, we found that SAT-based BMC did very well on three of them (C18, C13 and C17) but did not do as well on the other two at larger depths. The explicit state engine did extremely well on one of them (C17). We reached a fix-point in 9 cases but BDDs outperformed the other approaches on only 4 of them. SAT-based BMC outperformed the other two engines on 11 of the 25 benchmarks at depth 10 but as the depth was increased it did worse, and at depth 100 it did better on only 6 of them. Again, the SAT-engine was the most consistent and only timed out at a depth of 50 or greater. Figure 3 plots the number of benchmarks that each technique did better on versus the four depths checked, namely 10, 25, 50 and 100. For example, the plot shows that at depth 10, the BDD-based approach did better on 3 benchmarks while the other two engines did better on 11 benchmarks. The BDD-based method, as shown in the plot in Figure 3, appears to scale better on benchmarks where it does not fail to build the global transition structure (those that fail are indicated in Table 4 by a "-"). An interesting point to note is that at least one of the three algorithms finished on all but one of the benchmarks.

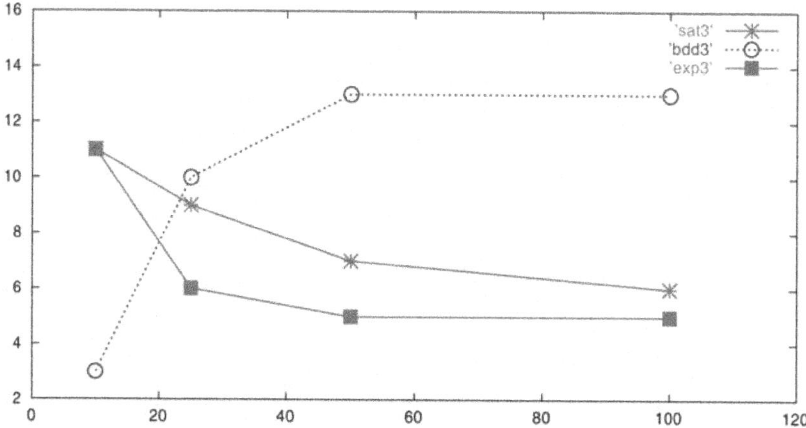

Fig. 3. Plot of the number of Group3 benchmarks that each engine did better on versus depth of BMC. X-axis: BMC depth at 10, 25, 50 and 100, Y-axis: Number of benchmarks (maximum is 25).

3.4 Choosing the Bound

In the results presented so far, we assumed that we knew the depth of the counterexample. This gave us a good measure of the performance of each engine. However, in general, the depth of the counterexample is unknown. There are two possible ways to choose the bound for BMC. One can choose a maximum bound and try to find the error within this bound. A disadvantage of this approach for SAT-based BMC is that the counterexample found will be of the specified length and this could make the counterexample harder to analyze. However, this approach seems to be the right one for both BDD-based and explicit state BMC since they stop as soon as they encounter the error. In order to investigate how this approach works with SAT-based BMC, and based on our results, we chose a maximum depth of 60 and ran the benchmarks in Groups 1 and 2 that had counterexamples of length at most 60. For each of these benchmarks, Figure 4 plots the time taken for BMC at the known depth of the counterexample versus the time taken at depth 60. We can see rather clearly that this approach is expensive and could take orders of magnitude more time. In fact three of the benchmarks that finished within 1000 seconds timed out at bound 60.

Alternatively we could employ an iterative approach, that starts at a minimum depth and systematically increases the depth until a counterexample is found. For our study, we used the following depths: 10, 25, 50 and 100. We applied this iterative method to benchmarks in Groups 1 and 2 that had counterexamples of length less than 100. Figure 5 plots the cumulative time taken versus the time taken at the depth of the counterexample. The X-axis represents the 29 benchmarks in increasing order based on the length of the counterexample and the Y-axis represents the cumulative time taken in seconds. This method appears to be more efficient and in most cases took approximately the same time

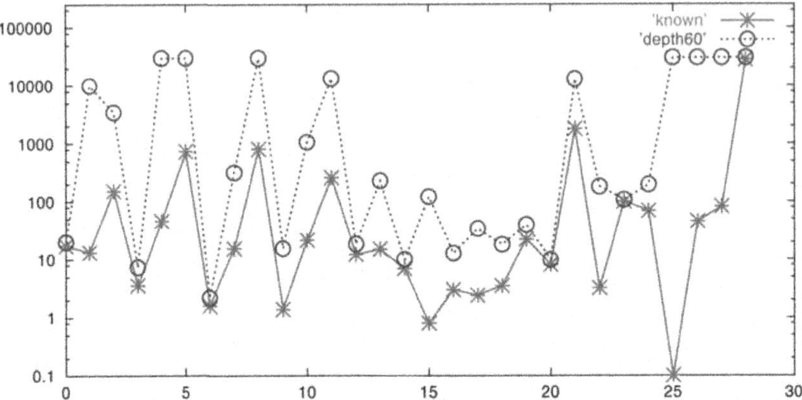

Fig. 4. Time taken for SAT BMC at the depth of counterexample versus depth=60. X-axis: benchmark, Y-axis: run time in seconds.

as BMC with the depth already known. The only three benchmarks where the difference was fairly significant had counterexamples of length 52 (B3) and 54 (B5 and B6 in Table 2) and therefore represent the worst case scenario. Only 2 of the 29 benchmarks with the iterative method changed the SAT BMC result in the comparison with BDDs and explicit state, and the difference in time in both cases was less than 30 seconds.

4 Conclusions

This paper presents a systematic performance analysis for BMC with three engines: SAT, BDDs and random explicit state. We used 62 industrial benchmarks that were partitioned into three groups based on the length of the counterexample and whether the property was falsified.

Our results demonstrate that for models with deep counterexamples, BDDs were the clear winner, while for models with shallow counterexamples, SAT and random explicit state performed comparably. The results were the same for both safety and liveness properties with the exception being that the random explicit state algorithm did much worse on the 13 liveness properties in our benchmark suite. The SAT-based approach was very consistent and completed within the timeout on all but 4 of the 62 benchmarks and, more importantly, all 4 timeouts were observed at a depth of 50 or greater. The SAT engine also seems to be less sensitive to the size of the design (number of state variables) and did well on the larger benchmarks. In cases when not much information is available about the design, running the engines in parallel until one of them completes is a sound idea.

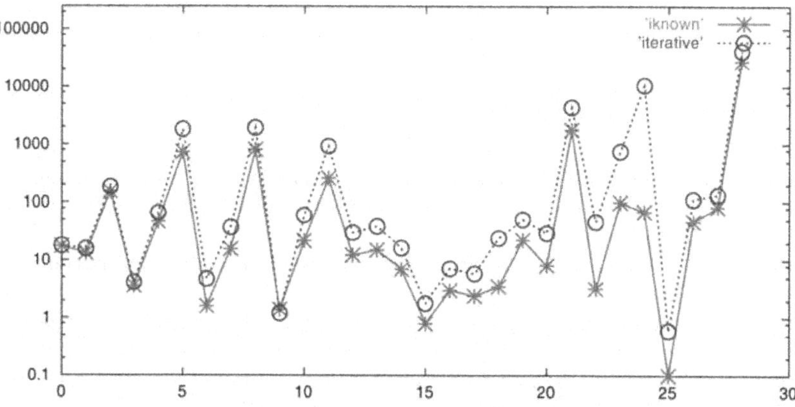

Fig. 5. Time taken for SAT BMC at the depth of counterexample versus cumulative time taken. X-axis: benchmark, Y-axis: run time in seconds.

References

[BC00] P. Bjesse and K. Claessen. SAT-based verification without state space traversal. In *FMCAD*, 2000.

[BCCZ99] A. Biere, A. Cimatti, E. Clarke, and Y. Zhu. Symbolic model checking without BDDs. In *Tools and Algorithms for the Construction and Analysis of Systems*, volume 1579 of *LNCS*, 1999.

[BCM+ 90] J. R. Burch, E. M. Clarke, K. L. McMillan, D.L. Dill, and J. Hwang. Symbolic model checking: 10^{20} states and beyond. In *LICS*, 1990.

[BCRZ99] A. Biere, E. Clarke, R. Raimi, and Y. Zhu. Verifying safety properties of a PowerPC microprocessor using symbolic model checking without BDDs. In *CAV*, 1999.

[BHSV+ 96] R. Brayton, G. Hachtel, A. Sangiovanni-Vincentelli, F. Somenzi, A. Aziz, S. Cheng, S. Edwards, S. Khatri, Y. Kukimoto, A. Pardo, S. Qadeer, R. Ranjan, S. Sarwary, T . Shiple, G. Swamy, and T. Villa. VIS. In *FMCAD*, 1996.

[BLM01] P. Bjesse, T. Leonard, and A. Mokkedem. Finding bugs in an Alpha microprocessor using satisfiability solvers. In *CAV*, volume 2102 of *LNCS*, 2001.

[Bor97] A. Boralv. The industrial success of verification tools based on stalmarck's method. In *CAV*, 1997.

[Bry86] R. E. Bryant. Graph-based algorithms for boolean function manipulations. *IEEE Transactions on Computers*, 1986.

[CCQ02] G. Cabodi, P. Camurati, and S. Quer. Can bdds compete with sat solvers on bounded model checking. In *DAC*, 2002.

[CE81] E.M. Clarke and E. A. Emerson. Design and synthesis of synchronization skeletons using branching time temporal logic. In *Workshop on Logics of Programs*, volume 131 of *LNCS*, 1981.

[CFF+01] Fady C., L. Fix, R. Fraer, E. Giunchiglia, G. Kamhi, A. Tacchella, and M. Y. Vardi. Benefits of bounded model checking at an industrial setting. In *CAV*, volume 2102 of *LNCS*, 2001.

[GN02] E. Goldberg and Y. Novikov. Berkmin: A fast and robust sat-solver. In *DATE*, 2002.

[HK90] Z. Har'El and R. P. Kurshan. Software for analytical development of communications protocols. *AT&T Technical Journal*, 69(1), 1990.

[KK97] A. Kuehlmann and F. Krohm. Equivalence checking using cuts and heaps. In *DAC*, 1997.

[KS02] D. Kroening and O. Strichman. Efficient computation of recurrence diameters. In *VMCAI*, 2002.

[Kur94] R. Kurshan. *Computer-aided Verification of Coordinating Processes: The Automata-Theoretic Approach.* Princeton University Press, 1994.

[McM93] K. McMillan. *Symbolic model checking: An approach to the state explosion problem.* Kluwer Academic Publishers, 1993.

[McM99] K. McMillan. Getting started with smv, 1999. URL: `http://www-cad.eecs.berkeley.edu/˜kenmcmil`.

[MMZ+01] M. W. Moskewicz, C. F. Madigan, Y. Zhao, L. Zhang, and S. Malik. Chaff: Engineering an Efficient SAT Solver. In *Proceedings of the 38th Design Automation Conference (DAC'01)*, 2001.

[MSS99] Marques-Silva and Sakallah. GRASP: A search algorithm for propositional satisfiability. *IEEETC: IEEE Transactions on Computers*, 48, 1999.

[QS82] J.P. Queille and J. Sifakis. Specification and verification of concurrent systems in CESAR. In *Proc. of the 5th International Symposium on Programming*, volume 137 of *LNCS*, 1982.

[SS98] M. Sheeran and G. Stålmarck. A tutorial on Stålmarck's proof procedure for propositional logic. In *CAV*, volume 1522 of *LNCS*, 1998.

[Str00] O. Strichman. Tuning SAT checkers for bounded model checking. In *CAV*, 2000.

[VB01] M. N. Velev and R. E. Bryant. Effective use of boolean satisfiability procedures in the formal verification of superscalar and VLIW. In *Proceedings of the 38th Conference on Design Automation Conference 2001*, 2001.

[Zha97] H. Zhang. SATO: An efficient propositional prover. In *Proceedings of the 14th International Conference on Automated deduction*, volume 1249 of *LNAI*, 1997.

5 Appendix

Table 3. Results for zChaff and BerkMin on benchmarks that passed.

Benchmark		depth 10		depth 25		depth 50		depth 100	
name	stvars	BerkMin	zChaff	BerkMin	zChaff	BerkMin	zChaff	BerkMin	zChaff
C1	51	**2.7**	**2.7**	**4.7**	5	**15.6**	50.1	**1002.1**	10529.8
C2	52	**3.3**	3.5	**3.8**	4.4	**5**	5.9	**7.4**	9.5
C3	53	3.3	**3.1**	**5.1**	15.1	**34.6**	219.2	**910.6**	7665.8
C4	58	**6.8**	46.5	**11.5**	145.7	**40**	1217.2	**414**	12284.2
C5	69	**1.6**	1.7	**2.6**	3.1	**5.8**	6.3	141.4	**131.9**
C6	70	**4.2**	4.4	**5.4**	11.6	**15.8**	67.7	**59.8**	495.2
C7	70	**6.8**	7.3	**7.1**	9.1	**9.7**	12.3	**14.8**	19.7
C8	77	13.3	**10**	17.7	**13.4**	25.3	**19.5**	40.4	**30.6**
C9	91	**10.3**	10.8	**14.4**	18.7	**22.6**	34.9	**96.8**	162.3
C10	95	10.7	**9.3**	**14.6**	14.8	**22.5**	24.1	57	**43.4**
C11	100	8.1	**5.3**	8.7	**7.6**	**15.2**	23.4	**1106.1**	6084.3
C12*	111	**35.4**	60.7	**4278.7**	23641.8	-	-	-	-
C13	114	**4.1**	5	**5.6**	7.2	**8.3**	11.5	**7.7**	20.3
C14	127	**70**	1723.4	**698**	-	**6960.9**	-	-	-
C15	131	**3.9**	**3.9**	6.3	**4**	**4**	6.2	6.5	**3.9**
C16	268	10	**8.8**	16.4	**16.3**	**34.3**	144.7	**460.9**	5026.3
C17	423	**15.6**	15.7	**23.5**	30.8	**38.6**	52.5	**71.4**	97.7
C18	423	14.6	**13.1**	21.2	**12.5**	**39**	2262.3	**98.9**	35340.3
C19	428	**54.7**	69.3	**78.2**	85.5	368.4	**133.3**	2356	**226.3**
C20	446	**22.1**	25.3	**27.9**	32.6	**37.7**	44.8	**60.4**	72.3
C21	455	22	**14.4**	33.8	**11**	52.2	**11**	100.5	**14.4**
C22	625	46.2	**42.7**	106.1	**58.3**	**3895.3**	12837.9	-	-
C23	600	**29**	29.8	**40.1**	45.9	**59.9**	72.4	**100.2**	125.7
C24	624	**43.9**	53.6	**61.7**	224.6	**69.6**	7977.9	**31753.6**	-
C25	644	**42.4**	46.8	**64.5**	80.8	152.6	**135**	**195**	255.4

Table 4. Results for benchmarks that passed.

Benchmark			depth 10			depth 25			depth 50			depth 100		
name	type	stvars	ES	BDD	BerkMin	ES	BDD	BerkMin	ES	BDD	BerkMin	ES	BDD	BerkMin
C1	S	51	118.9	**1.2**	2.7	2087.9	**0.9**	4.7	-	**1.5**	15.6	-	**51.7**	1002.1
C2	S	52	**0.09**	2.5	3.3	**0.08**	2.6	3.8	**0.13**	2.5	5	**0.12**	2.6(P)	7.4
C3	S	53	109.6	**1.3**	3.3	1588.2	**1.3**	5.1	-	**1.9**	34.6	-	**41.8**	910.6
C4	S	58	**2.6**	10.1	6.8	-	**10.1**	11.5	-	**10.1**	40	-	**10.3**	414
C5	S	69	**0.09**	1.1	1.6	**0.1**	1.4	2.6	**0.09**	2.5	5.8	**0.1**	2.7	141.4
C6	S	70	-	10.6	**4.2**	-	2164	**5.4**	-	9128.3	**15.8**	-	9586(P)	**59.8**
C7	S	70	-	7.7	**6.8**	-	111.2(P)	**7.1**	-	111.2(P)	**9.7**	-	111.2(P)	**14.8**
C8	S	77	**1.6**	15.5	13.3	**4.3**	7.8	17.7	8.9	**7.8**	25.3	17.9	**8.8**	40.4
C9	L	91	**0.14**	5.8	10.3	**0.15**	6.2	14.4	**0.14**	48.4	22.6	**0.14**	133.8(P)	96.8
C10	S	95	**2.3**	7	10.7	799.7	**7.1**	14.6	-	**9.5**	22.5	-	**10(P)**	57
C11	S	100	18.2	**3.2**	8.1	9326.3	**3.3**	8.7	-	**5.3**	15.2	-	**14.2**	1106.1
C12*	S	111	-	50	**35.4**	-	**370.4**	4278.7	-	**1872.4**	-	-	**4881.5**	-
C13	S	114	98.9	-	**4.1**	121.3	-	**5.6**	1568.5	-	**8.3**	-	-	**7.7**
C14	S	127	-	673.9	**70**	-	**664.4(P)**	698	-	**664.4(P)**	6960.9	-	**664.4(P)**	-
C15	S	131	-	49.1	**3.9**	-	7450.1	**6.3**	-	7869.5	**4**	-	8488.1	**6.5**
C16	S	268	**2.8**	6.2	10	182.5	**6.2**	16.4	9300.4	**6.4**	34.3	-	**12.6**	460.9
C17	S	423	**0.4**	12314(P)	15.6	**0.37**	12314(P)	23.5	**0.4**	12314(P)	38.6	**0.41**	12314(P)	71.4
C18	S	423	-	43.1	**14.6**	-	-	**21.2**	-	-	**39**	-	-	**98.9**
C19	L	428	**2.3**	34	54.7	57.8	**39.1**	78.2	3282.7	**96.9**	368.4	-	**297**	2356
C20	S	446	323.4	32.3	**22.1**	-	32.9	**27.9**	-	**33**	37.7	-	**34.9(P)**	60.4
C21	L	455	**7.1**	31.2	22	-	**31.3**	33.8	-	**33.6(P)**	52.2	-	**33.6(P)**	100.5
C22	S	457	-	-	**46.2**	-	-	**106.1**	-	-	**3895.3**	-	-	-
C23	S	600	364.6	53.4(P)	**29**	335.1	53.4(P)	**40.1**	357.4	**53.4(P)**	59.9	365	**53.4(P)**	100.2
C24	S	624	-	6705.3	**43.9**	-	-	**61.7**	-	-	**69.6**	-	-	**31753.6**
C25	S	644	**0.67**	32.6(P)	42.4	**0.6**	32.6(P)	64.5	**0.66**	32.6(P)	152.6	**0.67**	32.6(P)	195

On the Universal and Existential Fragments of the μ-Calculus*

Thomas A. Henzinger, Orna Kupferman, and Rupak Majumdar

Department of Electrical Engineering and Computer Science
University of California
Berkeley, CA 94720, USA
{tah,orna,rupak}@eecs.berkeley.edu

Abstract. One source of complexity in the μ-calculus is its ability to specify an unbounded number of switches between universal (AX) and existential (EX) branching modes. We therefore study the problems of satisfiability, validity, model checking, and implication for the universal and existential fragments of the μ-calculus, in which only one branching mode is allowed. The universal fragment is rich enough to express most specifications of interest, and therefore improved algorithms are of practical importance. We show that while the satisfiability and validity problems become indeed simpler for the existential and universal fragments, this is, unfortunately, not the case for model checking and implication. We also show the corresponding results for the alternation-free fragment of the μ-calculus, where no alternations between least and greatest fixed points are allowed. Our results imply that efforts to find a polynomial-time model-checking algorithm for the μ-calculus can be replaced by efforts to find such an algorithm for the universal or existential fragment.

1 Introduction

In model checking, we reason about systems and their properties by reasoning about formal models of systems and formal specifications of the properties [5]. The algorithmic nature of model checking makes it fully automatic, convenient to use, and attractive to practitioners. At the same time, model checking is very sensitive to the size of the formal model of the system and the formal specification. Commercial verification tools need to cope with the exceedingly large state spaces that are present in real-life designs. One of the most important developments in this area is the discovery of symbolic methods [2,27]. Typically, symbolic model-checking tools proceed by computing fixed-point expressions over the model's set of states. For example, to find the set of states from which a state satisfying some predicate p is reachable, the model checker starts with the set y of states in which p holds, and repeatedly adds to y the set EXy of states

* This work was supported in part by NSF grant CCR-9988172, the AFOSR MURI grant F49620-00-1-0327, and a Microsoft Research Fellowship.

H. Garavel and J. Hatcliff (Eds.): TACAS 2003, LNCS 2619, pp. 49–64, 2003.

that have a successor in y. Formally, the model checker calculates the least fixed point of the expression $y = (p \vee EXy)$.

Such fixed-point computations are described naturally in the *μ-calculus* [21], which is a logic that contains the existential and universal next modalities EX and AX, and the least and greatest fixed-point quantifiers μ and ν. The μ-calculus is an extremely general modal logic. It is as expressive as automata on infinite trees, and it subsumes most known specification formalisms, including dynamic logics such as PDL [13] and temporal logics such as LTL and CTL* [7, 8] (see [18] for a general result). The *alternation-free* fragment of the μ-calculus (AFMC, for short) [12] has a restricted syntax that does not allow the nesting of alternating least and greatest fixed-point quantifiers, which makes the evaluation of expressions very simple [6]. The alternation-free fragment subsumes the temporal logic CTL.

Four decision problems arise naturally for every specification formalism: the *satisfiability* problem (given a formula φ, is there a model that satisfies φ?) checks whether a specification can be implemented, and algorithms for deciding the satisfiability problem are the basis for program synthesis and control [3,29, 30]; the *validity* problem (given φ, do all models satisfy φ?) checks whether the specification is trivially satisfied, and is used as a sanity check for requirements [25]; the *model-checking* problem (given a formula φ and a model M, does M satisfy φ?) is the basic verification problem; and the *implication* problem (given two formulas φ and ψ, is $\varphi \to \psi$ valid?) arises naturally in the context of modular verification, where it must be shown that a module satisfies a property under an assumption about the environment [23,28].

The satisfiability, validity, and implication problems for the μ-calculus are all EXPTIME-complete [1,13] (since the μ-calculus is closed under negation, it is easy to get EXPTIME completeness for the validity and implication problems by reductions to and from the satisfiability problem). The model-checking problem for the μ-calculus was first considered in [12], which described an algorithm with complexity $O((mn)^{l+1})$, where m is the size of M, n is the size of φ, and l is the number of alternations between least and greatest fixed-point quantifiers in φ. In [11], the problem was shown to be equivalent to the nonemptiness problem for parity tree automata, and thus to lie in NP $\cap$ co-NP. Today, it is known that the problem is in UP $\cap$ co-UP [19][1], and the best known algorithm for μ-calculus model checking has a time complexity of roughly $O(mn^{\frac{l}{2}})$ [20,26,31], which is still exponential in the number of alternations. The precise complexity of the problem, and in particular, the question whether a polynomial time solution exists, is a long-standing open problem.

In this paper we study the complexity of the four decision problems for the *existential* and *universal* fragments of the μ-calculus. The existential fragment consists of formulas where the only allowed next modality is the existential one (EX), and the universal fragment consists of formulas where the only allowed next modality is the universal one (AX). We consider μ-calculus in positive

[1] The class UP is a subset of NP, where each word accepted by the Turing machine has a unique accepting run.

normal form, thus the strict syntactic fragments are also semantic fragments — there is no way of specifying an existential next in the universal fragment without negation, and vice versa. Both sublogics induce the state equivalence *similarity* (mutual simulation) [15], as opposed to bisimilarity, which is induced by the full μ-calculus [16]. The existential and universal fragments of the μ-calculus subsume the existential and universal fragments of the branching-time logics CTL and CTL*. For temporal logics, the universal and existential fragments have been studied (see, e.g., [23]). As we specify in the table in Figure 1, the satisfiability, validity, and implication problems for the universal and existential fragments of CTL and CTL* are all easier than the corresponding problems for the full logics [9,13,23,33]. On the other hand, the model-checking complexities for the universal and existential fragments of CTL and CTL* coincide with the complexities of the full logics, and the same holds for the system complexities of model checking (i.e., the complexities in terms of the size of the model, assuming the specification is fixed. Since the model is typically much bigger than the specification, system complexity is important) [4,24].

In contrast to CTL and CTL*, it is possible to express in the μ-calculus *unbounded switching* of AX and EX modalities. Such an unbounded switching is an apparent source of complexity. For example, the μ-calculus can express the reachability problem on And-Or graphs, which is PTIME-complete, while the reachability problem on plain graphs (existential reachability), and its universal counterpart, are NLOGSPACE-complete. Accordingly, the system complexity of the model-checking problem for the μ-calculus is PTIME-complete, whereas the one for CTL and CTL* is only NLOGSPACE-complete [12,17,24]. By removing the switching of modalities from the μ-calculus, one may hope that the algorithms for the four decision problems, and model checking in particular, will become simpler. Since most specifications assert what a system must or must not do in *all* possible futures, the universal fragment of the μ-calculus is expressive enough to capture most specifications of interest. Also, the problem of checking symbolically whether a model contains a computation that satisfies an LTL formula is reduced to model checking of an existential μ-calculus formula. Hence, our study is not only of theoretical interest —efficient algorithms for the universal and existential fragments of the μ-calculus are of practical interest.

We determine the complexities of the four decision problems for the universal and existential fragments of the μ-calculus, as well as for the corresponding alternation-free fragments. Our results are summarized in Figure 1. All the complexities in the figure, except for the NP$\cap$co-NP result for MC, $\exists MC$, and $\forall MC$ model checking are tight. It turns out that the hope to obtain simpler algorithms for the universal and existential fragments is only partially fulfilled. We show that while the satisfiability and validity problems become easier for the existential and universal fragments, both the model-checking and implication problems stay as hard as for the full μ-calculus (or its alternation-free fragment). In particular, our results imply that efforts to find a polynomial time model-checking algorithm for the μ-calculus can be replaced by efforts to find polynomial time model-checking algorithms for the universal or existential fragment. Note that the picture we obtain for the μ-calculus and its alternation-free fragment does not coincide with the picture obtained in the study of the universal and existential fragments of CTL and CTL*, where the restriction to the universal or existential fragments makes also the implication problem easier.

	Satisfiability	Validity	Implication	Model checking	system complexity
CTL*	2EXPTIME	2EXPTIME	2EXPTIME	PSPACE	NLOGSPACE
∀CTL*	PSPACE	PSPACE	EXPSPACE	PSPACE	NLOGSPACE
∃CTL*	PSPACE	PSPACE	EXPSPACE	PSPACE	NLOGSPACE
CTL	EXPTIME	EXPTIME	EXPTIME	PTIME (linear)	NLOGSPACE
∀CTL	PSPACE	co-NP	PSPACE	PTIME (linear)	NLOGSPACE
∃CTL	NP	PSPACE	PSPACE	PTIME (linear)	NLOGSPACE
MC	EXPTIME	EXPTIME	EXPTIME	NP ∩ co-NP	PTIME
∀MC	*PSPACE*	*co-NP*	*EXPTIME*	*NP ∩ co-NP*	*PTIME*
∃MC	*NP*	*PSPACE*	*EXPTIME*	*NP ∩ co-NP*	*PTIME*
AFMC	EXPTIME	EXPTIME	EXPTIME	PTIME (linear)	PTIME
∀AFMC	*PSPACE*	*co-NP*	*EXPTIME*	*PTIME (linear)*	*PTIME*
∃AFMC	*NP*	*PSPACE*	*EXPTIME*	*PTIME (linear)*	*PTIME*

Fig. 1. Summary of known and new (in italics) results

One key insight concerns the size of models for the existential and universal fragments of the μ-calculus. We prove that the satisfiability problem for the existential fragment of μ-calculus is in NP via a *linear-size model property*. This is in contrast to the full μ-calculus, which has only an exponential-size model property [22]. This shows that extending propositional logic by the EX modality and fixed-point quantifiers does not make the satisfiability problem harder. On the other hand, a similar extension with AX results in a logic for which the linear-size model property does not hold, and whose satisfiability problem is PSPACE-complete.

A second insight is that, in model-checking as well as implication problems, the switching of EX and AX modalities can be encoded by the boolean connectives $\vee$ and $\wedge$ in combination with either one of the two modalities and fixed-point quantifiers. Let us be more precise. The model-checking problem for the μ-calculus is closely related to the problem of determining the winner in games on And-Or graphs. The system complexity of μ-calculus model checking is PTIME-hard, because a μ-calculus formula of a fixed size can specify an unbounded number of switches between universal and existential branching modes. In particular, the formula $\mu y.(t \vee EXAXy)$ specifies winning for And-Or reachability games, and formulas with alternations between least and greatest fixed-point quantifiers can specify winning for And-Or parity games. One would therefore suspect that the universal and existential fragments of the μ-calculus, in which no switching between branching modes is possible, might not be sufficiently strong to specify And-Or reachability. Indeed, in [11] the authors define a fragment L_2 of the μ-calculus which explicitly bounds the number of switches between both AX and EX modalities and $\wedge$ and $\vee$ boolean operators. This fragment is as expressive as extended CTL* [11], and it cannot specify reachability in And-Or graphs (the system complexity of model checking is NLOGSPACE-complete). However, in model checking as well as implication problems, we can consider models in which the successors of a state are labeled in a way that enables the specification to directly refer to them. Then, it is possible to replace the existential next modality by a disjunction over all successors, and it is possible to replace the universal next modality by a conjunction that refers to each successor. More specifically, if we can guarantee that the successors of a state with branching degree two are labeled by l (left) and r (right), then the existential next formula EXy can be replaced by $AX(l \rightarrow y) \vee AX(r \rightarrow y)$, and the universal next formula AXy can be replaced by $EX(l \wedge y) \wedge EX(r \wedge y)$. While these observations are technically simple, they enable us to solve the open problems regarding the complexity of the universal and existential fragments of the μ-calculus.

2 Propositional μ-Calculus

The *propositional μ-calculus* (MC, for short) is a propositional modal logic augmented with least and greatest fixed-point quantifiers [21]. Specifically, we consider a μ-calculus where formulas are constructed from Boolean propositions with Boolean connectives, the temporal modalities EX and AX, as well as least (μ) and greatest (ν) fixed-point quantifiers. We assume without loss of generality that μ-calculus formulas are written in positive normal form (negation is applied only to atomic propositions). Formally, given a set AP of atomic propositions and a set V of variables, a μ-calculus formula is either:

- *true*, *false*, p, or $\neg p$, for $p \in AP$;
- y, for $y \in V$;
- $\varphi_1 \wedge \varphi_2$ or $\varphi_1 \vee \varphi_2$, where φ_1 and φ_2 are μ-calculus formulas;
- $AX\varphi$ or $EX\varphi$, where φ is a μ-calculus formula;
- $\mu y.\varphi$ or $\nu y.\varphi$, where $y \in V$ and φ is a μ-calculus formula.

We say that the variable y is *bound* in $\mu y.\varphi$ and $\nu y.\varphi$. A variable is *free* if it is not bound. A *sentence* is a formula that contains no free variables. We refer to AX and EX as the *universal* and *existential* next modalities, respectively. For a μ-calculus formula φ, define the *size* $|\varphi|$ of φ as the size of the DAG representation of φ.

The *universal μ-calculus* ($\forall MC$, for short) is the fragment of the μ-calculus in which the only next modality allowed is the universal one. Dually, the *existential μ-calculus* ($\exists MC$, for short) is the fragment in which the only next modality allowed is the existential one. Note that since μ-calculus formulas are written in positive normal form, there is no way to specify existential next in $\forall MC$ by negating universal next.

A μ-calculus formula is *alternation-free* if, for all $y \in V$, there are respectively no occurrences of ν (μ) on any syntactic path from an occurrence of μy (νy) to an occurrence of y. For example, the formula $\mu x.(p \vee \mu y.(x \vee EXy))$ is alternation-free, and the formula $\nu x.\mu y.((p \wedge x) \vee EXy)$ is not. The *alternation-free μ-calculus* ($AFMC$, for short) is the subset of the μ-calculus that contains only the alternation-free formulas. We also refer to the universal and existential fragments of $AFMC$, and denote them by $\forall AFMC$ and $\exists AFMC$, respectively.

A μ-calculus formula is *guarded* if for all $y \in V$, all occurrences of y that are in a scope of a fixed-point quantifier $\lambda \in \{\mu, \nu\}$ are also in a scope of a next modality which is itself in the scope of λ. For example, the formula $\mu y.(p \vee EXy)$ is guarded, and the formula $EX\mu y.(p \vee y)$ is not. We assume that all μ-calculus formulas are guarded. As proved in [24], every μ-calculus formula can be linearly translated to an equivalent guarded one, thus we do not lose generality with our assumption.

The semantics of μ-calculus formulas is defined with respect to Kripke structures. A *Kripke structure* $\mathcal{K} = \langle AP, W, R, w_0, L\rangle$ consists of a set AP of atomic propositions, a set W of states, a total transition relation $R \subseteq W \times W$, an initial state $w_0 \in W$, and a labeling $L : W \to 2^{AP}$ that maps each state to the set of atomic propositions true in that state.

Given a Kripke structure $\mathcal{K} = \langle AP, W, R, w_0, L\rangle$ and a set $\{y_1, \ldots, y_n\}$ of free variables, a *valuation* $\mathcal{V} : \{y_1, \ldots, y_n\} \to 2^W$ is an assignment of subsets of W to the variables in $\{y_1, \ldots, y_n\}$. For a valuation $\mathcal{V}$, a variable y, and a set $W' \subseteq W$, denote by $\mathcal{V}[y \leftarrow W']$ the valuation mapping y to W', and y' to $\mathcal{V}(y')$ for all $y' \neq y$. A formula φ with atomic propositions from AP and free variables $\{y_1, \ldots, y_n\}$ is interpreted over the structure $\mathcal{K}$ as a mapping $\varphi^{\mathcal{K}}$ from valuations to 2^W. Thus, $\varphi^{\mathcal{K}}(\mathcal{V})$ denotes the set of states that satisfy φ under the valuation $\mathcal{V}$. The mapping $\varphi^{\mathcal{K}}$ is defined inductively as follows:

- $true^{\mathcal{K}}(\mathcal{V}) = W$ and $false^{\mathcal{K}}(\mathcal{V}) = \emptyset$.
- For $p \in AP$, let $p^{\mathcal{K}}(\mathcal{V}) = \{w \in W \mid p \in L(w)\}$ and $(\neg p)^{\mathcal{K}}(\mathcal{V}) = \{w \in W \mid p \notin L(w)\}$.
- $(\varphi_1 \wedge \varphi_2)^{\mathcal{K}}(\mathcal{V}) = \varphi_1^{\mathcal{K}}(\mathcal{V}) \cap \varphi_2^{\mathcal{K}}(\mathcal{V})$.
- $(\varphi_1 \vee \varphi_2)^{\mathcal{K}}(\mathcal{V}) = \varphi_1^{\mathcal{K}}(\mathcal{V}) \cup \varphi_2^{\mathcal{K}}(\mathcal{V})$.
- $(AX\varphi)^{\mathcal{K}}(\mathcal{V}) = \{w \in W \mid \forall w'. \text{ if } (w, w') \in R \text{ then } w' \in \varphi^{\mathcal{K}}(\mathcal{V})\}$.
- $(EX\varphi)^{\mathcal{K}}(\mathcal{V}) = \{w \in W \mid \exists w'.(w, w') \in R \text{ and } w' \in \varphi^{\mathcal{K}}(\mathcal{V})\}$.
- $(\mu x.\varphi)^{\mathcal{K}}(\mathcal{V}) = \bigcap\{W' \subseteq W \mid \varphi^{\mathcal{K}}(\mathcal{V}[x \leftarrow W']) \subseteq W'\}$.
- $(\nu x.\varphi)^{\mathcal{K}}(\mathcal{V}) = \bigcup\{W' \subseteq W \mid W' \subseteq \varphi^{\mathcal{K}}(\mathcal{V}[x \leftarrow W'])\}$.

By the Knaster-Tarski theorem, the required fixed-points always exist. For a sentence, no valuation is required. For a state $w \in W$ of the Kripke structure $\mathcal{K}$, and a sentence φ, we write $\mathcal{K}, w \models \varphi$ iff $w \in \varphi^{\mathcal{K}}$.

3 Satisfiability and Validity

The satisfiability problem for a μ-calculus sentence φ is to decide whether there is a Kripke structure $\mathcal{K}$ and a state w in it such that $\mathcal{K}, w \models \varphi$. The validity problem is to decide whether $\mathcal{K}, w \models \varphi$ for all $\mathcal{K}$ and w. Note that φ is satisfiable iff $\neg\varphi$ is not valid. The satisfiability and validity problems for μ-calculus and its alternation-free fragment are EXPTIME-complete [1,13]. In this section we study the satisfiability and validity problems for the universal and existential fragments.

For a $\forall MC$ formula φ, let $[\varphi]$ denote the linear-time μ-calculus formula [21] obtained from φ by omitting all its universal path quantifiers. It is easy to see that φ is satisfiable iff $[\varphi]$ is satisfiable. Indeed, a model for $[\varphi]$ is also a model for φ, and each path in a model for φ is a model for $[\varphi]$. Since the satisfiability problem for the linear-time μ-calculus and its alternation-free fragment is PSPACE-complete [32], so is the satisfiability problem for $\forall MC$ and $\forall AFMC$.

Theorem 1. *The satisfiability problem for $\forall MC$ and $\forall AFMC$ is PSPACE-complete.*

Since both $\exists MC$ and $\exists AFMC$ subsume propositional logic, the satisfiability problem for these logics is clearly hard for NP. We show that the satisfiability problem is in fact NP-complete. To show membership in NP, we prove a *linear-size model property* for $\exists MC$.

Lemma 1. *Let φ be a formula of $\exists MC$. If φ is satisfiable, then it has a model with at most $O(|\varphi|)$ states and $O(|\varphi|)$ transitions.*

Proof. The proof is similar to the one used in [23] to show a linear-size model property for $\exists$CTL. We proceed by induction on the structure of $\exists MC$ formulas. With each $\exists MC$ formula φ, we associate a set S_φ of models (Kripke structures) that satisfy φ. We define S_φ by structural induction. The states of the models in S_φ are labeled by both the atomic propositions and the variables free in φ. We use $S_{\varphi_1} \to S_{\varphi_2}$ to denote the set of models obtained by taking a model M_1 from S_{φ_1}, a model M_2 from S_{φ_2}, adding a transition from the initial state of M_1 to the initial state of M_2, and fixing the initial state to be the one of M_1. We use $S_{\varphi_1} \cap^* S_{\varphi_2}$ to denote the set of models obtained by taking a model M_1 from S_{φ_1} and a model M_2 from S_{φ_2}, such that M_1 and M_2 agree on the labeling of their initial states, fixing the initial state to be the initial state of M_1, redirecting transitions to the initial state of M_2 into the initial state of M_1, and adding transitions from the initial state of M_1 to all the successors of the initial state of M_2. Finally, we use $S_{\varphi(\#)} \downarrow$, where $\#$ is an atomic proposition not in AP, to denote the set of models obtained from a model in $S_{\varphi(\#)}$ by adding transitions from states labeled by $\#$ to all the successors of the initial state, and removing $\#$ from the labels of states. We can now define S_φ as follows. Note that we do not consider the case where $\varphi = x$, for $x \in V$, as we assume that φ is a sentence.

- $S_{\mathbf{true}}$ is the set of all one-state models over AP.
- $S_{\mathbf{false}} = \emptyset$.
- S_p, for $p \in AP$, is the set of all one-state models over AP in which p holds.
- $S_{\neg p}$, for $\neg p \in AP$, is the set of all one-state models over AP in which p does not hold.

– $S_{\varphi_1 \vee \varphi_2} = S_{\varphi_1} \cup S_{\varphi_2}$.
– $S_{\varphi_1 \wedge \varphi_2} = S_{\varphi_1} \cap^* S_{\varphi_2}$.
– $S_{EX\varphi_1} = S_{\mathbf{true}} \to S_{\varphi_1}$.
– $S_{\mu x.\varphi_1(x)} = S_{\varphi_1(\varphi_1(false))}$.
– $S_{\nu x.\varphi_1(x)} = S_{\varphi_1(\# \wedge (\varphi_1(true)))} \downarrow$.

For example, if $AP = \{p\}$, and $\varphi = \nu x.\varphi_1(x)$ with $\varphi_1(x) = EX(p \wedge x) \wedge EX(\neg p \wedge x)$, then $\varphi_1(\# \wedge (\varphi_1(true))) = EX(p \wedge \# \wedge EXp \wedge EX\neg p) \wedge EX(\neg p \wedge \# \wedge EXp \wedge EX\neg p)$, and S_φ contains the two models obtained from the model M_1 described in the figure below by labeling the initial state by either p or $\neg p$. Also, if $AP = \{p, q\}$ and $\varphi = EXp \wedge (\mu y.q \vee (p \wedge EXy))$, then S_φ contains the models obtained from the models M_2 and M_3 described below by completing labels of p or q that are left unspecified.

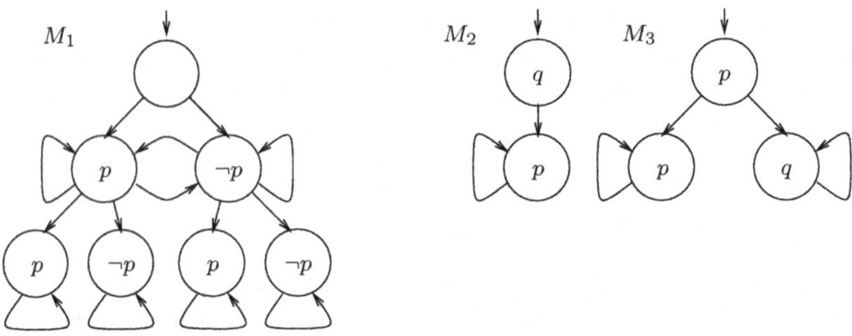

The models in S_φ are "economical" with respect to states that are required for satisfaction of formulas that refer to the strict future. For example, the initial state of models in $S_{EX\varphi_1}$ has a single successor that satisfies φ_1, and models in $S_{\mu y.\varphi(y)}$ that do not satisfy $\varphi(false)$ in the initial state, are required to satisfy $\varphi(false)$ in a successor state.

It is not hard to prove, by induction on the structure of φ, that each model in S_φ has $O(|\varphi|)$ states and $O(|\varphi|)$ transitions. We now prove, by an induction on the structure of φ, the following two claims.

1. For every model $M \in S_\varphi$, we have that M satisfies φ.
2. For every model M that satisfies φ, there is a model $M' \in S_\varphi$ such that M and M' agree on the labeling of their initial states.

Note that Claim (2) implies that if φ is satisfiable, then S_φ is not empty. Thus, the two claims together imply that if φ is satisfiable, then it has a satisfying model in S_φ, which is guaranteed to be of size linear in $|\varphi|$.

The proof for φ of the form *true*, *false*, p, $\neg p$, $\varphi_1 \vee \varphi_2$, and $\varphi_1 \wedge \varphi_2$ is easy. For the other cases, we proceed as follows.

Let $\varphi = EX\varphi_1$. By the induction hypothesis, all models in S_{φ_1} satisfy φ_1. Hence, (1) follows immediately from the definition of S_φ. To see (2), consider a model M that satisfies φ. Since $S_{\mathbf{true}}$ is the set of all one-state models over AP, it contains a model M' that agrees with M on the labeling of their initial states.

Let $\varphi = \mu x.\varphi_1(x)$. By the semantics of μ-calculus, a model that satisfies $\varphi_1(\varphi_1(\mathit{false}))$, satisfies φ as well. Hence, (1) follows immediately from the definition of S_φ. To see (2), consider a model M that satisfies φ. This means that for some $i > 0$, the model M satisfies $\varphi_1^i(\mathit{false})$. We construct a model M' that satisfies $\varphi_1(\varphi_1(\mathit{false}))$ and agrees with M on the label of the initial state. Let # be a proposition not in AP, and consider the formula $\varphi_1(\# \wedge \varphi_1^{i-1}(\mathit{false}))$. The model M can be attributed by # to satisfy $\varphi_1(\# \wedge \varphi_1^{i-1}(\mathit{false}))$. Moreover, since φ is guarded, the initial state of M is attributed by # only if there is a self loop in the initial state. Such a self loop can be unwound, so we can assume that the initial state of M is not attributed by #. Since φ is satisfiable, so is $\varphi_1(\mathit{false})$, and so there is a model N of $\varphi_1(\mathit{false})$. The structure M' is obtained from M by replacing all states attributed by # with N (i.e., all transitions leading into a state attributed by # are redirected to the initial state of N). Then, M' is a model of $\varphi_1(\varphi_1(\mathit{false}))$, and agrees with M in the labeling of the initial states.

Let $\varphi = \nu x.\varphi_1(x)$. By the semantics of μ-calculus, a model M satisfies φ iff M satisfies $\varphi_1^i(\mathit{true})$, for all $i \geq 0$. Consider a model $M \in S_\varphi$. By the definition of S_φ, the model M satisfies $\varphi_1(\mathit{true})$, and the states attributed # satisfy $\varphi_1(\mathit{true})$ as well. Since $\varphi_1(\mathit{true})$ is existential, the states attributed # continue to satisfy $\varphi_1(\mathit{true})$ after the new edges are added. In fact, it is not hard to see that after the new edges are added, the states attributed # also satisfy $\varphi_1(\#)$. Thus, for all $i \geq 1$, the model M can be unfolded $(i-1)$ times to show M satisfies $\varphi_1^i(\mathit{true})$, and we are done. To see (2), let M be a model of φ and let # be a proposition not in AP. Then, M satisfies $\varphi_1(\varphi_1(\mathit{true}))$, and it can be attributed by # to satisfy $\varphi_1(\# \wedge \varphi(\mathit{true}))$. As in the previous case, since φ is guarded, we can ensure that this leaves the labeling of the initial state unchanged, possibly after unwinding a self loop in the initial state. In addition, adding transitions from states attributed by # to all successors of the initial state, leaves the label of the initial state unchanged, and thus results in a model in S_φ that agrees with M on the labeling of their initial states. □

Note that the μ-calculus with both universal and existential next modalities has only an exponential-size model property (there is a μ-calculus sentence φ such that the smallest Kripke structure that satisfies φ is of size exponential in $|\varphi|$). Thus, the linear-size model property crucially depends on the fact that the only next modality that is allowed is the existential one. The linear-size model theorem shows that the satisfiability problem for $\exists MC$ and $\exists AFMC$ is in NP.

Theorem 2. *The satisfiability problem for $\exists MC$ and $\exists AFMC$ is NP-complete.*

Since a formula φ is satisfiable iff $\neg\varphi$ is valid, and since negating an $\exists MC$ formula results in a $\forall MC$ formula and vice versa, the following theorem is an immediate corollary of Theorems 1 and 2.

Theorem 3. *The validity problem is co-NP-complete for $\forall MC$ and $\forall AFMC$, and is PSPACE-complete for $\exists MC$ and $\exists AFMC$.*

4 Model Checking

The model-checking problem for the μ-calculus is to decide, given a Kripke structure $\mathcal{K}$ and a μ-calculus formula φ, the set of states in $\mathcal{K}$ that satisfy φ. In this section we study the model-checking problem for the universal and existential fragments of the μ-calculus. We show that in contrast to the case of satisfiability, the model-checking problem for the restricted fragments is not easier than the model-checking problem for the μ-calculus, and the same is true for the alternation-free fragments.

The model-checking problem for the μ-calculus is closely related to the problem of determining the winner in games on And-Or graphs. We first review here some definitions that will be used in the reduction of the model-checking problem for the full μ-calculus to the model-checking problem for the fragments. A *two-player game graph* is a directed graph $G = \langle V, E\rangle$, with a partition $V_e \cup V_u$ of V. The game is played between two players, player 1 and player 2. A position of the game is a vertex $v \in V$. At each step of the game, if the current position v is in V_e, then player 1 chooses the next position among the vertices in $\{w \mid \langle v, w\rangle \in E\}$. Similarly, if $v \in V_u$, then player 2 chooses the next position among the vertices in $\{w \mid \langle v, w\rangle \in E\}$. The game continues for an infinite number of steps, and induces an infinite path $\pi \in V^\omega$. The winner of the game depends on different conditions we can specify on words in V^ω. The simplest game is *reachability.* Then, the winning condition is some vertex $t \in V$, and player 1 wins the game if π eventually reaches the vertex t. Otherwise, player 2 wins. A richer game is *parity.* In parity games, there is a function $C : V \to \{0, \ldots, k-1\}$ that maps each vertex to a *color* in $\{0, \ldots, k-1\}$. Player 1 wins the parity game if the maximal color that repeats in π infinitely often is even.

A *strategy* for player 1 is a function $\xi_1 : V^* \times V_e \to V$ such that for all $u \in V^*$ and $v \in V_e$, we have $\xi_1(u \cdot v) \in \{w \mid \langle v, w\rangle \in E\}$. A strategy for player 2 is defined similarly, as $\xi_2 : V^* \times V_u \to V$. For a vertex $s \in V$, and strategies ξ_1 and ξ_2 for player 1 and player 2, respectively, the *outcome* of ξ_1 and ξ_2 from s, denoted $\pi(\xi_1, \xi_2)(s)$, is the trace $v_0, v_1, \ldots \in V^\omega$ such that $v_0 = s$ and for all $i \geq 0$, we have $v_{i+1} \in \xi_1(v_0 \ldots v_{i-1}, v_i)$ if $v_i \in V_e$, and $v_{i+1} \in \xi_2(v_0 \ldots v_{i-1}, v_i)$ if $v_i \in V_u$. Finally, a vertex $s \in V$ is winning for player 1 if there is a strategy ξ_1 of player 1 such that for all strategies ξ_2 of player 2, the outcome $\pi(\xi_1, \xi_2)(s)$ is winning for player 1. When G has an initial state s, we say that player 1 wins the game on G if s is winning for player 1 in G.

We start by considering the *system complexity* of the model-checking problem for the universal and existential fragments of the μ-calculus; that is, the complexity of the problem in terms of the model, assuming the formula is fixed. As discussed in Section 1, the system complexity of *AFMC* model checking is PTIME-complete, and hardness in PTIME [17] crucially depends on the fact that an *AFMC* formula of a fixed size can specify an unbounded number of switches between universal and existential branching modes. As we prove in Theorem 4 below, the setting of model checking enables us to trade an unbounded number of switches between universal and existential branching modes by an unbounded number of switches between disjunctions and conjunctions. The idea is that in model checking, unlike in satisfiability, we can consider models in which the successors of a state are labeled in a way that enables the formula to directly refer to them. Then, it is possible to replace the existential next modality by a disjunction over all successors, and it is possible to replace the universal next modality by a conjunction that refers to each successor.

Theorem 4. *The complexity and system complexity of $\forall AFMC$ (so, also of $\exists AFMC$) model checking is PTIME-complete.*

Proof. Membership in PTIME follows from the linear time algorithm for $AFMC$ [6]. For hardness, we reduce the problem of deciding a winner in a reachability game to model checking of a $\forall AFMC$ formula of a fixed size. Since one can model check a specification φ by checking $\neg\varphi$ and negating the result, the same lower bound holds for $\exists AFMC$.

Deciding reachability in two-player games is known to be PTIME-hard already for acyclic graphs with branching degree two, where universal and existential vertices alternate, and both s and t are in V_e [14]. Given a bipartite and acyclic game graph $G = \langle V, E\rangle$ with branching degree two, a partition of V to V_e and V_u, and two vertices s and t in V_e, we construct a Kripke structure $\mathcal{K} = \langle AP, W, R, w_0, L\rangle$ and a formula in $\forall AFMC$ such that $\mathcal{K}, w_0 \models \varphi$ iff player 1 wins the reachability game on G from state s and with target t.

We do the proof in two steps. First, we transform the graph G to another graph G', with some helpful properties, and then we construct the Kripke structure $\mathcal{K}$ from G'. Essentially, in G' each universal vertex is a left or right successor of exactly one existential vertex. Formally, $G' = \langle V', E'\rangle$, where $V' = V_e \cup V'_u$, and V'_u and E' are defined as follows. Let $E_e = E \cap (V_e \times V_u)$ and $E_u = E \cap (V_u \times V_e)$. Recall that each vertex in V_e has two successors. Let $E_e = E^l_e \cup E^r_e$ be a partition of E_e so that for each $v \in V_e$, one successor v_l of v is such that $\langle v, v_l\rangle \in E^l_e$ and the other successor v_r of v is such that $\langle v, v_r\rangle \in E^r_e$. Note that a vertex u may be the left successor of some vertex w_1 and the right successor of some other vertex w_2; thus $E^l_e(w_1, u)$ and $E^r_e(w_2, u)$. The goal of G' is to prevent such cases.

- $V'_u \subseteq V_u \times \{l, r\} \times V_e$ is such that $(v, l, w) \in V'_u$ iff $(w, v) \in E^l_e$ and $(v, r, w) \in V'_u$ iff $(w, v) \in E^r_e$. Thus, each edge $\langle w, v\rangle \in E_e$ contributes one vertex (v, l, w) or (v, r, w) to V'_u. Intuitively, visits to the vertex (v, l, w) correspond to visits to v in which it has been reached by following the left branch of w, and similarly for (v, r, w) and right.
- $E'_e = \{\langle v, (v_l, l, v)\rangle : \langle v, v_l\rangle \in E^l_e\} \cup \{\langle v, (v_r, r, v)\rangle : \langle v, v_r\rangle \in E^r_e\}$. Also, $E'_u = \{\langle (v, d, w), u\rangle : \langle v, u\rangle \in E_u\}$, and $E' = E'_e \cup E'_u$.

The size of G' is linear in the size of G. Indeed $|V'| = |V_e| + |E_e|$ and $|E'| = |E'_e| + |E'_u| \leq |E_e| + 2|E_u|$. It is not hard to see that player 1 can win the game in G iff he can win in G'. Note that the branching degree of G' remains two. The construction of G' ensures that the two successors of an existential vertex v can be referred to unambiguously as the left or the right successor of v.

The graph $G' = \langle V', E'\rangle$, together with s and t, induces the Kripke structure $\mathcal{K} = \langle AP, V', E', s, L\rangle$ described below. The set of atomic propositions $AP =$

$\{t, l\}$. For readability, we also introduce the shorthand r for $\neg l$.The proposition t holds in (and only in) the state t, and the propositions l and r hold in the left and right successor respectively for an existential node. Thus $l \in L(\langle v, l, w\rangle)$ and $r \in L(\langle v, r, w\rangle)$. Finally, let φ be the $\forall AFMC$ formula $\mu y.t \vee (AX(\neg l \vee AXy) \vee AX(\neg r \vee AXy))$. It is now easy to see that player 1 can win the reachability game for t from s in G' iff $\mathcal{K}, s \models \varphi$. □

Theorem 5. *The model-checking problem for* $\forall MC$ *(so, also for* $\exists MC$*) is as hard as the model-checking problem for the* μ*-calculus.*

Proof. The idea is similar to the proof of Theorem 4, only that instead of talking about winning a reachability game, we talk about winning a *parity game* [10], to which and from which μ-calculus model checking can be reduced [11]. Without loss of generality, we assume that existential and universal vertices alternate (the game graph is bipartite), and each node has exactly two successors. We also assume that each vertex in V_u has the same color as the incoming existential nodes (otherwise, we can duplicate nodes and get an equivalent game with this property). We assume that each vertex of G is labeled by the color $C(v)$, thus we can refer to G as a Kripke structure with $AP = \{0, \ldots, k-1\}$: the proposition i holds at vertex v iff $C(v) = i$. From [10], player 1 wins the parity game G at an existential vertex $s \in V_e$ iff

$$G, s \models \lambda_{k-1} x_{k-1} \ldots \mu x_1 . \nu x_0 . \; (\bigvee_{i \in [0 \ldots (k-1)]} (i \wedge EXAXx_i)),$$

where $\lambda_n = \nu$ if n is even, and $\lambda_n = \mu$ if n is odd.

The formula above uses both universal and existential next modalities. By transforming G to a Kripke structure $\mathcal{K}$ as in the proof of Theorem 4, we can use left and right labels to vertices in the graph and use only one type of branching mode. Formally, let $\mathcal{K}$ be the Kripke structure induced by G. Then, player 1 wins the parity game in G at a node s iff

$$\mathcal{K}, s \models \lambda_{k-1} x_{k-1} \ldots \mu x_1 . \nu x_0 . \; (\bigvee_{i \in [0 \ldots (k-1)]} (i \wedge ((AX(\neg l \vee AXx_i)) \vee (AX(\neg r \vee AXx_i)))$$

□

If the syntax of the μ-calculus is equipped with next modalities parameterized by action labels, then the above result follows immediately, because there is no distinction between existential and universal next modalities. Our proof shows that the result follows even if no such labeling is available.

5 Implication

The *implication problem* for a logic asks if one specification logically implies another specification; formally, given formulas φ and ψ of the logic, if the formula $\varphi \to \psi$ is valid. It arises naturally in *modular verification* [23,28], where the antecedent of the implication is the assumption about the behavior of a component's environment, and the consequent is a guarantee about the behavior of the component. For logics closed under negation, the implication problem is equivalent to validity: a formula φ is valid iff $true \rightarrow \varphi$. Thus, the implication problem for the μ-calculus is EXPTIME-complete. However, for the existential and universal fragments of the μ-calculus, this is not the case: the implication problem combines both universal and existential formulas, and is more general than satisfiability or validity.

Theorem 6. *The implication problem for $\exists MC$ and $\exists AFMC$ (so, also for $\forall MC$ and $\forall AFMC$) is EXPTIME-complete.*

Proof. For formulas φ_1 and φ_2 of $\exists MC$, we have that $\varphi_1 \rightarrow \varphi_2$ iff the formula $\varphi_1 \wedge \neg\varphi_2$ is not satisfiable. Membership in EXPTIME follows from the complexity of the satisfiability problem for the μ-calculus. Note that $\neg\varphi_2$ is a formula of $\forall MC$, thus we cannot apply the results of Section 3.

To prove hardness in EXPTIME, we do a reduction from the satisfiability problem of $AFMC$, proved to be EXPTIME-hard in [13]. Given an $AFMC$ formula ψ, we construct a formula φ_A of $\forall AFMC$ and a formula φ_E of $\exists AFMC$ such that the conjunction $\varphi = \varphi_E \wedge \varphi_A$ is satisfiable iff ψ is satisfiable. For simplicity, we assume that ψ is satisfied iff it is satisfied in a tree of branching degree two. Note that while our assumption does not hold for all $AFMC$ formulas, the EXPTIME-hardness of the satisfiability problem for $AFMC$ holds already for such formulas, which is sufficiently good for our goal here.

Intuitively, the formula φ_E would require the states of models of φ to be attributed by directions so that at least one successor is labeled by l and at least one successor is labeled by r. In addition, φ_A would contain a conjunct that requires each state to be labeled by at most one direction. Thus, states that are labeled by l cannot be labeled by r, and vice versa. Then, the other conjunct of φ_A is obtained from ψ by replacing an existential next modality by a disjunction over the successors of a state.

Formally, the formula $\varphi_E = \nu y.EX(l \wedge y) \wedge EX(r \wedge y)$ requires each state (except for the initial state) to have at least two successors, labeled by different directions, and the formula $\varphi_A^1 = \nu y.((\neg l) \vee (\neg r)) \wedge AXy$ requires each state to be labeled by at most one direction.

Then, the formula φ_A^2 is obtained from ψ by replacing a subformula of the form $EX\theta$ by the formula $AX(r \vee \theta) \vee AX(l \vee \theta)$. We show that for every ψ such that ψ is satisfiable iff it is satisfiable in a model of branching degree two, we have that ψ is satisfiable iff $\varphi_E \wedge \varphi_A^1 \wedge \varphi_A^2$ is satisfiable. First, if ψ is satisfiable, then there is a tree of branching degree two that satisfies it. This tree can be attributed with l and r so that it satisfies the formula $\varphi_E \wedge \varphi_A^1 \wedge \varphi_A^2$, by labeling the left successor of each node with $\{l, \neg r\}$ and the right successor of each node with $\{\neg l, r\}$. On the other hand, assume that the formula $\varphi_E \wedge \varphi_A^1 \wedge \varphi_A^2$ is satisfiable in a model M. The subformula $\varphi_E \wedge \varphi_A^1$ guarantees that each state of M has at least one successor that is not labeled l and at least one successor that is not labeled r. Accordingly, each subformula of the form $AX(r \vee \theta) \vee AX(l \vee \theta)$

is satisfied in a state w of M iff w has a successor that satisfies θ, thus w satisfies $EX\theta$. Hence, the model M also satisfies ψ. □

The above proof constructs, given a formula φ of the μ-calculus, two formulas φ_E and φ_A such that φ_E is an existential formula, φ_A is a universal formula, and φ is satisfiable iff $\varphi_E \wedge \varphi_A$ is satisfiable. However, one cannot in general construct formulas φ_E and φ_A such that $\varphi_E \wedge \varphi_A$ is equivalent to φ. This can be proved considering two states of a Kripke structure that are similar, but not bisimilar, and the formula of μ-calculus that distinguishes them.

Note that the implication problem for $\forall$CTL* and $\exists$CTL* is EXPSPACE-complete [23], and hence easier than the satisfiability problem for CTL*, which is 2EXPTIME-complete. The above construction does not work for $\exists$CTL*, as the formula φ_E used to label the states of a model by directions specifies an unbounded number of unfoldings of the structure. On the other hand, the number of unfoldings expressible by an $\exists$CTL* formula is bounded by the size of the formula; thus, the formula φ_E does not have an equivalent formula in $\exists$CTL*.

6 Discussion

We studied the complexity of the satisfiability, validity, model-checking, and implication problems for the universal and existential fragments of the μ-calculus and its alternation-free fragment. We proved that the linear-size model property, which is known for $\exists$CTL, holds also for $\exists MC$. Interestingly, the property does not hold for $\exists$CTL*, which is less expressive than $\exists MC$. Thus, the picture we obtain for $\exists MC$ and $\exists AFMC$ is different than the one known for $\exists$CTL* and $\exists$CTL. For the universal fragments $\forall MC$ and $\forall AFMC$, the picture does agree with the one known for $\forall$CTL* and $\forall$CTL, and the complexity of the satisfiability problem coincides with the complexity of the linear-time versions of the logics (obtained by omitting all universal path quantifiers).

We showed how labeling of states with directions makes the model-checking and implication problems for the universal and existential fragments as hard as for the full logics. While such a labeling is straightforward in the case of model checking, it is not always possible for implication. Indeed, in the case of CTL* and CTL, formulas cannot specify a legal labeling, making the implication problem for $\forall$CTL* and $\exists$CTL* strictly easier than the implication problem for CTL*, and similarly for CTL. In contrast, we were able to label the directions legally using a $\forall AFMC$ formula, making the implication problems for $\forall MC$ and $\exists MC$ as hard as the one for MC, and similarly for the alternation-free fragments. Another way to see the importance of the fixed-point quantifiers is to observe that the implication problems for Modal Logic (μ-calculus without fixed-point quantifiers) and its universal and existential fragments are co-NP-complete.

Finally, the *equivalence problem* for a logic asks, given formulas φ and ψ, if the formula $\varphi \leftrightarrow \psi$ is valid. The equivalence problem for the μ-calculus is EXPTIME-complete, by easy reductions to and from satisfiability. This gives an EXPTIME upper bound for the equivalence problem for $\exists MC$ and $\forall MC$.

By a reduction from satisfiability or validity (whichever is harder), we also get a PSPACE lower bound. However, the exact complexity for the equivalence problem for the universal and existential fragments of the μ-calculus remains open (also for the alternation-free fragments).

The gap above highlights the difficulty in studying the universal and existential fragments of the μ-calculus. It is easy to see that in all formalisms that are closed under complementation (in particular, full MC), equivalence is as hard as satisfiability. Indeed, φ and ψ are equivalent iff $(\varphi \wedge \neg\psi) \vee (\psi \wedge \neg\varphi)$ is not satisfiable. When a formalism is not closed under complementation, equivalence is not harder than implication, and is not easier than satisfiability or validity, whichever is harder. In the case of CTL, for example, it is easy to see that the equivalence problems for ∀CTL and ∃CTL are PSPACE-complete, as implication has the same complexity as satisfiability or validity (whichever is harder). The same holds for word automata: if we identify the existential fragment with nondeterministic automata, and the universal fragment with universal automata, then in both cases the language-containment problem (the automata-theoretic counterpart of implication) has the same complexity as the harder one of the nonemptiness and universality problems (the automata-theoretic counterparts of satisfiability and validity). Once we do not allow fixed-point quantifiers, the same holds for the μ-calculus: the equivalence problem for Modal Logic and its universal and existential fragments is co-NP-complete, as the co-NP-hardness of the implication problem applies already for the validity problem. So, in all the cases we know, except for the universal and existential fragments of CTL* and the μ-calculus and its alternation-free fragment, the above immediate upper and lower bounds do not induce a gap, and the exact complexity of the equivalence problem is known.

References

1. B. Banieqbal and H. Barringer. Temporal logic with fixed points. *Temporal Logic in Specification*, LNCS 398, pages 62–74. Springer-Verlag, 1987.
2. J. Burch, E. Clarke, K. McMillan, D. Dill, and L. Hwang. Symbolic model checking: 10^{20} states and beyond. *Information and Computation*, 98(2):142–170, June 1992.
3. E. Clarke and E. Emerson. Design and synthesis of synchronization skeletons using branching-time temporal logic. In *Logic of Programs*, LNCS 131, pages 52–71. Springer-Verlag, 1981.
4. E. Clarke, E. Emerson, and A. Sistla. Automatic verification of finite-state concurrent systems using temporal-logic specifications. *ACM Trans. on Programming Languages and Systems*, 8(2):244–263, 1986.
5. E. Clarke, O. Grumberg, and D. Peled. *Model Checking*. MIT Press, 1999.
6. R. Cleaveland and B. Steffen. A linear-time model-checking algorithm for the alternation-free modal μ-calculus. *Formal Methods in System Design*, 2:121–147, 1993.
7. M. Dam. CTL* and ECTL* as fragments of the modal μ-calculus. *Theoretical Computer Science*, 126:77–96, 1994.
8. E. Emerson and J. Halpern. Sometimes and not never revisited: On branching versus linear time. *Journal of the ACM*, 33(1):151–178, 1986.

9. E. Emerson and C. Jutla. The complexity of tree automata and logics of programs. In *Proc. Foundations of Computer Science*, pages 328–337. IEEE Press, 1988.
10. E. Emerson and C. Jutla. Tree automata, μ-calculus and determinacy. In *Proc. Foundations of Computer Science*, pages 368–377. IEEE Press, 1991.
11. E. Emerson, C. Jutla, and A. Sistla. On model-checking for fragments of μ-calculus. In *Computer Aided Verification*, LNCS 697, pages 385–396. Springer-Verlag, 1993.
12. E. Emerson and C.-L. Lei. Efficient model checking in fragments of the propositional μ-calculus. In *Proc. Logic in Computer Science*, pages 267–278. 1986.
13. M. Fischer and R. Ladner. Propositional dynamic logic of regular programs. *Journal of Computer and System Sciences*, 18:194–211, 1979.
14. R. Greenlaw, H. Hoover, and W. Ruzzo. *Limits of Parallel Computation.* Oxford University Press, 1995.
15. O. Grumberg and D.E. Long. Model checking and modular verification. *ACM Trans. on Programming Languages and Systems*, 16(3):843–871, 1994.
16. M. Hennessy and R. Milner. Algebraic laws for nondeterminism and concurrency. *Journal of the ACM*, 32:137–161, 1985.
17. N. Immerman. Number of quantifiers is better than number of tape cells. *Journal of Computer and System Sciences*, 22(3):384–406, 1981.
18. D. Janin and I. Walukiewicz. On the expressive completeness of the propositional μ-calculus with respect to the monadic second-order logic. In *Concurrency Theory*, LNCS 1119, pages 263–277. Springer-Verlag, 1996.
19. M. Jurdzinski. Deciding the winner in parity games is in UP $\cap$ co-UP. *Information Processing Letters*, 68(3):119–124, 1998.
20. M. Jurdzinski. Small progress measures for solving parity games. In *Theoretical Aspects of Computer Science*, LNCS 1770, pages 290–301. Springer-Verlag, 2000.
21. D. Kozen. Results on the propositional μ-calculus. *Theoretical Computer Science*, 27:333–354, 1983.
22. D. Kozen. A finite model theorem for the propositional μ-calculus. *Studia Logica*, 47(3):333–354, 1988.
23. O. Kupferman and M. Vardi. An automata-theoretic approach to modular model checking. *ACM Trans. on Programming Languages and Systems*, 22:87–128, 2000.
24. O. Kupferman, M. Vardi, and P. Wolper. An automata-theoretic approach to branching-time model checking. *Journal of the ACM*, 47(2):312–360, 2000.
25. R. Kurshan. *FormalCheck User's Manual.* Cadence Design Inc., 1998.
26. D. Long, A. Brown, E. Clarke, S. Jha, and W. Marrero. An improved algorithm for the evaluation of fixpoint expressions. In *Computer Aided Verification*, LNCS 818, pages 338–350. Springer-Verlag, 1994.
27. K. McMillan. *Symbolic Model Checking.* Kluwer Academic Publishers, 1993.
28. A. Pnueli. In transition from global to modular temporal reasoning about programs. In *Logics and Models of Concurrent Systems*, volume F-13 of *NATO Advanced Summer Institutes*, pages 123–144. Springer-Verlag, 1985.
29. A. Pnueli and R. Rosner. On the synthesis of a reactive module. In *Proc. Principles of Programming Languages*, pages 179–190. ACM Press, 1989.
30. P. Ramadge and W. Wonham. The control of discrete-event systems. *IEEE Trans. on Control Theory*, 77:81–98, 1989.
31. H. Seidl. Fast and simple nested fixpoints. *Information Processing Letters*, 59(6):303–308, 1996.
32. M. Vardi. A temporal fixpoint calculus. In *Proc. Principles of Programming Languages*, pages 250–259. ACM Press, 1988.
33. M. Vardi and L. Stockmeyer. Improved upper and lower bounds for modal logics of programs. In *Proc. Theory of Computing*, pages 240–251. ACM Press, 1985.

Resets vs. Aborts in Linear Temporal Logic*

Roy Armoni[1], Doron Bustan[2], Orna Kupferman[3], and Moshe Y. Vardi[2]

[1] Intel Israel Development Center
[2] Rice University
[3] Hebrew University

Abstract. There has been a major emphasis recently in the semiconductor industry on designing industrial-strength property specification languages. Two major languages are ForSpec and Sugar 2.0, which are both extensions of Pnueli's LTL. Both ForSpec and Sugar 2.0 directly support reset/abort signals, in which a check for a property ψ may be terminated and declared successful by a reset/abort signal, provided the check has not yet failed. ForSpec and Sugar 2.0, however, differ in their definition of failure. The definition of failure in ForSpec is syntactic, while the definition in Sugar 2.0 is semantic. In this work we examine the implications of this distinction between the two approaches, which we refer to as the *reset* approach (for ForSpec) and the *abort* approach (for Sugar 2.0). In order to focus on the reset/abort issue, we do not consider the full languages, which are quite rich, but rather the extensions of LTL with the reset/abort constructs.

We show that the distinction between syntactic and semantic failure has a dramatic impact on the complexity of using the language in a model-checking tool. We prove that Reset-LTL enjoys the "fast-compilation property": there is a linear translation of Reset-LTL formulas into alternating Büchi automata, which implies a linear translation of Reset-LTL formulas into a symbolic representation of nondeterministic Büchi automata. In contrast, the translation of Abort-LTL formulas into alternating Büchi automata is nonelementary (i.e., cannot be bounded by a stack of exponentials of a bounded height); each abort yields an exponential blow-up in the translation. This complexity bounds also apply to model checking; model checking Reset-LTL formulas is exponential in the size of the property, while model checking Abort-LTL formulas is nonelementary in the size of the property (the same bounds apply to satisfiability checking).

1 Introduction

A key issue in the design of a model-checking tool is the choice of the formal specification language used to specify properties, as this language is one of the *primary* interfaces to the tool [7]. (The other primary interface is the modelling language, which is typically the hardware description language used by the designers). In view of this, there has been a major emphasis recently in the semiconductor industry on designing industrial-strength property specification languages (PSLs), e.g., Cadence's FormalCheck Specification

* A full version of this paper is available at `http://www.cs.rice.edu/~vardi/`.

H. Garavel and J. Hatcliff (Eds.): TACAS 2003, LNCS 2619, pp. 65–80, 2003.

Language [8], Intel's ForSpec [1][1], IBM's Sugar 2.0 [2][2], and Verisity's Temporal ***e*** [11]. These languages are all *linear* temporal languages (Sugar 2.0 has also a branching-time extension), in which time is treated as if each moment in time has a unique possible future. Thus, linear temporal formulas are interpreted over linear sequences, and we regard them as describing the behavior of a single computation of a system. In particular, both ForSpec and Sugar 2.0 can be viewed as extensions of Pnueli's LTL [13], with regular connectives and hardware-oriented features.

The regular connectives are aimed at giving the language the full expressive power of Büchi automata (cf. [1]). In contrast, the hardware-oriented features, *clocks* and *resets/aborts*, are aimed at offering direct support to two specification modes often used by verification engineers in the semiconductor industry. Both clocks and reset/abort are features that are needed to address the fact that modern semiconductor designs consist of interacting parallel modules. Today's semiconductor design technology is still dominated by synchronous design methodology. In synchronous circuits, clock signals synchronize the sequential logic, providing the designer with a simple operational model. While the asynchronous approach holds the promise of greater speed ([5]), designing asynchronous circuits is significantly harder than designing synchronous circuits. Current design methodology attempt to strike a compromise between the two approaches by using multiple clocks. This methodology results in architectures that are globally asynchronous but locally synchronous. ForSpec, for example, supports local asynchrony via the concept of *local clocks*, which enables each subformula to sample the trace according to a different clock; Sugar 2.0 supports local clocks in a similar way.

Another aspect of the fact that modern designs consist of parallel modules interacting asynchronously is the fact that a process running on one module can be reset by a signal coming from another module. As noted in [15], reset control has long been a critical aspect of embedded control design. Both ForSpec and Sugar 2.0 directly support reset/abort signals. The ForSpec formula "accept a in ψ" asserts that the property ψ should be checked only until the arrival of the reset signal a, at which point the check is considered to have *succeeded*. Similarly, the Sugar 2.0 formula "ψ abort on a" asserts that property ψ should be checked only until the arrival of the abort signal a, at which point the check is considered to have succeeded. In both ForSpec and Sugar 2.0 the signal a has to arrive before the property ψ has "failed"; arrival after failure cannot "rescue" ψ. ForSpec and Sugar 2.0, however, differ in their definition of *failure*.

The definition of failure in Sugar 2.0 is semantic; a formula fails at a point in a trace if the prefix up to (and including) that point cannot be extended in a manner that satisfies the formula. For example, the formula " next **false**" fails semantically at time 0, because it is impossible to extend the point at time 0 to a trace that satisfies the formula. In contrast, the definition of failure in ForSpec is syntactic. Thus, " next **false**" fails syntactically at time 1, because it is only then that the failure is actually discovered. As another example, consider the formula "(globally $\neg p$) $\wedge$ (eventually p)". It fails semantically

[1] ForSpec 2.0 has been designed in a collaboration between Intel, Co-Design Automation, Synopsys, and Verisity, and has been incorporated into the hardware verification language Open Vera, see `http://www.open-vera.com`.

[2] See `http://www.haifa.il.ibm.com/projects/verification/sugar/` for description of Sugar 2.0. We refer here to Version 0.8 (Draft 1), Sept. 12, 2002.

at time 0, but it never fails syntactically, since it is always possible to wait longer for the satisfaction of the eventuality (Formally, the notion of syntactic failure correspond to the notion of *informative prefix* in [6].) Mathematically, the definition of semantic failure is significantly simpler than that of syntactic failure (see formal definitions in the sequel), since the latter requires an inductive definition with respect to all syntactical constructs in the language.

In this work we examine the implications of this distinction between the two approaches, which we refer as the *reset* approach (for ForSpec) and the *abort* approach (for Sugar 2.0). In order to focus on the reset/abort issue, we do not consider the full languages, which are quite rich, but rather the extensions of LTL with the reset/abort constructs. We show that while both extensions result in logics that are as expressive as LTL, the distinction between syntactic and semantic failure has a dramatic impact on the complexity of using the language in a model-checking tool. In linear-time model checking we are given a design M (expressed in an HDL) and a property ψ (expressed in a PSL). To check that M satisfies ψ we construct a state-transition system T_M that corresponds to M and a nondeterministic Büchi automaton $\mathcal{A}_{\neg\psi}$ that corresponds to the negation of ψ. We then check if the composition $T_M||\mathcal{A}_{\neg\psi}$ contains a reachable fair cycle, which represents a trace of M falsifying ψ [19]. In a symbolic model checker the construction of T_M is linear in the size of M [3]. For LTL, the construction of $\mathcal{A}_{\neg\psi}$ is also linear in the size of ψ [3,18]. Thus, the front end of a model checker is quite fast; it is the back end, which has to search for a reachable fair cycle in $T_M||\mathcal{A}_{\neg\psi}$, that suffers from the "state-explosion problem".

We show here that Reset-LTL enjoys that "fast-compilation property": there is a linear translation of Reset-LTL formulas into alternating Büchi automata, which are exponentially more succinct than nondeterministic Büchi automata [18]. This implies a linear translation of Reset-LTL formulas into a symbolic representation of nondeterministic Büchi automata. In contrast, the translation of Abort-LTL formulas into alternating Büchi automata is nonelementary (i.e., cannot be bounded by a stack of exponentials of a bounded height); each abort yields an exponential blow-up in the translation. These complexity bounds are also shown to apply to model checking; model checking Reset-LTL formulas is exponential in the size of the property, while model checking Abort-LTL formulas is nonelementary in the size of the property (the same bounds apply to satisfiability checking).

Our results provide a rationale for the syntactic flavor of defining failure in ForSpec; it is this syntactic flavor that enables alternating automata to check for failure. This approach has a more operational flavor, which could be argued to match closer the intuition of verification engineers. In contrast, alternating automata cannot check for semantic failures, since these requires coordination between independent branches of alternating runs. It is this coordination that yields an exponential blow-up per abort. Our lower bounds for model checking and satisfiability show that this blow-up is intrinsic and not a side-effect of the automata-theoretic approach.

2 Preliminaries

A *nondeterministic Büchi word automaton* (NBW) is $\mathcal{A} = \langle \Sigma, S, S_0, \delta, F \rangle$, where Σ is a finite set of alphabet letters, S is a set of states, $\delta : S \times \Sigma \to 2^S$ is a transition function, $S_0 \subseteq S$ is a set of initial states, and $F \subseteq S$ is a set of accepting states. Let $w = w_0, w_1, \ldots$ be an infinite word over Σ. For $i \in \mathbb{N}$, let $w^i = w_i, w_{i+1}, \ldots$ denote the suffix of w from its ith letter. A sequence $\rho = s_0, s_1, \ldots$ in S^ω is a *run* of $\mathcal{A}$ over an infinite word $w \in \Sigma^\omega$, if $s_0 \in S_0$ and for every $i > 0$, we have $s_{i+1} \in \delta(s_i, w_i)$. We use $inf(\rho)$ to denote the set of states that appear infinitely often in ρ. A run ρ of $\mathcal{A}$ is *accepting* if $inf(\rho) \cap F \neq \emptyset$. An NBW $\mathcal{A}$ accepts a word w if $\mathcal{A}$ has an accepting run over w. We use $L(\mathcal{A})$ to denote the set of words that are accepted by $\mathcal{A}$. For $s \in S$, we denote by $\mathcal{A}^s$ the automaton $\mathcal{A}$ with a single initial state s.

Before we define an alternating Büchi word automaton, we need the following definition. For a given set X, let $\mathcal{B}^+(X)$ be the set of positive Boolean formulas over X (i.e., Boolean formulas built from elements in X using $\wedge$ and $\vee$), where we also allow the formulas **true** and **false**. Let $Y \subseteq X$. We say that Y *satisfies* a formula $\theta \in \mathcal{B}^+(X)$ if the truth assignment that assigns *true* to the members of Y and assigns *false* to the members of $X \setminus Y$ satisfies θ. A tree is a set $X \subseteq \mathbb{N}^*$, such that for $x \in \mathbb{N}^*$ and $n \in \mathbb{N}$, if $xn \in X$ then $x \in X$. We denote the length of x by $|x|$.

An *alternating Büchi word automaton* (ABW) is $\mathcal{A} = \langle \Sigma, S, s^0, \delta, F \rangle$, where Σ, S, and F are as in NBW, $s^0 \in S$ is a single initial state, and $\delta : S \times \Sigma \to \mathcal{B}^+(S)$ is a transition function. A run of $\mathcal{A}$ on an infinite word $w = w_0, w_1, \ldots$ is a (possibly infinite) S-labelled tree τ such that $\tau(\varepsilon) = s^0$ and the following holds: if $|x| = i$, $\tau(x) = s$, and $\delta(s, w_i) = \theta$, then x has k children $x_1, \ldots, x_k$, for some $k \leq |S|$, and $\{\tau(x1), \ldots, \tau(xk)\}$ satisfies θ. The run τ is *accepting* if every infinite branch in τ includes infinitely many labels in F. Note that the run can also have finite branches; if $|x| = i$, $\tau(x) = s$, and $\delta(s, a_i) = \mathbf{true}$, then x need not have children.

An *alternating weak word automaton (AWW)* is an ABW such that for every strongly connected component C of the automaton, either $C \subseteq F$ or $C \cap F = \emptyset$. Given two AWW $\mathcal{A}_1$ and $\mathcal{A}_2$, we can construct AWW for $\Sigma^\omega \setminus L(\mathcal{A}_1)$, $L(\mathcal{A}_1) \cap L(\mathcal{A}_2)$, and $L(\mathcal{A}_1) \cup L(\mathcal{A}_2)$, which are linear in their size, relative to $\mathcal{A}_1$ and $\mathcal{A}_2$ [12].

Next, we define the temporal logic LTL over a set of atomic propositions AP. The syntax of LTL is as follows. An atom $p \in AP$ is a formula. If ψ_1 and ψ_2 are LTL formulas, then so are $\neg\psi_1$, $\psi_1 \wedge \psi_2$, $\psi_1 \vee \psi_2$, $\mathbf{X}\,\psi_1$, and $\psi_1 \,\mathbf{U}\, \psi_2$. For the semantics of LTL see [13]. Each LTL formula ψ induces a language $L(\psi) \subseteq (2^{AP})^\omega$ of exactly all the infinite words that satisfy ψ.

Theorem 1. [18] *For every* LTL *formula ψ, there exists an AWW $\mathcal{A}_\psi$ with $O(|\psi|)$ states such that $L(\psi) = L(\mathcal{A}_\psi)$.*

Proof. For every subformula φ of ψ, we construct an AWW $\mathcal{A}_\varphi$ for φ. The construction proceeds inductively as follows.

- For $\varphi = p \in AP$, we define $\mathcal{A}_p = \langle 2^{AP}, \{s_p^0\}, s_p^0, \delta_p, \emptyset \rangle$, where $\delta_p(s_p^0, \sigma) = \mathbf{true}$ if p is true in σ and $\delta_p(s_p^0, \sigma) = \mathbf{false}$ otherwise.
- Let ψ_1 and ψ_2 be subformulas of ψ and let $\mathcal{A}_{\psi_1}$ and $\mathcal{A}_{\psi_2}$ the automata for these formulas. The automata for $\neg\psi_1$, $\psi_1 \wedge \psi_2$, and $\psi_1 \vee \psi_2$ are the automata for $\Sigma^\omega \setminus L(\mathcal{A}_1)$, $L(\mathcal{A}_1) \cap L(\mathcal{A}_2)$, and $L(\mathcal{A}_1) \cup L(\mathcal{A}_2)$, respectively.

- For $\varphi = \mathbf{X}\psi_1$, we define $\mathcal{A}_\varphi = \langle 2^{AP}, \{s^0_\varphi\} \cup S_{\psi_1}, s^0_\varphi, \delta_0 \cup \delta_{\psi_1}, F_{\psi_1}\rangle$ where $\delta_0(s^0_\varphi, \sigma) = s^0_{\psi_1}$.
- For $\varphi = \psi_1 \mathbf{U} \psi_2$, we define $\mathcal{A}_\varphi = \langle 2^{AP}, \{s^0_\varphi\} \cup S_{\psi_1} \cup S_{\psi_2}, s^0_\varphi, \delta_0 \cup \delta_{\psi_1} \cup \delta_{\psi_2}, F_{\psi_1} \cup F_{\psi_2}\rangle$ where $\delta_0(s^0_\varphi, \sigma) = \delta_{\psi_2}(s^0_{\psi_2}, \sigma) \vee (\delta_{\psi_1}(s^0_{\psi_1}, \sigma) \wedge s^0_\varphi)$.

An automata-theoretic approach for LTL satisfiability and model-checking is presented in [20,21]. The approach is based on a construction of NBW for LTL formulas. Given an LTL formula ψ, satisfiability of ψ can be checked by first constructing an NBW $\mathcal{A}_\psi$ for ψ and then checking if $L(\mathcal{A}_\psi)$ is empty. As for model checking, assume that we want to check whether a system that is modelled by an NBW $\mathcal{A}_M$ satisfies ψ. First construct an NBW $\mathcal{A}_{\neg\psi}$ for $\neg\psi$, then check whether $L(\mathcal{A}_M) \cap L(\mathcal{A}_{\neg\psi}) = \emptyset$. (The automaton $\mathcal{A}_{\neg\psi}$ can also be used as a run-time monitor to check that ψ does not fail during a simulation run [6].)

Following [18], given an LTL formula ψ, the construction of the NBW for ψ is done in two steps: (1) Construct an ABW $\mathcal{A}'_\psi$ that is linear in the size of ψ. (2) Translate $\mathcal{A}'_\psi$ to $\mathcal{A}_\psi$. The size of $\mathcal{A}_\psi$ is exponential in the size of $\mathcal{A}'_\psi$ [10], and hence also in the size of ψ. Since checking for emptiness for NBW can be done in linear time or in nondeterministic logarithmic space [21], both satisfiability and model checking can be solved in exponential time or in polynomial space. Since both problems are PSPACE-complete [14], the bound is tight.

3 Reset-LTL

In this section we define and analyze the logic Reset-LTL. We show that for every Reset-LTL formula ψ, we can efficiently construct an ABW $\mathcal{A}_\psi$ that accepts $L(\psi)$. This construction allows us to apply the automata-theoretic approach presented in Section 2 to Reset-LTL. The logic Reset-LTL is an extension of LTL, with the operators accept in and reject in . Let ψ be a Reset-LTL formula over 2^{AP} and let b be a Boolean formula over AP. Then, accept b in ψ and reject b in ψ are Reset-LTL formulas. The semantic of Reset-LTL is defined with respect to tuples $\langle w, a, r\rangle$, where w is an infinite word over 2^{AP}, and a and r are Boolean formulas over AP. We refer to a and r as the *context* of the formula. Intuitively, a describes an *accept* signal, while r describes a *reject* signal. Note that every letter σ in w is in 2^{AP}, thus a and r are either true or false in σ. The semantic is defined as follows:

- For $p \in AP$, we have that $\langle w, a, r\rangle \models p$ if $w_0 \models a \vee (p \wedge \neg r)$.
- $\langle w, a, r\rangle \models \neg\psi$ if $\langle w, r, a\rangle \not\models \psi$.
- $\langle w, a, r\rangle \models \psi_1 \wedge \psi_2$ if $\langle w, a, r\rangle \models \psi_1$ and $\langle w, a, r\rangle \models \psi_2$.
- $\langle w, a, r\rangle \models \psi_1 \vee \psi_2$ if $\langle w, a, r\rangle \models \psi_1$ or $\langle w, a, r\rangle \models \psi_2$.
- $\langle w, a, r\rangle \models \mathbf{X}\,\psi$ if $w_0 \models a$ or $(\langle w^1, a, r\rangle \models \psi$ and $w_0 \not\models r)$.
- $\langle w, a, r\rangle \models \psi_1\, \mathbf{U}\, \psi_2$ if there exists $k \geq 0$ such that $\langle w^k, a, r\rangle \models \psi_2$ and for every $0 \leq j < k$, we have $\langle w^j, a, r\rangle \models \psi_1$.
- $\langle w, a, r\rangle \models$ accept b in ψ if $\langle w, a \vee (b \wedge \neg r), r\rangle \models \psi$.
- $\langle w, a, r\rangle \models$ reject b in ψ if $\langle w, a, r \vee (b \wedge \neg a)\rangle \models \psi$.

An infinite word w satisfies a formula ψ if $\langle w, \mathbf{false}, \mathbf{false}\rangle \models \psi$. The definition ensures that a and r are always disjoint, i.e., there is no $\sigma \in 2^{AP}$ that satisfies both a and r. It can be shown that this semantics satisfies a natural duality property: $\neg$accept a in ψ is logically equivalent to reject b in $\neg\psi$. For a discussion of this semantics, see [1]. Its key feature is that a formula holds if the accept signal is asserted before the formula "failed". The notion of failure is syntax driven. For example, **X false** cannot fail before time 1, since checking **X false** at time 0 requires checking **false** at time 1.

Before we analyze the complexity of Reset-LTL, we characterize its expressiveness.

Theorem 2. Reset-LTL *is as expressive as* LTL.

The proof of Theorem 2 relies on the fact that although the accept and reject conditions a and r of the subformulas are defined by the semantic of Reset-LTL, they can be determined syntactically. We can use this fact to rewrite Reset-LTL formulas into equivalent LTL formulas.

We now present a translation of Reset-LTL formulas into ABW. Note, that the context that is computed during the evaluation of Reset-LTL formulas depends on the part of the formula that "wraps" each subformula. Given a formula ψ, we define for each subformula φ of ψ two Boolean formulas $acc_\psi[\varphi]$ and $rej_\psi[\varphi]$ that represent the context of φ with respect to ψ.

Definition 1. *For a* Reset-LTL *formula ψ and a subformula φ of ψ, we define the* acceptance context of *φ, denoted $acc_\psi[\varphi]$, and the* rejection context of *φ, denoted $rej_\psi[\varphi]$. The definition is by induction over the structure of the formula in a top-down direction.*

- *If $\varphi = \psi$, then $acc_\psi[\varphi] =$ **false** and $rej_\psi[\varphi] =$ **false**.*
- *Otherwise, let ξ be the innermost subformula of ψ that has φ as a strict subformula.*
  - *If $\xi =$ accept b in φ, then $acc_\psi[\varphi] = acc_\psi[\xi] \vee (b \wedge \neg rej_\psi[\xi])$ and $rej_\psi[\varphi] = rej_\psi[\xi]$.*
  - *If $\xi =$ reject b in φ, then $acc_\psi[\varphi] = acc_\psi[\xi]$ and $rej_\psi[\varphi] = rej_\psi[\xi] \vee (b \wedge \neg acc_\psi[\xi])$.*
  - *If $\xi = \neg\varphi$, then $acc_\psi[\varphi] = rej_\psi[\xi]$ and $rej_\psi[\varphi] = acc_\psi[\xi]$.*
  - *In all other cases, $acc_\psi[\varphi] = acc_\psi[\xi]$ and $rej_\psi[\varphi] = rej_\psi[\xi]$.*

A naive tree representation of the Boolean formulas $acc_\psi[\varphi]$ and $rej_\psi[\varphi]$ can lead to an exponential blowup. This can be avoided by using DAG representation of the formulas. Note that two subformulas that are syntactically identical might have different contexts. E.g., for the formula $\psi =$ accept p_0 in $p_1 \vee$ accept p_2 in p_1, there are two subformulas of the form p_1 in ψ. For the left subformula we have $acc_\psi[p_1] = p_0$ and for the right subformula we have $acc_\psi[p_1] = p_2$.

Theorem 3. *For every* Reset-LTL *formula ψ, there exists an AWW $\mathcal{A}_\psi$ with $O(|\psi|)$ states such that $L(\psi) = L(\mathcal{A}_\psi)$.*

Proof. For every subformula φ of ψ, we construct an automaton $\mathcal{A}_{\psi,\varphi}$. The automaton $\mathcal{A}_{\psi,\varphi}$ accepts an infinite word w iff $\langle w, acc_\psi[\varphi], rej_\psi[\varphi]\rangle \models \varphi$. The automaton $\mathcal{A}_\psi$ is then $\mathcal{A}_{\psi,\psi}$. The construction of $\mathcal{A}_{\psi,\varphi}$ proceeds by induction on the structure of φ as follows.

- For $\varphi = p \in AP$, we define $\mathcal{A}_{\psi,p} = \langle 2^{AP}, \{s_p^0\}, s_p^0, \delta_p, \emptyset \rangle$, where $\delta_p(s_p^0, \sigma) = \mathbf{true}$ if $acc_\psi[\varphi] \vee (p \wedge \neg rej_\psi[\varphi])$ is true in σ and $\delta_p(s_p^0, \sigma) = \mathbf{false}$ otherwise.
- For Boolean connectives we apply the Boolean closure of AWW.
- For $\varphi = \mathbf{X}\,\psi_1$, we define $\mathcal{A}_{\psi,\varphi} = \langle 2^{AP}, \{s_\varphi^0\} \cup S_{\psi_1}, s_\varphi^0, \delta_0 \cup \delta_{\psi_1}, F_{\psi_1} \rangle$ where

$$\delta_0(s_\varphi^0, \sigma) = \begin{bmatrix} \mathbf{true} & \text{if } \sigma \models acc_\psi[\varphi], \\ \mathbf{false} & \text{if } \sigma \models rej_\psi[\varphi], \\ s_{\psi_1}^0 & \text{otherwise.} \end{bmatrix}$$

- For $\varphi = \psi_1 \,\mathbf{U}\, \psi_2$, we define $\mathcal{A}_{\psi,\varphi} = \langle 2^{AP}, \{s_\varphi^0\} \cup S_{\psi_1} \cup S_{\psi_2}, s_\varphi^0, \delta_0 \cup \delta_{\psi_1} \cup \delta_{\psi_2}, F_{\psi_1} \cup F_{\psi_2} \rangle$, where $\delta_0(s_\varphi^0, \sigma) = \delta_{\psi_2}(s_{\psi_2}^0, \sigma) \vee (\delta_{\psi_1}(s_{\psi_1}^0, \sigma) \wedge s_\varphi^0)$.
- For $\varphi = \mathsf{accept}\ b\ \mathsf{in}\ \psi_1$ we define $\mathcal{A}_{\psi,\varphi} = \mathcal{A}_{\psi,\psi_1}$
- For $\varphi = \mathsf{reject}\ b\ \mathsf{in}\ \psi_1$ we define $\mathcal{A}_{\psi,\varphi} = \mathcal{A}_{\psi,\psi_1}$

Note that $\mathcal{A}_{\psi,\varphi}$ depends not only on φ but also on $acc_\psi[\varphi]$ and $rej_\psi[\varphi]$, which depend on the part of ψ that "wraps" φ. Thus, for example, the automaton $\mathcal{A}_{\psi,\psi_1}$ we get for $\varphi = \mathsf{accept}\ b\ \mathsf{in}\ \psi_1$ is different from the automaton $\mathcal{A}_{\psi,\psi_1}$ we get for $\varphi = \mathsf{reject}\ b\ \mathsf{in}\ \psi_1$, and both automata depend on b.

The construction of ABW for Reset-LTL formulas allows us to use the automata-theoretic approach presented in Section 2. Accordingly, we have the following (the lower bounds follow from the known bounds for LTL).

Theorem 4. *The satisfiability and model-checking problems of* Reset-LTL *are PSPACE-complete.*

Theorems 3 and 4 imply that the standard automata-theoretic approach to satisfiability and model checking extends to Reset-LTL in a fairly straightforward fashion. In particular, translation to alternating automata underlies the standard approaches to compilation of LTL to automata. Current compilers of LTL to automata, either explicit [4] or symbolic [3], are syntax driven, recursively applying fairly simple rules to each formula in terms of it subformulas. For example, to compile the formula $X\varphi$ symbolically, the compiler generates symbolic variables z_φ and $z_{X\varphi}$, adds the symbolic invariance $z_{Xp} \leftrightarrow z'_\varphi$ (by convention primed variables refer to the next point in time), and proceeds with the processing of φ. As the proof of Theorem 3 shows, the same approach applies also to Reset-LTL.

Remark 1. Theorem 4 holds only for formulas that are represented as trees, where every subformula of ψ has a unique occurrence. It does not hold in DAG representation, where subformulas that are syntactically identical are unified. In this case one occurrence of a subformula could be related to many automata that differ in their context. Thus, the size of the automaton could be exponential in the length of the formula, and the automata-based algorithm runs in exponential space. An EXPSPACE lower bound for the satisfiability of Reset-LTL formulas that are represented as DAGs can be shown, so, the bounds are tight.

4 Abort-LTL

In this section we define and analyze the logic Abort-LTL. We first present a construction of AWW for Abort-LTL formulas with size nonelementary in the size of the formula. This implies nonelementary solutions for the satisfiability and model-checking problems, to which we later prove matching lower bounds.

The Abort-LTL logic extends LTL with an abort on operator. Formally, if ψ is an Abort-LTL formula over 2^{AP} and b is a Boolean formula over AP, then ψ abort on b is an Abort-LTL formula. The semantic of the abort operator is defined as follows:

- $w \models \psi$ abort on b iff $w \models \psi$ or there is a prefix w' of w and an infinite word w'' such that b is true in the last letter of w' and $w' \cdot w'' \models \psi$.

For example, the formula "$(\mathbf{G}\, p)$ abort on b" is equivalent to the formula $(p\,\mathbf{U}\,(p \wedge b)) \vee \mathbf{G}\, p$. Thus, in addition to words that satisfy $\mathbf{G}\, p$, the formula is satisfied by words with a prefix that ends in a letter that satisfies b and in which p holds in every state. Such a prefix can be extended to an infinite word where $\mathbf{G}\, p$ holds, and thus the word satisfies the formula.

Before we analyze the complexity of Abort-LTL, we characterized its expressiveness.

Theorem 5. Abort-LTL *is as expressive as* LTL.

The proof of Theorem 5 relies on the fact that for every LTL formula ψ there exists a counter-free deterministic Rabin word automaton (DRW) $\mathcal{A}_\psi$ such that $L(\psi) = L(\mathcal{A}_\psi)$, and vice versa [16]. Given an LTL formula ψ we use the counter-free DRW $\mathcal{A}_\psi$ to construct a counter-free DRW $\mathcal{A}'$ such that $L(\mathcal{A}') = L(\psi$ abort on $b)$. Thus, there exists an LTL formula ψ' that is equivalent to ψ abort on b.

We now describe a construction of AWW for Abort-LTL formulas. The construction involves a nonelementary blow-up. This implies nonelementary solutions for the satisfiability and model-checking problems, to which we later prove matching lower bounds. For two integers n and k, let $exp(1, n) = 2^n$ and $exp(k, n) = 2^{exp(k-1,n)}$. Thus, $exp(k, n)$ is a tower of k exponents, with n at the top.

Theorem 6. *For every* Abort-LTL *formula ψ of length n and* abort on *nesting depth k, there exists an AWW $\mathcal{A}_\psi$ with $exp(k, n)$ states such that $L(\psi) = L(\mathcal{A}_\psi)$.*

Proof. The construction of AWW for LTL presented in Theorem 1 is inductive. Thus, in order to extend it for Abort-LTL formulas, we need to construct, given b and an AWW $\mathcal{A}_\psi$ for ψ, an AWW $\mathcal{A}_\varphi$ for $\varphi = \psi$ abort on b. Once we construct $\mathcal{A}_\varphi$, the inductive construction is as described in Theorem 1. Given b and $\mathcal{A}_\psi$, we construct $\mathcal{A}_\varphi$ as follows.

- Let $\mathcal{A}_n = \langle 2^{AP}, S_n, s^{n0}, \delta_n, F_n \rangle$ be an NBW such that $L(\mathcal{A}_n) = L(\mathcal{A}_\psi)$. According to [10], $\mathcal{A}_n$ indeed has a single initial state and its size is exponential in $\mathcal{A}_\psi$.
- Let $\mathcal{A}'_n = \langle 2^{AP}, S'_n, s'^{n0}, \delta'_n, F'_n \rangle$ be the NBW obtained from $\mathcal{A}_n$ by removing all the states from which there are no accepting runs, i.e, all states s such that $L(\mathcal{A}^s_n) = \emptyset$.

- Let $\mathcal{A}_{fin} = \langle 2^{AP}, S'_n, s'^{n0}, \delta, \emptyset \rangle$, be an AWW where δ is defined, for all $s \in S$ and $\sigma \in \Sigma$ as follows.

$$\delta(s, \sigma) = \begin{bmatrix} \mathbf{true} & \text{if } \sigma \models b \text{ and } \delta_n(s, \sigma) \neq \emptyset, \\ \bigvee_{t \in \delta_n(s,\sigma)} t & \text{otherwise.} \end{bmatrix}$$

  Thus, whenever $\mathcal{A}'_n$ reads a letter that satisfies b, the AWW accepts. Intuitively, $\mathcal{A}_{fin}$ accepts words that contain prefixes where b holds in the last letter and ψ has not yet "failed".
- We define $\mathcal{A}_\varphi$ to be the automaton for $L(\mathcal{A}_\psi) \cup L(\mathcal{A}_{fin})$. Note that since both $\mathcal{A}_\psi$ and $\mathcal{A}_{fin}$ are AWW, so is $\mathcal{A}_\varphi$. The automaton $\mathcal{A}_\varphi$ accepts a word w if either $\mathcal{A}_\psi$ has an accepting run over w, or if $\mathcal{A}'_n$ has a finite run over a prefix w' of w, which ends in a letter σ that satisfies b.

For LTL, every operator increases the number of states of the automaton by one, making the overall construction linear. In contrast, here every abort on operator involves an exponential blow up in the size of the automaton. In the worst case, the size of $\mathcal{A}_\psi$ is $exp(k, n)$ where k is the nesting depth of the abort on operator and n is the length of the formula.

The construction of ABW for Abort-LTL formulas allows us to use the automata-theoretic approach presented in Section 2, implying nonelementary solutions to the satisfiability and model-checking problems for Abort-LTL.

Theorem 7. *The satisfiability and model-checking problems of* Abort-LTL *are in SPACE($exp(k, n)$)), where n is the length of the specification and k is the nesting depth of* abort on.

Note that the proof of Theorem 6, buttressed by lower bounds below, shows that to have a general compilation of Abort-LTL to automata one cannot proceed in a syntax-directed fashion; rather, to compile φ abort on b one has to construct in sequence $\mathcal{A}_\varphi$, $\mathcal{A}_n$, $\mathcal{A}'_n$, $\mathcal{A}_{fin}$, and finally $\mathcal{A}_{\varphi \text{ abort on } b}$ (of course, these steps can be combined).

We now prove matching lower bounds. We first prove that the nonelementary blow-up in the translation described in Theorem 6 cannot be avoided. This proves that the automata-theoretic approach to Abort-LTL has nonelementary cost. We construct infinitely many Abort-LTL formulas ψ_n^k such that every AWW that accept $L(\psi_n^k)$ is of size $exp(k, n)$. The formulas ψ_n^k, are constructed such that $L(\psi_n^k)$ is closely related to $\{ww\Sigma^\omega : |w| = exp(k, n)\}$. Intuitively, we use the abort on operator to require that every letter in the first word is identical to the letter at the same position in the next word. It is known that every AWW that accept this language has at least $exp(k, n)$ states. The proof that every AWW that accepts $L(\psi_n^k)$ has at least $exp(k, n)$ states is similar to the known proof for $\{ww\Sigma^\omega : |w| = exp(k, n)\}$ and is discussed later.

We then show that the nonelementary cost is intrinsic and is not a side-effect of the automata-theoretic approach by proving a nonelementary lower bounds for satisfiability and model checking of Abort-LTL.

We start by considering words of length 2^n; that is, when $k = 1$. Let $\Sigma = \{0, 1\}$. For simplicity, we assume that 0 and 1 are disjoint atomic propositions. Each letter of w_1 and w_2 is represented by block of n "cells". The letter itself is stored in the first cell of the block. In addition to the letter, the block stores its position in the word. The position is a number between 0 and $2^n - 1$, referred to as the *value* of the block, and we use an atomic proposition c_1 to encode it as an n-bit vector. For simplicity, we denote $\neg c_1$ by c_0. The vector is stored in the cells of the block, with the least significant bit stored at the first cell. The position is increased by one from one block to the next. The formulas in Γ requires that the first cell of each block is marked with the atomic proposition $\#$, that the first cell in the first block of w_2 is marked with the atomic proposition @, and that the first cell after w_2 is marked by \$. An example of a legal prefix (structure wise) is shown in Figure 1.

																$
								@								
#		#		#		#		#		#		#		#		#
0	?	0	?	1	?	1	?	1	?	0	?	1	?	1	?	?
c_0	c_0	c_0	c_1	c_1	c_0	c_1	c_1	c_0	c_0	c_0	c_1	c_1	c_0	c_1	c_1	?

Fig. 1. An example for $n = 2$ that represents the case where $w_1 = 0011$ and $w_2 = 1011$. Each row represents a unique atomic proposition, which should hold at exactly the cell in which it is marked. An exception are the propositions 0 and 1 whose values are checked only in the first cell in each block (other cells are marked ?)

Formally, Γ contains the following formulas.

- $\gamma_1 = \# \wedge (c_0 \wedge (Xc_0 \wedge \overset{n}{\cdots} \wedge Xc_0)$
  After every $\#$ before the first @ there are $n - 1$ cells without $\#$ or @, and then another $\#$.
- $\gamma_2 = (\# \rightarrow \bigwedge_{1 \leq i < n} \mathbf{X}^i(\neg\# \wedge \neg @) \wedge \mathbf{X}^n \#)\,\mathbf{U}\,@$
  The first cell is marked by $\#$ and the first block counter value is $000\ldots0$.

The following four formulas make sure that the position (that is encoded by c_0, c_1) is increased by one every $\#$. We use an additional proposition z that represents the carry. Thus, we add 1 to the least significant bit and then propagate the carry to the other bits. Note that the requirement holds until the last $\#$ before @.

- $\gamma_3 = (((\# \vee z) \wedge c_0) \rightarrow (\mathbf{X}(\neg z) \wedge \mathbf{X}^n\, c_1))\,\mathbf{U}\,(\# \wedge \mathbf{X}((\neg\#)\,\mathbf{U}\,@))$
- $\gamma_4 = ((\neg(\# \vee z) \wedge c_0) \rightarrow (\mathbf{X}(\neg z) \wedge \mathbf{X}^n\, c_0))\,\mathbf{U}\,(\# \wedge \mathbf{X}((\neg\#)\,\mathbf{U}\,@))$
- $\gamma_5 = (((\# \vee z) \wedge c_1) \rightarrow (\mathbf{X}\, z \wedge \mathbf{X}^n\, c_0))\,\mathbf{U}\,(\# \wedge \mathbf{X}((\neg\#)\,\mathbf{U}\,@))$
- $\gamma_6 = ((\neg(\# \vee z) \wedge c_1) \rightarrow (\mathbf{X}(\neg z) \wedge \mathbf{X}^n\, c_1))\,\mathbf{U}\,(\# \wedge \mathbf{X}((\neg\#)\,\mathbf{U}\,@))$

The following formulas require that the first @ is true immediately after w_1.

- $\gamma_7 = ((\# \wedge \bigvee_{0 \leq i < n} X^i c_0) \rightarrow ((\neg @)\,\mathbf{U}\,\mathbf{X}(\# \wedge \neg @)))\,\mathbf{U}\,@$
  as long as the counter is not $111\ldots1$ there not going to be @.
- $\gamma_8 = ((\# \wedge \bigwedge_{0 \leq i < n} X^i c_1) \rightarrow \mathbf{X}^n\, @)\,\mathbf{U}\,@$
  When the counter is $111\ldots1$ the next value going to be @.

The formulas for w_2 are similar, except that they begin with a $\neg@ \, \mathbf{U} \, (@ \wedge \ldots)$, and \$ replaces @. We add the formula $(\neg\$) \, \mathbf{U} \, @$ to make sure that the first \$ is immediately after w_2.

Next, we describe the formula θ, which requires that for all positions $0 \leq j \leq 2^{n-1}$, the j-th letter in w_1 is equal to the j-th position in w_2. While such a universal quantification on j is impossible in LTL, it can be achieved using the abort on operator.

We start with some auxiliary formulas:

$$\theta_= = \# \wedge \bigwedge_{i=0}^{n-1} ((\mathbf{X}^i \, c_0 \wedge ((\neg\$) \, \mathbf{U} \, (\$ \wedge \mathbf{X}^{i+1} \, c_0))) \vee (\mathbf{X}^i \, c_1 \wedge ((\neg\$) \, \mathbf{U} \, (\$ \wedge \mathbf{X}^{i+1} \, c_1))))$$

The formula requires the current position value to agree with the position value right after \$. Then, the formula

$$\theta_{next0} = (\theta_= \wedge ((\neg @) \, \mathbf{U} \, (@ \wedge (((\# \wedge \theta_=) \rightarrow 0) \, \mathbf{U} \, \$)))) \text{ abort on } \$.$$

requires that we are in a beginning of a block in w_1, and every block between @ and \$ whose position is equal to the position of the current block (note that there is exactly one such block) is marked with 0. Intuitively, let

$$\theta'_{next0} = \theta_= \wedge ((\neg @) \, \mathbf{U} \, (@ \wedge (((\# \wedge \theta_=) \rightarrow 0) \, \mathbf{U} \, \$)))$$

Then, θ'_{next0} requires that we are in a beginning of a block in w_1, the block position is equal to the position of the block that starts after \$, and every block between @ and \$ whose position is also equal to the position of the block that starts after \$ is marked with 0. Thus, θ'_{next0} is equivalent to θ_{next0} except that it fails when the current block does not match the block after \$. This is where the abort operator enters the picture. For every position, if the corresponding block is marked 0, the prefix of the word that ends at \$ can be extend such that the current block position match the position of the block that starts after \$. This extension would satisfy θ'_{next0}, thus the word satisfies θ_{next0}. The formula θ_{next1} is defined similarly.

Now, the formula θ requires that $w_1 = w_2$.

$$\theta = (((\# \wedge 0) \rightarrow \theta_{next0}) \wedge ((\# \wedge 1) \rightarrow \theta_{next1})) \, \mathbf{U} \, @$$

Words of length $exp(k, n)$. So far we have shown how to construct ψ_n^1, which defines equality between words of length $exp(1, n)$. We would like to scale up the technique to construct formulas ψ_n^k that define equality between words of length $exp(k, n)$. (As before, we use @ to mark the end of the first word and we use \$ to mark the end of the second word.) To do that, we encode such words by sequences consisting of $exp(k, n)$ $(k-1)$-blocks, of length $exp(k-1, n)$ each. Each such $(k-1)$-block, whose beginning is marked by $\#_{k-1}$, represents one letter, encoding both the letter itself as well as its position in the word, which requires $exp(k-1, n)$ bits. We need to require that (1) $(k-1)$-blocks behave as an $exp(k-1, n)$-counter, i.e., the first $(k-1)$-block is identically 0, and subsequent $(k-1)$-blocks count modulo $exp(k, n)$, and (2) if there are two $(k-1)$-blocks, b_1 in the first word and b_2 in the second word that encode the same position, then they must encode the same letter. To express (1) and (2), we have to refer to bits inside the $(k-1)$-blocks, which we encode using $(k-2)$-blocks, of length $exp(k-2,n)$.

Thus, we need an inductive construction. We start with 0-blocks, of length n, and use formulas Γ^0 to require that the 0-blocks behave as an n-bit counter (using the formulas $\gamma_1,\ldots,\gamma_8$ from earlier). Inductively, suppose we have already required the $(k-2)$-blocks to behave as an $exp(k-2,n)$ counter. We now want every sequence of $exp(k-1,n)$ $(k-2)$-blocks, initially marked with $\#_{k-1}$, to encode a $(k-1)$ block. We use the values of a proposition c^{k-1} at the start of each $(k-2)$-block to encode the bits of the $(k-1)$-block.

We now need to write formulas analogous to $\gamma_1,\ldots,\gamma_8$ to require that $(k-1)$-block to behave as an $exp(k-1,n)$-bit counter. The difficulty is in referring to bits in the same position of successive $(k-1)$-blocks using formulas of size polynomial in n (for $k=1$ we can use $\mathbf{X}^n$ to refer to corresponding bits in successive 0-blocks). To refer to corresponding bits in successive $(k-1)$-blocks, we use the fact that each such bit is encoded using $(k-2)$-blocks. Thus, referring to such bits require the comparison of $(k-2)$-blocks. Also, to say that the two words, each of length $exp(k,n)$ are equal we need to express the analog of θ, which requires the analogue of $\theta_=$. But the latter use a conjunction of size n to range over all the n-bits of a 0-block. Here we need to range over all $(k-2)$ blocks and compare pair of such blocks.

Thus, the key is to be able to compare i-blocks, for $i=0,\ldots,k-1$. Once we are able to compare i-blocks we can go ahead and construct and compare $(i+1)$-blocks. To compare i-blocks for $i\geq 1$ we use the marker $\$_i$. Instead of directly comparing two i-blocks, we compare them both to the i-block that come immediately after $\$_i$, just as in $\theta_=$ we compared two 0-blocks to the 0-block that comes immediately after the $ marker. By "aborting on" $\$_i$ we make sure that we are comparing the two i-blocks to *some* i-block that could come after $\$_i$; this way we are not bound to some specific i-block that actually comes after $\$_i$.

ψ_n^k is a conjunction of a sequence of sets of formulas. The construction of the sets of formulas is inductive, for every level i $(0\leq i\leq k)$, we define Γ^i and Θ^i that require level i to be "legal" and make some "tools" for level $i+1$. The set Γ^i requires the followings:

- γ_1^i requires that the counter value of the first i-block is $000\ldots0$.
- γ_2^i requires that after every $\#_i$ before the next $\#_i$ there are $exp(i,n)$ many $(i-1)$-blocks without $\#_i$. This formula is only needed in level 0, after that it is taken care of by γ_7^{i-1} and γ_8^{i-1}.
- The following four formulas (γ_3^i, γ_4^i, γ_5^i, and γ_6^i) make sure that the counter (that is encoded by c_0^i, c_1^i) value is increased by one every $\#_i$. We use an additional proposition z^i that represents the carry.
- In the following two formulas (γ_7^i and γ_8^i), the first $k-1$ levels are a bit different from the kth level. The first $k-1$ levels require that at the $\#_{i+1}$ proposition will be true only at the beginning of every $(i+1)$-block. The formulas of the kth level require that the @ will be true exactly at the beginning of w_2.

A similar set of formulas is used for w_2. In addition for $i>0$, we require that the first $\$_i$ marker appears after w_1 and w_2, and that the first $\$_i$ is proceeded by a legal i-block, and that i-block is proceeded by the first $\$_{i-1}$. These requirements can be formulated easily using formulas similar of formulas of Γ^i.

The Θ^i set requires two basic conditions:

1. A formula $\theta^i_{\#next0}$ that requires that the i-block between the next $\#_{(i+1)}$ and the one after, which has the same position value as the current i-block, represents the letter c_0^{i+1}. (A similar formula is needed for c_1^{i+1}).
2. A formula $\theta^i_{\$next0}$ that requires that the i-block in the $(i+1)$-block that starts after the first $\$_{(i+1)}$, and has the same position value as the current i-block, represents the letter c_0^{i+1}. (A similar formula is needed for c_1^{i+1}).

both formulas uses the auxiliary formula $\theta^i_=$ that requires the current i-block to be equivalent to the i-block that starts right after the first $\$_i$.

We present some examples that demonstrate the inductive construction. The base of the induction is the construction of Γ^0 and Θ^0. The formulas of Γ_0 are similar to the formulas that are presented in the former section, the main difference is that the 0-block with $11\ldots1$ value does not imply the end of the first word, but that the next 0-block should be marked with $\#_1$. Thus $\gamma_8^0 = ((\#_0 \wedge \bigwedge_{0\le i<n} X^i c_1^0) \rightarrow \mathbf{X}^n\, \#_1)\, \mathbf{U}\, @$
As for the formulas of Θ^0, they are similar to the formulas that presented in the former section, only here we also need formulas that determine the value of the matching address in the next 1-block. For example, $\theta^0_{\#next0}$ requires the matching 0-block in the next 1-block to represents c_0^1. Thus,
$\theta^0_{\#next0} = (\theta^0_= \wedge \mathbf{X}((\neg\#_1)\, \mathbf{U}\, (\#_1 \wedge (((\#_0 \wedge \theta^0_=) \rightarrow c_0^1)\, \mathbf{U}\, \mathbf{X}\, \#_1))))$ abort on $\$_0$

Assume that for some $1 < i \le k$, we already constructed Γ^j and Θ^j for every $j < i$. The structure of Γ^{i-1} is the base for Γ^i. For example, $\gamma_1^i = (\#_{i-1} \rightarrow c_0^i)\, \mathbf{U}\, \mathbf{X}\, \#_i$.

In the formulas that require the positions of the i-blocks to increased by one form one block to the next, we use the $\theta^{i-1}_{\#next0}$ and $\theta^{i-1}_{\#next1}$ formulas instead of the $\mathbf{X}^n$ operator. For example, $\gamma_3^i =$
$((\#_{i-1} \wedge (\#_i \vee z^i) \wedge c_0^i) \rightarrow (\mathbf{X}((\neg\#_{i-1})\mathbf{U}(\#_{i-1} \wedge (\neg z^i))) \wedge \theta^{i-1}_{\#next1}))\mathbf{U}(\#_i \wedge \mathbf{X}(\neg\#_i)\mathbf{U}@)$

Next, we describe Θ^i, the main change is in $\theta^i_=$, which requires that the current i-block position value is equal to the i-block that starts after $\$_i$. Thus,
$\theta^i_= = (((\#_{i-1} \wedge c_0^i) \rightarrow \theta^{i-1}_{\$next0}) \wedge ((\#_{i-1} \wedge c_1^i) \rightarrow (\theta^{i-1}_{\$next1})))\, \mathbf{U}\, \mathbf{X}\, \#_i$

In the rest of the formulas we use similar techniques. For example,
$\theta^i_{\#next0} = (\theta^i_= \wedge ((\neg\#_{i+1})\, \mathbf{U}\, (\#_{i+1} \wedge (((\#_i \wedge \theta^i_=) \rightarrow c_0^i)\, \mathbf{U}\, \mathbf{X}\, \#_{i+1}))))$ abort on $\$_i$,
which requires that the matching i-block in the next $(i+1)$-block represents c_0^{i+1}.

The last formula that we define requires w_1 and w_2 to be equivalent. First we define
$\theta^i_{@next0} = (\theta^{k-1}_= \wedge (\neg @)\, \mathbf{U}\, @ \wedge \mathbf{X}(((\#_{k-1} \wedge \theta^k_=) \rightarrow 0)\, \mathbf{U}\, \mathbf{X}\, @))$ abort on $\$_{k-1}$,
which requires that the matching $(k-1)$-block in w_2 represents 0. Next, we define $\theta^i_{@next1}$ in a similar way. Then, we define
$\theta_{=w} = (((\#_{k-1} \wedge 0) \rightarrow \theta^{k-1}_{@next0}) \wedge ((\#_{k-1} \wedge 1) \rightarrow (\theta^{k-1}_{@next1})))\, \mathbf{U}\, \mathbf{X}\, @$,
which requires that $w_1 = w_2$

We now discuss the length of the formulas in the above construction. For every $0 \le i \le k$, we have a constant number of formulas in Γ^i and Θ^i, thus the number of formulas is $O(k)$. The problem is in formulas that recursively use other formulas. Since formulas like $\theta^i_=$ contains four sub-formulas $\theta^{i-1}_=$, the length of $\theta^k_=$ is $O(4^k)$. Thus the total length of the formulas is $O(4^k + n)$.

Lemma 1. *Every ABW that accepts ψ_n^k has at least $exp(k,n)$ states.*

Lemma 1 shows that the the automata-theoretic approach to Abort-LTL has a nonelementary cost. We now show that this cost is intrinsic to Abort-LTL and is not an artifact of the automata-theoretic approach.

Satisfiability and model-checking for Abort-LTL. We now prove that satisfiability checking for Abort-LTL is SPACE($exp(k,n)$)-hard. We show a reduction from a hyper-exponent version of the *tiling problem* [22,9,17]. The problem is defined as follows relative to a parameter $k > 0$. We are given a finite set T, two relations $V \subseteq T \times T$ and $H \subseteq T \times T$, an initial tile t_0, a final tile t_a,and a bound $n > 0$. We have to decide whether there is some $m > 0$ and an a tiling of an $exp(k,n) \times m$-grid: such that: (1) t_0 is in the bottom left corner and t_a is in the top left corner, (2) Every pair of horizontal neighbors is in H, and (3) Every pair of vertical neighbors is in V. Formally: Is there a function $f : (exp(k,n) \times m) \rightarrow T$ such that (1) $f(0,0) = t_0$ and $t(0, m-1) = t_a$, (2) for every $0 \leq i < exp(k,n)$, and $0 \leq j < m$, we have that $(f(i,j), f(i+1,j)) \in H$, and (3) for every $0 \leq i < exp(k,n)$, and $0 \leq j < m-1$, we have that $(f(j,i), f(j,i+1)) \in V$. This problem is known to be SPACE($exp(k,n)$)-complete [9,17].

We reduce this problem to the satisfiability problem for Abort $-$ LTL. Given a tiling problem $\tau = \langle T, H, V.t_0, t_f, n \rangle$, we construct a formula ψ_τ such that τ admits tiling iff ψ_τ is satisfiable. The idea is to encode a tiling as a word over T, consisting of a sequence of blocks of length $l = exp(k,n)$, each encoding one row of the tiling. Such a word represents a proper tiling if it starts with t_0, ends with a block that starts with t_a, every pair of adjacent tiles in a row are in H, and every pair of tiles that are $exp(k,n)$ tiles apart are in V. The difficulty is in relating tiles that are far apart. To do that we represent every tile by a $(k-1)$-block, of length $exp(k-1,n)$, which represent the tiles position in the row. As we had earlier, to require that the $(k-1)$-blocks behave as a $exp(k-1,n)$-bit counter and to compare $(k-1)$-blocks, we need to construct them from $(k-2)$-blocks, which needs to be constructed from $(k-3)$-blocks, and so on. Thus, as we had earlier, we need an inductive construction of i-blocks, for $i = 1, \ldots, k-1$, and we need to adapt the machinery of the previous nonelementary lower-bound proof.

It can be shown that there exists an exponential reduction from the nonelementary domino problem to the satisfiability of Abort-LTL formulas. Thus the satisfiability problem of the Abort-LTL is non-elementary hard.

Theorem 8. *The satisfiability and model-checking problems for* Abort-LTL *formulas nesting depth k of* abort on *are SPACE($exp(k,n)$)-complete.*

5 Concluding Remarks

We showed in this paper that the distinction between reset semantics and abort semantics has a dramatic impact on the complexity of using the language in a model-checking tool. While Reset-LTL enjoys the "fast-compilation property"–there is a linear translation of Reset-LTL formulas into alternating Büchi automata, the translation of Abort-LTL formulas into alternating Büchi automata is nonelementary, as is the complexity of satisfiability and model checking for Abort-LTL. This raises a concern on the feasibility of implementing a model checker for logics based on Abort-LTL(such as Sugar 2.0). While the nonelementary blow-up is a worst-case prediction, one can conclude from our results that while Reset-LTL can be efficiently compiled using a rather modest extension to existing LTL compilers (e.g., [4,3]), a much more sophisticated automata-theoretic machinery is needed to implement an compiler for Abort-LTL.

It is important to understand that the issue here is not simply the complexity blow-up for some convoluted formulas of Abort-LTL. As noted earlier, the proof of Theorem 3 shows that the standard syntax-driven approach to compiling LTL to automata applies also to Reset-LTL; in fact, the ForSpec compiler applies syntax-driven processing to all ForSpec's constructs [1]. In contrast, the proof of Theorem 6, buttressed by Lemma 1, shows that to have a general compilation of Abort-LTL to automata one cannot proceed in a similar syntax-directed fashion. Thus, the sketchy description of a syntax-directed compilation scheme provided in the documentation of Sugar 2.0 is not only incomplete but also seriously underestimates the effort required to implement a compiler for full Sugar 2.0.

Acknowledgements. Work of Bustan and Vardi supported in part by NSF grants CCR-9988322, CCR-0124077, IIS-9908435, IIS-9978135, and EIA-0086264, by BSF grant 9800096, and by a grant from the Intel Corporation. Kupferman is visiting UC Berkeley and is supported by NSF grant CCR-9988172.

References

1. R. Armoni, L. Fix, R. Gerth, B. Ginsburg, T. Kanza, A. Landver, S. Mador-Haim, A. Tiemeyer, E. Singerman, M.Y. Vardi, and Y. Zbar. The ForSpec temporal language: A new temporal property-specification language. In *Proc. 8th Int'l Conf. on Tools and Algorithms for the Construction and Analysis of Systems (TACAS'02)*, Lecture Notes in Computer Science 2280, pages 296–311. Springer-Verlag, 2002.
2. I. Beer, S. Ben-David, C. Eisner, D. Fisman, A. Gringauze, and Y. Rodeh. The temporal logic sugar. In *Proc. Conf. on Computer-Aided Verification*, LNCS 2102, pages 363–367, 2001.
3. J.R. Burch, E.M. Clarke, K.L. McMillan, D.L. Dill, and L.J. Hwang. Symbolic model checking: 10^{20} states and beyond. *Information and Computation*, 98(2):142–170, June 1992.
4. R. Gerth, D. Peled, M.Y. Vardi, and P. Wolper. Simple on-the-fly automatic verification of linear temporal logic. In P. Dembiski and M. Sredniawa, editors, *Protocol Specification, Testing, and Verification*, pages 3–18. Chapman & Hall, August 1995.
5. S.M. Nowick K. van Berkel, M.B. Josephs. Applications of asynchronous circuits. *Proceedings of the IEEE*, 1999. special issue on asynchronous circuits & systems.
6. O. Kupferman and M.Y. Vardi. Model checking of safety properties. *Formal methods in System Design*, 19(3):291–314, November 2001.
7. R.P. Kurshan. Formal verification in a commercial setting. In *Proc. Conf. on Design Automation (DAC'97)*, volume 34, pages 258–262, 1997.
8. R.P. Kurshan. *FormalCheck User's Manual*. Cadence Design, Inc., 1998.
9. H.R. Lewis. Complexity of solvable cases of the decision problem for the predicate calculus. In *Foundations of Computer Science*, volume 19, pages 35–47, 1978.
10. S. Miyano and T. Hayashi. Alternating finite automata on ω-words. *Theoretical Computer Science*, 32:321–330, 1984.

11. M.J. Morley. Semantics of temporal *e*. In T. F. Melham and F.G. Moller, editors, Banff'99 *Higher Order Workshop (Formal Methods in Computation)*. University of Glasgow, Department of Computing Science Technic al Report, 1999.
12. D.E. Muller, A. Saoudi, and P.E. Schupp. Alternating automata, the weak monadic theory of the tree and its complexity. In *Proc. 13th Int. Colloquium on Automata, Languages and Programming*, LNCS 226, 1986.
13. A. Pnueli. The temporal logic of programs. In *Proc. 18th IEEE Symp. on Foundation of Computer Science*, pages 46–57, 1977.
14. A.P. Sistla and E.M. Clarke. The complexity of propositional linear temporal logic. *Journal ACM*, 32:733–749, 1985.
15. A comparison of reset control methods: Application note 11. `http://www.summitmicro.com/tech_support/notes/note11.htm`, Summit Microelectronics, Inc., 1999.
16. W. Thomas. A combinatorial approach to the theory of ω-automata. *Information and Computation*, 48:261–283, 1981.
17. P. van Emde Boas. The convenience of tilings. In *Complexity, Logic and Recursion Theory*, volume 187 of *Lecture Notes in Pure and Applied Mathetaics*, pages 331–363, 1997.
18. M.Y. Vardi. An automata-theoretic approach to linear temporal logic. In *Logics for Concurrency: Structure versus Automata*, LNCS 1043, pages 238–266, 1996.
19. M.Y. Vardi and P. Wolper. An automata-theoretic approach to automatic program verification. In *Proc. 1st Symp. on Logic in Computer Science*, pages 332–344, 1986.
20. M.Y. Vardi and P. Wolper. Automata-theoretic techniques for modal logics of programs. *Journal of Computer and System Science*, 32(2):182–221, April 1986.
21. M.Y. Vardi and P. Wolper. Reasoning about infinite computations. *Information and Computation*, 115(1):1–37, November 1994.
22. H. Wang. Dominoes and the aea case of the decision problem. In *Symposium on the Mathematical Theory of Automata*, pages 23–55, 1962.

A Generic On-the-Fly Solver for Alternation-Free Boolean Equation Systems*

Radu Mateescu

INRIA Rhône-Alpes / VASY, 655, avenue de l'Europe
F-38330 Montbonnot Saint Martin, France
Radu.Mateescu@inria.fr

Abstract. Boolean Equation Systems (BESs) offer a useful representation for various verification problems on finite-state concurrent systems, such as equivalence/preorder checking and model checking. In particular, on-the-fly resolution methods enable a demand-driven construction of the BES (and hence, of the state space) during verification. In this paper, we present a generic library dedicated to on-the-fly resolution of alternation-free BESs. Four resolution algorithms are currently provided by the library: A1, A2 are general, the latter being optimized to produce small-depth diagnostics, and A3, A4 are specialized for handling acyclic and disjunctive/conjunctive BESs in a memory-efficient way. The library is developed within the CADP toolbox and serves as engine for on-the-fly equivalence/preorder checking modulo five widely-used relations, and for model checking of alternation-free μ-calculus.

1 Introduction

Boolean Equation Systems (BESs) [15] are a well-studied framework for the verification of concurrent finite-state systems, by allowing to formulate model checking and equivalence/preorder checking problems in terms of BES resolution. Numerous algorithms for solving BESs have been proposed (see [15, chap. 6] for a survey). They can be basically grouped in two classes: *global* algorithms, which require the BES to be constructed entirely before the resolution, and *local* (or *on-the-fly*) algorithms, which allow the BES to be generated dynamically during the resolution. Local algorithms are able to detect errors in complex systems even when the corresponding BESs are too large to be constructed explicitly. Another feature is the generation of *diagnostics* (portions of the BES explaining the truth value of a variable), which provide considerable help for debugging applications and for understanding temporal logic formulas [16].

However, as opposed to the situation in the field of symbolic verification, for which a significant number of BDD-based packages are available [24], we are not aware of any generic environment for BES resolution available for on-the-fly verification. In this paper we present CÆSAR_SOLVE, a generic library for

* This research was partially funded by the IST-2001-32360 Project "ArchWare" and by Bull S.A.

H. Garavel and J. Hatcliff (Eds.): TACAS 2003, LNCS 2619, pp. 81–96, 2003.

BES resolution and diagnostic generation, created using the OPEN/CÆSAR environment for on-the-fly verification [14]. CÆSAR_SOLVE provides an application-independent representation of BESs as *boolean graphs* [1], much in the same way as OPEN/CÆSAR provides a language-independent representation of Labeled Transition Systems (LTSs). Four algorithms are currently available in the library. Algorithms A1 and A2 are general (they do not assume anything about the right-hand sides of the equations), A2 being optimized to produce small-depth diagnostics. Algorithms A3 and A4 are specialized for memory-efficient resolution of acyclic BESs and disjunctive/conjunctive BESs, which occur frequently in practice. CÆSAR_SOLVE serves as engine for two on-the-fly verification tools developed within the CADP toolbox [10]: the equivalence/preorder checker BISIMULATOR, which implements five widely-used equivalence relations, and the model checker EVALUATOR for regular alternation-free μ-calculus [18].

The paper is organized as follows. Section 2 defines alternation-free BESs. Section 3 presents algorithms A1–A4 and compares them according to three criteria which aim at improving time complexity. Section 4 outlines the encodings of various equivalence relations and temporal logics in terms of alternation-free BESs, identifying the particular cases suitable for algorithms A3 and A4. Section 5 shows the architecture of the library and some performance measures. Section 6 summarizes the results and indicates directions for future work.

2 Alternation-Free Boolean Equation Systems

A Boolean Equation System (BES) [1,15] is a tuple $B = (X, M_1, ..., M_n)$, where $X \in \mathcal{X}$ is a boolean variable and M_i are equation blocks ($i \in [1, n]$). Each block $M_i = \{X_j \stackrel{\sigma_i}{=} op_j \boldsymbol{X}_j\}_{j \in [1,m_i]}$ is a set of minimal (resp. maximal) fixed point equations of sign $\sigma_i = \mu$ (resp. $\sigma_i = \nu$). The right-hand side of each equation j is a pure disjunctive or conjunctive formula obtained by applying a boolean operator $op_j \in \{\vee, \wedge\}$ to a set of variables $\boldsymbol{X}_j \subseteq \mathcal{X}$. The boolean constants F and T abbreviate the empty disjunction $\vee\emptyset$ and the empty conjunction $\wedge\emptyset$.

The *main* variable X must be defined in block M_1. A variable X_j depends upon a variable X_l if $X_l \in \boldsymbol{X}_j$. A block M_i depends upon a block M_k if some variable of M_i depends upon a variable defined in M_k. A block is *closed* if it does not depend upon any other blocks. A BES is *alternation-free* if there are no cyclic dependencies between its blocks; in this case, the blocks are sorted topologically such that a block M_i only depends upon blocks M_k with $k > i$.

The semantics $[\![op_i\{X_1, ..., X_k\}]\!]\delta$ of a formula $op_i\{X_1, ..., X_k\}$ w.r.t. $\mathbf{Bool} = \{\mathsf{F}, \mathsf{T}\}$ and a context $\delta : \mathcal{X} \to \mathbf{Bool}$, which must initialize all variables $X_1, ..., X_k$, is the boolean value $op_i(\delta(X_1), ..., \delta(X_k))$. The semantics $[\![M_i]\!]\delta$ of a block M_i w.r.t. a context δ is the σ_i-fixed point of a vectorial functional $\Phi_{i\delta} : \mathbf{Bool}^{m_i} \to \mathbf{Bool}^{m_i}$ defined as $\Phi_{i\delta}(b_1, ..., b_{m_i}) = ([\![op_j \boldsymbol{X}_j]\!](\delta \oslash [b_1/X_1, ..., b_{m_i}/X_{m_i}]))_{j \in [1,m_i]}$, where $\delta \oslash [b_1/X_1, ..., b_n/X_n]$ denotes a context identical to δ except for variables $X_1, ..., X_n$, which are assigned values $b_1, ..., b_n$, respectively. The semantics of an alternation-free BES is the value of its main variable X given by the solution of M_1, i.e., $\delta_1(X)$, where the contexts δ_i are calculated as follows: $\delta_n = [\![M_n]\!][]$ (the context is empty because M_n is closed), $\delta_i = ([\![M_i]\!]\delta_{i+1}) \oslash \delta_{i+1}$ for $i \in [1, n-1]$ (a block M_i is interpreted in the context of all blocks M_k with $k > i$).

A block is *acyclic* if the dependency graph induced by its equations is acyclic. A variable X_j is called *disjunctive* (resp. *conjunctive*) if $op_j = \vee$ (resp. $op_j = \wedge$). A block M_i is disjunctive (resp. conjunctive) if each of its variables either is disjunctive (resp. conjunctive), or it depends upon at most one variable defined in M_i, its other dependencies being constants or variables defined in other blocks.

The on-the-fly resolution of an alternation-free BES $B = (X, M_1, ..., M_n)$ consists in computing the value of X by exploring the right-hand sides of the equations in a demand-driven way, without explicitly constructing the blocks. Several on-the-fly BES resolution algorithms are available [6,1,15,7]. Here we follow an approach proposed in [1], which proceeds as follows. To each block M_i is associated a resolution routine R_i responsible for computing the values of M_i's variables. When a variable X_j of M_i is computed by a call $R_i(X_j)$, the values of other variables X_l defined in other blocks M_k may be needed; these values are computed by calls $R_k(X_l)$ of the routine associated to M_k. This process always terminates, because there are no cyclic dependencies between blocks (the call stack of resolution routines has a size bounded by the depth of the dependency graph between blocks). Since a variable X_j of M_i may be required several times during the resolution process, the computation results must be kept persistent between subsequent calls of R_i to obtain an efficient overall resolution.

Compared to other algorithms like LMC [7], which consists of a single routine handling the whole BES, the scheme above presents two advantages: (a) the algorithms used in the resolution routines of individual blocks are simpler, since they must handle a single type of fixed point equations; (b) the overall resolution process is easier to optimize, simply by designing more efficient algorithms for blocks with particular structure (e.g., acyclic, disjunctive or conjunctive).

3 On-the-Fly Resolution Algorithms

This section presents four different algorithms implementing the on-the-fly resolution of individual equation blocks in an alternation-free BES. The algorithms are defined only for μ-blocks, those for ν-blocks being completely dual. Algorithms A1 and A2 are general (they do not depend upon the structure of the right-hand sides of the equations), whereas algorithms A3 and A4 are optimized for acyclic blocks and for disjunctive or conjunctive blocks, respectively.

We develop the resolution algorithms in terms of *boolean graphs* [1], which provide a graphical, more intuitive representation of BESs. Given an equation block $M_i = \{X_j \stackrel{\mu}{=} op_j \boldsymbol{X}_j\}_{j \in [1, m_i]}$, the corresponding boolean graph is a tuple $G = (V, E, L)$, where: $V = \{X_j \mid j \in [1, m_i]\}$ is the set of *vertices* (boolean variables), $E = \{X_j \to X_k \mid j \in [1, m_i] \wedge X_k \in \boldsymbol{X}_j\}$ is the set of *edges* (dependencies between variables), and $L : V \to \{\vee, \wedge\}$, $L(X_j) = op_j$ is the *vertex labeling* (disjunctive or conjunctive). The set of successors of a vertex x is noted $E(x)$. Sink $\vee$-vertices (resp. $\wedge$-vertices) represent variables equal to F (resp. T). During a call of the resolution routine R_i associated to block M_i, all variables

X_l defined in other blocks M_k and occurring free in M_i can be seen as constants, because their values are computed on-the-fly by calls to R_k.

As expected, the boolean graphs associated to acyclic blocks are acyclic. The graphs associated to disjunctive (resp. conjunctive) blocks may contain $\wedge$-vertices (resp. $\vee$-vertices) having at most one successor (these vertices correspond either to constants, or to variables having at most one non-constant successor in the current block), the other vertices being disjunctive (resp. conjunctive).

The algorithms we present are all based upon the same principle: starting at the variable of interest, they perform an on-the-fly, forward exploration of the boolean graph and propagate backwards the values of the "stable" variables (i.e., whose final value has been determined); the propagation of a T (resp. a F) backwards to a $\vee$-variable (resp. $\wedge$-variable) makes it T (resp. F). The algorithms terminate either when the variable of interest becomes stable, or the entire boolean graph is explored. To compare the different algorithms, we precise below three requirements desirable for obtaining a good time complexity:

(R1) The resolution of a variable (vertex of the boolean graph) must be carried out in a time linear in the size of the graph, i.e., $O(|V| + |E|)$. This is necessary for obtaining a linear time overall resolution of a multiple-block, alternation-free BES.

(R2) During the resolution of a variable, every new variable explored must be related to the variable of interest by (at least) a path of unstable variables in the boolean graph. This limits the graph exploration only to variables "useful" for the current resolution.

(R3) When a call of the resolution algorithm terminates, the portion of the boolean graph explored must be stable. This avoids that subsequent calls for solving the same variable lead to multiple explorations of the graph (which may destroy the overall linear time complexity).

3.1 Algorithm A1 (DFS, General)

Algorithm A1 is based upon a depth-first search (DFS) of the boolean graph. It satisfies all three aforementioned requirements: (R1) its worst-case time and space complexity is $O(|V| + |E|)$, because every edge in the boolean graph is traversed at most twice: forwards, when its source variable is explored, and backwards, when the value of its target variable (if it became stable) is back-propagated; (R2) new variables, explored from the top of the DFS stack, are related to the variable of interest, which is at the bottom of the DFS stack, via the unstable variables present on the stack; (R3) the portion of boolean graph explored after each call of the algorithm contains only stable variables, i.e., depending only upon variables already explored.

The algorithm can be seen as an optimized version of the Avoiding 1's algorithm proposed in [1]: it is implemented iteratively rather than recursively, it has a better average complexity because values of variables are back-propagated as soon as they become stable, and it has a lower memory consumption because dependencies between variables are discarded during back-propagation. A1 was initially developed for model-checking regular alternation-free μ-calculus [18].

3.2 Algorithm A2 (BFS, General)

Algorithm A2 (see Figure 1) is based upon a breadth-first search (BFS) of the boolean graph, starting from the variable of interest x. Visited vertices are stored in a set $A \subseteq V$ and visited but unexplored vertices are stored in a queue. To each vertex y are associated two informations: a counter $c(x)$, which keeps the number of y's successors that must become true in order to make y true ($c(y)$ is initialized to $|E(y)|$ if y is a $\wedge$-vertex and to 1 otherwise) and a set $d(y)$ containing the vertices that currently depend upon y. At each iteration of the main while-loop (lines 4–34), the vertex y in front of the queue is explored. If it is already stable (i.e., $c(y) = 0$), its value is back-propagated by the inner while-loop (lines 8–20) along the dependencies d; otherwise, all successors $E(y)$ are visited and (if they are stable or new) are inserted at the end of the queue.

The algorithm satisfies requirement (R1), since each call has a complexity $O(|V|+|E|)$. It does not satisfy (R2), because the back-propagation may stabilize vertices that "cut" all the paths relating x to vertices in the queue, and thus at some points the algorithm may explore vertices useless for deciding the truth value of x (however, the values of these vertices may be useful in later calls of A2). Finally, it satisfies (R3), since at the end of the main while-loop all visited vertices are stable (they depend only upon the vertices in A). These observations are confirmed experimentally, A2 being slightly slower than A1.

However, as regards the ability of generating positive diagnostics (examples) of small size, A2 performs better than A1. During the back-propagation carried out by the inner while-loop, to each $\vee$-vertex w that becomes stable is associated its successor $s(w)$ that made it stable (line 14). This information can be used to construct a diagnostic for x at the end of the algorithm, by performing another traversal of the subgraph induced by A and keeping the successors given by s (for $\vee$-vertices) or all successors (for $\wedge$-vertices) [16]. Being BFS-based, A2 generally produces examples of smaller depth than A1, and even of minimal depth when the examples are sequences (e.g., in the case of disjunctive blocks). Of course, the same situation occurs in the dual case, when A2 is used for producing negative diagnostics (counterexamples) for ν-blocks.

3.3 Algorithm A3 (DFS, Acyclic)

Algorithm A3 is based upon a DFS of the boolean graph and is specialized for solving acyclic equation blocks. It is quite similar to algorithm A1, except that it does not need to store dependencies between variables, since back-propagation takes place only along the DFS stack (the boolean graph being acyclic, variables become stable as soon as they are popped from the DFS stack). Therefore, algorithm A3 has a worst-case memory consumption $O(|V|)$, improving over the general algorithms A1 and A2.

Being DFS-based, algorithm A3 satisfies all requirements (R1)–(R3). A3 was initially developed for model-checking μ-calculus formulas on large traces obtained by intensive simulation of a system implementation [17].

```
function A2 (x, (V, E, L)) : Bool is
  c(x) := if L(x) = ∧ then |E(x)| else 1 endif;
  d(x) := ∅; A := {x}; queue := put(x, nil);
  while queue ≠ nil do
    y := head(queue); queue := tail(queue);
    if c(y) = 0 then
      B := {y};
      while B ≠ ∅ do
        let u ∈ B; B := B \ {u};
        forall w ∈ d(u) do
          if c(w) > 0 then
            c(w) := c(w) − 1;
            if c(w) = 0 then
              if L(w) = ∨ then s(w) := u endif;
              B := B ∪ {w}
            endif
          endif
        end;
        d(u) := ∅
      end
    else
      forall z ∈ E(y) do
        if z ∈ A then
          d(z) := d(z) ∪ {y};
          if c(z) = 0 then
            queue := put(z, queue)
          endif
        else
          c(z) := if L(z) = ∧ then |E(z)| else 1 endif;
          d(z) := {y}; A := A ∪ {z}; queue := put(z, queue)
        endif
      end
    endif
  end;
  return c(x) = 0
end
```

Fig. 1. Algorithm A2: BFS-based local resolution of a μ-block

3.4 Algorithm A4 (DFS, Disjunctive/Conjunctive)

Algorithm A4 (see Figure 2) is based upon a DFS of the boolean graph, performed recursively starting from the variable of interest x. A4 is specialized for solving disjunctive or conjunctive blocks; we show only its variant for disjunctive blocks, the other variant being dual. For simplicity, we assume that all $\wedge$-vertices of the disjunctive block have no successors (i.e., they are T): since each $\wedge$-vertex may have at most one non-constant successor in the block, it can be assimilated to a $\vee$-vertex if its other successors are evaluated first (possibly by calling the resolution routines of other blocks). In this case, solving a disjunctive block amounts to searching for a sink $\wedge$-vertex, since a T value will propagate back to x via $\vee$-vertices. This algorithm obviously meets requirements (R1) and (R2).

```
A := ∅; n := 0; stack := nil;
function A4 (x, (V, E, L)) : Bool is
  A := A ∪ {x}; n(x) := n; n := n + 1;
  stack := push(x, stack); low(x) := n(x);
  if |E(x)| = 0 then
    v(x) := if L(x) = ∧ then T else F endif; stable(x) := T
  else
    v(x) := F; stable(x) := F
  endif;
  forall y ∈ E(x) do
    if y ∈ A then
      val := v(y);
      if ¬stable(y) ∧ n(y) < n(x) then
        low(x) := min(low(x), n(y))
      endif
    else
      val := A4 (y, (V, E, L));
      low(x) := min(low(x), low(y))
    endif;
    if val then
      v(x) := T; stable(x) := T; break
    endif
  end;
  if v(x) ∨ low(x) = n(x) then
    repeat
      z := top(stack); v(z) := v(x); stable(z) := T;
      stack := pop(stack)
    until z = x
  endif;
  return v(x)
end
```

Fig. 2. Algorithm A4: DFS-based local resolution of a disjunctive μ-block

However, in order to guarantee requirement (R3), we must ensure that all visited vertices stored in $A \subseteq V$ are stable when x has been evaluated. This could be done by storing backward dependencies (as for algorithms A1 and A2), but for disjunctive blocks we can avoid this by computing the strongly connected components (SCCs) of the boolean graph. When x is evaluated to T, all vertices belonging to the SCC of x must become T (since they can reach x via a path of $\vee$-vertices) and the other ones must be stabilized to F.

Algorithm A4 combines the search for T vertices with a detection of SCC following Tarjan's classical algorithm. It proceeds as follows: for each successor y of vertex x (lines 10–23), it calculates its boolean value $v(y)$, its "lowlink" number $low(y)$, and a boolean $stable(y)$ which is set to F if y belongs to the current SCC and to T otherwise. Then, if $v(x) = \mathsf{T}$ or x is the root of a SCC, all vertices in the current SCC are stabilized to the value $v(x)$ (lines 24–29). In this way, algorithm A4 meets all requirements (R1)–(R3) and avoids to store transitions of the boolean graph, having a worst-case memory complexity $O(|V|)$.

4 Equivalence Checking and Model Checking

In this section we study two applications of BES resolution in the field of finite-state verification: equivalence/preorder checking and model checking, both performed on-the-fly. Various encodings of these problems in terms of BESs have been proposed in the literature [5,1,15]. Here we aim at giving a uniform presentation of these results and also at identifying particular cases where the algorithms A3 and A4 given in Sections 3.3 and 3.4 can be applied.

4.1 Encoding Equivalence Relations

Labeled Transition Systems (LTSs) are natural models for action-based languages describing concurrency, such as process algebras. An LTS is a quadruple $M = (Q, A, T, q_0)$, where: Q is the set of states, A is the set of actions ($A_\tau = A \cup \{\tau\}$ is the set of actions extended with the invisible action τ), $T \subseteq Q \times A_\tau \times Q$ is the transition relation, and $q_0 \in Q$ is the initial state. A transition $(q_1, a, q_2) \in T$ (also noted $q_1 \xrightarrow{a} q_2$) means that the system can evolve from state q_1 to state q_2 by performing action a. The notation is extended to transition sequences: if $l \subseteq {A_\tau}^*$ is a language defined over A_τ, $q_1 \xrightarrow{l} q_2$ means that from q_1 to q_2 there is a sequence of transitions whose actions concatenated form a word of l.

Let $M_i = (Q_i, A, T_i, {q_0}_i)$ be two LTSs ($i \in \{1, 2\}$). The table below shows the BES encodings of the equivalence between M_1 and M_2 modulo five widely-used equivalence relations: strong bisimulation [22], branching bisimulation [23], observational equivalence [19], $\tau^*.a$ equivalence [12], and safety equivalence [3]. These encodings are derived from the characterizations given in [12]. Each relation is represented as a BES with a single ν-block defining, for each couple of states $(p, q) \in Q_1 \times Q_2$, a variable $X_{p,q}$ which expresses that p and q are equivalent ($a \in A$ and $b \in A_\tau$). For each equivalence relation, the corresponding preorder relation is obtained simply by dropping either the second conjunct (for strong, $\tau^*.a$, and safety equivalence), or the third and fourth conjuncts (for branching and observational equivalence) in the right-hand sides of the equations defining $X_{p,q}$ (e.g., the strong preorder is defined by the BES $\{X_{p,q} \stackrel{\nu}{=} \bigwedge_{p \xrightarrow{b} p'} \bigvee_{q \xrightarrow{b} q'} X_{p',q'}\}$). Other equivalences, such as delay bisimulation [21] and η-bisimulation [2], can be encoded using a similar scheme. Note that for all weak equivalences, the computation of the right-hand sides of equations requires to compute transitive closures of τ-transitions in one or both LTSs.

RELATION	ENCODING
Strong	$\left\{ X_{p,q} \stackrel{\nu}{=} \left(\bigwedge_{p \xrightarrow{b} p'} \bigvee_{q \xrightarrow{b} q'} X_{p',q'}\right) \wedge \left(\bigwedge_{q \xrightarrow{b} q'} \bigvee_{p \xrightarrow{b} p'} X_{p',q'}\right) \right\}$
Branching	$\left\{ \begin{array}{l} X_{p,q} \stackrel{\nu}{=} \bigwedge_{p \xrightarrow{b} p'} \left((b = \tau \wedge X_{p',q}) \vee \bigvee_{q \xrightarrow{\tau^*} q' \xrightarrow{b} q''} (X_{p,q'} \wedge X_{p',q''})\right) \wedge \\ \qquad \bigwedge_{q \xrightarrow{b} q'} \left((b = \tau \wedge X_{p,q'}) \vee \bigvee_{p \xrightarrow{\tau^*} p' \xrightarrow{b} p''} (X_{p',q} \wedge X_{p'',q'})\right) \end{array} \right\}$
Observational	$\left\{ \begin{array}{l} X_{p,q} \stackrel{\nu}{=} \left(\bigwedge_{p \xrightarrow{\tau} p'} \bigvee_{q \xrightarrow{\tau^*} q'} X_{p',q'}\right) \wedge \left(\bigwedge_{p \xrightarrow{a} p'} \bigvee_{q \xrightarrow{\tau^* a \tau^*} q'} X_{p',q'}\right) \wedge \\ \qquad \left(\bigwedge_{q \xrightarrow{\tau} q'} \bigvee_{p \xrightarrow{\tau^*} p'} X_{p',q'}\right) \wedge \left(\bigwedge_{q \xrightarrow{a} q'} \bigvee_{p \xrightarrow{\tau^* a \tau^*} p'} X_{p',q'}\right) \end{array} \right\}$
$\tau^*.a$	$\left\{ X_{p,q} \stackrel{\nu}{=} \left(\bigwedge_{p \xrightarrow{\tau^* a} p'} \bigvee_{q \xrightarrow{\tau^* a} q'} X_{p',q'}\right) \wedge \left(\bigwedge_{q \xrightarrow{\tau^* a} q'} \bigvee_{p \xrightarrow{\tau^* a} p'} X_{p',q'}\right) \right\}$
Safety	$\left\{ \begin{array}{l} X_{p,q} \stackrel{\nu}{=} Y_{p,q} \wedge Y_{q,p} \\ Y_{p,q} \stackrel{\nu}{=} \left(\bigwedge_{p \xrightarrow{\tau^* a} p'} \bigvee_{q \xrightarrow{\tau^* a} q'} Y_{p',q'}\right) \end{array} \right\}$

In order to apply the resolution algorithms given in Section 3, the BESs shown in the table above must be transformed by introducing extra variables such that the right-hand sides of equations become disjunctive or conjunctive formulas. For example, the BES for strong bisimulation is transformed as follows:

$$\left\{ \begin{array}{l} X_{p,q} \stackrel{\nu}{=} \bigwedge_{p \xrightarrow{b} p'} Y_{b,p',q} \wedge \bigwedge_{q \xrightarrow{b} q'} Z_{b,p,q'} \\ Y_{b,p',q} \stackrel{\nu}{=} \bigvee_{q \xrightarrow{b} q'} X_{p',q'} \\ Z_{b,p,q'} \stackrel{\nu}{=} \bigvee_{p \xrightarrow{b} p'} X_{p',q'} \end{array} \right\}$$

This kind of BESs can be solved by using the general algorithms A1 and A2 (note that the encodings given above allow to construct both LTSs on-the-fly during BES resolution). However, when one or both LTSs M_1 and M_2 have a particular structure, the BESs can be simplified in order to make applicable the specialized algorithms A3 or A4.

Acyclic case. When M_1 or M_2 is acyclic, the BESs associated to strong bisimulation (and its preorder) become acyclic as well. This is easy to see for strong bisimulation: since the two-step sequences $X_{p,q} \rightarrow Y_{b,p',q} \rightarrow X_{p',q'}$ and $X_{p,q} \rightarrow Z_{b,p,q'} \rightarrow X_{p',q'}$ of the boolean graph correspond to transitions $p \xrightarrow{b} p'$ and $q \xrightarrow{b} q'$, a cycle $X_{p,q} \rightarrow \cdots X_{p,q}$ in the boolean graph would correspond to cycles $p \xrightarrow{b} \cdots p$ and $q \xrightarrow{b} \cdots q$ in both M_1 and M_2. For $\tau^*.a$ and safety equivalence (and their preorders), acyclic BESs are obtained when M_1 or M_2 contain no cycles going through visible transitions (but may contain τ-cycles): since two-step sequences in the boolean graph correspond to sequences of τ-transitions ended by a-transitions performed synchronously by the two LTSs, a cycle in the boolean graph would correspond to cycles containing an a-transition in both M_1 and M_2. For branching and observational equivalence (and their preorders), both LTSs M_1 and M_2 must be acyclic in order to get acyclic BESs, because τ-loops like $p \xrightarrow{\tau} p$ present in M_1 induce loops $X_{p,q} \rightarrow X_{p,q}$ in the boolean graph even if M_2 is acyclic.

If the above conditions are met, then the memory-efficient algorithm A3 can be used to perform equivalence/preorder checking. One practical application concerns the correctness of large execution traces produced by an implementation of a system w.r.t. the formal specification of the system [17]. Assuming the system specification given as an LTS M_1 and the set of traces given as an LTS M_2 (obtained by merging the initial states of all traces), the verification consists in checking the inclusion $M_1 \preceq M_2$ modulo the strong or safety preorder.

Conjunctive case. When M_1 or M_2 is deterministic, the BESs associated to the five equivalence relations considered and to their corresponding preorders can be reduced to conjunctive form. We illustrate this for strong bisimulation, the BESs of the other equivalences being simplified in a similar manner. If M_1 is deterministic, for every state $p \in Q_1$ and action $b \in A_\tau$, there is at most one transition $p \xrightarrow{b} p'_b$. Let $q \xrightarrow{b} q'$ be a transition in M_2. If there is no corresponding transition $p \xrightarrow{b} p'_b$ in M_1, the right-hand side of the equation defining $X_{p,q}$ trivially reduces to false (states p and q are not strongly bisimilar). Otherwise, the right-hand side of the equation becomes $\left(\bigvee_{q \xrightarrow{b} q'} X_{p'_b,q'}\right) \wedge \left(\bigwedge_{q \xrightarrow{b} q'} X_{p'_b,q'}\right)$, which reduces to $\bigwedge_{q \xrightarrow{b} q'} X_{p'_b,q'}$ since the first conjunct is absorbed by the second one. The same simplification applies when M_2 is deterministic, leading in both cases to a conjunctive BES.

For weak equivalences, further simplifications of the BESs can be obtained when one LTS is both deterministic and τ-free (i.e., without τ-transitions). For example, if M_1 is deterministic and τ-free, the BES for observational equivalence becomes $\{X_{p,q} \stackrel{\nu}{=} \bigwedge_{q \xrightarrow{\tau} q'} X_{p,q'} \wedge \bigwedge_{q \xrightarrow{a} q'} X_{p'_a,q'}\}$. These simplifications have been identified in [12]; we believe they can be obtained in a more direct way by using BES encodings.

When one of the above conditions is met, then the memory-efficient algorithm A4 can be used to perform equivalence/preorder checking. As pointed out in [12], when comparing the LTS M_1 of a protocol with the LTS M_2 of its service (external behaviour), it is often the case that M_2 is deterministic and/or τ-free.

4.2 Encoding Temporal Logics

Alternation-free BESs allow to encode the alternation-free μ-calculus [6,1,15]. The formulas of this logic, defined over an alphabet of propositional variables $X \in \mathcal{X}$, have the following syntax (given directly in positive form):

$$\varphi ::= \mathsf{F} \mid \mathsf{T} \mid \varphi_1 \vee \varphi_2 \mid \varphi_1 \wedge \varphi_2 \mid \langle a \rangle \varphi \mid [a] \varphi \mid X \mid \mu X.\varphi \mid \nu X.\varphi$$

The semantics of a formula φ on an LTS $M = (Q, A, T, q_0)$ denotes the set of states satisfying φ: boolean operators have the standard interpretation; possibility ($\langle a \rangle \varphi$) and necessity ($[a] \varphi$) operators denote the states from which some (resp. all) transitions labeled by a lead to states satisfying φ; minimal ($\mu X.\varphi$) and maximal ($\nu X.\varphi$) fixed point operators denote the least (resp. greatest) solution of the equation $X = \varphi$ interpreted over 2^Q. Fixed point operators act as binders for variables X in the same way as quantifiers in first-order logic. The alternation-free condition means that mutual recursion between minimal and maximal fixed point variables is forbidden.

Given an LTS M, the standard translation of an alternation-free formula φ into a BES [6,1,15] proceeds as follows. First, extra propositional variables are introduced at appropriate places of φ to ensure that in every subformula $\sigma X.\varphi'$ (where $\sigma \in \{\mu, \nu\}$) of φ, φ' contains a single boolean or modal operator (this is needed in order to obtain only disjunctive or conjunctive formulas in the right-hand sides of the resulting BES). Then, the BES is constructed in a bottom-up manner, by creating an equation block for each closed fixed point subformula $\sigma X.\varphi'$ of φ. The alternation-free condition ensures that once the fixed point subformulas of $\sigma X.\varphi'$ have been translated into equation blocks, all remaining variables in $\sigma X.\varphi'$ are of sign σ. Each closed fixed point subformula $\sigma X.\varphi'$ is translated into an equation block $\{X_p \stackrel{\sigma}{=} (\varphi')_p\}_{p \in Q}$, where variables X_p express that state p satisfies X and the right-hand side boolean formulas $(\varphi')_p$ are obtained using the translation shown in the table below.

φ	$(\varphi)_p$	φ	$(\varphi)_p$
F	F	T	T
$\varphi_1 \vee \varphi_2$	$(\varphi_1)_p \vee (\varphi_2)_p$	$\varphi_1 \wedge \varphi_2$	$(\varphi_1)_p \wedge (\varphi_2)_p$
$\langle a \rangle \varphi_1$	$\bigvee_{p \xrightarrow{a} q} (\varphi_1)_q$	$[a]\, \varphi_1$	$\bigwedge_{p \xrightarrow{a} q} (\varphi_1)_q$
X	X_p	$\sigma X.\varphi_1$	X_p

This kind of BES can be solved by the general algorithms A1 and A2 given in Section 3 (note that the translation procedure above allows to construct the LTS on-the-fly during BES resolution). However, when the LTS M and/or the formula φ have a particular structure, the BES can be simplified in order to make applicable the specialized algorithms A3 or A4.

Acyclic case. When M is acyclic and φ is guarded (i.e., every recursive call of a propositional variable in φ falls in the scope of a modal operator), the formula can be simplified in order to have only minimal fixed point operators, leading to an acyclic, single-block BES [17]. This procedure can be also applied when φ has higher alternation depth and/or is unguarded, in the latter case φ being first translated to guarded form (with a worst-case quadratic blow-up in size).

If the above conditions are met, then the memory-efficient algorithm A3 can be used to perform μ-calculus model checking. One practical application consists in verifying μ-calculus formulas on sets of large execution traces (represented as acyclic LTSs M by merging their initial states) produced by intensive random execution of a system implementation [17].

Disjunctive/conjunctive case. When φ is a formula of CTL [4], ACTL (Action-based CTL) [20] or PDL [13], the BES resulting after translation is in disjunctive or conjunctive form. The table below shows the translations of CTL and PDL operators into alternation-free μ-calculus [8] (here the '$-$' symbol stands for 'any action' of the LTS). For conciseness, we omitted the translations of PDL box modalities $[\beta]\,\varphi$, which can be obtained by duality. ACTL can be translated in a way similar to CTL, provided action predicates (constructed from action names and boolean operators) are used inside diamond and box modalities instead of simple action names [9].

Operator		Translation
CTL	$\mathsf{EX}\varphi$	$\langle - \rangle\, \varphi$
	$\mathsf{AX}\varphi$	$\langle - \rangle\, \mathsf{T} \wedge [-]\, \varphi$
	$\mathsf{E}[\varphi_1 \mathsf{U} \varphi_2]$	$\mu X.\varphi_2 \vee (\varphi_1 \wedge \langle - \rangle\, X)$
	$\mathsf{A}[\varphi_1 \mathsf{U} \varphi_2]$	$\mu X.\varphi_2 \vee (\varphi_1 \wedge \langle - \rangle\, \mathsf{T} \wedge [-]\, X)$
PDL	$\langle \alpha \rangle\, \varphi$	$\langle \alpha \rangle\, \varphi$
	$\langle \varphi_1 ? \rangle\, \varphi_2$	$\varphi_1 \wedge \varphi_2$
	$\langle \beta_1 ; \beta_2 \rangle\, \varphi$	$\langle \beta_1 \rangle\, \langle \beta_2 \rangle\, \varphi$
	$\langle \beta_1 \cup \beta_2 \rangle\, \varphi$	$\langle \beta_1 \rangle\, \varphi \vee \langle \beta_2 \rangle\, \varphi$
	$\langle \beta^* \rangle\, \varphi$	$\mu X.\varphi \vee \langle \beta \rangle\, X$

The translation of CTL formulas into BESs can be performed bottom-up, by creating a $\vee$-block (resp. a $\wedge$-block) for each subformula dominated by an operator $\mathsf{E}[\_\mathsf{U}\_]$ (resp. $\mathsf{A}[\_\mathsf{U}\_]$). For instance, the formula $\mathsf{E}[\varphi_1 \mathsf{U} \varphi_2]$ is translated, via the μ-calculus formula $\mu X.\varphi_2 \vee (\varphi_1 \wedge \langle - \rangle\, X)$, first into the formula $\mu X.\varphi_2 \vee \mu Y.(\varphi_1 \wedge \mu Z.\langle - \rangle\, X)$ by adding extra variables Y and Z, and then into the equation block $\{X_p \stackrel{\mu}{=} (\varphi_2)_p \vee Y_p, Y_p \stackrel{\mu}{=} (\varphi_1)_p \wedge Z_p, Z_p \stackrel{\mu}{=} \bigvee_{p \to q} X_q\}_{p \in Q}$. This block is disjunctive, because its only $\wedge$-variables are Y_p and their left successors $(\varphi_1)_p$ correspond to CTL subformulas encoded by some other block of the BES. The formula $\mathsf{A}[\varphi_1 \mathsf{U} \varphi_2]$ is translated, in a similar manner, into the equation block $\{X_p \stackrel{\mu}{=} (\varphi_2)_p \vee Y_p, Y_p \stackrel{\mu}{=} (\varphi_1)_p \wedge Z_p \wedge \bigwedge_{p \to q} X_q, Z_p \stackrel{\mu}{=} \bigvee_{p \to q} \mathsf{T}\}_{p \in Q}$. This block is conjunctive, because its $\vee$-variables X_p have their left successors $(\varphi_2)_p$ defined in some other block of the BES, and its $\vee$-variables Z_p have all their successors constant.

ACTL formulas can also be translated into disjunctive or conjunctive equation blocks, modulo their translations in μ-calculus [9]. In the same way, the translation of PDL formulas into BESs creates a $\vee$-block (resp. a $\wedge$-block) for each subformula $\langle \beta \rangle\, \varphi$ (resp. $[\beta]\, \varphi$): normal boolean operators can be factorized such that at most one of their successors belongs to the current block, and the conjunctions (resp. disjunctions) produced by translating the test-modalities $\langle \varphi_1 ? \rangle\, \varphi_2$ (resp. $[\varphi_1 ?]\, \varphi_2$) have their left operands defined in other blocks of the BES, resulting from the translation of the φ_1 subformulas.

Thus, the memory-efficient algorithm A4 can be used for model checking CTL, ACTL, and PDL formulas. This covers most of the practical needs, since many interesting properties can be expressed using the operators of these logics.

5 Implementation and Experiments

We implemented the BES resolution algorithms A1–A4 described in Section 3 in a generic software library, called CÆSAR_SOLVE, which is built upon the primitives of the OPEN/CÆSAR environment for on-the-fly exploration of LTSs [14]. CÆSAR_SOLVE is used by the BISIMULATOR equivalence/preorder checker and the EVALUATOR model checker. We briefly describe the architecture of these tools and give some experimental results concerning the A1–A4 algorithms.

5.1 Architecture of the Solver Library

The CÆSAR_SOLVE library (see Figure 3) provides an Application Programming Interface (API) allowing to solve on-the-fly a variable of a BES. It takes as input the boolean graph associated to the BES together with the variable of interest, and produces as output the value of the variable, possibly accompanied by a diagnostic (portion of the boolean graph). Depending on its particular form, each block of the BES can be solved using one of the algorithms A1–A4, which were developed using the OPEN/CÆSAR primitives (hash tables, stacks, etc.).

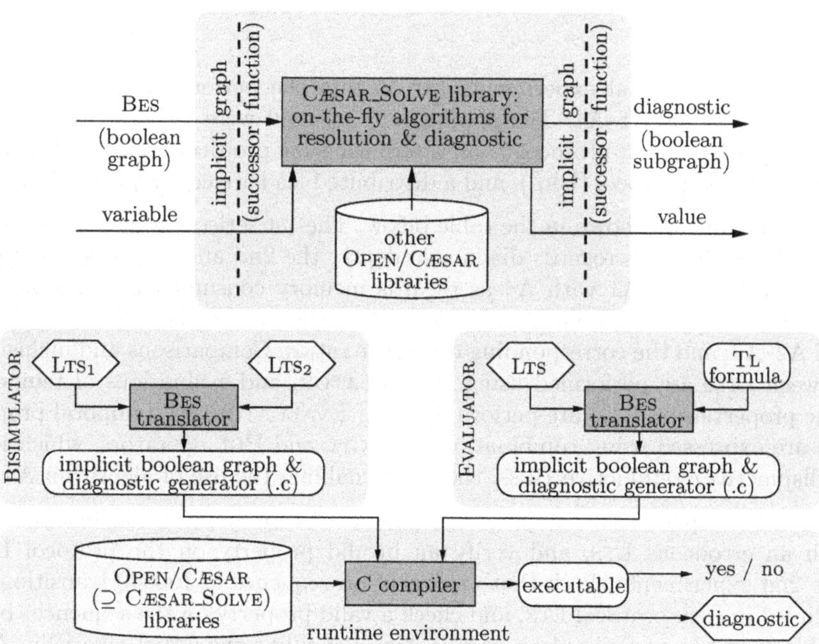

Fig. 3. The CÆSAR_SOLVE library and the tools BISIMULATOR and EVALUATOR

Both the input boolean graph and the diagnostic are represented implicitly by their successor functions, which allow to iterate over the outgoing edges (dependencies) of a given vertex (variable) and hence to perform on-the-fly traversals of the boolean graphs. This scheme is similar to the implicit representation of LTSs defined by the OPEN/CÆSAR environment [14]. To use the library, a user must provide the successor function of the BES (obtained by encoding some specific problem) and, if necessary, must interpret the resulting diagnostic by traversing the corresponding boolean subgraph using its successor function.

Two on-the-fly verification tools (see Figure 3) are currently using the CÆSAR_SOLVE library: BISIMULATOR, an equivalence/preorder checker between two LTSs modulo the five relations mentioned in Section 4.1, and EVALUATOR, a model checker for regular alternation-free μ-calculus [18] over LTSs. Each tool translates its corresponding verification problem into a BES resolution, identifying the particular cases suitable for algorithms A3–A4, and translates back the diagnostics produced by the library in terms of its input LTS(s).

5.2 Performance Measures

We performed several experiments to compare the performances of the resolution algorithms A1–A4. The applications selected were (several variants of) three communication protocols[1]: an alternating bit protocol (ABP), a bounded retransmission protocol (BRP), and a distributed leader election protocol (DLE).

The results are shown in the table below. The 1st series of experiments compares A1 with A2 as regards diagnostic depth; the 2nd and 3rd series compare A1 with A3, resp. A1 with A4 as regards memory consumption (measured in Kbytes). For each experiment, the table gives the measures obtained using A1 and A2–A4, and the corresponding difference ratios. Comparisons and inclusions between LTSs are performed using BISIMULATOR, and evaluations of temporal logic properties on LTSs are performed using EVALUATOR. All temporal properties are expressed using combinations of ACTL and PDL operators, which lead to disjunctive/conjunctive BESs, therefore enabling the use of algorithm A4.

The 1st experiments compare each protocol LTS modulo strong bisimulation with an erroneous LTS, and verify an invalid property on the protocol LTS. The 2nd experiments check that an execution sequence of 100000 transitions is included in each protocol LTS, and check a valid property on the sequence (both problems yield acyclic boolean graphs, hence enabling the use of algorithm A3). The 3rd experiments compare each protocol LTS modulo $\tau^*.a$ equivalence with its service LTS, which is deterministic (hence enabling the use of algorithm A4), and verify a valid property on the protocol LTS. We observe important reductions of diagnostic depth (up to 99%) whenever algorithm A2 can be used instead of A1, and reductions of memory consumption (up to 63%) whenever algorithms A3–A4 can be used instead of A1.

[1] All these examples can be found in the CADP distribution, available at the URL `http://www.inrialpes.fr/vasy/cadp`.

A2 versus A1			Diagnostic depth					
App.	Size		BISIMULATOR			EVALUATOR		
	States	Trans.	A1	A2	%	A1	A2	%
ABP	935000	3001594	235	19	91.9	50	12	76.0
BRP	355091	471119	1455	31	97.8	744	18	97.5
DLE	143309	220176	2565	25	99.0	147	14	90.4

A3 versus A1			Memory consumption					
App.	Size		BISIMULATOR			EVALUATOR		
	States	Trans.	A1	A3	%	A1	A3	%
ABP	935000	3001594	37472	32152	14.1	10592	8224	22.3
BRP	355091	471119	17656	13664	22.6	10240	7432	27.4
DLE	28710	73501	15480	11504	25.6	8480	6248	26.3

A4 versus A1			Memory consumption					
App.	Size		BISIMULATOR			EVALUATOR		
	States	Trans.	A1	A4	%	A1	A4	%
ABP	935000	3001594	178744	152672	14.5	163800	60248	63.2
BRP	355091	471119	35592	23608	33.6	26752	17432	34.8
DLE	18281	44368	107592	94584	12.0	3904	3224	17.4

6 Conclusion and Future Work

We presented a generic library, called CÆSAR_SOLVE, for on-the-fly resolution with diagnostic of alternation-free BESs. The library was developed using the OPEN/CÆSAR environment [14] of the CADP toolbox [10]. It implements an application-independent representation of BESs, precisely defined by an API. The library currently offers four resolution algorithms A1–A4, A2 being optimized to produce small-depth diagnostics and A3, A4 being memory-efficient for acyclic and disjunctive/conjunctive BESs. CÆSAR_SOLVE is used at the heart of the equivalence/preorder checker BISIMULATOR and the model checker EVALUATOR [18]. The experiments carried out using these tools assess the performance of the resolution algorithms and the usefulness of the diagnostic features.

We plan to continue our work along three directions. Firstly, in order to increase its flexibility, the CÆSAR_SOLVE library can be enriched with other BES resolution algorithms, such as LMC [7] or the Gauss elimination-based algorithm proposed in [15]. Due to the well-defined API of the library and the availability of the OPEN/CÆSAR primitives, the prototyping of new algorithms is quite straightforward; from this point of view, CÆSAR_SOLVE can be seen as an open platform for developing and experimenting BES resolution algorithms. Another interesting way of research is the development of parallel versions of the algorithms A1–A4, in order to exploit the computing resources of massively parallel machines such as PC clusters. Finally, other applications of the library can be envisaged, such as on-the-fly generation of test cases (obtained as diagnostics) from the LTS of a specification and the LTS of a test purpose, following the approach put forward in [11].

References

1. H. R. Andersen. Model checking and boolean graphs. *TCS*, 126(1):3–30, 1994.
2. J. C. M. Baeten and R. J. van Glabbeek. Another Look at Abstraction in Process Algebra. In *ICALP'87*, LNCS 267, pp. 84–94.
3. A. Bouajjani, J-C. Fernandez, S. Graf, C. Rodríguez, and J. Sifakis. Safety for Branching Time Semantics. In *ICALP'91*, LNCS 510.
4. E. M. Clarke, E. A. Emerson, and A. P. Sistla. Automatic Verification of Finite-State Concurrent Systems using Temporal Logic Specifications. *ACM Trans. on Prog. Lang. and Systems*, 8(2):244–263, April 1986.
5. R. Cleaveland and B. Steffen. Computing behavioural relations, logically. In *ICALP'91*, LNCS 510, pp. 127–138.
6. R. Cleaveland and B. Steffen. A Linear-Time Model-Checking Algorithm for the Alternation-Free Modal Mu-Calculus. In *CAV'91*, LNCS 575, pp. 48–58.
7. X. Du, S. A. Smolka, and R. Cleaveland. Local Model Checking and Protocol Analysis. *Springer STTT Journal*, 2(3):219–241, 1999.
8. E. A. Emerson and C-L. Lei. Efficient Model Checking in Fragments of the Propositional Mu-Calculus. In *LICS'86*, pp. 267–278.
9. A. Fantechi, S. Gnesi, and G. Ristori. From ACTL to Mu-Calculus. In *ERCIM'92 Ws. on Theory and Practice in Verification (Pisa, Italy)*, IEI-CNR, pp. 3–10, 1992.
10. J-C. Fernandez, H. Garavel, A. Kerbrat, R. Mateescu, L. Mounier, and M. Sighireanu. CADP (CÆSAR/ALDEBARAN Development Package): A Protocol Validation and Verification Toolbox. In *CAV'96*, LNCS 1102, pp. 437–440.
11. J-C. Fernandez, C. Jard, Th. Jéron, L. Nedelka, and C. Viho. Using On-the-Fly Verification Techniques for the Generation of Test Suites. In *CAV'96*, LNCS 1102.
12. J-C. Fernandez and L. Mounier. "On the Fly" Verification of Behavioural Equivalences and Preorders. In *CAV'91*, LNCS 575.
13. M. J. Fischer and R. E. Ladner. Propositional Dynamic Logic of Regular Programs. *J. of Comp. and System Sciences*, (18):194–211, 1979.
14. H. Garavel. OPEN/CÆSAR: An Open Software Architecture for Verification, Simulation, and Testing. In *TACAS'98*, LNCS 1384, pp. 68–84.
15. A. Mader. *Verification of Modal Properties Using Boolean Equation Systems.* VERSAL 8, Bertz Verlag, Berlin, 1997.
16. R. Mateescu. Efficient Diagnostic Generation for Boolean Equation Systems. In *TACAS'00*, LNCS 1785, pp. 251–265.
17. R. Mateescu. Local Model-Checking of Modal Mu-Calculus on Acyclic Labeled Transition Systems. In *TACAS'02*, LNCS 2280, pp. 281–295.
18. R. Mateescu and M. Sighireanu. Efficient On-the-Fly Model-Checking for Regular Alternation-Free Mu-Calculus. *Science of Comp. Programming*, 2002. To appear.
19. R. Milner. *Communication and Concurrency.* Prentice-Hall, 1989.
20. R. De Nicola and F. W. Vaandrager. *Action versus State based Logics for Transition Systems.* In *Semantics of Concurrency*, LNCS 469, pp. 407–419.
21. R. De Nicola, U. Montanari, and F. Vaandrager. Back and Forth Bisimulations. CS R9021, CWI, Amsterdam, May 1990.
22. D. Park. Concurrency and Automata on Infinite Sequences. In *Th. Comp. Sci.*, LNCS 104, pp. 167–183.
23. R. J. van Glabbeek and W. P. Weijland. Branching-Time and Abstraction in Bisimulation Semantics. In *Proc. IFIP 11th World Computer Congress*, 1989.
24. B. Yang, R.E. Bryant, D. R. O'Hallaron, A. Biere, O. Condert, G. Janssen, R.K. Ranjan, and F. Somenzi. A Performance Study of BDD-Based Model-Checking. In *FMCAD'98*, LNCS 1522, pp. 255–289.

Decidability of Invariant Validation for Paramaterized Systems*

Pascal Fontaine and E. Pascal Gribomont

University of Liège (Belgium)
{pfontain,gribomont}@montefiore.ulg.ac.be

Abstract. The control part of many concurrent and distributed programs reduces to a set $\Pi = \{p_1, \ldots, p_n\}$ of symmetric processes containing mainly assignments and tests on Boolean variables. However, the assignments, the guards and the program invariants can be Π-quantified, so the corresponding verification conditions also involve Π-quantifications. We propose a systematic procedure allowing the elimination of such quantifications for a large class of program invariants. At the core of this procedure is a variant of the Herbrand Theorem for many-sorted first-order logic with equality.

1 Introduction

At the heart of concurrent software are control-intensive concurrent algorithms, which solve a large class of problems, including mutual exclusion, termination detection, reliable communication through unreliable channels, synchronous communication through asynchronous channels, fault tolerance, leader election, Byzantine agreement, concurrent reading and writing, and so on. (See e.g. [8, 25] for many examples, with comments and formal or informal proofs). Many of those systems are composed of a parameterized number of identical processes or nearly identical processes[1]. Most variables are Booleans or arrays of Booleans, and operations on the remaining variables are elementary. The verification of such parameterized concurrent systems is the subject of many recent papers [1, 4,7,11,17,23,24,31].

Requirements of such algorithms usually fall in safety properties ("something bad never happens") and liveness properties ("something good eventually happens"). It is often possible to view a liveness property as the conjunction of a safety property and a fairness hypothesis ("progress is made") so, in practice, the verification of safety properties is the main part of formal methods and tools. The classical invariant method allows to reduce the verification of safety properties to the validity problem for first-order logic. It could happen that the

* This work was funded by a grant of the "Communauté française de Belgique – Direction de la recherche scientifique – Actions de recherche concertées"

[1] for example a process can compare its identifier with the identifier of another process. This somewhat breaks symmetry.

H. Garavel and J. Hatcliff (Eds.): TACAS 2003, LNCS 2619, pp. 97–112, 2003.

formula to be proved belongs to a well known decidable class (for instance, Presburger arithmetic), but this is rarely the case because Boolean arrays (modeled by uninterpreted predicates) are often used in these algorithms, together with interpreted predicates[2].

Quantifier-free first-order logic satisfiability checking is decidable for a very wide range of formulas with non-interpreted and interpreted predicates and functions. Thus decidability is often reached through quantifier elimination. We introduce here a simple quantifier elimination method for a large class of verification conditions. It is based on a many-sorted logic with equality variant of the Herbrand Theorem which allows to have some kind of finite model property [12] even when some functions (interpreted or not) and interpreted predicates are used in formulas. We then give criteria for verification conditions to benefit from this property. Those criteria allow to eliminate quantifiers in the proof by invariant of many reactive algorithms, and particularly for parameterized algorithms, leading to a powerful invariant validation procedure. It allows to reduce the invariant validation for a system with a parameterized number of processes to the invariant validation for a system with a known number of processes n_0 (Theorem 2). Our method can be seen as an extension of the invariant validation procedure presented in [3]: our approach does not restrict the use of functions and predicates to unary ones, and is not restricted to bounded variables.

Our implementation has given good results on several algorithms; in particular, it has been successful in proving all verification conditions for a parameterized railroad crossing system [21] used as benchmark for STeP, whereas STeP itself requires interactive verification for some of them [6].

We first present our variant of the Herbrand Theorem. Next, this variant is used to eliminate the quantifiers in verification conditions from invariant validation of parameterized systems. Last, two examples are presented.

2 Herbrand on Many-Sorted Logic

In this section, Theorem 1 and its context is introduced. This theorem will be used to eliminate quantifiers in verification conditions, which will lead to Theorem 2.

A many-sorted first-order language (a more complete introduction to many-sorted logic can be found in [13]) is a tuple $\mathcal{L} = \langle \mathcal{T}, \mathcal{V}, \mathcal{F}, \mathcal{P}, r, d \rangle$ such that $\mathcal{T}$ is a finite set of sorts (or types), $\mathcal{V}$ is the (finite) union of disjoint finite sets $\mathcal{V}_\tau$ of variables of sort τ, $\mathcal{F}$ and $\mathcal{P}$ are sets of function and predicate symbols, r $(\mathcal{F} \cup \mathcal{P} \to \mathbb{N})$ assigns an arity to each function and predicate symbol, and d $(\mathcal{F} \cup \mathcal{P} \to \mathcal{T}^\star)$ assigns a sort in $\mathcal{T}^{r(f)+1}$ to each function symbol $f \in \mathcal{F}$ and a sort in $\mathcal{T}^{r(p)}$ to each predicate symbol $p \in \mathcal{P}$. Nullary predicates are propositions, and nullary functions are constants.

The sets of τ-terms on language $\mathcal{L}$ contain all variables in $\mathcal{V}_\tau$, and for every function symbol $f \in \mathcal{F}$ of sort $\langle \tau_1, \dots \tau_n, \tau \rangle$, $f(t_1, \dots t_n)$ is a τ-term if $t_1, \dots t_n$ are $\tau_1, \dots \tau_n$-terms respectively. $Sort(t) = \tau$ if t is a τ-term.

[2] Presburger with (unary) uninterpreted predicates is undecidable [20].

An atomic formula is either $t = t'$ where t and t' are terms of the same sort, or a predicate symbol applied to arguments of appropriate sorts. Formulas are built (as usual) from atomic formulas, connectors ($\neg$, $\wedge$, $\vee$, $\Rightarrow$, $\equiv$), and quantifiers ($\forall$, $\exists$). The set of all variables used in formula Φ is noted $Vars(\Phi)$, and $Free(\Phi)$ is the set of all free variables in Φ. A formula Φ is closed if $Free(\Phi) = \emptyset$. A formula is τ-universally quantified if it is of the form $\forall x \Psi$ with x a variable of type τ.

A formula is in prenex form if it is of the form $Q_1 x_1 \ldots Q_n x_n(\Phi)$ where $Q_1, \ldots Q_n \in \{\exists, \forall\}$, $x_1, \ldots x_n \in \mathcal{V}$, and Φ is quantifier-free. A formula is in Skolem form if it is in prenex form without existential quantifier.

A (normal) interpretation of a formula on a many-sorted first-order language $\mathcal{L} = \langle \mathcal{T}, \mathcal{V}, \mathcal{F}, \mathcal{P}, r, d \rangle$ is a pair $\mathcal{I} = \langle D, I \rangle$ where

- D assigns a non-empty domain D_τ (set) to each type $\tau \in \mathcal{T}$. Those sets are not necessarily disjoint;
- I assigns an element in D_τ to each variable of sort τ;
- I assigns a function $D_{\tau_1} \times \ldots D_{\tau_n} \longrightarrow D_\tau$ to each function symbol $f \in \mathcal{F}$ of sort $\langle \tau_1, \ldots \tau_n, \tau \rangle$;
- I assigns a function $D_{\tau_1} \times \ldots D_{\tau_n} \longrightarrow \{\top, \bot\}$ to each predicate symbol $p \in \mathcal{P}$ of sort $\langle \tau_1, \ldots \tau_n \rangle$;
- the identity is assigned to the equality sign $(=)$.

$\mathcal{I}$ assigns a value in D_τ to every τ-term t. This value is noted $\mathcal{I}[t]$. Similarly, interpretation $\mathcal{I}$ assigns a value in $\{\top, \bot\}$ to every formula Φ, which is noted $\mathcal{I}[\Phi]$. An interpretation $\mathcal{I}$ is a model for formula Φ if $\mathcal{I}[\Phi] = \top$. A formula is satisfiable if there exists a model for it.

Given an interpretation $\mathcal{I}$, the congruence $\mathcal{C}_{\mathcal{I},=} = \{(t_i, t'_i) \mid \mathcal{I}[t_i] = \mathcal{I}[t'_i]\}$ is a reflexive, symmetric and transitive relation on the set of terms of language $\mathcal{L}$. This relation is important for the proof of the following theorem.

Theorem 1. *Given*

- *a closed formula S in* Skolem form *on the language $\mathcal{L} = \langle \mathcal{T}, \mathcal{V}, \mathcal{F}, \mathcal{P}, r, d \rangle$;*
- *$\tau \in \mathcal{T}$ such that there is no function symbol $f \in \mathcal{F}$ of sort $\langle \tau_1, \ldots \tau_n, \tau \rangle$ with $n > 0$, $\tau_1, \ldots \tau_n \in \mathcal{T}$;*

the set H_τ is the set of constant symbols of sort τ ($H_\tau = \{c \in \mathcal{F} \mid d(c) = \tau\}$). If $\{c \in \mathcal{F} \mid d(c) = \tau\} = \emptyset$, then $H_\tau = \{a\}$, where a is an arbitrary new constant symbol such that $a \notin \mathcal{F}$ and $a \notin \mathcal{V}$.

For every model $\mathcal{I} = \langle D, I \rangle$ of S, there is a model $\mathcal{I}' = \langle D', I' \rangle$ such that

- *D'_τ is the quotient of the set H_τ by congruence $\mathcal{C}_{\mathcal{I},=}$;*
- *$D'_{\tau'} = D_{\tau'}$ for every $\tau' \neq \tau$;*
- *$\mathcal{I}'[f] = \mathcal{I}[f]$ for every function symbol $f \in \mathcal{F}$ of sort $\langle \tau_1, \ldots \tau_n, \tau' \rangle$ such that $\tau_1 \neq \tau, \ldots \tau_n \neq \tau, \tau' \neq \tau$ ($n \geq 0$);*
- *$\mathcal{I}'[p] = \mathcal{I}[p]$ for every function symbol $p \in \mathcal{P}$ of sort $\langle \tau_1, \ldots \tau_n \rangle$ such that $\tau_1 \neq \tau, \ldots \tau_n \neq \tau$ ($n \geq 0$).*

Proof. Interpretation $\mathcal{I}'$ is built from $\mathcal{I}$:

- for every constant symbol c of sort τ in $\mathcal{F}$, $I'[c]$ is the class of c in D_τ;
- for every function symbol $f \in \mathcal{F}$ of sort $\langle \tau_1, \ldots \tau_n, \tau' \rangle$ $(n > 0)$, and every $d'_1 \in D'_{\tau_1}, \ldots d'_n \in D'_{\tau_n}$, $I'[f](d'_1, \ldots d'_n) = I[f](d_1, \ldots d_n)$ where $d_i = d'_i$ if $\tau_i \neq \tau$. If $\tau_i = \tau$, $d_i = I(d''_i)$ where d''_i is any element of the class $d'_i \in D_\tau$;
- for every predicate symbol $p \in \mathcal{P}$ of sort $\langle \tau_1, \ldots \tau_n \rangle$, and every elements $d'_1 \in D'_{\tau_1}, \ldots d'_n \in D'_{\tau_n}$, $I'[p](d'_1, \ldots d'_n) = I[p](d_1, \ldots d_n)$ where $d_i = d'_i$ if $\tau_i \neq \tau$. If $\tau_i = \tau$, $d_i = I(d''_i)$ where d''_i is any element of the class $d'_i \in D_\tau$.

It remains to show that $\mathcal{I}'$ is a model of S. Let us first introduce a notation: given an interpretation $\mathcal{J} = \langle D, J \rangle$, the interpretation $\mathcal{J}_{x_1/d_1, \ldots x_n/d_n} = \langle D, J' \rangle$ (where $x_1, \ldots x_n$ are variables) is such that $J'[x_i] = d_i$ for every $x_i \in \{x_1, \ldots x_n\}$ and $J'[t] = J[t]$ if $t \notin \{x_1, \ldots x_n\}$

Formula S is of the form $\forall x_1 \ldots \forall x_n(\Phi)$. Thus for all elements $d'_1, \ldots d'_n$ such that d'_i belongs to $D'_{\tau'}$ if x_i is a variable of sort τ', the following equality hold:

$$\mathcal{I}'_{x_1/d'_1, \ldots x_n/d'_n}[\Phi] = \mathcal{I}_{x_1/d_1, \ldots x_n/d_n}[\Phi]$$

with $d_i = \mathcal{I}[d''_i]$ where d''_i is any element of the class $d'_i \in D'_\tau$ if x_i is of sort τ, $d_i = d'_i$ otherwise.

Interpretation $\mathcal{I}$ is a model of formula S, that means $\mathcal{I}_{x_1/d_1, \ldots x_n/d_n}[\Phi] = \top$ for all elements $d_1, \ldots d_n$ where d_i belongs to $D_{\tau'}$ if x_i is a variable of sort τ'. It follows that $\mathcal{I}'_{x_1/d'_1, \ldots x_n/d'_n}[\Phi] = \top$ for all elements $d'_1, \ldots d'_n$ such that d'_i belongs to $D'_{\tau'}$ if x_i is a variable of sort τ'. So $\mathcal{I}'$ is a model of S. □

This theorem is not exactly an extension of the Herbrand theorem to many-sorted first-order logic. It is stronger than the Herbrand theorem (see for example [14] for the standard Herbrand theorem, or [16] for a version with equality) in the sense that the domain does not necessarily become infinite in the presence of functions. On the other hand, its restriction to one-sorted first-order logic gives back the Herbrand theorem, but restricted to the finite Herbrand universe case. Nevertheless this case is the most interesting one: having a finite domain means that quantifier elimination is possible. Consider the simple (unsatisfiable) formula

$$\forall i \forall j \, [f(i) > g(j)] \wedge g(a) = 3 \wedge \exists i \, [f(i) < 4] \tag{1}$$

where "<" and ">" are the usual order predicates on $\mathbb{N} \times \mathbb{N}$. Variables i and j and constants a and b are of sort $\tau \neq \mathbb{N}N$ whereas f and g are functions from τ to $\mathbb{N}N$. In this context, the preceding theorem states that formula (1) is satisfiable if and only if formula

$$f(a) > g(a) \wedge f(a) > g(b) \wedge f(b) > g(a) \wedge$$
$$f(b) > g(b) \wedge g(a) = 3 \wedge f(b) < 4$$

is. This last formula belongs to the decidable class of quantifier-free first-order logic with linear arithmetics on $\mathbb{N}N$ and uninterpreted function symbols.

Corollary 1. *A τ-universally quantified formula $\forall x \, \Phi(x)$ verifying the conditions of Theorem 1 is satisfiable if and only if the finite conjunction $\bigwedge_{c \in H_\tau} \Phi(c)$ is.*

3 Interpreted Predicates and Functions

A formula containing interpreted predicates and functions is satisfiable if and only if it has a model in a restricted subset of all interpretations, that is the set where interpretations associate a fixed domain to given sorts and a fixed meaning to those interpreted predicates and functions. In Theorem 1, both interpretations $\mathcal{I}$ and $\mathcal{I}'$ associate the same domain to every sort but τ, and give the same meaning to every predicate and function, provided none of their arguments is of sort τ. In other words, Theorem 1 is compatible with the use of interpreted predicates and functions provided none of their arguments is of sort τ. For instance, in the preceding example (i, j and a are of sort τ) the arguments of the order predicates ($f(i)$, $g(j)$, ...) are not of the sort τ. Using Theorem 1, interpretation $\mathcal{I}$ and $\mathcal{I}'$ are such that $\mathcal{I}[<] = \mathcal{I}'[<]$ and $\mathcal{I}[>] = \mathcal{I}'[>]$. And this allows to eliminate the quantifiers on the sort τ in presence of interpreted predicates with no argument of sort τ.

But it is also possible to use order predicates on the sort of quantified variables. Let φ be a formula with order predicates ("$\leq$", ...) on sort τ, and ψ be the conjunction of the axioms of total order theory,

$$\begin{aligned} \psi = \quad & \forall x\,(x \leq x) \\ & \wedge\ \forall x \forall y\,((x \leq y \wedge y \leq x) \Rightarrow x = y) \\ & \wedge\ \forall x \forall y \forall z\,((x \leq y \wedge y \leq z) \Rightarrow x \leq z) \\ & \wedge\ \forall x \forall y\,(x \leq y \vee y \leq x) \end{aligned}$$

with variables x, y, z of sort τ. An interpretation is a model of $\psi \wedge \varphi$ if and only if it is a model of φ interpreting "$\leq$", ... as the usual order predicates on D_τ. Putting $\psi \wedge \varphi$ in Skolem form does not introduce new Skolem functions. The conditions of Theorem 1 are met for $\psi \wedge \varphi$ if they are met for φ. Theorem 1 can be applied also if some comparisons are made between terms of the sort of quantified variables [3].

4 Quantifier Elimination in Invariant Validation

In order to verify that the assertion H is an invariant of the transition system $\mathcal{S}$, one has to validate the Hoare triple $\{H\}\sigma\{H\}$ for each transition[4] $\sigma \in \mathcal{S}$. This is first reduced to first-order logic proving, using Dijkstra [9] weakest precondition (wp) operator: Hoare tripe $\{H\}\sigma\{H\}$ is valid if and only if formula $H \Rightarrow wp[\sigma; H]$ can be proved. Weakest precondition calculus is easy, provided

[3] As in [3], "+1" and "$\oplus 1$" functions can sometimes be eliminated without introducing new Skolem functions, by noticing that $h = i + 1 \longleftrightarrow i < h \wedge \forall j\,(j \leq i \vee h \leq j)$ and $h = i \oplus 1 \longleftrightarrow [i < h \wedge \forall j\,(j \leq i \vee h \leq j)] \vee [h < i \wedge \forall j\,(h \leq j \vee j \leq i)]$.

[4] An example of transition is $(s_0[p]s_0[q], C \longrightarrow A, s_1[p]s_1[q])$ which allows the processes p and q to go from control point s_0 to control point s_1, executing the statements in A. The system transition can be executed from a state where formula C (the guard) is fulfilled.

transitions do not contain full loops in their statement part. The weakest precondition module in CAVEAT accepts assignments, conditional statements, sequences of statements, and some kind of quantified assignments. This is enough to model reactive algorithms from coarse to fine-grained versions.

In general, the invariant is a conjunction ($H = \bigwedge_{k \in K} h_k$) of relatively small assertions h_k. In parameterized systems, these assertions are often quantified over the (parameterized) set of processes. In order to avoid the appearance of Skolem functions when verification conditions are put in Skolem form, an assumption is made about these quantified assertions: they can be put both in prenex form $\exists^\star\forall^\star$ (called *hypothesis form* in the following, because this will be the allowed form in the antecedent of formulas of the form $A \Rightarrow B$) *and* in prenex form $\forall^\star\exists^\star$ (called *conclusion form* in the following, because this will be the allowed form in the conclusion of formulas of the form $A \Rightarrow B$). In practice, two particular cases of such formulas are met frequently:

- formulas in prenex form containing one type of quantifier;
- formulas containing only monadic predicates (and no equality)[5].

There is also an assumption for guards : guards must be formulas in hypothesis form. Guards met in practice fulfill this assumption as they are quantifier-free formulas or singly quantified formulas.

Taking the preceding conditions on quantifiers into account, proving formula $H \Rightarrow wp[\sigma; H]$ (with $H = \bigwedge_{k \in K} h_k$) reduces to prove a set of formulas (called verification conditions) of the form

$$(h_1 \wedge \ldots h_k \wedge G) \Rightarrow C_j$$

where G is the guard of σ. All formulas $h_1 \ldots h_k, G$ are in hypothesis form. There is one verification condition for each h_k ($k \in K$). Formula C_k comes from hypothesis h_k: $C_k \equiv wp\,[A; h_k]$, where A is the statement part of σ. C_k can be put in conclusion form: indeed, h_k can be put in conclusion form, and the weakest precondition operator does not modify the quantifier structure of a formula, in the language accepted by CAVEAT.

The last requirement is about functions: we require that no function used in the invariant H, or in the transition system $\mathcal{S}$ has the process set as domain. This may seem rather restrictive, but as reactive algorithms mainly use Boolean arrays (modeled by predicates, not functions), this requirement remains acceptable in practice.

Under those conditions, Theorem 1 can be used to eliminate the quantifiers:

Theorem 2. *If H is a conjunctive formula, and Σ is a transition system with a parameterized number n of processes, where*

[5] Indeed every monadic formula is logically equivalent to a Boolean combination of Skolem forms with one quantifier. So every monadic formula can be put in both hypothesis and conclusion forms.

- *all quantified variables in H and in the guard of the transitions of Σ range over the set of processes;*
- *every conjunct in H can be put both in hypothesis form ($\exists^\star\forall^\star$) and in conclusion form ($\forall^\star\exists^\star$);*
- *every transition guard can be put in hypothesis form;*
- *no interpreted predicate other than equality and order is used on the set of processes, neither in H nor in Σ;*
- *no function has the process set as domain, neither in H nor in Σ;*

then H is an invariant of Σ if and only if H is an invariant of the system Σ' with at most n_0 processes, where n_0 is the sum of

- *the number of existential quantifiers in H when put in hypothesis form;*
- *the maximum number of existential quantifiers in guards of transitions in Σ;*
- *the maximum number of universal quantifiers in the conjuncts of H, when put in conclusion form;*
- *the number of constants in H;*
- *the maximum number of processes taking part in a transition*[6]*.*

Proof. Indeed from the theorem conditions, every verification condition is of the form

$$(h_1 \wedge \ldots h_k \wedge G) \Rightarrow C$$

where formulas $h_1, \ldots h_k, G$ are in hypothesis form, and C is in conclusion form. When put prenex form, this formula is of the form

$$\forall x_1 \ldots \forall x_p \exists y_1 \ldots \exists y_q \, \varphi(x_1, \ldots x_p, y_1, \ldots y_q), \tag{2}$$

where p is the number of existential quantifiers in $h_1 \wedge \ldots h_k \wedge G$ plus the number of universal quantifiers in C. Otherwise stated, p cannot exceed the sum of

- the number of existential quantifiers in H ($h_1 \wedge \ldots h_k$) when put in hypothesis form;
- the maximum number of existential quantifiers in guards (G) of transitions in Σ;
- the maximum number of universal quantifiers in the conjuncts (h_k from which C is computed) of H, when put in conclusion form.

Formula (2) is provable if and only if formula

$$\exists x_1 \ldots \exists x_p \forall y_1 \ldots \forall y_q \, \neg\varphi(x_1, \ldots x_p, y_1, \ldots y_q) \tag{3}$$

is unsatisfiable or, using Skolemization, if and only if formula

$$\forall y_1 \ldots \forall y_q \, \neg\varphi(a_1, \ldots a_p, y_1, \ldots y_q) \tag{4}$$

is unsatisfiable, where $a_1, \ldots a_p$ are Skolem constants, i.e. constants which do not appear in $\varphi(x_1, \ldots x_p, y_1, \ldots y_q)$. Using Theorem 1, formula (4) is satisfiable if and only if there is a model with a finite process set, which contains all process constants in $\varphi(a_1, \ldots a_p, y_1, \ldots y_q)$, including $a_1, \ldots a_p$. So n_0 is the sum of

[6] usually at most two.

- p;
- the number of constants coming from H in φ;
- the maximum number of constants coming from the transitions through G and C, which is the maximum number of processes involved at the same time in a transition.

□

Comment. The satisfiability problem for the Schönfinkel-Bernays class, that is, the class of function-free first-order formulas of the form

$$\exists x_1 \ldots \exists x_p \forall y_1 \ldots \forall y_q \, \varphi(x_1, \ldots x_p, y_1, \ldots y_q),$$

has first been shown to be decidable by Bernays and Schönfinkel without equality [5] and by Ramsey with equality [29]. Theorem 1 extends this decidable class to allow the use of some functions (interpreted or not) and some interpreted predicates.

Corollary 2. *When conditions of Theorem 2 are met, checking if Σ preserves the invariant H is reduced to a quantifier-free first-order logic satisfiability checking problem.*

The quantifier-free satisfiability checking module [15] in CAVEAT is based on a modified version of the Nelson-Oppen algorithm [26,27]. It accepts linear arithmetic, as well as uninterpreted predicates and functions. When Theorem 2 applies, and when the quantifier-free formulas use only linear arithmetic, and uninterpreted predicates and functions, the invariant validation problem is decidable. This is the case for numerous algorithms. In the next section a simple one is presented.

5 Parameterized Burns Algorithm

In this well-known simple example only one type of variable is used. Theorem 1 thus reduces to the Herbrand theorem (with equality, without functions). This simple example allows to clearly exhibit the underlying fact which enables quantifier elimination: a finite Herbrand universe.

Burns algorithm [22], [25, p. 294] guarantees exclusive access to a critical section for a set of n identical processes. Each process p can be in one of six different location states (i.e. $s_0 \ldots s_5$). A rule expresses the trivial property that each process is in one and only one state at each time: one and only one variable in $s_0[p], \ldots, s_5[p]$ is true (for each p). A process p being in s_5 (i.e. $s_5[p]$ is true) is in the critical section.

Twelve transitions are possible between the six states:

$$\Big(\mathrm{s}_0[p],\ \mathrm{flag}[p]{:=}\mathrm{false},\ \mathrm{s}_1[p]\Big)$$

$$\Big(\mathrm{s}_1[p], \neg S[p,q] \wedge q < p \wedge \mathrm{flag}[q] \ \rightarrow\ \forall q : S[p,q]{:=}\mathrm{false},\ \mathrm{s}_0[p]\Big)$$

$$\Big(\mathrm{s}_1[p], \neg S[p,q] \wedge q < p \wedge \neg\mathrm{flag}[q] \ \rightarrow\ S[p,q]{:=}\mathrm{true},\ \mathrm{s}_1[p]\Big)$$

$$\Big(\mathrm{s}_1[p], \forall q\big(q < p \Rightarrow S[p,q]\big) \ \rightarrow\ \forall q : S[p,q]{:=}\mathrm{false},\ \mathrm{s}_2[p]\Big)$$

$$\Big(\mathrm{s}_2[p],\ \mathrm{flag}[p]{:=}\mathrm{true},\ \mathrm{s}_3[p]\Big)$$
$$\Big(\mathrm{s}_3[p], \neg S[p,q]\ \wedge\ q < p\ \wedge\ \mathrm{flag}[q]\ \rightarrow\ \forall q : S[p,q]{:=}\mathrm{false},\ \mathrm{s}_0[p]\Big)$$
$$\Big(\mathrm{s}_3[p], \neg S[p,q]\ \wedge\ q < p\ \wedge\ \neg\mathrm{flag}[q]\ \rightarrow\ S[p,q]{:=}\mathrm{true},\ \mathrm{s}_3[p]\Big)$$
$$\Big(\mathrm{s}_3[p], \forall q\Big(q < p \Rightarrow S[p,q]\Big)\ \rightarrow\ \forall q : S[p,q]{:=}\mathrm{false},\ \mathrm{s}_4[p]\Big)$$
$$\Big(\mathrm{s}_4[p], \neg S[p,q]\ \wedge\ p < q\ \wedge\ \mathrm{flag}[q]\ \rightarrow\ \forall q : S[p,q]{:=}\mathrm{false},\ \mathrm{s}_4[p]\Big)$$
$$\Big(\mathrm{s}_4[p], \neg S[p,q]\ \wedge\ p < q\ \wedge\ \neg\mathrm{flag}[q]\ \rightarrow\ S[p,q]{:=}\mathrm{true},\ \mathrm{s}_4[p]\Big)$$
$$\Big(\mathrm{s}_4[p], \forall q\Big(p < q \Rightarrow S[p,q]\Big)\ \rightarrow\ \forall q : S[p,q]{:=}\mathrm{false},\ \mathrm{s}_5[p]\Big)$$
$$\Big(\mathrm{s}_5[p],\ \mathrm{flag}[p]{:=}\mathrm{false},\ \mathrm{s}_0[p]\Big)$$

Mutual exclusion is obtained using two waiting rooms (s_3 and s_4). The first one ensures that when a process p has reached s_4, any other process q with $q < p$ and $\mathrm{flag}[q] = \mathrm{true}$ (trying to get access to critical section, or in the critical section) has gone through transition $s_2 \rightarrow s_3$ *after* p. The second waiting room guarantees that this process q (with $q < p$) will be blocked in s_4 at least until p resets flag[p] to false. Only the highest process (the one with the highest identifier) will thus get access to critical section[7].

The algorithm uses one single-writer shared register per process: flag[p] is set to true by process p when it wants to access to critical section. Each process p also uses a local array variable $S[p]$. This variable is used in three loops (s_1, s_3, s_4). In the loops for process p the value of the flag[q] variable of the other processes q is checked (processes q such that $q < p$ or $q > p$). $S[p]$ is used to keep track of processes already checked and those which still have to be checked. The algorithm makes also extensive use of a total order relation between processes.

Formula $H =_{\mathrm{def}} \forall p\ H_1(p) \wedge \forall p \forall q\, [H_2(p,q) \wedge H_3(p,q)]$, with

$$\begin{aligned} H_1(p) &=_{\mathrm{def}} \neg\mathrm{flag}[p] \Rightarrow (\mathrm{s}_0[p] \vee \mathrm{s}_1[p] \vee \mathrm{s}_2[p]) \\ H_2(p,q) &=_{\mathrm{def}} \mathrm{s}_2[p] \Rightarrow \neg S[p,q] \\ H_3(p,q) &=_{\mathrm{def}} \Big[q < p\ \wedge\ \mathrm{flag}[q]\ \wedge\ (\mathrm{s}_5[p] \vee \mathrm{s}_4[p] \vee (\mathrm{s}_3[p] \wedge S[p,q]))\Big] \\ &\qquad \Rightarrow \Big[\neg\mathrm{s}_5[q] \wedge \neg(\mathrm{s}_4[q] \wedge S[q,p])\Big] \end{aligned}$$

is an invariant. It entails[8] the mutual exclusion property:

$$\forall p \forall q \big[p \neq q \Rightarrow (\neg s_5[p] \vee \neg s_5[q])\big].$$

Every condition is met for Theorem 2 to be used. Indeed:

[7] Access to critical section will be easier for processes with high identifiers. This algorithm does not guarantee high-level-fairness.

[8] together with the rule which expresses the fact that each process is in one and only one state at a time.

- no function (at all) is used;
- every guard is in hypothesis form. In fact, every guard is at most once quantified;
- the invariant is a conjunction of formulas which are in both hypothesis and conclusion form, as they are universally quantified;
- the only interpreted predicates are equality and order; objects compared belong to a finite, but parameterized, domain: the set of processes.

From Theorem 2, if H is an invariant of this algorithm for $n_0 = 4$ *processes* then H will be an invariant of this algorithm *for any number of processes.*

Let's see how this work for a given verification condition: if H is an invariant, it is preserved by every transition, and in particular, by transition $\sigma_{1\to 2}$ from s_1 to s_2. Hoare triple $\{H\}\sigma_{1\to 2}\{H\}$ must be provable, so must be $\{H\}\sigma_{1\to 2}\{\forall p\ H_1(p)\}$, $\{H\}\sigma_{1\to 2}\{\forall p \forall q\ H_2(p,q)\}$ and $\{H\}\sigma_{1\to 2}\{\forall p \forall q\ H_3(p,q)\}$. In particular, from $\{H\}\sigma_{1\to 2}\{\forall p \forall q H_2(p,q)\}$ comes the verification condition

$$\varphi =_{\mathrm{def}} (h_1 \wedge h_2 \wedge h_3 \wedge g_1 \wedge g_2 \wedge l_1 \wedge l_2 \wedge l_3 \wedge l_4 \wedge l_5) \Rightarrow C$$

with

- $h_1 =_{\mathrm{def}} \forall p\ H_1(p)$
- $h_2 =_{\mathrm{def}} \forall p \forall q\ H_2(p,q)$
- $h_3 =_{\mathrm{def}} \forall p \forall q\ H_3(p,q)$
- $g_1 =_{\mathrm{def}} s_1[p]$
- $g_2 =_{\mathrm{def}} \forall q[q < p \Rightarrow S[p,q]]$
- $l_1 =_{\mathrm{def}} \forall p[s_0[p] \Rightarrow \neg(s_1[p] \vee s_2[p] \vee s_3[p] \vee s_4[p] \vee s_5[p])]$
- $l_2 =_{\mathrm{def}} \forall p[s_1[p] \Rightarrow \neg(s_2[p] \vee s_3[p] \vee s_4[p] \vee s_5[p])]$
- $l_3 =_{\mathrm{def}} \forall p[s_2[p] \Rightarrow \neg(s_3[p] \vee s_4[p] \vee s_5[p])]$
- $l_4 =_{\mathrm{def}} \forall p[s_3[p] \Rightarrow \neg(s_4[p] \vee s_5[p])]$
- $l_5 =_{\mathrm{def}} \forall p[s_4[p] \Rightarrow \neg s_5[p]]$
- $C =_{\mathrm{def}} \forall s \forall r[(s \neq p \Rightarrow s_2[s]) \Rightarrow \neg(s \neq p\ \wedge\ S[s,r])]$

Hypotheses $h_{1,2,3}$ come from the invariant, $g_{1,2}$ from the transition guards[9]. Formulas $l_{1,\ldots 5}$ state that each process is in one and only one state. The conclusion C is the result of applying the weakest precondition operator, i. e.,

$$C \equiv wp\ [\forall q : S[p,q]{:=}\text{false}; \mathrm{s}_1[p] := \text{false}; \mathrm{s}_2[p] := \text{true}; \forall p \forall q\ H_2(p,q)]$$

Every formula from h_1 to l_5 is in hypothesis form, and C is in conclusion form. The Herbrand universe for the negation of this verification condition contains four elements (p, q, and the new constants coming from the Skolemization of C). Every universal quantifier in hypotheses will then give rise to four instances, for a total of 61 hypotheses[10].

9 g_1 comes from the origin of the transition. Transition $(l_1, C \longrightarrow A, l_2)$ with origin l_1 and destination l_2 can be written as transition $((C \wedge l_1) \longrightarrow A; l_1 := \text{false}; l_2 := \text{true})$.

10 each formula h_1, g_2, $l_{1\ldots 5}$ generates four instances, whereas formulas h_2 and h_3 generate 16 instances. The 61st hypothesis is g_1.

CAVEAT took 5 seconds on a Pentium 1 GHz, to generate and verify 40 verification conditions. This includes the time to verify that the invariant entails the mutual exclusion property, and also that the invariant is made true by initial conditions.

6 Generalized Railroad Crossing

The Generalized Railroad Crossing benchmark [21] uses predicates and functions from arithmetic. It gives a general idea of what Theorem 1 allows to deal with.

A controller operates on a gate of a railroad crossing protecting N parallel railroad tracks. The gate must be down whenever a train takes the intersection, so that the intersecting road is closed. Each of the N trains can be in three different regions: in the intersection (I), in the section preceding the intersection (P), or anywhere else (not_here). The array variable "trains" records the position of each train: trains[i] can be one of the three values $I, P,$ not_here. The gate can be in four states: the value of variable "gate" can be $\text{down}, \text{up}, \text{going\_down}$ or going_up, with obvious meanings. The system should verify the safety property, which expresses the fact that the gate must be down when any of the N trains is passing the intersection:

$$\forall i\,(\text{trains}[i] = I \Rightarrow \text{gate} = \text{down})\,.$$

The gate takes some time to go from the state "up" to "down". This time must not exceed "gateRiseTime". Similarly the time to go from the "down" to the "up" states must not exceed "gateDownTime". Trains getting in P would take a minimum time "minTimeToI" and a maximum time "maxTimeToI" to get to the intersection. It is the controller job to know when to lower the gate, and when to raise it. Initially, the gate is up, and no train is either in the intersection or in the section preceding the intersection.

The system transitions are given on Figure 1. The first three transitions model the position changes of the train i. The two following ones express the controller decision to lower or raise the gate. The next two mean the gate reaches the up or down states. The last one models the time flow.

Only two transition guards are not quantifier-free. But they can easily be put in prenex form with a single quantifier. Functions are used (trains, firstEnter, lastEnter, schedTime, +) but they do not range over the process set. All requirements are thus met for Theorem 2 to be used, as long as the invariants to be checked also verify the requirements about quantifiers.

Figure 2 shows several invariance properties of the system. Together with the safety property, they give an invariant for the system. As the safety property is one conjunct of the invariant, it is trivially entailed by the invariant. In order to validate the invariant, it is necessary to take into account the constraints on constants (Figure 3) as well as the progress axioms[11] (Figure 4). They are supplementary hypotheses to be put in the verification conditions.

[11] For example, progress axiom P_1 states that the train does not stay indefinitely in section P before going in I.

$$\Big(\text{trains}[i] = \text{not\_here} \longrightarrow \text{begin} \quad \text{trains}[i] := P; \quad \text{firstEnter}[i] := T + \text{minTimeToI}; \quad \text{lastEnter}[i] := T + \text{maxTimeToI}; \quad \text{schedTime}[i] := T + \text{conMinI}; \quad \text{trainHere}[i] := \text{true} \quad \text{end}\Big)$$

$$\Big(\text{trains}[i] = P \wedge T \geq \text{firstEnter}[i] \longrightarrow \text{trains}[i] := I\Big)$$

$$\Big(\text{trains}[i] = I \longrightarrow \text{begin trains}[i] := \text{not\_here}; \ \text{trainHere}[i] := \text{false end}\Big)$$

$$\Big((\text{gate} = \text{up} \vee \text{gate} = \text{going\_up}) \wedge \text{gstatus} = \text{up} \wedge \exists i\,(\text{trainHere}[i] \wedge \text{schedTime}[i] \leq T + \gamma_{\text{down}} + \beta) \longrightarrow \text{begin} \quad \text{gate} = \text{going\_down}; \quad \text{lastDown} := T + \text{gateDownTime}; \quad \text{gstatus} := \text{down} \quad \text{end}\Big)$$

$$\Big((\text{gate} = \text{down} \vee \text{gate} = \text{going\_down}) \wedge \text{gstatus} = \text{down} \wedge \forall i\,(\text{trainHere}[i] \Rightarrow \text{schedTime}[i] > T + \gamma_{\text{down}} + \gamma_{\text{up}} + \text{carPassingTime}) \longrightarrow \text{begin} \quad \text{gate} := \text{going\_up}; \quad \text{lastUp} := T + \text{gateRiseTime}; \quad \text{gstatus} := \text{up} \quad \text{end}\Big)$$

$$\Big(\text{gate} = \text{going\_up} \longrightarrow \text{gate} := \text{up}\Big)$$

$$\Big(\text{gate} = \text{going\_down} \longrightarrow \text{gate} := \text{down}\Big)$$

$$\Big(T := T + \varepsilon\Big)$$

Fig. 1. The transitions modeling the General Railroad Crossing system

In the whole proof, only two properties (or guards) are existentially quantified, properties are at most once quantified, and at most one train take part in a transition. From Theorem 2, if the invariant (which guarantees that the algorithm is safe) is preserved *for four trains*, the algorithm will be safe *for any number of trains.*

CAVEAT took 87 seconds to generate and verify the 221 verification conditions necessary to prove the safety property.

$$T_1 =_{\text{def}} \forall i \left(T < \text{firstEnter}[i] \Rightarrow \text{trains}[i] \neq I \right)$$

$$T_2 =_{\text{def}} \forall i \Big(\text{trains}[i] = P \Rightarrow (\text{firstEnter}[i] \leq T + \text{minTimeToI} \ \wedge \ T \leq \text{lastEnter}[i] \ \wedge \text{lastEnter}[i] - \text{firstEnter}[i] = \text{maxTimeToI} - \text{minTimeToI}) \Big)$$

$$C_1 =_{\text{def}} \text{gstatus} = \text{up} \Rightarrow \forall i \left(\text{trainHere}[i] \Rightarrow T < \text{schedTime}[i] - \gamma_{\text{down}} \right)$$

$$GC_1 =_{\text{def}} \text{gstatus} = \text{down} \equiv (\text{gate} = \text{goingDown} \ \vee \ \text{gate} = \text{down})$$

$$GC_2 =_{\text{def}} \text{gstatus} = \text{down} \Rightarrow \text{lastDown} \leq T + \text{gateDownTime}$$

$$GC_3 =_{\text{def}} \text{gstatus} = \text{up} \Rightarrow \forall i \left(\text{trainHere}[i] \Rightarrow \text{lastDown} < \text{schedTime}[i] \right)$$

$$TC_1 =_{\text{def}} \forall i \left(\text{trainHere}[i] \equiv \text{trains}[i] \neq \text{notHere} \right)$$

$$TC_2 =_{\text{def}} \forall i \left(\text{trainHere}[i] \Rightarrow \text{schedTime}[i] < \text{firstEnter}[i] \right)$$

Fig. 2. Invariance properties

$$AC_1 = \gamma_{\text{down}} < \text{conMinI}$$

$$ACT_1 = \text{conMinI} < \text{minTimeToI}$$

$$AGC_1 = \text{gateDownTime} < \gamma_{\text{down}}$$

$$AGC_2 = \text{gateRiseTime} < \gamma_{\text{up}}$$

Fig. 3. Constraints on constants

$$G_1 =_{\text{def}} \text{gate} = \text{goingDown} \Rightarrow T \leq \text{lastDown}$$

$$G_2 =_{\text{def}} \text{gate} = \text{goingUp} \Rightarrow T \leq \text{lastUp}$$

$$P_1 =_{\text{def}} \forall i \, (\text{trains}[i] = P \Rightarrow T \leq \text{lastEnter}[i])$$

$$P_2 =_{\text{def}} \text{gstatus} = \text{up} \Rightarrow \forall i \left(\text{trainHere}[i] \Rightarrow T < \text{schedTime}[i] - \gamma_{\text{down}} \right)$$

$$P_3 =_{\text{def}} \text{gstatus} = \text{down} \Rightarrow \exists i \left(\text{trainHere}[i] \ \wedge \ \text{schedTime}[i] \leq T + \gamma_{\text{up}} + \text{carPassingTime} + \gamma_{\text{down}} \right)$$

Fig. 4. Progress axioms

7 Conclusions and Future Work

The invariant validation process often has an interactive part as well as an automatic part [6,30]. This interactive aspect (even if it is often easy) makes the proof process longer and tedious. This work is one step further to make the proof by invariants more applicable, either as a method by itself, or as an element of an automatic verification process.

The verification conditions obtained in the context of verification of parameterized algorithm are often quantified over the set of processes. We have presented here a quantifier elimination procedure based on an enhanced Herbrand Theorem, an adaptation of the classical Herbrand Theorem to many-sorted logic with equality. This quantifier elimination procedure is suitable for a large class of verification conditions including formulas coming from verification of parameterized systems. It has been successfully applied to the invariant validation for several algorithms included the bakery algorithm (with or without bounded tickets), a railroad crossing system, Burns, Dijkstra, Ricart & Agrawala, Szymanski... As the quantifier-free validity problem is usually decidable, this quantifier elimination procedure is a key to automatic validation of invariants.

With bigger algorithms, instantiation itself may become a problem. Finding simple and effective heuristics to selectively instantiate formulas is also in our concern. A rigorous hypothesis selection and elimination method has already been found in the pure propositional case [19], and the results are promising. We plan to adapt it to the present framework.

References

1. P. A. Abdulla, A. Bouajjani, B. Jonsson, and M. Nilsson. Handling global conditions in parametrized system verification. In *Computer Aided Verification Conference*, volume 1633 of *Lecture Notes in Computer Science*, pages 134–145. Springer-Verlag, July 1999.
2. K. R. Apt and D. C. Kozen. Limits for automatic verification of finite-state concurrent systems. *Information Processing Letters*, 22(6):307–309, May 1986.
3. T. Arons, A. Pnueli, S. Ruah, J. Xu, and L. Zuck. Parameterized verification with automatically computed inductive assertions. In *Computer Aided Verification*, volume 2102 of *Lecture Notes in Computer Science*, pages 221–234. Springer-Verlag, July 2001.
4. K. Baukus, Y. Lakhnech, and K. Stahl. Verification of Parameterized Protocols. *Journal of Universal Computer Science*, 7(2):141–158, Feb. 2001.
5. P. Bernays and M. Schönfinkel. Zum Entscheidungsproblem der mathematischen Logik. *Math. Annalen*, 99:342–372, 1928.
6. N. S. Bjørner, Z. Manna, H. B. Sipma, and T. E. Uribe. Deductive verification of real-time systems using STeP. *TCS: Theoretical Computer Science*, 253, 2001.
7. A. Bouajjani, B. Jonsson, M. Nilsson, and T. Touili. Regular model checking. In *Computer Aided Verification*, volume 1855 of *Lecture Notes in Computer Science*, pages 403–418. Springer-Verlag, July 2000.
8. K. M. Chandy and J. Misra. *Parallel Program Design*. Addison-Wesley, Reading, Massachusetts, 1988.

9. E. W. Dijkstra. *A Discipline of Programming.* Prentice-Hall, 1976.
10. B. Dreben and W. D. Goldfarb. *The Decision Problem: Solvable Classes of Quantificational Formulas.* Addison-Wesley, Reading, Massachusetts, 1979.
11. E. A. Emerson and K. S. Namjoshi. Automatic verification of parameterized synchronous systems. In *Computer Aided Verification*, volume 1102, pages 87–98. Springer-Verlag, July 1996.
12. H.-D. Ebbinghaus and J. Flum. *Finite Model Theory.* Perspectives in Mathematical Logic. Springer-Verlag, Berlin, 1995.
13. H. B. Enderton. *A Mathematical Introduction to Logic.* Academic Press, Inc., Orlando, Florida, 1972.
14. M. Fitting. *First-Order Logic and Automated Theorem Proving.* Springer-Verlag, Berlin, 1990.
15. P. Fontaine and E. P. Gribomont. Using BDDs with combinations of theories. In *Logic for Programming, Artificial Intelligence, and Reasoning*, volume 2514 of *Lecture Notes in Computer Science.* Springer, 2002.
16. J. Gallier, P. Narendran, S. Raatz, and W. Snyder. Theorem proving using equational matings and rigid E–unification. *Journal of the ACM*, 39(2):377–429, Apr. 1992.
17. S. M. German and A. P. Sistla. Reasoning about systems with many processes. *Journal of the ACM*, 39(3):675–735, July 1992.
18. S. Graf and H. Saïdi. Verifying invariants using theorem proving. In *Computer Aided Verification*, volume 1102 of *Lecture Notes in Computer Science*, pages 196–207. Springer Verlag, 1996.
19. E. P. Gribomont. Simplification of boolean verification conditions. *Theoretical Computer Science*, 239(1):165–185, May 2000.
20. J. Y. Halpern. Presburger arithmetic with unary predicates is Π_1^1 complete. *The Journal of Symbolic Logic*, 56(2):637–642, June 1991.
21. C. Heitmeyer and N. A. Lynch. The generalized railroad crossing — a case study in formal verification of real-time systems. In *Proceedings 15th IEEE Real-Time Systems Symposium,* San Juan, Puerto Rico, pages 120–131, Dec. 1994.
22. H. E. Jensen and N. A. Lynch. A proof of burns n-process mutual exclusion algorithm using abstraction. In *Tools and Algorithms for Construction and Analysis of Systems*, volume 1384 of *Lecture Notes in Computer Science*, pages 409–423. Springer-Verlag, Mar. 1998.
23. Y. Kesten, O. Maler, M. Marcus, A. Pnueli, and E. Shahar. Symbolic model checking with rich assertional languages. In *Computer Aided Verification*, volume 1254 of *Lecture Notes in Computer Science*, pages 424–435. Springer-Verlag, 1997.
24. R. P. Kurshan and K. McMillan. A structural induction theorem for processes. In *Principles of Distributed Computing*, pages 239–248. ACM Press, Aug. 1989.
25. N. Lynch. *Distributed Algorithms.* Morgan Kaufmann, San Francisco, CS, 1996.
26. G. C. Necula. *Compiling with Proofs.* PhD thesis, Carnegie Mellon University, Oct. 1998. Available as Technical Report CMU-CS-98-154.
27. G. Nelson and D. C. Oppen. Simplifications by cooperating decision procedures. *ACM Transactions on Programming Languages and Systems*, 1(2):245–257, Oct. 1979.
28. A. Pnueli, S. Ruah, and L. D. Zuck. Automatic deductive verification with invisible invariants. In *Tools and Algorithms for the Construction and Analysis of Systems*, Lecture Notes in Computer Science, pages 82–97, 2001.
29. F. Ramsey. On a Problem of Formal Logic. *Proceedings of the London Mathematical Society*, 30:264–286, 1930.

30. N. Shankar. Verification of Real-Time Systems Using PVS. In *Computer Aided Verification*, volume 697 of *Lecture Notes in Computer Science*, pages 280–291. Springer-Verlag, June 1993.
31. P. Wolper and V. Lovinfosse. Verifying properties of large sets of processes with network invariants. In *Automatic Verification Methods for Finite State Systems*, volume 407 of *Lecture Notes in Computer Science*, pages 68–80. Springer-Verlag, June 1989.

Verification and Improvement of the Sliding Window Protocol*

Dmitri Chkliaev[1], Jozef Hooman[2], and Erik de Vink[1]

[1] Department of Mathematics and Computer Science,
Technische Universiteit Eindhoven,
P.O. Box 513, 5600 MB Eindhoven, The Netherlands
{dmitri, evink}@win.tue.nl

[2] Computing Science Institute, University of Nijmegen, The Netherlands
hooman@cs.kun.nl

Abstract. The well-known Sliding Window protocol caters for the reliable and efficient transmission of data over unreliable channels that can lose, reorder and duplicate messages. Despite the practical importance of the protocol and its high potential for errors, it has never been formally verified for the general setting. We try to fill this gap by giving a fully formal specification and verification of an improved version of the protocol. The protocol is specified by a timed state machine in the language of the verification system PVS. This allows a mechanical check of the proof by the interactive proof checker of PVS. Our modelling is very general and includes such important features of the protocol as sending and receiving windows of arbitrary size, bounded sequence numbers and channels that may lose, reorder and duplicate messages.

1 Introduction

Reliable transmission of data over unreliable channels is an old and well-studied problem in computer science. Without a satisfactory solution, computer networks would be useless, because they transmit data over channels that often lose, duplicate, or reorder messages. One of the most efficient protocols for reliable transmission is the Sliding Window (SW) protocol [Ste76]. Many popular communication protocols such as TCP and HDLC are based on the SW protocol.

Communication protocols usually involve a subtle interaction of a number of distributed components and have a high degree of parallelism. This is why their correctness is difficult to ensure, and many protocols turned out to be erroneous. One of the most promising solutions to this problem is the use of formal verification, which requires the precise specification of the protocol in some specification language and a formal proof of its correctness by mathematical techniques. Formal verification is especially useful when it uses some form of mechanical support, such as a model checker or an interactive theorem prover.

* This research is supported by the Dutch PROGRESS project EES5202, "Modelling and performance analysis of telecommunication systems".

H. Garavel and J. Hatcliff (Eds.): TACAS 2003, LNCS 2619, pp. 113–127, 2003.

However, formal verification of communication protocols is notoriously difficult. Even verification of a version of the Alternating Bit protocol [BSW69] (which is one of the simplest communication protocols), namely the Bounded Retransmission Protocol (BRP) of Philips Electronics, turned out to be non-trivial. The use of model checking for verification of the BRP is problematic due to the infinite state space of the protocol (caused by unboundedness of the message data, the retransmission bound, and the file length). In [DKRT97], only restricted versions of the protocol could be model-checked; the manually derived constraints have been checked by parametric model-checking in [HRSV01], revealing a small error. More general correctness proofs by theorem provers also encounter many technical difficulties [GP96,HSV94,HS96].

Despite the practical significance of the Sliding Window protocol, the work on its formal verification had only a limited success so far. Stenning [Ste76] only gave an informal manual proof for his protocol. A semi-formal manual proof is also presented in [Knu81]. A more formal, but not fully automated proof for the window size of one is given in [BG94], and for the arbitrary window size in [FGP03]. Some versions of the protocol have been model-checked for small parameter values in [RRSV87,Kai97]. The combination of abstraction techniques and model-checking in [SBLS99] allowed to verify the SW protocol for a relatively large window size of 16 (which is still a few orders less than a possible window size in TCP). Almost all of these verifications assume *data link channels*, which can only lose messages. The protocols for such channels, called *data link protocols*, are important (they include, e.g., HDLC, SLIP and PPP protocols), but they are only used for transmission of data over relatively short distances.

In this paper, we study the verification of sliding window protocols for more general *transport channels*, which can also reorder and duplicate messages. Such channels are already considered in the original paper on the SW protocol by Stenning [Ste76]. The protocols for such channels (called *transport protocols*), such as TCP, can transmit data over very large networks such as the Internet.

Note that an SW protocol does not exists for all types of transport channels. As [AAF+94] shows, for a fully asynchronous system and channels that can both lose and reorder messages, it is impossible to design an efficient transmission protocol that uses bounded sequence numbers. A similar result is proved for systems that can both reorder and duplicate messages [WZ89]. In [SK00], unbounded sequence numbers are assumed for verification of the SW protocol for transport channels. This makes the verification rather simple, because it is known that the repetition of sequence numbers is the main source of errors for SW protocols [Tan96].

Unfortunately, transmission protocols that use unbounded sequence numbers are usually not practical. Because of the impossibility results mentioned above, a SW protocol for transport channels with bounded sequence numbers can only be designed for systems, in which each message in a channel has a maximum lifetime[1]. Such a SW protocol is a part of the TCP protocol, which operates over

[1] Such protocols can also be designed for untimed systems which limit the reordering of messages [Knu81], but such systems seem to be only of theoretical interest.

transport channels with a given maximum packet lifetime. The theoretical basis of that protocol is presented in [SD78]. TCP uses 2^{32} sequence numbers, which is enough to represent 4 gigabytes of data. The transmission mechanism of TCP uses a complicated timing mechanism to implement sequence numbers in such a way that their periodical repetition does not cause ambiguity. It often requires the sender and the receiver to synchronize on the sequence numbers they use. Such synchronization is provided by the three-way handshake protocol, which is not a part of the SW protocol and correctness of which is not easy to ensure. In general, the transmission mechanism of TCP seems too complicated and too specific for TCP to serve as a good starting point for verification of SW protocols for transport channels.

Another approach is chosen in [Sha89]. Shankar presents a version of the SW protocol for transport channels with the maximum packet lifetime, which does not require any synchronization between the sender and the receiver, and also does not impose any restrictions on the transmission policy. However, the range of sequence numbers, required to ensure the correctness of his protocol, depends on the maximum transmission rate of the sender. In the case of TCP, his protocol would only work correctly if the sender did not send into the channel more than some 30 megabytes of data per second (if we take 120 seconds for the maximum packet lifetime in TCP, as in [Tan96]). Such restriction may not be practical for modern networks, which are getting faster every year. Indeed, the range of sequence numbers in a large industrial protocol like TCP is fixed. Therefore, if the available transmission rate at some point exceeds our expectations, we would need to re-design the whole protocol to allow for faster transmission, which may be costly.

In this paper, we present a new version of the SW protocol for transport channels. In our opinion, it combines some of the best features of the transmission mechanism of TCP and Shankar's protocol. We do not require any synchronization between the sender and the receiver. Maximum packet lifetime and appropriate transmission and acknowledgment policies are used to ensure the correct recognition of sequence numbers. These policies are rather simple; roughly speaking, they require the sender (receiver) to stop and wait for the maximum packet lifetime after receiving acknowledgment for (delivering) the maximum sequence number, respectively. Unlike some previous works [Ste76,Sha89], the range of sequence numbers used by our protocol does not depend on the transmission rate of the sender. Therefore, between the required periods of waiting, the sender may transmit data arbitrarily fast, even if the range of sequence numbers is fixed[2], e.g. as in TCP. If implemented for TCP, our protocol would allow to transmit files up to 4 gigabytes arbitrarily fast.

Even for relatively simple communication protocols, manual formal verification is so lengthy and complicated that it can easily be erroneous. This is why we need some form of mechanical support. Our protocol highly depends on com-

[2] Of course, the *average* transmission rate of our protocol over the long run does depend on the range of sequence numbers, because the fewer sequence numbers the protocol has, the more often it has to stop and wait after the maximum number.

plex data structures and uses several parameters of arbitrary size, such as the window size and the range of sequence numbers. Hence completely automatic verification is not feasible for us. This is why we use an interactive theorem prover. We have chosen PVS [PVS], because we have an extensive experience with it and successfully applied the tool to verification of several complicated protocols [Chk01]. PVS, which is based on a higher-order logic, has a convenient specification language and is relatively easy to learn and to use.

The rest of the paper is organized as follows. In section 2, we give an informal description of our protocol. In section 3, we formalize the protocol by a timed state machine. Section 4 outlines the proof of correctness property for our protocol. Some concluding remarks are given in section 5.

2 Protocol Overview

In section 2.1 we present the basics of a sliding window protocol. The required relation between sequence numbers and window size is described in section 2.2. Timing restrictions are discussed in section 2.3.

2.1 Basic Notions

Sender and receiver. In a SW protocol, there are two main components: the sender and the receiver. The sender obtains an infinite sequence of data from the *sending host.* We call indivisible blocks of data in this sequence "frames", and the sequence itself the "input sequence". The input sequence must be transmitted to the receiver via an unreliable network. After receiving a frame via the channel, the receiver may decide to *accept* the frame and eventually *deliver* it to the *receiving host.* The correctness condition for a SW protocol says that the receiver should deliver the frames to the receiving host in the same order in which they appear in the input sequence.

Messages and channels. In order to transmit a frame, the sender puts it into a *frame message* together with some additional information, and sends it to the *frame channel.* After the receiver eventually accepts the frame message from this channel, it sends an *acknowledgment message* for the corresponding frame back to the sender. This acknowledgment message is transmitted via the *acknowledgment channel.* After receiving an acknowledgment message, the sender knows that the corresponding frame has been received by the receiver.

Sequence numbers. The sender sends the frames in the same order in which they appear in its input sequence. However, the frame channel is unreliable, so the receiver may receive these frames in a very different order (if receive at all). Therefore it is clear that each frame message must contain some information about the order of the corresponding frame in the input sequence. Such additional information is called "sequence number". In the SW protocol, instead of the exact position of the frame in the input sequence, the sender sends the remainder of this position with respect to some fixed modulus K. The value of K varies greatly among protocols: it is only 16 for the Mascara protocol for wireless ATM networks, but 2^{32} for TCP. To acknowledge a frame, in the acknowledgment message the receiver sends the sequence number with which the frame was received. Acknowledgments are "accumulative"; for example, when the sender acknowledges a frame with sequence number 3, it means that frames with sequence numbers 0, 1 and 2 have also been accepted.

Sending window. At any time, the sender maintains a sequence of sequence numbers corresponding to frames it is permitted to send. These frames are said to be a part of the *sending window.* Similarly, the receiver maintains a *receiving window* of sequence numbers it is permitted to accept. In our protocol, the sizes of sending and receiving windows are equal and represented by an arbitrary integer N.

At some point during the execution it is possible that some frames in the beginning of the sending window have been already sent, but not yet acknowledged, and the remaining frames have not been sent yet. When an acknowledgment arrives for a frame in the sending window that has been already sent, this frame and all preceding frames are removed from the window as acknowledgments are accumulative. Simultaneously, the window is shifted forward, such that it again contains N frames. As a result, more frames can be sent. Acknowledgments that fall outside the window are discarded. If a sent frame is not acknowledged for a long time, it usually means that either this frame or an acknowledgment for it has been lost. To ensure the progress of the protocol, such a frame is eventually *resent.* Many different policies for sending and resending of frames exist [Tan96], which take into account, e.g., the efficient allocation of resources and the need to avoid network congestion. Here we abstract from such details of the transmission policy and specify only those restrictions on protocol's behaviour that are needed to ensure its safety property.

Receiving window. During the execution, the receiving window is usually a mix of sequence numbers corresponding to frames that have been accepted out of order and sequence numbers corresponding to "empty spaces", i.e. frames that are still expected. When a frame arrives with a sequence number corresponding to some empty space, it is accepted, i.e. inserted in the window, otherwise it is discarded. At any time, if the first element of the receiving window is a frame, it can be delivered to the receiving host, and the window is shifted by one. The sequence number of the last delivered frame can be sent back to the sender to acknowledge the frame (for convenience reasons, in this version we acknowledge delivered frames instead of accepted frames). Not every frame must be acknowledged; it is possible to deliver a few frames in a row and then acknowledge only the last of them. If the receiver does not deliver any new frames for a long time, it may resend the last acknowledgment to ensure the progress of the protocol.

2.2 Relating Sequence Numbers and Window Size

It is explained in [Tan96], that for data link channels we need $K \geq 2 * N$ to ensure the unambiguous recognition of sequence numbers. However, for transport channels this condition is not sufficient. Indeed, suppose that window size $N = 1$ and we use $K = 2$ sequence numbers, so we only have sequence numbers 0 and

1. Suppose the sender sends the first two frames $f0$ and $f1$ to the receiver, which are successfully accepted, delivered and acknowledged. Suppose, however, that $f0$ has been duplicated in the frame channel and subsequently reordered with $f1$, so the channel still contains frame $f0$ with sequence number 0. The receiver now has a window with an empty space and sequence number 0, so it can receive frame $f0$ for the second time, violating the safety property. In this case, the error is caused by the combination of message reordering and duplication; a similar erroneous scenario can be constructed using reordering and loss.

This simple example clearly shows that we need additional restrictions on the protocol to recognize sequence numbers correctly. Traditional approaches [Ste76,Sha89] introduce a stronger restriction on K, which essentially has the form $K \geq 2*N + f(Rmax, Lmax)$, where $Rmax$ is the maximum transmission rate of the sender, $Lmax$ is the maximum message lifetime, and f is some function. As we already explained in the introduction, such dependence between the range of sequence numbers and the maximum transmission rate is undesirable. This is why in our protocol we only require $K \geq 2 * N$, but introduce some timing restrictions on the transmission and acknowledgment policies (explained below) to ensure that frames and acknowledgments are not received more than once.

2.3 Timing Restrictions

In our protocol, the sender is allowed to reuse sequence number 0 and all subsequent sequence numbers only after more than $Lmax$ time units have passed since the receipt of the acknowledgment with the maximum sequence number $K - 1$. This is necessary to ensure that when sequence number 0 is resent, all "old" acknowledgments, i.e. those for frames preceding the current frame, are already removed from the acknowledgment channel (because their timeouts expired), and cannot be mistaken for "new" acknowledgments, i.e. those for the current frame and its successors.

Similarly, the receiver is allowed to accept sequence number 0 (or any subsequent sequence numbers) only after more than $Lmax$ time units have passed since the delivery of a frame with the maximum sequence number $K - 1$. This is necessary to ensure that all "old" frames have been removed from the frame channel and cannot be mistaken for "new" frames. To implement these restrictions, our protocol keeps two variables $tackmax$ and $tdelmax$, expressing the time when we received an acknowledgment for sequence number $K - 1$, and delivered a frame with sequence number $K - 1$, respectively.

We were surprised to discover during the verification that these restrictions are not quite sufficient. It is the acknowledgment for the maximum sequence number $K - 1$ that causes the problem. In the initial version of the protocol, acknowledgments for a particular frame could be resent at any time. Suppose that between the receipt of an acknowledgment for sequence number $K - 1$ and the sending of sequence number 0 by the sender, the acknowledgment for sequence number $K - 1$ is resent by the receiver. Then this acknowledgment may still be in the channel at the time when sequence number $K - 1$ is sent by the sender again (assuming the fast and correct transmission of all $K-1$ frames within $Lmax$ time units). As a result, this "old" acknowledgment may be mistaken for a newly sent acknowledgment. So, the sender will think that a frame with sequence number $K-1$ is acknowledged, whereas in fact it could have been lost.

We constructed a (lengthy) scenario in which such incorrect receipt of acknowledgments eventually leads to incorrect receipt of frames and violation of the safety property. To fix this error, in the revised version of the protocol the acknowledgment with sequence number $K-1$ must be sent immediately after the corresponding frame is delivered, and it cannot be resent. Considering that acknowledgments can be lost, this results in a possibility of deadlock. We are not very concerned about this, since any reasonable implementation of the SW protocol also does not allow to resend acknowledgments at any time (only if there is a strong suspicion that the original message has been lost). In our protocol, we prefer to abstract away from such implementation details. However, we also constructed a modification of our protocol (presented below) that does not suffer from this deadlock problem.

Possible improvement. The simplest way to prevent the acknowledgment with sequence number $K-1$ from being accepted again is to introduce the additional waiting period for the sender. Before the sender resends sequence number $K-1$, it should wait for more than $Lmax$ time units after accepting the acknowledgment with sequence number $K-2$. This ensures the elimination of all "old" acknowledgments with sequence number $K-1$. As a result, it becomes possible to acknowledge a particular frame with sequence number $K-1$ more than once, and this resolves the deadlock problem. However, it is obvious that this additional waiting period greatly reduces the performance of the protocol.

We specified this modification of our protocol in PVS, but we did not verify it for two reasons. Firstly, it is not clear whether the degradation in performance is justified. In a complex distributed system, it is not reasonable to avoid deadlock at any cost. It may be more efficient to allow a deadlock in some rare situations, and to use an additional protocol to resolve it. Secondly, this additional waiting period would make the verification of the protocol even more complex without adding much theoretical value to it.

3 Formal Specification

Formally, in our approach a protocol is defined by the notion of a *state*, representing a snapshot of the state-of-affairs during protocol execution, and a set of actions. For the SW protocol, we have actions of sender and receiver, and a delay action. Our timing model can be considered a simplified version of timed automata of Alur and Dill [AD94], in which there is only one clock (called *time*) that is never reset. Actions are specified by a precondition and an effect predicate which relates the states before and after action execution. An execution of our protocol, or a *run*, is represented by an infinite sequence of the form $s_0 \stackrel{a_0}{\rightarrow} s_1 \stackrel{a_1}{\rightarrow} \ldots \stackrel{a_{i-1}}{\rightarrow} s_i \stackrel{a_i}{\rightarrow} s_{i+1} \stackrel{a_{i+1}}{\rightarrow} \ldots$, where s_i are states, a_i are executed actions, s_0 is the initial state, each s_i satisfies the precondition of a_i, and every pair (s_i, s_{i+1}) corresponds to the effect of a_i. In this section, we describe the structure of states and actions in our specification.

First we define the data structure of the protocol. For the sender, the window "slides" over the infinite input sequence *input*. We do not specify the nature of the frames in the input sequence. Variable $first$ denotes the first frame in the sending window, *ftsend* is the first frame that has not been sent yet, and we always have $\mathit{first} \leq \mathit{ftsend} \leq \mathit{first}+N$. Thus, at any moment of time, frames with indices from $first$ to $ftsend-1$ (if any) have been sent but not yet acknowledged, and frames with indices from $ftsend$ to $first+N-1$ (if any) are in the sending window but not sent yet. Variable *tackmax* expresses the time when we received the acknowledgment with the maximum sequence number $K-1$ for the last time. As a time domain $Time$, we take the set of non-negative real numbers.

Sender:
1) $\mathit{input} \ : \ \mathit{sequence}[Frames]$,
2) $\mathit{first} \ : \ \mathit{nat}$,
3) $\mathit{ftsend} \ : \ \mathit{nat}$,
4) $\mathit{tackmax} \ : \ Time$

For the receiver, *output* is the finite output sequence, *rwindow* is the receiving window with N elements (which are either frames or empty spaces, denoted by ε), $lastdel$ is the last delivered sequence number, *acklastdel* is a boolean variable which tells whether we are allowed to send the acknowledgment for $lastdel$ to the sender, and variable *tdelmax* expresses the time when we delivered the frame with the maximum sequence number $K-1$ for the last time (the importance of variables $acklastdel$ and *tdelmax* is explained in subsection 2.3).

Receiver:
1) $\mathit{output} \ : \ \mathit{finite\_sequence}[Frames]$,
2) $\mathit{rwindow} \ : \ \{0,\ 1,\ \ldots\ N-1\} \longrightarrow$
$(\mathit{snumber} \ : \ \{0,\ 1,\ \ldots\ K-1\},\ \mathit{frn} \ : \ Frames \cup \{\varepsilon\})$,
3) $\mathit{lastdel} \ : \ \{0,\ 1,\ \ldots\ K-1\}$,
4) $acklastdel \ : \ \mathit{bool}$,
5) $\mathit{tdelmax} \ : \ Time$

The frame channel and the acknowledgment channel are represented by its contents, namely a set of frame messages and a set of acknowledgment messages, respectively. Besides a sequence number and possibly a frame, in our model each message includes its *timeout*, i.e. the latest time when it must be removed from the channel. When a message is sent, we assign as its timeout the current time plus *Lmax*, where *Lmax* is the maximum message lifetime. Note that timeout is only used to model maximum message lifetime, it cannot be used by the recipient of a message.

FrameMessage:
1) *snumber* : $\{0, 1, \ldots K-1\}$,
2) *frame* : $Frames$,
3) *timeout* : $Time$

AckMessage:
1) *snumber* : $\{0, 1, \ldots K-1\}$,
2) *timeout* : $Time$

The complete state of the protocol consists of the sender, the receiver and the two channels *fchannel* and *achannel*, together with the variable $time$, indicating the current time. The initial state of the protocol is defined in a rather obvious way, i.e. 0 is assigned to most fields.

State:
1) *sender* : $Sender$,
2) *receiver* : $Receiver$,
3) *fchannel* $\subseteq FrameMessage$,
4) *achannel* $\subseteq AckMessage$,
5) *time* : $Time$

There are seven atomic actions in our protocol: one general ($Delay$), three for the sender ($Send$, *Resend* and *Receiveack*) and three for the receiver (*Receive*, $Sendack$ and *Deliver*). Due to space limitations, we only give an informal description of these actions. The full specification of the protocol can be found in the PVS files, available via [URL]. In the rest of the paper, operator mod K gives a remainder to a modulus K.

Note that actions for sending and receiving messages are nondeterministic. Actions for sending messages ($Send$, *Resend* and $Sendack$) either add a message to the channel (which models its successful sending) or let the channel unchanged (which models loss of a message). Actions for receiving messages (*Receiveack* and *Receive*) either remove a message from the channel (which models its "normal" reception) or let the channel unchanged (which models duplication of a message). The reordering of messages is modelled by representing both channels by unordered sets.

Also note that the sender and the receiver are "input enabled" (e.g., as in I/O automata of Lynch [Lyn96]); they are always willing to receive a message from the channel. This is necessary to ensure that all messages can be received before their timeouts expire. If certain conditions are met, the received message is accepted, changing the state of the sender (receiver), otherwise it is discarded.

3.1 The Delay Action

Action $Delay(t)$ expresses the passing of t units of time. The precondition of this action expresses that time cannot be advanced above the minimal time-out value in channels. Hence, any message in a channel must be removed from the channel before its timeout expires. The effect predicate expresses that the new state equals the old state except for the value of time which is incremented by t.

3.2 Actions of the Sender

- **Send.** This action sends the first frame that has not been sent yet, i.e. the frame with index $ftsend$, and $ftsend\ \underline{mod}\ K$ is included into the message as its sequence number. The precondition of this action expresses that sequence number 0 can be reused only after more than $Lmax$ time units have passed since the last acknowledgment of sequence number $K-1$, and only if 0 is the first sequence number in the window, i.e. if $ftsend\ \underline{mod}\ K = 0$, then we require 1) $time > tackmax + Lmax$ and 2) $first = ftsend$.

- **Resend(i).** This action resends a frame that has already been sent but not yet acknowledged, i.e. a frame with index i such as $i \geq first$ and $i < ftsend$.

- **Receiveack(am).** This action receives acknowledgment message am and checks whether $snumber(am)$ lies within the sending window. If so, the frames with sequence numbers up to $snumber(am)$ are removed from the window and the window is shifted accordingly, and if $snumber(am) = K-1$, then the current time is assigned to the variable $tackmax$. Otherwise, the message is discarded.

3.3 Actions of the Receiver

- **Receive(fm).** This action receives frame message fm and checks whether $snumber(fm)$ corresponds to some empty space in the receiving window. If so, it accepts the message if more than $Lmax$ time units have passed since the last delivery of a frame with sequence number $K-1$. The exact formalization of this requirement is subtle because frames can be accepted and delivered in different order; it is defined by giving a restriction on the position of $snumber(fm)$ in the window in addition to the timing restriction $time > tdelmax + Lmax$ (see [URL] for details). If these conditions for acceptance are satisfied, then the frame from the message is inserted into the corresponding place in the window; otherwise the message is discarded.

- **Sendack.** This action sends an acknowledgment for the last delivered frame, i.e. the frame with sequence number $lastdel$. If $lastdel = K-1$, it changes the value of variable $acklastdel$ to false. The precondition of Sendack requires $acklastdel$ to be true, and this prevents the acknowledgment for $K-1$ from being resent.

- **Deliver**. The precondition of this action requires that the first element of the receiving window is a frame. If it is the case, the frame is appended to the output sequence and removed from the window, i.e. the window is shifted by one. Also, the sequence number of the frame is assigned to $lastdel$, if this sequence number is $K-1$, then the current time is assigned to $tdelmax$, and $acklastdel$ becomes equal to true.

In addition to the preconditions of individial actions, we also specify an additional assertion expressing that each delivery of the sequence number $K-1$ is immediately followed by action $Sendack$ acknowledging this sequence number.

4 Formal Verification

A SW protocol is correct with respect to safety, if the receiver always delivers the frames to the receiving host in the same order in which they appear in the input sequence. In our model, we prefer to define correctness in terms of states rather than actions. Note that in each state, frames that have already been delivered to the receiving host are represented by the output sequence. Therefore, the safety property for a particular state s can be expressed by a predicate, which says that the output sequence is the prefix of the input sequence:

$$Safe(s) = \forall\, i:\ i < length(output(s)) \Longrightarrow output(s)(i) = input(s)(i)$$

Let $st(r)$ and $act(r)$ denote the sequence of states and sequence of actions of a run r, respectively. Run r is safe if it is safe in each state, i.e. we define

$$Safety(r) = \forall\, i : Safe(st(r)(i))$$

To verify our SW protocol, we proved $Safety(r)$ for each run r, using the interactive theorem prover of PVS. The proof was performed by the first author in about 4 months (from scratch, without hand-written proofs). It consists of about 150 PVS lemmas and theorems and some 10 thousand PVS commands, see [URL]. Our experience with PVS has been very positive, e.g., there are more than sufficient lemmas about modulo arithmetic in the PVS prelude file.

Our verification efforts are comparable with the efforts to verify the BRP protocol in [GP96,HSV94]. However, our proof seems to be much more involved, and includes some lemmas that are far from trivial. In general, this is not surprising, considering that our protocol tolerates more types of channel faults, and it has several parameters, a relatively complex data structure and timing aspects. It is reported in [HSV94] that they could prove most invariants by simple induction on the length of the execution. For our proof, this is certainly not the case. The proof of many lemmas about the current state required a rather subtle analysis of all states and actions preceeding this state in a run. Another problem we faced is that correctness of one difficult invariant for the receiver depended on a similar invariant for the sender, and vice versa. Significant efforts and some advanced techniques were needed to break this cycle in the proof. In the next subsection, we briefly outline the proof of the main correctness condition.

4.1 Proof of Correctness Condition

We need to prove the following theorem:

$$\forall\, r :\ Safety(r) \qquad\qquad Main$$

The following abbreviations are used for a run r: bn is a variable for an integer not greater than $N-1$, $rwindow_r(i, bn) = rwindow(st(r)(i))(bn)$ (i.e. $rwindow_r(i, bn)$ is the bn-th element of the receiving window in state i), $first_r(i) = first(st(r)(i))$, $ftsend_r(i) = ftsend(st(r)(i))$, and $LO_r(i)$ is the length of the output sequence in state i. It is easy to prove that all actions of our protocol don't change the input sequence, so we denote by $input_r$ the input sequence in each state of r.

The proof of $Main$ is based on the following important invariant $OriginOK$:

$$\forall\, r,\ i,\ bn :\ frn(rwindow_r(i, bn)) \neq \varepsilon \Longrightarrow$$
$$frn(rwindow_r(i, bn)) = input_r(LO_r(i) + bn) \qquad\qquad OriginOK$$

Invariant $OriginOK$ determines the "origin" of each frame in the receiving window: a frame in the position bn was sent by the sender from the position in the input sequence, that is equal to the sum of bn and the current length of the output sequence. Assuming $OriginOK$, it is easy to prove theorem $Main$.

Proof of $Main$. Let r be an arbitrary run. The proof is by induction on the length of the output. If it is 0, the statement is trivially true. Now suppose that the theorem has been proved for any output length not greater than k, and that we are in the state with index i such that $LO_r(i) = k+1$. It is easy to see that action $Deliver$ increases the length of the output exactly by one, and all other actions of our protocol don't change the output. Therefore, there exists index l such that $l < i$, $LO_r(l) = k$, $act(r)(l) = Deliver$ and $output(st(r)(l+1)) = output(st(r)(i))$. By the induction hypothesis, it follows that in state $st(r)(l)$, the input is the prefix of the output. We can now apply invariant $OriginOK$ for r, l and 0, and obtain that the frame delivered by action $act(r)(l)$ originates from position $LO_r(l)$ in the input. Thus in state $st(r)(l)$, output includes frames $input_r(0)$, $input_r(1)$, ... $input_r(LO_r(l) - 1)$, and frame $input_r(LO_r(l))$ is added to it by action $act(r)(l)$. Therefore, in states $st(r)(l+1)$ and $st(r)(i)$ the output is still the prefix of the input, which completes the proof.

To prove invariant $OriginOK$, the following important invariants $AckOK$ and $FrOK$ are needed:

$$\forall\, r,\ i :\ first_r(i) \leq LO_r(i) \qquad\qquad AckOK$$

Intuitively, invariant $AckOK$ implies that acknowledgments are accepted only once. Indeed, the value of $first$ is equal to the number of frames for which acknowledgments from the receiver have been accepted. But the receiver acknowledges only delivered frames which are included in the output. Therefore, $first$ can become greater than the length of the output only if the sender accepts some acknowledgments more than once.

$\forall\ r,\ i,\ bn:\ frn(rwindow_r(i, bn)) \neq \varepsilon \Longrightarrow LO_r(i) + bn < ftsend_r(i)$ $FrOK$

Invariant $FrOK$ informally means that frames are accepted only once. Indeed, if the receiving window has a frame in position bn, it implies that at least $LO_r(i) + bn + 1$ frames have been sent by the sender, but the exact number of such frames is represented by variable $ftsend$. Therefore, the invariant can only be violated if the receiver accepts some frames more than once.

Together, invariants $AckOK$ and $FrOK$ mean that the length of the output is always within the borders of the sending window. Despite the clear intuitive meaning of these invariants, their proofs are fairly large and complicated, and they use some advanced techniques, such as counting of the number of certain actions preceeding the current state. Due to space limitations, we cannot present these proofs here. In this paper, we only show how to use invariants $AckOK$ and $FrOK$ to prove invariant $OriginOK$. Below we give a brief sketch of the proof, which is based on dozens of PVS lemmas.

Proof of $OriginOK$. Let's consider arbitrary r, i and bn, and suppose there is a frame in the receiving window in position bn. It is easy to prove that as long as a frame stays in the window, the sum of its position and the length of the output remains the same. Therefore, we can assume without loss of generality that this frame has just been put into the window, i.e. action $act(r)(i-1)$ is a receive action that accepts message with frame $frn(rwindow_r(i, bn))$ from the channel. It is also easy to prove that a frame in position bn has a sequence number $LO_r(i) + bn\ \underline{mod}\ K$. Thus in state $st(r)(i-1)$, the frame channel includes a message with frame $frn(rwindow_r(i, bn))$ and sequence number $LO_r(i) + bn\ \underline{mod}\ K$. We can prove that each message in the frame channel was sent by the sender at some moment in the past. This implies that the message originates from some frame with position j in the input sequence, i.e. $input_r(j) = frn(rwindow_r(i, bn))$, and from the way in which messages are constructed we obtain $j\ \underline{mod}\ K = LO_r(i) + bn\ \underline{mod}\ K$. To finish the proof, it is now sufficient to show $j = LO_r(i) + bn$.

It is easy to see that $j < ftsend_r(i-1)$. We can also prove $ftsend_r(i-1) - j \leq K$. Indeed, it is obvious that in state $st(r)(i-1)$, all frames in positions from $j+1$ to $ftsend_r(i-1) - 1$ have already been sent. If $ftsend_r(i-1) - j > K$, then there are at least K such positions, so at least one of them has a remainder 0 with respect to K. Thus after sending the frame in position j, we sent a frame with sequence number 0 at least once. But our protocol waits for $Lmax$ time units before resending sequence number 0, and this ensures that by the time of this resending all preceding messages disappear from the channel. Contradiction, because in state $st(r)(i-1)$ we received a message originating from position j in the input.

Now we use invariants $AckOK$ and $FrOK$. Invariant $AckOK$ gives $first_r(i) \leq LO_r(i)$, hence $first_r(i) \leq LO_r(i) + bn$. We know that $ftsend_r(i) - first_r(i) \leq N$, so $ftsend_r(i) - (LO_r(i) + bn) \leq N$. Invariant $FrOK$ implies $LO_r(i) + bn <$

$ftsend_r(i)$. Action $act(r)(i-1)$ is not a send action, so we have $LO_r(i) + bn < ftsend_r(i-1)$ and $ftsend_r(i-1) - (LO_r(i)+bn) \leq N$. Comparing this with our results about j, we obtain that both j and $LO_r(i)+bn$ are less than $ftsend_r(i-1)$, and the difference between each of them and $ftsend_r(i-1)$ is not greater than K. Therefore the difference between j and $LO_r(i) + bn$ is less than K. But we already know that these two numbers have the same remainder with respect to K. Thus they are equal, and this completes the proof.

5 Conclusions

We presented the formal specification and verification of the Sliding Window protocol for transport channels. Our version of the protocol offers an interesting improvement over some previously published versions (as it tolerates arbitrary transmission rates), and can potentially be used as a part of the TCP protocol. Unlike most previous papers, our modelling of the protocol is very general, and the verification is supported by the interactive theorem prover PVS.

An interesting lesson we learned from this project is that the traditional (untimed) Sliding Window protocol cannot correctly handle the combination of message reordering and duplication, or reordering and loss, as explained in section 2.2. The timed version of the protocol presented in this paper eliminates the potential errors arising from such a combination, but at a cost of a significant performance loss. It should be noted, however, that some performance loss seems to be unavoidable for any Sliding Window protocol operating over transport channels. E.g., the complicated timing mechanism of TCP, as mentioned in the introduction, also requires waiting if there is a danger of overlap of sequence numbers. For a good comparison of performances, in our future work we would like to analyse the performance of our protocol for different retransmission policies, possibly using simulations, and to study its compatibility with TCP. It would be also interesting to apply our verification techniques (which have already been used for several concurrency control protocols in [Chk01]) to other types of communication protocols.

References

[AAF+94] Y. Afek, H. Attiya, A. Fekete, M. Fischer, N. Lynch, Y. Mansour, D. Wang, and L. Zuck. Reliable communication over unreliable channels. *Journal of the ACM*, 41:1267–1297, 1994.

[AD94] R. Alur and D.L. Dill. A theory of timed automata. *Theoretical Computer Science*, 126:183–235, 1994.

[BG94] M.A. Bezem and J.F. Groote. A correctness proof of a one-bit sliding window protocol in μCRL. *The Computer Journal*, 37:1–19, 1994.

[BSW69] K.A. Barlett, R.A. Scantlebury, and P.C. Wilkinson. A note on reliable transmission over half duplex links. *Communications of the ACM*, 12:260–261, 1969.

[Chk01] D. Chkliaev. *Mechanical Verification of Concurrency Control and Recovery Protocols*. PhD thesis, Technische Universiteit Eindhoven, 2001.

[DKRT97] P.R. D'Argenio, J.-P. Katoen, T.C. Ruys, and J. Tretmans. The bounded retransmission protocol must be on time! In *TACAS'97*, pages 416 – 431. LNCS 1217, 1997.

[FGP03] W. Fokkink, J.F. Groote, and J. Pang. Verification of a sliding window protocol in μCRL. *Unfinished article*, 2003.

[GP96] J.F. Groote and J.C. van de Pol. A bounded retransmission protocol for large data packets. A case study in computer-checked verification. In *AMAST'96*, pages 536–550. LNCS 1101, 1996.

[HRSV01] T. Hune, J.M.T. Romijn, M.I.A. Stoelinga, and F.W. Vaandrager. Linear parametric model checking of timed automata. In *TACAS'01*, pages 189–203. LNCS 2031, 2001.

[HS96] K. Havelund and N. Shankar. Experiments in Theorem Proving and Model Checking for Protocol Verification. In *FME'96: Industrial Benefit and Advances in Formal Methods*, pages 662–681. LNCS 1051, 1996.

[HSV94] L. Helmink, M.P.A. Sellink, and F.W. Vaandrager. Proof-checking a data link protocol. In *International Workshop TYPES'93*, pages 127–165. LNCS 806, 1994.

[Kai97] R. Kaivola. Using compositional preorders in the verification of sliding window protocol. In *Computer Aided Verification*, pages 48–59. LNCS 1254, 1997.

[Knu81] D.E. Knuth. Verification of link-level protocols. *BIT*, 21:31–36, 1981.

[Lyn96] N. Lynch. *Distributed Algorithms.* Morgan Kaufmann Publishers, 1996.

[PVS] *PVS Specification and Verification System, http://pvs.csl.sri.com/.*

[RRSV87] J.L. Richier, C. Rodriguez, J. Sifakis, and J. Voiron. Verification in Xesar of the sliding window protocol. In *Protocol specification, testing and verification 7*, pages 235–248, 1987.

[SBLS99] K. Stahl, K. Baukus, Y. Lakhnech, and M. Steffen. Divide, abstract, and model-check. In *The 5th International SPIN Workshop on Theoretical Aspects of Model Checking*, pages 57–76. LNCS 1680, 1999.

[SD78] C. Sunshine and Y. Dalal. Connection management in transport protocols. *Computer Networks*, 2:454–473, 1978.

[Sha89] A. Udaya Shankar. Verified data transfer protocols with variable flow control. *ACM Transactions on Computer Systems*, 7:281–316, 1989.

[SK00] M. Smith and N. Klarlund. Verification of a sliding window protocol using IOA and MONA. In *Formal methods for distributed system development*, pages 19–34. Kluwer Academic Publishers, 2000.

[Ste76] N.V. Stenning. A data transfer protocol. *Computer Networks*, 1:99–110, 1976.

[Tan96] A.S. Tanenbaum. *Computer Networks.* Third Edition, Prentice-Hall International, 1996.

[URL] *PVS specifications and proofs, http://www.cs.kun.nl/~hooman/SWP.html.*

[WZ89] D. Wang and L. Zuck. Tight bounds for the sequence transmission problem. In *The 8th ACM Symposium on Principles of Distributed Computing*, pages 73–83. ACM, 1989.

Simple Representative Instantiations for Multicast Protocols

Javier Esparza and Monika Maidl

School of Informatics, University of Edinburgh
{jav+monika}@inf.ed.ac.uk

Abstract. We present a formal model for multicast network protocols working on arbitrary tree structures. We give sufficient conditions under which correctness of the protocol for all structures reduces to correctness for the structures with at most one layer of internal nodes. If additional conditions hold, we can reduce further to correctness for one single structure. All these results can be applied to (an abstract version of) the Pragmatic General Multicast protocol.

In the last years, much effort has been devoted to the verification of parameterised distributed systems, i.e., distributed systems designed to work correctly independently of the number of processes taking part in them. Classical examples of these systems are distributed algorithms for leader election, byzantine agreement, or distributed termination, and communication protocols, like cache coherence or network protocols. In this paper we study multicast network protocols working on tree structures.[1] In these protocols, data are exchanged between a sender (the root of the tree) and several receivers (the leaves) via network elements (the internal nodes). Messages flowing from sender to receivers can be multicasted, i.e., simultaneously sent to several successors. Examples of such multicast network protocols are PGM (Pragmatic General Multicast) [S$^+$00] and LMS (Light-weight Multicast Services) [PPV].

Verifying a property ϕ of a parameterised system consists of checking that ϕ for all possible structures (in our case, for all possible trees). This may be difficult, and so a common approach is to first reduce the task to checking ϕ for a restricted class of structures (see for instance [EN95]). This is also the approach of this paper.

We first provide a general formal model for multicast networks. The only assumption is that messages can overtake other messages and can get lost, but cannot be duplicated. This is a reasonable assumption for protocols in which channels are just an abstraction for a routing mechanism that may send different messages—or different fragments of the same message—through various routes, as in the PGM and LMS protocols. For protocols in which messages cannot overtake others or get lost, the assumption overapproximates the behaviour of the protocol. In this case, correctness in our model still implies correctness of

[1] Actually, these protocols run on arbitrary networks, but use a distribution tree to broadcast messages. We assume that this tree has already been established.

H. Garavel and J. Hatcliff (Eds.): TACAS 2003, LNCS 2619, pp. 128–143, 2003.

the protocol. We define a notion of simulation that preserves stuttering-invariant linear-time properties, i.e., if the simulating structure satisfies the property, then the simulated structure also satisfies it.

Equipped with this formal setting, we identify general sufficient conditions for a protocol P to be *collapsable*, meaning that a property holds for all instantiations $\mathcal{N}(P)$ of P if and only if it holds for the set of instantiations $\mathcal{N}^1(P)$ with at most one level of internal elements. We prove that for every instantiation T in $\mathcal{N}(P)$ there is an instantiation T' in $\mathcal{N}^1(P)$ that simulates T.[2] Then, all instantiations in $\mathcal{N}^1(P)$ satisfy ϕ if and only if all instantiations in $T \in \mathcal{N}(P)$ satisfy ϕ, because simulation preserves properties and $\mathcal{N}^1(P) \subseteq \mathcal{N}(P)$.

In particular, our conditions are satisfied by network elements that only perform 'forwarding', i.e., only forward messages down from the parent to all children, and up from some child to the parent. Hence, our result can be applied to telecommunication protocols that do not assume that router support can be used and that use a fixed distribution tree. We show that they are also satisfied by the PGM protocol, where network elements have a much richer functionality, which is used to make communication between the sender and receivers more reliable and efficient.

While the collapse of $\mathcal{N}(P)$ to $\mathcal{N}^1(P)$ removes the problem of dealing with different tree topologies, it still leaves us with an infinite number of possible instantiations. This cannot be avoided as long as more receivers can generate more behaviour. However, we prove that if the number of different messages that can circulate is finite and receivers and network elements can repeatedly send the same message upwards, then the verification task can be further reduced: Given a property ϕ, all instantiations of $\mathcal{N}^1(P)$ satisfy ϕ if and only if one single universal instantiation U, which depends on Φ. Again, we prove that if the number of messages in the PGM protocol is bounded, then the result can be applied, and the protocol has a universal instantiation.

The paper is structured as follows. In section 1 we introduce (a version of) the PGM protocol, in order to introduce network protocols and have a rich running example for our definitions and results. Section 2 contains our formal model. Our notions of property and simulation are given in Section 3. Section 4 presents the sufficient conditions for a network to be collapsable. This section is divided into two parts; the first part deals with the special case, in which network elements can only forward messages, and the second deals with the general case. The section also shows that the PGM protocol satisfies the conditions. Finally, section 5 presents the universal instance that can simulate any other instantiation of a collapsable protocol, assuming that the number of messages is finite. The paper is accompanied by a technical report [EM02] which contains full proofs.

[2] Notice that we always speak of instantiations *of the same protocol*. Given a protocol P, one can always find another protocol P' such that every $T \in \mathcal{N}(P)$ is simulated by some $T' \in \mathcal{N}^1(P')$ by making the sender, receiver and internal processes more complicated.

1 The PGM Protocol

The Pragmatic General Multicast (PGM) protocol is a reliable multicast protocol for the distribution of information from multiple senders to multiple receivers. It is designed in order to minimize loading of the network due to acknowledgment messages or retransmissions of lost packets, and has been presented to the Internet Engineering Task Force as an open reference specification. We consider the following abstract, untimed variant of the protocol for one sender. We have a tree of processes connected by bidirectional channels. Messages can get lost and can overtake each other (i.e., can be delivered in a different order than they are sent), but cannot be duplicated. The root of the tree is the sender, and the leaves the receivers. The other processes are internal *network elements*. The source multicasts a numbered sequence of data packets called odata(*nr*,*trl*) (for original data) within a transmit window; *nr* is the number of the package, and *trl* is the left-hand edge of the sender's window at the moment of sending it. Network elements forward these packets down the distribution tree. If a receiver detects that packet *nr* is missing from the sequence, it repeatedly sends a *primary negative acknowledgment* (pnak(*nr*)) to its parent, requesting a repair. Each network element that receives a pnak forwards it to its parent, and multicasts a nak-confirmation (ncf(*nr*)) to its children; it then keeps sending secondary nak (snak(*nr*)) to its parent (which are forwarded upwards, but do not generate confirmations) until it receives a *nak-confirmation* itself. When the source receives a pnak or snak it provides a repair (rdata(*nr*,*trl*)), which is multicasted downwards to the processes that requested them. There is a final feature called *nak-anticipation*: A receiver may receive a confirmation to a pnak sent by *another* receiver. Anticipating its own future need for a repair, it repeatedly sends snak's to its parent, until either the original data or the repair arrives. Notice that odata-, rdata- and ncf-messages travel *downwards* (from sender to receivers) while pnak- and snak-messages travel *upwards* (from receiver to sender).

Formally, the protocol is given by three agents describing the sender, the receivers, and the network elements, whose descriptions can be found in Table 1. Every agent has a set of *variables* and a set of (atomic) *transitions*. Transitions are guarded by either boolean expressions over the process variables or by the delivery of a message. In the initial state, all sets are empty, *odata*, *txw_trail* and *rxw_trail* are 0, and *WIN_SIZE* has some fixed value (window size).

Our version of the PGM protocol differs slightly from [S$^+$00] in that we distinguish between primary and secondary nak messages. While our result also holds for the original version, as shown in [Mai02], our version allows for a generic proof, and it can simulate the original version except for a behaviour which is not desirable according to the specification: Our version is more economic in the number of nak messages sent than the original one. All these points are discussed in detail in the full version [EM02] of this paper.

Table 1. Agents of the PGM protocol

```
agent source
odata, WIN_SIZE, TXWTR: ℕ; rec_nak: set of ℕ
s1: in pnak(nr) ∨ in snak(nr) → out ncf(nr) downwards;
                                  txw_trail < nr → rec_nak := add(rec_nak, nr);
s2: is_in(nr, rec_nak) → nr > txw_trail → out rdata(nr, txw_trail) downwards;
                         rec_nak := remove(rec_nak, nr);
s3: length(rec_nak) = 0 → out odata(odata, txw_trail) downwards;
                          odata := odata + 1;
                          odata + 1 > WIN_SIZE + txw_trail
                              → txw_trail := txw_trail + WIN_SIZE;
endagent;

agent network_element
set_repair: set of ℕ; set_interf: set of (ℕ, channel_name)
e1: in pnak(nr) → set_repair := add(set_repair, nr);
                  set_interf := add(set_interf, (nr, c));   [c reception channel]
                  pnak ∉ set_repair → out pnak(nr) upwards;
                  out ncf(nr) downwards;
e2: in snak(nr) → set_interf := add(set_interf, (nr, c));   [c reception channel]
                  snak ∉ set_repair → out  snak(nr) upwards;
e3: in rdata(nr, trl) → set_repair := remove(set_repair, nr);
                        out  rdata(nr,trl)  to all channels c' s.t. (nr, c') ∈ set_interf
                        set_interf := remove((nr, c'), set_interf)
e4: in ncf(nr) → set_repair := remove(set_repair, nr);
e5: in odata(nr, trl) → out  odata(nr, trl) downwards;
e6: is_in(nr, set_repair) → out  snak(nr) upwards;
endagent;

agent receiver
rxw_trail, set_nr, set_missing: set of ℕ
r1: in odata(nr, trl) ∧ rxw_trail< nr→ rxw_trail <  trl → rxw_trail := trl;
                                       set_nr := add(set_nr, nr);
                                       for all (rxw_trail < i < nr ∧ i ∉ set_nr)
                                           set_missing := add(set_missing, i);
                                       set_missing := remove(set_missing, nr);
                                       set_smissing := remove(set_smissing, nr)
r2: in ncf(nr) ∧ rxw_trail< nr∧ nr∉ set_nr→ set_smissing := add(set_smissing, nr)
                                            for all (rxw_trail < i < nr ∧ i ∉ set_nr)
                                                set_smissing := add(set_smissing, i);
r3: in rdata(nr, trl) ∧ rxw_trail< nr→ rxw_trail <  trl → rxw_trail := trl;
                                       set_nr := add(set_nr, nr);
                                       set_missing := remove(set_missing, nr);
                                       set_smissing := remove(set_smissing, nr)
r4: is_in(nr, set_missing) → nr > rxw_trail →  out pnak (nr) upwards;
                             nr ≤ rxw_trail → set_missing := remove(set_missing, nr);
r5: is_in(nr, set_smissing) → nr > rxw_trail → out snak(nr) upwards;
                              nr≤ rxw_trail→ set_smissing := remove(set_smissing, nr);
endagent;
```

2 A Formal Model of Network Protocols

In this section we formalise the notions of tree networks, and of families of tree networks defined by a protocol.

2.1 Messages, Actions, Events, and Histories

Let M be a (possibly infinite) set of *messages*. We assume that M contains an 'empty' message, denoted by $\bot$. We assume that $M = M{\uparrow} \cup M{\downarrow} \cup \bot$ [3] where $M{\uparrow}$ and $M{\downarrow}$ are sets of *upward* and *downward* messages such that $M{\uparrow} \cap M{\downarrow} = \emptyset$. We model receiving or sending no message as receiving or sending the "empty" message $\bot$. An *abstract action*, or just an *action*, is a triple $(i, o_1, o_2) \neq (\bot, \bot, \bot)$ of messages such that $o_1 \in M{\uparrow} \cup \bot$ and $o_2 \in M{\downarrow} \cup \bot$. Intuitively, an action models receiving a message i, and sending a message o_1 upwards and a message o_2 downwards. A *trace* is a finite sequence of actions. We denote the set of all traces by TR.

Let Ch be a set of *downward channels*, and let $ch \notin Ch$ be an *upward channel*. A *concrete action* or *event* over ch, Ch is a fivetuple (i, c, o_1, o_2, C), where (i, o_1, o_2) is an abstract action, $c \in \{ch\} \cup Ch$, $C \subseteq Ch$, and moreover, either $c = ch$ and $i \in M{\downarrow} \cup \bot$, or $c \in Ch$ and $i \in M{\uparrow} \cup \bot$. (The intuition is that ch is the channel communicating with the parent, and Ch the channels communicating with the children.) An event corresponds to a process receiving message i through channel c, sending o_1 through the upward channel ch, and sending o_2 through a subset C of downward channels. We denote the set of all events by E. A *history* is a finite sequence of events. We denote the set of all histories by H.

Given an event $e = (i, c, o_1, o_2, C)$ over ch, Ch, we define the *action corresponding to e* as (i, o_1, o_2), and denote it by $a(e)$. Given a channel c', we define the *c'-action* corresponding to e, denoted by $c'(e)$, as the pair $(c'(i), c'(o_1, o_2))$ given by: (1) $c'(i) = i$ if $c' = c$ and $c'(i) = \bot$ otherwise, and (2) $c'(o_1, o_2) = o_1$ if $c' = ch$, $c'(o_1, o_2) = o_2$ if $c' \in C$, and $c'(o_1, o_2) = \bot$ otherwise.

Given a history $h = e_1 \ldots e_n$, we define its *associated trace* as the sequence $tr(h) = a(e_1) \ldots a(e_n)$. Given a channel c, at most one message is sent through c during an action, and hence the projection of history h onto channel c is a sequence $tr(h, c) = c(e_1) \ldots c(e_n)$. We call such sequences *projected traces* and denote them by $TRproj$.

2.2 Agents and Processes

In multicast protocols, like the PGM, agents are defined to work independently of the identity and number of their upward and downward channels, because the architecture of the network is not known *a priori*. Our notion of *agents* intends to be very general, while respecting this limitation.

An *agent* is a pair $A = (\rho, f)$, where $\rho \colon TR \times M \to 2^{M{\uparrow} \times M{\downarrow}}$ is the *input/output relation*, and $f \colon TRproj \times Act \times Bool \to Bool$ is the *filter*. Let us explain

[3] Throughout the paper we identify $\bot$ and the set $\{\bot\}$. This should cause no confusion.

this definition. Intuitively, an agent A selects the events that can be executed as a function of the past history, and of the current input message i. After receiving i, the agent selects an event in two steps. First, it nondeterministically selects the messages o_1, o_2 to be sent upwards and downwards, respectively, as a function of the current trace tr of actions and the input message i. Formally, $(o_1, o_2) \in \rho(tr, i)$. In the second step, the agent determines the subset of downward channels through which the message o_2 is sent. The agent examines each channel $c \in Ch$, and decides whether to send o_2 through it or not depending on the action $a = (i, o_1, o_2)$, the projection $tr(h, c)$ of h on channel c, and on whether the input i came via the channel c or not. Formally, o_2 is sent through c if $f(tr(h,c), a, b) = true$, where b is true iff i arrived through channel c.

A *process* is a triple $P = (ch, Ch, A)$, where A is an agent, Ch is a set of channels, and ch is a channel that does not belong to Ch. The set of *transitions* of the process P is the subset of $H \times E \times H$ containing the triples $(h, e, h \cdot e)$ (also denoted by $h \xrightarrow{e} h \cdot e$), such that e is an event that can be selected by A when h is the past history of the process.

Example: We formalise the input/output relation ρ_n of the network element agent of the PGM protocol in our framework. (The filter can be formalised analogously.)

$$\begin{aligned}
\rho_n(tr, \mathrm{rdata}(nr, trl)) &= \{(\bot, \mathrm{rdata}(nr, trl))\} \\
\rho_n(tr, \mathrm{pnak}(nr)) &= \{(\mathrm{pnak}(nr), \mathrm{ncf}(nr))\} \\
\rho_n(tr, \mathrm{snak}(nr)) &= \{(\mathrm{snak}(nr), \bot)\} \\
\rho_n(tr, \mathrm{odata}(nr, trl)) &= \{(\bot, \mathrm{odata}(nr, trl))\} \\
\rho_n(tr, \mathrm{ncf}(nr)) &= \{(\bot, \bot)\} \\
\rho_n(tr, \bot) &= \begin{cases} \{(\mathrm{snak}(nr), \bot)\} & \text{if } nr \in \mathit{set_repair}(tr) \\ \emptyset & \text{otherwise} \end{cases}
\end{aligned}$$

Note that the value of *set_repair* is fully determined by tr; $nr \in \mathit{set\_repair}(tr)$ if and only if tr contains the action $(\mathrm{pnak}(nr), \mathrm{pnak}(nr), \mathrm{ncf}(nr))$ (which adds nr to *set_repair*) and no later occurrence of the actions $(\mathrm{ncf}(nr), \bot, \mathrm{ncf}(nr))$ or $(\mathrm{rdata}(nr), \bot, \mathrm{rdata}(nr))$ (which remove nr). So *set_repair* provides an abstract view on a trace sufficient to define ρ_n.

2.3 Tree Networks and Protocols

Loosely speaking, a tree network is a network of processes with a tree topology; every process is connected to its parent and children by bidirectional channels.

Syntax. A finite tree T is a set of nodes together with a partial order $\leq_T$ satisfying the usual tree condition: if $\mathbf{n}_1 \leq_T \mathbf{n}$ and $\mathbf{n}_2 \leq_T \mathbf{n}$, then $\mathbf{n}_1 \leq_T \mathbf{n}_2$ or $\mathbf{n}_2 \leq_T \mathbf{n}_1$. We denote the child relation by $\prec$ (i.e., $\mathbf{n} \prec \mathbf{n}'$ if $\mathbf{n} <_T \mathbf{n}'$ and there is no $\mathbf{n}''$ such that $\mathbf{n} <_T \mathbf{n}'' <_T \mathbf{n}'$). We write $p(n)$ for the *parent* of $\mathbf{n}$, i.e., for the unique $\mathbf{n}'$ such that $\mathbf{n}' \prec \mathbf{n}$ or for the symbol "_" if there is not such $\mathbf{n}'$. If $\mathbf{n} \prec \mathbf{n}'$, then we call the pair $[\mathbf{n}, \mathbf{n}']$ a *channel.* We define the sets of downward channels of $\mathbf{n}$ in T as $Ch(\mathbf{n}, T) = \{[\mathbf{n}, \mathbf{n}'] \mid \mathbf{n} \prec \mathbf{n}'\}$, and let $ch(\mathbf{n}, T) = [p(\mathbf{n}), \mathbf{n}]$. If $\mathbf{n}$ is the root, then the channel $[\_, \mathbf{n}]$ is considered to connect to the environment. If no confusion is possible, we shorten $ch(\mathbf{n}, T)$ and $Ch(\mathbf{n}, T)$ to $ch(\mathbf{n})$ and $Ch(\mathbf{n})$, respectively. Throughout this paper, for simplicity we assume that the sender only uses its downward channels and receivers only use their upward channel.

A *tree network* is a pair (T, A), where T is a finite tree, and A is a mapping that associates to each node $\mathbf{n} \in N$ an agent $A(\mathbf{n})$. The mapping *Proc* associates to each node $\mathbf{n}$ the process $Proc(\mathbf{n}) = (ch(\mathbf{n}), Ch(\mathbf{n}), A(\mathbf{n}))$.

We call the root of the tree the *sender* of the network, and denote it by $\mathbf{s}$. Maximal nodes w.r.t. $\leq_T$ are called *receivers*. All other nodes are called *internal*.

A tree network (T, A) is *homogeneous* if $A(\mathbf{n}) = A(\mathbf{n}')$ for every two internal nodes $\mathbf{n}, \mathbf{n}'$, and $A(\mathbf{r}) = A(\mathbf{r}')$ for every two receivers $\mathbf{r}$ and $\mathbf{r}'$. A *protocol* P is a set of three agents A_s, A_n, A_r. A protocol P defines a family $\mathcal{N}(P)$ of homogeneous tree networks, namely the tree networks (T, A) satisfying $A(\mathbf{s}) = A_s$, $A(\mathbf{n}) = A_n$ for all internal elements $\mathbf{n}$, and $A(\mathbf{r}) = A_r$ for all receivers $\mathbf{r}$.

Semantics. A *network event* of a tree network (T, A) is a pair $(\mathbf{n}, e)$, where $\mathbf{n}$ is a node of T and e is an event of $Proc(\mathbf{n})$. Intuitively, a network event models that the process $Proc(\mathbf{n})$ executes the event e. We denote the set of all network events by *Nev*. A *network history* is a finite sequence of network events. Given a network history $nh = (\mathbf{n}_1, e_1) \ldots (\mathbf{n}_n, e_n)$ and a node $\mathbf{n}$, we define by $nh(\mathbf{n})$ the projection of nh onto the events executed by $\mathbf{n}$. Notice that $nh(\mathbf{n})$ is a history of the process $Proc(\mathbf{n})$.

Since messages can overtake other messages, a channel behaves like a multiset, which only retains the multiplicity of each message, but not their order. Loss of a message need not be modelled explicitely, because it can be simulated by never taking the message from the channel. The multiset of messages that are waiting for delivery in the channel c after the execution of nh is denoted by $M(nh, c)$. Formally, $M(nh, [\mathbf{n}, \mathbf{n}'])$ is the multiset of messages sent through channel c by $Proc(\mathbf{n})$ and $Proc(\mathbf{n}')$ during the network history nh, minus the multiset of messages received through c by the same processes, also during nh.

A triple $(nh, (\mathbf{n}, e), nh')$, where nh, nh' are network histories and $(\mathbf{n}, e)$ is a network event, is a transition of (T, A) if there is a transition $h \xrightarrow{e} h'$ of $Proc(\mathbf{n})$ satisfying the following conditions:

(1) $nh(\mathbf{n}) = h$, $nh'(\mathbf{n}) = h'$, and $nh(\mathbf{n}') = nh(\mathbf{n})$ for every $\mathbf{n}' \neq \mathbf{n}$.
(2) Let i be the message received by $Proc(\mathbf{n})$ in e, and let c be the channel through which i arrived. Then, either $i = \perp$, or $i \in M(nh, c)$. I.e., the message received by $Proc(\mathbf{n})$ in the event e was either empty or it was waiting for delivery in the channel c.

If $(nh, (\mathbf{n}, e), nh')$ is a transition of (T, A), then we write $nh \xrightarrow[\mathbf{n}]{e} nh'$. We write $nh \xrightarrow[\mathbf{n}_1 \ldots \mathbf{n}_n]{e_1 \ldots e_n} nh'$ if there are transitions $nh \xrightarrow[\mathbf{n}_1]{e_1} nh_1 \ldots nh_{n-1} \xrightarrow[\mathbf{n}_n]{e_n} nh'$. W.l.o.g, we assume that every network history has at least one successor (if not, just add self-looping transitions with some special label).

Fair executions. In our framework, a state of a tree network is given by a network history. An *execution* of T is an infinite sequence $\pi = nh_0\, nh_1\, nh_2 \ldots$ of network histories (i.e., of states) such that for every $i \geq 0$ there is a network event $(e_i, \mathbf{n}_i)$ satisfying $nh_i \xrightarrow[\mathbf{n}_i]{e_i} nh_{i+1}$. An execution is *fair* with respect to a subset $\tilde{T} \subseteq T$ if for every node $\mathbf{n} \in \tilde{T}$ in the network, $\mathbf{n}_i = \mathbf{n}$ for infinitely many $i \geq 0$, i.e., if every node in $\tilde{T}$ executes infinitely many events.

3 Fair Stuttering Simulations for Tree Networks

Fix a protocol P. We are interested in properties that concern only the behaviours of the sender and the receivers, since these are the 'visible' elements of the protocol. So we consider properties Φ of the form $\Phi = \forall \mu \forall \sigma \phi$, where μ is a tuple of *message variables*, σ is a tuple of *receiver variables*, and ϕ is a stuttering invariant LTL temporal logic formula [Lam83,PW97]. The atomic propositions of ϕ can be indexed by the variables of μ, σ.

Example: Informally, the main property that the PGM protocol should satisfy is "for every receiver $\mathbf{r}$ and for every message m sent by the sender, eventually one of the following two holds: $\mathbf{r}$ receives m, or $\mathbf{r}$ knows that m is lost, and that the sender is not going to resend it in the future". The second possibility means that $\mathbf{r}$ finds out that the lower end of the sender's retransmission window (given by *txw_trail*) is larger than the number of messages m.

Given a tree network $T \in \mathcal{N}(P)$, we interpret atomic propositions over sets of network histories of T.[4] We say that T satisfies Φ if for all valuations *val* of the variables μ, σ, and for all executions π of T that are fair with respect to $\mathbf{s}$ and to all receivers in the image of *val*, $\pi \models \phi[\mu := val(\mu),\ \sigma := val(\sigma)]$.

Note that executions in which some processes not mentioned in the property are not scheduled infinitely often are fair, and so the property must also hold for them. But we exclude as unfair those executions in which the sender or some receiver mentioned in the property is 'cut off from the network' after a certain time point, i.e. does no longer receive messages due, say, to a connection breakdown. We say that P satisfies Φ if T satisfies Φ for all $T \in \mathcal{N}(P)$, i.e., P satisfies a property if all the homogeneous tree networks of $\mathcal{N}(P)$ satisfy it.

A simulation of T by T' preserves a property Φ if $T' \models \Phi$ implies $T \models \Phi$. Our goal is to prove that all the tree networks of $\mathcal{N}(P)$ can be simulated by those in a subset $\mathcal{N}'(P) \subseteq \mathcal{N}(P)$, according to a notion of simulation that preserves properties. Once this is achieved, we can prove that P satisfies Φ by showing that the networks of $\mathcal{N}'(P)$ satisfy Φ.

We now define a stuttering version of simulation, similar to stuttering bisimulation [BCG88]. In the simulations used in our proofs all actions of the simulated network T have a corresponding sequence of actions in the simulating network T', and so we do not have to consider stuttering in T, which simplifies

[4] Once P is fixed, all networks (T, A) of $\mathcal{N}(P)$ share the same agent function A. So we shorten (T, A) to T.

the definition. Since we only require fair paths to satisfy a property, we adapt the definition accordingly, like in fair simulation as introduced in [GL94], the coarsest simulation that preserves fair-ACTL*.

Given two networks T and T', let Im be a mapping that assigns to each receiver $\mathbf{r}$ of T a receiver $Im(\mathbf{r})$ of T', called the *image* of $\mathbf{r}$. Let $Match(nh, nh')$ be the relation between histories of T and T' given by $tr(nh(\mathbf{s})) = tr(nh'(\mathbf{s}')))$, where $\mathbf{s}$ and $\mathbf{s}'$ are the senders of T and T', respectively, and $tr(nh(\mathbf{r})) = tr(nh'(Im(\mathbf{r})))$ for all receivers $\mathbf{r}$.

Definition 1
A *fair stuttering simulation of T by T' with respect to Im* is a relation $R \subseteq NH \times NH'$ such that $R(nh, nh')$ implies:

- $Match(nh, nh')$.
- For every subset $\tilde{T}$ of T consisting of the sender and receivers, and for every execution π of T starting at nh which is fair with respect to $\tilde{T}$ there is an execution π' of T' starting at nh', fair with respect to $Im[\tilde{T}]$, and an increasing mapping $\sigma\colon \mathbb{N} \longrightarrow \mathbb{N}$ such that (a) for all $n \geq 0$, $R(\pi(n), \pi'(\sigma(n)))$, and (b) for all $\sigma(n) < j \leq \sigma(n+1)$, $Match(\pi(n+1), \pi'(j))$.

We say that T is simulated by T' (with respect to Im) if there is a mapping Im and a fair stuttering simulation R of T by T' with respect to Im such that $R(nh_0, nh'_0)$, where nh_0 and nh'_0 are the empty network histories of T and T'.

The following theorem describes properties that are preserved by fair stuttering simulation. It follows easily from the fact that for every execution π in T that is fair with respect to a subset $\tilde{T}$ there is an execution π' in T', fair with respect to $Im[\tilde{T}]$, such that the states of π and π' pointwise (up to stuttering) satisfy *Match*. This implies that π' satisfies the same stuttering-invariant LTL properties as π.

Theorem 1 *Let T and T' be tree networks such that T is simulated by T' with respect to Im. Let $\Phi = \forall\mu\forall\sigma\phi$ be a formula such that (1) ϕ is stuttering-invariant, and (2) for all atomic propositions p of ϕ and for all network histories nh and nh', $Match(nh, nh')$ implies $nh \models p \iff nh' \models p$. Then, $T' \models \Phi$ implies $T \models \Phi$.*

Finally, we have the result we were looking for:

Theorem 2 *Let $\mathcal{N}' \subseteq \mathcal{N}(P)$ such that each $T \in \mathcal{N}(P)$ is simulated by some $T' \in \mathcal{N}'$, and let Φ as is Theorem 1. Then $\mathcal{N}' \models \Phi$ implies $\mathcal{N}(P) \models \Phi$.*

4 Collapsable Tree Networks

In this section, we explore conditions on protocols that allow to flatten the tree hierarchy, i.e. conditions implying that any tree network can be simulated by one with at most one layer of internal elements.

Throughout this section we fix a protocol P consisting of agents (ρ_s, f_s), (ρ_n, f_n) and (ρ_r, f_r). Let $\mathcal{N}^0(P)$ be the set of tree networks in $\mathcal{N}(P)$ without internal elements, and let $\mathcal{N}^1(P)$ be the set of tree networks in $\mathcal{N}(P)$ with only one layer of internal elements. For simplicity, we only consider sender agents that always sends downward messages through all their downward channels.

We are interested in protocols like the PGM, where the sender exchanges messages with the receivers, and the primary functionality of internal elements is to *forward* these messages. Transition $\mathbf{e_5}$ of the PGM provides an example. However, in order to deal with lost messages and to improve the efficiency, internal elements can also perform other tasks. First, they can *filter* downward messages: Instead of sending a message to all its successors, they select a subset of them as recipients. An example is transition $\mathbf{e_3}$. Moreover, besides forwarding with or without filtering, internal elements can also *generate* messages. Transition $\mathbf{e_6}$ is an example of 'spontaneous' generation, while in transition $\mathbf{e_1}$ reception of pnak(nr) triggers the generation of ncf(nr). The generation of messages can in general depend on the internal state of the component, i.e., its history. For example, generation of snak(nr) depends on whether nr is contained in the set set_repair.

We present our main result in two steps. First, in section 4.1 we consider internal agents that have only forwarding transitions (but possibly with filtering). We then consider protocols in which network elements can also generate messages. It is easy to see that for general protocols of this form there is no $n \geq 0$ such that $\mathcal{N}^n(P)$ simulates $\mathcal{N}(P)$. We identify a class of protocols P for which $\mathcal{N}(P)$ can be simulated by $\mathcal{N}^1(P)$, and show that the PGM belongs to it.

4.1 Forwarding Agents

Intuitively, a forwarding agent is an agent that forwards incoming upward messages through its upward channel, and multicasts incoming downward messages through some of its downward channels. We also allow the agent to 'swallow' messages.

Definition 2
Formally, an agent (ρ, f) is a *forwarding agent* if for every trace tr and every message $i \in M$:

- If $i \in M\!\uparrow$, then $\rho(tr, i) \subseteq \{(i, \bot), (\bot, \bot)\}$;
- if $i \in M\!\downarrow$, then $\rho(tr, i) \subseteq \{(\bot, i), (\bot, \bot)\}$; and
- if $i = \bot$, then $\rho(tr, \bot) = \{(\bot, \bot)\}$.

A *forwarding protocol* is a protocol whose network element agent (but not necessarily its sender or receiver agents) is forwarding.

Let T be a tree network. We define the tree $\underline{T}$ as follows: $\underline{T}$ contains a sender $\underline{\mathbf{s}}$ and a receiver $\underline{\mathbf{r}}$ for every receiver $\mathbf{r}$ of T, but no internal elements; $\leq_{\underline{T}}$ is the projection of $\leq_T$ onto $\underline{T}$. So in $\underline{T}$, every receiver is a child of the sender.

In the full version [EM02], we define a relation $nh \lhd \underline{nh}$ between network histories nh and $\underline{nh}$, and show that $\lhd$ is a fair stuttering simulation of T by $\underline{T}$. We get as corollary:

Theorem 3 *If P is a forwarding protocol and Φ is like in Theorem 1, then $\mathcal{N}^0(P) \models \Phi$ if and only if $\mathcal{N}(P) \models \Phi$.*

4.2 Forwarding and Generating Agents

In this section, we consider internal agents that can not only forward but also generate messages. Clearly, we can no longer expect $\mathcal{N}(P)$ to be simulated by $\mathcal{N}^0(P)$, unless the messages generated by the internal elements have no effects whatsoever. We give conditions under which $\mathcal{N}(P)$ can be simulated by $\mathcal{N}^1(P)$. We then show that these conditions are satisfied by the PGM protocol.

Let $M_{gen} \subseteq M$ be the set of messages that can be generated by internal network elements. (Notice that the sender and the receivers can also generate messages, but these do not have to be in M_{gen}.)

Definition 3
A *forwarding and generating agent* (*f&g agent* for short) is an agent (ρ, f) such that for every trace $tr \in TR$ and for every message $i \in M$, the following conditions hold:

- If $i \in M\!\uparrow$ and $(o_1, o_2) \in \rho(tr, i)$, then $o_1 \in \{i, \bot\}$ and $o_2 \in M_{gen} \cup \{\bot\}$;
- if $i \in M\!\downarrow$ and $(o_1, o_2) \in \rho(tr, i)$, then $o_1 \in M_{gen} \cup \{\bot\}$ and $o_2 \in \{i, \bot\}$; and
- if $i = \bot$ and $(o_1, o_2) \in \rho(tr, \bot)$, then $o_1, o_2 \in M_{gen} \cup \{\bot\}$.

A *f&g protocol* is a protocol with a f&g internal element agent.

These definition allows messages to be generated as 'side-effects' of forwarding other messages, or spontaneously, i.e. without receiving input. In the PGM protocol, ncf-messages are generated as side-effects, while snak-messages are generated spontaneously.

Conditions on the Protocol. We define the class of *simple protocols*, for which we prove that $\mathcal{N}^1(P)$ simulates $\mathcal{N}(P)$. This requires some preliminaries.

Receiving a message has two effects. The first, immediate effect is that some messages are sent. The second effect is that the internal state of the process (given in our model by the history) changes. This change may enable the process to send messages, but these may not be sent immediately. The change of state may also disable the emission of messages. An example of an enabling effect is given by transitions **e1** and **e6** of the PGM: Transition **e1** adds *nr* to *set_repair*, which enables the process to send snak through transition **e6**.

We need a definition implying the following intuitive idea: Receiving a message i in a subset M' may have arbitrary disabling effects, but it can only enable upward forwarding of i, or generation of messages in another subset M''.

Definition 4
Let (ρ, f) be an agent, tr be a trace of it, $M' \subseteq M$, and $M'' \subseteq M\uparrow$. Let $Rem(tr, M', M'')$ be the set of all traces resulting from tr by removing arbitrarily many actions of the form (i, o_1, o_2) such that either $i \in M'$ or $i = o_2 = \bot$ and $o_1 \in M''$. We say that M' *only enables* M'' in the agent (ρ, f) if for every trace tr and every $tr' \in Rem(tr, M', M'')$ the following conditions hold:

(1) If $i \in M' \cap M\uparrow$ and $(o_1, o_2) \in \rho(tr, i)$, then $o_1 \in M'' \cup \{i, \bot\}$ and $o_2 = \bot$; if $i \in M' \cap M\downarrow$ and $(o_1, o_2) \in \rho(tr, i)$, then $o_1 \in M'' \cup \bot$ and $o_2 = \bot$;
(2) if $i \in M \setminus \bot$, then $\rho(tr, i) \subseteq \rho(tr', i)$; and $\rho(tr, \bot) \setminus \rho(tr', \bot) \subseteq \{(o, \bot) \mid o \in M''\}$.

Let us see why this definition captures the intuition above. Condition (1) expresses that the *immediate* effect of receiving $i \in M'$ can only be forwarding i up, or the generation of an upward message $o_1 \in M''$. Condition (2) expresses that the *long-term* effect of receiving i can only the be generation of upward messages in M'', let us see why. Suppose first that $M'' = \emptyset$. Then (2) implies that receiving messages in M' can only have disabling effects: Whatever we can do after receiving the messages (given by $\rho(tr, i)$), we can also do without receiving them (given by $\rho(tr', i)$). Now consider the general case. Since $\rho(tr, \bot) \setminus \rho(tr', \bot) \subseteq \{(o, \bot) \mid o \in M''\}$, receiving messages in i may now enable actions $(\bot, o, \bot)$ for $o \in M''$. And since in $Rem(tr, M, M'')$ we now allow to remove actions $(\bot, o, \bot)$ for $o \in M''$, we make sure that such actions themselves only enable actions of the same kind.

We are almost ready to present the definition of simple protocols. Let M_{fil} be the subset of $M\downarrow$ containing the messages that can be filtered when being forward downwards. More precisely, for all actions a in which the downwards output message belongs to $M\downarrow \setminus M_{fil}$, there is no filtering, i.e., $f(tr, a, b) = true$ for all traces tr and all boolean values b. We now define:

Definition 5
Let $P = (A_s, A_n, A_r)$ be a f&g protocol. P is *simple* if:

(a) In A_n (the network element agent), M_{gen} only enables $\emptyset$, and
(b) in A_r (the receiver agent), $M_{fil} \cup M_{gen}$ only enables $M_{gen} \cap M\uparrow$.

If condition (a) is dropped, the following scenario becomes possible: A network element $\mathbf{n}$ spontaneously generates a message o_1 and sends it upwards to its parent. The parent forwards it up and, in the next step, generates itself another copy of o_1; all predecessors of $\mathbf{n}$ behave in the same way. This produces a cascade of upward messages, and the number of o_1's received by the sender depends on the position of $\mathbf{n}$ in the tree structure. It is easy to see that this makes it impossible to simulate arbitrary structures by structures with at most one layer of internal elements.

If condition (b) is dropped, the following scenario becomes possible: A downward message $m \in M_{fil}$ is filtered out by a network element $\mathbf{n}$, i.e., $\mathbf{n}$ does not forward m down to any of its successors. The receivers that get m react by sending upwards a message $o_1 \notin M_{gen}$. Network elements that receive o_1 forward it up and, in the next step, generate a message $o'_1 \in M_{gen}$ and send it upwards. Again, the number of o'_1 messages received by the sender depends on the position of $\mathbf{n}$ in the tree structure.

The simulation. We show that $\mathcal{N}^1(P)$ simulates $\mathcal{N}(P)$ if P is simple. Let T be a tree network. We define the tree $\underline{T}$ as follows: $\underline{T}$ contains a sender $\underline{\mathbf{s}}$. As network elements can generate messages, the simulating tree network now has to contain a network element $\underline{\mathbf{n}}$ for every network element $\mathbf{n}$ in T and $\underline{\mathbf{n}}$ is a child of $\underline{\mathbf{s}}$. Moreover, a network element $\underline{\mathbf{n}}$ has to have the same receivers below itself as $\mathbf{n}$ does, because the actions of all these receivers can affect $\mathbf{n}$. So for every $\mathbf{r} > \mathbf{n}$, $\underline{\mathbf{n}}$ needs to have a child $\underline{\mathbf{r}}(\mathbf{n})$ that acts like $\mathbf{r}$. Thereby, we assume for simplicity that all receivers have an internal element as parent.

Figure 1 displays an example tree T and its flattening $\underline{T}$. In the full version [EM02], we define a simulation relation $nh \lhd \underline{nh}$ between network histories nh of T and $\underline{nh}$ of $\underline{T}$. The receiver $\underline{\mathbf{r}}(p(\mathbf{r}))$ exactly simulates $\underline{\mathbf{r}}$, and so we abbreviate $\underline{\mathbf{r}}(p(\mathbf{r}))$ by $\underline{\mathbf{r}}$. The other copies $\underline{\mathbf{r}}(\mathbf{n})$ are guaranteed to be able to execute the same actions as $\mathbf{r}$ except actions (i, o_1, o_2) such that $i \in M_{fil} \cup M_{gen}$ or actions $(\perp, o, \perp)$ such that $o \in M_{gen}$.

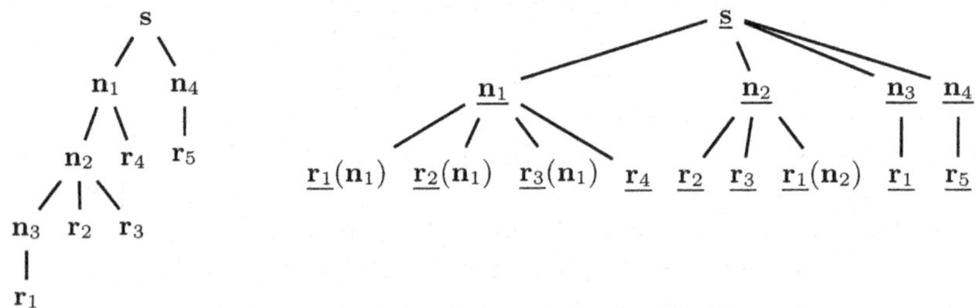

Fig. 1. Example of a tree T and its flattening $\underline{T}$

We obtain that for simple f&g protocols, it suffices to consider trees with only one level of internal elements:

Theorem 4 *If P is a simple f&g protocol and Φ is as in Theorem 1 then $\mathcal{N}^1(P) \models \Phi$ holds if and only if $\mathcal{N}(P) \models \Phi$.*

The PGM protocol. We sketch why the PGM example as presented in Section 1 is simple in the sense of Definition 5. In the PGM protocol, M_{gen} consists of the messages of form snak(nr) and ncf(nr), and M_{fil} consists of the messages of form rdata(nr, trl). Let us show that the protocol satisfies the conditions of Definition 5.

First, the network element agent (ρ_n, f_n) of page 133 is f&g by definition. For (a): When forwarding snak(nr), only a message in M_{gen} (namely snak(nr)) is sent upwards, and nothing downwards, and on reception of ncf(nr) nothing is sent. This shows that condition (1) of Definition 4 holds. In order to see that messages in M_{gen} do not have long-term enabling effects (condition (2)), first note that ρ_n can be defined in terms of the variable *set_repair*, as explained on 133.[5] Reception of snak(nr) does not change *set_repair*, and on reception of ncf(nr), nr is removed from *set_repair*: So if $tr' \in Rem(tr, M_{gen}, \emptyset)$, i.e., if tr' is obtained by removing actions with input snak(nr) or ncf(nr) then in tr' the same actions as in tr (and possibly more) are enabled. For (b): On reception of rdata(nr,trl) or ncf(nr), nothing is sent (condition (1)). In order to see that messages in M_{gen} do not have long-term enabling effects, notice first that ρ_n can be defined in terms of the variables of the agent. Since reception of rdata(nr,trl) adds nr to *set_nr* and removes it from *set_missing* and *set_smissing*, it only disables actions. Reception of ncf(nr) only enables actions of the form ($\perp$, snak(nr'), $\perp$). Finally, sending of ($\perp$, snak(nr'), $\perp$) does not change the variables of the receiver, and so it does not enable or disable actions. So the only actions that can be enabled in tr but not in $tr' \in Rem(tr, M_{fil} \cup M_{gen}, M_{gen} \cap M\!\uparrow)$ are of the form ($\perp$, snak(nr'), $\perp$).

5 Reduction of One-Layer Tree Networks

Given a simple protocol P and a property Φ, we have shown that checking Φ reduces to proving that $\mathcal{N}^1(P) \models \Phi$. We now introduce the class of *iteration protocols*, and show that for them $\mathcal{N}^1(P) \models \Phi$ reduces to proving $U_k \models \Phi$, where U_k is a particular instantiation of $\mathcal{N}^1(P)$ that depends on the number k of receiver variables used in Φ. Combining the two results we have that a simple iteration protocol P satisfies Φ if and only if $U_k \models \Phi$.

A trace tr is *reachable* by an agent (ρ, f) if it is empty or if $tr = tr' \cdot (i, o_1, o_2)$ where tr' is reachable and $(o_1, o_2) \in \rho(tr', i)$. An agent *can resend upward messages* if for every reachable trace $tr \cdot (i, o_1, o_2)$ and for every $n \geq 1$, the trace $tr \cdot (i, o_1, o_2) \cdot (\perp, o_1, \perp)^n$ is also reachable.

Definition 6
A protocol is an *iteration protocol* if $M\!\uparrow$ is a finite set, and both the receiver and the network element agents can resend upward messages.

If we bound the number of possible message numbers in the PGM protocol, i.e., instead of $nr \in \mathbb{N}$ we say $nr \in [1..n]$ for some number n, then we obtain a simple iteration protocol: The conditions of Definition 6 hold because of transitions **e6**, **r4** and **r5**.

Definition 7
Let P be an iteration protocol P, and let u and g be the sizes of $M\!\uparrow$ and $M\!\uparrow \cap M_{gen}$, respectively. For each $n \geq 1$, we define the *universal instance* U_k of $\mathcal{N}^1(P)$ as follows: The sender has $k + g + u$ children, all of them network elements; each of the first $k + u$ network elements has $u + 1$ children; and each of the other g network elements has u children. For $1 \leq i \leq k$, we denote the first child of the i-th network element by $\underline{\mathbf{r}}_i$. We also denote the tuple $(\underline{\mathbf{r}}_1, \ldots, \underline{\mathbf{r}}_k)$ by $\underline{\mathbf{R}}$.

[5] The variable *set_interf* is irrelevant for ρ_n, it only affects the filter function f_n.

In order to prove that U_k can simulate the behaviour of instances T in $\mathcal{N}^1(P)$, we use the following notion: Let *Im* be a function mapping a k-sized subset $\tilde{R} = \{\mathbf{r}_1, \ldots, \mathbf{r}_k\}$ of receivers of T to receivers of U_k. Let $Match(nh, nh')$ hold if $tr(nh)(\mathbf{r}) = trl(nh'(Im(\mathbf{r})))$ for all $\mathbf{r} \in \tilde{R}$. We say that fair executions of T are *stuttering-included* in the fair executions of U_k if for any execution π which is fair with respect to $\tilde{R}$, there is an execution π' of U_k, fair with respect to $Im[\tilde{R}]$, and an increasing mapping $\sigma : \mathbb{N} \rightarrow \mathbb{N}$ such that $Match(\pi(i), \pi'(\sigma(i)))$ holds for all i, and for all $\sigma(i) < j \leq \sigma(i+1)$, $Match(\pi(i+1), \pi'(j))$.

Intuitively, in an iteration protocol, u-many receivers can mimic the behaviour of any set R of receivers as follows: For every $m \in M\uparrow$ there is a receiver $\mathbf{r}(m) \in R$ that first outputs m. We simulate all transitions of $\mathbf{r}(m)$ until the first output of m, and switch to iterating $(\bot, m, \bot)$ afterwards, and so can simulate all actions of receivers in R. By using this observation, we obtain:

Theorem 5 *Let P be a simple f&g iteration protocol and let $T \in \mathcal{N}^1(P)$. Let $\{\mathbf{r}_1, \ldots, \mathbf{r}_k\}$ be a subset of the receivers of T. The fair executions of T are stuttering-included in the fair executions of U_k with respect to the mapping Im given by $Im(\mathbf{r}_i) = \underline{\mathbf{r}}_i$.*

Analogously to Theorem 1, stuttering-inclusion of fair executions implies that any formula Φ with k receiver variables that holds for U_k also holds for T. As U_k is in $\mathcal{N}^1(P)$, we obtain:

Theorem 6 *Let P be a simple f&g iteration protocol, and let Φ be a property $\Phi = \forall\mu\forall\sigma\phi$ as in Theorem 1 such that σ is a tuple of n receiver variables. Then, $\mathcal{N}^1(P) \models \Phi$ if and only if $U_n \models \Phi[\sigma := \underline{\mathbf{R}}]$ and so, by Theorem 4, P satisfies Φ if and only if $U_n \models \Phi[\sigma := \underline{\mathbf{R}}]$.*

6 Conclusions and Related Work

We have provided a general formal model of multicast network protocols with which tree-based multicast protocols can be modelled appropriately. We have proved a general theorem showing that for a simple class of protocols, the verification problem reduces to the analysis of instantiations with at most one layer of internal elements between sender and receivers. For a smaller class we have also proved that the verification reduces to the analysis of one single instantiation. Protocols whose internal elements just forward messages fit easily in our class. In fact, we have shown that the PGM protocol, whose internal elements exhibit a far more complicated behaviour, also fits in it.

As future work, we plan to explore whether our results can also be used for protocols that use local error recovery, which is a possible extension of the PGM protocol, and whether our approach can be extended to the analysis of timed protocols.

Related work. Some work on regular model-checking has addressed the problem of automatically verifying systems with a parameterised tree structure

[BT02]. However, these techniques still seem far from being able to attack systems of the complexity of the PGM. There are also some papers on the analysis of the PGM protocol. However, so far they have concentrated on analysing the behaviour of a fixed instance, and so this work has a different nature to the work carried out here. In [BBP02], the timed behaviour of a small instance of a simplified model is analysed. In the ADVANCE project, the untimed behaviour of a system that can simulate the universal instance U_1 has been studied. By our results this system can simulate *any* instance with respect to the main property of the protocol, since this property only involves one receiver variable. Unfortunately, at the time of writing this paper this instance is still out of the reach of the automatic tools.

Acknowledgements. This work has been supported by the FP5 Project ADVANCE, contract No IST-1999-29082.

References

[BBP02] Bérard, B., Bouyer, P. and Petit, A. *Analysing the PGM protocol with UPPAAL.* In: *2nd Workshop on Real-Time Tools.* Dep. Information Technology, Uppsala Univ., 2002, Tech. Report 2002-025.

[BCG88] Browne, M. C., Clarke, E. and Grumberg, O. *Characterizing finite Kripke structures in propositional temporal logic.* Theoretical Computer Science, 59: 115–131, 1988.

[BT02] Bouajjani, A. and Touili, T. *Extrapolating tree transformations.* In: *Proc. 14th Intl. Conf. on Computer Aided Verification.* 2002, LNCS 2404.

[EM02] Esparza, J. and Maidl, M. *Simple representative instantiations for multicast protocols*, 2002. Available at `http://www.dcs.ed.ac.uk/monika`.

[EN95] Emerson, E. A. and Namjoshi, K. S. *Reasoning about rings.* In: *Proc. 22th ACM Conf. on Principles of Programming Languages.* 1995.

[GL94] Grumberg, O. and Long, D. E. *Model checking and modular verification.* TOPLAS, 16(3): 843–871, 1994.

[Lam83] Lamport, L. *What good is temporal logic?* In: *Proc. IFIP 9th World Computer Congress.* 1983.

[Mai02] Maidl, M. *Simple representative instantiations for the PGM protocol*, 2002. Available at `http://www.dcs.ed.ac.uk/monika`.

[PPV] Papadopoulos, C., Parulkar, G. and Varghese, G. *LMS: A router assisted scheme for reliable multicast.* To appear in: IEEE/ACM Transactions on Networking.

[PW97] Peled, D. and Wilke, T. *Stutter-invariant temporal properties are expressible without the next-operator.* Information Processing Letters, 63: 243–246, 1997.

[S+00] Speakman, T. et al. *PGM reliable transport protocol specification*, 2000. RFC 3208 (experimental) of the IETF. Available at: `http://www.ietf.org/rfc.html`.

Rapid Parameterized Model Checking of Snoopy Cache Coherence Protocols*

E. Allen Emerson and Vineet Kahlon

Department of Computer Sciences and Computer Engineering Research Center
The University of Texas, Austin TX78712, USA
{emerson,kahlon}@cs.utexas.edu

Abstract. A new method is proposed for *parameterized* reasoning about snoopy cache coherence protocols. The method is distinctive for being exact (sound and complete), fully automatic (algorithmic), and tractably efficient. The states of most cache coherence protocols can be organized into a hierarchy reflecting how *tightly* a memory block in a given cache state is bound to the processor. A broad framework encompassing snoopy cache coherence protocols is proposed where the hierarchy implicit in the design of protocols is captured as a *pre-order*. This yields a new solution technique that hinges on the construction of an *abstract history graph* where a global concrete state is represented by an abstract state reflecting the occupied local states. The abstract graph also takes into account the history of local transitions of the protocol that were fired along the computation to get to the global state. This permits the abstract history graph to exactly capture the behaviour of systems with an arbitrary number of homogeneous processes. Although the worst case size of the abstract history graph can be exponential in the size of the transition diagram describing the protocol, the actual size of the abstract history graph is small for standard cache protocols. The method is applicable to all 8 of the most common snoopy cache protocols described in Handy's book [19] from Illinois-MESI to Dragon. The experimental results for parameterized verification of each of those 8 protocols document the efficiency of this new method in practice, with each protocol being verified in just a fraction of a second. It is emphasized that this is parameterized verification.

1 Introduction

Cache protocols provide a vital buffer between the ever growing performance of processors and lagging memory speeds making them indispensable for applications such as shared memory multi-processors. Unfortunately, cache protocols are behaviorally complex. Ensuring their correct operation, in particular that they maintain the fundamental safety property of *coherence* so that different processes agree on their view of shared data items, can be subtle. The difficulty of the problem is often magnified as the number n of coordinating caches increases. Moreover, it is highly desirable that a cache protocol be correct independent of the magnitude of n. There is thus great practical as well as theoretical interest in uniform parameterized reasoning about systems comprised of n

* This work was supported in part by NSF grants CCR-009-8141 & CCR-020-5483, and SRC contract 2002-TJ-1026.

H. Garavel and J. Hatcliff (Eds.): TACAS 2003, LNCS 2619, pp. 144–159, 2003.

homogeneous cache protocols so as to ensure correctness for systems of *all* sizes n. This general problem is known in the literature as the *Parameterized Model Checking Problem (PMCP)*. It is in general algorithmically undecidable. Prior attempts to address the PMCP for cache protocols (cf. Section 5) have had a number of limitations, ranging from incompleteness to the need for considerable human intervention and ingenuity to potentially catastrophic inefficiency.

In this paper, we present a general method for solving the PMCP over snoopy cache coherence protocols of the sort commonly used in shared memory multiprocessors. Our framework includes all of the protocols in the book of Handy [19]. Our method is specialized to dealing with *safety* properties, as is appropriate for reasoning about coherence. We give a solution for this PMCP over our cache framework for safety that is distinguished by being exact (sound and complete), fully automatic (algorithmic), and having complexity bounds that are quite tractable. The worst case complexity of our general algorithm is single exponential time in the size of the state diagram of a single cache unit; however, our experimental results show that our algorithm performs *very* efficiently in practice. We have applied our method to verify parameterized versions of the MSI, MESI, MOESI, Illinois (MESI-type), Berkeley, N+1, Dragon, and Firefly cache coherence protocols.

In our framework, we model cache coherence protocols using a specialized variant of broadcast protocols [14] that we call *pre-ordered broadcast protocols*, where processes coordinate using broadcast primitives plus boolean guards. A broadcast transmission corresponds to a cache protocol putting a message on the bus; reception of such a message corresponds to snooping the bus and taking appropriate action. Boolean guards make it possible to model protocols (e.g., Illinois, Firefly, Dragon) that need to determine the presence or absence of the required memory block in other caches. Our approach exploits a key feature common to most snoopy cache coherence protocols [8]: their states can be organized into a *hierarchy* based on how *tightly* a memory block in a given state is bound to the processor. Consider, for example, the MSI cache coherence protocol (cf. Figure 1). A memory block in the *modified* state is intended to be used by at most one processor and can be written to by that processor locally without generating any memory transactions across the bus. So it is tightly bound to the processor. However, a block in the *shared* state can potentially be shared by multiple processes and cannot be modified locally. Hence it is less tightly bound to the processor. We make precise this notion of tightness by capturing it as a *pre-order*[1] on the state set of an individual cache protocol. Intuitively, a state higher in the order is more tightly bound to the processor than a state that is comparably lower in the order. For instance, in the case of the MSI protocol, the pre-order, $\preceq$, is given by $I \prec S \prec M$.

Our technique involves the construction of an *abstract history graph* over nodes of the form $(a, A) \in S \times 2^S$, where S is the set of states of the given cache protocol. The key idea is the following: We represent global state s of a system with n caches by a tuple of the form $(a, A) \in S \times 2^S$. Here a denotes the local state of the process

[1] A *pre-order* on finite set S is a reflexive and transitive binary relation $\preceq$ on S. There are several associated relations. We say x is equivalent to y, written $x \approx y$, iff $x \preceq y \wedge y \preceq x$; x strictly precedes y, written $x \prec y$, iff $x \preceq y \wedge \neg(y \preceq x)$; x is incomparable to y, written $x \not\sim y$, iff $\neg(x \preceq y) \wedge \neg(y \preceq x)$.

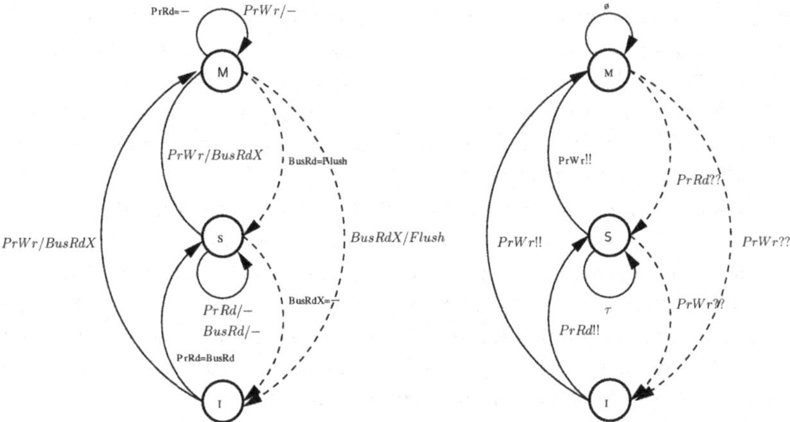

Fig. 1. The MSI Cache Coherence Protocol and its template

executing the most recent transition in the computation leading up to s that flushes all the other processes into some unique fixed state. The set A denotes the maximal set of states of S that could potentially be filled given arbitrarily many processes by firing (a stuttering of the) the sequence of local transitions that were fired in the system with n caches to get to s. The standard abstract graph construction used in, e.g., [25] just stores the set of local states occurring in a global state. Our new construction's extra historical information permits us to reason about an arbitrary number of caches in an *exact* fashion with respect to safety properties. In the worst case, the size of the abstract graph may be exponential in the size of the state diagram of the given cache protocol. But in practice the abstract graph tends to be small as documented by our empirical results. In our experiments, protocols with k states had abstract graphs with ck abstract states, for small $c \leq 2$. We believe this may be a reflection of the tendency for broadcast transitions to drive recipients from a wider range of cache states to a narrower (lower in the pre-order) range of cache states, thereby reducing the number of degrees of freedom possible for abstract states. Finally, we discuss how our technique enables us to generate error traces once an error is detected.

The rest of the paper is organized as follows. We begin by introducing the system model in section 2. In section 3, we present a model checking algorithm for verifying parameterized safety properties based on the construction of the abstract history graph. Applications and experimental results are discussed in section 4, while a comparison with related works and some concluding remarks are given in the final section 5.

2 Preliminaries

2.1 A Motivating Example

We use as an example the simple MSI cache coherence protocol. The state transition diagram for the MSI protocol is shown in figure 1. The symbols M, S and I stand for

$modified$, $shared$ and $invalid$ states, respectively. The states are organized so that the closer the state is to the top, the more *tightly* is the memory block in that state bound to the processor. In our system model we capture this notion of tightness as a *pre-order*, $\preceq$, on the states of the cache protocol. The notation A/B means that if the controller observes the event A from the processor side of the bus then in addition to the state change it generates the bus transaction or action B. The null action is denoted by "-". Transitions due to observed bus transactions are shown as dashed arcs, while those due to local processor actions are shown in bold arcs. The $Bus\ Read$ ($BusRd$) transaction is generated by a process read ($PrRd$) request when the memory block is not in the cache. The newly loaded block is *promoted*, viz., moved up in the state diagram, from invalid to the shared state in the requesting cache. If any other cache has the block in the modified state and it observes a $BusRd$ transaction on the bus, then its copy is stale and so it *demotes* its copy to the shared state. We call such a transition a *low-push* broadcast. More generally broadcast transition $a \rightarrow b$ is a low-push transition with respect to $\preceq$ iff it forces every other process in a local that is strictly higher in the pre-order $\preceq$ than b to a state that is at most as high as b. The $Bus\ Read\ Exclusive$ ($BusRdX$) transaction is generated by a $PrWr$ to a block that is either not in the cache or is in the cache but not in the modified state. The cache controller puts the address on the bus and asks for an exclusive copy that it intends to modify. All other caches are invalidated. Once the cache obtains the exclusive copy, the write can be performed in the cache. This is an example of a *flush* broadcast transition, that forces every process other than the one firing the transition and in its non-initial state into a unique fixed state defined by the transition.

The template U for a protocol, such as MSI, is obtained from its state transition diagram through a simple abstraction, treating the behavior of the processors as purely nondeterministic. The transformation is straightforward, syntactic, and mechanical: Each transition generated by processor actions (represented by a bold line) and labeled by A/B, where $B \neq -$, is labeled with the broadcast send label $A!!$ while every transition generated by bus actions (represented by dashed lines) and labeled with B/C is labeled with the matching broadcast receive label $A??$. In the original diagram the relationship between a broadcast send A/B and its corresponding receive B/C was established with the common symbol B, while in the template it is established by the common symbol A in the labels $A!!$ and $A??$. Every bold transition labeled with $A/-$ represents a local action and is therefore labeled with the local transition label τ. The natural[2] pre-order $\preceq$ on U is $\mathsf{I} \prec \mathsf{S} \prec \mathsf{M}$. All transitions labeled with $PrRd$ are low-pushes with respect to $\preceq$, while those labeled with $PrWr$ are flushes.

2.2 The System Model: Pre-ordered Broadcast Protocols

In this paper we consider families of systems of the form U^n, such that a pre-order, $\preceq$, can be imposed on the states of *template* U such that each transition of U is either a local transition or a flush broadcast or a low-push broadcast with respect to $\preceq$. Furthermore the transition could also be labeled with the specialized disjunctive guard $\bigvee \neg(\mathsf{i})$ or the specialized conjunctive guard $\bigwedge(\mathsf{i})$. We call such systems *pre-ordered broadcasts*.

[2] There is usually a natural and visually obvious pre-order, but there may be more than one suitable pre-order. A suitable pre-order can be constructed as shown in the section 3.4.

The process template U is formally defined by the 4-tuple $(S, \Sigma, R, \mathsf{i})$, where

- S is a finite, non-empty set of *states*.
- Σ is a finite set of *labels* including the local transition label τ, broadcast labels $l!!$ and receive labels $l??$.
- The local transition relation R is such that each transition tr is either local $a \xrightarrow{g:\tau} b$, or a broadcast, $a \xrightarrow{g:l!!} b$, or a receive $a \xrightarrow{g:l??} b$.

We assume that receives are deterministic: for each label $l!!$ appearing in some broadcast send and for each state s in S, there is a unique corresponding receive transition on $l??$ out of s.

The guard g labeling each transition tr of R is either the boolean expression *true* or the *specialized conjunctive* guard $\bigwedge(\mathsf{i})$, or the *specialized disjunctive* guard $\bigvee \neg(\mathsf{i})$. We assume that the guard is *true* for receive transitions. In practice, the above mentioned guards suffice in modeling cache coherence protocols as each cache only needs to know whether another cache has the memory block it requires, expressed using the specialized disjunctive guard, or whether no other cache has it, expressed using the specialized conjunctive guard.

We further stipulate a pre-ordering, $\preceq$, on the state set S of U such that i is the minimum element, i.e., for all local states $a \neq \mathsf{i}$, we have $a \succ \mathsf{i}$, and such that each broadcast transition tr is of either of the two forms

1. *Flush*: Given state a of U, transition $b \xrightarrow{l!!} c \in R$, where $c \neq \mathsf{i}$, is called an *a-flush* transition provided that there exists the matching receive transition $\mathsf{i} \xrightarrow{l??} \mathsf{i}$ in R and for each state $d \neq \mathsf{i}$ of U, there is a matching receive transition of the form $d \xrightarrow{l??} a$ in R; a *flush* transition is an a-flush for some a. Intuitively, an a-flush transition pushes every process in its non-initial state, other than the one firing the transition, into local state a.
2. *Low-push*: Transition $a \xrightarrow{l!!} b$ is a *low-push* transition provided that, $b \neq \mathsf{i}$, $\neg(b \prec a)$, and for each state c such that $b \prec c$ there is a matching receive transition of the form $c \xrightarrow{l??} d$ such that $d \preceq b$; and, for all other states c, there is a matching self-loop receive transition $c \xrightarrow{l??} c$. Intuitively transition $a \xrightarrow{l!!} b$ is a low-push if it pushes every process in a local state strictly higher than b in the pre-order $\preceq$ into a state at most as high as b while leaving the rest of the processes untouched.

In practice, a natural pre-order $\preceq$ is normally supplied along with the diagram of U as it drawn in appropriate levels. If not, there is given in the section 3.4 an efficient algorithm ($O(|U|^2)$) to compute an appropriate pre-order if one exists.

To capture block replacement behavior, we also require that templates be *initializable*[3]. This means that from each state a of a protocol, there is a local transition of the form $a \xrightarrow{\tau} \mathsf{i}$. Such initializations model block replacement behavior, where a cache is non-deterministically pushed into its invalid state, irrespective of the current state of the block. For simplicity, re-initialization transitions and self-loop receptions are not drawn in state transition diagrams of cache protocols (cf. [8]).

[3] Initializability is not needed for the mathematical results of section 3.1; however, it is needed for the results of section 3.2.

Given U, the state transition digram for $U^n = (S^n, \Sigma, R^n, \mathfrak{i}^n)$, the system with n copies of U, is based on interleaving semantics in the standard way.

A *path* $x = x_0 x_1 ...$ of U^n is a sequence of states of S^n starting at the initial state $\mathfrak{i}^n$ of U^n such that for every $i \geq 0$, $(x_i, a, x_{i+1}) \in R^n$ for some $a \in \Sigma$. For global state s of U^n, and $i \in [1:n]$, we use $s[i]$ to denote the local state of process U_i in s and for computation path z of U^n, we use $z[i]$ to denote the local computation path of U_i in z, viz., the sequence $z_0[i]z_1[i]....$ We write $x.s \in U^n$ to mean that finite computation path x of U^n ends in global state s. In this paper we will focus on finite paths and computations as they suffice for safety. Finally, given global state s of U^n, and local state a of U, we let $num(a, s)$ denote the number of copies of a in s, viz., the number of processes in local state a in global state s.

3 Safety Properties

Given a state a of U, we say that a is *reachable* iff there exists n such that there is a finite computation of U^n leading to a state with a process in local state a. For cache coherence protocols, we are typically interested in *pairwise reachability*, viz., given a pair (a, b) of local states a and b of template U, deciding whether for some n, there exists a reachable global state of U^n, with a process in each of the local states a and b. For instance, in the case of the MSI protocol, we are interested in showing that none of the pairs in the set $\{(M, M), (M, S)\}$ is pairwise reachable.

3.1 Systems without Conjunctive Guards

In this section, we assume that U is a template without conjunctive guards; guards of the form *true* or $\bigvee \neg(\mathrm{i})$ are permitted. This allows us to handle the MSI, MOESI, MESI (not the Illinois version which is handled in the next section), Berkeley and N+1 protocols.

A standard technique for reasoning about parameterized systems involves the construction of an abstract graph to capture the behaviour of a system instance of arbitrary size. Classically, the abstract graph is defined to be a transition diagram over the set 2^S with a given concrete global state s of a system instance U^n being mapped via mapping ϕ, say, onto the set $A = \{a_i | num(a_i, s) \geq 1\}$. For $B, C \in 2^S$, a transition is introduced from B to C in the abstract graph iff there exists m and concrete states t and u of U^m such that $\phi(t) = B$, $\phi(u) = C$ and u results from t by firing a concrete transition of U^m. There is a loss of information in the mapping ϕ which is reflected in the fact that it might not be possible to identify a unique successor B of A in the abstract graph that results by firing a transition $tr = a \to b$, where $a \in A$. For instance if tr is a local transition, then two different successors are possible: $B_1 = A \setminus \{a\} \cup \{b\}$ and $B_2 = A \cup \{b\}$ depending, respectively, on whether there is exactly one or at least 2 copies of a in the concrete state that maps onto A. To preserve soundness we cover for both cases and introduce both B_1 and B_2 as possible successors. However this may generate bogus paths in the abstract graph, viz., paths for which there do not exist matching concrete computations. Thus there might exist paths in the abstract graph that don't "lift" to concrete computations and hence the above technique though sound is not complete.

In this paper to check pairwise reachability, we use the *abstract history graph* of U, denoted by $\mathcal{A}_U$, where we bypass the above problem by mapping each concrete state s onto a tuple of the form (a, A), that denotes a formal state with at least one copy of state a and finite but arbitrarily many copies of each state in A. As we later show this permits us to reason about safety properties in a sound and complete fashion.

Definition (representative). Given template $U = (S, \Sigma, R, \mathsf{i})$, and a finite computation $x.s$ of U^n, we define *rep*$(x.s)$ to be the tuple $(a, A) \in S \times 2^S$, where, if no flush transition was fired along x, then $a = \mathsf{i}$ and $A = \{s[j] \| j \in [1:n]\}$; and if U_i is the process to last fire a flush transition along x, then $s[i] = a$ and $A = \{s[j] \| j \in [1:n] \wedge j \neq i\}$.

Given template U, the *abstract history graph*, $\mathcal{A}_U = (\mathcal{S}_U, \mathcal{R}_U, (\mathsf{i}, \{\mathsf{i}\}))$, is a transition diagram defined over tuples of the form $(a, A) \in S \times 2^S$. For $x.s \in U^n$, for some n, we will show how to map $x.s$ onto a tuple of the form (a, A). This mapping depends not only on the global state s but also on x, viz., the history of the computation leading to s and thus the term *abstract history graph*. Essentially in tuple (a, A), state a records the local state in s of the process executing the last flush along x, whereas A is a superset of the set of the local states of the remaining processes. This dichotomy is justified on the basis of the fact that we can pump up the multiplicity of each local state in s to any desired value except possibly of the current local state in s of the process to last execute a flush along x which could have multiplicity exactly one as we later show.

We now define the transition relation $\mathcal{R}_U$. Towards that end, given a tuple (a, A) and a local or a broadcast send transition $tr = c \rightarrow d$, we define the successor of (a, A) via tr as either the *state-successor*, denoted by *state-succ*$((a, A), tr)$ or the *set-successor* of (a, A), denoted by *set-succ*$((a, A), tr)$. As mentioned above, we think of (a, A) as a state with finite but arbitrarily many copies of each state in A plus one copy of a. The case of the *state-successor* captures the scenario when a process in local state a that possibly has multiplicity only one fires tr while the case of the *set-successor* captures the scenario when a process in local state $c \in A$ with arbitrarily large multiplicity fires enabled transition tr.

Definition (state-successor). Let $(a, A) \in S \times 2^S$ and let transition $tr = a \rightarrow b \in R$ labeled by guard g, be enabled in (a, A), viz., if $g = \bigvee \neg(\mathsf{i})$, then $\exists a' \in A : a' \neq \mathsf{i}$. Then *state-succ*$((a, A), tr) = (b, B)$, where if tr is a local transition then $B = A$ and if tr is a broadcast send transition then $B = \{b' | \exists a' \in A : \exists a' \longrightarrow b' \in R$ *that is a matching receive for tr* $\}$.

As an example, since firing the transition $tr = \mathsf{I} \overset{PrRd!!}{\longrightarrow} \mathsf{S}$ of the MSI protocol affects only processes in state M by causing them to transit to state S, therefore *state-succ*$((\mathsf{I}, \{\mathsf{I}, \mathsf{S}\}), tr) = (\mathsf{S}, \{\mathsf{I}, \mathsf{S}\})$.

Definition (set-successor). Let $(a, A) \in S \times 2^S$ and let transition $tr = b \rightarrow c \in R$, where $b \in A$, be such that if tr is labeled by guard g then it is enabled in (a, A), viz., if $g = \bigvee \neg(\mathsf{i})$, then for some $a' \in \{a\} \cup A$: $a' \neq \mathsf{i}$. Then, *set-succ*$((a, A), tr)$, is defined as the tuple

- $(c, \{c', \mathsf{i}\})$ if tr is a c'-flush transition
- $(a, A \cup \{c\})$ if tr is a local transition. Note that since we had arbitrarily many copies of b to start with so even after firing local transition tr we are guaranteed arbitrarily

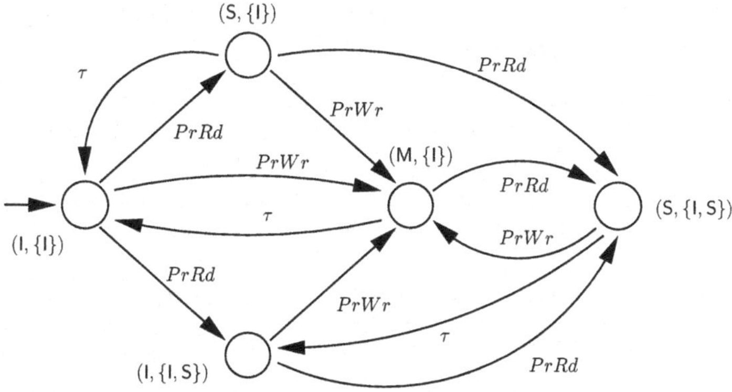

Fig. 2. The abstract history graph for the MSI Cache Coherence Protocol

many processes in local state b which is therefore not excluded from the second component of the resulting tuple.

- (d, B) if tr is a low-push broadcast transition, where $a \longrightarrow d$ is the (unique) matching receive for tr from a and $B = \{c\} \cup \{b' | \exists a' \in A : \exists a' \longrightarrow b' \in R$ that is a matching receive for tr $\}$. As in the previous case since we have arbitrarily many copies of b so in B we include the local state that results from firing the matching receive for tr from b which by definition of a low push transition (and the fact that $b \preceq b$) is b itself.

As an example, since firing the transition $tr = \mathsf{S} \overset{PrWr!!}{\longrightarrow} \mathsf{M}$ of the MSI protocol flushes every other process into state I, therefore *set-succ*$((\mathsf{I}, \{\mathsf{I}, \mathsf{S}\}), tr) = (\mathsf{M}, \{\mathsf{I}\})$. We now formally define the abstract history graph of a template U.

Definition (Abstract History Graph). Given template $U = (S, \Sigma, R, \mathsf{i})$, the *abstract history graph* of U, is defined to be the tuple $\mathcal{A}_U = (\mathcal{S}_U, \mathcal{R}_U, (\mathsf{i}, \{\mathsf{i}\}))$, where $\mathcal{S}_U = S \times 2^S$ and $\mathcal{R}_U = \{((a, A), (b, B)) | (b, B) =$ *state-succ*$((a, A), tr))$ *or* $(b, B) =$ *set-succ*$((a, A), tr))$ *for some local or broadcast send transition tr of* $U\}$.

As an example, the abstract history graph for the MSI protocol is shown in figure 3. Self loops are omitted for the sake of simplicity. For convenience, we have labeled each transition of the graph by the label of the transition responsible for "firing" it.

Note that as opposed to the classical construction, given a tuple (a, A) and transition tr both the set-successor and state-successor of (a, A) via tr are uniquely defined. This is because as will be shown in proposition 3.3, we can have arbitrarily many copies of each state in A thereby alleviating the problem of considering the different successors that may arise from concrete states with different counts of local states as was the case with the classical abstract graph construction. This permits us to give exact path correspondences between the parameterized family of concrete systems and the abstract history graph as we now show. Since we are dealing with systems of a "disjunctive" nature having (arbitrarily many) extra copies does not disable any transitions.

Given $x.s \in U^n$, the precise mapping of $x.s$ onto a tuple of $\mathcal{A}_U$ is given by the ω-representative of $x.s$, denoted by ω-*rep*$(x.s)$.

Definition (ω-representative). Let $x = x_0...x_l$ be a finite computation path of U^n. Then we define the *ω-representative* of $x.x_l$, denoted by ω-*rep*$(x.x_l)$, as the tuple $(a, A) \in S \times 2^S$, defined as follows: If $l = 0$, then $(a, A) = (\mathsf{i}, \{\mathsf{i}\})$, else suppose that transition $x_{l-1} \to x_l$ is initiated by transition tr of U, fired locally by process U_j and let U_k be the process to last execute a flush transition in $x_0...x_{l-1}$. Then

$$(a, A) = \begin{cases} state\text{-}succ(\omega\text{-}rep(x_0...x_{l-1}.x_{l-1}), tr) \ \ if\ j = k \\ \ \ set\text{-}succ(\omega\text{-}rep(x_0...x_{l-1}.x_{l-1}), tr) \ \ otherwise \end{cases}$$

The tuple *rep*$(x.s)$ specifies the actual set of states present in the global state s, having followed path x through U^m. In contrast, the ω-representative ω-*rep*$(x.s)$ incorporates not only the local states present in s but also the states that could potentially be present, given sufficiently many processes n, in a global state of U^n that results from firing (a stuttering of) the same local transitions as were fired along x to get to s. Thus, ω-*rep*$(x.s)$ drags along some "history" of the computation x leading to s, and thereby stores more information than *rep*$(x.s)$. This is formalized as follows.

Proposition 3.1 (Containment Property). Given $x.s \in U^n$, such that *rep*$(x.s) = (a, A)$ and ω-*rep*$(x.s) = (b, B)$, we have $a = b$ and $A \subseteq B$.

We now establish a "path correspondence" between finite computations of U^n and between finite paths of $\mathcal{A}_U$ starting at $(\mathsf{i}, \{\mathsf{i}\})$.

Proposition 3.2 (Projection). For any finite path $x.s$ in U^n, there exists a finite path $y.t$ in $\mathcal{A}_U$ starting at $(\mathsf{i}, \{\mathsf{i}\})$ such that $t = \omega$-*rep*$(x.s)$.

For the other direction, we have

Proposition 3.3 (Lifting). Let x be a path of $\mathcal{A}_U$ starting at $(\mathsf{i}, \{\mathsf{i}\})$ and leading to tuple (a, A) of $\mathcal{A}_U$. Then, given $p \geq 1$, there exists $y.t \in U^n$, for some n, such that *rep*$(y.t) = (a, A)$ and t has at least p copies of each state in A plus a copy of a.

Combining the previous three results, we have

Theorem 3.4 (Decidability Result). Pair $(a, b) \in S \times S$ is pairwise reachable iff there exists a path in $\mathcal{A}_U$ starting at $(\mathsf{i}, \{\mathsf{i}\})$ to a tuple of the form (c, C) where either $a = c$ and $b \in C$; or $b = c$ and $a \in C$; or $a \in C$ and $b \in C$.

Thus we have reduced the problem of pairwise reachability for a pair of local states of a given template U to the problem of reachability in $\mathcal{A}_U$, the abstract history graph constructed from U. Since the size of the abstract graph is $O(|U|2^{|U|})$, we have .

Corollary 3.5. The pairwise reachability problem for a pair of local states of a given template U can be solved in time $O(|U|2^{|U|})$, where $|U|$ is the size of template U as measured by the number of states and transitions in U.

Note that in the construction of $\mathcal{A}_U$, it suffices to consider only the set of tuples reachable from the initial tuple $(\mathsf{i}, \{\mathsf{i}\}))$. In practice, the number of states of this graph may be much smaller than the worst case scenario where it could be $|S| \times 2^{|S|}$. This is illustrated clearly by our experimental results in section 4.2.

3.2 Adding the Specialized Conjunctive Guard

To reason about systems wherein the templates are augmented with the specialized conjunctive guard along with the assumption of initializability, we use a modification of the abstract history graph. Broadly speaking, the intuition behind the modification is that we can make the specialized conjunctive guard of a process evaluate to true starting at any global state by driving all the other processes into their respective initial states by making use of the local initializing transition mentioned above. Thus for every tuple (a, A) in the abstract history graph, we add a transition of the form $(a, A) \rightarrow (a', \{\mathsf{i}\})$ where either $a' = a$ or $a' \in A$ to $\mathcal{A}_U$.

Definition (Modified Abstract History Graph). Given template $U = (S, \Sigma, R, \mathsf{i})$ and its abstract graph $\mathcal{A}_U = (\mathcal{S}_U, \mathcal{R}_U, (\mathsf{i}, \{\mathsf{i}\}))$, define the modified abstract graph $\mathcal{A}_U^{\mathcal{I}}$ to be the tuple $(\mathcal{S}_U, \mathcal{R}_U^{\mathcal{I}}, (\mathsf{i}, \{\mathsf{i}\})))$, where $\mathcal{R}_U^{\mathcal{I}}$ is the set of all transitions $((a, A), (b, B))$, where

- $B = \{\mathsf{i}\}$ and either $b = a$ or $b \in A$. This transition corresponds to the successive firing of the local initializing transition that leaves one process in state $b \in \{a\} \cup A$ and the rest of the processes in their initial states, thereby enabling guard $\bigwedge(\mathsf{i})$ labeling its transitions.
- $A = \{\mathsf{i}\} = B$ and $\exists tr = a \rightarrow b \in R$ labeled by $\bigwedge(\mathsf{i})$. This corresponds to the firing of a transition labeled with $\bigwedge(\mathsf{i})$.
- $\exists tr \in R$ labeled either by $\bigvee \neg(\mathsf{i})$ or by true such that either $(b, B) =$ *state-succ*$((a, A), tr)$ or $(b, B) =$ *set-succ*$((a, A), tr)))\}$ This correspond to the firing of transitions labeled with $\bigvee \neg(\mathsf{i})$ or true.

Then, as in section 3.1, we can show a "path correspondence" between concrete finite computations of U^n and finite paths in $\mathcal{A}_U^{\mathcal{I}}$ starting at $(\mathsf{i}, \{\mathsf{i}\})$. The proofs are similar and are therefore omitted. Thus as in section 3.1, we have the following decidability result from which it follows, as before, that for this model of computation, pairwise reachability can be decided in time $O(|U|2^{|U|})$, where $|U|$ is the size of the template U.

Theorem 3.6 (Decidability Result). Pair $(a, b) \in S \times S$ is pairwise reachable iff there exists a path in $\mathcal{A}_U^{\mathcal{I}}$ starting at $(\mathsf{i}, \{\mathsf{i}\})$ to a tuple of the form (c, C) where either $a = c$ and $b \in C$; or $b = c$ and $a \in C$; or $a \in C$ and $b \in C$.

3.3 Generating Error Traces

A critical part of the verification process, once an error is detected, is the generation of a concrete computation of the system at hand leading to an erroneous global state. Till now, we have shown how to reduce the verification process for safety properties

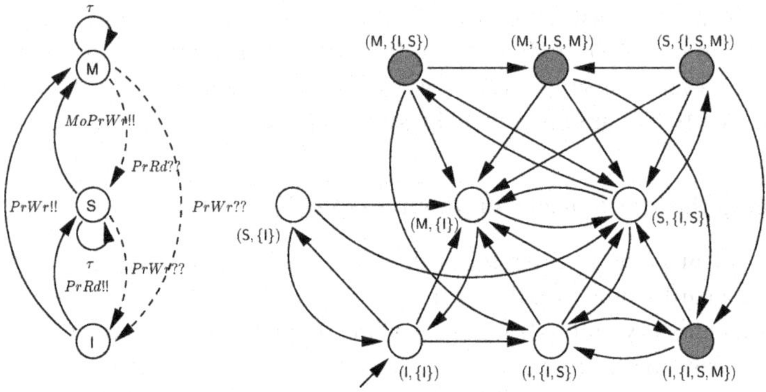

Fig. 3. The template for the Broken MSI Protocol and its abstract history graph

of the parameterized version of a given cache protocol to reachability analysis over the corresponding abstract history graph. This only allows us to detect an erroneous state in the abstract history graph and thereby construct a path in the abstract graph to an erroneous state. To get back a concrete computation of an instance of an original system leading to a concrete erroneous state, we make use of the construction used in proving proposition 3.3. Given a path x starting at the initial tuple $(\mathsf{i}, \{\mathsf{i}\})$ leading to an erroneous tuple (a, A) of the abstract history graph, this construction can be used to give a fully automated procedure to construct a finite computation y of a concrete system U^n, for some n, ending in a state t such that $rep(y.t) = (a, A)$. In general, n is of size linear in the length of x, viz., $O(|S|2^{|S|})$ in the worst case. But, as mentioned above, in practice, the number of states of the abstract history graph reachable from its initial state tend to be small and consequently so does the length of y. The ability to automatically generate error traces distinguishes our work from [9], where no effective way to generate error traces was given.

We now illustrate the construction with a broken version of the MSI protocol (figure 3). The MSI protocol is clobbered by replacing the flush transition labeled with $PrWr$!! from the shared state to the modified state by a low push transition labeled with $MoPrWr$!!. In the abstract history graph, self loops are omitted for simplicity reasons and erroneous tuples are shaded. Note that the erroneous pair $(\mathsf{I}, \{\mathsf{I}, \mathsf{S}, \mathsf{M}\})$ can be reached via the path $(\mathsf{I}, \{\mathsf{I}\}) \rightarrow (\mathsf{I}, \{\mathsf{I}, \mathsf{S}\}) \rightarrow (\mathsf{I}, \{\mathsf{I}, \mathsf{S}, \mathsf{M}\})$ by firing a transition labeled with $PrRd$ followed by a transition labeled with $MoPrWr$. From this path we can get back a concrete computation of a system with 3 caches by firing transitions labeled with $PrRd$, $PrRd$ and $MoPrWr$ in the order listed, a stuttering of the sequence $PrRd$, $MoPrWr$. The resulting concrete computation is: $(\mathsf{I}, \mathsf{I}, \mathsf{I}) \stackrel{PrRd_1!!}{\longrightarrow} (\mathsf{S}, \mathsf{I}, \mathsf{I}) \stackrel{PrRd_2!!}{\longrightarrow} (\mathsf{S}, \mathsf{S}, \mathsf{I}) \stackrel{MoPrWr_1!!}{\longrightarrow} (\mathsf{M}, \mathsf{S}, \mathsf{I})$. Here symbol a_i labeling a transition indicates that process U_i fires a transition of template U labeled with a.

3.4 Automatic Construction of Pre-order

In practice, one can usually obtain the natural pre-order by drawing the diagram in levels, reflecting how tightly a memory block in a given cache state is bound to the processor. Such levels are used in the textbook by Culler [8] et al. If not, we can efficiently exhibit a feasible pre-order, $\preceq$, that can be imposed, or determine that none exists.

We proceed by constructing the labeled, directed graph $Q_U = (S, \{\preceq, \prec, \neg\prec\}, E)$, where $E \subseteq S \times \{\preceq, \prec, \neg\prec\} \times S$ is its edge set. For $a, b \in S$, an edge of the form $(a, \preceq, b)$ represents $a \preceq b$, $(a, \prec, b)$ indicates $a \prec b$ and $(a, \neg\prec, b)$ means $\neg(a \prec b)$. We construct Q_U as follows.

1. Initially, $E = \{(\mathsf{i}, \prec, a) | a \neq \mathsf{i}, a \in S\}$. This is because of the assumption we made in the system model that for each $a \neq \mathsf{i}$, we have $\mathsf{i} \prec a$.

2. For each non-local transition or non-flush broadcast send transition[4], $tr = (a, l!!, b)$, we have $\neg(b \prec a)$. Thus we augment E by adding the edge $(b, \neg\prec, a)$. Furthermore if $(c, l??, d)$ is a matching receive for tr such that $c \neq d$, then we have that $d \preceq b \prec c$ and so we add the edges $(d, \preceq, b)$ and $(b, \prec, c)$ to E. On the other hand if $(d, l??, d)$ is a matching receive for tr, then we have that $\neg(b \prec d)$ and so we add the edge $(b, \neg\prec, d)$ to E. If E already contains an edge of the form $(e, \preceq, f)$, then in case we add the edge $(e, \prec, f)$ to E in the above step, we remove $(e, \preceq, f)$ to ensure that there is only one edge from e to f labeled with $\preceq$ or $\prec$.

Let Q'_U be the subgraph of Q_U that we get by deleting all edges labeled with $\neg\prec$. Then we can impose a pre-order $\preceq$ on the states of U compatible with its transitions iff

(1) there does not exist a cycle in Q'_U containing an edge labeled with $\prec$; and

(2) for each edge $(a, \neg\prec, b)$ of Q_U, there do not exist two distinct maximal strongly connected components of Q'_U, one containing state a and the other one containing state b such that there is path from a to b in Q'_U.

Since the maximal strongly connected components of Q'_U can be constructed in time linear in the size of Q_U, viz., linear in $|U|$, therefore the above mentioned conditions 1 and 2 can be checked in time quadratic in the size of U. Thus we can decide in $O(|U|^2)$ time whether a desired pre-order can be imposed on S or not.

4 Applications

As applications, we consider model checking parameterized versions of all of the snoop based cache protocols presented in [19]. The translation from the state transition diagram of a given protocol to its template is straightforward and syntactic and can be performed in the same mechanical fashion as was done for the MSI protocol in section 2.1: Firing a bold transition labeled with $A/-$ and/or one that requires that no other cache currently possesses the desired memory block does not affect the status of the memory block in any other cache. Such a transition is therefore labeled with the local transition label τ and in the second case also guarded with the $\bigwedge(\mathsf{i})$. Otherwise, a transition labeled by A/B, where $B \neq -$, is labeled with the broadcast send label $A!!$ while every transition

[4] Flush broadcast send transitions can be identified syntactically as all their matching receives from every non-initial state transit to a unique state with the matching receive from i self-looping on itself. Local transitions can be identified by the absence of matching receives.

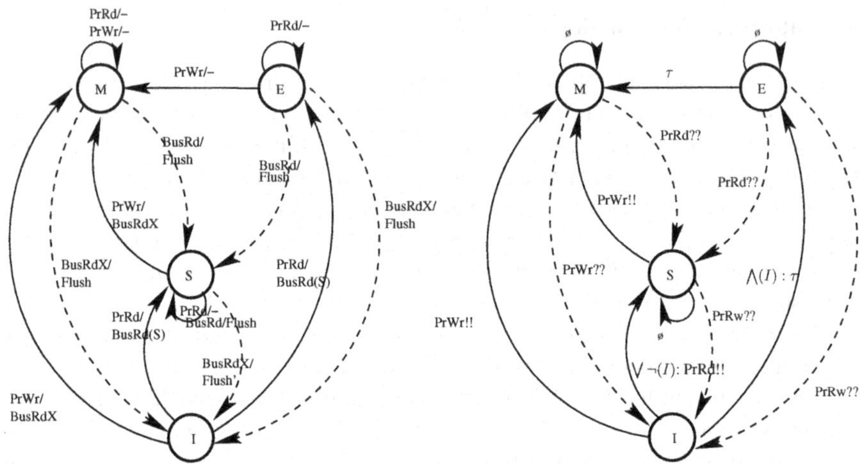

Fig. 4. The Illinois MESI Cache Coherence Protocol and its template

generated by bus actions (represented by dashed lines) and labeled with B/C is labeled with the matching broadcast receive label $A??$. If to fire the transition additionally requires some other cache to possess the desired memory block then it is also guarded by $\bigvee \neg(\mathsf{i})$. Below we consider only the *Illinois MESI* protocol in detail, with some others being handled in the full report [10].

4.1 The Illinois MESI Cache Coherence Protocol

The transition digram and the template for the Illinois MESI cache coherence protocol is shown in figure 4. Formally the template is defined as $U = (S, \Sigma, R, \{\mathsf{i}\})$ where, $S = \{\mathsf{I}, \mathsf{S}, \mathsf{E}, \mathsf{M}\}$ with the pre-order being given by $\mathsf{I} \prec \mathsf{S} \prec \mathsf{E} \approx \mathsf{M}$. The set $\Sigma = \{\tau, \mathsf{PrRd!!}, \mathsf{PrRd??}, \mathsf{PrWr!!}, \mathsf{PrWr??}\}$. The transitions are as defined below.

Empty Broadcasts (Local Transitions): $(\mathsf{M}, \tau, \mathsf{I})$, $(\mathsf{E}, \tau, \mathsf{I})$, $(\mathsf{S}, \tau, \mathsf{I})$, $(\mathsf{I}, \tau, \mathsf{E})$, $(\mathsf{S}, \tau, \mathsf{S})$, $(\mathsf{E}, \tau, \mathsf{E})$, $(\mathsf{M}, \tau, \mathsf{M})$. Note that the first three transitions are included because of the assumption of initializability and are for simplicity reasons not shown in figure 4 nor are broadcast receive transitions that are self loops.

Low-push sends: $(\mathsf{I}, \mathsf{PrRd!!}, \mathsf{S})$.

Low-push receives: $(\mathsf{M}, \mathsf{PrRd??}, \mathsf{S})$, $(\mathsf{E}, \mathsf{PrRd??}, \mathsf{S})$.

Flush sends: $(\mathsf{I}, \mathsf{PrWr!!}, \mathsf{M})$, $(\mathsf{S}, \mathsf{PrWr!!}, \mathsf{M})$.

Flush receives: $(\mathsf{M}, \mathsf{PrWr??}, \mathsf{I})$, $(\mathsf{E}, \mathsf{PrWr??}, \mathsf{I})$, $(\mathsf{S}, \mathsf{PrWr??}, \mathsf{I})$.

The transitions $(\mathsf{I}, \mathsf{PrRd!!}, \mathsf{S})$ and $(\mathsf{I}, \tau, \mathsf{E})$ are labeled with $\bigvee \neg(\mathsf{i})$ and $\bigwedge(\mathsf{i})$ respectively, with the rest of the transitions being labeled with the *true* guard.

We need to decide whether the following pairs are pairwise reachable: (M, M), (M, E), (M, S), (E, E), (E, S).

4.2 Experimental Results

Here we summarize the results for a wide range of examples of cache coherence protocols. For detailed descriptions of these protocols refer to [19]. The column under *# of Abstract States* refers to the number of reachable states in the abstract history graph for protocols that don't use conjunctive guards, viz., MSI, MESI, MOESI, Berkeley and N+1; and in the modified abstract history graph for ones that use conjunctive guards, viz., Illinois-MESI, Firefly and Dragon. It is worth noting that although in the worst case the number of reachable abstract states in the modified abstract history graph corresponding to the template $U = (S, R, \Sigma, \mathrm{i})$ could be as large as $|S|2^{|S|}$, in practice it typically turns out to be much smaller. For instance in the MESI protocol, the number of reachable abstract states were 6, against a worst case possibility of $4 \times 2^4 = 64$ states. A similar scenario holds for the other protocols. Thus, in conclusion, the abstract history graph construction seems to work well in practice. The experiments were carried out on a machine with a 797MHz Intel Pentium III processor and 256 Mb RAM. Below, we tabulate the results for a variety of cache coherence protocols. The user time for verifying each of the cache coherence protocols was less than 0.01 seconds.

Protocol	*Pre-Order*	*# of Abstract States*
MSI	*Invalid* $\prec$ *Shared* $\prec$ *Modified*	5
MESI	*Invalid* $\prec$ *Shared* $\prec$ *Exclusive* $\approx$ *Modified*	6
Illinois	*Invalid* $\prec$ *Shared* $\prec$ *Exclusive* $\approx$ *Modified*	6
MOESI	*Invalid* $\prec$ *Owned* $\approx$ *Shared* $\prec$ *Exclusive* $\approx$ *Modified*	7
N+1	*Invalid* $\prec$ *Valid* $\prec$ *Dirty*	5
Berkeley	*Invalid* $\prec$ *Owned Non-exclusively* $\approx$ *Unowned*; *Unowned* $\prec$ *Owned Exclusively*	5
Firefly	*Invalid* $\prec$ *Shared* $\prec$ *Dirty* $\approx$ *Valid Exclusive*	6
Dragon	*Invalid* $\prec$ *Shared Clean* $\approx$ *Shared Modified* $\prec$ *Exclusive*; *Exclusive* $\approx$ *Modified*	8

5 Concluding Remarks

The generally undecidable PMCP has received a good deal of attention in the literature. A number of interesting proposals have been put forth, and successfully applied to certain examples ([7,6,26,20,2,3,27,21]). Most of these works, however, suffer from the drawbacks of being either only partially automated or being sound but not guaranteed complete. Much human ingenuity may be required to develop, e.g., network invariants; the method may not terminate; the complexity may be intractably high; and the underlying abstraction may only be conservative, rather than exact.[5]

Similar limitations apply to prior work on PMCP for cache protocols. Pong and Dubois [25] described methods that were sound but not complete, as they were based on conservative, inexact abstractions. In [14] a general framework of parameterized *broadcast protocols* was introduced and it was shown how certain simple cache protocols

[5] However for frameworks that handle specialized applications domains decisions procedures can be given that are both sound and complete and fully automatic and in some cases efficient ([13,15,11,12,5,24]).

could be modeled. That framework, however, did not admit guarded transitions, necessary to model many cache protocols such as Illinois (MESI). In [16], it was shown that showed that PMCP for safety over such broadcast protocols of [14] is decidable using the general backward reachability procedure of [1]. However, the backward reachability algorithm of [1] that [16], makes use of, although general, suffers from the handicap that the best known bound for its running time is not known to be primitive recursive [23]. In [22], Maidl, using a proof tree based construction, shows decidability of the PMCP for a broad class of systems including broadcast protocols, but again the decision procedure is not known to be primitive recursive. Moreover [22,16,14] do not report experimental results for cache protocols.

More recently, Delzanno [9] uses arithmetical constraints to model global states of systems with many identical caches. This method uses invariant checking via backward reachability analysis of [1] and provides a broad framework for reasoning about cache coherence protocols but the procedure does not terminate on some examples. Furthermore, this technique does not provide a way to generate *error traces* when a bug is detected. In [17], it was shown that for a sub class of broadcast protocols called *entropic* broadcast protocols, a generalization of the Karp-Miller procedure for Petri nets terminates. While mathematically elegant, the model does not allow for boolean guards necessary for modeling protocols like Illinois-MESI, Firefly and Dragon. Also, no explicit bounds were provided on the size of the resulting coverability tree (cf. [23]).

In this paper we have exploited the hierarchical organization inherent in the design of snoopy cache protocols, representing and generalizing this organization using preorders. We then present a specialized variant of the broadcast protocols model called *pre-ordered protocols* tailored to capture snoopy cache coherence protocols. This has allowed us to provide a unified, fully automated and efficient method to reason about parameterized snoopy cache coherence protocols. Our method is unique in meeting all these important criteria: (a) it is sound and complete; (b) it is algorithmic; (c) it is *rapid* meaning reasonably efficient in principle: worst case complexity single exponential. (d) it has broad modeling power: handles all 8 examples from Handy's book; (e) it is *rapid* also meaning demonstrably efficient in experimental practice; each example protocol was verified — for parameterized correctness — in a fraction of a second; and (f) it caters for error trace recovery.

References

1. P. Abdulla, K. Cerans, B. Jonsson, Y. K. Tsay. General Decidability Theorems for Infinite State Systems. *LICS*. 1996.
2. P. Abdulla, A. Boujjani, B. Jonsson and M. Nilsson. Handling global conditions in parameterized systems verification. CAV 1999.
3. P. Abdulla and B. Jonsson. On the existence of network invariants for verifying parameterized systems. In *Correct System Design - Recent Insights and Advances*, 1710, LNCS, pp 180–197, 1999.
4. K. Apt and D. Kozen. Limits for automatic verification of finite-state concurrent systems. *Information Processing Letters*, 15, pages 307-309, 1986.
5. T. Arons, A. Pnueli, S. Ruah, J, Xu and L. Zuck. Parameterized Verification with Automatically Computed Inductive Assertions. CAV 2001, LNCS 2102, 2001.

6. M.C. Browne, E.M. Clarke and O. Grumberg. Reasoning about Networks with Many Identical Finite State Processes. *Information and Control*, 81(1), pages 13–31, April 1989.
7. E.M. Clarke, O. Grumberg and S. Jha. Verifying Parameterized Networks using Abstraction and Regular Languages. CONCUR. LNCS 962, pages 395–407, Springer-Verlag, 1995.
8. D. E. Culler and J. P. Singh. Parallel Computer Architecture: A Hardware/Software Approach. Morgan Kaufmann Publishers, 1998.
9. G. Delzanno. Automatic Verification of Parameterized Cache Coherence Protocols. CAV 2000, 51–68.
10. E.A. Emerson and V. Kahlon. This paper, full version. Available at `http://www.cs.utexas.edu/users/{emerson,kahlon}/tacas03/`
11. E.A. Emerson and V. Kahlon. Reducing Model Checking of the Many to the Few. CADE-17. LNCS , Springer-Verlag, 2000.
12. E.A. Emerson and V. Kahlon. Model Checking Large-Scale and Parameterized Resource Allocation Systems. TACAS, 2002.
13. E.A. Emerson and K.S. Namjoshi. Reasoning about Rings. POPL. pages 85–94, 1995.
14. E.A. Emerson and K.S. Namjoshi. On Model Checking for Non-Deterministic Infinite-State Systems. LICS 1998.
15. E.A. Emerson and K.S. Namjoshi. Automatic Verification of Parameterized Synchronous Systems. CAV. LNCS , Springer-Verlag, 1996.
16. J. Esparza, A Finkel and R. Mayr, On the Verification of Broadcast Protocols. LICS 1999.
17. A. Finkel and J. Leroux. A finite covering tree for analyzing entropic broadcast protocols. Proc. VCL 2000. Report DSSE-TR-2000-6, Univ. Southampton, GB.
18. S.M. German and A.P. Sistla. Reasoning about Systems with Many Processes. *J. ACM*, 39(3), July 1992.
19. J. Handy. The Cache Memory Book. Academic Press, 1993.
20. R. P. Kurshan and K. L. McMillan. A Structural Induction Theorem for Processes. PODC. pages 239–247, 1989.
21. D. Lesens, N. Halbwachs and P. Raymond. Automatic Verification of Parameterized Linear Network of Processes. POPL 1997. pp 346–357, 1997.
Parallel Coordination Programs I.*Acta Informatica 21*, 1984.
22. M. Maidl. A Unifying Model Checking Approach for Safety Properties of Parameterized Systems. CAV 2001.
23. K. McAloon. Petri Nets and Large Finite Sets. *Theoretical Computer Science 32*, pp. 173–183, 1984.
24. A. Pnueli, S. Ruah and L. Zuck. Automatic Deductive Verification with Invisible Invariants. TACAS 2001, LNCS, 2001.
25. F. Pong and M. Dubois. A New Approach for the Verification of Cache Coherence Protocols. *IEEE Transactions on Parallel and Distributed Systems*, Vol. 6, No. 8, August 1995.
26. A. P. Sistla, Parameterized Verification of Linear Networks Using Automata as Invariants, CAV, 1997.
27. P. Wolper and V. Lovinfosse. Verifying Properties of Large Sets of Processes with Network Invariants. In J. Sifakis(ed) *Automatic Verification Methods for Finite State Systems*, Springer-Verlag, LNCS 407, 1989.

Proof-Like Counter-Examples

Arie Gurfinkel and Marsha Chechik

Department of Computer Science, University of Toronto,
Toronto, ON M5S 3G4, Canada.
{arie,chechik}@cs.toronto.edu

Abstract. Counter-examples explain why a desired temporal logic property fails to hold, and as such considered to be the most useful form of output from model-checkers. Reported explanations are typically short and described in terms of states and transitions of the model; as a result, they can be effectively used for debugging. However, counter-examples are not available for every CTL property and are often inadequate for explaining exactly what the answer means [CLJV02].
In this paper, we present the approach of annotating counter-examples with additional proof steps. This approach does not sacrifice any of the advantages of traditional counter-examples, yet allows the user to understand and navigate through the counter-example better. We describe our proof system, discuss how to connect it with counter-example generators, and present KEGVis – a tool for visualizing and browsing the annotated counter-examples.

1 Introduction

A model-checker can tell the user not only whether a desired temporal property holds, but also generate a counter-example, explaining the reasons why this property failed. Typically, counter-examples are fairly small and are given in terms of states and transitions of the model; thus, they are readily understood by engineers and can be effectively used for debugging the model. The counter-example generation ability has been one of the major advantages of model-checking in comparison with other verification methods.

Counter-examples are a form of mathematical proof: to disprove that some property φ holds on all elements of some set S, it is sufficient to produce a single element $s \in S$ such that $\neg\varphi$ holds on s. For model-checking, this has two ramifications. First, counter-examples are restricted to universally-quantified formulas, and second, counter-examples have been viewed as infinite or finite *paths*, starting from the initial state, that illustrate failure of a given property. This notion of path-like counter-examples has been implemented in SMV [McM93,CGMZ95]. Yet only a subset of universally-quantified CTL (ACTL), namely ACTL $\cap$ LTL, has linear counter-examples [CLJV02]. Recent work by Clarke et. al. [CLJV02] has extended this notion to *tree-like* counter-examples. This method generates trees instead of paths as counter-examples and is complete for ACTL. For example, a counter-example for $AF(\neg y \ \wedge \ AX\neg x)$, where shaded areas indicate which subformula is being disproved, is shown in Figure 1. This example is taken from [CLJV02]. Note that tree-like counter-examples are fairly hard to understand: different parts of the counter-example correspond to different parts of the property; thus, local information is insufficient to understand what each branch is attempting to disprove.

H. Garavel and J. Hatcliff (Eds.): TACAS 2003, LNCS 2619, pp. 160–175, 2003.

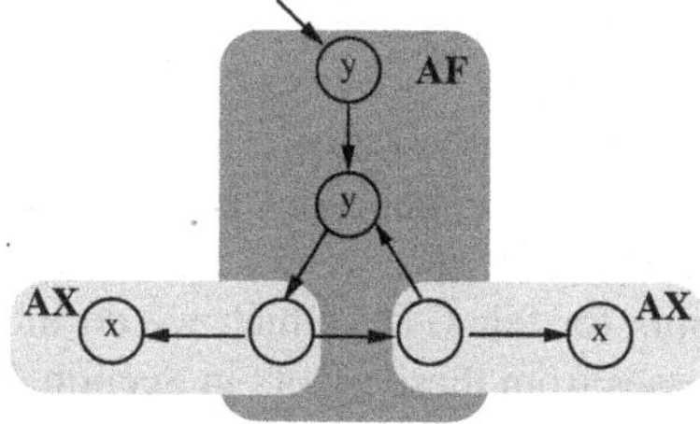

Fig. 1. Counter-example for $AF(\neg y \ \wedge \ AX\neg x)$ (from [CLJV02]).

This makes it difficult to navigate to "interesting" parts of the counter-example, so the user has to understand the counter-example in its entirety.

The typical approach of existing counter-example generators is to give a complete explanation, if it is available. Yet the model-checker cannot explain why an existential property is false or why a universal one is true, and gives no feedback to the user in these cases. Such an explanation could include the entire model! Thus, in general, we say that a counter-example is not available if it is too large to be practical. Certainly, the problem gets even more difficult when temporal quantifiers are nested, e.g., $EFAX\varphi$ (is there a reachable state from which φ holds in all successors?). Counter-example generators, conventional or tree-like, do not give the user any feedback for such properties, even though counter-examples are available for parts of the formula.

The goals of the work reported in this paper are as follows: (1) to preserve the desired usability aspects of counter-examples, i.e., their short length and the close correspondence to the model; (2) to provide some feedback even if in general the counter-example is not available; (3) to help the user in *understanding* complex counter-examples.

Our results follow from the primary observation that counter-examples are simply proofs by example; yet they are the *coarsest* type of proofs which skips all steps except those that result in the transition to the next state. Additional proof steps that explain *why* the model-checker chose this sequence of states for presentation can be added as means of annotating the counter-examples. With this approach, short linear counter-examples remain intuitive, but long and bushy counter-examples become significantly easier to understand because the user can refer to the proof for the explanation. Further, when counter-examples are not available, they can be replaced by proof obligations which are either discharged by a theorem-prover or taken on faith. For example, if the model-checker determines that a property $AX\varphi$ holds, we (1) show which states are successors of the current state; (2) indicate that φ holds in these states; and (3) generate a proof obligation that the current state has no additional successors. The user might check the last claim by using a theorem-prover or simply by eye-balling the model. We call the resulting construction *proof-like counter-examples*.

In this paper, we present and formalize the concept of proof-like counter-examples and show how to generate them from a run of a model-checker. We also describe a system for visualizing and browsing such counter-examples. Here, we concentrate on the problem of computing witnesses to existential properties. This problem is dual to the one of computing counter-examples. We choose witnesses for our presentation because we find it more natural to talk about why a property is true as opposed to why a negation of a property is false [CGMZ95].

The rest of this paper is organized as follows: Section 2 introduces our notation and gives some background on CTL model-checking. Before we can describe the generation and the presentation of proof-like witnesses, we have to develop a proof system that allows us to generate proofs for fair CTL, which we do in Section 3. We show how to extract proof-like witnesses from these proofs in Section 4. Section 4 also discusses tool support for browsing these witnesses. Our primary goal is not to produce proofs for all possible temporal properties. In that, we differ from the work that uses model-checking for proof generation [PZ01,PPZ01,Nam01,TC02]. Instead, we concentrate on annotating counter-examples with proof steps. We compare our results with related work in Section 5. Section 6 concludes the paper with the summary of our approach and venues for future work.

2 Background

We assume that the reader is familiar with the basics of model checking and CTL; this information is available in [CGP99]. Below, we recall some specific concepts and fix the notation.

We use $\top$ and $\bot$ to represent *True* and *False*, respectively. $\mathbb{B}$ and $\mathbb{N}$ are the set of boolean values $\{\top, \bot\}$ and all natural numbers, respectively. An unnamed function over the domain D is denoted by $\lambda x \in D \cdot$ *F-n Body*. $\mu Z \cdot f(Z)$ and $\nu Z \cdot f(Z)$ are the least and the greatest fixpoints of a function f, respectively.

A Kripke structure is a tuple $M = (S, R, s_0, A, I)$ where S is a set of states; $R : S \times S \to \mathbb{B}$ is a (total) transition function; $s_0 \in S$ is an initial state, A is a set of atomic propositions; and $I : S \to 2^A$ is a (total) labeling function. CTL formulas are evaluated over infinite trees of computations produced by M . We write $[\![\varphi]\!]^M(s)$ to indicate the value of φ in state s of M. If M is clear from the context, we omit it from our notation. If a formula φ holds in the initial state, i.e. $[\![\varphi]\!](s_0) = \top$, it is considered to hold in the model.

We use EG, EX and EU as our adequate set for CTL [CGP99]. These operators are defined as follows:

$$\begin{array}{rll} EX\varphi & \triangleq \lambda s \cdot \exists t \in S \cdot R(s,t) \wedge [\![\varphi]\!](t) & \text{def. of } EX \\ EG\varphi & \triangleq \nu Z \cdot \varphi \wedge EXZ & \text{def. of } EG \\ E[\varphi\, U\, \psi] & \triangleq \mu Z \cdot \psi \vee (\varphi \wedge EXZ) & \text{def. of } EU \end{array}$$

We also explicitly define the bounded versions of EU:

$$\begin{array}{ll} E[\varphi\, U_0\, \psi] \triangleq \psi & \text{def. of } EU_0 \\ E[\varphi\, U_i\, \psi] \triangleq \psi \vee (\varphi \wedge EXE[\varphi\, U_{i-1}\, \psi]) & \text{def. of } EU_i \end{array}$$

Note that

$$E[\varphi\, U\, \psi] = E[\varphi\, U_\infty\, \psi]$$

The remaining operators can be computed from these, as shown in [CGP99].

Fig. 2. A simple Kripke structure.

A computation of M on which all of the given fairness conditions $C = \{c_1, ..., c_k\}$ occur infinitely often is called a *fair computation*. Model-checking restricted to fair computations of M is called *fair*, and the resulting language is called FCTL. This language can be obtained by providing a fair version of EG ($E_C G$) as follows:

$$E_C G\varphi \triangleq \nu Z \cdot \varphi \wedge \bigwedge_{i=1}^{k} EXE[\varphi U \varphi \wedge c_i \wedge Z] \quad \text{def. of } E_C G$$

Thus, $[\![E_C G\top]\!](s) = \top$ if and only if s is a starting state of some fair computation of M. Computing $E_C X\varphi$ in s amounts to restricting successors of s to the ones at the start of some fair computation, and evaluating $EX\varphi$ using only these successors. Computing $E_C U$ is similar:

$$\begin{array}{lll} E_C X\varphi & \triangleq EX(\varphi \wedge E_C G\top) & \text{def. of } E_C X \\ E_C[\varphi\, U\, \psi] & \triangleq E[\varphi\, U\, (\psi \wedge E_C G\top)] & \text{def. of } E_C U \end{array}$$

ECTL is the universal fragment of CTL where every path is existentially quantified and negation is restricted to atomic propositions. ACTL is the dual universal fragment of CTL, i.e., only universal quantification is allowed. Their fair counterparts are referred to as FECTL and FACTL, respectively.

In this paper, we use p and q to stand for arbitrary atomic propositions, s and t to represent states, and φ and ψ to represent CTL formulas. We also use the notation $\{s\}$ to express a formula that evaluates to $\top$ at state s and $\bot$ otherwise, i.e. $[\![\{s\}]\!](t) \triangleq (s = t)$. We use $\overline{\{s\}}$ for the negation of $\{s\}$.

3 Generating Proofs

In this section, we develop a proof system that allows us to generate proofs for fair CTL. We start with ECTL and then extend our framework to deal with fairness, universal quantification, and negation, resulting in fair CTL. We show how to extract proof-like witnesses from these proofs in Section 4.

3.1 Proof Rules for ECTL

Our initial goal is to develop a sound and complete proof system that allows us to prove validity of sentences of the form $[\![\varphi]\!](s)$, where φ is an ECTL formula, and s is a state of a given Kripke structure M.

We assume that our proof system includes all axioms of boolean and propositional logic. Several of such axioms are shown in Figure 3. For example, in the one-point rule, also known as the $\exists$ introduction rule, f is a predicate and d is some element of D. Intuitively, the one-point rule states that to justify an existential statement $\exists x \in D \cdot f(x)$,

$$\frac{a}{a \vee b}\ \vee\text{-intro} \qquad \frac{a \quad b}{a \wedge b}\ \wedge\text{-intro}$$

$$\frac{b}{a \vee b}\ \vee\text{-intro} \qquad \frac{f(d)}{\exists x \in D \cdot f(x)}\ \text{one-point rule}$$

$$\frac{f(d_1) \qquad f(d_2) \qquad \ldots \qquad f(d_n)}{\forall d \in D \cdot f(d)}\ \text{finite quantification, with } \bigcup_{i=1}^{n}\{d_i\} = D$$

$$\frac{\forall x \in D_1 \cdot f(x) \wedge g(x) \qquad \forall x \in D \setminus D_1 \cdot \neg f(x)}{\forall x \in D \cdot f(x) \rightarrow g(x)}\ \text{universal case splitting}$$

Fig. 3. Some axioms of propositional and boolean logic.

$$\frac{\top}{[\![\top]\!](s)}\ \text{value-rule} \qquad \frac{[\![\varphi]\!](s) \quad [\![\psi]\!](s)}{[\![\varphi \wedge \psi]\!](s)}\ \wedge\text{-rule}$$

$$\frac{I(s,p)}{[\![p]\!](s)}\ \text{atomic-rule} \qquad \frac{[\![\varphi]\!](s) \vee [\![\psi]\!](s)}{[\![\varphi \vee \psi]\!](s)}\ \vee\text{-rule}$$

$$\frac{\neg I(s,p)}{[\![\neg p]\!](s)}\ \text{neg-atomic-rule} \qquad \frac{\exists t \in S \cdot R(s,t) \wedge [\![\varphi]\!](t)}{[\![EX\varphi]\!](s)}\ EX$$

Fig. 4. Proof rules for non-temporal operators and EX.

one simply needs to exhibit an element $d \in D$ for which $f(d)$ holds. Note also we only consider quantification over finite domains.

In addition, we assume that all axioms of the theory of Kripke structures and the axiomatization of a particular Kripke structure M are available. The latter includes statements about M's transition relation R and its labeling function I. For example, some of the axioms describing the Kripke structure in Figure 2 are:

$$\begin{array}{ll} R(s_0, s_1) = \top & I(s_0, p) = \top \\ R(s_0, s_0) = \bot & I(s_0, q) = \bot \end{array}$$

The proof rules for non-temporal operators and EX are shown in Figure 4. They follow directly from the definition of the corresponding operators. The EX-rule introduces an existential quantifier, which is typically eliminated by the one-point rule shown in Figure 3.

The proof rules for the bounded EU are given in Figure 5 and follow directly from the definition of this operator. To derive the rule for the unbounded EU, we start by noting the monotonicity of EU_i:

$$\frac{[\![\psi]\!](s)}{[\![E[\varphi\; U_0\; \psi]]\!](s)}\; EU_0 \qquad \frac{\exists n \in \mathbb{N} \cdot [\![E[\varphi\; U_n\; \psi]]\!](s)}{[\![E[\varphi\; U\; \psi]]\!](s)}\; EU$$

$$\frac{[\![\psi \vee (\varphi \wedge EXE[\varphi\; U_{i-1}\; \psi])]\!](s)}{[\![E[\varphi\; U_i\; \psi]]\!](s)}\; EU_i$$

$$\frac{[\![(\varphi \wedge EXE[\varphi\; U\; \varphi \wedge \{s\}]) \vee (\varphi \wedge EXEG(\varphi \wedge \overline{\{s\}}))]\!](s)}{[\![EG\varphi]\!](s)}\; EG$$

Fig. 5. Proof rules for EU and EG.

Proposition 1 *Let φ, ψ be ECTL formulas and $i, j \in \mathbb{N}$. Then,*

$$i \geq j \Rightarrow \forall s \in S \cdot ([\![E[\varphi\; U_i\; \psi]]\!](s) \Leftarrow [\![E[\varphi\; U_j\; \psi]]\!](s))$$

Since we assume that the state space is finite, the rule is actually bi-directional. That is, for a given Kripke structure M, there always exists a natural number n, which depends on the diameter of the directed graph induced by M, such that $E[\varphi\; U\; \psi] = E[\varphi\; U_n\; \psi]$. The proof rule for the unbounded EU is given in Figure 5.

To complete our proof system, we need to find a proof rule for EG. Unfortunately, we cannot proceed in the same manner as before and use the ECTL equivalence $EG\varphi = \varphi \wedge EXEG\varphi$. Doing so would result in a proof system which is not complete, since this proof rule can potentially be applied an infinite number of times.

Instead, note that $[\![EG\varphi]\!](s)$ is the result of evaluating $G\varphi$ on all infinite paths emanating from the state s. Moreover, since we are dealing with finite state systems, every infinite path can be decomposed into a finite (possibly empty) prefix and a finite repeating suffix. Thus, we can decompose $[\![EG\varphi]\!](s)$ into EG restricted to all non-trivial cycles around s, and EG restricted to all infinite paths that do not contain s in the future.

First, we consider the restriction of $[\![EG\varphi]\!](s)$ to all non-trivial cycles around s. Essentially, this is simply a fair-EG, where the fairness condition is given by a single formula $\{s\}$. That is, the set of non-trivial cycles around s is exactly the set of paths along which s occurs infinitely often. Furthermore, since our starting state is s, any infinite path along which s occurs infinitely often is equivalent to a finite path from s to itself. Thus, to evaluate $[\![EG\varphi]\!](s)$ restricted to cycles around s, it is sufficient to consider only finite paths from s to s. This intuition is formalized in the following theorem, the proof of which is available in [Gur02]:

Theorem 1 *Let φ be an ECTL formula and s be a state of a Kripke structure. Then,*

$$[\![EG\varphi]\!](s) = [\![(\varphi \wedge EXE[\varphi\; U\; \varphi \wedge \{s\}]) \vee (\varphi \wedge EXEG(\varphi \wedge \overline{\{s\}}))]\!](s)$$

A proof rule for EG is given in Figure 5.

Theorem 2 *The proof system for ECTL is sound and complete.*

Proof:
The proof of soundness comes from the fact that our proof rules have been derived using definitions and equivalences between ECTL operators.

To prove completeness, we show that any valid statement of the form $[\![\varphi]\!](s)$ can be proven by a finite number of applications of our proof rules. The proof proceeds on the structure of the formula φ. A proof sketch follows:

(1) Let φ be a propositional temporal formula, that is, φ does not contain EU and EG. Each rule given in Figure 4 reduces φ to its subformulas. Thus, the rest of the proof for this case proceeds by induction on the number of subformulas of φ.

(2) If in addition to (1), φ can also contain EU_i, EU_i can be removed by expanding it using rules for EU_0 and EU_i given in Figure 5.

(3) If φ can contain bounded or unbounded EU, we note that for a given Kripke structure, there exists an equivalent formula in which all unbounded EU operators are replaced by their bounded versions, reducing the resulting formula to case (2) considered above.

(4) If φ can also contain EG, i.e., $\varphi \in$ ECTL, the EG-rule reduces a formula with EG to two formulas: (a) the one with EU, handled by the above case, and (b) a new formula containing EG, where the EG operator is restricted to a subset of the state space which does not contain the current state s. Therefore, this rule can only be applied up to $|S|$ times, ensuring that a valid statement $[\![\varphi]\!](s)$ can be proven by a finite number of applications of our proof rules. □

3.2 Automatic Proof Generation

Given a statement $[\![\varphi]\!](s)$, we are interested in an automated proof of its validity. We can achieve this by embedding the proof system of Section 3.1 into an automated theorem prover, such as PVS [OSR93], and use its facilities for generating the proof. Yet we can do so more efficiently if we use the model-checker as a decision procedure for (a) deciding the validity of a given subformula (so that our proof generator avoids exploring irrelevant proof branches) and for (b) applying the one-point rule. We call this decision procedure `modelCheck` and assume that `modelCheck`(φ, s) computes $[\![\varphi]\!](s)$.

We start with the boolean connective $\vee$. Given a statement of the form $[\![\varphi \vee \psi]\!](s)$, we apply the $\vee$-rule:

$$\frac{[\![\varphi]\!](s) \vee [\![\psi]\!](s)}{[\![\varphi \vee \psi]\!](s)} \ \vee\text{-rule}$$

Next, we must apply the $\vee$-introduction rule, using either φ or ψ. Since the choice depends on the validity of $[\![\varphi]\!](s)$ and $[\![\psi]\!](s)$, this suggests a simple proof strategy: if $[\![\varphi]\!](s)$ is valid, apply the $\vee$-introduction rule with φ; otherwise, if $[\![\psi]\!](s)$ is valid, apply the $\vee$-introduction rule with ψ; otherwise, terminate declaring that the statement is invalid. This proof strategy is implemented by an algorithm shown in Figure 6(a).

We now examine the case of the unbounded until (EU) operator. Given the statement $[\![E[\varphi\ U\ \psi]]\!](s)$, we first apply the EU-rule:

$$\frac{\exists n \in \mathbb{N} \cdot [\![E[\varphi\ U_n\ \psi]]\!](s)}{[\![E[\varphi\ U\ \psi]]\!](s)} \ EU$$

(a)
```
proc orRule(φ, ψ, s)
  k_φ := modelCheck(φ, s)
  k_ψ := modelCheck(ψ, s)
  if k_φ then
    apply ∨-introduction with φ
  else if k_ψ then
    apply ∨-introduction with ψ
  else
    terminate with invalid
  end if
end proc
```

(c)
```
proc exOnePoint(φ, s, ℓ)
  k := modelCheck(EX φ, s)
  if not k then
    terminate with invalid
  end if
  t̂ := exWitness(φ, s)
  apply the one-point rule substituting t̂ for t
end proc
```

(b)
```
proc euOnePoint(φ, ψ, s, ℓ)
  i := 0
  eu := modelCheck(E[φ U ψ], s)
  eui = ⊥
  while eui ≠ eu do
    eui := modelCheck(E[φ U_i ψ], s)
    i := i + 1
  end while
  if eui then
    apply the one-point rule substituting i for n
  else
    terminate with invalid
  end if
end proc
```

Fig. 6. Algorithms for generating proof-like witnesses.

The next step is to find an instantiation of n for the one-point rule. Recall that the bounded EU_i is monotone when viewed as a function of i (by Proposition 1). Moreover, it is bounded above by the unbounded EU. Therefore, we can find the instantiation of n by a linear search, starting from $n = 0$. The algorithm for the application of the one-point rule is given in Figure 6(b). The intermediate computations performed by this algorithm are exactly the same as the ones done by a symbolic model-checking algorithm. Thus, if the results of the intermediate computations performed by modelCheck$(E[\varphi\ U\ \psi], s)$ are available, a more efficient binary search can be used instead of the linear one.

For example, consider the Kripke structure in the Figure 2 and assume that we want to prove that $[\![E[p\ U\ q]]\!](s_0)$. After the application of the EU-rule, we get

$$\exists n \in \mathbb{N} \cdot [\![E[p\ U_n\ q]]\!](s_0)$$

To apply the one-point rule, we first try $[\![E[p\ U_0\ q]]\!](s_0) = [\![q]\!](s_0)$. This yields $\bot$. Increasing the bound, we get $[\![E[p\ U_1\ q]]\!](s_0) = \top$ and therefore can apply the one-point rule by instantiating n to 1.

Finally, given the statement $[\![EX\varphi]\!](s)$, we start by applying the EX rule:

$$\frac{\exists t \in S \cdot R(s,t) \wedge [\![\varphi]\!](t)}{[\![EX\varphi]\!](s)}\ EX$$

Then, we need to eliminate the existential quantifier by applying the one-point rule. First, let us define a function *img* : $S \to \mathbb{B}$ as

$$img(x) \triangleq R(s,x) \wedge [\![\varphi]\!](x)$$

Clearly,

$$\exists t \in S \cdot R(s,t) \wedge [\![\varphi]\!](t) \Leftrightarrow \exists t \in S \cdot img(t) = \top$$

Thus, to apply the one-point rule, we need to find an element $\hat{t} \in img^{-1}(\top)$. Unfortunately, unlike the previous cases, we cannot obtain this element by only using the model-checker as a black box. Note, however, that if a path $s, \hat{t}$ is a witness to $[\![EX\varphi]\!](s)$, then the element $\hat{t} \in img^{-1}(\top)$. Thus, we assume the availability of a function $\texttt{exWitness}(\varphi, s)$ which computes a witness to $[\![EX\varphi]\!](s)$. A version of this function can be easily obtained from any symbolic model-checker. The algorithm for the application of the one-point rule in the case of EX is given in Figure 6(c).

3.3 Extention to FCTL

Here we extend the results presented earlier in this section: to fair ECTL (FECTL), to ACTL, and finally to full FCTL.

Extention to ECTL with fairness Let a set of fairness conditions $C = \{c_1, ..., c_k\}$ be given. $E_C G$, a fair version of EG, is defined as a restriction of EG to paths where each fairness condition occurs infinitely often (see Section 2). This intuition is formalized below:

Theorem 3 *Let $C = \{c_1, \ldots, c_k\}$ be a set of fairness conditions, and $F_i(Z) = EX\ E[\varphi\ U\ \varphi \wedge c_i \wedge Z]$. Then,*

$$E_C G\varphi = \nu Z \cdot \varphi \wedge (F_1 \circ \ldots \circ F_k)(Z)$$

For example, if $C = \{c_1, c_2\}$, then

$$E_C G\varphi = \nu Z \cdot \varphi \wedge EXE[\varphi\ U\ \varphi \wedge c_1 \wedge EXE[\varphi\ U\ \varphi \wedge c_2 \wedge Z]]$$

The proofs of this and the remaining theorems in this paper are available in [Gur02].

The proof rule for $E_C G$ is obtained similarly to the EG-rule. We show how $[\![E_C G\varphi]\!](s)$ can be decomposed into (1) $E_C G$ restricted to fair cycles around s and (2) fair paths that do not contain s, and then use this result to define the proof rule.

Theorem 4 *Let φ be a FECTL formula, s be a state of a Kripke structure, $C = \{c_1, \ldots, c_k\}$ be a set of fairness conditions, and F_i be defined as in Theorem 3. Then*

$$[\![E_C G\varphi]\!](s) = [\![(\varphi \wedge (F_1 \circ \cdots \circ F_k)(EXE[\varphi\ U\ \varphi \wedge \{s\}])) \vee (\varphi \wedge EXE_C G(\varphi \wedge \overline{\{s\}}))]\!](s)$$

This theorem gives rise to the proof rule for $E_C G$, shown in Figure 7.

Recall from Section 2 that other FECTL operators are defined through $E_C G$, so no additional proof rules are required.

Theorem 5 *The proof system for FECTL is sound and complete.*

The proof is similar to the one for ECTL.

$$\frac{[\![(\varphi \wedge (F_1 \circ \cdots \circ F_k)(EXE[\varphi\, U\, \varphi \wedge \{s\}])) \vee (\varphi \wedge EXE_CG(\varphi \wedge \overline{\{s\}}))]\!](s)}{[\![E_CG\varphi]\!](s)}\ E_CG$$

Fig. 7. A proof rule for E_CG.

$$\frac{\forall t \in S \cdot R(s,t) \rightarrow [\![\varphi]\!](t)}{[\![AX\varphi]\!](s)}\ AX$$

$$\frac{[\![\varphi \wedge AXAG(\{s\} \vee \varphi)]\!](s)}{[\![AG\varphi]\!](s)}\ AG$$

$$\frac{[\![\psi]\!](s)}{[\![A[\varphi\, U_0\, \psi]]\!](s)}\ AU_0$$

$$\frac{[\![\psi \vee (\varphi \wedge AXA[\varphi\, U_{i-1}\, \psi])]\!](s)}{[\![A[\varphi\, U_i\, \psi]]\!](s)}\ AU_i$$

$$\frac{\exists n \in \mathbb{N} \cdot [\![A[\varphi\, U_n\, \psi]]\!](s)}{[\![A[\varphi\, U\, \psi]]\!](s)}\ AU$$

Fig. 8. Proof rules for ACTL.

Extension to ACTL The ACTL subset of CTL is very similar to ECTL. The essential difference is that the EX operator in the fixpoint definition of the ECTL temporal operators is replaced by its dual AX. The proof rules are derived similarly to the ones for ECTL, and are summarized in Figure 8.

The AX-rule introduces universal quantification over the state space. Although the state-space is finite, the result is too large to present to the user explicitly and thus forms the basis of a proof obligation. Yet sometimes it is possible to reduce the complexity of such proof obligations. The application of the universal case splitting rule

$$\frac{\forall t \in S_1 \cdot R(s,t) \wedge [\![\varphi]\!](t) \qquad \forall t \in S \setminus S_1 \cdot \neg R(s,t)}{\forall t \in S \cdot R(s,t) \rightarrow [\![\varphi]\!](t)}\ \text{universal case splitting}$$

tells us that we can show that φ holds for all successors of s, and no other states are successors of s. If the set S_1 is relatively small, it is demonstrated to the user via the finite quantification rule:

$$\frac{R(s,t_1) \wedge [\![\varphi]\!](t_1) \quad \ldots \quad R(s,t_n) \wedge [\![\varphi]\!](t_n)}{\forall t \in S_1 \cdot R(s,t) \wedge [\![\varphi]\!](t)}\ \text{finite quantification, with } \bigcup_{i=1}^{n}\{t_i\} = S_1$$

and the fact that the elements of $S \setminus S_1$ are not successors of s is retained as a proof obligation.

ACTL proofs that do not involve the use of AX, such as proving $[\![A[\varphi\ U\ \psi]]\!](s)$ when $[\![\psi]\!](s)$ holds, are generated automatically.

Extension to FCTL To extend the proof rules to full CTL, we need to extend the neg-atomic-rule to temporal operators. Using the well-known dualities between ECTL and ACTL operators [CGP99], we obtain the negation rules summarized in Figure 9. Note that the negation applied to the EU operator (neg-EU rule) is handled differently. Since

$$\frac{[\![AX\neg\varphi]\!](s)}{[\![\neg EX\varphi]\!](s)}\ \text{neg-}EX \qquad \frac{[\![A[\top\ U\ \neg\varphi]]\!](s)}{[\![\neg EG\varphi]\!](s)}\ \text{neg-}EG$$

$$\frac{[\![EX\neg\varphi]\!](s)}{[\![\neg AX\varphi]\!](s)}\ \text{neg-}AX \qquad \frac{[\![E[\top\ U\ \neg\varphi]]\!](s)}{[\![\neg AG\varphi]\!](s)}\ \text{neg-}AG$$

$$\frac{[\![(\neg\psi \wedge \neg\varphi) \vee (\neg\psi \wedge \neg EXE[\varphi \wedge \overline{\{s\}}\ U\ \psi \wedge \neg\overline{\{s\}}])]\!](s)}{[\![\neg E[\varphi\ U\ \psi]]\!](s)}\ \text{neg-}EU$$

$$\frac{[\![EG\neg\psi \vee E[\neg\varphi\ U\ \neg\varphi \wedge \neg\psi]]\!](s)}{[\![\neg A[\varphi\ U\ \psi]]\!](s)}\ \text{neg-}AU$$

Fig. 9. Proof rules for negation.

(a) $$\cfrac{\cfrac{R(s,\hat{t}) \qquad [\![\varphi]\!](\hat{t})}{\exists t \in S \cdot R(s,t) \wedge [\![\varphi]\!](t)}\ \text{one-point rule}}{[\![EX\varphi]\!](s)}\ EX$$

(c) $$\begin{array}{c}[\![\varphi]\!](\hat{t})\\ \uparrow\\ [\![EX\varphi]\!](s)\end{array}$$

(b) $$\frac{[\![\varphi]\!](\hat{t})}{[\![EX\varphi]\!](s)}$$

(d) $$\begin{array}{c}\hat{t}\\ \uparrow\\ s\end{array}$$

Fig. 10. From proofs to witnesses.

any adequate set for CTL must contain the EU operator [Lar95], it is not possible to express its negation as a combination of only ACTL operators.

Finally, to yield the proof system for FCTL, we combine the above proof rules with the one for $E_C G$.

4 Generating Proof-Like Counter-Examples

In this section we describe how to use the proof system introduced in Section 3 to generate annotated witnesses and counter-examples. We also discuss and illustrate the tool support for this approach.

4.1 From Proofs to Counter-Examples

There is a clear one-to-one correspondence between witnesses and proofs for CTL. Note, however, that proofs are finite, whereas witnesses can be infinite and are typically

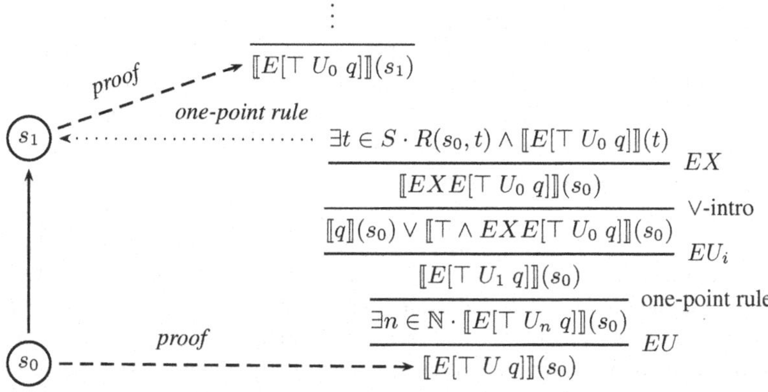

Fig. 11. Proof-like witness for $\llbracket E[\top\ U\ q]\rrbracket(s_0)$.

represented using a finite prefix and a finite repeating suffix. We return to this subject below.

Consider the proof for $\llbracket EX\varphi\rrbracket(s)$ shown in Figure 10(a). Here, $\hat{t}$ is some state in S obtained by the model-checking procedure `exWitness`(φ, s) as part of the one-point rule for EX (see line 6 of the algorithm in Figure 6(c)). The witness can be visually obtained from the proof of EX via the following steps:

1. remove all nodes from the proof tree except for: (a) the root node, and (b) nodes that are the result of the application of the one-point rule to EX and that do not correspond to the axioms of the transition relation (see Figure 10(b));
2. replace horizontal bars by directed edges (see Figure 10(c));
3. relabel the root node by s and each node of the form $\llbracket\varphi\rrbracket(\hat{t})$ by $\hat{t}$ (see Figure 10(d)).

Clearly, the result of the application of the above procedure to the proof of $\llbracket EX\varphi\rrbracket(s)$ is a path through the Kripke structure that is a witness to $\llbracket EX\varphi\rrbracket(s)$. A similar procedure that uses finite quantification instead of the one-point rule also exists for AX.

Note that a sequence of steps in a Kripke structure is the only information given by the witness generators. We referred to it as the *coarsest* type of proof in Section 1. All of such steps are results of the application of the one-point rule to EX or the finite quantification rule to AX. Other proof steps do not result in state transitions and are not shown by conventional witness generators. When extracting the witness from our proofs, we label each state in a witness with these missing proof steps. Branches in the witness result from applications of $\wedge$-intro and finite quantification rules. Loops can be identified by merging states with the same label, allowing the representation of nested loops. The resulting structures are called *proof-like witnesses* or *counter-examples*.

For example, a proof-like witness for $\llbracket E[\top\ U\ q]\rrbracket(s_0)$ on the Kripke structure in Figure 2 is shown in Figure 11. In this figure, the circled nodes represent states and solid arrows between them represent state transitions. Thus, the witness for $\llbracket E[\top\ U\ q]\rrbracket(s_0)$ consists of two states: s_0 followed by s_1. Each state is labeled with the part of the proof that directly depends on it. This is indicated by the dashed *proof* arrows. Finally, each step in the proof that adds new states to the witness is labeled with the states it introduces, indicated by the dotted *one-point rule* (finite quantification rule) arrows.

As can be seen from this example, a proof-like witness is essentially a composition of two trees: the witness state tree, and the proof tree. This allows the user to either ignore the proof part and only explore the witness, or ignore the witness part and only explore the proof, or switch between the two representations at will.

In Section 1, we set out three goals for our work. The first goal, preserving usability aspects of witnesses, is achieved by our ability to generate conventional witnesses. The second goal, providing some feedback even if the complete counter-example is not available, is satisfied by generating proof obligations for universal properties and combining them with other proof steps so that users can understand the reasons behind these. The last goal, helping users in understanding complex counter-examples, is achieved by providing *complete* information necessary to justify the result of the model-checker. Yet proof-like counter-examples often end up being quite large. Automated support for *browsing* these counter-examples is a key for the effective use of this information for understanding and debugging the model. We address the tool support and browsing strategies below.

4.2 Tool Support for Browsing Counter-Examples

We have developed a prototype proof/witness browser tool called KEGVis (Kounter-example generator and visualizer). The tool uses the symbolic model-checker NuSMV [CCGR99] to generate proof-like witnesses for CTL formulas, and the daVinci [FW94] graph visualization package for their visual presentation. KEGVis can give the user a high-level overview of proof-like witnesses and allow him/her to skip certain steps, fast forward to "interesting" parts of the witness, determine whether the current state is part of a loop, etc.

Figure 12 lists several examples of strategies for efficient navigation through proof-like counter-examples. We distinguish between static and dynamic modes of navigation. In the former, the witness is generated prior to browsing, while in the latter, it is generated in response to user actions.

In the static mode, the exploration can proceed either in the forward direction, convenient for discovering why a particular path in a witness justifies a given subformula, or in the backward direction, used for identifying why a particular "suspicious" state is part of the witness. In both cases, the user can restrict the part of the witness of property φ to be displayed by selecting subformulas or operators of φ. This restriction is implemented in KEGVis by letting the user specify the initial condition, i.e. the one that should hold in the beginning of a path to explore, and the final condition, i.e. the one that tells KEGVis when to stop the exploration. For example, to restrict the witness to the EF operator of property $P = EGEF(x \wedge EXx)$, we set the initial and the final conditions to $EF(x \wedge EXx)$ and $x \wedge EXx$, respectively. Note that there are several paths satisfying the initial condition; all of them will be displayed. If a chosen subformula or operator φ occurs in multiple places in the temporal formula (e.g., x in property P above), then paths satisfying φ can be found by the following algorithm: (1) find the smallest unique subformula ψ that contains φ; (2) find all states that justify ψ; (3) for each state t found in step (2), follow the proof to a state labeled with φ. For example, the smallest unique subformula that contains the second occurrence of x in P is EXx. Thus, this x can be justified by successors of states labelled with EXx.

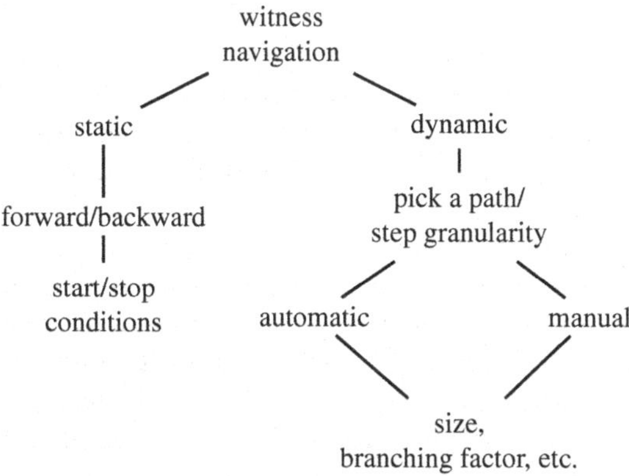

Fig. 12. Browsing strategies for proof-like witnesses/counter-examples.

Witness generation is usually quite expensive. The dynamic mode of witness exploration allows the user to control which path of the witness is to be generated, or what should be the granularity of the logical step before further user input is solicited. These choices are based on the information available from the proof part of the proof-like witness, and can be taken manually or by a user-supplied heuristic function. Consider exploring the witness for the formula $[\![EFx \wedge EFy]\!](s)$. After a few steps of the exploration, the proof labeling state s may indicate that fixpoints for EFx and EFy have been achieved in 3 and 5 iterations, respectively:

$$\dfrac{\dfrac{[\![E[\top\ U_3\ x]]\!](s)}{[\![EFx]\!](s)} \qquad \dfrac{[\![E[\top\ U_5\ y]]\!](s)}{[\![EFy]\!](s)}}{[\![EFx \wedge EFy]\!](s)}\ \wedge\text{-intro}$$

The user can then use this information to guide the witness generation in the direction of the shorter path.

Current implementation of KEGVis supports static exploration only; the dynamic exploration mode is still under development.

5 Related Work

The proof system developed in this paper is similar to the tableaux used for local model-checking [SW91]. In fact, the automated proof-generation technique can be seen as a simulation of a run of a local model-checker, where the information collected from the run of a global model-checker is used to guide the construction of the proof.

Several other researches have explored the idea of generating proofs from the model-checking runs [PZ01,PPZ01,Nam01,TC02]. Their common motivation is to use proofs to provide *complete* information justifying the result of the model-checker, in particular, in cases where a witness, or a counter-example, is not feasible.

The work of Namjoshi [Nam01] concentrates on generating a proof of validity of a run of a global μ-calculus model-checker. This is accomplished by augmenting the model-checker to record the set of states satisfying each subformula and the convergence bound for each fixpoint operator. In cases where the formula has a finite witness, this information can also be used to produce proof-like witnesses, using techniques similar to the one described in Section 3.2. Tan and Cleaveland [TC02] extend Namjoshi's work to local model-checking.

An approach of Peled et. al. [PZ01,PPZ01] is similar to ours in spirit. The main goal is to generate proofs that are as easy to understand as possible, and use them to communicate the reasons behind the model-checking result to the user. The technique developed in [PZ01,PPZ01] generates proofs of satisfaction for LTL properties. Note that this is similar to providing witnesses for ACTL; thus, the approach is complimentary to ours, as it addresses the problem of discharging proof obligations that we generate in the case of AX.

In this paper, we have only explored how proofs can be used to aid in understanding witnesses, yet other applications are also possible. For example, Namjoshi [Nam01] suggests that one can use proofs extracted from the model-checker to debug the model-checker itself, or use them as a basis for integration between model-checking and theorem proving. Since proof-like witnesses are effectively proofs, they can be used in any application that calls for a proof of satisfaction of a temporal property.

6 Conclusion

The main contribution of this paper is the concept of *proof-like witnesses* (and counter-examples) that bridges the gap between proofs and witnesses. Our proof-like witnesses are expressed in terms of computations of the model (thus making them easy to understand), yet allow us to provide some feedback to the user even if in general the witness is not available. Overall, we have shown that expressing witnesses as proofs, in combination with an intelligent browser tool, provides a significant support for understanding complex witnesses.

In order to create proof-like witnesses, we have developed a sound and complete proof system for CTL. This makes our approach a logical, rather than an algorithmic, one. The main advantage here is that a proof of correctness of our witness generator is significantly simplified; furthermore, the technique can be easily extended to other, non-traditional, applications such as witness generation for temporal-logic queries [GDC02].

The major limitation of our approach is that it provides only limited information in the case of witnesses for ACTL and properties that use both universal and existential quantifiers. In the future, we plan to explore possible solutions to this problem along the lines of [PPZ01]. We also plan to enhance our tool, KEGVis, to support dynamic witness exploration.

References

[CCGR99] A. Cimatti, E.M. Clarke, F. Giunchiglia, and M. Roveri. NuSMV: a new Symbolic Model Verifier. In N. Halbwachs and D. Peled, editors, *Proceedings of 11th Conference on Computer-Aided Verification (CAV'99)*, number 1633 in Lecture Notes in Computer Science, pages 495–499, Trento, Italy, July 1999. Springer.

[CGMZ95] E.M. Clarke, O. Grumberg, K.L. McMillan, and X. Zhao. Efficient Generation of Counterexamples and Witnesses in Symbolic Model Checking. In *Proceedings of 32nd Design Automation Conference (DAC 95)*, pages 427–432, San Francisco, CA, USA, 1995.

[CGP99] E. Clarke, O. Grumberg, and D. Peled. *Model Checking*. MIT Press, 1999.

[CLJV02] E.M. Clarke, Y. Lu, S. Jha, and H. Veith. Tree-Like Counterexamples in Model Checking. In *Proceedings of the Seventeenth Annual IEEE Symposium on Logic in Computer Science (LICS'02)*, pages 19–29, Copenhagen, Denmark, July 2002. IEEE Computer Society.

[FW94] M. Fröhlich and M. Werner. The Graph Visualization System daVinci – A user interface for applications. Technical Report 5/94, Department of Computer Science, Bremen University, 1994.

[GDC02] A. Gurfinkel, B. Devereux, and M. Chechik. "Model Exploration with Temporal Logic Query Checking". In *Proceedings of SIGSOFT Conference on Foundations of Software Engineering (FSE'02)*, Charleston, South Carolina, November 2002. ACM Press.

[Gur02] A. Gurfinkel. Multi-valued symbolic model-checking: Fairness, counter-examples, running time. Master's thesis, University of Toronto, Department of Computer Science, October 2002.

[Lar95] F. Laroussinie. "About the Expressive Power of CTL Combinators". *Information Processing Letters*, 54:343–345, 1995.

[McM93] K.L. McMillan. *Symbolic Model Checking*. Kluwer Academic, 1993.

[Nam01] K. Namjoshi. Certifying Model Checkers. In *Proceedings of 13th International Conference on Computer-Aided Verification (CAV'01)*, volume 2102 of *LNCS*. Springer-Verlag, 2001.

[OSR93] S. Owre, N. Shankar, and J. Rushby. "User Guide for the PVS Specification and Verification System (Draft)". Technical report, Computer Science Lab, SRI International, Menlo Park, CA, 1993.

[PPZ01] D. Peled, A. Pnueli, and L. Zuck. From falsification to verification. In *FST&TCS*, volume 2245 of *LNCS*. Springer-Verlag, 2001.

[PZ01] D. Peled and L. Zuck. From model checking to a temporal proof. In *Proceedings of the 8th International SPIN Workshop (SPIN'2001)*, volume 2057 of *LNCS*, pages 1–14, Toronto, Canada, May 2001. Springer.

[SW91] C. Stirling and D. Walker. Local model-checking in the modal mu-calculus. *Theoretical Computer Science*, 89, 1991.

[TC02] L. Tan and R. Cleaveland. Evidence-Based Model Checking. In *Proceedings of 14th Conference on Computer-Aided Verification (CAV'02)*, volume 2404 of *LNCS*, pages 455–470, Copenhagen, Denmark, July 2002. Springer-Verlag.

Multiple-Counterexample Guided Iterative Abstraction Refinement: An Industrial Evaluation

Marcelo Glusman[1,2], Gila Kamhi[2], Sela Mador-Haim[2], Ranan Fraer[2], and Moshe Y. Vardi[3*]

[1] Computer Science Department, The Technion, Haifa, Israel
marce@cs.technion.ac.il
[2] Formal Property Verification, Intel Corporation, Haifa, Israel
{gila.kamhi,sela.mador-haim,ranan.fraer}@intel.com
[3] Department of Computer Science, Rice University
vardi@cs.rice.edu

Abstract. In this paper, we describe a completely automated framework for iterative abstraction refinement that is fully integrated into a formal-verification environment. This environment consists of three basic software tools: Forecast, a BDD-based model checker, Thunder, a SAT-based bounded model checker, and MCE, a technology for multiple-counterexample analysis. In our framework, the initial abstraction is chosen relative to the property under verification. The abstraction is model checked by Forecast; in case of failure, a counterexample is returned. Our framework includes an abstract counterexample analyzer module that applies techniques for bounded model checking to check whether the abstract counterexample holds in the concrete model. If it does, it is extended to a concrete counterexample. This important capability is provided as a separate tool that also addresses one of the major problems of verification by manual abstraction. If the counterexample is spurious, we use a novel refinement heuristic based on MCE to guide the refinement. After the part of the abstract model to be refined is chosen, our refinement algorithm computes a new abstraction that includes as much logic as possible without adding too many new variables, therefore striking a balance between refining the abstraction and keeping its size manageable. We demonstrate the effectiveness of our framework on challenging Intel designs that were not amenable to BDD-based model-checking approaches.

1 Introduction

One of the most significant recent developments in the area of formal design verification is the discovery of algorithmic methods for verifying properties of *finite-state* systems. In temporal-logic *model checking*, we verify the correctness of a finite-state system with respect to a desired temporal property by checking whether a labeled state-transition graph that models the system satisfies a temporal logic formula that specifies this property [9,27,33,37]. With the advent of symbolic techniques [7], model-checking tools have enjoyed a substantial and growing use over the last few years, showing ability to discover

* Supported in part by NSF grants CCR-9700061, CCR-9988322, IIS-9908435, IIS-9978135, and EIA-0086264, by BSF grant 9800096, and by a grant from the Intel Corporation.

H. Garavel and J. Hatcliff (Eds.): TACAS 2003, LNCS 2619, pp. 176–191, 2003.

subtle flaws that result from extremely improbable events. While until recently these tools were viewed as of academic interest only, they are now routinely used in industrial applications [5,16]. Nevertheless, model checking is still limited with respect to the size of the designs it can handle, due to the so-called *state-explosion problem*, which refers to the exponential complexity of model checking with respect to the number of state variables in the model. One of the most fundamental techniques for dealing with the state explosion problem is that of *abstraction*, in which the concrete model is abstracted to a simpler model that has a smaller state space, and, hopefully, retains the essential features of the concrete model [11]. The abstract model is typically an overapproximation of the concrete model–it allows behaviors that are not allowed in the concrete model. Thus, with respect to universal properties (properties that are defined in terms of universal quantification over traces), model checking the abstract model is *sound*–if the abstract model satisfies the property, then so does the concrete model. Since the abstract model, however, is an overapproximation, "false negatives" are possible; one can get *spurious* counterexamples, which cannot be extended to allowed behaviors in the concrete model.

Consequently, without automation, model checking by abstraction requires a fair amount of manual labor. First, one has to decide how to abstract the concrete model. If the model checker shows that the abstract model satisfies the property under verification, then so does the concrete model and we are done. Otherwise, the model checker returns a counterexample with respect to the abstract model. One then has to analyze the counterexample to see if it is real or spurious. If the counterexample is real, then it has to be extended to a counterexample of the concrete model, which is then returned to the verification engineer for debugging. If the counterexample is spurious, one has to refine the abstract model in order to bring it closer to the concrete model, so that the spurious counterexample is eliminated. This labor-intensive process reduces dramatically the productivity of the verification engineer. As a result, the usefulness of model checking to the formal verification of large industrial designs is seriously hampered. Over the last decade, there has been a consistent effort to automate the above process of model checking by abstraction, offering algorithmic support to *iterative abstraction refinement*. This consists of three basic steps: *abstract* the design's model, *analyze* the counterexample, *refine* the abstraction (see Figure 1). Starting with Balarin and Sangiovanni-Vincentelli [2], researchers described several ways in which these steps can be automated [11,25, 31,28,10,30,17,38] (see Related Work).

In this paper, we describe a completely automated prototype framework for iterative abstraction refinement that is integrated into a formal-verification environment consisting of three basic software tools: Forecast, a BDD-based model checker [16], Thunder, a SAT-based bounded model checker [13], and MCE, a technology for multiple-counterexample analysis [14]. As in [25], to abstract the model, we automatically cut (prune) the design logic, by turning chosen circuit nodes (not necessarily latches) into free, i.e., unconstrained inputs, therefore pruning the logic that drives them; also, the initial abstraction is chosen relative to the property under verification. Our framework applies bounded model checking techniques [4] to analyze the counterexample. The key insight here is that the abstract counterexample has a bounded length, which enables us to reduce this problem to a bounded model checking problem. Clarke et al in [8] have proposed similar SAT-based techniques to address this problem. In addition to being an

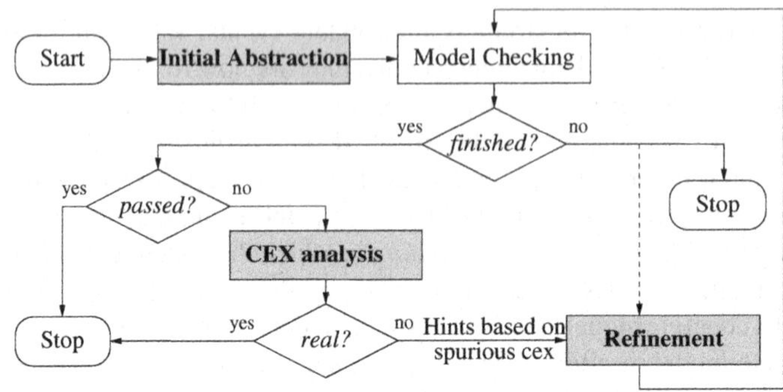

Fig. 1. Framework for automated abstraction and iterative counterexample-guided refinement

integral part of the automatic refinement framework, this capability in our solution is also crucial to support manual abstraction methods, so it is also provided as a stand-alone utility. In summary, the task is to check whether an abstract counterexample holds in the concrete model. If it does, it has to be extended to a concrete counterexample, which the verification engineer can use for debugging.

If the analysis step indicates that the abstract counterexample is spurious, then the abstraction is too "loose" and it has to be refined. Some freed nodes have to be un-freed, adding new logic to the abstract model. This increases the model's logical complexity, which raises the computational complexity of model checking it. Thus, there is a tradeoff here between eliminating spurious behaviors and increasing the size of the abstract model. One of our two main contributions is a novel heuristic to choose the nodes to be un-freed. A recent work shows how Multiple Counterexample (MCE) technology [14] supports the analysis of many counterexamples simultaneously. We show how an MCE-based heuristic can be used to guide the refinement process by selecting for un-freeing nodes that are more relevant for eliminating the spurious counterexamples.

Our second main contribution is to show how, after the nodes to be un-freed are chosen, we can refine the model by including as much logic as possible without adding too many new variables (freed nodes). Other iterative refinement frameworks [38] perform the refinement only at latch level. In many real-life designs, however, replacing a latch with all the new latches in its transitive fan-in can cause sudden addition of huge amounts of logic. Therefore it is desirable to be able to prune at the intermediate nodes. We describe a heuristic that analyzes the logic between the un-freed nodes and their fan-in latches to find a balance between refining the abstraction and keeping the abstract model's size manageable.

The rest of the paper is structured as follows: Section 2 describes related work in the published literature. Section 3 introduces the model checking environment in which our tool operates, and the way an initial abstraction is chosen. Sections 4 and 5 describe, respectively, the counterexample analysis module, and the refinement algorithm. In Section 6 we evaluate the effectiveness of our prototype on a set of challenging Intel designs that were not amenable to BDD-based model-checking approaches.

We follow with concluding remarks in Section 7.

2 Related Work

The *cone-of-influence* (COI) *reduction* [12] is the most common abstraction technique, used today as a core component in most model-checking tools. The COI of a property consists of all the variables that affect the property directly or indirectly, based on the dependencies between the variables of the model. Variables that are not in the COI cannot influence the validity of the specification and can therefore be removed from the model. COI reduction is an *exact* abstraction, in the sense that the abstract model satisfies the property *if and only if* the concrete model does. More aggressive abstractions, which are the ones we consider in this paper, go one step further by eliminating parts of the COI that are believed to be irrelevant to the property being checked. In doing so, they create an overapproximation, as the abstract model might introduce spurious behaviors that were not present in the concrete one. A significant effort has been invested in automating the whole process, resulting in various *iterative refinement* frameworks [25,2,26,31,32,28, 22,10,17,38,35]. We now discuss some of these works.

An early such framework is the *localization reduction* of Kurshan [25], defined in the context of ω-regular language containment, and implemented in COSPAN [19]. This reduction keeps the nodes (both latches and intermediate nodes) that are topologically close (in the node dependency graph) to the property being verified, while the other nodes are abstracted away with non-deterministic assignments. The refinement is counterexample guided, with each step adding additional nodes, again according to the dependency graph. Unfortunately, not enough details (for an effective implementation) are provided in [25] on the check for spurious counterexamples or the selection of a small set of nodes to eliminate such counterexamples.

Balarin and Sangiovanni-Vincentelli [2] present a similar iterative framework for checking language emptiness of communicating automata. To check for spurious counterexamples they synthesize an automaton from the error trace and intersect it with the automaton of the concrete model. The resulting language emptiness problem is submitted to a BDD-based model checker. Our experience shows that BDD-based methods have little chance of coping with the size of the concrete model. By contrast, SAT-based solutions like ours for counterexample analysis scale much better with the model size. Moreover, we avoid compiling the error trace into an automaton, to avoid introducing auxiliary variables. Instead, our reduction to bounded model checking translates the error trace into new constraints added to the SAT instance.

Clarke et al. [10] use counterexample-guided refinement for ACTL* model checking. Their abstraction exploits the control structure of a HDL (Hardware Description Language) design rather than the dependency graph. This provides finer control by allowing several degrees of abstraction for each variable. Relying on such syntactic information, however, hampers the application of this technique to gate-level designs. To check for spurious counterexamples, BDD-based reachability analysis is performed on the concrete model constrained with the information provided by the error trace. This suffers from the same scalability problem mentioned above. This last issue is addressed in [3], where the analysis and reconstruction of counterexamples is performed on an intermediate model that is midway between the concrete model and the abstract one. The intermediate model is itself refined in an incremental way. As the other BDD-based approaches, this approach still has limited capacity as the examples reported in the paper do not exceed 400 variables. Today it is widely accepted that SAT or ATPG are more appropriate for the analysis of spurious counterexamples. That is the approach taken in [8] where SAT is used for this task. This paper suggests also two new refinement heuristics, one based on Integer Linear Programming and the other based on Machine Learning. Both heuristics try to find a minimal set of variables that separates between a set of dead states and a set of bad states. To that purpose, one needs to sample sufficiently many states in both sets. In the worst case we might have to sample an exponential number of states, so the sampling itself can be quite expensive.

The iterative refinement tool described in [38] was the first one to employ different verification engines. A hybrid BDD-ATPG engine is used for model checking, sequential ATPG is used for detecting spurious counterexamples, and a combination of 3-valued simulation and sequential ATPG is used to obtain refinement hints. We strongly believe that using additional engines in addition to BDD-based ones is, indeed, the only way to overcome the limitations of BDD-based model checking.

A distinguishing feature of our approach is the fine control over successive refinements' size growth. This stems from two critical aspects: First, our refinement does not attempt to eliminate one single error trace at all price. Our experience shows that this tends to push the refinement in the wrong direction by adding more logic than necessary. Instead, our refinement analyzes simultaneously all the error traces (of a given length) and adds a small number of nodes that are likely to be the root cause of all such spurious counterexamples. Second, we do not limit our pruning to the level of latches, but we also prune at the level of intermediate nodes in the design. This strategy was found to be critical in coping with nodes that have a large fan-in cone by avoiding to bring in the whole cone of these nodes at once. By carefully choosing the nodes to be pruned, we get fine control over the growth of the successive refinements' size. The Min-Cut technique we apply to achieve this effect and the flow problem we generate from the circuit when using this technique are quite standard, but their use for the specific purpose of choosing the next pruning of the model is new. In [38], a Min-Cut is computed in the counterexample analysis phase, but as we said, in that work only latches are chosen for pruning. A similar technique is also used in the Ketchum tool [21], when checking for unreachability of coverage states, as an optimization of automatic test-pattern generation. It is known (even though no details have been published) that in the FormalCheck tool a Min-Cut is used for refinement, but to our best knowledge, it is computed on a completely different flow problem.

3 Model Checking Environment and Initial Abstraction

The set-up: The hardware design being verified is given in a high-level hardware description language and compiled into a logical model, on which the model abstraction and refinement process takes place. The logical models on which we operate consist of a set V of Boolean variables used to represent the system states, a Boolean formula I representing the set of initial states, a collection *TR* of Boolean formulas representing transition constraints, and a collection F of formulas representing fairness constraints. All the formulas are over the variables in V, except for the formulas in *TR*, which are over the variables in $V \cup V'$, where $V' = \{x' \mid x \in V\}$. Given an assignment s to the variables in V, let s' denote the corresponding assignment to the variables in V'. A *fair trace* of this model is an infinite sequence $s_0, s_1, \ldots$ of assignments to the variables in V, such that s_0 satisfies I, for every $i \in \mathbb{N}$ and for all $\tau \in TR$ $s_i \cup s'_{i+1}$ satisfies τ, and for every $\varphi \in F$ there are infinitely many i such that s_i satisfies φ [29].

In our set-up, the specification and assumptions are given in Intel's ForSpec language [1], which is linear-time temporal logic augmented with regular expressions, clocks, and resets. Given a temporal assumption f and a temporal assertion g, the requirement we must check is that the model satisfies $f \rightarrow g$. This check is implemented via the automata-theoretic approach [36]. Both f and $\neg g$ are compiled into logical models of their respective Büchi automata. These models are conjoined with the logical model of the design under verification, and the model checker then tests the combined model for language emptiness.

The abstraction method we chose consists of selecting certain nodes in this combined model, and turning them into free inputs. The constraints in *TR* are typically of the form "$v' = \ldots$" or "$v = \ldots$", so we can turn v into a free input by removing from *TR* any constraints with v or v' on the left side. We call this operation *freeing v*. After it is done, part (or all) of the logic that drives v stops influencing the variables that define the property, thus allowing the COI reduction to prune that part of the logic from the model. The freed nodes therefore define a *frontier* that separates, in the concrete model, the logic included in the current abstract model from the logic that is pruned out.

Initial Abstraction: The first step is automatic generation of an initial abstract model, i.e., the first frontier. The specification and assumption's logic are probably very relevant to the property being checked, so pruning them is likely to cause spurious counterexamples. Moreover, the part of the model generated by the ForSpec compiler is relatively small. Our initial abstract model is thus obtained by freeing the first nodes of the original design's logic model that are connected to the ForSpec-generated logic (See Figure 2). Model checking this first abstract model usually takes very little time and finds only spurious counterexamples, unless the property is directly implied by the provided assumption, regardless of the design being verified.

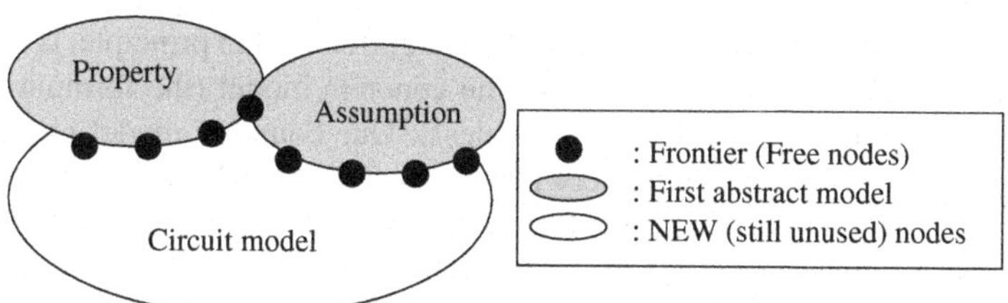

Fig. 2. Initial Abstraction

Model Checking: Forecast, Intel's BDD-based model checker, searches for a counterexample trace, which is represented by a prefix and a fair cycle (i.e., one in which every fairness constraint is satisfied at least in one state). In this paper we focus on safety properties, for which only a prefix of a trace is needed [24]. In case an abstract counterexample is found, Forecast provides a trace that must be analyzed to determine if it is real (see Section 4). Forecast also provides Multiple-Counterexample (MCE) information [14], to be used by the refinement module (See Section 5.2).

We should note that Forecast is run using all the usual reductions and optimizations, such as the Cone of Influence reduction [12] and Dynamic Variable Reordering [34], which means that the order of the logic variables in the BDDs evolves during the model checking session. Every run's final variable order is saved in a file and later incorporated by the model checker in the next iteration, as part of its initial variable ordering. Every iteration's abstract model includes all the variables that appear in the preceding ones, so by incorporating the previously computed variable order we can obtain smaller BDDs.

4 Counterexample Analysis

Automatic abstractions as well as manual abstractions can result in false negatives. Therefore, the efficiency of any framework that supports abstractions highly depends on the ability to detect whether the abstract counterexamples resulting from a verification session are spurious or not. In this section, we describe a counterexample analysis method (hereafter called "CexAn") for determining whether an abstract counterexample is real, i.e., can be extended to the concrete model. If this is the case, CexAn extends the abstract counterexample to a concrete one. Hence, the benefits of CexAn are both in determining spurious failures and, in case of valid failure reports, easing the debugging of the abstract counterexamples since the provided concrete counterexamples include assignments for the concrete model's inputs.

CexAn is built on SAT-based bounded model checking technology. The inputs to CexAn are the concrete model M, and the abstract counterexample *AbstCex*. The counterexample analysis problem is translated to a k-bounded model checking problem, where $k + 1$ is the length of AbstCex. As in bounded model checking, the concrete model is unrolled k steps and a propositional formula is generated. The formula describes paths from s_0 to s_k such that s_0 is an initial state and for all $0 \leq i < k$, there is a transition from s_i to s_{i+1}: $Path(s_0, \ldots, s_k) = I(s_0) \wedge \bigwedge_{i=0}^{k-1} TR(s_i, s_{i+1})$
The construction of $Path(s_0, \ldots, s_k)$, while straightforward in principle, is a nontrivial computational task because of the size of the concrete model (the formula may have hundreds of thousands propositional variables!). Our bounded model checking tool, Thunder, implements the unrolling very efficiently. The AbstCex is also translated to a propositional formula *CexForm*, in the following way: Let $Phase_i$ be a Boolean formula describing the i-th phase ($0 \leq i \leq k$) in AbstCex. Every $Phase_i$ restricts the variables corresponding to abstract model nodes, to the values they take in the corresponding phase of CexForm. Then, we define: $CexForm(s_0, \ldots, s_k) = \bigwedge_{i=0}^{k} Phase_i$
The SAT engine looks for a satisfying assignment for the formula:

$$Path(s_0, \ldots, s_k) \wedge CexForm(s_0, \ldots, s_k).$$

In case a satisfying assignment is found, we report that the counterexample is real and provide the extended counterexample in terms of the concrete model's signals. If a satisfying assignment does not exist, we conclude that the concrete model does not display a counterexample agreeing with AbstCex on the signals present in the abstract model, so we report that the counterexample is spurious.

5 Refinement Algorithm

5.1 Rationale

For abstractions by freeing and pruning, refining an abstraction means moving the frontier of freed nodes, therefore defining a bigger abstract model. This involves two main steps: i) choosing the nodes in the frontier that will be "un-freed", therefore adding their whole "cone of influence" back into the model, and ii) choosing the nodes in the newly added logic that will be freed, to keep the abstract model small. In the new abstraction, the un-freed nodes' values are constrained by the added logic, so fewer behaviors will be possible. The refinement iterations terminate since we do not apply backtracking.

The goal of an iterative refinement process is to find an abstraction that does not display *any* spurious counterexamples. It may have no counterexamples at all, or it may reveal a real one. To achieve this goal in fewer iterations, every refinement step should add as much logic as possible. However, our search for this goal is carried out within the capacity limits of the model checking phase, so we must only add the logic that has the best chance to (eventually) eliminate *all* the spurious counterexamples.

Given a spurious counterexample, it is computationally difficult to find a minimal set of nodes that need to be un-freed to eliminate it [10]. One approach is to greedily add nodes to the abstract model until the spurious counterexample at hand is eliminated. This greedy approach may be quite suboptimal and lead to significant growth of the abstract model. Another approach is to overapproximate and add a large "chunk" of logic in one refinement step to guarantee elimination of the spurious counterexample. This may cause the sudden addition of too much logic to the abstract model. Thus, eliminating the spurious counterexample at hand in a single refinement step is not necessarily the best way of refining the abstraction.

The next section presents a new heuristic that, at every iteration, guides the refinement by hinting at nodes in the frontier that should be un-freed to eliminate all or many of the spurious counterexamples of a given length. For the reasons just described, we prefer to limit the amount of logic added in a single iteration, and decide on the next refinement steps based on fresh hints from the guiding heuristic. The tradeoff between adding more logic in a single iteration and limiting the abstract model's size is present throughout the rest of this section.

5.2 Choosing the Nodes in the Frontier to Be Un-freed

In counterexample-guided refinement frameworks, spurious counterexamples are analyzed, looking for hints as to which elements of the abstraction cause the spurious counterexamples. In our case, the hints we need should suggest which nodes in the frontier must be un-freed first. Our tool's refinement module implements a new technique for obtaining such hints. The new heuristic exploits Multiple Counterexample (MCE) information [14] provided as a multi-valued counterexample annotation by our BDD-based symbolic model checker, Forecast. A multi-valued annotation of a counterexample represents *all* the counterexamples of the same length. The use of MCE information facilitates the simultaneous elimination of several spurious counterexamples in a few refinement steps. This makes the new heuristic specially suited for attaining the goal defined in Section 5.1.

Multi-valued counterexample annotation. Traditional symbolic model checkers provide a single counterexample as the output of a failing verification. It is specially difficult to diagnose a verification failure reported as a single counterexample trace. On one hand, the verification engineer has too much data, all the signal's values along the whole counterexample trace. On the other hand, he has too little data, only one counterexample among many possible ones. Forecast addresses the counterexample diagnosis problem by providing MCE information in the form of "multi-valued counterexample annotation", a concise and intuitive counterexample data representation. In this annotation, a counterexample trace is enhanced with a classification of signal values along the trace into three types: (a) *Strong* 0/1: indicates that in all counterexamples, the value of the signal at the given phase of the trace is 0 or 1, respectively. (b) *Conditional* 0/1: indicates that although the value of the signal at this phase is 0 or 1 for this counterexample, this value can be different for another counterexample illustrating the failure. (c) *Irrelevant* 0/1: indicates that the value of the signal at this phase is probably unrelated to the verification failure. Thus a single multi-valued annotated counterexample also provides information on all the other possible counterexamples of the same length.

Using MCE to obtain hints for refining abstractions. The strong values provide insight on the pertinent signals causing the counterexample. For example, if the value of a signal at a certain phase of a counterexample is a strong zero, this means that correcting the design so that the value of the signal will be one at that phase often gets rid of all counterexamples of the same length as the counterexample at hand. Hence, the error rectification problem is often reduced to determining how to cause a strong-valued signal to take on a different value. We first assign a unique fixed weight to each of the three value types, where strong values get a higher weight. Then, given a multi-valued annotated spurious counterexample, we compute, for every node, the average weight of the values assigned to it along the whole trace. The nodes with the highest average weight are chosen for refinement.

The decision on how many nodes in the current frontier should be un-freed at every iteration involves the tradeoff described in Section 5.1. Choosing only the node with the highest average weight yields the most cautious refinement process, but a longer one. Experimentation, and examination of the list of frontier nodes sorted by decreasing weight, suggest that good results can be obtained by un-freeing only a few nodes at a time. In Section 6, we elaborate on experimental results that lead to a decision on the number of nodes to un-free at each iteration.

5.3 Choosing the New Frontier

In some iterative abstraction refinement frameworks in which the abstractions consist of pruning the model (e.g., [38]), only latches (i.e., registers) are chosen to become part of the frontier. After choosing the latches to be un-freed, the new latches that replace them in the frontier are those in their transitive fan-in (except for those that already appear within the current abstract model). Our experiments on real-life examples showed that this refinement policy causes, in many cases, a sudden increase in the abstract model's size, bigger than what we would like to have in a controlled refinement process – usually

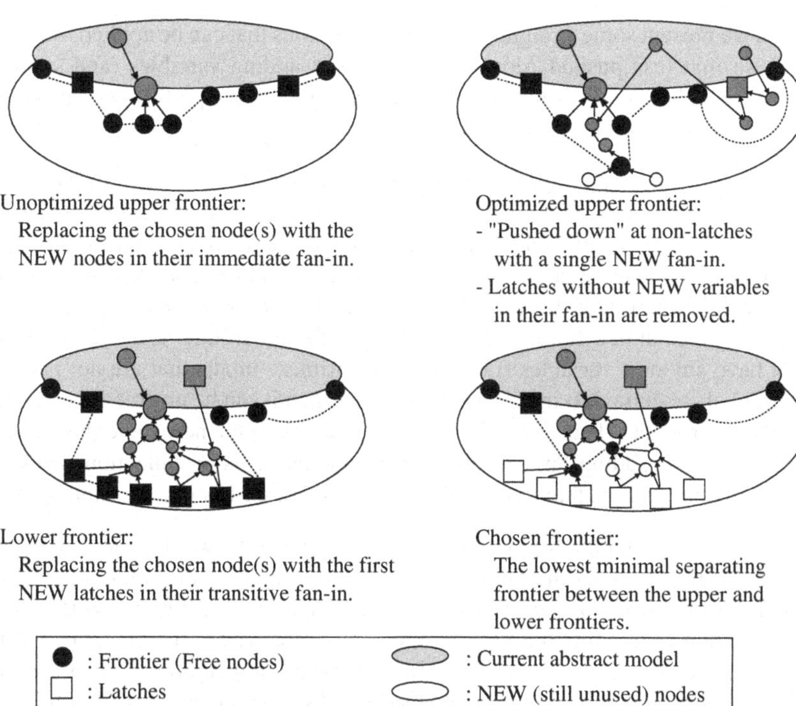

Unoptimized upper frontier:
Replacing the chosen node(s) with the NEW nodes in their immediate fan-in.
Optimized upper frontier:
- "Pushed down" at non-latches with a single NEW fan-in.
- Latches without NEW variables in their fan-in are removed.
Lower frontier:
Replacing the chosen node(s) with the first NEW latches in their transitive fan-in.
Chosen frontier:
The lowest minimal separating frontier between the upper and lower frontiers.
: Frontier (Free nodes)
: Latches
: nodes within current abstract model
: Current abstract model
: NEW (still unused) nodes

Fig. 3. Choosing a new frontier

causing lots of irrelevant logic to be taken into the current abstract model, and therefore slowing down the model checking phase or even reaching its capacity limit. To keep the growth rate of the number of variables under control, we realized that it is crucial to be able to add any node to the free nodes frontier, without restricting ourselves to freeing only latches. The most cautious approach is to replace a node in the frontier with those nodes in its *immediate* fan-in (only the new ones, i.e., those which do not appear in the previous model). This yields a very slow refinement process. In the sequel, we refer to this frontier as the *upper frontier*, and we call the frontier that passes through the latches and input signals in the transitive fan-in – *lower frontier* (see Figure 3). Obviously, a tradeoff (based on the discussion in Section 5.1) has to be found between the upper frontier and the lower frontier. It is desirable to allow the model to grow as much as possible, while minimizing the number of variables in the BDDs, since this typically minimizes the size of the BDDs describing sets of reachable states. However, the addition of intermediate nodes increases the number of constraints, which may in turn increase the time cost of computing image sets. Between the upper and lower frontiers there are no latches, so the number of variables added depends on the number of nodes in the chosen frontier itself (because they are turned into free inputs). This means that we must seek the smallest frontier, and among those with minimal size, the one that has the most constraints on the transition relation.

First, we present some straightforward optimizations that can be applied to the upper frontier, so that it is pushed "downwards" without adding variables (and sometimes saving some). These optimizations (illustrated in Figure 3) are performed repeatedly on the upper frontier, until they are no longer applicable:

- Single-new-fan-in propagation: At every given moment, the nodes in the fan-in of a node in the frontier can be divided into two sets: those that already appear in the current abstract model, and those that do not (we call them *new* nodes). If a node n_1 in the frontier is not a latch, and it has a *single* new fan-in node n_2, then n_1 can be replaced in the frontier by n_2 without adding variables to the model.
- Latches without new fan-in variables: If a node in the frontier is a latch, and it does not have any new variables (i.e., latches or primary inputs that are not part of the current abstract model) in its transitive fan-in, then it can be un-freed (i.e., removed from the frontier). This adds to the abstract model all the new logic that drives the latch, without adding any variables to the model. This optimization saves many refinement iterations that would otherwise be spent un-freeing this kind of latches.

The frontier we are looking for must *separate* the upper and lower frontiers, in the sense that every path (following the fan-in relation) connecting a node in the lower frontier to a node in the upper one must include at least one node belonging to the frontier. This means that we are looking for a minimal cut in the part of the model between the optimized upper frontier and the lower frontier. The computation of such a minimal cut is a standard procedure in circuit analysis [23,18], implemented by first translating the part of the model between the frontiers into a simple flow problem based on the fan-in relation, then executing a Maxflow algorithm [15], and finally applying the Max-Flow Min-Cut Theorem [6] to derive a minimal cut from the maximal flow found. If several such minimal cuts exist, we prefer the lowest one, i.e., the one that takes as much intermediate logic as possible into the next abstract model.

6 Results

We now report how our iterative refinement prototype performs in experiments carried out on Intel designs. Some are verification test cases, i.e., the model checker answers "true", and some are falsification test cases, where a real counterexample is reported. All the selected test cases are way beyond the capacity of Forecast, our BDD-based model checker (they did not complete within the timeout bound of 48 hours, even with COI reduction).

Table 1 records, for each test case, the number of iterations required to reach a definite result (pass or fail), the number of variables (latches and inputs) in the concrete model and in the abstract model of the last iteration (both after the COI reduction), Forecast CPU time for the last iteration, and total Forecast CPU time.

A significant problem in industrial-size projects is ensuring that the properties that are satisfied by a snapshot of the design under development, are also satisfied by later versions. In the context of conventional testing this is checked through regression testing. By saving the set of nodes that belong to the frontier defining the last abstraction (as well as the generated BDD variable order) we provide support for regression verification

Table 1. Results on ten real-life test cases beyond the capacity of BDD-based symbolic model checking. *Real1-Real9* are verification cases, *Real10* is a falsification case.

	Iterations	Variables in concrete vs. last abstract model	Forecast CPU time (secs) Last iteration	Total
Real1	1	627/132	215	215
Real2	10	627/167	1390	8008
Real3	10	627/161	112	1653
Real4	5	627/149	251	914
Real5	5	627/148	310	915
Real6	5	627/155	240	809
Real7	5	635/157	291	975
Real8	18	627/244	2983	9558
Real9	77	903/192	2100	19800
Real10	8	669/218	22	227

[20], which attempts to repeat a verification result after the design has been modified (e.g., if the changes affect only parts of the model that are pruned out after the nodes in the frontier are freed). For regression verification purposes, one would expect the running time to be quite close to Forecast CPU time on the last iteration. As is shown in Table 1, Forecast CPU times on the last iterations are negligible (less than 3000 seconds) in comparison to the original timeout bound (48 hours).

We also applied our prototype to five other designs: *Real11*, *Real2'*, *Real3'*, *Real4'*, *Real8'*. The results, reported in Table 2, demonstrate three points:

Robustness: The latter four designs are later versions of designs *Real2*, *Real3*, *Real4*, *Real8* from Table 1. As can be seen by the reported number of variables in the concrete models, these designs are larger than the earlier versions by about 50 variables. Such growth can pose a significant hurdle to a BDD-based model checker. In contrast, this growth did not have a marked impact on our prototype.

Regression: As discussed above, for regression verification a good starting point is the abstraction and variable order obtained from the last refinement iteration. To see the impact of variable order reuse, we ran the last iteration of the refinement both with the order obtained from prior iterations and without that order (in that case Forecast supplied an initial order based on static analysis). As can be seen in designs *Real11* and *Real8'*, order reuse can have a dramatic impact on performance.

MCE hints: To assess the power of MCE hints, we ran the prototype with different settings, un-freeing at each iteration 4, 16, or 24 variables. As is seen in the table, going from 4 to 16 reduced the number of iterations (and consequently also total running time) significantly, but going from 16 to 24 did not have such an effect. We also checked for each iteration whether the spurious counterexample has been eliminated and reported on the fraction of iterations in which this happened. Again, as is seen in the table, a significant effect occurred only in the transition from 4 to 16 un-freed variables. Note that this transition typically did not increase the number of variables in the final abstraction. Our experience shows that for each design there is a balance point between counterexample

Table 2. Results on five real-life verification test cases that were beyond the capacity of Forecast, when the number of nodes un-freed at every iteration was 4, 16 or 24. The Forecast time is also shown when the last iteration is rerun without reusing initial variable order information.

	Un-freed nodes	Iterations	Variables (concrete vs. last abstract model)	Forecast time (secs) Last iteration		Iterations that removed the CEX
				reused order	no reuse	
Real1'	4	26	652/302	1902	10229	8/26
	16	7	652/221	2276		5/7
	24	6	652/331	1714		4/6
Real2'	4	10	677/222	1529	1757	7/10
	16	5	677/218	1381		3/5
	24	5	677/218	1492		3/5
Real3'	4	10	652/187	430	426	5/10
	16	6	652/221	1250		5/6
	24	6	652/223	2762		4/6
Real4'	4	6	677/209	656	814	3/6
	16	4	677/211	265		3/4
	24	4	677/256	256		3/4
Real8'	4	17	677/290	1307	3692	5/17
	16	7	677/293	6053		5/7
	24	6	677/293	timeout(3 hrs.)		4/6

Table 3. Comparison between refining to the lower frontier vs. to the mincut frontier

	No-Mincut				Mincut			
	Iterations	Latches	Inputs	time	Iterations	Latches	Inputs	time
Test1	1	0	140	111	1	0	126	48
Test2	t/o			16571	9	38	154	1171
Test3	19	36	180	5003	9	40	151	2241
Test4	18	34	147	4185	8	30	129	897
Test5	14	26	142	2391	6	25	130	1305
Test6	22	42	286	4543	8	36	151	653
Test7	15	28	152	1549	5	27	121	555
Test8	1	0	141	115	1	0	138	62
Test9	1	0	141	116	6	19	136	528
Test10	1	0	141	117	1	0	138	60
Test11	1	0	146	69	1	0	139	86
Test12	1	0	141	111	6	18	138	1246

elimination and abstraction growth rate. This point depends only on the design and not on the property, since the design is the major contributor to state explosion.

We applied our iterative refinement flow on 12 distinct real-life test cases, comparing the results of using the lower frontier vs. the min-cut frontier,. The results, reported in Table 3, clearly demonstrate three advantages of the Min-Cut optimization:

- The run-time of the iterative refinement flow can be significantly reduced. In all but 3 tests, we achieved reduction in run time. In one case, Test2, the run did not complete at all without applying the Min-Cut optimization, timing-out after several hours. Applying Min-Cut, the verification completed in 1171 seconds.
- When Min-Cut optimizations are not used, un-freeing more than 2 latches at a time adds too much redundant logic and have a negative impact on the quality of the abstraction as well as run time, whereas when Min-Cut is applied the frontier can pass through non-latch elements so the addition of logic for every un-freed frontier node can be more conservative. We were able to un-free more frontier nodes (8) at each iteration. As a result, the number of iterations is reduced, as seen in the table.
- The Min-Cut technique may not reduce significantly the number of latches in the final abstractions, but it reduced the number of inputs significantly, as seen in Test6.

7 Concluding Remarks

Automatic generation of abstractions and their iterative refinement is a successful method that expands the applicability of current model-checking tools. Our work contributes to this area in several ways: First, we describe an automatic counterexample analysis tool, which is integrated with a SAT-based bounded model checker. Besides detecting spurious abstract counterexamples for the iterative refinement framework, this tool can be used in isolation for analyzing the results of manual abstractions. Most useful is its ability to provide a concrete version for real counterexamples. Second, our work departs from the way counterexamples have been used to guide the refinement process until now, in that the refinement step need not necessarily eliminate the spurious counterexample at hand. Instead, the refinement is done so that *all* the spurious counterexamples are eventually eliminated. While doing it, one must choose only the most relevant logic in order to avoid reaching the capacity limits of the model checker before a successful abstraction is found. We present a novel heuristic based on Multiple Counterexample (MCE) technology, that specifically addresses this goal. The MCE heuristic hints at the nodes in the frontier that are most relevant for all the counterexamples of the same length as the one at hand. Third, our refinement algorithm achieves fine control over the abstract models' size growth by allowing the frontier to include intermediate logic nodes, and by applying optimizations aimed at minimizing the number of added variables while maximizing the constraints added to the abstract model.

Our experiments show the success of this approach for real-life test cases that were beyond the capacity of a state-of-the-art BDD-based model checker, and provide insight on how various tool configuration parameters can be tuned for a given set of test cases.

One possible avenue for future work is to combine hints from different sources when deciding which nodes will be un-freed. Other possible direction for development is to allow the refinement process to backtrack and try other refinement directions when the capacity limits of the model checker are reached.

References

1. R. Armoni, L. Fix, A. Flaisher, R. Gerth, B. Ginsburg, T. Kanza, A. Landver, S. Mador-Haim, E. Singerman, A. Tiemeyer, M.Y. Vardi, and Y. Zbar. The ForSpec temporal logic: A new temporal property-specification language. In *Tools and Algorithms for the Construction and Analysis of Systems (TACAS'02)*, LNCS. Springer-Verlag, 2002.
2. F. Balarin and A.L. Sangiovanni-Vincentelli. An iterative approach to language containment. In *CAV'93*, LNCS, pages 29–40. Springer-Verlag, 1993.
3. S. Barner, D. Geist, and A. Gringauze. Symbolic localization reduction with reconstruction layering and backtracking. In E. Brinksma and K. G. Larsen, editors, *CAV'02*, volume 2404 of *LNCS*, pages 65–77. Springer-Verlag, 2002.
4. A. Biere, A. Cimatti, E.M. Clarke, and Y. Zhu. Symbolic model checking without BDDs. In *Tools and Algorithms for Construction and Analysis of Systems (TACAS'99)*, volume 1579 of *LNCS*, pages 193–207. Springer-Verlag, 1999.
5. P. Biesse, T. Leonard, and A. Mokkedem. Finding bugs in an alpha microprocessors using satisfiability solvers. In *CAV'01*, volume 2102 of *LNCS*, pages 454–464. Springer-Verlag, 2001.
6. B. Bollobas. *Graph Theory*. Springer-Verlag, 1979.
7. J.R. Burch, E.M. Clarke, K.L. McMillan, D.L. Dill, and L.J. Hwang. Symbolic model checking: 10^{20} states and beyond. *Information and Computation*, 98(2):142–170, June 1992.
8. E. M. Clarke, A. Gupta, J. Kukula, and O. Strichman. SAT based abstraction-refinement using ILP and machine learning techniques. In E. Brinksma and K. G. Larsen, editors, *CAV'02*, volume 2404 of *LNCS*, pages 265–279. Springer-Verlag, 2002.
9. E.M. Clarke, E.A. Emerson, and A.P. Sistla. Automatic verification of finite-state concurrent systems using temporal logic specifications. *ACM Transactions on Programming Languages and Systems*, 8(2):244–263, January 1986.
10. E.M. Clarke, O. Grumberg, S. Jha, Y. Lu, and H. Veith. Counterexample-guided abstraction refinement. In *CAV'00*, volume 1855 of *LNCS*, pages 154–169. Springer-Verlag, 2000.
11. E.M. Clarke, O. Grumberg, and D.E. Long. Model checking and abstraction. *ACM Transactions on Programming Languages and Systems*, 16(5):1512–1542, September 1994.
12. E.M. Clarke, O. Grumberg, and D. Peled. *Model Checking*. MIT Press, 1999.
13. F. Copty, L. Fix, R. Fraer, E. Giunchiglia, G. Kamhi, A. Tacchella, and M.Y. Vardi. Benefits of bounded model checking at an industrial setting. In *CAV'01*, volume 2102 of *LNCS*, pages 436–453. Springer-Verlag, 2001.
14. F. Copty, A. Irron, O. Weissberg, N.P. Kropp, and G. Kamhi. Efficient debugging in a formal verification environment. In T. Margaria et. al., editor, *Correct Hardware Design and Verification Methods (CHARME'01)*, volume 2144 of *LNCS*, pages 275–292. Springer-Verlag, 2001.
15. L.R. Ford and D.R. Fulkerson. Maximal flow through a network. *Canadian Journal of Mathematics*, 8:399–404, 1956.
16. R. Fraer, G. Kamhi, B. Ziv, M. Vardi, and L. Fix. Prioritized traversal: efficient reachability analysis for verication and falsification. In *CAV'00*, volume 1855 of *LNCS*, pages 389–402. Springer-Verlag, 2000.
17. G.S. Govindaraju and D.L. Dill. Counterexample-guided choice of projections in approximate symbolic model checking. In *ICCAD'00*, 2000.
18. G. Hachtel and F. Somenzi. *Synthesis and Verification Algorithms*. Kluwer, 1996.
19. R.H. Hardin, Z. Har'el, and R.P. Kurshan. COSPAN. In *CAV'96*, volume 1102 of *LNCS*, pages 423–427. Springer-Verlag, 1996.
20. R.H. Hardin, R.P. Kurshan, K.L. McMillan, J.A. Reeds, and N.J.A. Sloane. Efficient regression verification. *IEE Proc. WODES'96*, pages 147–150, 1996.

21. P.H. Ho, T. Shiple, K. Harer, J.H. Kukula, R. Damiano, V. Bertacco, J. Taylor, and J. Long. Smart simulation using collaborative formal simulation engines. In *ICCAD'00*, pages 120–126, 2000.
22. J. Jang, I. Moon, and G. Hachtel. Iterative abstraction-based CTL model checking, 2000.
23. B. Krishnamurthy. An improved Min-Cut algorithm for partitioning VLSI networks. *IEEE Transactions on Computers*, 33(5):438–446, 1984.
24. O. Kupferman and M.Y. Vardi. Model checking of safety properties. *Formal Methods in System Design*, 19:291–314, 2001.
25. R.P. Kurshan. *Computer Aided Verification of Coordinating Processes*. Princeton Univ. Press, 1994.
26. W. Lee, A. Pardo, J. Jang, G. Hachtel, and F. Somenzi. Tearing based abstraction for CTL model checking. In *ICCAD'96*, pages 76–81, 1996.
27. O. Lichtenstein and A. Pnueli. Checking that finite state concurrent programs satisfy their linear specification. In *Proc. 12th ACM Symp. on Principles of Programming Languages*, pages 97–107, 1985.
28. J. Lind-Nielsen and H.R. Andersen. Stepwise CTL model checking of state/event systems. In *CAV'99*, volume 1633 of *LNCS*, pages 316–327. Springer-Verlag, 1999.
29. Z. Manna and A. Pnueli. *The Temporal Logic of Reactive and Concurrent Systems: Specification*. Springer-Verlag, January 1992.
30. K.S. Namjoshi and R.P. Kurshan. Syntactic program transformations for automatic abstraction. In *CAV'00*, volume 1855 of *LNCS*, pages 435–449. Springer-Verlag, 2000.
31. A. Pardo and G. Hachtel. Automatic abstraction techniques for propositional μ-calculus model checking. In *CAV'97*, volume 1254 of *LNCS*, pages 12–23. Springer-Verlag, 1997.
32. A. Pardo and G. Hachtel. Incremental CTL model checking using BDD subsetting. In *Design Automation Conference*, pages 457–462, 1998.
33. J.P. Queille and J. Sifakis. Specification and verification of concurrent systems in Cesar. In *Proc. 5th International Symp. on Programming*, volume 137 of *LNCS*, pages 337–351. Springer-Verlag, 1981.
34. R. Rudell. Dynamic Variable Ordering for Ordered Binary Decision Diagrams. In *ICCAD'93*, pages 42–47. IEEE Computer Society Press, 1993.
35. V. Rusu and E. Singerman. On proving safety properties by integrating static analysis, theorem proving and abstraction. In W.R. Cleaveland, editor, *TACAS'99*, volume 1579 of *LNCS*, pages 178–192. Springer-Verlag, 1999.
36. M.Y. Vardi. An automata-theoretic approach to linear temporal logic. In F. Moller and G. Birtwistle, editors, *Logics for Concurrency: Structure versus Automata*, volume 1043 of *LNCS*, pages 238–266. Springer-Verlag, 1996.
37. M.Y. Vardi and P. Wolper. An automata-theoretic approach to automatic program verification. In *1st Symp. on Logic in Computer Science*, pages 332–344, Cambridge, June 1986.
38. D. Wang, P.H. Ho, J. Long, J.H. Kukula, Y. Zhu, T. Ma, and R. Damiano. Formal property verification by abstraction refinement with formal, simulation and hybrid engines. In *Design Automation Conference*, pages 35–40, 2001.

Verification of Hybrid Systems Based on Counterexample-Guided Abstraction Refinement*

Edmund Clarke[1], Ansgar Fehnker[2], Zhi Han[2], Bruce Krogh[2], Olaf Stursberg[2,3], and Michael Theobald[1]

[1] Computer Science, Carnegie Mellon University, Pittsburgh, PA
[2] Electrical and Computer Engineering, Carnegie Mellon University, Pittsburgh, PA
[3] Process Control Lab, University of Dortmund, Germany

Abstract. Hybrid dynamic systems include both continuous and discrete state variables. Properties of hybrid systems, which have an infinite state space, can often be verified using ordinary model checking together with a finite-state abstraction. Model checking can be inconclusive, however, in which case the abstraction must be refined. This paper presents a new procedure to perform this refinement operation for abstractions of infinite-state systems, in particular of hybrid systems. Following an approach originally developed for finite-state systems [1,2], the refinement procedure constructs a new abstraction that eliminates a counterexample generated by the model checker. For hybrid systems, analysis of the counterexample requires the computation of sets of reachable states in the continuous state space. We show how such reachability computations with varying degrees of complexity can be used to refine hybrid system abstractions efficiently. A detailed example illustrates our counterexample-guided refinement procedure. Experimental results for a prototype implementation of the procedure indicate its advantages over existing methods.

1 Introduction

Hybrid systems are formal models that include both continuous and discrete state variables. With the increasing use of hybrid systems to design embedded controllers for complex systems such as manufacturing processes, automobiles, and transportation networks, there is an urgent need for more powerful analysis tools, especially for safety critical applications. Tools developed so far for automated analysis of hybrid systems are restricted to low-dimensional continuous dynamics [3]. The reason for this limitation is the difficulty of representing and computing sets of reachable states for continuous dynamic systems. Recent publications have proposed two general approaches to deal

* This research was supported by the Defense Advanced Research Project Agency (DARPA) MoBIES project under contracts no. F3361500C1701 and F33615-02-C-0429, by the Army Research Office (ARO) under contract no. DAAD19-01-1-0485, by the National Science Foundation (NSF) under grants no. CCR-0121547 and CCR-0098072. The views and conclusions contained in this document are those of the authors and should not be interpreted as representing the official policies, either expressed or implied, of DARPA, ARO, NSF, the U.S. Government or any other entity.

H. Garavel and J. Hatcliff (Eds.): TACAS 2003, LNCS 2619, pp. 192–207, 2003.

with the complexity of hybrid system analysis, namely, modular analysis (e.g., [4,5]) and abstraction (e.g., [6,7,8]). This paper focuses on the latter approach.

Abstraction maps a given model into a less complex model that retains the behaviors of interest [6]. In the context of hybrid system verification, abstraction transforms the inherently infinite state system into a finite-state model [7,8]. Existing tools often do not consider the property itself when building an abstract model. Rather, an abstract representation is constructed for the entire hybrid system using a degree of detail which seems to be appropriate. If the abstraction is not appropriate to analyze the property, the whole abstraction process is started again, or the abstract model is globally refined [9].

As an alternative, we suggest a procedure that (a) starts from a coarse abstract model and a safety property, (b) identifies parts of the hybrid system which potentially violate the property, and (c) iteratively refines the abstract model until verification reveals whether or not the property in question is satisfied. A framework that follows this general scheme of abstraction, refinement, and analysis, is *counterexample-guided abstraction refinement (CEGAR)* [1,10,2]: For a given system the initial abstraction leads to a conservative model that is guaranteed to include all behaviors of the original system. Model checking is then applied to the abstract model. If the property is violated, the model checker produces a *counterexample* as an *execution path* for the abstract model for which the property is not true. If the counterexample corresponds to a behavior of the original system, then the property does not hold for the original system. Otherwise, the information provided by the counterexample is then used to *refine* the abstract model, i.e., some detail is added to the abstract model in order to obtain a more accurate, yet conservative, representation of the original model. In particular, the refined model is constructed so that it is guaranteed to exclude the *spurious* counterexample. The procedure of alternating between model checking and refinement is continued until the property is confirmed or refuted.

This procedure has recently been applied successfully to finite discrete systems in a variety of domains, particularly for the verification of digital circuits [1,10]. Earlier work that is based on the use of counterexamples includes the localization reduction in the context of concurrent systems [2], and recent work has applied the technique to the verification of C-programs [11,12]. Another related abstraction refinement approach for programs [13] is not based on counterexamples but uses backward and forward reachability to decide how to refine an abstract model.

This paper makes two important contributions. First, we extend counterexample-guided model refinement to *infinite-state* systems. Second, we show how our new approach can be applied to hybrid systems, which include both continuous and discrete state variables and thus have an infinite-state space. We provide effective means of coping with the difficulties of computing reachable sets for infinite state systems. In particular, we employ reachable set computations with varying degrees of complexity to refine hybrid system abstractions efficiently. This flexibility cannot easily be achieved with other verification tools for hybrid systems. We note that using counterexamples to guide generation of discrete abstractions is being pursued independently by Alur et al. at University of Pennsylvania [14].

The paper is structured as follows. Section 2 presents preliminaries on abstraction and counterexample-guided refinement. In Section 3 we describe a new verification approach that refines abstract models of infinite state systems based on counterexamples.

We introduce hybrid systems in Section 4, and apply our new verification approach to hybrid systems in Section 5. Section 6 presents conclusions.

2 Preliminaries

We introduce the notions of abstraction and counterexample-guided refinement in a general setting for infinite state systems. The type of model we are working with throughout the section is a transition system defined as follows:

Definition 1 *Transition System.* A *transition system* is a 3-tuple $TS = (S, S_0, E)$ with a (possibly infinite) state set S, an initial set $S_0 \subset S$, and a set of transitions $E \subset S \times S$. $\diamond$

Given two transition systems A and C, A is said to be an *abstract model* of C if the following relation can be established.

Definition 2 *Abstraction.* A transition system $A = (\hat{S}, \hat{S}_0, \hat{E})$ with a finite set of states $\hat{S}$ is an *abstract model* of a transition system $C = (S, S_0, E)$, denoted $A \succeq C$, if there exists an *abstraction function* $\alpha : S \to \hat{S}$ such that:

- the initial set is $\hat{S}_0 = \{\hat{s}_0 |\ \exists s_0 \in S_0 : \hat{s}_0 = \alpha(s_0)\}$
- and $\hat{E} \supseteq \{(\hat{s}_1, \hat{s}_2) |\ \exists s_1, s_2 \in S\ : (s_1, s_2) \in E, \hat{s}_1 = \alpha(s_1), \hat{s}_2 = \alpha(s_2)\}$. $\diamond$

Sometimes the term *simulation* is used in the literature to describe the abstraction relation. In contrast to the definitions of abstraction in [1,10], Defn. 2 allows that A includes *spurious transitions*, i.e., the set $\hat{E}$ may contain elements that do not correspond to transitions in C. As a consequence the abstraction function in Defn. 2 does not uniquely define A. Spurious transitions arise in the construction of abstractions of hybrid systems because in most cases sets of reachable states for continuous systems can not be represented and computed exactly.

Abstract models will be used to analyze properties of a given transition system. Throughout the paper, we will call the given system C the *concrete system*.

In order to construct a more detailed model from a given abstract model, we define the following concept of *model refinement*.

Definition 3 *Refinement of Abstract Models.* Given a concrete system $C = (S, S_0, E)$ and an abstract model $A = (\hat{S}, \hat{S}_0, \hat{E})$ such that $C \preceq A$, with abstraction function $\alpha : S \to \hat{S}$, a model $A' = (\hat{S}', \hat{S}'_0, \hat{E}')$ is called a *refined abstract model of C with respect to A* if two abstraction functions $\alpha' : S \to \hat{S}'$ and $\alpha'' : \hat{S}' \to \hat{S}$ exist, i.e., $C \preceq A' \preceq A$. $\diamond$

A property is verified for the concrete model C using an abstract model A. In this paper we will consider the verification of safety properties, defined as follows.

Definition 4 *Safety.* Given a transition system $TS = (S, S_0, E)$, let the set $B \subset S$ specify a set of *bad states* such that $S_0 \cap B = \emptyset$. We say that TS *is safe with respect to* B, denoted by $TS \models \mathbf{AG}\neg B$ iff there is no path in the transition system from an initial state in S_0 to a bad state in B. Otherwise we say TS *is unsafe*, denoted by $TS \not\models \mathbf{AG}\neg B$. $\diamond$

Definition 5 *Counterexamples.* A path $\sigma = (s_0, s_1, \ldots, s_m)$ of $TS = (S, S_0, E)$ with $s_m \in B$ is called a *counterexample* of TS with respect to the safety property $TS \models$ **AG**$\neg B$. Given a concrete transition system C, an abstract transition system A, and a counterexample σ in C, we say that $\hat{\sigma} = (\hat{s}_0, \hat{s}_1, \hat{s}_2, \ldots, \hat{s}_m)$ is the *corresponding abstract counterexample* of the abstract system A, if $\hat{s}_i = \alpha(s_i)$ holds for all $i \in \{0, \ldots, m\}$. Given a counterexample $\hat{\sigma}$ of A, σ is called a *corresponding concrete counterexample* if $\hat{s}_i = \alpha(s_i)$ and $(s_i, s_{i+1}) \in E$. If a counterexample $\hat{\sigma}$ of A has no corresponding concrete counterexample for C, $\hat{\sigma}$ is called a *spurious counterexample*.$\diamond$

Lemma 1. *Given a concrete model* $C = (S, S_0, E)$*, and an abstract model* $A = (\hat{S}, \hat{S}_0, \hat{E})$ *of* C *with an abstraction function* α*, let* $B \subseteq S$*, and* $\hat{B} = \{\hat{b} \mid \exists\, b \in B : \hat{b} = \alpha(b)\}$*. If* $A \models$ ***AG***$\neg\hat{B}$*, then* $C \models$ ***AG***$\neg B$*.* □

If $A \models$ **AG**$\neg\hat{B}$ can be verified, it can immediately be concluded from Lemma 1 (i.e., without applying verification to the concrete system C) that $C \models$ **AG**$\neg B$. On the other hand, the converse of Lemma 1 with respect to the **AG**-property does not hold. If the verification of A reveals $A \not\models$ **AG**$\neg\hat{B}$, then we cannot conclude that C is not safe with respect to B, since the counterexample for A may be spurious. We call a method that checks whether or not a counterexample is spurious a *validation method*. If the validation method discovers that the counterexample is spurious, then the counterexample is used to refine A. We now introduce a scheme for *counterexample-guided refinement of abstractions* to verify safety properties for a given concrete model. The basic principle is to repeat the following sequence of steps until the property is verified or refuted [1]. The starting point is a concrete model C and an abstract model A (we propose in Sec. 5.1 one specific way to obtain an initial abstract model for hybrid systems). For a set $B \subseteq S$ of bad states for C, we assume for simplicity that $\alpha(s) \in \hat{B}$ implies $s \in B$. The first step is then to analyze $A \models$ **AG**$\neg\hat{B}$ by model checking. If this property holds it can immediately be concluded from Lemma 1 that C is safe, too. Otherwise a counterexample is obtained, and it must be validated whether it has a corresponding concrete counterexample in C. If there is a corresponding concrete counterexample, then the safety property does not hold for C. In the other case, i.e. the counterexample is spurious, the counterexample is used to refine the model A. That is, a new and more detailed model A' with $C \preceq A' \preceq A$ is determined, which excludes the spurious counterexample.

The procedure of model checking, validation of the counterexample, and refinement of the abstract model is repeated until the safety property is proved or refuted for C. The pseudo-code in Fig. 1 summarizes this procedure:

The crucial steps in the CEGAR procedure are *validation*, *refinement*, and *model checking*. With respect to model checking, standard algorithms for **AG**-properties can be used [15].

The important step in validating a counterexample is the computation of successors of states. We define an operator $succ$ that determines the successor states from a given set $\tilde{S} \subseteq S$ by $succ(\tilde{S}) = \{s \in S | \exists \tilde{s} \in \tilde{S} : (\tilde{s}, s) \in E\}$. This set may not be exactly computable for a given concrete model C, i.e. only over-approximations $\overline{succ}(\tilde{S}) \supset succ(\tilde{S})$ may be available. We first assume that $succ(\tilde{S})$ is computable.

ALGORITHM: Counterexample-Guided Abstraction Refinement: CEGAR
INPUT: Concrete model C and a set of bad states B
OUTPUT: B is (or is not) reachable

```
Generate initial abstract model A (bad states are called B̂)
Generate counterexample σ̂ by model checking A wrt. B̂
WHILE σ̂ exists DO
        Validation of σ̂
        IF σ̂ validated THEN terminate with "B reachable"
        ELSE
                Generate refined model A' using counterexample σ̂
                A := A'
                Generate next σ̂ by model checking A wrt. B̂
        ENDIF
ENDDO
Terminate with "B not reachable"
```

Fig. 1. CEGAR: Scheme for verifying/falsifying $C \models \mathbf{AG}\neg B$ based on counterexample-guided abstraction refinement

A counterexample $\hat{\sigma} = (\hat{s}_0, \ldots, \hat{s}_m)$ of A is then validated as follows: Let $S_k = \alpha^{-1}(\hat{s}_k)$, $k \in \{0, \ldots, m\}$ denote the set of concrete states corresponding to an element of $\hat{\sigma}$. The reachable parts of these sets are recursively defined by $S_0^{reach} := S_0$, $S_k^{reach} := succ(S_{k-1}^{reach}) \cap S_k$, $k \in \{1, \ldots, m\}$. The counterexample is spurious iff $S_k^{reach} = \emptyset$ applies for at least one k, and we say *the counterexample is refuted.* Otherwise, the counterexample is *validated*, and B is reachable.

If the counterexample is refuted with $S_k^{reach} = \emptyset$, the model A is refined to a new finite abstract model $A' = (\hat{S}', \hat{S}'_0, \hat{E}')$ (cf. Defn. 3). The refined model should take into account that there are no concrete transitions from states in S_{k-1}^{reach} to states in S_k. We therefore require that the set $\hat{E}'$ of A' does **not** contain transitions in the set $\{(\alpha'(s_1), \alpha'(s_2)) \mid \exists\, s_1 \in S_{k-1}^{reach}, s_2 \in S_k\}$. Thus, succeeding refined models will exclude previously explored counterexamples. A method for the refinement of abstract models for infinite-state systems will be presented in the next section.

3 Refinement of Abstract Models for Infinite State Systems

This section presents a specific method for refining an abstract model A for an infinite state system. The main idea is to directly use the information obtained from the validation procedure to refine some abstract states: Assume that the abstract model includes a transition between $\hat{s}_1$ and $\hat{s}_2$, while the validation of the counterexample has revealed that only a subset of concrete states in $S_2 := \alpha^{-1}(\hat{s}_2)$ is reachable from concrete states in $S_1 := \alpha^{-1}(\hat{s}_1)$. In this case we refine A by splitting $\hat{s}_2$ into two new states. The first one, denoted by $\hat{s}_2^{reach}$, represents the reachable subset of S_2, given by $S_2^{reach} := succ(S_1) \cap S_2$. The second one, denoted by $\hat{s}_2^{comp}$, represents the complement of the reachable part, given by $S_2^{comp} := S_2 \setminus S_2^{reach}$. In addition, the abstraction function that maps concrete states to abstract ones has to be refined, too.

Definition 6 *Refinement by State Splitting.* Given a concrete model $C = (S, S_0, E)$ and an abstract model $A = (\hat{S}, \hat{S}_0, \hat{E})$ with an abstraction function $\alpha : S \rightarrow \hat{S}$. Let $(\hat{s}_1, \hat{s}_2) \in \hat{E}$ be a transition of a counterexample $\hat{\sigma}$. Then, we define ρ_{split} as a refinement function that maps A, α, and $(\hat{s}_1, \hat{s}_2) \in \hat{E}$ onto the refined abstract model $A' = (\hat{S}', \hat{S}'_0, \hat{E}')$ and the refined abstraction function $\alpha' : S \rightarrow \hat{S}'$, i.e., $(A', \alpha') = \rho_{split}(A, \alpha, (\hat{s}_1, \hat{s}_2))$, defined as follows:

- $\hat{S}' = (\hat{S} \setminus \hat{s}_2) \cup \{\hat{s}_2^{reached}, \hat{s}_2^{comp}\}$
- $\alpha'(s) = \begin{cases} \alpha(s) & \text{if } s \notin S_2 \\ \hat{s}_2^{reach} & \text{if } s \in S_2^{reach} \\ \hat{s}_2^{comp} & \text{if } s \in S_2^{comp} \end{cases}$
- $\hat{S}'_0 = \{\hat{s}' \in \hat{S}' | \alpha''(\hat{s}') \in \hat{S}_0\}$
- $\hat{E}' = \{(\hat{s}'_1, \hat{s}'_2) \in \hat{S}' \times \hat{S}' | \exists \hat{s}_1, \hat{s}_2 \in \hat{S} \ : (\hat{s}_1, \hat{s}_2) \in \hat{E} \wedge \hat{s}_1 = \alpha''(\hat{s}'_1) \wedge \hat{s}_2 = \alpha''(\hat{s}'_2)\} \setminus (\hat{s}_1, \hat{s}_2^{comp})$

where $\alpha'' : \hat{S}' \rightarrow \hat{S}$ maps $\hat{s}'$ onto itself if $\hat{s}' \notin \{\hat{s}_2^{reached}, \hat{s}_2^{comp}\}$, and on $\hat{s}_2$ otherwise. ◇

Lemma 2. *Let $A = (\hat{S}, \hat{S}_0, \hat{E})$ be an abstract model of $C = (S, S_0, E)$ with the abstraction function $\alpha : S \rightarrow \hat{S}$. For a given transition $(\hat{s}_1, \hat{s}_2) \in \hat{E}$, assume that $S_2^{reach} \neq \emptyset$ holds. Then, $(A', \alpha') := \rho_{split}(A, \alpha, (\hat{s}_1, \hat{s}_2))$ satisfies $A \succeq A' \succeq C$.* □

The idea of splitting an abstract state has also been considered by Jeannet et al. [13]. However, their method does not address hybrid systems, and it uses forward and backward reachability on the abstract model rather than counterexamples to decide which state to split. One advantage (among others) of a counterexample-based approach is that it terminates quickly when a discovered counterexample is not spurious and thus proving that the safety property does not hold for the concrete system.

As a next step, we consider the case where the set of successors of S_1 and the set S_2 are disjoint. In this case, we can simply omit the corresponding abstract transition.

Definition 7 *Refinement by Eliminating a Transition.* The function ρ_{purge} is a refinement that maps an abstract model $A = (\hat{S}, \hat{S}_0, \hat{E})$, an abstraction function $\alpha : S \rightarrow \hat{S}$ and a transition $(\hat{s}_1, \hat{s}_2) \in \hat{E}$ onto $A' = (\hat{S}, \hat{S}_0, \hat{E}')$ with $\hat{E}' = \hat{E} \setminus (\hat{s}_1, \hat{s}_2)$. ◇

Lemma 3. *Let $A = (\hat{S}, \hat{S}_0, \hat{E})$ be an abstract model of $C = (S, S_0, E)$ with the abstraction function $\alpha : S \rightarrow \hat{S}$. For a given transition $(\hat{s}_1, \hat{s}_2) \in \hat{E}$, assume that $S_2^{reach} = \emptyset$ holds. Then, $A' := \rho_{purge}(A, \alpha, (\hat{s}_1, \hat{s}_2))$ satisfies $A \succeq A' \succeq C$.* □

Based on these results, we now present a more specific formulation of the CEGAR algorithm in Fig. 2, called INFINITE-STATE-CEGAR, which uses the functions ρ_{split} and ρ_{purge} for refinement.

Correctness of the algorithm is implied by the following two lemmas[1]. Note that termination of the algorithm cannot be guaranteed as the number of states in the concrete model may be infinite, and a finite abstract model to verify (or disprove) the given property may not exist.

[1] The proofs of all lemmas in the paper can be found in [16].

```
ALGORITHM: INFINITE-STATE-CEGAR
INPUT: Concrete model C and a set of bad states B
OUTPUT: B is (or is not) reachable

Generate initial abstract model A and abstraction function α
B̂ := α(B)
Generate counterexample σ̂ = (ŝ_0, ... , ŝ_m) by model checking of A wrt. B̂
S_0^reach := α^{-1}(ŝ_0)
WHILE σ̂ exists DO
    // validation of counterexample
    k := 0
    WHILE S_k^reach ≠ ∅ AND k < m DO
        k := k + 1
        S_k^reach := succ(S_{k-1}^reach) ∩ α^{-1}(ŝ_k)
    ENDDO
    // if counterexample is validated, then terminate, else refine
    IF S_k^reach ≠ ∅ THEN terminate with "B reachable"
    ELSE
        FOR l = 1, ... , k - 1
            // split abstract state ŝ_l into two: one that corresponds
            // to S_l^reach and one that corresponds to α^{-1}(ŝ_l) \ S_l^reach
            IF S_l^reach ≠ α^{-1}(ŝ_l)
            THEN (A, α) := ρ_split(A, α, ŝ_{l-1}, ŝ_l)
            ENDIF
        ENDFOR
        // remove spurious transition between ŝ_{k-1} and ŝ_k
        A := ρ_purge(A, α, ŝ_{k-1}, ŝ_k)
        Generate σ̂ by model checking of A wrt. B̂
    ENDIF
ENDDO
Terminate with "B not reachable"
```

Fig. 2. INFINITE-STATE-CEGAR.

Lemma 4. *If the algorithm terminates with "B reachable", then* $C \not\models \mathbf{AG}\neg B$. □

Lemma 5. *If the algorithm terminates with "B not reachable", then* $C \models \mathbf{AG}\neg B$. □

The proposed procedure of validating counterexamples and refining abstract models is based on the computation of successor states. Alternatively, one could formulate a similar algorithm that uses sets of predecessors, or even a combination of both as presented in [1] and [10].

The INFINITE-STATE-CEGAR algorithm in Fig. 2 is based on the assumption that sets of successor states are exactly computable. Lemma 5 holds, however, also if successor states are not exactly computable, and instead only *over*-approximations of the set of successor states can be computed. If only under-approximations of successor sets can be computed, Lemma 5 will not hold, but Lemma 4 will.

4 Hybrid Systems

Hybrid systems are a class of infinite state systems that include both continuous and discrete state variables. This section presents hybrid automata, which are used to model hybrid systems. We illustrate these definitions with an example that models a simple car controller, which is also used in later sections to illustrate our new verification approach.

4.1 Definition of Hybrid Automata

Definition 8 *Syntax of the Hybrid Automaton HA.* A *hybrid automaton* is a tuple $HA = (Z, z_0, X, inv, X_0, T, g, j, f)$ where

- Z is a finite set of *locations* with an *initial location* $z_0 \in Z$.
- $X \subseteq \mathbb{R}^n$ is the continuous state space.
- $inv : Z \to 2^X$ assigns to each location $z \in Z$ an invariant of the form $inv(z) \subseteq X$.
- $X_0 \subseteq X$ is the set of initial continuous states. The set of initial hybrid states of *HA* is thus given by the set of states $\{z_0\} \times X_0$.
- $T \subseteq Z \times Z$ is the set of *discrete transitions* between locations.
- $g : T \to 2^X$ assigns a *guard* set $g((z_1, z_2)) \subseteq X$ to $t = (z_1, z_2) \in T$.
- $j : T \times X \to 2^X$ assigns to each pair $(z_1, z_2) \in T$ and $x \in g((z_1, z_2))$ a *jump* set $j((z_1, z_2), x) \subseteq X$.
- $f : Z \to (X \to \mathbb{R}^n)$ assigns to each location $z \in Z$ a continuous vector field $f(z)$. We use the notation f_z for $f(z)$. The evolution of the continuous behavior in location z is governed by the differential equation $\dot{\chi}(t) = f_z(\chi(t))$. We assume that the differential equation has a unique solution for each initial value $\chi(0) \in X_0$. $\diamond$

The semantics of HA is defined as a trace transition system. A state (z, x) corresponds to a continuous state x within location z. Two states, (z_1, x_1) and (z_2, x_2), are connected by a transition if and only if state (z_2, x_2) can be reached from state (z_1, x_1) by a continuous evolution within location z_1 followed by a discrete transition to location z_2.

Definition 9 *Semantics of the Hybrid Automaton HA.* The semantics of a Hybrid automaton HA is a *transition system* $TTS = (S, S_0, E)$ with:

- the set of all *hybrid states* (z, x) of HA,

$$S = \bigcup_{z \in Z} \bigcup_{x \in inv(z)} (z, x) \tag{1}$$

- the set of *initial hybrid states* $S_0 = \{z_0\} \times X_0$,
- transitions $(s_1, s_2) \in E$ with $s_1 = (z_1, x_1)$, $s_2 = (z_2, x_2)$, iff there exists $(z_1, z_2) \in T$ and a trajectory $\chi : [0, \tau] \to X$ for some $\tau \in \mathbb{R}^{>0}$ such that:
  - $x_1 = \chi(0)$, $\chi(\tau) \in g((z_1, z_2))$,
  - $x_2 \in j((z_1, z_2), \chi(\tau))$,
  - $\dot{\chi}(t) = f_{z_1}(\chi(t))$ for $t \in [0, \tau]$,
  - $\chi(t) \in inv(z_1)$ for $t \in [0, \tau]$,
  - $x_2 \in inv(z_2)$.

A path $\sigma = \{s_0, s_1, s_2, \ldots\}$ of TTS is called a *trace* of HA, and we refer to TTS as the *trace transition system* of HA. ◇

Definition 10 *Safety of a Hybrid Automaton.* For a hybrid automaton HA with a semantics as in Defn. 9, let $z_b \in Z \setminus \{z_0\}$ denote an *unsafe* location. HA is said to be *safe* with respect to z_b, denoted by $TTS \models \mathbf{AG}\neg z_b$ iff for all traces σ applies: $\nexists s \in \sigma$ with $s = (z_b, x)$ for some $x \in X$. We write $TTS \not\models \mathbf{AG}\neg z_b$ otherwise. ◇

The extension of the analysis task to multiple initial locations and/or multiple unsafe locations is straightforward but is omitted here for simplicity.

4.2 Example

As a motivating example, we use a simple controller that steers a car along a straight road. The car is assumed to drive at a constant speed $r = 2$, and its motion is modeled by the distance x ($x = 0$ corresponds to the middle of the road) from the middle of the road and the heading angle γ ($\gamma = 0$ corresponds to moving straight ahead). Fig. 3 shows a scenario in which the car drives initially on the road. The controller is able to detect whether the car is on the left or right border (i.e. $x \leq -1$, $x \geq 1$) – whenever the car enters the left border, the controller forces it to turn right until the car is back on the road again. Then a left turn is initiated, and continued until the car is again going straight ahead in the direction of the road, i.e. when the heading is aligned with the road ($\gamma = 0$). A similar strategy is employed when the car enters the right border.

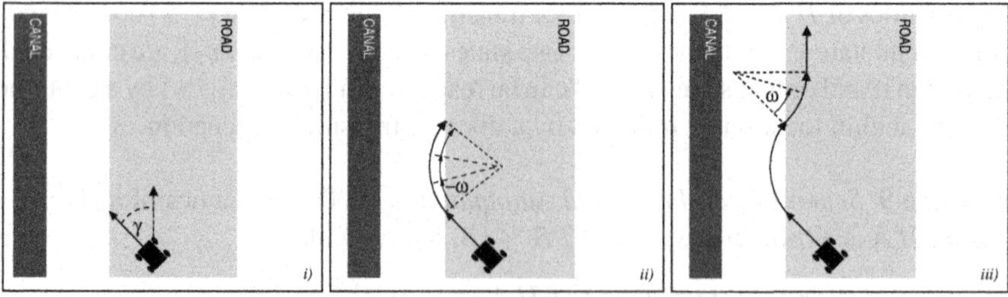

Fig. 3. *i)* Initially, the car drives on the road with heading angle γ. *ii)* If the controller detects that the car left the road, it corrects the heading by turning right to avoid the canal. *iii)* Once the car is back on the road, a left turn is initiated until the car moves straight again.

Fig. 4 shows a hybrid automaton model of the controlled behavior for the car. Besides the position x and the heading angle γ, the description includes an internal timer c, that the controller uses to time the steering manoeuvres. The differential equations for these three continuous variables depend on the location: we have $\dot{x} = -r \cdot sin(\gamma)$ in all locations except of `in_canal`. The derivative of γ varies when a border is reached. On the border the motion of the car describes an arc with the angular velocity $\dot{\gamma} = -\omega = -\pi/4$ (or $\omega = \pi/4$ respectively), i. e., the arc is part of a circle with radius r/ω. The timer

c measures the time period which the car spends on a borders. In the correction modes the timer decreases with double rate, i.e., the correction takes half the time as the car was on the border before. Since the sign of $\dot{\gamma}$ is reversed when the car moves back on the road, the angle has the value zero when the correction mode is left ($c = 0$), i.e., the car moves then along the road. During this correction it might, however, happen that the other border is reached, which means that the controller then switches to the strategy of the corresponding location.

The three continuous variables are initialized to $-1 \leq x \leq 1$ (the car is on the road), $-\pi/4 \leq \gamma \leq \pi/4$, and $c = 0$. It has to be verified for this set of initial states whether the given control strategy guarantees that the unsafe location `in_canal` (z_b) is never reached. The following sections present how this task can be solved by abstraction-based and counterexample-guided verification.

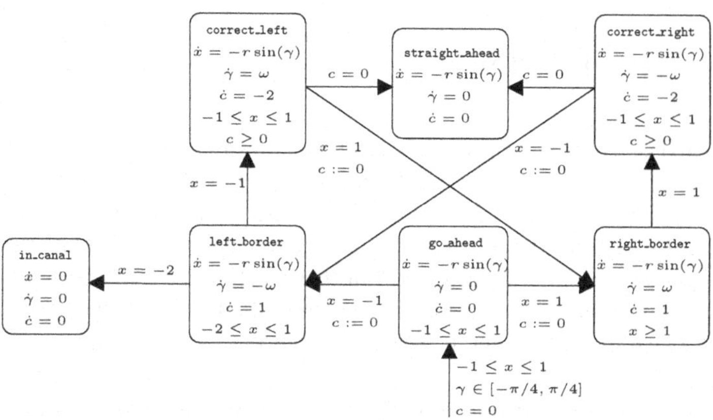

Fig. 4. Hybrid automaton that models the car steering example. Location `in_canal` has to be avoided. For each location, the continuous dynamics of the three variables x, γ and c is described by differential equations, and invariants are specified as inequalities. Guards and jumps are assigned to the transitions, e.g., a transition from location `go_ahead` to `left_boarder` is possible if the value of x is 1, and then the value of c is set to zero.

5 Refinement of Abstractions for Hybrid Systems

This section applies the general concepts of Section 3 to the particular class of infinite state systems of hybrid systems.

We present specific solutions for the two crucial steps, the validation of counterexamples and the refinement of abstract models. The key to the validation step is the computation of successor states for a given set of states in the trace transition system. Starting from the initial set, the validation procedure computes the successors along the counterexample until either the unsafe location z_{sp} is reached or a transition is determined to be spurious. The computation of sets of successors states is usually the most expensive step in hybrid system verification. Moreover, successor sets can be computed and represented *exactly* only for certain sub-classes of hybrid systems [17,18]. However, several approaches to over-approximate successor sets have been published, as e. g., approximations by orthogonal polyhedra [19], general polyhedra [20], projections to lower dimensional polyhedra [21], or ellipsoids [22]. Most of these approaches aim at providing an efficient way to obtain conservative but tight approximations.

The verification framework presented here can include different techniques to over-approximate the set of successors. The idea of using different methods is motivated by the trade-off between the accuracy and the computational complexity of different methods. If, e.g., a faster but maybe less accurate technique is sufficient to refute a counterexample, there is no need to use a computationally more expensive method.

In the following, we first describe how an initial abstraction for a hybrid automaton can be obtained, and then focus on the validation of counterexamples and the refinement based on the use of different methods for computing successor states.

5.1 Abstraction of Hybrid Systems

For the first step of INFINITE-STATE-CEGAR, the construction of an initial abstraction, we introduce one abstract state for each location of HA. This means that two hybrid states (z_i, x_i) and (z_j, x_j) of TTS are mapped to the same abstract state if and only if $z_i = z_j$. This rule applies for all but the initial location, which we split into two abstract states to separate the initial hybrid states in that location from the non-initial hybrid states: we introduce one abstract state $\hat{s}_0$ to represent all initial hybrid states of TTS, and another one ($\hat{s}'_0$) to represent the remaining hybrid states in location z_0.

Definition 11 *Initial Abstraction of Hybrid Systems.* Given a hybrid automaton HA with $Z = \{z_0, z_1, \dots, z_{n_z}\}$, let S denote the set of hybrid states as defined in (1). For $i \in \{0, 1, \dots, n_z\}$, we define the abstraction function $\alpha : S \to \hat{S}$ by:

$$\alpha(z_i, x) = \begin{cases} \hat{s}_0 \text{ if } i = 0 \wedge x \in X_0 \\ \hat{s}'_0 \text{ if } i = 0 \wedge x \notin X_0 \\ \hat{s}_i \text{ otherwise} \end{cases} \tag{2}$$

and the initial abstract model $A = (\hat{S}, \hat{S}_0, \hat{E})$ is defined by ($i \in \{0, 1, \dots, n\}$, $j \in \{0, 1, \dots, n_z\}$):

- $\hat{S} = \{\hat{s}'_0, \hat{s}_0, \hat{s}_1, \dots, \hat{s}_n\}$
- $\hat{S}_0 = \{\hat{s}_0\}$
- $\hat{E} = \{(\hat{s}_i, \hat{s}_j) | (z_i, z_j) \in T\} \cup \{(\hat{s}'_0, \hat{s}_j) | (z_0, z_j) \in T\} \cup \{(\hat{s}_i, \hat{s}'_0) | (z_i, z_0) \in T\}$ ◇

The initial abstract model represents the discrete structure of the hybrid system without regarding the continuous dynamics and guards. It has to be shown that A is indeed an abstract model of the underlying trace transition system, i.e., that it fulfills Defn. 2:

Lemma 6. *For HA with trace transition system $TTS = (S, S_0, E)$, let $A = (\hat{S}, \hat{S}_0, \hat{E})$ denote the initial abstract model for TTS. Then, $A \succeq TTS$.* □

Example (cont.) Fig. 5 depicts the initial abstract model of the hybrid system in Fig. 4. It is a copy of the discrete part of the hybrid system, except that the initial location is divided into two parts: $\hat{s}_0$ represents the states in location `go_ahead` with $x \in [-1, 1]$, $\gamma \in [-\pi/4, \pi/4]$ and $c = 0$, and $\hat{s}'_0$ all other states in `go_ahead`. The abstract states $\hat{s}_1$ to $\hat{s}_6$ represent the hybrid states of the other locations (`left_border`, `right_border`, `correct_left`, `correct_right`, `straight_ahead` and `in_canal`, respectively). ♦

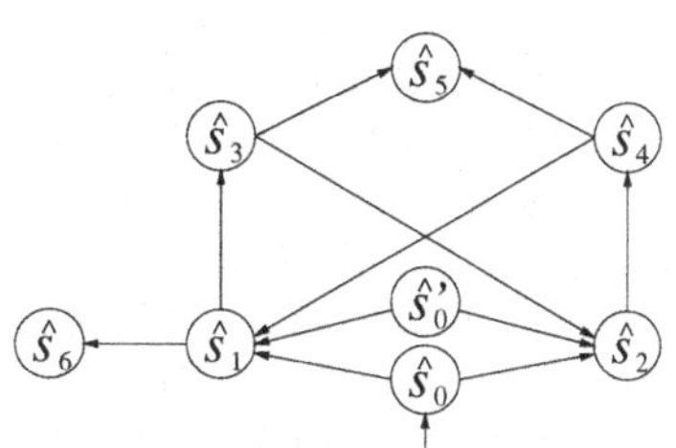

Fig 5. Initial abstract model of the hybrid system depicted in Fig. 4

5.2 Over-Approximation of the Sets of Successors

Computing sets of successor states is required in the validation and refinement steps. The goal is to use different over-approximations with different precisions and different computational needs. We first define an over-approximation operator of the successor relation for a tuple of sets of states. The operator conservatively approximates which states in the second set (target set) are successors of states in the first set (source set).

Definition 12 *Over-approximation of successor states.* Let HA be a hybrid automaton with the trace transition system $TTS = (S, S_0, E)$, and let A and α be defined as in Defn. 11. For a transition $(\hat{s}_1, \hat{s}_2) \in \hat{E}$ of A, we call $S_1 := \alpha^{-1}(\hat{s}_1)$ the set of *hybrid source states* and $S_2 := \alpha^{-1}(\hat{s}_2)$ the set of *potential hybrid successor states*. Then, $\overline{succ} : (2^S \times 2^S) \to 2^S$ is an *over-approximation* of the hybrid successor states in S_2 iff the following holds:

- $\overline{succ}(S_1, S_2) \subseteq S_2$,
- for all $s_1 \in S_1$ and $s_2 \in S_2 \setminus \overline{succ}(S_1, S_2)$, $(s_1, s_2) \notin E$. ◇

A possible explicit realization of the operator $\overline{succ}$ combines the following steps: (a) By approximating the continuous evolution for all states in S_1, the reachable subset of the guard set $g(t)$ is determined, where $t = (z_1, z_2) \in T$ is the transition of HA that corresponds to the transition $(\hat{s}_1, \hat{s}_2) \in \hat{E}$ of A. Usually, this step is the most costly of the whole verification procedure; (b) the jump function $j(t, x)$ is applied to all hybrid states (z_1, x) which are in the reachable subset of $g(t)$; (c) the image of $j(t, x)$ is intersected with the set S_2 of potential hybrid successor states.

Example (cont.) Our prototype implementation employs two different methods, $\overline{succ}_{coarse}$ and $\overline{succ}_{tight}$, to over-approximate the set of successor states. For example, for the discrete transition from `correct_right` to `left_border`, we choose S_1 as subset of the plane $x = 1$ for location `correct_right`, and S_2 as all states of location `left_border` that satisfy the invariant $-2 \leq x \leq -1$. The transition is not spurious, if there exists a trajectory that starts in S_1, and ends in S_2 without leaving the invariant of `correct_right` $(-1 \leq x \leq 1 \wedge c \geq 0)$.

The first method $\overline{succ}_{coarse}$ poses the existence question for a trajectory between S_1 and S_2 as an optimization problem. The distance between a trajectory and S_2 is defined as the minimum distance between all points on the trajectory and S_2. If the global minimum over all trajectories that start in S_1 is strictly greater than zero, then no successor state of S_1 exists in S_2. In this case $\overline{succ}_{coarse}$ returns an empty set. If the minimum distance is zero, at least one corresponding concrete path exists, and $\overline{succ}_{coarse}$ returns the complete set S_2 as an over-approximation of the set of successor states. In the considered example, the distance of the optimal trajectory to S_2 is greater than zero, and there is hence no trajectory from S_1 to S_2[2]. The second method $\overline{succ}_{tight}$ computes polyhedra that enclose all trajectories that originate in S_1 [20]. The set of successor states $\overline{succ}_{tight}(S_1, S_2)$ is then obtained by intersecting the polyhedra with S_2. In the considered example, there are no successors of S_1 in S_2. ♦

5.3 Validation and Refinement

INFINITE-STATE-CEGAR makes a clear distinction between the validation of a counterexample, and the refinement of the abstract model. For hybrid systems, we propose a slightly different approach, in which the steps of validation and refinement are interleaved. We assume to have a set of over-approximation techniques $\overline{succ}_1, \ldots, \overline{succ}_p$ that can (but do not need to) establish a hierarchy of coarse to tight approximations.

The algorithm for the combined validation and refinement steps of a counterexample is as follows. Let $\sigma = (\hat{s}_0, \ldots, \hat{s}_m)$ be a counterexample of the abstract model A. The algorithm consists of two nested loops. The outer loop corresponds to checking each transition of the counterexample. The inner loop applies each of the over-approximation techniques to the current transition of the counterexample, and, depending on the result, executes one of the two refinement operations: If an over-approximation technique $\overline{succ}_l$, $l \in \{1, \ldots, p\}$, reveals that the current transition is spurious, i.e. $S_k^{reach} = \emptyset$, then the transition is removed from the abstract model by ρ_{purge}. When a transition is removed, the set of behaviors of A does not include the current counterexample anymore, and thus the combined validation and refinement step is completed.

If on the other hand, $\overline{succ}_l$ returns a non-empty set S^k_{reach} and this set is a true subset of the states corresponding to $\hat{s}_k$, the function ρ_{split} divides $\hat{s}_k$ into two states $\hat{s}_k^{reach}$ and $\hat{s}_k^{comp}$ (cf. Defn. 6). In this case however $\sigma = (\hat{s}_0, \ldots, \ldots, \hat{s}_{k-1}, \hat{s}_k^{reach}, \hat{s}_{k+1} \ldots, \hat{s}_m)$ remains a counterexample of the refined model. Thus, the algorithm continues with the next transition $(k+1)$ until either $S_k^{reach} = \emptyset$ or until the last transition of the counterexample is validated. There is some freedom in combining the steps of validation and refinement. One alternative is to apply the coarsest method for validation first to all transitions in the abstract counterexample, or to apply state splitting (ρ_{split}) only based on the result of the most accurate approximation method $\overline{succ}_p$.

The proposed algorithm has two possible outcomes: either it is proved that a forbidden state cannot be reached or that there exists a counterexample that cannot be refuted. Since the validation procedure relies on over-approximations, it can not be guaranteed that this abstract counterexample corresponds to a concrete one. In this case, under-approximations of sets of successor states can possibly be used to prove that a counterexample exists: Assume that the procedure terminates with a counterexample $\sigma = (\hat{s}_0, \hat{s}_1, \ldots, \hat{s}_k, \ldots, s_m)$, no transition of which could be refuted. Similar to Defn. 12, we can define an *under-approximation* of successor states

[2] Illustrating figures can be found in [16]

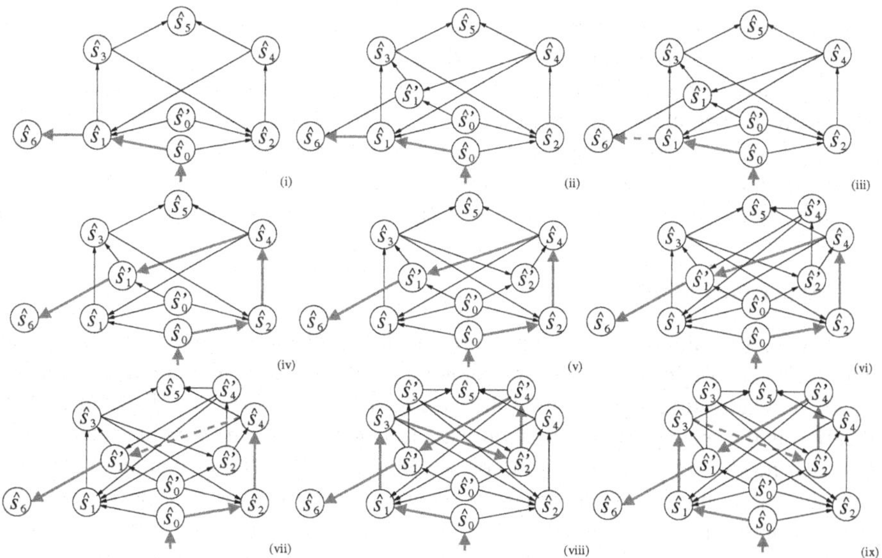

Fig. 6. Counterexample guided abstraction illustrated for the car steering problem.

$S_k^{reach} = \underline{succ}(S_{k-1}^{reach}, \alpha^{-1}(\hat{s}_k))$ which returns a set $S_k^{reach} \subseteq \alpha^{-1}(\hat{s}_k)$ for which it is ensured that it only contains true successors of S_{k-1}^{reach}. If this operator is applied along the counterexample (from $k = 1$ to $k = m$) and $S_m^{reach} \neq \emptyset$ applies, there exists at least one path for the hybrid system which violates the safety property.

Example (cont) The requirement that the hybrid model in Fig. 4 should never enter the location `in_canal` translates into the reachability question for state $\hat{s}_6$ of the abstract model in Fig. 5. The first counterexample for the initial abstract model is $\sigma_1 = (\hat{s}_0, \hat{s}_1, \hat{s}_6)$ (see Fig. 6(i)). The validation procedure considers first the transition $(\hat{s}_0, \hat{s}_1)$ which corresponds to the transition between `go_ahead` and `left_border` in the hybrid automaton. As a first step, $\overline{succ}_{coarse}(S_0, \alpha^{-1}(\hat{s}_1))$ is computed with the result that the minimum distance over all initial states is zero. This is obvious from the fact that those states of the initial set for which $x = -1$ enable the transition guard immediately. Thus, $\overline{succ}_{coarse}$ returns the entire invariant of location `left_border` as set S_2. The next step is to compute $S_2^{reach} = \overline{succ}_{tight}(S_0, \alpha^{-1}(\hat{s}_1))$. The algorithm then splits $\hat{s}_1$ such that $\hat{s}_1$ represents the set S_2^{reach}, and the new abstract state $\hat{s}_1'$ represents $S_2 \setminus S_2^{reach}$ (Fig. 6 (ii)). Since the counterexample has not been eliminated yet, the transition $(\hat{s}_1, \hat{s}_6)$ is considered next. $\overline{succ}_{coarse}$ finds that the minimal distance between the trajectories that start in S_2^{reach}, and the guard $x = -2$ is greater than zero. Thus, no trajectory reaches the guard, and the corresponding transition is removed (Fig. 6 (iii)).

The procedure continues with the next counterexample $\sigma_2 = (\hat{s}_0, \hat{s}_2, \hat{s}_4, \hat{s}_1', \hat{s}_6)$, as depicted in Fig. 6 (iv). As for the first counterexample, the abstract state $\hat{s}_2$ is split into the states that are reachable from the initial set S_0, and the remainder (Fig. 6 (v)). Then, the procedure moves one transition ahead and splits state $\hat{s}_4$ as a result of applying $\overline{succ}_{tight}$. The reachable part is represented by $\hat{s}_4$ in Fig. 6 (vi). Method $\overline{succ}_{coarse}$ then finds that one cannot reach any state that is represented by $\hat{s}'_1$ from this set, and the transition $(\hat{s}_4, \hat{s}'_1)$ can be deleted from A (Fig. 6 (vii)).

The final counterexample is $\sigma_3 = (\hat{s}_0, \hat{s}_1, \hat{s}_3, \hat{s}'_2, \hat{s}'_4, \hat{s}'_1, \hat{s}_6)$. The state $\hat{s}_1$ was already split for the first counterexample. Similarly to the procedure for the counterexample σ_2, state $\hat{s}_3$ is split as depicted in Fig. 6 (viii). It can be shown that transition $(\hat{s}_3, \hat{s}'_2)$ is spurious, which eliminates the last counterexample (Fig. 6 (ix)). Consequently, the state $\hat{s}_6$ is not reachable, and thus the same applies for the location `in_canal`. ♦

5.4 Experimental Results

Experimental results for a prototype implementation of the procedure indicate its advantages over existing methods. We compare INFINITE-STATE-CEGAR with a method based on breadth-first application of the successor operator $\overline{succ}_{tight}$. Breadth-first application is the most prevalent method used for model checking hybrid systems. This approach needs 175 second cputime on a Pentium 4, 1.4GHz, to compute that location `in_canal` is not reachable. INFINITE-STATE-CEGAR together with only one of the two over-approximation methods, $\overline{succ}_{tight}$, takes 120 seconds. As in the case of the breadth-first methods, 99% of the cputime is spent on computing $\overline{succ}_{tight}$. If INFINITE-STATE-CEGAR employs both approximation methods, then the time is cut in about half. The verification takes 68 seconds, of which 64 seconds are used to compute $\overline{succ}_{tight}$, and 3 seconds to solve the optimization problems of $\overline{succ}_{coarse}$.

6 Conclusions

This paper presents a new method for using counterexamples to refine abstractions of hybrid systems. The principal alternative to verifying safety properties of hybrid systems by counterexample-guided verification is to compute the reachable states using a breadth-first application of the successor operator *succ*. It is apparent that the INFINITE-STATE-CEGAR procedure can be faster than breadth-first reachability when the safety property does not hold for the concrete system, since in this case it is possible that the model checker will quickly find a true counterexample. On the other hand, if the safety property holds, refuting one counterexample may implicitly refute others. However, the INFINITE-STATE-CEGAR procedure may continue until all possible counterexamples have been explored (and indeed, may not terminate), which is in some cases equivalent to the breadth-first reachability computation. Nevertheless, INFINITE-STATE-CEGAR allows to use multiple methods for computing approximations to the successor states. Further evaluation of the INFINITE-STATE-CEGAR procedure and a comparison to breadth-first reachability and other alternatives is currently underway.

References

1. Clarke, E., Grumberg, O., Jha, S., Lu, Y., Veith, H.: Counterexample-guided abstraction refinement. In: CAV. Volume 1855 of LNCS, Springer (2000) 154–169
2. Kurshan, R.: Computer-Aided Verification of Coordinating Processes: The Automata-Theoretic Approach. Princeton University Press (1994)

3. Silva, B., Stursberg, O., Krogh, B., Engell, S.: An assessment of the current status of algorithmic approaches to the verification of hybrid systems. In: IEEE Conf. on Decision and Control. (2001) 2867–2874
4. Henzinger, T., Minea, M., Prabhu, V.: Assume-guarantee reasoning for hierarchical hybrid systems. In: HSCC. Volume 2034 of LNCS, Springer (2001) 275–290
5. Frehse, G., Stursberg, O., Engell, S., Huuck, R., Lukoschus, B.: Modular analysis of discrete controllers for distributed hybrid systems. In: IFAC World Congress. (2002)
6. Alur, R., Henzinger, T., Lafferriere, G., Pappas, G.: Discrete abstractions of hybrid systems. Proceedings of the IEEE **88** (2000) 971–984
7. Alur, R., Dang, T., Ivancic, F.: Reachability analysis of hybrid systems via predicate abstraction. In: HSCC. Volume 2289 of LNCS, Springer (2002) 35–48
8. Tiwari, A., Khanna, G.: Series of abstractions for hybrid automata. In: HSCC. Volume 2289 of LNCS, Springer (2002) 465–478
9. Chutinan, A., Krogh, B.: Verification of infinite-state dynamic systems using approximate quotient transition systems. IEEE Transactions on Automatic Control **46** (2001) 1401–1410
10. Clarke, E., Gupta, A., Kukula, J., Strichman, O.: Sat based abstraction-refinement using ilp and machine learning techniques. In: CAV. LNCS, Springer (2002)
11. Ball, T., Majumdar, R., Millstein, T.D., Rajamani, S.K.: Automatic predicate abstraction of c programs. In: PLDI. SIGPLAN 36(5) (2001)
12. Henzinger, T., Jhala, R., Majumdar, R., Sutre, G.: Lazy abstraction. In: Symp. on Principles of Programming Languages, ACM Press (2002) 58–70
13. Jeannet, B., Halbwachs, N., Raymond, P.: Dynamic Partitioning in Analyses of Numerical Properties. In: Static Analysis Symposium (1999), 39–50
14. Alur, R., Dang, T., Ivančić, F.: Counter-Example Guided Predicate Abstraction of Hybrid Systems. In: TACAS, Springer (2003)
15. Clarke, E., Grumberg, O., Peled, D.: Model Checking. MIT Press (1999)
16. Clarke, E., Fehnker, A., Han, Z., Krogh, B., Ouaknine, J., Stursberg, O., Theobald, M.: Abstraction and Counterexample-Guided Refinement in Model Checking of Hybrid Systems. Technical report CMU-CS-03-104. Download from *http://www.cs.cmu.edu/~theobald.*
17. Lafferriere, G., Pappas, G., Yovine, S.: A new class of decidable hybrid systems. In: HSCC. LNCS 1569, Springer (1999) 103–116
18. Henzinger, T., Kopke, P., Puri, A., Varaiya, P.: What's decidable about hybrid automata? In: Symposium on Theory of Computing, ACM Press (1995) 373–382
19. Dang, T., Maler, O.: Reachability analysis via face lifting. In: HSCC. LNCS 1386 (1998)
20. Chutinan, A., Krogh, B.: Verification of polyhedral-invariant hybrid automata using polygonal flow pipe approximations. In: HSCC. LNCS 1569, Springer Verlag (1999) 76–90
21. Greenstreet, M., Mitchell, I.: Reachability analysis using polygonal projections. In: HSCC. LNCS 1569, Springer (1999) 103–116
22. Kurzhanski, A., Varaiya, P.: Ellipsoidal techniques for reachability analysis. In: HSCC. LNCS 1790, Springer (2000) 203–213

Counter-Example Guided Predicate Abstraction of Hybrid Systems*

Rajeev Alur[1], Thao Dang[2], and Franjo Ivančić[1]

[1] University of Pennsylvania
[2] VERIMAG

Abstract. Predicate abstraction has emerged to be a powerful technique for extracting finite-state models from infinite-state systems, and has been recently shown to enhance the effectiveness of the reachability computation techniques for hybrid systems. Given a hybrid system with linear dynamics and a set of linear predicates, the verifier performs an on-the-fly search of the finite discrete quotient whose states correspond to the truth assignments to the input predicates. The success of this approach depends on the choice of the predicates used for abstraction. In this paper, we focus on identifying these predicates automatically by analyzing spurious counter-examples generated by the search in the abstract state-space. We present the basic techniques for discovering new predicates that will rule out closely related spurious counter-examples, optimizations of these techniques, implementation of these in the verification tool, and case studies demonstrating the promise of the approach.

1 Introduction

Inspired by the success of model checking in hardware verification and protocol analysis [12,20], there has been increasing research on developing tools for automated verification of hybrid (mixed discrete-continuous) models of embedded controllers [1,4,6,9,16,19,22]. Model checking requires the computation of the set of reachable states of a model, and in presence of continuous dynamics, this is typically undecidable. Consequently, contemporary tools for model checking of hybrid systems, such as CheckMate[9] and d/dt[6], approximate the set of reachable states by polyhedra. It has been shown that effectiveness of the reachability computation for hybrid systems can be enhanced using predicate abstraction [3]. Predicate abstraction is a powerful technique for extracting finite-state models from complex, potentially infinite-state, discrete systems (see, for instance, [14,23]), and tools such as Bandera [13], SLAM [7], and Feaver [21] have used it for analysis of C or Java programs. The input to our verification tool consists of the concrete system modeled by a hybrid automaton, the safety property to be verified, and a finite set of predicates over system variables to

* This research was supported in part by ARO URI award DAAD19-01-1-0473, DARPA Mobies award F33615-00-C-1707, NSF award ITR/SY 0121431, and European IST project CC (Computation and Control).

H. Garavel and J. Hatcliff (Eds.): TACAS 2003, LNCS 2619, pp. 208–223, 2003.

be used for abstraction. For the sake of efficiency, we require that all invariants, guards, and discrete updates of the hybrid automaton are specified by linear expressions, the continuous dynamics is linear, possibly with bounded input, and the property as well as the abstraction predicates are linear. An abstract state is a valid combination of truth values to the predicates, and thus, corresponds to a polyhedral set of the concrete state-space. The verifier performs an on-the-fly search of the abstract system by symbolic manipulation of polyhedra.

The core of the verifier is the computation of the transitions between abstract states that capture both discrete and continuous dynamics of the original system. Computing discrete successors is relatively straightforward, and involves computing weakest preconditions, and checking non-emptiness of intersection of polyhedral sets. For computing continuous successors of an abstract state A, we use a strategy inspired by the techniques used in CheckMate and `d/dt`. However, while tools such as `d/dt` are designed to compute a "good" approximation of the continuous successors of A, we are interested in checking if this set intersects with a new abstract state permitting many optimizations. Postulating the verification problem for hybrid systems as a search problem in the abstract system has many benefits compared to the traditional approach of computing approximations of reachable sets, and our experiments indicate significant improvements in time and space requirements compared to a tool such as `d/dt`.

The success of our scheme crucially depends on the choice of the predicates used for abstraction. In this paper, we focus on identifying such predicates automatically by analyzing spurious counter-examples generated by the search in the abstract state-space. Counter-example guided refinement of abstractions has been used in multiple contexts before, for instance, to identify the relevant timing constraints in verification of timed automata [5], to identify the relevant boolean predicates in verification of C programs [7], and to identify the relevant variables in symbolic model checking [11]. We present the basic techniques for analyzing counter-examples, techniques for discovering new predicates that will rule out spurious counter-examples, optimizations of these techniques, implementation of these in our verifier, and case studies demonstrating the promise of the approach. Counter-example guided refinement of abstractions for hybrid systems is being independently explored by the hybrid systems group at CMU [10].

The abstract counter-example consists of a sequence of abstract states leading from an initial state to a state violating the property. The analysis problem is to check if the corresponding sequence can be traversed in the concrete system. We perform a forward search from the initial abstract state following the given counter-example. The analysis relies on techniques for polyhedral approximations of the reachable sets under continuous dynamics. We also implemented a local test that checks for feasibility of *pairwise transitions*, and this proves to be effective in many cases. If the counter-example is found to be infeasible, then we wish to identify new predicates that would rule out this sequence in the refined abstract space. This reduces to the problem of finding predicates that *separate* two sets of polyhedra. We present a greedy strategy for identifying such predicates. After discovering new predicates, we include these to the set of predicates used before, and rerun the search in the refined abstract state-space. We demonstrate the feasibility using three case studies. The first one involves verification of a parametric version of Fischer's protocol. The second one involves analysis of a thermostat model, and the third analyzes a model of an adaptive cruise controller. In each of these cases, we show how counter-example analysis can be effective in discovering the predicates that are needed for establishing safety.

2 Predicate Abstraction for Linear Hybrid Systems

In this section, we briefly recap the definitions of predicate abstraction for linear hybrid systems and the search strategy in the abstract space as outlined in [3].

2.1 Mathematical Model

We denote the set of all n-dimensional linear expressions $l : \mathbb{R}^n \to \mathbb{R}$ with Σ_n and the set of all n-dimensional linear predicates $\pi : \mathbb{R}^n \to \mathbb{B}$, where $\mathbb{B} := \{0, 1\}$, with $\mathcal{L}_n$. A linear predicate is of the form $\pi(x) := \sum_{i=1}^{n} a_i x_i + a_{n+1} \sim 0$, where $\sim \in \{\geq, >\}$ and $\forall i \in \{1, \dots, n+1\} : a_i \in \mathbb{R}$. The set of finite sets of n-dimensional linear predicates is denoted by $\mathcal{C}_n$, where an element of $\mathcal{C}_n$ represents the conjunction of its elements.

Definition 1 (Linear Hybrid System). *An n-dimensional* **linear hybrid system** *is a tuple $H = (\mathcal{X}, L, X_0, I, f, T)$ with the following components:*

- *$\mathcal{X} \subseteq \mathbb{R}^n$ is a convex polyhedron representing the* **continuous state-space**.
- *L is a finite set of* **locations**. *The* **state-space** *of H is $X = L \times \mathcal{X}$. Each state thus has the form (l, x), where $l \in L$ is the discrete part of the state, and $x \in \mathcal{X}$ is the continuous part.*
- *$X_0 \subseteq X$ is the set of* **initial states**. *It is assumed that for all locations $l \in L$, the set $\{x \in \mathcal{X} \mid (l, x) \in X_0\}$ is a convex polyhedron.*
- *$I : L \to \mathcal{C}_n$ assigns to each location $l \in L$ a finite set of linear predicates $I(l)$ defining the* **invariant** *conditions that constrain the value of the continuous part of the state while the discrete location is l. The hybrid automaton can only stay in location l as long as the continuous part of the state x satisfies $I(l)$, i.e. $\forall \pi \in I(l) : \pi(x) = 1$. We write $\mathcal{I}_l$ for the invariant set of location l, that is the set of all points x satisfying all predicates in $I(l)$.*
- *$f : L \to (\mathbb{R}^n \to \mathbb{R}^n)$ assigns to each location $l \in L$ a* **continuous vector field** *$f(l)$ on x. While at location l the evolution of the continuous variable is governed by the differential equation $\dot{x} = f(l)(x)$. We restrict our attention to hybrid automata with linear continuous dynamics, that is, for every location $l \in L$, the vector field $f(l)$ is linear, i.e. $f(l)(x) = A_l x$ where A_l is an $n \times n$ matrix. The analysis can also be applied to systems having linear continuous dynamics with uncertain, bounded input of the form $\dot{x} = A_l x + B_l u$.*
- *$T \subseteq L \times L \times \mathcal{C}_n \times (\Sigma_n)^n$ is a relation capturing discrete transition jumps between two discrete locations. A transition $(l, l', g, r) \in T$ consists of an initial location l, a destination location l', a set of* **guard** *constraints g and*

a linear **reset** *mapping* r. *From a state* (l, x) *where all predicates in* g *are satisfied the hybrid automaton can jump to location* l' *at which the continuous variable* x *is reset to a new value* $r(x)$. *We write* $\mathcal{G}_t \subseteq \mathcal{I}_l$ *for the guard set of a transition* $t = (l, l', g, r) \in T$ *which is the set of points satisfying all linear predicates of* g *and the invariant of the location* l.

2.2 Transition System Semantics

We define the semantics of a hybrid automaton by formalizing its underlying transition system. For simplicity we consider the system $\dot{x} = A_l x$, and we denote the flow of this system with $\Phi_l(x, t) = e^{A_l t}x$. The underlying transition system of H is $T_H = \{X, \rightarrow, X_0\}$. The state-space of the transition system is the state-space of H, i.e. $X = L \times \mathcal{X}$. The transition relation $\rightarrow \subseteq X \times X$ between states of the transition system is defined as the union of two relations $\rightarrow_C, \rightarrow_D \subseteq X \times X$. The relation $\rightarrow_C$ describes transitions due to continuous flows, whereas $\rightarrow_D$ describes transitions due to discrete jumps.

$$
\begin{aligned}
(l, x) \rightarrow_C (l, y) \;\; &\text{iff} \;\; \exists t \in \mathbb{R}_{\geq 0} : \Phi_l(x, t) = y \wedge \forall t' \in [0, t] : \Phi_l(x, t') \in \mathcal{I}_l. \\
(l, x) \rightarrow_D (l', y) \;\; &\text{iff} \;\; \exists (l, l', g, r) \in T : x \in \mathcal{G}_t \wedge y = r(x) \wedge y \in \mathcal{I}_{l'}.
\end{aligned}
$$

2.3 Discrete Abstraction

We define a discrete abstraction of the hybrid system $H = (\mathcal{X}, L, X_0, I, f, T)$ with respect to a given k-dimensional vector of n-dimensional linear predicates $\Pi = (\pi_1, \pi_2, \ldots, \pi_k) \in (\mathcal{L}_n)^k$. We can partition the continuous state-space $\mathcal{X} \subseteq \mathbb{R}^n$ into at most 2^k states, corresponding to the 2^k possible boolean evaluations of Π; hence, the infinite state-space X of H is reduced to $|L|2^k$ states in the abstract system. From now on, we refer to the hybrid system H as the *concrete system* and its state-space X as the *concrete state-space*.

Definition 2 (Abstract state-space). *Given an* n*-dimensional hybrid system* $H = (\mathcal{X}, L, X_0, f, I, T)$ *and a* k*-dimensional vector* $\Pi \in (\mathcal{L}_n)^k$ *of* n*-dimensional linear predicates we can define an* **abstract state** *as a tuple* $(l, \boldsymbol{b})$, *where* $l \in L$ *and* $\boldsymbol{b} \in \mathbb{B}^k$. *The abstract state-space for a* k*-dimensional vector of linear predicates hence is* $Q_\Pi := L \times \mathbb{B}^k$. *We define a* **concretization function** $C_\Pi : \mathbb{B}^k \rightarrow 2^{\mathcal{X}}$ *for a vector of linear predicates* $\Pi = (\pi_1, \ldots, \pi_k) \in (\mathcal{L}_n)^k$ *as* $C_\Pi(\boldsymbol{b}) := \{x \in \mathcal{X} \mid \forall i \in \{1, \ldots, k\} : \pi_i(x) = b_i\}$.

Definition 3 (Discrete Abstraction). *Given a hybrid system* $H = (\mathcal{X}, L, X_0, f, I, T)$, *we define its abstract system with respect to a vector of linear predicates* Π *as the transition system* $H_\Pi = (Q_\Pi, \overset{\Pi}{\rightarrow}, Q_0)$ *where*

- *the set of initial states is* $Q_0 = \{(l, \boldsymbol{b}) \in Q_\Pi \mid \exists x \in C_\Pi(\boldsymbol{b}) : (l, x) \in X_0\}$;
- *the abstract transition relation* $\overset{\Pi}{\rightarrow} \subseteq Q_\Pi \times Q_\Pi$ *is defined as the union of the following two relations* $\overset{\Pi}{\rightarrow}_D, \overset{\Pi}{\rightarrow}_C \subseteq Q_\Pi \times Q_\Pi$. *The relation* $\overset{\Pi}{\rightarrow}_D$ *represents*

transitions in the abstract state-space due to discrete jumps, whereas $\xrightarrow{\Pi}_C$ *represents transitions due to continuous flows:*

$$
\begin{aligned}
(l, \boldsymbol{b}) \xrightarrow{\Pi}_D (l', \boldsymbol{b}') \;\; \textit{iff} \;\; & \exists (l, l', g, r) \in T, x \in C_\Pi(\boldsymbol{b}) \cap \mathcal{G}_t : \\
& (l, x) \rightarrow_D (l', r(x)) \wedge r(x) \in C_\Pi(\boldsymbol{b}'); \\
(l, \boldsymbol{b}) \xrightarrow{\Pi}_C (l, \boldsymbol{b}') \;\; \textit{iff} \;\; & \exists x \in C_\Pi(\boldsymbol{b}), t \in \mathbb{R}_{\geq 0} : \Phi_l(x, t) \in C_\Pi(\boldsymbol{b}') \wedge \\
& \forall t' \in [0, t] : \Phi_l(x, t') \in \mathcal{I}_l.
\end{aligned}
$$

2.4 Searching the Abstract State-Space

Given a hybrid system H we want to verify certain safety properties. We define a property by specifying a set of *unsafe locations* $U \subseteq L$ and a set $\mathcal{B} \subseteq \mathcal{X}$ of *unsafe continuous states*. The property is said to hold for the hybrid system H iff there is no valid trace that leads to some state in $\mathcal{B}$ while in an unsafe location. We implemented an on-the-fly search of the abstract state-space giving priority to computing discrete successors rather than continuous successors, as this is generally much faster. Computing discrete successors is relatively straightforward, and involves computing weakest preconditions, and checking non-emptiness of intersection of polyhedral sets. For computing continuous successors of an abstract state A, we compute the polyhedral slices of states reachable at fixed times $r, 2r, 3r, \ldots$ for a suitably chosen r, and then, take convex-hull of all these polyhedra to over-approximate the set of all states reachable from A. We are only interested in checking if this set intersects with a new abstract state. This approach has many benefits compared to the traditional approach of computing approximations of reachable sets, one of them being the fact that the expensive operation of computing continuous successors is applied only to abstract states, and not to intermediate polyhedra of unpredictable shapes and complexities.

We include an optimization technique in the search strategy. For each concrete counter-example in the concrete hybrid system, there exists an equivalent counter-example that has the additional constraint that there are no two consecutive transitions due to continuous flow. This is due to the additivity of flows of hybrid systems, namely $(l, x) \rightarrow_C (l, x') \wedge (l, x') \rightarrow_C (l, x'') \Rightarrow (l, x) \rightarrow_C (l, x'')$. We are hence searching only for counter-examples in the abstract system that do not have two consecutive transitions due to continuous flow.

3 Counter-Example Analysis

An abstract counter-example consists of a sequence of abstract states and transitions leading from an initial state to a state violating the property. The analysis problem is to check if the corresponding sequence of modes and discrete switches can be traversed in the concrete system. The analysis relies on techniques for polyhedral approximations of the reachable sets under continuous dynamics. To speed up the feasibility analysis, we also implemented a local test that checks for feasibility of *pairwise transitions*, and this often proves to be effective.

3.1 Global Analysis Algorithm

We denote the set of transition labels Σ_T as $\Sigma_T = T \cup \{C\}$, denoting that either a discrete transition or a continuous transition occurred. For the subsequent definitions of counter-examples in the abstract state-space we use the following notation for transitions due to discrete jumps for $t = (l, l', g, r) \in T$:

$$(l, \boldsymbol{b}) \overset{\Pi}{\to}_t (l', \boldsymbol{b'}) \text{ iff } \exists x \in C_\Pi(\boldsymbol{b}) \cap \mathcal{G}_t : (l, x) \to_D (l', r(x)) \wedge r(x) \in C_\Pi(\boldsymbol{b'}).$$

Definition 4. *An* **abstract path** *p in the abstract state-space given by the vector of predicates Π of length $n \geq 0$ is a pair $(\boldsymbol{a}, \boldsymbol{t}) \in (Q_\Pi)^{n+1} \times (\Sigma_T)^n$, such that $\boldsymbol{a} = (a_0, \ldots, a_n)$ and $\boldsymbol{t} = (t_0, \ldots, t_{n-1})$ with $t_i \in \Sigma_T$, $a_0 = (l_0, \boldsymbol{b_0}) \in Q_0$, and $\forall 0 \leq i \leq n-1 : a_i \overset{\Pi}{\to}_{t_i} a_{i+1}$. The set of abstract paths of length n given by the vector of predicates Π is denoted by $\mathcal{P}_n^\Pi$. A* **counter-example** *is an abstract path $p = (\boldsymbol{a}, \boldsymbol{t}) = ((a_0, \ldots, a_n), (t_0, \ldots, t_{n-1}))$, such that a_n is a violation of the property to be proven. We call the sequence of abstract states $\boldsymbol{a} = (a_0, \ldots, a_n)$ of a counter-example $p = (\boldsymbol{a}, \boldsymbol{t})$ an unlabeled counter-example.*

The counter-example analysis problem is twofold. The first objective is to check whether a counter-example in the abstract system corresponds to a counter-example in the concrete system. In case that the analysis finds that this particular counter-example cannot be traversed in the concrete system, we want the analysis to identify one or more new predicates that would rule out *closely related* counter-examples in the refined abstract state-space. The refined abstract state-space is defined by adding these predicates to the previous set of predicates used in the abstract state-space search. We define the notion of refinement between abstract paths to formalize the concept of closely related abstract paths.

Definition 5. *A vector of predicates $\Pi' \in (\mathcal{L}_n)^{k'}$ refines a vector of predicates $\Pi \in (\mathcal{L}_n)^k$, if its corresponding set of predicates includes all predicates in Π.*

Definition 6. *An abstract state $a' = (l', \boldsymbol{b'}) \in Q_{\Pi'}$ for the vector of predicates Π' refines another abstract state $a = (l, \boldsymbol{b}) \in Q_\Pi$ for the vector of predicates Π, iff $l = l'$ and $C_{\Pi'}(\boldsymbol{b'}) \subseteq C_\Pi(\boldsymbol{b})$.*

Definition 7. *An abstract path $p' = ((a'_0, \ldots, a'_n), (t'_0, \ldots, t'_{n-1})) \in \mathcal{P}_n^{\Pi'}$ for a vector of predicates Π' refines another abstract path $p = ((a_0, \ldots, a_n), (t_0, \ldots, t_{n-1})) \in \mathcal{P}_n^\Pi$ for a vector of predicates Π, with $a_i = (l_i, \boldsymbol{b_i})$ and $a'_i = (l'_i, \boldsymbol{b'_i})$, iff Π' refines Π, $\forall 0 \leq i \leq n : a'_i$ refines a_i, and $\forall 0 \leq i \leq n-1 : t'_i = t_i$.*

During the counter-example analysis we define $\texttt{Pre} : Q_\Pi \times \Sigma_T \times Q_\Pi \to 2^{\mathcal{X}}$ and $\texttt{Post} : 2^{\mathcal{X}} \times \Sigma_T \times Q_\Pi \to 2^{\mathcal{X}}$ functions that consider only the abstract states or the concretely reachable state space rather than the whole continuous state-space $\mathcal{X}$. The computation of these takes into consideration the concretization of the abstract state, as well as the invariants and guards of the system. We define the functions Pre and Post with $a = (l, \boldsymbol{b})$ and $a' = (l', \boldsymbol{b'})$ as:

$$\text{Pre}(a,t,a') = \begin{cases} \left\{ \begin{array}{c} x \in C_\Pi(\boldsymbol{b}) \cap \mathcal{G}_t | \\ r(x) \in C_\Pi(\boldsymbol{b}') \cap \mathcal{I}_{l'} \end{array} \right\} & : \ t = (l,l',g,r); \\ \left\{ \begin{array}{c} x \in C_\Pi(\boldsymbol{b}) \cap \mathcal{I}_l | \exists \tau \in \mathbb{R}_{\geq 0} \\ \Phi_l(x,\tau) \in C_\Pi(\boldsymbol{b}') \cap \mathcal{I}_{l'} \\ \wedge \forall \tau' \in [0,\tau] : \Phi_l(x,\tau') \in \mathcal{I}_{l'} \end{array} \right\} & : \ t = C. \end{cases}$$

$$\text{Post}(P,t,a') = \begin{cases} \text{Post}\left(\left\{ \begin{array}{c} x \in C_\Pi(\boldsymbol{b}') \cap \mathcal{I}_{l'} | \\ \exists y \in \mathcal{G}_t \cap P : x = r(y) \end{array} \right\}, C, a' \right) & : \ t = (l,l',g,r); \\ \left\{ \begin{array}{c} x \in C_\Pi(\boldsymbol{b}') \cap \mathcal{I}_{l'} | \exists \tau \in \mathbb{R}_{\geq 0} \\ \exists y \in P : \Phi_{l'}(y,\tau) = x \\ \wedge \forall \tau' \in [0,\tau] : \Phi_{l'}(y,\tau') \in \mathcal{I}_{l'} \end{array} \right\} & : \ t = C. \end{cases}$$

Our counter-example analysis algorithm is presented in algorithm 1. The set R_0 is the part of the initial state-space that is covered by the abstract state $(l, \boldsymbol{b_0})$. We then compute the concretely reachable state-space of each abstract state of the counter-example. For each $1 \leq i \leq n$ we compute R_i as the reachable region after i transitions according to the counter-example. It is hence clear that if $R_i = \emptyset$ for some i then the counter-example is spurious.

Algorithm 1 Analyzing a counter-example $p \in \mathcal{P}_n^\Pi$

```
R_0 = C_Π(b_0) ∩ {x ∈ I_{l_0} | (l_0, x) ∈ X_0}
for 1 ≤ i ≤ n do
  R_i = Post(R_{i-1}, t_{i-1}, a_i)
  if R_i = ∅ then
    return "Counter-example is spurious!"
  end if
end for
return "Counter-example is concrete!"
```

In the case that we found that the counter-example is spurious, we want to use the counter-example to find new predicates. Consider a counter-example $p \in \mathcal{P}_n^\Pi$, such that $R_{k+1} = \emptyset$ and $R_k \neq \emptyset$ for $0 \leq k < n$. We call t_k the failing transition of the counter-example p. Then we can prove the following lemma.[1]

Lemma 1. *Given a counter-example* $p = (\boldsymbol{a}, \boldsymbol{t}) = ((a_0, \ldots, a_n), (t_0, \ldots, t_{n-1})) \in \mathcal{P}_n^\Pi$ *where* t_k *is the failing transition, we have* $R_k \cap \text{Pre}(a_k, t_k, a_{k+1}) = \emptyset$.

We want to add new predicates to the vector Π, so that the refined vector Π' does not allow a refined (unlabeled) counter-example of p to reappear. Consider a strategy that adds predicates to the set Π that correspond to a separation of R_k from $\text{Pre}(a_k, t_k, a_{k+1})$ for a failing transition t_k. This means that we are looking for a refined set of predicates Π' of Π, such that every refined abstract

[1] Please note, that we omit all the proofs in this paper for the sake of brevity.

state intersects at most with one of the two sets R_k and $\texttt{Pre}(a_k, t_k, a_{k+1})$. We define the notion of separation in terms of polyhedral sets, since we approximate the set of reachable states by polyhedral slices in the implementation of the tool. It should be noted here that we use under-approximations of the reachable sets of states during the analysis of counter-examples while we over-approximated the reachable sets of states during the search in the abstract state-space.

Definition 8 (Separating predicates). *Let $\mathcal{P} = \{P_1, \dots, P_n\}$ and $\mathcal{Q} = \{Q_1, \dots, Q_m\}$ be two disjoint sets of convex polyhedra. We denote by $\bigcup \mathcal{P}$ and $\bigcup \mathcal{Q}$ the union of all polyhedra in $\mathcal{P}$ and $\mathcal{Q}$. A finite vector of linear predicates $\Pi = (\pi_1, \pi_2, \dots, \pi_k)$ separates $\mathcal{P}$ and $\mathcal{Q}$ iff for all $\boldsymbol{b} \in \mathbb{B}^k$, at least one of the two sets $(C_\Pi(\boldsymbol{b}) \cap \bigcup \mathcal{P})$ and $(C_\Pi(\boldsymbol{b}) \cap \bigcup \mathcal{Q})$ is empty.*

The predicates in Π are called *separating predicates.* Note that such a vector Π always exists[2], but it is often not unique.

Theorem 1. *Assume a counter-example $p \in \mathcal{P}_n^\Pi$ for a vector of predicates Π such that t_k is the failing transition. If Π' refines Π and additionally contains predicates corresponding to a separation of R_k from $\texttt{Pre}(a_k, t_k, a_{k+1})$, and we find a refined counter-example $p' \in \mathcal{P}_n^{\Pi'}$ of p, then there exists a failing transition t_j in p', such that $j < k$.*

As a single counter-example p is of finite length, the above theorem assures us that after a finite number of iterations, a refinement of p will not be possible.

3.2 Locally Infeasible Abstract States

In this section we present a second counter-example analysis algorithm, which checks a counter-example quickly for a common cause of spurious counter-examples. We also show that this analysis produces new predicates with stronger implications for subsequent searches in the refined abstract state-space.

Definition 9. *For a path $p = (\boldsymbol{a}, \boldsymbol{t}) \in \mathcal{P}_{n+1}^\Pi$ given the vector of predicates Π, with $\boldsymbol{a} = (a_0, \dots, a_{n+1}) = ((l_0, \boldsymbol{b_0}), \dots, (l_{n+1}, \boldsymbol{b_{n+1}}))$ and $\boldsymbol{t} = (t_0, \dots, t_n)$, we say that an abstract state a_i for $1 \le i \le n$ is* **locally infeasible**, *iff*

$$\texttt{Post}(C_\Pi(\boldsymbol{b_{i-1}}), t_{i-1}, a_i) \cap \texttt{Pre}(a_i, t_i, a_{i+1}) = \emptyset.$$

The detection of locally infeasible abstract states can be implemented in a straight-forward fashion. In addition, we can easily compute new predicates that disallow refined counter-examples. If a state a_i is locally infeasible, then we can use the fact that our implemented optimization technique guarantees that either t_{i-1} or t_i is a discrete transition. If t_{i-1} is discrete, one reasonable choice is to use the predicates corresponding to the constraints of the polyhedral sets representing $\texttt{Post}(C_\Pi(\boldsymbol{b_{i-1}}), t_{i-1}, a_i)$ in the refined search. Otherwise, a possible approach is to use the predicates corresponding to $\texttt{Pre}(a_i, t_i, a_{i+1})$ in the refined search. We denote this strategy of picking new predicates by `LocalStrategy`.

[2] It is easy to see that we can simply take the linear constraints of all polyhedra from P or from Q to determine Π.

We can now prove the following two theorems about using the strategy `LocalStrategy` in case we find a locally infeasible abstract state. The theorems formalize that by using this strategy we can assure that a refinement of the (unlabeled) counter-example will not be found in subsequent searches.

Theorem 2. *Assume a counter-example $p \in \mathcal{P}_n^{\Pi}$ for a vector of predicates Π, such that there is a locally infeasible abstract state a_i in p. A search in the refined abstract state-space given by the strategy* `LocalStrategy` *to find new predicates will not find a counter-example that is a refinement of p.*

Theorem 3. *Assume a hybrid system $H = (\mathcal{X}, L, X_0, I, f, T)$ with the properties that $\forall l \in L : (l, l', g, r) \in T \Rightarrow l \neq l'$, and $\forall (l, l', g_1, r_1), (l, l', g_2, r_2) \in T : g_1 = g_2 \wedge r_1 = r_2$. Additionally assume a counter-example $p = (\boldsymbol{a}, \boldsymbol{t}) \in \mathcal{P}_n^{\Pi}$ for a vector of predicates Π, such that there is a locally infeasible abstract state a_i in p. Then a search in the refined abstract state-space obtained using the strategy* `LocalStrategy` *to refine the set of predicates Π will not produce a refined unlabeled counter-example.*

4 Computing Separating Predicates

In the previous section we described two counter-example analysis algorithms. If the counter-example is found to be infeasible, then we wish to identify one or more new predicates that would rule out this sequence in the refined abstract space. This reduces to the problem of finding one or more predicates that *separate* two sets of polyhedra. We present a greedy strategy for identifying the separating predicates. After discovering new predicates, we then include these predicates to the set of predicates used before, and rerun the search in the refined abstract state-space defined by the enriched predicate set.

4.1 Separating Two Disjoint Convex Polyhedra

Let P and Q be two disjoint convex polyhedra. To separate them, we define the distance between P and Q as follows: $d(P,Q) = \inf\{d(p-q) \mid p \in P \wedge q \in Q\}$ where $d(\cdot)$ denotes the Euclidean distance. Since P and Q are disjoint, $d(P,Q)$ is positive. Let $p^* \in P$ and $q^* \in Q$ be points that form a pair of closest points. We denote by $s(p^*, q^*)$ the line segment with extreme points p^* and q^*. The half-space $\mathcal{H}$ which is normal to $s(p^*, q^*)$ and has q^* as a supporting point can be written as: $\mathcal{H} = \{x \mid \langle p^* - q^*, x\rangle \geq \langle p^* - q^*, q^*\rangle\}$. We denote by $\overline{\mathcal{H}}$ the complement of $\mathcal{H}$.

Lemma 2. *The polyhedron Q is contained in $\mathcal{H}$ and P is contained in $\overline{\mathcal{H}}$.*

We remark that Lemma 2 also holds for any half-space which is normal to $s(p^*, q^*)$ and passes through an arbitrary point in $s(p^*, q^*)$. Hence, any such half-space can be used to define a separating predicate. To compute $d(P,Q)$ as well as p^* and q^*, there exist efficient algorithms [8] which take time $\mathcal{O}(K_P + K_Q)$ where K_P and K_Q are the number of vertices of P and Q.

4.2 Separating Two Disjoint Sets of Convex Polyhedra

We proceed with the problem of finding a set Π of separating predicates for two sets of convex polyhedra $\mathcal{P}_1$ and $\mathcal{P}_2$. In order to keep the size of the abstract state space as small as possible, we want to find Π with the smallest number of predicates. Many related polyhedral separation problems have been considered in literature [17,18]. However, the solutions proposed in these works are only for two and three dimensional polyhedra. On the other hand, even in low dimensions most separation problems were shown to be intractably hard. In three dimensions the problem of finding a minimum facet-separator for two polyhedral solids is NP-complete [15]. Our objective is not to find an optimal solution but to develop methods which are effective on the problem of separating reachable sets of hybrid systems for abstraction refinement purposes.

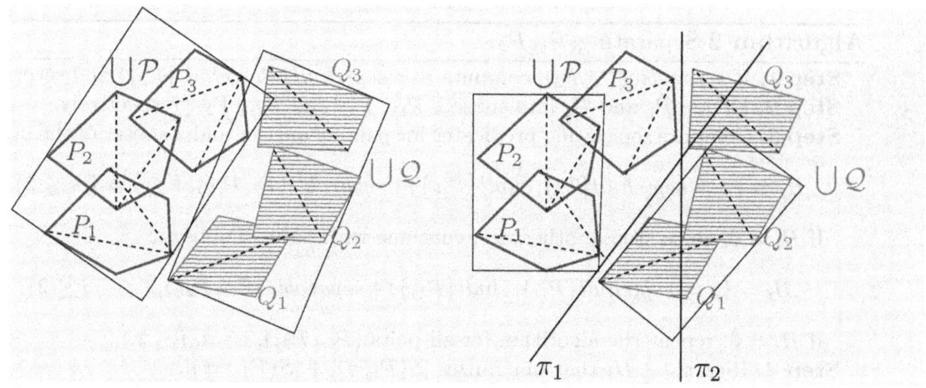

Fig. 1. Subdividing the sets $\mathcal{P} = \{P_1, P_2, P_3\}$ and $\mathcal{Q} = \{Q_1, Q_2, Q_3\}$ respectively into $\{P_1, P_2\}$, $\{P_3\}$ and $\{Q_1, Q_2\}$, $\{Q_3\}$ allows to find two separating predicates π_1 and π_2.

Our solution is based on the following observation. Given two set of polyhedra $\mathcal{P}_1$ and $\mathcal{P}_2$, if the convex hulls of $\mathcal{P}_1$ and $\mathcal{P}_2$ are disjoint, then one can apply the method presented in the previous section to find a separating predicate. If the convex hulls intersect, it is clear that $\mathcal{P}_1$ and $\mathcal{P}_2$ cannot be separated by a single hyperplane. The main idea is to divide $\mathcal{P}_1$ and $\mathcal{P}_2$ into subsets of polyhedra such that their convex hulls do not intersect allowing to find a separating predicate. The procedure of subdivision can be done in a hierarchical way. We begin with all polyhedra in $\mathcal{P}_1$ and $\mathcal{P}_2$ and recursively subdivide until the convex hulls are pairwise disjoint. Moreover, for efficiency purposes, instead of convex hulls, we can use approximations by non-axis-aligned bounding boxes which are easier to compute and test for overlaps (see figure 1). One way to compute tight fitting bounding boxes is to align the axes of the box in the directions along which the vertices of the polyhedra tend to lie. From the vertices of the polyhedra we can determine the matrix of covariance and take its largest eigenvectors to define the orientation of the box.

Our method for computing separating predicates is summarized in algorithm 2. We denote by $\mathcal{H}(\pi)$ the half-space defined by predicate π. Given a set $\mathcal{P}$ of polyhedra, *chull*$(\mathcal{P})$ and *bbox*$(\mathcal{P})$ are respectively the convex hull and the non-axis-aligned bounding box of $\mathcal{P}$. The set $\mathcal{S}(\mathcal{P}, \pi) = \{s \in \mathcal{P} \mid s \subseteq \mathcal{H}(\pi)\}$ is the largest subset of $\mathcal{P}$ lying entirely inside $\mathcal{H}(\pi)$, and $Int(\mathcal{P}, \pi) = \{s \cap \mathcal{H}(\pi) \mid s \in \mathcal{P} \ \wedge \ s \cap \mathcal{H}(\pi) \neq \emptyset\}$ is the intersection of $\bigcup \mathcal{P}$ with $\mathcal{H}(\pi)$. The core of the algorithm is a procedure, called *sep*, which computes a separating predicate for two disjoint polyhedra using the method presented in section 4.1. Two sets of polyhedra $\mathcal{P}_1$ and $\mathcal{P}_2$ are called *separable* if $conv\{\mathcal{P}_1\} \cap conv\{\mathcal{P}_2\} = \emptyset$ where *conv* is a convex-approximation operation which can be *chull* or *bbox*. The notation $separable(\mathcal{P}_1, \mathcal{P}_2)$ in the algorithm indicates that $\mathcal{P}_1$ and $\mathcal{P}_2$ are separable.

Algorithm 2 Separating$(\mathcal{P}_1, \mathcal{P}_2)$

Step 1. If $separable(\mathcal{P}_1, \mathcal{P}_2)$, compute $\pi = sep(chull\{\mathcal{P}_1\}, chull\{\mathcal{P}_2\})$ and return π.
Step 2. Divide $\mathcal{P}_1$ and $\mathcal{P}_2$ into subsets $\mathcal{P}_{11}$, $\mathcal{P}_{12}$ and $\mathcal{P}_{21}$, $\mathcal{P}_{22}$, respectively.
Step 3. Compute separating predicates for pairs of one set and a subset of the other:

$$\Pi_t = \{\pi = sep(chull\{\mathcal{P}_i\}, chull\{\mathcal{P}_{jk}\}) \mid separable(\mathcal{P}_i, \mathcal{P}_{jk}), 1 \leq i \neq j, k \leq 2\}.$$

If $\Pi_t \neq \emptyset$, go to step 4; otherwise, continue with pairs of subsets:

$$\Pi_t = \{\pi = sep(chull\{\mathcal{P}_{1i}\}, chull\{\mathcal{P}_{2j}\}) \mid separable(\mathcal{P}_{1i}, \mathcal{P}_{2k}), 1 \leq i, j \leq 2\}.$$

If $\Pi_t = \emptyset$, repeat the algorithm for all pairs $(\mathcal{P}_{1i}, \mathcal{P}_{2j}), 1 \leq i, j \leq 2$.
Step 4. Pick $\pi_m \in \Pi_t$ that maximizes $|\mathcal{S}(\mathcal{P}_1, \pi)| + |\mathcal{S}(\mathcal{P}_2, \neg\pi)|$.
Step 5. Compute pairs $(Int(\mathcal{P}_1, \pi_m), Int(\mathcal{P}_2, \pi_m))$, $(Int(\mathcal{P}_1, \neg\pi_m), Int(\mathcal{P}_2, \neg\pi_m))$. For each pair, if both sets are non-empty, repeat the algorithm for the pair.

We briefly sketch the proof of the correctness of algorithm 2. As one can see from step 4, we use a greedy strategy to choose separating predicates, that is we select the one that can separate the largest number of polyhedra. The goal of step 5 is to exclude the subsets of $\bigcup \mathcal{P}_1$ and $\bigcup \mathcal{P}_2$ that the selected predicate π_m can separate. Indeed, if one of the sets $Int(\mathcal{P}_1, \pi_m)$ and $Int(\mathcal{P}_2, \pi_m)$ is empty, then either $\mathcal{P}_1$ or $\mathcal{P}_2$ lies entirely outside the half-space $\mathcal{H}(\pi_m)$. This means that the predicate π_m can separate a part of one set from the other, and we only need to continue with the remaining part.

One factor that determines the number of separating predicates is the subdivision in step 2. The way we subdivide the sets $\mathcal{P}_1$ with view of avoiding interference of the resulting subsets with $\mathcal{P}_2$ is as follows. We first try to split $\mathcal{P}_1$ into two subsets such that one contains all the polyhedra entirely outside $conv(\mathcal{P}_2)$. If this subset is empty, then we split $\mathcal{P}_1$ with respect to a hyperplane which is perpendicular to the longest side of $bbox(\mathcal{P}_1)$ and passes through its centroid. Another option for the normal of the splitting hyperplane is the line passing through the two most distant points.

We now briefly discuss the bound on the number of predicates algorithm 2 can produce. It is easy to see that the upper bound corresponds to the case where no splitting can produce separable subsets, which requires to consider all pairs of polyhedra. In other words, in this case, each time algorithm 2 finds a separating predicate π_m, $|(Int(\mathcal{P}_1, \pi_m)| = |\mathcal{P}_1| - 1$ and $|(Int(\mathcal{P}_2, \pi_m)| = |\mathcal{P}_2|$; similarly, $|(Int(\mathcal{P}_1, \neg\pi_m)| = |\mathcal{P}_1|$ and $|(Int(\mathcal{P}_2, \neg\pi_m)| = |\mathcal{P}_2| - 1$. This means that in each side of the half-space of π_m, two sets of polyhedra remain to be separated and the size of one set is decreased by 1. For example, if $|\mathcal{P}_1| = |\mathcal{P}_2| = K$, we can prove that algorithm 2 produces in worst case $2^{K+1} - 1$ predicates. It is important to note that this worst case typically happens when the polyhedra in each set are all disjoint and intertwine with those in the other set. However, in this context, reachable sets to be separated are often connected. Hence, in many practical cases, convex hulls or non-axis-aligned bounding boxes are relatively good approximations and the number of separating predicates produced by algorithm 2 is often much smaller than this bound. Finally, we can use the following lemma to achieve better efficiency.

Lemma 3. *If a set of predicates Π separates the boundaries of $\mathcal{P}_1$ and $\mathcal{P}_2$ then it separates $\mathcal{P}_1$ and $\mathcal{P}_2$.*

To prove the lemma, we remark that Π separates $\mathcal{P}_1$ and $\mathcal{P}_2$ iff any line segment between a point in $\mathcal{P}_1$ and another point in $\mathcal{P}_2$ intersects with the hyperplane of at least one predicates in Π. Hence if Π separates the boundaries of $\mathcal{P}_1$ and $\mathcal{P}_2$ then it separates $\mathcal{P}_1$ and $\mathcal{P}_2$ since any line segment connecting points in the interior of two disjoint sets must cross the boundaries of both sets. Using lemma 3 we can consider only some boundary layer of $\mathcal{P}_1$ and $\mathcal{P}_2$, which allows to obtain tighter convex approximations and thus reduces splitting.

5 Implementation and Experimentation

We presented foundations for automated verification of safety properties of hybrid systems by combining the ideas of counter-example guided predicate abstraction and polyhedral approximation of reachable sets of linear continuous dynamics. The presented counter-example analysis tool extends previous work on predicate abstraction of hybrid systems [3]. Our current prototype implementation of the predicate abstraction model checking and the counter-example analysis tool are both implemented in C++ using library functions of the hybrid systems reachability tool `d/dt` [6]. We implemented a translation procedure from CHARON [2] source code to the predicate abstraction input language which is based on the `d/dt` input language. Our tool uses the polyhedral libraries CDD and QHull. We have implemented the global analysis algorithm, the local feasibility check, as well as the computation of separating predicates as part of the counter-example analysis tool.

5.1 Fischer's Mutual Exclusion

We first look at an example of mutual exclusion which uses time-based synchronization in a multi-process system. We want to implement a protocol that allows a shared resource to be used exclusively by at most one of two processes at any given time. The state machines for the two processes are shown in figure 2. The example is small enough to be used effectively for an illustration of our approach.

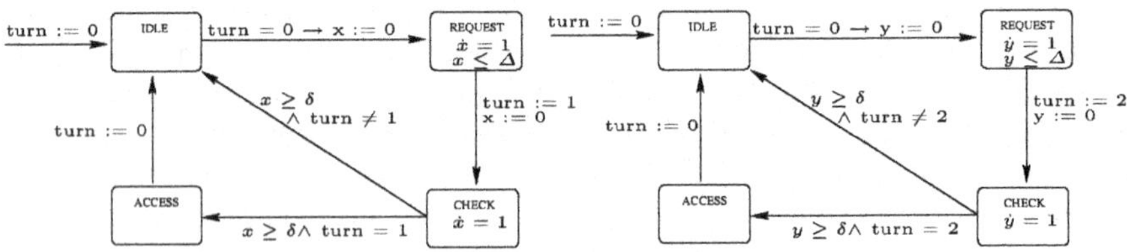

Fig. 2. The two processes for the mutual exclusion example

The possible execution traces depend on the two positive parameters Δ and δ. If the parameters are such that $\Delta \geq \delta$ is true, we can find a counter-example that proves the two processes may access the shared resource at the same time. On the other hand, if $\delta > \Delta$, then the system preserves mutual exclusive use of the shared resource. We use this example to illustrate the use of the local feasibility check of counter-examples for the case that $\delta > \Delta$. Consider the abstract system defined by the predicates used in the description of the 2-process Fischer's mutual exclusion protocol. These are: $x \geq \delta, y \geq \delta, x \leq \Delta, y \leq \Delta, \delta > \Delta, \Delta > 0, \delta > 0, x \geq 0$ and $y \geq 0$. The search in the abstract state-space finds a counter-example of length nine. The third abstract state a_3 in the counter-example has both processes in their respective `Request` locations, `turn` $= 0$, and $0 \leq x \leq \Delta, 0 \leq y \leq \Delta$. The following state a_4 can be reached by a discrete transition t_d, and the first process is now in its `Check` location, while `turn` $= 1$ and $0 \leq x \leq \Delta, 0 \leq y \leq \Delta$. The fifth abstract state a_5 can then be reached by a continuous transition t_c, so that the locations and the `turn` variable are unchanged, but now we have $x > \delta, 0 \leq y \leq \Delta$. Then, a_4 is locally infeasible, as shown by projection onto the variables x and y:

$$\texttt{Post}_{|(x,y)}(a_3, t_d, a_4) = \{(x,y)^T \in \mathbb{R}^2 \,|\, 0 \leq x \leq y \leq \Delta < \delta\} \text{ and}$$
$$\texttt{Pre}_{|(x,y)}(a_4, t_c, a_5) = \{(x,y)^T \in \mathbb{R}^2 \,|\, 0 \leq y < x \leq \Delta < \delta\};$$

hence, we know that $\texttt{Post}(a_3, t_d, a_4) \cap \texttt{Pre}(a_4, t_c, a_5) = \emptyset$. Following the strategy `LocalStrategy` we include the only one new predicate $x \leq y$ to the set of predicates. In the next iteration with this refinement of the abstract state-space, we obtain a symmetrical locally infeasible counter-example. The strategy `LocalStrategy` then suggests the symmetric predicate $y \leq x$. The subsequent reachability analysis finds 54 reachable abstract states in the refined abstract state-space, which all maintain the mutual exclusion property.

5.2 Thermostat

We have also successfully applied our counter-example guided predicate abstraction technique to verify a thermostat example. We present this case study to illustrate the global counter-example analysis algorithm as well as the procedure to separate two disjoint sets of polyhedra. The single hybrid automaton in this case study is shown in figure 3. It contains a timer `clock` and a temperature `Temp`. The initial location is `Heat` and the initial set is $\texttt{clock} = 0, 5 \leq \texttt{Temp} \leq 10$, and the bad set is $\texttt{Temp} < 4.5$ in any location. The model can be proven correctly by adding the predicate $\texttt{clock} \leq 0$ to the predicates that are already mentioned in the model as transition guards and location invariants. In this case, the abstraction uses ten predicates and finds 35 reachable abstract states.

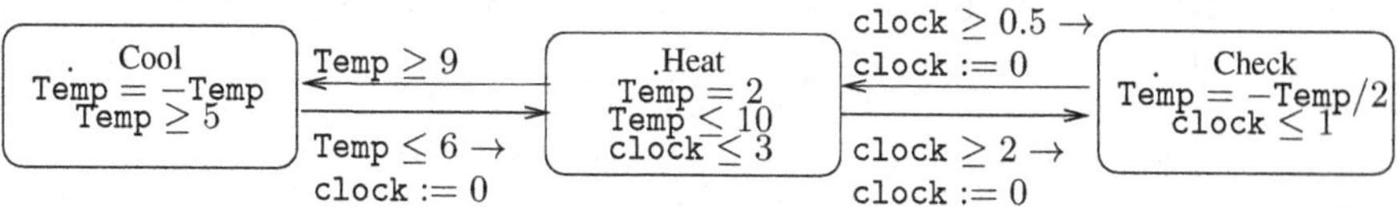

Fig. 3. The Thermostat example. We omit the differential equation $\dot{\texttt{clock}} = 1$ in all three locations.

For purposes of illustration, we start the verification using our counter-example guided predicate abstraction toolkit with the predicates mentioned in the model; that means, we are searching for a set of predicates that can be used to refine this initial set to be able to prove the safety of the given model. Note that picking the aforementioned predicate $\texttt{clock} \leq 0$ would suffice. In addition, to illustrate the global analysis algorithm and the separating routine only, we skip the local feasibility checking algorithm. The first iteration of our algorithm produces a spurious counter-example of length 7 after 11 abstract states have been discovered by the search of the abstract state-space. The separation routine suggests the following four linear predicate to refine the abstract state-space:

```
 0.979265*Temp +  0.202584*clock <=  9.34423
 0.872555*Temp +  0.488515*clock <=  8.16961
 0.428587*Temp +  0.9035   *clock <=  4.11184
-0.0680518*Temp +  0.997682*clock <= -0.439659
```

Please notice the last suggested predicate and its similarity to the predicate mentioned before. The model designer may have been able to use this suggested set of predicates to refine the abstract state space by adding the predicate $\texttt{clock} \leq 0$.

Following our example, after refining the predicates with the help of these four predicates, the system still finds a spurious counter-example, and suggest four more predicates. In a third round after discovering another spurious counter-example, the system generates eleven more predicates, one of which is `0.0139043*Temp + 0.999903*clock <= 0.152558`. The total set of 28 predicates is in the following iteration enough to prove the thermostat example safe. The search in the abstract state-space finds 358 reachable abstract states.

5.3 Coordinated Adaptive Cruise Control

We have also successfully applied our predicate abstraction technique to verify a model of the *Coordinated Adaptive Cruise Control* mode of a vehicle-to-vehicle coordination system. This case study is provided by the PATH project (see `http://www-path.eecs.berkeley.edu`). We first briefly describe the model omitting a more detailed discussion for the sake of brevity. The goal of this mode is to maintain the car at some desired speed v_d while avoiding collision with a car in front. Let x and v denote the position and velocity of the car. Let x_l, v_l and a_l denote respectively the position, velocity and acceleration of the car in front. Since we want to prove that no collision happens regardless of the behavior of the car in front, this car is treated as disturbance, more precisely, the derivative of its acceleration is modeled as uncertain input ranging in $[da_{lmin}, da_{lmax}]$.

The closed-loop system can be modeled as a hybrid automaton with 5 continuous variables and 8 locations.The invariants of the locations and the transition guards are specified by the operation regions and switching conditions of the controller together with the bounds on the speed and acceleration. In order to prove that the controller can guarantee that no collision between the cars can happen, we specify an unsafe set as $x_l - x \leq 0$ in all locations. To define initial predicates, in addition to the constraints of the invariants and guards, we use the predicate of the bad set allowing to distinguish safe and unsafe states and predicates representing the initial set. Assuming that the follower car is faster than the preceding car, and a too small initial separation of the two cars, the tool finds a counter-example that corresponds to a real trace in the concrete system. On the other hand, if the two cars start with a large enough initial separation, the combined verification approach enabled us to prove safety of the abstract system which implies safety of the concrete system.

References

1. R. Alur, C. Courcoubetis, N. Halbwachs, T.A. Henzinger, P. Ho, X. Nicollin, A. Olivero, J. Sifakis, and S. Yovine. The algorithmic analysis of hybrid systems. *Theoretical Computer Science*, 138:3–34, 1995.
2. R. Alur, T. Dang, J. Esposito, Y. Hur, F. Ivančić, V. Kumar, I. Lee, P. Mishra, G. Pappas, and O. Sokolsky. Hierarchical modeling and analysis of embedded systems. *Proceedings of the IEEE*, 91(1), January 2003.
3. R. Alur, T. Dang, and F. Ivančić. Reachability analysis of hybrid systems via predicate abstraction. In *Hybrid Systems: Computation and Control, Fifth International Workshop*, LNCS 2289. Springer-Verlag, 2002.
4. R. Alur and D.L. Dill. A theory of timed automata. *Theoretical Computer Science*, 126:183–235, 1994.
5. R. Alur, A. Itai, R.P. Kurshan, and M. Yannakakis. Timing verification by successive approximation. *Information and Computation*, 118(1):142–157, 1995.

6. E. Asarin, O. Bournez, T. Dang, and O. Maler. Approximate reachability analysis of piecewise-linear dynamical systems. In *Hybrid Systems: Computation and Control, Third International Workshop*, LNCS 1790, pages 21–31. 2000.
7. T. Ball and S. Rajamani. Bebop: A symbolic model checker for boolean programs. In *SPIN 2000 Workshop on Model Checking of Software*, LNCS 1885. 2000.
8. S. Cameron. A comparison of two fast algorithms for computing the distance between convex polyhedra. *IEEE Transactions on Robotics and Automation*, 13(6):915–920, 1997.
9. A. Chutinan and B.K. Krogh. Verification of polyhedral-invariant hybrid automata using polygonal flow pipe approximations. In *Hybrid Systems: Computation and Control, Second International Workshop*, LNCS 1569, pages 76–90. 1999.
10. E. Clarke, A. Fehnker, Z. Han, B. Krogh, O. Stursberg, and M. Theobald. Verification of hybrid systems based on counterexample-guided abstraction refinement. In *Tools and Algorithms for the Construction and Analysis of Systems*, 2003.
11. E. Clarke, O. Grumberg, S. Jha, Y. Lu, and H. Veith. Counterexample-guided abstraction refinement. In *Computer Aided Verification*, pages 154–169, 2000.
12. E.M. Clarke and R.P. Kurshan. Computer-aided verification. *IEEE Spectrum*, 33(6):61–67, 1996.
13. J.C. Corbett, M.B. Dwyer, J. Hatcliff, S. Laubach, C.S. Pasareanu, Robby, and H. Zheng. Bandera: Extracting finite-state models from Java source code. In *Proceedings of 22nd International Conference on Software Engineering*. 2000.
14. P. Cousot and R. Cousot. Abstract interpretation: a unified lattice model for static analysis of programs by construction or approximation of fixpoints. In *Proceedings of the 4th ACM Symposium on Principles of Programming Languages*, 1977.
15. G. Das and D. Joseph. The complexity of minimum convex nested polyhedra. In *Canadian Conference on Computational Geometry*, 1990.
16. C. Daws, A. Olivero, S. Tripakis, and S. Yovine. The tool KRONOS. In *Hybrid Systems III: Verification and Control*, LNCS 1066. Springer-Verlag, 1996.
17. D. Dobkin and D. Kirkpatrick. Determining the separation of preprocessed polyhedra – a unified approach. In *Proc. of ICALP'90*, pages 400–413, 1990.
18. H. Edelsbrunner and F.P. Preparata. Minimum polygon separation. *Information and Computation*, 77:218–232, 1987.
19. T.A. Henzinger, P. Ho, and H. Wong-Toi. HyTech: the next generation. In *Proceedings of the 16th IEEE Real-Time Systems Symposium*, pages 56–65, 1995.
20. G.J. Holzmann. The model checker SPIN. *IEEE Transactions on Software Engineering*, 23(5):279–295, 1997.
21. G.J. Holzmann and M.H. Smith. Automating software feature verification. *Bell Labs Technical Journal*, 5(2):72–87, 2000.
22. K. Larsen, P. Pettersson, and W. Yi. Uppaal in a nutshell. *Springer International Journal of Software Tools for Technology Transfer*, 1, 1997.
23. C. Loiseaux, S. Graf, J. Sifakis, A. Bouajjani, and S. Bensalem. Property preserving abstractions for the verification of concurrent systems. *Formal Methods in System Design Volume 6, Issue 1*, 1995.

Schedulability Analysis Using Two Clocks

Elena Fersman, Leonid Mokrushin, Paul Pettersson, and Wang Yi

Uppsala University
Department of Information Technology
P.O. Box 337, S-751 05 Uppsala, Sweden
{elenaf,leom,paupet,yi}@it.uu.se

Abstract. In classic scheduling theory, real-time tasks are usually assumed to be periodic, i.e. tasks arrive and compute with fixed rates periodically. To relax the stringent constraints on task arrival times, we propose to use timed automata to describe task arrival patterns. In a previous work, it is shown that the general schedulability checking problem for such models is a reachability problem for a decidable class of timed automata extended with subtraction. Unfortunately, the number of clocks needed in the analysis is proportional to the maximal number of schedulable task instances associated with a model, which in many cases is huge.

In this paper, we show that for fixed priority scheduling strategy, the schedulability checking problem can be solved by reachability analysis on standard timed automata using only *two* extra clocks in addition to the clocks used in the original model to describe task arrival times. The analysis can be done in a similar manner to response time analysis in classic Rate-Monotonic Scheduling. We believe that this is the optimal solution to the problem, a problem that was suspected undecidable previously. We also extend the result to systems in which the timed automata and the tasks may read and update shared data variables. Then the release time-point of a task may depend on the values of the shared variables, and hence on the time-point at which other tasks finish their exection. We show that this schedulability problem can be encoded as timed automata using $n+1$ extra clocks, where n is the number of tasks.

1 Introduction

In the area of real time scheduling methods such as rate monotonic scheduling are widely applied in the analysis of periodic tasks with deterministic behaviours. For non-periodic tasks with non-deterministic behaviours, there are no satisfactory procedures. In reality control tasks are often triggered by sporadic events coming from the environment. The common approach to analyze schedulability of such systems with non-periodic tasks is to consider the minimal inter-arrival time of a task as its period and then follow the ordinary technique used for periodic tasks. Obviously such an approximate method is quite pessimistic since the task control structures are not considered. A major advantage can be gained

H. Garavel and J. Hatcliff (Eds.): TACAS 2003, LNCS 2619, pp. 224–239, 2003.

using timed automata to specify relaxed timing constraints on events and model other behavioural aspects such as concurrency and synchronization. In order to perform schedulability analysis with timed automata the model of Extended Timed Automata (ETA) has been suggested in [FPY02]. It unifies timed automata [AD94] with the classic task models from scheduling theory allowing to execute tasks asynchronously and specify hard time constraints on computations. Furthermore, the problem of schedulability analysis for this model has been proven to be decidable for any scheduling policy and the algorithm for schedulability analysis was presented. It is based on translation of the schedulability problem into reachability for the decrementation automata [MV94]. A remaining challenge is to make the result applicable for schedulability analysis of systems with non-uniformly recurring tasks that scale up to industrial systems. In this paper we present an efficient algorithm for schedulability analysis of systems with relaxed timing constraints, which uses only two additional clocks. The algorithm also allows to compute the worst-case response time for non-periodic tasks.

The rest of this paper is organized as follows: Section 2 describes the syntax and semantics of ETA and defines scheduling problems related to the model. In Section 3, we present the main result of this paper – an algorithm to perform schedulability analysis of systems with relaxed timing constraints. Section 4 is devoted to schedulability analysis of systems with fixed priorities and data-dependent control. In Section 5, we describe implementation issues and how to perform worst-case response time analysis. Section 6 concludes the paper with summary and related work.

2 Preliminaries

2.1 Timed Automata with Tasks

A timed automaton [AD94] is a standard finite-state automaton extended with a finite collection of real-valued clocks. One can interpret timed automata as an abstract model of a running system that describes the possible events occurring during its execution. Those events must satisfy given timing constraints. To clarify how events, accepted by a timed automaton, should be handled or computed we extend timed automata with asynchronous processes [FPY02], i.e. tasks triggered by events asynchronously. The idea is to associate each location of a timed automaton with an executable program called a task. We assume that the execution times and hard deadlines of the tasks are known[1].

Syntax. Let $\mathcal{P}$ ranged over by P, Q, R, denote a finite set of task types. A task type may have different instances that are copies of the same program with different inputs. Each task P is characterized as a pair of natural numbers denoted

[1] Task may have other parameters such as fixed priority for scheduling and other resource requirements, e.g. memory requirement.

$P(C, D)$ with $C \leq D$, where C is the execution time (or computation time) of P and D is the deadline for P. The deadline D is relative, meaning that when task P is released, it should finish within D time units. We shall use $C(P)$ and $D(P)$ to denote the worst case execution time and relative deadline of P respectively.

As in timed automata, assume a finite set of alphabets *Act* for actions and a finite set of real-valued variables $\mathcal{C}$ for clocks. We use a, b etc. to range over *Act* and x_1, x_2 etc. to range over $\mathcal{C}$. We use $\mathcal{B}(\mathcal{C})$ ranged over by g to denote the set of conjunctive formulas of atomic constraints in the form: $x_i \sim C$ or $x_i - x_j \sim D$ where $x_i, x_j \in \mathcal{C}$ are clocks, $\sim \in \{\leq, <, \geq, >\}$, and C, D are natural numbers. The elements of $\mathcal{B}(\mathcal{C})$ are called *clock constraints.*

Definition 1. *A timed automaton extended with tasks, over actions Act, clocks $\mathcal{C}$ and tasks $\mathcal{P}$ is a tuple $\langle N, l_0, E, I, M \rangle$ where*

- *$\langle N, l_0, E, I \rangle$ is a timed automaton where*
  - *N is a finite set of locations ranged over by l, m, n,*
  - *$l_0 \in N$ is the initial location, and*
  - *$E \subseteq N \times \mathcal{B}(\mathcal{C}) \times Act \times 2^{\mathcal{C}} \times N$ is the set of edges.*
  - *$I : N \mapsto \mathcal{B}(\mathcal{C})$ is a function assigning each location with a clock constraint (a location invariant).*
- *$M : N \hookrightarrow \mathcal{P}$ is a partial function assigning locations with tasks*[2]*.*

Intuitively, a discrete transition in an automaton denotes an event triggering a task and the guard (clock constraints) on the transition specifies all the possible arrival times of the event (or the associated task). Whenever a task is triggered, it will be put in a scheduling (or task) queue for execution (corresponding to the ready queue in operating systems).

Operational Semantics. Extended timed automata may perform two types of transitions just as standard timed automata. The difference is that delay transitions correspond to the execution of running tasks with highest priority and idling for the other tasks waiting to run. Discrete transitions corresponds to the arrival of new task instances.

We represent the values of clocks as functions (called clock assignments) from $\mathcal{C}$ to the non–negative reals. A state of an automaton is a triple (l, u, q) where l is the current control location, u the clock assignment, and q is the current task queue. We assume that the task queue takes the form: $[P_1(c_1, d_1), \ldots, P_n(c_n, d_n)]$ where $P_i(c_i, d_i)$ denotes a released instance of task type P_i with remaining computing time c_i and relative deadline d_i

A scheduling strategy Sch e.g. FPS (fixed priority scheduling) or EDF (earliest deadline first) is a sorting function which changes the ordering of the task queue elements according to the task parameters. For example, EDF($[P(3.1, 10)$,

[2] Note that M is a partial function meaning that some of the locations may have no task. Note also that we may associate a location with a set of tasks instead of a single one. It will not cause technical difficulties.

$Q(4, 5.3)]) = [Q(4, 5.3),\ P(3.1, 10)])$. We call such sorting functions scheduling strategies that may be preemptive or non-preemptive [3].

Run is a function which given a real number t and a task queue q returns the resulted task queue after t time units of execution according to available computing resources. For simplicity, we assume that only one processor is available. Then the meaning of $\mathsf{Run}(q, t)$ should be obvious and it can be defined inductively. For example, let $q = [Q(4, 5), P(3, 10)]$. Then $\mathsf{Run}(q, 6) = [P(1, 4)]$ in which the first task is finished and the second has been executed for 2 time units.

Further, for non-negative a real number t, we use $u + t$ to denote the clock assignment which maps each clock x to the value $u(x) + t$, $u \models g$ to denote that the clock assignment u satisfies the constraint g and $u[r \mapsto 0]$ for $r \subseteq \mathcal{C}$, to denote the clock assignment which maps each clock in r to 0 and agrees with u for the other clocks (i.e. $\mathcal{C} \backslash r$).

Definition 2. *Given a scheduling strategy* Sch[4]*, the semantics of an extended timed automaton* $\langle N, l_0, E, I, M \rangle$ *with initial state* (l_0, u_0, q_0) *is a transition system defined by the following rules:*

- $(l, u, q) \xrightarrow{a}_{\mathsf{Sch}} (m, u[r \mapsto 0], \mathsf{Sch}(M(m) :: q))$ *if* $l \stackrel{g,a,r}{\longrightarrow} m$ *and* $u \models g$
- $(l, u, q) \xrightarrow{t}_{\mathsf{Sch}} (l, u + t, \mathsf{Run}(q, t))$ *if* $(u + t) \models I(l)$

where $M(m) :: q$ *denotes the queue with* $M(m)$ *inserted in* q.

2.2 Schedulability and Decidability

In this section we briefly review the verification problems of ETA. For more details, we refer the reader to [FPY02]. We first mention that we have the same notion of reachability as for ordinary timed automata.

Definition 3. *We shall write* $(l, u, q) \longrightarrow (l', u', q')$ *if* $(l, u, q) \xrightarrow{a} (l', u', q')$ *for an action* a *or* $(l, u, q) \xrightarrow{t} (l', u', q')$ *for a delay* t. *For an automaton with initial state* (l_0, u_0, q_0), (l, u, q) *is reachable iff* $(l_0, u_0, q_0)(\longrightarrow)^*(l, u, q)$.

Note that the reachable state-space of an ETA is infinite not only because of the real-valued clocks, but also unbounded size of the task queue.

Definition 4. *(Schedulability) A state* (l, u, q) *where* $q = [P_1(c_1, d_1), \ldots, P_n(c_n, d_n)]$ *is a failure denoted* (l, u, Error) *if there exists* i *such that* $c_i \geq 0$ *and* $d_i < 0$, *that is, a task failed in meeting its deadline. Naturally an automaton* A *with initial state* (l_0, u_0, q_0) *is non-schedulable with* Sch *iff* $(l_0, u_0, q_0)(\longrightarrow_{\mathsf{Sch}})^*(l, u, \mathsf{Error})$ *for some* l *and* u. *Otherwise, we say that* A *is schedulable with* Sch. *More generally, we say that* A *is schedulable iff there exists a scheduling strategy* Sch *with which* A *is schedulable.*

[3] A non-preemptive strategy will never change the position of the first element of a queue. A preemptive strategy may change the ordering of task types only, but never change the ordering of task instances of the same type.

[4] Note that we fix Run to be the function that represents a one-processor system.

The schedulability of a state may be checked by the standard schedulability test. We say that (l, u, q) is schedulable with Sch if $\mathsf{Sch}(q) = [P_1(c_1, d_1) \ldots P_n(c_n, d_n)]$ and $(\sum_{i \leq k} c_i) \leq d_k$ for all $k \leq n$. Alternatively, an automaton is schedulable with Sch if all its reachable states are schedulable with Sch.

Theorem 1. *The problem of checking schedulability for extended timed automata is decidable.*

Proof. The proof is given in [FPY02]. □

3 Main Result: Two Clocks Encoding

In this section we present the main result of this paper. It shows that for timed automata extended with tasks executed according to fixed priorities, the scheduling problem can be encoded into a reachability problem of ordinary timed automata using only two additional clocks.

Our analysis technique is inspired by Joseph and Pandya's rate-monotonic analysis of periodic tasks [JP86], where the worst-case response time of each task is calculated as the sum of the task's execution time, and the blockings imposed by other tasks. Similar to Joseph and Pandya, we check for each task type independently that it meets its deadline. However, the model of ETA gives rise to a more general scheduling problem than systems with periodic tasks only. As a result, we can not base our analysis on the existence of an a priori known worst-case scenario for a given task. Instead, it will be part of the analysis to find all situations in which a task may execute.

Assume an ETA A and a fixed priority scheduling strategy Sch. To solve the scheduling problem, for each $P_i \in \mathcal{P}$ we construct automata $E_i(\mathsf{Sch})$ and $E(A)$, and check for reachability of a predefined error state in the product automaton of the two. If the error state is reachable, task P_i of automaton A is not schedulable with Sch. The check is performed in priority order for each task in $\mathcal{P}$, starting with the task of highest priority.

To construct the $E(A)$, the automaton A is annotated with distinct synchronization actions $\mathsf{release}_i$ on all edges leading to locations labeled with the task name P_i. The actions will allow the scheduler to observe when tasks are released for execution in A. The rest of this section is devoted to show that $E_i(\mathsf{Sch})$ can be constructed as a timed automaton using only two clocks.

Theorem 2. *Given a fixed priority scheduling strategy* Sch*,* $E_i(\mathsf{Sch})$ *can be encoded as a timed automaton containing two clocks.*

Proof. Follows from Lemma 1 and 2 shown later in this section. □

In the encoding of $E_i(\mathsf{Sch})$, we shall use $C(i)$, $D(i)$ and $\mathsf{Prio}(i)$ to denote the worst-case execution time, the deadline, and the priority of task type P_i, respectively. $E_i(\mathsf{Sch})$ uses the following variables:

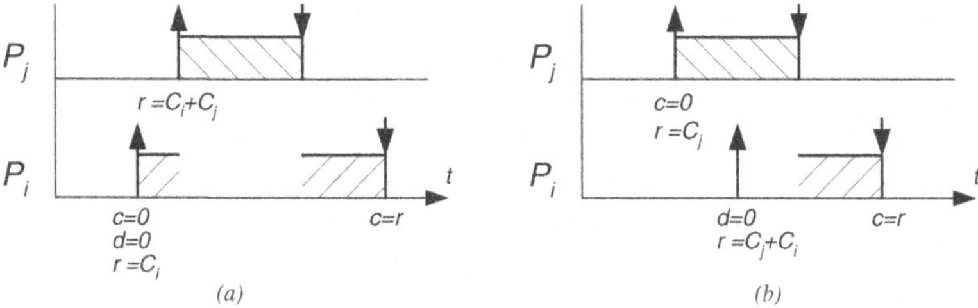

Fig. 1. Task execution schemes for tasks P_i and P_j with $\mathsf{Prio}(j) > \mathsf{Prio}(i)$. The symbols $\uparrow$ and $\downarrow$ indicate release and completion of tasks, respectively.

- d - a clock measuring the time since the analysed task instance of P_i was released for execution,
- c - a clock accumulating the time since the task queue last empty (or containing only tasks P_k with $\mathsf{Prio}(k) < \mathsf{Prio}(i)$).
- r - a data variable used to sum up the time needed to complete all tasks released since the processor was last idle (i.e. not executing instances of P_i and all higher priority tasks).

The clock d is reset when the analysis of a task instance begins, and will be used to check that it completes before its deadline. The clock c is used to compute the time point when the analysed task instance of P_i completes. The variable r will be assigned so that P_i completes when $\mathsf{c} = \mathsf{r}$. Fig.1 shows in two Gantt charts how the variables are used in $E_i(\mathsf{Sch})$. In Fig.1(a) task P_i executes immediately but is preempted by P_j. In Fig.1(b) task P_i is released when task P_j is already executing. Note how the clocks c and d are reset, and variable r is updated in the two scenarios so that task P_i is completed when the condition $\mathsf{c} = \mathsf{r}$ is satisfied. Note also that the deadline of P_i is reached when $\mathsf{d} = D(i)$ (as d is reset when P_i is released for execution).

The encoding of $E_i(\mathsf{Sch})$ is shown in Fig.2. Intuitively, the locations have the following interpretations:

- Idle_i - denotes a situation where no task P_j with $\mathsf{Prio}(j) \geq \mathsf{Prio}(i)$ is being executed (or ready to be executed).
- Check_i - an instance of task type P_i is currently ready for execution (possibly executing) and is being analysed for schedulability.
- Busy_i - a task of type P_j with priority $\mathsf{Prio}(j) \geq \mathsf{Prio}(i)$ is currently executing.
- Error_i - the analysed task queue is not schedulable with Sch.

The analysis of an instance of P_i starts when a transition from Idle_i or Busy_i to Check_i is taken. The transitions in $E_i(\mathsf{Sch})$ have the following intuitive interpretations:

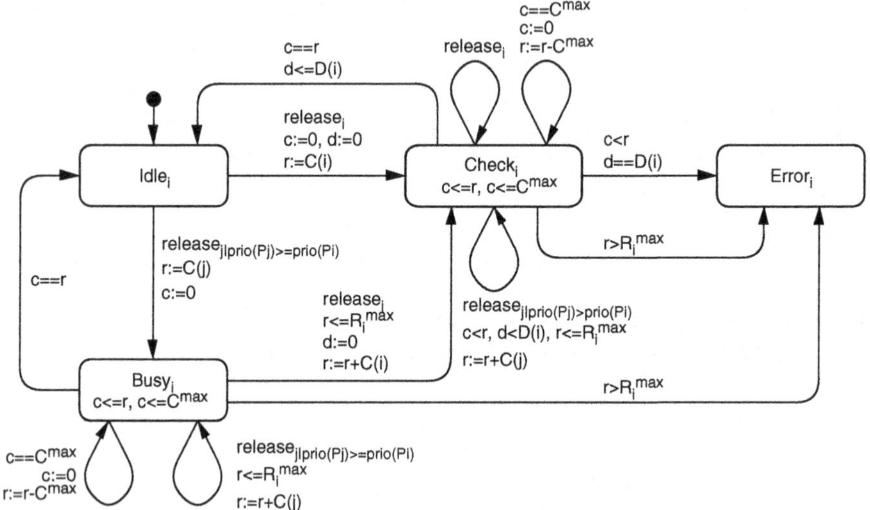

Fig. 2. Encoding of schedulability problem.

- Idle_i - is (re-)entered when the task instance being checked in Check_i, or a sequence of tasks arrived in Busy_i, has finished execution. In both cases the enabling condition c=r ensures that the location is reached when all tasks P_j with $\mathsf{Prio}(j) \geq \mathsf{Prio}(i)$ have finished their executions.
- Busy_i - the ingoing transitions to Busy_i are taken when a task P_j such that $\mathsf{Prio}(j) \geq \mathsf{Prio}(i)$ is released. The additional self-loop, is taken to decrement both c and r with the constant value C^{max}. This does not change the truth-value of any of the guards in which c and r appear, as the values are always compared to each other.
- Check_i - transitions entering Check_i from Idle_i or Busy_i are taken when a task instance of P_i is (non-deterministically) chosen for checking. Self-loops in Check_i are taken to update r at the release of higher-priority tasks. New instances of P_i in Check_i are ignored as they are considered by the non-deterministic choice in location Busy_i.
- Error_i - is reached when the analysed task instance reaches its deadline (encoded $\mathsf{d} = \mathsf{D}(i)$) before completion (encoded $\mathsf{c} < \mathsf{r}$). In addition, Error_i is entered if the set of released tasks is guaranteed to be non-schedulable (encoded $\mathsf{r} > \mathsf{R}_i^{max}$, the value of R_i^{max} is discussed below).

In addition to these transitions, in Fig 2 we have omitted self-loops in all locations, which synchronize with $E(A)$ whenever a task of priority lower than $\mathsf{Prio}(i)$ is released. They can be ignored as these tasks do not affect the response time of P_i.

The constant C^{max} can be any value greater than 0. We use $\mathsf{C}^{max} = \max_i(C(i))$. To find a value for R_i^{max}, we need the result of the previous analysis steps. Recall that the analysis of all $P_i \in \mathcal{P}$ is performed in priority order, starting with the highest priority. Thus, when P_i is analysed we can find the maximum value assigned to r in the previous analysis steps. Let r^{max} denote this value. Recall that $\mathsf{r} - \mathsf{c}$ is always the time remaining until the released tasks complete their executions (except in location Idle_i and Error_i where r is not updated). For the set of released tasks to be schedulable we have that $\mathsf{r} - \mathsf{c} < \mathsf{r}^{max} + D(i)$. It follows that $\mathsf{r} < \mathsf{r}^{max} + D(i) + \mathsf{C}^{max}$ since $\mathsf{c} \leq \mathsf{C}^{max}$. We set the constant $\mathsf{R}_i^{max} = \mathsf{r}^{max} + D(i) + \mathsf{C}^{max}$ and use $\mathsf{r} > \mathsf{R}_i^{max}$ to detect non-schedulable task sets in $E_i(\mathsf{Sch})$.

The last step of the encoding is to construct the product automata $E(A)||E_i(\mathsf{Sch})$ for each $P_i \in \mathcal{P}$, and check by reachability analysis that location Error_i is not reachable in the product automaton. We now show that $E(A)||E_i(\mathsf{Sch})$ is bounded.

Lemma 1. *The clocks* c *and* d*, and the data variable* r *of* $E_i(\mathsf{Sch})$ *in* $E(A)||E_i(\mathsf{Sch})$ *are bounded.*

Proof. The clocks d and c are bounded by the constants $D(i)$ and C^{max} respectively. The data variable r is bounded by $\mathsf{R}_i^{max} + \max_{\{j \,:\, \mathsf{Prio}(j) > \mathsf{Prio}(i)\}} C(j)$. □

Lemma 2. *Let* A *be an extended timed automaton and* Sch *a fixed-priority scheduling strategy. Assume that* (l_0, u_0, q_0) *and* $(\langle l_0, \mathsf{Idle}_i\rangle, v_0)$ *are the initial states of* A *and the product automaton* $E(A)||E_i(\mathsf{Sch})$ *respectively where* l_0 *is the initial location of* A*,* u_0 *and* v_0 *are clock assignments assigning all clocks with* 0 *and* q_0 *is the empty task queue. Then the following holds:*

$$(l_0, u_0, q_0)(\longrightarrow)^*(l, u, \mathsf{Error}) \text{ iff } (\langle l_0, \mathsf{Idle}_i\rangle, v_0)(\longrightarrow)^*(\langle l', \mathsf{Error}_i\rangle, v)$$

for some l, u, l', v, i.

Proof. It is by induction on the length of transition sequence (i.e. reachability steps). □

Thus, we have shown that the scheduling problem can be solved by a reachability problem for timed automata, and from Lemma 1 we know that the reachability problem is bounded. This completes the proof of Theorem 2.

4 Analysing Data-Dependent Control

In this section we extend the result of the previous section to handle extended time automata in which the tasks may use (read and update) data variables, shared between the tasks and the automata. This results in a model with *data-dependent control* in the sense that the behaviour of the control automaton, and the release time-point of tasks may depend on the values of the shared variables, and hence on the time-points at which other tasks complete their executions. We first present the model of ETA extended with data variables [AFP+03].

4.1 Extended Timed Automata with Data Variables

Syntax. Assume a set of variables $\mathcal{D}$ ranged over by u, which takes their values from finite data domains, and are updated by assignments in the form $u := \mathcal{E}$, where $\mathcal{E}$ is a mathematical expression. We use $\mathcal{R}$ to denote the set of all possible assignments. A task P is now characterized by a triple $P(C, D, R)$, where C and D are the execution time and the deadline as usual, and $R \subseteq \mathcal{R}$ is a set of assignments. We use $R(P)$ to denote the set of assignments of P, and we assume that a task assigns the variables according to $R(P)$ by the end of its execution.

The data variables assigned by tasks may also be updated and tested (or read) by the extended timed automata. Let $\mathcal{A} = \mathcal{R} \cup \{x := 0 \mid x \in \mathcal{C}\}$ be the set of updates. We use r to stand for a subset of $\mathcal{A}$. To read and test the values of the data variables, let $\mathcal{B}(\mathcal{D})$ be a set of predicates over $\mathcal{D}$. Let $\mathcal{B} = \mathcal{B}(\mathcal{D}) \cup \mathcal{B}(\mathcal{C})$ be ranged over by g called guards.

Operational Semantics. To define the semantics, we use valuations to denote the values of variables. A valuation is a function mapping clock variables to the non-negative reals, and data variables to the data domain. We denote by $\mathcal{V}$ the set of valuations ranged over by σ. For a non-negative real number t, we use $\sigma + t$ to denote the valuation which updates each clock x with $\sigma(x) + t$, and $\sigma[r]$ to denote the valuation which maps each variable α to the value of $\mathcal{E}$ if $\alpha := \mathcal{E} \in r$ (note that $\mathcal{E}$ is zero if α is a clock) and agrees with σ for the other variables. We are now ready to present the semantics of extended timed automata with data variables by the following rules:

- $(l, \sigma, q) \xrightarrow{a}_{\mathsf{Sch}} (m, \sigma[r], \mathsf{Sch}(M(m) :: q))$ if $l \xrightarrow{g,a,r} m$ and $\sigma \models g$
- $(l, \sigma, q) \xrightarrow{t}_{\mathsf{Sch}} (l, \sigma + t, \mathsf{Run}(q, t))$ if $(\sigma + t) \models I(l)$ and $C(\mathsf{Hd}(q, t)) > t$
- $(l, \sigma, q) \xrightarrow{t}_{\mathsf{Sch}} (l, (\sigma[A(\mathsf{Hd}(q))]) + t, \mathsf{Run}(q, t))$ if $(\sigma + t) \models I(l)$ and $C(\mathsf{Hd}(q)) = t$

where $M(m) :: q$ denotes the queue with $M(m)$ inserted in q and $\mathsf{Hd}(q)$ denotes the first element of q.

4.2 Schedulability Analysis

As in the previous section, we shall encode the ETA A and the fixed-priority scheduling strategy Sch into timed automata and check for reachability of predefined error states. The encoding $E(A)$ is the same as in the previous section. However, the encoding of Sch will be different with data-depended control, as the result of the schedulability analysis depends on the data-variables that may be updated whenever a task completes its execution. In the rest of this section we describe how to construct $E(\mathsf{Sch})$:

Theorem 3. *For an extended timed automaton A with data variables, and a fixed priority scheduling strategy* Sch*, $E(\mathsf{Sch})$ can be constructed as timed automaton containing $n+1$ clocks, where n is a number of task types used in A.*

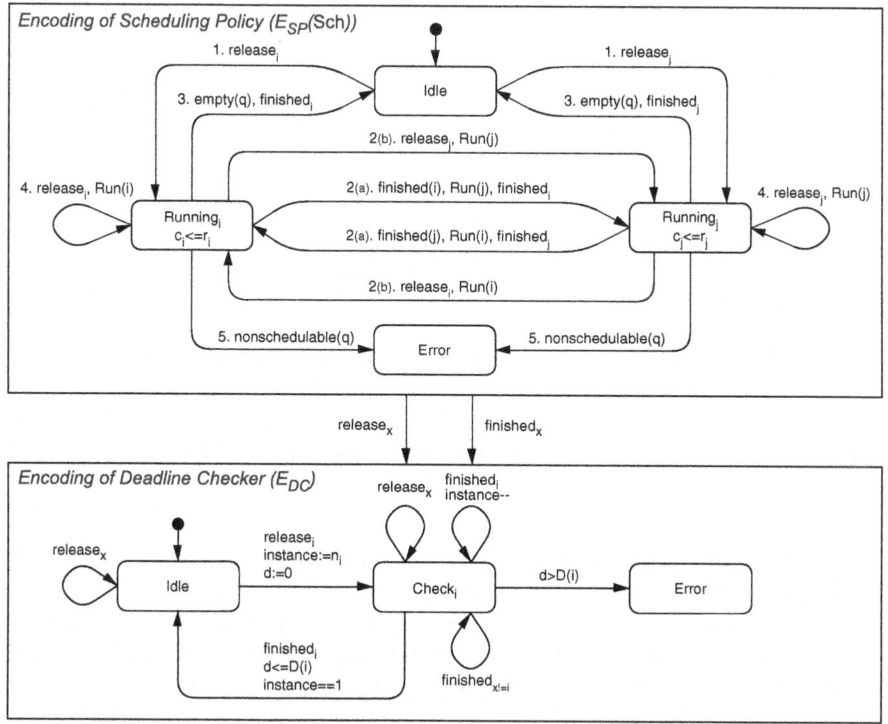

Fig. 3. Encoding of schedulability problem.

Proof. Follows from Lemma 3 and 4 shown later in this section. □

The construction of $E(\mathsf{Sch})$ is illustrated in Fig.3. It is consists of two parallel automata: $E_{\mathsf{SP}}(\mathsf{Sch})$ - encoding the scheduling policy (containing n clocks), and E_{DC} - encoding a generic deadline checker (containing one clock). As in the previous section, the two scheduling automata (in this case both $E_{\mathsf{SP}}(\mathsf{Sch})$ and E_{DC}) synchronize with $E(A)$ on the action $\mathsf{release}_i$ when an instance of task P_i is released. In addition, $E_{\mathsf{SP}}(\mathsf{Sch})$ and E_{DC} synchronize on $\mathsf{finished}_i$ whenever an instance of P_i finishes its execution.

Encoding of Scheduling Policy $E_{\mathsf{SP}}(\mathsf{Sch})$. We first introduce some notation. Let P_{ij} denote instance j of task P_i. For each P_{ij}, $E_{\mathsf{SP}}(\mathsf{Sch})$ has a state variable $\mathsf{status}(i,j)$ that is initially set to free. Let $\mathsf{status}(i,j) = \mathsf{running}$ denote that P_{ij} is executing on the processor, $\mathsf{preempted}$ that P_{ij} is started but not running, and $\mathsf{released}$ that P_{ij} is released but not yet started. We use $\mathsf{status}(i,j) = \mathsf{free}$ to denote that P_{ij} is not released yet. Note that for all (i,j) there can be only one j such that $\mathsf{status}(i,j) = \mathsf{preempted}$ (i.e. only one instance of the same task type is started), and for all (i,j) there can only be one pair (k,l) such that

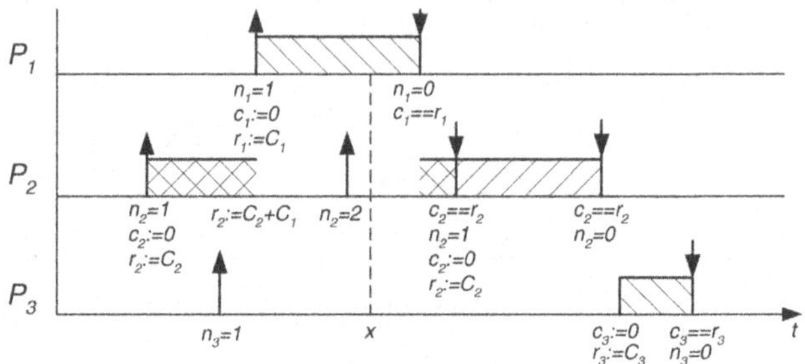

Fig. 4. Task execution scheme where $\mathsf{Prio}(1) > \mathsf{Prio}(2) > \mathsf{Prio}(3)$.

$\mathsf{status}(k, l) = \mathsf{running}$ (i.e. only one task is running in a one-processor system). For each task type P_i we use three variables:

- c_i - clock measuring the time passed since P_i started its execution. We reset c_i whenever an instance of P_i is started.
- r_i - data variable accumulating the response time of P_i from the moment it starts to execute. r_i is set to $C(i)$ when an instance of P_i is started, and updated to $\mathsf{r}_i + C(j)$ when a higher-priority task P_j is released.
- n_i - data variable keeping track of the number of P_i currently released.

In Fig. 4, we show how the above variables are used in $E_{\mathsf{SP}}(\mathsf{Sch})$. At time point x state variable status has the values $\mathsf{status}(1, 1) = \mathsf{running}$, $\mathsf{status}(2, 1) = \mathsf{preempted}$, $\mathsf{status}(2, 2) = \mathsf{released}$, and $\mathsf{status}(3, 1) = \mathsf{released}$.

To represent each task instance in $E_{\mathsf{SP}}(\mathsf{Sch})$ we use a triple $\langle c_i, r_i, \mathsf{status}(i, j)\rangle$, and the task queue q will contain such triples. Note that the maximal number of instances of P_i appearing in a schedulable queue is $\lceil D(i)/C(i)\rceil$. Thus, the size of the queue is bounded to $\sum_{P_i \in \mathcal{P}} \lceil D(i)/C(i)\rceil$. We shall say that queue is empty, denoted $\mathsf{empty}(q)$, if $\mathsf{status}(i, j) = \mathsf{free}$ for all (i, j).

For a given scheduling strategy Sch, we use the predicate $\mathsf{Run}(m, n)$ to denote that task instance P_{mn} is scheduled to run according to Sch. For a given fixed priority scheduling policy Sch, it can be coded as a constraint over the state variables. For example, for deadline-monotonic scheduling[5], $\mathsf{Run}(m, n)$ is the conjunction of the following constraints:

- $\mathsf{r}_k \leq D(k)$ for all k, l such that $\mathsf{status}(k, l) \neq \mathsf{free}$: all response time integers are less than deadlines
- $\mathsf{status}(m, n) \neq \mathsf{free}$: P_{mn} is released or preempted
- $D(m) \leq D(i)$ for all i: P_m has the highest priority

[5] In deadline-monotonic scheduling, task priorities are assigned according to deadlines, such that $\mathsf{Prio}(i) > \mathsf{Prio}(j)$ iff $D(i) < D(j)$.

We use $\mathsf{Run}(m)$ to denote that a task instance of P_m is scheduled to run according to Sch. The predicate $\mathsf{finished}(m,n)$ denotes that P_{mn} has finished its execution. We define $\mathsf{finished}(m,n)$ to $(c_m = r_m) \wedge (\mathsf{status}(m,n) \neq \mathsf{free})$. Finally, we use $\mathsf{nonschedulable}(q)$ to denote that the queue q is non-schedulable in a sense that there exists a pair (i,j) for which $r_i > D(i)$ and $\mathsf{status}(i,j) \neq \mathsf{free}$.

The automaton $E_{\mathsf{SP}}(\mathsf{Sch})$ contains three type of locations: Idle, $\mathsf{Running}_i$ and Error. Note that $\mathsf{Running}_i$ is parameterized with i representing the running task type. Location Idle denotes that the task queue is empty. $\mathsf{Running}_i$ denotes that task instance of type P_i is running, that is, for some j $\mathsf{status}(i,j) = \mathsf{running}$. For each $\mathsf{Running}_i$ we have the location invariant $c_i \leq r_i$. Error denotes that the task queue is non-schedulable with Sch. There are five types of edges labeled as follows:

1. Idle to $\mathsf{Running}_i$: edges labeled with action $\mathsf{release}_i$, and reset $\{r_i := C(i), c_i := 0, \mathsf{n}_i := 1, \mathsf{status}(i,j) := \mathsf{running}\}$.
2. $\mathsf{Running}_i$ to Idle: edges labeled with guard $\mathsf{empty}(q)$ and reset $\{\mathsf{n}_i := 0, R(P_i)\}$.
3. $\mathsf{Running}_i$ to $\mathsf{Running}_m$: two types of edges:
   a) the running task P_{ij} is finished and P_{mn} is scheduled to run by $\mathsf{Run}(m,n)$. There are two cases:
      i. P_{mn} was preempted earlier: encoded by guard $\mathsf{finished}(i,j) \wedge \mathsf{status}(m, n) = \mathsf{preempted} \wedge \mathsf{Run}(m,n)$, action $\mathsf{finished}_i$, and reset $\{\mathsf{status}(i,j) := \mathsf{free}, \mathsf{n}_i := \mathsf{n}_i - 1, \mathsf{status}(m,n) := \mathsf{running}, R(P_i)\}$
      ii. P_{mn} was released, but never preempted (not started yet): encoded by guard $\mathsf{finished}(i,j) \wedge \mathsf{status}(m,n) = \mathsf{released} \wedge \mathsf{Run}(m,n)$ action $\mathsf{finished}_i$, and reset $\{\mathsf{status}(i,j) := \mathsf{free}, \mathsf{n}_i := \mathsf{n}_i - 1, r_m := C(m), c_m = 0, \mathsf{status}(m,n) := \mathsf{running}, R(P_i)\}$
   b) a new task P_{mn} is released, which preempts the running task P_{ij}: encoded by guard $\mathsf{status}(m,n) = \mathsf{free} \wedge \mathsf{Run}(m,n)$, action $\mathsf{release}_m$, and reset $\{\mathsf{status}(m,n) := \mathsf{running}, \mathsf{n}_m := \mathsf{n}_m + 1, r_m := C(m), c_m := 0, \mathsf{status}(i,j) := \mathsf{preempted}\} \cup \{r_k := r_k + C(m) \mid \mathsf{status}(k,l) = \mathsf{preempted}\}$ (we increment the response times of all preempted tasks by the execution time of the released higher-priority task).
4. $\mathsf{Running}_i$ to $\mathsf{Running}_i$: edges representing the case when a task release does not preempt the running task P_{ij}: encoded by guard $\mathsf{status}(k,l) = \mathsf{free} \wedge \mathsf{Run}(i,j)$, action $\mathsf{released}_k$, and reset $\{\mathsf{status}(k,l) := \mathsf{released}, \mathsf{n}_k := \mathsf{n}_k + 1\} \cup \{r_k := r_k + C(m) \mid \mathsf{status}(k,l) = \mathsf{preempted}\}$
5. $\mathsf{Running}_i$ to Error: an edge labeled by the guard $\mathsf{nonschedulable}(q)$.

Encoding of Deadline Checker E_{DC}. It is similar to the encoding of $E_i(\mathsf{Sch})$ described in the previous section, in the sense that it checks for deadline violations of each task instance independently. The clock d is used in E_{DC} to measure the time since the analysed instance of P_i was released for execution. E_{DC} also uses a data variable, named instance. From location Idle the automaton nondeterministically starts to analyse a task on the edge to Check_i, at which clock d is reset and instance is set to n_i, i.e. the current number of released instances of task P_i. In Check_i, $\mathsf{instance}$ is decremented whenever an instance of P_i finishes its execution. The analysed task finishes when $\mathsf{instance} = 1$ and the location Idle is reentered. However, if d is greater than $D(i)$, the task failed to meet its deadline and the location Error is reached.

The next step of the encoding is to construct the product automaton $E(A)|| E_{\mathsf{SP}}(\mathsf{Sch})||E_{\mathsf{DC}}$ in which the automata can only synchronize on identical action symbols. We now show that the product automaton is bounded.

Lemma 3. *The clocks* c_i *and* d, *and the data variables* r_i *and* n_i *of* $E_{\mathsf{SP}}(\mathsf{Sch})||E_{\mathsf{DC}}$ *in* $E(A)||E_{\mathsf{SP}}(\mathsf{Sch})||E_{\mathsf{DC}}$ *are bounded.*

Proof. First note that the integers r_k are bounded by $D(k) + \max_i(C(i))$ due to the fact that all edges incrementing r_k (by some $C(i)$) are guarded by the constraint $\mathsf{Run}(m,n)$ requiring $\mathsf{r}_k \leq D(k)$. The bound for n_k is $\lceil D(k)/C(k) \rceil$. The clocks d and c_k are bounded by $\max_i(D(i))$ and r_k, respectively. □

Lemma 4. *Let* A *be an extended timed automaton and* Sch *a fixed-priority scheduling strategy. Assume that* (l_0, u_0, q_0) *and* $(\langle l_0, \mathsf{Idle}, \mathsf{Idle}\rangle, v_0)$ *are the initial states of* A *and the product automaton* $E(A)||E_{\mathsf{SP}}(\mathsf{Sch})||E_{\mathsf{DC}}$ *respectively where* l_0 *is the initial location of* A, u_0 *and* v_0 *are clock assignments assigning all clocks with* 0 *and* q_0 *is the empty task queue. Then the following holds:*

$$(l_0, u_0, q_0)(\longrightarrow)^*(l, u, \mathsf{Error}) \text{ iff } (\langle l_0, \mathsf{Idle}\rangle, v_0)(\longrightarrow)^*(\langle l', \mathsf{Error}, m\rangle, v) \text{ or } (\langle l_0, \mathsf{Idle}\rangle, v_0)(\longrightarrow)^*(\langle l'', m', \mathsf{Error}\rangle, v')$$

for some $l, u, l', l'', m, m', v, v'$.

Proof. It is by induction on the length of transition sequence (i.e. reachability steps). □

5 Implementation

The algorithm described in Section 3 has been implemented in TIMES, a tool for modeling and schedulability analysis of embedded real-time systems [AFM+02]. The modeling language of TIMES is ETA as described in Section 4.1 of this paper. The tool currently supports simulation, schedulability analysis, checking of safety and liveness properties, and synthesis of executable C-code [AFP+03].

A screenshot of the TIMES tool analysing a simple control system with data-dependent control consisting of tasks with fixed priorities is shown in Fig.5. The schedulability analysis is performed as described in Section 3.

The system analysed in Fig.5 is a simple controller of a motor, periodically polling a sensor and at requests providing a user with sensor statistics. In the initial location, an instance of task ReadSensor is released. The controller waits 10 time units for a user to push the button. If the button is not pushed, the controller releases the two tasks AnalyzeData and ActuateMotor. If the button is

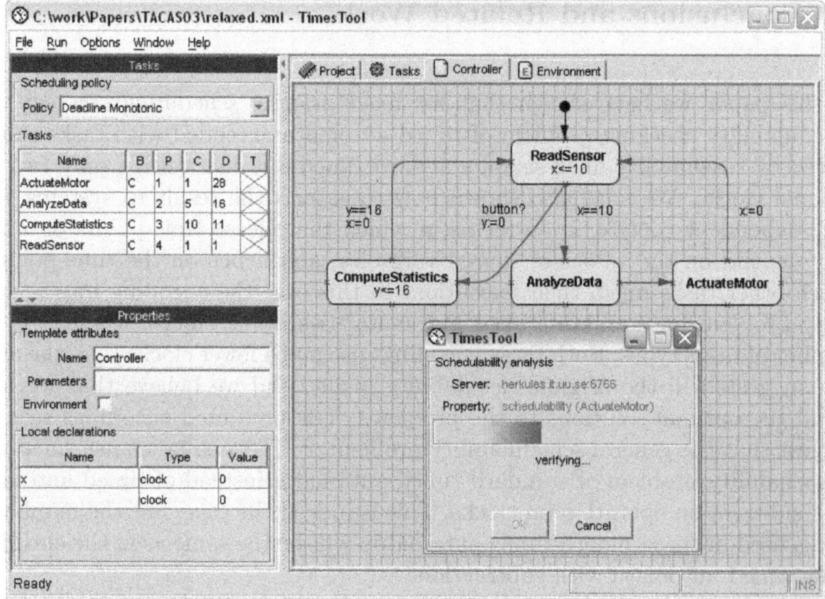

Fig. 5. The TIMES tool performing schedulability analysis.

pushed when the controller operates in its initial location, an instance of task ComputeStatistics is released for execution, and the controller waits 16 time units before releasing task ReadSensor again.

The system has been analysed with two algorithms implemented in the TIMES tool. An implementation based on the original decidability result described in [FPY02] consumes 2.7 seconds, whereas an implementation of the algorithm presented in Section 3 of this paper terminates in 0.1 seconds on the same machine[6]. Thus, the time consumption is reduced significantly for this system.

In addition to schedulability analysis, it is possible to adjust the algorithms presented in this paper, and implemented in TIMES, to compute the worst-case response time of tasks in a schedulable system. In general, the response time of a task is a non-integer value. We take the worst-case response time to be the lowest integer value greater or equal to the longest response time of a task. The worst-case response time of task P_i can be obtained from the maximum value appearing in the upper bound on the clock d[7] in the symbolic states generated during the schedulability analysis of task P_i (i.e. in the reachability analysis). In Fig.5 the numbers in the task table column D are the worst-case response times of the tasks in the system. Thus, if any of them is decreased, the system becomes non-schedulable.

[6] The measurements were made on a Sun Ultra-80 running SunOS 5.7. The UNIX program `time` was used to measure the time consumption.

[7] Here we refer to clock d described in Section 3.

6 Conclusions and Related Work

In this paper we have shown that for fixed priority scheduling strategy, the schedulability checking problem of timed automata extended with tasks can be solved by reachability analysis on standard timed automata using only two additional clocks. We have also shown how to extend the result to systems with data-dependent control, i.e. systems in which the release time-points of a task may depend on the values of shared variables, and hence on the time-point at which other tasks finish their execution. In this case the encoding into reachability problem for standard timed automata uses $n+1$ clocks, where n is the number of tasks types. Both these encodings use much fewer clocks than the analysis suggested in the original decidability result, and we believe that we have found the optimal solutions to the problems. The presented encodings seem to suggest that the general schedulability problem of ETA can be transformed into a reachability problem of standard timed automata, instead of timed automata with subtraction operation on clocks. This is indeed the case, but the number of clocks used in the standard timed automaton will be the same as in the encoding using timed automata with subtraction.

The schedulability checking algorithms described in this paper have been implemented in the TIMES tool. An experiment shows that the new techniques substantially reduce the computation time needed to analyse an example systems with fixed priority scheduling strategy.

Related work. Well established scheduling theory and scheduling algorithms are described in various publications. In the area of real time scheduling methods such as rate monotonic scheduling [But97] are widely applied in the analysis of systems with deterministic behaviours restricted to periodic tasks. However, for systems with non-periodic tasks and non-deterministic behaviours, there are still no satisfactory procedures to perform schedulability analysis. One of the approaches to achieve schedulability is based on controller synthesis paradigm [AGS02,AGP+99]. The methodology described in [AGS02] relies on the idea that one can build schedulable system successively restricting guards of the controllable actions in its model in an appropriate way. However, concepts related to implementation description are not addressed in this work. In the area of non-preemptive scheduling timed automata has been used mainly for job-shop scheduling [Feh99,AM01,HLP01]. The idea is to get schedules out of traces produced during reachability analysis for pre-defined locations specifying scheduling goal. Stop-watch automata have been used to solve preemptive scheduling problem [MV94,Cor94,CL00]. But since reachability analysis problem for this class of automata is undecidable in general there is no guarantee of termination for the analysis without the assumption that task preemptions occur only at integer points. Tools have been developed to support the design and analysis of embedded systems with tasks. Examples hereof include TAXYS [CPP+01] and TIMES [AFM+02].

References

[AD94] R. Alur and D. L. Dill. A theory of timed automata. *Theoretical Computer Science*, 126(2):183–235, 1994.

[AFM+02] T. Amnell, E. Fersman, L. Mokrushin, P. Pettersson, and W. Yi. Times – a tool for modelling and implementation of embedded systems. In *In Proc.TACAS'02*, volume 2280 of *LNCS*, pages 460–464. Springer, 2002.

[AFP+03] T. Amnell, E. Fersman, P. Pettersson, H. Sun, and W. Yi. Code synthesis for timed automata. To appear in Nordic Journal of Computing, 2003.

[AGP+99] K. Altisen, G. Gößler, A. Pnueli, J. Sifakis, S. Tripakis, and S. Yovine. A framework for scheduler synthesis. In *In Proc. IEEE RTSS'99*, pages 154–163, 1999.

[AGS02] K. Altisen, G. Gößler, and J. Sifakis. Scheduler modeling based on the controller synthesis paradigm. *Journal of Real-Time Systems, special issue on Control Approaches to Real-Time Computing*, 23:55–84, 2002.

[AM01] Y. Abdeddaïm and O. Maler. Job-shop scheduling using timed automata. In *In Proc. CAV'01*, volume 2102 of *LNCS*, pages 478–492. Springer, 2001.

[But97] G. C. Buttazzo. *Hard Real-Time Computing Systems. Predictable Scheduling Algorithms and Applications.* Kulwer Academic Publishers, 1997.

[CL00] F. Cassez and F. Laroussinie. Model-checking for hybrid systems by quotienting and constraints solving. In *In Proc. CAV'00*, volume 1855 of *LNCS*, pages 373–388. Springer, 2000.

[Cor94] J. Corbett. Modeling and analysis of real-time ada tasking programs. In *In Proc. IEEE RTSS'94*, pages 132–141, 1994.

[CPP+01] E. Closse, M. Poize, J. Pulou, J. Sifakis, P. Venier, D. Weil, and S. Yovine. Taxys: a tool for the development and verification real-time embedded systems. In *In Proc. CAV'01*, volume 2102 of *LNCS*. Springer, 2001.

[Feh99] A. Fehnker. Scheduling a steel plant with timed automata. In *In Proc. IEEE RTCSA'99*, 1999.

[FPY02] E. Fersman, P. Pettersson, and W. Yi. Timed automata with asynchronous processes: Schedulability and decidability. In *In Proc.TACAS'02*, volume 2280 of *LNCS*, pages 67–82. Springer, 2002.

[HLP01] Thomas Hune, Kim G. Larsen, and Paul Pettersson. Guided Synthesis of Control Programs using UPPAAL. *Nordic Journal of Computing*, 8(1):43–64, 2001.

[JP86] M. Joseph and P. Pandya. Finding response times in a real-time system. *BSC Computer Journal*, 29(5):390–395, October 1986.

[MV94] J. McManis and P. Varaiya. Suspension automata: A decidable class of hybrid automata. In *In Proc. CAV'94*, volume 818, pages 105–117. Springer, 1994.

On Optimal Scheduling under Uncertainty*

Yasmina Abdeddaïm, Eugene Asarin, and Oded Maler

VERIMAG, Centre Equation, 2, av. de Vignate 38610 Gières, France
{Yasmina.Abdeddaim,Eugene.Asarin,Oded.Maler}@imag.fr

Abstract. In this work we treat the problem of scheduling under two types of temporal uncertainty, set-based and probabilistic. For the former we define appropriate optimality criteria and develop an algorithm for finding optimal scheduling strategies using a backward reachability algorithm for timed automata. For probabilistic uncertainty we define and solve a special case of continuous-time Markov Decision Process. The results have been implemented and were applied to benchmarks to provide a preliminary assessment of the merits of each approach.

1 Introduction

The problem of evaluating or optimizing the performance of an open reactive system, that is, a system that interacts with an external environment, raises some serious conceptual problems. Given such a system S, each instance d of the environment can potentially induce a different behavior $S(d)$, and the question is how to take all these behaviors into account while evaluating the system performance. Several approaches to this problem are commonly used:
1) *Worst-case*: the system is evaluated according to its worst behavior.
2) *Average-case*: the set of all environment instances is considered as a probability space and this induces a probability over all system behaviors. The system is then evaluated according to the expected value (over all its behaviors) of the performance measure.
3) *Nominal-case*: the system is evaluated according to its performance with respect to one behavior which corresponds to one "typical" instance of the environment.

Each of these approaches has its advantages and shortcomings. The worst-case approach is often used for safety-critical systems where the cost associated with bad behaviors is too high to tolerate, even if they constitute a negligible fraction of the possible behaviors. This is implicitly the approach taken in verification, where the performance measure is discrete and consists of a binary classification into "correct" and "incorrect", and this means that a system is incorrect if one of its behaviors violates the property in question. On the negative side, this approach might lead to an over-pessimistic allocation of resources which can be very inefficient during most of the system lifetime.[1]

The probabilistic approach is more appropriate when the performance measure is more "continuous" in nature, e.g. the waiting time in a queue, and one can tolerate

* This work was partially supported by the European Community Projects IST-2001-35304 AMETIST (Advanced Methods for Timed Systems), `http://ametist.cs.utwente.nl` and IST-2001-33520 CC (Control and Computation), `http://www.dii.unisi.it/~hybrid/cc/`

[1] A good analogy is to live all your life wearing a helmet fearing a meteorite rain, or going to the airport a day before the flight to counteract all conceivable traffic jams.

H. Garavel and J. Hatcliff (Eds.): TACAS 2003, LNCS 2619, pp. 240–253, 2003.

graceful degradation in moments of extreme pressure from the environment. The implicit assumption underlying the nominal approach is somewhat similar to the probabilistic one, namely, the nominal behavior is "close" to most of the behaviors we are likely to see in the system life-time and the performance of other behaviors varies "continuously" with the distance from the nominal one. This approach is widely used in control theory.

From a computational standpoint the nominal approach is the easiest because when d is fixed the system is closed and $S(d)$ can be computed by simple simulation. Moreover, the comparison of two candidate systems S and S' is based on the same d. In the worst-case approach when it is not known a-priori which d induces the worst behavior, one has to "simulate exhaustively" with all instances in order to find that behavior. This is the inherent difficulty of verification compared to testing/simulation. Moreover, when we want to compare S and S' for optimality, it might be that each of them attains its worst performance on a different instance. The probabilistic approach is generally[2] the most difficult because not only do we need to explore all behaviors but also keep track of their probabilities in order to compute the overall evaluation of the system.

In this work we treat the problem of job-shop scheduling under temporal uncertainty. The system to be designed is a scheduler, i.e. a mechanism that controls the allocation of resources to competing tasks. The environment consists of tasks, all known in advance, that need to be executed on certain machines while satisfying some ordering constraints. The only source of uncertainty is the *duration* of the tasks which is known to be bounded within an interval of the form $[l, u]$. Alternatively, the duration of each task can be given as a continuous random variable. Each *instance* (also called *realization*) of the environment consists of selecting a number $d \in [l, u]$ for every task. The behavior induced by the scheduler on this instance is evaluated according to the length of the schedule, i.e. the termination time of the last task executed.

As a running example consider two jobs

$$J_1 = (m_1, 10) \prec (m_3, [2,4]) \prec (m_4, 5) \qquad J_2 = (m_2, [2,8]) \prec (m_3, 7)$$

with the intended meaning that J_1 has to use m_1 for 10 time, then m_3 for a period between 2 and 4 time, then m_4 for 5, etc. In this example the only resource under conflict is m_3 and the order of its usage is the only decision the scheduler needs to take. The uncertainties concern the durations of the first task of J_2 and the second task in J_1. Hence an instance is a pair $d = (d_1, d_2) \in [2,4] \times [2,8]$. It is very important to note that in our example (and in "reactive" systems in general) instances reveal themselves progressively during execution — the value of d_1, for example, is known *only after the termination of* m_2.

Each instance defines a deterministic scheduling problem admitting one or more optimal solutions. Such a solution specifies the start time of every task. Figure 1-(a) depicts optimal schedules for the instances $(8,4)$, $(8,2)$ and $(4,4)$. Of course, such an optimal schedule can only be generated by a *clairvoyant* scheduler who knows the whole instance in advance.

For this type of problems, worst-case optimization reduces to nominal-case because there is one specific instance, namely the one where each task terminates the latest possible, such that the performance of any scheduler on this instance will be at least

[2] At least when the approach is applied naively without using additional mathematical information that can simplify the solution in some special cases.

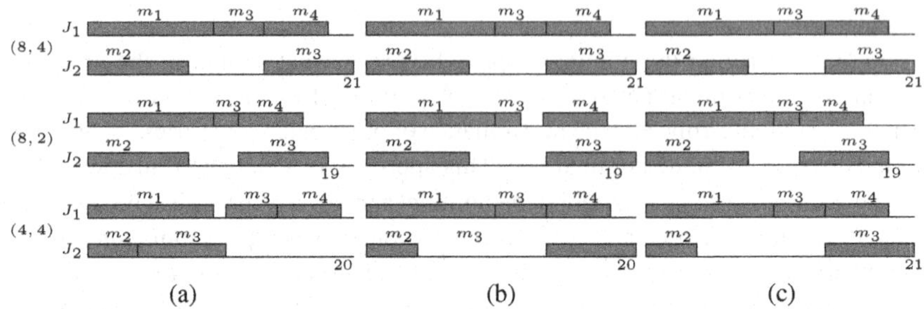

Fig. 1. (a) Optimal schedules for three instances. For the first two the optimum is obtained with $J_1 \prec J_2$ on m_3 while for the third — with $J_2 \prec J_1$; (b) A static schedule based on the worst instance $(8, 4)$. It gives the same length for all instances; (c) The behavior of a hole filling strategy based on instance $(8, 4)$.

as bad as on any other instance. This trivializes the problem of worst-case optimization because we can do the following: find an optimal schedule for the worst instance, extract the start time for each task and stick to the schedule regardless of the actual instance. The behavior of a static scheduler for our example, based on instance $(8, 4)$ is depicted in Figure 1-(b), and one can see that it is rather wasteful for other instances. Intuitively we will prefer a smarter adaptive scheduler that reacts to the evolution of the environment and uses additional information revealed during the execution of the schedule. This is the essential difference between a schedule (a plan, an open-loop controller) and a scheduling *strategy* (a reactive plan, a closed-loop controller). The latter is a mechanism that observes the state of the system (which tasks have terminated, which are executing and for how long) and decides accordingly what to do. When there is no uncertainty, the scheduler knows exactly what will be the state at every time instant, so the strategy can be reduced to a simple assignment of start times to tasks.

One of the simplest ways to be adaptive is the following. First we choose a *nominal instance* d and find a schedule S which is optimal for that instance. Rather than taking S "literally", we extract from it only the qualitative information, namely the order in which conflicting tasks utilize each resource. In our example the optimal schedule for the worst instance $(8, 4)$ is associated with the ordering $J_1 \prec J_2$ on m_3. Then, during execution, we start every task as soon as its predecessors have terminated, provided that the ordering is not violated (a similar strategy was used in [NY00] and probably elsewhere). As Figure 1-(c) shows, such a strategy is better than the static schedule for instances such as $(8, 2)$ where it takes advantage of the earlier termination of the second task of J_1 and "shifts forward" the start times of the two tasks that follow. On the other hand, instance $(4, 4)$ cannot benefit from the early termination of m_2, because shifting m_3 of J_2 forward will violate the $J_1 \prec J_2$ ordering on m_3.

Note that this "hole-filling" strategy is not restricted to the worst-case. One can use any nominal instance and then shift tasks forward or backward as needed while maintaining the order. On the other hand, a static schedule (at least when interpreted as a function from time to actions) can only be based on the worst-case — a schedule based on another nominal instance may assume a resource available at some time point, while in reality it will be occupied.

While the hole filling strategy can be shown to be optimal for all those instances whose optimal schedule has the same ordering as that of the nominal instance, it is not good for instances such as $(4, 4)$, where a more radical form of adaptiveness is required. If we look at the optimal schedules for $(8, 4)$ and $(4, 4)$ (Figure 1-(a)) we see that the decision whether or not to execute the second task of J_2 is done in both cases in the same qualitative state, namely m_1 is executing and m_2 has terminated. The only difference is in the elapsed execution time of m_1 at the decision point. Hence an adaptive scheduler should base its decisions also on such quantitative information which, in the case of timed automata models, is represented by clock values.

Consider the following approach: initially we find an optimal schedule for some nominal instance. During the execution, whenever a task terminates (before or after the time it was assumed to) we re-schedule the "residual" problem, assuming nominal values for the tasks that have not yet terminated. In our example, we first build an optimal schedule for $(8, 4)$. If task m_2 in J_2 has terminated after 4 time we have the residual problem

$$J_1' = (\mathbf{m_1}, \mathbf{6}) \prec (m_3, 4) \prec (m_4, 5) \qquad J_2' = (m_3, 7)$$

where the boldface letters indicate that m_1 must be scheduled immediately (it is already executing and we assume no preemption). For this problem the optimal solution will be to start m_3 of J_2. Likewise if m_2 terminates at 8 we have

$$J_1' = (\mathbf{m_1}, \mathbf{2}) \prec (m_3, 4) \prec (m_4, 5) \qquad J_2' = (m_3, 7)$$

and the optimal schedule consists of waiting for the termination of m_1 and then starting m_3 of J_1. The property of the schedules obtained this way, is that at any moment in the execution they are optimal with respect to the nominal assumption concerning the *future*. A similar idea is used in *model-predictive control* where at each time actions at the current "real" state are re-optimized while assuming some nominal prediction of the future.

This approach involves a lot of *on-line* computation, namely solving a new scheduling problem each time a task terminates. The alternative approach that we propose in this paper is based on expressing the scheduling problem using timed automata and synthesizing a controller *off-line*. In this framework [AMPS98,AM99,AGP+99] a strategy is a function from states and clock valuations to controller actions (in this case starting tasks). After computing such a strategy and representing it properly, the execution of the schedule may proceed while keeping track of the state of the corresponding automaton. Whenever a task terminates, the optimal action is quickly computed from the strategy look-up table and the results are identical to those obtained via on-line re-scheduling. Of course, there is a trade-off between what we gain in reducing on-line computation time and what we pay in terms of the time and space needed to compute and store the strategy, but this is outside the scope of the current paper.

The rest of the paper is organized as follows. In Section 2 we describe the model and characterize the properties of the dynamic schedulers we want to compute. In section 3 we show how to model the problem using timed automata. The algorithm for synthesizing optimal strategies is described in Section 4 along with its implementation using the zone library of Kronos. In Section 5 we formulate and solve the same scheduling problem where tasks durations are known to be distributed probabilistically. Section 6 concludes the paper with a brief review of the experimental results and future directions. Due to time and space limitation, large parts of the paper are written at an informal intuitive level. Readers interested in more precise definitions or in the details of the experimental results may consult the expanded version of this paper.[3]

2 The Model

We will use a formulation which is slightly more general than the standard job-shop problem by allowing a partial-order relation between tasks. We denote by $Int(\mathbb{N})$ the set of intervals with integer endpoints.

Definition 1 (Uncertain Job-Shop Specification).
An uncertain job-shop specification is $\mathcal{J} = (P, M, \prec, \mu, D, U)$ where P is a finite number of tasks, M is a finite set of machines, $\prec$ is a partial-order precedence relation on tasks, $\mu : P \to M$ assigns tasks to machines, $D : P \to Int(\mathbb{N})$ assigns an integer-bounded interval to each task and $U \subseteq P$ is a subset of immediate tasks consisting of some $\prec$-minimal elements.

The set U is typically empty in the initial definition of the problem and we need it to define residual problems. We use D^l and D^u to denote the the lower- and upper-bounds of the intervals, respectively. The set $\Pi(p) = \{p' : p' \prec p\}$ denotes all the predecessors of p, namely the tasks that need to terminate before p starts. In the standard job-shop scheduling problem, $\prec$ decomposes into a disjoint union of chains (linear orders) called jobs.

An *instance* of the environment is any function $d : P \to \mathbb{R}_+$, such that $d(p) \in D(p)$ for every $p \in P$. The set of instances admits a natural partial-order relation: $d \leq d'$ if $d(p) \leq d'(p)$ for every $p \in P$. Any environment instance induces naturally a deterministic instance of $\mathcal{J}$, denoted by $\mathcal{J}(d)$, which is a classical job-shop scheduling problem. The worst-case is defined by the maximal instance $d(p) = D^u(p)$ for every p.

Definition 2 (Schedule). *Let $\mathcal{J} = (P, M, \prec, \mu, D, U)$ be an uncertain job-shop specification and let $\mathcal{J}(d)$ be a deterministic instance. A feasible schedule for $\mathcal{J}(d)$ is a function $s : P \to \mathbb{R}_+$, where $s(p)$ defines the start time of task p, satisfying:*
1) Precedence*: For every p, $s(p) \geq \max_{p' \in \Pi(p)}(s(p') + d(p'))$.*
2) Mutual exclusion*: For every p, p' such that $\mu(p) = \mu(p')$*
$$[s(p), s(p) + d(p)] \cap [s(p'), s(p') + d(p')] = \emptyset.$$
3) Immediacy*: For every $p \in U$, $s(p) = 0$.*

The schedule length is the termination time of the last task, i.e. $\max_{p \in P}(s(p) + d(p))$. An *optimal schedule* for $\mathcal{J}(d)$ is a schedule having a minimal length.

In order to be adaptive we need a *scheduling strategy*, i.e. a rule that may induce a different schedule for every d. However, this definition is not simple because we need to restrict ourselves to *causal* strategies, strategies that can base their decisions only on information available at the time they are made. In our case, the value of $d(p)$ is revealed only when p terminates.

[3] It can be found in `www-verimag.imag.fr/~maler/Papers/uncertain.ps`

Definition 3 (State of Schedule). *The state of a schedule s at time t is $S = (P^f, P^a, c, P^e)$ such that P^f is a downward-closed subset of $(P, \prec)$ indicating the tasks that have terminated (those satisfying $s(p) + d(p) \leq t$), P^a is a set of active tasks currently being executed (those satisfying $s(p) \leq t \leq s(p) + d(p)$), $c : P^a \rightarrow \mathbb{R}_+$ is a function such that $c(p) = t - s(p)$ indicates the time elapsed since the activation of p and P^e is the set of enabled tasks consisting of those whose predecessors are in P^f. The set of all possible states is denoted by $\mathcal{S}$.*

Definition 4 (Scheduling Strategy). *A (state-based) scheduling strategy is a function $\sigma : \mathcal{S} \rightarrow P \cup \{\bot\}$ such that for every $S = (P^f, P^a, c, P^e)$, $\sigma(S) = p \in P^e \cup \{\bot\}$ and for every $p' \in P^a$, $\mu(p) \neq \mu(p')$.*

In other words a strategy decides at each state whether to do nothing and let time pass ($\bot$) or to choose an enabled task, not being in conflict with any active task, and start executing it. An operational definition of the interaction between a strategy and an instance will be given later using timed automata, but intuitively one can see that the evolution of the state of a schedule consists of two types of transitions: uncontrolled transitions where an active task p terminates after $d(p)$ time and moves from P^a to P^f, leading possibly to adding new tasks to P^e, and a decision of the scheduler to start an enabled task. The combination of a strategy and an instance yields a unique schedule $s(d, \sigma)$ and we say that a state is (d, σ)-reachable if it occurs in $s(d, \sigma)$.

Next we formalize the notion of a residual problem, namely a specification of what remains to be done in an intermediate state of the execution.

Definition 5 (Residual Problem). *Let $\mathcal{J} = (P, M, \prec, \mu, D, U)$ and let $S = (P^f, P^a, c, P^e)$ be a state. The residual problem starting from S is $\mathcal{J}_S = (P - P^f, M, \prec', \mu', D', P^a)$ where $\prec'$ and μ' are, respectively, the restrictions of $\prec$ and μ, to $P - P^f$ and D' is constructed from D by letting*

$$D'(p) = \begin{cases} D(p) \dot{-} c(p) & \text{if } p \in P^a \\ D(p) & \text{otherwise} \end{cases}$$

Likewise a residual instance d_S is an instance restricted to $P^a \cup P^e$ defined as

$$d_S(p) = \begin{cases} d(p) \dot{-} c(p) & \text{if } p \in P^a \\ d(p) & \text{otherwise} \end{cases}$$

Let d be an instance. A strategy σ is *d-future-optimal* if for every instance d' and from every (σ, d')-reachable state S, it produces the optimal schedule for $\mathcal{J}_S(d_S)$. If we take d to be the maximal instance, this is exactly the property of the on-line re-scheduling approach described informally in the previous section.

3 Timed Automata for Scheduling Problems

In this section we model the problem using timed automata based on definitions that can be found in [AM01]. We construct for every task p with $D(p) = [l, u]$ a 3-state timed automaton $\mathcal{A}_D$ (Figure 2-(a)) with a waiting state $\overline{p}$, an active state p where the task is executing and a final state $\underline{p}$. The automaton has one clock which is reset to zero upon entering p ("start") and its value determines when a transition to $\underline{p}$ ("end") is taken. This automaton captures all instances: it can stay in p as long as $c \leq u$ and can leave p as soon as $c \geq l$. It represents the possible behaviors of the task *in isolation*, i.e. ignoring precedence and resource constraints. The transition from $\overline{p}$ to p is triggered by a decision of the scheduler, respecting those constraints, while the time of the transition from p to $\underline{p}$ is determined by the instance. When an instance d is given, all the non-determinism is related to scheduler decisions and the behaviors are captured by the automaton $\mathcal{A}_d$ of Figure 2-(b). The automaton $\mathcal{A}_{D,d}$ of Figure 2-(c) will be used later for computing d-future optimal strategies: it can terminate as soon as $c \geq d$ but can stay in p until $c = u$.

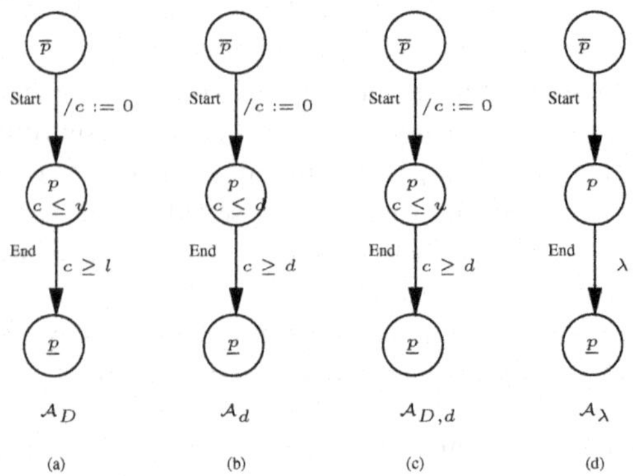

Fig. 2. The generic automaton $\mathcal{A}_D$ for a task p such that $D(p) = [l, u]$. The automaton $\mathcal{A}_d$ for a deterministic instance d. The automaton $\mathcal{A}_{D,d}$ for computing d-future optimal strategies and the automaton $\mathcal{A}_\lambda$ for an exponentially distributed duration. Staying conditions for $\overline{p}$ and $\underline{p}$ are **true** and are omitted from the figure.

The timed automaton for the whole job-shop specification is the composition of the automata for the individual tasks.[4] The composition is rather standard, the only particular feature is the enforcement of precedence and mutual exclusion constraints. This is achieved by forbidding global states in which a task is active before all its predecessors have terminated or in which two or more tasks that use the same resource are active (see [AM01]).

The result of applying this composition to the automata corresponding to the example[5] appears in Figure 3. Since in this example $\prec$ decomposes into two disjoint chains, we can annotate global discrete states with tuples of the form (α^1, α^2) where α^j is either

[4] In the following we will not distinguish between $\mathcal{A}_D$, $\mathcal{A}_d$ and $\mathcal{A}_{D,d}$ — the definitions are the same for all of them.

[5] To make things simpler we change J_1 to be completely deterministic, i.e. $J_1 = (m_1, 10) \prec (m_3, 4) \prec (m_4, 5)$.

$\overline{m}$ or m where $m = \mu(p)$ and p is the maximal enabled or active task in the jth chain (or f when the last task in the chain has terminated). For example $(\underline{p}_1, \overline{p}_2, \overline{p}_3, p_4, \overline{p}_5)$ is written as $(\overline{m}_3, m_2)$ and $(\underline{p}_1, \overline{p}_2, \overline{p}_3, \underline{p}_4, \underline{p}_5)$ as $(\overline{m}_3, f)$. For the same reason we can re-use the same clock for all tasks that share the same chain.[6] Note that the automaton is acyclic.

The relation between runs of the automaton and feasible schedules was elaborated in [AM01,A02] where it was shown that solving the (deterministic) job-shop scheduling problem amounts to finding the shortest run (in terms of elapsed time) from the initial to the final state. A configuration of the timed automaton corresponds to a state of the schedule and the residual problem associated with such a state is represented by the sub-automaton rooted in the corresponding configuration.

The automaton can be viewed as specifying a *game* between the scheduler and the environment. The environment can decide whether or not to take an "end" transition and terminate an active task and the scheduler can decide whether or not to take some enabled "start" transition. A strategy is a function that maps any configuration of the automaton either into one of its transition successors or to the waiting "action". For example, at $(m_1, \overline{m}_3)$ there is a choice between moving to (m_1, m_3) by giving m_3 to J_2 or waiting until J_1 terminates m_1 and letting the environment take the automaton to $(\overline{m}_3, \overline{m}_3)$, from where the conflict concerning m_3 can be resolved in either of the two possible ways.

A strategy is d-future optimal if from every configuration reachable in $\mathcal{A}_{D,d}$ it gives the shortest path to the final state (assuming that future uncontrolled transitions are taken according to d). In the next section we use a simplified form of the definitions and the algorithm of [AM99] to find such strategies.

4 Optimal Strategies for Timed Automata

Let $\mathcal{J}$ be a job-shop specification and let $\mathcal{A}_{D,d} = (Q, C, s, f, I, \Delta)$ be the automaton corresponding to an instance d, that is, "end" transitions are guarded by conditions of the form $c_i \geq d(p_i)$. Let $h : Q \times V \rightarrow \mathbb{R}_+$ be a function with the intended meaning that $h(q, \mathbf{v})$ is the length of the minimal run from $(q, \mathbf{v})$ to f, assuming that all uncontrolled future transitions will be taken according to d. This function admits the following recursive backward definition:

$$h(f, \mathbf{v}) = 0 \quad h(q, \mathbf{v}) = \min\{t + h(q', \mathbf{v}') : (q, \mathbf{v}) \xrightarrow{t} (q, \mathbf{v} + t\mathbf{1}) \xrightarrow{0} (q', \mathbf{v}')\}.$$

In other words, $h(q, \mathbf{v})$ is the minimum over all immediate successors q' of q of the time it takes from $(q, \mathbf{v})$ to satisfy the transition guard to q' plus the time to reach f from the resulting configuration $(q', \mathbf{v}')$. In [AM99] it has been shown that h ranges over a class of "nice" functions closely related to the zones used in the verification of timed automata and that this class is well-founded and, hence, the computation of h terminates even for automata with cycles, a fact that we do not need here as h is computed in one sweep through all (acyclic) paths from the final to the initial state.

[6] More on the relation between jobs and partially-ordered tasks can be found in [AKM03].

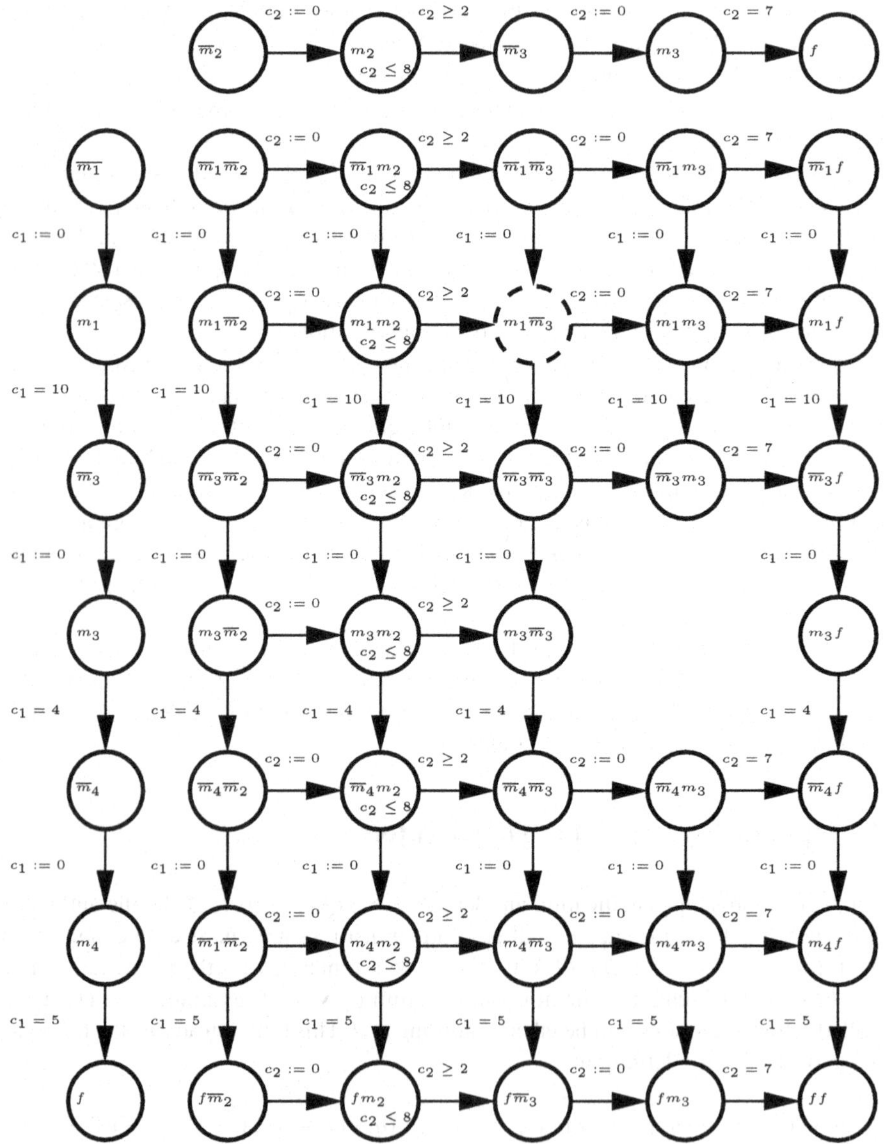

Fig. 3. The global automaton for the job-shop specification. The automata on the left and upper parts of the figure are the partial compositions of the automata for the tasks of J_1 and J_2, respectively. The "hole" at the right stands for the illegal state (m_3, m_3). The dashed state is where a decision of the scheduler is needed.

Let us illustrate the computation of h on our example. We write h in the form $h(\alpha^1, \alpha^2, c_1, c_2)$ and use $\bot$ to denote cases where the value of the corresponding clock is irrelevant (its task is not active). We start with

$$h(f, f, \bot, \bot) = 0 \quad h(m_4, f, c_1, \bot) = 5 \dot{-} c_1 \quad h(f, m_3, \bot, c_2) = 7 \dot{-} c_2$$

because the time to reach (f, f) from (m_4, f) is the time it takes to satisfy the guard $c_1 = 5$, etc. The value of h at (m_4, m_3) depends on the values of both clocks which determine what will terminate before, m_4 or m_3 and whether the shorter path goes via (m_4, f) or (f, m_3).

$$h(m_4, m_3, c_1, c_2) = \min \begin{Bmatrix} 7 \dot{-} c_2 + h(m_4, f, c_1 + 7 \dot{-} c_2, \bot), \\ 5 \dot{-} c_1 + h(f, m_3, \bot, c_2 + 5 \dot{-} x1) \end{Bmatrix}$$

$$= \min\{5 \dot{-} c_1, 7 \dot{-} c_2\} = \begin{cases} 5 \dot{-} c_1 \text{ if } c_2 \dot{-} c_1 \geq 2 \\ 7 \dot{-} c_2 \text{ if } c_2 \dot{-} c_1 \leq 2 \end{cases}$$

Note that the corresponding transitions are both uncontrolled "end" transitions and no decision of the scheduler is required in this state.

This procedure goes higher and higher in the graph, computing h for the whole state-space $Q \times V$. In particular, for state $(m_1, \overline{m}_3)$ where we need to decide whether to start m_3 of J_2 or to wait, we obtain:

$$h(m_1, \overline{m}_3, c_1, \bot) = \min\{16, 21 \dot{-} c_1\} = \begin{cases} 16 & \text{if } c_1 \leq 5 \\ 21 \dot{-} c_1 & \text{if } c_1 \geq 5 \end{cases}$$

The extraction of a strategy from h is straightforward: if the optimum of h at $(q, \mathbf{v})$ is obtained via a controlled transition to q' we let $\sigma(q, \mathbf{v}) = q'$ otherwise, when it is obtained via an uncontrolled transition we let $\sigma(q, \mathbf{v}) = \bot$. At $(m_1, \overline{m}_3)$ the optimal result is obtained by giving m_3 immediately to J_2 and moving to (m_1, m_3) when $c_1 \leq 5$ or by waiting to the termination of m_1, reaching $(\overline{m}_3, \overline{m}_3)$ and then moving to $(m_3, \overline{m}_3)$ if $c_1 \geq 5$. Note that if we assume that J_1 and J_2 started their first tasks simultaneously, the value of c_1 upon entering $(m_1, \overline{m}_3)$ is exactly the duration of m_2 in the instance.

The results of [AM01] concerning "non-lazy" schedules imply that there exist an optimal strategy having the additional property that if $\sigma(q, \mathbf{v}) = \bot$ then $\sigma(q, \mathbf{v}') = \bot$ for every $\mathbf{v}' \geq \mathbf{v}$. In other words, if an enabled controlled transition gives the optimum it can be taken as soon as possible. This fact will be used later in the implementation of the strategy.

Existing algorithms for timed automata work on sets, not on functions, and in order to apply them to the computation of h we do the following.[7] Let $\mathcal{A}'$ be an auxiliary automaton obtained from $\mathcal{A}$ by adding a clock T which is never reset to zero. Clearly, if $(q, (\mathbf{v}, T))$ is reachable in $\mathcal{A}'$ from the initial state $(s, (\mathbf{0}, 0))$ then $(q, \mathbf{v})$ is reachable in $\mathcal{A}$ in time T. Let Θ be a positive integer larger then the longest path in the automaton. Starting from $(f, (\bot, \ldots, \bot, \Theta))$ and doing backward reachability we can construct a relational representation of h. More precisely, if $(q, (\mathbf{v}, T))$ is backward reachable from $(f, (\bot, \ldots, \bot, \Theta)$in $\mathcal{A}'$ then f is forward reachable in $\mathcal{A}$ from $(q, \mathbf{v})$ within $\Theta - T$ time.

We recall some commonly-used definitions in the verification of timed automata [HNSY94]. A *zone* is a subset of V consisting of points satisfying a conjunction of inequalities of the form $c_i - c_j \geq k$ or $c_i \geq k$. A *symbolic state* is a pair (q, Z) where q is a discrete state and Z is a zone. It denotes the set of configurations $\{(q, \mathbf{v}) : \mathbf{v} \in Z\}$.

[7] A similar construction was proposed in [NTY00] to implement shortest path algorithm for cyclic timed automata using forward reachability.

Zones and symbolic states are closed under various operations including the following:

1) The *time predecessors* of (q, Z) is the set of configurations from which (q, Z) can be reached by letting time progress:

$$Pre^t(q, Z) = \{(q, \mathbf{v}) : \mathbf{v} + r\mathbf{1} \in Z, r \geq 0\}.$$

2) The δ*-transition predecessor* of (q, Z) is the set of configurations from which (q, Z) is reachable by taking the transition $\delta = (q', \phi, \rho, q) \in \Delta$:

$$Pre^\delta(q, Z) = \{(q', \mathbf{v}') : \mathbf{v}' \in \text{Reset}_\rho^{-1}(Z) \cap \phi\}.$$

3) The *predecessors* of (q, Z) is the set of all configuration from which (q, Z) is reachable by any transition δ followed by passage of time:

$$Pre(q, Z) = \bigcup_{\delta \in \Delta} Pre^t(Pre^\delta(q, Z)).$$

The result can be represented as a set of symbolic states.

Algorithm 1 is based on the standard backward reachability algorithm for timed automata. It starts with the final state of $\mathcal{A}'$ in a waiting list and outputs the set R of all backward-reachable symbolic states. In order to be able to extract strategies we store tuples of the form (q, Z, q') such that Z is a zone of $\mathcal{A}'$ and q' is the successor of q from which (q, Z) was reached backwards.

Algorithm 1 (Backward Reachability for Timed Automata)
Waiting:$=\{(f, (\bot, \ldots, \bot, \Theta))\}, \emptyset)\}$;
Explored:$=\emptyset$;
while *Waiting* $\neq \emptyset$ **do**
  Pick $(q, Z, q'') \in$ *Waiting;*
  For every $(q', Z') \in Pre(q, Z)$*;*
    Insert (q', Z', q) *into Waiting;*
  Move (q, Z, q'') *from Waiting to Explored*
end
R:=Explored;

The set R gives sufficient information for implementing the strategy. Whenever a transition to $(q, \mathbf{v})$ is done during the execution we look at all the symbolic states with discrete state q and find

$$h(q, \mathbf{v}) = \min\{\Theta - T : (\mathbf{v}, T) \in Z \wedge (q, Z, q') \in R\}.$$

If q' is a successor via a controlled transition, we move to q', otherwise we wait until a task terminates and an uncontrolled transition is taken. Non-laziness guarantees that we need not revise a decision to wait until the next transition. This concludes our major contribution, an algorithm for computing d-future optimal strategies for the problem of job-shop scheduling under uncertainty.

Theorem 1 (Computing d-future Optimal Strategies). *The problem of finding d-future optimal strategies for job-shop scheduling problem under uncertainty is solvable using timed automata reachability algorithms.*

5 Probabilistic Uncertainty

In this section we sketch the formulation and the solution of the same problem where uncertainty in task durations is considered to be probabilistically distributed. We use exponential distribution and associate with each task a parameter λ such that the time t that the task spends in its active state p satisfies:

$$P(t \geq T) = e^{-\lambda T}.$$

The automaton for a task, depicted in Figure 2-(d), is a mixture of a non-deterministic automaton and a continuous time Markov chain. The decision when to make the transition from $\overline{p}$ to p is to be made by the scheduler and is *not* probabilistically distributed. Hence, before the construction of the scheduler we cannot assign probabilities to the runs of the automaton, which are of the form $\overline{p} \xrightarrow{r} \overline{p} \xrightarrow{0} p \xrightarrow{t} p \xrightarrow{0} \underline{p} \xrightarrow{\infty}$, where r is the time chosen by the scheduler to wait before starting p.

A probabilistic version of the example used in the previous section looks like this:

$$J_1 = (m_1, \lambda_1) \prec (m_3, \lambda_2) \prec (m_4, \lambda_3) \qquad J_2 = (m_2, \lambda_4) \prec (m_3, \lambda_5)$$

and it induces a probability distribution on the space of instances, $\mathbb{R}_+^5$. A scheduling strategy is, as before, a mechanism for deciding at every instance whether to start an enabled task or to wait. A strategy together with an instance determines the length of the obtained schedule and our goal is to find a strategy that optimizes the *expected value* (over all instances) of this length.

The automata for the example are similar to those in Figure 3 with λ replacing $[l, u]$. The states of the product automaton admit combinations of controlled and probabilistic transitions. A state like $(\overline{m}_3, \overline{m}_3)$ has two controlled transitions that can be taken immediately. A scheduling strategy will determine which of them should be taken. A state like (m_1, m_2) has two outgoing probabilistic transitions and the instance determines which of them will be taken. However it is possible to compute the expected staying time in the state and the probability of each transition to win the "race". In a state having both types of transitions, such as $(\overline{m}_3, m_2)$, the outcome depends on the strategy. If it decides to wait, the controlled transitions are erased and the evolution depends on the probabilistic race. Otherwise if the strategy chooses a start transition, the rest of the transitions disappear. The important thing is that after determining the strategy the system becomes an ordinary continuous time Markov process with a well-defined expected length for a path from beginning to termination, and our goal is to find a strategy that optimizes this expected length.

The exponential distribution is memoryless, which means that the probability of a transition to be taken does not change with the passage of time.[8] Hence an optimal strategy, like the hole filling strategy of the previous section, depends only on the discrete state and does not need to record clock values.

The optimal strategy, like the future-d-optimal strategies of the previous section, is found by a variant of dynamic programming value iteration. Let $h : Q \to \mathbb{R}_+$ be a function such that $h(q)$ is the best achievable expected value of the time from q to the final state f. By definition, $h(f) = 0$ and its value for the other states is computed backwards as follows. Let q be a state having k outgoing "end" transitions

[8] This property is a source for both the analytic simplicity of this distribution as well as its modest relevance to certain real-world situations.

with parameters $\lambda_1, \ldots, \lambda_k$, leading to states $q_1, \ldots, q_k$, respectively, and l outgoing "start" transitions leading to states $q'_1, \ldots, q'_l$, respectively. A strategy that takes one of the start transitions to a state q'_j spends no time at q and hence the expected time to reach f will be like that of q'_j. On the other hand a strategy that waits might make the environment take any of the "end" transition. Hence

$$h(q) = \min\{h^{\perp}(q), h(q'_1), \ldots h(q'_l)\}$$

where $h^{\perp}(q)$ is the expected value of h over all possible outcomes of waiting, computed as:

$$h^{\perp}(q) = d + \sum_{j=1}^{k} \gamma_j \cdot h(q_j)$$

where d is the expected duration (over all instances) of staying in q and γ_j is the probability that the transition to q_j will be the one taken. These are:

$$d = \frac{1}{\sum_{a=1}^{k} \lambda_a} \text{ and } \gamma_j = \frac{\lambda_j}{\sum_{a=1}^{k} \lambda_a}.$$

The strategy chooses to wait or to take one of the start transitions according to where the minimum is obtained. To the best of our knowledge, this as an unexplored class of continuous-time Markov decision processes for which we can show:

Theorem 2 (Optimal Strategies for Probabilistic Uncertainty). *The problem of finding an optimal strategy for a job-shop specification with exponentially distributed durations is solvable.*

6 Discussion

We have implemented Algorithm 1 using the zone library of Kronos[BDM+98], as well as the hole-filling strategy and the algorithm for the exponential distribution. In our first set of experiments, a d-future optimal strategy based on the worst-case produced schedules that, on the average, are only 2.39% longer than optimal schedules produced by a clairvoyant scheduler. For comparison, the static worst-case strategy deviates from the optimum by an average of 16.18%. The hole-filling strategy based on worst-case prediction achieves good performance (3.73% longer than the optimum). On the other hand, if these strategies are based on nominal instances other than the worst-case, the results are poor, sometimes even worse than a static schedule. So one may conclude that *adaptive pessimism* is a reasonable strategy for this class of problems.

The question of scaling-up the results to larger problems remains open. Currently we can compute d-future optimal strategies for problems with up to 4 jobs, each with 6 tasks. The computation of the strategy for exponential distribution is faster (no clocks and zones) but it is subject to the same type of state explosion. For the deterministic case, we have shown in [AM01] that rather large problems can be solved using forward reachability algorithms that do not use zones (only points in the clock space) and that can use intelligent search strategies to prune the search space (see also [BFH+01]). This is not the case for uncertain problems where backward computations on zones seem unavoidable: Under uncertainty the environment can lead the automaton to a large portion of the discrete state-space and to uncountably-many clock valuations, on which the strategy should be defined. The sub-optimal hole-filling strategy produces good results with much more modest computation by solving a deterministic problem. More details concerning the experimental results and the computational difficulty appear in the expanded version of the paper along with some suggestions for future work.

Acknowledgment. We thank Marius Bozga for his help in the implementation. Comments by Stavros Tripakis, Ed Brinksma and Albert Benveniste improved the presentation.

References

[A02] Y. Abdedadïm, *Scheduling with Timed Automata*, PhD Thesis, INPG, 2002.

[AKM03] Y. Abdedadïm, A. Kerbaa and O. Maler Task Graph Scheduling using Timed Automata, *Proc. FMPPTA'03*, to appear, 2003.

[AM01] Y. Abdedadïm and O. Maler, Job-Shop Schedusling using Timed Automata in *Proc. CAV'01*, 478–492, LNCS 2102, Springer 2001.

[AGP+99] K. Altisen, G. Goessler, A. Pnueli, J. Sifakis, S. Tripakis and S. Yovine, A Framework for Scheduler Synthesis, *Proc. RTSS'99*, 154–163, IEEE, 1999.

[AM99] E. Asarin and O. Maler, As Soon as Possible: Time Optimal Control for Timed Automata, in *Proc. HSCC'99* 19–30, LNCS 1569, Springer, 1999.

[AMPS98] E. Asarin, O. Maler, A. Pnueli and J. Sifakis, Controller Synthesis for Timed Automata, *Proc. IFAC Symposium on System Structure and Control*, 469–474, 1998.

[BFH+01] G. Behrmann, A. Fehnker T.S. Hune, K.G. Larsen, P. Pettersson and J. Romijn, Efficient Guiding Towards Cost-Optimality in UPPAAL, in *Proc. TACAS 2001*, 174–188, LNCS 2031, Springer, 2001.

[BDM+98] M. Bozga, C. Daws, O. Maler, A. Olivero, S. Tripakis, and S. Yovine, Kronos: a Model-Checking Tool for Real-Time Systems, *Proc. CAV'98*, LNCS 1427, Springer, 1998.

[HNSY94] T. Henzinger, X. Nicollin, J. Sifakis, and S. Yovine, Symbolic Model-checking for Real-time Systems, *Information and Computation* 111, 193–244, 1994.

[NTY00] P. Niebert, S. Tripakis S. Yovine, Minimum-Time Reachability for Timed Automata, *IEEE Mediteranean Control Conference*, 2000.

[NY00] P. Niebert and S. Yovine, Computing Optimal Operation Schemes for Chemical Plants in Multi-batch Mode, *Proc. HSCC'00*, 338–351, LNCS 1790, Springer, 2000.

Static Guard Analysis in Timed Automata Verification

Gerd Behrmann[1], Patricia Bouyer[2*], Emmanuel Fleury[1], and Kim G. Larsen[1]

[1] BRICS***, Aalborg University Denmark
Fredrik Bajers Vej 7, 9220 Aalborg Ø – Denmark
{behrmann,fleury,kgl}@cs.auc.dk
[2] LSV, CNRS UMR 8643, ENS de Cachan
61, av. du Prés. Wilson, 94235 Cachan Cedex – France
bouyer@lsv.ens-cachan.fr

Abstract. By definition Timed Automata have an infinite state-space, thus for verification purposes, an exact finite abstraction is required. We propose a *location-based finite zone abstraction*, which computes an abstraction based on the *relevant* guards for a particular state of the model (as opposed to *all* guards). We show that the location-based zone abstraction is sound and complete with respect to location reachability; that it generalises *active-clock reduction*, in the sense that an inactive clock has no relevant guards at all; that it *enlarges* the class of timed automata, that can be verified. We generalise the new abstraction to the case of *networks* of timed automata, and experimentally demonstrate a potentially exponential speedup compared to the usual abstraction.

1 Introduction

Since their introduction by Alur and Dill [3], timed automata have become one of the most well-studied and well-established models for real-time systems. By their definition timed automata models describe infinite state-spaces. Thus, to enable algorithmic verification, exact finite abstractions are required. Here, the original region-graph construction of Alur and Dill provides a "universal" such abstraction. However, whereas indispensable as a key to decidability for several timed automata related decision problems, the enormous size of the region-graph construction makes it highly impractical for tool-implementation. In fact, most real-time verification tools (*e.g.* UPPAAL [20,6], KRONOS [12] and CMC [19]) apply abstractions based on so-called zones and in a highly model-dependent manner in order to be as coarse (and hence small and efficient) as possible.

To insure finiteness, it is essential for the (region- as well as zone-based) abstractions to take into account the maximum constants to which clocks are compared. In particular, the abstractions identify states which are identical except for the values of clocks exceeding the (relevant) maximum constants. Obviously, the smaller we choose

* Supported by a BRICS grant. The work has been mainly carried out while the author had a post-doctoral position at Aalborg University.

*** Basic Research in Computer Science (www.brics.dk), funded by the Danish National Research Foundation.

H. Garavel and J. Hatcliff (Eds.): TACAS 2003, LNCS 2619, pp. 254–270, 2003.

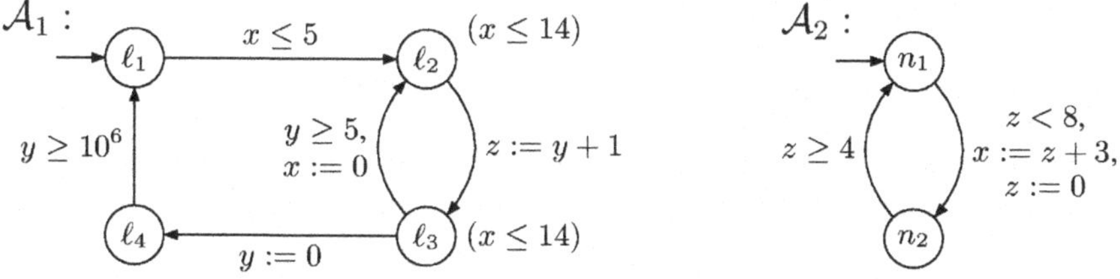

Fig. 1. *Network of timed automata* $\mathcal{A}_1 \parallel \mathcal{A}_2$.

these maximum constants, the coarse the abstraction will be. So far, the maximum constants have been determined by a global examination of *all* guards in the model. In this paper we propose a coarser *location-based* abstraction, using location-dependent (and smaller) maximum constants based on the *relevant* guards for a particular state of the timed automaton.

Consider the timed automata network in Fig. 1. Here, global examination identifies 10^6 as a maximum constant for y. However, the guard $y \geq 10^6$ is clearly irrelevant in ℓ_2 and ℓ_3 as any path from these locations to the guard must pass through a reset of y. Thus, it should be possible to choose valid maximum constants, $\max_2$ and $\max_3$, for y in ℓ_2 and ℓ_3 substantially smaller than 10^6. Obviously, $\max_2, \max_3 \geq 5$, due to the relevant guard $y \geq 5$. However, 5 may not necessarily be a valid maximum constant for y in ℓ_2 and ℓ_3: the combination of the update $z := y + 1$ with the guard $z < 8$ in $\mathcal{A}_2$ suggests the relevance of the derived guard $y < 8 - 1$. Thus $\max_2, \max_3 \geq 7$. In fact realizing that also the update $x := z + 3$ and the invariant $x \leq 14$ are relevant in ℓ_2 and ℓ_3 yields $\max_2, \max_3 = 10$ as smallest valid maximal constants for y in ℓ_2 and ℓ_3.

In this paper, we will offer efficient methods for identification of location-dependent maximal constants based on a static analysis for determining and combining *relevant* guards and updates for a given location. In particular, we prove that the maximal constants determined are valid in the sense that the resulting relevant guard abstraction is exact with respect to location reachability. Furthermore, to keep the static analysis as light as possible, we offer a computational method allowing valid location-dependent maximal constants of a network to be derived from the component automata. We further experimentally demonstrate that the use of location-dependent maximal constants in abstractions provides a potential exponential speedup[1].

The closest related work to our static analysis method for relevant guards and updates is the *active-clock reduction* technique for timed automata presented in [15]. In fact, active-clock reduction is a special case of our relevant guard abstraction, in the sense that an inactive clock has no relevant guards at all. Also related is the work in [13] on using precomputed influence information.

[1] *E.g.* an exponential speedup is obtained for the reachability of the network in Fig. 1.

2 The Model and Its Semantics

The model used in this paper is that of networks of timed automata. Let X be a set of non-negative real-valued variables called *clocks*, and $\mathcal{A}\mathrm{ct}$ a set of actions and co-actions (denoted $a!$ and $a?$) and the non-synchronising action (denoted τ). The set of *guards*, denoted by $\mathcal{G}(X)$, and the set of updates, denoted by $\mathcal{U}(X)$, are generated by the grammars

$$g ::= x \bowtie c \mid g_1 \wedge g_2 \qquad \mathsf{up} ::= x := c \mid x := y + c \mid \mathsf{up}_1 \wedge \mathsf{up}_2 \ ,$$

where $x, y \in X$, $c \in \mathbb{N}$, $\bowtie \in \{<, \leq, =, \geq, >\}$, $\mathsf{base}(\mathsf{up}_1) \cap \mathsf{base}(\mathsf{up}_2) = \emptyset$, and base is a function such that $\mathsf{base}(x := c) = \mathsf{base}(x := y + c) = \{x\}$ and $\mathsf{base}(\mathsf{up}_1 \wedge \mathsf{up}_2) = \mathsf{base}(\mathsf{up}_1) \cup \mathsf{base}(\mathsf{up}_2)$. For the static analysis to follow we also define the function used such that $\mathsf{used}(x \bowtie c) = \{x\}$, $\mathsf{used}(x := y + c) = \{y\}$ and $\mathsf{used}(\varphi_1 \wedge \varphi_2) = \mathsf{used}(\varphi_1) \cup \mathsf{used}(\varphi_2)$, where φ_i is either a guard or an update.

Definition 1. *A timed automaton over $(\mathcal{A}\mathrm{ct}, X)$ is a tuple (L, ℓ^0, I, E), where L is a set of locations, $\ell^0 \in L$ is an initial location, $I : L \to \mathcal{G}(X)$ assigns invariants to locations, and E is a set of edges such that $E \subseteq L \times \mathcal{G}(X) \times \mathcal{A}\mathrm{ct} \times \mathcal{U}(X) \times L$.* A network of timed automata $\mathcal{A}_1 \parallel \cdots \parallel \mathcal{A}_n$ *over $(\mathcal{A}\mathrm{ct}, X)$ is defined as the parallel composition of n timed automata over $(\mathcal{A}\mathrm{ct}, X)$. Let $\mathcal{A}_i = (L_i, \ell_i^0, I_i, E_i)$ for $1 \leq i \leq n$. We write $\ell \xrightarrow{g,a,u}_i \ell'$ iff $(\ell, g, a, u, \ell') \in E_i$ and $I(\boldsymbol{\ell}) = \bigwedge_{1 \leq i \leq n} I_i(\ell_i)$, where $\boldsymbol{\ell}$ is our standard notation for a vector $\boldsymbol{\ell} = (\ell_1, \ldots, \ell_n)$.*

The semantics of a network of timed automata is defined in terms of a transition system over states of the network. Intuitively, there are three kinds of transitions: delay transitions, internal transitions, and synchronisations. Before formally stating the semantics, we introduce a few definitions. A clock valuation $\sigma \in \mathbb{R}_{\geq 0}^X$ is a function which assigns values to clocks. If $d \in \mathbb{R}_{>0}$ is a delay, then $\sigma + d$ denotes the clock valuation such that for each clock x, $(\sigma + d)(x) = \sigma(x) + d$. If $\mathsf{up} \in \mathcal{U}(X)$ is an update, then $\mathsf{up}(\sigma)$ denotes the valuation which maps x to c if $x := c$ is in up, maps x to $\sigma(y) + c$ if $x := y + c$ is in up, and agrees with σ in all other cases. We write $\sigma \models g$ if and only if the clock valuation σ satisfies the guard g (defined in the natural way).

Definition 2. *The semantics of a network of timed automata $\mathcal{A}_1 \parallel \cdots \parallel \mathcal{A}_n$ is defined by a transition system $(S, s_0, \longrightarrow)$, where $S = (L_1 \times \cdots \times L_n) \times \mathbb{R}_{\geq 0}^X$ is the set of states, $s_0 = (\boldsymbol{\ell}^0, \sigma^0)$ is the initial state, $\forall x \in X$: $\sigma^0(x) = 0$, and $\longrightarrow \subseteq S \times S$ is the set of transitions defined by:*

$$\frac{\forall 0 \leq d' \leq d : \sigma + d' \models I(\boldsymbol{\ell})}{(\boldsymbol{\ell}, \sigma) \xrightarrow{d} (\boldsymbol{\ell}, \sigma + d)} \quad \text{if } d \in \mathbb{R}_{>0}$$

$$\frac{\ell_i \xrightarrow{g,\tau,\mathsf{up}}_i \ell_i' \qquad \sigma \models g \qquad \mathsf{up}(\sigma) \models I(\boldsymbol{\ell}[\ell_i'/\ell_i])}{(\boldsymbol{\ell}, \sigma) \xrightarrow{\tau} (\boldsymbol{\ell}[\ell_i'/\ell_i], \mathsf{up}(\sigma))}$$

$$\frac{\begin{array}{l}\ell_i \xrightarrow{g_i,a!,\mathsf{up}_i}_i \ell_i' \\ \ell_j \xrightarrow{g_j,a?,\mathsf{up}_j}_j \ell_j'\end{array} \qquad \sigma \models g_i \wedge g_j \qquad \sigma' \models I(\boldsymbol{\ell}')}{(\boldsymbol{\ell}, \sigma) \xrightarrow{\tau} (\boldsymbol{\ell}', \sigma')} \quad \begin{array}{l}\text{if } i \neq j, \\ \boldsymbol{\ell}' = \boldsymbol{\ell}[\ell_i'/\ell_i, \ell_j'/\ell_j], \\ \sigma' = (\mathsf{up}_i \wedge \mathsf{up}_j)(\sigma)\end{array}$$

In contrast to UPPAAL and KRONOS, we allow updates of the form $x := y + c$. In the next section, we restrict ourselves to individual timed automata (*i.e.* consider only τ actions). Extensions to networks of timed automata will be considered in section 6.

3 Forward Analysis

A standard forward breadth-first or depth-first state-space exploration based directly on the transition relation '$\longrightarrow$' defined in section 2 is unlikely to terminate, since the state space is uncountably infinite. The classical approach used to prove decidability of the reachability problem for timed automata involves the construction of a region graph [3]. Intuitively, regions are sets of clock valuations indistinguishable by arbitrary guards and behaving identical under delay and update operations. In practice, tools like UPPAAL and KRONOS use zones rather than regions to build a coarser representation of the state-space. Zones are sets of clock valuations definable by conjunctions of constraints of the forms $x \bowtie c$ and $x - y \bowtie c$, where x and y are clocks and c is an integer. Using zones makes the state-space countable, but not finite. In order to make it finite, an abstraction of the state-space is needed. In the following, we will use Z to refer to zones and W to arbitrary sets of valuations.

In this section we will recall the symbolic semantics of timed automata, the DBM representation of zones, and the DBM based abstraction used in order to obtain a finite state-space.

Symbolic Semantics. For universality, the definition of the symbolic semantics uses arbitrary sets of clock valuations, rather than zones.

Definition 3. *The symbolic semantics of a timed automaton $\mathcal{A} = (L, \ell^0, I, E)$ is based on the abstract transition system $(S, s_0, \Longrightarrow)$, where $S = L \times \mathcal{P}(\mathbb{R}^X_{\geq 0})^2$, $s_0 = (\ell^0, \{\sigma^0\})$, and '$\Longrightarrow$' is defined by the following two rules:*

DELAY: $(\ell, W) \Longrightarrow (\ell, W')$,
where $W' = \{\sigma + d \mid \sigma \in W \land d \geq 0 \land \forall 0 \leq d' \leq d : \sigma + d' \models I(\ell)\}$

ACTION: $(\ell, W) \Longrightarrow (\ell', W')$ *if there exists a transition* $\ell \xrightarrow{g,a,\mathsf{up}} \ell'$ *in* $\mathcal{A}$,
such that $W' = \{\mathsf{up}(\sigma) \mid \sigma \in W \land \sigma \models g \land \mathsf{up}(\sigma) \models I(\ell')\}$.

Example 1. The timed automaton in the following figure illustrates that although the symbolic semantics results in a countable state-space, it is not necessarily finite. Whenever one time unit has passed, the loop will be taken and y will be reset to zero. However x keeps growing thus resulting in an infinite state-space.

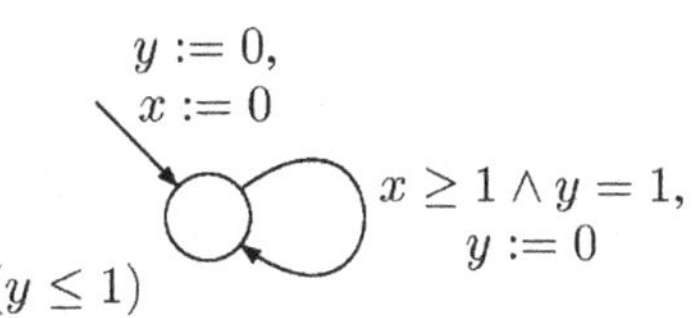

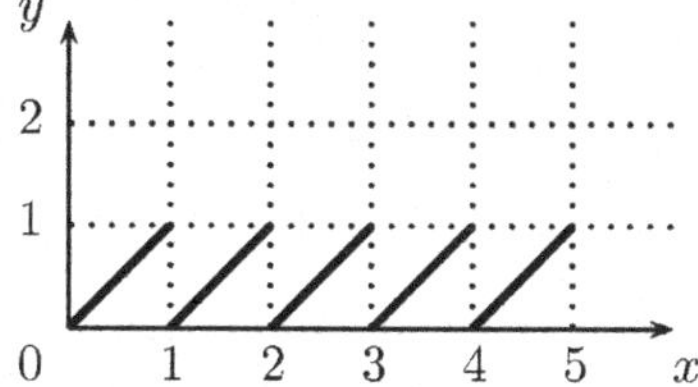

[2] $\mathcal{P}(A)$ denotes the power set of A.

To obtain a finite graph, we suggest to apply some abstraction $\mathfrak{a} : \mathcal{P}(\mathbb{R}^X_{\geq 0}) \hookrightarrow \mathcal{P}(\mathbb{R}^X_{\geq 0})$, such that $W \subseteq \mathfrak{a}(W)$. The abstract transition system '$\Longrightarrow_\mathfrak{a}$' will then be given by the following induction rules:

$$\frac{(\ell, W) \Longrightarrow (\ell', W')}{(\ell, W) \Longrightarrow_\mathfrak{a} (\ell', \mathfrak{a}(W'))} \quad \text{if } W = \mathfrak{a}(W)$$

A simple way to assure that the reachability graph induced by '$\Longrightarrow_\mathfrak{a}$' is finite is to establish that there is only finitely many abstractions of sets of valuations, that is, the set $\{\mathfrak{a}(W) \mid \mathfrak{a} \text{ defined on } W\}$ is finite. In this case $\mathfrak{a}$ is said to be a *finite abstraction*. Moreover, $\Longrightarrow_\mathfrak{a}$ is said to be *sound* and *complete* whenever:

SOUND: $(\ell^0, \{\sigma^0\}) \Longrightarrow_\mathfrak{a}^* (\ell, W)$ implies $\exists \sigma \in W : (\ell^0, \sigma^0) \longrightarrow^* (\ell, \sigma)$

COMPLETE: $(\ell^0, \sigma^0) \longrightarrow^* (\ell, \sigma)$ implies $\exists W : \sigma \in W \wedge (\ell^0, \{\sigma^0\}) \Longrightarrow_\mathfrak{a}^* (\ell, W)$

Completeness follows trivially from the definition of abstraction. Of course, if $\mathfrak{a}$ and $\mathfrak{b}$ are two abstractions such that for any set of valuations W, $\mathfrak{a}(W) \subseteq \mathfrak{b}(W)$, we prefer to use abstraction $\mathfrak{b}$, because the graph induced by it, is *a priori* smaller than the one induced by $\mathfrak{a}$. Our aim is thus to propose an abstraction which is finite and which induces a sound abstract transition system. We also require that this abstraction is *effective*, in the sense that it can be efficiently computed.

Zones. A First step in finding an effective abstraction is realizing that W will always be a zone for any $(\ell^0, \{\sigma^0\}) \Longrightarrow^* (\ell, W)$. Zones can be represented using *Difference Bound Matrices* (DBM). We will briefly recall the definition of DBMs, but refer to [16, 14,5,8] for more details.

A DBM is a square matrix $M = \langle m_{i,j}, \prec_{i,j} \rangle_{0 \leq i,j \leq n}$ such that $m_{i,j} \in \mathbb{Z}$ and $\prec_{i,j} \in \{<, \leq\}$ or $m_{i,j} = \infty$ and $\prec_{i,j} = <$. M represents the zone $[\![M]\!]$ which is defined by $[\![M]\!] = \{\sigma \mid \forall 0 \leq i,j \leq n : \sigma(x_i) - \sigma(x_j) \prec_{i,j} m_{i,j}\}$, where $\{x_i \mid 1 \leq i \leq n\}$ is the set of clocks, and x_0 is a clock which is always 0, (*i.e.* $\forall \sigma$: $\sigma(x_0) = 0$). DBMs are not a canonical representation of zones, but a normal form can be computed by considering the DBM as an adjacency matrix of a weighted directed graph and computing all shortest paths. In particular, if $M = \langle m_{i,j}, \prec_{i,j} \rangle_{0 \leq i,j \leq n}$ is a DBM in normal form, then it satisfies the *triangular inequality*, that is, for every $0 \leq i,j,k \leq n$, we have that $(m_{i,j}, \prec_{i,j}) \leq (m_{i,k}, \prec_{i,k}) + (m_{k,j}, \prec_{k,j})$ where comparisons and additions are defined in a natural way (see [8]). All operations needed to compute '$\Longrightarrow$' can be implemented by manipulating the DBM.

The 'Maximum Constants' Abstraction. The abstraction currently in use in model-checkers, is based on the idea that the automaton is only sensitive to changes on a clock if its value is below a certain constant. That is, for each clock there is a maximum constant and once the value of a clock has passed this constant, its exact value is no longer relevant – only the fact that it is larger than the maximum constant matters. Transforming a DBM to reflect this idea is often referred to as *extrapolation* or *normalisation* [15].

Definition 4 (Extrapolation). *Given a set of clocks $\{x_i \mid 1 \leq i \leq n\}$, a maximum constant k_i for each clock x_i, and a DBM $M = \langle m_{i,j}, \prec_{i,j} \rangle_{0 \leq i,j \leq n}$, the* extrapolation *of M is $M' = \langle m'_{i,j}, \prec'_{i,j} \rangle_{0 \leq i,j \leq n}$ such that:*

$$(m'_{i,j}, \prec'_{i,j}) = \begin{cases} (\infty, <) & \textit{if } m_{i,j} > k_i, \\ (-k_j, <) & \textit{if } m_{i,j} < -k_j, \\ (m_{i,j}, \prec_{i,j}) & \textit{otherwise.} \end{cases}$$

Let $\Lambda_{\boldsymbol{k}}$ denote the extrapolation operator corresponding to the tuple of constants $\boldsymbol{k} = (k_1, \ldots, k_n)$. In an abuse of notation, we use $\Lambda_{\boldsymbol{k}}$ as an abstraction function.

The actual choice of constants $\boldsymbol{k}$ is based on the guards, invariants, and updates of the system. For the simple subset of timed automata without guards on clock differences and with clock updates limited to reset to a constant, the constant k_i for clock x_i is simply the maximum constant in any guard or invariant that x_i is ever compared to. In the general case, finding $\boldsymbol{k}$ requires solving a system of simple linear Diophantine inequalities [10,8], having one variable, p_x, for each clock x. The inequalities are on the form $p_x \leq p_y + c$ whenever there is an update $x := y + c$ in the automaton, or $p_x \geq d$ whenever there is a guard $x \bowtie d$ in the automaton. The system of inequalities has the nice property that whenever it has a solution $\boldsymbol{k}$, then it is safe to use $\Lambda_{\boldsymbol{k}}$ as an abstraction. The graph induced by the transition relation '$\Longrightarrow_{\Lambda_{\boldsymbol{k}}}$' is obviously finite and has an effective implementation. Its soundness has been proved in [9].

4 Location-Dependent Abstractions

The symbolic transition relation '$\Longrightarrow_{\Lambda_{\boldsymbol{k}}}$' defined in the previous section is based on a location-independent abstraction of zones. That is, for a given symbolic state (ℓ, Z) the abstraction applied to Z is independent of ℓ, but merely uses global information of the constants to which clocks are compared throughout the automaton. However, for a given location not all of these comparisons may be of relevance: if all paths in the automaton from a location ℓ to a guard $x \bowtie c$ passes through an update of x, then intuitively the guard is not relevant or active in ℓ.

To illustrate this, consider the timed automaton in Fig. 2. Here the guard $y \geq 10^6$ is irrelevant in ℓ_2 as any path from ℓ_2 to the guard necessarily must pass through the reset of y. In contrast the guard $y \geq 5$ is relevant in ℓ_2. It is easy to see that for any pair $(\ell_2, v_x, v_y), (\ell_2, v_x, w_y)$, where $v_y, w_y > 5$, the set of reachable locations is identical, stipulating the irrelevance of the guard $y \geq 10^6$. Now using '$\Longrightarrow_{\Lambda_{\boldsymbol{k}}}$', observing that

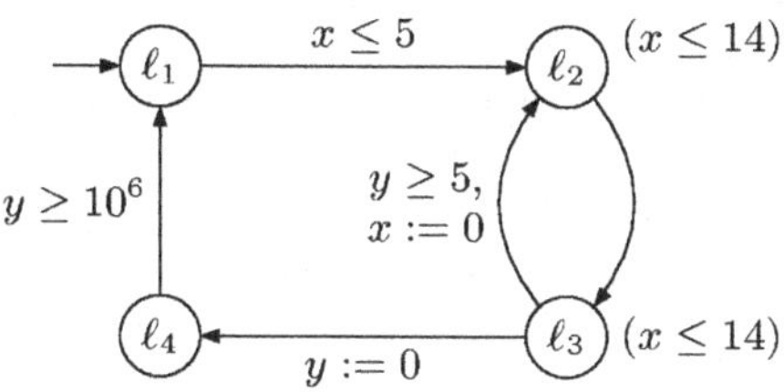

Fig. 2. Timed Automaton A.

$k_x = 5$ and $k_y = 10^6$, iteration of the cycle between ℓ_2 and ℓ_3 leads to the following sequence of symbolic states for the timed automaton in Fig. 2:

$$\begin{aligned}
&(\ell_1, x = 0 \wedge y = 0) \\
&\Longrightarrow_{\Lambda_k} (\ell_1, x = y) \Longrightarrow_{\Lambda_k} (\ell_2, 5 \leq x, y \leq 14 \wedge x = y) \\
&\Longrightarrow^2_{\Lambda_k} (\ell_2, x \in [0, 14] \wedge y \in [5, 28] \wedge y - x \in [5, 14]) \\
&\ldots\ldots \\
&\Longrightarrow^n_{\Lambda_k} (\ell_2, x \in [0, 14] \wedge y \in [5, 14n] \wedge y - x \in [5, 14n - 14]) \\
&\ldots\ldots \\
&\Longrightarrow^*_{\Lambda_k} (\ell_2, 0 \leq x \leq 14 \wedge 5 \leq y \wedge 5 \leq y - x);
\end{aligned}$$

where $n \leq \lceil 10^6/14 \rceil + 1$. We observe that the symbolic states in this sequence are strictly increasing, and hence termination of a forward symbolic exploration using '$\Longrightarrow_{\Lambda_k}$' occurs only extremely slowly. Obviously, we look for a more abstract '$\Longrightarrow_{\Lambda_k}$' which will take into account the irrelevance of the guard $y \geq 10^6$ in location ℓ_2. In the remainder of this section we suggest three such abstractions, all ignoring location-irrelevant guards and sound and complete *w.r.t.* location reachability, but differing in efficiency of representation. Let us consider for the rest of this section a given timed automaton $\mathcal{A} = (L, \ell^0, I, E)$.

Location-based Bisimulation. In Fig. 2, states of the form (ℓ_2, v_x, v_y) with $v_y > 5$ and $v_x \leq 14$, do not only agree on location-reachability but are *location-bisimilar*. We define *location-based bisimularity*, $\equiv$, as the largest relation *s.t.*:

- $(\ell, \sigma) \equiv (\ell', \sigma')$ implies $\ell = \ell'$,
- if $(\ell_1, \sigma_1) \equiv (\ell_2, \sigma_2)$ and $(\ell_1, \sigma_1) \xrightarrow{\tau} (\ell_1', \sigma_1')$,
  then $\exists \sigma_2'$, such that $(\ell_2, \sigma_2) \xrightarrow{\tau} (\ell_2', \sigma_2')$ and $(\ell_1', \sigma_1') \equiv (\ell_2', \sigma_2')$,
- if $(\ell_1, \sigma_1) \equiv (\ell_2, \sigma_2)$ and $(\ell_1, \sigma_1) \xrightarrow{d_1} (\ell_1', \sigma_1')$,
  then $\exists \sigma_2'$, $\exists d_2$, such that $(\ell_2, \sigma_2) \xrightarrow{d_2} (\ell_2', \sigma_2')$ and $(\ell_1', \sigma_1') \equiv (\ell_2', \sigma_2')$,
- *vice-versa* (for the two last conditions).

If W is a set of valuations, we denote by $W_{\equiv,\ell}$ the set $\{\sigma \mid \exists \sigma' \in W \text{ s.t. } (\ell, \sigma) \equiv (\ell, \sigma')\}$ and we define the induced symbolic transition relation $\Longrightarrow_{\equiv}$ by the rule:

$$\frac{(\ell, W) \Longrightarrow (\ell', W')}{(\ell, W) \Longrightarrow_{\equiv} (\ell', W'_{\equiv,\ell'})} \quad \text{if } W = W_{\equiv,\ell}$$

Lemma 1. *$\Longrightarrow_{\equiv}$ is* sound *and* complete *w.r.t. location-reachability.*

Though inducing a sound and complete symbolic transition relation, there is no simple way to represent $\equiv$-closures. In particular, as shown in the following example, for a given location ℓ and zone Z, the set $Z_{\equiv,\ell}$ might not be a zone.

Example 2. Assume that we reach state ℓ with the zone $Z = (0 \leq x, y \leq 1)$. The set $Z_{\equiv,\ell}$ is $\{\sigma \mid \sigma(x) \leq 3 \text{ or } \sigma(y) \geq 2\}$, which is not a zone (non-convex).

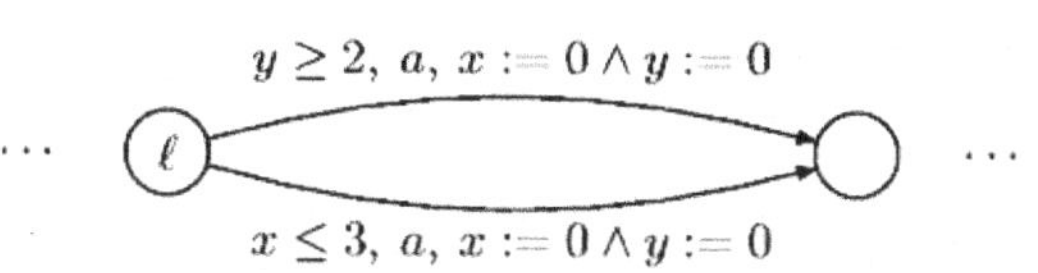

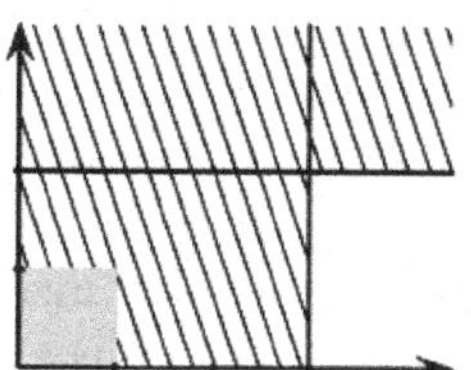

Location-Dependent Maximal Constants. Even with a suitable representation of the $\equiv$-closed sets (*e.g.* using lists of zones or structures as CDDs [4], DDDs [21]), the actual computation of the closure would be at least as difficult as solving the location-reachability problem itself [1,2]. What we are looking for is an alternative abstraction obtained by a more efficient analysis of the relevance of guards. The method proposed in the following determines for each clock x and each location ℓ a maximum constant $\max_x^\ell$ beyond which the actual value of x in ℓ is irrelevant. Let $\{\max_x^\ell \mid x \in X, \ell \in L\}$ be a set of variables and define the system of inequalities, $\mathcal{S}_\mathcal{A}$, as follows:

Definition 5 (Location-dependent max constants). *For each transition* $\ell \xrightarrow{g,\tau,\mathsf{up}} \ell'$ *of* $\mathcal{A}$*, we have the following inequalities in* $\mathcal{S}_\mathcal{A}$*:*

$$\begin{cases} \max_x^\ell \geq c, & \text{if } (x \bowtie c) \text{ is in the constraints } g \text{ or } I(\ell), \\ \max_x^\ell \geq \max_y^{\ell'} - c, & \text{if } (y := x + c) \text{ is in } \mathsf{up} \text{ and } x \leq d \text{ or } x < d \text{ is not in } g, \\ \max_x^\ell \geq \max_x^{\ell'}, & \text{if } x \notin \mathsf{base}(\mathsf{up}). \end{cases}$$

Example 3. Consider the timed automaton $\mathcal{A}$ of Fig. 2. Then $\mathcal{S}_\mathcal{A}$ consists of the following inequalities:[3]

$$\left\{ \begin{array}{llll} \max_x^{\ell_1} \geq 5, \max_x^{\ell_2} & \max_x^{\ell_2} \geq 14, \max_x^{\ell_3} & \max_x^{\ell_3} \geq 14, \max_x^{\ell_4} & \max_x^{\ell_4} \geq \max_x^{\ell_1} \\ \max_y^{\ell_1} \geq \max_y^{\ell_2} & \max_y^{\ell_2} \geq \max_y^{\ell_3} & \max_y^{\ell_3} \geq 5 & \max_y^{\ell_4} \geq 10^6, \max_y^{\ell_1} \end{array} \right\}$$

Let $\alpha = (\max_x^\ell)_{x \in X, \ell \in L}$ be a solution of $\mathcal{S}_\mathcal{A}$. The equivalence $\cong_\alpha$ is defined by $(\ell, \sigma) \cong_\alpha (\ell', \sigma') \overset{\text{def}}{\iff} \ell = \ell'$ and $\forall x : \sigma(x) = \sigma'(x)$ or $\sigma(x), \sigma'(x) > \max_x^\ell$.

Lemma 2. *Whenever* $(\ell, \sigma) \cong_\alpha (\ell, \sigma')$ *then* $(\ell, \sigma) \equiv (\ell, \sigma')$.

For W a set of valuations, let $W_{\cong_\alpha, \ell} = \{\sigma' \mid \exists \sigma \in W \text{ s.t. } (\ell, \sigma) \cong_\alpha (\ell, \sigma')\}$ and let '$\Longrightarrow_{\cong_\alpha}$' be the induced abstracted symbolic transition relation. From the previous Lemma 2 it follows that $W_{\cong_\alpha, \ell} \subseteq W_{\equiv, \ell}$ for any set of valuations W. As clearly $W \subseteq W_{\cong_\alpha, \ell}$, we have immediately:

Lemma 3. $\Longrightarrow_{\cong_\alpha}$ *is* sound *and* complete *w.r.t. location-reachability.*

Note that, if α and β are two solutions, it is clear that $W_{\cong_\beta, \ell} \subseteq W_{\cong_\alpha, \ell}$ whenever $\alpha \leq \beta$.[4] Thus, to maximize abstraction in the interest of early termination, we look for

[3] We write $a \geq b, c$ as a shorthand for the set of inequalities $a \geq b$, $a \geq c$.

[4] Here $\alpha \leq \beta$ is defined componentwise, *i.e.* $\alpha \leq \beta$ iff $\forall \ell \in L$, $\forall x \in X : \alpha_x^\ell \leq \beta_x^\ell$.

a smallest solution of $\mathcal{S}_{\mathcal{A}}$. For example, given the automaton $\mathcal{A}$ of Fig. 2, the smallest solution of $\mathcal{S}_{\mathcal{A}}$, as described in Example 3, is $\max_x^{\ell_i} = 14$ for $i \in \{1, 2, 3, 4\}$, $\max_y^{\ell_i} = 5$ for $i \in \{1, 2, 3\}$ and $\max_y^{\ell_4} = 10^6$.

However, as for $\equiv$, there is no efficient way to represent $\cong_\alpha$-closures. Indeed, even if Z is a zone, it is not guaranteed that $Z_{\cong_{\alpha,\ell}}$ will be. For example, consider the zone Z (hashed) depicted in the figure on the right and let $\alpha^\ell = (2, 1)$. Then the set of valuations $Z_{\cong_{\alpha,\ell}}$ is obtained by adding the right part (gray). As a result, the union of these two is non-convex.

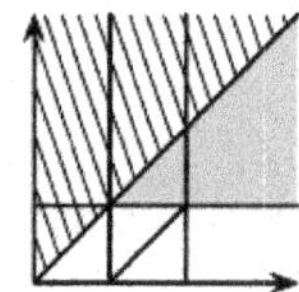

Location-Dependent Abstraction Using DBMs. The (sound and complete) symbolic transition relations induced by the two abstractions considered so far, unfortunately do not preserve convexity of valuation-sets. In order to allow for valuation-sets to be represented *efficiently* as zones, we consider a slightly finer abstraction. In fact, we use a location-dependent version of the maximal constant abstraction on DBMs.

Given a timed automaton $\mathcal{A} = (L, \ell^0, I, E)$, let $\mathcal{S}_{\mathcal{A}}$ be the system of inequalities associated with $\mathcal{A}$ and $\alpha = (\max_x^\ell)_{x \in X, \ell \in L}$ be a solution to this system. For Z a zone, we define Z_α^ℓ as $\Lambda_{\alpha_{|\ell}}(Z)$ where $\alpha_{|\ell}$ is the tuple $(\max_x^\ell)_{x \in X}$ (see Definition 4 for Λ). The following non-trivial Lemma demonstrates that this zone-based abstraction is indeed finer than the two previously considered:

Lemma 4. *Let Z be a zone, $\ell \in L$ and α a solution to $\mathcal{S}_{\mathcal{A}}$, then $Z_\alpha^\ell \subseteq Z_{\cong_{\alpha,\ell}}$.*

The abstract transition system '$\Longrightarrow_\alpha$' is now induced in the obvious manner:

$$\frac{(\ell, Z) \Longrightarrow (\ell', Z')}{(\ell, Z) \Longrightarrow_\alpha (\ell', \Lambda_{\alpha_{|\ell'}}(Z'))} \qquad \text{if } \Lambda_{\alpha_{|\ell}}(Z) = Z$$

Note that, this transition system is well-defined (and consistent) because whenever Z is a zone, then also Z_α^ℓ is a zone. We may now state our main-theorem:

Theorem 1. *Let $\mathcal{A}$ be a timed automaton and $\mathcal{S}_{\mathcal{A}}$ the system of linear inequalities associated with $\mathcal{A}$. If α is a solution of $\mathcal{S}_{\mathcal{A}}$, then '$\Longrightarrow_\alpha$' is* sound *and* complete *w.r.t. location-reachability.*

$$S_{\mathcal{B}}^g = \begin{cases} \max_x \geq 2 \\ \max_x \leq \max_x - 1 \\ \max_x \geq 3 \end{cases} \qquad S_{\mathcal{B}}^l = \begin{cases} \max_x^\ell \geq 2 \\ \max_x^{\ell'} \leq \max_x^\ell - 1 \\ \max_x^{\ell'} \geq 3 \end{cases}$$

ℓ — $x \geq 2,\ a,\ x := x - 1$ → ℓ' (self-loop: $x \leq 3$, b, $x := 0$)

Fig. 3. Decrementing Timed Automaton, $\mathcal{B}$.

Moreover, the symbolic reachability graph induced by '$\Longrightarrow_\alpha$' is obviously finite and is useful as the basis for a terminating, forward reachability algorithm. It should be noted that the use of location-dependent maximal constant abstraction *enlarges* the class of timed automata for which we may decide location-reachability compared with the previous method. For example, whereas the automaton of Fig. 3 may be analysed using the new location-dependent abstractions, the global maximal constant abstraction from [10] does not apply:

$$\mathcal{S}^g_{\mathcal{B}} = \begin{cases} \max_x \geq 2 \\ \max_x \leq \max_x -1 \\ \max_x \geq 3 \end{cases} \qquad \mathcal{S}^l_{\mathcal{B}} = \begin{cases} \max^\ell_x \geq 2 \\ \max^{\ell'}_x \leq \max^\ell_x -1 \\ \max^{\ell'}_x \geq 3 \end{cases}$$

Here $\mathcal{S}^g_{\mathcal{B}}$ is the inequality system for global maximal constants and $\mathcal{S}^l_{\mathcal{B}}$ is the system for location-dependent maximal constants. Trivially, $\mathcal{S}^g_{\mathcal{B}}$ has no solutions, and $\mathcal{B}$ may consequently not be analysed using the methods of [10]. In contrast $\mathcal{S}^l_{\mathcal{B}}$ has the (minimal) solution α with $\max^\ell_x = 4$ and $\max^{\ell'}_x = 3$. Hence location-reachability is decidable for $\mathcal{B}$ using '$\Longrightarrow_\alpha$'.

5 Solving Simple Diophantine Constraints

We know from [17,7] that the problem of solving a system of inequalities like $\mathcal{S}_\mathcal{A}$ is decidable, but the study done in these papers is much more general ([7] deals with general Presburger formulae) and the complexity is 3EXPTIME-complete. In this section, we provide, both, a polynomial and a linear algorithm for solving specific Diophantine inequality systems.

Minimal solutions. The interest of computing small solutions to $\mathcal{S}_\mathcal{A}$ appears clearly. Small solutions give large abstractions, and thus a smaller state-space to explore. The following lemma asserts that there is a unique minimal solution to the simple inequality systems we generate.[5]

Lemma 5. *Let $\mathcal{A}$ be a timed automaton and $\mathcal{S}_\mathcal{A}$ the inequality system associated to $\mathcal{A}$. If $\mathcal{S}_\mathcal{A}$ has a solution, then it has a unique minimal solution.*

Our aim is to provide efficient algorithms to find the minimal solution. We will reduce the problem to computing the longest paths in a digraph.

Reduction to a graph problem. We consider the system $\mathcal{S}_\mathcal{A}$ and we construct the directed graph $\mathcal{G}_\mathcal{A}$, having a vertex for each variable $\max^\ell_x$ in addition to the special vertex **0**, and with the set of edges defined as follows:

- There is an edge $\max^\ell_x \xrightarrow{c} \mathbf{0}$ in $\mathcal{G}_\mathcal{A}$ if $\max^\ell_x \geq c$ is in $\mathcal{S}_\mathcal{A}$.
- There is an edge $\max^\ell_x \xrightarrow{c} \max^{\ell'}_y$ in $\mathcal{G}_\mathcal{A}$ if $\max^\ell_x \geq \max^{\ell'}_y + c$ is in $\mathcal{S}_\mathcal{A}$.

An edge labeled with $-\infty$ is equivalent to having no edge between two vertices. The relation between the graph $\mathcal{G}_\mathcal{A}$ and $\mathcal{S}_\mathcal{A}$ is stated by the following result:

[5] This is not the case for general linear Diophantine inequality systems, see [17,7].

Proposition 1. *The system $S_\mathcal{A}$ has a solution iff the graph $\mathcal{G}_\mathcal{A}$ has no positive cycle. Moreover, the minimal solution to the system $S_\mathcal{A}$ corresponds to the longest paths in $\mathcal{G}_\mathcal{A}$ from each vertex "$\max_x^\ell$" to* **0**.

The problem thus reduces to a graph problem: we compute the longest paths in a graph without positive cycles, which is equivalent (by inversing the edges) to compute shortest paths in graphs without negative cycles. We can thus use, for example, Floyd-Warshall's algorithm, which is polynomial ($\mathcal{O}(n^3)$) in the number of variables of the system, which is $n = |X| \cdot |L|$ where $|X|$ is the number of clocks of the automaton and $|L|$ the number of locations.

A particular simpler case. We restrict to timed automata that use only updates of the form $x := c$ and $x := y$. The inequalities that we have to consider in this particular case are only of the two following forms: either $\max_x^\ell \geq \max_y^{\ell'}$ or $\max_x^\ell \geq c$ for a constant c. The graph that corresponds to such a system has a form like the one described below. Two vertices (different from **0**) are either not linked or the label of the edge is 0. There are moreover edges from non-**0** vertices to **0** that can be labeled by any positive integer.

In this (special) case, a simpler algorithm can be used:

- Compute the 0-cycles (*i.e.*, in this special case, the strongly connected components of the graph)
- The new graph, where we replace each 0-cycle by a single vertex, is a *DAG*. Longest paths can be computed in linear time (in the number of strongly connected components, *i.e.* the number of variables of the system).

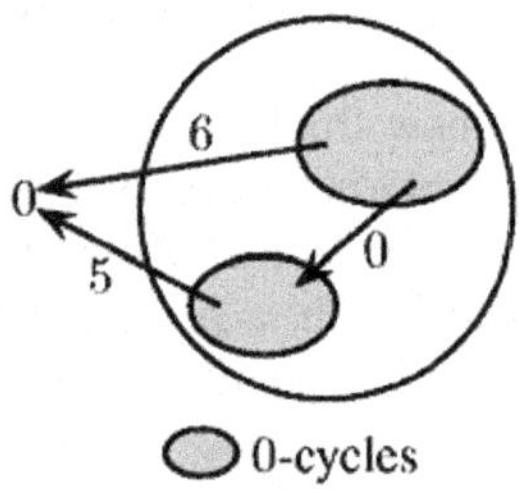

This algorithm has the nice property to be linear in the number of variables of the system (keep in mind that the number of variables is $|X| \cdot |L|$).

Active-Clock Reduction. A notion of active-clock reduction has been proposed in [15] for classical timed automata and has demonstrated a significant reduction in numerous case studies. This notion even makes sense for our more general model of timed automata, as defined in Section 2. Let $\mathcal{A}$ be a timed automaton. The active-clock reduction is computed as a (minimal) fix point by:

$$Act(\ell) = \bigcup_{(\ell \xrightarrow{g,a,u} \ell') \text{ in } \mathcal{A}} \mathsf{used}(g) \cup \mathsf{used}(u) \cup (Act(\ell') \setminus \mathsf{base}(u))$$

The following theorem states that active-clock reduction is a special case of our location-dependent abstraction technique.

Theorem 2. *Let $x \in X$, $\ell \in L$, and $(\max_x^\ell)_{x \in X, \ell \in L}$ be the minimal solution of $S_\mathcal{A}$. Then $x \in Act(\ell)$ iff $\max_x^\ell > -\infty$.*

6 Dealing with Composition

Having so far developed a method for location-based abstraction for individual timed automata, it is now necessary to study its extension to the general case of *networks* of timed automata (see Section 2) in order to be applicable in tools such as UPPAAL. A simple solution would be to construct (at least logically) a single automaton having the same behaviour as the network and then apply our method to this product automaton. However, this approach would suffer from an exponential explosion in the size of the inequality system (e.g. the number of variables) to be solved w.r.t. the number of components of the network.

To avoid this explosion, we will develop *compositional* methods allowing (valid) location-dependent maximal constants of the product automaton to be efficiently derived from location-dependent maximal constants of the components of the network. However, the fact that clocks may be shared (read and written) by several component automata of a network, complicates the combination of maximal constant information of components. To illustrate this reconsider the network of Fig. 1 from the introduction, where the clocks x and z are shared between $\mathcal{A}_1$ and $\mathcal{A}_2$. Considering the automaton $\mathcal{A}_2$ in isolation, the maximal constant(s) for z, $c_z^{n_i}$, seems to be 8 in both n_1 and n_2. However, the presence of the update $x := z + 3$ in $\mathcal{A}_2$ together with the invariants $(x \leq 14)$ in $\mathcal{A}_1$ requires that the value(s) of $c_z^{n_i}$ must take the maximal constants for x in $\mathcal{A}_1$ into account in order to be valid. How to make such transfer in a valid, yet efficient manner will be dealt with in this section.

For the sake of clarity, we fix some notation. For each network $\boldsymbol{\mathcal{A}}$, for each location vector $\boldsymbol{\ell}$ of this network and for each clock x, we denote by $\max_{\boldsymbol{\ell},x}^{\boldsymbol{\mathcal{A}}}$ the minimal solution for the system $\mathcal{S}_{\boldsymbol{\mathcal{A}}}$.

A First Simple Case. As a first simple case assume that $\boldsymbol{\mathcal{A}} = \mathcal{A}_1 \parallel \cdots \parallel \mathcal{A}_n$ and that each automaton $\mathcal{A}_i$ only uses updates of the form $x := c$, and no update of the form $x := y+c$. In addition, clocks may (or may not) be local in the sense that any clock is used (read and written) by at most one automaton. Now, consider the obvious combination of location-dependent maximal constants of components obtained by maximality, *i.e.* if c_i is the maximal constant for x in ℓ_i (of $\mathcal{A}_i$) then $\max\{c_1, \ldots, c_n\}$ will be the suggested maximal constant for x in $\boldsymbol{\ell}$ (of $\boldsymbol{\mathcal{A}}$) or formally:

$$\mathrm{Max}_{\boldsymbol{\ell},x}^{\boldsymbol{\mathcal{A}}} = \max\left\{\max_{\ell_i,x}^{\mathcal{A}_i} \mid i = 1 \ldots n\right\}. \qquad (\star)$$

This combination yields a valid solution to $\mathcal{S}_{\boldsymbol{\mathcal{A}}}$ as stated in the following:

Proposition 2. *Let $\boldsymbol{\mathcal{A}}$ be a network only using updates of the form $x := c$, then* $\mathrm{Max}_{\boldsymbol{\ell},x}^{\boldsymbol{\mathcal{A}}} \geq \max_{\boldsymbol{\ell},x}^{\boldsymbol{\mathcal{A}}}$. *If moreover clocks are local, then* $\mathrm{Max}_{\boldsymbol{\ell},x}^{\boldsymbol{\mathcal{A}}} = \max_{\boldsymbol{\ell},x}^{\boldsymbol{\mathcal{A}}}$

The General Case. In the general case the component automata may have updates of the form $x := y + c$ as well as sharing of clocks. In particular, the case where one component, $\mathcal{A}_i$, contains a general update $x := y + c$ of x and another component, $\mathcal{A}_j$, a test $x \bowtie d$ on x requires a *transfer* of maximal constants for x (in certain locations) in $\mathcal{A}_j$ to maximal constants for y (in certain locations) in $\mathcal{A}_i$. Thus, the simple combination

$(*)$ will not be valid. As an example consider the network of Fig. 1 and the corresponding inequality systems, $\mathcal{S}_{\mathcal{A}_1}$ and $\mathcal{S}_{\mathcal{A}_2}$[6]:

$$\mathcal{S}_{\mathcal{A}_1} = \left\{ \begin{array}{ll} \max_x^{\ell_1} \geq 5, \max_x^{\ell_2} & \max_y^{\ell_1} \geq \max_y^{\ell_2} \\ \max_x^{\ell_2} \geq 14, \max_x^{\ell_3} & \max_y^{\ell_2} \geq \max_y^{\ell_3} \\ \max_x^{\ell_3} \geq 14, \max_x^{\ell_4} & \max_y^{\ell_3} \geq 5 \\ \max_x^{\ell_4} \geq \max_x^{\ell_1} & \max_y^{\ell_4} \geq 10^6, \max_y^{\ell_1} \end{array} \right\}, \quad \mathcal{S}_{\mathcal{A}_2} = \left\{ \begin{array}{l} \max_z^{n_1} \geq 8 \\ \max_z^{n_2} \geq 4, \max_z^{n_1} \end{array} \right\}$$

Calculations give $\max_{\ell_2,z}^{\mathcal{A}_1} = -\infty$ and $\max_{n_1,z}^{\mathcal{A}_2} = 8$ and hence $\mathrm{Max}_{(\ell_2,n_1),z}^{\boldsymbol{\mathcal{A}}} = 8$ by $(*)$. However, this combination is invalid as it ignores the invariant $(x \leq 14)$ in $\mathcal{A}_1$, which combined with the update $x := z + 3$ in $\mathcal{A}_2$ will require $\max_{(\ell_2,n_1),z}^{\boldsymbol{\mathcal{A}}} \geq 11$. To obtain a valid inequality system, we take the transfer-update $x := z + 3$ (say) into account in the following way: for each location ℓ_i of $\mathcal{A}_1$ we add the constraint $\max_z^{n_1} \geq \max_x^{\ell_i} - 3$. Thus, to make the method compositional, we make no assumptions as to the location $\mathcal{A}_1$ might be in simultaneously with $\mathcal{A}_2$ being in location n_1. We add similar constraints to $\max_y^{\ell_2}$ to take the transfer-update $z := y + 1$ into account. The two added transfer equation systems are thus: $\mathcal{T}_{1\to 2} = \{ \max_z^{n_1} \geq \max_x^{\ell_i} - 3 : 1 \leq i \leq 4 \}$, and $\mathcal{T}_{2\to 1} = \{ \max_y^{\ell_2} \geq \max_z^{\ell_i} - 1 : i = 1, 2 \}$.

Applying $(*)$ to the solutions found from the inequality system obtained by combining $\mathcal{S}_{\mathcal{A}_1}, \mathcal{S}_{\mathcal{A}_2}$ with $\mathcal{T}_{1\to 2}$ and $\mathcal{T}_{2\to 1}$ yields a valid solution to $\mathcal{S}_{\mathcal{A}_1 \| \mathcal{A}_2}$. In the remainder we formalize the method, state its correctness and complexity.

In general, for two different component automata $\mathcal{A}_i$ and $\mathcal{A}_j$ (with $i \neq j$), the transfer inequality system $\mathcal{T}_{i\to j}$ is obtained by adding for each update of the form $x := y + c$ in $\mathcal{A}_j$ with source-location ℓ a constraint $\max_{\ell,y}^{\mathcal{A}_j} \geq \max_{n,x}^{\mathcal{A}_i} - c$ for *any* location n of $\mathcal{A}_i$. Now, by combining the component inequality systems with the transfer inequality systems into $\mathcal{M} = \bigcup \{ \mathcal{S}_{\mathcal{A}_i} : 1 \leq i \leq n \} \cup \bigcup \{ \mathcal{T}_{i\to j} : i \neq j \}$ and defining: $\mathrm{MAX}_{\ell,x}^{\boldsymbol{\mathcal{A}}} = \max\{ \max_{\ell_i,x}^{\mathcal{M}} \mid i = 1 \ldots n \}$, where $(\max_{\ell_i,x}^{\mathcal{M}})$ is the minimal solution to $\mathcal{M}$, the following proposition holds:

Proposition 3. *Let $\boldsymbol{\mathcal{A}}$ be a network of timed automata. Then* $\mathrm{MAX}_{\ell,x}^{\boldsymbol{\mathcal{A}}} \geq \max_{\ell,x}^{\boldsymbol{\mathcal{A}}}$.

Thus from the (minimal) solution to $\mathcal{M}$ we may obtain valid location-dependent constants. It is important to note that the size of the system of inequalities $\mathcal{M}$ grows polynomial with the number of components of the network[7] thus allowing for our solution methods from the previous section to scale up. The computation of the maximal constants corresponding to particular location-vectors (and clocks) will be obtained from the minimal solution to $\mathcal{M}$ in an on-the-fly fashion.

7 Experiments with UPPAAL

A first prototype of the location-dependent abstraction technique has been implemented in UPPAAL. The fragment considered for this prototype can deal with networks of au-

[6] Note, that as $\mathcal{A}_2$ has no guards on x, there are no constraints on maximal constants involving x in $\mathcal{S}_{\mathcal{A}_2}$. Similar holds for $\mathcal{A}_1$ and z.

[7] Assuming a fixed number of locations and clocks for each component the number of variables grows linearly and the number or inequalities grows quadraticly.

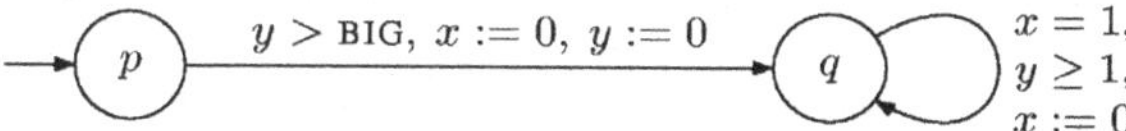

Fig. 4. Naive Example.

tomata and resets to a constant ($x := c$). The algorithms are those described in section 5 and section 6. Our algorithm is expected to beat the standard approaches for timed automata in which we have a tremendous difference on clock constraints from one location to another one. In order to demonstrate this, let us consider a *naive example* (Fig. 4). In such an automaton, and considering a global approach of the maximum constants on clocks, the constant BIG plays a crucial role in the analysis of the system. The bigger the constant BIG is, the longer the analysis will last. Indeed, one can notice the fact that applying the location-dependent analysis on this automaton reduces the maximum constants of y to BIG in the initial location p and to 1 in the location q. These results have a huge impact on the analysis of the model. In Table 1, this naive example and the resources of its analysis are displayed for several values of the constant BIG. The *Global Method* refers to the classical approach, the *Active-clock Reduction* refers to the algorithm which only considers the clocks which are active in the locations [15], and finally, the *Local Constants* refers to our method. The time performance of our method is insensitive to the size of constant BIG.

Two Processes is the example from the introduction (see Fig. 1), but slightly modified: the updates of the form $x := y+c$ have been rewritten into $x := y$ and hard coded into the automaton[8]. The constant BIG is the constraint on the clock y valued 10^6. Once again, our abstraction is coarser than the ones traditionally applied, and therefore performs better on the verification.

The next example, namely *Asymmetric Fischer*, refers to a classical two process Fischer example where the constants of one of the processes have been changed to the constant BIG. Experiments show a gain of 50% in time. The final example, referred to as *Bang & Olufsen*, is an industrial case study [18]. The Bang & Olufsen Power Down Protocol controls the transitions between stand-by mode and power-on mode in the company's products, where power consumption minimization is an important feature. The UPPAAL model of this protocol heavily uses a clock c and introduces a certain amount of guards with constants from 1 to 25000. The way the model is built introduces a lot of locations where the maximum constant of c can be reduced from 25000 to some lower constants. Without any modification of the model we have noticed an improvement of 25% in the speed and 20% of the memory usage.

Finally, it is crucial to point out that, as expected by the theory, our algorithm is performing as well as the active-clock reduction technique in all other examples that we tried (including the total suite of UPPAAL benchmarks). Location-dependent abstraction out performs active-clock reduction only when it deals with models in which there is a big difference on the value of the maximum constants from state to state (as demonstrated in this section), but has no effect on models which do not have this sort of property. We

[8] The technique used to transform timed automata with $x := c$ and $x := y$ into timed automata with only resets is described in [11].

Table 1. *Experimental Results (Intel PentiumIV@1.8GHz).*

	Constant BIG	*Global Method*	*Active-clock Reduction*	*Local Constants*
Naive Example	10^3	0.05s/1MB	0.05s/1MB	0.00s/1MB
	10^4	4.78s/3MB	4.83s/3MB	0.00s/1MB
	10^5	484s/13MB	480s/13MB	0.00s/1MB
	10^6	stopped	stopped	0.00s/1MB
Two Processes	10^3	3.24s/3MB	3.26s/3MB	0.01s/1MB
	10^4	5981s/9MB	5978s/9MB	0.37s/2MB
	10^5	stopped	stopped	72s/5MB
Asymmetric Fischer	10^3	0.01s/1MB	0.01s/1MB	0.01s/1MB
	10^4	2.20s/3MB	2.20s/3MB	0.85s/2MB
	10^5	333s/19MB	333s/19MB	160s/13MB
	10^6	33307s/122MB	33238s/122MB	16330s/65MB
Bang & Olufsen	25000	stopped	159s/243MB	123s/204MB

also emphasize the fact that our experiments did not exhibit any significant difference between the performance of the active-clock reduction and our method.

8 Conclusions and Further Work

In this paper, we have shown that the classical zone construction used to obtain a finite abstraction of a timed automaton is sensitive to large differences in the constants to which clocks are compared. We have contributed a *location-dependent zone abstraction*, which uses static analysis to identify the *relevant guards and invariants* in a given location. We have shown that this abstraction generalises the well-known active-clock reduction technique. In addition, we have extended the concept to the case of networks of timed automata and to the case of more general updates of clocks. Experiments have demonstrated, that our abstraction in some cases can result in an exponential speedup. On real-world cases, we either match or surpass the performance of active-clock reduction, depending on whether the system compares clocks to different constants or not.

There are a number of open questions, that need further work. Our experiments do not evaluate the quality of the heuristic described in Section 6 used for networks of timed automata, *i.e.*, whether computing the maximum constants based on the product automaton would yield significantly smaller constants. Also, we have not tested with systems containing non-trivial updates ($x := y + c$). This is partly due to lack of realistic systems using these kind of updates.

In UPPAAL, clocks (and clock differences) may be compared to expressions over bounded integer variables. Extending the active guard reduction technique to this case involves finding the smallest upper bound of an integer expression in a given location. Also, the idea of active-clock reduction could equally be applied to integer variables. In the sequential case, this has been studied in the field of compiler theory and is also related to slicing techniques (recently added to SPIN). Finally, we have not yet explored the fact, that we can verify a broader class of timed automata compared to the classic approach. A case-study demonstrating the usefulness of this claim is needed.

References

1. R. Alur, C. Courcoubetis, D. Dill, N. Halbwachs, and H. Wong-Toi. An Implementation of Three Algorithms for Timing Verification Based on Automata Emptiness. In *Proc. 13th IEEE Real-Time Systems Symp. (RTSS'92)*, pp. 157–166. IEEE Computer Society Press, 1992.
2. R. Alur, C. Courcoubetis, N. Halbwachs, D. Dill, and H. Wong-Toi. Minimization of Timed Transition Systems. In *Proc. 3rd Int. Conf. on Concurrency Theory (CONCUR'92)*, vol. 630 of *LNCS*, pp. 340–354. Springer, 1992.
3. R. Alur and D. Dill. A Theory of Timed Automata. *Theoretical Computer Science*, 126(2):183–235, 1994.
4. G. Behrmann, K. G. Larsen, J. Pearson, C. Weise, and W. Yi. Efficient Timed Reachability Analysis Using Clock Difference Diagrams. In *Proc. 11th Int. Conf. on Computer Aided Verification (CAV'99)*, vol. 1633 of *LNCS*, pp. 341–353. Springer, 1999.
5. J. Bengtsson. *Clocks, DBMs ans States in Timed Systems*. PhD thesis, Dept. of Information Technology, Uppsala Univ., Uppsala, Sweden, 2002.
6. J. Bengtsson, K. G. Larsen, Fredrik Larsson, P. Pettersson, W. Yi, and Carsten Weise. New Generation of UPPAAL. In *Proc. Int. Workshop on Software Tools for Technology Transfer (STTT'98)*, BRICS Notes, pp. 43–52, 1998.
7. A. Boudet and H. Comon. Diophantine Equations, Presburger Arithmetic and Finite Automata. In *Proc. 21st Int. Coll. on Trees in Algebra and Programming (CAAP'96)*, vol. 1059 of *LNCS*, pp. 30–43. Springer, 1996.
8. P. Bouyer. Timed Automata May Cause Some Troubles. Research Report LSV–02–9, LSV, ENS de Cachan, France, 2002.
9. P. Bouyer. Untameable Timed Automata! In *Proc. 20th Annual Symp. on Theoretical Aspects of Computer Science (STACS'2003)*, 2003. To appear.
10. P. Bouyer, C. Dufourd, E. Fleury, and A. Petit. Are timed automata updatable? In *Proc. 12th Int. Conf. on Computer Aided Verification (CAV'2000)*, vol. 1855 of *LNCS*, pp. 464–479. Springer, 2000.
11. P. Bouyer, C. Dufourd, E. Fleury, and A. Petit. Expressiveness of updatable timed automata. In *Proc. 25th Int. Symp. on Mathematical Foundations of Computer Science (MFCS'2000)*, vol. 1893 of *LNCS*, pp. 232–242. Springer, 2000.
12. M. Bozga, C. Daws, O. Maler, A. Olivero, S. Tripakis, and S. Yovine. KRONOS: a Model-Checking Tool for Real-Time Systems. In *Proc. 10th Int. Conf. on Computer Aided Verification (CAV'98)*, vol. 1427 of *LNCS*, pp. 546–550. Springer, 1998.
13. V. Braberman, D. Garbervetsky, and A. Olivero. Improving the Verification of Timed Systems Using Influence Information. In *Proc. 8th Int. Conf. on Tools and Algorithms for the Construction and Analysis of Systems (TACAS'02)*, vol. 2280 of *LNCS*, pp. 21–36. Springer, 2002.
14. E. Clarke, O. Grumberg, and D. Peled. *Model-Checking*. The MIT Press, 1999.
15. C. Daws and S. Tripakis. Model-Checking of Real-Time Reachability Properties using Abstractions. In *Proc. 4th Int. Conf. on Tools and Algorithms for the Construction and Analysis of Systems (TACAS'98)*, vol. 1384 of *LNCS*, pp. 313–329. Springer, 1998.
16. D. Dill. Timing Assumptions and Verification of Finite-State Concurrent Systems. In *Proc. of the Workshop on Automatic Verification Methods for Finite State Systems*, vol. 407 of *LNCS*, pp. 197–212. Springer, 1989.

17. E. Domenjoud. Solving Systems of Linear Diophantine Equations: an Algebraic Approach. In *Proc. 16th Int. Symp. on Mathematical Foundations of Computer Science (MFCS'91)*, vol. 520 of *LNCS*, pp. 141–150. Springer, 1991.
18. K. Havelund, A. Skou, K.G. Larsen, and K. Lund. Formal Modeling and Analysis of an Audio/Video Protocol: an Industrial Case Study using UPPAAL. In *Proc. 18th IEEE Real-Time Systems Symp. (RTSS'97)*, pp. 2–13. IEEE Computer Society Press, 1997.
19. F. Laroussinie and K.G. Larsen. CMC: a Tool for Compositional Model-Checking of Real-Time Systems. In *Proc. IFIP Int. Conf. on Formal Description Techniques & Protocol Specification, Testing, and Verification (FORTE-PSTV'98)*, pp. 439–456. Kluwer Academic, 1998.
20. K. G. Larsen, P. Pettersson, and W. Yi. UPPAAL in a Nutshell. *Software Tools for Technology Transfer*, 1(1–2):134–152, 1997.
21. J. Møller, J. Lichtenberg, H.R. Andersen, and H. Hulgaard. Difference Decision Diagrams. In *Proc. 13th Int. Workshop on Computer Science Logic (CSL'99)*, vol. 1683 of *LNCS*, pp. 111–125. Springer, 1999.

MOBY/DC – A Tool for Model-Checking Parametric Real-Time Specifications

Henning Dierks[1] and Josef Tapken[2]

[1] University of Oldenburg,
Department of Computer Science,
P.O.Box 2503
26111 Oldenburg, Germany
[2] cewe digital GmbH,
Meerweg 30-32,
26133 Oldenburg, Germany

Abstract. We define an operational subset of Duration Calculus, called phase automata, which serves as an intermediate language for the analysis and verification of real-time system descriptions that contain timing parameters. We introduce the tool MOBY/DC which implements a model-checking algorithm for phase automata. The algorithm applies compositional model-checking techniques and handles parameters by built-in procedures or by a link to $CLP(R)$. Due to the parameters the model-checking problem is undecidable in general. Hence, we have to accept that the results are overapproximations only in order to guarantee termination. The overapproximation together with the compositional technique makes the model-checker especially well suited for proving the absence of error traces instead of finding them.

1 Introduction

Most timed automata model-checkers demand concrete values for the timing bounds. However, in high-level system descriptions often parameters are used for the timing bounds. To cope with parameters we designed and implemented a new model-checking algorithm for parametric phase automata. As an option the tool solves the parametric constraints by translation of the parametric timing bounds into fragments of constraint logic programs [JM94] which are fed into the interpreter $CLP(R)$ [HJM$^+$92]. Due to an undecidability result for our parametric language [Tap01], we have to pay a certain price. Therefore, we chose an approximation technique in order to guarantee the termination of the model-checking procedure (in contrast to the semi-decision procedure of HYTECH [HHW97]).

Our model-checking algorithm was designed to complement the approaches provided by the timed automata model-checkers UPPAAL and KRONOS. The experiences with these model-checkers have shown that the strength of their approaches is to find errors in the specification rather than to prove their absence. We chose a compositional model-checking technique [And95] which is also implemented in the timed automata tool CMC [LL98]. Our algorithm often performs better for correctness proofs because it can happen that only few of the parallel components of the model are needed to prove

H. Garavel and J. Hatcliff (Eds.): TACAS 2003, LNCS 2619, pp. 271–277, 2003.

the absence of an error. To show the presence of an error always the whole network has to be examined.

2 Phase Automata

In this section we explain phase automata by an example[1]. The phase automata build an operational subset of the Duration Calculus [HZ97] since the semantics is given in Duration Calculus.

Example: Generalized Railroad Crossing: In [HL94] the case study of a "Generalized Railroad Crossing" (GRC for short) is proposed as a benchmark for the comparison of formal methods. The task is to develop a gate controller which shall secure a railroad crossing. The system is modeled by two observables. The first one describes the environment of the gate controller, which includes tracks and trains. The observable is called Track and has the range $\{\mathsf{E}, \mathsf{A}, \mathsf{Cr}\}$ with the following meaning: $\mathsf{Cr} \stackrel{\text{df}}{=}$ at least one train is in the crossing, $\mathsf{A} \stackrel{\text{df}}{=}$ at least one train is approaching the crossing but no train is in it, and $\mathsf{E} \stackrel{\text{df}}{=}$ no train is approaching or crossing, i.e. the track is empty. The second observable Gate describes the gate on an abstract level by the following three values: $\mathsf{Cl} \stackrel{\text{df}}{=}$ the gate is fully closed, $\mathsf{O} \stackrel{\text{df}}{=}$ the gate is fully open, and $\mathsf{I} \stackrel{\text{df}}{=}$ the gate is not open and not closed.

Two formal approaches [ORS96,DD97] to this case study using Duration Calculus based methods assume the following properties for trains:

1. It cannot happen that a train passes through the approaching area in less than ε_1 time units if the track was empty before.
2. The slowest train needs at most ξ_1 time units to approach the crossing.

In Fig. 1 a phase automaton is given (lhs) that expresses the first property. The automaton consists of four phases ($p_1, \ldots, p_4$) and several transitions between them. Phases are inscribed by a DC state assertion (e.g. p_4 with $\lceil \mathsf{Cr} \rceil$). The assertions can be built over all observables of the system and do not have to be disjoint (cf. phase p_2 and p_3). Initial phases are marked by an incoming edge (see p_1, p_2, and p_4). To express timing aspects a phase automaton is equipped with a set of clocks (here c_1) each of them being inscribed by a time interval over the reals (in this example $[\varepsilon_1, \infty]$ for clock c_1). The bounds of the interval can be specified as ∞ or as a linear contraint, ie. $c + \sum c_i \cdot x_i$ where the c's are constants and the x's are parameters. Finally, clock scopes are defined by associating to each clock an arbitrary set of phases. Here, the scope of clock c_1 comprises only the phase p_2.

The informal behaviour of the left automaton in Fig. 1 is as follows. Initially, the automaton allows an arbitrary interpretation of the observables due to the state assertions of the initial phases. If the automaton is in phase p_1 with the track being empty ($\lceil \mathsf{E} \rceil$) and an approaching phase shall succeed, then the automaton has to change to p_2 (and not to p_3 due to the missing transition). The clock c_1 requires that the phase p_2 is stable for at least ε_1 time units. Thus, it is not allowed that an $\lceil \mathsf{A} \rceil$-phase is shorter than ε_1 time units if $\lceil \mathsf{E} \rceil$ precedes.

[1] For a full and formal treatment we refer the reader to [Tap01].

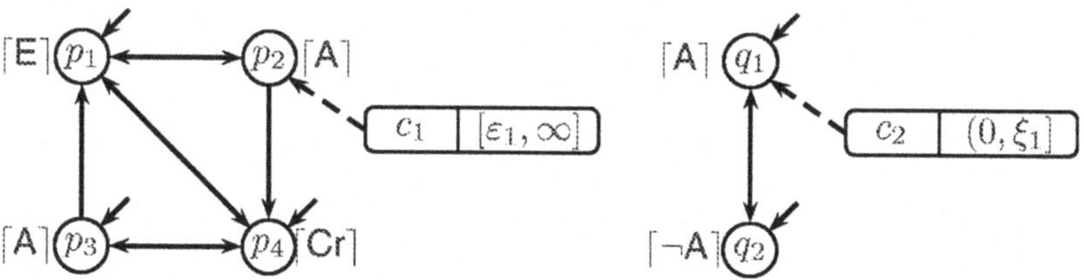

Fig. 1. Phase automaton for (1) and (2).

The property (2) is described by the right automaton in Fig. 1. The semantics of the parallel composition of these automata is simply the intersection of all interpretations of Track and Gate that belong to the semantics of the components. Thus, the parallel composition corresponds directly to the conjunction in Duration Calculus. The semantics of the cross product[2] of phase automata is equivalent to the semantics of the parallel composition. Phase automata without parameters can be transformed into timed automata [Mru00] and vice versa [Sch01].

3 Moby/DC

In Fig. 2 the specification of the GRC in MOBY/DC is presented. The description contains several text nodes with declarations of observables, parameters, and given constraints on those. Moreover, several phase automata are defined which either belong to the description of the system or describe *negated properties* of the system. Above we specified properties (1) and (2) by the phase automata in Fig. 1. Both are shown in Fig. 2 and named `Stab` resp. `Prog` with ε_1, ξ_1 as `e1` and `x1`.

In MOBY/DC each phase has as default a single clock with interval $(0, \infty]$ (written as `(0,w]`) allowing the system to stay there arbitrarily long — even forever. In case of $(0, \infty)$ the phase has to be left eventually. The requirements of the GRC are given in [HL94] as follows:

Safety: The gate is down during all occupancy intervals.
Utility: The gate is up if no train was crossing during the last ξ_2 seconds and no train will cross during the next ξ_1 seconds.

Both requirements are represented in Fig. 2 (`Safety` and `Utility`) as negations, i.e. as phase automata which express counter examples of these properties. The parameters ξ_1, ξ_2 (`x1`,`x2`) appear in `Utility` and in some of the specification automata.

The compositional model-checking algorithm is sketched in Fig. 3. It utilizes a function `isEmpty` that tests some sufficient conditions for emptiness. Hence, only the return value `true` is reliable. The procedure `minimise` applies reductions on a phase automaton which simplify the automaton in terms of phases and clocks. It returns a smaller automaton which possibly allows more behaviour.

[2] The syntactic cross product operation on phase automata is defined as expected except for the transition relation. Transitions (p, p') and (q, q') in the corresponding automata leads to transitions $((p, q), (p', q))$, $((p, q), (p, q'))$, *and* $((p, q), (p', q'))$.

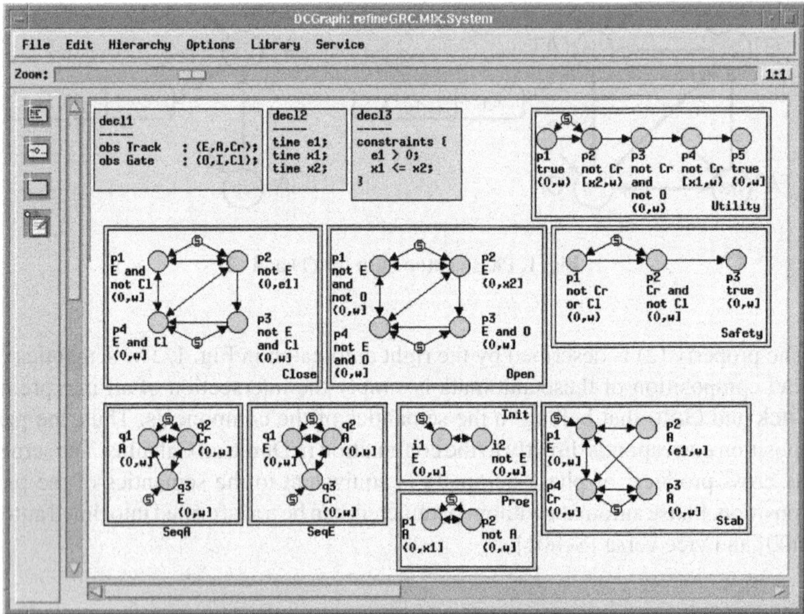

Fig. 2. A screenshot of MOBY/DC.

```
Procedure: semantics of 𝒜₁||...||𝒜ₙ = ∅?
Input: 𝒜₁,...,𝒜ₙ;
    𝒜 := 𝒜₁; i := 2;
    minimise(𝒜);
    while ( i ≤ n and not isEmpty(𝒜) ) do
        𝒜 := 𝒜 × 𝒜ᵢ; i := i + 1;
        minimise(𝒜);
    od
Output: isEmpty(𝒜);
```

Fig. 3. Basic model-checking algorithm

To prove that a system $\mathcal{A}_1 || \ldots || \mathcal{A}_k$ satisfies a requirement *Req*, the user has to provide a phase automaton $\mathcal{N}$ that describes (or overapproximates) $\neg Req$. If the model-checking computes that the semantics of $\mathcal{N} || \mathcal{A}_1 || \ldots || \mathcal{A}_k$ is empty, then the system satisfies *Req*. Due to the construction of `isEmpty` and `minimise` only the positive result is reliable, i.e. the tool might produce false-negatives but no false-positives.

Due to space limitations we cannot explain `isEmpty` and `minimise` in detail. The analysis of the parameters is done in `minimise` where the model-checker tries to find superfluous transitions and phases in the products. This is the place where (optionally) $CLP(R)$ is employed. Its input is a set of constraints over the parameters and a partial execution path of the product phase automaton. If $CLP(R)$ cannot find a solution of these constraints then the model-checker can identify a superfluous transition or phase.

4 Comparison

Now we use the GRC example for a performance comparison of MOBY/DC with the timed automata model-checker KRONOS (version 2.4.4[3]) and CMC (version 1.5). In order to apply the timed automata model-checkers we have to replace the parameters by concrete values. Therefore, we choose $\varepsilon_1 \stackrel{\text{df}}{=} 2$, $\xi_1 \stackrel{\text{df}}{=} 4$, and $\xi_2 \stackrel{\text{df}}{=} 4$ whereas MOBY/DC was working with the constraints $\varepsilon > 0$ and $\xi_1 \leq \xi_2$.

Table 1. Performance comparison for the GRC-example

phase automata	CMC	KRONOS	MOBY/DC
Safety, Close, SeqE, Init, Stab	1.5s	0.1s	0.7s
Safety, Close, SeqE, Init, Stab, Open, SeqA, Prog	2.1s	37.1s	0.7s
Safety, Open, SeqA, Prog, Close, SeqE, Init, Stab	29.8s	15.3s	0.9s
Utility, Open, SeqA, Prog, Stab	50.4s	0.2s	0.9s
Utility, Open, SeqA, Prog, Stab, Close, SeqE, Init	445.9s	5.3s	0.9s
Utility, Close, SeqE, Init, Open, SeqA, Prog, Stab	426.8s	8.3s	1.3s

Furthermore, we employ the translations of phase automata into timed automata [Mru00]. In both tools we check for the non-zenoness of the parallel composition of the timed automata. If it is non-zeno then the semantics is not empty. Both translations are similar and produce networks of timed automata instead of building the cross product. For this purpose the translations exploit the multisynchronisation concepts of the timed automata tools[4].

For the performance comparison we measured the execution times on an UltraSPARC-II with 296 MHz. The results are shown in Table 1. For both requirements we made checks with three different models. First we checked the smallest model which is necessary to prove the requirement. Then, we added the remaining automata which are not needed for the proof. Adding them at the end is better for the checkers which are based on compositional techniques. In contrast to CMC the performance of MOBY/DC is not at all influenced by automata added at the end. The reason for this difference is that CMC always examines the whole model and MOBY/DC can benefit from the monotonicity of the parallel composition of phase automata. KRONOS first builds the cross product of the given automata and then starts the reachability check. The KRONOS-entries in Table 1 comprises the time spent on model-checking and for building the cross product.

[3] using breadth first with the parameters -ai (inclusion abstraction) and -ax (extrapolation abstraction)

[4] Due to this fact the translations cannot be ported directly to Uppaal.

5 Related Work

Based on linear hybrid automata or parametric timed automata several tools have been developed: HyTech [HHW97] applies a semi-decision procedure on linear hybrid automata whereas LMPC [LTA98], TReX [ABS01] and a parametric extension of Uppaal work on parametric timed automata [HRSV02]. None of these tools apply compositional techniques for verification.

Acknowledgements. The authors thank E.-R. Olderog and the members of the "semantics group" in Oldenburg for fruitful discussions on the subject of this paper. Furthermore we thank the anonymous referees for their helpful suggestions and hints.

References

[ABS01] A. Annichini, A. Bouajjani, and M. Sighireanu. TReX: A Tool for Reachability Analysis of Complex Systems. In G. Berry, H. Comon, and A. Finkel, editors, *Proceedings of CAV 2001*, number 2102 in LNCS. Springer, 2001.

[And95] H.R. Andersen. Partial Model Checking. In *Proc. of the 10th Annual IEEE Symp. on Logic in Computer Science*, pages 398–407. IEEE Press, 1995.

[DD97] H. Dierks and C. Dietz. Graphical Specification and Reasoning: Case Study "Generalized Railroad Crossing". In J. Fitzgerald, C.B. Jones, and P. Lucas, editors, *FME'97*, volume 1313 of *LNCS*, pages 20–39, Graz, Austria, September 1997. Springer.

[HHW97] T.A. Henzinger, P.-H. Ho, and H. Wong-Toi. HyTech: a model checker for hybrid systems. *STTT*, 1(1+2):110–122, December 1997.

[HJM+92] N.C. Heintze, J. Jaffar, S. Michaylov, P.J. Stuckey, and R.H.C. Yap. *The CLP(R) Programmer's Manual, Version 1.2*, September 1992.

[HL94] C. Heitmeyer and N. Lynch. The Generalized Railroad Crossing. In *IEEE Real-Time Systems Symposium*, 1994.

[HRSV02] T. Hune, J. Romijn, M. Stoelinga, and F. Vaandrager. Linear Parametric Model Checking of Timed Automata. *Journal of Logic and Algebraic Programming*, 2002.

[HZ97] M.R. Hansen and Zhou Chaochen. Duration Calculus: Logical Foundations. *FAC*, 9:283–330, 1997.

[JM94] J. Jaffar and M. J. Maher. Constraint logic programming: A survey. *The Journal of Logic Programming*, 19/20:503–582, May–July 1994.

[LL98] F. Laroussinie and K.G. Larsen. CMC: A Tool for Compositional Model-Checking of Real-Time Systems. In *Proceedings of IFIP Joint Int. Conf. Formal Description Techniques & Protocol Specification, Testing, and Verification (FORTE-PSTV'98)*, pages 439–456. Kluwer Academic, November 1998.

[LTA98] R. Lutje Spelberg, H. Toetenel, and M. Ammerlaan. Partition Refinement in Real-Time Model Checking. In A.P. Ravn and H. Rischel, editors, *Formal Techniques in Real-Time and Fault-Tolerant Systems*, volume 1486 of *LNCS*, pages 143–157, Lyngby, Denmark, September 1998. Springer.

[Mru00] C. Mrugalla. Transformation of phase automata into timed automata. Master's thesis, University of Oldenburg, Department of Computer Science, Oldenburg, Germany, 2000. (in German).

[ORS96] E.-R. Olderog, A.P. Ravn, and J.U. Skakkebæk. Refining System Requirements to Program Specifications. In C. Heitmeyer and D. Mandrioli, editors, *Formal Methods for Real-Time Computing*, volume 5 of *Trends in Software*, pages 107–134. Wiley, 1996.

[Sch01] A. Schäfer. Fault tree analysis and real-time model-checking. Master's thesis, University of Oldenburg, Department of Computer Science, Oldenburg, Germany, 2001. (in German).

[Tap01] J. Tapken. *Model-Checking of Duration Calculus Specifications*. PhD thesis, University of Oldenburg, June 2001.

$\sqrt{}$erics: A Tool for Verifying Timed Automata and Estelle Specifications*

Piotr Dembiński[1], Agata Janowska[2], Paweł Janowski[2], Wojciech Penczek[1,5], Agata Półrola[3], Maciej Szreter[1], Bożena Woźna[4], and Andrzej Zbrzezny[4]

[1] Institute of Computer Science, PAS, Ordona 21, 01-237 Warsaw, Poland
{piotrd,penczek,mszreter}@ipipan.waw.pl
[2] Institute of Informatics, Warsaw University, Banacha 2, 02-097 Warsaw, Poland
{janowska,janowski}@mimuw.edu.pl
[3] Faculty of Mathematics, University of Lodz, Banacha 22, 90-238 Lodz, Poland
polrola@math.uni.lodz.pl
[4] Institute of Mathematics and Computer Science, Pedagogical University of Częstochowa, Armii Krajowej 13/15, 42-200 Częstochowa, Poland
{b.wozna,a.zbrzezny}@wsp.czest.pl
[5] Podlasie Academy, 3 Maja 54, 08-110 Siedlce, Poland

Abstract. The paper presents a new tool for automated verification of Timed Automata as well as protocols written in the specification language Estelle. The current version offers an automatic translation from Estelle specifications to timed automata, and two complementary methods of reachability analysis. The first one is based on Bounded Model Checking (BMC), while the second one is an on-the-fly verification on an abstract model of the system.

1 Introduction

We present a new tool for automated verification of Timed Automata as well as protocols written in the specification language Estelle. The main novelty of our tool consists in combining the translation from a subset of Estelle to Timed Automata [6] with the translation of the reachability problem for Timed Automata to the satisfiability problem of propositional formulas (SAT-problem) [20]. The latter problem is very efficiently solved by the SAT-solver ZChaff [13] that is exploited in our tool. Since the above approach is mainly applicable for finding errors, i.e., disproving safety properties, we extend our tool $\sqrt{}$erics with another module, which is used when the correctness is to be proved. This module is based on our original method [17] of building a pseudo-bisimulating model for a timed automaton, which preserves the reachability properties. Reachability over a pseudo-bisimulating model is checked on-the-fly, i.e., while building the model.

The architecture of $\sqrt{}$erics is composed of the following modules (see also Fig. 1):

* Partly supported by the State Committee for Scientific Research under the grant No. 8T11C 01419.

H. Garavel and J. Hatcliff (Eds.): TACAS 2003, LNCS 2619, pp. 278–283, 2003.

- **Language Translator** from the fragment of Estelle to the intermediate language,
- **TA Translator** from the intermediate language to timed automata,
- **BBMC Reachability Analyser** that verifies reachability properties over timed automata,
- **Splitter** that generates pseudo-bisimulating models for timed automata,
- **Verifier** that verifies reachability properties over pseudo-bisimulating models.

2 Related Tools

The high-level modelling languages, among which Estelle [10], SDL [11], and LOTOS [9] belong to most widely used, were defined to describe logical circuits, distributed systems and communication protocols. Many tools supporting design in these languages have been produced, but tools for formal verification still need to be developed. On the other hand, for a long time the model-checking tools have been designed for testing new scientific ideas, without paying much attention to their applicability for verification of real-world complex concurrent systems.

The first generation of model-checking tools consists of explicit state-space checkers, prone to the *state explosion problem*. Model checkers based on an explicit state space representation are still developed (SPIN [8], Kronos [21], Uppaal [2] etc.), exploiting various methods of overcoming this drawback. Another methodology is *symbolic model checking*, in which an explicit representation of states is replaced by a symbolic one. Symbolic representations in a form of decision diagrams are exploited in many packages, like Rabbit [3], SMV [12] and Uppaal2k [16]. The next branch of symbolic model checking tools, represented by NuSMV [5] and a MathSAT-related environment [18], is based on a concept of Bounded Model Checking.

Several solutions for integrating the above languages and tools have been proposed. IF [4] uses an intermediate language IF, to which higher-level specifications can be translated, enabling further verification using one of the above tools. Another example of a development environment is CADP [7], which allows to transform a LOTOS system description to the formats accepted by model checkers.

3 Theory Behind $\surd$erics

The theoretical background for our implementation has been presented in several papers [6,14,20]. In this section we sketch the main ideas.

Our tool accepts three kinds of input: specifications written in a subset of Estelle or in the intermediate language, or timed automata. **Estelle** [10] is an ISO standard specification language designed for describing communication protocols and distributed systems. The **intermediate language (IL)** [6] allows for describing a system as a set of processes, which exchange information by message passing (via bounded or unbounded channels) or memory sharing (using global variables). A process is described in terms of states and transitions similarly like in Estelle.

The translation from the subset of Estelle to the intermediate language is quite straightforward, as the execution models and the syntax of these formalisms are similar, although some Estelle language constructions require special and careful treatment. The details about the translation can be found in [6].

A system described in the intermediate language can be further translated either to a set of **timed automata** [1], each of which represents a component of the system, or to a global (product) **timed automaton** (for the description see [6]). The automata that are obtained are then passed to other components of $\surd$erics, which are aimed at performing reachability model checking.

Given a property p, reachability model checking consists in an exploration of the state space of the system, testing whether there exists a reachable state where p holds. Our tool offers two complementary methods of reachability analysis, the first of which is based on Bounded Model Checking (BMC) and a SAT-solver, while the second one is an on-the-fly verification on an abstract model of the system. The BMC-based method combines the well-known *forward reachability* analysis and the bounded model checking method for Timed Automata [14,15, 19,20]. The forward reachability algorithm searches the state space by moving from a state to its successors in the breadth-first mode, whereas BMC performs a verification on a part of the model exploiting a SAT-solver. The detailed description of the above method can be found in [19,20]. In case when no state satisfying a tested property is reachable, the SAT-based method can be ineffective. Therefore, in parallel to the BMC-based reachability analysis, $\surd$erics offers a verification method consisting in generating finite *abstract models* for Timed Automata (the pseudo-bisimulating ones [17]), using a partitioning algorithm, and performing an on-the-fly reachability verification. The detailed description of the above algorithm can be found in [17].

4 Tool Overview

As it has been already stated, $\surd$erics allows for an input in Estelle. Moreover, the system to be verified can be given in the intermediate language or in the form of timed automata in the Kronos-like format. Below, we present a short description of the case, where an Estelle specification is given as an input.

An Estelle specification is automatically translated to a description in the intermediate language (by the Language Translator). The obtained specification usually requires additional (manual) modifications, aimed at adding properties to states or bounds on sizes of buffers (all these features are not handled in the Estelle standard). Then, the enriched specification is passed to the TA Translator, which generates either a set of timed automata corresponding to the components of the system, or a global timed automaton. The automata are returned in the Kronos-like format. Then, they are passed to another component of $\surd$erics aimed at reachability model checking, i.e., BBMC or Splitter. The connection between the modules of $\surd$erics is presented in Fig. 1.

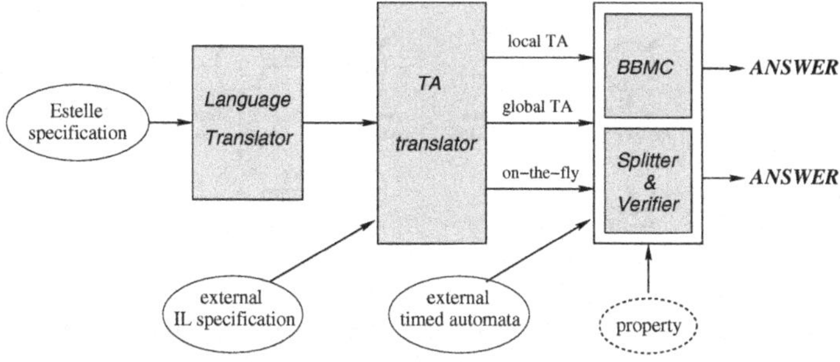

Fig. 1. The modules of $\surd$erics

5 Case Studies

We provide experimental results for three well-known examples: the Alternating Bit Protocol, Fischer's Mutual Exclusion Protocol and Railroad Crossing System (RCS). As the input for the first example we have used an Estelle specification. Two properties have been tested: "whenever the sender receives an acknowledgement and its bit is set to 0, then the receiver's bit is set to 0 as well" (false), and "whenever the sender receives an acknowledgement, its bit is set to 0 and the receiver managed to change its bit, then the receiver's bit is set to 0" (true). In

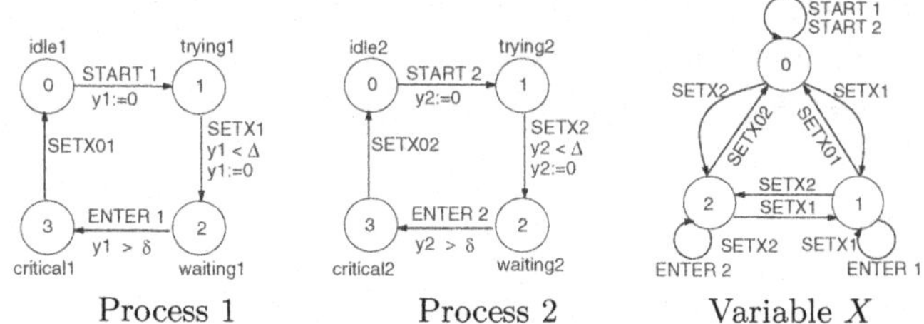

Fig. 2. Fischer's Mutual Exclusion Protocol for two processes

the case of the Mutual Exclusion Protocol we have used an input in the intermediate language. The timed automata returned by the $\surd$erics translation of this specification are presented in Fig. 2. We have tested them for various values of the parameters, as only if $\Delta < \delta$, then the mutual exclusion property is ensured. In case of the system RCS, the three system automata of the train, gate and controller, and the automaton for a property (see Fig. 3) have been used as the input. The property automaton describes that "whenever the gate is down it is moved back up within K seconds", which is satisfied for $K < 700$.

The experimental results are presented in Fig. 4. In all the examples, the BBMC Reachability Analyser has been used to show that a state satisfying a tested property is reachable, while the Splitter module has been applied to

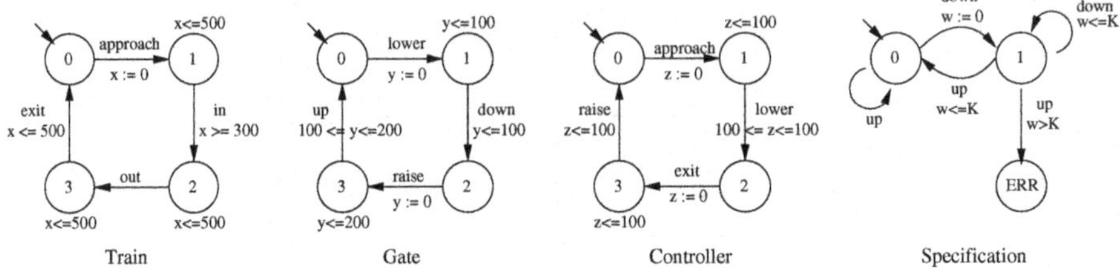

Fig. 3. The automata for the railroad crossing system and a specification

	Alternating Bit				Mutex							RCS				
	ARG		ZChaff					ARG		ZChaff			ARG		ZChaff	
	min	MB	min	MB	NP	δ	Δ	min	MB	min	MB	K	min	MB	min	MB
BBMC	0.21	1.38	0.16	5.62	39	1	2	34.30	382.10	168.3	684.8	500	0.67	5.94	0.08	10.62
	states		edges		NP	δ	Δ	states		edges		K	states		edges	
Splitter	2332		8267		5	2	1	9849		38545		800	18		24	

Fig. 4. Experimental results

generate the whole model of the system, i.e., to show that no state satisfying the property can be reached. We provide the times and the amounts of memory needed for BBMC Reachability Analyser to prove reachability of the state, and the sizes of pseudo-bisimulating models generated by Splitter. For the Mutual Exclusion Protocol, NP denotes the number of processes which have been tested.

A web page of our tool is available at
`http://www.ipipan.waw.pl/~penczek/verics`.

References

1. R. Alur and D. Dill. Automata for modelling real-time systems. In *Proc. of the International Colloquium on Automata, Languages and Programming (ICALP'90)*, volume 443 of *LNCS*, pages 322–335. Springer-Verlag, 1990.
2. J. Bengtsson, K. Larsen, F. Larsson, P. Pettersson, W. Yi, and C. Weise. New generation of UPPAAL. In *Proc. of the Int. Workshop on Software Tools for Technology Transfer*, 1998.
3. D. Beyer. Rabbit: Verification of real-time systems. In *Proc. of the Workshop on Real-Time Tools (RT-TOOLS'01)*, pages 13–21, 2001.
4. M. Bozga, J-C. Fernandez, L. Ghirvu, S. Graf, J.P. Krimm, L. Mounier, and J. Sifakis. IF: An intermediate representation for SDL and its applications. In *Proc. of SDL Forum'99*, pages 423–440, 1999.
5. A. Cimatti, E. M. Clarke, F. Giunchiglia, F. Giunchiglia, M. Pistore, M. Roveri, R. Sebastiani, and A. Tacchella. NuSMV 2: An open-source tool for symbolic model checking. In *Proc. of CAV'02*, volume 2404 of *LNCS*, pages 359–364. Springer-Verlag, 2002.

6. A. Doroś, A. Janowska, and P. Janowski. From specification languages to Timed Automata. In *Proc. of the Int. Workshop on Concurrency, Specification and Programming (CS&P'02)*, volume 161(1) of *Informatik-Berichte*, pages 117–128. Humboldt University, 2002.
7. H. Garavel, F. Lang, and R. Mateescu. An overview of CADP 2001. Technical Report RT-254, INRIA Rhône-Alpes, 655, avenue de l'Europe, 38330 Montbonnot-St-Martin, December 2001.
8. G. J. Holzmann. The model checker SPIN. *IEEE Trans. on Software Eng.*, 23(5):279–295, 1997.
9. ISO 8807 – information processing systems – Open System Interconnection. LOTOS – a formal description technique based on the temporal ordering of observational behaviour, 1989.
10. ISO/IEC 9074(E), Estelle – a formal description technique based on an extended state-transition model. International Standards Organization, 1997.
11. ITU-T Recommendation Z.100(11/99): Languages for telecommunication applications – Specification and Description Language, 1999.
12. K. McMillan. The SMV system. Technical Report CMU-CS-92-131, Carnegie-Mellon University, February 1992.
13. M. Moskewicz, C. Madigan, Y. Zhao, L. Zhang, and S. Malik. Chaff: Engineering an efficient SAT solver. In *Proc. of the 38th Design Automation Conference (DAC'01)*, pages 530–535, June 2001.
14. W. Penczek, B. Woźna, and A. Zbrzezny. SAT-based bounded model checking for the universal fragment of TCTL. Technical Report 947, ICS PAS, Ordona 21, 01-237 Warsaw, August 2002.
15. W. Penczek, B. Woźna, and A. Zbrzezny. Towards bounded model checking for the universal fragment of TCTL. In *Proc. of the 7th Int. Symp. on Formal Techniques in Real-Time and Fault Tolerant Systems (FTRTFT'02)*, volume 2469 of *LNCS*, pages 265–288. Springer-Verlag, 2002.
16. P. Pettersson and K. G. Larsen. UPPAAL2k. *Bulletin of the European Association for Theoretical Computer Science*, 70:40–44, February 2000.
17. A. Półrola, W. Penczek, and M. Szreter. Reachability analysis for Timed Automata based on partitioning. Technical report, ICS PAS, Ordona 21, 01-237 Warsaw, 2003. to appear.
18. R. Sebastiani. Integrating SAT solvers with math reasoners: Foundations and basic algorithms. Technical Report 0111-22, ITC-IRST, Sommarive 16, 38050 Povo, Trento, Italy, November 2001.
19. B. Woźna, W. Penczek, and A. Zbrzezny. Checking reachability properties for Timed Automata via SAT. Technical Report 949, ICS PAS, Ordona 21, 01-237 Warsaw, October 2002.
20. B. Woźna, W. Penczek, and A. Zbrzezny. Reachability for timed systems based on SAT-solvers. In *Proc. of the Int. Workshop on Concurrency, Specification and Programming (CS&P'02)*, volume 161(2) of *Informatik-Berichte*, pages 380–395. Humboldt University, 2002.
21. S. Yovine. KRONOS: A verification tool for real-time systems. *Springer International Journal of Software Tools for Technology Transfer*, 1(1/2):123–133, 1997.

A New Knowledge Representation Strategy for Cryptographic Protocol Analysis

Ivan Cibrario B.[1], Luca Durante[1], Riccardo Sisto[2], and Adriano Valenzano[1]

[1] Istituto di Elettronica e di Ingegneria dell'Informazione e delle Telecomunicazioni
c/o Politecnico di Torino, C.so Duca degli Abruzzi 24
I-10129 Torino, Italy
durante,valenzano,ivan.cibrario@polito.it
[2] Dipartimento di automatica e Informatica
Politecnico di Torino, C.so Duca degli Abruzzi 24
I-10129 Torino, Italy
sisto@polito.it

Abstract. The formal verification of security properties of a cryptographic protocol is a difficult, albeit very important task as more and more sensible resources are added to public networks. This paper is focused on model checking; when adopting this approach to the problem, one challenge is to represent the intruder's knowledge in an effective way. We present an intruder's knowledge representation strategy that supports the full term language of spi calculus and does not pose artificial restrictions, such as atomicity or limited maximum size, to language elements. In addition, our approach leads to practical implementation because the knowledge representation is incrementally computable and is easily amenable to work with various term representation languages.

1 Introduction

The formal verification of security properties of cryptographic protocols is a difficult task; one possible approach is to use model checking, which has already been explored in previous papers such as [5,8,10,11]. When using this approach, one of the challenges is to find a compact and efficient representation of the intruder's knowledge, which plays a central role in modeling the protocol behavior in an hostile environment, without sacrificing the expressive power of the specification language. Previous papers only give partial solutions to this problem, the most common approach being to restrict the way in which intruder messages can be built. For example, a common restriction is to force encryption keys to be atomic [5,16].

This paper presents a novel intruder's knowledge representation strategy that achieves both the goals of compactness and implementation efficiency; in particular, the proposed representation is largely independent from the term representation language chosen, i.e. supports all main cryptographic message contruction operators, including the full term language of spi calculus [1]. Moreover, it keeps

H. Garavel and J. Hatcliff (Eds.): TACAS 2003, LNCS 2619, pp. 284–298, 2003.

the intruder's knowledge in a minimized, canonical form, and is shown to be incrementally computable.

Having a canonical intruder's knowledge representation is especially important when state exploration techniques are used to check security properties. In fact, simpler non-canonical representations, such as for example the plain set of messages the intruder has access to when eavesdropping honest agents, may lead to state proliferation, because different sets of known messages may correspond to the same intruder knowledge. For example, knowing a symmetric key k and the encryption of a data item m under k is equivalent to knowing the cleartext m and k.

This representation has been used in a broader framework, presented in [9] and sketched in [8], where automatic testing equivalence verification of spi calculus specifications is described. There, the intruder's knowledge representation is further empowered by symbolic techniques; one of their functions is to prevent state space explosion associated with the intruder's ability to synthesize complex keys.

This paper presents the proposed intruder's knowledge representation by means of the spi calculus specification language. Since the expressive power of the message specification section of this language is better than or equivalent to the one of most other formalisms for cryptographic protocols, the adoption of spi calculus as our reference specification language is not restrictive.

The paper assumes that the reader is familiar with basic cryptography, and is structured as follows: section 2 presents the syntax of spi calculus, and informally describes its semantics. In section 3, we discuss our knowledge representation strategy, while in sections 4 and 5 we outline its computational complexity and work out some examples, respectively. Last, section 6 discusses related works and draws some conclusions.

2 Spi Calculus

The spi calculus is defined in [1] as an extension of the π calculus [15] with cryptographic primitives. It is a process algebraic language designed for describing and analyzing cryptographic protocols. These protocols heavily rely on cryptography and on message exchange through communication channels; accordingly, the spi calculus provides powerful primitives to express cryptography and communication.

This section summarizes the syntax and describes the language's semantics informally; the language used in this paper fully conforms to the spi calculus definition found in [1], with the naming conventions outlined in Tab. 1.

A spi calculus specification is a system of independent processes, executing in parallel; they synchronize via message-passing through named communication channels. The spi calculus has two basic language elements: terms, to represent data, and processes, to represent behaviors.

Terms can be either atomic elements, i.e. names, including the special name 0 representing the integer constant zero, and variables, or compound terms built

Table 1. Naming Conventions

m	ranges over names
x and y	range over variables
P, Q and R	range over processes
σ and ρ	range over terms
Σ	ranges over sets of terms

using the term composition operators listed in Tab. 2. Names may represent communication channels, atomic keys and key pairs, nonces (also called *fresh names*) and any other unstructured data.

If a term σ occurs as a sub-expression of another term ρ, then σ is called a *subterm* of ρ; moreover, any term σ is a subterm of itself.

Table 2. Term syntax of spi calculus

σ, ρ	terms
m	name
(σ, ρ)	pair
0	zero
$\mathrm{suc}(\sigma)$	successor
x	variable
$\mathrm{H}(\sigma)$	hashing
$\{\sigma\}_\rho$	shared-key encryption
σ^+, σ^-	public/private part
$\{[\sigma]\}_\rho$	public-key encryption
$[\{\sigma\}]_\rho$	private-key signature

The informal meaning of the composition operators is as follows:

- (σ, ρ) is the *pairing* of σ and ρ. It is a compound term whose components are σ and ρ. Pairs can always be freely split into their components.
- $\mathrm{suc}(\sigma)$ is the *successor* of σ. This operator has been introduced mainly to represent successors over integers, but it can be used, more generally, as the abstract representation of an invertible function on terms.
- $\mathrm{H}(\sigma)$ is the *hashing* of σ. $\mathrm{H}(\sigma)$ represents a function of σ that cannot be inverted.
- Term $\{\sigma\}_\rho$ is the ciphertext obtained by encrypting σ under key ρ using a shared-key cryptosystem.
- σ^+ and σ^- represent respectively the public and private half of a key pair σ. σ^+ cannot be deduced from σ^- and vice versa.
- $\{[\sigma]\}_\rho$ is the result of the public-key encryption of σ with ρ.
- $[\{\sigma\}]_\rho$ is the result of the signature (private key encryption) of σ with the private key ρ.

Besides term specification, spi calculus also offers a set of operators to build behavior expressions that, in turn, represent processes. For example, Fig. 1 shows the spi calculus specification of a very simple protocol inspired by [10]. The left hand side of the figure shows the message exchanges involved in the protocol, using the informal, intuitive representation often encountered in the literature, whereas the right hand side of the figure shows the corresponding spi calculus specification. In this protocol, two agents A and B sharing a secret key k and represented by spi calculus processes P_A and P_B, exchange two messages:

- First, A sends to B message M encrypted under key k over public channel c. This is represented, in spi calculus, by the output statement $\overline{c}\langle\{M\}_k\rangle$ in process P_A and by the corresponding input statement $c(y_1)$ in P_B; the latter statement assigns the datum just received to variable $y1$ of P_B.
- Then, B tries to decrypt the message with key k, as specified by the statement $case\ y_1\ of\ \{y_2\}_k$ in P_B and, when successful, sends back to A the hashed cleartext of M on the same channel c, with the output statement $\overline{c}\langle H(y_2)\rangle$. Process A receives this message with the input statement $c(x)$.
- Finally, A checks that the hash just received is correct with the statement $[x\ is\ H(M)]$ and proceeds with further operations on message M, represented by the unspecified process $F(M)$.

The role of the spi calculus process P_{sample} in the example is twofold:

- With the restriction operator (νk), it generates a restricted, private name k, only known to P_A, P_B and itself, to be used as the encryption key.
- It instantiates both P_A and P_B to run in parallel, by means of the parallel composition operator $|$, so that an instance of P_{sample} represents all agents involved in a session of the protocol.

$A \rightarrow B : \{M\}_k$	$P_A(M) \triangleq \overline{c}\langle\{M\}_k\rangle.\ c(x).\ [x\ is\ H(M)]\ F(M)$
$B \rightarrow A : H(M)$	$P_B \triangleq c(y_1).\ case\ y_1\ of\ \{y_2\}_k\ in\ \overline{c}\langle H(y_2)\rangle.\ 0$
	$P_{\text{sample}} \triangleq (\nu k)(P_A(M) \mid P_B)$

Fig. 1. A simple spi calculus specification

3 Intruder's Knowledge Representation

Our approach to the representation of the knowledge that an intruder can acquire borrows some of the notation and concepts introduced in [5], and has some similarities with [10] and [11] as section 6 points out; however, it is more sophisticated in some respects:

- encryption and decryption keys are not restricted to be atomic.
- we focus on spi calculus to its full extent, including public/private key cryptosystems, and the related operators.
- the intruder's knowledge is always kept in a minimized form that both speeds up and simplifies processing.

Moreover, as most other researchers do, our method relies on the following well-known, *perfect encryption* assumptions:

- to extract the cleartext m from the encrypted messages $\{m\}_k$, $\{[m]\}_{k^+}$ and $[\{m\}]_{k^-}$, the corresponding decryption keys k, k^- and k^+ must be known.
- the cryptosystem has enough redundancy so that the decryption algorithm can determine whether its task succeeded in, and to prevent encryption collisions.
- it is not possible for an attacker to guess or forge any secret data item.

The intruder's model we adopted is the so-called *Dolev-Yao model*, and has been inspired by [7]. In other words, we assume that the intruder is able to:

- eavesdrop on, remove, replay and arbitrarily reorder messages sent over public communication channels.
- forge new messages with the pieces of messages already intercepted, possibly from previous protocol sessions, and inject them into the public channels.
- generate its own nonces.
- decrypt encrypted messages, provided it has got the appropriate key, and split compound cleartext messages into pieces.

Let $\mathcal{A}$ be the set of spi calculus names, including the integer constant 0, and $\mathcal{M}(\mathcal{A})$ the set of all spi calculus terms that can be built by combining the elements of $\mathcal{A}$ by means of the operators defined in Tab. 2. For simplicity, and without loss of generality, name overloading is forbidden, i.e. it is assumed that distinct elements are always identified by distinct names.

The closure of a set of terms $\Sigma \subseteq \mathcal{M}(\mathcal{A})$ is denoted $\widehat{\Sigma}$ and is defined as the set of all spi calculus terms that can be built by combining the elements of Σ by means of the operators defined in Tab. 2 and their inverses. Formally, $\widehat{\Sigma}$ is the least set of terms such that, for each σ, σ_1 and $\sigma_2 \in \mathcal{M}(\mathcal{A})$, the following closure rules hold:

$$\sigma \in \Sigma \quad \Rightarrow \sigma \in \widehat{\Sigma} \tag{1}$$

$$\sigma \in \widehat{\Sigma} \quad \Rightarrow \quad \mathrm{suc}(\sigma) \in \widehat{\Sigma} \quad \text{(successor)} \tag{2}$$

$$\sigma_1 \in \widehat{\Sigma} \wedge \sigma_2 \in \widehat{\Sigma} \quad \Rightarrow \quad (\sigma_1,\, \sigma_2) \in \widehat{\Sigma} \quad \text{(pairing)} \tag{3}$$

$$\sigma_1 \in \widehat{\Sigma} \wedge \sigma_2 \in \widehat{\Sigma} \quad \Rightarrow \quad \{\sigma_1\}_{\sigma_2} \in \widehat{\Sigma} \quad \text{(sh. key encryption)} \tag{4}$$

$$\sigma \in \widehat{\Sigma} \quad \Rightarrow \quad \mathrm{H}(\sigma) \in \widehat{\Sigma} \quad \text{(hashing)} \tag{5}$$

$$\sigma_1 \in \widehat{\Sigma} \wedge \sigma_2^+ \in \widehat{\Sigma} \quad \Rightarrow \quad \{[\sigma_1]\}_{\sigma_2^+} \in \widehat{\Sigma} \quad \text{(pub. key encryption)} \tag{6}$$

$$\sigma_1 \in \widehat{\Sigma} \wedge \sigma_2^- \in \widehat{\Sigma} \quad \Rightarrow \quad [\{\sigma_1\}]_{\sigma_2^-} \in \widehat{\Sigma} \quad \text{(private key signature)} \tag{7}$$

$$\sigma \in \widehat{\Sigma} \quad \Rightarrow \sigma^+ \in \widehat{\Sigma} \wedge \sigma^- \in \widehat{\Sigma} \quad \text{(key projection)} \tag{8}$$

$$\mathrm{suc}(\sigma) \in \widehat{\Sigma} \Rightarrow \sigma \in \widehat{\Sigma} \quad \text{(prec)} \tag{9}$$

$$(\sigma_1,\, \sigma_2) \in \widehat{\Sigma} \Rightarrow \sigma_1 \in \widehat{\Sigma} \wedge \sigma_2 \in \widehat{\Sigma} \quad \text{(projection)} \tag{10}$$

$$\{\sigma_1\}_{\sigma_2} \in \widehat{\Sigma} \wedge \sigma_2 \in \widehat{\Sigma} \Rightarrow \sigma_1 \in \widehat{\Sigma} \quad \text{(sh. key decryption)} \tag{11}$$

$$\{[\sigma_1]\}_{\sigma_2^+} \in \widehat{\Sigma} \wedge \sigma_2^- \in \widehat{\Sigma} \Rightarrow \sigma_1 \in \widehat{\Sigma} \quad \text{(pub. key decryption)} \tag{12}$$

$$\{[\sigma_1]\}_{\sigma_2^-} \in \widehat{\Sigma} \wedge \sigma_2^+ \in \widehat{\Sigma} \Rightarrow \sigma_1 \in \widehat{\Sigma} \quad \text{(signature check)} \tag{13}$$

$$\sigma^+ \in \widehat{\Sigma} \wedge \sigma^- \in \widehat{\Sigma} \Rightarrow \sigma \in \widehat{\Sigma} \quad \text{(key pairing)} \tag{14}$$

In principle, if Σ is the set of messages the intruder has intercepted so far, the generation of individual elements of $\widehat{\Sigma}$ (informally, the set of all messages the intruder can generate at a given point) starting from Σ can be viewed as a derivation in a natural deduction system [17].

In this respect, closure rule (1) represents the ability to derive an element from itself, closure rules (2)-(8) are equivalent to the introduction rules of the natural deduction system ($\mathcal{I}$ rules), and closure rules (9)-(14) are equivalent to its elimination rules ($\mathcal{E}$ rules).

For example, using the rule notation of [17], closure rule (4) is equivalent to the introduction rule:

$$\frac{\sigma_1 \quad \sigma_2}{\{\sigma_1\}_{\sigma_2}} \ \{\}\text{-}\mathcal{I} \text{ rule} \ . \tag{15}$$

Informally, we can read this rule as: "when both σ_1 and σ_2 are known to the intruder, then the intruder also knows about $\{\sigma_1\}_{\sigma_2}$."

Similarly, closure rule (11) is equivalent to the elimination rule:

$$\frac{\{\sigma_1\}_{\sigma_2} \ \sigma_2}{\sigma_1} \ \{\}\text{-}\mathcal{E} \text{ rule} \ . \tag{16}$$

Informally, we can read this rule as: "when the intruder knows both $\{\sigma_1\}_{\sigma_2}$ and σ_2, then it can succesfully perform a decryption and add σ_1 to its knowledge."

In an elimination rule, the premise that contains the operator removed by the rule is called the *major premise*, while all other premises are called *minor premises*. For example, in rule (16), $\{\sigma_1\}_{\sigma_2}$ is the major premise and σ_2 is the minor premise.

The theory of natural deduction [17] implies that, if $\sigma \in \widehat{\Sigma}$, then σ can be deduced from Σ with a *natural* deduction in *normal* form, that is, a chain of applications of $\mathcal{E}$ rules followed by a chain of applications of $\mathcal{I}$ rules, along the rules' major premises. This is not necessarily true along minor premises, so the closure of Σ under $\mathcal{E}$ rules only is not a suitable candidate to represent the intruder's knowledge, unless some additional constraints are imposed, such as the atomicity of encryption keys; this is exactly the approach adopted, for example, in [5,16]. In the following, we show that this difficulty can be overcome by introducing the concept of *minimal closure seed of* Σ and by suitably refining the derivation rules of the deduction system.

We say that a set of terms is *finite* if it contains a finite number of finite length elements. Given a finite set of terms Σ, we define the *minimal closure seed of* Σ, and denote it as $\overline{\Sigma}$, the subset of $\widehat{\Sigma}$ that satisfies the following predicates for each $a \in \mathcal{A}$, and for each σ, σ_1, $\sigma_2 \in \mathcal{M}(\mathcal{A})$:

$$a \in \overline{\Sigma} \quad \Leftrightarrow \quad a \in \widehat{\Sigma} \tag{17}$$

$$\mathrm{suc}(\sigma) \notin \overline{\Sigma} \tag{18}$$

$$(\sigma_1, \sigma_2) \notin \overline{\Sigma} \tag{19}$$

$$\{\sigma_1\}_{\sigma_2} \in \overline{\Sigma} \quad \Leftrightarrow \quad \sigma_2 \notin \widehat{\Sigma} \tag{20}$$

$$\mathrm{H}(\sigma) \in \overline{\Sigma} \quad \Leftrightarrow \quad \sigma \notin \widehat{\Sigma} \tag{21}$$

$$\{[\sigma_1]\}_{\sigma_2^+} \in \overline{\Sigma} \quad \Leftrightarrow \quad \sigma_2^+ \notin \widehat{\Sigma} \vee \sigma_1 \notin \widehat{\Sigma} \tag{22}$$

$$[\{\sigma_1\}]_{\sigma_2^-} \in \overline{\Sigma} \quad \Leftrightarrow \quad \sigma_2^- \notin \widehat{\Sigma} \vee \sigma_1 \notin \widehat{\Sigma} \tag{23}$$

$$\sigma^+ \in \overline{\Sigma} \quad \Leftrightarrow \quad \sigma \notin \widehat{\Sigma} \tag{24}$$

$$\sigma^- \in \overline{\Sigma} \quad \Leftrightarrow \quad \sigma \notin \widehat{\Sigma} \tag{25}$$

For example, if $\Sigma = \{\{[m]\}_{a^+}, a^-\}$, then $\overline{\Sigma} = \{\{[m]\}_{a^+}, a^-, m\}$, because:

- $a^- \in \overline{\Sigma}$, by rule (25), because $a \notin \widehat{\Sigma}$ and is therefore impossible to represent the key pair (a^+, a^-) with the key name a alone.
- $m \in \overline{\Sigma}$: since $a^- \in \overline{\Sigma} \subset \widehat{\Sigma}$, then a^- can be used to decrypt $\{[m]\}_{a^+}$, by rule (12). Then, being m a name, by rule (17), $m \in \overline{\Sigma}$.
- $\{[m]\}_{a^+} \in \overline{\Sigma}$, by rule (22), because $a^+ \notin \widehat{\Sigma}$, so there is no way to construct $\{[m]\}_{a^+}$ starting from other members of $\overline{\Sigma}$.

Before discussing the basic properties of $\overline{\Sigma}$, let us preliminarily define $\mathtt{r}(\sigma, \Sigma)$ as the boolean value obtained by executing the following algorithm:

```
boolean r(σ, Σ) {
  if σ ∈ Σ                  then return TRUE;
  else if σ = suc(σ₁)       then return r(σ₁, Σ);
  else if σ = (σ₁, σ₂)      then return r(σ₁, Σ) ∧ r(σ₂, Σ);
  else if σ = {σ₁}σ₂        then return r(σ₁, Σ) ∧ r(σ₂, Σ);
  else if σ = H(σ₁)         then return r(σ₁, Σ);
  else if σ = {[σ₁]}σ₂⁺     then return r(σ₁, Σ) ∧ r(σ₂⁺, Σ);
  else if σ = [{σ₁}]σ₂⁻     then return r(σ₁, Σ) ∧ r(σ₂⁻, Σ);
  else if σ = σ₁⁺           then return r(σ₁, Σ);
  else if σ = σ₁⁻           then return r(σ₁, Σ);
  else (σ ∈ A \ Σ)          return FALSE;
}
```

Informally, this algorithm recursively checks whether σ can be deduced from the set Σ using *introduction* rules (2)-(7) only; in this respect, an introduction rules is a rule that builds a new term by introducing an operator between one or more simpler terms. The basic properties of $\overline{\Sigma}$ are then expressed by the following theorems:

Theorem 1. *(Finiteness) For each finite set of terms $\Sigma \subseteq \mathcal{M}(\mathcal{A})$, $\overline{\Sigma}$ is finite.*

Proof. By inspection of rules (17)-(25) it is clear that any structured element of $\overline{\Sigma}$ has at least a subterm that does not belong to $\widehat{\Sigma}$, i.e. a subterm that cannot be built by combining the elements of Σ. This means that any element of $\overline{\Sigma}$ is necessarily a subterm of an element of Σ. But since Σ is finite, the subterms of its elements are also finite. This implies that $\overline{\Sigma}$ is finite. □

Theorem 2. *(Minimality) Let $\Sigma \subseteq \mathcal{M}(\mathcal{A})$ be a finite set of terms, and $\sigma \in \overline{\Sigma}$. Then $\widehat{(\overline{\Sigma} \setminus \{\sigma\})} \subset \widehat{\overline{\Sigma}}$.*

Proof. From rules (1)-(14) it is clear that $\widehat{(\overline{\Sigma} \setminus \{\sigma\})} \subseteq \widehat{\overline{\Sigma}}$. So, it is enough to show that there is at least an element of $\widehat{\overline{\Sigma}}$ that does not belong to $\widehat{(\overline{\Sigma} \setminus \{\sigma\})}$. Such an element is σ. It belongs to $\widehat{\overline{\Sigma}}$ by rule (1), but it does not belong to $\widehat{(\overline{\Sigma} \setminus \{\sigma\})}$ because by rules (17)-(25) it is either a name or a structured term with at least a subterm that cannot be built from the elements of $\widehat{\Sigma}$ (which includes $\widehat{\overline{\Sigma}}$ by definition). □

Theorem 3. *(Decidability) Let $\sigma \in \mathcal{M}(\mathcal{A})$ be any finite term, $\Sigma \subseteq \mathcal{M}(\mathcal{A})$ be a finite set of terms, and let us assume that $\overline{\Sigma}$ is known. Then, determining if $\sigma \in \widehat{\Sigma}$ is decidable.*

Proof. We claim that $\sigma \in \widehat{\Sigma}$ iff $\mathbf{r}(\sigma, \overline{\Sigma})$ is true. This claim can be proved by induction, proving directly the cases $\sigma \in \overline{\Sigma}$ and $\sigma \in \mathcal{A} \setminus \overline{\Sigma}$, and proceeding inductively for the other cases. Once the claim is proved, it remains to be shown that the computation of $\mathbf{r}(\sigma, \overline{\Sigma})$ takes a finite number of steps, but this descends directly from the fact that σ and $\overline{\Sigma}$ are finite, and at each recursion step the function $\mathbf{r}$ is invoked on proper subterms of its argument σ. □

The minimal closure seed $\overline{\Sigma}$ enjoys some additional properties, that make it a good candidate as a finite and minimized representation of the term generation capabilities of an intruder that has learned the set of terms Σ:

Theorem 4. *(Closure preservation) For each finite set of terms $\Sigma \subseteq \mathcal{M}(\mathcal{A})$, $\widehat{\overline{\Sigma}} = \widehat{\Sigma}$.*

Theorem 5. *(Computability) For each finite set of terms $\Sigma \subseteq \mathcal{M}(\mathcal{A})$, $\overline{\Sigma}$ can be computed in a finite number of steps.*

An obvious corollary of the above theorems is:

Corollary 1. *Let $\sigma \in \mathcal{M}(\mathcal{A})$ be any finite term and $\Sigma \subseteq \mathcal{M}(\mathcal{A})$ be a finite set of terms. Then, determining whether $\sigma \in \widehat{\Sigma}$ is decidable.*

Proof. We claim that the computation of $\overline{\Sigma}$ from Σ can be carried out by repeatedly applying closure rules (1)-(14). More precisely, let us define a *reduction rule* as a triple $R = \langle \Sigma_I,\ C,\ \Sigma_O \rangle$, where Σ_I and Σ_O are sets of terms representing respectively premises and conclusions of closure rule C.

Applying reduction step R to a finite set of terms Σ means eliminating the premises from and adding the conclusions to Σ. This is written $\Sigma \xrightarrow{R} \Sigma'$, where $\Sigma' = (\Sigma \setminus \Sigma_I) \cup \Sigma_O$ is the resulting set.

Given a finite set of terms Σ, a *reduction of* Σ is a finite sequence of application of reduction rules R_i to finite sets of terms Σ_i, denoted:

$$\Sigma_0 \xrightarrow{R_0} \Sigma_1 \xrightarrow{R_1} \Sigma_2 \ \cdots \ \Sigma_{k-1} \xrightarrow{R_{k-1}} \Sigma_k \ ,$$

such that $\Sigma_0 = \Sigma$ and $R_i \in \mathcal{R}(\Sigma_i)$, where $\mathcal{R}(\Sigma_i)$ is the set of reduction rules whose pre-conditions are satisfied by Σ_i. Below, the notation $a \to b$ means that if the pre-condition a is true, then the reduction rule b can be applied in Σ_i, that is, $b \in \mathcal{R}(\Sigma_i)$. The set $\mathcal{R}(\Sigma_i)$ is the least set such that the following relations hold:

$$\mathrm{H}(\sigma) \in \Sigma_i \ \wedge \ \mathtt{r}(\sigma, \Sigma_i) \to \langle \{\mathrm{H}(\sigma)\}, (5), \emptyset \rangle \tag{26}$$

$$\begin{array}{r} \{[\sigma_1]\}_{\sigma_2^+} \in \Sigma_i \\ \wedge\, \mathtt{r}(\sigma_1, \Sigma_i) \ \wedge \ \mathtt{r}(\sigma_2^+, \Sigma_i) \end{array} \to \langle \{\{[\sigma_1]\}_{\sigma_2^+}\}, (6), \emptyset \rangle \tag{27}$$

$$\begin{array}{r} [\{\sigma_1\}]_{\sigma_2^-} \in \Sigma_i \\ \wedge\, \mathtt{r}(\sigma_1, \Sigma_i) \ \wedge \ \mathtt{r}(\sigma_2^-, \Sigma_i) \end{array} \to \langle \{[\{\sigma_1\}]_{\sigma_2^-}\}, (7), \emptyset \rangle \tag{28}$$

$$\sigma^+ \in \Sigma_i \ \wedge \ \mathtt{r}(\sigma, \Sigma_i) \to \langle \{\sigma^+\}, (8), \emptyset \rangle \tag{29}$$

$$\sigma^- \in \Sigma_i \ \wedge \ \mathtt{r}(\sigma, \Sigma_i) \to \langle \{\sigma^-\}, (8), \emptyset \rangle \tag{30}$$

$$\mathrm{suc}(\sigma) \in \Sigma_i \to \langle \{\mathrm{suc}(\sigma)\}, (9), \{\sigma\} \rangle \tag{31}$$

$$(\sigma_1, \sigma_2) \in \Sigma_i \to \langle \{(\sigma_1, \sigma_2)\}, (10), \{\sigma_1, \sigma_2\} \rangle \tag{32}$$

$$\{\sigma_1\}_{\sigma_2} \in \Sigma_i \ \wedge \ \mathtt{r}(\sigma_2, \Sigma_i) \to \langle \{\{\sigma_1\}_{\sigma_2}\}, (11), \{\sigma_1\} \rangle \tag{33}$$

$$\begin{array}{r} \{[\sigma_1]\}_{\sigma_2^+} \in \Sigma_i \\ \wedge\, \mathtt{r}(\sigma_2^-, \Sigma_i) \ \wedge \ \neg\mathtt{r}(\sigma_1, \Sigma_i) \end{array} \to \langle \{\{[\sigma_1]\}_{\sigma_2^+}\}, (12), \{\sigma_1, \{[\sigma_1]\}_{\sigma_2^+}\} \rangle \tag{34}$$

$$\begin{array}{r} [\{\sigma_1\}]_{\sigma_2^-} \in \Sigma_i \\ \wedge\, \mathtt{r}(\sigma_2^+, \Sigma_i) \ \wedge \ \neg\mathtt{r}(\sigma_1, \Sigma_i) \end{array} \to \langle \{[\{\sigma_1\}]_{\sigma_2^-}\}, (13), \{\sigma_1, [\{\sigma_1\}]_{\sigma_2^-}\} \rangle \tag{35}$$

$$\sigma^+ \in \Sigma_i \ \wedge \ \sigma^- \in \Sigma_i \to \langle \{\sigma^+, \sigma^-\}, (14), \{\sigma\} \rangle \tag{36}$$

It can be shown by inspection that reductions preserve closures, i.e. that the following proposition holds:

Proposition 1. *if* $\Sigma \xrightarrow{R} \Sigma'$ *is a one-step reduction, then* $\widehat{\Sigma} = \widehat{\Sigma'}$.

Our initial claim can be proved by proving the following proposition:

Proposition 2. *Given a finite set of terms* Σ*, there exists a finite reduction of* Σ*:*

$$\Sigma = \Sigma_0 \xrightarrow{R_0} \Sigma_1 \cdots \Sigma_{k-1} \xrightarrow{R_{k-1}} \Sigma_k \ ,$$

such that $\Sigma_k = \overline{\Sigma}$.

A reduction that leads from Σ to $\overline{\Sigma}$ can be found if we keep applying reduction rules $R_i \in \mathcal{R}(\Sigma_i)$ as long as some can be applied. It can be verified by inspection that reduction rules $R_i \in \mathcal{R}(\Sigma_i)$ always add subterms of terms that are already included in Σ_i, and that the application of each $R_i \in \mathcal{R}(\Sigma_i)$ cannot produce loops. Since Σ is finite, it is guaranteed that in a finite number of steps we reach a Σ_k on which no reduction rule can be applied. When this happens, $\Sigma_k = \overline{\Sigma}$, because all the pre-conditions of relations (26)-(36) are false, which implies that Σ_k satisfies the minimal closure seed definition predicates (17)-(25).

Theorem 4 directly descends from propositions 1 and 2, while theorem 5 descends from the above two propositions and from the fact that the computation of $\mathbf{r}(\sigma, \Sigma_i)$ takes a finite number of steps. □

In analogy with the natural deduction system, and unlike [5], we allow *both* $\mathcal{I}$ and $\mathcal{E}$ rules to be applied in the computation of $\overline{\Sigma}$ from Σ, under the constraint of their pre-condition and at the expense of a greater computational complexity, which will be analyzed in section 4. However, as entailed by these theorems, this approach does neither sacrifice decidability nor computability.

Theorems 1, 2 and 4 state that the closure seed representation of a finite set of terms Σ is finite and is the minimal set of terms having the same closure of Σ, where minimality means that any element cannot be built from the other ones by means of term composition operators only, i.e. there are no redundant elements. This is a significant departure from the approach of [11,14], whose methods accumulate all the terms the intruder knows about without aiming to minimize their representation.

The proof of theorems 4 and 5 entails that if a new term ρ is added to a minimal closure seed $\overline{\Sigma}$, e.g. as a consequence of an output process, the new minimal closure seed $\overline{\overline{\Sigma} \cup \{\rho\}}$ can be incrementally computed by a reduction that starts from $\overline{\Sigma} \cup \{\rho\}$, without restarting from scratch; it can be expected that the incremental computation is far less expensive in terms of computing power.

In general, the net effect of such a reduction is to eliminate some elements from and add some other new elements to the former $\overline{\Sigma}$. We denote $\delta^{-}_{\overline{\Sigma}}(\rho)$ the set of eliminated elements and $\delta^{+}_{\overline{\Sigma}}(\rho)$ the set of added elements. Formally:

$$\delta^{-}_{\overline{\Sigma}}(\rho) = \overline{\Sigma} \setminus \left(\overline{\overline{\Sigma} \cup \{\rho\}}\right) \tag{37}$$

$$\delta^{+}_{\overline{\Sigma}}(\rho) = \left(\overline{\overline{\Sigma} \cup \{\rho\}}\right) \setminus \overline{\Sigma} \tag{38}$$

Let us now define formally how the intruder's knowledge representation is updated when a new term ρ is received by the intruder: an algorithm that computes the updated intruder's knowledge $\overline{\Sigma'}$ is the one that computes a reduction of

$\overline{\Sigma} \cup \{\rho\}$, thus determining $\delta^{+}_{\overline{\Sigma}}(\rho)$ and $\delta^{-}_{\overline{\Sigma}}(\rho)$ as sketched in the proof of theorems 4 and 5, then computes $\overline{\Sigma'} = (\overline{\Sigma} \cup \delta^{+}_{\overline{\Sigma}}(\rho)) \setminus \delta^{-}_{\overline{\Sigma}}(\rho)$.

We have now shown that $\overline{\Sigma}$ is an adequate, minimal representation of the intruder's knowledge, it is incrementally computable, and the question $\sigma \in \widehat{\Sigma}$ is decidable $\forall \sigma \in \mathcal{M}(\mathcal{A})$. So, given an intruder knowledge $\overline{\Sigma}$ and a finite term $\sigma \in \mathcal{M}(\mathcal{A})$, we can say that the intruder can produce σ iff $\sigma \in \widehat{\overline{\Sigma}}$, i.e. iff $\mathtt{r}(\sigma, \overline{\Sigma})$.

4 Computational Complexity

4.1 On the Computation of the Question $\sigma \in \Sigma$

In this and in the following sections, let $\mathrm{op}(\sigma)$ be the number of operators in term σ and $\mathrm{n}(\Sigma)$ the number of elements in set Σ. Moreover, we extend the domain of the operator $\mathrm{op}(\cdot)$ to sets of terms, by defining it as:

$$\mathrm{op}(\Sigma) = \max_{\sigma \in \Sigma}(\mathrm{op}(\sigma))$$

in that case. Assuming that the comparison between atomic terms can be carried out in constant time, and the lookup of a term in Σ is sequential, then the computational complexity to check whether $\sigma \in \Sigma$ is $O(nm)$, where $n = \mathrm{n}(\Sigma)$ and $m = \mathrm{op}(\sigma)$.

4.2 On the Computation of $\mathtt{r}(\sigma, \Sigma)$

The worst case happens when the operator's tree in σ is fully unbalanced, that is, each invocation of $\mathtt{r}(\sigma, \Sigma)$ on a compound term σ with m operators entails the recursive computation of $\mathtt{r}(\sigma_1, \Sigma)$ and $\mathtt{r}(\sigma_2, \Sigma)$, where σ_1 is atomic, and σ_2 has $m-1$ operators.

In this case, each recursion step executes in $O(nm)$, where $n = \mathrm{n}(\Sigma)$ and $m = \mathrm{op}(\sigma)$ as shown above, and the recursion depth is m. So, the computational complexity of $\mathtt{r}(\sigma, \Sigma)$ is $O(nm^2)$, as it has also been proven in [13], in the more general framework of local inference rule sets.

4.3 On the Incremental Computation of $\overline{\Sigma}$

For the sake of this discussion, and without loss of generality, let us define a *reduction step* as the simultaneous application of all independent reduction rules and let us denote it with $\rightarrow$. The incremental reduction of $\overline{\Sigma}$ after the addition of the new term ρ can be seen as a finite sequence of reduction steps starting from $\overline{\Sigma} \cup \{\rho\} = \Sigma_0$; reduction step i acts on set Σ_i and produces the (partially) reduced set Σ_{i+1}:

$$\overline{\Sigma} \cup \{\rho\} = \Sigma_0 \rightarrow \ldots \rightarrow \Sigma_i \rightarrow \Sigma_{i+1} \rightarrow \ldots$$

Let $n_i = \mathrm{n}(\Sigma_i)$ be the number of terms in Σ_i, and $m_i = \mathrm{op}(\Sigma_i)$ the maximum number of operators of terms in Σ_i. Then, we have the initial condition:

$$\begin{cases} n_0 = \mathrm{n}(\overline{\Sigma} \cup \{\rho\}) \\ m_0 = \mathrm{op}(\overline{\Sigma} \cup \{\rho\}) \end{cases}$$

In the worst case, up to n_i reduction rules can be applied at step i, one for each term in Σ_i; assuming that we can determine which reduction rule must be applied in constant time, each application of such rule entails one invocation of the $\in$ operator and up to two invocations of $\mathtt{r}(\cdot,\cdot)$; therefore, each application of a reduction rule at reduction step i has a computational complexity of $O(n_i m_i) + O(n_i m_i^2) = O(n_i m_i^2)$, and the computational complexity of reduction step i is $O(n_i^2 m_i^2)$.

At each reduction step i, whenever we remove a term a from Σ_i, and add some other terms $a_1 \ldots a_n$ derived from it, the added terms will always have one operator less than the term they originated from, that is, $\mathrm{op}(\{a_1 \ldots a_n\}) = \mathrm{op}(a) - 1$.

Therefore, as a result of reduction step i we remove n_i terms with m_i operators and add up to $2n_i$ terms with up to $m_i - 1$ operators; rules (34) and (35) are the only exceptions in this respect, because they do not remove any term. However, their application does not lead to the worst-case complexity because they leave in Σ_{i+1} the compound term $\{[\sigma_1]\}_{\sigma_2^+}$ or $\{[\sigma_1]\}_{\sigma_2^-}$ that cannot be further reduced, because $\sigma_1 \in \Sigma_{i+1}$ as a consequence of the application of the rule itself. So, we can write:

$$\begin{cases} n_{i+1} = 2n_i \\ m_{i+1} = m_i - 1 \end{cases}$$

After a maximum of m_0 reduction steps, Σ_{m_0} is reduced to contain only atoms and no further reductions are possible. So the computational complexity of the reduction as a whole is:

$$\sum_{i=0}^{m_0} O(n_i^2 m_i^2) = \sum_{i=0}^{m_0} O((2^i n_0)^2 (m_0 - i)^2) = O(n_0^2 2^{2m_0}) \ . \tag{39}$$

4.4 Comparison with Normal, Natural Deductions

When we assume that encryption keys are atomic, neglect public/private cryptosystems, and restrict our scope to normal, natural deductions only, as in [5], we can replace all invocations of $\mathtt{r}(\sigma, \Sigma)$ in pre-conditions (26)-(36) with the simpler check $\sigma \in \Sigma$, and we can drop out reduction rules (27)-(30) and (34)-(36).

Accordingly, the complexity of a reduction step as defined in the previous section is reduced to $O(n_i m_i)$, because function $\mathtt{r}(\cdot,\cdot)$ is never invoked in this case. So, the complexity of the reduction process as a whole reduces to:

$$\sum_{i=0}^{m_0} O(n_i m_i^2) = \sum_{i=0}^{m_0} O(2^i n_0 (m_0 - i)^2) = O(n_0 2^{m_0}) \ . \tag{40}$$

5 Examples

As an example, let us start with the minimal closure seed

$$\overline{\Sigma} = \{c, \{\{k_1\}_{k_2}\}_{k_3}, \{[m]\}_{k_1{}^+}, k_1{}^+, k_2\} \ ,$$

and let us observe the reduction process described above when the new term $\rho = k_3$ is added; in Tab. 3 the second column lists the contents of the partially reduced sets Σ_i at each reduction step, the next column recalls the reduction rule applied in that step, and the rightmost two columns list the set of elements removed from and added to Σ_i by the application of the rule, denoted Σ_I and Σ_O, respectively.

Table 3. An example of reduction

i	Σ_i	Rule	Σ_I	Σ_O
0	$\{c, \{\{k_1\}_{k_2}\}_{k_3}, \{[m]\}_{k_1{}^+}, k_1{}^+, k_2, k_3\}$	(33)	$\{\{\{k_1\}_{k_2}\}_{k_3}\}$	$\{\{k_1\}_{k_2}\}$
1	$\{c, \{[m]\}_{k_1{}^+}, k_1{}^+, k_2, k_3, \{k_1\}_{k_2}\}$	(33)	$\{\{k_1\}_{k_2}\}$	$\{k_1\}$
2	$\{c, \{[m]\}_{k_1{}^+}, k_1{}^+, k_2, k_3, k_1\}$	(29)	$\{k_1{}^+\}$	$\emptyset$
3	$\{c, \{[m]\}_{k_1{}^+}, k_2, k_3, k_1\}$	(34)	$\emptyset$	$\{m\}$
4	$\{c, \{[m]\}_{k_1{}^+}, k_2, k_3, k_1, m\}$	(27)	$\{\{[m]\}_{k_1{}^+}\}$	$\emptyset$
5	$\{c, k_2, k_3, k_1, m\}$			

In the table, rule applications are serialized, i.e. only one rule is applied at each step for clarity; in an actual implementation, all independent rules can be applied simultaneously, as outlined in the complexity analysis carried out in section 4.

Table 4 presents a reduction involving a non-atomic symmetric key; the initial intruder's knowledge is $\overline{\Sigma} = \{\{k_A\}_{k_S}, \{m\}_{\{k_B\}_{k_A}}, k_B, \mathrm{H}(m)\}$ and the added term is $\rho = k_S$. Note that in the second step, the premises of rule (33) are indeed satisfied, because $\mathtt{r}(\{k_B\}_{k_A}, \Sigma_1)$ is true, even if $\{k_B\}_{k_A} \notin \Sigma_1$.

Table 4. A reduction involving a non-atomic key

i	Σ_i	Rule	Σ_I	Σ_O
0	$\{\{k_A\}_{k_S}, \{m\}_{\{k_B\}_{k_A}}), k_B, \mathrm{H}(m), k_S\}$	(33)	$\{\{k_A\}_{k_S}\}$	$\{k_A\}$
1	$\{\{m\}_{\{k_B\}_{k_A}}, k_B, \mathrm{H}(m), k_S, k_A\}$	(33)	$\{\{m\}_{\{k_B\}_{k_A}}\}$	$\{m\}$
2	$\{k_B, \mathrm{H}(m), k_S, k_A, m\}$	(26)	$\{\mathrm{H}(m)\}$	$\emptyset$
3	$\{k_B, k_S, k_A, m\}$			

6 Concluding Remarks

Most finite [5,6,12] and infinite-state [2,3,4] protocol analysis methods based on model checking restrict encryption operators to atomic keys only.

For example, in [5] and [16], this restriction comes from the adoption of the closure of Σ under $\mathcal{E}$ rules as a representation of the intruder's knowledge.

Other approaches based on theorem proving do not pose this restriction but the tradeoff typically is between incompletness and possible non-termination of the analysis [14].

It is worth noting that support for constructed, non-atomic keys is becoming increasingly important to be able to analyze real-world protocols, since it is common for such protocols to build a symmetric key from shared secrets and other data exchanged between parties during a run of the protocol itself.

Other papers, such as [10,11], relax this restriction but neither explicitly introduce the notion of $\overline{\Sigma}$, that is, the minimized, canonical representation of the intruder's knowledge, nor analyze and exploit its properties.

The free term algebra of [14], too, allows any term to be used as an encryption key for both public-key and symmetric key encryption; however, the attacker's knowledge representation is not minimized and some other slight restrictions are in effect, such as for example the assumption that private keys are never leaked.

This assumption seems quite reasonable, but cannot easily be guaranteed by hand for complex protocols; so, we believe that such property is best checked with the aid of a formal, automated method.

By contrast, our approach does not pose any restriction on the internal structure and construction operators of encryption keys, besides those implied by spi calculus, thus supporting the full term language of spi calculus itself, even though at the expense of a greater computational complexity, as can be seen by comparing equations (39) and (40).

However, we believe that the additional expressive power and flexibility of our method more than outweighs this disadvantage in the range of values found in practice for n_0 and m_0.

Last, it should be noted that, even if we adopted the term syntax of spi calculus in this paper, our method is easily amenable to work with other term representation languages with similar sets of term composition operators.

Acknowledgments. The authors wish to thank the anonymous referees, whose valuable comments and suggestions helped to improve the quality of this paper. This work has been partially funded by the Italian National Research Council, grant number CNRC00FE45.

References

1. M. Abadi, and A. D. Gordon, "A Calculus for Cryptographic Protocols The Spi Calculus", *Digital Research Report*, vol. 149, January 1998, pp. 1–110.

2. R. Amadio, and D. Lugiez, "On the Reachability Problem in Cryptographic Protocols", *Proc. of CONCUR'2000, LNCS 1877*, pp. 380–394, Springer-Verlag, 2000.
3. M. Boreale, R. De Nicola, and R. Pugliese, "Proof Techniques for Cryptographic Processes", *Proc. of the 14th IEEE Symposium Logic In Computer Science (LICS'99)*, IEEE Computer Society Press, pp. 157–166, 1999.
4. M. Boreale, "Symbolic Trace Analysis of Cryptographic Protocols", In *Proc. 28th ICALP*, Vol. 2076 of *Lecture Notes in Computer Science*, Springer-Verlag, pp. 667–681, 2001.
5. E. M. Clarke, S. Jha, and W. Marrero, "Using state space exploration and a natural deduction style message derivation engine to verify security protocols", *Proc. of IFIP PROCOMET*, Chapman & Hall, London, 1998, pp. p.87–106.
6. E. M. Clarke, S. Jha, and W. Marrero, "Verifying security protocols with Brutus", ACM Trans. on Software Engineering and Methodology Vol. 9, No. 4, October 2000, pp. 443–487.
7. D. Dolev, and A. Yao, "On the security of public key protocols", *IEEE Transactions on Information Theory*, 29(2):198–208, 1983.
8. L. Durante, R. Sisto, and A. Valenzano, "A state-exploration technique for spi-calculus testing equivalence verification", *Proc. of FORTE/PSTV 2000*, Pisa, October 2000, pp. 155–170.
9. L. Durante, R. Sisto, and A. Valenzano, "Automatic testing equivalence verification of spi-calculs specifications", Politecnico di Torino I.R. DAI/ARC 1-02.
10. M. Fiore, and M. Abadi, "Computing Symbolic Models for Verifying Cryptographic Protocols", *Proc. of 14th IEEE Computer Security Foundations Workshop*, pp. 160–173, June 2001.
11. A. Huima, "Efficient Infinite-State Analysis of Security Protocols", *Proc. of FLOC Workshop on Formal Methods and Security Protocols*, 1999.
12. G. Lowe, "Breaking and fixing the Needham-Schroeder public-key protocol using FDR", *Proc. of TACAS'97*, Springer LNCS 1055, 1996.
13. D. A. McAllester, "Automatic Recognition of Tractability in Inference Relations", *Journal of the ACM*, Vol. 40, No. 2, April 1993, pp. 284–303.
14. J. Millen, and V. Shmatikov, "Constraint solving for Bounded-Process Cryptographic Protocol Analysis", *8th ACM Conference on Computer and Communication Security*, pages 166–175, November 2001.
15. R. Milner, J. Parrow, and D. Walker, "A Calculus of mobile processes, parts I and II", *Information and Computation*, pages 1–40 and 41–77, September 1992.
16. L. C. Paulson, "The inductive approach to verifying cryptographic protocols", *Journal of Computer Security*, Vol. 6, pp. 85–128, 1998.
17. D. Prawitz, "Natural Deduction: A Proof-Theoretical Study", Almqvist & Wiskell, 1965.

Pattern-Based Abstraction for Verifying Secrecy in Protocols*

Liana Bozga, Yassine Lakhnech, and Michael Périn

Verimag
2 av. de Vignate 38610 Gieres, France.
{lbozga,lakhnech,perin}@imag.fr

Abstract. We present a method based on abstract interpretation for verifying secrecy properties of cryptographic protocols. Our method allows to verify secrecy properties in a general model allowing an unbounded number of sessions, an unbounded number of principals and an unbounded size of messages. As abstract domain we use sets of so-called *pattern terms*, that is, terms with an interpreted constructor, *Sup*, where a term *Sup*(t) is meant for the set of terms that contain t as sub-term. We implemented a prototype and were able to verify well-known protocols such as for instance Needham-Schroeder-Lowe (0.02 sec), Yahalom (12.67 sec), Otway-Rees (0.02 sec), Skeme (0.06 sec) and Kao-Chow (0.07 sec).

1 Introduction

At the heart of almost every computer security architecture is a set of cryptographic protocols that use cryptography to encrypt and sign data. They are used to exchange confidential data such as pin numbers and passwords, to authentify users or to guarantee anonymity of principals. It is well known that even under the idealized assumption of perfect cryptography, logical flaws in the protocol design may lead to incorrect behavior with undesired consequences. Maybe the most prominent example showing that cryptographic protocols are notoriously difficult to design and test is the Needham-Schroeder protocol for authentication. It has been introduced in 1978 [23]. An attack on this protocol has been found by G. Lowe using the CSP model-checker FDR in 1995 [18]; and this led to a corrected version of the protocol [19]. Consequently there has been a growing interest in developing and applying formal methods for validating cryptographic protocols [20,8]. Most of this work adopts the so-called Dolev and Yao model of intruders. This model assumes perfect cryptographic primitives and a nondeterministic intruder that has total control of the communication network and capacity to forge new messages. It is known that reachability is undecidable for cryptographic protocols in the general case [13], even when a bound is put on the size of messages [12]. Because of these negative results, from the point of view of verification, the best we can hope for is either to identify decidable sub-classes

* This work has been partially supported by the RNTL project EVA.

H. Garavel and J. Hatcliff (Eds.): TACAS 2003, LNCS 2619, pp. 299–314, 2003.

as in [3,24,21] or to develop correct but incomplete verification algorithms as in [22,17,15].

In this paper, we present a correct but, in general, incomplete verification algorithm to prove secrecy without putting any assumption on messages nor on the number of sessions. Proving secrecy means proving that secrets are not revealed to unauthorized agents. The main contribution of our paper is an original method for proving that a secret is not revealed by a set of rules that model how the initial set of messages known by the intruder evolves. The method is based on the notion of "the secret being *guarded*, or *kept under the hat* of a safe message". For example, suppose that our secret is the nonce N_B and that the key K_B^{-1} – the inverse of K_B – is not known by the intruder. Then, any message that contains N_B and that is encrypted with K_B is a guard for N_B. For instance, N_B is guarded in the message $\{\{N_A, N_B\}_{K_B}\}_{K_I}$ by the sub-message $\{N_A, N_B\}_{K_B}$. The idea is then to compute a set of guards that will keep the secret unrevealed in all sent messages and such that the inverses of the keys used in the guards are also secrets. The difficulty here is that the set of guards is, in general, infinite. Therefore, we use *terms* to represent sets of guards. For instance the term $\{x, x_s\}_{K_B}$ says that the secret will be guarded in any message $\{m, m'\}_{K_B}$, where the secret is not a sub-message of m [1] but may be a sub-message of m'. The problem is, however, that there might be a rule $\{I, y\}_{K_B} \to y$ that will send y unencrypted to the intruder if (s)he produces the message $\{I, y\}_{K_B}$. Hence, the term $\{x, x_s\}_{K_B}$ will guard the secret except when x is I. Thus, our abstract domain consists of pairs $(\mathcal{G}, \mathcal{B})$ of terms. Those in $\mathcal{G}$ correspond to good messages that guard the secrets, whereas those in $\mathcal{B}$ denote "bad exceptions", that is, the particular instances of terms in $\mathcal{G}$ that do not guard the secrets. A weakness of terms is, however, that variables appear only at the leafs, and hence, they do not allow to describe, for instance, the set of terms that share a common sub-term. To mitigate this weakness, we introduce *pattern terms*, that is, terms with an interpreted constructor, *Sup*, where a term *Sup*(t) is meant for the set of terms that contain t as sub-term.

We developed a prototype in Caml that implements this method. We have been able to verify several protocols taken from [6] including, for instance, Needham-Schroeder-Lowe (0.02 sec), Yahalom (12.67 sec), Otway-Rees (0.02 sec), Skeme (0.06 sec) and Kao-Chow (0.07 sec).

Related work. Dolev, Even and Karp introduced [10] the class of ping-pong protocols and showed its decidability. The restriction put on these protocols are too restrictive and none of the protocols of [6] falls in this class. Recently, Comon, Cortier and Mitchell [7] extended this class allowing pairing and binary encryption while the use of nonces still cannot be expressed in their model. Reachability is decidable for the bounded number of sessions [3,24,21] or when nonce creation is not allowed and the size of messages is bounded [12]. These assumptions are rarely justified in practice.

---

[1] unless it is guarded by an other term.

Type systems and type-checking have also been advocated as a method for verifying security protocols (e.g. [1,16,2]). Although, these techniques can handle unbounded protocols they are as far as we know not yet completely automatic. Closest to our work are partial algorithms based on abstract interpretation and tree automata that have been presented in [22,17,15]. The main difference is, however, that we do not compute the set of messages that can be known by the intruder but a set of guards as explained above. Our method can handle unbounded protocols fully automatically with the price that it may discover false attacks. Interesting enough is that does not happen on any of the practical protocols we tried (see Table 1).

2 Preliminary

If $n \in \mathbb{N}$ then we denote by $\mathbb{N}_n$ the set $\{1, \cdots, n\}$. Let $\mathcal{X}$ be a countable set of variables and let $\mathcal{F}^i$ be a countable set of function symbols of arity i, for every $i \in \mathbb{N}$. Let $\mathcal{F} = \bigcup_{i \in \mathbb{N}} \mathcal{F}^i$. The set of *terms over* $\mathcal{X}$ *and* $\mathcal{F}$, denoted by $\mathcal{T}(\mathcal{X}, \mathcal{F})$, is the smallest set containing $\mathcal{X}$ and closed under application of the function symbols in $\mathcal{F}$, i.e., $f(t_1, \cdots, t_n)$ is a term in $\mathcal{T}(\mathcal{X}, \mathcal{F})$, if $t_i \in \mathcal{T}(\mathcal{X}, \mathcal{F})$, for $i = 1, \cdots, n$, and $f \in \mathcal{F}^n$. As usual, function symbols of arity 0 are called constant symbols. *Ground terms* are terms with no variables. We denote by $\mathcal{T}(\mathcal{F})$ the set of ground terms over $\mathcal{F}$.

A tree *tr* is a function from a finite subset of ω^* to $\mathcal{X} \cup \mathcal{F}$ such that $tr(u) \in \mathcal{F}^n$ iff $u \cdot j \in dom(tr)$, for every $j \in \{0, \cdots, n-1\}$. We identify terms with trees by associating to each term t a tree $Tr(t)$ as follows: (1) if x is a variable, then $dom(Tr(x)) = \{\epsilon\}$ and $Tr(x)(\epsilon) = x$, (2) if f is a constant symbol, then $dom(Tr(f)) = \{\epsilon\}$ and $Tr(f)(\epsilon) = f$ and (3) for a term $t = f(t_0, \cdots, t_{n-1})$, $dom(Tr(t)) = \{\epsilon\} \cup \bigcup_{i=0}^{n-1} i \cdot dom(Tr(t_i))$, where $\cdot$ is word concatenation extended to sets, $Tr(t)(\epsilon) = f$ and $Tr(t)(i \cdot u) = Tr(t_i)(u)$. Henceforth, we tacitly identify the term t with $Tr(t)$. The elements of $dom(t)$ are called *positions* in t. We use $\prec$ to denote the prefix relation on ω^*. We write $t(p)$ to denote the symbol at position p in t and $t_{|p}$ to denote the subterm of t at position p, which corresponds to the tree $t_{|p}(x) = t(p \cdot x)$ with $x \in dom(t_{|p})$ iff $x \cdot p \in dom(t)$.

3 Models for Cryptographic Protocols

In this section, we describe how we model cryptographic protocols and give a precise definition of the properties we want to verify. We begin by describing the messages involved in a protocol model.

3.1 Messages

The set of messages is denoted by $\mathcal{M}$ and contains terms constructed from constant symbols and the function symbols **encr** $: \mathcal{M} \times \mathcal{K} \to \mathcal{M}$ and **pair** $: \mathcal{M} \times \mathcal{M} \to \mathcal{M}$. Constant symbols are also called atomic messages and are defined as follows:

1. *Principle names* are used to refer to the principles in a protocol. The set of all principles is $\mathcal{P}$.
2. *Nonces* can be thought as randomly generated numbers. As no one can predict their values, they are used to convince for the freshness of a message. We denote by $\mathcal{N}$ the set of nonces.
3. *Keys* are used to encrypt messages. We have the following atomic keys for each $p_1, \cdots, p_r \in \mathcal{P}^r$ where *pbk*, *pvk* and *smk* stand respectively for *public*, *private* and *symmetric* keys:

$$pbk(p_1, \cdots, p_r) \mid pvk(p_1, \cdots, p_r) \mid smk(p_1, \cdots, p_r).$$

   We denote by $\mathcal{AK}(p_1, \cdots, p_r)$ this set of keys and let $\mathcal{K} = \bigcup_{\boldsymbol{p} \in \mathcal{P}^+} \mathcal{AK}(\boldsymbol{p})$ denote the set of all keys. The key $pbk(p_1, \cdots, p_r)$ is an inverse of the key $pvk(p_1, \cdots, p_r)$ and vice versa; and a key $smk(p_1, \cdots, p_r)$ is its self-inverse. If k is a key then we use k^{-1} to denote its inverse. Moreover, as usual, we write K_A instead of $pbk(A)$, K_A^{-1} instead of $pvk(A)$ and K_{AB} instead of $smk(A, B)$.

For the sake of simpicity we left out the signatures and hash functions but we can easlily handle them in our model.

Let $\mathcal{A} = \mathcal{P} \cup \mathcal{N} \cup \mathcal{K}$ and $\mathcal{F} = \mathcal{A} \cup \{\mathbf{encr}, \mathbf{pair}\}$. As usual, we write (m_1, m_2) for $\mathbf{pair}(m_1, m_2)$ and $\{m\}_k$ instead of $\mathbf{encr}(m, k)$. *Message terms* are the elements of $\mathcal{T}(\mathcal{X}, \mathcal{F})$, that is, terms over the atoms $\mathcal{A}$, a set of variables $\mathcal{X}$ and the binary function symbols **encr** and **pair**. *Messages* are ground terms in $\mathcal{T}(\mathcal{X}, \mathcal{F})$, i.e, $\mathcal{M} = \mathcal{T}(\mathcal{F})$.

3.2 The Intruder Model

In this section, we describe how an intruder can create new messages from already known messages. We use the most commonly used model, introduced by Dolev and Yao [11], which is given by a formal system $\vdash$. The intruder capabilities for intercepting messages and sending (fake) messages are fixed by the operational semantics. Thus, the *derivability of a message* m from a set E of messages, denoted by $E \vdash m$, is described by the following axiom and rules:

- If $m \in E$ then $E \vdash m$.
- If $E \vdash m_1$ and $E \vdash m_2$ then $E \vdash \mathbf{pair}(m_1, m_2)$. This rule is called pairing.
- If $E \vdash m$ and $E \vdash k \in \mathcal{K}$ then $E \vdash \mathbf{encr}(m, k)$. This is called encryption.
- If $E \vdash \mathbf{pair}(m_1, m_2)$ then $E \vdash m_1$ and $E \vdash m_2$. This is called projection.
- If $E \vdash \mathbf{encr}(m, k)$, $E \vdash k'$ and k and k' are inverses then $E \vdash m$. This is called decryption.

Notations. For a term t, we use the notation $E \not\vdash t$ to denote that no instance of t is derivable from E, that is, for no substitution $\sigma : \mathcal{X} \to \mathcal{M}$, we have $E \vdash \sigma(t)$.

We now define *critical* and *non-critical* positions in a message. The idea is that since there is no way to deduce from an encrypted message the key with which it has been encrypted, the key position in messages of the form $\mathbf{encr}(m, k)$

is not critical[2]. Formally, given a term t, a position p in t is called *non-critical*, if there is a position q such that $p = q \cdot 2$ and $t(q) = \mathbf{encr}$; otherwise it is called *critical*. We will also use the notation $s \in_c m$ to denote that s appears in m at a critical position, i.e., there exists $p \in dom(m)$ such that p is critical and $m_{|p} = s$.

We also use the notation $E \not\vdash^{\in_c} t$ to denote that no message derivable from E contains an instantiation of t at a critical position, that is, for every message m if $E \vdash m$ then $\sigma(t) \not\in_c m$, for any σ. The relation $\not\vdash^{\in_c}$ is naturally extended to set of terms.

3.3 Representation of the Protocol

We use in this paper a simple protocol representation that can be proved to be a safe approximation of a more realistic model [5]. The main idea behind this representation is the following abstraction. First, we fix an arbitrary session where the same principal, say A, plays the (say two) different roles in the protocol. Then, we identify the intruder I with all principles other than A. Moreover, we identify all sessions in which A is not involved. Concerning the other sessions, that is, those where A is involved, we identify:

- all sessions where A plays both roles and which are different from the fixed session,
- all sessions where A plays the first role while the second role is played by an other principal,
- all sessions where A plays the second role while the first role is played by a different principal.

Identifying sessions means also identifying the nonces and keys used in these sessions. This leaves us with a system where we still have unbounded number of messages as the size of the messages is not bounded. To summarize: We model a protocol as a set of transitions that can be taken in any order and any number of times. We also apply the safe and exact abstraction that consists in considering only one honest principal and one dishonest principal (the intruder). The proof that this abstraction is safe and actually also exact is given in [9].

Thus, a protocol is represented by a pair $(\mathcal{C}, \mathcal{R})$ consisting of:

- a predicate $\mathcal{C}$ on sets of messages describing the messages that the intruder may initially know, and
- a finite set $\mathcal{R}$ of rule schemata of the form $t_1 \rightarrow t_2$, where the t_i's are terms.

The constraint $\mathcal{C}$ can be used to describe freshness properties. For instance, if N is a nonce then the condition $E \not\vdash^{\in_c} N$ states that N is fresh with respect to E. In a companion paper [5], we describe how an abstract procotol description $(\mathcal{C}, \mathcal{R})$ is derived from a concrete one by abstract interpretation.

Notice that we do not lose generality by considering transitions of the form $t \rightarrow t'$ instead of transitions with more than one term on the left-hand side, as

[2] For the insider, the critical position corresponds, for instance, to the subterm relation in the strand space model [14,25].

a transition $t_1, \cdots, t_n \to t'$ can be encoded as $(t_1, (t_2, \cdots, (t_{n-1}, t_n) \cdots) \to t'$. Actually, our verification tool uses this encoding as it increases precision of the results.

Let us turn our attention to the semantics of a protocol $(\mathcal{C}, \mathcal{R})$. A *run* of $(\mathcal{C}, \mathcal{R})$ is given by a finite sequence of sets of messages E_i of the form

$$E_0 \stackrel{r_1}{\to} E_1 \cdots E_{n-1} \stackrel{r_n}{\to} E_n$$

with $n \geq 0$ such that E_0 satisfies the constraint $\mathcal{C}$ and such that, for each $i = 1, \cdots n$, there is a substitution $\rho_i : \mathcal{X} \to \mathcal{M}$ such that $E_{i-1} \vdash \rho(t_1)$ and $E_i = E_{i-1} \cup \{\rho(t_2)\}$, where $t_1 \to t_2 = r_i$.

In other words, considering E_{i-1} as the current knowledge of the intruder, a rule $t_1 \to t_2 = r_i$ can be taken if there is an instance $\rho(t_1)$ of t_1 that is derivable from E_{i-1}. The effect of applying the rule culminates in adding the message $\rho(t_2)$ to the knowledge of the intruder. Notice how following Bolignano [4] communication is modeled through the knowledge of the intruder. That is, the intruder can intercept messages use them to create fake messages and deliver these to the principals.

3.4 Secrecy Modeling

Our goal is to determine whether secrecy property holds: for instance whether the intruder can get a secret s. That is, does a run exist that leads to a set E of messages from which s is derivable.

A *secret* is given by a message m. A protocol P satisfies the secrecy property defined by m, denoted by $\not\vdash_P m$, if it does not admit any run $E_0 \stackrel{r_1}{\to} E_1 \cdots E_{n-1} \stackrel{r_n}{\to} E_n$ such that $E_n \vdash m$. The definition of secrecy can be pointwisely extended to a set of secrets.

Example 1. The Needham-Schroeder protocol for authentification can be described as follows using the usual informal notation for cryptographic protocols:

$$\begin{array}{l} A \to B : \{A, N_1\}_{K_B} \\ B \to A : \{N_1, N_2\}_{K_A} \\ A \to B : \{N_2\}_{K_B} \end{array}$$

Intuitively, A plays the role of the initiator of the session; while B is a responder.

In our model which yields an over-approximation of the possible runs of the protocol, we can describe the Needham-Schroeder protocol by the following rules. We write $\frac{t_1}{t_2}$ *instead of* $t_1 \to t_2$.

session (A, I)	*session* (I, A)	*the fixed session* (A, A)	*other sessions* (A, A)
$\frac{-}{\{A,N_1^{AI}\}_{pbk(I)}}$;	$\frac{-}{\{I,N_I\}_{pbk(A)}}$;	$\frac{-}{\{A,N_1\}_{pbk(A)}}$;	$\frac{-}{\{A,N_1^{AA}\}_{pbk(A)}}$;
$\frac{\{A,y\}_{pbk(I)}}{\{y,N_I\}_{pbk(A)}}$;	$\frac{\{I,y\}_{pbk(A)}}{\{y,N_2^{IA}\}_{pbk(I)}}$;	$\frac{\{A,y\}_{pbk(A)}}{\{y,N_2\}_{pbk(A)}}$;	$\frac{\{A,y\}_{pbk(A)}}{\{y,N_2^{AA}\}_{pbk(A)}}$;
$\frac{\{N_1^{AI},z\}_{pbk(A)}}{\{z\}_{pbk(I)}}$;	$\frac{\{N_I,z\}_{pbk(I)}}{\{z\}_{pbk(A)}}$;	$\frac{\{N_1,z\}_{pbk(A)}}{\{z\}_{pbk(A)}}$;	$\frac{\{N_1^{AA},z\}_{pbk(A)}}{\{z\}_{pbk(A)}}$;

Each rule corresponds to a transition of the Needham-Schroeder protocol instantiated w.r.t. the nonces and the principals of an abstract session.

Beyond these rules, the verification problem is defined by a constraint $\mathcal{C}(E)$ *on the initial knowledge of the intruder, e.g.,* $E \not\vdash^{\in_c} \{ N_1,\ N_2,\ pvk(A) \}$ *and a secrecy property defined by the set of messages* $\{N_2, pvk(A)\}$.

4 Verification Based on Patterns Keeping Secrets

Throughout this section we assume that we are given a protocol $P = (\mathcal{C}, \mathcal{R})$ and a set of secrets defined by a set $\mathcal{S}$ of messages. We present an algorithm that allows to verify that a protocol preserves a set of secrets.

4.1 Hat-Messages: Messages Keeping Secrets under a Hat

If a principal A wants to protect a secret s, then he has to use a key whose inverse is not known by the intruder in order to encrypt every occurence of s in every message sent. The secret s itself need not be directly encrypted. Indeed, it should be enough that it only appears as part of encrypted messages. The basic idea of our method is to compute the set of encrypted messages that protect the secrets. As we will see, encryption with a safe key is not always sufficient to protect a secret in every message, as honest principals following the protocol can unwillingly help the intruder in decrypting the message.

In order to develop this idea formally we need to introduce a few definitions. Recall that critical and non-critical positions as well as the notation $\in_c$ has been introduced in Section 3.2.

Definition 1. *We call* hat-term *any term of the form* $\mathbf{encr}(t, k)$. *It is called* hat-message *if it is a ground term. Then, a secret s is protected by a set of hat-messages H in a set of messages M, denoted by* $M\langle H\rangle s$, *if the following condition is satisfied:*

> *for all messages* $m \in M$, *for all critical positions* p *in* m *with* $m_{|p} = s$, *there exists a position* $q \prec p$ *such that* $m_{|q} \in H$. □

Example 2. According to our definition, the hat-message $\mathbf{encr}(s, k)$ protects the secret s in the messages $\mathbf{encr}(\mathbf{encr}(s, k), k')$ but it does not protect it neither in the message $\mathbf{encr}(\mathbf{encr}(s, k'), k)$ nor in $\mathbf{pair}(\mathbf{encr}(s, k), s)$. Furthermore, even if the key k is part of the secrets, it does not need to be protected in the previous messages for it never appears in critical position. □

The notion of a message being protected by a hat-message introduced above does not take into account the capabilities of the intruder to decompose and compose new messages. We have to give particular care to the treatment of composed secrets as they can be obtained either by composition or decomposition. To do so, let us define the weak closure under decomposition of a term. Let T be a set terms. Then, T is called *weakly closed under decomposition*, or just weakly closed for short, if for any term $f(t_1, \cdots, t_n) \in T$ there is some $i \in \mathbb{N}_n$ such that $t_i \in T$. Then, a set T' is called a *weak closure* of T, if it is weakly closed, contains T and no proper sub-set of it satisfies these properties. Now, we are ready to extend the notion of a message being protected by a hat-message taking into account the intruder.

Definition 2. *A set $\mathcal{S}$ of messages is called* strongly protected *by $\mathcal{H}$ in M, denoted by $M[\mathcal{H}]\mathcal{S}$, if the following conditions are satisfied:*

1. *$M \vdash m \Rightarrow m\langle\mathcal{H}\rangle\mathcal{S}$, i.e., the secrets in $\mathcal{S}$ must be protected in any message that the intruder can deduce from M.*
2. *$\mathcal{S}$ is weakly closed.*
3. *$Keys(\mathcal{H})^{-1} \subseteq \mathcal{S}$ where $Keys(H)^{-1} = \{k^{-1} \mid \mathbf{encr}(t,k) \in H\}$, i.e., the inverses of all the keys used in hat-messages are also secrets.* □

Intuitively, Condition (2) ensures that the intruder will always miss at least one part of a secret preventing him from deducing it by composition. Condition (3) ensures that the intruder will not be able to decrypt a secret protected by a hat-message.

Our main motivation in introducing $M[\mathcal{H}]\mathcal{S}$ lays in the following proposition that states that adding a message m in which the secrets of $\mathcal{S}$ are protected preserves strong protection of $\mathcal{S}$.

Proposition 1. *Let $M, \mathcal{S} \subseteq \mathcal{T}(\mathcal{F})$ be sets of messages, $\mathcal{H}$ be a set of hat-messages and m be a message. If $M[\mathcal{H}]\mathcal{S}$ and $m\langle\mathcal{H}\rangle\mathcal{S}$ then $M \cup \{m\}[\mathcal{H}]\mathcal{S}$.* □

The proof of this proposition is presented in [5]; it does not rely on the fact that keys are atomic. Actually, our method can be extended to cover the case of non atomic keys.

Let now $r = t_1 \to t_2$ be a rule in $\mathcal{R}$ (recall that we have fixed an arbitrary protocol $P = (\mathcal{C}, \mathcal{R})$. We say that the pair $(\mathcal{S}, \mathcal{H})$ composed of a set of secrets and a set of hat-messages is *stable w.r.t. a rule* r, if for every subtitution σ, we have $\sigma(t_2)\langle\mathcal{H}\rangle\mathcal{S}$. It is stable w.r.t. a set of rules $\mathcal{R}$ if it stable w.r.t. to each rule in $\mathcal{R}$. Then, using Proposition 1, we can prove by induction the following theorem:

Theorem 1. *Let $\mathcal{S}$ be a set of secrets and $\mathcal{H}$ be a set of hat-messages. If $(\mathcal{S}, \mathcal{H})$ is stable w.r.t. all rules in $\mathcal{R}$ and $E_0[\mathcal{H}]\mathcal{S}$, for every set of messages E_0 that satisfies $\mathcal{C}$, then $\not\vdash_P \mathcal{S}$, i.e., the secrets in $\mathcal{S}$ are preserved by P.*

According to Theorem 1, given a protocol $P = (\mathcal{C}, \mathcal{R})$ and a set $\mathcal{S}$ of secrets, if we can find a set $\mathcal{H}$ of hat-messages and a set $\mathcal{S}'$ of secrets such that:

- the constraint $\mathcal{C}$ on E_0 – the messages initially known by the intruder – implies $E_0[\mathcal{H}]\mathcal{S}'$,
- $\mathcal{S} \subseteq \mathcal{S}'$, and
- $(\mathcal{S}', \mathcal{H})$ is stable w.r.t. $\mathcal{R}$.

we can conclude that the secrets in $\mathcal{S}$ are preserved by $P = (\mathcal{C}, \mathcal{R})$. In this section, we develop an algorithm that computes a stable pair $(\mathcal{S}', \mathcal{H})$. This is done in two steps. First, we develop a semantic version of the algorithm in which we do not consider questions related to representing sets of hat-messages. Then, we define a symbolic representation for hat-messages and develop a symbolic algorithm.

4.2 A Semantic Version of the Verification Algorithm

In Figure 1, we present an algorithm that computes a pair $(\mathcal{S}, \mathcal{H})$ which is stable w.r.t. the rules of the protocol. It uses the function *Closure* that associates to a set T of terms a weak closure of T. The algorithm takes a set of rules $\mathcal{R}$, a set of secrets $\mathcal{S}$ and a set of hat-messages $\mathcal{H}$ as input. It is a fixpoint computation, starting with $(\mathcal{S}, \mathcal{H})$. If it terminates, it returns an augmented set of secrets $\mathcal{S}'$ and a set $\mathcal{H}'$ such that $\mathcal{H}' \subseteq \mathcal{H}$. We now explain intuitively the clue point of the algorithm. Let us take a rule $t_p \to t_c$ in $\mathcal{R}$, a substitution $\sigma : \mathcal{X} \to \mathcal{T}(\mathcal{F})$ and a hat-message h such that h protects a secret in $\sigma(t_p)$. If the secret is not protected by any hat-messages in $\sigma(t_c)$ – the conclusion of the instanciated rule, then the hat-message h is not safe indeed and it must be removed from the set of hat-messages. Actually, even when the inverse of the keys used in the hat-messages are unknown by the intruder, the secret can be unwillingly revealed by a principal. Think for instance of a protocol with $\{(y, x)\}_{pbk(A)} \to \{x\}_{pbk(y)}$ as a rule of principal A. On reception of the message $\{(I, \mathit{Secret})\}_{pbk(A)}$, the principal A will respond $\{\mathit{Secret}\}_{pbk(I)}$ thus unwillingly decrypting the secret for the intruder. So, $\{(I, \mathit{Secret})\}_{pbk(A)}$ is a particular case where $pbk(A)$ does not protect the secret and it must be removed from the set of hat-messages. Case 2 in the algorithm considers the case where a secret is not protected in the conclusion and the premisse does not contain a secret. In this case, the apparently harmless premise is as compromising as the secret, and hence, is added to the set of secrets. The following proposition summarizes the properties of the algorithm.

Proposition 2. *If the algorithm of Figure 1 applied to $(\mathcal{R}, \mathcal{S}, \mathcal{H})$ terminates, it returns $\mathcal{S}'$ and $\mathcal{H}'$ which satisfy the following conditions:*

1. *$(\mathcal{S}', \mathcal{H}')$ is stable w.r.t. $\mathcal{R}$,*
2. *$\mathcal{S} \subseteq \mathcal{S}'$, and*
3. *$Keys(\mathcal{H}')^{-1} \subseteq \mathcal{S}'$.* □

Using Proposition 2 and Theorem 1, we can prove the following corollary.

Corollary 1. *If the algorithm of Figure 1 terminates with $(\mathcal{S}', \mathcal{H}')$ as result and each set of messages E_0 that satisfies $\mathcal{C}(E_0)$ also satisfies $E_0[\mathcal{H}']\mathcal{S}'$, we can conclude $\not\models_P \mathcal{S}'$, and hence, $\not\models_P \mathcal{S}$.* □

4.3 A Symbolic Representation of Hat-Messages: Pattern Terms

To develop an effective version of our semantic algorithm, we need to represent (potentially infinite) sets of hat-messages. To do so, we introduce a symbolic representation that consists in a pair $(\mathcal{G}, \mathcal{B})$ of sets of terms over variables in $\mathcal{X} \cup \mathcal{X}_s$. Here, $\mathcal{X}_s$ denotes a new disjoint set of variables. We use $x_s, y_s, \cdots$ as typical variables in $\mathcal{X}_s$. Roughly speaking, a hat-message for a secret is an instance of a term in $\mathcal{G}$ that is not an instance of any term in $\mathcal{B}$. Therefore, we call the terms in $\mathcal{G}$ *good patterns* and those in $\mathcal{B}$ *bad patterns*. In good patterns, we use the variables in $\mathcal{X}_s$ to mark the positions in which a term containing a secret is

input: $\mathcal{R}$, a weakly closed $\mathcal{S}$ and $\mathcal{H}$
output: $\mathcal{S}'$, $\mathcal{H}'$ such that $(\mathcal{S}', \mathcal{H}')$ is stable w.r.t. $\mathcal{R}$.
  $\mathcal{S}' := \mathcal{S}$; $\mathcal{H}' := \mathcal{H}$;
repeat
  — *first, add to the secrets the inverse of the keys used in hat-messages then,*
  — *compute the closure that adds to S' one subpart of each compound secret of $\mathcal{S}'$*
  $\mathcal{S}' := \mathcal{S}' \cup Keys(\mathcal{H}')^{-1}$; $\mathcal{S}' := Closure(\mathcal{S}')$; $\mathcal{S}_c := \mathcal{S}'$; $\mathcal{H}_c := \mathcal{H}'$;
  for each $t_p \to t_c \in \mathcal{R}$
    — *compute all Dangerous Substitutions of rule $t_p \to t_c$ where a secret is*
    — *not kept in the conclusion*
    $DS := \{\sigma : \mathcal{X} \to \mathcal{M} \mid \neg\big(\sigma(t_c)\langle\mathcal{H}'\rangle\mathcal{S}'\big)\}$;
    — *compute the corresponding Dangerous Premisses*
    $DP := \{\sigma(t_p) \mid \sigma \in DS\}$;
    — *update the secret and hat-messages according to the dangerous premisses:*
    — *case 1 removes the hat-messages that appear in dangerous premisses*
    for each $s \in \mathcal{S}'$, $m \in DP$ **do**
      — *the bad hat-messages of s are those which protect a secret*
      — *that can be disclosed by a rule*
      $BHat := \{m_{|q} \mid \exists p.\ q \prec p \wedge m_{|p} = s \wedge m_{|q} \in \mathcal{H}'\}$
      — *select a subset of hat-messages to be removed*
      choose $BHat' \subseteq BHat$ **with** $BHat \neq \emptyset \Rightarrow BHat' \neq \emptyset$
      — *update the set of hat-message $\mathcal{H}$*
      $\mathcal{H}' := \mathcal{H}' \setminus BHat'$;
    od
    — *case 2 adds to the secrets all bad premisses than do not contain any secret*
    $newS := \{m \in DP \mid \forall s \in \mathcal{S}'.\ s \notin_c m\}$; $\mathcal{S}' := \mathcal{S}' \cup newS$
  od
until $(\mathcal{S}', \mathcal{H}') = (\mathcal{S}_c, \mathcal{H}_c)$

Fig. 1. The semantic version of the verification algorithm

allowed to appear. While in bad patterns, they are used to mark positions where it is not guaranteed that the secret is protected. For instance, if $\mathcal{G}$ contains the term $\{x_s\}_K$ and $\mathcal{B}$ contains the term $\{(A, x_s)\}_K$ then the message $\{(B, Secret)\}_K$ will be in the set represented by $(\mathcal{G}, \mathcal{B})$, while the message $\{(A, Secret)\}_K$ will not. Let us now define this symbolic representation formally.

To do so, we introduce *pattern terms* defined by the following BNF:

$$pt ::= N \mid P \mid K \mid x \mid x_s \mid \mathbf{pair}(pt_1, pt_2) \mid \mathbf{encr}(pt, K) \mid Sup\,(pt)$$

where $N \in \mathcal{N}$, $P \in \mathcal{P}$, $K \in \mathcal{K}$, $x \in \mathcal{X}$, and $x_s \in \mathcal{X}_s$. The set of pattern terms is denoted by $\mathcal{PT}(\mathcal{X} \cup \mathcal{X}_s, \mathcal{F})$. Notice that every term in $\mathcal{T}(\mathcal{X} \cup \mathcal{X}_s, \mathcal{F})$ is also a pattern term in $\mathcal{PT}(\mathcal{X} \cup \mathcal{X}_s, \mathcal{F})$. The difference between the two is that patterns terms make use of the special *Sup* function symbol.

Intuitively, as can be seen from the following definition, $Sup\,(t)$ represents all terms containing the term t as a sub-term. For instance, the terms A, $\mathbf{pair}(x, A)$, $\mathbf{encr}(A, K)$, $\cdots$ all belong to $[\![Sup\,(A)]\!]$.

Definition 3. *Given a pattern term* pt, *let* $[\![\mathrm{pt}]\!]$ *be defined as follows:*

$$\begin{aligned} [\![\mathrm{pt}]\!] &= \{\mathrm{pt}\} \quad \textit{if } \mathrm{pt} \textit{ is a constant or a variable} \\ [\![\mathbf{pair}(\mathrm{pt}_1, \mathrm{pt}_2)]\!] &= \{\mathbf{pair}(t_1, t_2) \mid t_1 \in [\![\mathrm{pt}_1]\!], t_2 \in [\![\mathrm{pt}_2]\!]\} \\ [\![\mathbf{encr}(\mathrm{pt}_1, k)]\!] &= \{\mathbf{encr}(t_1, k) \mid t_1 \in [\![\mathrm{pt}_1]\!]\} \\ [\![Sup(\mathrm{pt})]\!] &= \{t \mid \textit{ there is a position } p \textit{ in } t \textit{ s.t. } t_{|p} \in [\![\mathrm{pt}]\!]\} \end{aligned}$$

We then represent a pair $(\mathcal{S}, \mathcal{H})$ by triple $\langle \mathcal{S}, \mathcal{G}, \mathcal{B} \rangle$ of finite sets of secrets, good and bad patterns. Good patterns correspond to "maybe safe" hat terms and bad patterns define "really unsafe" hat terms. The formal definition of the concretization of $\langle \mathcal{S}, \mathcal{G}, \mathcal{B} \rangle$ is given in [5].

5 A Symbolic Verification Algorithm

The symbolic algorithm is obtained from the algorithm of Figure 1 by replacing each operation by a corresponding symbolic one that operates on $\langle \mathcal{S}, \mathcal{G}, \mathcal{B} \rangle$. For the sake of presentation, we explain the symbolic algorithm in the particular case where $\mathcal{B}$ consists of terms rather than pattern terms, i.e., *Sup* does not occur in any term in $\mathcal{B}$. The extension of the algorithm to pattern terms is explained in a technical report [5].

Before presenting the algorithm we need to introduce the following definitions. Let t and t' be terms and let q be a position in t. A substitution $\sigma : \mathcal{X} \cup \mathcal{X}_s \to \mathcal{T}(\mathcal{X} \cup \mathcal{X}_s, \mathcal{F})$ is called *a q-matcher* of t' on t, if $\sigma(t') = t$ and there is a position $q' \preceq q$ such that $t'_{|q'} \in \mathcal{X}_s$. Given a set $\mathcal{G}$ of terms, we say that t q-matches in $\mathcal{G}$, if there is a term $t' \in \mathcal{G}$ and a q-matcher of t' on t. Moreover, a substitution $\sigma : \mathcal{X} \cup \mathcal{X}_s \to \mathcal{T}(\mathcal{X} \cup \mathcal{X}_s, \mathcal{F})$ is called *a q-unifier* of t' with t, if $\sigma(t') = \sigma(t)$ and one of the following conditions is satisfied: 1.) $t_{|q} \in \mathcal{X}_s$ and there is a variable $y_s \in \mathcal{X}_S$ such that $y_s \in_c t'_{|q}$ and in case y_s is in the domain of σ, a secret or a secret variable appears at a critical position in $\sigma(y_s)$ or 2.) there exists a position $q' \preceq q$ such that $t'_{|q'} \in \mathcal{X}_s$. Also, q-unification can be extended to sets of terms.

The symbolic algorithm takes as input a set of rules $\mathcal{R}$, a set of secrets $\mathcal{S}$, a set of good terms $\mathcal{G}$ and an empty set of bad terms $\mathcal{B} = \emptyset$. It computes new bad terms and secrets until the concretization of $\langle \mathcal{S}, \mathcal{G}, \mathcal{B} \rangle$ becomes stable w.r.t. all rules in $\mathcal{R}$. Let us now sketch its main steps:

1. The set $\mathcal{S}$ of secrets becomes $\mathcal{S} \cup Keys(\mathcal{G})^{-1}$, where $Keys(\mathcal{G})^{-1}$ is the set of keys of the form k^{-1} such that $\mathbf{encr}(t, k)$ is in $\mathcal{G}$.
2. Given a rule $t_p \to t_c$ in $\mathcal{R}$, we have to consider all possible critical occurrences of a secret in the conclusion t_c. This is done by replacing variables in t_c by secret variables. In other words, we consider all rules in $\mathcal{R}' = \{\sigma(t_p) \to \sigma(t_c) \mid t_p \to t_c \in \mathcal{R},\ \sigma : var(t_c) \to \mathcal{X}_s\}$.
3. Given a rule $t_p \to t_c$ in $\mathcal{R}'$, the algorithm computes the set of dangerous substitution DS as follows. A substitution $\sigma : var(t_c) \to \mathcal{T}(\mathcal{X} \cup \mathcal{X}_s, \mathcal{F})$ is *dangerous* if there is a critical position p in t_c such that $t_{c|p} \in \mathcal{X}_s \cup \mathcal{S}$ and the following condition holds: for every positions p_i, q_i such that $q_i.p_i = p$, if

$t_{c|q_i}$ p_i-matches in $\mathcal{G}$, then σ can be completed into a p_i-unifier of $t_{c|q_i}$ in $\mathcal{B}$, meaning there are $b \in \mathcal{B}$ and σ' with $dom(\sigma') \subseteq var(b)$ such that $\sigma \cup \sigma'$ is a p_i-unifier of $t_{c|q_i}$ with b. Then,

$$DS := \{\sigma : var(t_c) \to \mathcal{T}(\mathcal{X} \cup \mathcal{X}_s, \mathcal{F}) \mid \sigma \text{ is dangerous}\}$$

Example 3 below illustrates the computation of dangerous substitutions.

4. The set of *dangerous premises* is given by $DP = \{\sigma(t_p) \mid \sigma \in DS\}$. The new bad terms are the subterms of a dangerous premise $t \in DP$ that were supposed to protect a secret in t. So, bad terms are particular instances of terms in $\mathcal{G}$ that must be removed. Formally,

$$BHat = \{t_{|q} \mid t \in DP,\ \exists p\ q.p \text{ critical in } t, t_{|q.p} \in \mathcal{X}_s \cup \mathcal{S},\ t_{|q}\ p\text{-matches with } \mathcal{G}\}$$

Each occurrence of $\mathcal{H}'$ in the semantic algorithm is now replaced by the set of bad terms $\mathcal{B}'$ and computing the restriction of $\mathcal{H}'$ now corresponds to the instruction $\mathcal{B}' := \mathcal{B}' \cup BHat$.

5. Finally, $newS$ is replaced by

$$newS := \{t \in DP \mid var(t) \cap \mathcal{X}_s = \emptyset,\ \forall s \in \mathcal{S}'.\ s \notin_c t\}$$

Example 3. We illustrates the computation of dangerous substitutions on the rule $t_p \to t_c$ *given in Figure 2 and the sets of terms:*

$$\mathcal{G} = \{\ \mathbf{encr}(x_s, K_B),\ \mathbf{encr}(x_s, K_A)\ \}$$
$$\mathcal{B} = \{\ \mathbf{encr}(\mathbf{pair}(I, x'_s), K_B),\ \mathbf{encr}(\mathbf{pair}(\mathbf{pair}(A, x''), x''_s), K_B)\ \}$$

We consider the conclusion of the rule. The first step consists in looking for all the critical positions in the conclusion where a secret or a secret variable appears. We find one variable $y_s \in \mathcal{X}_s$ *at position* 01101 *in the term* t_c. *For* y_s, *there are two protecting positions* ϵ *and* 011*: the term* $\mathbf{encr}(x_s, K_B)$ 01101-*matches with* $t_{c|\epsilon}$ *and it also* 01-*matches with* $t_{c|011}$. *Then, we search for all substitutions that* 01101-*unify* $t_{c|\epsilon}$ *and* 01-*unify* $t_{c|011}$ *with the bad terms. Starting with position* $p_1 = \epsilon$, $t_{c|\epsilon}$ 01101-*unifies with the bad term* $\mathbf{encr}(\mathbf{pair}(I, x'_s), K_B)$ *for the unifier* $\sigma' = [z = I, x'_s = t_{c|01}]$. *This cancels the top most protection. Then, we attempt to complete the substitution* σ' *so that it also cancels the protection at position* $p_2 = 011$. *To do so, we try to* 01-*unify the term* $\sigma'(t_c)_{|p_2} = \mathbf{encr}(\mathbf{pair}(\mathbf{pair}(y, I), y_s), K_B)$ *with a bad term and succeed with the bad term* $\mathbf{encr}(\mathbf{pair}(\mathbf{pair}(A, x''), x''_s), K_B)$ *and the unifier* $\sigma'' = [y = A, x'' = I, y_s = x''_s]$. *The two unifiers are then composed and restricted to the domain* $var(t_c)$ *resulting in the substitution* $\sigma = (\sigma' \cup \sigma'')_{/var(t_c)} = [y = A, z = I]$. *Pursuing this process does not provide other substitutions and finally* σ *appears to be the only dangerous substitutions. We now look at the premise of the rule to compute the new bad terms induced by* σ. *The position of the secret variable* y_s *in* t_p *is protected by the good term* $\mathbf{encr}(x_s, K_A)$ *that* 01-*matches on* $t_{p|0}$. *However, the dangerous substitution* σ *tells that this protection will not work in case where* y *is* A *and* z *is* I. *Consequently, we refine the set of hat messages by removing this particular case. In our symbolic representation, this comes out to add* $\sigma(t_{p|0}) = \mathbf{encr}(\ \mathbf{pair}(\mathbf{pair}(A, I), y_s),\ K_A)$ *to the set of bad terms.* □

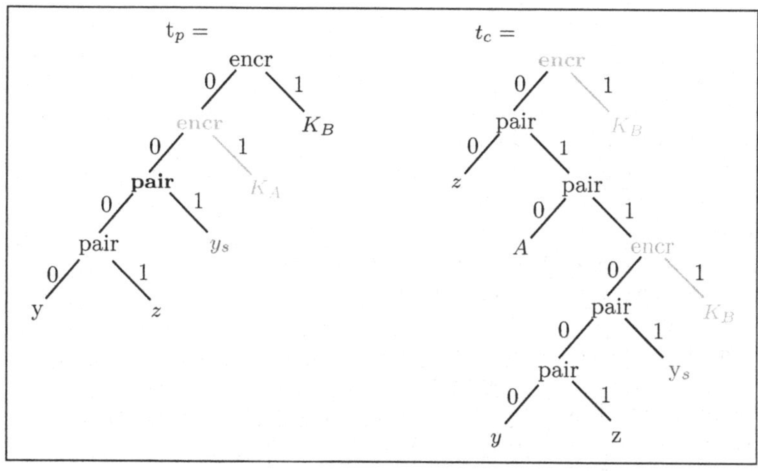

Fig. 2. Illustration of computing dangerous substitutions.

6 An Example of Verification and Experimentations

We illustrate our approach on the verification of the corrected version of the Needham-Schroeder protocol, also called Needham-Schroeder-Lowe. The correction bears on the second transition of principal B in Example 1, which becomes:

$$\begin{aligned} A \rightarrow B &: \{A, N_1\}_{K_B} \\ B \rightarrow A &: \{B, N_1, N_2\}_{K_A} \\ A \rightarrow B &: \{N_2\}_{K_B} \end{aligned}$$

We run our prototype implementation, named HERMES, with the secrets $\{N_2, K_A^{-1}, K_B^{-1}\}$, the empty set of bad patterns and the set $\mathcal{G} = \{\{x_s\}_{K_A}, \{x_s\}_{K_B}\}$ of good patterns. It terminates with the set of secrets unchanged and the set $\mathcal{B}$ of bad patterns : $\{I, x_s\}_{K_A}$, $\{A, (N_1^{AA}, Sup(I, x_s))\}_{K_A}$, $\{A, (N_1, Sup(I, x_s))\}_{K_A}$.

From this, we can conclude that the Needham-Schroeder-Lowe protocol preserves the secret N_2. Concerning, the uncorrected version of Example 1, during computation of new secrets and bad patterns, we arrive at a situation where we have to add $\{A, N_1^{AI}\}_{K_I}$ as a secret. As this message contains neither a fresh nonce nor a secret, it can not be a secret. We stop the computation and follow it back to reconstruct the attack known as "man in the middle".

6.1 On the Termination of the Symbolic Algorithm

In this section, we present a technique that makes a depth-first implementation of the symbolic verification algorithm always terminate, at a price of safe approximation of the results. In fact, our prototype implementation of our verification

Table 1. This figure has been obtainded by running HERMES on a Pentium III 600Mhz PC under Linux 2.2.19.

Protocol Name	Result	Time (sec)
Yahalom	OK	12.67
Needham-Schroeder Public Key	Attack	0.01
Needham-Schroeder Public Key (with a key server)	Attack	0.90
Needham-Schroeder-Lowe	OK	0.02
Otway-Rees	OK*	0.02
Denny Sacco Key Distribution with Public Key	Attack	0.02
Wide Mouthed Frog (modified)	OK	0.01
Kao-Chow	OK	0.07
Neumann-Stubblebine	OK*	0.04
Needham-Schroeder Symmetric Key	Attack	0.04
ISO Symmetric Key One-Pass Unilateral Authentication	Attack	0.01
ISO Symmetric Key Two-Pass Unilateral Authentication	OK	0.01
Andrew Secure RPC	Attack	0.04
Woo and Lam	OK	0.06
Skeme	OK	0.06

* There is a known attack of the untyped version of the protocol. Discovering this type attack automatically requires to deal with non-atomic keys. This is not yet implemented in HERMES.

algorithm, named HERMES, terminates with precise results on all pratical examples of protocols we tried. That is, the results did not show any false attack (see Table 1).

A sequence $(t_i)_{i\geq 0}$ of pattern terms is called *increasing at a sequence* $(p_i)_{i\geq 0}$ of positions, if the following conditions are satisfied for every $i \geq 0$:

1. $p_i \in dom(t_i)$ and $p_i \preceq p_{i+1}$,
2. $t_0[z/p_0] = t_i[z/p_0]$, where z is fresh variable.
3. $t_{i|p_i} = t_{0|p_0}$.

Let us consider an example to clarify these definitions.

Example 4. Consider the following rule from the session (A, A) of Needham-Schroeder-Lowe protocol presented in Section 6:

$$r = \frac{\{(A, (N_1^{AA}, y))\}_{K_A}}{\{y\}_{K_A}}.$$

Consider the sequence $(\{\theta^i(I, x)\}_{K_A})_{i\geq 0}$, where $\theta(z) = (A, (N_1^{AA}, z))$. The first three terms of the sequence are $\{\theta^0(I, x)\}_{K_A} = \{(I, x)\}_{K_A}$, $\{\theta^1(I, x)\}_{K_A} = \{(A, (N_1^{AA}, (I, x)))\}_{K_A}$ and $\{\theta^2(I, x)\}_{K_A} = \{(A, (N_1^{AA}, (A, (N_1^{AA}, (I, x)))))\}_{K_A}$. The whole sequence can be obtained by iteratively computing the bad patterns induced by the rule r starting from the bad term $\{(I, x)\}_{K_A}$. Thus, a naive application of our symbolic algorithm will not terminate. On the other hand, this sequence is increasing at $(p_i = 0(11)^i)_{i\geq 0}$. Indeed, $\{\theta^i(I, x)\}_{K_A}[z/p_0] = \{z\}_{K_A}$

and $\left(\{\theta^i(I,x)\}_{K_A}\right)_{|p_i} = (I,x)$, for every $i \geq 0$. We will see now how this fact can be exploited to make the algorithm to converge. □

The clue of our technique for enforcing termination of the symbolic algorithm is expressed by the following proposition:

Proposition 3. *Let* $(t_i)_{i\geq 0}$ *be increasing at* $(p_i)_{i\geq 0}$. *Then,*

$$\bigcup_{i\geq 0}[\![t_i]\!] \subseteq \bigcup_{i<j}[\![t_i]\!] \cup [\![t_j[Sup(t_{j|p_j})/p_j]]\!], \text{ for every } j \geq 0.$$

Example 5. Consider again our Example 4. Then, if we choose $j=1$, we obtain a set consisting of the two pattern terms $\{(I,x)\}_{K_A}$ and $\{(A,(N_1^{AA}, Sup(I,x)))\}_{K_A}$ which approximates the whole sequence $\left(\{\theta^i(I,x)\}_{K_A}\right)_{i\geq 0}$.

7 Conclusion

In this paper, we presented a method based on abstract interpretation for verifying secrecy properties of cryptographic protocols in a general model. Our method deals with unbounded number of sessions, unbounded number of principals, unbounded message depth and unbounded creation of fresh nonces. The main contribution of this paper is a verification algorithm that consists of computing an inductive invariant using patterns as symbolic representation. In case the given protocol is correct, our method provides a proof tree that can be exploited for certification. More precisely, from the obtained proof tree we can automatically deduce a proof, for instance in Coq or PVS, that can serve for certification. We are actually working on implementing this idea.

Our method can already deal with models in which we distinguish between long term and short term keys and which contain variables ranging over keys. The idea here is that short term keys can be revealed to the intruder when a session has terminated. This is not the case for long term keys. This allows a more faithful modeling of some protocols.

Our tool together with the examples of Table 1 can be experimented at the url: `http://www-verimag.imag.fr/~Liana.Bozga/eva/hermes.php`.

References

1. Martín Abadi. Secrecy by typing in security protocols. In *Theoretical Aspects of Computer Software*, volume 1281 of *LNCS*, p. 611–638, 1997.
2. Martín Abadi and Bruno Blanchet. Secrecy Types for Asymmetric Communication. In *Foundations of Software Science and Computation Structures*, volume 2030 of *LNCS*, p. 25–41, 2001.
3. Roberto M. Amadio and Denis Lugiez. On the reachability problem in cryptographic protocols. In *International Conference on Concurrency Theory*, volume 1877 of *LNCS*, p. 380–394, 2000.

4. D. Bolignano. An approach to the formal verification of cryptographic protocols. In *ACM Conference on Computer and Communications Security*, p. 106–118, 1996.
5. L. Bozga, Y. Lakhnech, and M. Périn. Abstract interpretation for secrecy using patterns. Technical report, Verimag, 2002.
6. J. Clark and J. Joacob. A survey on authentification protocol. Available at the url http://www.cs.york.ac.uk/~jac/papers/drareviewps.ps, 1997.
7. H. Comon, V. Cortier, and J. Mitchell. Tree automata with one memory, set constraints, and ping-pong protocols. In *International Colloquium on Automata, Languages and Programming*, volume 2076 of *LNCS*, 2001.
8. H. Comon, V. Shmatikov. Is it possible to decide whether a cryptographic protocol is secure or not? *Journal of Telecommunications and Information Technology*, 2002.
9. H. Comon-Lundh and V. Cortier. Security properties: Two agents are sufficient. Technical report, LSV, 2002.
10. D. Dolev, S. Even, and R. M. Karp. On the security of ping-pong protocols. In *Advances in Cryptology*, p. 177–186, 1982.
11. D. Dolev and A. C. Yao. On the security of public key protocols. *IEEE Transactions on Information Theory*, 29(2):198–208, 1983.
12. N. Durgin, P. Lincoln, J. Mitchell, and A. Scedrov. Undecidability of bounded security protocols. In *Workshop on Formal Methods and Security Protocols*, 1999.
13. S. Even and O. Goldreich. On the security of multi-party ping pong protocols. Technical report, Israel Institute of Technology, 1983.
14. F.J.T. Fábrega, J.C. Herzog, and J.D. Guttman. Strand Spaces: Why is a Security Protocol Correct? In *IEEE Conference on Security and Privacy*, p. 160–171, 1998.
15. T. Genet and F. Klay. Rewriting for cryptographic protocol verification. In *International Conference on Automated Deduction*, volume 1831 of *LNCS*, 2000.
16. A. Gordon and A. Jeffrey. Authenticity by typing for security protocols. In *IEEE Computer Security Foundations Workshop*, p. 145–159, 2001.
17. Jean Goubault-Larrecq. A method for automatic cryptographic protocol verification. In *International Workshop on Formal Methods for Parallel Programming: Theory and Applications*, volume 1800 of *LNCS*, 2000.
18. G. Lowe. An attack on the Needham-Schroeder public-key authentification protocol. *Information Processing Letters*, 56(3):131–133, 1995.
19. G. Lowe. Breaking and fixing the Needham-Schroeder Public-Key protocol using FDR. In *Tools and Algorithms for the Construction and Analysis of Systems*, volume 1055 of *LNCS*, p. 147–166, 1996.
20. C. Meadows. Invariant generation techniques in cryptographic protocol analysis. In *Computer Security Foundations Workshop*, 2000.
21. J. Millen and V. Shmatikov. Constraint solving for bounded-process cryptographic protocol analysis. In *ACM Conference on Computer and Communications Security*, p. 166–175, 2001.
22. David Monniaux. Abstracting Cryptographic Protocols with Tree Automata. In *Static Analysis Symposium*, volume 1694 of *LNCS*, p. 149–163, 1999.
23. R.M. Needham and M.D. Schroeder. Using encryption for authentication in large networks of computers. *Communications of the ACM*, 21(12):993–999, 1978.
24. M. Rusinowitch and M. Turuani. Protocol insecurity with finite number of sessions is NP-complete. In *IEEE Computer Security Foundations Workshop*, 2001.
25. J. Thayer, J. Herzog, and J. Guttman. Honest Ideals on Strand Spaces. In *IEEE Computer Security Foundations Workshop*, p. 66–78, 1998.

Compositional Analysis for Verification of Parameterized Systems

Samik Basu and C.R. Ramakrishnan

Department of Computer Science
SUNY at Stony Brook
Stony Brook, NY 11794-4400
{bsamik, cram}@cs.sunysb.edu

Abstract. Many safety-critical systems that have been considered by the verification community are parameterized by the number of concurrent components in the system, and hence describe an infinite family of systems. Traditional model checking techniques can only be used to verify specific instances of this family. In this paper, we present a technique based on compositional model checking and program analysis for automatic verification of infinite families of systems. The technique views a parameterized system as an expression in a process algebra (CCS) and interprets this expression over a domain of formulas (modal mu-calculus), considering a process as a property transformer. The transformers are constructed using partial model checking techniques. At its core, our technique solves the verification problem by finding the limit of a chain of formulas. We present a widening operation to find such a limit for properties expressible in a subset of modal mu-calculus. We describe the verification of a number of parameterized systems using our technique to demonstrate its utility.

1 Introduction

Model checking is a widely used approach for verifying whether a system specification possesses a property expressed in temporal logic [CES86,QS82]. Many efficient verification tools been developed based on approaches such as explicit-state [Hol97], symbolic [BCM+90] and compositional [ASW94] techniques. Traditionally, model checkers have been restricted to the verification of finite-state systems, although recent research on constraint-based techniques (e.g. [DP99]), symmetry reduction [ID96], data independence [Wol86], and symbolic checking with rich assertional languages [KP00] have extended model checking techniques to certain classes of infinite-state systems.

The Driving Problem. One class of infinite-state systems called *parameterized systems* is particularly interesting. A parameterized system describes an infinite family of (typically finite-state) systems; instances of the family can be obtained by fixing the parameters. Consider a simple example of parameterized producer-consumer system shown in Figure 1. A producer process P performs an action

H. Garavel and J. Hatcliff (Eds.): TACAS 2003, LNCS 2619, pp. 315–330, 2003.

$$\begin{aligned} \mathtt{P} &\stackrel{def}{=} \mathtt{a.P} \\ \mathtt{C} &\stackrel{def}{=} \overline{\mathtt{a}}.\mathtt{C} \\ \mathtt{sys}(N) &\stackrel{def}{=} (\mathtt{P}^N|\mathtt{C})\backslash\{\mathtt{a}\} \end{aligned}$$
(a)

$$\begin{aligned} \varphi &\equiv X \;\; where \;\; X =_\nu \langle\tau\rangle\mathtt{tt} \wedge [\tau]X \\ \varphi_c &\equiv Y \;\; where \;\; Y =_\nu \langle\tau,\mathtt{a}\rangle\mathtt{tt} \wedge [\tau,\mathtt{a}]Y \\ \varphi_1 &\equiv Z_1 \;\; where \;\; Z_1 =_\nu [\tau,\mathtt{a},\overline{\mathtt{a}}]Z_1 \\ \varphi_2 &\equiv Z_2 \;\; where \;\; Z_2 =_\nu [\tau,\mathtt{a},\overline{\mathtt{a}}]Z_2 \end{aligned}$$
(b)

Fig. 1. (a) Parameterized System with one consumer and arbitrary number of producers. (b) Deadlock-freedom formula φ and property transformation results

a and continues to behave as P. Similarly, the consumer process C repeatedly performs action $\overline{\mathtt{a}}$. The processes communicate by synchronization on $\overline{\mathtt{a}}$ and a actions. The parameterized system Sys(M, N) is specified as parallel composition of M producers and N consumers. Our objective is to verify deadlock-freedom property for *all instances* of the system Sys.

Models of many safety-critical systems are parameterized: e.g., resource arbitration protocols, communication protocols, etc. Traditionally, model checkers have been used to verify specific instances of the infinite family described by a parameterized system: e.g., to verify that a mutual exclusion protocol is correct for fixed numbers of objects and threads [BSW00]. Clearly, this strategy cannot be used to verify *all instances* of the infinite family of systems.

Our Solution. In this paper we present an automatic technique for checking whether any or all arbitrary instances of an infinite family of systems possess a given temporal property. At a high level, our solution to the verification problem is analogous to program analysis. Each instance of a parameterized system is viewed as an expression in a process algebra (specifically, CCS [Mil89]). We then interpret these process algebraic expressions over a domain consisting of formulas in an expressive temporal logic (specifically, the alternation free modal mu-calculus [Koz83]). The interpretation is based on associating a *property transformer* Π for each process p in the parameterized system. Given a system s consisting of p concurrently composed with an arbitrary environment e, Π captures the relationship between properties that hold in the environment e and the properties that hold in the system s. For instance, consider the process P in Figure 1(a). The process can move on a transition only if there is a concurrent process ready to move on $\overline{\mathtt{a}}$ transition. In order for the process P to execute the a action, the environment must be capable of synchronizing with an $\overline{\mathtt{a}}$ action. Thus the process P can be seen as transforming the property ("eventually do a transition") to its environment ("eventually do $\overline{\mathtt{a}}$ transition").

The property transformer for a given process is generated based on the notion of *quotienting* due to [And95]. Based on the property transformer, we define a chain of mu-calculus formulas whose limit characterizes the behavior of an arbitrary instance of the parameterized system. Consider the problem of verifying deadlock-freedom for the parameterized system sys(n) for all $n \geq 1$. The formula to be checked for the entire system is given in Figure 1(b) as φ.

Consider the system sys(n) with one consumer (C) and n producer processes($\mathtt{P}^n$). We compute the property expected of the producers alone, by transforming the property φ using the property transformer for C process. The resulting "quotient" property is the formula φ_c in the figure. Intuitively, φ_c states that φ can be modeled by an environment composed in parallel to process C if the environment can perform infinitely many a or τ actions. Therefore, if $\mathtt{P}^n \models \varphi_c$ then $\mathtt{sys}(n) \models \varphi$. Next, transform φ_c using the property transformer for process P. The resultant property left for the environment ($\mathtt{P}^{n-1}$) to satisfy is φ_1. Quotienting further using process P, the residue obtained is φ_2. Further transformation of φ_2 using the property transformer for P will leave it unaltered. Thus, we have reached the limit φ_ω of formula sequence generated by iterative transformation using property transformer of process P. Then $\mathtt{0} \models \varphi_\omega$ implies $\forall n \in N$ $\mathtt{sys}(n) \models \varphi$. The above discussion presents a high level view of the technique used to verify properties for all or any members of a parameterized system. Actual technique, however, keeps track of various restriction and relabeling operations applied to the processes. See Section 3,4 for details.

Note that the domain of interpretation, the modal mu-calculus, has infinite ascending chains, and hence the limit computation may not terminate. Nevertheless, we find that the iterative computation of the limit does converge for a number of example parameterized systems. To handle a larger class of systems, we also define a widening operation to accelerate the convergence, and in some cases guarantee termination.

Related Work. A number of techniques have been proposed to verify parameterized systems with varying amounts of user intervention ranging from fully automatic techniques (such as [KP00]) which focus on the domain of representations of system states, to program-transformation-based systems capable of inferring the structure of certain underlying induction proofs [RKR+00,RR01].

One of the approaches is to reduce the infinite-state verification problem to an equivalent finite-state one, by identifying a representative finite-state system corresponding to a given parameterized system and temporal property (e.g. see [EN95,EN96,ID99]). Cache coherence protocols and unidirectional token ring protocols have been successfully verified using this approach. Recently there have been efforts to verify infinite families by choosing an appropriate finite representation (e.g. using regular languages or counting the number of components in particular states, see [EN98,EFM99,Del00,PS00]). All these approaches require a specialized way of specifying processes: as grammars [CGJ97], logic programs [RKR+00], or rewrite rules [KP00]. In contrast, out technique directly manipulates parameterized process specifications written in a standard process algebraic representation that is typically used by finite-state model checking tools. Moreover, being based on program analysis, our technique can be applied with little or no knowledge of the internals of the system under consideration. This is in contrast to representation-based techniques [EN98,EFM99, Del00,KP00] whose success depends on a clever choice of representations. Another approach, which requires considerable user intervention, is to generate a network invariant for a system consisting of arbitrary number of identical components [CGJ97,LHR97]. For chains and circular networks [SG99] presents a method to generate such invariants automatically using a fixed point iteration procedure over two-dimensional strings automata. Our technique is also based on computing the limit of an infinite chain, but one of mu-calculus formulas, and does not restrict the network topology of the system to be verified.

An important aspect of our work is the generation of property transformers using techniques from compositional model checking. Considerable amount of research has been done on using assume-guarantee reasoning for constructing compositional proofs [GL94,AH96,McM97,BG97,HQR98]. However, these methods typically need considerable user guidance. Closely related to our work are the compositional model checker of [ASW94] and the partial model checker of [And95]. The latter work defines property transformers for parallel composition of sequential automata, while we generalize the transformers to arbitrary CCS processes. We also present a bisimulation-based procedure to reduce the size of formulas generated by property transformers that results in smaller formulas than the method used in [And95].

Contributions. We present a technique for automatic verification of parameterized systems, representing an infinite family of finite-state systems. The technique views processes as property transformers and is based on computing the limit of a sequence of mu-calculus formula generated by these transformers.

1. We develop a compositional model checker for CCS [Mil89] and use this model checker to generate property transformers (Section 3).
2. We use the property transformers to define a sequence of mu-calculus formula. The limit of this sequence is used to verify properties over infinite families of systems. (Section 4).
3. To guarantee convergence of iterative procedure, we define acceleration and widening operators (based on widening techniques used in type analysis) for mu-calculus formula. (Section 4.1).
4. We show the usefulness of the technique by presenting its application in verifying protocols over token passing rings (Milner's cycle of schedulers [And95]), mutual exclusion protocols (Java metalock [ADG+99]), and cache coherence protocols [Del00] (Section 5). Details of the examples are available at `http://www.cs.sunysb.edu/~lmc/compose`.

2 Preliminaries

We briefly outline the syntax of the process algebra CCS [Mil89] and the logic modal mu-calculus [BS01] used in the rest of the paper.

2.1 CCS and Labeled Transition Systems

CCS is a simple process algebra that can be used to specify a variety of systems. Below we describe the syntax of expressions in *basic* CCS:

$$\mathcal{P} \rightarrow 0 \mid A \mid a.\mathcal{P} \mid \mathcal{P} + \mathcal{P} \mid \mathcal{P}'|'\mathcal{P} \mid \mathcal{P}\backslash L \mid \mathcal{P}[f]$$

In the above, 0 denotes a deadlocked process. A ranges over process names (agents) and a ranges over a set of actions $Act = \mathcal{L} \cup \overline{\mathcal{L}} \cup \tau$, where τ represents an internal action and $\mathcal{L}$ is a set of labels and $\overline{\mathcal{L}}$ is such that $a \in \mathcal{L} \Leftrightarrow \overline{a} \in \overline{\mathcal{L}}$. Finally, L ranges over the powerset of $\mathcal{L}$, and $f : \mathcal{L} \rightarrow \mathcal{L}$. The operators '.', '+', '|', '\' and '[·]' are called prefix, choice, parallel, restriction and relabeling respectively. A CCS specification consists of a set of process definitions, denoted by D, of the form $A \stackrel{def}{=} P$, where $P \in \mathcal{P}$. Each agent used in P, in turn, appears on the left hand side of some process definition in D. Note that process definitions may be recursive.

A labeled transition system $(S, \rightarrow)$ is specified by a set of *states* S and a transition relation $\rightarrow \subseteq S \times Act \times S$. The operational semantics of CCS expressions is given in terms of labeled transition systems where states represent CCS expressions. See [Mil89] for a full definition of the semantics of CCS.

2.2 The Modal mu-Calculus

The modal mu-calculus [Koz83] is an expressive temporal logic with explicit greatest and least fixed point operators. Following [CS93,And95], we use the *equational* form of mu-calculus. The syntax of *formulas* in modal mu-calculus over a set of propositional variables X and actions Act is given by the following grammar : $\Phi \rightarrow tt \mid ff \mid X \mid \Phi \vee \Phi \mid \Phi \wedge \Phi \mid \langle\alpha\rangle\Phi \mid [\alpha]\Phi$.

In the above, α specifies a set of actions in positive form (as $\beta \subseteq Act$) or negative form (as $-\beta$, where $\beta \subseteq Act$). $\langle\alpha\rangle\Phi$ states that there exists an action in α following which formula Φ holds true, while $[\alpha]\Phi$ states that after every action in α, Φ is satisfied. The variables used in a mu-calculus formula are *defined* using a *sequence* of simultaneous equations where the ith equation has the form: $X_i =_\mu \varphi_i$ or $X_i =_\nu \varphi_i$, where $\varphi_i \in \Phi$. The least and greatest fixed point symbols μ and ν are said to represent the *sign* of the equation. In the remainder of the paper,we use σ, ranging over $\{\mu, \nu\}$ to denote the sign of an arbitrary equation. We assume that each variable occurs exactly once on the left hand side of an equation. The variable X_1 defined by the first equation is called the *top variable.* The set of equations representing some property is denoted by F. The set of all mu-calculus equations is denoted by $\mathcal{E}$.

Model Checking. Given a labeled transition system $(S, \rightarrow)$, the semantics of mu-calculus formulas are stated such that each formula denotes a subset of S. Refer to [BS01] for semantics of mu-calculus. We say that a mu-calculus formula φ holds at a state s, if s is in the model of φ (denoted by $s \models \varphi$).

3 Partial Model Checking

Our technique for verification of parameterized systems is based on viewing a process as a property transformer. We generate property transformers using a partial model checker [And95]. Consider the verification of a formula φ over a process expression of the form $P|Q$. Given φ and P we generate the obligation

φ' on Q such that $P|Q \models \varphi$ whenever $Q \models \varphi'$. Thus we view P as *transforming* the obligation φ on $P|Q$ to the obligation φ' on Q. This transformation is called *quotienting* in [And95], where it is defined for modal mu-calculus properties and systems specified by a LTSs.

In Figure 2 we define the property transformer using a function $\Pi : (\mathcal{P} \times \mathcal{L} \times \mathcal{F}) \rightarrow \Phi \rightarrow \Phi$ where $\mathcal{L}$ is 2^{Act} and $\mathcal{F}$ is a set of partial functions $f : Act \rightarrow Act$ such that $f(x) \neq x$. We use $\perp$ to denote empty relabeling function which is undefined everywhere. We define composition of two relabeling functions $h = f \circ g$ such that $h(x)$ is undefined if $f(x)$ and $g(x)$ are undefined, $h(x) = f(x)$ if $g(x)$ is undefined, $h(x) = g(x)$ if $f(x)$ is undefined; if both are defined, then $h(x) = f(g(x))$. Φ is the set of modal mu-calculus formulas. Finally $\mathcal{P}$ is the set of all CCS process expressions. A process expression is said to be *well-named* if all relabeling operations of the form $Q[f]$ are such that set of visible actions of process Q is disjoint from the range of function f.

The transformer $\Pi_f^L(P)$ considers process P under a set of restricted actions (L) and a relabeling function (f). The transformer generates a formula ψ as the obligation of the environment of process P such that (a) modal actions are suitably relabeled by f and (b) environment is not allowed to synchronize on any actions in L. The transformer $\Pi_f^L(P)$ transforms φ and generates ψ defined over fixed point variables $X_{P,f,L}$, where φ is defined over variables in X.

The set of visible actions of process P is denoted by $vn(P)$. The names of formula φ, denoted by $n(\varphi)$, are the set of all actions in the modal subformulas of φ and the names of all the formula variables appearing in φ; The names of formula variable X are the names of formula φ that defines X (i.e. $X =_\sigma \varphi$). Range of relabeling f is the set of actions v such that $f : x \rightarrow v$. The function $f' = f \backslash L$ is such that $f'(x) = f(x)$ if $f(x) \notin L$ and $f'(x)$ is undefined otherwise.

Rules 1 through 5 in Figure 2 define the property transformer for propositional constants, boolean connectives, formula variables. Rule 6 states that the property transformer for the zero (deadlocked) process, which is the identity of the parallel composition operator of CCS, has the identity function as its property transformer. Rule 7 states that the property transformer for an agent is the property transformer of the process expression used to define the agent.

Property transformer of a process with relabeling function f_p is property transformer of the process under new relabeling function by composing the existing relabeling function with f_p (Rule 8). Rule 9 presents the property transformer for a process with restriction L_p. The restricted actions are mapped to a set of new names. This set is disjoint from the set of actions in the formula $(n(\varphi))$, visible actions of process $(vn(P))$ and restricted(L) and relabeled$(range(f))$ actions of the transformer.

Rule 10 captures the compositionality of property transformers: the property transformer for a parallel composition of processes is simply the function composition of the individual property transformers with appropriate restriction and relabels. First, consider process P_1 in Rule 10. The transformer function for P_1 is restricted on actions in L_1, which are not visible to the environment of P_1, *i.e.* P_2. Therefore, transformer function for P_2 is restricted on actions in L_2

1. $\Pi_f^L(P)(tt) = tt$
2. $\Pi_f^L(P)(ff) = ff$
3. $\Pi_f^L(P)(\varphi_1 \vee \varphi_2) = \Pi_f^L(P)(\varphi_1) \vee \Pi_f^L(P)(\varphi_2)$
4. $\Pi_f^L(P)(\varphi_1 \wedge \varphi_2) = \Pi_f^L(P)(\varphi_1) \wedge \Pi_f^L(P)(\varphi_2)$
5. $\Pi_f^L(P)(X) = X_{P,f,L}$
6. $\Pi_f^L(0)(\varphi) = \varphi$
7. $\Pi_f^L(A)(\varphi) = \Pi_f^L(P)(\varphi) \quad \texttt{if } A \stackrel{def}{=} P \in D$
8. $\Pi_f^L(P[f_p])(\varphi) = \Pi_{f \circ f_p}^L(P)(\varphi)$
9. $\Pi_f^L(P \backslash L_p)(\varphi) = \Pi_f^{L \cup L'}(P[L'/L_p])(\varphi)$ $\texttt{where } L' \cap (n(\varphi) \cup vn(P) \cup range(f) \cup L) = \{\}$
10. $\Pi_f^L(P_1|P_2)(\varphi) = \Pi_{f_2}^{L_2}(P_2)(\Pi_f^{L_1}(P_1)(\varphi))$ $\texttt{where } L_1 = L - vn(P_2),\ L_2 = L - L_1,\ f_2 = f \backslash L_1$
11. $$\Pi_f^L(a.P)(\langle\alpha\rangle\varphi) = \langle\alpha\rangle\Pi_f^L(a.P)(\varphi) \vee \left\{\begin{array}{ll} \Pi_f^L(P)(\varphi) & \texttt{if } f(a) \in \alpha \\ ff & \texttt{otherwise} \end{array}\right\} \vee \left\{\begin{array}{ll} \langle\overline{f(a)}\rangle\Pi_f^L(P)(\varphi) & \texttt{if } \tau \in \alpha \ \wedge \ \overline{f(a)} \notin L \\ ff & \texttt{otherwise} \end{array}\right\}$$
12. $$\Pi_f^L(a.P)([\alpha]\varphi) = [\alpha]\Pi_f^L(a.P)(\varphi) \wedge \left\{\begin{array}{ll} \Pi_f^L(P)(\varphi) & \texttt{if } f(a) \in \alpha \\ tt & \texttt{otherwise} \end{array}\right\} \wedge \left\{\begin{array}{ll} [\overline{f(a)}]\Pi_f^L(P)(\varphi) & \texttt{if } \tau \in \alpha \ \wedge \ \overline{f(a)} \notin L \\ tt & \texttt{otherwise} \end{array}\right\}$$
13. $\Pi_f^L(P_1 + P_2)(\langle\alpha\rangle\varphi) = \langle\alpha\rangle\Pi_f^L(P_1 + P_2)(\varphi) \vee \Pi_f^L(P_1)(\langle\alpha\rangle\varphi) \vee \Pi_f^L(P_2)(\langle\alpha\rangle\varphi)$
14. $\Pi_f^L(P_1 + P_2)([\alpha]\varphi) = [\alpha]\Pi_f^L(P_1 + P_2)(\varphi) \wedge \Pi_f^L(P_1)([\alpha]\varphi) \wedge \Pi_f^L(P_2)([\alpha]\varphi)$

A. $$\Pi_f^L(P)(X =_\sigma \varphi \cup E) = X_{P,f,L} =_\sigma \Pi_f^L(P)(\varphi) \ \cup \ \Pi_f^L(P)(E) \ \cup \{\bigcup(\Pi_{F'}^{L'}(P')(X' =_{\sigma'} \varphi') \texttt{ s.t } X'_{P',F',L'} \texttt{is subformula of } \Pi_f^L(P)(\varphi),\ X' =_{\sigma'} \varphi' \in F\}$$

B. $\Pi_f^L(P)(\{\}) = \{\}$

Fig. 2. Partial Model Checker for CCS

$(= L - L_1)$. Further, note that, relabel mapping on process P_2 is transformed by projecting off the mappings concerning names in L_1.

Rule 11 arises from the fact that $a.P|Q$ may satisfy $\langle\alpha\rangle\varphi$ in one of the following three ways:

1. Q does an α action to Q' leaving $a.P|Q'$ to satisfy φ. In this case, the obligation on Q is to do an α action, followed by satisfying the obligation left by $a.P$ due to φ (first disjunct in the rhs of Rule 11).
2. $a \in \alpha$ and P does the a action, leaving $P|Q$ to satisfy φ. In this case the obligation on Q is simply the obligation left by P due to φ (second disjunct in the rhs of Rule 11).
3. $\tau \in \alpha$, P does an a action that synchronizes with an $\overline{a}$ action by Q to produce the necessary τ action. This means that the obligation on Q is to first produce an $\overline{a}$ action and then satisfy whatever obligation is left by P due to φ (third disjunct of Rule 11).

Note that, property transformer of P, under a set of restricted actions L, does not permit the environment Q to synchronize on any action present in L. The third disjunct generates modal obligation for the environment on the action $\overline{f(a)}$ only when $\overline{f(a)} \notin L$. Rule 12 is the dual of Rule 11.

Rule 13 presents the property transformer for process with choice operator $(P_1 + P_2)$. It is defined by considering three different cases. In the first disjunct, selection of the processes P_1 and P_2 is postponed and the environment is provided with the obligation to satisfy diamond modality. The second and third disjunct represents the cases when the choices are made in favor of process P_1 and process P_2 respectively. Rule 14 is the dual of Rule 13.

Rules A and B define a function $\Pi : (\mathcal{P} \times \mathcal{L} \times \mathcal{F}) \to \mathcal{E} \to \mathcal{E}$ which defines property transformers over mu-calculus *equations*. To transform a sequence of equations E, we construct the set of equations as per Rules A and B.

The correctness of the quotienting operation, formally stated below, can be proved by induction on the structure of formula and process expressions.

Theorem 1 *Given a well-named process expression P the following identity holds*

$$\forall Q \quad Q|P \models \varphi \;\Leftrightarrow\; Q \models \Pi_{\perp}^{\{\}}(P)(\varphi)$$

4 Verification of Parameterized Systems

Consider a parameterized system P_n defined by parallel composition of processes P. The parameter (n) represents the number of processes P present in the system. Consider verifying whether the ith instance of the above system possesses property φ: *i.e.* whether $P_i \models \varphi$. Let

$$\varphi_i = \Pi_f^L(P_i)(\varphi),$$

where f and L are the relabelings and restrictions applied to the process P_i. Therefore, from Theorem 1, $0 \models \varphi_i \Leftrightarrow P_i \models \varphi$.

Now consider verifying whether $\forall i.\ P_i \models \varphi$. Let φ'_i be defined as follows

$$\varphi'_i = \begin{cases} \varphi_1 & \textit{if } i = 1 \\ \varphi'_{i-1} \wedge \varphi_i & \textit{if } i > 1 \end{cases} \tag{1}$$

By definition of φ'_i, $\forall 1 \leq j \leq i.0 \models \varphi_j \Leftrightarrow 0 \models \varphi'_i$. Hence, $0 \models \varphi'_i$ means that $\forall 1 \leq j \leq i.P_j \models \varphi$. If φ'_ω is the limit of sequence $\varphi'_1, \varphi'_2 \ldots$, then, $0 \models \varphi'_\omega \Leftrightarrow \forall i \geq 1.P_i \models \varphi$.

A dual method can be used to determine whether $\exists i \geq 1.\ s_i \models \varphi$ simply by defining

$$\varphi'_i = \begin{cases} \varphi_1 & \textit{if } i = 1 \\ \varphi'_{i-1} \vee \varphi_i & \textit{if } i > 1 \end{cases} \tag{2}$$

We say that φ'_i is said to be *contracting* if $\varphi'_i \Rightarrow \varphi'_{i-1}$ and *relaxing* if $\varphi'_{i-1} \Rightarrow \varphi'_i$. For systems indexed by a single parameter, the limit of the sequence of φ'_is can be computed by a fixed point iteration procedure. For details of the proof refer to `http://www.cs.sunysb.edu/~lmc/compose`.

Two problems need to be solved before this method can be implemented. First of all, we need a procedure to check if the limit φ_ω has been reached: that is to determine the equivalence of two mu-calculus formulas. Checking equivalence between mu-calculus properties is EXPTIME-hard [EJ88] and hence we need an efficient procedure to compute an approximate equivalence relation. Moreover, as remarked in [And95] the formulas resulting from property transformers tend to be large and effective simplification procedures are needed before this method becomes practical. While we use the simplification rules from [And95], we use a more powerful procedure to test for equivalence between mu-calculus formulas by constructing graphs from the formulas and checking for their bisimilarity.

The second problem arises due to the existence of infinite ascending chains in the domain of modal mu-calculus formulas: the iteration procedure may not always terminate. We describe a widening operator (based on definitions of widening operators over type domains) to guarantee the termination of iteration procedure at the expense of completeness in Section 4.1. In [PS00], similar idea has been applied on regular transition relations to ensure convergence of transitive closures of parameterized systems. The distinguishing feature of our work is that widening (acceleration) is tailored to property representation (mu-calculus) unlike the acceleration on transition relations [PS00].

The approach presented above can be be easily applied to infinite families of systems specified by two or more parameters by considering a multi-parameter system as a nesting of single parameter systems. This cannot be done if the parameters are interdependent; a method capable of handling such infinite families remains to be developed.

4.1 Accelerating Fixed Point Iterations

Widening [CC77] is a well-known technique for accelerating and guaranteeing termination over domains with infinite ascending chains. We first present an acceleration operation, inspired by the widening operators defined over type graphs in the area of type analysis [HCC94], to accelerate the convergence, but this still does not guarantee termination. This operation can be modified to yield a widening operator for a class of mu-calculus formulas.

Let $\psi_0, \psi_1, \ldots$ be a sequence of mu-calculus formulas such that $\psi_{i+1} = f(\psi_i)$. Furthermore, let the sequence be such that $\forall i.\ \psi_{i+1} \Rightarrow \psi_i$ (contracting sequence) or $\forall i.\ \psi_{i+1} \Leftarrow \psi_i$ (relaxing sequence). We now consider the problem of computing the limit of such a sequence. The acceleration operation, *accel*, is a monotonic function that determines a new formula $\psi' = accel(\psi_i, \psi_{i+1})$ based on the differences between ψ_i and ψ_{i+1} such that $\psi' \geq \psi_{i+1}$. The acceleration operation is defined by considering a graph representation of mu-calculus formulas as described below.

Formula Graph. A formula graph, called *F-graph*, is an and/or graph that captures the structure of a mu-calculus formula, and is defined as follows:

Special Transition Rule for top variable X

$[X]^{\#,\sigma} \overset{\#,\gamma,\sigma}{\circ\!\!\longrightarrow} [\phi]^{\#,\sigma}$ if $X =_\sigma \phi$

General Transition Rules

1(a).	$[\varphi_1\ b\ \varphi_2]^{b',\sigma} \overset{b,m,\sigma}{\circ\!\!\longrightarrow} [\psi]^{b,\sigma}$	if $[\varphi_1]^{b,\sigma} \overset{b,m,\sigma}{\circ\!\!\longrightarrow} [\psi]^{b,\sigma} \wedge (b = b' \vee b' = \#)$
1(b).	$[\varphi_1\ b\ \varphi_2]^{b',\sigma} \overset{b,m,\sigma}{\circ\!\!\longrightarrow} [\psi]^{b,\sigma}$	if $[\varphi_2]^{b,\sigma} \overset{b,m,\sigma}{\circ\!\!\longrightarrow} [\psi]^{b,\sigma} \wedge (b = b' \vee b' = \#)$
2.	$[\varphi_1\ b\ \varphi_2]^{b',\sigma} \overset{b,\gamma,\sigma}{\circ\!\!\longrightarrow} [\varphi_1\ b\ \varphi_2]^{b,\sigma}$	if $b' \neq b \wedge b' \neq \#$
3(a).	$[\langle a\rangle\varphi]^{b,\sigma} \overset{b,\langle a\rangle,\sigma}{\circ\!\!\longrightarrow} \varphi^{b,\sigma}$	
3(b).	$[[a]\varphi]^{b,\sigma} \overset{b,[a],\sigma}{\circ\!\!\longrightarrow} \varphi^{b,\sigma}$	
4.	$[Y]^{b,\sigma} \overset{b,\gamma,\sigma}{\circ\!\!\longrightarrow} \varphi^{b,\sigma_1}$	if $Y =_{\sigma_1} \varphi$

Fig. 3. Transition relation for F-graph

Definition 1 *F-graph is defined as a tuple* $FG = (S, \circ\!\!\longrightarrow, A)$*, where* S *is the set of states labeled by a pair* (α, σ)*,* $A \subseteq \alpha \times \beta \times \sigma$ *is the set of labels on transitions, where* $\alpha \in \{\#, \vee, \wedge\}$*,* $\beta \in \{[a], \langle a\rangle, \gamma\}$ *and* $\sigma \in \{\mu, \nu\}$*.* $\circ\!\!\longrightarrow \subseteq S \times A \times S$ *is the labeled transition relation between pairs of states. The transition relation* $\circ\!\!\longrightarrow$ *is a least relation as defined in Figure 3.*

Each state in formula graph is labeled by (i) a boolean connective (b) stating whether the state is a part of "and" or "or" structure and (ii) a fixed point operator (σ) keeping track of fixed point nature of the current state's ancestor. Note that the top variable X, thus, has no inherited attributes. We use a special symbol # as its b label and synthesize the fixed point attribute from the definition of X. Rules 1 to 4 complete the definition of transition relation for all other cases. Rules 1(a) and 1(b) are defined by transitive closure relation and captures action label m present in identical boolean structures and under same fixed point operators. Note that the special symbol # can match with both $\wedge$ and $\vee$ boolean operators. Rule 2 presents the nesting of boolean structures. In this case, we use another special marker γ to identify toggling between boolean operators. γ is also used to mark the first transition from a formula variable.

Note that F-graphs capture only some of the structure of a mu-calculus formula: for instance, the order of conjuncts in a disjunction is omitted. F-graphs can be viewed as labeled transition systems. This permits us to check for equivalence between two mu-calculus formulas based on the bisimulation [Mil89] of their respective F-graphs.

Proposition 1 *Two mu-calculus formula* φ_1 *and* φ_2 *are equivalent if their corresponding F-graphs* F_1 *and* F_2 *are bisimilar.*

Acceleration based on F-graphs. The widening operator over type graphs [Mil99,HCC94] identifies topological differences between two graphs and

```
procedure widen(Fφ1, Fφ2)
clash-set := null;
visited := null;
topoclash(N1, N2);
//N1, N2 are start nodes of Fφ1, Fφ2
visited := null
foreach Nc ∈ clash-set do
    Na := anc-of(Nc, Fφ2);
    rearrange(Na, Nc);
endforeach
return(Fφ2);
```

```
procedure anc-of(Nc, Fφ2)
foreach Na ∈ Fφ2 do
if Na o--*-->Nc ∧ sim(Na, Nc) then
    return(Na);
endforeach
return(null);
```

```
procedure topoclash(N1, N2)
if (N1, N2) ∈ visited then
    return;
if ∃N2 o--b,m,σ--> M2 ∧ ¬∃N1 o--b,m,σ--> M1 then
  clash-set := clash-set ∪ {N2}
  return;
foreach N2 o--b,m,σ--> M2 do
  foreach N1 o--b,m,σ--> M1 do
    visited:=visited ∪ (N1, N2);
    remove N2 from clash-set;
    topoclash(M1, M2);
  endforeach
endforeach
```

```
procedure sim(Na, Nc)
if (Na, Nc) ∈visited then
  return 1;
ret-val := 1;
foreach Nc o--b,m,σ--> Mc do
  ret-val1 := 0;
  foreach Na o--b,γ,σ--> * o--b,m,σ--> o--b,γ,σ--> * Ma do
    visited:=visited ∪ (Na, Nc);
    ret-val1:=ret-val1|sim(Ma, Mc);
  endforeach
  ret-val := ret-val & ret-val1;
endforeach
return(ret-val);
```

Fig. 4. Widening Algorithm

detects the state (in the graph to be widened) which leads to such a disparity between the two graphs. This node is termed as witness to *topological clash*. In the next step, an ancestor of the witness is selected with some specific property. Finally all the transitions from the witness is directed to the ancestor resulting in a loop. This removes the sub-graph of the witness and shortens the graph.

Following the same line, we develop an acceleration operator over mu-calculus formulas expressing safety and reachability properties as follows. Let F_φ be the formula graph corresponding to the formula φ. We first formalize the notion of a topological clash between the formula graphs of two formulas φ_1 and φ_2.

Definition 2 *Formula φ_2 clashes with φ_1 (denoted by $\varphi_1 \ominus \varphi_2$) if there exists states N_1 in F_{φ_1} and N_2 in F_{φ_2}, such that the states N_1 and N_2 are reachable from the start states of F_{φ_1} and F_{φ_2} by identical sequences of transitions and there exists a transition from N_2 that has no matching transition from N_1. This is called topological clash and N_2 is said to be a witness to the clash.*

Intuitively, the above relation identifies the situation when φ_2 has an new sub-formula that is not present in φ_1. This type of divergence in the formula arises when a formula keeps a count of modal operators needed to reach a distinguished state. We discard such counters as follows. We identify an ancestor of witness node such that the ancestor simulates the witness (see [Mil89] for definition of simulation). Finally, the accelerated graph $F_{\varphi'}$ is constructed from F_{φ_2} by removing the witness node and redirecting all its incoming edges to ancestor node and introducing outgoing transitions of witness to ancestor. Figure 4 presents the pseudo-code for our acceleration operation. Procedure `widen` takes in two formula graphs F_{φ_1} and F_{φ_2} and performs acceleration of the latter. Procedure `topoclash` constructs the set (`clash-set`) of witness nodes to topological clash. In the next step, for each node N_c in the `clash-set` a suitable ancestor N_a is detected using the procedure `anc-of`. Finally, procedure `rearrange` (Line 7 of `widen`) removes the node N_c and redirects its incoming and outgoing edges to and from N_a respectively. The acceleration operation defined here is only applicable if the selected witness node is an $\wedge$ or $\vee$ node and the sequence of φ_i is contracting (Equation 1) or relaxing (Equation 2) respectively.

Note that such acceleration shortens the formula graph by merging one or more witness nodes with their respective ancestors. In terms of abstraction of formula, such merging amounts to discarding the exact sequence of modal actions that is preserved in un-abstracted formula.

Note however that the acceleration operator is not a widening operator and its range contains infinite ascending chains. Two factors prevent it from being a widening operator. First, the nodes selected for discarding are restricted by the definition of generated formula (contraction or relaxation) and hence not all growth in formula graphs are even considered for pruning. For instance, sequence may be contracting but a formula can grow under an '$\vee$' node. This factor for divergence disappears when we restrict the mu-calculus formulas under consideration to those whose F-graphs have all and-nodes or all or-nodes. Simple reachability and safety properties are of this form. Secondly, the selected witness N_2 may not have an ancestor N_a such that N_a simulates N_2. Under this circumstance, we can simply replace N_2 with *tt* if N_2 is a '$\vee$' node and *ff* if N_2 is a '$\wedge$' node. This approximation, combined with the restriction of mu-calculus formulas proposed above, makes the acceleration operation a widening operation. The approximation, however appears to be very coarse and results in considerable information loss (see Section 5).

5 Case Studies

In this section, we discuss the applicability of our technique for automatic verification of mu-calculus properties for single-parameter systems. The examples show that our technique can be used to verify parameterized systems with different control structures like ring, chain and star networks.

Milner Scheduler. Milner's Scheduler [Mil89] consists of `cell` processes connected in the form of a cycle where the ith cell waits on synchronization with $(i-1)^{th}$ cell and then communicates with the $(i+1)^{th}$ cell. Further each `cell` is also capable of performing autonomous actions. Initially all cells except `cell(0)` are waiting to synchronize on an `out` action from the previous cell in ring.

We consider the verification of the following mu-calculus property that encodes the existence of a deadlock : $\varphi_d : X =_\mu [\tau]\mathtt{ff} \vee \langle\tau\rangle X$. Consider a system consisting of `N+1` `cell` processes, denoted by `sys(N)`, and the problem of verifying $\exists$`Nsys(N)` $\models \varphi_d$. The sequence of formula as defined in Equation 2 does not converge. This is because ψ_i, the ith formula in the chain explicitly represents all possible interleavings between actions of the `cell(i)` and the `cell(0)`. Equivalence reduction alone cannot discard such interleavings. When the acceleration operator (Section 4.1) is used, the resulting chain converges; the acceleration operator ignores the exact nature of interleaving between the actions. The limit after acceleration, φ_f, leaves for the environment the obligation to satisfy φ_d after an `out` action of the `cell(N)` or an `in` action of `cell(0)`. As `0` has no outgoing transition, `0` $\not\models \varphi_f$. This implies $\forall$`N sys(N)` $\not\models \varphi_d$.

Similar behavior is exhibited by *token-ring* protocol and *queues* with two or more buffers. In all these cases, while the iterative procedure for limit computation does not converge directly, the acceleration operator forces termination.

Cache Coherence. Cache coherence protocols [AB86] are used in multiprocessor systems with shared memory, where each processor possesses its own private cache. The protocol we considered (from [Del00]) defines four distinct states for each processor – invalid, valid, shared and exclusive. Processors in invalid state have an outdated copy of the memory block in their cache; processors in valid and shared states have the current copy of memory block in their cache; a processor in exclusive state is the exclusive owner of the memory block.

Previous efforts [Del00] to verify data consistency involved abstracting the parameterized system into a single infinite state system by counting the number of processors in various states. Model checking was performed by reachability analysis of this system. In contrast, we modeled the parameterized system and used a least fixed point formula φ to detect the presence of more than one processor in each of valid, shared or exclusive states – objective being to check $\exists$`N sys(N)` $\models \varphi$ where `sys(N)` consists of `N` processors. The limit φ_f is obtained after three iterations, since at any point of time at most two processors can share the ownership of cached data. Finally `0` $\not\models \varphi_f$ implying data consistency is maintained for system consisting of any number of processors.

Java Meta-lock. The Java Meta-lock is a distributed algorithm that ensures fast mutually exclusive access of objects by Java threads [ADG+99]. The protocol involves synchronous communication between objects and threads and also between the threads themselves.

We first consider the system consisting of fixed number of threads and arbitrary number of objects and a least fixed point deadlock formula φ_d. Our objective is to check $\exists$`N sys(k, N)` $\models \varphi_d$, where `k` is the fixed number of threads and `N` is the number of objects. In this example, the limit computation converges in two iterations to yield φ_f, since each `object` process behaves independently of any other `object`. Finally, `0` $\not\models \varphi_f$ ensuring freedom from deadlock for all the members of the parameterized system `sys(k, N)`.

Let us now consider the dual case with an arbitrary number of thread processes and a fixed number of objects. Using the same φ_d, our aim is to verify $\exists$`M sys(M, k)` $\models \varphi_d$. The sequence of formulas generated by property transformer for the threads does not converge even with application of acceleration operator. The sequence converges only after the coarse approximation performed by the widening operator. The reason is that in case of meta-lock protocol each `thread` process can directly communicate with any other `thread` process. Hence ψ_i, the ith formula in the sequence contains actions related to synchronization between the ith thread and any other thread. When attempting to accelerate the convergence of the limit computation, we find that the selected witnesses of topological clashes (see Section 4.1) do not have an ancestor that simulates them, and hence no reduction is possible. In this case, the widening operator approximates the witness state with *tt*. Intuitively, this approximation implies that any transition sequence leading to interaction between threads will satisfy φ_d. However this approximation is too coarse since the resultant limit φ_f is such that $\mathtt{0} \models \varphi_f$. Due to the approximation, we cannot determine whether φ_d is modeled by the `sys(M, k)`.

6 Conclusion

We described an automatic technique, based on program analysis techniques, for the verification of infinite families of concurrent systems. At the core of the technique is the use of partial model checking for generating property transformers over modal mu-calculus formulas from system specifications in CCS. In our technique, the problem of verifying an infinite family is posed as a problem of finding the limit of a chain of modal mu-calculus formulas. We also presented a widening operator to guarantee termination of the analysis for a subclass of modal mu-calculus formulas. We have implemented this technique in the XSB tabled logic programming system [XSB00]. The utility of the technique has been demonstrated by verifying a number of example parameterized systems with diverse characteristics in a uniform manner. The technique, however, is too approximate to provide useful results in certain cases where induction-based verification techniques have been successful (metalock with multiple threads and single object [RR01]). Development of abstractions of property transformers and widening operators which perform more fine-grained approximations is a topic of future research.

Acknowledgments. We would like thank to Dr. K. Narayan Kumar for discussion and guidance. We are also thankful to the anonymous reviewers for their valuable comments. This work is supported in part by NSF grants EIA-9705998, CCR-9876242, EIA-9805735, IIS-0072927, CCR-0205376, and ONR grant N000140110967.

References

[AB86] J. Archibald and J.L. Baer. Cache coherence protocols: Evaluation using a multi-processor simulation model. In *ACM TOCS*, 1986.

[ADG+99] O. Agesen, D. Detlefs, A. Garthwaite, R. Knippel, Y.S. Ramakrishna, and D. White. An efficient meta-lock for ubiquitous synchronization. In *OOPSLA*, 1999.

[AH96] R. Alur and T. Henzinger. Reactive modules. In *LICS*, 1996.

[And95] H. R. Andersen. Partial model checking. In *LICS*, 1995.

[ASW94] H. R. Andersen, C. Stirling, and G. Winskel. A compositional proof system for the modal mu-calculus. In *LICS*, 1994.

[BCM+90] J. R. Burch, E. M. Clarke, K. L. McMillan, D. L. Dill, and L. J. Hwang. Symbolic model checking: 10^{20} states and beyond. In *LICS*, 1990.

[BG97] S. Berezin and D. Gurov. A compositional proof system for the modal mu-calculus and CCS. Technical Report CMU-CS-97-105, CMU, 1997.

[BS01] J. Bradfield and C. Stirling. Modal logics and mu-calculi: an introduction. In *Handbook of Process Algebra*. Elsevier, 2001.

[BSW00] S. Basu, S. A. Smolka, and O. R. Ward. Model checking the Java Meta-Locking algorithm. In *ECBS*, 2000.

[CC77] P. Cousot and R. Cousot. Abstract interpretation: A unified lattice model for static analysis of programs by construction or approximation of fixpoints. In *POPL*, 1977.

[CES86] E. M. Clarke, E. A. Emerson, and A. P. Sistla. Automatic verification of finite-state concurrent systems using temporal logic specifications. *ACM TOPLAS*, 1986.

[CGJ97] E.M. Clarke, O. Grumberg, and S. Jha. Verifying parameterized networks. In *ACM transactions on programming languages and systems*, 1997.

[CS93] R. Cleaveland and B. Steffen. A linear-time model checking algorithm for the alternation-free modal mu-calculus. *FMSD*, 1993.

[Del00] G. Delzanno. Automatic verification of parameterized cache coherence protocols. In *CAV*, 2000.

[DP99] G. Delzanno and A. Podelski. Model checking in CLP. In *TACAS*, 1999.

[EFM99] J. Esparza, A. Finkel, and R. Mayr. On the verification of broadcast protocols. In *LICS*, 1999.

[EJ88] E. A. Emerson and C. S. Jutla. The complexity of tree automata and logics of programs. In *FOCS*, pages 328–337, 1988.

[EN95] E.A. Emerson and K.S. Namjoshi. Reasoning about rings. In *POPL*, 1995.

[EN96] E.A. Emerson and K.S. Namjoshi. Automated verification of parameterized synchronous systems. In *CAV*, 1996.

[EN98] E.A. Emerson and K.S. Namjoshi. On model checking for non-deterministic infinite state systems. In *LICS*, 1998.

[GL94] O. Grumberg and D.E. Long. Model checking and modular verification. In *TOPLAS*, 1994.

[HCC94] P. Van Hentenryck, A. Cortesi, and B. Le Charlier. Type analysis of prolog using type graphs. In *JLP*, 1994.

[Hol97] G. J. Holzmann. The model checker SPIN. *IEEE TSE*, 1997.

[HQR98] T. Henzinger, S. Qadeer, and S.K. Rajamani. You assume, we guarantee. In *CAV*, 1998.

[ID96] C. N. Ip and D. L. Dill. Better verification through symmetry reduction. In *FMSD*, 1996.

[ID99] C.N. Ip and D.L. Dill. Verifying systems with replicated components in murphi. In *FMSD*, 1999.

[Koz83] D. Kozen. Results on the propositional μ-calculus. *TCS*, 1983.

[KP00] Y. Kesten and A. Pnueli. Control and data abstraction:the cornerstones of pratical formal verification. In *Intl. Journal on STTT*, 2000.

[LHR97] D. Lesens, N. Halbwachs, and P. Raymond. Automatic verification of linear networks processes. In *POPL*, 1997.

[McM97] K.L. McMillan. Compositional rule for hardware design refinement. In *CAV*, 1997.

[Mil89] R. Milner. *Communication and Concurrency*. International Series in Computer Science. Prentice Hall, 1989.

[Mil99] P. Mildner. *Type Domains form Abstract interpretation: A critical study.* PhD thesis, Uppsala University, 1999.

[PS00] A. Pnueli and E. Shahar. Liveness and acceleration in parameterized verification. In *CAV*, 2000.

[QS82] J. P. Queille and J. Sifakis. Specification and verification of concurrent systems in Cesar. In *Proceedings of the International Symposium in Programming*, 1982.

[RKR+00] A. Roychoudhury, K.N. Kumar, C.R. Ramakrishnan, I.V. Ramakrishnan, and S.A. Smolka. Verification of parameterized systems using logic-program transformations. In *TACAS*, 2000.

[RR01] A. Roychoudhury and I.V. Ramakrishnan. Automated inductive verification of parameterized protocols. In *CAV*, 2001.

[SG99] A. P. Sistla and V. Gyuris. Parameterized verification of linear networks using automata as invariants. *Formal Aspects of Computing*, 1999.

[Wol86] P. Wolper. Expressing interesting properties in propositional temporal logic. In *POPL*, 1986.

[XSB00] The XSB Group. The XSB logic programming system v2.1, 2000. Available from `http://www.cs.sunysb.edu/~sbprolog`.

Learning Assumptions for Compositional Verification

Jamieson M. Cobleigh[1]*, Dimitra Giannakopoulou[2,3], and Corina S. Păsăreanu[3]

[1] Department of Computer Science, University of Massachusetts, Amherst, MA 01003-9264, USA
jcobleig@cs.umass.edu
[2] RIACS/USRA
[3] Kestrel Technology LLC, NASA Ames Research Center, Moffett Field, CA 94035-1000, USA
{dimitra,pcorina}@email.arc.nasa.gov

Abstract. Compositional verification is a promising approach to addressing the state explosion problem associated with model checking. One compositional technique advocates proving properties of a system by checking properties of its components in an assume-guarantee style. However, the application of this technique is difficult because it involves non-trivial human input. This paper presents a novel framework for performing assume-guarantee reasoning in an incremental and fully automated fashion. To check a component against a property, our approach generates assumptions that the environment needs to satisfy for the property to hold. These assumptions are then discharged on the rest of the system. Assumptions are computed by a learning algorithm. They are initially approximate, but become gradually more precise by means of counterexamples obtained by model checking the component and its environment, alternately. This iterative process may at any stage conclude that the property is either true or false in the system. We have implemented our approach in the LTSA tool and applied it to a NASA system.

1 Introduction

Our work is motivated by an ongoing project at NASA Ames Research Center on the application of model checking to the verification of autonomous software. Autonomous software involves complex concurrent behaviors for reacting to external stimuli without human intervention. Extensive verification is a prerequisite for the deployment of missions that involve autonomy.

Given some formal description of a system and of a required property, model checking automatically determines whether the property is satisfied by the system. The limitation of the approach, referred to as the "state explosion" prob-

* This author is grateful for the support received from RIACS to undertake this research while participating in the Summer Student Research Program at the NASA Ames Research Center.

H. Garavel and J. Hatcliff (Eds.): TACAS 2003, LNCS 2619, pp. 331–346, 2003.

lem [8], is that it needs to store the explored system states in memory, which is impossible for most realistic systems.

Compositional verification presents a promising way of addressing state explosion. It advocates a "divide and conquer" approach where properties of the system are decomposed into properties of its components, so that if each component satisfies its respective property, then so does the entire system. Components are therefore model checked separately. It is often the case, however, that components only satisfy properties in specific contexts (also called environments). This has given rise to the assume-guarantee style of reasoning [18,21].

Assume-guarantee reasoning first checks whether a component M guarantees a property P, when it is part of a system that satisfies an assumption A. Intuitively, A characterizes all contexts in which the component is expected to operate correctly. To complete the proof, it must also be shown that the remaining components in the system, i.e., M's environment, satisfy A. Several frameworks have been proposed [18,21,7,16,24,17] to support this style of reasoning. However, their practical impact has been limited because they require non-trivial human input in defining assumptions that are strong enough to eliminate false violations, but that also reflect the remaining system appropriately.

In contrast, this paper presents a novel framework for performing assume-guarantee reasoning in an *incremental* and *fully automatic* fashion. Our approach iterates a process based on gradually *learning* assumptions. The learning process is based on queries to component M and on counterexamples obtained by model checking M and its environment, alternately. Each iteration may conclude that the required property is satisfied or violated in the system analyzed. This process is guaranteed to terminate; in fact, it converges to an assumption that is necessary and sufficient for the property to hold in the specific system.

Our approach has been implemented in the Labeled Transition Systems Analyzer (LTSA) [20], and applied to the analysis of the Executive module of an experimental Mars Rover (K9) developed at NASA Ames. We are currently in the process of also implementing it in Java Pathfinder (JPF) [23]. In fact, as our approach relies on standard features of model checkers, it is fairly straightforward to add in any such tool.

The remainder of the paper is organized as follows. We first provide some background in Section 2, followed by a high level description of the framework that we propose in Section 3. The algorithms that implement this framework are presented in Section 4. We discuss the applicability of our approach in practice and extensions that we are considering in Section 5. Section 6 describes our experience with applying our approach to the Executive of the K9 Mars Rover. Finally, Section 7 presents related work and Section 8 concludes the paper.

2 Background

The presentation of our approach is based on techniques for modeling and checking concurrent programs implemented in the LTSA tool [20]. The LTSA supports Compositional Reachability Analysis (CRA) of a software system based on its

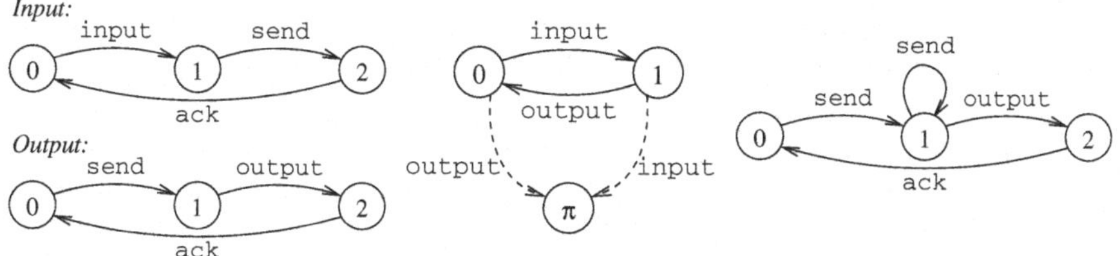

Fig. 1. Example LTSs **Fig. 2.** *Order* Property **Fig. 3.** LTS for *Output′*

architecture, which, in general, has a hierarchical structure. CRA incrementally computes and abstracts the behavior of composite components based on the behavior of their immediate children in the hierarchy [13]. The flexibility that the LTSA provides in selecting any component in the hierarchy for analysis or abstraction makes it ideal for experimenting with our approach.

Labeled Transition Systems (LTSs). The LTSA tool uses LTSs to model the behavior of communicating components in a concurrent system. In the following, we present LTSs and semantics of their operators in a typical process algebra style. However note that our goal here is not to define a process algebra.

Let $\mathcal{A}ct$ be the universal set of observable actions and let τ denote a local action *unobservable* to a component's environment. We use π to denote a special *error state*, which models the fact that a safety violation has occurred in the associated system. We require that the error state has no outgoing transitions. Formally, an LTS M is a four tuple $\langle Q, \alpha M, \delta, q_0 \rangle$ where:

- Q is a finite non-empty set of states
- $\alpha M \subseteq \mathcal{A}ct$ is a set of observable actions called the *alphabet* of M
- $\delta \subseteq Q \times \alpha M \cup \{\tau\} \times Q$ is a transition relation
- $q_0 \in Q$ is the initial state

We use Π to denote the LTS $\langle \{\pi\}, \mathcal{A}ct, \emptyset, \pi \rangle$. An LTS $M = \langle Q, \alpha M, \delta, q_0 \rangle$ is *non-deterministic* if it contains τ-transitions or if $\exists (q, a, q'), (q, a, q'') \in \delta$ such that $q' \neq q''$. Otherwise, M is *deterministic.*

Consider a simple communication channel that consists of two components whose LTSs are shown in Fig. 1. Note that the initial state of all LTSs in this paper is state 0. The *Input* LTS receives an input when the action `input` occurs, and then sends it to the *Output* LTS with action `send`. After some data is sent to it, *Output* produces output using the action `output` and acknowledges that it has finished, by using the action `ack`. At this point, both LTSs return to their initial states so the process can be repeated.

Traces. A *trace* σ of an LTS M is a sequence of observable actions that M can perform starting at its initial state. For example, $\langle \texttt{input} \rangle$ and $\langle \texttt{input}, \texttt{send} \rangle$ are both traces of the *Input* LTS in Fig. 1. The set of all traces of M is called the *language* of M, denoted $\mathcal{L}(M)$. For $\Sigma \subseteq \mathcal{A}ct$, we use $\sigma \upharpoonright \Sigma$ to denote the trace obtained by removing from σ all occurrences of actions $a \notin \Sigma$.

Parallel Composition. Let $M = \langle Q, \alpha M, \delta, q_0 \rangle$ and $M' = \langle Q', \alpha M', \delta', q'_0 \rangle$. We say that M *transits* into M' with action a, denoted $M \xrightarrow{a} M'$, if and only if $(q_0, a, q'_0) \in \delta$ and either $Q = Q'$, $\alpha M = \alpha M'$, and $\delta = \delta'$ for $q'_0 \neq \pi$, or, in the special case where $q'_0 = \pi$, $M' = \Pi$.

The parallel composition operator $\|$ is a commutative and associative operator that combines the behavior of two components by synchronizing the actions common to their alphabets and interleaving the remaining actions. For example, in the parallel composition of the *Input* and *Output* components from Fig. 1, actions `send` and `ack` will each be synchronized.

Formally, let $M_1 = \langle Q^1, \alpha M_1, \delta^1, q_0^1 \rangle$ and $M_2 = \langle Q^2, \alpha M_2, \delta^2, q_0^2 \rangle$ be two LTSs. If $M_1 = \Pi$ or $M_2 = \Pi$, then $M_1 \| M_2 = \Pi$. Otherwise, $M_1 \| M_2$ is an LTS $M = \langle Q, \alpha M, \delta, q_0 \rangle$, where $Q = Q^1 \times Q^2$, $q_0 = (q_0^1, q_0^2)$, $\alpha M = \alpha M_1 \cup \alpha M_2$, and δ is defined as follows, where a is either an observable action or τ (note that the symmetric rules are implied by the fact that the operator is commutative):

$$\frac{M_1 \xrightarrow{a} M'_1,\ a \notin \alpha M_2}{M_1 \| M_2 \xrightarrow{a} M'_1 \| M_2} \qquad \frac{M_1 \xrightarrow{a} M'_1,\ M_2 \xrightarrow{a} M'_2,\ a \neq \tau}{M_1 \| M_2 \xrightarrow{a} M'_1 \| M'_2}$$

Properties. We call a deterministic LTS that contains no π states a *safety LTS.* A *safety property* is specified as a safety LTS P, whose language $\mathcal{L}(P)$ defines the set of acceptable behaviors over αP. An LTS M satisfies P, denoted as $M \models P$, if and only if $\forall \sigma \in \mathcal{L}(M) : (\sigma \upharpoonright \alpha P) \in \mathcal{L}(P)$.

When checking a property P, an *error LTS* denoted P_{err} is created, which traps possible violations with the π state. Formally, the error LTS of a property $P = \langle Q, \alpha P, \delta, q_0 \rangle$ is $P_{err} = \langle Q \cup \{\pi\}, \alpha P_{err}, \delta', q_0 \rangle$, where $\alpha P_{err} = \alpha P$ and

$$\delta' = \delta \cup \{(q, a, \pi) \mid a \in \alpha P \text{ and } \nexists q' \in Q : (q, a, q') \in \delta\}$$

Note that the error LTS is *complete*, meaning each state other than the error state has outgoing transitions for every action in the alphabet.

For example, the *Order* property shown in Fig. 2 captures a desired behavior of the communication channel shown in Fig. 1. The property comprises states 0, 1 and the transitions denoted by solid arrows. It expresses the fact that `inputs` and `outputs` come in matched pairs, with the `input` always preceding the `output`. The dashed arrows illustrate the transitions to the error state that are added to the property to obtain its error LTS.

To detect violations of property P by component M, the parallel composition $M \| P_{err}$ is computed. It has been proved that M violates P if and only if the π state is reachable in $M \| P_{err}$ [5]. For example, state π is not reachable in $Input \| Output \| Order_{err}$, so we conclude that $Input \| Output \models Order$.

Assume-Guarantee Reasoning. In the assume-guarantee paradigm a formula is a triple $\langle A \rangle\ M\ \langle P \rangle$, where M is a component, P is a property, and A is an assumption about M's environment [21]. The formula is true if whenever M is part of a system satisfying A, then the system must also guarantee P.

The LTSA is particularly flexible in performing assume-guarantee reasoning. Both assumptions and properties are defined as safety LTSs[1]. In fact, a safety LTS A can be used as an assumption *or* as a property. To be used as an assumption for module M, A itself is composed with M, thus playing the role of an abstraction of M's environment. To be used as a property to be checked on M, A is turned into A_{err} and then composed with M.

To check an assume-guarantee formula $\langle A \rangle\ M\ \langle P \rangle$, where both A and P are safety LTSs, the LTSA computes $A \parallel M \parallel P_{err}$ and checks if state π is reachable in the composition. If it is, then $\langle A \rangle\ M\ \langle P \rangle$ is violated, otherwise it is satisfied.

Deterministic Finite State Automata (DFAs) and Safety LTSs. One of the components of our framework is a learning algorithm that produces DFAs, which our framework then uses as safety LTSs. A DFA M is a five tuple $\langle Q, \alpha M, \delta, q_0, F \rangle$ where $Q, \alpha M, \delta$, and q_0 are defined as for *deterministic* LTSs, and $F \subseteq Q$ is a set of accepting states.

For a DFA M and a string σ, we use $\delta(q, \sigma)$ to denote the state that M will be in after reading σ starting at state q. A string σ is said to be *accepted* by a DFA $M = \langle Q, \alpha M, \delta, q_0, F \rangle$ if $\delta(q_0, \sigma) \in F$. The *language accepted by* M, denoted $\mathcal{L}(M)$ is the set $\{\sigma \mid \delta(q_0, \sigma) \in F\}$.

The DFAs returned by the learning algorithm in our context are *complete*, *minimal*, and *prefix-closed* (an automaton M is prefix-closed if $\mathcal{L}(M)$ is prefix-closed, i.e., for every $\sigma \in \mathcal{L}(M)$, every prefix of σ is also in $\mathcal{L}(M)$). These DFAs therefore contain a single non-accepting state. They can easily be transformed into safety LTSs by removing the non-accepting state, which corresponds to state π of an error LTS, and all transitions that lead into it.

3 Framework for Incremental Compositional Verification

Consider the case where a system is made up of two components, M_1 and M_2. As mentioned in the previous section, a formula $\langle A \rangle\ M\ \langle P \rangle$ is true if, whenever M is part of a system satisfying A, then the system must also guarantee property P. The simplest compositional proof rule shows that if $\langle A \rangle\ M_1\ \langle P \rangle$ and $\langle true \rangle\ M_2\ \langle A \rangle$ hold, then $\langle true \rangle\ M_1 \parallel M_2\ \langle P \rangle$ is true. This proof strategy can also be expressed as an inference rule as follows:

$$\frac{\begin{array}{l}\text{(Step 1) } \langle A \rangle\ M_1\ \langle P \rangle \\ \text{(Step 2) } \langle \mathit{true} \rangle\ M_2\ \langle A \rangle\end{array}}{\langle \mathit{true} \rangle\ M_1 \parallel M_2\ \langle P \rangle}$$

Note that this rule is not symmetric in its use of the two components, and does not support circularity. Despite its simplicity, our experience with applying compositional verification to several applications has shown it to be the most useful rule in the context of checking safety properties. For the use of the compositional rule to be justified, the assumption must be more abstract than M_2,

[1] Any LTS without π states can be transformed into a safety LTS by determinization.

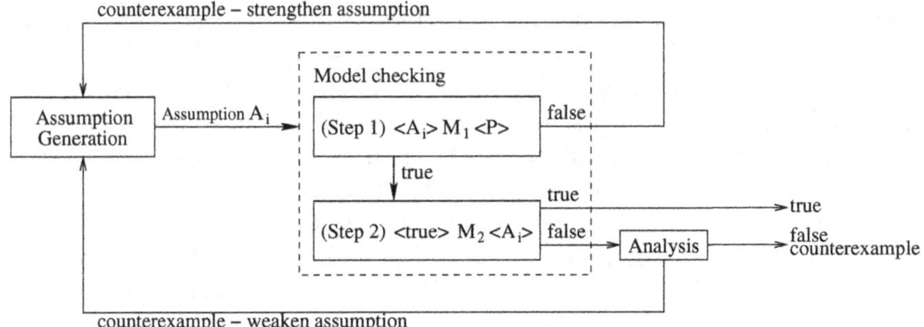

Fig. 4. Incremental compositional verification during iteration i

but still reflect M_2's behavior. Additionally, an appropriate assumption for the rule needs to be strong enough for M_1 to satisfy P in Step 1. Developing such an assumption is a non-trivial process.

To obtain appropriate assumptions, our framework applies the compositional rule in an iterative fashion as illustrated in Fig. 4. At each iteration i, an assumption A_i is provided based on some knowledge about the system and on the results of the previous iteration. The two steps of the compositional rule are then applied. Step 1 is applied first, to check whether M_1 guarantees P in environments that satisfy A_i. If the result is false, it means that this assumption is too *weak*, i.e., A_i does not restrict the environment enough for P to be satisfied. The assumption therefore needs to be *strengthened* (which corresponds to removing behaviors from it) with the help of the counterexample produced by Step 1. In the context of the next assumption A_{i+1}, component M_1 should at least not exhibit the violating behavior reflected by this counterexample.

If Step 1 returns true, it means that A_i is strong enough for the property to be satisfied. To complete the proof, Step 2 must be applied to discharge A_i on M_2. If Step 2 returns true, then the compositional rule guarantees that P holds in $M_1 \parallel M_2$. If it returns false, further analysis is required to identify whether P is indeed violated in $M_1 \parallel M_2$ or whether A_i is stronger than necessary. Such analysis is based on the counterexample returned by Step 2. If A_i is too strong it must be *weakened* (i.e., behaviors must be added) in iteration $i+1$. The result of such weakening will be that at least the behavior that the counterexample represents will be allowed by assumption A_{i+1}. The new assumption may of course be too weak, and therefore the entire process must be repeated.

To implement this iterative, incremental process in a fully automated way, our framework uses a learning algorithm for assumption generation and a model checker for the application of the two steps in the compositional rule. The learning algorithm is described in detail in the next section.

```
(1) let S = E = {λ}
    loop {
(2)    Update T using queries
       while (S, E, T) is not closed {
(3)       Add sa to S to make S closed where s ∈ S and a ∈ Σ
(4)       Update T using queries
       }
(5)    Construct candidate DFA C from (S, E, T)
(6)    Make the conjecture C
(7)    if C is correct return C
       else
(8)       Add e ∈ Σ* that witnesses the counterexample to E
    }
```

Fig. 5. The L* Algorithm

4 Algorithms

4.1 The L* Algorithm

The learning algorithm used by our approach was developed by Angluin [3] and later improved by Rivest and Schapire [22]. In this paper, we will refer to the *improved* version by the name of the original algorithm, L*. L* learns an unknown regular language and produces a DFA that accepts it. Let U be an unknown regular language over some alphabet Σ. In order to learn U, L* needs to interact with a *Minimally Adequate Teacher*, from now on called *Teacher*. A Teacher must be able to correctly answer two types of questions from L*. The first type is a *membership query*, consisting of a string $\sigma \in \Sigma^*$; the answer is *true* if $\sigma \in U$, and *false* otherwise. The second type of question is a *conjecture*, i.e., a candidate DFA C whose language the algorithm believes to be identical to U. The answer is *true* if $\mathcal{L}(C) = U$. Otherwise the Teacher returns a counterexample, which is a string σ in the symmetric difference of $\mathcal{L}(C)$ and U.

At a higher level, L* creates a table where it incrementally records whether strings in Σ^* belong to U. It does this by making membership queries to the Teacher. At various stages L* decides to make a conjecture. It constructs a candidate automaton C based on the information contained in the table and asks the Teacher whether the conjecture is correct. If it is, the algorithm terminates. Otherwise, L* uses the counterexample returned by the Teacher to extend the table with strings that witness differences between $\mathcal{L}(C)$ and U.

In the following more detailed presentation of the algorithm, line numbers refer to L*'s illustration in Fig. 5. L* builds an observation table (S, E, T) where S and E are a set of prefixes and suffixes, respectively, both over Σ^*. In addition, T is a function mapping $(S \cup S \cdot \Sigma) \cdot E$ to {true, false}, where the operator "$\cdot$" is defined as follows. Given two sets of event sequences P and Q, $P \cdot Q = \{pq \mid p \in P \text{ and } q \in Q\}$, where pq represents the concatenation of the event sequences p and q. Initially, L* sets S and E to $\{\lambda\}$ (line 1), where λ represents the empty string. Subsequently, it updates the function T by making membership queries so that it has a mapping for every string in $(S \cup S \cdot \Sigma) \cdot E$ (line 2). It then checks whether the observation table is *closed*, i.e., whether

$$\forall s \in S, \forall a \in \Sigma, \exists s' \in S, \forall e \in E : T(sae) = T(s'e)$$

If (S, E, T) is not closed, then sa is added to S where $s \in S$ and $a \in \Sigma$ are the elements for which there is no $s' \in S$ (line 3). Once sa has been added to S, T needs to be updated (line 4). Lines 3 and 4 are repeated until (S, E, T) is closed.

Once the observation table is closed, a candidate DFA $C = \langle Q, \alpha C, \delta, q_0, F \rangle$ is constructed (line 5), with states $Q = S$, initial state $q_0 = \lambda$, and alphabet $\alpha C = \Sigma$, where Σ is the alphabet of the unknown language U. The set F consists of the states $s \in S$ such that $T(s) =$ true. The transition relation δ is defined as $\delta(s, a) = s'$ where $\forall e \in E : T(sae) = T(s'e)$. Such an s' is guaranteed to exist when (S, E, T) is closed. The DFA C is presented as a conjecture to the Teacher (line 6). If the conjecture is correct, i.e., if $\mathcal{L}(C) = U$, L* returns C as correct (line 7), otherwise it receives a counterexample $c \in \Sigma^*$ from the Teacher.

The counterexample c is analyzed by L* to find a suffix e of c that witnesses a difference between $\mathcal{L}(C)$ and U; e must be such that adding it to E will cause the next conjectured automaton to reflect this difference[2] (line 8). Once e has been added to E, L* iterates the entire process by looping around to line 2.

Characteristics of L*. L* is guaranteed to terminate with a minimal automaton M for the unknown language U. Moreover, for each closed observation table (S, E, T), the candidate DFA C that L* constructs is smallest, in the sense that any other DFA consistent[3] with the function T has at least as many states as C. This characteristic of L* makes it particularly attractive for our framework. The conjectures made by L* strictly increase in size; each conjecture is smaller than the next one, and all incorrect conjectures are smaller than M. Therefore, if M has n states, L* makes at most $n - 1$ incorrect conjectures. The number of membership queries made by L* is $\mathcal{O}\left(kn^2 + n \log m\right)$, where k is the size of the alphabet of U, n is the number of states in the minimal DFA for U, and m is the length of the longest counterexample returned when a conjecture is made.

4.2 Learning for Assume-Guarantee Reasoning

Assume a system $M_1 \parallel M_2$, and a property P that needs to be satisfied in the system. In the context of the compositional rule presented in Section 3, the learning algorithm is called to guess an assumption that can be used in the rule to prove or disprove P. An assumption with which the rule is guaranteed to return conclusive results is the *weakest assumption* A_w under which M_1 satisfies

[2] The procedure for finding e is beyond the scope of this paper, but is described in [22].

[3] A DFA C is consistent with function T if, for every σ in $(S \cup S \cdot \Sigma) \cdot E$, $\sigma \in \mathcal{L}(C)$ if and only if $T(\sigma) =$ true.

P. Assumption A_w describes exactly those traces over $\Sigma = (\alpha M_1 \cup \alpha P) \cap \alpha M_2$ which, when simulated on $M_1 \parallel P_{err}$ cannot lead to state π. The language $\mathcal{L}(A_w)$ of the assumption contains at least *all* traces of M_2 abstracted to Σ that prevent M_1 from violating P. Formally, A_w is such that, for any environment component M_E, $\langle true \rangle\ M_1 \parallel M_E\ \langle P \rangle$ if and only if $\langle true \rangle\ M_E\ \langle A_w \rangle$ [14].

In our framework, L* learns the traces of A_w through the iterative process described in Section 3. The process terminates as soon as compositional verification returns conclusive results, which is often before the weakest assumption A_w is computed by L*. For L* to learn A_w, we need to provide a Teacher that is able to answer the two different kinds of questions that L* asks. Our approach uses model checking to implement such a Teacher.

Membership Queries. To answer a membership query for $\sigma = \langle a_1, a_2, \ldots, a_n \rangle$ in Σ^* the Teacher simulates the query on $M_1 \parallel P$. For clarity of presentation we will reduce such simulations to model checking, although we have implemented them more efficiently, directly as simulations. So for string σ, the Teacher first builds $A_\sigma = \langle Q, \alpha A_\sigma, \delta, q_0 \rangle$ where $Q = \{q^0, q^1, \ldots, q^n\}$, $\alpha A_\sigma = \Sigma$, $\delta = \{(q^i, a^{i+1}, q^{i+1}) \mid 0 \leq i < n\}$, and $q_0 = q^0$. The Teacher then model checks $\langle A_\sigma \rangle\ M_1\ \langle P \rangle$. If true is returned, it means that $\sigma \in \mathcal{L}(A_w)$, because M_1 does not violate P in the context of σ, so the Teacher returns true. Otherwise, the answer to the membership query is false.

Conjectures. Due to the fact that in our case the language $\mathcal{L}(A_w)$ that is being learned is prefix-closed, all conjectures returned by L* are also prefix-closed. Our framework transforms these conjectures into safety LTSs (see Section 2), which constitute the intermediate assumptions A_i. In our framework, the first priority is to guide L* towards a conjecture that is strong enough to make Step 1 of the compositional rule return true. Once this is accomplished, the resulting conjecture may be too strong, in which case our framework guides L* towards a conjecture that is weak enough to make Step 2 return conclusive results about whether the system satisfies P. The way the Teacher that we have implemented reflects this approach is by using two oracles and counterexample analysis to answer conjectures as follows.

Oracle 1 performs Step 1 in Fig. 4, i.e., it checks $\langle A_i \rangle\ M_1\ \langle P \rangle$. If this does not hold, the model checker returns a counterexample c. The Teacher informs L* that its conjecture A_i is not correct and provides $c \upharpoonright \Sigma$ to witness this fact. If, instead, $\langle A_i \rangle\ M_1\ \langle P \rangle$ holds, the Teacher forwards A_i to Oracle 2.

Oracle 2 performs Step 2 in Fig. 4 by checking $\langle true \rangle\ M_2\ \langle A_i \rangle$. If the result of model checking is true, the teacher returns true. Our framework then terminates the verification because, according to the compositional rule, P has been proved on $M_1 \parallel M_2$. If model checking returns a counterexample, the Teacher performs some analysis to determine the underlying reason (see Section 3 and Fig. 4).

Counterexample analysis is performed by the Teacher in a way similar to that used for answering membership queries. Let c be the counterexample returned by Oracle 2. The Teacher computes $A_{c \upharpoonright \Sigma}$ and checks $\langle A_{c \upharpoonright \Sigma} \rangle\ M_1\ \langle P \rangle$. If true, it means that A_i is too strong since M_1 does not violate P in the context of

Table 1. Mapping T_1

	T_1	E_1: λ
S_1	λ	true
	output	false
$S_1 \cdot \Sigma$	ack	true
	output	false
	send	true
	output, ack	false
	output, output	false
	output, send	false

Table 2. Mapping T_2

	T_2	E_2: λ	E_2: ack
S_2	λ	true	true
	output	false	false
	send	true	false
$S_2 \cdot \Sigma$	ack	true	true
	output	false	false
	send	true	false
	output, ack	false	false
	output, output	false	false
	output, send	false	false
	send, ack	false	false
	send, output	true	true
	send, send	true	true

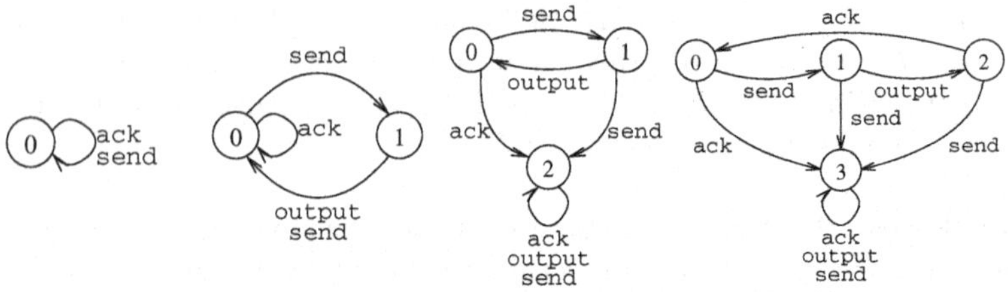

Fig. 6. A_1 **Fig. 7.** A_2 **Fig. 8.** A_3 **Fig. 9.** A_4

c, and $c \upharpoonright \Sigma$ is returned as a counterexample for conjecture A_i. If the model checker returns false with some counterexample c', it means that P is violated in $M_1 \parallel M_2$. To generate a counterexample for $\langle true \rangle\ M_1 \parallel M_2\ \langle P \rangle$ our framework composes c and c' in a way similar to the parallel composition of LTSs. That is, common actions in c and c' are synchronized and some interleaving instance of the remaining actions is selected.

4.3 Example

Given components *Input* and *Output* as shown in Fig. 1 and the property *Order* shown in Fig. 2, we will check $\langle true \rangle$ *Input* $\parallel$ *Output* $\langle Order \rangle$ by using our approach. The alphabet of the assumptions that will be used in the compositional rule is $\Sigma = ((\alpha Input \cup \alpha Order) \cap \alpha Output) = \{\texttt{send}, \texttt{output}, \texttt{ack}\}$.

As described, at each iteration L* updates its observation table and produces a candidate assumption whenever the table becomes closed. The first closed table obtained is shown in Table 1 and its associated assumption, A_1, is shown in Fig. 6. The Teacher answers conjecture A_1 by first invoking Oracle 1, which checks $\langle A_1 \rangle$ *Input* $\langle Order \rangle$. Oracle 1 returns false, with counterexample

$\sigma = \langle \texttt{input}, \texttt{send}, \texttt{ack}, \texttt{input} \rangle$, which describes a trace in $A_1 \parallel Input \parallel Order_{err}$ that leads to state π.

The Teacher therefore returns counterexample $\sigma \upharpoonright \Sigma = \langle \texttt{send}, \texttt{ack} \rangle$ to L*, which uses queries to update its observation table until it is closed. From this table, shown in Table 2, the assumption A_2, shown in Fig. 7, is constructed and conjectured to the Teacher. This time, Oracle 1 reports that $\langle A_2 \rangle$ *Input* $\langle Order \rangle$ is true, meaning the assumption is not too weak. The Teacher calls Oracle 2 to determine if $\langle true \rangle$ *Output* $\langle A_2 \rangle$. This is also true, so our algorithm reports that $\langle true \rangle$ *Input* $\parallel$ *Output* $\langle Order \rangle$ holds.

This example did not involve weakening of the assumptions produced by L*, since the assumption A_2 was sufficient for the compositional proof. This will not always be the case. For example, let us substitute *Output* by *Output'* illustrated in Fig. 3, which allows multiple `send` actions to occur before producing `output`. The verification process will be identical to the previous case, until Oracle 2 is invoked by the Teacher for conjecture A_2. Oracle 2 returns that $\langle true \rangle$ *Output'* $\langle A_2 \rangle$ is false, with counterexample $\langle \texttt{send}, \texttt{send}, \texttt{output} \rangle$. The Teacher analyzes this counterexample and determines that in the context of this trace, *Input* does not violate *Order*. The trace is returned to L*, which will weaken the conjectured assumption. The process involves two more iterations, during which assumptions A_3 (Fig. 8) and A_4 (Fig. 9), are produced. Using A_4, which is the weakest assumption A_w, both Oracles report true, so our framework reports that $\langle true \rangle$ *Input* $\parallel$ *Output'* $\langle Order \rangle$ holds.

5 Discussion

5.1 Correctness

Theorem 1. *Given components M_1 and M_2, and property P, the algorithm implemented by our framework terminates and it returns true if P holds on $M_1 \parallel M_2$ and false otherwise.*

Proof. To prove the theorem we will first argue correctness of our approach, and then the fact that it terminates.

Correctness: The Teacher in our framework uses the two steps of the compositional rule to answer conjectures. It only returns true when both steps return true, and therefore correctness is guaranteed by the compositional rule. Our framework reports an error when it detects a trace σ of M_2 which, when simulated on M_1, violates the property, which implies that $M_1 \parallel M_2$ violates P.

Termination: At any iteration, our algorithm returns true or false and terminates, or continues by providing a counterexample to L*. By correctness of L*, we are guaranteed that if it keeps receiving counterexamples, it will eventually, at some iteration i, produce A_w. During this iteration, Step 1 will return true by definition of A_w. The Teacher will therefore apply Step 2, which will return either true and terminate, or a counterexample. This counterexample represents a trace of M_2 that is not contained in $\mathcal{L}(A_w)$. Since, as discussed in Section 4, A_w is both necessary and sufficient, analysis of the counterexample will return false, and the algorithm will terminate. □

5.2 Practical Considerations

In our context, the languages queried by L* are prefix-closed. This is because our technique applies to purely safety properties; any finite prefix of a trace that satisfies such a property must also satisfy the property. Therefore, when for some string σ a membership query $\langle A_\sigma \rangle\ M_1\ \langle P \rangle$ returns false, we know that for any extension of σ the answer will also be false. We can thus improve the efficiency of the algorithm by reducing the cost of some of the membership queries that are answered by the Teacher. For example, in the observation table shown in Table 1, the entry for $\langle \texttt{output} \rangle$ is false. The Teacher can return false for the queries $\langle \texttt{output}, \texttt{ack} \rangle$, $\langle \texttt{output}, \texttt{send} \rangle$, and $\langle \texttt{output}, \texttt{output} \rangle$ without invoking the model checker.

In our framework, membership queries, conjectures, and counterexample analysis all involve model checking, which is performed on-the-fly. The assumptions that are used in these steps are increasing in size, and grow no larger than the size of A_w. In our experience, for well-designed systems, the interfaces between components are small. Therefore, assumptions are expected to be significantly smaller than the environment that they represent in the compositional rules. Although L* needs to maintain an observation table, this table does not need to be kept in memory while the model checking is performed.

Note that our framework provides an "any time" [11] approach to compositional verification. If memory is not sufficient to reach termination, intermediate assumptions are generated, which may be useful in approximating the requirements that a component places on its environment to satisfy certain properties.

5.3 Extensions

Generalization. Our approach has been presented in the context of two components. Assume now that a system consists of n components $M_1 \parallel \cdots \parallel M_n$. The simplest way to generalize our approach is to group these components into two higher level components, and apply the compositional rules as already discussed. Another possibility is to handle the general case without computing the composition of any components directly. Our algorithm provides a way of checking $\langle true \rangle\ M_1 \parallel M_2\ \langle P \rangle$ in a compositional way. If M_2 consists of more than one component, our algorithm could be applied recursively for Step 2. This is an interesting future direction, in particular since the membership queries concentrate on a single component at a time. However, we need to further investigate how meaningful such an approach would be in practice.

Computing the Weakest Assumption. L* can also be used to learn the weakest possible assumption A_w that will prevent a component M_1 from violating a property P. This assumption will be generated without knowing M_2, the component M_1 interacts with. The only place in our assume-guarantee framework where M_2 is used is in Oracle 2, when the Teacher tries to determine if the Assumption generated is too strong. Oracle 2 can be replaced by a conformance checker, for example the W-Method [6], which is designed to expose a

Table 3. Results for the Rover Example

Iteration	$\|A_i\|$	States	Transitions	Result
1 - Oracle 1	1	5	24	Too weak
2 - Oracle 1	2	268	1,408	Too weak
3 - Oracle 1	3	235	1,209	Too weak
4 - Oracle 1	5	464	2,500	Not too weak
4 - Oracle 2	5	32	197	False

difference between a specification and an implementation. This will produce a set of sequences that are guaranteed to expose an error in the conjectured assumption if one exists. The sequence of intermediate assumptions conjectured by the Teacher are approximate and become more refined the longer L* runs. As discussed before, approximate assumptions can still be useful.

6 Experience

We implemented the assume-guarantee framework described above in the LTSA tool, and experimented with our approach in the analysis of a design-level model of the executive subsystem for the K9 Mars Rover, developed at NASA Ames. The executive is a multi-threaded system that receives plans from a Planner, which it executes according to a plan language semantics.

We used our framework to check one property that refers to a subsystem of the executive consisting of two components: the main coordinating component named *Executive*, and a component responsible for monitoring state conditions named *ExecCondChecker*. The property states that for a specific variable of the *ExecCondChecker* shared with the *Executive*, if the *Executive* reads the value of the variable, then the *ExecCondChecker* should not read this value before the *Executive* clears it first. We set M_1 = *ExecCondChecker* and M_2 = *Executive*. The experiment was conducted on a Pentium III 500 MHz with 1 Gb of memory running RedHat Linux 7.2 using Sun's Java SDK version 1.4.0_01. To check the property directly by composing the two modules with the property required searching 3,630 states and 34,653 transitions.

Table 3 shows the results of using our framework on this example. The $|A_i|$ column gives the number of states of the assumptions generated. The table also shows the number of states and transitions explored during the analysis of the assumption. In iterations 1-3, Oracle 1 determined that the learned assumptions were too weak. In iteration 4, the learned assumption was not too weak so it was given to Oracle 2, which returned a counterexample. When simulated on the *ExecCondChecker*, this counterexample led to an error state. The analysis therefore concluded that the property does not hold.

The largest state space involved in the application of our approach was explored by Oracle 1 during iteration 4, and consisted of 464 states and 2,500 transitions. This is approximately one order of magnitude smaller than the state space explored when checking the property directly on $M_1 \parallel M_2$. On the other hand, our approach took 8.639 seconds as compared to 0.535 seconds for checking the property directly. This is due to the iterative learning of assumptions. However, we believe that the potential benefits of our approach in terms of memory outweigh the time overhead that it may incur. Our experimental work is of course preliminary, and we are planning to carry out larger case studies to validate our approach.

7 Related Work

One way of addressing both the design and verification of large systems is to use their natural decomposition into components. Formal techniques for support of component-based design are gaining prominence, see for example [9,10]. In order to reason formally about components in isolation, some form of assumption (either implicit or explicit) about the interaction with, or interference from, the environment has to be made. Even though we have sound and complete reasoning systems for assume-guarantee reasoning, see for example [18,21,7,16,24], it is always a mental challenge to obtain the most appropriate assumption [17].

It is even more of a challenge to find automated techniques to support this style of reasoning. The thread modular reasoning underlying the Calvin tool [12] is one start in this direction. In the framework of temporal logic, the work on Alternating-time Temporal Logic ATL [1] was proposed for the specification and verification of open systems together with automated support via symbolic model checking procedures. The Mocha toolkit [2] provides support for modular verification of components with requirement specifications based on the ATL.

In previous work [14], we presented an algorithm for automatically generating the weakest possible assumption for a component to satisfy a required property. Although the motivation of that work is different, the ability to generate the weakest assumption can also be used to automate assume-guarantee reasoning. The algorithm in [14] does not compute partial results, meaning no assumption is obtained if the computation runs out of memory. This may happen if the state space of the component is too large. The approach presented here generates assumptions incrementally and may terminate before A_w is computed. Moreover, even if it runs out of memory before reaching conclusive results, intermediate assumptions may be used to give some indication to the developer of the requirements that the component places on its environment.

The problem of generating an assumption for a component is similar to the problem of generating component interfaces to deal with intermediate state explosion in CRA. Several approaches have been defined for automatically abstracting a component's environment to obtain interfaces [4,19]. These approaches do not address the issue of incrementally refining interfaces, as needed for carrying out an assume-guarantee proof.

Learning in the context of model checking has also been investigated in [15], but with a different goal. In that work, the L* Algorithm is used to generate a model of a software system which can then be fed to a model checker. A conformance checker determines if the model accurately describes the system.

8 Conclusions

Although theoretical frameworks for sound and complete assume-guarantee reasoning have existed for decades, their practical impact has been limited because they involve non-trivial human interaction. In this paper, we presented a novel approach to performing such reasoning in a fully automatic fashion. Our approach uses a learning algorithm to generate and refine assumptions based on queries and counterexamples, in an iterative process. The process is guaranteed to terminate, and return true if a property holds in a system, and a counterexample otherwise. If memory is not sufficient to reach termination, intermediate assumptions are generated, which may be useful in approximating the requirements that a component places on its environment to satisfy certain properties.

One advantage of our approach is its generality. It relies on standard features of model checkers, and could therefore easily be introduced in any such tool. For example, we are currently in the process of implementing it in JPF for the analysis of Java code. The architecture of our framework is modular, so its components can easily be substituted by more efficient ones. To evaluate how useful our approach is in practice, we are planning its extensive application to real systems. However, our early experiments provide strong evidence in favor of this line of research.

In the future, we plan to investigate a number of topics including whether the learning algorithm can be made more efficient in our context; whether different algorithms would be more appropriate for generating the assumptions; whether we could benefit by querying a component and its environment at the same time or by implementing more powerful compositional rules. An interesting challenge will also be to extend the types of properties that our framework can handle to include liveness, fairness, and timed properties.

Acknowledgments. The authors would like to thank Alex Groce for his help with the L* Algorithm, Willem Visser and Flavio Lerda for their help with JPF, and Zhendong Su and the anonymous referees for useful comments.

References

1. R. Alur, T. A. Henzinger, and O. Kupferman. Alternating-time temporal logic. In *Compositionality: The Significant Difference – An International Symposium*, 1997.
2. R. Alur, T. A. Henzinger, F. Y. C. Mang, S. Qadeer, S. K. Rajamani, and S. Tasiran. MOCHA: Modularity in model checking. In *Proc. of the 10th Int. Conf. on Computer-Aided Verification*, pages 521–525, June 28–July 2, 1998.
3. D. Angluin. Learning regular sets from queries and counterexamples. *Information and Computation*, 75(2):87–106, Nov. 1987.
4. S. C. Cheung and J. Kramer. Context constraints for compositional reachability analysis. *ACM Transactions on Software Engineering and Methodology*, 5(4):334–377, Oct. 1996.
5. S. C. Cheung and J. Kramer. Checking safety properties using compositional reachability analysis. *ACM Transactions on Software Engineering and Methodology*, 8(1):49–78, Jan. 1999.

6. T. S. Chow. Testing software design modeled by finite-state machines. *IEEE Transactions on Software Engineering*, SE-4(3):178–187, May 1978.
7. E. M. Clarke, D. E. Long, and K. L. McMillan. Compositional model checking. In *Proc. of the 4th Symp. on Logic in Computer Science*, pages 353–362, June 1989.
8. E. M. Clarke, O. Grumberg, and D. A. Peled. *Model Checking*. MIT Press, 1999.
9. L. de Alfaro and T. A. Henzinger. Interface automata. In *Proc. of the 8th European Software Engineering Conf. held jointly with the 9th ACM SIGSOFT Symp. on the Foundations of Software Engineering*, pages 109–120, Sept. 2001.
10. L. de Alfaro and T. A. Henzinger. Interface theories for component-based design. In *Proc. of the 1st Int. Workshop on Embedded Software*, pages 148–165, Oct. 2001.
11. T. Dean and M. S. Boddy. An analysis of time-dependent planning. In *Proc. of the 7th National Conf. on Artificial Intelligence*, pages 49–54, Aug. 1988.
12. C. Flanagan, S. N. Freund, and S. Qadeer. Thread-modular verification for shared-memory programs. In *Proc. of the 11th European Symp. on Programming*, pages 262–277, Apr. 2002.
13. D. Giannakopoulou, J. Kramer, and S. C. Cheung. Behaviour analysis of distributed systems using the Tracta approach. *Automated Software Engineering*, 6(1):7–35, July 1999.
14. D. Giannakopoulou, C. S. Păsăreanu, and H. Barringer. Assumption generation for software component verification. In *Proc. of the 17th IEEE Int. Conf. on Automated Software Engineering*, Sept. 2002.
15. A. Groce, D. Peled, and M. Yannakakis. Adaptive model checking. In *Proc. of the 8th Int. Conf. on Tools and Algorithms for the Construction and Analysis of Systems*, pages 357–370, Apr. 2002.
16. O. Grumberg and D. E. Long. Model checking and modular verification. In *Proc. of the 2nd Int. Conf. on Concurrency Theory*, pages 250–265, Aug. 1991.
17. T. A. Henzinger, S. Qadeer, and S. K. Rajamani. You assume, we guarantee: Methodology and case studies. In *Proc. of the 10th Int. Conf. on Computer-Aided Verification*, pages 440–451, June 28–July 2, 1998.
18. C. B. Jones. Specification and design of (parallel) programs. In R. Mason, editor, *Information Processing 83: Proc. of the IFIP 9th World Congress*, pages 321–332. IFIP: North Holland, 1983.
19. J.-P. Krimm and L. Mounier. Compositional state space generation from Lotos programs. In *Proc. of the 3rd Int. Workshop on Tools and Algorithms for the Construction and Analysis of Systems*, pages 239–258, Apr. 1997.
20. J. Magee and J. Kramer. *Concurrency: State Models & Java Programs*. John Wiley & Sons, 1999.
21. A. Pnueli. In transition from global to modular temporal reasoning about programs. In K. Apt, editor, *Logic and Models of Concurrent Systems*, volume 13, pages 123–144, New York, 1984. Springer-Verlag.
22. R. L. Rivest and R. E. Schapire. Inference of finite automata using homing sequences. *Information and Computation*, 103(2):299–347, Apr. 1993.
23. W. Visser, K. Havelund, G. Brat, and S.-J. Park. Model checking programs. In *Proc. of the 15th IEEE Int. Conf. on Automated Software Engineering*, Sept. 2000.
24. Q. Xu, W. P. de Roever, and J. He. The rely-guarantee method for verifying shared variable concurrent programs. *Formal Aspects of Computing*, 9(2):149–174, 1997.

Automated Module Composition*

Stavros Tripakis

VERIMAG, Centre Equation, 2, rue de Vignate, 38610 Gières, France.
www-verimag.imag.fr, tripakis@imag.fr.

Abstract. We define an abstract problem of module composition (MC). In MC, modules are seen as black boxes with input and output ports. The objective is, given a set of available modules, to instantiate some of them (one or more times) and connect their ports, in order to obtain a target module. A general compatibility relation defines which ports can be connected to each other. Constraints are imposed on the number of instances of each module and the number of copies of each port. A linear objective function can be given to minimize the total cost of module instances and port copies.

The MC problem is motivated by the need to automate the composition of legacy modules used in the development of software embedded in cars. Due to the large number of modules, composition "by hand" is tedious and error-prone, and its automation would lead to significant cost reduction.

We show that the MC problem is NP-complete, by formulating an equivalent integer optimization problem. We also identify a number of special cases where the MC problem can be solved in polynomial time. Finally, we suggest techniques that can be used for the general cases.

1 Introduction

In this paper we introduce a problem of *module composition* and provide algorithms and fundamental worst-case complexity results for it.

The setting is as follows. We are given a set of available module types. Each module type is characterized simply by a set of input ports and a set of output ports. A binary compatibility relation between input and output ports models which input port can be connected to which output port. The problem is to (1) generate zero or more instances of each module type, (2) generate zero or more copies of each port in each module instance, and (3) connect all ports in a compatible way so that no port remains disconnected. As we show below, this problem is general enough to capture the problem of finding a composition of available modules that "implements" a given target module.

Constraints can be imposed on the number of instances of each module type (e.g., "at least 2 copies of A, at most 1 copy of B", etc) and the number of copies of each port in an instance (e.g., "can fan-out port p at most 10 times,

* This work has been supported in part by the European project "Next TTA" under project No IST-2001-32111.

H. Garavel and J. Hatcliff (Eds.): TACAS 2003, LNCS 2619, pp. 347–362, 2003.

port q needs at least 2 inputs", etc). A linear objective function can be given to minimize the total cost of module instances, port copies and connections.

To motivate the reader, we give an example, shown in Figure 1. The figure shows two available module types A and B and a target module T. The goal is to instantiate and connect A and B to obtain T. The only compatible ports are output port q_1 of A with input port p_3 of B (we use an arrow from p_3 to q_1 to denote that). For simplicity, we assume there are no bounds on the number of instances of modules or the number of copies of ports. By instantiating each of A and B and their ports once and connecting q_1 to p_3, we achieve our goal.

Now, it is easy to see that the above problem is equivalent to the following slightly modified problem. Given A, B and T^{-1} (the "inverted" version of T, that is, where input ports are turned into outputs and outputs into inputs), find a composition which includes exactly one instance of T^{-1} and results in the "closed" module (that is, where all ports are connected). Therefore, in the rest of this paper, we consider this modified version of the problem where there are only available modules and the goal is to reach a closed composition. We call this the module composition problem (MC).

The results we obtain for MC are the following. First, we give an equivalent formulation as an integer programming optimization problem. Second, we show that MC is NP-complete. Third, we identify a number of special cases where MC can be solved in polynomial time, by solving an equivalent network flow problem. Finally, we suggest methods to be used in the general case.

Applications. We believe that the abstract problem introduced and studied in this paper has a number of practical applications. For example, in a circuit layout context, modules might represent chips and ports might represent wires. In a software engineering context, modules and ports might represent software components and their interfaces. Automatic composition can be especially useful in a dynamic and distributed environment, such as programs communicating over the Internet using middleware like CORBA or JINI: in such an environment, it is important for fault tolerance and reconfiguration to dispose of fast automatic composition techniques.

The application that has initially motivated our work comes from the domain of automotive embedded software development [12,2]. The problem there is to "design a software tool that automatically composes a fully executable model from a list of components and an architectural description of the final model" (quote from [12]). The components are used for simulation and eventually code generation. Due to the large number of legacy components (hundreds or more, often developed by different groups), the current practice of composition "by hand" is extremely tedious, as well as error prone. It is obvious that an automatic composition technique would greatly reduce the software production cost.

Related work. Automating software composition is not a new idea. Tools such as `make` are widely used to automate compilation or any other software transformation, taking into account dependencies, and so on. The major difference

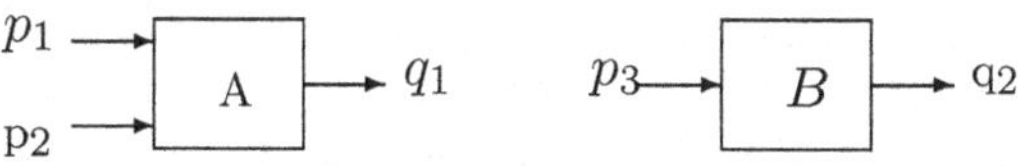

Two available module types, A and B

The target module T The "inverse" of the target module

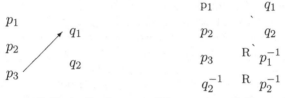

The compatibility relation between ports The compatibility relation after adding the inverted ports

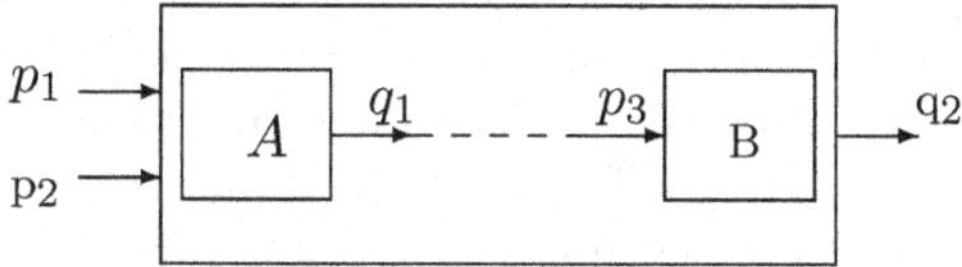

A composition of two instances of A and B which implements the target T

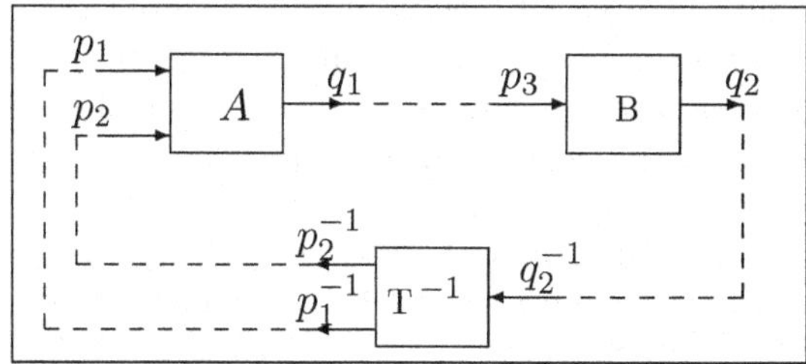

A composition of three instances of A, B and T^{-1} which implements the "closed" module

Fig. 1. Module composition example.

of these tools with our approach is, however, that in make, all alternative rules (i.e., possible solution chains) have to be *a-priori* known and hardcoded in the `makefile`. Another drawback is that hardcoding preferences among alternative solutions is not always easy in tools like `make`.

Our work is obviously related to Architecture Description Languages[1] as well as to Software Architectures (e.g., see [15]) and other component models (e.g., see [18]). Our approach is independent of methodological and language-specific aspects. We have focused in defining a basic formal problem (with obvious practical applications) and obtaining fundamental complexity results. We have also been interested in a "light-weight" approach. Our framework is intentionally simple: for example, it cannot impose global constraints on a solution and modules do not have operational semantics. This simplicity makes automation in the large possible.

[16,11] propose the tool *Metaframe*, based on *linear temporal logic* and using a variant of the synthesis algorithm of [10] (of exponential worst-case complexity). The major difference with our framework is that they build only *linear* compositions (i.e., chains) rather than general graphs, as we do. Other differences are that in Metaframe, all possible solutions can be obtained, whereas in our case, we obtain only one solution. In Metaframe, constraints on the order of modules in a chain can be expressed (e.g., A must appear before B), however, it is not clear how to specify preference constraints or bounds on the number of modules.

The problem in [7,8] is to automatically generate all possible configurations of middleware architectures. Here, too, all possible solutions are found. Their framework is not restricted to linear architectures, however, the number of components to be used in a solution is fixed in advance, and preference constraints cannot be expressed. Like Steffen et al, Kloukinas et al. also use algorithms inspired by *model-checking* and *formal verification* techniques.

Also related is the dataflow composition based framework implemented in the tool *Sword* [6,14]. The problem is quite similar to ours: the synthesis of a composite service based on available services. As with the above works, it is not clear whether multiple copies of each service can be used and whether preferences or bounds can be expressed. The algorithm used in Sword is also quite different from ours: it uses rule-based techniques from the domain of artificial intelligence.

Finally, related is the component-modeling language *Alloy*, for which it is possible to perform automatic analysis in a first-order logic [5]. The analysis is sound but not complete, since the logic is undecidable. We do not know yet whether it is possible to express some type of module composition and automate it within the Alloy framework.

This work extends the results of [17] which deal with the problem of automatically composing modules in a chain.

2 Module Composition Problem

Let N denote the set of natural numbers $\{0, 1, 2, ...\}$.

[1] E.g., see www.sei.cmu.edu/architecture/adl.html for a list of ADLs.

We consider a finite set of *ports*, $P = \{p_1, ..., p_k\}$. We assume that $P = \mathsf{P_{in}} \cup \mathsf{P_{out}}$, where $\mathsf{P_{in}} \cap \mathsf{P_{out}} = \emptyset$. $\mathsf{P_{in}}$ is the set of *input* ports, $\mathsf{P_{out}}$ is the set of *output* ports.

We also consider a *compatibility relation* $\mathsf{C} \subseteq \mathsf{P_{in}} \times \mathsf{P_{out}}$, between input and output ports. The understanding is that input port p can be connected to output port q iff $(p, q) \in \mathsf{C}$.

A *module type* is a tuple $A = (In, Out, f_{in}, f_{out})$, where $In \subseteq \mathsf{P_{in}}$, $Out \subseteq \mathsf{P_{out}}$, $f_{in} : In \rightarrow 2^N$ and $f_{out} : Out \rightarrow 2^N$. An *instance* of A is a tuple $(In, Out, g_{in}, g_{out})$, where $g_{in} : In \rightarrow N$ and $g_{out} : Out \rightarrow N$, such that for all $p \in In$, $g_{in}(p) \in f_{in}(p)$, and for all $q \in Out$, $g_{out}(q) \in f_{out}(q)$. The meaning is that $f_{out}(p)$ defines the possible *fan-out* factors of output port p, namely, how many (compatible) input ports can be connected to p. For example, if $f_{out}(p) = \{1, 2\}$ then at least one and at most two ports should be connected to p. We can view $f_{out}(p)$ as specifying how many *copies* of p an instance of module A can have. Each copy of p will be connected to a single copy of another port. Then, in a given instance of A, $g_{out}(p)$ fixes exactly how many copies of p there are, within the range specified by $f_{out}(p)$. The meanings of f_{in} and g_{in} are symmetric.

We will use the following notation and assumptions. For a module type $A = (In, Out, f_{in}, f_{out})$, $in(A)$, $out(A)$, $f_{in}(A)$ and $f_{out}(A)$ denote In, Out, f_{in} and f_{out}, respectively. Similarly for module instances. We will assume that $f_{in}(p)$ and $f_{out}(q)$ are non-negative integer intervals, e.g., $[0, 5]$, $[1, 1]$, and so on. We will also assume that the set of input and output ports of a module type are disjoint. Finally, we will assume that given a set of module types, they all have disjoint sets of input ports and disjoint sets of output ports.

Given a multiset of module instances $\mathcal{I}$ (not necessarily all of the same module type), a *composition* on $\mathcal{I}$ is defined as a multiset X of tuples of the form (A, p, B, q), where $A, B \in \mathcal{I}$, $p \in in(A)$ and $q \in out(B)$. The meaning of (A, p, B, q) is that input port p of A is connected to output port q of B.

We say that a composition X on $\mathcal{I}$ is *closed* if the following conditions hold:

$$\forall A \in \mathcal{I}, \forall p \in in(A), |\{(A, p, \_, \_) \in \mathsf{X}\}| = g_{in}(A)(p) \tag{1}$$

$$\forall A \in \mathcal{I}, \forall q \in out(A), |\{(\_, \_, A, q) \in \mathsf{X}\}| = g_{out}(A)(q) \tag{2}$$

Conditions 1 and 2 say that X connects a port to exactly as many ports as specified by its fan factor.

We say that a composition X on $\mathcal{I}$ *respects a compatibility relation* C if

$$\forall p \in \mathsf{P_{in}}, q \in \mathsf{P_{out}}, (\_, p, \_, q) \in \mathsf{X} \Rightarrow (p, q) \in \mathsf{C} \tag{3}$$

The last element we need is a set of constraints on how many instances of a module type we can have. We formalize that as a function $\mathsf{N_{inst}} : \mathcal{M} \rightarrow 2^N$, where $\mathcal{M}$ is the set of module types and for each module type A in $\mathcal{M}$, $\mathsf{N_{inst}}(A)$ is an interval. For example, if $\mathsf{N_{inst}}(A) = [1, 10]$, this means that at most 10 instances of A are available and at least 1 instance should be used, whereas if $\mathsf{N_{inst}}(A) = N$, then an arbitrary number of instances of A can be used, possibly none. We say that a set of module instances $\mathcal{I}$ *respects* $\mathsf{N}_{\mathsf{inst}}$ if for each module type A, if n_A is the number of instances of A in $\mathcal{I}$ (notice that $\mathcal{I}$ is a multiset), then $n_A \in \mathsf{N}_{\mathsf{inst}}(A)$.

We are now ready to state the module composition problem.

Definition 1 (Module Composition Problem (MC)). *Given*
(a) disjoint sets of input and output ports $\mathsf{P}_{\mathsf{in}}, \mathsf{P}_{\mathsf{out}}$,
(b) a compatibility relation $\mathsf{C} \subseteq \mathsf{P}_{\mathsf{in}} \times \mathsf{P}_{\mathsf{out}}$,
(c) a set of module types $\mathcal{M}$, *and*
(d) constraints on the number of module instances

$$\mathsf{N}_{\mathsf{inst}} : \mathcal{M} \to 2^{N},$$

find
(e) a set of module instances $\mathcal{I}$ *that respects* $\mathsf{N}_{\mathsf{inst}}$, *and*
(f) a composition X *on* $\mathcal{I}$ *that respects* C *and is closed.*

Example 2. Consider the set of module types shown at the top of Figure 2. For the sake of simplicity, we assume that two ports are compatible iff they have the same name.[2] We require that exactly one instance of module A_0 be present in the composition, while there are no constraints on the number of instances of A_1, A_2, A_3. In our framework this can be modeled by setting $\mathsf{N}_{\mathsf{inst}}(A_0) = \{1\}$ and $\mathsf{N}_{\mathsf{inst}}(A_1) = \mathsf{N}_{\mathsf{inst}}(A_2) = \mathsf{N}_{\mathsf{inst}}(A_3) = N$. The fan factors of all ports are constrained to be exactly 1, except for output port a of module A_0, which can have from 0 up to 3 copies. That is, $f_{out}(A_0)(a) = [0, 3]$, and $f_{in}(p) = f_{out}(q) = [1, 1]$, for all other ports p, q in the system. A solution of this MC is shown at the bottom of the figure. In the solution, there is one instance of A_0, A_2, A_3 and two instances of A_1. Also, there are two copies of output port a of A_0, each connected to a copy of input port a of a different instance of A_1.

Remark 3 (The compatibility relation). We assume that the compatibility relation is given. Indeed, how compatibility of ports is derived is application specific, and out of the scope of this paper. Still, we give some examples of the range of expressiveness of the compatibility relation below. Note that the compatibility relation can be derived (possibly automatically) independently of the composition problem: this can be done once and used in many composition instances.

As in Example 2, compatibility could be simply based on names: two ports are compatible iff they have the same name (note that our framework is strictly more expressive than naming, see footnote 2). Another possibility is type matching: each port represents a type, and two ports are compatible iff their types match (for example, p_{int} matches q_{int} and q_{real}). Note that *polymorphic* types can be handled as well: for example, a module computing the length of a list of objects of any type can have an input port p which is compatible with all output ports

[2] There exist compatibility relations which can be expressed in our framework, i.e., as a binary relation $\mathsf{C} \subseteq \mathsf{P}_{\mathsf{in}} \times \mathsf{P}_{\mathsf{out}}$, yet cannot be reduced to naming. Section 3.2 contains an example of such a relation (Figure 3). The algorithm we present in Section 3 can handle any relation $\mathsf{C} \subseteq \mathsf{P}_{\mathsf{in}} \times \mathsf{P}_{\mathsf{out}}$.

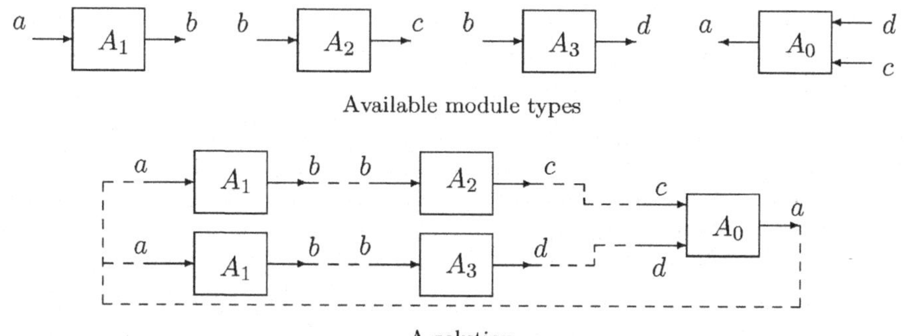

Fig. 2. A module composition problem and a solution.

representing lists.[3] Ports could also represent interfaces (i.e., sets of functions defined by their signatures), in which case port p is compatible with port q if the interface defined by p is a subset of the one defined by q.[4]

Ports could even be given semantics in terms of automata (as in [9] or [3]) which can express, for instance, the acceptable order of function calls in an interface[5] (e.g., "before you call *get()* you must call *init()*"). Here, compatibility can be defined as a *simulation* relation between automata and can be derived automatically by testing offline, for every pair of input/output ports (p, q), whether the automaton of p simulates the one of q.

Non-uniqueness of solutions, optimality. We observe that an MC does not necessarily have a unique solution. This is because of the following reasons:

- If a set of instances works, then doubling the instances will work too (provided the constraints on number of instances are met).
- Even if we require the number of elements in $\mathcal{I}$ to be minimal, there might be more than one minimal solutions.
- Even if we fix the number of instances, there might be multiple ways to instantiate the fan factors of some ports. For example, if $(p, q) \in \mathsf{C}$ and $f_{in}(p) \cap f_{out}(q) = [1, 2]$, then we could let $g_{in}(p) = g_{out}(q) = 1$ or $g_{in}(p) = g_{out}(q) = 2$, which amounts to creating one or two copies of each port and connecting them.

[3] When polymorphism is allowed, it is sometimes desirable, in case type p is compatible with many types $q_1, ..., q_k$, to select the type q_i that is "closest" to p. This can be done in our framework through the use of an objective function to be minimized, see below.

[4] We see the module having input p as the *caller* component and the module having output q as the *called-upon* component.

[5] For example, see the *RosettaNet* project (www.rosettanet.org), where every "Partner Interface Process" (i.e. every interaction between two entities) is standardized, its syntax given in XML and its semantics described by an automaton.

- Even if we fix both the number of module instances and port copies, there may be different compositions (i.e., different ways to "wire" the modules) possible.

The algorithm that we give in the following section finds an *optimal* solution to an MC, provided a solution exists. The solution is optimal with respect to a given (linear) *objective function* which represents the sum of the costs of creating instances of a module (an instance of module type A_i will add a cost c_i), creating copies of ports (a copy of port p will add a cost c_p), and connecting ports (connecting port p to port q will add a cost $c_{p,q}$). This is useful, since we can express the fact that some modules might be more costly than others, as well as express preferences/priorities in connecting pairs of ports.

3 Automated Module Composition

In this section we present the main results of our study of MC:

- The general MC is decidable and NP-complete.
- In a number of special cases (e.g., when the number of instances for each module type is known), MC can be solved in polynomial time.

The basic idea for proving decidability is to formulate an integer program, such that MC has a solution iff the integer program has a solution. Moreover, an optimal solution of the integer program with respect to a linear objective function corresponds to an optimal set of instances $\mathcal{I}$ for MC. Given $\mathcal{I}$, finding a composition X is straightforward. NP-hardness is proved by reducing the Knapsack problem to MC. We start by illustrating our approach with a simple example.

3.1 A Simple Example

Consider again the MC problem of Figure 2. Initially, let us assume that the fan factors of all ports are equal to 1 (we relax this assumption later). That is, $f_{in}(p) = f_{out}(q) = [1, 1]$, for all ports p, q in the system. We will also assume throughout this example that all costs are equal to 1, that is, a solution is optimal if it minimizes the sum of module instances, port copies and connections.

We begin by creating integer variables x_0, x_1, x_2, x_3, where x_i represents the number of instances of module A_i in the solution. From $\mathsf{N}_{\mathsf{inst}}$, we obtain the constraints $x_0 = 1$, $x_i \geq 0$, $i = 1, 2, 3$.

Viewing the port names as independent vectors, we can represent each module type by a simple linear expression on these vectors. Doing so, we get the expressions $-c - d + a$ for A_0, $-a + b$ for A_1, $-b + c$ for A_2, and $-b + d$ for A_3.

Now, it is easy to see that the requirement that the composition be closed is equivalent to the following constraint:

$$x_0 \cdot (-c - d + a) + x_1 \cdot (-a + b) + x_2 \cdot (-b + c) + x_3 \cdot (-b + d) = 0 \qquad (4)$$

or equivalently:

$$a \cdot (x_0 - x_1) + b \cdot (x_1 - x_2 - x_3) + c \cdot (-x_0 + x_2) + d \cdot (-x_0 + x_3) = 0 \quad (5)$$

Indeed, module A_0 will "contribute" x_0 copies of its output port named a (since the fan factors are set to 1), and each of these has to be connected to a copy of the input port of A_1 named a, therefore, x_0 must be equal to x_1 in order to have a closed composition.

Since a, b, c, d are independent vectors, equation (5) is equivalent to the set of equations:

$$x_0 - x_1 = 0 \quad (6)$$

$$x_1 - x_2 - x_3 = 0 \quad (7)$$

$$-x_0 + x_2 = 0 \quad (8)$$

$$-x_0 + x_3 = 0 \quad (9)$$

Thus, we ended up with a simple system of linear equations on integer variables, namely, equations (6)-(9), along with the initial constraint $x_0 = 1$. Solving the system (e.g., by Gaussian elimination), we find that it is infeasible. This means that there exists no solution to the above instance of MC.

We now relax the constraint that the fan factors of all ports should be 1. For example, suppose that $f_{out}(A_0)(a) = [0, 3]$. To model this, we create an additional variable y_0^a, which represents the fan-out factor of port a of A_0. Since each instance of A_0 can contribute from 0 up to 3 copies of a, we have the constraint:

$$x_0 \cdot 0 \leq y_0^a \leq x_0 \cdot 3 \quad (10)$$

Equation (4) now becomes:

$$y_0^a \cdot a + x_0 \cdot (-c - d) + x_1 \cdot (-a + b) + x_2 \cdot (-b + c) + x_3 \cdot (-b + d) = 0 \quad (11)$$

We can transform constraints (10) and (11) to an equivalent set of equations:

$$y_0^a - 3x_0 + s = 0 \quad (12)$$

$$y_0^a - x_1 = 0 \quad (13)$$

$$x_1 - x_2 - x_3 = 0 \quad (14)$$

$$-x_0 + x_2 = 0 \quad (15)$$

$$-x_0 + x_3 = 0 \quad (16)$$

where $s \geq 0$ is a *slack* variable that transforms the inequality constraint into an equality. Solving equations $x_0 = 1$ and (12)-(16) by Gaussian elimination, we obtain the optimal solution $x_0 = x_2 = x_3 = 1$, $y_0^a = x_1 = 2$, $s = 1$. This corresponds to the set of module instances shown in the bottom of Figure 2.

Once the set of module instances is determined, connecting the ports (i.e., finding a composition) is trivial: pick any unconnected copy of an input port and connect it to an unconnected copy of a compatible output port; repeat until all ports are connected. Notice that this procedure is guaranteed to terminate with all ports connected, since the above constraints ensure that a closed composition exists. Also notice that since connections are made at random, there might be more than one compositions possible.

3.2 Formulation as an Integer Programming Problem

Let $\mathcal{M} = \{A_0, A_1, ..., A_n\}$ be the set of module types. The integer program contains the following non-negative integer variables and constraints.

- x_i, $i = 0, ..., n$, represents the number of instances of module A_i. Let $\mathsf{N}_{\mathsf{inst}}(A_i) = [l_i, u_i]$. For each x_i, we have the constraint
$$l_i \le x_i \le u_i. \tag{17}$$
If $u_i = \infty$, then the constraint becomes $l_i \le x_i$.
- y_p, $p \in \mathsf{P}_{\mathsf{in}}$, represents the total number of copies of input port p of a module A_i, in all instances of A_i. Letting $f_{in}(A_i)(p) = [a_p, b_p]$, each instance of A_i can "contribute" from a_p up to b_p copies of p. Therefore, for each p, we have the constraint
$$x_i \cdot a_p \le y_p \le x_i \cdot b_p. \tag{18}$$
If $b_p = \infty$, then the constraint becomes $x_i \cdot a_p \le y_p$.
- z_q, $q \in \mathsf{P}_{\mathsf{out}}$, represents the total number of copies of output port q of a module A_i, in all instances of A_i. Letting $f_{out}(A_i)(q) = [a_q, b_q]$, each instance of A_i can "contribute" from a_q up to b_q copies of q. Therefore, for each q, we have the constraint
$$x_i \cdot a_q \le z_q \le x_i \cdot b_q. \tag{19}$$
If $b_q = \infty$, then the constraint becomes $x_i \cdot a_q \le z_q$.
- $w_{p,q}$, $(p,q) \in \mathsf{C}$, represents the number of connections between a copy of p and a copy of q. We relate the $w_{p,q}$ with the y_p and z_q variables with the following sets of constraints, for each $p \in \mathsf{P}_{\mathsf{in}}$, $q \in \mathsf{P}_{\mathsf{out}}$:
$$y_p = \sum_{(p,q)\in \mathsf{C}} w_{p,q} \quad \text{and} \quad z_q = \sum_{(p,q)\in \mathsf{C}} w_{p,q} \tag{20}$$
Constraints (20) ensure that a closed connection exists.

Proposition 4. *There is a solution to MC iff there exist non-negative integers x_i, for $i = 0, ..., n$, y_p, for $p \in \mathsf{P}_{\mathsf{in}}$, z_q, for $q \in \mathsf{P}_{\mathsf{out}}$, $w_{p,q}$, for $(p,q) \in \mathsf{C}$, such that constraints (17)-(20) are satisfied.*

Regarding optimality, it can be easily incorporated in the above formulation, by introducing an objective function to be minimized. Let $c_i \ge 0$ be the cost of an instance of module A_i, $c_p \ge 0$ be the cost of a copy of port p, $c_q \ge 0$ be the cost of a copy of port q, and $c_{p,q} \ge 0$ be the cost of connecting a copy of p to a copy of q. We define the objective function to be:

$$f(\boldsymbol{x}, \boldsymbol{y}, \boldsymbol{z}, \boldsymbol{w}) = \textstyle\sum_{i=0,\ldots,n} c_i x_i + \sum_{p\in\mathsf{P}_{\mathsf{in}}} c_p y_p + \sum_{q\in\mathsf{P}_{\mathsf{out}}} c_q z_q + \sum_{q\in\mathsf{P}_{\mathsf{out}}} c_{p,q} w_{p,q},$$

where $\boldsymbol{x}, \boldsymbol{y}, \boldsymbol{z}, \boldsymbol{w}$ are the vectors of variables $x_i, y_p, z_q, w_{p,q}$, respectively.

Then, we get an integer optimization problem:

minimize $f(\boldsymbol{x}, \boldsymbol{y}, \boldsymbol{z}, \boldsymbol{w})$, subject to constraints (17)-(20), and $x_i, y_p, z_q, w_{p,q}$ are non-negative integers.

It is worth observing that, first, if $l_i = 0$ for all $i = 0, ..., n$, then the trivial solution $x_i = y_p = z_q = w_{p,q} = 0$ is both feasible and optimal. Second, if for all i such that $l_i \geq 1$, for all $p \in in(A_i)$, $a_p = 0$, and for all $q \in out(A_i)$, $a_q = 0$, then the solution $x_i = l_i$, $y_p = z_q = w_{p,q} = 0$ is both feasible and optimal. Therefore, the interesting cases arise when there exists some i such that $l_i \geq 1$ and for some $p \in in(A_i)$, $a_p \geq 1$, or for some $q \in out(A_i)$, $a_q \geq 1$.

Eliminating redundancy in the integer program. In many cases, there may be a lot of redundancy in the above integer program, in the sense that the number of variables and constraints can be reduced. We have seen such a case in the example of section 3.1, where we used not all of the y_p or z_q variables and none of the $w_{p,q}$ variables. We now explain which variables and constraints can be eliminated and when. Our discussion on eliminating $w_{p,q}$ variables also shows that not all compatibility relations can be reduced to naming.

Eliminating y_p or z_q variables. In the case where $f_{in}(p) = [1, 1]$ for some input port p (i.e., the fan factor of p is 1), constraint (18) above becomes $x_i \cdot 1 \leq y_p \leq x_i \cdot 1$, or $y_p = x_i$. In that case, we can eliminate variable y_p and use x_i in its place. Similarly, for some output port q, we can eliminate variable z_q if $f_{out}(q) = [1, 1]$.

Eliminating $w_{p,q}$ variables. The reason why we did not have to use any $w_{p,q}$ variables in the example of section 3.1 is that we assumed that the compatibility relation of that example can be reduced to port naming, such that two ports are compatible iff they have the same name. This cannot always be done. For example, look at Figure 3. For the compatibility relation on the left, we cannot find a naming that works. Indeed, assume we give p_1 the name a. Then we have to name q_1 and q_2 by a too. Since q_2 is named a and is compatible with p_2, we have to name p_2 by a as well. But now p_2 and q_1 have the same name, even though they are not compatible. On the other hand, for the compatibility relation on the right of the figure, we can find a naming (just name all ports a) that works.

Formally, we say that a compatibility relation $\mathsf{C} \subseteq P_{in} \times P_{out}$ *has the Z property* if for any $p_1, p_2 \in P_{in}$ and any $q_1, q_2 \in P_{out}$

$$(p_1, q_1) \in \mathsf{C} \wedge (p_1, q_2) \in \mathsf{C} \wedge (p_2, q_2) \in \mathsf{C} \Rightarrow (p_2, q_1) \in \mathsf{C}. \Rightarrow (p_2, q_1) \in \mathsf{C}.$$

Then, we can show the following:

Lemma 5. *We can find a function* $\mathsf{name} : P_{in} \cup P_{out} \to N$ *such that* $\forall p \in P_{in}, q \in P_{out}, \mathsf{name}(p) = \mathsf{name}(q) \Leftrightarrow (p, q) \in \mathsf{C}$*, iff* C *has the Z property.*

Thus, if C has the Z property, we can partition $\mathsf{P_{in}}$ and $\mathsf{P_{out}}$ into disjoint subsets $\mathsf{P_{in}} = \mathsf{P_{in}}^0 \cup \mathsf{P_{in}}^1 \cup \cdots \mathsf{P_{in}}^k$, $\mathsf{P_{out}} = \mathsf{P_{out}}^0 \cup \mathsf{P_{out}}^1 \cup \cdots \mathsf{P_{out}}^k$, such that $p \in \mathsf{P_{in}}^i$ iff $\mathsf{name}(p) = i$ and $q \in \mathsf{P_{out}}^i$ iff $\mathsf{name}(q) = i$. Then, we can eliminate variables

$w_{p,q}$, and replace the set of constraints (20)-(20) by one constraint as follows, for each $i = 0, ..., k$:

$$\sum_{p \in \mathsf{P_{in}}^i} y_p = \sum_{q \in \mathsf{P_{out}}^i} z_q. \tag{21}$$

In fact, even if C does not have the Z property, "parts" of it might possess it. In such a case, we can perform the above optimization for these parts, eliminating the corresponding $w_{p,q}$ variables.

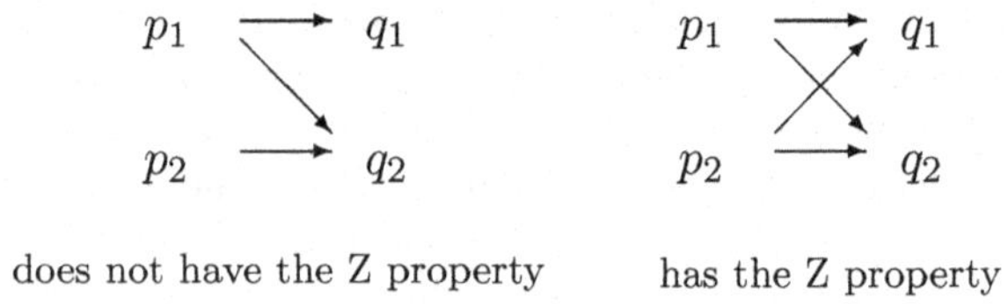

p_1 → q_1 p_1 → q_1

p_2 → q_2 p_2 → q_2

does not have the Z property has the Z property

Fig. 3. Illustration of the Z property.

3.3 NP-Completeness

Theorem 6. *The Module Composition Problem is NP-Complete.*

Proof: First we show that MC is in NP. It has been shown that any integer programming problem can be transformed in polynomial time into a 0-1 integer programming problem, that is, where all variables take the values 0 or 1 (e.g., see chapter I.5 of [13]). Since there is a polynomial number of 0-1 variables, say k, there are 2^k possible solutions. For each solution, it can be checked in polynomial time whether it is feasible. If a feasible solution is found, the composition can be computed in linear time in the number of ports, as discussed in section 3.5. Therefore, MC is in NP.

To prove that MC is NP-hard, we reduce a variant of the *Knapsack problem* (KP) to MC. KP is defined as follows. We are given a set of numbers $S = \{c_1, ..., c_n\} \subset N$, and some $M \in N$. We are asked whether there exists a subset $S' \subseteq S$, such that $\sum_{x \in S'} x = M$. The problem is known to be NP-complete [4].

We reduce KP to MC as follows. Let $A_0, A_1, ..., A_n$ be module types, where:

- $\mathsf{N_{inst}}(A_0) = \{1\}$ and $\mathsf{N_{inst}}(A_i) = \{0, 1\}$, for each $i = 1, ..., n$.
- A_0 has no output ports, M input ports, and $f_{in}(A_0)(p) = [1, 1]$ for each input port p of A_0.
- For each $i = 1, ..., n$, A_i has no input ports, c_i output ports, and $f_{out}(A_i)(q) = [1, 1]$ for each output port q of A_i.
- Every input port is compatible with every output port.

It is easy to see that KP has a solution iff the above MC has a solution. ■

3.4 Special Cases of Polynomial Complexity

Although the worst-case complexity of the general MC is exponential, there are many interesting special cases where MC can be solved in polynomial time. This is when the integer program of section 3.2 can be transformed to an equivalent *network flow problem*, which can be solved in polynomial time using a variety of algorithms (e.g., see [1]). We now identify some of these cases.

Special case I: known number of module instances. Suppose that the number of module instances are known, that is, $l_i = u_i$, for all $i = 0, ..., n$. In this case the problem is equivalent to a *min-cost flow problem*, in a network defined as follows. There is one node for each input port p, one node for each output port q, a source node s and a sink node t. There is a directed link from s to each node p, and the flow along this link corresponds to y_p. There is a directed link from each node q to t, and the flow along this link corresponds to z_q. There is a directed link from p to q, for each $(p,q) \in \mathsf{C}$, and the flow along this link corresponds to $w_{p,q}$. There is a directed link from t to s. Finally, there are lower and upper *capacity bounds* on the links (s,p) and (q,t), corresponding to constraints (18) and (19). The objective function is similar to the one given in section 3.2, namely, minimize $(\sum_{p \in \mathsf{P}_{\mathsf{in}}} c_p \cdot y_p) + (\sum_{q \in \mathsf{P}_{\mathsf{out}}} c_q \cdot z_q)$.

A number of min-cost flow algorithms can be used in this case. For example, the *enhanced capacity scaling algorithm* has complexity $O((e \log v) \cdot (e + v \log v))$, where v is the number of nodes and e the number of edges. Notice that in the network construction above, we have $v = |\mathsf{P}_{\mathsf{in}}| + |\mathsf{P}_{\mathsf{out}}| + 2$ and $e = |\mathsf{P}_{\mathsf{in}}| + |\mathsf{P}_{\mathsf{out}}| + |\mathsf{C}|$.

Special case II: modules with single input/output ports. Suppose that each module type has at most one input port and at most one output port, that is, $|in(A_i)| \leq 1$ and $|out(A_i)| \leq 1$, for all $i = 0, ..., n$, and $f_{in}(p) = f_{out}(q) = [1, 1]$, for all ports p, q. Then, the problem can be again transformed into a min-cost network flow problem, where the network is defined as follows. There are two nodes, s_i and t_i, for each $i = 0, ..., n$. There is a directed link from s_i to t_i with capacity $x_i \in [l_i, u_i]$. If A_i has an input port p and A_j has an output port q, such that $(p,q) \in \mathsf{C}$, then there is a directed link from t_i to s_j. The objective function is similar to the one given in section 3.2, namely, minimize $\sum_{i=0,...,n} c_i \cdot x_i$.

Again, any min-cost flow algorithm can be used. In this case, the number of nodes is $2n$ and the number of edges is $n + |\mathsf{C}|$.

3.5 Overall Algorithm for the Module Composition Problem

Based on the results of the previous sections, the overall algorithm to solve MC has three stages.

In Stage 1, we try to find an optimal solution to the integer optimization program given in section 3.2. If no feasible solution exists, then MC has no solution (by proposition 4). If an optimal solution is found, we proceed to stage 2.

In Stage 2, we know the x_i's, y_p's, z_q's and $w_{p,q}$'s. From these, we can build a set of module instances $\mathcal{I}$ as follows. There will be x_i instances of module A_i. For each input port p of A_i, there will be a total of y_p copies of p in all instances of A_i. How many copies are assigned to each instance does not matter, as long as there are between a_p and b_p copies of p in each instance. Therefore, we can assign copies to instances at random, making sure the above constraints are met.[6] Similarly, we assign a total of z_q copies of port q.

Finally, in Stage 3, we build the composition as follows. Initially all copies of all ports are disconnected. We repeat the following, until all copies of all ports are connected: pick any unconnected copy of an input port and connect it to an unconnected copy of a compatible output port.[7]

Obviously, the hard part is Stage 1: solving the integer program. For this, the following strategy can be employed. First, check whether the problem instance belongs to one of the special cases given in section 3.4. These tests can be done automatically. If the problem belongs to a special case, apply a min-cost flow algorithm of choice.

If the problem does not belong to any special case, apply a heuristic of choice. There is a large number of heuristics for integer optimization problems developed in the literature. We just mention a few here, referring the reader to [1,13] for details.

1. Apply *Lagrangian relaxation*, by removing the constraints (17)-(19) from the feasible region and adding the following term to the objective function:

$$\begin{aligned} g(\boldsymbol{\lambda}, \boldsymbol{\mu}, \boldsymbol{x}, \boldsymbol{y}, \boldsymbol{z}, \boldsymbol{w}) = & \left(\sum_i \lambda_i(u_i - x_i) + \mu_i(x_i - l_i)\right) \\ & + \left(\sum_p \lambda_p(b_p x_i - y_p) + \mu_p(y_p - a_p x_i)\right) \\ & + \left(\sum_q \lambda_q(b_q x_i - z_q) + \mu_q(z_q - a_q x_i)\right), \end{aligned}$$

   where the λ's and μ's are the Lagrange multipliers. By doing this, we end-up with a min-cost network flow problem, which can be iteratively solved to obtain a strict bound on the optimal solution and perhaps also find one.
2. Use *branch-and-bound* to iteratively solve *linear relaxations* of the integer program (i.e., where the variables are not restricted to be integers), and converge to an integer solution.
3. Use a *cutting-plane* algorithm to do the above.

4 Summary, Discussion, and Perspectives

We have introduced an abstract problem of module composition and showed how its solution can be computed effectively. We believe that the problem arises in many instances in practice, in particular in the development of large software

---

[6] By proposition 4, it is guaranteed that we can assign copies such that the above constraints are met.

[7] Again, by proposition 4, this procedure is guaranteed to terminate with all ports connected.

systems or the deployment of dynamic systems. We also believe that an automated procedure can result to significant cost savings, both by speeding-up the assembly process and by facilitating component re-use.

One question about our work might be, what is the behavior of the composite module and how is it ensured that this behavior is correct? It has been our conscious decision not to associate detailed semantics with our model. We could, for instance, specify the behavior of a module by an automaton and define the composition of modules in terms of automata composition. This would permit us to express desirable properties of the global system in a formal specification language (e.g., temporal logic) and use formal verification techniques (e.g., model checking) to check whether the property holds or not. Instead of doing this, we opted for a more "light-weight" approach, where modules are "black boxes" with no internal semantics and composition only guarantees local port compatibility. The motivations behind our choice have been the following:

1. We care about scalability of our method. State-of-the-art formal verification techniques cannot cope with more than in the order of tens of modules, thus are not sufficient for large systems.
2. We argue that (local) port compatibility can be made as expressive as necessary, thereby capturing the intended semantics and ensuring that systems that "compose well" are also "correct by construction" to a certain degree. (See Remark 3 for examples of compatibility relations.)
3. Even in the case where the semantics of ports are not strong enough to capture all necessary global properties, we believe that our algorithms are still useful as a "first pass" of module composition, which is automated, therefore fast. After this first pass, the designer can examine the result using more sophisticated techniques in order to verify all properties of interest. The first pass is still useful since it has relieved the designer from the tedious process of composing a large number of components "by hand".

Regarding future work, we intend to apply our methods in the particular context of embedded software development for cars. In order to make the approach more usable, we plan to develop techniques to automate the resolution of the compatibility relation: deciding whether two ports are compatible can be done automatically based on a set of rules such name matching, type matching, matching of sampling rates, etc. Finally, we intend to investigate the power of local port compatibility with respect to global properties of the composite system.

References

1. R.K. Ahuja, T.L. Magnanti, and J.B. Orlin. *Network Flows – Theory, Algorithms and Applications*. Prentice-Hall, 1993.
2. K. Butts, D. Bostic, A. Chutinan, J. Cook, B. Milam, and Y. Wang. Usage scenarios for a model compiler. In *EMSOFT'01*. Springer, LNCS 2211, 2001.
3. L. de Alfaro and T.A. Henzinger. Interface theories for component-based design. In *EMSOFT'01*. Springer, LNCS 2211, 2001.

4. M. Garey and D. Johnson. *Computers and Intractability: a guide to the theory of NP-completeness.* Freeman, 1979.
5. D. Jackson. Automating first-order relational logic. In *Foundations of Software Engineering*, 2000.
6. E. Kiciman, L. Melloul, and A. Fox. Towards zero-code service composition. In *8th Workshop on Hot Topics in Operating Systems (HotOS VIII)*, 2001.
7. C. Kloukinas and V. Issarny. Automating the composition of middleware configurations. In *Automated Software Engineering*, 2000.
8. C. Kloukinas and V. Issarny. SPIN-ning Software Architectures: A Method for Exploring Complex Systems. In *Working IEEE/IFIP Conference on Software Architecture (WICSA2001)*, 2001.
9. E.A. Lee and Y. Xiong. System-level types for component-based design. Technical report, Technical Memorandum UCB/ERL M00/8, University of California, Berkeley, 2000.
10. Z. Manna and P. Wolper. Synthesis of communicating processes from temporal logic specifications. *ACM TOPLAS*, 6(1), January 1984.
11. T. Margaria and B. Steffen. Backtracking-free design planning by automatic synthesis in metaframe. In *Fundamental Aspects of Software Engineering*, 1998.
12. W. Milam and A. Chutinan. Model composition and analysis challenge problems. Technical report of Mobies project. Available at: http://vehicle.me.berkeley.edu/mobies, 2001.
13. G.L. Nemhauser and L.A. Wolsey. *Integer and Combinatorial Optimization.* Wiley, 1988.
14. S. R. Ponnekanti and A. Fox. Sword: A developer toolkit for web service composition. In *11th World Wide Web Conference (Web Engineering Track)*, 2002.
15. M. Shaw and D. Garlan. *Software Architecture: Perspectives on an Emerging Discipline.* Prentice Hall, 1996.
16. B. Steffen, T. Margaria, and M. von der Beeck. Automatic synthesis of linear process models from temporal constraints: An incremental approach. In *ACM/SIGPLAN Int. Workshop on Automated Analysis of Software (AAS'97)*, 1997.
17. S. Tripakis. Automated composition of module chains. In *ETAPS'02 Workshop on Software Composition.* Volume 65, issue 4 of ENTCS, Elsevier, 2002.
18. R. van Ommering, F. van der Linden, J. Kramer, and J. Magee. The Koala component model for consumer electronics software. *IEEE Computer*, March 2000.

Modular Strategies for Recursive Game Graphs* **

Rajeev Alur[1], Salvatore La Torre[2], and Parthasarathy Madhusudan[1]

[1] University of Pennsylvania
[2] Università degli Studi di Salerno

Abstract. In this paper, we focus on solving games in recursive game graphs that can model the control flow in sequential programs with recursive procedure calls. While such games can be viewed as the pushdown games studied in the literature, the natural notion of winning in our framework requires the strategies to be modular with only local memory; that is, resolution of choices within a module does not depend on the context in which the module is invoked, but only on the history within the current invocation of the module. While reachability in (global) pushdown games is known to be EXPTIME-complete, we show reachability in modular games to be NP-complete. We present a fixpoint computation algorithm for solving modular games such that the worst-case number of iterations is exponential in the total number of returned values from the modules. If the strategy within a module does not depend on the global history, but can remember the history of the past invocations of this module, that is, if memory is local but persistent, we show that reachability becomes undecidable.

1 Introduction

The original motivation for studying games in the context of formal analysis of systems comes from the controller synthesis problem. Given a description of the system where some of the choices depend upon the input and some of the choices represent uncontrollable internal non-determinism, designing a *controller* that supplies inputs to the system so that the product of the controller and the system satisfies the correctness specification corresponds to computing winning strategies in two-player games. This question has been studied extensively in the literature (see [5,15,10] for sample research and [19] for a survey). Besides the long-term dream of synthesizing correct programs from formal specifications, games are relevant in two different contemporary contexts. First, model checking for branching-time logics such as μ-calculus, as well as several procedures that

* This research was supported in part by ARO URI award DAAD19-01-1-0473, NSF CAREER award CCR97-34115, and NSF award ITR/SY 0121431. The second author was also supported by the MIUR in the framework of the project "Metodi Formali per la Sicurezza" (MEFISTO) and MIUR grant 60% 2002.

** For the details of the proofs of this paper we refer the reader to the technical report available at the URL:"`http://www.cis.upenn.edu/~madhusud/`".

H. Garavel and J. Hatcliff (Eds.): TACAS 2003, LNCS 2619, pp. 363–378, 2003.

use tree automata emptiness for deciding various logics, can be reduced to solving games [9,18]. Second, games have been shown to be relevant for verification of open systems. For instance, the *Alternating Temporal Logic* allows specification of requirements such as "module A can ensure delivery of the message no matter how module B behaves" [2]; *module checking* deals with the problem of checking whether a module behaves correctly no matter in which environment it is placed [11]; and the framework of interface automata allows assumptions about the usage of a component to be built into the specification of the interface of the component, and formulates compatibility of interfaces using games [8].

In traditional model checking, the model is a finite state machine whose vertices correspond to states, and whose edges correspond to transitions. To define two-player games in this model, the vertices are partitioned into two sets corresponding to the two players, where a player gets to choose the transition when the current state belongs to its own partition [1]. In this paper, we consider the richer system model of *recursive state machines* (RSMs), in which vertices can either be ordinary states or can correspond to invocations of other state machines in a potentially recursive manner. Recursive state machines can model the control flow in typical sequential imperative programming languages with recursive procedure calls.

More precisely, a recursive state machine consists of a set of component machines called *modules*. Each module has a set of *nodes* (atomic states) and *boxes* (each of which is mapped to a module), a well-defined interface consisting of *entry* and *exit* nodes, and edges connecting nodes/boxes. An edge entering a box models the invocation of the module associated with the box, and an edge leaving a box corresponds to a return from that module. To define two-player games on recursive state machines, we partition the nodes into two sets such that a player gets to choose the transition when the current node belongs to its own partition. We focus on solving the *reachability* game, that is, deciding if one of the players has a strategy to force the system starting from a specified node to enter one of the target nodes.

Due to recursion, the underlying global state-space is infinite and behaves like a *pushdown* system. While reachability in pushdown games is already studied [20,6], we are interested in developing algorithms for games on RSMs for two reasons. First, RSMs is a more natural model of recursive systems, and studying reachability (without games) on RSMs has led to refined bounds on complexity in terms of parameters such as the number of entry and exit nodes of modules [1]. Second, existing algorithms for solving pushdown games assume that each player has access to the entire global history which includes the information of the play in all modules. The first contribution of the paper is the notion of *modular* strategies for games on RSMs. A modular strategy is a strategy that has only local memory, and thus, resolution of choices within a module does not depend on the context in which the module is invoked, but only on the history

[1] More interesting forms of interactions between the two players are possible, for instance, see alternating transition systems [2], but we will use a simple game model for this paper.

within the current invocation of the module. This permits a natural definition of synthesis of recursive controllers: a controller for a module can be plugged into any context where the module is invoked. Clearly, there are cases where there is no modular strategy, but there is a global one. Recent work on the interface compatibility checking for software modules implements the global games on pushdown systems [7], but we believe that checking for existence of modular strategies matches better with the intuition for compatibility.

After formulating the notion of modular strategies, we show that deciding existence of modular winning strategies for reachability games is NP-complete. In contrast, global reachability games are EXPTIME-complete [20]. Then, we proceed to formulate a fixpoint computation algorithm that generalizes the symbolic solution to reachability games. For ordinary game graphs, the fixpoint algorithm, starting with the target vertices, iteratively grows the set of vertices from which winning is ensured. In our case, when a node is found to be winning, the algorithm also needs to keep track of the strategies within different modules that were used. This labeling is needed to make sure that the same set of module strategies is used consistently everywhere to ensure modularity. It turns out that the only relevant information about a strategy used within a module is the set of exit nodes of the module that the strategy can restrict the game into. Consequently, in the worst-case, the number of iterations of our fixpoint computation is exponential in the number of exit nodes of the modules.

We also consider *safety* winning conditions for recursive game graphs. Since we restrict to modular strategies of the protagonist, on recursive game graphs safety is not dual to reachability. We prove that determining the existence of a modular strategy for a safety recursive game is also NP-complete.

Finally, we consider the case when the strategy within a module is required to have only local memory, and does not depend on the global history, but this memory can be persistent, and can remember the history of the past invocations of this module. In this case, we prove the reachability games to be undecidable by a reduction from the undecidability of multi-player games with incomplete information [14].

Related work: We have already explained the relation to the global games on pushdown systems [4,6,20]. The notion of modular strategies may remind the reader of games with partial information, but this is technically quite different from the standard notion of partial information, and, in fact, lowers the complexity class of the decision problem, while introducing partial information typically adds an exponential to the complexity. Another context where modular strategies have been studied is in the realm of concurrent or distributed games where the intention is to come up with distributed controllers for a system (see [16,12,17] and references therein). In that setting, however, looking for modular strategies quickly leads to undecidability. There are some restricted architectures that are decidable, a prominent one being the *hierarchic architectures* [14,16]. Our problem, however, is quite different from these works since in our setting the control is always in one module, while in the concurrent setting, control can be in several modules at any given time.

2 Games on Recursive Graphs

In this section we introduce recursive games and the decision problem we wish to solve. We start recalling the notion of flat games which are the standard games on And-Or graphs.

2.1 Flat Game Graphs

A *flat game graph* is a tuple $G = \langle V, V_0, V_1, \gamma \rangle$ where V is a finite set of vertices, V_0 and V_1 define a partition of V, and $\gamma : V \to 2^V$ is a function giving for each vertex $u \in V$ the set of its *successors* in G. The game is played by two players, player 0 (the *protagonist*) and player 1 (the *adversary*). For $p = 0, 1$, the vertices in V_p are those from which only player p can move and the allowed moves are given by the function γ. A *play* of a game graph G is a (finite or infinite) path in G constructed in turns by the two players. A play $u_0 u_1 \ldots$ starting at a vertex u_0 is constructed as follows: if $u_0 \in V_p$, player p chooses a successor vertex u_1; at each step j, player p (where $u_j \in V_p$) chooses a successor vertex u_{j+1}.

A *strategy* for player p is a function $f : V^* \to V$ mapping sequences (and hence plays) to vertices. The idea is that when a play πu has been played, where $u \in V_p$, the strategy f recommends the move $f(\pi u)$. A play $\pi = u_1 u_2 \ldots$ is *according to* f if for every $j < |\pi|$ such that $u_j \in V_p$, $f(u_0 \ldots u_j) = u_{j+1}$. When a strategy for player p depends only on the current vertex of a play, i.e., if $f(\pi x) = f(\pi' x)$, for all plays π, π' and $x \in V_p$, it is called a *memoryless strategy*. A play π according to a strategy is said to be *maximal* if it cannot be continued (i.e. if π is infinite or there is no $v \in V$ such that πv is a play according to the strategy).

Since we are interested in *reachability* games in this paper, we have a *winning condition* for the game given by a subset of *target* vertices X. A flat reachability game is then a tuple $\langle G, v_0, X \rangle$ where G is a flat game graph, v_0 is the initial vertex where the plays start, and X, a subset of the vertices, is the target set. A play is winning for the protagonist if it contains a vertex in X (i.e. a play $\pi = u_0 u_1 \ldots$, where $u_0 = v_0$, is winning if there is an $i < |\pi|$ such that $u_i \in X$). A strategy for the protagonist is winning if all maximal plays according to it are winning, while a strategy for the adversary is winning if all maximal plays according to it are not winning. Hence, a winning strategy for the protagonist is one which forces the play to the target set X, no matter how the adversary chooses. Flat reachability games are PTIME-complete and if a player has a winning strategy, it also has a memoryless winning strategy [13].

2.2 Recursive Game Graphs

In this paper, our main objective is to study reachability games in hierarchical and recursive graph structures that are defined using several interacting component game graphs (or game modules). Our model is a generalization to game graphs of the recursive state machines model defined in [1].

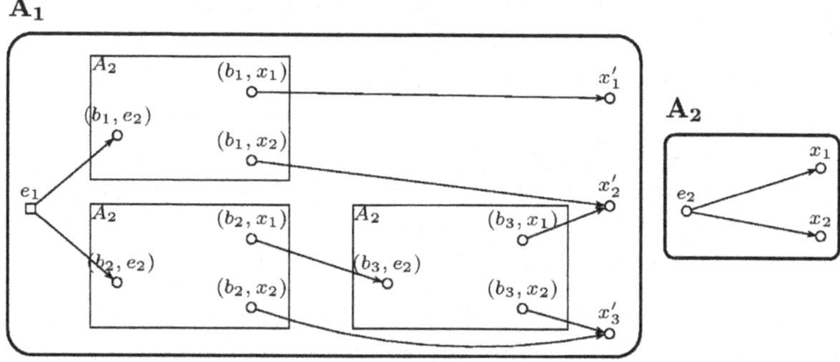

Fig. 1. A recursive game graph

A *recursive game graph* A is given by a tuple $\langle A_1, \ldots, A_n \rangle$, where each *game module* $A_i = (N_i, B_i, V_i^0, V_i^1, Y_i, En_i, Ex_i, \delta_i)$ consists of the following components:

- A set of nodes N_i which we call the *nodes* of module A_i.
- A nonempty set of *entry* nodes $En_i \subseteq N_i$ and a nonempty set of *exit* nodes $Ex_i \subseteq N_i$.
- A set of *boxes* B_i.
- Two disjoint sets V_i^0 and V_i^1 that partition the set of nodes and boxes into two sets, i.e. $V_i^0 \cup V_i^1 = N_i \cup B_i$ and $V_i^0 \cap V_i^1 = \emptyset$. The set V_i^0 (V_i^1) denotes the places where it is the turn of player 0 (resp. player 1) to play.
- A labeling $Y_i : B_i \rightarrow \{1, \ldots, n\}$ that assigns to every box an index of the game modules $A_1, \ldots, A_n$.
- Let $Calls_i = \{(b, e) \mid b \in B_i, e \in En_j, j = Y_i(b)\}$ denote the set of *calls* of module A_i and let $Retns_i = \{(b, x) \mid b \in B_i, x \in Ex_j, j = Y_i(b)\}$ denote the set of *returns* in A_i. Then, $\delta_i : N_i \cup Retns_i \rightarrow 2^{N_i \cup Calls_i}$ is a *transition function.*

We also refer to entry (exit) nodes simply as entry (exit). Nodes of N_i, for any i, which are in V_i^p are called p-nodes while returns of the form (b, u), where $b \in V_i^p$, for some i, are called *p-returns.* An element in $Calls_i$ of the form (b, e) represents a call from A_i to the module A_j, where $j = Y_i(b)$ and e is an entry of A_j. An element in $Retns_i$ of the form (b, x) corresponds to the associated return of control from A_j to A_i when the call exits from A_j at exit x. The transition function hence defines moves from nodes and returns to a set of nodes and calls.

To illustrate the definitions, consider the example shown in Figure 1. It comprises two modules A_1 and A_2, where A_1 has three boxes that invoke A_2. The only adversary node is e_1, the initial node of A_1.

We make some assumptions of these graphs in the sequel that enable a more readable presentation (these will turn out to be without loss of generality for the problems we consider):

- There is only *one* entry point to every module, i.e. $|E_i| = 1$ for every i. We refer to this unique entry point of A_i as e_i.
- For every $u \in N_i$, $e_i \notin \delta_i(u)$ holds, and for every $x \in Ex_i$, $\delta_i(x)$ is empty. That is, there are no transitions from a module to its own entry nodes and no transitions from its exits.
- The nodes and boxes of all agents are disjoint. Let $B = \bigcup_i B_i$ denote the set of all boxes and $N = \bigcup_i N_i$ denote the set of all nodes. We extend the functions $\{Y_i\}_{i=1}^n$ to a single function $Y : B \to \{1, \ldots, n\}$.

Note that the above definition allows recursive calls—a module can call itself directly or indirectly. We say that a recursive game graph is *hierarchic* if this cannot happen. Formally, a recursive game graph $\langle A_1, \ldots A_n \rangle$ is hierarchic if there is an ordering $\leq$ on the modules such that for every A_i, A_i has no calls to any A_j where $A_j \leq A_i$ (i.e. there is no box b in A_i such that $A_{Y(b)} \leq A_i$). For example, the game graph in Figure 1 is hierarchic.

To define the notions of play and strategy for a recursive game graph, we first give the semantics of our model by defining a flat game graph associated with it. This is similar to the way one associates a flat model that describes the behavior of a recursive state machine. A (global) *state* of a recursive game graph $A = \langle A_1, \ldots, A_n \rangle$ is a tuple $\langle \bar{b}, u \rangle$ where $\bar{b} = b_1, \ldots, b_r$ is a finite (perhaps empty) sequence of boxes from B, and u is a node in N. Consider a state $\langle b_1, \ldots, b_r, u \rangle$ such that $b_i \in B_{j_i}$ for $1 \leq i \leq r$ and $u \in N_j$. Such a state is well-formed if $Y(b_i) = j_{i+1}$ for $1 \leq i < r$, and if $r \geq 1$, $Y(b_r) = j$. If τ denotes the empty sequence, note that any state of the form $\langle \tau, u \rangle$ is well-formed; we henceforth use $\langle u \rangle$ to denote $\langle \tau, u \rangle$. Intuitively, a well-formed state $\langle b_1, b_2, u \rangle$ denotes the configuration where b_1 is a call to a module which in turn called another module using b_2 in which the current node is u. When the last module exits, the control goes back to the corresponding return of b_2, and so on. Henceforth, we assume states to be well-formed and denote by Q_A the set of global states of A.

According to the partition of nodes and boxes in the recursive game graph, the states are also classified as protagonist and adversary states. For $p = 0, 1$, a state $\langle b_1, \ldots, b_r, u \rangle$ is a p-state if either u is not an exit and is a p-node, or, (b_r, u) is a p-return. (If $r = 0$ and u is an exit, the definition will not matter since there are no transitions from it; we hence choose these states to be, say, 0-states.) We denote by Q_p the set of p-states.

The *global game graph* corresponding to a recursive game graph A is $G_A = (Q_A, Q_0, Q_1, \delta)$ where the global transition function δ is given as follows. Let $s = \langle b_1, \ldots, b_r, u \rangle$ be a state with $u \in N_j$ and $b_r \in B_m$. Then, $s' \in \delta(s)$ provided one of the following holds:

1. $u' \in \delta_j(u)$ for a node u' of A_j, and $s' = \langle b_1, \ldots, b_r, u' \rangle$.
2. $(b', e) \in \delta_j(u)$ for a box b' of A_j, and $s' = \langle b_1, \ldots, b_r, b', e \rangle$.
3. u is an exit node of A_j, $u' \in \delta_m(b_r, u)$ for a node u' of A_m, and $s' = \langle b_1, \ldots, b_{r-1}, u' \rangle$.
4. u is an exit node of A_j, $(b', e) \in \delta_m(b_r, u)$ for a box b' of A_m, and $s' = \langle b_1, \ldots, b_{r-1}, b', e \rangle$.

The first case above is when the control stays within the module A_j, the second case is when a new module is entered via a box of A_j, the third is when the control exits A_j and returns to A_m, and the last case is when the control exits A_j and immediately enters a new module via a box of A_m. Note that the set of reachable states from, say, a state $\langle e_i \rangle$ ($e_i \in En_i$) could be infinite if the recursive game graph is not hierarchic (if it is hierarchic, the global reachable graph is finite).

A *recursive game* is a tuple $\langle A, e_1, X \rangle$ where $A = \langle A_1, \ldots A_n \rangle$ is a game graph, e_1 is the entry node of A_1, and $X \subseteq Ex_1$ is the target set, which is a subset of the exits of A_1. The *global recursive game* corresponding to $\langle A, e_1, X \rangle$ is the flat game $\langle G_A, \langle e_1 \rangle, X' \rangle$ where X' is the set of all global states $s = \langle b_1, \ldots, b_r, u \rangle$ where $u \in X$. A (winning) *global strategy* in a recursive game is a (winning) strategy in the global recursive game.

If we use the notion of global strategies, it will lead us to the definition of games equivalent to pushdown games [20]. One can show that for every recursive game, there is a polynomial-sized pushdown automaton whose configuration game graph (as in [20]) is isomorphic to the global graph of the recursive game, and vice-versa. We depart from pushdown games at this point in that we require a particular kind of strategy (namely a modular strategy) that wins these games. In the next section, we introduce this class of strategies and define the corresponding decision problem.

2.3 Modular Strategies

We are interested in *modular strategies* for the protagonist in each game module such that when the strategies are put together, the protagonist wins the game. Such strategies are restricted in that they can only refer to the "local history" of each module, that is, the portion of the play corresponding to the "current" invocation of the module.

To define formally a modular strategy for a recursive game graph A, we introduce some notation. For a play π, the control after π is in A_i if the current node is in A_i; however, if the current node is an exit node, then the control is in the module that made the last call. Formally, for a play πs, we say that the *control after* πs *is in* A_i if $s = \langle b_1, \ldots, b_r, u \rangle$, with $u \in N_i \backslash Ex_i$ or $(b_r, u) \in Retns_i$. Note that the control after a play can be in at most one module.

Consider a play $\pi = s_0 s_1 \ldots s_k$ and let the control after π be in A_i. Let $s_k = \langle b_1, \ldots, b_r, u \rangle$. Then we define the current stack of π to be $\beta(\pi) = \langle b_1, \ldots, b_r \rangle$, if $u \notin Ex$ and $\beta(\pi) = \langle b_1, \ldots, b_{r-1} \rangle$, otherwise. Now, let j be the *largest* index $0 \leq j \leq k$ such that $s_j = \langle \beta(\pi), e_i \rangle$. Intuitively, s_j corresponds to the activation of A_i that led to s_k. The states $s_{j'}$, where $j \leq j' \leq k$ are all of the form $\langle \beta(\pi), b'_1, \ldots, b'_{r'}, u' \rangle$, for some $r' \geq 0$. Note that there may be states $s_{j'}$, $j < j' \leq k$ such that $s_{j'} = \langle \beta(\pi), b'_1, \ldots, b'_{r'}, e_i \rangle$, with $r' \geq 1$, which denote recursive entries into A_i, but which have returned before s_k. We will now be interested in $\alpha(\pi) = s_j \ldots s_k$, the suffix of π from s_j.

What we want to do now is to project $\alpha(\pi)$ to the nodes, calls and returns in A_i, discarding fragments of runs in modules called from A_i. To do this, let us define a projection function ρ^i_β, for a sequence $\beta = \langle b_1, \ldots, b_r \rangle$, of any state s as follows: if $s = \langle \beta, u \rangle$, where $u \in N_i$, then $\rho^i_\beta(s) = u$; if $s = \langle \beta, b, u \rangle$, where $(b, u) \in Calls_i \cup Retns_i$, then $\rho^i_\beta(s) = (b, u)$; in all other cases, $\rho^i_\beta(s) = \varepsilon$, the empty word. We extend ρ^i_β to sequences of states: $\rho^i_\beta(s'_1 \ldots s'_l) = \rho^i_\beta(s'_1) \ldots \rho^i_\beta(s'_l)$.

We can now define a function μ_i that extracts the *local memory* from the play π: $\mu_i(\pi) = \rho^i_{\beta(\pi)}(\alpha(\pi))$. Thus the local memory of a play π ending in a state s_k stands for the fragment of the play in the current module that gives the sequence of nodes, calls and returns in A_i that led to the state s_k, ignoring the sub-plays in called modules (including recursive calls to itself).

A *modular* strategy f for player 0 is a strategy for player 0 such that for all plays π, π' of A, if the control after π and π' are both in A_i and $\mu_i(\pi) = \mu_i(\pi')$ then $f(\pi) = f(\pi')$ holds. In other words, the advice of the strategy f for any play π which is currently in A_i depends only on the local memory $\mu_i(\pi)$.

Since a modular strategy depends only on the local memories, we can alternatively view the modular strategy as a set of strategies, one for each game module. A strategy for a game module A_i is a function $f_i : (N_i \cup Calls_i \cup Retns_i)^* \rightarrow (N_i \cup Calls_i)$. A *local strategy* $\widehat{f}$ is $\{f_i\}_{i=0}^n$ where f_i is a strategy for A_i. A play π is according to $\widehat{f}$ if for every prefix $\pi' s s'$ of π, if the control after $\pi' s$ is in A_i and s is in Q_0, then the following holds: let $\mu_i(\pi' s) = w$, then $\mu_i(\pi s s') = wu$ where $u = f_i(w)$.

For a modular strategy f, we can associate with it a local strategy. Let π be a play consistent with f. Set $\beta = \beta(\pi)$ and let the control after π be in A_i. Then, $f_i(\mu_i(\pi)) = \rho^i_\beta(f(\pi))$ (the function f_i on other values can be defined arbitrarily). Then it is easy to see that the plays according to f are precisely the plays according to the local strategies. Conversely, given a local strategy $\widehat{f} = \{f_1, \ldots, f_n\}$, we can associate a modular strategy f with it. Let πs be a play consistent with $\widehat{f}$, let the control after πs be in A_i, and let $\beta(\pi s) = \beta$. Then $f(\pi s) = s'$ where s' is the unique successor of s such that $\rho^i_\beta(s') = f_i(\mu_i(\pi s))$. Again, it is easy to see that f is modular and that the sets of plays according to f and $\widehat{f}$ are the same. In the sequel, we freely switch between modular strategies and the corresponding local strategies.

We consider the following decision problem.

> Given a recursive game $\langle A, e_1, X \rangle$, is there a modular winning strategy (or equivalently, a local strategy that is winning) for the protagonist?

Consider the game graph in Figure 1. Note that the only place where the protagonist has a choice is in picking the move from e_2. If the target set is $\{x'_2, x'_3\}$ then the protagonist has a winning modular strategy where it chooses to move to the exit node x_2 in A_2. For the target set $\{x'_1, x'_3\}$, there is no modular strategy for the protagonist that is winning. However, it is easy to see that there is a global winning strategy.

The idea behind modular strategies is that it is more appropriate to look for strategies for the modules rather than a monolithic strategy. However, rather than allowing a strategy for a module A_i to remember only the play from the *last* call to A_i, we could allow the strategy to remember *all* parts of the play when it was inside A_i. That is, we could allow strategies to have a *persistent* memory where it is allowed to remember how the play evolved in all the previous calls to the module. For example, in the recursive game in Figure 1, though there is no modular strategy for the protagonist for the target set $\{x'_1, x'_3\}$, there is a persistent strategy (the strategy for A_2 picks x_1 when it is first called and picks x_2 on the second call). Checking for persistent strategies, however, turns out to be undecidable (see Section 5 for details).

From now on, when the context is clear, we use the term *strategy* to mean modular strategies.

3 Solving Recursive Games

Let us fix a reachability game $\langle A, e_1, X\rangle$ for the rest of this section, where $A = \langle A_1, \ldots, A_k\rangle$, and each $A_i = (N_i, B_i, V_i^0, V_i^1, Y_i, En_i, Ex_i, \delta_i)$.

Consider f, a modular strategy for $\langle A, e_1, X\rangle$. The key to deciding recursive games is the observation that whether f is winning or not is primarily determined by finding, for each A_i, the set of exit nodes of A_i which the local strategy f_i will lead a play entering A_i to. Let X_i^f denote the set of exits a play can reach if it enters A_i and continues according to f; that is, an exit point $x \in Ex_i$ is in X_i^f if there is a play according to f of the form $\pi\langle\bar{b}, e_i\rangle\pi'\langle\bar{b}, x\rangle$. Since the strategy f is modular, such exits x are the ones for which there is a play according to f of the form $\langle e_i\rangle\pi''\langle x\rangle$. In fact, if we take a winning strategy $\widehat{f}$ and replace an f_i in $\widehat{f}$ with a different strategy f'_i which calls the same modules that f_i calls and leads to the same set of exit nodes of A_i, then this will also be a winning strategy. This motivates the following definitions.

For a modular strategy f for $\langle A, e_1, X\rangle$, the *call graph of f* is $C_f = (V, \rightarrow, \lambda)$ such that $(V, \rightarrow)$ is a graph where:

- $V \subseteq \{A_1, \ldots, A_n\}$ is the set of all A_i such that there is a play according to f that enters A_i.
- $A_i \rightarrow A_j$ iff there is some play according to f from $\langle e_1\rangle$ where there is a call from A_i to A_j (i.e. there is a play of the form $\langle e_1\rangle\pi\langle b_1, \ldots, b_r, e\rangle$ with $b_r \in B_i$ and $Y(b_r) = A_j$).
- For every $A_i \in V$, let $\lambda(A_i) = X_i^f$.

We first make a simple observation:

Lemma 1. *Let f be a winning strategy for $\langle A, e_1, X\rangle$ and let $C_f = (V, \rightarrow, \lambda)$ be the call graph of f. Then, $(V, \rightarrow)$ is acyclic.*

Proof. If f is a strategy whose call graph has a cycle, then one can show that there is a play according to f that makes calls to the modules recursively according to the cycle in the call graph, and hence never reaches the target set. Such an f will not be winning. □

For a strategy f on $\langle A, e_1, X\rangle$, we say that f is hierarchic if the plays according to f make no recursive calls (i.e., no play according to f reaches a state of the form $s = \langle b_1, \ldots, b_i, u\rangle$, where $\exists l \in \{1, \ldots, n\}$ such that $u \in N_l$ and $b_j \in N_l$, for some $j \in \{1, \ldots i\}$). The following is immediate from the above lemma:

Corollary 1. *Reachability games admit only hierarchic winning strategies.*

We recall that the target set X is a subset of the exits of module A_1. An interesting consequence of the above result is that when we consider modular strategies, the only global states of the target set which can be reached on a winning modular strategy are $\langle x \rangle$, $x \in X$.

Motivated by the above lemma, we give a general definition of a call graph: a *call graph* is a tuple $C = (V, \rightarrow, \lambda)$ where $V \subseteq \{A_1, \ldots, A_n\}$, $(V, \rightarrow)$ is an acyclic graph and $\lambda(A_i) \subseteq Ex_i$, for each $A_i \in V$.

Let $C = (V, \rightarrow, \lambda)$ be a call graph for the game $\langle A, e_1, X \rangle$. Let A_i be a module of the game. We now define a game graph A_i^C which is a flat game graph associated with A_i and C, where, intuitively, we replace each call (b, e_j) to a module A_j by a vertex where player 1 can take the game to any return (b, x_j) where x_j is in $\lambda(A_j)$. In other words, we are defining a game graph under the assumption that a call to a module A_j could result in returns corresponding to $\lambda(A_j)$ and we want to solve the game for A_i under these assumptions. The game graph A_i^C will also prohibit any calls to modules that it is not supposed to call, in accordance with the call graph C.

Formally, A_i^C is defined as follows: $A_i^C = (S_i, S_i^0, S_i^1, \gamma_i)$ where

- $S_i = N_i \cup \mathit{Calls}_i \cup \mathit{Retns}_i$.
- $S_i^0 = (V_i^0 \cap N_i) \cup \{(b, x) \in \mathit{Retns}_i \mid b \in V_i^0\}$.
- $S_i^1 = (V_i^1 \cap N_i) \cup \{(b, x) \in \mathit{Retns}_i \mid b \in V_i^1\} \cup \mathit{Calls}_i$.
- The transition function γ_i is defined as follows:
  1. If $u \in N_i \cup \mathit{Retns}_i$, $\gamma_i(u) = \delta_i(u)$.
  2. If $(b, e) \in \mathit{Calls}_i$ and $A_{Y(b)}$ is a successor of A_i in C, then $\gamma_i((b, e)) = \{(b, x) \mid x \in \lambda(A_{Y(b)})\}$.
  3. If $(b, e) \in \mathit{Calls}_i$ and $A_{Y(b)}$ is not a successor of A_i in C, then $\gamma_i((b, e)) = \emptyset$.

The graph A_i^C is thus obtained by taking the vertices as the nodes, calls and returns of A_i. The nodes and returns are partitioned into 0-nodes and 1-nodes as in A_i. Also, the calls are all deemed to be 1-nodes. The transition function follows the transition function of A_i for nodes and returns. For a call (b, e), the transition function maps it to an empty set if A_i is not permitted to call $A_{Y(b)}$ according to the call graph C. Note that if a play reaches such a call, then it is maximal and hence losing for player 0. If A_i is permitted to call $A_{Y(b)}$, then we take the expected set of exit nodes $\lambda\left(A_{Y(b)}\right)$ from the call graph and have edges to each of the returns corresponding to these exits.

We can now state the main result for which we have developed the definitions above:

Lemma 2. *There exists a winning strategy for $\langle A, e_1, X \rangle$ if and only if there exists a call graph $C = (V, \rightarrow, \lambda)$ such that $\lambda(A_1) \subseteq X$ and for every $A_i \in V$, player 0 wins the reachability game $\langle A_i^C, e_i, \lambda(A_i) \rangle$.*

Proof. If f is a winning strategy for $\langle A, e_1, X\rangle$, we show that its call graph C_f satisfies the requirements of the lemma. In fact, the strategy f_i for A_i itself serves as a winning strategy in $\langle A_i^{C_f}, e_i, \lambda(A_i)\rangle$, for each A_i in the call graph C_f.

Conversely, if there is a call graph $C = (V, \rightarrow, \lambda)$ that satisfies the properties of the lemma, then the strategy for any $A_i^C \in V$ serves as a strategy for A_i in the recursive game and these strategies in fact constitute a winning strategy. □

We say that a local strategy $\{f_i\}_{i=1}^n$ is *memoryless* if for every pair of sequences $\sigma u, \sigma' u \in (N_i \cup Calls_i \cup Retns_i)^*$, $f_i(\sigma u) = f_i(\sigma' u)$. That is, if the local strategies' selection depends only on the current node of the play.

As a corollary to the above lemma we have:

Corollary 2. *If there is winning strategy for a recursive game, then there is a local memoryless winning strategy for it.*

We can now show that solving reachability games is NP-complete:

Theorem 1. *Reachability on recursive (as well as hierarchic) game graphs is* NP*-complete.*

Proof. The NP procedure works as follows. First, we guess a calling graph $C = (V, \rightarrow, \lambda)$ such that $A_1 \in V$ and $\lambda(A_1) \subseteq X$, where X is the target set. Then, for every module A_i, we check if there is a winning strategy for player 1 in $\langle A_i^C, e_i, \lambda(A_i)\rangle$. If all the games are winning for player 0, we report that player 0 wins the recursive game. It is easy to see that this works in polynomial time. Correctness follows from Lemma 2.

For the lower bound, we reduce the satisfiability problem of 3-CNF formulas to solving a reachability game on hierarchic game graphs. The intuition is that there is a module for each variable, where player 0 has to pick a valuation for the variable by picking an exit point. The initial module enables player 1 to pick any clause and call a module corresponding to that clause. In the module for each clause, player 0 points to a literal that witnesses the clause satisfaction by calling the module of the corresponding variable. Player 0 wins if all clauses are satisfied. Since a modular strategy picks essentially a valuation of the variables independent of the context in which it is called, player 0 wins iff the formula is satisfiable. □

4 A Labeling Algorithm

In this section, we describe an exponential-time realization of the nondeterministic procedure sketched in the previous section. The algorithm we present is an extension of the usual *attractor set* construction on flat graphs [13] adapted to our setting, and, it computes the vertices where player 0 can win in an incremental on-the-fly fashion.

Our algorithm iteratively labels vertices of a recursive game graph with tuples of sets of exit nodes according to some initialization and update rules. The

Algorithm Reach

Initially, each exit $u \in X$ is labeled by tuples $\langle E_1, \ldots, E_n \rangle$, where $E_1 = \{x\}$ and $E_i = \top$, for every $i > 1$. All the other nodes, calls, and returns are unlabeled.

Labels are updated according to the following rules:

Rule 1: For a 0-node (or a 0-return) v of A_i, if $\langle E_1, \ldots, E_n \rangle$ labels $v' \in \delta_i(v)$ then add $\langle E_1, \ldots, E_n \rangle$ to labels of v.

Rule 2: For a 1-node (or a 1-return) v of A_i, $\delta_i(v) = \{v_1, \ldots, v_k\}$, if (a) $\langle E_1^h, \ldots, E_n^h \rangle$ labels v_h for $h = 1, \ldots, k$, and (b) for every $l \neq i$, $E_l^1, \ldots, E_l^k$ are pairwise consistent, then add $\langle E_1', \ldots, E_n' \rangle$ to labels of v, where $E_j' = \bigcup_{h=1}^k E_j^h$ for $j = 1, \ldots, n$.

Rule 3: For a return (b, x) of A_i labeled by $\langle E_1, \ldots, E_n \rangle$ where $Y_i(b) = j$, add $\langle E_1', \ldots, E_k' \rangle$ to labels of x where $E_j' = \{x\}$ and $E_l' = \top$ for $l \neq j$.

Rule 4: For a call (b, e) of A_i such that $Y_i(b) = j$, let $(b, x_1), \ldots, (b, x_k)$ be any k distinct returns from (b, e). Suppose that for $h = 1, \ldots, k$, $\langle E_1^h, \ldots, E_n^h \rangle$ labels (b, x_h) and $\langle E_1^0, \ldots, E_n^0 \rangle$ labels e in A_j. If $E_i^0 = \top$, $E_j^0 = \{x_1, \ldots, x_k\}$, and $E_l^0, \ldots, E_l^k$ are pairwise consistent for $l \neq i$, then add $\langle E_1, \ldots, E_n \rangle$ to labels of (b, e), where $E_l = \bigcup_{h=0}^k E_l^h$ for $l = 1, \ldots, n$.

The algorithm halts when there are no more labels that can be added. Then, it gives an affirmative answer if and only if e_1 is labeled with a tuple $\langle E_1, \ldots, E_k \rangle$ such that $E_1 \subseteq X$.

Fig. 2. Algorithm Reach.

algorithm halts when the computed labeling reaches its fixed-point, i.e., there are no new labels that can be added.

Let $A = \langle A_1, \ldots, A_n \rangle$ be a recursive game graph. Consider the reachability game $\langle A, e_1, X \rangle$. We use a special symbol $\top$ and we overload the set union operator with the rule $\top \cup E = E$, for any set E. We use v to denote a node, a call, or a return of A_j, for any j. We describe now the algorithm Reach (Figure 2) that solves the modular reachability problem. Algorithm Reach consists of labeling iteratively each v, with tuples of the form $\langle E_1, \ldots, E_n \rangle$, where each E_i is either a subset of Ex_i or is the symbol $\top$. Each v could be labeled at any time with a *set* of such labels.

The reason we need to keep these labels, as opposed to just a set in the attractor-set computation, is to ensure that the strategy we construct is modular. Since the exit nodes which a strategy f_i takes us to in A_i is the important information we need to know, these labels will ensure that we can consistently pick a single strategy f_i for each A_i in the end.

For a set of maximal finite plays Π, let $Final(\Pi) = \{s \mid$ there is a play of the form $\pi s \in \Pi\}$. Intuitively, $Final(\Pi)$ is the exact set of states the plays in Π end in.

When $v \in N_i \cup Calls_i \cup Retns_i$ gets a label $\langle E_1, \ldots, E_n \rangle$, it is supposed to mean that there exists a local strategy $\widehat{f} = \{f_i\}$ such that the following hold:

A1. If Π_v is the set of all maximal plays starting at $\langle v \rangle$ and consistent with $\widehat{f}$, then Π_v contains only finite plays and $Final(\Pi) = \{\langle x_i \rangle \mid x_i \in E_i\}$. Further, the plays in Π_v do not enter any A_j, where $E_j = \top$, nor does it re-enter A_i.

A2. Let l be such that $E_l \neq \top$ and $l \neq i$. Let Π_l be the set of maximal plays starting at $\langle e_l \rangle$ and consistent with $\widehat{f}$. Then Π_l consists of only finite plays and $Final(\Pi) = \{\langle x_l \rangle \mid x_l \in E_l\}$. Further, the plays in Π_l never enter any module A_j, where $E_j = \top$, nor does it enter A_i.

Intuitively, when a node in A_i is labeled with $\langle E_1, \ldots, E_n \rangle$, it signifies that there is a set of strategies for each module A_j, where $E_j \neq \top$, such that the strategies drive the play from the current node to some node in E_i. Moreover, these strategies never make the play enter a module $A_{j'}$ for which strategies are not assumed (i.e. where $E_{j'} = \top$). Also, the strategy for A_j drives any play entering it to the set E_j. Finally, the strategies are guaranteed not to call A_i

For any $E', E'' \in 2^{Ex_i} \cup \{\top\}$, we say that E' and E'' are *consistent* if $E' = \top$, or $E'' = \top$, or $E' = E''$.

Rule 1 makes a 0-node or 0-return u inherit a label of a successor. The idea is that there is a strategy from u, where the protagonist picks this successor and plays then according to the strategy assured at the successor, inductively. At a 1-node or a 1-return u, the protagonist has no choice—it can be taken to any of the successor nodes. The rule hence labels u only if all the successors agree upon the exit-nodes that they assume for all components. Rule 3 activates an exit of a module when a return corresponding to that exit is activated in some module; the activation is similar to the way we initialized our algorithm by activating the exits corresponding to the target. Calls are labeled using Rule 4: we check whether the assumptions on all modules by both the called module's entry point as well as the returns corresponding to the call are consistent, check whether the called module does not call A_i and label the call by an appropriate label. We prove now that REACH solves the reachability problem for recursive games.

Lemma 3 (Soundness). *Let $A = \langle A_1, \ldots, A_n \rangle$ be a recursive game graph. If a node, a call, or a return v of A_i is labeled by* REACH *with $\langle E_1, \ldots, E_n \rangle$, then there exists a local strategy $\widehat{f} = \{f_i\}$ such that (A1) and (A2) hold.*

Proof. The lemma is proved by induction on the number of applications of the update rules. For the initial labeling the lemma is trivially true. The induction step is fairly straightforward from the inductive hypothesis and the intuition behind the labeling. For example, if Rule 2 is applied to label a node u in A_i, then we can pick strategies for the modules from the set of strategies of its successors whose existence is guaranteed by the induction hypothesis. The only subtle point is that the selection of local strategies needs to be done carefully to ensure that the constructed strategy is not recursive (i.e. their call graph is not recursive). For Rule 2, we pick a strategy for a module A_j ($j \neq i$) as the strategy for A_j at a successor v'; however, we ensure that for every $A_{j'}$ which is called by this strategy, we pick the strategy for $A_{j'}$ using the strategy at v'. □

Lemma 4 (Completeness). *Let $A = \langle A_1, \ldots, A_n \rangle$ be a recursive game graph and $X \subseteq Ex_1$. If there exists a winning strategy for the protagonist in the reachability game $\langle A, e_1, X \rangle$, then e_1 is labeled by algorithm* Reach *with $\langle E_1, \ldots, E_n \rangle$ where $E_1 \subseteq X$.*

Proof. The gist of the proof is as follows. Let f be a winning strategy of the protagonist in the reachability game $\langle A, e_1, X \rangle$, and let $C_f = (V, \rightarrow, \lambda)$ be its call graph. We can then define a finite strategy tree with f that encodes all the plays according to f as labels of paths in the tree. One can also associate each vertex of the tree with a node in the recursive game—namely, the node reached on the play corresponding to the vertex. We then show by induction on this tree, from the leaves to the root, that for every vertex v in the tree, if the node corresponding to it is u in A_i, then u gets a label $\langle E_1^u, \ldots, E_m^u \rangle$ such that: $E_i \subseteq \lambda(A_i)$ and for every $j \neq i$, E_j is consistent with $\lambda(A_j)$, if $A_j \in V$, and $E_j = \top$, for every $A_j \notin V$. The lemma then holds from the fact that the root gets such a label. □

The soundness of Reach follows from Lemma 3, by condition A1 (with $v = e_1$), while Lemma 4 proves its completeness. Reach can require exponential time since it can generate exponentially many labels. A careful analysis shows that it works in fact in time exponential in the total number of exit nodes, exponential in the maximum out-degree of the underlying graphs, but polynomial in the size of the recursive game graph. Also, note that Reach can stop once the initial node gets the appropriate label, even before reaching the fixpoint.

5 Extensions

Safety recursive games: Consider a recursive game graph A. A safety condition requires that the plays stay within a set of *good* vertices, or equivalently that *bad* vertices are avoided. A *safety recursive game* is $\langle A, e_1, X_{good} \rangle$, where A is a recursive game graph, e_1 is the entry point of the game module A_1, and X_{good} is a subset of A nodes (let us assume that all exits are good). A play of such a game is winning if all the visited states are of the form $\langle b_1, \ldots, b_r, x \rangle$ where $x \in X_{good}$. If we restrict to modular strategies, safety recursive games are not dual to reachability recursive games. This is because in both definitions, while the protagonist is forced to use a modular strategy, the adversary is allowed to use an arbitrary strategy. In contrast with reachability, winning modular strategies in safety recursive games may not be hierarchic (in particular Lemma 1 and thus Corollary 1 do not hold). Despite this, deciding safety recursive games is also NP-complete. The hardness result is directly obtained from the reduction given in the proof of Theorem 1. For membership to NP, we can prove that the existence of a winning strategy f can be witnessed by a (possibly cyclic) call graph and a tuple $\langle E_1, \ldots, E_n \rangle$, where E_i is a subset of the exits of A_i, with the meaning that: 1) in each module A_i, we can visit only calls to modules that are successors in the call graph, and 2) the winning local strategy in A_i stays within the safe set X_{good} and it either never exits A_i or it exits through an exit in E_i. Once this is guessed, checking that indeed a strategy is winning reduces to solving safety games on flat graphs whose total size is polynomial in the size of the recursive game graph.

Handling multiple entries: Consider a recursive game $\langle A, e_1, X\rangle$ where each module is allowed to have multiple entry nodes. The semantics of the game and modular strategies are the natural extensions of those for the single-entry setting. When a play enters a module, since the strategy for the module knows the entry point where the module enters, it could follow completely different strategies for the different entry nodes and still remain modular. Hence, we can replace every module which has, say, m entry nodes with a set of m modules, one for each entry point, but where each new module has only one entry. We suitably change the calls from other modules so that they call the corresponding modules with the appropriate entry point. It is easy to see that one can check for a modular strategy on the original game by checking for a modular strategy in this game. Consider a recursive game G with n modules and let m_e be the maximum number of entries to any module. Then, it is easy to see that the above reduction produces a game graph with at most $n \cdot m_e$ modules and the overall size of the game graph is at most $|G|^3$, where $|G|$ is the size of G.

Recursive games with variables: In modeling programs, it is natural to have variables over a finite domain that are abstractions of actual variables and which can be passed from module to module (see, for instance, the SLAM model checker [3]). We can extend our setup to handle this by augmenting nodes with the values of variables. These variables can be local, global or passed as parameters when calls are made to other modules. If a module A_i has r_i input variables, r_o output variables and s internal variables, then we can model this by having $2^{r_i} \cdot |En_i|$ entry nodes, $2^{r_o} \cdot |Ex_i|$ exits, and $2^{r_i+r_o+k} \cdot |N_i|$ internal nodes (we assume all variables be boolean). Note that a modular strategy will be such that the strategy for a module can take into account the parameters that are sent and returned when calling the module, but cannot know the exact evolution of the of the called program. This makes our setting a very natural setup where we can deal with the construction of skeletons of program modules which achieve a particular specification.

Persistent memory strategies: As mentioned in Section 2.3, we can relax the condition of modular strategies and instead ask for a *persistent strategy*, where a strategy for a module can remember not only the play from the last call to the module, but *all* parts of the play when the play entered into this module. The idea is that we can realize the strategy for a module as a program which has a static memory to store all that happens within the module, and use this information to drive the play. However, it turns out that checking whether there is a persistent strategy in a given recursive game is *undecidable*. The reduction is from the undecidability of solving multi-player games with incomplete information [14]. We have:

Theorem 2. *The problem of checking whether there is a winning persistent strategy in a given hierarchical game is undecidable.*

References

1. R. Alur, K. Etessami, and M. Yannakakis. Analysis of recursive state machines. In *Proc. of the 13th International Conference on Computer Aided Verification, CAV'01*, LNCS 2102, pages 207–220. Springer, 2001.
2. R. Alur, T. Henzinger, and O. Kupferman. Alternating-time temporal logic. *Journal of the ACM*, 49(5):1–42, 2002.
3. T. Ball and S. Rajamani. Bebop: A symbolic model checker for boolean programs. In *Proceedings of the SPIN 2000 Workshop on Model Checking of Software*, LNCS 1885, pages 113–130. Springer, 2000.
4. A. Bouajjani, J. Esparza, and O. Maler. Reachability analysis of pushdown automata: Application to model-checking. In *Proc. 8th Conference on Concurrency Theory*, volume 1243 of *LNCS*, pages 135–150, Warsaw, July 1997. Springer.
5. J. Büchi and L. Landweber. Solving sequential conditions by finite-state strategies. *Trans. AMS*, 138:295–311, 1969.
6. T. Cachat. Symbolic strategy synthesis for games on pushdown graphs. In *Automata, Languages and Programming, 29th Int'l Coll., ICALP, Malaga, Spain, July 8-13, 2002, Proceedings*, volume 2380 of *LNCS*, pages 704–715. Springer.
7. A. Chakrabarti, L. de Alfaro, T. Henzinger, M. Jurdzinski, and F. Mang. Interface compatibility checking for software modules. In *Proceedings of the 14th Int'l Conf. on Computer-Aided Verification*, LNCS 2404, pages 428–441. Springer, 2002.
8. L. de Alfaro and T. A. Henzinger. Interface automata. In *Proceedings of the Ninth Annual Symposium on Foundations of Software Engineering (FSE)*, pages 109–120. ACM Press, 2001.
9. E. A. Emerson. Model checking and the mu-calculus. In N. Immerman and P. Kolaitis, editors, *Proceedings of the DIMACS Symposium on Descriptive Complexity and Finite Models*, pages 185–214. American Mathematical Society Press, 1997.
10. O. Kupferman and M. Vardi. Church's problem revisited. *The Bulletin of Symbolic Logic*, 5(2):245–263, June 1999.
11. O. Kupferman, M. Vardi, and P. Wolper. Module checking. *Information and Computation*, 164(2):322–344, 2001.
12. P. Madhusudan and P. S. Thiagarajan. A decidable class of asynchronous distributed controllers. In *Proceedings of the 13th International Conference on Concurrency Theory (CONCUR '02)*, LNCS 2421, pages 145–160. Springer, 2002.
13. R. McNaughton. Infinite games played on finite graphs. *Annals of Pure and Applied Logic*, 65:149–184, 1993.
14. G. Peterson and J. Reif. Multiple-person alternation. In *Proc. 20st IEEE Symposium on Foundation of Computer Science*, pages 348–363, 1979.
15. A. Pnueli and R. Rosner. On the synthesis of a reactive module. In *Proc. 16th ACM Symposium on Principles of Programming Languages*, Austin, January 1989.
16. A. Pnueli and R. Rosner. Distributed reactive systems are hard to synthesize. In *Proc. 31st IEEE Symposium on Foundation of Computer Sc.*, pages 746–757, 1990.
17. K. Rudie and W. Wonham. Think globally, act locally: Decentralized supervisory control. *IEEE Transactions on Automatic Control*, 37(11):1692–1708, 1992.
18. W. Thomas. Languages, automata, and logic. *Handbook of Formal Language Theory*, III:389–455, 1997.
19. W. Thomas. Infinite games and verification. In *Proceedings of the International Conference on Computer Aided Verification CAV'02*, volume 2404 of *Lecture Notes in Computer Science*, pages 58–64. Springer, 2002.
20. I. Walukiewicz. Pushdown processes: Games and model-checking. *Information and Computation*, 164(2):234–263, January 2001.

Saturation Unbound*

Gianfranco Ciardo, Robert Marmorstein, and Radu Siminiceanu

College of William and Mary, Williamsburg, Virginia 23187
{ciardo,rmmarm,radu}@cs.wm.edu

Abstract. In previous work, we proposed a "saturation" algorithm for symbolic state-space generation characterized by the use of multi-valued decision diagrams, boolean Kronecker operators, event locality, and a special iteration strategy. This approach outperforms traditional BDD-based techniques by several orders of magnitude in both space and time but, like them, assumes a priori knowledge of each submodel's state space. We introduce a new algorithm that merges explicit local state-space discovery with symbolic global state-space generation. This relieves the modeler from worrying about the behavior of submodels in isolation.

1 Introduction

Since their introduction, implicit methods for symbolic model checking, such as decision diagrams, in particular BDDs [5,6,8], have been enormously successful. However, the systems targeted have been mainly synchronous VLSI designs and protocols, where the possible values of each state variable can be easily determined a priori. For arbitrary systems modeled in a high-level formalism such as Petri nets or pseudocode, determining the range of the state variables is more difficult. Traditionally, the burden of this task has been placed on the user. In NuSMV [14], for example, the domain of multi-valued variables must be explicitly specified as a set or integer range. In our own previous work [11,12,23], the input (a Petri net) must be partitioned so that the state space of each "local subnet" can be generated in isolation. This practice requires careful addition of inhibitor arcs or other constructs to ensure correct local behavior without affecting the global behavior, a difficult and error-prone endeavor.

In this paper, we address this problem with an algorithm that produces a multi-valued decision diagram (MDD) [21] representation of the final state-space and a separately stored representation of the "minimal" local state spaces. The algorithm interleaves explicit local exploration of each submodel with symbolic exploration of the global state space. The new algorithm is based on our *saturation* algorithm [12], which uses an MDD to store the global states and boolean Kronecker matrices to encode the transition relation. By using a *disjunctively-partitioned transition relation* [20], exploiting *event locality* [23], performing *in-place updates* [11] of MDD nodes, and using an innovative iteration strategy,

* Work supported in part by the National Aeronautics and Space Administration under grants NAG-1-2168 and NAG-1-02095 and by the National Science Foundation under grants CCR-0219745 and ACI-0203971.

H. Garavel and J. Hatcliff (Eds.): TACAS 2003, LNCS 2619, pp. 379–393, 2003.

saturation showed massive time and space improvements over traditional symbolic state-space generation approaches. Our new algorithm exploits these same ideas, but can be applied to a more general class of models. The inherent asynchronicity of software models makes them ideal candidates for our new approach.

Section 2 gives the necessary background on symbolic state-space generation and the rationale behind our contribution. Section 3 presents our new algorithm. We discuss theoretical and practical issues of design and implementation in Section 4, and provide experimental results in Section 5. Section 6 discusses related work and Section 7 concludes by suggesting further research directions.

2 State Space Generation

A discrete-state model is a triple $(\widehat{\mathcal{S}}, \mathbf{s}, \mathcal{N})$, where $\widehat{\mathcal{S}}$ is the set of *potential states* of the model, $\mathbf{s}$ is the *initial state* (a set of initial states could be easily handled), and $\mathcal{N} : \widehat{\mathcal{S}} \to 2^{\widehat{\mathcal{S}}}$ is the *next-state function* specifying which states can be reached from a given state in a single step. Since we target asynchronous systems, we partition $\mathcal{N}$ into a union of next-state functions [20]: $\mathcal{N}(s) = \bigcup_{e \in \mathcal{E}} \mathcal{N}_e(s)$, where $\mathcal{E}$ is a finite set of *events*, $\mathcal{N}_e$ is the next-state function associated with event e, i.e., $\mathcal{N}_e(s)$ is the set of states the system can enter when e occurs, or *fires*, in state s. An event e is said to be *disabled* in s if $\mathcal{N}_e(s) = \emptyset$; otherwise, it is *enabled*.

The *reachable state space* $\mathcal{S} \subseteq \widehat{\mathcal{S}}$ is the smallest set containing $\mathbf{s}$ and closed with respect to $\mathcal{N}$: $\mathcal{S} = \{\mathbf{s}\} \cup \mathcal{N}(\mathbf{s}) \cup \mathcal{N}(\mathcal{N}(\mathbf{s})) \cup \cdots = \mathcal{N}^*(\mathbf{s})$, where "$*$" denotes the reflexive and transitive closure, and we let $\mathcal{N}(\mathcal{X}) = \bigcup_{s \in \mathcal{X}} \mathcal{N}(s)$. Thus, $\mathcal{S}$ is the smallest fixed point of the equation $\mathcal{S} = \mathcal{N}(\mathcal{S})$ in which $\mathcal{S}$ contains $\{\mathbf{s}\}$. Since $\mathcal{N}$ is composed of several functions $\mathcal{N}_e$, we can build $\mathcal{S}$ by applying each function in any order, as long as we consider each event often enough [17].

The systems we target can be partitioned into interacting submodels. For a model composed of K *submodels*, a *global* system state is a K-tuple $(i_K, \ldots, i_1)$, where i_k is the *local* state of submodel k, for $K \geq k \geq 1$. Thus, the potential state space $\widehat{\mathcal{S}}$ is given by the cross-product $\mathcal{S}_K \times \cdots \times \mathcal{S}_1$ of K *local* state spaces. For example, the places of a Petri net can be partitioned into K subsets, with the marking written as a vector of the K corresponding submarkings. Partitioning enables us to use techniques targeted at exploiting system structure, including *symbolic* state space storage techniques based on decision diagrams.

Multi-valued decision diagrams for the state space. If each local state space $\mathcal{S}_k$ is known, we can use mappings $\psi_k : \mathcal{S}_k \to \{0, 1, \ldots, n_k - 1\}$, where $n_k = |\mathcal{S}_k|$, and encode $\mathcal{S} \subseteq \widehat{\mathcal{S}}$ via a (*quasi-reduced ordered*) MDD, i.e., a directed acyclic edge-labeled multi-graph where:

- Nodes are organized into $K + 1$ *levels*. We write $\langle k{:}p \rangle$ to denote a generic node, where k is the level and p is a unique index for that level.
- Level K contains only a single *non-terminal* node $\langle K{:}r \rangle$, the *root*, whereas levels $K-1$ through 1 contain one or more non-terminal nodes.
- Level 0 consists of two *terminal* nodes, $\langle 0{:}0 \rangle$ and $\langle 0{:}1 \rangle$.

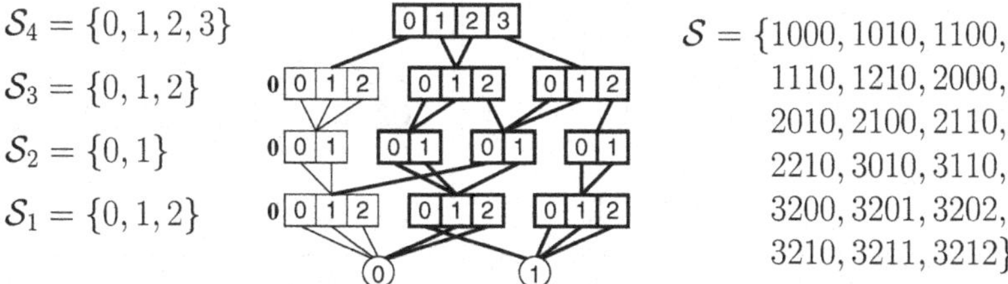

S4 = {0, 1, 2, 3}
S3 = {0, 1, 2}
S2 = {0, 1}
S1 = {0, 1, 2}
S = {1000, 1010, 1100, 1110, 1210, 2000, 2010, 2100, 2110, 2210, 3010, 3110, 3200, 3201, 3202, 3210, 3211, 3212}

Fig. 1. An example MDD and the state space $\mathcal{S}$ encoded by it.

- A non-terminal node $\langle k{:}p\rangle$ has n_k arcs pointing to nodes at level $k-1$. If the ith arc, for $i \in \mathcal{S}_k$, is to node $\langle k-1{:}q\rangle$, we write $\langle k{:}p\rangle[i] = q$. *Duplicate* nodes are not allowed but, unlike *reduced ordered* MDDs, *redundant* nodes where all arcs point to the same node are allowed (both versions are canonical).

Let $\mathcal{B}(\langle k{:}p\rangle)$ be the set of (sub-)states encoded by the MDD rooted at $\langle k{:}p\rangle$. As in [12], we reserve the node index 0 at each level k, so that $\mathcal{B}(\langle k{:}0\rangle) = \emptyset$. In previous work, we also reserved the index 1, so that $\mathcal{B}(\langle k{:}1\rangle) = \mathcal{S}_k \times \cdots \mathcal{S}_1$, but as discussed in Section 4, this optimization can no longer be used. Fig. 1 shows a four-level MDD and the set $\mathcal{S}$ it encodes. The lightly bordered nodes represent the empty set and are not explicitly stored in the MDD.

Kronecker encoding for the next-state function. Effective symbolic state space generation requires an efficient encoding of the next-state function. Unlike BDD approaches, where $\mathcal{N}$, or each $\mathcal{N}_e$, is encoded in a $2K$-level BDD, we adopt a Kronecker representation inspired by work on Markov chains [2,7,25]. As in [11,12,23], we use a *consistent* model partition, where each $\mathcal{N}_e$ is decomposed into K local next-state functions $\mathcal{N}_{e,k}$, for $K \geq k \geq 1$, which satisfy

$$\forall (i_K, \ldots, i_1) \in \widehat{\mathcal{S}},\ \mathcal{N}_e(i_K, \ldots, i_1) = \mathcal{N}_{e,K}(i_K) \times \cdots \times \mathcal{N}_{e,1}(i_1).$$

By defining matrices $\mathbf{W}_{e,k} \in \{0,1\}^{n_k \times n_k}$, where $\mathbf{W}_{e,k}[i_k, j_k] = 1 \Leftrightarrow j_k \in \mathcal{N}_{e,k}(i_k)$, the next-state function is encoded as the incidence matrix given by the (boolean) sum of Kronecker products $\sum_{e \in \mathcal{E}} \bigotimes_{K \geq k \geq 1} \mathbf{W}_{e,k}$. The $\mathbf{W}_{e,k}$ matrices are extremely sparse (for standard Petri nets, each row contains at most one nonzero entry), and are indexed using the same mapping ψ_k used to index $\mathcal{S}_k$.

In addition to efficiently representing $\mathcal{N}$, the Kronecker encoding allows us to exploit event *locality* [11,23] and employ *saturation* [12]. Locality means that most events depend on few submodels, hence few levels of the MDD (event e is *independent* of level k if $\mathbf{W}_{e,k} = \mathbf{I}$, the identity). If we let $Top(e)$ and $Bot(e)$ denote the highest and lowest levels on which e depends, respectively, the saturation strategy iterates until node $\langle k{:}p\rangle$ has reached a fixed point with respect to all $\mathcal{N}_e$ such that $Top(e) \leq k$, collectively written as $\mathcal{N}_{\leq k}$, without examining the nodes above $\langle k{:}p\rangle$ in the MDD.

Local state spaces. Traditional symbolic state-space generation assumes a priori knowledge of the local state spaces. For BDDs, each $\mathcal{S}_k$ is simply $\{0,1\}$; in our previous MDD work [11,12,23], each $\mathcal{S}_k$ is finite and built prior to state-space generation. Since $\mathcal{S}_k$ is known, we can store its elements in a search structure,

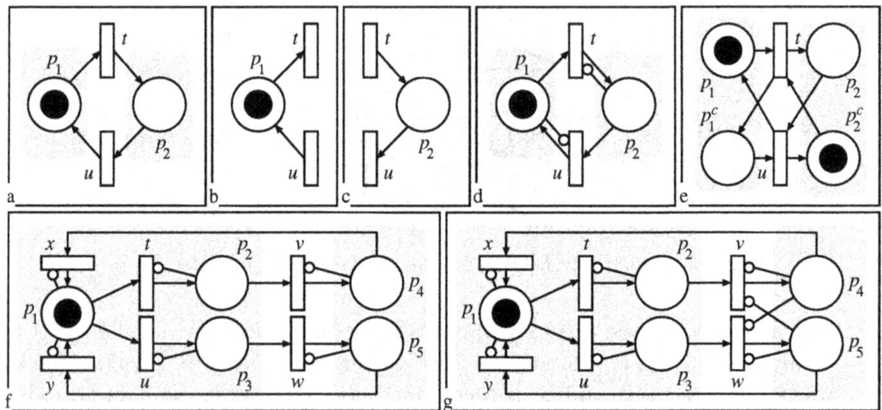

Fig. 2. Local state spaces built in isolation can be strict supersets of the actual ones.

which encodes the mapping ψ_k. Local states in the MDD may then be referenced exclusively through their integer indices in ψ_k.

For a given high-level formalism, each $\mathcal{S}_k$ can be *pregenerated* with an explicit traversal of the local state-to-state transition graph of the submodel obtained by considering all the variables associated with the submodel and all the events affecting those variables. Unfortunately, this pregeneration may create spurious local states. For example, if the two places of the Petri net in Fig. 2(a) are partitioned into two subsets, the corresponding subnets, (b) and (c), have unbounded local state spaces when considered in isolation. In subnet (b), transition u can keep adding tokens to place p_1 since, without the input arc from p_2, u is always locally enabled. Hence, in isolation, p_1 may contain arbitrarily many tokens. The same can be said for subnet (c). However, $\mathcal{S} = \{(1,0),(0,1)\}$, so we would ideally like to define $\mathcal{S}_2 = \mathcal{S}_1 = \{0,1\}$. This can be enforced by adding either inhibitor arcs, (d), or complementary places, (e). Consider now the Petri net of Fig. 2(f), partitioned into two subnets, one containing p_1, p_2, and p_3, the other containing p_4 and p_5. The inhibitor arcs shown avoid unbounded local state spaces in isolation, but they don't ensure that the local state spaces are as small as possible. For example, the local state space built in isolation for the subnet containing p_4 and p_5 is $\{(0,0),(1,0),(0,1),(1,1)\}$, while only the first three states are actually reachable in the overall net, since p_4 and p_5 can never contain a token at the same time. This is corrected in (g) by adding two more inhibitor arcs, from p_5 to v and from p_4 to w. An analogous problem exists for the other subnet as well, and correcting it with inhibitor arcs is even more cumbersome.

Thus, there are two problems with pregeneration: a local state space in isolation might be unbounded (causing pregeneration to fail) or contain spurious states (causing inefficiencies in the symbolic state-space generation). Asking the modeler to cope with this by adding constraints to the original model (e.g., the inhibitor arcs in Fig. 2) is at best burdensome, since it requires a priori knowledge of $\mathcal{S}$, the output of state-space generation, and at worst dangerous, since doing so might "mask" undesirable behaviors that are present in the overall model.

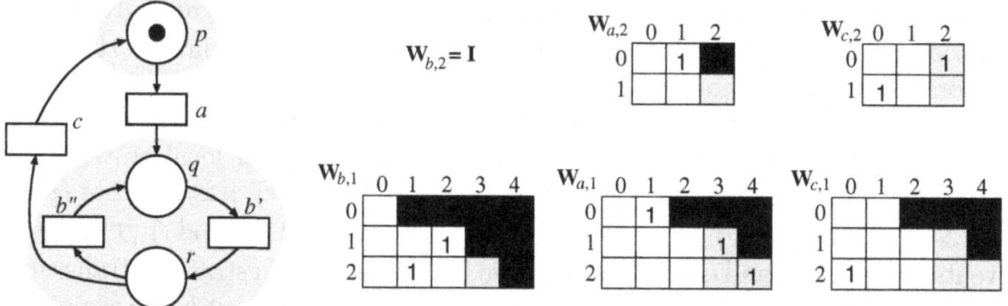

Fig. 3. An example snapshot of transition matrices $\mathbf{W}_{e,k}$.

3 Local State Spaces with Unknown Bounds

We now describe an *on-the-fly* algorithm that merges explicit local state with symbolic global state explorations and builds the *smallest* local state spaces $\mathcal{S}_k$ needed to encode the correct global state space $\mathcal{S} \subseteq \widehat{\mathcal{S}} = \mathcal{S}_K \times \cdots \times \mathcal{S}_1$. Ideally, the additional time spent exploring local state spaces on-the-fly should be comparable to that spent in the pregeneration phase of our old algorithm. This is, in fact, the case for our new algorithm, which incrementally discovers a set $\widehat{\mathcal{S}}_k$ of *locally-reachable* local states, of which only a subset $\mathcal{S}_k$ is also globally reachable. When our algorithm determines that a local state is globally reachable, it labels it as *confirmed*. Since *unconfirmed* local states in $\widehat{\mathcal{S}}_k \setminus \mathcal{S}_k$ are limited to a "rim" around the confirmed ones, and since unconfirmed states do not increase the size of MDD nodes, memory overhead is small in practice.

Expanding local state spaces. Initially, for $K \geq k \geq 1$, $\widehat{\mathcal{S}}_k = \mathcal{S}_k = \{\mathbf{s}_k\}$, the kth component of the initial state $\mathbf{s}$. The iteration strategy of [12] saturates nodes bottom-up through an exhaustive symbolic reachability analysis: it fires globally enabled events on a node as long as new global states are found. In our new version, the MDD encodes only confirmed states, but our Kronecker encoding describes all possible transitions from confirmed local states to both confirmed and unconfirmed local states. Thus, we only explore *global symbolic firings* originating in confirmed states. The next-state function for event e in local state i of node $\langle k{:}p \rangle$ (Fig. 4, lines 9 of *Saturate* and 9 of *RecFire*) may lead to a state $j \in \mathcal{S}_k$ or $j \in \widehat{\mathcal{S}}_k \setminus \mathcal{S}_k$. In the former case, j is already confirmed and row j of $\mathbf{W}_{e,k}$ has been built (thus the local states reachable from j are in $\widehat{\mathcal{S}}_k$). In the latter case, j is unconfirmed: it is locally, but not necessarily globally, reachable, thus it appears as a column index but has no corresponding row in $\mathbf{W}_{e,k}$. Local state j will be confirmed if the global symbolic firing that used the entry $\mathbf{W}_{e,k}[i,j]$ is actually possible, i.e., if e can fire in an MDD path from *Top*(e) to *Bot*(e) through node $\langle k{:}p \rangle$. Only when j is confirmed, its rows in $\mathbf{W}_{e,k}$ (for all events e that depend on k) are built, using one forward step of *explicit local reachability analysis*. This step must consult the description of the model itself, and thus works on actual submodel variables, not state indices. This is the only operation that may discover new unconfirmed local states.

Transition matrices. The on-the-fly algorithm uses "rectangular" Kronecker matrices over $\{0,1\}^{\mathcal{S}_k \times \widehat{\mathcal{S}}_k}$ where only confirmed local states "know" their successors, confirmed or not.

Fig. 3 shows an example. The net is partitioned into subnet 2, containing place p, and subnet 1, with places q and r. The potential local state spaces discovered with the saturation algorithm are $\widehat{\mathcal{S}}_2 = \{0 \equiv (p^1), 1 \equiv (p^0), 2 \equiv (p^2)\}$, and $\widehat{\mathcal{S}}_1 = \{0 \equiv (q^0r^0), 1 \equiv (q^1r^0), 2 \equiv (q^0r^1), 3 \equiv (q^2r^0), 4 \equiv (q^1r^1)\}$. The model events are grouped and ordered as dictated by the saturation strategy: transitions that are local to subnet 1, b' and b", are merged into macroevent b, the remaining two being the "synchronizing" events a and c. There are two Kronecker matrices for each event, $\mathbf{W}_{e,k}$, $e \in \{a,b,c\}$, $k \in \{1,2\}$, hence six in total, among which $\mathbf{W}_{b,2}$ is the identity, since macroevent b does not affect subnet 2.

Three regions of the matrices are highlighted: the white portion corresponds to moves between confirmed states and those are kept in the final matrices; the shaded area corresponds to moves from confirmed to unconfirmed states; the black region means that the corresponding column indices were out of range at the time the row was built. The actual evolution of the matrices is:

1. The initial state is inserted, with index 0, in each local state space. The row for local state 0 of $\widehat{\mathcal{S}}_1$ in each of the corresponding three matrices is built explicitly: only event a leads to a new local state (q^1r^0), which is indexed 1. Similarly at level 2, a new local state (p^0) is discovered by locally firing a and another, (p^2), by locally firing c, these are indexed 1 and 2, respectively.
2. MDD saturation starts; in the initial MDD node at level 1, no events are enabled, but at level 2, event a is successfully (globally) fired, leading to global state $(1,1) \equiv (p^0, q^1r^0)$. As a result, local states 1 at both levels are confirmed. Their corresponding rows are built with an explicit exploration in each subnet. At level 1, local state 1 can move to $2 \equiv (q^0r^1)$ by firing the b' component of b, or to $3 \equiv (q^2r^0)$ by locally firing a. At level 2, only event c can fire in local state 1, leading to local state $0 \equiv (p^1)$.
3. Event b is globally fired resulting in the confirmation of local state 2 of $\widehat{\mathcal{S}}_1$ as globally reachable. Its row is built in $\mathbf{W}_{b,1}, \mathbf{W}_{a,1}, \mathbf{W}_{c,1}$. During this phase, one more local state is discovered, $4 \equiv (q^1r^1)$, corresponding to a potential firing of event a in state 2, as well as the already confirmed states 1, by firing the b" component of b, and 0 by firing c.
4. Event c is globally fired from global state $(1,2) \equiv (p^0, q^0r^1)$, leading to global state $(0,0) \equiv (p^1, q^0r^0)$, whose local states are both confirmed, hence no explicit exploration is needed for either of them.
5. Saturation ends, with the final local state spaces $\mathcal{S}_2 = \{0,1\}$, $\mathcal{S}_1 = \{0,1,2\}$ and global state-space $\mathcal{S} = \{(0,0),(1,1),(1,2)\}$. The matrices are trimmed to their final "square" shape: 2×2 at level 2, and 3×3 at level 1, by discarding the unconfirmed local states along with their corresponding columns.

The algorithm. The pseudocode of our new algorithm, in Fig. 4, uses the data types *ev* (model event), *local* (local state), *level*, and *idx* (node index within

```
GenerateSS():idx
Build the MDD encoding N*_E(s).

declare p,r:idx, k:level, s:state,i:local;
p ← 1;
for k = 1 to K do
  s ← InitialState(k);
  i ← InsertState(k, s);
  Confirm(k, i);
  r ← NewNode(k);
  ⟨k:r⟩[i] ← p;
  Saturate(k, r);
  CheckIn(k, r);
  p ← r;
return r;     • ⟨K:r⟩ is the MDD root
```

```
Saturate(in k:level, p:idx)
Update ⟨k:p⟩, to encode N*_≤k(B(⟨k:p⟩)).

declare L:set of local, i,j,j':local;
declare e:ev, f,u:idx; pChng:bool;
repeat
  pChng ← false;
  foreach e ∈ E s.t. Top(e) = k do
    L ← Locals(e, k, p);
    while L ≠ ∅ do
      pick and remove i from L;
      f ← RecFire(e, k−1, ⟨k:p⟩[i]);
      if f ≠ 0 then
        foreach j s.t. W_e,k[i, j]=1 do
          u ← Union(k−1, f, ⟨k:p⟩[j]);
          if u≠⟨k:p⟩[j] then
            if j ∉ S_k then Confirm(k, j);
            ⟨k:p⟩[j] ← u; pChng ← true;
            if ∃j', W_e,k[j, j'] = 1 then
              L ← L∪{j};
until pChng = false;
```

```
Union(in k:level, p:idx, q:idx):idx
Build the MDD for B(⟨k:p⟩) ∪ B(⟨k:q⟩).

if p = 0 or p = q then return q;
if q = 0 then return p;
if Find(UC[k], {p, q}, s) then return s;
s ← NewNode(k);
for i = 0 to |S_k| − 1
  u ← Union(k−1, ⟨k:p⟩[i], ⟨k:q⟩[i]);
  ⟨k:s⟩[i] ← u;
CheckIn(k, s);
Insert(UC[k], {p, q}, s);
return s;
```

```
RecFire(in e:ev, l:level, q:idx):idx
Build the MDD for N*_≤l(N_e(B(⟨l:q⟩))).

declare L:set of local, i,j:local;
declare f,u,s:idx, sChng:bool;
if l < Bot(e) then return q;
if Find(FC[e, l], q, s) then return s;
s ← NewNode(l); sChng ← false;
L ← Locals(e, l, q);
while L ≠ ∅ do
  pick and remove i from L;
  f ← RecFire(e, l−1, ⟨l:q⟩[i]);
  if f ≠ 0 then
    foreach j s.t. W_e,l[i, j] = 1 do
      u ← Union(l−1, f, ⟨l:s⟩[j]);
      if u≠⟨l:s⟩[j] then
        if j ∉ S_l then Confirm(l, j);
        ⟨l:s⟩[j] ← u; sChng ← true;
if sChng then Saturate(l, s);
CheckIn(l, s);
Insert(FC[e, l], q, s);
return s;
```

```
Confirm(in k:level, i:local)
Add i to S_k and build its rows in all W_e,k
where e depends on submodel k.

declare e:ev, j:local, n:int, s, u:state;
s ← GetState(k, i);
foreach e dependent on submodel k
  foreach u ∈ NextState(e, k, s)
    j ← InsertState(k, u);
    W_e,k[i, j] ← 1;
S_k ← S_k ∪ {i};
```

```
Locals(in e:ev, k:level, p:idx):set of local
Local indices of ⟨k:p⟩ locally enabling e:
{i∈S_k:⟨k:p⟩[i]≠0 ∧ ∃j, W_e,k[i, j] = 1}.
```

```
CheckIn(in k:level, inout p:idx)
If ∀i ∈ S_k, ⟨k:p⟩[i] = 0, delete ⟨k:p⟩ and
set p to 0. If ⟨k:p⟩ duplicates ⟨k:q⟩, delete
⟨k:p⟩ and set p to q. Else, insert ⟨k:p⟩ in
the unique table UT[k].
```

```
NewNode(in k:level):idx
Create a new MDD node at level k, with
its arcs set to 0.
```

Fig. 4. Pseudocode for the on-the-fly version of our saturation algorithm [12].

a level); in practice, these are simply integers in appropriate ranges. In addition, the model-specific type *state* represents the explicit description of a local state. We assume the existence of the following dynamically-sized global hash tables: $UT[k]$, for $K \geq k \geq 1$, the *unique table* for nodes at level k, to retrieve p given $\langle k{:}p\rangle[0], \ldots, \langle k{:}p\rangle[n_k - 1]$; $UC[k]$, for $K > k \geq 1$, the *union cache* for nodes at level k, to retrieve s given p and q, where $\mathcal{B}(\langle k{:}s\rangle) = \mathcal{B}(\langle k{:}p\rangle) \cup \mathcal{B}(\langle k{:}q\rangle)$; and $FC[e,k]$, for $Top(e) > k \geq Bot(e)$, the *firing cache* for event e and nodes at level k, to retrieve s given node p, where $\mathcal{B}(\langle k{:}s\rangle) = \mathcal{N}^*_{\leq k}(\mathcal{N}_e(\mathcal{B}(\langle k{:}p\rangle)))$, where $\mathcal{N}_e(i_k, \ldots, i_1)$ is to be interpreted as $\mathcal{N}_{e,k}(i_k) \times \cdots \times \mathcal{N}_{e,1}(i_1)$. Hash-table access is provided by *Insert*(*key*,*val*), which associates *val* to *key*, and *Find*(*key*,*res*), which returns *true* if *key* is in the cache and sets *res* to the associated value. Furthermore, we use K dynamically-sized arrays to store nodes, so that $\langle k{:}p\rangle$ can be efficiently retrieved as the pth entry of the kth array. The two-dimensional array of sparse matrices $\mathbf{W}_{e,k}$ is a global variable. We also assume a global variable of type *model* with the following functional interface: *InsertState*(*level*, *state*) : *local*, *GetState*(*level*, *local*) : *state*, *NextState*(*ev*, *level*, *state*) : *state*, and *InitialState*(*level*) : *state*.

4 Comments

We now discuss some details of the on-the-fly algorithm, especially the challenges raised by its design and implementation.

MDD nodes of variable size. With pregeneration, the size of MDD nodes at level k is fixed, easing their creation, deletion, and reuse. With our on-the-fly expansion of $\mathcal{S}_k$, we might instead allocate nodes of increasing size. Fortunately, a saturated node $\langle k{:}p\rangle$ remains saturated when a new state i is added to $\mathcal{S}_k$, as long as the semantic of the missing arc $\langle k{:}p\rangle[i]$ is taken to be an arc to $\langle k-1{:}0\rangle$. However, the growth of $\mathcal{S}_k$ implies that we cannot reserve a special meaning for node $\langle k{:}1\rangle$, as done with pregeneration [12], where $\mathcal{B}(\langle k{:}1\rangle) = \mathcal{S}_k \times \cdots \times \mathcal{S}_1$. In [12], this optimization could speed-up the computation whenever node $\langle k{:}1\rangle$ is involved in a union, since we could immediately conclude that $\mathcal{B}(\langle k{:}1\rangle) \cup \mathcal{B}(\langle k{:}p\rangle) = \mathcal{B}(\langle k{:}1\rangle)$. Indeed, such nodes were not even stored explicitly in [12]. To reserve index 1 for the same purpose with the on-the-fly approach is problematic, since, whenever we increase $\mathcal{S}_l$, for $l \leq k$, the meaning of $\mathcal{B}(\langle k{:}1\rangle)$ implicitly changes. We can still reserve index 0 for the empty set, and exploit the relation $\mathcal{B}(\langle k{:}0\rangle) \cup \mathcal{B}(\langle k{:}p\rangle) = \mathcal{B}(\langle k{:}p\rangle)$, since the representation of the empty set is the same as that in [12].

This observation led us to use *quasi-reduced* (instead of *reduced*) MDDs. The latter eliminates redundant nodes and is potentially more efficient, but its arcs can span multiple levels. As discussed in [11], such arcs are more difficult to manage and can yield a slower state-space generation when exploiting locality. With the on-the-fly algorithm, they create an even worse problem: they become "incorrect" when a local state space grows. For example, both the reduced and the quasi-reduced 3-level MDDs in Fig. 5(a) and (c) encode the state space $\mathcal{S} = \{(0,0,2), (0,1,2), (1,0,2), (1,1,2), (3,0,2)\}$, when $\mathcal{S}_3 = \{0,1,2,3\}$, $\mathcal{S}_2 = \{0,1\}$, and $\mathcal{S}_1 = \{0,1,2\}$. If we want to add global state $(3,2,2)$ to $\mathcal{S}$, we need to add

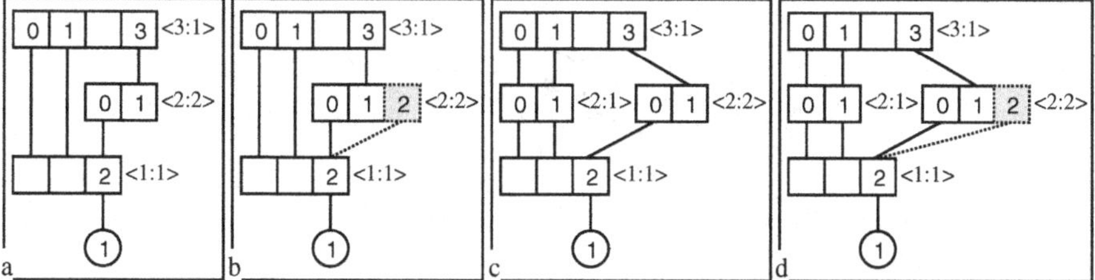

Fig. 5. Before and after, with reduced (a-b) vs. quasi-reduced (c-d) MDDs.

local state 2 to $\mathcal{S}_2$ and set arc $\langle 2{:}2\rangle[2]$ to $\langle 1{:}1\rangle$. However, while the resulting quasi-reduced MDD in (d) is correct, the reduced one in (b) is not, since now it also encodes global states $(0, 2, 2)$ and $(1, 2, 2)$. To fix the problem, we could reintroduce the formerly-redundant node $\langle 2{:}1\rangle$ so that the new reduced and quasi-reduced MDDs coincide. While it would be possible to modify the MDD to obtain a correct reduced ordered MDD in this manner whenever a local state space grows, the cost of doing so is unjustifiably high.

Compacting the arc arrays. To facilitate dynamically-sized nodes, we use indirection. Node $\langle k{:}p\rangle$ is associated with entry p of array $nodes_k$, as we need direct access to it, given p. However, the arcs of all nodes at level k are stored together in a second array $arcs_k$. Entry $nodes_k[p]$ has fixed size and stores, among other information, fields bg, the beginning location where the "chunk" of arcs for $\langle k{:}p\rangle$ begins in $arcs_k$, and sz, the chunk's size, since n_k changes over time. Saturation "updates-in-place" a node $\langle k{:}p\rangle$ when exploring the firing of an event e such that $Top(e) = k$. Fortunately, this implies that only the currently unsaturated node at level k (there is at most one such node at any point in time) might cause $\mathcal{S}_k$ to grow: if we store the arcs of this node as the last chunk in $arcs_k$, we never need to grow any "internal" chunk.

However, saturated nodes may still become obsolete and need to be recycled. Deleting $\langle k{:}p\rangle$ leaves a "hole" of size $nodes_k[p].sz$ in $arcs_k$. Since these holes may be smaller than the chunks needed for new nodes, we cannot easily reuse them as-is. Instead, we mark them as invalid and periodically clean them by "compacting to the left" the entire $arcs_k$ array. The space opened at the right end of $arcs_k$ can then be reused for new nodes. Shifting chunks of arcs requires that the values $nodes_k[p].bg$ pointing to these chunks be updated as well. There are several ways to do this. Our implementation stores, together with the chunk for $\langle k{:}p\rangle$ in $arcs_k$, a back pointer to the node itself, i.e., the value p. This allows us to compact $arcs[k]$ via a linear scan: valid values are shifted to the left over invalid values until all holes have been removed. Simultaneously, using the back pointer p, we access and update the value $nodes_k[p].bg$ after shifting the corresponding chunk. With respect to our pregeneration implementation where arc chunks are stored directly in $nodes_k$ as arrays of fixed size n_k, this requires 12 additional bytes per node, for bg and sz in $nodes_k$ and for the back pointer in $arcs_k$. However, it can also save memory, since chunks can be smaller than for pregeneration and could be stored with sparse techniques.

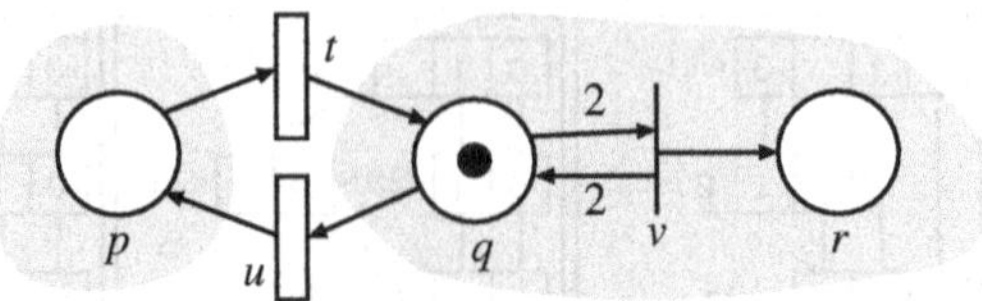

Fig. 6. Potential but not actual overflow of a local state space.

We keep track of the number of invalid entries, and trigger compaction whenever a portion of the entries in $arcs_k$ become invalid (50% in our experiments).

Overflowing of potential local state spaces. Our new algorithm eliminates the need to specify additional constraints for any formalism where each state can reach a finite number of states in a single step. A subtle problem remains, however, if an infinite number of states can be reached in one step. For example, in Generalized Stochastic Petri Nets [1], *immediate* transitions, such as v in Fig. 6, are processed not by themselves, but as events that can take place instantaneously after the firing of *timed* transitions, such as t and u (somewhat analogous to *internal* events in process algebra). In Fig. 6, we partition the net into subnet 2, containing place p, and subnet 1, containing places q and r. The initial local states are (p^0) and (q^1r^0) respectively. When the latter state is confirmed into $\mathcal{S}_1$, an explicit local exploration begins. Transition t can fire in subnet 1 in isolation, leading to marking (q^2r^0). This enables immediate transition v which, processed right away as part of the firing of t, leads to markings (q^2r^1), (q^2r^2), (q^2r^3), ... and so on. Thus, the explicit local exploration fails with an overflow in place r, while a traditional explicit global exploration would not, since it would never reach a global marking with two tokens in q. This situation is quite artificial, however. It can occur only if the formalism allows a state to reach an infinite number of states in one "timed step".

BDDs vs. MDDs. Our choice of MDDs over BDDs for modeling asynchronous systems is prompted by the success of the saturation strategy, which exploits event locality and gives flexibility in the choice of partitioning. MDDs are an excellent match for our Kronecker encoding of the next-state function; indeed, the two, in conjunction with a "good" partition, allow us to *increase* the amount of locality. However, the issues addressed in our work are not exclusive to MDDs.

It is true that determining the potential state space for BDDs "simply" means deciding the number K of boolean variables. However, when the actual model has integer variables, the modeler needs to know how many bits are needed for their encoding, and this is just as difficult as determining the size of our local state spaces a priori. Just as with our MDDs, then, choosing too many bits can lead to inefficiencies, choosing too few can mask errors. An on-the-fly algorithm for BDDs would have to expand the decision diagrams "vertically", creating more levels of binary variables to cope with a growing range for an integer variable, while MDDs can simply extend local state spaces "horizontally". Furthermore, in our approach, unconfirmed local states appear only in the columns of the Kronecker matrices encoding the next-state function, not in the MDD.

Table 1. Generation of the state space: On-The-Fly vs. PREgeneration vs. NuSMV

N	Reachable states	Final memory (KB)			Peak memory (KB)			Time (sec)		
		OTF	PRE	NuSMV	OTF	PRE	NuSMV	OTF	PRE	NuSMV
Dining Philosophers: $K=N$, $\|\mathcal{S}_k\|=34$ for all k										
20	3.46×10^{12}	4	3	4,178	5	4	4,192	0.01	0.01	0.4
50	2.23×10^{31}	11	10	8,847	14	12	8,863	0.03	0.02	13.1
100	4.97×10^{62}	24	20	8,891	28	25	15,256	0.06	0.05	990.8
200	2.47×10^{125}	48	40	21,618	57	50	59,423	0.15	0.11	18,129.3
5,000	6.53×10^{3134}	1,210	1,015	—	1,445	1,269	—	65.55	51.29	—
Slotted Ring Network: $K=N$, $\|\mathcal{S}_k\|=15$ for all k										
5	5.39×10^{4}	1	1	502	5	5	507	0.01	0.01	0.1
10	8.29×10^{9}	5	5	4,332	28	27	8,863	0.06	0.04	6.1
15	1.46×10^{15}	10	9	771	80	77	11,054	0.18	0.13	2,853.1
100	2.60×10^{105}	434	398	—	15,753	14,486	—	41.72	25.78	—
Round Robin Mutual Exclusion: $K=N+1$, $\|\mathcal{S}_k\|=10$ for all k except $\|\mathcal{S}_1\|=N+1$										
10	2.30×10^{4}	5	5	917	6	7	932	0.01	0.01	0.2
20	4.72×10^{7}	18	17	5,980	20	21	5,985	0.04	0.03	1.4
30	7.25×10^{10}	37	36	2,222	41	41	8,716	0.09	0.07	5.6
100	2.85×10^{32}	357	355	13,789	372	372	21,814	2.11	1.55	2,836.5
150	4.82×10^{47}	784	781	—	807	807	—	7.04	5.07	—
FMS: $K=19$, $\|\mathcal{S}_k\|=N+1$ for all k except $\|\mathcal{S}_{17}\|=4$, $\|\mathcal{S}_{12}\|=3$, $\|\mathcal{S}_7\|=2$										
5	1.92×10^{4}	5	6	2,113	6	9	2,126	0.01	0.01	1.0
10	2.50×10^{9}	16	19	1,152	26	31	8,928	0.02	0.02	41.6
25	8.54×10^{13}	86	135	17,045	163	239	152,253	0.16	0.11	17,321.9
150	4.84×10^{23}	6,291	15,459	—	16,140	29,998	—	18.50	10.92	—

5 Results

We compare the space and runtime required by our new algorithm with those of its pregeneration predecessor [12] and of NuSMV [14], a symbolic verifier built on top of the CUDD library [27]. We use a 2.4 Ghz Pentium IV with 1GB of memory. Our examples include four models from [12], parametrized by an integer N: dining philosophers, slotted ring, round robin mutual exclusion, and flexible manufacturing system (FMS). The first three models are safe Petri nets: N affects the height of the MDD but not the size of the local state spaces (except for $\mathcal{S}_1$ in the round robin model, which grows linearly in N). The FMS has instead an MDD with fixed height but size of the nodes increasing linearly in N. In the pregeneration and NuSMV models, additional constraints are manually imposed to ensure that the correct local state spaces are built in isolation.

Table 1 lists the peak and final memory and the runtime for these algorithms. For comparison's sake, we assume that a BDD node in NuSMV uses 16 bytes. To be fair, we point out that our memory consumption refers to the MDD only, while we believe that the number of nodes reported by NuSMV includes also those for the next-state function; however, our Kronecker encoding for $\mathcal{N}$ is extremely efficient, requiring at most 300KB in any model, except for the model with 5,000 dining philosophers, where it requires 5.2MB. The memory for the operation caches is not included in either our or NuSMV results (for our algorithms, caches never exceeded 20MB on these examples). Both the on-the-fly and the pregeneration MDD algorithms are able to handle significantly larger models than NuSMV. We show the largest value of N for each of the four models where generation was possible, in the penultimate row for NuSMV and the last row for SMART. When comparisons with NuSMV can be made, our algorithms show speed-up ratios over 100,000 and memory reduction ratios over 1,000.

The results demonstrate that the overhead of the on-the-fly algorithm versus pregeneration is acceptable. Moreover, the additional 12-byte per node memory overhead required to manage dynamically-sized nodes at a given level k can be offset by the ability to store nodes with $m < n_k$ arcs (because they were created when $\mathcal{S}_k$ contained only m states, or because the last $n_k - m$ arcs point to $\langle k-1{:}0 \rangle$ and are truncated). In fact, for the FMS model, this results in smaller memory requirements than with pregeneration, suggesting that the use of sparse nodes is advantageous in models with large local state spaces. Even if our on-the-fly implementation is not yet as optimized as that of pregeneration, the runtime of the on-the-fly algorithm is still excellent, at most 70% over that of pregeneration. This is a good tradeoff, given the increase in modeling ease and safety afforded by not having to worry about local state space generation in isolation.

6 Related Work

Symbolic analysis of unbounded discrete-event systems has been considered before in a more general setting than ours: in most cases, the goal is the study of systems with infinite but regular state spaces. For example, the Queue BDDs of [18] allow one to model systems with a finite number of boolean variables plus one or more unbounded queues, as long as the contents of the queue can be represented by a DFA. The MONA system [19], implementing *monadic second-order logic*, can be used to verify *parametric* systems without relying on a proof by induction. These types of approach can be generally classified under the umbrella of *regular model checking* [4].

Our goal in this paper is more modest, since we only target models with a finite state space, but it is also very different. The saturation approach we introduced in [12] has been shown to be vastly superior to traditional breadth-first approaches for globally-asynchronous locally-synchronous systems (see also [13] for its application to edge-valued decision diagrams). However, it was limited to models for which bounds on the state variables are known a priori. Here, we extended it to bounded models with unknown bounds, such as those arising when modeling distributed software, one of the most challenging problems in symbolic methods. Our description formalism of choice, Petri nets with inhibitor arcs, self-modifying behavior, and non-deterministic decision, is Turing-equivalent, thus we can only hope that the state space of a given model is finite. Even when it is finite, though, it can still have a highly "irregular" pattern. It is in these patterns that the efficiency of our approach is particularly desirable. To our knowledge, the algorithm we presented is the first to combine symbolic generation of the global state space with exact explicit generation of the local state spaces, but the issue is related, at least for Petri nets, to the existence of invariants [24]. Indeed, we could use *place invariants* to bound our local state spaces and proceed using pregeneration, but our on-the-fly approach is superior because it has a small overhead, while invariant analysis is very expensive in pathological cases [22]. More importantly, the invariant approach is limited: a net might not be fully covered by invariants yet be bounded because of inhibitor arcs or other constructs; invariant analysis alone might suggest that a place is unbounded because it concludes that a transition t can keep "pumping" tokens into it, while in reality t might never be enabled given the particular initial marking. Indeed, invariant analysis does not take into account the presence of inhibitor arcs, and it can deal only with a limited class of marking-dependent arc cardinalities used in *self-modifying nets* [9], yet both constructs are very useful in practice to define compact and realistic models. Our solution is fast, general, user-friendly, and terminates in at least all cases where previous algorithms terminate.

The idea of a disjunctively-partitioned transition relation is natural for asynchronous systems [15,20], and in particular for Petri nets. However, our inspiration for its (boolean) Kronecker encoding comes from the field of Markov chains, where (real) Kronecker operators are increasingly used to encode the infinitesimal generators of large Markov models described compositionally [2,7,25]. Thanks to this encoding, we can exploit the presence of locality in the transition relation of each individual event, achieving much greater efficiency.

With regard to the saturation approach itself, several works proposed abandoning the breadth-first approach of traditional symbolic state-space generation, with the goal of reducing the peak number of nodes, but they often still have some vestiges of breadth-first search. For example, [3,26] improve efficiency by exploring only a portion of the newly-found states, those encoded by the "densest" nodes in the decision diagram. The closest to our saturation approach is the "modified breadth-first search" mentioned in [20]. We believe that our saturation approach is the first one to fully avoid any flavor of a global breadth-first iteration and, for globally-asynchronous locally-synchronous models, its locality-based ordering of the events appears to be much more effective, at times even optimal: cases where the peak number of nodes is only $O(1)$ larger than the final number of nodes were reported in [12].

7 Conclusion and Future Work

Traditional symbolic state-space generation approaches require a priori knowledge of the range of the state variables. In practice this puts a considerable burden on the modeler who must add artificial constraints and may risk masking actual errors in the original model. In this paper, we presented a new approach that avoids this requirement by integrating explicit local state-space generation with symbolic global state-space generation, and building a Kronecker representation of the next-state function "on-the-fly". Our algorithm provides this new capability at a small overhead cost with respect to our previous "pregeneration" algorithm, but it remains enormously more efficient than other approaches in which the next-state function is encoded as a BDD.

We stress that the data structure we employ, MDDs whose nodes can be expanded at runtime, may have useful applications beyond state-space generation. On the other hand, while our saturation algorithm is very efficient, it should be clear that its use is not a prerequisite to the on-the-fly exploration of the local state spaces we presented; however, we showed how the two can be seamlessly integrated, and this enhances the usefulness and applicability of saturation.

In the future, we plan to investigate reordering, splitting, and merging of MDD levels. These are more general than the reordering of BDD variables, but we hope to extend some heuristics already known for that problem [16]. Also, our algorithms are currently implemented in SMART [10], a simulation and modeling tool for logic and stochastic analysis. Eventually, we intend to make them available as C++ libraries.

References

1. M. Ajmone Marsan, G. Balbo, G. Conte, S. Donatelli, and G. Franceschinis. *Modelling with Generalized Stochastic Petri Nets.* John Wiley & Sons, New York, 1995.
2. V. Amoia, G. De Micheli, and M. Santomauro. Computer-oriented formulation of transition-rate matrices via Kronecker algebra. *IEEE Trans. Rel.*, 30:123–132, June 1981.
3. R. Bloem, K. Ravi, and F. Somenzi. Symbolic guided search for CTL model checking. In *Proc. 37th Conf. on Design Automation*, p. 29–34. ACM Press, 2000.
4. A. Bouajjani, B. Jonsson, M. Nilsson, and T. Touili. Regular model checking. In *Computer Aided Verification*, pages 403–418, 2000.
5. R. E. Bryant. Graph-based algorithms for boolean function manipulation. *IEEE Trans. Comp.*, 35(8):677–691, Aug. 1986.
6. R. E. Bryant. Symbolic boolean manipulation with ordered binary-decision diagrams. *ACM Comp. Surv.*, 24(3):393–318, 1992.
7. P. Buchholz, G. Ciardo, S. Donatelli, and P. Kemper. Complexity of memory-efficient Kronecker operations with applications to the solution of Markov models. *INFORMS J. Comp.*, 12(3):203–222, 2000.
8. J. R. Burch, E. M. Clarke, K. L. McMillan, D. L. Dill, and L. J. Hwang. Symbolic model checking: 10^{20} states and beyond. In *Proc. 5th Annual IEEE Symp. on Logic in Computer Science*, pages 428–439, Philadelphia, PA, 4–7 June 1990. IEEE Comp. Soc. Press.
9. G. Ciardo. Petri nets with marking-dependent arc multiplicity: properties and analysis. In R. Valette, editor, *Proc. 15th Int. Conf. on Applications and Theory of Petri Nets*, LNCS 815, pages 179–198, Zaragoza, Spain, June 1994. Springer-Verlag.
10. G. Ciardo, R. L. Jones, A. S. Miner, and R. Siminiceanu. SMART: Stochastic Model Analyzer for Reliability and Timing. In P. Kemper, editor, *Tools of Int. Multiconference on Measurement, Modelling and Evaluation of Computer-Communication Systems*, pages 29–34, Aachen, Germany, Sept. 2001.
11. G. Ciardo, G. Luettgen, and R. Siminiceanu. Efficient symbolic state-space construction for asynchronous systems. In M. Nielsen and D. Simpson, editors, *Proc. 21th Int. Conf. on Applications and Theory of Petri Nets*, LNCS 1825, pages 103–122, Aarhus, Denmark, June 2000. Springer-Verlag.

12. G. Ciardo, G. Luettgen, and R. Siminiceanu. Saturation: An efficient iteration strategy for symbolic state space generation. In T. Margaria and W. Yi, editors, *Proc. Tools and Algorithms for the Construction and Analysis of Systems (TACAS)*, LNCS 2031, pages 328–342, Genova, Italy, Apr. 2001. Springer-Verlag.
13. G. Ciardo and R. Siminiceanu. Using edge-valued decision diagrams for symbolic generation of shortest paths. In M. D. Aagaard and J. W. O'Leary, editors, *Proc. Fourth International Conference on Formal Methods in Computer-Aided Design (FMCAD)*, LNCS 2517, pages 256–273, Portland, OR, USA, Nov. 2002. Springer-Verlag.
14. A. Cimatti, E. Clarke, F. Giunchiglia, and M. Roveri. NuSMV: A new symbolic model verifier. In *CAV '99*, LNCS 1633, pages 495–499. Springer-Verlag, 1999.
15. O. Coudert and J. C. Madre. Symbolic computation of the valid states of a sequential machine: algorithms and discussion. In *1991 Int. Workshop on Formal Methods in VLSI Design*, pages 1–19, Miami, FL, USA, 1991.
16. M. Fujita, H. Fujisawa, and Y. Matsunaga. Variable ordering algorithms for ordered binary decision diagrams and their evaluation. *IEEE Trans. on Computer–Aided Design of Integrated Circuits and Systems*, 12(1):6–12, 1993.
17. A. Geser, J. Knoop, G. Lüttgen, B. Steffen, and O. Rüthing. Chaotic fixed point iterations. Technical Report MIP-9403, Univ. of Passau, 1994.
18. P. Godefroid and D. E. Long. Symbolic protocol verification with queue BDDs. *Formal Methods in System Design*, 14(3):257–271, May 1999.
19. J. G. Henriksen, J. L. Jensen, M. E. Jørgensen, N. Klarlund, R. Paige, T. Rauhe, and A. Sandholm. Mona: Monadic second-order logic in practice. In E. Brinksma, R. Cleaveland, K. G. Larsen, T. Margaria, and B. Steffen, editors, *Tools and Algorithms for the Construction and Analysis of Systems*, volume 1019, pages 89–110. Springer, 1995.
20. J.R. Burch, E.M. Clarke, and D.E. Long. Symbolic model checking with partitioned transition relations. In A. Halaas and P.B. Denyer, editors, *Int. Conference on Very Large Scale Integration*, pages 49–58, Edinburgh, Scotland, Aug. 1991. IFIP Transactions, North-Holland.
21. T. Kam, T. Villa, R. Brayton, and A. Sangiovanni-Vincentelli. Multi-valued decision diagrams: theory and applications. *Multiple-Valued Logic*, 4(1–2):9–62, 1998.
22. J. Martinez and M. Silva. A simple and fast algorithm to obtain all invariants of a generalised Petri net. In *Proc. 2nd European Workshop on Application and Theory of Petri Nets*, pages 411–422, Bad Honnef, Germany, 1981.
23. A. S. Miner and G. Ciardo. Efficient reachability set generation and storage using decision diagrams. In H. Kleijn and S. Donatelli, editors, *Proc. 20th Int. Conf. on Applications and Theory of Petri Nets*, LNCS 1639, pages 6–25, Williamsburg, VA, USA, June 1999. Springer-Verlag.
24. T. Murata and R. Church. Analysis of marked graphs and Petri nets by matrix equations. Research report MDC 1.1.8, Department of information engineering, Univeristy of Illinois, Chicago, IL, Nov. 1975.
25. B. Plateau. On the stochastic structure of parallelism and synchronisation models for distributed algorithms. In *Proc. ACM SIGMETRICS*, pages 147–153, Austin, TX, USA, May 1985.
26. K. Ravi and F. Somenzi. Efficient fixpoint computation for invariant checking. In *Proc. Int. Conference on Computer Design (ICCD)*, pages 467–474, Austin, TX, Oct. 1999. IEEE Comp. Soc. Press.
27. F. Somenzi. CUDD: CU Decision Diagram Package, Release 2.3.1. http://vlsi.colorado.edu/~fabio/CUDD/cuddIntro.html.

Construction of Efficient BDDs for Bounded Arithmetic Constraints*

Constantinos Bartzis and Tevfik Bultan

Department of Computer Science
University of California
Santa Barbara CA 93106, USA
{bar,bultan}@cs.ucsb.edu

Abstract. Most symbolic model checkers use BDDs to represent arithmetic constraints over bounded integer variables. The size of such BDDs can be exponential on the number and size (in bits) of the integer variables in the worst case. In this paper we show how to construct linear-sized BDDs for linear integer arithmetic constraints. We present basic constructions for atomic equality and inequality constraints and extend them to handle arbitrary linear arithmetic formulas. We also present three alternative ways of handling out-of-bounds transitions, and discuss multiple bounds on integer variables. We experimentally compare our approach to other BDD-based symbolic model checkers and demonstrate that the algorithms presented in this paper can be used to improve their performance significantly.

1 Introduction

Performance of a symbolic model checker depends on the efficiency of the algorithms for the BDD construction and the sizes of the generated BDD representations. In this paper we address both these issues for linear arithmetic constraints on bounded integer variables. BDD-based model checkers represent bounded integer variables by mapping them to a set of Boolean variables using a binary encoding. Our experiments show that the state of the art BDD-based model checkers use inefficient algorithms for BDD construction from linear arithmetic constraints and fail to generate compact BDD representations for them [11,8,1]. Handling linear arithmetic constraints efficiently is an important problem since such constraints are common in reactive system specifications. For example, the distribution files for the BDD-based model checker NuSMV contain specifications with linear arithmetic constraints, however, the verification time for these specifications for NuSMV does not scale when the bounds on integer variables are increased. The algorithms and complexity results presented in this paper demonstrate that this inefficiency is not inherent to the BDD data structure and can be avoided.

* This work is supported in part by NSF grant CCR-9970976 and NSF CAREER award CCR-9984822.

H. Garavel and J. Hatcliff (Eds.): TACAS 2003, LNCS 2619, pp. 394–408, 2003.

We present algorithms for constructing efficient BDD representations from atomic arithmetic constraints of the form $\sum_{i=1}^{v} a_i \cdot x_i \# a_0$, where $\# \in \{=, \neq, >, \geq, \leq, <\}$. We show that the size of the resulting BDD is linear in the number of variables and the number of bits used to encode each variable. We also show that the time complexity of the construction algorithm is the same. We also give bounds for BDDs for linear arithmetic formulas which can be obtained by combining atomic arithmetic constraints with boolean connectives. We show that the resulting BDDs for linear arithmetic formulas are still linear in the number of variables and the number of bits used to encode each variable. We extend the construction algorithms to handle transitions which can take the bounded integer variables out-of-bounds. We present three different approaches for handling out-of-bounds transitions and show that all of them preserve the complexity results. We also generalize the construction algorithms to multiple bounds on integer variables. We show that as long as all the bounds are powers of two the complexity results are preserved. One interesting result is that multiple bounds which are not powers of two cause the BDD size to be exponential in the number of variables in the worst case.

The problem of inefficient BDD representation of arithmetic constraints in symbolic model checkers has been pointed out in [7,12]. In [7], the problem for SMV is handled by writing a preprocessor and fixing the BDD variable order. However, as we show in this paper, this extra step is not necessary since efficient BDDs can be directly constructed from a set of linear arithmetic constraints. In [12], the problem is solved only for constraints of the form $x + y = z$, where x, y and z can be variables or constants. Even though such constraints arise very often in practice, our algorithms are more general without sacrificing efficiency. Binary Moment Diagrams (BMDs) [4] and Hybrid Decision Diagrams (HDDs) [9] are data structures designed to represent arithmetic expressions and handle arithmetic operations on word-level verification where an array of binary bits can be referred as an integer. These data structures can also be used to construct linear-sized BDDs from linear arithmetic constraints. However, in this paper, we show that one can construct linear-sized BDDs from linear arithmetic constraints directly, without using these data structures. Hence, the algorithms we present can be easily integrated to a BDD-based model checker.

2 Atomic Equality Constraints

Given a set of v integer variables $x_i, 1 \leq i \leq v$ such that $0 \leq x_i < 2^b$ and a linear equation of the form $\sum_{i=1}^{v} a_i \cdot x_i = a_0$ we construct a BDD with $v \cdot b$ boolean variables $x_{i,j}, 1 \leq i \leq v, 0 \leq j < b$ which evaluates to **1** iff $\sum_{i=1}^{v} a_i \cdot (\sum_{j=0}^{b-1} x_{i,j} \cdot 2^j) = a_0$. In other words the BDD variables $x_{i,j}$ represent the binary digits of the integer variables and the BDD evaluates to **1** iff the equation is satisfied by the valuation $x_i = \sum_{j=0}^{b-1} x_{i,j} \cdot 2^j$ for $1 \leq i \leq v$. We show that such a BDD has $O(v \cdot b \cdot \sum_{i=1}^{v} |a_i|)$ nodes, i.e. the size of the BDD is linear on the number of boolean variables. Note that in general the size of a BDD can be exponential on

BDD construction algorithm for equations $\sum_{i=1}^{v} a_i \cdot x_i = a_0$ *on b-bit variables*

```
Procedure: node(i, j, c)
//Constructs a node in level i of layer j with label c
BDDnode n
    n.index := j · v + i
    if (i = v and j = b − 1)
        if (c = 0) n.low := 1
        else n.low := 0
        if (c + a_v = 0) n.high := 1
        else n.high := 0
    else if (i = v)
        if (c is even) n.low := node(1, j + 1, c/2)
        else n.low := 0
        if (c + a_v is even) n.high := node(1, j + 1, (c + a_v)/2)
        else n.high = 0
    else
        n.low := node(i + 1, j, c)
        n.high = node(i + 1, j, c + a_v)
    return n

Main: return node(1, 0, −a_0)
```

Fig. 1. BDD construction algorithm for equations

the number of boolean variables and experimental results show that state of the art model checkers produce exponentially large BDDs.

The algorithm is given in Figure 1. The constructed BDD consists of b layers of v levels each. The j_{th} layer corresponds to the j_{th} least significant bit of each integer variable and the i_{th} level in a layer corresponds to the i_{th} integer variable. Every node in a level is labeled with an integer c between $-\sum_{i=0}^{v} |a_i|$ and $\sum_{i=0}^{v} |a_i|$. In particular, the label of a node in the 1_{st} level of the j_{th} layer corresponds to a value of the carry c resulting from the computation of $\sum_{i=1}^{v} a_i \cdot (\sum_{n=0}^{j-1} x_{i,j} \cdot 2^n) - a_0$, where $x_{i,j}$s are the values of the BDD variables along one of the paths from the root to that node. Furthermore, the label of a node in the k_{th} level, $2 \leq k \leq v$, of the j_{th} layer is the value $c + \sum_{i=1}^{k-1} a_i \cdot x_{i,j}$, where $x_{i,j}$s are the values of the BDD variables along one of the paths from the node in the 1_{st} level of the j_{th} layer with label c to that node.

As an example consider the linear equation $2x - 3y = 1$, where x and y are 4 bits long. Figure 2 shows the structure of a complete intermediate layer (inside the dashed rectangle) of the corresponding BDD. The nodes outside the rectangle comprise the first level of the next layer. The complete BDD is shown in Figure 3. For all Figures, edges not shown point to **0** terminal node. Note that the BDDs constructed by the algorithms in this paper are not necessarily reduced. Standard BDD reduction needs to be applied after the construction.

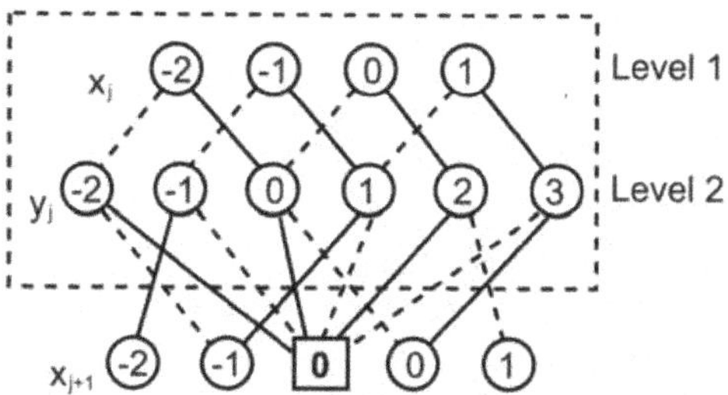

Fig. 2. Layer of a BDD for $2x - 3y = 1$

Theorem 1. *The algorithm given in Figure 1 constructs a BDD representing the linear equation* $\sum_{i=1}^{v} a_i \cdot x_i = a_0$ *on b-bit non-negative integer variables. The time complexity of the algorithm and the size of the resulting BDD is* $O(v \cdot b \cdot \sum_{i=1}^{v} |a_i|)$.

Proof. For the purposes of the proof we can think of a BDD as a bit-serial processor as described in [3]. Such a processor computes a Boolean function by examining the arguments x_1, x_2, and so on in order, producing output 0 or 1 after the last bit has been read. It requires internal storage to store enough information about the arguments it has already seen to correctly deduce the value of the function from the values of the remaining arguments. Trivially it can store all the values of the arguments it has already seen by using exponentially large storage. In our case we can show that linear storage is needed. The size of the storage consumed by the processor translates to the number of nodes in the BDD.

The ordering of the boolean variables $x_{i,j}$ is lexicographical primarily on j and secondarily on i or equivalently the index of variable $x_{i,j}$ is $j \cdot v + i$. The *index* of the root is 1. One can easily verify that any internal node with index *index* points to a node with index *index* + 1, except for the nodes with index $b \cdot v$ that point to the terminal nodes. Thus the constructed BDD is consistent with the ordering mentioned above. Therefore the bit-serial processor equivalent of the BDD first processes the least significant bit of the integer variables $x_1, x_2, ..., x_v$ in this order, then it processes the second least significant bits and so on. In the end the processor needs to verify whether or not $\sum_{i=1}^{v} a_i \cdot x_i = a_0$ or equivalently $\sum_{i=1}^{v} a_i \cdot (\sum_{j=0}^{b-1} x_{i,j} \cdot 2^j) = a_0$ or

$$- a_0 + \sum_{j=0}^{b-1} 2^j \cdot (\sum_{i=1}^{v} a_i \cdot x_{i,j}) = 0 \tag{1}$$

To accomplish this the processor gradually computes the left hand side of equation (1) bit by bit and compares it against zero. If at any point the comparison fails it immediately evaluates to **0**, otherwise it continues. It starts with an initial value of $-a_0$ and then gradually adds to it $a_i \cdot x_{i0}$ as it reads the values of $x_{1,0}$ up to $x_{v,0}$ and stores the intermediate result $-a_0 + \sum_{i=1}^{l} a_i \cdot x_{i,0}$ every time. Note

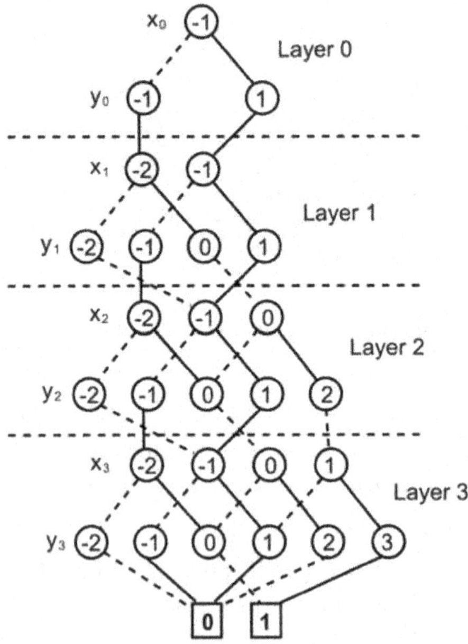

Fig. 3. BDD for $2x - 3y = 1$ for 4-bit variables

that the value stored is shown as the label of each BDD node in the Figures. At the end of processing layer 0, if the result is an odd number (or the resulting bit is 1) the processor immediately evaluates to **0**, since what remains to add, namely $\sum_{j=1}^{b-1} 2^j \cdot (\sum_{i=1}^{v} a_i \cdot x_{i,j})$, is an even number and there is no chance that the final result will be zero. Otherwise, the intermediate result at this point divided by two is equal to the remaining carry c, i.e. $c = (-a_0 + \sum_{i=1}^{v} a_i \cdot x_{i,0})/2$. The value of the carry is the only piece of information that needs to be stored at this point. If we divide both sides of equation (1) by 2 we will get:

$$c + \sum_{j=1}^{b-1} 2^{j-1} \cdot (\sum_{i=1}^{v} a_i \cdot x_{i,j}) = 0 \quad (2)$$

Now the processor needs to verify equation (2) and this task is similar to the initial one, so the processor continues to operate in a similar manner. In the end, in order for the final result to be 0 the final carry has to be also 0. In that case the processor evaluates to **1**, otherwise it evaluates to **0**. This concludes the proof of correctness of our construction algorithm.

For the proof of termination and complexity, the fundamental question that needs to be answered is how many different intermediate results need to be stored at any point during the operation of the bit-serial processor or in other words how many BDD nodes are there at any level. The number of nodes at any level is bounded by the size of the range defined by the least and the greatest label in that level. If the labels of the nodes at level $j \cdot v + 1$ belong to a range of size $n_{1,j}$,

BDD construction algorithm for inequations $\sum_{i=1}^{v} a_i \cdot x_i < a_0$ *on b-bit variables*

```
Procedure: node(i, j, c)
//Constructs a node in level i of layer j with label c
BDDnode n
    n.index := j · v + i
    if (i = v and j = b − 1)
        if (c < 0) n.low := 1
        else n.low := 0
        if (c + a_v < 0) n.high := 1
        else n.high := 0
    else if (i = v)
        if (c is even) n.low := node(1, j + 1, c/2)
        else n.low := node(1, j + 1, (c − 1)/2
        if (c + a_v is even) n.high := node(1, j + 1, (c + a_v)/2)
        else n.high = node(1, j + 1, (c + a_v − 1)/2)
    else
        n.low := node(i + 1, j, c)
        n.high = node(i + 1, j, c + a_v)
    return n

Main: return node(1, 0, −a_0)
```

Fig. 4. BDD construction algorithm for inequations

then level $j \cdot v + 2$ has at most $n_{2,j} = n_{1,j} + |a_1|$ nodes, level $j \cdot v + 3$ has at most $n_{3,j} = n_{1,j} + |a_1| + |a_2|$ nodes and so on. Finally level $j \cdot v + v + 1 = (j+1) \cdot v + 1$ has at most $n_{1,j+1} = (n_{1,j} + \sum_{i=1}^{v} |a_i|)/2$ nodes because that many are the different values of the carry that need to be stored, as described earlier. Initially $n_{1,0} = 1$ and by induction one can prove that no $n_{i,j}$ is larger than $2 \cdot \sum_{i=1}^{v} |a_i|$. There are $v \cdot b$ levels in the BDD so the total number of nodes is $O(v \cdot b \cdot \sum_{i=1}^{v} |a_i|)$, i.e. the size of the constructed BDD is linear on both v and b. Each node is created once if we store each of them in a hash table indexed by i, j and c and the creation of a node requires a fixed amount of work, so the complexity of our algorithm is $O(v \cdot b \cdot \sum_{i=1}^{v} |a_i|)$. Note that a tighter bound for the BDD size is $O(b \cdot \sum_{i=1}^{v} |a_i| \cdot (1 + v - i))$. Interestingly this indicates that the size of the BDD is minimized if the integer variables are ordered in increasing order of the absolute values of their coefficients.

3 Atomic Inequality Constraints

Next we show how to construct BDDs for inequations of the form $\sum_{i=1}^{v} a_i \cdot x_i < a_0$, $0 \le x_i < 2^b$. Note that we can transform all other kinds of linear inequations $(\le, >, \ge)$ to this form by changing the signs of the coefficients and/or adding 1 to the constant term a_0. The algorithm is similar to the one for equations and is

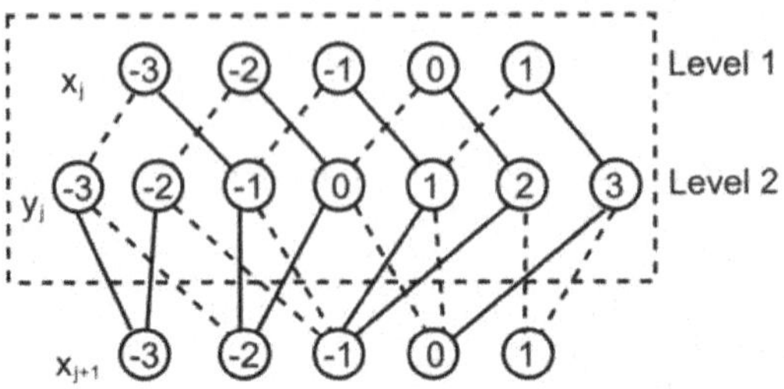

Fig. 5. Layer of a BDD for $2x - 3y < 1$

shown in Figure 4. There are only two differences. First, after having processed an equal number of bits from all integer variables (lines 9-13 of the algorithm) we do not require the resulting bit to be 0. The bit-serial processor only computes the correct value of the remaining carry and proceeds to the next level. Second, in order for the inequality to hold after all bits have been processed (lines 4-8 of the algorithm), the remaining carry has to be negative. Obviously, these two modifications do not change the bound on the number of nodes in the BDD, which is again $O(v \cdot b \cdot \sum_{i=1}^{v} |a_i|)$. This proves the following theorem.

Theorem 2. *The algorithm given in Figure 4 constructs a BDD representing the linear inequation $\sum_{i=1}^{v} a_i \cdot x_i < a_0$ on b-bit non-negative integer variables. The time complexity of the algorithm and the size of the resulting BDD is $O(v \cdot b \cdot \sum_{i=1}^{v} |a_i|)$.*

As an example consider the linear inequation $2x - 3y < 1$, where x and y are 4 bits long. Figures 5 and 6 show the structure of an intermediate layer and the complete BDD before being reduced.

4 Linear Arithmetic Formulas

In symbolic model checking BDDs are subjected to operations such as intersection, union, negation, etc. as well as subsumption and equivalence tests. The time and space complexity of these operations depends on the size of the operands. The complexity of negation is $O(1)$, as it involves only swapping the terminal nodes **0** and **1**, but the complexity of intersection and union which are very frequently used operations is $O(n_1 \cdot n_2)$, where n_1 and n_2 are the sizes of the operands. Suppose that one performs one of these operations on two BDDs representing the constraints $\sum_{i=1}^{v} a_i \cdot x_i = a_0$ and $\sum_{i=1}^{v} b_i \cdot x_i = b_0$ whose sizes are $O(v \cdot b \cdot \sum_{i=1}^{v} |a_i|)$ and $O(v \cdot b \cdot \sum_{i=1}^{v} |b_i|)$ respectively, as proved earlier. One would expect the size of the resulting BDD to be $O(v^2 \cdot b^2 \cdot \sum_{i=1}^{v} |a_i| \cdot \sum_{i=1}^{v} |b_i|)$. Actually this is a pessimistic estimation. The resulting BDD will have again $v \cdot b$ layers, corresponding to a bit-serial processor that examines each of the $x_{i,j}$s one by one as before. The only difference is that now it needs to remember the intermediate results from both BDDs and thus every layer will have $O(\sum_{i=1}^{v} |a_i| \cdot \sum_{i=1}^{v} |b_i|)$

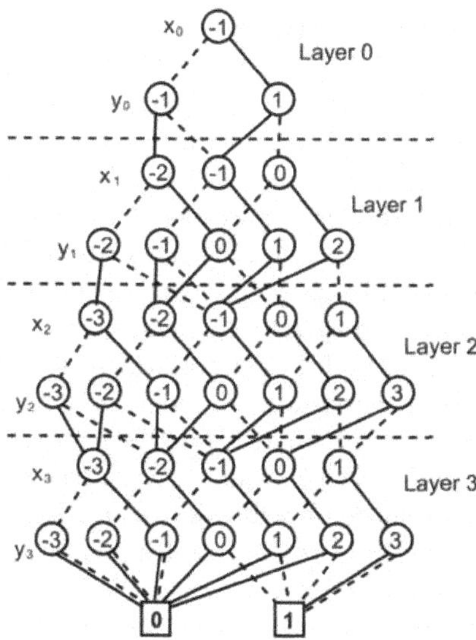

Fig. 6. BDD for $2x - 3y < 1$ for 4-bit variables

nodes and there will be $O(v \cdot b \cdot \sum_{i=1}^{v} |a_i| \cdot \sum_{i=1}^{v} |b_i|)$ nodes in total. Clearly the same argument holds for more than two linear constraints, which proves the following Theorem.

Theorem 3. *Given a linear arithmetic formula on b-bit non-negative integer variables consisting of n atomic constraints of the form* $\sum_{i=1}^{v} a_{i,j} \cdot x_i = a_{0,j}$, $1 \leq j \leq n$ *and boolean connectives* $\neg, \wedge, \vee$, *one can construct a BDD of size* $O(v \cdot b \cdot \prod_{j=1}^{n} \sum_{i=1}^{v} |a_{i,j}|)$ *representing the formula in time* $O(v \cdot b \cdot \prod_{j=1}^{n} \sum_{i=1}^{v} |a_{i,j}|)$.

The conclusion is that when basic operations are performed by a model checker on BDDs representing linear arithmetic constraints on bounded integers, the size of intermediate BDD representations remains linear on the number and size of the integer variables, i.e. the space and time complexity of operations does not blow up with respect to these two parameters. This is very important since such "blow ups" are a common drawback of BDD based model checking.

Note that since satisfiability checking for BDDs can be performed in constant time, one can decide the satisfiability of n linear constraints on v b-bit integer variables in time $O(v \cdot b \cdot \prod_{j=1}^{n} \sum_{i=1}^{v} |a_{i,j}|)$, using our construction algorithm. Hence, the complexity is linear in v and b, and only exponential in the number of atomic constraints n. This problem is NP-complete even if $b = 1$ [10], which implies that there is no algorithm which is polynomial in v, b and n, unless P=NP.

5 Handling Multiplication

An inherently unavoidable shortcoming of BDDs is their inability to efficiently represent arithmetic constraints involving multiplication between variables. In [3] it has been proven that the size of such BDDs has a lower bound exponential on b, the size of the integer variables, regardless of the variable ordering. The good news is that by choosing the variable ordering we defined earlier and by slightly modifying our construction algorithm one can accommodate multiplication and keep the size of the produced BDD exponential only in b and the number of integer variables involved in multiplications which is in many cases less than v, the total number of integer variables. The idea supporting this argument is the following. Suppose we want to construct a BDD for an arithmetic formula on $v = m + l$ integer variables, in which only m variables are multiplied with other variables in the formula (which we will call m-variables) and the rest l variables (which we will call l-variables) are only multiplied with constants, forming the "linear part" of the formula. In the worst case, the bit-serial processor equivalent of the BDD will need to remember the exact values of the m variables and the intermediate results c of the computation of the "linear part", as described earlier. The number of levels remains the same $v \cdot b$. At any level, when an m-variable is processed all nodes are doubled in the next level, thus remembering the new bit of the m-variable and the various cs are propagated properly. When an l-variable is processed, the processor behaves exactly as in the linear case. The number of nodes is doubled $m \cdot b$ times and consequently the size of the BDD will be $O(2^{m \cdot b} \cdot l \cdot b \cdot \sum_{i=1}^{v} |a_i|)$. Of course this is not an impressive result but nevertheless indicates a complexity that is exponentially dependent on m and not v. In many practical cases if m is non-zero it is at least much less than v. Note that by choosing a different variable ordering one can end up with BDDs of exponential size in both b and v.

6 Handling Overflows

When constructing BDDs to represent the transition relation of a system, special care is needed in order to handle possible overflows. For example consider a transition labeled by $x' = x + 1$, where x is the current state variable and x' is the next state variable. They are both 2-bit non-negative integers ranging between 0 and 3. When $x = 3$ and the transition is taken, what is an appropriate value of x in the next state, since it cannot be 4? We consider three alternatives:

1. The transition is not taken and the next state is empty.
2. Modular arithmetic is performed and $x = 0$ in the next state.
3. An "Out of bounds" error is detected and reported.

BDD construction for the transition relation depends on the choice of one of these three alternative approaches. For our example, an intermediate layer and the complete BDDs for all three approaches are shown in Figure 7. The construction algorithm described earlier follows the first approach. The difference between the

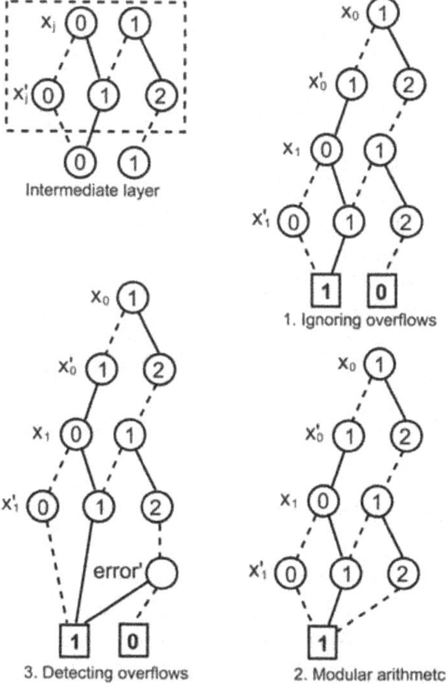

Fig. 7. Alternative ways to handle overflows

three approaches is in the edges generated by lines 6 and 8 of the construction algorithm, which correspond to the case where the b least significant bits of the variables (in our example $b = 2$) satisfy the equation but there is a remaining non-zero carry indicating an overflow. The first approach points all such edges to the **0** terminal node, thus making the BDD to evaluate to **0** whenever an overflow occurs. The second approach points all such edges to **1**, thus ignoring overflows and performing modular arithmetic. The third approach is a bit more involved. There is an extra global boolean variable *error* in the end of the variable ordering. All edges generated by lines 6 and 8 of the construction algorithm point to a node with the *index* of $error'$ and $low = \mathbf{0}$ and $high = \mathbf{1}$. Initially *error* is false. When an overflow occurs, *error* will become true in the next state. Note that for all three approaches Theorems 1, 2, and 3 still hold.

In all versions of SMV out-of-bounds errors are checked statically which means that even unreachable out-of-bound transitions are reported as out-of-bounds errors. By using alternative 3 presented above one can check if an out-of-bounds error is reachable and report an out-of-bounds error only when an out-of-bounds error occurs on some execution path. One can also implement the static out-of-bounds error check used in SMV by reporting a potential out-of-bounds error if a node with the *index* of the boolean variable $error'$ appears in the transition relation BDD.

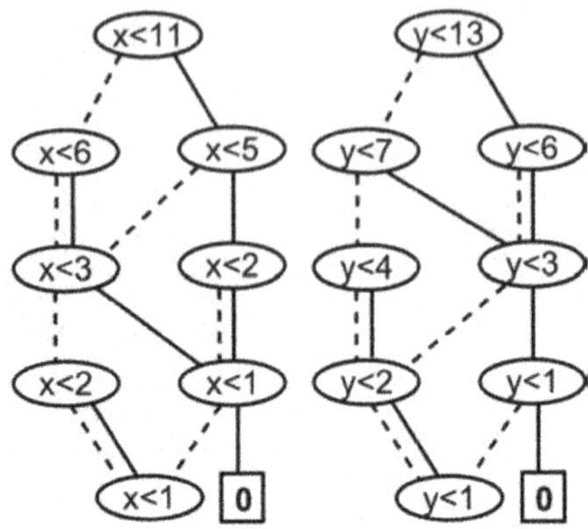

Fig. 8. Bounds information for $0 \leq x < 11$ and $0 \leq y < 13$

7 Handling Multiple Bounds on Variables

So far we have studied the construction of BDDs for linear arithmetic constraints on v integer variables $x_i, 1 \leq i \leq v$ such that $0 \leq x_i < 2^b$, i.e. all variables were non-negative and bounded by the same power of two. Now consider the case where each variable x_i has its own general bounds $l_i \leq x_i < h_i$, where l_i and h_i are (possibly negative) integer constants. As a first step we can eliminate the lower bounds by replacing every variable x_i in every constraint by the variable $X_i = x_i - l_i$. Now any constraint of the form $\sum_{i=1}^{v} a_i \cdot x_i \# a_0$, where $\# \in \{=, \neq, >, \geq, \leq, <\}$, becomes $\sum_{i=1}^{v} a_i \cdot X_i \# a_0 - \sum_{i=0}^{v} a_i \cdot l_i$ and $0 \leq X_i < h_i - l_i = d_i$. Now the lower bound of all variables is again 0 as it was initially but the upper bounds are different and not necessarily powers of two.

Here we will show how to construct BDDs for equations of the form $\sum_{i=1}^{v} a_i \cdot x_i = a_0$, where $0 \leq x_i < d_i$ for $1 \leq i \leq v$. The construction of BDDs for inequations is similar. Since there are extra constraints $0 \leq x_i < d_i$ that have to be satisfied in order for the BDD to evaluate to **1**, extra information has to be "stored" in the nodes: the valid range for the part of every variable that has not yet been processed. Since the lower bound for every variable is 0, only the upper bound needs to be stored. At the root node, the upper bound for each variable x_i is d_i. After the least significant bit $x_{i,0}$ of variable x_i has been processed, the upper bound for the rest of x_i (i.e. the value of x_i with the least significant bit removed) becomes $\lceil (d_i - x_{i,0})/2 \rceil$. In general, if the upper bound u for x_i at a node n in level i of layer j is d, then at $n.low$ $u = \lceil d/2 \rceil$ and at $n.high$ $u = \lceil (d-1)/2 \rceil$. As an example, consider the equation $2x - 3y = 1$, where $0 \leq x < 11$ and $0 \leq y < 13$. Figure 8 shows the bounds information for x and y as described earlier. Figure 9 shows the complete BDD for the equation.

We can prove that at any level there are at most two different upper bounds, which differ by one, for each variable. Initially, there is only one bound for each variable. If at some level the two different upper bounds for a variable are d and $d+1$, then in the next layer those bounds will become $\lceil (d-1)/2 \rceil$

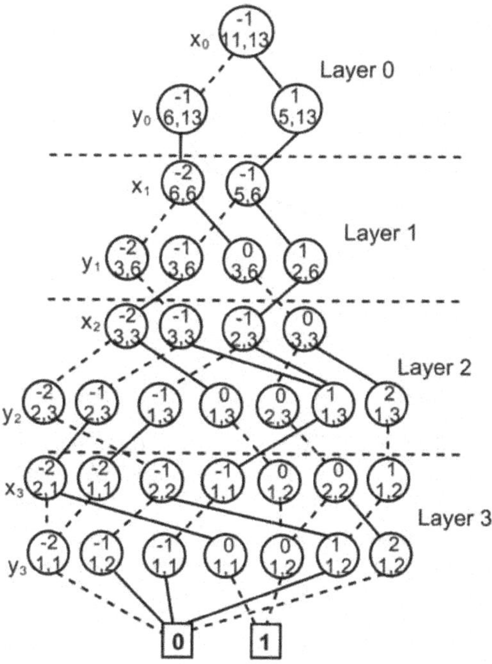

Fig. 9. BDD for $2x - 3y = 1$ when $0 \leq x < 11$ and $0 \leq y < 13$

and $\lceil (d+1)/2 \rceil$. In general, there can be at most 2^v different combinations of bounds for all v variables at any level. The maximum number of layers is $\log_2(\max(d_i))$. Consequently, the size of the BDD representing the equation is $O(v \cdot \log_2(\max(d_i)) \cdot 2^v \cdot \sum_{i=1}^{v} |a_i|)$, which is exponential in the number of variables v. Remember that when the upper bounds are powers of two 2^b the size of the BDD is only $O(v \cdot b \cdot \sum_{i=1}^{v} |a_i|)$. Interestingly, this indicates that when modeling a system and the choice of bounds for the integer variables is independent of the input specification, it is better to choose bounds that are powers of two.

8 Experimental Results

We integrated our construction algorithms to Composite Symbolic Library and Action Language Verifier [6,13]. Action Language Verifier is an infinite state CTL model checker and it uses Composite Symbolic Library as its symbolic manipulator. We created a new version of the Action Language Verifier (ALV) by using BDDs as symbolic representations for bounded integers and integrating our BDD construction algorithms for linear arithmetic constraints.

We experimented with two specification examples, `Bakery` and `Barber`, available at: http://www.cs.ucsb.edu/~bultan/composite/. `Bakery` is a mutual exclusion protocol for 2 processes. `Barber` is a monitor specification for the Sleeping

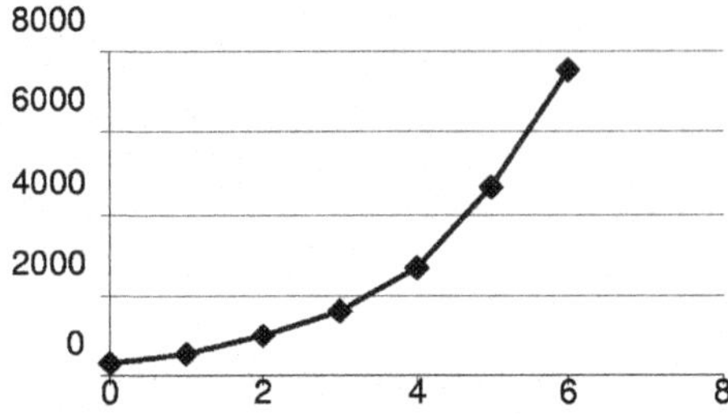

Fig. 10. Size of the BDD for $x_1 + x_2 - x_3 - x_4 + x_5 - x_6 = 7$ versus the number of variables with upper bound different than 2^8

Table 1. Bakery

bits	CMU SMV	Cadence SMV	NuSMV	ALV
4	0.04	0.17	0.07	0.17
5	0.23	0.27	0.26	0.17
6	1.27	0.5	1.71	0.17
7	9.37	1.39	20.52	0.18
8	78.87	6.12	142.82	0.18
9	673.11	21.67	1186.45	0.18
10	↑	84.1	↑	0.19
11	↑	329.93	↑	0.19
12	↑	1503.83	↑	0.19
100	↑	↑	↑	0.31

Table 2. Barber

bits	CMU SMV	Cadence SMV	NuSMV	ALV
4	0.15	0.36	0.3	0.23
5	0.46	0.86	1.09	0.25
6	2.03	2.97	13.47	0.29
7	14.14	10.42	1185.92	0.3
8	274.89	38.29	↑	0.35
9	↑	157.58	↑	0.39
10	↑	721.25	↑	0.42
11	↑	↑	↑	0.44
12	↑	↑	↑	0.48
100	↑	↑	↑	5.12

Barber problem from [2]. We also verified three specification examples, **abp**, **p-queue** and **prod-cons**, included in the NuSMV distribution. Example **abp** is an alternating bit protocol, and **p-queue** and **prod-cons** are two different implementations of a buffer where data is inserted, sorted and consumed. We were able to verify safety and liveness properties for these examples. We run these experiments using three different implementations of the SMV, namely CMU SMV (version 2.5.4.3), Cadence SMV (version 08-20-01p2) and NuSMV (version 2). We obtained the experimental results on a SUN ULTRA 10 work station with 768 Mbytes of memory, running SunOs 5.7.

We measured the time required to verify each of the examples for different sizes of the integer variables from 4 bits to 100 bits. The results are shown in Tables 1-5. Entries ↑ signify that the according experiment did not finish in 4000 seconds. It is clear that for all current implementations of SMV, the recorded times are exponential in the size of the integer variables, while for ALV which uses the construction algorithms presented earlier, the recorded times are linear in the size of the integer variables. Note that ALV is not a BDD based model checker, hence SMV may be better optimized for BDD based verification. However, our point is that the advantages of our construction algorithms can be exploited by integrating them to any BDD based model checker.

Table 3. Alternating Bit Protocol. The property checked is independent of the integer data field. Since Cadence SMV can detect and verify data independent properties efficiently, we also verified a data dependent property. The verification time for the data dependent property stays almost the same for the Action Language Verifier.

bits	CMU SMV	Cadence SMV		NuSMV	ALV	
		data independent	data dependent		data independent	data dependent
4	0.12	0.21	3.91	2.69	0.23	0.24
5	0.26	0.2	7.56	2.71	0.23	0.25
6	1.26	0.23	24.11	2.63	0.24	0.24
7	30.24	0.18	84.33	3.05	0.23	0.26
8	147.96	0.19	343.47	3.61	0.23	0.24
9	693.67	0.2	↑	6.6	0.25	0.26
10	3755.46	0.24	↑	24.12	0.23	0.27
11	↑	0.27	↑	87.62	0.27	0.27
12	↑	0.36	↑	342.89	0.24	0.27
100	↑	↑	↑	↑	0.69	0.72

Table 4. Queue

bits	CMU SMV	Cadence SMV	NuSMV	ALV
4	0.3	0.57	0.33	3.21
5	1.75	1.23	1.21	5.63
6	24.47	5.37	12.07	8.14
7	2159.69	38.8	122.3	10.77
8	↑	318.39	1125.34	13.06
100	↑	↑	↑	440.87

Table 5. Producer – Consumer

bits	CMU SMV	Cadence SMV	NuSMV	ALV
2	5.49	4.61	23.27	210.44
3	216.94	73.98	3264.97	698.93
4	↑	1430.54	↑	2600
5	↑	↑	↑	6062.34

Finally, Figure 10 illustrates the effect of arbitrary bounds on variables as described in Section 7. We used our construction algorithm to build a BDD for the equation $x_1+x_2-x_3-x_4+x_5-x_6=7$, where $0 \le x_1, x_2, x_3, x_4, x_5, x_6 < 2^8$ and recorded the size of the resulting reduced BDD. Then we gradually changed the upper bound of each of the variables to some arbitrary unique value less than 2^8 and recorded the size of the resulting reduced BDD each time. The results shown in Figure 10 demonstrate the exponential growth of the size of the BDD described in Section 7.

9 Conclusions

In this paper we have shown experimentally that current implementations of BDD based symbolic model checkers are inefficient in representing linear arithmetic constraints on bounded integer variables. We solved this problem by giving efficient BDD construction algorithms, proving their complexity and experimentally demonstrating their efficiency. These algorithms can be used to improve the performance of existing BDD based symbolic model checkers. Finally, we have shown that powers of 2 are a good choice for variable bounds, and choosing arbitrary bounds for integer variables can cause exponential blow-up in the BDD size.

References

1. Cadence SMV. `http://www-cad.eecs.berkeley.edu/~kenmcmil/smv`.
2. G. R. Andrews. *Concurrent Programming: Principles and Practice.* The Benjamin/Cummings Publishing Company, Redwood City, California, 1991.
3. R. Bryant. Graph-based algorithms for boolean function manipulation. In *Proceedings of the 27th ACM/IEEE Design Automation Conference*, 1990.
4. R.E Bryant and Y.A. Chen. Verification of arithmetic functions with binary moment diagrams. In *Proceedings of the 32nd ACM/IEEE Design Automation Conference*, June 1995.
5. T. Bultan, R. Gerber, and C. League. Composite model checking: Verification with type-specific symbolic representations. *ACM Transactions on Software Engineering and Methodology*, 9(1):3–50, January 2000.
6. T. Bultan and T. Yavuz-Kahveci. Action language verifier. In *Proceedings of the 16th IEEE International Conference on Automated Software Engineering*, 2001.
7. W. Chan, R. J. Anderson, P. Beame, S. Burns, F. Modugno, D. Notkin, and J. D. Reese. Model checking large software specifications. *IEEE Transactions on Software Engineering*, 24(7):498–520, July 1998.
8. A. Cimatti, E.M. Clarke, E.Giunchiglia, F. Giunchiglia, M. Pistore, M. Roveri, R. Sebastiani, and A. Tacchella. Nusmv 2: An opensource tool for symbolic model checking. In *Proceedings of the International Conference on Computer-Aided Verification*, 2002.
9. E.M. Clarke, M. Fujita, and X. Zhao. Hybrid decision diagrams – overcoming the limitations of mtbdds and bmds. In *In International Conference of Computer-Aided Design*, pages 159–163, 2000.
10. M. Garey and D.Jonson. *Computers and Intractability: A Guide to the Theory of NP-completeness.* Freeman, 1979.
11. K. L. McMillan. *Symbolic model checking.* Kluwer Academic Publishers, Massachusetts, 1993.
12. J. Yang, A. K. Mok, and F. Wang. Symbolic model checking for event-driven real-time systems. *ACM Transactions on Programming Languages and Systems*, 19(2):386–412, March 1997.
13. T. Yavuz-Kahveci, M. Tuncer, and T. Bultan. Composite symbolic library. In *Proceedings of the 7th International Conference on Tools and Algorithms for the Construction and Analysis of Systems*, volume 2031 of *Lecture Notes in Computer Science*, pages 335–344. Springer-Verlag, April 2001.

Modeling and Analysis of Power-Aware Systems*

Oleg Sokolsky[1], Anna Philippou[2], Insup Lee[1], and Kyriakos Christou[1]

[1] University of Pennsylvania, USA. {sokolsky,lee,christou}@cis.upenn.edu
[2] University of Cyprus, Cyprus. annap@ucy.ac.cy

Abstract. The paper describes a formal approach for designing and reasoning about power-constrained, timed systems. The framework is based on *process algebra*, a formalism that has been developed to describe and analyze communicating concurrent systems. The proposed extension allows the modeling of probabilistic resource failures, priorities of resource usages, and power consumption by resources within the same formalism. Thus, it is possible to model alternative power-consumption behaviors and analyze tradeoffs in their timing and other characteristics. This paper describes the modeling and analysis techniques, and illustrates them with examples, including a dynamic voltage-scaling algorithm.

1 Introduction

In recent years, great technological advances in wireless communication and mobile computing have given rise to sophisticated embedded devices (e.g., PDA, cell phones, smart sensors) and wireless network infrastructures that are becoming widespreadly available. In addition, new applications with powerful functionalities are being developed to meet the ever-increasing demand by the users. A serious limitation of the mobile embedded devices is the battery life available to them. Although a great deal of power-intensive computation has to be performed to carry out application-specific functionalities such as video streaming, this has to be done on a limited amount of power. To cope with this fact, a number of power-aware algorithms and protocols have been proposed aiming to make energy savings by dynamically altering the power consumed by a processor while still achieving the required behavior. However, in time-constrained applications often found in embedded systems, applying power-saving techniques can lead to serious problems. This is because changing the power available to tasks can affect their execution time which may lead to violation of timing constraints and other undesirable properties. A challenge presented by such systems is the development of algorithms that incorporate power-saving techniques and task management without sacrificing timing and performance guarantees, see e.g. [14].

The main purpose of this paper is to present a unified formal framework and associated toolset for designing and reasoning about power-constrained, timed

* This research was supported in part by NSF CCR-9988409, NSF CCR-0086147, NSF CCR-0209024, ARO DAAD19-01-1-0473, and by the EU Future and Emerging Technologies programme IST-1999-14186 (ALCOM-FT).

H. Garavel and J. Hatcliff (Eds.): TACAS 2003, LNCS 2619, pp. 409–424, 2003.

systems. The framework we propose is based on *process algebra*, a formalism which has been developed to describe and analyze communicating, concurrent systems. The most salient aspect of process algebras is that they support the *modular* specification and verification of systems. Process algebras are being used widely in specifying and verifying concurrent systems and they have been extended to account for time and probabilistic behavior.

The formal framework we propose is based on the process algebra P^{2}ACSR which extends our previous work on formal methods for real-time [10] and probabilistic systems [13] by incorporating the ability of reasoning about power consumption. The Algebra of Communicating Shared Resources (ACSR) [10] is a timed process algebra which represents a real-time system as a collection of concurrent processes. Each process can engage in two kinds of activities: communication with other processes by means of instantaneous *events* and computation by means of timed *actions*. Executing an action requires access to a set of resources and takes a non-zero amount of time measured by an implicit global clock. The notion of a resource, which is already important in the specification of real-time systems, additionally provides a convenient abstraction for a variety of aspects of systems behavior. One such aspect is the failure of physical devices: in a probabilistic extension of ACSR, PACSR [13], resources are extended with the ability to fail, and are associated with a probability of failure. In P^{2}ACSR, the resource model of PACSR is further extended to reason about power consumption. Resources in P^{2}ACSR specifications are accompanied with information about the power consumption of each resource use. Thus, we can compute the power consumed by system executions requiring access to a set of power-consuming resources. We provide an operational semantics of P^{2}ACSR via *labeled concurrent Markov chains* [17], which are transition systems containing both probabilistic and nondeterministic behavior. Probabilistic behavior is present in the model due to resource failure and nondeterministic behavior due to the fact that P^{2}ACSR specifications typically consist of several parallel processes producing events concurrently.

We are interested in being able to specify and verify high-level requirements of P^{2}ACSR specifications, and, in particular, to study their power-consumption behavior and tradeoffs in their timing and other characteristics. To do this we extend model-checking analysis techniques to allow reasoning about power consumption properties. First, we present a probabilistic, power-aware temporal logic for expressing properties of P^{2}ACSR expressions by associating power-consumption constraints with temporal operators. Second, the analysis technique allows us to compute bounds on power consumption in executions of the model. We present model-checking algorithms both for the logic and for bound computations. In order to allow the automatic analysis of P^{2}ACSR specifications, we have extended the PARAGON toolset [16], which previously allowed the specification and analysis of ACSR and PACSR processes, to accept P^{2}ACSR specifications and construct the probabilistic transition systems emanating from them, and we have augmented the toolset with the model-checking algorithms both for the logic and for the bounds computations.

We illustrate the usefulness of the proposed formalism using a dynamic voltage-scaling algorithm for real-time, power-aware systems [14]. In this example, we use resources to model the power-consuming processing unit which can be used at different power levels with different execution speeds. We model the probabilistic nature of task execution time in the system by employing probabilistic resources. The expected savings in power consumption that the algorithm offers were computed automatically using the PARAGON toolset extension.

Related work. This work extends our earlier work on probabilistic process algebra PACSR [13]. Similar approaches process models have been considered by [8] and [15]. Similar logics and model checking approaches were presented in [15] and [8]. Extensions made in this work allow us to reason quantitatively about power consumption using resource attributes as rewards. Much work on reward-based modeling and analysis has been done in the context of performance modeling using the formalisms of stochastic process algebras [2] and continuous-time Markov chains [1]. The approach taken in this paper uses discrete time and yields coarser but easier to analyze models. A difference in the modeling approach, compared to all these papers, is that we use resource attributes to capture probabilistic aspects of behavior as well as rewards, which offers us a flexible and easily extensible framework.

The rest of the paper is organized as follows: the next section present the P^2ACSR syntax and semantics. Section 3 describes analysis techniques for P^2ACSR processes, and Section 4 presents the case study in which a power-aware real-time scheduling algorithm is modeled and analyzed. We conclude with some final remarks and discussion of future work.

2 The General Framework

We assume that a system contains a finite set of serially reusable resources drawn from a countable infinite set of resources $\mathcal{R}$ and we let r range over $\mathcal{R}$. Resources correspond to physical entities, such as processor units and communication channels, or to abstract notions such as message arrival. They can have a set of numerical attributes that let us capture quantitative aspects of resource-constrained computations. We use three resource attributes. One attribute captures the probability of resource failure, which remains constant for each resource throughout a system specification. The other two attributes may change with each resource use and represent access priority and power consumption.

Probabilistic resource failures. We associate with each resource a probability [13]. This probability captures the rate at which the resource may fail. A failure may correspond to either a physical failure, such as a processor failure, or a failure of some abstract condition, for example no message arrival when one was expected. We assume that in each execution step, resources fail independently. To capture the notion of a failed resource we also consider the set $\overline{\mathcal{R}}$ that contains, for each $r \in \mathcal{R}$, its dual element $\overline{r}$, representing the *failed* resource r. For each $r \in \mathcal{R}$, we use $\pi(r) \in [0, 1]$ to denote the probability of resource r being

up in a given step, while $\pi(\overline{r}) = 1 - \pi(r)$ is the probability of r failing in a given step. Failed resources are useful when we need to model recovery from failures.
Resources and power consumption. In order to reason about power consumption in distributed settings, the set of resources $\mathcal{R}$ is partitioned into a finite set of disjoint classes $\mathcal{R}_i$, for some index set I. Intuitively, each $\mathcal{R}_i$ corresponds to a distinct power source which can provide a limited amount of power at any given time. This limit is denoted by c_i. Each resource $r \in \mathcal{R}_i$ consumes a certain amount of power from the source $\mathcal{R}_i$. As we will see below, the rate of power consumption is specified in *timed actions*.

2.1 The Syntax

As PACSR, P^{2}ACSR has three types of actions: instantaneous events, timed actions, and probabilistic actions. We discuss these three concepts below.
Instantaneous events. Instantaneous actions are called *events*, and provide the basic synchronization primitives in the process algebra. An event is denoted as a pair (a, p), where a is the label of the event and p, a natural number, is the priority of the event. Labels are drawn from the set $\mathsf{L} = \mathcal{L} \cup \overline{\mathcal{L}} \cup \{\tau\}$, where if $a \in \mathcal{L}$, $\overline{a} \in \overline{\mathcal{L}}$ is its *inverse* label. The special label τ, also called the silent action, arises when two events with inverse labels are executed concurrently. Thus, events are similar to actions in CCS, with the distinction that here we also impose priorities. We use $\mathcal{D}_E$ to denote the set of events.
Timed actions. A timed action consists of several resources, each resource being used at some priority and at some level of power consumption, and consumes one unit of time. Formally, an action is a finite set of triples of the form (r, p, c), where r is a resource, p is the priority of the resource usage and c is the rate of power consumption, with the restriction that each resource is represented at most once.

An example of an action is given by $\{(cpu, 2, 3),(msg, 1, 0)\}$. This action takes one unit of time and uses resource *cpu* representing a processor unit, at priority level two, consuming three units of power. This action also assumes that the processor receives a message, represented by resource msg. The fact that the processor may fail or that the message may or may not arrive is modeled by assigning probabilities of failures to resources *cpu* and msg. The action takes place only if none of the resources *cpu* and msg fail. On the other hand, action $\{(cpu, 2, 3), (\overline{msg}, 1, 0)\}$ takes place when resource msg fails and resource *cpu* does not. Such an action may be used to describe the behavior of the processor when it does not receive a message. The action $\emptyset$ represents idling for one unit of time, since no resource is consumed. We denote the set of resources used in an action A as $\rho(A)$. We use $\mathcal{D}_R$ to denote the set of actions.
Probabilistic transitions. As already mentioned resources are associated with a probability of failure. Thus, the behavior of a resource-consuming system has certain probabilistic aspects to it. Consider the action $\{(cpu, 2, 3), (msg, 1, 0)\}$, where resources *cpu* and msg have probabilities of failure 0 and 1/3, respectively, that is $\pi(cpu) = 1$ and $\pi(msg) = 2/3$. This action takes place with probability $\pi(cpu) \cdot \pi(msg) = 2/3$ and fails with probability 1/3.

Processes. We let P, Q range over processes and we assume a set of process constants, each with an associated definition of the kind $X \stackrel{\text{def}}{=} P$. We write Proc for the set of P^{2}ACSR processes. The following grammar describes the syntax of P^{2}ACSR processes. We present only those operators that are used in the examples in the paper. The complete set of operators can be found in [11].

$$P ::= \text{NIL} \mid (a,n).P \mid A{:}P \mid b \rightarrow P \mid P + P \mid P \| P \mid P\backslash F \mid X$$

Process NIL represents the inactive process. There are two prefix operators, corresponding to the two types of actions. The first, $(a,n).P$, executes the instantaneous event (a,n) and proceeds to P. When it is not relevant for the discussion we omit the priority of an event in a process and simply write $a.P$. The second, $A : P$, executes a resource-consuming action A during the first time unit and proceeds to P. An action can take place if none of the resources used by it fail and also if it does not violate the power constraints of the system. Otherwise, $A : P$ cannot execute the action and behaves as NIL. As a shorthand notation, we will write $A^n : P$ for a process that performs n consecutive actions A and then behaves as P. Process $b \rightarrow P$ behaves as P if condition b is true, otherwise it behaves as NIL. Process $P + Q$ represents a nondeterministic choice between the two summands. Process $P \| Q$ describes the concurrent composition of P and Q: the component processes may proceed independently or interact with one another while executing events, and they synchronize on timed actions. In $P\backslash F$, where $F \subseteq L$, the scope of labels in F is restricted to process P; that is, components of P may use these labels to interact with one another but not with P's environment.

As an example of a process, consider the process

$$P \stackrel{\text{def}}{=} \{(cpu,2,3),(msg,1,0)\} : P_1 + \{(cpu,2,2),(\overline{msg},1,0)\} : P_2 \ .$$

Process P represents a processor that can accept messages from a channel. Depending on whether the message arrives or not, P has two alternative behaviors. If the message arrives, that is, resource msg is up, P processor receives the message, consuming 3 units of power, and proceeds to process it as P_1. Otherwise, $\overline{msg}$ is up, P consumes only 2 units of power and continues as P_2.

As a syntactic convenience, we allow P^{2}ACSR processes to be parameterized by a set of index variables, allowing us to represent collections of similar processes concisely. Each index variable is given a fixed range of values. For example, the parameterized process $P_t \stackrel{\text{def}}{=} t < 2 \rightarrow (a_t, p_t).P_{t+1}, \quad t \in \{0..2\}$ is equivalent to the following three processes: $P_0 \stackrel{\text{def}}{=} (a_0,p_0).P_1, \quad P_1 \stackrel{\text{def}}{=} (a_1,p_1).P_2, \quad P_2 \stackrel{\text{def}}{=} \text{NIL}$.

2.2 Operational Semantics

In this section we give an informal account of the operational semantics for P^{2}ACSR. The detailed account can be found in [11] and is an extension of the PACSR semantics presented in [13]. The behavior of a P^{2}ACSR process depends on the status of the resources it requires during its first time step. For example, the process P in the previous section, will evolve depending of whether the processor is available or failed and whether or not a message arrives. In order to capture this relation between process behavior and resource status we introduce the notion of a *world*. A *world* is a set of resources W such that it cannot contain both a resource and its failed counterpart. When $r \in W$, r is known to be available, when $\overline{r} \in W$, r is known to be failed. Then, we introduce the notion of a *configuration* as a pair of the form $(P, W) \in \mathsf{Proc} \times 2^{\mathsf{R}}$, representing a P^{2}ACSR process P in world W. We write S for the set of all configurations. Further, given world W we write $\mathcal{W}(W)$ for the set of worlds that give status to the same resources as W, and $\pi(W)$ is the probability of the world, given by the product of $\pi(r), r \in W$.

The intuition for the semantics is as follows: for a process P, we begin with the configuration $(P, \emptyset)$. As computation proceeds two types of transitions may be performed: (1) for any configuration (P, W) where the world W does not contain information regarding the status of *all* of P's immediately relevant resources, probabilistic transitions are taken to a number of new configurations each of which spells out a possible world of these resources. Such configurations are called probabilistic and denoted S_p. Otherwise, (2) for all configurations holding all necessary information about the status of resources, nondeterministic transitions (which can involve events or actions) are taken. Such configurations are called nondeterministic and denoted S_n. The set of immediately relevant resources, denoted $\mathsf{imr}(P)$, is defined inductively on the structure of the process. Intuitively, immediately relevant resources are contributed by the timed actions that may be taken by the process in the first step and also resources added by the resource closure operator. After the status of a resource is determined by a probabilistic transition, it cannot change until the next timed action occurs. Once a timed action occurs, the state of resources has to be determined anew, since in each time unit resources can fail independently from any previous failures.

Thus the semantics is given in terms of a labeled transition system whose states are configurations and whose transitions are either probabilistic or nondeterministic. Each probabilistic transition originates from configurations in S_p and leads to a configuration in S_n. Probabilistic transitions are labeled with the probability of reaching a new world with the updated resource status. The rule for the probabilistic transition relation describes the manipulation of the worlds as a result of the transition.

As an example, consider the process $P \stackrel{\text{def}}{=} \{(r_1, 2, 1), (r_2, 2, 2)\} : P_1 + (e, 1).P_2$ in the initial configuration $(P, \emptyset)$. The immediate resources of P are $\{r_1, r_2\}$. Since there is no knowledge in the configuration's world regarding these resources, the configuration belongs to the set of probabilistic configurations S_p, from where we have four probabilistic transitions that determine the status of r_1 and r_2:

$$(P, \emptyset) \stackrel{\pi(r_1)\cdot\pi(r_2)}{\longrightarrow_p} (P, \{r_1, r_2\}), (P, \emptyset) \stackrel{\pi(r_1)\cdot\pi(\overline{r_2})}{\longrightarrow_p} (P, \{r_1, \overline{r_2}\}),$$
$$(P, \emptyset) \stackrel{\pi(\overline{r_1})\cdot\pi(r_2)}{\longrightarrow_p} (P, \{\overline{r_1}, r_2\}), (P, \emptyset) \stackrel{\pi(\overline{r_1})\cdot\pi(\overline{r_2})}{\longrightarrow_p} (P, \{\overline{r_1}, \overline{r_2}\}).$$

All of the resulting configurations are nondeterministic since they contain full information about P's immediate resources.

Nondeterministic transitions are labeled with either an event or a timed action. The rules for nondeterministic transitions are, for the most part, the same as for PACSR and can be found in [13]. The difference comes in the side conditions in the rules for action prefix and parallel composition. An action can take place if it does not violate the power consumption constraints. The predicate $\mathsf{valid}(A) = \bigwedge_{i \in I}(\sum_{r \in \mathcal{R}_i} \mathsf{pc}_r(A) \leq c_i)$ captures this requirement. The action prefix rule requires that the action appearing in the action prefix be valid. The rule for parallel composition requires that processes in a parallel composition need to synchronize on a timed action, that is, a process advances only if both of its subprocesses can take action steps labeled by actions A_1 and A_2 that use disjoint resources, and the resulting action $A_1 \cup A_2$ is valid.

In the example, the nondeterministic configuration $(P, \{r_1, r_2\})$, where $P \stackrel{\text{def}}{=} \{(r_1, 2, 1), (r_2, 2, 2)\} : P_1 + (e, 1).P_2$ has two nondeterministic transitions:

$$(P, \{r_1, r_2\}) \stackrel{\{(r_1,2,1),(r_2,2,2)\}}{\longrightarrow} (P_1, \emptyset) \qquad \text{and} \qquad (P, \{r_1, r_2\}) \stackrel{e}{\longrightarrow} (P_2, \{r_1, r_2\}).$$

The other configurations, $(P, \{r_1, \overline{r_2}\})$, $(P, \{\overline{r_1}, r_2\})$, and $(P, \{\overline{r_1}, \overline{r_2}\})$, allow only the e-labeled transition since either r_1 or r_2 is failed and the action cannot occur.

The prioritized transition system for P^{2}ACSR is based on the notion of *preemption* and refines the unprioritized transition relation $\longrightarrow$ by taking priorities into account. It is given by the pair of transition relations $\longrightarrow_p$ and $\longrightarrow_n$, the latter of which is defined below. The preemption relation $\prec$ on *Act* is defined as for ACSR, specifying when two actions are comparable with respect to priorities. For example, $\emptyset \prec A$ for all actions A, that is, the idle action $\emptyset$ is preempted by all other timed actions, and $(a, p) \prec (a, p')$, whenever $p < p'$. For the precise definition of $\prec$ we refer to [10]. The basic idea behind $\longrightarrow_n$ is that a nondeterministic transition of the form $(P, W) \stackrel{\alpha}{\longrightarrow} (P', W')$ is included in $\longrightarrow_n$ if and only if there are no higher-priority transitions enabled in (P, W). Thus, the prioritized nondeterministic transition system is obtained from the unprioritized one by pruning away preemptable transitions.

3 Analysis

In this section we discuss possible analysis that can be performed on P^{2}ACSR specifications. We begin by presenting the formal model underlying P^{2}ACSR processes which is that of *labeled concurrent Markov chains* [17].

Definition 1. A *labeled concurrent Markov chain* (LCMC) is a tuple $\langle S_n, S_p, Act, \longrightarrow_n, \longrightarrow_p, s_0 \rangle$, where S_n is the set of nondeterministic states, S_p is the set of probabilistic states, *Act* is the set of labels, $\longrightarrow_n \subset S_n \times Act \times (S_n \cup S_p)$ is the nondeterministic transition relation, $\longrightarrow_p \subset S_p \times [0,1] \times S_n$ is the probabilistic transition relation, satisfying $\Sigma_{(s,\pi,t) \in \longrightarrow_p} \pi = 1$ for all $s \in S_p$, and $s_0 \in S_n \cup S_p$ is the initial state. □

We may see that the operational semantics of P^{2}ACSR yields transition systems that are LCMCs with $Act = \mathcal{D}_E \cup \mathcal{D}_R$, and the sets S_n, S_p are the sets of nondeterministic and probabilistic configurations, respectively. In what follows, we let ℓ range over $Act \cup [0,1]$.

A *computation* in $T = \langle S_n, S_p, Act, \longrightarrow_n, \longrightarrow_p, s_0 \rangle$ is either a finite sequence $c = s_0\,\ell_1\,s_1 \ldots \ell_k\,s_k$, where s_k has no transitions, or an infinite sequence $c = s_0\,\ell_1\,s_1 \ldots \ell_k\,s_k \ldots$, such that $s_i \in S_n \cup S_p$, $\ell_{i+1} \in Act \cup [0,1]$ and $(s_i, \ell_{i+1}, s_{i+1}) \in \longrightarrow_p \cup \longrightarrow_n$, for all $0 \leq i$. We denote by $\mathsf{comp}(T)$ the set of all computations of T and by $\mathsf{Pcomp}(T)$ the set of all partial computations of T, that is the set of initial subsegments of computations of T.

To define probability measures on computations of an LCMC the nondeterminism present must be resolved. To achieve this, the notion of a *scheduler* has been employed [17,8]. A scheduler σ is an entity that, given a partial computation ending in a nondeterministic state, chooses the next transition to be executed. This gives rise to computation trees that can be viewed as labeled Markov chains. Each path through a computation tree is a *scheduled computation* of the LCMC and can be assigned a probability by taking a product of the probabilistic labels along the path. See [11] for the details.

3.1 Model Checking for P^{2}ACSR

The first technique we propose for analyzing P^{2}ACSR specifications is that of model-checking. Model checking is a verification technique aimed at determining whether a system specification satisfies a property typically expressed as a temporal logic formula. To allow model checking on P^{2}ACSR specifications, in this section we introduce a probabilistic temporal logic that allows one to associate power consumption constraints with fragments of behaviors. Behavioral fragments of interest are expressed in terms of regular expressions over *Act*, the set of observable actions. The associated model-checking algorithm, also presented in this section, is used to check whether these constraints are satisfied and thus whether formulae of the logic are satisfied by system specifications.

Our logic for P^{2}ACSR is an extension of the logic of [13], which, in turn, is based on the Hennessy-Milner Logic (HML) with *until* [7]. The extension established allows for quantitative analysis of power consumption properties of a system by associating a condition with the *until* operator. The condition takes a form such as $\leq pc$ or $\geq pc$ for a constant pc. In this way we can express a property that an execution, timed or untimed, satisfies a power consumption constraint, with a certain probability (which may be equal to one). We also include a second construct that allows a similar type of reasoning but specifying the power sources for which analysis is to be performed.

Definition 2. *(Power-aware PHML with until)* The syntax of $\mathcal{L}^{pc}_{PHMLu}$ is defined by the following grammar, where f, f', range over $\mathcal{L}^{pc}_{PHMLu}$-formulae, Φ is a regular expression over *Act*, R is a subset of the set of resources $\mathcal{R}$, p a number in $[0,1]$ representing a probability, t a number representing a time limit, pc a number representing a power consumption, and $\bowtie \in \{\leq, <, \geq, >\}$:

$$f \;::=\; tt \;\mid\; \neg f \;\mid\; f \wedge f' \;\mid\; f\langle\Phi\rangle^{\bowtie' pc}_{\bowtie p} f' \;\mid\; f\langle\Phi\rangle^{\bowtie' pc}_{\bowtie p,t} f' \;\mid\; f\langle\Phi\rangle^{\bowtie' pc,R}_{\bowtie p} f' \;\mid\; f\langle\Phi\rangle^{\bowtie' pc,R}_{\bowtie p,t} f'. \;\Box$$

$\mathcal{L}^{pc}_{PHMLu}$-formulae are interpreted over states of LCMCs. Informally, formulae of the form $f\langle\Phi\rangle f'$ state that there is some execution and some integer l such that f holds for the first $l-1$ steps and f' becomes true in the l-th step and the observable behavior of the l-step execution involves some behavior from Φ. The subscript $\bowtie p$ denotes that the probability of paths fulfilling the formula is $\bowtie p$ and the use of subscript t denotes that the paths of interest are only those that achieve the goal in at most t time units. Finally, the superscript $\bowtie' pc$ requires paths to use $\bowtie' pc$ units of power, and the use of R, restricts power consumption calculations to the set of resources R. For instance, formula $tt\langle Act^*\rangle^{\leq pc}_{\geq 1} f$ expresses that there is some execution of the system for which eventually f becomes true, with probability 1, without consuming more than pc units of power. Similarly, $\neg(tt\langle Act^*\rangle^{\geq pc}_{>0} tt)$, specifies that the power consumption never exceeds the threshold of pc units, whereas $\neg(tt\langle Act^*\rangle^{\geq pc,\{cpu\}}_{>0} tt)$, specifies that the power consumption of resource cpu never exceeds the threshold of pc units.

In order to present the semantics of the four until operators, we need to compute the probabilities that certain behaviors occur. Consider now the formula $f\langle\Phi\rangle^{\leq pc,R}_{\bowtie p,t} f'$. Given two sets of states A, B of an LCMC T and a sequence of actions $\Phi \subseteq Act^*$, we consider following set of partial computations of T. The computations lead to a state in B via Φ, with intermediate states in A, and take less than time t and consume no more than pc units of power on resources in R. Given a scheduler σ, the set of complete scheduled computations that are extensions of the partial computations above is measurable in the probability space of T. We denote its probability $\Pr_A(T, \Phi, B, \leq pc, R, t, \sigma)$. Similarly, we can define probabilities for other kinds of formulas.

Finally, the satisfaction relation $\models \subseteq (S_n \cup S_p) \times \mathcal{L}^{pc}_{PHMLu}$, stating when an LCMC state satisfies a given formula, is defined inductively as follows. Let $T = (S_n, S_p, Act, \longrightarrow_n, \longrightarrow_p, s_0)$, be an LCMC. Then:

$s \models tt$ always

$s \models \neg f$ *iff* $s \not\models f$

$s \models f \wedge f'$ *iff* $s \models f$ and $s \models f'$

$s \models f\langle\Phi\rangle^{\bowtie' pc,R}_{\bowtie p,t} f'$ *iff* there is $\sigma \in \mathsf{Sched}(s)$ such that $\Pr_A(s, \Phi, B, \bowtie' pc, R, t, \sigma) \bowtie p$, where $A = \{s' \mid s' \models f\}$, $B = \{s' \mid s' \models f'\}$

Similar definitions are given for the other variants of the until operator.

The Model-Checking Algorithm. Let *closure*(f) denote the set of formulae $\{\ f', \neg f' \mid f'$ is a subformula of $f\ \}$. Our model-checking algorithm is similar to the CTL model-checking algorithm of [5]. In order to check that LCMC T satisfies some formula $f \in \mathcal{L}^{pc}_{PHMLu}$, the algorithm labels each state s of T with a set $F \subseteq$ *closure*(f), such that for every $f' \in F$, $s \models f'$. T satisfies f if and only if s_0, the initial state of T, is labeled with f. The algorithm starts with the atomic subformulae of f and proceeds to more complex subformulae. The labeling rules are straightforward from the semantics of the operators, with the exception of the *until* operator.

In order to decide whether a state s satisfies one of the four until operators, we compute the maximum or minimum probability of the specified behavior Φ.

The maximum value of $\Pr_A(s, \Phi, B, \leq pc, \sigma)$ over all σ is computed by solving a linear programming problem. Specifically, it is given as the smallest value of the variable $X^s_{f\langle\Phi\rangle\leq^{pc} f'}$ satisfying the following set of equations:

$$X^s_{f\langle\Phi\rangle\leq^{pc} f'} = \begin{cases} \sum\limits_{s \xrightarrow{\pi}_p s'} \pi \cdot X^{s'}_{f\langle\Phi\rangle\leq^{pc} f'} & \text{if } s \in S_p \\ \max(\{X^{s'}_{f\langle\Phi-\alpha\rangle\leq^{pc-\mathsf{pow}(\alpha)} f'} \mid s \xrightarrow{\alpha}_n s'\}) & \text{if } s \in S_n, s \models f \\ 1 & \text{if } s \in S_n, s \models f', \varepsilon \in \Phi, pc \geq 0 \\ 0 & \text{otherwise} \end{cases}$$

where $\Phi - \alpha$ is $\{\phi \mid \alpha\phi \in \Phi\}$ if $\alpha \neq \tau$ and Φ, otherwise. A solution for this set of equations can be computed as follows: for all equations of the form $X = \max\{X_1, \ldots X_n\}$, we introduce, the set of inequalities $X \geq X_i$ aiming to minimize the function $\sum_i X_i$. Using algorithms based on the ellipsoid method, this problem can be solved in time polynomial in the number of variables (see, e.g. [9]). The number of variables is $O(|T| \times 2^{|f|})$. Clearly, for each state s of T, there is one variable labeled s for each subformula of f that is considered by the algorithm. However, the number of subformulae of an *until* formula $f\langle\Phi\rangle f'$ depends on the number of regular expressions derived by the operation $\Phi - \alpha$, which is exponential in the size of Φ in the worst case. We think that it is possible to make the algorithm polynomial in the size of the formula by constructing equations differently. However, this is still left for future research.

Example. Consider two systems requiring the use of a resource. Suppose the first system employs a highly reliable resource r that never fails, $\pi(r) = 1$, but consumes a large amount of power during each of its uses. On the other hand the second system opts on using a less reliable resource r' with probability of failure 1/2 but consumes less power. The description of these systems is as follows:

$$P \stackrel{\text{def}}{=} rec\ X.\{(r,1,2)\} : \overline{succ}.X$$
$$Q \stackrel{\text{def}}{=} rec\ X.(\{(r',1,1)\} : \overline{succ}.X + \{(\overline{r'},1,0)\} : X)$$

We observe that Q attempts to use resource r' and if it is up then it consumes r', performs the event $\overline{succ}$ and returns to its initial state, otherwise, if r' is down, it retries to use r' until it succeeds. The LCMCs corresponding to processes P, Q are given in Figure 1.

We may see that although Q risks a delay in successfully using resource r', on average, it consumes less power than P per successful resource use. Specifically, it is easy to show that letting Φ be the regular expression $\{\{(r,1,2)\,\{(r',1,1)\},\{(\overline{r'},1,0)\}\}^*\ \overline{succ}$, we have that $(Q,\emptyset) \models tt\langle\Phi\rangle^{\leq 1}_{\geq 1} tt$, since, with probability 1, configuration $(Q,\emptyset)$ can eventually successfully use resource r' using 1 unit of power. On the other hand, $(P,\emptyset) \not\models tt\langle\Phi\rangle^{\leq 1}_{\geq 1} tt$, since a successful usage of resource r consumes two units of power. Introducing a time limit to the property to be checked we can see the tradeoff with respect to the time delay between using resource r' and using resource r: although $(P,\emptyset) \models tt\langle\{\Phi\rangle^{\leq 2}_{\geq 1,1} tt$, $(Q,\emptyset) \not\models tt\langle\Phi\rangle^{\leq 2}_{\geq 1,1} tt$, instead $(Q,\emptyset) \models tt\langle\Phi\rangle^{\leq 1}_{\geq 0.5,1} tt$, and $(Q,\emptyset) \models tt\langle\Phi\rangle^{\leq 2}_{\geq 0.75,2} tt$.

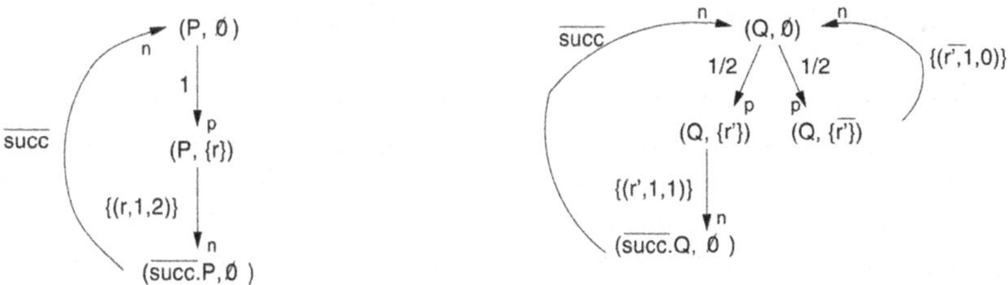

Fig. 1. The LCMCs of processes P and Q

3.2 Probabilistic Bounds on Power Consumption

Model checking P[2]ACSR processes with respect to logical formulae allows us to verify important properties of a process. A disadvantage of this approach, however, is that to reason about power consumption we need to guess and specify a bound on power consumption in the formula. These bounds may come from the requirements for the process, but often we do not have them *a priori*. In this case, we need to compute bounds on power consumption of a process over a fixed interval of time. In this section we show how such bounds can be calculated.

Let T be an LCMC and σ a finite scheduler, where by σ being finite we mean that it can schedule a finite number of transitions. We consider the set of scheduled computations of σ and would like to compute their expected power consumption, which we denote by $Pow(T, \sigma)$. This expected value is $Pow(s_0, \sigma, \sigma_0)$, where s_0 is the initial state of T, given by the solution to the following set of equations:

$$Pow(s, \sigma, c) = \begin{cases} 0 & \sigma(c) = \perp \\ \mathsf{pow}\,(\alpha) + Pow(s', \sigma, c\alpha s') & s \in S_n, \sigma(c) = (s, \alpha, s') \\ \Sigma_{s'} \pi(s, s') \cdot Pow(s', \sigma, c\pi(s, s')s') & s \in S_p \end{cases}$$

Given a finite P[2]ACSR process P, we may use the same scheme to compute the maximum expected power consumption $pow(P)$ over the set of all its schedulers. This can be achieved by the following algorithm for the initial state s_0. Minimum expected power consumption is obtained by replacing function max() with min(). By replacing $\mathsf{pow}\,(\alpha)$ by $\mathsf{pow}\,(\alpha, R)$, we can also compute the expected power-consumption bounds regarding the set of resources R.

compute_bounds(s)
    if $s \in S_n$ **then**
        if s has no outgoing transitions **then** $pow(s) = 0$
        else for each s', $s \xrightarrow{\alpha}_n s'$
            compute_bounds(s'); $pow(s) = \max_{s \xrightarrow{\alpha}_n s'} (\mathsf{pow}\,(\alpha) + pow(s'))$;
    if $s \in S_p$ **then**
        for each s', $s \xrightarrow{\alpha}_n s'$
            compute_bounds(s'); $pow(s) = \Sigma_{s \xrightarrow{p}_p s'} p \cdot pow(s')$

4 Case Study: Power-Aware Real-Time Scheduling

In this section, we describe the case study of a power-aware application, based on the work of [14] and concerning the use of dynamic voltage scaling [3] in an embedded real-time system. Dynamic voltage scaling allows to make a trade-off between performance and power consumption. A processor can lower its operating frequency, using a lower supply voltage and thus consuming less power. At the same time, a lower-frequency execution means that tasks take longer to compute. A power-aware real-time operating system has to decide when it can to operate at a lower frequency while maintaining the system's real-time requirements.

In [14], Pillai and Shin propose extensions to real-time scheduling algorithms to make use of dynamic voltage scaling. We concentrate on the extension of the Earliest Deadline First (EDF) scheduling algorithm [12] that utilizes cycles unused by the tasks to lower the operating frequency for other tasks. The algorithm assumes a set of independent periodic tasks $T_1, \ldots, T_n$ to be executed on the same processor. Each task T_i has a *period* p_i, a *worst-case execution time* c_i, and a deadline d_i by which execution must be completed. The ratios of execution time to period in each task define the nominal utilization of the processor by the task set that determines whether the tasks can be scheduled. In reality, tasks often take much less than the worst case to execute. Thus effective utilization of the task set may be much lower than the nominal one.

When the processor operates at a lower frequency, execution times of tasks grow accordingly, increasing nominal utilization so that the task set may become unschedulable. However, the effective utilization may be small enough even for a lower frequency. The power-aware scheduling algorithm of [14] computes effective utilization during execution and switches frequencies to use the lowest frequency for which the task set remains effectively schedulable.

For the case study, we use the example from [14]. The task set contains three tasks with the following parameters: $c_1 = 3$, $p_1 = 8$; $c_2 = 3$, $p_2 = 10$; $c_3 = 1$, $p_3 = 14$. In each case, the deadline of the task is the same as its period. Execution times are shown for the maximum processor frequency. We assume that the processor has two possible operating frequencies. For simplicity, we assume that at the reduced frequency tasks take twice as long to execute and consume half of the power. We demonstrate that the timing constraints of the tasks are maintained even at the lower frequency and compute the savings in power consumption offered by the power-aware scheduling.

The ACSR representation of the EDF scheduling algorithm has been presented in [4]. Here, we extend that representation in P^{2}ACSR to incorporate probabilistic completion time of the tasks. An instance of the scheduling problem is modeled as a collection of processes $T_1, \ldots, T_n$. Process T_i is shown in Figure 2. A task is represented as a parallel composition of two processes: Job_i and $Activator_i$.

The role of the activator is to keep track of the timing constraint of the task. At the beginning of every period, $Activator_i$ sends the signal $start_i$ to Job_i, releasing the task for execution, and then idles until the end of the period. If, by the end of the period, the task has not finished its execution, it will not be able accept the next $start_i$ signal, resulting in a deadlock that will signify the scheduling failure.

The other process, Job_i, upon receiving the $start_i$ signal, begins its execution. At each time step, the task has a priority that is increased as the task approaches its deadline. The task that has been released t time units ago, has $p_i - t$ time units remaining until the deadline and has priority $p_{max} - (p_i - t)$, where $p_{max} = max(p_1, \ldots, p_n) + 1$. When the task receives the processor resource, it executes for one time unit and its accumulated execution time e, is increased together with the elapsed time t. At any time step, the task can be interrupted by another task that has a closer deadline. In this case, the task makes an idling step and its accumulated execution time stays the same while the elapsed time is increased.

In order to model the potential for early termination, we associate, with each task, a probability distribution on the time it takes to complete the task. For simplicity, we assume that the execution time of a task conforms to the geometric distribution. That is, after every execution step, the task may terminate with probability π and continue its execution with probability $1 - \pi$. Thus the probability that the task takes i time units to execute is $(1 - \pi)^{i-1} \cdot \pi$. We assume that this distribution is the same for all tasks. We introduce an additional resource *cont* that represents continuation of the task execution. When the resource fails, the task terminates its execution, becoming Job_i. Otherwise, the execution continues, up to the worst-case execution time.

To model slower or faster execution of the task, depending on the operating frequency, we introduce events *fast* and *slow* to determine whether the processor is in the fast or slow mode. If the processor is in the slow mode, the next computation step takes two time units. The task also uses two additional events, $release_i$ and $end_{i,j}$, which are used to drive the voltage scaling algorithm and correspond to the release of task T_i and the completion of T_i after j time units, respectively.

The algorithm of [14] recomputes effective utilization every time a task is released for execution or ends its execution. Then, it selects the least operating frequency for the processor that would still guarantee schedulability of the task set. The algorithm maintains, for each task T_i its effective utilization U_i, which is set initially, and also whenever the task T_i is released, to c_i/p_i. When T_i completes its execution for the current period, U_i is set to c_i^{act}/p_i, where c^{act} is the actual time used by the task. Every time one of the U_i values is changed, the algorithm selects the lowest operating frequency f from the set of possible frequencies such that $U_1 + \ldots + U_n \leq f/f_{max}$, where f_{max} is the highest operating frequency.

Resources used in the model of the task do not consume power since both represent abstract notions: scheduling priorities and probabilistic completion. Power consumed by the processor is captured by a separate resource *power* that is used by the process DVS, shown in Figure 3, consists of two parallel parts. The first part, represented by the process $Scale_{e_1,e_2,e_3}$, represents the voltage scaling algorithm itself. Triggered by an event $release_i$ or $end_{i,c}$ that correspond

$$
\begin{aligned}
Job_i &= \emptyset : Job_i + (start_i, 0).(\overline{release_i}, i).Exec_{i,0,0} \\
Exec_{i,e,t} &= e < c_i \rightarrow ((fast, i).(\{(cpu, p_{max} - (p_i - t), 0), (cont, 1, 0)\} : Exec_{i,e+1,t+1} \\
&\qquad + \{(cpu, p_{max} - (p_i - t), 0), (\overline{cont}, 1, 0)\} : (\overline{end_{i,e+1}}, i).Job_i \\
&\qquad + \emptyset : Exec_{i,e,t+1}) \\
&\quad + (slow, i).(\{(cpu, p_{max} - (p_i - t), 0)\} : \\
&\qquad (\{(cpu, p_{max} - (p_i - t), 0), (cont, 1, 0)\} : Exec_{i,e+1,t+2} \\
&\qquad + \{(cpu, p_{max} - (p_i - t), 0), (\overline{cont}, 1, 0)\} : (\overline{end_{i,e+1}}, i).Job_i) \\
&\qquad + \emptyset : Exec_{i,e,t+1}) \\
&+ e = c_i \rightarrow (\overline{end_{i,c_i}}, i).Job_i \qquad e \in \{0..c_i\}, t \in \{0..p_i\}
\end{aligned}
$$

Fig. 2. A speed-sensitive task

to the release or, respectively, completion of the task T_i after executing for c time units, the process *SetNew* computes the effective utilization and sends signal f_{down} if a lower operating frequency is possible and signal f_{up} otherwise. The other component of the process DVS keeps the information at the current operating frequency. It has two states, DVS_{fast} and DVS_{slow}. In the former state, the process uses the resource *power* at the power consumption level of pw_{fast} and in the latter state the same resource is used with power consumption of pw_{slow}, where pw_{fast} and pw_{slow} are parameters of the model.

$$
\begin{aligned}
DVS &= (Scale_{c_1,c_2,c_3} \| DVS_{fast}) \backslash \{f_{up}, f_{down}\} \\
Scale_{e_1,e_2,e_3} &= (release_1, 0).SetNew_{c_1,e_2,e_3} + (release_2, 0).SetNew_{e_1,c_2,e_3} \\
&+ (release_3, 0).SetNew_{e_1,e_2,c_3} \\
&+ \Sigma_{c \in \{1..c_1\}}(end_{1,c}, 0).SetNew_{c,e_2,e_3} + \Sigma_{c \in \{1..c_2\}}(end_{2,c}, 0).SetNew_{e_1,c,e_3} \\
&+ \Sigma_{c \in \{1..c_3\}}(end_{3,c}, 0).SetNew_{e_1,e_2,c} + \emptyset : Scale_{e_1,e_2,e_3} \\
SetNew_{e_1,e_2,e_3} &= e_1/p_1 + e_2/p2 + e_3/p_3 < 1/2 \rightarrow (\overline{f_{down}}, 4).Scale_{e_1,e_2,e_3} \\
&+ e_1/p_1 + e_2/p2 + e_3/p_3 >= 1/2 \rightarrow (\overline{f_{up}}, 4).Scale_{e_1,e_2,e_3}) \\
DVS_{fast} &= \{(power, 1, pw_{fast})\} : DVS_{fast} + (\overline{fast}, 1).DVS_{fast} \\
&+ (f_{down}, 0).DVS_{slow} + (f_{up}, 0).DVS_{fast} + \\
DVS_{slow} &= \{(power, 1, pw_{fast})\} : DVS_{slow} + (\overline{slow}, 1).DVS_{slow} \\
&+ (f_{down}, 0).DVS_{slow} + (f_{up}, 0).DVS_{fast}
\end{aligned}
$$

Fig. 3. P^{2}ACSR representation of voltage scaling

Analysis. We began the analysis of the case study by checking that the task set remains schedulable by the power-aware scheduling algorithm. The resulting system does not have any deadlocks, which means that all timing constraints are satisfied. Then we used the algorithm described in Section 3.2 to compute the expected power consumption of our task set for the duration of one major frame, that is, the product of periods of all tasks, $p_1 \cdot p_2 \cdot p_3$ (1120 time units).

The probability of the task completion after a computation step was taken to be 0.3, and parameters pw_{fast} and pw_{slow} were 2 and 1, respectively.

The expected minimum and maximum power consumption were calculated to be 1906.66 and 1922.65, respectively. Without the dynamic voltage scaling, when each step would take pw_{fast} power units, the power consumption for the same period would be 2240 units. As a result, expected savings from the dynamic voltage scaling are between 14% and 14.8%.

We also verified several obvious properties of the task set. For example, consider the first iteration of the first task in the set. The system, which starts in the fast mode, will switch into the slow mode if the first task finishes after the first step, which happens with probability 0.3. Executions of the other two tasks will not then affect the power mode, and the first eight steps of the system will consume only 9 units of power. All other executions will consume more power. Thus, the system satisfies the property $tt\langle power^8 \rangle^{\leq 10}_{\leq 0.3} tt$. Here, expression $power^8$ denotes eight consecutive actions that utilize the resource $power$.

5 Conclusions

We have presented P^{2}ACSR, a process algebra for resource-constrained real-time systems. The formalism allows one to model the power consumption of resources and perform power-oriented analysis of a system's behavior. We have also described two techniques for analysing P^{2}ACSR specifications. First, we have presented a probabilistic temporal power-aware logic in which one can express properties of interest regarding the behavior of power-aware, real-time systems. Second, we have presented an algorithm for computing probabilistic bounds on power consumption.

Furthermore, to allow for the automatic analysis of power-aware real-time systems, we have extended the PARAGON toolset [16], which previously allowed the specification and analysis of ACSR and PACSR processes, to handle the power consumption model of P^{2}ACSR. The toolset may accept P^{2}ACSR specifications, construct the LCMCs emanating from them, and perform model-checking as well as compute probabilistic bounds on power consumption. We have successfully applied our techniques for modeling and analysing a couple of examples, including a dynamic-voltage algorithm.

Another useful measure to be computed on P^{2}ACSR specifications which is currently being implemented in PARAGON, is that of long-run average performance. Average power consumption can be computed per unit of time or, if desired, per user-defined periods of interest, as shown in [6]. Finally, we intend to define ordering relations by which to relate processes that, although behaviorally similar, differ in their power consumption rates.

References

1. C. Baier, B.R. Haverkort, H. Hermanns, and J.-P. Katoen. On the logical characterisation of performability properties. In *Proceedings of ICALP 00*, volume 1853 of *LNCS*, pages 780–792, 2000.

2. M. Bernardo. An algebra-based method to associate rewards with empa terms. In *Proceedings of ICALP 97*, volume 1256 of *LNCS*, pages 358–368, July 1997.
3. T. D. Burd and R. W. Brodersen. Energy efficient CMOS microprocessor design. In *Proceedings of IEEE Hawaii International Conference on System Sciences. Volume 1: Architecture*, pages 288–297, 1995.
4. J-Y. Choi, I. Lee, and H.-L. Xie. The specification and schedulability analysis of real-time systems using ACSR. In *Proceedings of Real-Time Systems Symposium*, December 1995.
5. E. Clarke, E. Emerson, and A. Prasad Sistla. Automatic verification of finite state concurrent systems using temporal logic specifications. *ACM Transactions on Programming Languages and Systems*, 8(2), 1986.
6. L. de Alfaro. How to specify and verify the long-run average behavior of probabilistic systems. In *Proceedings of IEEE Symposium on Logic in Computer Science*, pages 454–465, 1998.
7. R. De Nicola and F. W. Vaandrager. Three logics for branching bisimulation. In *Proceedings of LICS '90*, 1990.
8. H. Hansson. Time and probability in formal design of distributed systems. In *Real-Time Safety Critical Systems*, volume 1. Elsevier, 1994.
9. H. Karloff. *Linear Programming.* Progress in Theoretical Computer Science. Birkhauser, 1991.
10. I. Lee, P. Brémond-Grégoire, and R. Gerber. A process algebraic approach to the specification and analysis of resource-bound real-time systems. *Proceedings of the IEEE*, pages 158–171, Jan 1994.
11. I. Lee, A. Philippou, and O. Sokolsky. Formal modeling and analysis of power-aware real-time systems. Technical Report MIS-CIS-02-12, Department of Computer and Information Science, University of Pennsylvania, 2002.
12. C. L. Liu and J. W. Layland. Scheduling algorithms for multiprogramming in a hard real-time environment. *Journal of the ACM 20*, 1:46–61, 1973.
13. A. Philippou, O. Sokolsky, R. Cleaveland, I. Lee, and S. Smolka. Probabilistic resource failure in real-time process algebra. In *Proceedings of CONCUR 98*, pages 389–404, 1998.
14. P. Pillai and K. G. Shin. Real-time dynamic voltage scaling for low-power embedded operating systems. In *Proceedings of ACM Symposium on Operating Systems Principles*, 2001.
15. R. Segala and N. Lynch. Probabilistic simulations for probabilistic processes. In *Proceedings CONCUR 94,* Uppsala, Sweden, volume 836 of *LNCS*, pages 481–496, 1994.
16. O. Sokolsky, I. Lee, and H. Ben-Abdallah. Specification and analysis of real-time systems with PARAGON. *Annals of Software Engineering*, 7:211–234, 1999.
17. M. Vardi. Automatic verification of probabilistic concurrent finite-state programs. In *Proceedings of the Symposium on Foundations of Computer Science*, pages 327–338, 1985.

A Set of Performance and Dependability Analysis Components for CADP

Holger Hermanns[1,2] and Christophe Joubert[3]

[1] Department of Computer Science, University of Twente, P.O. Box 217, NL-7500 AE Enschede, The Netherlands
[2] Department of Computer Science, Saarland University, Im Stadtwald, D-66123 Saarbrücken, Germany
[3] INRIA Rhône-Alpes / VASY, 655, avenue de l'Europe F-38330 Montbonnot Saint-Martin, France

Abstract. This paper describes a set of analysis components that open the way to perform performance and dependability analysis with the CADP toolbox, originally designed for verifying the functional correctness of LOTOS specifications. Three new tools (named BCG_STEADY, BCG_TRANSIENT and DETERMINATOR) have been added to the toolbox. The approach taken fits well within the existing architecture of CADP which doesn't need to be altered to enable performance evaluation.

1 Introduction

The design of models suited for performance and dependability analysis of systems is difficult because of their ever increasing size and complexity, in particular for systems with a high degree of irregularity. The potential of formal methods and tools to support the modelling and analysis of performance and dependability aspects has led to various techniques and tools, mostly based on stochastic Petri nets (SPN for short, e.g. [2,22,3,4]), or stochastic process algebras (e.g. [12, 1,15]), or both [7].

This paper describes PDAC (Performance and Dependability Analysis Components), a set of components that enable the study of performance and dependability for specifications developed by means of the CADP toolbox [10]. The latter is a widespread tool set for the design and verification of complex systems. CADP supports the process algebra LOTOS for specification, and offers various tools for simulation and formal verification, including equivalence checkers (bisimulations) and model checkers (temporal logics and modal μ-calculus). The toolbox is designed as an open platform for the integration of other specification, verification and analysis techniques. This is realized by means of application programming interfaces (API) which on different levels provide means to extend or exploit the functionalities of the toolbox. These APIs have been used by others to link CADP to other specification languages as well as other verification/testing tools.

Here we describe how these APIs have been used to support performance and dependability analysis based on Markov modelling and numerical algorithms. Our efforts have been driven by the intention to avoid changes to the

H. Garavel and J. Hatcliff (Eds.): TACAS 2003, LNCS 2619, pp. 425–430, 2003.

existing components as much as possible, while providing a sound and efficient framework for performance and dependability analysis, including state-of-the-art stochastic model checking techniques. To achieve this we use the theory of interactive Markov chains [13], a conservative extension of both process algebra and *continuous-time Markov chains* (CTMC for short), the latter being a well-investigated and frequently used class of stochastic models. More details on the modelling philosophy can be found in [13,8], while here we focus on the tool architectural aspects. The resulting set of tool components (`http://fmt.cs.utwente.nl/tools/pdac/`) will be part of the forthcoming CADP 2003 (`http://www.inrialpes.fr/vasy/cadp`).

The paper is organised as follows. Section 2 briefly explains how the process algebra LOTOS can be used for modelling Markovian aspects. Section 3 describes extensions of CADP to support performance evaluation.

2 Interactive Markov Chains in CADP

Many stochastic models derived from state-transition diagrams have been proposed. Our approach is based on the *interactive Markov chain* model (IMC), which can be considered as simply a *labelled transition system* (LTS) whose transitions can be either labelled with an action (as in an 'ordinary' LTS) or with special labels of the form "$\texttt{rate}\ \lambda$", where λ is a positive real value. A transition "$\xrightarrow{\texttt{rate}\ \lambda}$" going out of some state S is called a *delay transition* and expresses an internal delay in state S (henceforth called a Markov delay). It indicates that the time t spent in S follows a so-called *negative exponential distribution function* $Prob\{t \leq x\} = 1 - e^{-\lambda x}$, to be read as: the probability that state S is exited at time x the latest equals $1 - e^{-\lambda x}$. The IMC model contains as two particular cases the LTS model and the well-known CTMC model (which is obtained when there are only delay transitions). The latter model has been extensively studied in the literature and is equipped with various efficient evaluation strategies (see, e.g. [23]). Similar to Markov decision processes [20], the IMC model allows nondeterminism in states, i.e., two identical action transitions leaving the same state.

To extend the CADP tool towards IMC, the approach chosen [8] is a lightweight one, which does not modify the syntax of LOTOS and requires no change in the CADP compilers for LOTOS (CÆSAR.ADT and CÆSAR). The approach has two steps. Starting from a (functionally verified) LOTOS specification, the user can insert, wherever a Markov delay λ_i should occur, a new (fresh) LOTOS gate Λ_i. After the special gates Λ_i have been inserted in the specification, CÆSAR and CÆSAR.ADT are invoked as usual to generate the corresponding LTS, which is stored in the BCG (Binary Coded Graphs) format. This LTS is then turned into an IMC (still encoded in the BCG format) by replacing all its action transitions Λ_i with delay transitions "$\texttt{rate}\ \lambda_i$". This is done using the BCG_LABELS tool of CADP.

So, by this two step methodology, we can generate an IMC model corresponding to a LOTOS specification with inserted delays and store this model in the

BCG format. Another, less manual, possibility to specify IMC has been suggested in [16] where a constraint-oriented style is used to incorporate Markov delays (or more complex phase-type distributions) between the actions of an existing (and verified) LOTOS specification. Again, the result is an IMC model stored in the BCG format. We refer to [8] for a discussion of the soundness of this approach, and for more details and options in the process of generating an IMC with CADP.

3 Analysis Components

The PDAC set encompasses two sorts of tools to analyse IMC models generated via CADP. (i) The DETERMINATOR tool and the CADP component tool BCG_MIN provide different means to distill a CTMC from an IMC model. (ii) The main analysis components, BCG_STEADY and BCG_TRANSIENT, enable numerical inspection of the behavior CTMCs encoded in the BCG format. We discuss the tools in reverse order.

Analysing a Markov Chain. Two analysis tools provide standard numerical algorithms to compute the distribution of probability in a CTMC.

- BCG_TRANSIENT implements the uniformisation method [23], calculating the time-dependent probability to be in each of the Markov Chain states at a user-specified point in time (relative to the initialisation of the system). The time point is a command-line parameter.
- BCG_STEADY computes the time-independent, long run equilibrium probabilities for each of the system states, using the Gauss-Seidel algorithm [23]. This equilibrium is known to exist for arbitrary finite CTMCs.

Both tools accept a BCG file as input. Unless the file contains action transitions, the graph is accepted for analysis. First, the tool transforms the given graph into the generator matrix representation of a CTMC using the sparse matrix package of [18]. Then, the respective computational procedure is launched. In either case, this results in a vector of state probabilities.

Dependent on the option selected by the user, the solution vector is written to file (option `-sol`) or is further processed, to compute so-called transition throughputs. A transition throughput indicates the average number of transition executions per time unit, for a user-specified set of transitions of interest. These measures can provide important high-level information to assess the system performance, reliability or productivity. BCG_TRANSIENT and BCG_STEADY support throughput calculations if the BCG file contains tagged delay transitions of the form "*tag* `; rate` λ", where *tag* can be an arbitrary label. In this case the throughput is computed for each syntactic tag occuring in the BCG file (if the option `-thr` is selected).

To allow postprocessing and visualisation of computed measures, BCG_TRANSIENT and BCG_STEADY give output results in a CSV-like format (Comma Separated Values). Thus data can be directly conveyed as input to table-oriented applications such as GNUPLOT or EXCEL, which can read CSV files.

Distilling the Markov Chain. Since the numerical analysis components take a CTMC as input, tools are needed to distill a CTMC from an IMC model. Due to the presence of nondeterminism in IMC this is infeasible in general, and the toolset only provides two partial solutions to this. Both are based on the observation that nondeterminism – while being essential for compositional specification – can often be factored out in the final state space being subject to performance and dependability analysis.

- DETERMINATOR implements an on-the-fly algorithm for the *well-specified* condition [11,6] of a stochastic process. Roughly, an IMC is said to be well-specified, if – whatever nondeterministic decisions are taken – the resulting CTMC is unique. The algorithm implemented is a variant of the one described in [5,6].
- BCG_MIN is the bisimulation minimiser of CADP. It can also be used for distilling a CTMC from an IMC: If for a given IMC it holds that – whatever nondeterministic decisions are taken – the resulting *lumped* CTMC chain is unique, then this lumped CTMC will be returned by (the stochastic branching bisimulation option of) BCG_MIN applied to the original IMC model with all actions hidden.

BCG_MIN provides a more powerful way of resolving nondeterministic compared to the DETERMINATOR tool (which does not check the quotient under lumping), but it is computationally more expensive (and is not an on-the-fly algorithm). It is possible to use DETERMINATOR as a preprocessor to BCG_MIN. In the practical cases we considered, this combination turned out to be rather beneficial. Typically the time needed for distilling a lumped CTMC from IMC was decreased by a factor of eight, compared to applying BCG_MIN directly.

Other specification formalisms. When designing the extension to CADP, care has been taken to exploit the features of the BCG API in a way that as far as possible also other formalisms are supported by the toolset. We refer to the manual pages (see `http://fmt.cs.utwente.nl/tools/pdac/` and `http://www.inrialpes.fr/vasy/cadp/man`) for a complete description of the possibilities and limitations, and highlight only a few specific options we have implemented:

- Both BCG_TRANSIENT and BCG_STEADY can handle state spaces where delay transitions and probabilistic transitions coexist. The latter are encoded using distinguished labels of the form "`prob` p_i", where p_i is a real value from the interval $(0, 1]$. These models often appear in the context of generalized SPN and similar models [19].
- DETERMINATOR is able to handle models with delay transitions, nondeterministic transitions and also probabilistic transitions. Such models occur in the context of stochastic activity networks or other SPN like models [21,5].

These options allow the tool components to be used in the context of other modelling formalisms, provided that a link to the BCG format exists (via the API). The tool BCG_IO provides encoding and decoding functionality from/to various tool formats, including simple text-based formats. As one particular application of the BCG API, a conversion from the BCG format to the ETMCC model checker [17] has been implemented. This allows one to perform stochastic model checking of CTMCs encoded in the BCG format.

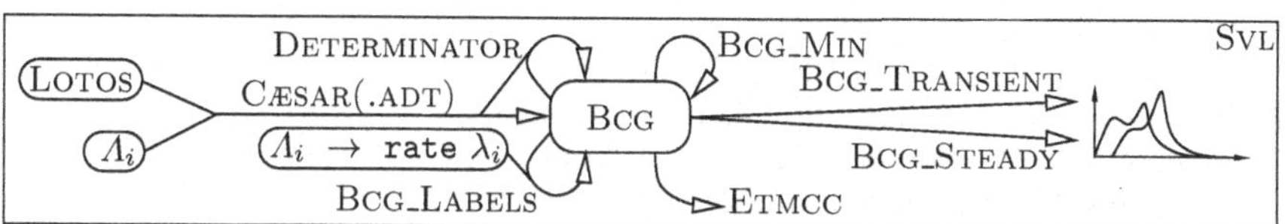

Fig. 1. Tool chain of CADP with PDAC.

Using the scripting language SVL. The diagram in Figure 1 summarizes the position of each component inside the tool chain, where Λ_i refers to the fresh LOTOS gates which are later (using BCG_LABELS) replaced by "`rate` λ_i". The tools BCG_MIN and/or DETERMINATOR are used to distill a CTMC (the latter being an *on-the-fly* algorithm), and BCG_STEADY or BCG_TRANSIENT are used for numerical analysis.

To drive a whole set of performance studies, the scripting language SVL[9] turned out to be very useful. It allows one to conveniently execute the required sequence of tool invocations, and to iterate the numerical analysis on a (possibly multidimensional) list of performance parameters. With SVL we have mechanised the analysis of the SCSI II protocol [8] and of the HUBBLE space telescope [14].

Acknowledgements. We are grateful to Hubert Garavel and Radu Mateescu (INRIA Rhône-Alpes) for their insightful comments about the design of the PDAC. The BCG_MIN tool is a co-development of Damien Bergamini (INRIA Rhône-Alpes), Moëz Cherif (formerly at INRIA Rhône-Alpes), Hubert Garavel, and Holger Hermanns. The tools BCG_TRANSIENT and BCG_STEADY are based on code provided by Vassilis Mertsiotakis (LUCENT TECHNOLOGIES) as part of the TIPPTOOL, which was developed at the University of Erlangen-Nürnberg. This work is supported by the Dutch foundation for scientific research NWO under the VERNIEUWINGSIMPULS program, and has been carried out during a stay of the second author at the University of Twente.

References

1. M. Bernardo, W.R. Cleaveland, S.T. Sims, and W.J. Stewart. TwoTowers: A Tool Integrating Functional and Performance Analysis of Concurrent Systems. In *Proc. FORTE/PSTV'98*, p. 457–467, Kluwer, 1998.
2. G. Chiola, G. Franceschinis, R. Gaeta, and M. Ribaudo. GreatSPN 1.7: GRaphical Editor and Analyzer for Timed and Stochastic Petri Nets. *Perf. Eval.*, 24(1,2):47–68, 1995.

3. G. Ciardo, A.S. Miner. SMART: Simulation and Markovian Analyzer for Reliability and Timing. In *Proc. IPDS'96*, p. 60, IEEE CS Press, 1996.
4. G. Ciardo, J. Muppala, and K. Trivedi. SPNP: stochastic Petri net package. In *Proc. PNPM'89*, p. 142–151, IEEE CS Press, 1989.
5. G. Ciardo and R. Zijal. Well-defined stochastic Petri nets. In *Proc. MASCOTS'96*, p. 278–284, IEEE CS Press, 1996.
6. D.D. Deavours and W.H. Sanders. An efficient well-specified check. In *Proc. PNPM'99*, p. 124–133, IEEE CS Press, 1999.
7. D.D. Deavours, G. Clark, T. Courtney, D. Daly, S. Derisavi, J.M. Doyle, W. H. Sanders, and P.G. Webster. The Möbius Framework and Its Implementation. *IEEE Trans. on Softw. Eng.*, 28(10):956–969, 2002.
8. H. Garavel and H. Hermanns. On Combining Functional Verification and Performance Evaluation using CADP. In *Proc. FME'02*. LNCS 2391:410–429, 2002.
9. H. Garavel and F. Lang. SVL: A Scripting Language for Compositional Verification. In *Proc. FORTE/PSTV 2001*, p. 377–394, Kluwer, 2001.
10. H. Garavel, F. Lang, and R. Mateescu. An Overview of CADP 2001. *EASST Newsletter*, 4:13–24, 2002.
11. R. German, A. van Moorsel, M.A. Qureshi, and W.H. Sanders. Algorithms for the Generation of State-Level Representations of Stochastic Activity Networks with General Reward Structures. *IEEE Trans. on Softw. Eng.*, 22(9):603–614, 1996.
12. S. Gilmore and J. Hillston. The PEPA Workbench: A Tool to Support a Process Algebra-Based Approach to Performance Modelling. In *Proc. TOOLS'94*. LNCS 794:353–368, 1994.
13. H. Hermanns. *Interactive Markov Chains and the Quest for Quantified Quality.* LNCS 2428, 2002.
14. H. Hermanns. Construction and Verification of Performance and Reliability Models. *Bulletin of the EATCS*, 74:135-154, 2001.
15. H. Hermanns, U. Herzog, U. Klehmet, V. Mertsiotakis, and M. Siegle. Compositional performance modelling with the TIPPtool. *Perf. Eval.*, 39(1-4):5–35, January 2000.
16. H. Hermanns and J.P. Katoen. Automated compositional Markov chain generation for a plain-old telephony system. *Sci. of Comp. Prog.*, 36(1):97–127, 2000.
17. H. Hermanns, J.-P. Katoen, J. Meyer-Kayser, and M. Siegle. A Markov Chain Model Checker. In *Proc. TACAS'00*. LNCS 1785:347–362, 2000.
18. K.S. Kundert. Sparse matrix techniques. In *Circuit analysis, Simulation and Design 3*, North-Holland, 1986.
19. A. Marsan, G. Balbo, and G. Conte. A Class of Generalized Stochastic Petri Nets for the Performance Evaluation of Multiprocessor Systems. *ACM Trans. on Comp. Sys.*, 2(2):93–122, 1984.
20. M.L. Puterman. *Markov Decision Processes.* John Wiley, 1994.
21. W.H. Sanders and J.F. Meyer. Stochastic Activity Networks: Formal Definitions and Concepts. In *Proc. FMPA 2000*. LNCS 2090:315–343, 2001.
22. W.H. Sanders, W.D. Oball, M.A. Qureshi, and F.K. Widjanarko. The UltraSAN modeling environment. *Perf. Eval.*, 24(1):89–115, 1995.
23. W.J. Stewart. *Introduction to the numerical solution of Markov chains.* Princeton University Press, 1994.

The Integrated CWB-NC/PIOATool for Functional Verification and Performance Analysis of Concurrent Systems*

Dezhuang Zhang, Rance Cleaveland, and Eugene W. Stark

Department of Computer Science
State University of New York at Stony Brook
Stony Brook, NY 11794-4400 USA
{dezhuang, rance, stark}@cs.sunysb.edu

Abstract. This paper reports on an effort to integrate two verification tools, the Concurrency Workbench of the New Century (CWB-NC) and PIOATool. Our aim is to build a single tool that combines the "functional" analysis capabilities of the CWB-NC with the compositional performance-analysis features of PIOATool. We discuss some of the issues involved in the integration, highlighting a particular integration paradigm in which one tool becomes a *subshell* of the other.

1 Introduction

This paper describes a tool integration effort involving the combination of two system-analysis tools, the Concurrency Workbench of the New Century (CWB-NC) [4,5,6] and PIOATool [9,12]. The goal of this project is to build a new tool combining support for checking both correctness and performance properties of system models.

The two tools in question have the following characteristics. The **CWB-NC** is a retargetable tool that implements a number of "functional correctness" routines, including a variety of semantic equivalences and preorders and a model checker for the modal μ-calculus. The **PIOATool** implements compositional performance analysis methods [9, 10] for *probabilistic I/O automata* (PIOA) [14]. PIOAs extend the well-known I/O automaton model for nondeterministic computation [8] with two kinds of performance information: probability distributions representing the relative likelihood with which transitions from a given state labeled by the same *input* are performed; and rate information describing how long, on average, outputs / internal actions take. PIOAs are also equipped with notion of parallel composition. The PIOATool computes a variety of transient performance measures on parallel compositions of PIOAs.

An important requirement for the integrated tool is that users should be able to provide system models on which both functional and performance analyses could be undertaken. However, the CWB-NC and PIOATool have very different internal model formats. The former generally supports compositional specification notations based on process algebras. Internally, systems are represented as terms in a modeling language;

* Research supported by NSF grants CCR-9988155, CCR-9988489, and CCR-0098037 and Army Research Office grants DAAD190110003 and DAAD190110019.

H. Garavel and J. Hatcliff (Eds.): TACAS 2003, LNCS 2619, pp. 431–436, 2003.

semantic routines are then used by the verification procedures such as the model checker in order to compute the semantic content of these terms. The PIOATool, on the other hand, includes procedures that are highly optimized for handling systems given as parallel compositions of semantic objects in the form of PIOAs.

We address these issues by: defining a process algebra for PIOA systems, implementing a translation for terms in this algebra into sequential compositions of "pure" PIOAs, and introducing a *subshell* for running PIOATool analyses. The rest of this paper discusses each of these in turn and concludes with a case study and related work.

2 A Process Algebra for PIOAs

The notation for PIOAs [11] has a two-level syntax. The lower level comprises so-called *sequential* terms, which denote transition systems annotated with probability and rate information. At this level, PIOA requirements such as "input-enabledness" (every state must be capable of processing any input) are not enforced. The upper level defines *PIOA agents*, which denote probabilistic I/O automata that satisfy all the input-enabledness, stochasticity, and compatibility properties that systems of PIOA must possess.

To define the language, let L be a set of labels, and let $\tau \notin L$ be the internal action; we use $a \in L$ and $b \in L \cup \tau$ in what follows. Let $p_1, \ldots, p_n$ denote probabilities summing to 1 and r a positive real number denoting a rate, and let X come from a set of *process names*. Then sequential terms are defined via the following BNF grammar.

$$s ::= nil \mid a?[p_1 : s_1, \ldots, p_n : s_n] \mid b(r)!s \mid s_1 + s_2 \mid X$$

Intuitively nil has no transitions, while $a?[p_1 : s_1, \ldots, p_n : s_n]$ can perform the input action $a?$ and subsequently evolve to term s_i with probability p_i, $b(r)!s$ denotes a process that can perform output/internal action $b!$ with rate r and then evolve to term s, and s_1+s_2 is a nondeterministic choice. Finally, X represents an "invocation" of the process term bound to X in the environment.

The upper level of the language syntax is as follows, where $I \subseteq L$ and $O \subseteq L$ are sets of labels of input and output actions, respectively, and $a, a' \in L$.

$$t ::= \langle I, O \rangle s \mid [I, O]t \mid t_1 \parallel t_2 \mid t\{a \leftarrow a'\}$$

These operators have the following interpretation. $\langle I, O \rangle s$ represents a "type cast": provided every state reachable from s enables all, and only, inputs in I, and only outputs in O, and stochasticity requirements are met, then $\langle I, O \rangle s$ is a PIOA term. Term $[I, O]t$ denotes a "coercion" of t so that inputs come from I and outputs come from O. Term $t_1 \parallel t_2$ is the parallel composition of t_1 and t_2: for it to be well-formed, t_1 and t_2 must not share output actions. The resulting term has as inputs the intersection of the inputs of t_1 and t_2 and as outputs the union of the output sets of t_1 and t_2. Outputs of t_1 sharing a label with inputs of t_2 are "fed into" t_2 and also made available to the environment of $t_1 \parallel t_2$. Finally, $t\{a \leftarrow a'\}$ relabels the actions involving a to ones involving a'.

As the previous discussion implies, PIOA terms have a type system that ensures input-enabledness and compatibility of parallel compositions. The definition of this system, and of the SOS rules defining the transitions of PIOA terms, are omitted. The PAC [3] is applied to these rules to build the single-step "transition engine" used by the CWB-NC and PIOATool. Exhaustively applying the engine to a type-correct PIOA term yields a single PIOA describing the global behavior of the system.

3 Translating PIOA Terms to Parallel Compositions

The PIOA language fits easily within the CWB-NC framework: terms in the language represent systems, and the SOS rules define a transition relation. For the CWB-NC semantic analyses (which are insensitive to stochastic information) the probability and rate information on the transitions is ignored. However, for these terms to be processable by the PIOATool they must be converted into parallel compositions of "pure" PIOA. This entails the elimination of coercion and renaming and the replacement of sequential terms by PIOAs. The latter may be easily accomplished by applying the operational semantics exhaustively to these terms, yielding PIOAs. Coercion may also be eliminated, since in the PIOA language it turns out to distribute over parallel composition and may be "absorbed" easily into PIOAs. Somewhat surprisingly, the well-formedness conditions for PIOAs also license the distribution of renaming over parallel composition. Thus the basic conversion routine may be defined as follows. (1) "Push" all coercions and renamings inside all parallel compositions; (2) To the sequential + coercion + renaming terms embedded inside the parallel compositions, apply the SOS rules to generate PIOAs. Because parallel composition is associative, the resulting term containing PIOAs and parallel composition can be converted into a list of PIOAs. Note that no special semantic routines need to be implemented for this transformation; the existing PIOA semantic routines, and the algebraic properties of the language, suffice.

4 The PIOA Subshell

The final conceptual issue we confront involves the integration of the tool functionalities. The paradigm we adopt is based on the notion of a *subshell*, i.e. an "inner" command line, or *mode*, that has access to the data structures of the "outer" command line. In our case, we make the PIOATool a subshell of the CWB-NC. Once inside this subshell, the user may invoke the performance-analysis routines of PIOATool.

As was mentioned earlier, the two tools use different internal representations for systems. While there are routines for converting terms into sequences of PIOAs, these are computationally expensive. Consequently, we want to minimize the number of times these routines are called, while still providing a user with the analytical capabilities of both tools. Our solution to this issue is to introduce a separate environment for the PIOA-Tool subshell. This environment maps identifiers to sequences of PIOAs. We also add a command to the subshell that allows PIOA terms to be "imported" into the PIOATool environment. This command translates the term given as an argument and binds it to an identifier. Once this importation takes place, the associated sequence of PIOAs may be subjected to PIOATool commands.

The PIOATool computes performance statistics for user-defined *observables*, which are rules for mapping PIOA execution sequences to numeric values. The PIOATool subshell also includes commands for binding observables to identifiers.

5 Case Study: A Distributed Mutual Exclusion Protocol

We now consider the application of the integrated tool to a "tournament-style" distributed mutual-exclusion protocol. Our example supposes a collection of *user* processes that are located at the leaves of a binary tree. Each user process requires from time to time the exclusive use of a resource, the allocation of which is managed by *arbiter* processes located at the interior nodes of the tree.

A user process requests the resource by performing a *request* output action, which synchronizes with a corresponding *request* input action of the user's parent arbiter. If the resource is currently held by the arbiter, and the arbiter has not already committed the resource to the user's sibling, then the arbiter will respond with a *grant* output, which synchronizes with a corresponding *grant* input to the user process. When the user is finished using the resource, it performs a *release* output to return the resource to its parent. The user must then wait for a *reset* input from the parent before it is permitted to make a new request.

If a user process makes a request and the resource is already committed to its sibling, then the arbiter ignores the request. When the sibling has finished with the resource and issued a *release* to the arbiter, then the subsequent *reset* action performed by the arbiter also resets the pending request, which must then be reissued by the user. If a user process requests the resource from its parent and the resource is not currently in the possession of any process in the subtree rooted at the parent, then the parent arbiter must request the resource from its own parent. This is done in exactly the same way as for a user process requesting the resource from its parent.

```
seq U_IDLE = request(1)!U_WAITING + reset?[1: U_IDLE] + grant?[1: U_ERROR]
seq U_WAITING = reset?[1: U_IDLE] + grant?[1: U_USING]
seq U_USING = release(1)!U_DONE + reset?[1: U_ERROR] + grant?[1: U_ERROR]
seq U_DONE = reset?[1: U_IDLE] + grant?[1: U_ERROR]
seq U_ERROR = error(1)!U_ERROR + reset?[1: U_ERROR] + grant?[1: U_ERROR]
proc USER = <{reset,grant},{request,release}>U_IDLE
```

The above shows the PIOA code for a user process. The code defines five sequential terms (introduced by the `seq` keyword), followed by the definition of PIOA term USER.

In the remainder of this section we step through a session in which we analyze a four-user system organized as a complete binary tree. This system has $1,264,375$ global states, of which $1,700$ are reachable. The session was run on a 1.8GHz Intel Xeon processor with 2Gb of on-board memory. Throughout, we quote the commands issued verbatim while simply summarizing the output produced by the tool.

```
cwb-nc> load mutex.pioa
cwb-nc> load mutex.mu
cwb-nc> chk MUTEX root_can_error
```

We begin the session by loading the file `mutex.pioa`, which contains the PIOA declarations needed to define MUTEX, the overall system. We then load file `mutex.mu`, which contains declarations of mu-calculus formulas defining various properties to be checked of MUTEX. One such property, `root_can_error`, asserts that the root arbiter is capable of entering an error state due to the arrival of an unexpected input (e.g. `release` before a `grant`). To check this property , we use the `chk` command, which invokes the CWB-NC's model checker. After 2.3 seconds, the CWB-NC responds with FALSE: the root arbiter cannot enter an error state.

```
cwb-nc> pioa
cwb-nc-pioa> sys S = MUTEX
cwb-nc-pioa> obs awaitRequest1 = await { R.SUBTREE[2].L.[].request_1 }
cwb-nc-pioa> obs awaitGrant1 = await { R.SUBTREE[2].L.[].grant_1 }
cwb-nc-pioa> obs req1ToGrant1Prob = (prob * (awaitRequest1 ; awaitGrant1))
cwb-nc-pioa> obs result = apply S req1ToGrant1Prob
cwb-nc-pioa> obs req1ToGrant1Time = (prob * (awaitRequest1 ; (time * awaitGrant1)))
cwb-nc-pioa> obs result = apply S req1ToGrant1Time
cwb-nc-pioa> eval result
```

The next part of the session shows the use of PIOATool to calculate two different quantities concerning the first request issued by the leftmost user in the system. The first such quantity is the measure ("probability") that this request will eventually be granted. To obtain this number, we first enter the PIOA subshell using the `pioa` command. Then, the PIOA term `MUTEX` is compiled into a system of PIOAs and bound to the identifier `S`. We next define an "observable" `request1ToGrant1Prob` using primitives `await`, `prob`, `;`, and `*` provided by PIOATool. The long string inside of the braces is an action pathname that is generated automatically by the tool to ensure that internal actions are given unique names. The PIOA system `S` is then "applied" to `request1ToGrant1Prob` to produce a new observable: `result`. The application of `S` actually proceeds in a component-at-a-time fashion. Finally `result` is "evaluated" to extract the resulting probability. This phase, which involves the solution of a system of linear equations in 537 unknowns, is performed using straight LU decomposition. The reported result, 1, is obtained after 149.1 seconds of computation, and represents the likelihood that the leftmost user does not "starve". This result is in contrast to what would be obtained a model checker, which would report that starvation is possible. The quantitative analysis indicates that the "likelihood" of starvation is 0.

Given that the leftmost user cannot, probabilistically speaking, starve, the next quantity we compute is the expected time that elapses between the user's `request` and the subsequent `grant`. To calculate this, we form the observable `req1ToGrant1Time`, apply S to it, and evaluate the result. After 72.2 seconds, the answer 15.85 is returned.

6 Conclusions, and Related and Future Work

In this paper we have studied issues surrounding the integration of a performance-analysis tool, PIOATool, and a functional-analysis tool, the Concurrency Workbench of the New Century. Central to our integration architecture is the notion of *subshell*, which allows the integrated tools to share data structures and routines while retaining their separate analytical capabilities. The subshell idea efficiently addresses the *data transfer* problem among integrating tools: how can the tools exchange information? A common approach involves the use of files to store this information. While this has the advantage of enabling tools to be loosely coupled, it does suffer from the following drawbacks. (a) An intermediate format must be defined. This can be subtle and time-consuming. (b) The intermediate formats must be parsed and unparsed repeatedly, slowing down tool performance. (c) The files can become quite large and require significant processing time when tools must exchange intermediate data structures.

The two existing efforts most closely related to this project include TwoTowers [2] and the performance integration work in CADP [7]. TwoTowers is also built on two existing tools, the CWB-NC and MarCA [13] with EMPAr [1] as the specification language. Aside from the specification formalisms, the key distinction between that work and this involves the tool architecture. TwoTowers isolates the CWB-NC and MarCA from one another; the tool kernel is responsible for translating EMPAr terms into a format suitable for either tool. The kernel therefore implements a semantics of (a subset of) EMPAr for the MarCA tool, and another semantics (embedded in the CWB-NC using PAC) for the functional interpretation of EMPAr. In contrast, our tool implements a single base semantics used by both tools. The CADP project uses files to transfer data between tools; our integration is tighter and therefore avoids overhead associated with accessing secondary storage to retrieve intermediate results.

As for future work, we would like to study how the CWB-NC/PIOATool can be modified to support performance analyses for value-passing systems.

References

1. M. Bernardo. An algebra-based method to associate rewards with EMPA terms. In *ICALP'97*, vol. 1256 of *LNCS*, pages 358–368, Jul. 1997.
2. M. Bernardo, R. Cleaveland, S. Sims, and W. Stewart. TwoTowers: A tool integrating functional and performance analysis of concurrent systems. In *FORTE XI/PSTV XVIII '98*, pages 457–467, Nov. 1998.
3. R. Cleaveland, E. Madelaine, and S. Sims. A front-end generator for verification tools. In *TACAS'95*, vol. 1019 of *LNCS*, pages 153–173, May 1995.
4. R. Cleaveland, J. Parrow, and B. Steffen. The Concurrency Workbench: A semantics-based tool for the verification of finite-state systems. *ACM TOPLAS*, 15(1):36–72, Jan. 1993.
5. R. Cleaveland and S. Sims. The NCSU Concurrency Workbench. In *Computer Aided Verification (CAV '96)*, vol. 1102 of *LNCS*, pages 394–397, Jul. 1996.
6. R. Cleaveland and S. Sims. Generic tools for verifying concurrent systems. *Science of Computer Programming*, 42(1):39–47, Jan. 2002.
7. H. Garavel and H. Hermanns. On combining functional verification and performance evaluation using CADP. In *FME*, vol. 2391 of *LNCS*, pages 410–429, 2002.
8. N. Lynch and M. Tuttle. Hierarchical correctness proofs for distributed algorithms. In *6th ACM PODC*, pages 137–151, 1987.
9. E. Stark and G. Pemmasani. Implementation of a compositional performance analysis algorithm for probabilistic I/O automata. In *7th PAPM*, pages 3–24, 1999.
10. E. Stark and S. Smolka. Compositional analysis of expected delays in networks of probabilistic I/O automata. In *Proc. 13th LICS*, pages 466–477, Jun. 1998.
11. E. Stark, S. Smolka, and R. Cleaveland. A process-algebraic language for PIOA. Unpublished draft, 2003.
12. E. Stark. Compositional performance analysis using probabilistic I/O automata. In *CONCUR 2000*, vol. 1877 of *LNCS*, pages 25–28, Aug. 2000.
13. W. Stewart. *Introduction to the Numerical Solution of Markov Chains*. Princeton University Presss, 1994.
14. S. Wu, S. Smolka, and E. Stark. Composition and behaviors of probabilistic I/O automata. *Theoretical Computer Science*, 176(1–2):1–38, Apr. 1997.

Banana – A Tool for Boundary Ambients Nesting ANAlysis *

Chiara Braghin[1], Agostino Cortesi[1], Stefano Filippone[1], Riccardo Focardi[1], Flaminia L. Luccio[2], and Carla Piazza[1]

[1] Dipartimento di Informatica, Università Ca' Foscari di Venezia,
{braghin,cortesi,sfilippo,focardi,piazza}@dsi.unive.it
[2] Dipartimento di Scienze Matematiche, Università di Trieste,
luccio@dsm.univ.trieste.it

1 Introduction

Banana is a tool for the analysis of information leakage in mobile agent specifications. The language considered is Mobile Ambient calculus, initially proposed by Cardelli and Gordon with the main purpose of explicitly modeling mobility [5]. Sites and agents (i.e., processes) are modeled as nested boxes (i.e., ambients), provided with capabilities for entering, exiting and dissolving other boxes. This specification language provides a very simple framework to reason about information flow and security when mobility is an issue [1].

The main features of Banana are:

- A textual and graphical editor for Mobile Ambients, to specify and modify the process by setting ambient nesting capabilities and security attributes in a very user-friendly fashion.
- A parser which checks for syntax errors and builds the syntax tree out of the Mobile Ambient process.
- An analyzer which computes an over approximation of all possible nestings occurring at run-time. The tool supports two different control flow analyses, namely the one of Nielson et al. [6] and the one by Braghin et al. [1].
- A post-processing module, that interprets the results of the analysis in terms of the boundary-based information-flow model proposed in [1], where information flows correspond to leakages of high-level (i.e., secret) ambients out of protective (i.e., boundary) ambients, toward the low-level (i.e., untrusted) environment.
- A detailed output window reporting both the analysis and the security results obtained by the post-processing module, and some statistics about the computational costs of the performed analysis.

* Partially supported by MIUR Project "Modelli formali per la sicurezza", the EU Contract IST-2001-32617 "Models and Types for Security in Mobile Distributed Systems", and project "Matematica per le scienze e la tecnologia", Università di Trieste.

H. Garavel and J. Hatcliff (Eds.): TACAS 2003, LNCS 2619, pp. 437–441, 2003.

BANANA is implemented in Java and strongly exploits the modularity of object-oriented technology, thus allowing scalability to other analyses (e.g., the one in [3]) and extensions of the target language (e.g., [7]). Moreover, BANANA is conceived as an applet based on AWT and thus compatible with the majority of current web browsers supporting Java.

2 Security of Mobile Ambients

The Mobile Ambient calculus has been introduced in [5] with the main purpose of explicitly modeling mobility. Indeed, ambients are arbitrarily nested boundaries which can move around through suitable capabilities. The syntax of processes is given as follows, where $n \in \mathbf{Amb}$ denotes an ambient name.

$P, Q ::= (\nu n)P$	restriction	$\mid n^{\ell^a}[P]$	ambient
$\mid \mathbf{0}$	inactivity	$\mid \mathbf{in}^{\ell^t}\, n.P$	capability to enter n
$\mid P \mid Q$	composition	$\mid \mathbf{out}^{\ell^t}\, n.P$	capability to exit n
$\mid\ !P$	replication	$\mid \mathbf{open}^{\ell^t}\, n.P$	capability to open n

Intuitively, the restriction $(\nu n)P$ introduces the new name n and limits its scope to P; $P \mid Q$ is P and Q running in parallel; replication provides recursion and iteration. By $n^{\ell^a}[P]$ we denote the ambient named n with the process P running inside it. The capabilities $\mathbf{in}^{\ell^t}\, n$ and $\mathbf{out}^{\ell^t}\, n$ move their enclosing ambients in and out ambient n, respectively; the capability $\mathbf{open}^{\ell^t}\, n$ is used to dissolve a sibling ambient n. Labels on ambients and on transitions are introduced as it is customary in static analysis to indicate "program points".

The operational semantics of a process P is given through a suitable reduction relation $\rightarrow$ and a structural congruence $\equiv$ between processes. Intuitively, $P \rightarrow Q$ represents the possibility for P of reducing to Q through some computation (see also [5]).
For instance, let P_1 be a process modeling an *envelope* sent from *venice* to *warsaw*:

$$venice[\, envelope[\mathbf{out}\ venice.\mathbf{in}\ warsaw.\mathbf{0}] \mid Q] \mid warsaw[\mathbf{open}\ envelope.\mathbf{0}]$$

Initially, *envelope* is in site *venice*. Then, it exits *venice* and enters site *warsaw* by applying its capabilities **out** *venice* and **in** *warsaw*, respectively. Once site *warsaw* receives *envelope*, it reads its content by consuming its **open** *envelope* capability. Finally, process P_1 reaches the state: $venice[\mathbf{0}] \mid warsaw[Q]$.

To deal with security issues, information is classified into different levels of confidentiality. This is obtained by exploiting the labelling of ambients. In particular, the set of ambient labels is partitioned into three disjoint sets: *high*, *low* and *boundary* labels. Ambients labelled with boundary labels (*boundary ambients*) are the ones responsible for confining confidential information. Information leakage occurs if a high level ambient exits a boundary, thus becoming possibly exposed to a malicious ambient attack. For instance, let P_2 be an extension of process P_1, in which the *envelope* contains confidential data *hdata* (labelled *high*) which needs to be safely sent from *venice* to *warsaw*.

$venice^{b_1}[\ envelope^{b_2}[\mathbf{out}^{c_1}\ venice.\mathbf{in}^{c_2}\ warsaw.\mathbf{0} \mid hdata^{h}[\mathbf{in}^{c_3}\ translator.\mathbf{0}]\ ]\ ] \mid$
$warsaw^{b_3}[\mathbf{open}^{c_4}\ envelope.\mathbf{0}] \mid translator^{m}[\mathbf{in}^{c_5}\ envelope.\mathbf{0}] \mid \mathbf{open}^{c_6}\ translator$

In this case, *venice*, *warsaw* and *send* must be labelled *boundary* to protect *hdata* during the whole execution. (See [1,2] for more detail.)

The tool verifies that in every execution of process P no direct information leakage occurs, by implementing the control flow analyses described in [6] and [1]. Both analyses aim at modeling the possible nesting of processes occurring at run-time. The analysis presented in [1] is a refinement of [6]: it separately considers nestings inside and outside boundaries, thus leading to a more accurate result with respect to security issues.

3 Tool Overview

A screen-shot of the BANANA tool is shown in Figure 1, while Figure 2 gives an overview of the architecture of the tool.

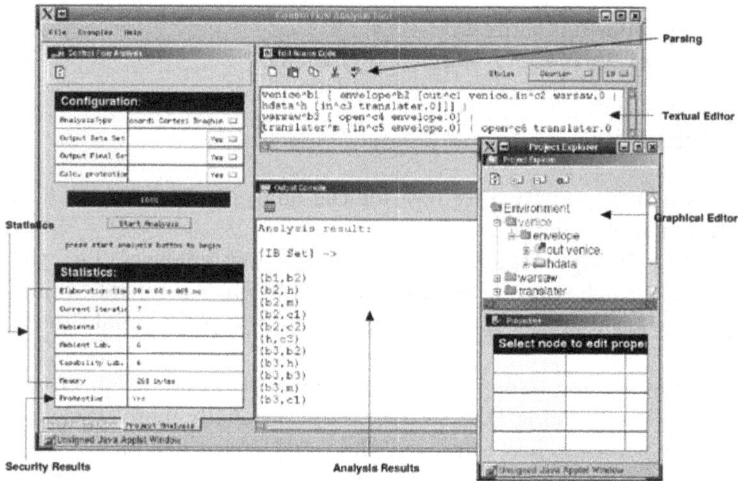

Fig. 1. Screen-shot of the BANANA tool.

A user can edit the process to be analyzed by using either the Textual or the Graphical Editor. The security labelling (i.e., the labels denoting untrusted, confidential, and boundary ambients) can be inserted directly by the user, or automatically derived by the tool during the parsing phase. In the latter case, ambients starting with letter 'b' are labelled boundaries, while ambients starting with 'h' are labelled high. By selecting an item in the Project Explorer window, the user can check/modify the properties of the ambient/capability. The user can also check the syntax correctness of the process by selecting the Parsing button.

The user can then choose to launch either the Nielson or the Braghin et al. analysis. Once the analysis has started the tool parses the process, builds a

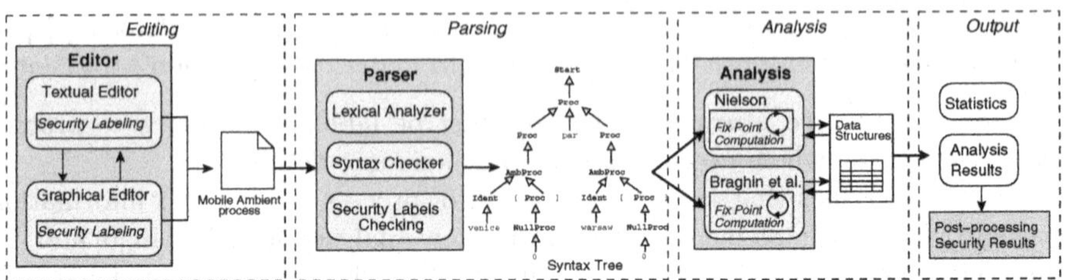

Fig. 2. Overview of the BANANA tool.

syntax tree and computes the fix point algorithm yielding an over-approximation of all possible ambient nestings. The result of the analysis is reported in the Output Console as a list of pairs of labels.

By post-processing the analysis results, BANANA reports in the filed Protective the sure absence of information leakages.

The BANANA tool has been accurately tested using a suite of use cases consisting of processes differing in the size and number of capabilities. It is available on-line at the following address:
`http://www.dsi.unive.it/~dbraghin/banana/`

4 Conclusion

BANANA is a very user-friendly tool for the analysis of information leakage in Mobile Ambient specifications.

It allows to compare two different control flow analyses, i.e., the one by Nielson et al. and the one by Braghin et al., run on non-trivial examples. This also shows the feasibility of these analyses, that have polynomial time and space complexities.

Another interesting issue is the scalability of this tool: as an on-going work we are currently extending BANANA to computationally more efficient analyses, as the one in [3] that has improved time and space complexities. This task is particularly simple, because of the modularity of the object-oriented Java technology.

The scalability is also possible toward variants of the Mobile Ambient calculus and extensions of the analysis, such as the one of [4] where a minimal set of security boundaries is inferred.

References

1. C. Braghin, A. Cortesi, and R. Focardi. Security Boundaries in Mobile Ambients. *Computer Languages*, Elsevier, to appear, vol. 18, 2002.
2. C. Braghin, A. Cortesi, and R. Focardi. Control Flow Analysis of Mobile Ambients with Security Boundaries. In B. Jacobs and A. Rensink, editors, *Proc. of Fifth Int. Conf. on Formal Methods for Open Object-Based Distributed Systems (FMOODS'02)*, pages 197–212, Kluwer Academic Publisher, 2002.

3. C. Braghin, A. Cortesi, R. Focardi, F.L. Luccio, and C. Piazza A New Algorithm for Control Flow Analysis of Mobile Ambients. In *Proc. of The 4th International Conference on Verification, Model Checking and Abstract Interpretation (VMCAI'03)*, LNCS, to appear, 2003.
4. C. Braghin, A. Cortesi, R. Focardi, and S. van Bakel. Boundary Inference for Enforcing Security Policies in Mobile Ambients. In *Proc. of The 2nd IFIP Int. Conf. on Theoretical Computer Science (TCS'02)*, pages 383–395. Kluwer Academic Publisher, August 2002.
5. L. Cardelli and A.D. Gordon. Mobile Ambients. Theoretical Computer Science (TCS), 240(1):177–213, 2000.
6. R. R. Hansen, J. G. Jensen, F. Nielson, and H. Riis Nielson. Abstract Interpretation of Mobile Ambients. In *Proc. of Static Analysis Symposium (SAS)*, volume 1694 of Lecture Notes in Computer Science, pages 134–148. Springer-Verlag, September 1999.
7. Francesca Levi and Davide Sangiorgi. Controlling Interference in Ambients. In *Proc. 28th ACM Symposium on Principles of Programming Languages (POPL'01)*, pages 352–364, 2000.

State Class Constructions for Branching Analysis of Time Petri Nets*

Bernard Berthomieu and François Vernadat

LAAS-CNRS, 7, avenue du Colonel Roche, 31077 Toulouse Cedex, France
fax: +33 5.61.33.64.11, tel: +33. 5.61.33.63.63
{Bernard.Berthomieu,Francois.Vernadat}@laas.fr

Abstract. This paper is concerned with construction of some state space abstractions for Time Petri nets. State class spaces were introduced long ago by Berthomieu and Menasche as finite representations for the typically infinite state spaces of Time Petri nets, preserving their linear time temporal properties. This paper proposes a similar construction that preserves their branching time temporal properties. The construction improves a previous proposal by Yoneda and Ryuba. The method has been implemented, computing experiments are reported.

Keywords: Time Petri nets, state classes, branching time temporal properties, model-checking, bisimulation, real-time systems modeling and verification.

1 Introduction

Many techniques for analysis of Petri nets or Time Petri nets proceed by building a labeled transition system (LTS) preserving the properties of interest (e.g. reachability set, deadlocks), in a first step, and then checking on this LTS the properties to be proven, in a second step. We are interested here in building labeled transition systems that preserve the branching properties of Time Petri nets. The branching properties are those one can express in modal logics like HML or branching time temporal logics like CTL^*, for instance; they are checked on the LTS produced using standard techniques not described here.

A technique for reachability analysis of Time Petri nets has been available for a long time [BM83,BD91]. This method computes state classes, which are finite representations for some infinite sets of states. State classes capture a marking and a convex firing time space for the transitions enabled at that marking. The state class graph preserves markings, as well as traces and complete traces of the state graph, and so is suitable for reachability analysis and LTL model checking. But, as it does not preserve the branching structure of the state graph (it is deterministic, by construction), it does not allow CTL^* model checking.

A state class graph construction preserving branching structure was proposed by Yoneda and Ryuba in [YR98]. Starting from an alternative definition of state

* This work was partially supported by RNTL Projet COTRE (www.laas.fr/COTRE)

H. Garavel and J. Hatcliff (Eds.): TACAS 2003, LNCS 2619, pp. 442–457, 2003.

classes, classes are split by linear constraints so that each state captured in a class has a successor in each of the following classes, such classes are called "Atomic". The authors show that atomicity of all classes ensures preservation of CTL^* properties. Though effective, the construction of [YR98] suffers some drawbacks that lead to class spaces larger than necessary. This paper proposes an alternative construction of the graph of atomic classes that does not suffer these drawbacks, is faster to compute, and is applicable to a larger class of nets.

The paper is organized as follows. Section 2 reviews the terminology of Time Petri nets and the available approaches for building state space abstractions that preserve LTL and CTL^* properties. Section 3 introduces strong classes, suitable as starting point for refinement into atomic classes. Section 4 discusses preservation of branching properties and introduces the revisited construction of atomic state classes. Section 5 completes the technical treatment. Computing experiments are reported Section 6.

2 Time Petri Nets, States, State Classes

2.1 Time Petri Nets

Let $\mathbf{I}^+$ be the set of nonempty real intervals with nonnegative rational end-points. For $i \in \mathbf{I}^+$, $\downarrow i$ denotes its left end-point, and $\uparrow i$ its right end-point (if i bounded) or ∞. For any $\theta \in \mathbf{R}^+$, $i \dot{-} \theta$ denotes the interval $\{x - \theta | x \in i \wedge x \geq \theta\}$.

Definition 1. *A* Time Petri net *(or* TPN*) is a tuple* $\langle P, T, \mathbf{Pre}, \mathbf{Post}, m_0, I_s \rangle$, *in which* $\langle P, T, \mathbf{Pre}, \mathbf{Post}, m_0 \rangle$ *is a Petri net, and* $I_s : T \rightarrow \mathbf{I}^+$ *is a function called the* Static Interval *function.*

Function I_s associates a temporal interval $I_s(t) \in \mathbf{I}^+$ with every transition of the net. $Eft_s(t) = \downarrow I_s(t)$ and $Lft_s(t) = \uparrow I_s(t)$ are called the static earliest and latest firing times of t, respectively. A Time Petri net is shown in Figure 1.

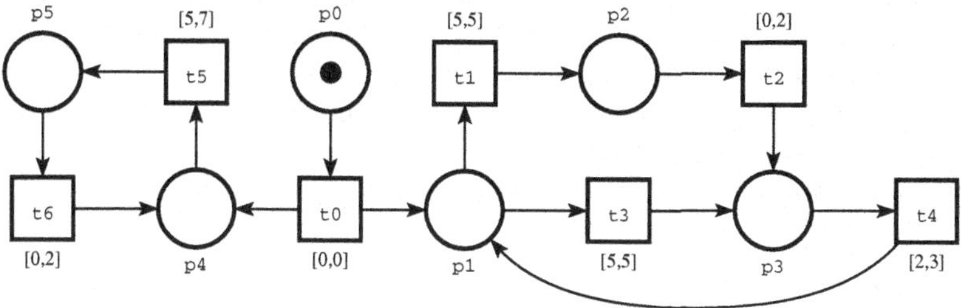

Fig. 1. A Time Petri net

2.2 States and Firing Schedules

States, and the temporal state transition relation $\xrightarrow{t@\theta}$, are defined as follows:

Definition 2. *A* state *of a TPN is a pair $s = (m, I)$ in which m is a marking and I is a function called the* interval *function. Function $I : T \to \mathbf{I}^+$ associates a temporal interval with every transition enabled at m.*
We write $(m, I) \stackrel{t@\theta}{\longrightarrow} (m', I')$ iff $\theta \in \mathbf{R}^+$ and:

1. $m \geq \mathbf{Pre}(t) \ \wedge \ \theta \geq \downarrow I(t) \ \wedge \ (\forall k \in T)(m \geq \mathbf{Pre}(k) \Rightarrow \theta \leq \uparrow I(k))$
2. $m' = m - \mathbf{Pre}(t) + \mathbf{Post}(t)$
3. $(\forall k \in T)(m' \geq \mathbf{Pre}(k) \Rightarrow$
   $I'(k) = \textbf{if } k \neq t \wedge m - \mathbf{Pre}(t) \geq \mathbf{Pre}(k) \textbf{ then } I(k) \dot{-} \theta \textbf{ else } I_s(k))$

We have $s \stackrel{t@\theta}{\longrightarrow} s'$ if firing transition t from s at time θ after t became last enabled leads to state s'. (1) ensures that transitions fire in their temporal interval, unless disabled by firing some other transition. (2) is the standard marking transformation. From (3), transitions persistent wrt t have their interval shifted by θ and truncated to nonnegative times, and newly enabled transitions are assigned their static intervals. A transition that remained enabled during its own firing is considered newly enabled (alternative interpretations of multi-enabledness are investigated in [Ber01a]). Firing a transition takes no time.

In the sequel, $s \stackrel{t}{\rightarrow} s'$ stands for $(\exists\theta)(s \stackrel{t@\theta}{\longrightarrow} s')$, $s \stackrel{t_1 \ldots t_n}{\longrightarrow} s'$ for $(\exists s_1 \ldots s_{n-1})(s \stackrel{t_1}{\rightarrow} s_1 \stackrel{t_2}{\rightarrow} \ldots \stackrel{t_{n-1}}{\rightarrow} s_{n-1} \stackrel{t_n}{\rightarrow} s')$, $s \rightarrow s'$ for $(\exists t)(s \stackrel{t}{\rightarrow} s')$, and $\stackrel{*}{\rightarrow}$ for the reflexive and transitive closure of $\rightarrow$.

Definition 3. *The* state graph *of a TPN is the structure*
$SG = (S, \stackrel{t@\theta}{\longrightarrow}, s_0)$, *where:*

$S = \{s | s_0 \stackrel{*}{\rightarrow} s\}$ *is the set of states reachable from the initial state* s_0
$s_0 = (m_0, I_0)$, *where* $I_0(t) = I_s(t)$ *for any* t *enabled at* m_0.

A *firing schedule* is a sequence of successively firable transitions, called its *support*, together with their relative firing times.

It is often convenient to see the temporal information in states as a firing domain, instead of an interval function: The *firing domain* of state (m, I) is the set of vectors $\{\underline{\phi} | (\forall k)(\underline{\phi}_k \in I(k))\}$, with components indexed by the enabled transitions. Given a state s, $\mathcal{M}(s)$ denotes its marking, and $\mathcal{F}(s)$ its firing domain.

Transitions may fire at any time in their temporal intervals, so states typically admit an infinity of successors. Finitely representing state spaces involves grouping states into sets, called state classes. All class space constructions discussed in this paper can be explained from the following characteristic systems.

2.3 Characteristic Systems

The times at which transitions in a firing sequence σ can fire (ranged over by the *path variables* $\underline{\theta}$) and the firing domain of the state reached (ranged over by the *state variables* $\underline{\phi}$) are related in a system of linear inequalities, called here the *characteristic system* of σ, written K_σ. K_σ has shape:

(1) $P\underline{\theta} \leq \underline{p}$
(2) $\underline{0} \leq \underline{\phi}$, $\underline{e} \leq \underline{\phi} + M\underline{\theta} \leq \underline{l}$, where $\underline{e}_k = Eft_s(k)$ and $\underline{l}_k = Lft_s(k)$

These systems are computed by the following algorithm, easily proven correct from Definition 2. Variable θ_ν stands for the possible firing times of transition t:

Algorithm 1 (Computing characteristic systems)

- *The initial system is* $K_\epsilon = \{Eft_s(t) \leq \underline{\phi}_t \leq Lft_s(t) \mid \mathbf{Pre}(t) \leq m_0\}$
- *Assume* σ *is firable and* $m_0 \xrightarrow{\sigma} m$. *Then* $\sigma.t$ *is firable iff:*
  (i) $m \geq \mathbf{Pre}(t)$ *(*t *is enabled at* m*)*
  (ii) system $K_\sigma \wedge \{\underline{\phi}_t \leq \underline{\phi}_i \mid i \neq t \wedge m \geq \mathbf{Pre}(i)\}$ *is consistent*
- *If* $\sigma.t$ *is firable, then* $K_{\sigma.t}$ *is computed from* K_σ *by:*
  1. *The firability constraints for t in (ii) above are added to* K_σ.
  2. *Variable* $\underline{\phi}_t$ *is renamed into a new path variable :* $\underline{\theta}_\nu$
  3. *For each* k *enabled at m', a new variable* $\underline{\phi}'_k$ *is introduced, obeying:*
     $\underline{\phi}'_k = \underline{\phi}_k - \underline{\theta}_\nu$, *if* $k \neq t$ *and* $m - \mathbf{Pre}(t) \geq \mathbf{Pre}(k)$
     $Eft_s(k) \leq \underline{\phi}'_k \leq Lft_s(k)$, *otherwise*
  4. *Variables* $\underline{\phi}$ *are eliminated.*

Characteristic systems constitute a labeled tree KG, rooted at K_ϵ. Node K_σ characterizes the set of states (generally infinite) reachable from the initial state by firing schedules of support σ. The characteristic system tree is finitely branching and deterministic, but it is still in general infinite. The next step towards finite representations of state spaces is to consider these systems modulo some equivalence relation. Several relations can be used, depending on the properties of the state space to be preserved.

2.4 State Classes That Preserve Linear Properties

State classes were proposed in [BM83] for finitely representing the state graphs of bounded Time Petri nets, preserving markings and complete traces. To distinguish them from the other constructions discussed in this paper, those state classes will be referred to as the *linear state classes*.

Linear state classes stem from the following observation: Assume sequences σ and σ' lead to the same marking from m_0, and characteristic systems K_σ and $K_{\sigma'}$ have equal solution sets after projection on their state variables $\underline{\phi}$. Then the subtrees of KG rooted at K_σ and $K_{\sigma'}$, respectively, are isomorphic. Linear state classes are characteristic systems considered modulo this equivalence.

We first give an abstract definition of linear state classes, in terms of states, helpful for relating these classes with the other sorts of classes discussed in the paper. Then, their construction and properties are recalled.

Definition 4. *The* linear state class graph *of a TPN is the structure*
$LSCG = (C/\cong, \xrightarrow{t}, [\{s_0\}]_\cong)$, *where*

C is the cover[1] *of S inductively defined by:*
$$C = \bigcup_{\sigma \in T^*} C_\sigma, \text{where } C_\epsilon = \{s_0\}, C_{\sigma.t} = \{s | (\exists s' \in C_\sigma)(s' \xrightarrow{t} s)\}$$

[1] A cover of e is a set of non-empty subsets of e whose union contains e

$$c \cong c' \text{ iff } (\exists s \in c)(\exists s' \in c')(\mathcal{M}(s) = \mathcal{M}(s') \wedge \bigcup_{s \in c} \mathcal{F}(s) = \bigcup_{s' \in c'} \mathcal{F}(s'))$$

$$c \xrightarrow{t} c' \text{ iff } (\exists s \in c)(\exists s' \in c')(s \xrightarrow{t} s')$$

Each C_σ captures all states reachable from the initial state by firing schedules of support σ. A state may belong to several classes. All states in a class have the same marking. State classes are considered modulo equivalence $\cong$: Defining the marking of a class as the marking of its states, and the firing domain of a class as the union of the firing domains of all states captured in the class, two classes are equivalent by $\cong$ iff their markings and firing domains are equal.

Linear state classes are exactly represented by the characteristic systems of Section 2.3, after elimination of path variables $\underline{\theta}$. They are computed by an algorithm similar to Algorithm 1, Section 2.3, except that the path variable $\underline{\theta}_\nu$ introduced at step 2 is eliminated at step 4. The resulting systems are difference systems.

The set of linear state classes of a TPN is finite iff the TPN is bounded [BM83]. This latter property is undecidable but there are decidable sufficient conditions for it [Ber01a]. Boundedness aspects will not be discussed further in this paper, where all TPNs considered are assumed bounded.

The $LSCG$ and SG hold the same markings and firing sequences (omitting time annotations for SG). In addition, no deadlock state may belong to the same class than a non-deadlock state, since all states in a class have same marking and the "deadlocked" property for a state only depends on its marking. So, seen as labeled transition systems, the SG and $LSCG$ are complete-trace equivalent. In terms of temporal logics, the $LSCG$ preserves LTL formulas, but clearly not CTL^* formulas, since, by construction, the $LSCG$ is deterministic.

The $LSCG$ of the net Figure 1 admits 83 classes and 160 transitions.

2.5 Atomic State Classes [YR98]

Assume each state class denotes some set of states. A class c is *Atomic* if, for each class c', whenever a state in c has a successor in c' then all states of c have successors in c'. The authors show that if linear properties are preserved, and all classes are atomic, then CTL^* properties are preserved too. They also propose a two-step construction for such a graph: An initial graph is first built, that preserves linear properties, then an iterative algorithm splits non atomic classes.

It is essential for the second step that class equivalence preserves atomicity. This makes the $LSCG$ of the previous section unsuitable as the first step, for instance, as two $LSCG$ classes may be equivalent by $\cong$ while one is atomic and the other is not. The authors start from an alternative concept of state class. Though formalized differently, their treatment can be explained as follows.

First, state classes are associated with firing sequences, as follows. The class associated with σ is represented by a pair (m, Θ) in which m is the marking reached by firing σ from m_0 and system Θ is subsystem (1) of the characteristic system K_σ. Classes are considered modulo an equivalence relation: Each transition k enabled at m has a "parent", which is the last transition in σ the firing of which enabled k (or the special v if k was enabled from the start). Then classes (m, Θ) and (m', Θ') are considered equivalent if $m = m'$, their enabled transitions have same "parents", and these parents could be fired at the same absolute times (this can be checked from Θ and Θ' after a simple transformation).

Next, classes are split until all of them are atomic. The authors show that, if $c = (m, \Theta)$ is non atomic, then there must exist some linear constraint ρ, nonredundant in Θ and such that, for some successor c' of c, ρ is necessary for a state in c to have a successor in c'. Class c is then split into subclasses $(m, \Theta \wedge \rho)$ and $(m, \Theta \wedge \neg\rho)$. Their descendant classes are computed from copies of those of c, by constraining their systems by ρ and $\neg\rho$, respectively. Their algorithm has been implemented, and some computational results produced.

Though effective, this construction suffers some drawbacks:

1. Their equivalence relation relies on the history of firings rather than the state contents of classes. As firing schedules of different supports may well lead to the same state, it is too weak to identify all classes that denote equal sets of states. As a result, their initial state class graph is typically larger than necessary. An alternative notion of classes, called "strong classes", suitable as a starting point for the splitting process but not suffering this drawback, is proposed in Section 3.

2. In addition to enforcing atomicity, their refinement algorithm maintains the invariant that each class captures exactly the successors of the states in its predecessor classes. This invariant is in fact unnecessary, maintaining it generally increases the number of classes. An alternative refinement algorithm will be proposed in Section 4, that typically yields smaller graphs. Computing atomic classes amounts to refine an initial partition of states into a bisimulation, the issue has been widely investigated in the literature.

3 Strong State Classes

3.1 Abstract Definition

In terms of state sets, Strong classes coincide with the cover C of the set of reachable states introduced in Definition 4 (before being quotiented by $\cong$):

Definition 5. *The* strong state class graph *of a TPN is the structure*

$$SSCG = (C, \xrightarrow{t}, \{s_0\}), \text{ where}$$

$$C = \bigcup_{\sigma \in T^*} C_\sigma, \text{ where } C_\epsilon = \{s_0\},\ C_{\sigma.t} = \{s | (\exists s' \in C_\sigma)(s' \xrightarrow{t} s)\}$$

$$c \xrightarrow{t} c' \text{ iff } (\exists s \in c)(\exists s' \in c')(s \xrightarrow{t} s')$$

For LTL model checking, the $SSCG$ brings nothing more than brought by the $LSCG$. But, since atomicity is expressed in terms of states, the $SSCG$ is clearly an adequate starting point for refinement of classes into atomic classes.

For building the $SSCG$, we need means of representing strong classes and checking their equality. Clock domains are adequate for this purpose.

3.2 Clock Domains and Their Equivalence

With any firing schedule, one may associate a *clock function* γ. With each transition enabled at the marking reached, function γ associates the time elapsed since that transition was last enabled. The clock function (seen as a vector) associated with a schedule of support σ and times $\underline{\theta}$ is exactly component $M\underline{\theta}$ in characteristic system K_σ: M_{ik} has value 1 if transition σ_i was fired after transition k was last enabled, and 0 otherwise. Adding equations $\underline{\gamma} = M\underline{\theta}$ to K_σ, and eliminating variables $\underline{\theta}$, it comes a system that relates clocks with firing domains (or states):

(1') $G\underline{\gamma} \leq \underline{g}$
(2') $\underline{0} \leq \underline{\phi}$, $\underline{e} \leq \underline{\phi} + \underline{\gamma} \leq \underline{l}$ where $\underline{e}_k = Eft_s(k)$ and $\underline{l}_k = Lft_s(k)$

Now, as for time vectors, different clock vectors may yield the same state. A suitable equivalence relation is much easier to obtain, however, as will be shown.

Let $\langle Q \rangle$ denote the solution set of inequation system Q. The set of states denoted by a marking m and a clock system $Q = \{G\underline{\gamma} \leq \underline{g}\}$ is the set $\{(m, \Phi(\underline{\gamma})) | \underline{\gamma} \in \langle Q \rangle\}$, where firing domain $\Phi(\underline{\gamma})$ is the solution set in $\underline{\phi}$ of subsystem (2') above.

Definition 6 (equivalence $\equiv$). *Given two pairs $c = (m, Q = \{G\underline{\gamma} \leq \underline{g}\})$ and $c' = (m', Q' = \{G'\underline{\gamma}' \leq \underline{g}'\})$, we write $c \equiv c'$ iff they denote equal sets of states.*

Equivalence $\equiv$ is easily decided in a particular case:

Theorem 1 ($\equiv$, bounded static intervals case). *Consider $c = (m, Q = \{G\underline{\gamma} \leq \underline{g}\})$ and $c' = (m', Q' = \{G'\underline{\gamma}' \leq \underline{g}'\})$. If all transitions enabled at m or m' have bounded static intervals, then $c \equiv c'$ iff $m = m' \wedge \langle Q \rangle = \langle Q' \rangle$.*

Proof. Consider system (2') above. For any k, we have $0 \leq \underline{\gamma}_k$, $0 \leq \underline{l}_k$, and $0 \leq \underline{l}_k - \underline{\gamma}_k$. So, given $\underline{\gamma}$, and if all $\underline{l}_k$ are finite, (2') admits exactly one solution $\underline{\phi}$. □

This theorem identifies an important class of TPNs for which clock systems exactly characterize state sets: the nets in which all transitions have bounded static intervals. Though some authors do so (e.g. [YR98]), we do not wish to enforce that restriction, however, for it would prevent to mix timed and untimed transitions in specifications. Now, for ease of explanation of the constructions to come, and since constructions in the general case can be explained from those in the particular case, we will assume this restriction enforced until the end of Section 4. The treatment will be generalized to arbitrary TPNs in Section 5.

We now propose an algorithm for building the graph of strong state classes.

3.3 Construction of the *SSCG*

Strong classes are represented by pairs (m, Q), where m is a marking and Q is a clock system $G\underline{\gamma} \leq \underline{g}$. Clock variables $\underline{\gamma}$ are bijectively associated with the transitions enabled at m. Equivalence $\equiv$ is implemented as in Theorem 1.

Algorithm 2 (Computing strong state classes)
For each firable firing sequence σ, a pair R_σ can be computed as explained below. Compute the smallest set C including R_ϵ and such that, whenever $R_\sigma \in C$ and $\sigma.t$ is firable, then either $R_{\sigma.t} \in C$ or $R_{\sigma.t}$ is equivalent by $\equiv$ to some pair in C.

- *The initial pair is* $R_\epsilon = (m_0, \{0 \leq \underline{\gamma}_t \leq 0 \mid \mathbf{Pre}(t) \leq m_0\})$
- *If σ is firable and $R_\sigma = (m, Q)$, then $\sigma.t$ is firable iff:*
  (i) t is enabled at m, that is : $m \geq \mathbf{Pre}(t)$
  (ii) Q augmented with the following constraints is consistent:
  $0 \leq \theta\ ,\ Eft_s(t) - \underline{\gamma}_t \leq \theta,\ \{\theta \leq Lft_s(i) - \underline{\gamma}_i \mid m \geq \mathbf{Pre}(i)\}$
- *If $\sigma.t$ is firable, then $R_{\sigma.t} = (m', Q')$ is computed from $R_\sigma = (m, Q)$ by:*
  $m' = m - \mathbf{Pre}(t) + \mathbf{Post}(t)$
  Q' obtained by:
  1. *A new variable is introduced, θ, constrained by conditions (ii);*
  2. *For each i enabled at m', a new variable $\underline{\gamma}'_i$ is introduced, obeying:*
     $\underline{\gamma}'_i = \underline{\gamma}_i + \theta$, *if $i \neq t$ and* $m - \mathbf{Pre}(t) \geq \mathbf{Pre}(i)$
     $0 \leq \underline{\gamma}'_i \leq 0$, *otherwise*
  3. *Variables $\underline{\gamma}$ and θ are eliminated.*

The temporary variable θ stands for the possible firing times of transition t. There is an arc labeled t between classes R_σ and c if $c \equiv R_{\sigma.t}$. Each R_σ computed coincides with characteristic system K_σ, with subsystem (2) replaced by $\underline{\gamma} = M\underline{\theta}$, and then variables $\underline{\theta}$ eliminated. By Theorem 1, assuming enforced the "bounded static intervals" restriction, R_σ denotes exactly the set of states reachable from s_0 by schedules of support σ.

The set of clock systems Q with distinct solution sets one can built by Algorithm 2 is finite, whether the TPN is bounded or not, so the $SSCG$ is finite iff the TPN is bounded. The proof relies on similar arguments than used for proving finiteness of the set of linear classes in [BM83]. One may easily add on the fly boundedness checks to Algorithm 2, enforcing sufficient conditions, as done for the construction of the $LSCG$ there.

Equivalence $\equiv$ is checked by putting clock systems into canonical forms, and then checking their identity. Clock systems are difference systems; their canonical forms can be computed in polynomial time and space using e.g. Floyd/Warshall's algorithm for computing all pairs shortest paths.

The $SSCG$ of the net Figure 1 admits 107 classes and 205 transitions.

The first purpose of the $SSCG$ is to serve as initial graph for refinement into the atomic state class graph. Now, it clearly preserves LTL properties too. For the purpose of LTL model checking, the $SSCG$ would be a poor substitute for the $LSCG$, however, as the latter is typically smaller and is faster to compute.

Before introducing our revisited construction for the graph of atomic state classes, let us summarize the benefits of the $SSCG$ over the proposal of [YR98] for the initial state class graph: (1) Clock systems modulo $\equiv$ canonically represent state sets, while two non equivalent Yoneda classes may denote the same set of states. (2) The number of variables in clock systems is, on average, smaller than that of the corresponding systems in [YR98]. (3) With the extension of the method introduced Section 5, the "bounded static interval" restriction is removed (Yoneda's construction requires it).

4 Atomic State Classes Revisited

4.1 Preserving Branching Properties

Let us state three properties of state class graphs (c and c' are classes):

(EE) $(\forall t \in T)(\forall c, c')(c \xrightarrow{t} c' \Leftrightarrow (\exists s \in c)(\exists s' \in c')(s \xrightarrow{t} s'))$
(AE) $(\forall c')(c \xrightarrow{t} c' \Rightarrow (\forall s \in c)(\exists s' \in c')(s \xrightarrow{t} s'))$
(EA) $(\forall c')(c' \xrightarrow{t} c \Rightarrow (\forall s \in c)(\exists s' \in c')(s' \xrightarrow{t} s))$

In their most general definition, state class graphs, or spaces, are covers of the set of states of the TPN such that all states in each class bear the same marking, equipped with a transition relation satisfying (EE). State class spaces are similar to the abstract state spaces of [PP01], except that we allow a concrete state to belong to several classes.

Our goal is to build state class graphs that preserve the branching properties of a TPN, that is of its state graph. Branching properties are those expressed in modal logics like HML or in branching time temporal logics like CTL^*. In absence of silent transitions, bisimilarity is known to preserve such properties [BCG88,NV95]. So, we just want to build state class graphs which are bisimilar with the state graph of the TPN, omitting time information in the latter.

The graph of atomic classes of [YR98] satisfies this property. Their algorithm enforces (EE), (AE) and (EA). It is easily shown that (AE) and (EE) imply bisimilarity with the state graph. Maintaining (EA) is unnecessary however.

Bisimulations can be computed with an algorithm initially aimed at solving the *relational coarsest partition* problem [PT87]. Let $\rightarrow$ be a binary relation over a finite set U, and for any $S \subseteq U$, let $S^{-1} = \{x | (\exists y \in S)(x \rightarrow y)\}$. A partition P of U is *stable* if, for any pair (A, B) of blocks of P, either $A \subseteq B^{-1}$ or $A \cap B^{-1} = \emptyset$ (A is said *stable wrt* B). Computing a bisimulation, starting from an initial partition P of states, is computing a stable refinement Q of P [KS90,ACH+96]. An algorithm is the following [PT87]:

Initially : $Q = P$
while there exists $A, B \in Q$ such that $\emptyset \not\subseteq A \cap B^{-1} \not\subseteq A$ **do**
    replace A by $A_1 = A \cap B^{-1}$ and $A_2 = A - B^{-1}$ in Q

So, building a graph of atomic classes from the $SSCG$ is computing a stable refinement of it. Our algorithm is based on the above, differences include:

– As timed systems may admit infinitely many states, these are not handled individually, but as part of particular, convex, sets. The coarsest bisimulation does not necessary yields convex blocks. Our treatment enforces convexity of blocks when it conflicts with the "coarsest" property. The stability condition in the above algorithm is rephrased into a more primitive one based on nonredundancy of some linear constraint, explained in the next Section.

– Our refinement process starts from a cover of states, rather than a partition. Refinements are still sound, but the "coarsest" property is lost, again.

Compared to Yoneda's treatment, our construction enforces (AE), clearly equivalent to stability wrt successor classes, but not (EA). So, notwithstanding the differences in the definition of classes, it yields smaller graphs, in general.

4.2 Splitting Strong Classes

Let $c = (m, Q)$ be some class and assume $c \xrightarrow{t} c' = (m', Q')$. We want to check if c is stable wrt c' by t (that is if all states of c have a successor in c' by t), and, if not the case, to compute a partition of c in which all blocks are stable wrt c' by t. This is done as follows : if c is not stable wrt c' by t, then a linear constraint ρ is computed such that it is non redundant[2] in Q and ρ is necessary for a state of c to have a successor in c' by t. c is then split into subclasses $l = (m, Q \wedge \{\neg\rho\})$ and $r = (m, Q \wedge \{\rho\})$. Subclass l is stable wrt c' by t as it has no successor in c' by t; iterating this process from r until all subclasses of c found are stable wrt c' by t yields a partition of c stable wrt c'.

It remains to be shown how to find splitting constraints. Let us review how Algorithm 2 computes the successors of the states in c by t (omitting markings): Starting from the clock system Q of c, the firability conditions for t from c are added (subsystem (F) below). Next, new variables $\underline{\gamma}'_i$ are introduced for the persistent transitions (subsystem (N)) and for the newly enabled transitions. Finally, variables $\underline{\gamma}$ and θ are eliminated.

$$(Q)\ \ G\underline{\gamma} \leq \underline{g} \qquad (F)\ \ A(\underline{\gamma}|\theta) \leq \underline{b} \qquad (N)\ \ \underline{\gamma}'_i = \underline{\gamma}_i + \theta$$

For the sake of computing splitting constraints, newly enabled transitions may be omitted, as their variables do not appear in Q. Let Q'' be system Q' with these variables eliminated. Stability of c wrt c' can be rephrased then:

$$(\forall \underline{\gamma})(Q \Rightarrow (\exists \theta, \underline{\gamma}')(F \wedge N \wedge Q''))$$

This formula asserts that the solution set of Q is included in that of $F \wedge N \wedge Q''$, projected on variables $\underline{\gamma}$. It can be checked by building system $F \wedge N \wedge Q''$ and then verifying that all constraints of this system are redundant in Q. Any non-redundant one provides a splitting constraint for c. Since there are finitely many constraints in $F \wedge N \wedge Q''$, the partitioning process described above terminates.

Convexity of partition members has been favored over the "coarsest" property of the partition. Depending on the order in which splitting constraints are considered, one may obtain different partitions of c, of possibly different sizes.

4.3 The Revisited Atomic State Class Graph

Definition 7. *Given a bisimulation relation $\approx$ on states, the* atomic state class graph, *over $\approx$, of a TPN is the structure*

$$\begin{aligned} ASCG &= (A, \xrightarrow{t}, \{s_0\}), \textit{ where} \\ A &= \bigcup_{c \in C} (c/\approx), \textit{ where } C \textit{ is the set of strong state classes} \\ c &\xrightarrow{t} c' \textit{ iff } (\exists s \in c)(\exists s' \in c')(s \xrightarrow{t} s') \end{aligned}$$

[2] ρ is non-redundant in Q iff both systems $Q \wedge \{\rho\}$ and $Q \wedge \{\neg\rho\}$ are consistent.

For any TPN, its $ASCG$ and state graph SG are bisimilar. In practice, the $ASCG$ will be built over the bisimulation obtained by the splitting method of Section 4.2. An algorithm is the following:

Algorithm 3 (Computing atomic state classes)

Start from the SSCG
while *some class c is unstable wrt one of its successors c′* **do**
  split c wrt c′
  restore property (EE)
Collect all classes reachable from the initial class.

Splitting c replaces it by a pair $\{l, r\}$. Each of the l and r inherits the predecessors and successors of c, including themselves and excluding c if c was successor of itself. Classes, including those obtained as results of splits, are considered modulo $\equiv$. Checking (EE) can be done with an algorithm similar to atomicity detection: some state of class a has a successor in b iff the clock set of the potential predecessors of b, computed as in Section 4.2, intersects with the clock set of a. This amounts to checking consistency of an inequation system. Details and optimizations are left out.

Termination of Algorithm 3 follows from finiteness of the $SSCG$ and of partitions of classes by the stability condition.

The $ASCG$ of the net Figure 1 admits 101 classes and 431 transitions. For that example, the $ASCG$ has less classes than the $SSCG$, but more transitions.

5 Handling Unbounded Static Intervals

We assumed from Section 3.2 that all transitions of nets had bounded static intervals. In practice, this prevents to mix timed and untimed transitions in specifications, as the latter would be represented by transitions bearing static interval $[0, \infty[$. Removing that restriction has thus important practical benefits.

Applied to arbitrary TPNs, and with equivalence $\equiv$ implemented as in Theorem 1, Algorithm 2 would not always terminate. Consider the net below:

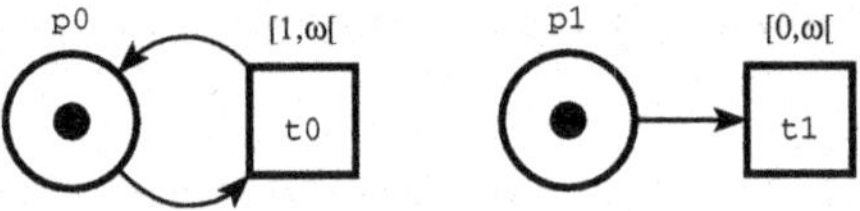

Its initial strong class is $(m_0 = \{p_0, p_1\}, \{0 \leq \underline{\gamma}_{t_0} \leq 0,\ 0 \leq \underline{\gamma}_{t_1} \leq 0\})$. Firing $k > 0$ times t_0 from it leads to $C_k = (m_k = \{p_0, p_1\}, \{0 \leq \underline{\gamma}_{t_0} \leq 0,\ k \leq \underline{\gamma}_{t_1}\})$. Since their clock systems have different solution sets, C_0 and all the C_k are distinct.

Now, it should be observed that C_0 and all C_k denote exactly the same set of states since their clock systems define the same interval function: $I = \{1 \leq I(t_0),\ 0 \leq I(t_1)\}$. These classes are actually equivalent by $\equiv$ (cf. Definition 6), but $\equiv$ in the general case cannot be implemented simply as in Theorem 1.

The most general clock system that yields that interval function is $\widehat{Q} = \{0 \leq \underline{\gamma}_{t_0} \leq 0,\ 0 \leq \underline{\gamma}_{t_1}\})$. Replacing clock systems in C_0 and the C_k by it produces a graph bisimilar to the previous as the future of a class only depends on its state contents, but finite. We now discuss computation of such "largest" clock systems.

Definition 8 (relaxation of clock systems).
Let (m, Q) represent some strong state class, and E^ω be the set of transitions enabled at m that have unbounded static interval. The relaxation *of system Q is the disjunction of systems $\widehat{Q} = \bigvee\{Q_e | e \subseteq E^\omega\}$, with Q_e obtained by:*

(i) First, Q is augmented with constraints:
$\gamma_t < Eft_s(t), \forall t \in e$
$\gamma_t \geq Eft_s(t), \forall t \in E^\omega - e$
(ii) Then all variables $t \in E^\omega - e$ are eliminated
(iii) Finally, constraints $\gamma_t \geq Eft_s(t), \forall t \in E^\omega - e$, are added again

Clock space Q is recursively partitioned according to whether $\underline{\gamma}_k \geq Eft_s(k)$ or not, for some k corresponding to a transition with unbounded Lft_s. Then, in the half space in which $\underline{\gamma}_k \geq Eft_s(k)$, the upper bound of $\underline{\gamma}_k$ is relaxed.

Relation $\equiv$ can now be decided in the general case. The solution set $\langle\widehat{Q}\rangle$ of $\widehat{Q}$ is the union of the solution sets of its components. Intuitively, each equivalence class of state classes by $\equiv$ admits a largest element which is obtained from any state class in the equivalence class by relaxation of its clock system.

Theorem 2 ($\equiv$ in arbitrary TPNs). *Let $c = (m, Q = \{G\underline{\gamma} \leq \underline{g}\})$ and $c' = (m', Q' = \{G'\underline{\gamma}' \leq \underline{g}'\})$. Then $c \equiv c' \Leftrightarrow m = m' \wedge \langle\widehat{Q}\rangle = \langle\widehat{Q'}\rangle$.*

Proof. If $m \neq m'$, then the property is clearly true. Assume thus $m = m'$ and let us prove property (P): $(\forall m, Q, Q')((m, Q) \equiv (m, Q') \Leftrightarrow \langle\widehat{Q'}\rangle = \langle\widehat{Q}\rangle)$. We have:
(1) $(\forall(m, Q))((m, Q) \equiv (m, \widehat{Q}))$:

For each $e \subseteq E^\omega$, let Q^e be the system obtained after step (i) in Definition 8. $(m, Q) \equiv (m, \bigvee\{Q^e | e \subseteq E^\omega\})$ since the Q^e constitute a partition of Q. (1) holds if $(\forall e)((m, Q^e) \equiv (m, Q_e))$, with Q_e as in Definition 8. By construction, each $\underline{\gamma} \in \langle Q_e\rangle$ either belongs to Q^e, or only differs from some $\underline{\gamma}' \in \langle Q^e\rangle$ by its components k in $E^\omega - e$. Since, for each k, $\underline{\gamma}_k \geq Eft_s(k)$ and $\underline{\gamma}'_k \geq Eft_s(k)$, both $\underline{\gamma}$ and $\underline{\gamma}'$ define interval $[0, \infty[$ for k, so they define the same interval function.
(2) $(\forall m, Q, Q')(\langle Q'\rangle \not\subseteq \langle\widehat{Q}\rangle \Rightarrow (m, Q) \not\equiv (m, Q'))$:

Assume $\underline{\gamma}' \in Q'$ and $\underline{\gamma}' \notin \widehat{Q}$. The only case when two clock vectors may denote the same interval function is when they differ by some components corresponding to transitions with unbounded static intervals, and these components are larger or equal than the Eft_s of those transitions. If this was the case for $\underline{\gamma}'$ and $\underline{\gamma}$, then both would belong to $\widehat{Q}$, by construction. So, no $\underline{\gamma} \in Q$ may denote the same interval function than $\underline{\gamma}'$, and $(m, Q) \not\equiv (m, Q')$.
(3) $(\forall m, Q, Q')(\langle Q\rangle = \langle Q'\rangle \Rightarrow (m, Q) \equiv (m, Q'))$: obvious, proof omitted.
(4) $(\forall m, Q, Q')((m, Q) \equiv (m, Q') \Rightarrow \langle\widehat{Q}\rangle = \langle\widehat{Q'}\rangle)$:

since $(m, Q) \equiv (m, Q') \Rightarrow (m, Q) \equiv (m, \widehat{Q'}) \wedge (m, \widehat{Q}) \equiv (m, Q')$, by (1)
$\Rightarrow \langle\widehat{Q'}\rangle \subseteq \langle\widehat{Q}\rangle \wedge \langle\widehat{Q}\rangle \subseteq \langle\widehat{Q'}\rangle$, by (2)

(5) $(\forall m, Q, Q')(\langle \widehat{Q} \rangle = \langle \widehat{Q'} \rangle \Rightarrow (m, Q) \equiv (m, Q'))$:
since $\langle \widehat{Q} \rangle = \langle \widehat{Q'} \rangle \Rightarrow (m, \widehat{Q}) \equiv (m, \widehat{Q'})$, by (3)
$\Rightarrow (m, Q) \equiv (m, Q')$, by (1)

(P) by (4) and (5). □

It remains to show how to update the construction algorithms for the *SSCG* and *ASCG* to handle arbitrary static intervals. Simply implementing $\equiv$ as in Theorem 2, rather than as in Theorem 1, would be satisfying for building the *SSCG*, but it would obscure split operations for construction of the *ASCG*. A better alternative is to keep $\equiv$ implemented as in Theorem 1 throughout, and integrate relaxation into Algorithm 2 as follows: after computation of $R_{\sigma.t} = (m', Q')$, $\widehat{Q'}$ is computed, and R_σ is assigned as many successors classes by t as $\widehat{Q'}$ has components, each pairing m' with a single component of $\widehat{Q'}$. This does not incur any significant time or space penalty, compared to the first alternative, as relaxations would be computed anyway, and stored for speeding equivalence checks. The *ASCG* for an arbitrary TPN is then built exactly as in Algorithm 3, except that refinement starts from the *SSCG* obtained by the updated Algorithm 2. The classes obtained by splits need not be relaxed.

6 Computing Experiments

Preliminary implementations of the algorithms for building strong and atomic state class graphs have been integrated in a tool named *Tina* [Ber01b]. Beside these constructions, *Tina* offers various other reachability graph constructions for Petri nets and Time Petri nets, including the *LSCG*.

We first compared our treatment with that of [YR98], on their examples. The results in number of classes, edges, and computing times, are reported in Table 1. The last column shows the size of the minimization of the *ASCG* under bisimulation, computed with *Aldebaran* [FGK+96]. The results confirm the expected benefits of our construction, in terms of size and cost.

Table 1. Yoneda's experiments.

Example		*ASCG*	*Yoneda*	*Optimal*
	Classes	36	53	26
(*Fig.* 5*a*)	*Edges*	61	95	47
	CPU(*s*)	0.01	0.02	
	Classes	62	64	46
(*Fig.* 5*b*)	*Edges*	163	178	135
	CPU(*s*)	0.06	0.41	
	Classes	80	168	80
(*Fig.* 5*c*)	*Edges*	204	363	204
	CPU(*s*)	0.10	11.93	

Figure 2 shows more challenging examples. The examples are Time Petri net versions of the classical level crossing example. The nets are obtained by parallel composition of n train models (lower left), synchronized with a controller model (upper left, n instantiated), and a barrier model (upper right). The specifications mix timed and untimed transitions (those labeled *App*).

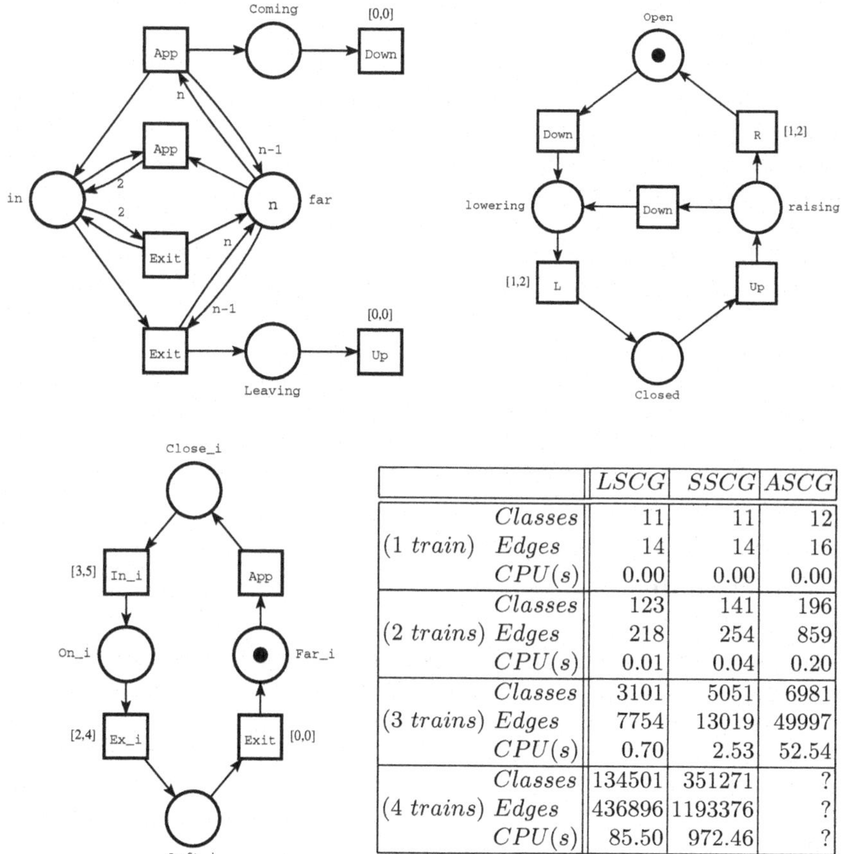

		$LSCG$	$SSCG$	$ASCG$
	Classes	11	11	12
(1 *train*)	*Edges*	14	14	16
	$CPU(s)$	0.00	0.00	0.00
	Classes	123	141	196
(2 *trains*)	*Edges*	218	254	859
	$CPU(s)$	0.01	0.04	0.20
	Classes	3101	5051	6981
(3 *trains*)	*Edges*	7754	13019	49997
	$CPU(s)$	0.70	2.53	52.54
	Classes	134501	351271	?
(4 *trains*)	*Edges*	436896	1193376	?
	$CPU(s)$	85.50	972.46	?

Fig. 2. Level crossing example.

For each model, we built with *Tina* its $LSCG$, $SSCG$ and $ASCG$, their sizes are also shown in Figure 2 (no figures are available for Yoneda's construction). Computing times for the $ASCG$ are much larger than for the $LSCG$ or $SSCG$, but it preserves more properties. Safety properties like "the barrier is closed when a train crosses the road" can be checked on any graph, but liveness properties like "when no train approaches, the barrier eventually opens" must be checked on the $ASCG$. Temporal properties like "when a train approaches, the barrier closes within some given delay" generally translate to safety or liveness properties of the net composed with "observer nets" deduced from the properties.

Note the fast increase in number of classes with the number of trains, for all constructions. For this particular example, this number could be greatly reduced by exploiting the symmetries of the state space resulting from replication of the train model. An adhoc solution at modeling level would be e.g. to prevent train $i+1$ to approach when trains $1 \dots i$ are not in state Far. For linear state classes, an alternative is allowed by a variant of the $LSCG$ construction discussed in [Ber01a], in which a transition enabled k times (i.e. st. $m \geq k * \mathbf{Pre}(t)$) is associated with k distinct intervals, instead of one. These intervals are ordered and, when firing transitions, the oldest is considered first. For our example, symmetries could be handled by modeling trains by a single copy of the train model in Figure 2, marked with n, instead of n copies, and using that interpretation of multi-enabledness. Extending the approach to the $ASCG$ is being investigated.

Finally, we compared our constructions with the "time-abstracting bisimulations" [TY96] built by the tool *Kronos* [Yov97] for a similar level crossing example modeled with timed automata. The figures we obtained for building the time-abstracting bisimulations are similar to those we obtained for building the $ASCG$, both in terms of sizes and computing times. These constructions serve the same purposes and are here equally expensive. No equivalent of the much faster $LSCG$ construction is available for timed automata. More generally, comparisons between these two modeling techniques should be taken with care, they have different modeling abilities and require different analysis techniques. Some examples may favor one, while others, or slight changes, may favor the other. In both cases, running times are very sensitive to changes in time constraints.

7 Conclusion

We proposed in this paper a construction of a state space abstraction for Time Petri nets that allows to prove properties relying on their branching structure, like liveness properties or those expressed in logics HML or CTL^*. It improves an existing construction in [YR98] by producing more abstract graphs, being faster to compute, and being applicable to a larger class of Time Petri nets. This construction complements the "standard" state classes method of [BM83], suitable for LTL model checking and reachability analysis.

We believe the constructions in [YR98] and those proposed here open interesting research paths in analysis and model-checking of Time Petri nets, that we intend to explore further. For generality, we focused our attention to preservation of "full" branching properties, as, in our context, this implies preservation of truth values of formulas of the strongest available temporal logics. The $ASCG$ construction can be further refined to only preserve formulas of weaker logics, like the sublogics of CTL^* considered in [PP01], using the techniques developed in their paper.

Our immediate goals are to improve the algorithmics for construction of the $ASCG$. Longer term goals include investigation of partial order techniques [PP01] to reduce further its size, and systematic methods for checking formulas of logics with time, such as $TCTL$ [ACD90]. Many formula in such logics do not actually require to build the $ASCG$ but can be more efficiently proved on the

LSCG of the TPN composed with some observer net built from the formula. An in-depth study of this proof technique is needed for Time Petri nets.

Acknowledgments. The authors are grateful to Tomohiro Yoneda for many discussions and making his experimental software available to us, and to Agata Półrola for her comments on the original draft of this paper.

References

[ACD90] R. Alur, C. Courcoubetis, and D. Dill. Model-checking for real-time systems. In *Proc. 5th IEEE Symposium on Logic in Computer Science*, pages 414–425, june 1990.

[ACH+96] R. Alur, C. Courcoubetis, N. Halbwachs, D.L. Dill, and H. Wong-Toi. Minimization of timed transition systems. In *CONCUR 92: Theories of Concurrency, Springer LNCS 630*, pages 340–354, 1996.

[BCG88] M. C. Browne, E. M. Clarke, and O. Grümberg. Characterizing finite kripke structures in propositional temporal logics. *Theoretical Computer Science*, 59:115–131, 1988.

[BD91] B. Berthomieu and M. Diaz. Modeling and verification of time dependent systems using time Petri nets. *IEEE Transactions on Software Engineering*, 17(3):259–273, March 1991.

[Ber01a] B. Berthomieu. La méthode des classes d'états pour l'analyse des réseaux temporels – mise en œuvre, extension à la multi-sensibilisation. In *Proc. Modélisation des Systèmes Réactifs, Toulouse, France*, October 2001.

[Ber01b] B. Berthomieu. *The Tina V2 Toolbox.* http://www.laas.fr/tina, LAAS/CNRS, 2001.

[BM83] B. Berthomieu and M. Menasche. An enumerative approach for analyzing time Petri nets. *IFIP Congress Series*, 9:41–46, 1983.

[FGK+96] J-C. Fernandez, H. Garavel, A. Kerbrat, R. Mateescu, L. Mounier, and M. Sighireanu. CADP: A protocol validation and verification toolbox. In *8th Conference on Computer-Aided Verification, CAV'96, Springer LNCS 1102*, July 1996.

[KS90] P. K. Kanellakis and S. A. Smolka. Ccs expressions, finite state processes, and three problems of equivalence. *Information and Computation*, 86:43–68, 1990.

[NV95] R. De Nicola and F. Vandrager. Three logics for branching bisimulation. *Journal of the ACM*, 42(2):458–487, 1995.

[PP01] W. Penczek and A. Półrola. Abstraction and partial order reductions for checking branching properties of time petri nets. In *Proc. of ICATPN, Springer LNCS 2075*, pages 323–342, 2001.

[PT87] P. Paige and R. E. Tarjan. Three partition refinement algorithms. *SIAM Journal on Computing*, 16(6):973–989, 1987.

[TY96] S. Tripakis and S. Yovine. Analysis of timed systems based on time–abstracting bisimulations. In *8th Conference Computer-Aided Verification, CAV'96, Springer LNCS 1102*, pages 232–243, jul 1996.

[Yov97] S. Yovine. Kronos: A verification tool for real-time systems. *International Journal of Software Tools for Technology Transfer*, 1(1), 1997.

[YR98] T. Yoneda and H. Ryuba. CTL model checking of Time Petri nets using geometric regions. *IEEE Transactions on Information and Systems*, E99-D(3):1–10, 1998.

Branching Processes of High-Level Petri Nets

Victor Khomenko and Maciej Koutny

School of Computing Science, University of Newcastle
Newcastle upon Tyne NE1 7RU, U.K.
{Victor.Khomenko, Maciej.Koutny}@ncl.ac.uk

Abstract. In this paper, we define branching processes and unfoldings of high-level Petri nets and propose an algorithm which builds finite and complete prefixes of such unfoldings. The advantage of our method is that it avoids a potentially expensive translation of a high-level Petri net into a low-level one. The approach is conservative as all the verification tools employing the traditional unfoldings can be reused with prefixes derived directly from high-level nets. We show that this is often better than the usual explicit construction of the intermediate low-level net.

Keywords: Verification, model checking, high-level Petri nets, unfolding.

1 Introduction

A distinctive characteristic of reactive concurrent systems is that their sets of local states have descriptions which are both short and manageable, and the complexity of their behaviour comes from highly complicated interactions with the external environment rather than from complicated data structures and manipulations thereon. One way of coping with this complexity problem is to use formal methods and, especially, computer aided verification tools implementing model checking (see, e.g., [4]) — a technique in which the verification of a system is carried out using a finite representation of its state space.

The main drawback of model checking is that it suffers from the state space explosion problem. That is, even a relatively small system specification can yield a very large state space. To cope with this, a number of techniques have been proposed, which can roughly be classified as aiming at a compact representation of the full state space of a reactive system, or at an explicit generation of its reduced (though sufficient for a given verification task) representation.

McMillan's (finite prefixes of) Petri Net unfoldings (see, e.g., [20,21]) rely on the partial order view of concurrent computation, and represent system's actions and local states implicitly, using an acyclic net. In view of the development of fast model checking algorithms employing unfoldings ([11,14]), the problem of efficiently building them is becoming increasingly important. Recently, [7,8, 10,12,15,22] addressed this issue — considerably improving the original McMillan's technique — but we feel that generating net unfoldings deserves further investigation. In particular, it is highly desirable to generalize this technique to

H. Garavel and J. Hatcliff (Eds.): TACAS 2003, LNCS 2619, pp. 458–472, 2003.

more expressive formalisms, such as high-level (or 'coloured') Petri nets. This formalism allows one to model in quite a natural way many constructs of high-level specification languages used to describe concurrent systems (see, e.g., [1, 9]). Though it is possible to translate a high-level net into a low-level one and then unfold the latter, it is often the case that the intermediate low-level net is much larger than the resulting prefix.

In this paper, we propose an approach which allows one to build the prefix directly from a high-level net. Such a method is often superior to the traditional one, involving the explicit construction of an intermediate low-level net.

Notation. A *multiset* over a set X is a function $\mu : X \to \mathbb{N} \stackrel{\text{df}}{=} \{0, 1, 2, \ldots\}$ (any subset of X may be viewed through its characteristic function as a multiset over X). We denote $x \in \mu$ if $\mu(x) \geq 1$, and for two multisets over X, μ and μ', we write $\mu \leq \mu'$ if $\mu(x) \leq \mu'(x)$ for all $x \in X$. $\varnothing$ denotes the *empty multiset* defined by $\varnothing(x) \stackrel{\text{df}}{=} 0$, for all $x \in X$. A finite multiset may be represented by explicitly listing its elements between the $\{\!\!\{ \ldots \}\!\!\}$ brackets, e.g., $\{\!\!\{y, y, z\}\!\!\}$ denotes μ such that $\mu(y) = 2$, $\mu(z) = 1$ and $\mu(x) = 0$, for $x \in X \setminus \{y, z\}$. The sum of two multisets μ and μ' over X is given by $(\mu + \mu')(x) \stackrel{\text{df}}{=} \mu(x) + \mu'(x)$, the difference by $(\mu - \mu')(x) \stackrel{\text{df}}{=} \max\{0, \mu(x) - \mu'(x)\}$, and the intersection by $(\mu \cap \mu')(x) \stackrel{\text{df}}{=} \min\{\mu(x), \mu'(x)\}$, for all $x \in X$. A multiset μ is finite if there are finitely many $x \in X$ such that $\mu(x) \geq 1$. In such a case, the cardinality of μ is defined as $|\mu| \stackrel{\text{df}}{=} \sum_{x \in X} \mu(x)$. $\{\!\!\{P(x) \mid x \in \mu\}\!\!\}$, where μ is a multiset and $P(x)$ is an object constructed from $x \in X$, will be used to denote the multiset μ' such that $\mu'(y) \stackrel{\text{df}}{=} \sum_{x \in X \wedge P(x) = y} \mu(x) \cdot y$, where $\mu(x) \cdot y$ is the multiset consisting of exactly $\mu(x)$ copies of y, e.g., $\{\!\!\{x^2{+}1 \mid x \in \{\!\!\{-1, 0, 0, 1\}\!\!\}\}\!\!\} = \{\!\!\{1, 1, 2, 2\}\!\!\}$. For a mapping $h : X \to Y$ and a multiset μ over X, we denote $h\{\!\!\{\mu\}\!\!\} \stackrel{\text{df}}{=} \{\!\!\{h(x) \mid x \in \mu\}\!\!\}$.

2 Low-Level Petri Nets

In this section, we first present basic definitions concerning Petri nets, and then recall (see also [6,8,16]) notions related to net unfoldings.

A *net (with weighted arcs)* is a triple $N \stackrel{\text{df}}{=} (P, T, W)$ such that P and T are disjoint sets of respectively *places* and *transitions*, and W is a multiset over $(P \times T) \cup (T \times P)$ called the *weight function.* A net N is called *ordinary* if W is a set; in such a case, W can be considered as a *flow relation* on $(P \times T) \cup (T \times P)$. A *marking* of N is a multiset M over P, and the set of all markings of N will be denoted by $\mathcal{M}(N)$. (Note that M is finite whenever P is.) We adopt the standard rules about drawing nets, viz. places are represented as circles, transitions as boxes, the weight function by arcs with the indicated weight (we do not draw arcs whose weight is 0, and we do not indicate the weight if it is 1), and markings are shown by placing tokens within circles. The multisets ${}^\bullet z \stackrel{\text{df}}{=} \{\!\!\{y \mid (y, z) \in W\}\!\!\}$ and $z^\bullet \stackrel{\text{df}}{=} \{\!\!\{y \mid (z, y) \in W\}\!\!\}$, denote the *pre-* and *postset* of $z \in P \cup T$. (Note that for an ordinary net, both ${}^\bullet z$ and $z^\bullet$ are sets.) We will assume that ${}^\bullet t \neq \varnothing \neq t^\bullet$, for every $t \in T$.

A *net system* is a pair $\Sigma \stackrel{\text{df}}{=} (N, M_0)$ comprising a finite net $N = (P, T, W)$ and an *initial* marking M_0. A transition $t \in T$ is *enabled* at a marking M if ${}^\bullet t \le M$. Such a transition can be *fired*, leading to the marking $M' \stackrel{\text{df}}{=} M - {}^\bullet t + t^\bullet$; we denote this by $M[t\rangle M'$. The set of *reachable* markings of Σ is the smallest (w.r.t. $\subset$) set $\mathcal{RM}(\Sigma)$ containing M_0 and such that if $M \in \mathcal{RM}(\Sigma)$ and $M[t\rangle M'$, for some $t \in T$, then $M' \in \mathcal{RM}(\Sigma)$.

Σ is *k-bounded* if, for every reachable marking M and every place $p \in P$, $M(p) \le k$, and *safe* if it is 1-bounded. Moreover, Σ is *bounded* if it is k-bounded for some $k \in \mathbb{N}$. One can show that the set $\mathcal{RM}(\Sigma)$ is finite iff Σ is bounded.

Places $p_1, \ldots, p_k$ of a net system Σ are *mutually exclusive* if no reachable marking puts tokens on more than one of them, i.e., for every $M \in \mathcal{RM}(\Sigma)$, $M(p_i) \ge 1$ implies $M(p_j) = 0$, for all $j \in \{1, \ldots, k\} \setminus \{i\}$.

Low-level branching processes. Two nodes (places or transitions), y and y', of an ordinary net $N = (P, T, W)$ are *in conflict*, denoted by $y \# y'$, if there are distinct transitions $t, t' \in T$ such that ${}^\bullet t \cap {}^\bullet t' \neq \varnothing$ and (t, y) and (t', y') are in the reflexive transitive closure of the flow relation W, denoted by $\preceq$. A node y is in *self-conflict* if $y \# y$.

An *occurrence net* is an ordinary net $ON \stackrel{\text{df}}{=} (B, E, G)$, where B is the set of *conditions* (places), E is the set of *events* (transitions) and G is a flow relation, satisfying the following: ON is acyclic (i.e., $\preceq$ is a partial order); for every $b \in B$, $|{}^\bullet b| \le 1$; for every $y \in B \cup E$, $\neg(y \# y)$ and there are finitely many y' such that $y' \prec y$, where $\prec$ denotes the transitive closure of G. $Min(ON)$ will denote the set of minimal (w.r.t. $\prec$) elements of $B \cup E$. The relation $\prec$ is the *causality relation*. Two nodes are *concurrent*, denoted $y \ co\ y'$, if neither $y \# y'$ nor $y \preceq y'$ nor $y' \preceq y$.

A *homomorphism* from an occurrence net $ON = (B, E, G)$ to a net system Σ is a mapping $h : B \cup E \to P \cup T$ such that: $h(B) \subseteq P$ and $h(E) \subseteq T$ (conditions are mapped to places, and events to transitions); for each $e \in E$, $h\{\!|{}^\bullet e|\!\} = {}^\bullet h(e)$ and $h\{\!|e^\bullet|\!\} = h(e)^\bullet$ (transition environments are preserved); $h\{\!|Min(ON)|\!\} = M_0$ (minimal conditions are mapped to the initial marking); and for all $e, f \in E$, if ${}^\bullet e = {}^\bullet f$ and $h(e) = h(f)$ then $e = f$ (there is no redundancy). A *branching process* of Σ is a pair $\pi \stackrel{\text{df}}{=} (ON, h)$ such that ON is an occurrence net and h is a homomorphism from ON to Σ.

If an event e is such that $h(e) = t$ then we will often refer to it as being *t-labelled.* A branching process $\pi' = (ON', h')$ of Σ is a *prefix* of a branching process $\pi = (ON, h)$, denoted by $\pi' \sqsubseteq \pi$, if $ON' = (B', E', G')$ is a subnet of $ON = (B, E, G)$ containing all minimal elements and such that: if $e \in E'$ and $(b, e) \in G$ or $(e, b) \in G$ then $b \in B'$; if $b \in B'$ and $(e, b) \in G$ then $e \in E'$; and h' is the restriction of h to $B' \cup E'$. For each Σ there exists a unique maximal (w.r.t. $\sqsubseteq$) branching process Unf_Σ^{max}, called the *unfolding* of Σ (see [6]).

Sometimes it is convenient to start a branching process with a (virtual) initial event $\perp$, which has the postset $Min(ON)$, empty preset, and no label; we will use such an event, without drawing it in figures or treating it explicitly in algorithms.

Configurations and cuts. A *configuration* of an occurrence net ON is a set of events C such that for all $e, f \in C$, $\neg(e \# f)$ and, for every $e \in C$, $f \prec e$

implies $f \in C$; since we assume the initial event $\bot$, we additionally require that $\bot \in C$. For every $e \in E$, the configuration $[e] \stackrel{\mathrm{df}}{=} \{f \mid f \preceq e\}$ is called the *local configuration* of e, and $\langle e \rangle \stackrel{\mathrm{df}}{=} [e] \setminus \{e\}$ denotes the set of *causal predecessors* of e. Moreover, for a set of events E', we denote by $C \oplus E'$ the fact that $C \cup E'$ is a configuration and $C \cap E' = \varnothing$. Such an E' is a *suffix* of C, and $C \oplus E'$ is an *extension* of C.

The set of all finite (resp. local) configurations of a branching process π is denoted by $\mathcal{C}^{\pi}_{fin}$ (resp. $\mathcal{C}^{\pi}_{loc}$), and we will drop the superscript π if $\pi = Unf^{max}_{\Sigma}$.

A set of events E' is *downward-closed* if all causal predecessors of the events in E' also belong to E'. Such a set *induces* a unique branching process π whose events are exactly the events in E', and whose conditions are the conditions adjacent to the events in E' (including $\bot$).

A set of conditions B' such that for all distinct $b, b' \in B'$, $b \; co \; b'$, is called a *co-set*. A *cut* is a maximal (w.r.t. $\subset$) co-set. Every marking reachable from $Min(ON)$ is a cut.

Let C be a finite configuration of a branching process π. Then the set $Cut(C) \stackrel{\mathrm{df}}{=} (\bigcup_{c \in C} c^{\bullet}) \setminus (\bigcup_{c \in C} {}^{\bullet}c)$ is a cut (note that $\bot \in C$); moreover, the multiset of places $Mark(C) \stackrel{\mathrm{df}}{=} h\{\!|\, Cut(C) |\!\}$ is a reachable marking of Σ, called the *final marking* of C. A marking M of Σ is *represented* in π if there is $C \in \mathcal{C}^{\pi}_{fin}$ such that $M = Mark(C)$. Every marking represented in π is reachable in the original net system Σ, and every reachable marking of Σ is represented in Unf^{max}_{Σ}.

Complete prefixes of Petri net unfoldings. Though unfoldings are infinite whenever the original net systems have infinite runs, it turns out that often they can be truncated in such a way that the resulting prefixes, though finite, contain enough information to decide a certain behavioural property, e.g., deadlock freeness. We then say that the prefixes are *complete* for this property.

There exist several different methods of truncating Petri net unfoldings. The differences are related to the kind of information about the original unfolding one wants to preserve in the prefix, as well as to the choice between using only local configurations (which can improve the running time of an unfolding algorithm), or all finite configurations (which can result in a smaller prefix), to cut the unfolding. In [16], a uniform approach to truncating unfoldings, based on *cutting contexts*, was proposed.

Cutting contexts. For greater flexibility, the approach proposed in [16] is parametric. The first parameter determines the information to be preserved in a complete prefix (in the standard case, the set of reachable markings). The main idea there was to shift the emphasis from the reachable markings of Σ to the finite configurations of Unf^{max}_{Σ}. Formally, the information to be preserved in the prefix corresponds to the equivalence classes of some equivalence relation $\approx$ on $\mathcal{C}_{fin}$. The other two parameters are more technical: they specify under which circumstances an event can be designated as a cut-off event (intuitively, this means that all its causal successors in the full unfolding can be removed).

A *cutting context* is a triple $\Theta \stackrel{\mathrm{df}}{=} (\approx, \lhd, \{\mathcal{C}_e\}_{e \in E})$, where:

1. $\approx$ is an equivalence relation on $\mathcal{C}_{fin}$.

2. $\lhd$, called an *adequate* order, is a strict well-founded partial order on $\mathcal{C}_{fin}$ refining $\subset$, i.e., $C' \subset C''$ implies $C' \lhd C''$.
3. $\approx$ and $\lhd$ are *preserved by finite extensions*, i.e., for every pair of configurations $C' \approx C''$, and for every suffix E' of C', there exists a finite suffix E'' of C'' such that: $C'' \oplus E'' \approx C' \oplus E'$, and if $C'' \lhd C'$ then $C'' \oplus E'' \lhd C' \oplus E'$.
4. $\{\mathcal{C}_e\}_{e \in E}$ is a family of subsets of $\mathcal{C}_{fin}$, i.e., $\mathcal{C}_e \subseteq \mathcal{C}_{fin}$, for all $e \in E$. $\diamond$

The main idea behind the adequate order is to specify which configurations will be preserved in the complete prefix; it turns out that all $\lhd$-minimal configurations in each equivalence class of $\approx$ will be preserved. The last parameter is needed to specify the set of configurations used later to decide whether an event can be designated as a cut-off event. For example, $\mathcal{C}_e$ may contain all finite configurations of Unf_Σ^{max}, or, as it is usually the case in practice, only the local ones. We will say that a cutting context Θ is *dense (saturated)* if $\mathcal{C}_e \supseteq \mathcal{C}_{loc}$ (resp. $\mathcal{C}_e = \mathcal{C}_{fin}$), for all $e \in E$.

In practice, Θ is usually dense (or even saturated, see [10]), the adequate order is either McMillan's one (see [8,21]) or the total order proposed in [8], and at least the following equivalences $\approx$ have been shown to be of interest:

- $C' {\approx_{mar}} C''$ if $Mark(C') = Mark(C'')$. This is the most widely used equivalence (see [8,10,12,20]). Note that the equivalence classes of $\approx_{mar}$ correspond to the reachable markings of Σ.
- $C' {\approx_{code}} C''$ if $Mark(C') = Mark(C'')$ and $Code(C') = Code(C'')$, where *Code* is the signal coding function. Such an equivalence is used in [23] for unfolding Signal Transition Graphs (STGs) specifying asynchronous circuits.
- $C' {\approx_{sym}} C''$ if $Mark(C')$ and $Mark(C'')$ are symmetric markings according to some suitable notion (see [5,13]). This equivalence is the basis of the approach aimed at reducing the size of prefix described in [5].

We will write $e \lhd f$ whenever $[e] \lhd [f]$. Clearly, $\lhd$ is a well-founded partial order on the set of events refining $\prec$. Hence, one can use the Noetherian induction for definitions and proofs, i.e., it suffices to define or prove something for an event under the assumption that it has already been defined or proven for all its $\lhd$-predecessors. In the rest of this section, we assume that the cutting context Θ is fixed.

A branching process π of Σ is *complete w.r.t. a set E_{cut}* (see also [16]) of events of Unf_Σ^{max} if the following hold:

1. If $C \in \mathcal{C}_{fin}$, then there is $C' \in \mathcal{C}_{fin}^{\pi}$ such that $C' \cap E_{cut} = \varnothing$ and $C \approx C'$.
2. If $C \in \mathcal{C}_{fin}^{\pi}$ is such that $C \cap E_{cut} = \varnothing$, and e is an event such that $C \oplus \{e\} \in \mathcal{C}_{fin}$, then $C \oplus \{e\} \in \mathcal{C}_{fin}^{\pi}$.

A branching process π is *complete* if it is complete w.r.t. some set E_{cut}.

Note that π remains complete following the removal of all events e for which $\langle e \rangle \cap E_{cut} \neq \varnothing$, after which the events from E_{cut} (usually referred to as *cut-off* events) will be either maximal events of the prefix or not in the prefix at all. Note also that the last definition depends only on the equivalence $\approx$, and not on the other components of the cutting context.

For the relation $\approx_{mar}$, each reachable marking is represented by a configuration in $\mathcal{C}_{fin}$ and, hence, also by a configuration in $\mathcal{C}^{\pi}_{fin}$, provided that π is complete. This is what is usually expected from a correct prefix. Moreover, the definition of completeness implies that all firings enabled by the configurations from $\mathcal{C}^{\pi}_{fin}$ containing no events from E_{cut} are preserved (see [16] for the explanation why this property is desirable).

Static cut-off events. Here we recall (see also [16]) the definition of static cut-off events. They are defined w.r.t. the whole unfolding, so that they are independent on an algorithm (hence the term 'static'), together with *feasible* events, which are precisely those events whose causal predecessors are not cut-off events, and as such must be included in the prefix determined by the static cut-off events.

The sets of *feasible* events, denoted by $fsble_{\Theta}$, and *static cut-off* events, denoted by cut_{Θ}, of Unf^{max}_{Σ} are defined thus:

1. An event e is a feasible event if $\langle e \rangle \cap cut_{\Theta} = \varnothing$.
2. An event e is a static cut-off event if it is feasible, and there is a configuration $C \in \mathcal{C}_e$ such that $C \subseteq fsble_{\Theta} \setminus cut_{\Theta}$, $C \approx [e]$, and $C \lhd [e]$. Any C satisfying these conditions will be called a *corresponding* configuration of e.

It turns out that, due to the well-foundedness of $\lhd$, $fsble_{\Theta}$ and cut_{Θ} are well-defined sets (see [16]). Since $\langle \perp \rangle = \varnothing$, $\perp \in fsble_{\Theta}$ by the above definition. Furthermore, $\perp \notin cut_{\Theta}$, since $\perp$ cannot have a corresponding configuration. Indeed, $[\perp] = \{\perp\}$ is the smallest (w.r.t. $\subset$) configuration, and so $\lhd$-minimal by the definition of a cutting context.

Canonical prefix. Once the feasible events are defined, the following notion arises quite naturally. The *canonical* prefix of Unf^{max}_{Σ} is the branching process Unf^{Θ}_{Σ} induced by $fsble_{\Theta}$. Thus Unf^{Θ}_{Σ} is uniquely determined by the cutting context Θ. In [16], it is proven that the canonical prefix is always complete, and the conditions which guarantee its finiteness are investigated. Further in this paper we will show that all these results can be imported to the theory of branching processes of high-level Petri nets.

Algorithms for generating canonical prefixes. It turns out that canonical prefixes can be constructed by straightforward generalizations of the existing unfolding algorithms (see, e.g., [8,12]). The *slicing* algorithm from [12], parameterized by a cutting context Θ, is shown in Figure 1. (The algorithm proposed in [8] is its special case.) It is assumed that the function PotExt(π) finds the set of *possible extensions* of a branching process π, according to the following. For a branching process π of Σ, a *possible extension* is a pair (D, t), where D is a co-set in π and t is a transition of Σ, such that $h\{\!|D|\!\} = {}^{\bullet}t$ and π contains no t-labelled event with preset D. We will take the pair (D, t) as a t-labelled event having D as its preset.

Compared to the standard unfolding algorithm in [8], the slicing algorithm has the following modifications in its main loop. A set of events Sl, called a *slice*, is chosen on each iteration and processed as a whole, without taking or adding any events from or to pe. A slice must satisfy the following conditions:

- Sl is a non-empty subset of the current set of possible extensions pe.

```
input : Σ = (N, M₀) — a net system
output : Pref_Σ — the canonical prefix of Σ's unfolding (if it is finite)

Pref_Σ ← the empty branching process
add instances of the places from M₀ to Pref_Σ
pe ← PotExt(Pref_Σ)
cut_off ← ∅
while pe ≠ ∅ do
    choose Sl ∈ Slices(pe)
    if ∃e ∈ Sl : [e] ∩ cut_off = ∅
    then
        for all e ∈ Sl in any order refining ◁ do
            if [e] ∩ cut_off = ∅
            then
                add e together with its postset to Pref_Σ
                if e is a cut-off event of Pref_Σ then cut_off ← cut_off ∪ {e}
        pe ← PotExt(Pref_Σ)
    else pe ← pe \ Sl
```

Fig. 1. Unfolding algorithm with slices (e is a cut-off event of $Pref_\Sigma$ if there is $C \in \mathcal{C}_e$ such that the events of C belong to $Pref_\Sigma$ but not to cut_off, $C \approx [e]$, and $C \lhd [e]$).

- For every $e \in Sl$ and every event $f \lhd e$ of Unf_Σ^{max}, $f \notin pe \setminus Sl$ and $pe \cap \langle f \rangle = \varnothing$.

In particular, if $f \in pe$ and $f \lhd e$ for some $e \in Sl$, then $f \in Sl$. The set $\text{Slices}(pe)$ is chosen so that it is non-empty whenever pe is non-empty. Note that this algorithm, in general, exhibits more non-determinism than the one from [8]: it may be non-deterministic even if the order $\lhd$ is total. Since the events in the current slice can be processed independently, the slicing algorithm admits efficient parallelization (along the lines proposed in [12]). A crucial property of the slicing unfolding algorithm is that it generates the canonical prefix (see [12, 16]).

3 High-Level Petri Nets

In this paper we use M-nets (see [1]) as the main high-level Petri net model, as we believe that it is general enough to cover many other existing relevant formalisms. The full definition of M-nets can be found in [1]. Here, in order to match the presentation of low-level nets as closely as possible, we give a suitably adapted short description omitting those details which are not directly related to our purposes. In particular, [1] devotes a lot of attention to the composition rules, which are relevant only at the construction stage of an M-net, but not for model checking of an already constructed one.

M-nets. It is assumed that there exists a (finite or infinite) set Tok of elements (or 'colours') and a set VAR of variable names, such that $Tok \cap VAR = \varnothing$. An *M-net* N is a quadruple $N \stackrel{\text{df}}{=} (P, T, W, \iota)$ such that P and T are disjoint sets of respectively *places* and *transitions*, W is a multiset over $(P \times VAR \times T) \cup (T \times VAR \times P)$ of arcs, and ι is an inscription function with the domain $P \cup T$. It is assumed that, for every place $p \in P$, $\iota(p) \subseteq Tok$ is the *type* of p and, for every transition $t \in T$, $\iota(t)$ is a boolean expression over $Tok \cup VAR$, called the *guard* of t. We assume that the types of all places are finite.[1] In what follows, we assume that $N = (P, T, W, \iota)$ is a fixed M-net.

For a transition $t \in T$, let ${}^\bullet t \stackrel{\mathrm{df}}{=} \{\!|p^v \mid (p, v, t) \in W|\!\}$, $t^\bullet \stackrel{\mathrm{df}}{=} \{\!|p^v \mid (t, v, p) \in W|\!\}$, and $VAR(t) \stackrel{\mathrm{df}}{=} \{v \mid (p, v, t) \in W\} \cup VAR(\iota(t))$, where $VAR(\iota(t))$ is the set of variables appearing in $\iota(t)$. A *firing mode* of t is a mapping $\sigma : VAR(t) \to Tok$ such that $\sigma(v) \in \iota(p)$, for all p^v in ${}^\bullet t + t^\bullet$, and $\iota(t)$ evaluates to **true** under the substitution given by σ. (The notation p^v, similarly as p^x and t^σ used later on, is a shorthand for the pair (p, v).)

We define the set of *legal place instances* as $\mathcal{P} \stackrel{\mathrm{df}}{=} \{p^x \mid p \in P \wedge x \in \iota(p)\}$ and the set of *legal firings* as $\mathcal{T} \stackrel{\mathrm{df}}{=} \{t^\sigma \mid t \in T \text{ and } \sigma \text{ is a firing mode of } t\}$. For every $t^\sigma \in \mathcal{T}$, we will also denote ${}^\bullet t^\sigma \stackrel{\mathrm{df}}{=} \{\!|p^{\sigma(v)} \mid p^v \in {}^\bullet t|\!\}$ and $t^{\sigma\bullet} \stackrel{\mathrm{df}}{=} \{\!|p^{\sigma(v)} \mid p^v \in t^\bullet|\!\}$. According to the definitions given below, all valid markings of an M-net will be composed of legal place instances, and its firing sequences will be composed of legal firings. Furthermore, the sets $\mathcal{P}$ and $\mathcal{T}$ will provide the basis for the construction of the low-level net corresponding to a high-level one.

A *marking* M of N is a multiset over $\mathcal{P}$. We will denote the set of all such markings by $\mathcal{M}(N)$. (Traditionally, a marking is a mapping which, to every place $p \in P$, associates a multiset over $\iota(p)$. Clearly, such a representation is equivalent to that we chose to use.)

The *transition relation* is a ternary relation on $\mathcal{M}(N) \times \mathcal{T} \times \mathcal{M}(N)$ such that a triple (M, t^σ, M') belongs to it (denoted $M[t^\sigma\rangle M'$) if ${}^\bullet t^\sigma \le M$ and $M' = M - {}^\bullet t^\sigma + t^{\sigma\bullet}$. Note that σ is a firing mode of t, which guarantees that M' is a valid marking of N.

M-net systems. An *M-net system* is a pair $\Upsilon \stackrel{\mathrm{df}}{=} (N, M_0)$ comprising a finite M-net N and an *initial* marking M_0. The set of *reachable* markings of an M-net system Υ is the smallest (w.r.t. $\subset$) set $\mathcal{RM}(\Upsilon)$ containing M_0 and such that if $M \in \mathcal{RM}(\Upsilon)$ and, for some $t^\sigma \in \mathcal{T}$, $M[t^\sigma\rangle M'$ in N then $M' \in \mathcal{RM}(\Upsilon)$.

An M-net system Υ is *k-bounded* if, for every marking $M \in \mathcal{RM}(\Upsilon)$ and every $p^x \in \mathcal{P}$, $M(p^x) \le k$; *safe* if it is 1-bounded; and *bounded* if it is k-bounded for some $k \in \mathbb{N}$. Moreover, Υ is *strictly k-bounded* if, for every marking $M \in \mathcal{RM}(\Upsilon)$ and every place $p \in P$, $|\{\!|x \mid p^x \in M|\!\}| \le k$, and *strictly safe* if it is strictly 1-bounded. One can show that strictly k-bounded M-net systems are k-bounded, strictly safe ones are safe, and the set $\mathcal{RM}(\Upsilon)$ is finite iff Υ is bounded. Note that according to the above definitions, a safe M-net system can have a reachable marking which places several tokens on the same place, provided that their 'colours' are all distinct. The rational behind our choice of the definition is that the low-level *expansion* (defined below) of an M-net system is safe iff the original M-net system is safe, and so the total adequate order proposed in [8] for safe net systems can be re-used (see the end of Section 4).

[1] In general, allowing infinite types yields a Turing-powerful model. Nevertheless, this restriction can be omitted in certain important cases (see Section 5).

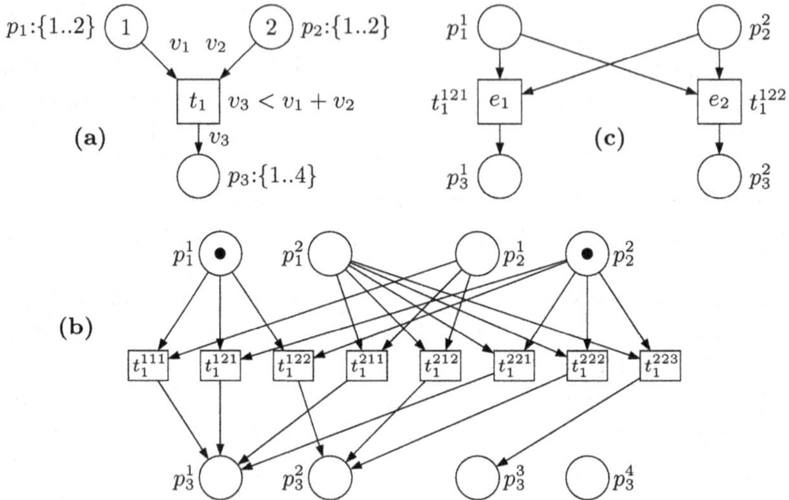

Fig. 2. An M-net system **(a)**, its expansion **(b)**, and its unfolding **(c)**. Note that a firing mode σ of t is represented as a three-element string $\sigma(v_1)\sigma(v_2)\sigma(v_3)$.

Consider the M-net system shown in Figure 2(a). At the initial marking, t_1 can fire with the firing mode $\sigma \stackrel{\mathrm{df}}{=} \{v_1 \mapsto 1, v_2 \mapsto 2, v_3 \mapsto 1\}$ or $\sigma' \stackrel{\mathrm{df}}{=} \{v_1 \mapsto 1, v_2 \mapsto 2, v_3 \mapsto 2\}$, consuming the tokens from p_1 and p_2 and producing respectively the token 1 or 2 on p_3. Formally, we have $\{\!|p_1^1, p_2^2|\!\}[t_1^\sigma\rangle\{\!|p_3^1|\!\}$ and $\{\!|p_1^1, p_2^2|\!\}[t_1^{\sigma'}\rangle\{\!|p_3^2|\!\}$.

Transforming M-net systems into low-level nets. For each M-net it is possible to build an 'equivalent' low-level one. Such a transformation is called 'unfolding' in [1], but since this term is already used in this paper with a different meaning (see Section 2), we will use the term 'expansion' instead. The *expansion* $\mathcal{E}(N)$ of an M-net $N = (P, T, W, \iota)$ is a low-level net $\mathcal{E}(N) \stackrel{\mathrm{df}}{=} (\mathcal{P}, \mathcal{T}, W')$ where $W' \stackrel{\mathrm{df}}{=} \sum_{t^\sigma \in \mathcal{T}}(\{\!|(p^{\sigma(v)}, t^\sigma) \mid (p, v, t) \in W|\!\} + \{\!|(t^\sigma, p^{\sigma(v)}) \mid (t, v, p) \in W|\!\})$. The expansion $\mathcal{E}(M)$ of a marking M of N is M itself, i.e., $\mathcal{E}(M) \stackrel{\mathrm{df}}{=} M$ (this is possible since there is no difference between the markings of $\mathcal{E}(N)$ and N). Finally, the expansion of an M-net system $\Upsilon = (N, M_0)$ is defined as $\mathcal{E}(\Upsilon) \stackrel{\mathrm{df}}{=} (\mathcal{E}(N), \mathcal{E}(M_0))$ (see Figure 2(a,b)).

Proposition 1 ([1]). *Let N be an M-net, and $M', M'' \in \mathcal{M}(N)$. Then $M'[t^\sigma\rangle M''$ in Υ iff $M'[t^\sigma\rangle M''$ in $\mathcal{E}(\Upsilon)$.*

Proposition 2. *Let $\Upsilon = (N, M_0)$ be an M-net system.*

- *For every $k \in \mathbb{N}$, $\mathcal{E}(\Upsilon)$ is k-bounded (safe) iff Υ is k-bounded (safe).*
- *If Υ is strictly safe and p is a place of Υ then the places p^x, $x \in \iota(p)$, are mutually exclusive in $\mathcal{E}(\Upsilon)$.*

Though, by Proposition 1, the expansion of an M-net system faithfully models the original system, the disadvantage of this transformation is that it usually yields a very large net. Moreover, the resulting net system is usually *unnecessarily* large, in the sense that it contains many places which cannot be marked and many dead transitions. This is so because the place types are usually overapproximations, and the transitions of the original M-net system may have many firing modes, only few of which are realized when executing the net from the initial marking. E.g., only two out of eight transitions of the expansion of the M-net system in Figure 2(a), shown in Figure 2(b), can actually fire. Therefore, though the M-net expansion is a neat theoretical construction, it is often impractical.

4 Branching Processes of High-Level Nets

In this section, we develop the main results of this paper, namely the notions of a branching process of an M-net system, the associated unfolding, and its canonical prefix. We also show that there is a strong correspondence between the branching processes of an M-net system and those of its expansion. This allows for importing many results from the theory of branching processes of low-level Petri nets.

A *homomorphism* from an occurrence net $ON = (B, E, G)$ to an M-net system Υ is a mapping $h : B \cup E \to \mathcal{P} \cup \mathcal{T}$ such that: $h(B) \subseteq \mathcal{P}$ and $h(E) \subseteq \mathcal{T}$ (conditions are mapped to legal place instances, and events to legal firings); for every $e \in E$, $h\{\!|{}^\bullet e|\!\} = {}^\bullet h(e)$ and $h\{\!|e^\bullet|\!\} = h(e)^\bullet$ (the environments of legal firings are preserved); $h\{\!|Min(ON)|\!\} = M_0$ (minimal conditions are mapped to the initial marking); and for all $e, f \in E$, if ${}^\bullet e = {}^\bullet f$ and $h(e) = h(f)$, then $e = f$ (there is no redundancy). A *branching process* of Υ is a pair $\pi \stackrel{\text{df}}{=} (ON, h)$ such that ON is an occurrence net and h is a homomorphism from ON to Υ. (See Figure 2.)

This definition closely follows the definition of a (low-level) branching process of $\mathcal{E}(\Upsilon)$, and constitutes the main contribution of this paper. Because of this similarity, most of the definitions for branching processes of low-level net systems can now be lifted to branching processes of M-net systems. In particular, this is the case for the notions of a *configuration*, *cut*, *final marking*, the relation $\sqsubseteq$, *cutting context*, and the *completeness* of a prefix. Also, most of the results proven for branching processes of low-level Petri nets can also be lifted to branching processes of M-net systems. In particular, for each M-net system Υ there exist a unique (up to isomorphism) maximal (w.r.t. $\sqsubseteq$) branching process Unf_Υ^{max} of Υ, called the *unfolding* of Υ. Moreover, for any cutting context Θ there exists unique *canonical* prefix Unf_Υ^Θ (coinciding with $Unf_{\mathcal{E}(\Upsilon)}^\Theta$) of Unf_Υ^{max}, and the theory of canonical prefixes (see [16]) can be transferred without any changes.

It is straightforward to give an upper bound on the size of Unf_Υ^Θ, since the results of [8,16] regarding the size of the canonical prefix are still applicable. In particular, if the cutting context $\Theta = (\approx, \lhd, \{\mathcal{C}_e\}_{e\in E})$ is dense, $\lhd$ is total, and $C' \approx C'' \Leftrightarrow Mark(C') = Mark(C'')$, then the number of non-cut-off events in Unf_Υ^Θ does not exceed $|\mathcal{RM}(\Upsilon)|$.

5 M-net Unfolding Algorithm

Due to the results developed in the previous section, it is now possible to suggest a suitable modification of the standard unfolding algorithms, e.g., that in Figure 1, which is capable of building canonical prefixes of M-net unfoldings. It turns out that the only thing which has to be changed is the notion of a possible extension (so all the modifications are inside the PotExt function and thus are not visible in the top-level description of the algorithm).

For a branching process π of an M-net system Υ, a *possible extension* is a pair (D, t^σ), where D is a co-set in π and t^σ is a legal firing, such that $h\{\!|D|\!\} = {}^\bullet t$ and π contains no t^σ-labelled event with the preset D. Similarly as in the low-level case, we will take the pair (D, t^σ) as a new event of the prefix, with the preset D. After it is inserted into the prefix, its postset D' consisting of new conditions such that $h\{\!|D'|\!\} = t^{\sigma\bullet}$ is also inserted.

It is worth noting that most of the existing heuristics aiming at speeding up the prefix generation can be applied. In particular, the total adequate order for safe net systems proposed in [8] can be used to unfold safe M-net systems. It is still adequate, since Unf_Υ^{max} coincides with $Unf_{\mathcal{E}(\Upsilon)}^{max}$ and the expansion of a safe M-net system is safe. Moreover, the *concurrency relation* (see [7,22]) can also be employed, even for non-safe systems. As for the *preset trees* (see [15]), they can be used without any modifications to unfold strictly safe M-net systems (and we work now on generalizing them to wider net classes).

It turns out that direct unfolding a high-level net not only avoids the generation of its (potentially, very large) expansion, but often is also more efficient than unfolding its expansion. Indeed, the most time-consuming part of the algorithm is computing the possible extensions (see [15]). Since one high-level transition usually corresponds to several low-level ones, less transitions have to be tried each time possible extensions are computed, which may lead to considerable savings in the running time.

It is often the case that the information about the firing mode of an event needs not be explicitly stored. Indeed, this information almost always can be discarded, since one is usually not interested what was the precise firing mode of a transition, as long as the consumed and produced tokens are the same.

An important extension of our approach allows for M-nets with places having infinite types. For example, it is often convenient to assign to a place the type $\mathbb{N}$ rather than $\{1, \ldots, n\}$, since n might be not known in advance. Even when the set of reachable markings of such an M-net system is finite, its expansion is infinite and so of little use for model checking, whereas with our direct approach we still can build the canonical prefix and complete the verification. The only thing which needs to be ensured is that at any stage of prefix construction only a finite number of legal firings needs to be considered. This will be the case if, for every transition t and every finite multiset Z over $\mathcal{P}$, the set of all firing modes σ of t such that ${}^\bullet t^\sigma \leq Z$ is both finite and computable.

Having built a canonical prefix, one can easily construct the refined version of the low-level expansion of the original M-net system, with unreachable places

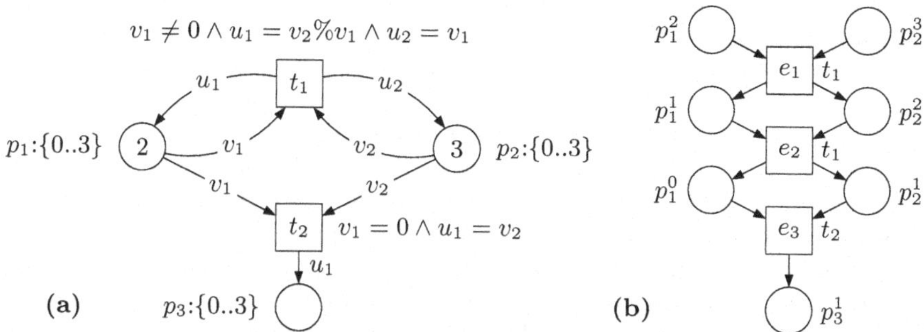

Fig. 3. An M-net system modelling Euclid's algorithm for computing the greatest common divisor of two non-negative integers **(a)**, and its unfolding **(b)**. Firing modes are not shown, but can easily be determined from events' presets and postsets.

and dead transitions removed. This may be important, e.g., for directly mapping a Petri net to a circuit simulating its behaviour (see, e.g., [3]).

Finally, it is worth mentioning that since our method constructs exactly the same prefix which would have been generated from the corresponding expansion of the M-net system, all the existing model checkers employing unfolding prefixes derived from low-level nets can be used without any changes when dealing with prefixes generated directly from M-net systems.

6 Case Studies

In this section, we compare our approach with the traditional one, viz. the unfolding of M-net expansions. We used the unfolding engine described in [12,15] which after suitable modifications was able to unfold both low-level and high-level nets. For building M-net expansions, we used the `hl2ll` utility from the PEP tool (see [2]). The experiments were conducted on a PC with a *Pentium*^{TM} III/500MHz processor and 128M RAM.

The meaning of the columns in the tables is as follows (from left): the 'size' of the problem; the number of places and transitions in the original M-net system; the number of places and transitions in the corresponding expansion, together with the time required by the `hl2ll` utility to build the expansion; the number of conditions, feasible events, and cut-off events in the canonical prefix; the times (in seconds) required to unfold the expansion of the M-net system and the M-net system itself, respectively.

The first example is data-intensive, and so the traditional (via low-level nets) approach is extremely inefficient, whereas we expected our algorithm to perform well. The second example is control-intensive, so the M-net expansions are just slightly larger that the original M-nets. It was chosen to test the worst-case performance of our method relatively to unfolding of the low-level expansion.

Greatest common divisor (GCD). An M-net simulating Euclid's algorithm for computing the greatest common divisor of two non-negative integers, together with its unfolding, is shown in Figure 3. In this net, t_1 fires until the number in p_1 becomes 0, replacing the number in p_2 by that in p_1, and the number in p_1 by the residual of division of these two numbers. Then t_2 fires copying the result from p_2 to p_3. In our experiments, for each N we computed the greatest common divisor of F_N and F_{N-1}, where F_i denotes the i-th Fibonacci's number (such numbers are known to produce the longest sequences of computational steps for Euclid's algorithm). The results of our experiments are summarized in Table 1. From the structure of the M-net, it is easy to calculate that its expansion contains $3(F_N + 1)$ places and $(F_N + 1)^2$ transitions. These values are reported in the corresponding columns of the table, even though `hl2ll` failed to produce the expansions when they became large.

The experimental results show that for this example the high-level unfolding is clearly superior. Though the M-net expansion grows very quickly, the resulting prefix has only $2N - 1$ conditions and $N - 1$ events. Therefore, our algorithm was able to build it for relatively large N (we had to stop the experiments after $N = 45$ since F_{50} overflows 4-bytes integer, but it is a limitation of the current implementation rather than of the method itself).

Mutual exclusion algorithm. The previous example was rather favourable for our algorithm, since the expansions of the M-net systems were very large. We therefore checked the performance of our approach in a totally opposite case, when the expansion of an M-net is relatively small. This happens when the transitions of the M-net are connected to few places and the cardinality of most place types is 1. Such M-nets arise when modelling Lamport's mutual exclusion algorithm (see [13,19]), which employs 'very small' atomic actions. We encoded it in the $B(PN)^2$ language supported by the PEP tool, and the corresponding experimental results are shown in Table 1. As one can see, our algorithm performs almost as well as the algorithm for low-level nets. Though there is some overhead when computing transition guards and more complicated final states, it is relatively small, because the most time-consuming operation is computing the possible extensions of a current prefix. Moreover, this overhead becomes relatively smaller as the size of the prefix grows (it is just 0.5% for the last example in the table).

After the prefixes had been build, we verified using the efficient model checker described in [14] that the M-net system is deadlock free, and that the places corresponding to the critical sections of the processes are mutually exclusive. This was done without recompiling the model checker, since our unfolding algorithm generates prefixes which are indistinguishable from those generated by a low-level net unfolder from the corresponding expansions of the M-nets.

It is worth noting that in this example partial-order methods have advantage over the state-space ones. In [13], this mutual exclusion algorithm was verified for $N = 3$ by building a reachability graph of the Petri net model and for $N = 4$ by applying symmetry reductions. We managed to verify the case $N = 4$ without applying symmetry reductions, using a PC with smaller memory (128M rather than 256M), for a net which was generated from a relatively high-level description

Table 1. Experimental results for the M-net systems simulating Euclid's GCD algorithm and Lamport's mutex algorithm.

	M-net		Expansion			Unfolding			Time[s]	
N	$\|P\|$	$\|T\|$	$\|P\|$	$\|T\|$	Time[s]	$\|B\|$	$\|E\|$	$\|E_{cut}\|$	LL	HL
5	3	2	18	36	<1	9	4	0	<1	<1
10	3	2	168	3136	1	19	9	0	6	<1
15	3	2	1833	$>10^5$	—	29	14	0	—	<1
20	3	2	$>10^4$	$>10^7$	—	39	19	0	—	<1
25	3	2	$>10^5$	$>10^9$	—	49	24	0	—	<1
30	3	2	$>10^6$	$>10^{11}$	—	59	29	0	—	<1
35	3	2	$>10^7$	$>10^{13}$	—	69	34	0	—	<1
40	3	2	$>10^8$	$>10^{16}$	—	79	39	0	—	<1
45	3	2	$>10^9$	$>10^{18}$	—	89	44	0	—	<1

	M-net		Expansion			Unfolding			Time[s]	
N	$\|P\|$	$\|T\|$	$\|P\|$	$\|T\|$	Time[s]	$\|B\|$	$\|E\|$	$\|E_{cut}\|$	LL	HL
2	52	50	58	88	<1	711	368	102	<1	<1
3	77	76	86	154	<1	23424	12026	4562	29	30
4	104	104	116	236	<1	736507	375983	167780	28772	28917

($B(PN)^2$ language) rather than built by hand. Moreover, our specification was not optimal since we had to replicate parts of the code, because $B(PN)^2$ does not currently have the **goto** operator (see [17] for more details). In principle, it is also possible to apply partial-order methods together with symmetry reductions (see [5,16]) to achieve even better results, but we have not implemented the combined method yet.

7 Conclusions

We defined branching processes and unfoldings of high-level Petri nets and proposed an algorithm which builds finite and complete prefixes. We established an important relation between the branching processes of a high-level net and those of its low-level expansion, viz. that the sets of their branching processes are the same, allowing us to import results proven for low-level nets. Among such results are the canonicity of the prefix for different cutting contexts, the usability of the total adequate order proposed in [8], and the parallel unfolding algorithm proposed in [12]. Our approach is conservative in the sense that all the verification tools employing the traditional unfoldings can be reused with such prefixes. The conducted experiments demonstrated that it is, on one hand, superior to the traditional approach on data-intensive application, and, on the other hand, has the same performance on control-intensive ones. The full version of this paper ([17]) contains a comparison with a similar work reported in [18].

Acknowledgements. This research was supported by an ORS Awards Scheme grant ORS/C20/4, and by EPSRC grants GR/M99293 and GR/M94366 (MOVIE).

References

1. E. Best, H. Fleischhack, W. Fraczak, R. Hopkins, H. Klaudel, and E. Pelz: A Class of Composable High Level Petri Nets. *ICATPN'1995*, LNCS 935 (1995) 103–120.
2. E. Best and B. Grahlmann: PEP — more than a Petri Net Tool. *TACAS'96*, LNCS 1055 (1996) 397–401.
3. A. Bystrov and A. Yakovlev: Asynchronous Circuit Synthesis by Direct Mapping: Interfacing to Environment. *ASYNC'02*, IEEE Comp. Soc. Press (2002) 127–136.
4. E. M. Clarke, O. Grumberg, and D. Peled: *Model Checking*. MIT Press (1999).
5. J.-M. Couvreur, S. Grivet, and Denis Poitrenaud: Unfolding of Products of Symmetrical Petri Nets. *ICATPN'2001*, LNCS 2075 (2001) 121–143.
6. J. Engelfriet: Branching processes of Petri Nets. *Acta Inf.* 28 (1991) 575–591.
7. J. Esparza and S. Römer: An Unfolding Algorithm for Synchronous Products of Transition Systems. *CONCUR'99*, LNCS 1664 (1999) 2–20.
8. J. Esparza, S. Römer and W. Vogler: An Improvement of McMillan's Unfolding Algorithm. *TACAS'96*, LNCS 1055 (1996) 87–106. Full version: *Formal Methods in System Design* 20(3) (2002) 285–310.
9. H. Fleischhack, B. Grahlmann: A Petri Net Semantics for $B(PN)^2$ with Procedures. *PDSE'97*, IEEE Computer Society Press (1997) 15–27.
10. K. Heljanko: Minimizing Finite Complete Prefixes. *CS&P'99*, Workshop Concurrency, Specification and Programming (1999) 83–95.
11. K. Heljanko: Using Logic Programs with Stable Model Semantics to Solve Deadlock and Reachability Problems for 1-Safe Petri Nets. *Fund. Inf.* 37(3) (1999) 247–268.
12. K. Heljanko, V. Khomenko and M. Koutny: Parallelisation of the Petri Net Unfolding Algorithm. *TACAS'02*, LNCS 2280 (2002) 371–385.
13. K. Jensen: *Colored Petri Nets. Basic Concepts, Analysis Methods and Practical Use.* EATCS Monographs on Theoretical Computer Science (1992).
14. V. Khomenko and M. Koutny: LP Deadlock Checking Using Partial Order Dependencies. *CONCUR'2000*, LNCS 1877 (2000) 410–425.
15. V. Khomenko and M. Koutny: Towards An Efficient Algorithm for Unfolding Petri Nets. *CONCUR'2001*, LNCS 2154 (2001) 366–380.
16. V. Khomenko, M. Koutny, and V. Vogler: Canonical Prefixes of Petri Net Unfoldings. *CAV'02*, LNCS 2404 (2002) 582–595.
17. V. Khomenko and M. Koutny: Branching Processes of High-Level Petri Nets. Techn. Rep. CS-TR-763, Department of Computing Science, University of Newcastle (2002).
18. V. E. Kozura: Unfolding of Colored Petri Nets. Techn. Rep. 80, A. P. Ershov Institute of Informatics Systems (2000).
19. L. Lamport: A Fast Mutual Exclusion Algorithm. *ACM Transactions on Computer Systems* 5(1) (1987) 1–11.
20. K. L. McMillan: Using Unfoldings to Avoid State Explosion Problem in the Verification of Asynchronous Circuits. *CAV'92*, LNCS 663 (1992) 164–174.
21. K. L. McMillan: *Symbolic Model Checking*. PhD thesis, CMU-CS-92-131 (1992).
22. S. Römer: *Entwicklung und Implementierung von Verifikationstechniken auf der Basis von Netzentfaltungen.* PhD thesis, Technische Universitat Munchen (2000).
23. A. Semenov: *Verification and Synthesis of Asynchronous Control Circuits Using Petri Net Unfolding.* PhD Thesis, University of Newcastle upon Tyne (1997).

Using Petri Net Invariants in State Space Construction

Karsten Schmidt

Institut für Informatik, Humboldt-Universität zu Berlin, D-10099 Berlin
kschmidt@informatik.hu-berlin.de

Abstract. The linear algebraic invariant calculus is a powerful technique for the verification of Petri nets. Traditionally it is used for structural verification, i.e. for avoiding the explicit construction of a state space. In this paper, we study the use of Petri net invariants for reducing the memory resources required *during* state space construction. While place invariants help to reduce the amount of memory needed for each single state (without reducing the number of states as such), transition invariants can be used to reduce the number of states to be stored. Interestingly, our approach does not require computing invariants in full, let alone storing them permanently. All information we need can be deduced from an upper triangular form of the Petri net's incidence matrix. Experiments prove that the place invariant technique leads to improvements in both memory and run time costs while transition invariants lead to a space/time tradeoff that can be controlled heuristically.

1 Introduction

Petri net invariants are a well understood and broadly used concept in the verification of Petri nets. Place invariants can be used to closely over-approximate the state space thus being useful for verifying various safety properties. Transition invariants give hints to cycles, other than this they have been of some limited use in verification [13]. So far, invariants have been mainly studied as structural analysis techniques, i.e. as a tool to *replace* explicit state space verification. In this paper, we propose methods to use them for *improving* state space verification. The general ideas are not very deep from a theoretical perspective, but turned out to lead to significant improvements in run time and space of explicit state space verification.

For place invariants, we use the fact that a place invariant corresponds to a linear equation that involves the markings of several places. Given such an equation, the marking of one of the places is therefore determined by the marking of the remaining places. Consequently, it is not necessary to store the marking of that particular place in the state space data structure. Given n linearly independent place invariants, only $|P| - n$ places need to be stored to uniquely identify a state. Our experiments suggest that a vector to be stored can be shrunk to 50-70 percent of its original size. Since many state space related operations operate then on the shrunk vector, we obtain significant run time improvements

H. Garavel and J. Hatcliff (Eds.): TACAS 2003, LNCS 2619, pp. 473–488, 2003.

that more than compensate the overhead for acquiring the necessary information about place invariants.

Techniques for compressing state representations based on place invariants have been proposed, for instance, in [14]. There, they use specific place invariants that allow us to deduce that exactly one place in the support of the invariant contains exactly one token while the remaining places are empty. In such a situation (assuming n places in the support of the invariant) they can shrink the n places to a representation of size $\log n$. However, this approach requires full computation of particular invariants (which can be done by linear programming) while our approach is based on much simpler information about place invariants which can be computed even more efficiently.

For transition invariants, we use their capability of hinting at cycles in the state graph. Every transition sequence that can occur in some state and returns to the same state, corresponds to a transition invariant. Now it is easy to verify that for termination of reachability graph generation it is sufficient to store as many states as are necessary to cover all cycles of the graph (i.e. to have one state of the cycle stored). The other states will be generated over and over again (without storing them, thus without detecting that they have been generated before) but since these states do not form cycles they do not pose any threat for termination of reachability graph generation. We show that, given some knowledge about transition invariants, a set of states can be characterized that covers all cycles of the net. This number is reasonably small thus allowing for a significant state space reduction. Unfortunately, the repeated generation of states leads to an exponential blow up in the run time. This blow up is not as bad when partial order reduction is applied in connection with the transition invariant reduction (since partial order reduced graphs have smaller branching factors). However, we found it necessary to implement a configurable tradeoff between space and time. Given a user configurable number k, we store, in addition to the states required by the invariant method, all states that are encountered in a distance from the initial marking that is divisible by k. This way, the amount of repeated encounters of other states can be limited, for the price of more space costs.

Only few Petri net tools use a state compression based on place invariants (in fact, besides our own tool LoLA [20] we only know of INA [15] using this technique). The reason might be that most other Petri net tools have high level Petri nets as their base formalisms, in contrast to INA's and LoLA's low level Petri net languages. Computing invariants for high level nets [9,3,23,16,19] is a much more involved task than computing low level net invariants where we "only" need to solve a system of linear equations with integer coefficients.

An approach similar to the transition invariant approach has been reported for the real time verification tool UPPAAL [12]. They verify systems that are parallel compositions of timed state machines and use depth first search on the component state machines for identifying cycles in the components. Those cycles are used to characterize a set of states covering all cycles in the reachability graph.

As the actual contribution of this paper, we show that both our approaches do not even depend on the actual computation of invariants, let alone having the invariants explicitly stored in memory. All information we need can be deduced from transforming the matrix that defines the system of linear equations to be solved into an upper triangular form. On models with 10,000 Petri net nodes, this task does still take less than one second, so the preprocessing overhead can be neglected.

We first introduce Petri nets, related state spaces, and state equations. The latter concept is the starting point for both invariant calculi. We then sketch an algorithm for depth first state space generation and present the two reductions. We continue with a method that can deduce all information we need about invariants from upper triangular forms of the involved systems of equations. We conclude with some experimental results and a discussion on compatibility with other state space reduction techniques.

2 Petri Nets, State Space, and State Equation

Let $\mathbf{N}$ denote the set of natural numbers, including 0. Consider a Petri net $N = [P, T, F, W, m_0]$ with a finite set P of places, a finite set T of transitions, a set $F \subseteq (P \times T) \cup (T \times P)$ of arcs, an arc weight function $W : (P \times T) \cup (T \times P) \longrightarrow \mathbf{N}$ such that $W([x, y]) = 0$ if and only if $[x, y] \notin F$, and a marking m_0, the initial marking. A marking is a mapping $m : P \longrightarrow \mathbf{N}$ which is usually interpreted as a distribution of tokens on the places, with p carrying $m(p)$ tokens. A transition t is interpreted as changing the distribution of tokens by removing $W([p, t])$ tokens from p (for all places p), and producing $W([t, p])$ tokens on p (for all places p). Thus, a marking m' is immediately reachable by a transition t from a marking m (written $m \xrightarrow{t} m'$) iff, for all p, $m(p) \geq W([p, t])$, and $m'(p) = m(p) - W([p, t]) + W([t, p])$.

The Petri net depicted in Fig. 1 models the well known dining philsophers example. In the picture, places are represented by circles, transitions by rectangles, arcs as arrows. In the example, weights are 0 (no arrow) or 1 (arrow present). The initial marking is represented by black dots on places.

Reachability can be extended to sequences of transitions by letting $m \xrightarrow{\varepsilon} m$ for all markings m and the empty sequence ε, and $m \xrightarrow{wt} m'$ iff there is a marking m_1 such that $m \xrightarrow{w} m_1$ and $m_1 \xrightarrow{t} m'$ (with w being a sequence of transitions and t a transition). m' is just reachable from m ($m \xrightarrow{*} m'$) iff there is a transition sequence w such that $m \xrightarrow{w} m'$.

The state space of a Petri net consists of the set $R_N(m_0) = \{m \mid m_0 \xrightarrow{*} m\}$ of states reachable from the initial marking. It can be extended to a graph by letting $R_N(m_0)$ be the vertices and $. \xrightarrow{t} .$ be the edges labeled with transitions. Most properties of interest are defined, and can be verified, as patterns of the state graph. Therefore, we present our technique, without discussing particular properties, using an algorithm that just generates the state graph.

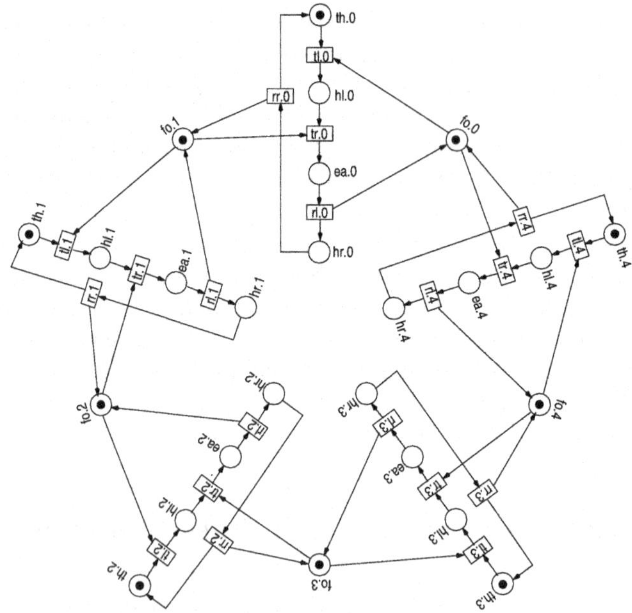

Fig. 1. This Petri net models the 5 dining philosophers system. The internal state of philospher i is marked by a token on th.i (thinking), hl.i (has left fork), ea.i (eating), or hr.i (has right fork). A token on fo.i models an available fork. Transitions shift states by removing the token representing the current state, producing a token representing the next state, and consuming or producing (or: taking or releasing) a fork.

The incidence matrix C of a Petri net N has a row for each place $p \in P$ and a column for each transition $t \in T$. It is defined by $C(p,t) = W(t,p) - W(p,t)$.

From the definition of reachability, it follows that $m \xrightarrow{w} m'$ (for a sequence w) implies

$$m' = m + C \cdot \Psi(w)$$

where $\Psi(w)$ (the count vector of w) is a column indexed by T where $\Psi(w)(t)$ corresponds to the number of occurrences of t in w, and markings are considered as P-indexed columns. This equation is called the *Petri net state equation.* Throughout this paper, $A \cdot B$ denotes the inner product between two matrices $A : I_1 \times I_2 \longrightarrow \mathbb{Q}$ and $B : I_2 \times I_3 \longrightarrow \mathbb{Q}$ (including vectors as matrices with 1 as one of their dimensions), and $A \cdot B(i,k) = \sum_{j \in I_2} A(i,j) \cdot B(j,k)$ for all $i \in I_1$ and $k \in I_3$.

3 Invariants

A place invariant is an integer row vector i such that $i \cdot C = \underline{0}$ where $\underline{0}$ is a null vector of appropriate dimension, and i has P as its index set. The requirement of having an integer vector can be relaxed to rational, or real numbers without

Table 1. Depth first generation of state graph for $N = [P, T, F, W, m_0]$; t^- and t^+ are P-indexed vectors with $t^-(p) = W([p,t])$ and $t^+(p) = W([t,p])$

```
var V: set of markings initial ∅;
var E: set of edges initial ∅;
var current: marking initial m0;
procedure StateGraph()
var t : transition;
var Enabled: set of transitions;
begin
    V := V ∪ {current};
    Enabled := {t | t ∈ T ∧ current ≥ t⁻};
    for t in Enabled do
        E := E ∪ [current,current −t⁻ + t⁺];
        current := current +t⁺ − t⁻;
        if current ∉ V then
            StateGraph();
        fi
        current := current +t⁻ − t⁺;
    done end.
```

significant impact on our approach. The main property of an invariant i is that, for a marking m' reachable from another marking m, it holds that $i \cdot m' = i \cdot m$. Thus, every reachable state has the same product with i as the initial marking. The main property can be easily verified by multiplying i from the left to the state equation.

One example for a place invariant in Fig. 1 is the vector assigning 1 to places fo.0, hl.0, ea.0, ea.4, and hr.4 while assigning 0 to the remaining places.

A transition invariant is an integer column vector i such that $C \cdot i = \underline{0}$ where i has T as its index set. It follows directly from the state equation that for every transition sequence w where $m \xrightarrow{w} m$ for some m (forms a cycle), $\Psi(w)$ is a transition invariant.

One example for a transition invariant in Fig. 1 is the vector assigning 1 to transitions tl.0, tr.0, rl.0, and rr.0 while assigning 0 to all remaining transitions.

4 Place Invariant Based State Compression

Let i be a place invariant and p be a place such that $i(p) \neq 0$. Let m be a marking. From the main property of place invariants, we have

$$m(p) = \frac{i \cdot m_0 - \sum_{p' \in P \setminus \{p\}} i(p') \cdot m(p')}{i(p)}$$

Thus, $m(p)$ can be completely determined from m on the remaining places, i, and the (constant) initial marking m_0. Consequently, it is not necessary to store $m(p)$ explicitly for any reachable marking m. Using the place invariant mentioned in the previous section, we can, in every reachable marking, deduce the token count in fo.0 from the token counts on hl.0, ea.0, ea.4, and hr.4: if any of those places contains a token then fo.0 does not, otherwise it contains exactly one token.

A net usually has more than one place invariant. Consequently, n linearly independent invariants can be used to exempt n components of a marking from explicit storage.

Assume that P is partitioned into a set S of significant places and R of redundant places ($P = S \cup R$, $S \cap R = \emptyset$) such that for each $p \in R$ there is a place invariant i_p holding $i_p(p) \neq 0$ and $i_p(p') = 0$ for $p' \in R \setminus \{p\}$. This means, according to previous considerations, the marking on all redundant places can be reconstructed from the marking on significant places. Notice that $\{i_p \mid p \in R\}$ is a linearly independent set of invariants. Furthermore, due to the ability of uniquely reconstructing the whole vector, we have that for two reachable markings m and m', $m = m'$ if and only if $m(p) = m'(p)$ for all $p \in S$.

In other words, the portion of m that corresponds to S uniquely identifies a reachable state. This comparison is the only operation that is ever done with states other than the current state. A further look at the depth first search algorithm in Tab. 1 shows that the current state itself is never loaded from the set V of known states but always computed from firing transitions forward or backward.[1] This is an efficient solution anyway since firing a transition (forward or backward) involves only places in the immediate F-neighborhood of the transition while copying a state involves the whole P.

Thus, assuming that we only store the S-portion of m in the set of known states, we can preserve the full functionality of the sketched depth first search. All we need to know is a set S of significant places satisfying the above requirements, the actual vectors i_p are completely irrelevant (beyond the determination of S). Search and insert operations to the set V now involve only S-vectors rather than P-vectors which speeds up both operations. Our experiments show that the additional run time to determine S more than pays off through these speed ups.

The actual determination of S and R is left to Sec. 6.

In the model in Fig. 1, one possible partition has all places hl.i, ea.i, and hr.i as significant places, all remaining places are redundant. Thus, the size of every state vector shrinks from 25 components to 15 components.

Actually, there are several possibilities to partition P. Correctness of our approach is independent of the particular choice. The maximum number of elements in R is equal to the number of linearly independent place invariants in the system. The construction below does always yield such a maximum size set R.

[1] Backward firing refers to step 16 of the algorithm presented in Sec. 3. This is the step where we backtrack from a completely processed state to one of its predecessor state during (forward) reachability analysis. This step should not be confused with backward reachability analysis.

5 Transition Invariant Based Reduction

As already sketched in the introduction, we aim at identifying a set $Z \subseteq R_N(m_0)$ of states such that every cycle in the reachability graph contains at least one element of Z. Transition invariants characterize count vectors of transition sequences that corresponds to cycles: if a transition sequence returns to the start state, its count vector is a transition invariant.

In Fig. 1, the sequence tl.1, tr.1, rl.1, rr.1 can be executed in the initial state and reproduces the initial state. The vector assigning 1 to the mentioned transitions and 0 to the remaining transitions is a transition invariant.

Consider a set U of transitions such that every transition invariant (other than the vector of all zeros) is non-zero for at least one element in U. Then, consequently, every cycle in the state graph contains a state m where an edge labeled with an element t of U springs off, i.e. t is enabled at m. Thus, the set of states where at least one element of U is enabled satisfies the condition posed on Z above.

Applying transition invariant based reduction means that states that enable elements of U are stored in the set V of known states while other states are computed and explored, but not stored permanently. Given a set U, determining whether or not a marking m enables an element of U can be embedded efficiently into the calculation of enabled transitions at m. If we explore, for a second time, a state that does not enable a transition in U, we do not find this state in V, so we compute its successors a second time. However, since ignored states do not form complete cycles, termination of reachability graph generation is still guaranteed.

In preprocessing, only U needs to be determined while, as in the case of place invariants, it is not necessary to know the actual invariants.

While the place invariant based technique leads to gains in both space and time efficiency, the transition invariant based technique can become extremely slow, since states that are not stored permanently can be visited and explored a large (up to exponential) number of times. This problem is less grave when the transition invariant technique is combined with partial order reduction. Partial order reduction narrows the number of successors to be computed in each state. Thus, the average number of predecessors of a states shrinks as well, and that number determines how often not permanently stored states would be re-explored. Still, first experiments suggested that it is necessary to further improve the time efficiency of the method. We decided to gain time efficiency by storing more states permanently (thus re-exploring less states). We experimented with a criterion that stores states if they are explored in a distance that is divisible by some user specified number k. Thus, regarding the depth first search tree, certain layers of the tree are stored completely, in addition to the states that potentially close cycles. In this combination, the choice of k controls a space/time tradeoff where large values mean trading time for getting better space efficiency while small numbers increase time efficiency while requiring more space.

With not saving all states, it does not make sense to store edges. Therefore the sketch of the transition invariant based reduction in Tab. 2 does not contain edges at all. Nevertheless every state will be eventually visited by the algorithm. Thus, simple safety properties such as reachability, deadlocks, etc., can still be exhaustively verified.

Table 2. Depth first generation of state graph with transition invariant based reduction for $N = [P, T, F, W, m_0]$; t^- and t^+ are P-indexed vectors with $t^-(p) = W([p,t])$ and $t^+(p) = W([t,p])$; let k be a nonzero natural number and U as described in the text

```
var V: set of P-vectors initial ∅;
var current: marking initial m0;
var depth: integer initial 0;
procedure TStateGraph()
var t : transition;
var Enabled: set of transitions;
begin
    Enabled := {t | t ∈ T ∧ current ≥ t⁻};
    if Enabled ∩U ≠ ∅ or depth ≡ 0  mod k then
        V := V ∪{current};
    fi
    for t in Enabled do
        current := current +t⁺ − t⁻; depth := depth + 1;
        if current ∉ V then
            TStateGraph();
        fi
        current := current +t⁻ − t⁺; depth := depth - 1;
    done end.
```

6 Upper Triangular Form

In this section, we demonstrate how efficiently a partition of P into sets S of significant and R of redundant places can be computed based on well known linear algebra. Determining a set U of transitions needed for the transition invariant technique is equally simple.

Consider a homogeneous system $A \cdot x = \underline{0}$ of linear equations (A can be the incidence matrix C for transition invariant, or the transposed of C for place invariant calculation). It is well known that exchanging rows in A, adding a row of A to another, or multiplying a row by a scalar, are operations that preserve the space of solutions and can be used to transform the matrix into an upper triangular form, that is into a form where the leftmost nonzero element of a row is always right of the leftmost nonzero element of the previous row. Call the columns that contain the leftmost nonzero element of some row *head* columns, and call columns that do not contain a leftmost nonzero element of any row *tail* columns.

Example. The matrix

$$\begin{pmatrix} 1 & 0 & 1 & 1 & 0 & 2 & 3 \\ 0 & 1 & 1 & 2 & 2 & 1 & 1 \\ 0 & 0 & 0 & 0 & 2 & 1 & 0 \\ 0 & 0 & 0 & 0 & 0 & 0 & 1 \end{pmatrix}$$

is in upper triangular form. Columns 1, 2, 5, and 7 are head columns while columns 3, 4, and 6 are tail columns.

Columns of A correspond to variables in x. Thus, we can partition variables correspondingly into head variables and tail variables. In the example, we would have head variables x_1, x_2, x_5, and x_7, and tail variables x_3, x_4, and x_6. The partition into head and tail variables depends on the particular upper triangular form, especially on the order of indices in the index sets of the involved matrix. The number of head and tail variables is, however, determined by the rank of the matrix.

Now, consider a tail variable x_j, a partial assignment to x where $x_j = 1$, and $x_k = 0$ for all remaining tail variables. We can easily see that every such partial assignment can be extended to a solution of the whole system of equations. For this purpose, start at the bottom row of A. This row has, besides some of the tail columns, only its own head column as nonzero entry. Thus, the partial assignment can be extended, by assigning some rational value (zero or nonzero), to a solution for the bottom equation of the upper triangular form. Values of other head variables are irrelevant since they have zero coefficients in the bottom equation. Now, going up step by step, we have always a partial assignment to all variables that have nonzero entries, except the head variable of the considered row, and an appropriate assignment to that variable solves the new equation without interfering with equations below. Consequently, every partial solution that assigns 1 to some tail variable and 0 to the remaining tail variables, can be extended to a unique rational solution (and, by multiplying by a common divisor, to an integer solution) of the system of equations that is unique up to multiplying all components by a scalar. Rank considerations show, that the set of solutions obtained this way forms a basis of the whole solution space (the number of head variables corresponds to the rank of A, the number of all variables to the dimension of x).

Without knowing the values of solutions on the head variables, we have sufficient information for both invariant based state space techniques. For the place invariant approach, we need to partition P into significant and redundant places. Since places correspond to variables in the system of equations corresponding to place invariants, we can let S be the head variables of the upper triangular form, and R be the tail variables. This setting matches exactly the definition of significant and redundant places.

For transition invariants, we can observe that there cannot be any nonzero transition invariant that assigns 0 to all tail variables. Since the set of invariants that can be obtained by the above procedure forms a basis for the set of all solutions to the system of equations (the solutions are obviously linearly independent), a solution that assigns 0 to all tail variables must be representable as a linear combination of the base vectors. By construction, only the zero vector can be a linear combination of the described solutions that assigns 0 to all tail variables. Thus, the set U of all transitions that correspond to tail variables in the system of equations has the property that every nonzero transition invariant has a nonzero element in U. Moreover, this set is minimal at least with respect to set inclusion, since for every proper subset of this U, one of the generators we described would have all its nonzero entries outside U.

In conclusion, gaining the knowledge needed for our techniques requires less effort than even computing the actual invariants!

7 Compatibility with Other Reduction Techniques

Place invariant based compression is compatible with most other frequently used reduction techniques. For all known *partial order reduction* techniques (see [24] for a survey), it is sufficient to investigate the current state. For some advanced techniques, the state graph as such must be investigated for strongly connected components and transitions occurring in strongly connected components. None of this information is altered by our compression technique based on place invariants.

For *symmetry reduction* [7,22,8,2,4,1,10,17,18], the test whether the current state is in V must be replaced by a test whether there is a symmetry such that the symmetric image of the current state is in V. There are different solutions to this problem, [18] lists several of them. One solution is to iterate all symmetries, apply a symmetry to the current state and check for containment of the resulting symmetric image of the state. In this solution, the projection of the current state to S can be done after the application of the symmetry, so there is no compatibility problem. A second solution uses symmetries to transform the current state into a canonical representative of its class and checks whether the representative is in V. Again, there is no problem since the projection to S can be applied to the representative. A third solution proposed in [21] proposes to iterate through V (more precisely, the subset of V that matches the hash value of the current state), and tries to calculate a symmetry from the iterated states to the current state. This approach would require restoring elements of V to full markings which is not covered by our approach. Thus, symmetry reduction can be used in connection with place invariant compression, but not all of the existing methods for checking containment of a symmetric image can be applied.

Coverability graph generation [11,5] involves checking whether the current state covers any predecessor state on the path back to the initial state. If so, the coverability graph algorithm assigns the value ω to every properly covering component. In order to be compatible with place invariant based reduction, we can store information about ω-introductions separated from the actual marking vectors. So, we can attach to each state a list of places where a ω is introduced exactly at that state, together with the old (finite) value that is replaced with ω. This way, we can generate all states on the path from the initial state to the current state, by starting with the current state, firing transitions backwards in connection with updating a pointer to the corresponding S-vector in V. If that pointer points to a state with attached information about ω-introductions, that information can be used to restore the value of the vector before introduction of the new ω. This way, all states on the path from the initial state to the current state can be generated without actually retrieving states from V. Since two subsequent states differ in only few components (the environment of the fired transition), this method of iterating states is very efficient anyway. In conclusion, place invariant based state compression is compatible with coverability graph generation. This result holds, however, only for the original coverability graph algorithm proposed in [11]. For the minimal coverability graph algorithm proposed in [5], not only states on the path back to the initial state, but *all* states in V are checked for covering. For this covering check it is neither sufficient to use only the S-projection of states in V, nor is there an efficient way to restore those states without knowing the actual values of place invariants.

There are other compression techniques than place invariants. Most of them [6,25] rely on hash functions on the states. Applying these techniques to the S-projection of a marking instead of the full marking can speed up the calculation of hash values. Moreover, since the components removed by the place invariant compression are functionally dependent on the remaining components, applying hash techniques to the compressed vector can even lead to a more perfect (i.e. more uniformly spreading) behavior of the hash function based techniques. So far, we have not verified this conjecture experimentally.

For symbolic state spaces, for instance, based on BDDs, the compression might be of little value. Reducing the BDD to S is no solution since we need the full state in order to compute enabled transitions and successor markings. In explicit state space analysis, this is fully covered by having the current state available in uncompressed form. In symbolic state space analysis, enabledness and successors are computed from the BDD, so the reduced information is insufficient. Remember that an important pre-requisite of our technique is to restore current states by firing transitions forward or backward, rather than copying them from V.

Since the transition invariant based technique only controls which markings are permanently stored, but not which successors are explored at a marking, there are no compatibility problems with basic partial order reduction techniques. With basic partial order reduction methods we mean techniques where the determination of the set of transitions to be fired at a state can be determined from the current state and the net structure. The original deadlock preserving stubborn set technique, and several of the stubborn set approaches for Petri net standard properties are in this class of partial order reduction methods. For advanced techniques (such that rely on investigations on connected components of the state graph, for instance the LTL preserving and CTL* preserving methods; refer to the survey [24] for details), we need some future research to check whether the necessary information can be retrieved from the reduced graph (the original edge relation is unavailable due to the removal of states). Basic partial order reduction techniques, however, increase the performance of the transition invariant technique by reducing the average branching factor in the state graph. Cycles in a graph reduced by partial order reduction, are definitely cycles in the original graph, so the transition invariant technique works correctly for partial order reduced graphs (in the sense that reduced graph generation terminates).

For symmetries, we need to be careful since cycles in a symmetrically reduced graph do not necessarily correspond to cycles in the original graph. The reason is that a marking can have an edge to a symmetric image of its actual successor marking. However, a cycle in the reduced graph can be extended to a cycle in the original graph since for every sequence executable in a state, a sequence consisting of equivalent transitions can be executed at a symmetric state. Thus, for every cycle in the reduced graph there is a cycle in the original graph (maybe longer) that consists of the transitions occurring in the reduced graph's cycle and transitions equivalent to them. Therefore, enlarging U by all transitions that are equivalent w.r.t. symmetry to elements in U can guarantee that the enlarged U contains at least one transition for each cycle in the symmetrically reduced state graph.

Transition invariant based reduction and coverability graph reduction according to [11] are compatible when the technique described earlier is used to generate all states from the current state back to the initial state.

Application of hash function based compression techniques does not interfere with the transition invariant based reduction; a combination with BDD based techniques seems not to be feasible.

8 Experiments

As examples, we use a sequence of n dining philosophers examples, and a sequence of a semaphore based scheme for concurrent read and exclusive write access to a data base for n writing and n reading processes.

An n dining philosophers system, in the version we use, has $5n$ places and $2n$ linearly independent place invariants. Thus, the reduction in terms of vector length is 40%. The data base scheme with n reading and n writing processes has $6n + 1$ places and $3n + 1$ independent place invariants. Thus, the vector length is reduced to approximately 50%. In several other examples, we got reductions from 30% to 50%. In run time (all numbers are measured on one and the same computer and include the whole task including reading the net, processing invariants (for reduced version), and generating the full state graph), we got the following numbers[2].

The reported systems are tiny since we wanted to compare run times between place invariant reduction and brute force state space generation. In connection with other reduction techniques, the speed up is comparable. For instance, verifying a 500 philosophers system (with an overall of $3^{500} - 1$ states, the partial

[2] All reported run times relate to the implementation of both methods in the tool LoLA [20], running on a LINUX machine equipped with a 650MHz Pentium processor and 256 MByte of RAM.

Table 3. Speedup introduced by place invariant compression.

	10 phil	11 phil	12 phil	14 data	16 data	18 data
states	59048	117146	531440	16398	65552	262162
time (sec) without red.	2.7	9.8	37.7	2.0	10.4	53.8
time (sec) with red.	2.1	7.7	30.3	1.3	6.7	35.8

order reduced state space consists of 751502 states. It takes 149 sec. to compute it with place invariant compression, compared to 238 sec. without. Using both partial order and symmetry reduction on the 1000 dining philosophers system, the reduced state space consists of 2997 states (compared to 3^{1000} states of the full state space). Computation requires 189.4 sec. with place invariants involved, compared to 189.7 without. In this case, numbers are almost equal since most of the time is spent for investigating symmetries.

For the transition invariant technique, it is interesting to study the impact of the heuristical parameter k that controls the amount of additionally stored states. An n philosophers system has n independent transition invariants. With n writing and n reading processes, the data base scheme has $2n$ independent transition invariants.

The first two tables show the limited capabilities of transition invariant based reduction without combining it with partial order reduction. The first table shows the impact of k. For the data base example, larger values of k do not change the number of states which can be blamed to very tight cycles in that net.

Table 4. State reduction and time overhead in transition invariant reduction on the dining philosophers system.

	5 phil	6 phil	7 phil	8 phil	9 phil
states without red.	242	728	2186	6560	19682
time (sec) without red.	0.03	0.04	0.08	0.23	0.76
states with red., $k = 5000$	160	530	1708	5417	16952
time (sec) with red., $k = 5000$	0.09	0.7	9.7	136.0	2177.6
states with red., $k = 20$	186	591	1828	5664	17545
time (sec) with red., $k = 20$	0.05	0.1	0.36	3.19	10.8
states with red., $k = 10$	201	629	1947	5984	18289
time (sec) with red., $k = 10$	0.04	0.07	0.19	0.59	1.8

The last table shows the behavior of transition invariant based reduction in connection with partial order reduction. We use deadlock preserving stubborn sets as the partial order reduction technique. The numbers show a significantly better performance of the transition invariance technique.

Table 5. State reduction and time overhead in transition invariant reduction on the data base system.

	14 data	16 data	18 data
states	16398	65552	262162
time (sec) without red.	2.0	10.4	53.8
states with red. $k = 10$	16384	65536	262144
time (sec.) with red. $k = 10$	2.1	10.4	55.1

Table 6. Combination of transition invariant reduction with partial order reduction.

	100 phil	200 phil	200 data	300 data	400 data
states (p.o. red. only)	29702	119402	401	601	801
time (sec) (p.o. red. only)	2.2	16.4	8.2	25.1	61.0
states both red., $k = 5000$	10311	41093	1	1	1
time (sec.) both red., $k = 5000$	45.3	395.3	13.0	26.8	64.6
states both red., $k = 20$	14502	59002	1	1	1
time (sec.) both red., $k = 20$	3.5	26.5	8.0	26.7	64.4
states both red., $k = 10$	17702	71402	1	1	1
time (sec.) both red., $k = 10$	2.8	21.4	8.3	26.7	64.0

9 Discussion

The place invariant technique yields improvements in both space and time. It is compatible with many other reduction techniques. Thus, no special care needs to be taken when applying the method. The transition invariant based approach turns out to be unfeasible as a standalone technique but can be rather valuable when applied in connection with partial order reduction. It requires that the parameter k that controls the space/time tradeoff of the technique be chosen carefully. Then, however, it can make the difference between getting a state graph into the available memory or not.

Feasibility of both methods relies on the fact that we do not need the actual values of the invariants but only information that, in a generating set, certain elements are guaranteed to be 0 or nonzero. This way, no space is required for storing invariants, and preprocessing can be reduced to just generating an upper triangular form out of the net's incidence matrix (or its transposed).

Besides the fact that the linear algebraic approach to invariance is already rather Petri net specific (even low level net specific), our approach relies essentially on the Petri net specific fact that we can backtrack from a successor state by firing a transition backwards. Many other system description languages are based on programming language like notations where constant assignments (for example, $x := 0$) cannot be applied backwards that easily. In such a situation, it would be more difficult to live without the ability to re-construct complete states.

For high level nets, several obstacles make the place invariant technique unfeasible. First, an automatic calculation of place invariants is a computationally involved task. The approach would therefore need to rely on user supplied invariants. Second, the supplied invariants must enable the system to deduce a partition into significant and redundant place instances (colours). Finally, many high level net tools compute successor states by executing programming language style code attached to arcs or transitions. In that framework, it is usually impossible to backtrack to a predecessor marking other than by restoring it from the depository of known states since the attached code cannot be executed "backwards".

In contrast, the transition invariant technique can be adapted to high level nets without major problems, at least when the high level net formalism is such that all bindings of a high level net transition cause the same *number* of tokens to be produced or consumed at every pre- and post-place of the transition. In that case, the skeleton of the high level net (replacing all coloured tokens by black tokens) is well defined and every cycle in the high level net state space corresponds to a cycle in its skeleton. Then, computing U in the skeleton, and storing all states of the high level net that enable at least one binding of some transition in U solves the problem connected with our transition invariant based reduction method.

References

1. G. Chiola and G. Franceschinis. Colored gspn models and automatic symmetry detection. In *Proceedings of the 3rd Int. Workshop on Petri Nets and Performance Models 1989, Kyoto, Japan – Los Alamitos, CA, USA*, pages 50–60. IEEE Computer Society Press, 1990.
2. E.M. Clarke, R. Enders, T. Filkorn, and S. Jha. Exploiting symmetry in temporal logic model checking. *Formal Methods in System Design*, 9:77–104, 1996.
3. J.M. Couvreur. The general computations of flows for coloured nets. *Proc. of the 11th int. Workshop on Application and Theory of Petri nets*, 1990.
4. E.A. Emerson and A. P. Sistla. Symmetry and model checking. *Formal Methods in System Design*, 9:105–131, 1996.
5. A. Finkel. A minimal coverability graph for petri nets. *Proc. of the 11th International Conference on Application and Theory of Petri nets*, pages 1–21, 1990.
6. G. Holzmann. On limits and possibilities of automated protocol analysis. *Proc. 7th IFIP WG 6.1 Int. Workshop on Protocol Specification, Testing, and Verification*, pages 137–161, 1987.
7. Huber, A. Jensen, Jepsen, and K. Jensen. Towards reachability trees for high–level petri nets. In *Advances in Petri Nets 1984, Lecture Notes on Computer Science 188*, pages 215–233, 1984.
8. C. Norris Ip and D. L. Dill. Better verification through symmetry. *Formal Methods in System Design*, 9:41–75, 1996.
9. K. Jensen. How to find invariants for coloured petri nets. *Lecture Notes In Computer Science*, 118:327–338, 1981.

10. K. Jensen. Condensed state spaces for symmetrical coloured petri nets. *Formal Methods in System Design*, 9:7–40, 1996.
11. R. M. Karp and R. E. Miller. Parallel programm schemata. *Journ. Computer and System Sciences 4*, pages 147–195, Mai 1969.
12. K. Larsen, F. Larsen, P. Pettersen, and W. Yi. Efficient verification of real-time systems: compact data structure and state-space reduction. *Proc. 18th IEEE Real-Time Systems Symp., LNCS*, pages 14–24, 1997.
13. K. Lautenbach and H. Ridder. Liveness in bounded petri nets which are covered by t–invariants. *Proc. of the 15th international Conference on Theory and Application of Petri nets, Zaragoza, LNCS 815*, pages 358–375, 1994.
14. E. Pastor and J. Cortadella. Efficient encoding schemes for symbolic analysis of petri nets. *Proc. Proc. DATE '98*, pages 790–795, 1998.
15. S. Roch and P. Starke. *INA – Integrierter Netz-Analysator Version 1.7. Handbuch.* Humboldt-University Berlin, Institute of Computer Science, 1997.
16. K. Schmidt. On the computation of place invariants for algebraic petri nets. *Proceedings of the STRICT workshop Berlin*, 1995.
17. K. Schmidt. How to calculate symmetries of petri nets. *Acta Informatica 36*, pages 545–590, 2000.
18. K. Schmidt. Integrating low level symmetries into reachability analysis. *Proc. of the 6th International Conference Tools and Algorithms for the Construction and Analysis of Systems, LNCS 1785*, pages 315–331, 2000.
19. K. Schmidt. T–invariants of algebraic petri nets. *Informatik–Bericht*, 31, 1994.
20. K. Schmidt. Lola: A low level analyser. *Proc. Int. Conf. Application and Theory of Petri net, LNCS*, 1825:465–474, 1999.
21. K. Schmidt. Integrating low level symmetries into reachability analysis. *Proc. TACAS 2000, LNCS*, 1785:315–331, 2000.
22. P. Starke. Reachability analysis of petri nets using symmetries. *J. Syst. Anal. Model. Simul.*, 8:294–303, 1991.
23. J. Toksvig. Design and implementation of a place invariant tool for coloured petri nets. Master's thesis, University of Aarhus, 1995.
24. A. Valmari. The state explosion problem. In *Lectures on Petri Nets I – Basic Models, LNCS 1491*, pages 429–528, 1998.
25. P. Wolper and D. Leroy. Reliable hashing without collision detection. *Proc. CAV, LNCS*, pages 59–70, 1993.

Optimistic Synchronization-Based State-Space Reduction

Scott D. Stoller[1]* and Ernie Cohen[2]

[1] State University of New York at Stony Brook
Computer Science Dept., SUNY at Stony Brook, Stony Brook, NY 11794-4400.
stoller@cs.sunysb.edu, http://www.cs.sunysb.edu/~stoller
[2] Microsoft Research, Cambridge, UK, ernie.cohen@acm.org

Abstract. Reductions that aggregate fine-grained transitions into coarser transitions can significantly reduce the cost of automated verification, by reducing the size of the state space. We propose a reduction that can exploit common synchronization disciplines, such as the use of mutual exclusion for accesses to shared data structures. Exploiting them using traditional reduction theorems requires checking that the discipline is followed in the original (*i.e.*, unreduced) system. That check can be prohibitively expensive. This paper presents a reduction that instead requires checking whether the discipline is followed in the reduced system. This check may be much cheaper, because the reachable state space is smaller.

1 Introduction

For many concurrent software systems, a straightforward model of the system has such a large and complicated state space that automated verification, by automated theorem-proving or state-space exploration (model checking), is infeasible. *Reduction* is an important technique for reducing the size of the state space by aggregating transitions into coarser-grained transitions.

When exploring the state space of a concurrent system, context switches between threads are typically allowed before each transition. A simple example of a reduction for concurrent systems is to inhibit context switches within sequences of transitions that access only unshared variables. This effectively increases the granularity of transitions. Thus, one can regard this and similar reductions as defining a *reduced system*, which is a coarser-grained version of the original system. The reduced system may have dramatically fewer states than the original system. A *reduction theorem* asserts that certain properties are preserved by the transformation.

We consider a more powerful reduction that exploits common synchronization disciplines. For example, in a system that uses mutual exclusion on accesses to some shared variables—called *protected variables*—our reduction inhibits context switches within sequences of transitions that access only unshared variables

* The author gratefully acknowledges the support of NSF under Grant CCR-9876058 and the support of ONR under Grants N00014-01-1-0109 and N00014-02-1-0363.

H. Garavel and J. Hatcliff (Eds.): TACAS 2003, LNCS 2619, pp. 489–504, 2003.

and protected variables. The model-checking experiments reported in [Sto02] are based on a similar reduction, which decreased memory usage (which is proportional to the number of states) by a factor of 25 or more. Such reductions can also significantly decrease the computational cost of the automated theorem-proving needed for thread-modular verification [FQS02].

Traditional reduction theorems, such as [Lip75,CL98,Coh00], can also exploit such synchronization disciplines. However, a hypothesis of these traditional theorems is that the allegedly protected variables are indeed protected (by synchronization that enforces mutual exclusion) in the original (*i.e.*, unreduced) system. How can we establish this? Static analyses like [BR01,FF01] can automatically provide a conservative approximation but sometimes return "don't know". For general finite-state systems, it might seem that the only way to automatically obtain exact information about whether selected variables are actually protected is to express this condition as a history property and check it by state-space exploration of the original system. If this were the case, then the reduction would be almost pointless.

Our reduction theorem implies that one can determine exactly during state-space exploration of the *reduced* system whether the synchronization discipline is followed in the original system.

Our reduction theorem is designed to be used together with traditional reduction theorems. Suppose a traditional reduction theorem asserts that some property ϕ is preserved by the reduction if the original system follows the synchronization discipline. After checking that the reduced system follows the discipline and satisfies ϕ, one can use our reduction theorem to conclude that the original system follows the discipline, and then use the traditional reduction theorem to conclude that the original system satisfies ϕ.

The reduction in [Sto02] is similar in spirit to the one in this paper. The main contributions of this paper relative to [Sto02] are: (1) a reduction that applies to systems that use arbitrary synchronization mechanisms to achieve mutual exclusion (the results in [Sto02] apply only when monitors are used); (2) separation of a general reduction theorem that justifies checking hypotheses of traditional reduction theorems in the reduced system from the application of this technique to mutual-exclusion synchronization disciplines; (3) allowing non-determinism in invisible transitions (in the notation of Section 3, [Sto02] requires that u be deterministic); (4) significantly shorter and cleaner proofs, based on ω-algebra. The first author initially tried to prove similar results in a transition-system framework, like the one in [God96]; that should be possible, but our experience suggests that the algebraic framework facilitates the task.

Operations on monitors are not analyzed specially in this paper. As a result, for systems that mainly use monitors for synchronization, this reduction is not as effective as the one in [Sto02]. It should be possible to integrate the specialized treatment of monitor operations in [Sto02] into this paper's broader framework.

Our method and traditional partial-order methods (*e.g.*, ample sets [CGP99], stubborn sets [Val97], and persistent sets [God96]) both exploit independence (commutativity) of transitions, but our method can establish independence of transitions—and hence achieve a reduction—in many cases where traditional partial-order methods cannot. Traditional partial-order methods, as implemented in tools such as Spin [Hol97] and VeriSoft [God97], use two kinds of information to determine independence of transitions: program-specific information about which processes may perform which operations on which objects (*e.g.*, only process P_2 sends messages on channel C_1), and manually supplied program-independent information about dependencies between operations on selected datatypes (*e.g.*, a send operation on a full channel is disabled until a receive operation is performed on that channel). Our method also exploits more complicated program-specific information to determine independence of transitions, *e.g.*, the invariant that a particular variable is always protected by particular synchronization constructs.

Traditional partial-order methods rely on static analysis to conservatively determine dependencies between transitions. As a result, those methods are less effective for programs that contain references (or pointers) and arrays, because static analysis cannot in general determine exactly which locations are accessed by each transition, and the static analysis of dependencies between transitions is correspondingly imprecise. Our method does not rely on conservative static analysis of dependencies and has no difficulty with references, *etc.*

2 Omega Algebra

An *omega algebra* is an algebraic structure over the operators (in order of increasing precedence) 0 (nullary), 1 (nullary), + (binary infix), $\cdot$ (binary infix, usually written as simple juxtaposition), $\star$ (binary infix, same precedence as $\cdot$), * (unary suffix), and $^\omega$ (unary suffix), satisfying the following axioms[1]:

$$
\begin{array}{rlrl}
(x+y)+z = x+(y+z) & & x \le y \Leftrightarrow x+y=y & \\
x+y = y+x & & & \\
x+x = x & & x^* = 1+x+x^*\,x^* & \\
0+x = x & & x\,y \le x \Rightarrow x\,y^* = x & (^*\text{ ind}) \\
x\,(y\,z) = (x\,y)\,z & & x\,y \le y \Rightarrow x^*\,y = y & (^*\text{ ind}) \\
0\,x = x\,0 = 0 & & & \\
1\,x = x\,1 = x & & x \star y = x^\omega + x^*\,y & \\
x\,(y+z) = x\,y + x\,z & & x^\omega = x\,x^\omega & \\
(x+y)\,z = x\,z + y\,z & & x \le y\,x + z \Rightarrow x \le y \star z & (\star\text{ ind})
\end{array}
$$

In parsing formulas, $\cdot$ and $\star$ associate to the right; e.g., $u\ v \star x \star y$ parses to $(u \cdot (v^\omega + v^* \cdot (x^\omega + x^* \cdot y)))$. In proofs, we use the hint "(dist)" to indicate application of the distributivity laws, and the hint "(hyp)" to indicate the use of hypotheses. If x_i is a finite collection of terms, we write $(+i : x_i)$ and $(\cdot i : x_i)$ for the sum and product, respectively, of these terms.

These axioms are sound and complete for the usual equational theory of omega-regular expressions. (Completeness holds only for *standard* terms, where

[1] The axioms are equivalent to Kozen's axioms for Kleene algebra [Koz94], plus the three axioms for omega terms.

the first arguments to $\cdot$, $^\omega$, and $\star$ are regular.) Thus, we make free use, without proof, of familiar equations from the theory of (omega-)regular languages (e.g., $x^*\ x^* = x^*$).

y is a *complement* of x iff $x\ y = 0 = y\ x$ and $x + y = 1$. It is easy to show that complements (when they exist) are unique and that complementation is an involution; a *predicate* is an element of the algebra with a complement. In this paper, p and q range over predicates, with complements $\overline{p}$ and $\overline{q}$. It is easy to show that the predicates form a Boolean algebra, with $+$ as disjunction, $\cdot$ as conjunction, 0 as *false*, 1 as *true*, complementation as negation, and $\leq$ as implication. Common properties of Boolean algebras (e.g., $p\ q = q\ p$) are used silently in proofs, as is the fact $x\ p\ y = 0 \implies x\ y = x\ \overline{p}\ y$.

The omega algebra axioms support several interesting programming models, where (intuitively) 0 is magic[2], 1 is skip, $+$ is chaotic nondeterministic choice, $\cdot$ is sequential composition, $\leq$ is refinement, x^* is executed by executing x any finite number of times, and x^ω is executed by executing x an infinite number of times. The results of this paper are largely motivated by the *relational model*, where terms denote binary relations over a state space, 0 is the empty relation, 1 is the identity relation, $\cdot$ is relational composition, $+$ is union, * is reflexive-transitive closure, $\leq$ is subset, and x^ω relates an input state s to an output state if there is an infinite sequence of states starting with s, with consecutive states related by x. (Thus, x^ω relates an input state to either all states or none, and $x^\omega = 0$ iff x is well-founded.) Predicates are identified with the set of states in their domain (i.e., the states from which they can be executed). We define $\top = 1^\omega$; it is easy to see that $\top$ is the maximal element under $\leq$, and in the relational model, it relates all pairs of states.

In addition to equational identities of regular languages, we will use the following two standard theorems (proofs of these theorems and more sophisticated theorems of this type appear in [Coh00]):

$$x\ y \leq y\ z \implies x^*\ y \leq y\ z^* \tag{1}$$

$$y\ x \leq x\ y \implies (x + y)^* \leq x^*\ y^* \tag{2}$$

3 A Reduction Theorem

We consider systems composed of a fixed, finite set of concurrent processes (each perhaps internally concurrent and nondeterministic). Variables i and j range over process indices. Each process i has a visible action v_i and an invisible action u_i[3], where the invisible action is constrained to neither receive information from other processes nor to send information to other processes so as to create a race condition in the recipient. This constraint is guaranteed only so long as some global synchronization policy is followed. For example, in a system

[2] magic is the program that has no possible executions (and so satisfies every possible specification). Of course, it cannot be implemented.

[3] Note that u_i and v_i can be sums of nondeterministic actions that correspond to individual transitions of process i.

where processes are synchronized using locks, either visible or invisible actions of process i might modify variables that are either local to process i or protected by locks held by process i, or send asynchronous messages to other processes; but only visible actions can acquire locks or wait for a condition to hold. Note that violation of the synchronization discipline (e.g., an action accessing a shared variable without first obtaining an appropriate lock) might cause a race condition between an invisible action and the actions of another process, violating the constraint on invisible actions.

To avoid introducing temporal operators, we introduce a Boolean history variable q that records whether the synchronization discipline has been violated at some point in the execution. Predicate p_i means that process i cannot perform an invisible action, *i.e.*, that u_i is disabled. Let p be the conjunction of the p_i's, *i.e.*, $p = (\cdot i : p_i)$. A state satisfying p is called *visible*; thus, in a visible state, all invisible transitions are disabled.

We now define several actions, formalized in the definitions (3)–(9) below. An M_i action consists of a visible action of process i followed by a sequence of invisible actions of process i. An N_i action is an M_i action that is "maximal" (i.e., further u_i actions are disabled) and that finishes in a state where the synchronization discipline has not been violated. N_i is effectively the transition relation of thread i in the reduced system. (Additional conditions will imply that executing an N action in a visible state results in a visible state; thus, in the reduced system, context switches occur only in visible states.) A u (respectively v, M, N) action is a u_i (respectively, v_i, M_i, N_i) action of some process i. Finally, an R action is executable iff (*i*) the discipline has been violated, or (*ii*) such a violation is possible after execution of a single M action. (Like x^ω, R relates each initial state to either all final states or none.)

$$M_i = v_i \; u_i^* \tag{3}$$
$$N_i = M_i \; p_i \; \overline{q} \tag{4}$$
$$u = (+i : u_i) \tag{5}$$
$$v = (+i : v_i) \tag{6}$$
$$M = (+i : M_i) \tag{7}$$
$$N = (+i : N_i) \tag{8}$$
$$R = (1 + M) \; q \; \top \tag{9}$$

Our reduction theorem says that if the original system can reach a violation of the synchronization discipline starting from some visible state, then the reduced system can also reach a violation starting from the same initial state, except that the violation might occur partway through the last transition of the reduced system (*i.e.*, the last transition might be an M action rather than an N action). The transition relations of the original and reduced systems are $u + v$ and N, respectively. Thus, the conclusion of the reduction theorem, (19), is

$$p \; (u + v)^* \; q \leq N^* \; R \tag{10}$$

The hypotheses of our reduction theorem are as follows, formalized in formulas 11–(18) below. It is impossible to execute invisible actions of a single process forever without violating the discipline (11). An action cannot enable or disable an invisible action of another process (12),(13), and in the absence of a discipline violation, it commutes to the right of such an action (14),(15). Visible and invisible actions of a process cannot be simultaneously enabled (16). u_i is enabled whenever p_i is *false* (17). Invisible actions cannot hide violations of the discipline (18).

$$(u_i\ \overline{q})^{\omega} = 0 \tag{11}$$

$$i \neq j \implies u_j\ p_i = p_i\ u_j \tag{12}$$

$$i \neq j \implies v_j\ p_i = p_i\ v_j \tag{13}$$

$$i \neq j \implies u_j\ u_i \leq u_i\ (q\ \top + u_j + u_j\ q\ \top) \tag{14}$$

$$i \neq j \implies v_j\ u_i \leq u_i\ (q\ \top + v_j + v_j\ q\ \top) \tag{15}$$

$$\overline{p}_i\ v_i = 0 = p_i\ u_i \tag{16}$$

$$1 \leq p_i + u_i\ \top \tag{17}$$

$$q\ u_i \leq u_i\ q \tag{18}$$

Our reduction theorem can be used to check not only the synchronization discipline, but also the invariance of any other predicate I such that violations of I cannot be hidden by invisible actions. To see this, note that, except for (18), the conditions above are all monotonic in q. Thus, if all the conditions above (including (18)) are satisfied for a predicate q, and there is a predicate I such that $I\ u_i \leq u_i\ I$ for each i, then all the conditions are still satisfied if q is replaced with $q + I$.

The proof below can be viewed as formalizing the following construction, which starts from an execution that violates the discipline and produces an execution of the reduced system that also violates the discipline. First, we try to move invisible u_i actions to the left of u_j and v_j actions, where $i \neq j$, starting from the left (*i.e.*, from the leftmost u_i action that immediately follows a u_j or v_j action). The u_i action cannot make it all the way to the beginning of the execution (since $p\ u_i = 0$), so it must eventually run into either another u_i or a v_i. Repeating this produces an execution in which a sequence of M actions leads to a violation of the discipline.

Next, we try to turn all but the last of these M actions into N actions, starting from the next to last M action. In general, we will have done this for some number of M actions, so we will have an execution that ends with $N^*\ R$. Now try to convert the last M_i before the $N^*\ R$ suffix into an N action. Suppose this M_i action ends with u_i enabled. u_i must then also be enabled later when the discipline is first violated (because (12) and (13) imply N_j does not affect enabledness of u_i, and (16) implies N_i is disabled when u_i is enabled), so we add a u_i action just after the violation and try to push it backward (through the $N^*\ (1 + M)$). This may create additional violations of the discipline, but there will always be an $N^*\ R$ to the right of the new u_i. Eventually, u_i makes it back to the M_i, extending M_i with another u_i. By (11), u_i's cannot continue forever without violating the discipline, so repeating this extension process eventually either gives us a violation right after M_i (in which case we have produced a new $N^*\ R$ action, so we can discard everything after it) or lead to the u_i's being disabled, in which case we have succesfully turned the M_i action into an N action and again turned the extended execution into an execution that ends with $N^*\ R$. Repeating this for each M_i action, moving from right to left, produces the desired execution of the reduced system.

We now turn to the formal proof of the reduction theorem (19). We push u's left (lines 1-2) where they are eliminated by the initial p (line 3), push M's to the left of R's (line 4), condense the R's to a single R (lines 5-6), and finally turn the M's into N's (lines 7-8):

$$p\ (u+v)^*\ q \leq N^*\ R \tag{19}$$

$$\begin{array}{lll}
p\ (u+v)^*\ q & \leq & \{v \leq M \leq M+R \} \\
p\ (u+M+R)^*\ q & \leq & \{(M+R)\ u \leq (1+u)\ (M+R)\ (20); (2)\} \\
p\ u^*\ (M+R)^*\ q & \leq & \{p\ u = 0\ (16); p \leq 1 \} \\
(M+R)^*\ q & \leq & \{R\ M \leq R;\ (2) \} \\
M^*\ R^*\ q & \leq & \{R\ R \leq R, \ \text{so}\ \ R^* = (1+R) \} \\
M^*\ (1+R)\ q & \leq & \{(1+R)\ q = R \} \\
M^*\ R & \leq & \{1 \leq N^* \} \\
M^*\ N^*\ R & = & \{M\ N^*\ R \leq N^*\ R\ (21);\ (^*\ \text{ind}) \} \\
N^*\ R & &
\end{array}$$

(20) says that a u moves to the left of an M or R (but may disappear in the process):

$$(M+R)\ u \leq (1+u)\ (M+R) \tag{20}$$

$$\begin{array}{lll}
(M+R)\ u & \leq & \{(\text{dist}) \} \\
M\ u + R\ u & \leq & \{R = R\ \top, \ \text{so}\ R\ u = R\ \top\ u \leq R\ \top = R\} \\
M\ u + R & = & \{(7), (5), (\text{dist}) \} \\
(+i, j : M_j\ u_i) + R & \leq & \{M_j\ u_i \leq (1+u_i)\ (M_j+R))\ (25) \} \\
(+i, j : (1+u_i)\ (M_j+R)) + R & \leq & \{(7), (5), (\text{dist}) \} \\
(1+u)\ (M+R) & &
\end{array}$$

(21) shows that $N^*\ R$ actions act as a factory for u_i actions until they either produce a discipline violation (q) or until they produce enough u_i's to turn the M_i to their left into an N.

$$M_i\ N^*\ R \leq N^*\ R \tag{21}$$

$$\begin{array}{lll}
M_i\ N^*\ R & \leq & \{N^*\ R \leq (u_i\ \overline{q})N^*\ R + (p_i + u_i\ q)N^*\ R \ \} \\
 & & \{(22); (\star\ \text{ind}) \} \\
M_i\ (u_i\ \overline{q}) \star (p_i + u_i\ q)\ N^*\ R & \leq & \{(u_i\ \overline{q})^\omega = 0\ (11) \} \\
M_i\ (u_i\ \overline{q})^*\ (p_i + u_i\ q)\ N^*\ R & \leq & \{\overline{q} \leq 1;\ M_i\ u_i^* = M_i\ (3) \} \\
M_i\ (p_i + u_i\ q)\ N^*\ R & = & \{(\text{dist}) \} \\
(M_i\ p_i + M_i\ u_i\ q)\ N^*\ R & \leq & \{M_i\ u_i \leq M_i\ (3);\ M_i\ p_i \leq M_i\ p_i\ \overline{q} + M_i\ q\} \\
(M_i\ p_i\ \overline{q} + M_i\ q)\ N^*\ R & \leq & \{M_i\ p_i\ \overline{q} = N_i\ (4);\ N_i \leq N(8) \} \\
(N + M_i\ q)\ N^*\ R & \leq & \{(\text{dist}) \} \\
N\ N^*\ R + M_i\ q\ N^*\ R & \leq & \{M_i\ q\ N^*\ R \leq M_i\ q\ \top \leq R\ (9) \} \\
N\ N^*\ R + R & \leq & \{N\ N^* \leq N^*,\ 1 \leq N^* \} \\
N^*\ R & &
\end{array}$$

(22) and (23) show that $N^*\ R$ generates a u_i (unless p_i already holds, or the discipline has already been violated).

$$N^*\ R \leq (u_i\ \overline{q})\ N^*\ R + (p_i + u_i\ q)\ N^*\ R \tag{22}$$

$$\begin{array}{lll}
N^*\ R & \leq & \{N^*\ R \leq (p_i + u_i)\ N^*\ R (23)\} \\
(p_i + u_i)\ N^*\ R & \leq & \{u_i = u_i\ \overline{q} + u_i\ q \} \\
(p_i + u_i\ \overline{q} + u_i\ q)\ N^*\ R & \leq & \{(\text{dist}) \} \\
(u_i\ \overline{q})\ N^*\ R + (p_i + u_i\ q)\ N^*\ R & &
\end{array}$$

$$N^*\ R \leq (p_i + u_i)\ N^*\ R \tag{23}$$

$$\begin{array}{lll}
N^*\ R & = & \{(9) \} \\
N^*\ (1 + M)\ q\ \top & \leq & \{1 \leq p_i + u_i\ \top\ (17) \} \\
N^*\ (1 + M)\ q\ (p_i + u_i)\ \top & \leq & \{q\ p_i = p_i\ q;\ q\ u_i \leq u_i\ q\ (18) \} \\
N^*\ (1 + M)\ (p_i + u_i)\ q\ \top & \leq & \{M\ (p_i + u_i) \leq (p_i + u_i)\ (M + R),\ (25)\} \\
N^*\ (p_i + u_i)\ (1 + M + R)\ q\ \top & \leq & \{(1 + M + R)\ q\ \top \leq R\ (9) \} \\
N^*\ (p_i + u_i)\ R & \leq & \{N\ (p_i + u_i) \leq (p_i + u_i)\ (N + R)\ (24); \} \\
 & & \{(1) \} \\
(p_i + u_i)\ (N + R)^*\ R & \leq & \{R\ N \leq R;\ (2) \} \\
(p_i + u_i)\ N^*\ R^*\ R & = & \{R\ R \leq R;\ (^*\ \text{ind}) \} \\
(p_i + u_i)\ N^*\ R & &
\end{array}$$

Finally, (24) and (25) show that $(p_i + u_i)$ commutes left past an N or M (possibly changing them into R's).

$$N_j\ (p_i + u_i) \leq (p_i + u_i)\ (N + R) \tag{24}$$

$$\begin{array}{lll}
N_j\ (p_i + u_i) & \leq & \{N_j \leq M_j\ p_j\ (4) \} \\
M_j\ p_j (p_i + u_i) & \leq & \{p_j\ p_i = p_i\ p_j;\ p_j\ u_i \leq u_i\ p_j\ (12)(16) \} \\
M_j\ (p_i + u_i)\ p_j & \leq & \{M_j\ (p_i + u_i) \leq (p_i + u_i)\ (M_j + R),\ (25)\} \\
(p_i + u_i)\ (M_j + R)\ p_j & \leq & \{1 = q + \overline{q} \} \\
(p_i + u_i)\ (M_j + R)\ p_j\ (\overline{q} + q) & \leq & \{M_j\ p_j\ \overline{q} \leq N\ (4)(8);\ M_j\ q \leq R\ (9) \} \\
(p_i + u_i)\ (N + R) & &
\end{array}$$

$$M_j\ (p_i + u_i) \leq (p_i + u_i)\ (M_j + R) \tag{25}$$

$i = j$:

$$\begin{array}{lll}
M_i\ (p_i + u_i) & \leq & \{p_i \leq 1;\ M_i\ u_i \leq M_i\ (3) \} \\
M_i & \leq & \{v_i = p_i\ v_i\ (16),\ \text{ so }\ M_i = p_i\ M_i\ (3)\} \\
(p_i + u_i)\ (M_i + R) & &
\end{array}$$

$i \neq j$:

Let $[x] = x + x\ q\ \top + q\ \top$; then

$$\begin{array}{lll}
M_j\ (p_i + u_i) & = & \{(3) \} \\
v_j\ u_j^*\ (p_i + u_i) & \leq & \{u_j\ (p_i + u_i) \leq (p_i + u_i)\ [u_j]\ (12)(14);\ (1)\} \\
v_j\ (p_i + u_i)\ [u_j]^* & = & \{[u_j]^* = [u_j^*]\ (2) \} \\
v_j\ (p_i + u_i)\ [u_j^*] & \leq & \{v_j\ (p_i + u_i) \leq (p_i + u_i)\ [v_j]\ (13)(15) \} \\
(p_i + u_i)\ [v_j]\ [u_j^*] & \leq & \{[v_j]\ [u_j]^* \leq M_j + R \} \\
(p_i + u_i)\ (M_j + R) & &
\end{array}$$

4 System Model and Synchronization Discipline

We define a simple model of concurrent systems that use mutual exclusion for access to selected variables, and we prove that our reduction theorem applies to these systems. This model is intended to be the simplest one that retains all relevant aspects of concurrent programming languages, such as Java. It can be modified and generalized in various ways with little effect on our results.

Each shared variable is classified as *protected* or *unprotected*. There are no constraints on how unprotected variables are accessed. The synchronization discipline requires that mutual exclusion be used for access to protected variables. Any combination of synchronization mechanisms (locks, condition variables, semaphores, barriers, *etc.*) can be used to provide the mutual exclusion, provided the scheme can be captured by *exclusive access predicates*. For each protected variable x and each thread i, there is an exclusive access predicate e_i^x. The synchronization discipline requires that e_i^x hold in states from which thread i can execute a transition that accesses x. Mutual exclusion is expressed by the requirement that, for every variable x and every two distinct threads i and j, e_i^x and e_j^x are mutually exclusive (*i.e.*, cannot hold simultaneously).

Formally, a system is a tuple $\langle \Theta, V_{unsh}, V_{prot}, V_{unprot}, T, I, e \rangle$ where

Θ is a set of threads (thread identifiers). i and j range over Θ.

V_{unsh} is a set of unshared variables, *i.e.*, variables that appear in transitions of at most one thread.

V_{prot} is a set of variables declared (possibly incorrectly) to be "protected", *i.e.*, there are synchronization mechanisms that ensure mutual exclusion for accesses to these variables. For each variable $x \in V_{prot}$ and each thread i, there is an exclusive access predicate e_i^x.

V_{unprot} is a set of (possibly shared) variables, called "unprotected variables". No assumptions are made regarding synchronization for accesses to them.

$T = \bigcup_i T_i$ is a set of transitions, where T_i is the set of transitions of thread i. Let $V = V_{unsh} \cup V_{prot} \cup V_{unprot}$ and $V_{guard} = V_{unsh} \cup V_{unprot}$. A transition t is a guarded command $g \to c$, where the guard g is a predicate over V_{guard}, and c is built from assignments over V, sequential composition, and conditionals (if-then and if-then-else).

I is a predicate over V. I characterizes the initial states.

e is a family of (possibly incorrect) exclusive access predicates e_i^x over V.

Guards are used for synchronization (blocking). Conditionals in commands are used for sequential control flow. For convenience of analysis, protected variables cannot appear in guards. This is reasonable because the synchronization mechanisms that protect the variables, not the protected variables themselves, should be used to achieve the necessary synchronization. The value of a protected variable v can be copied into an unshared or unprotected variable, and the latter variable can be used in a guard, or v can be moved from V_{prot} to V_{unprot} and then used in a guard directly.

Fix a system. A *state* is a mapping from variables to values. Let Σ be the set of states. We also use states as maps from expressions to values, with the usual meaning (homomorphic extension).

A transition t is *enabled* in state s if its guard is true in s. An *execution* is a finite or infinite sequence σ of states such that $\sigma(0)$ satisfies I and every pair of consecutive states in σ is in $[\![t]\!]$ for some transition t.

A transition is *visible* if it (*i*) contains an occurrence of a variable in V_{unprot} or (*ii*) might change the value of an exclusive access predicate. Other transitions are *invisible*. This classification of transitions determines the transition relations u_i and v_i and the predicates p_i.

A system is well-formed if the following conditions hold.

WF-initVis. The initial transitions of each thread are visible, *i.e.*, $I \Rightarrow p$. (This ensures that the conclusion of the reduction theorem applies to all reachable states of the original system.)

WF-sep. Visible and invisible transitions of each thread are separate, *i.e.*, cannot be executed from the same state. Formally, $(\forall i : \text{domain}(u_i) \cap \text{domain}(v_i) = \emptyset)$.

WF-acc. Internal non-determinism in a transition (*i.e.*, non-deterministic choices that do not affect the ending state) does not affect the set of variables accessed by the transition or the order in which those variables are first accessed. (This ensures well-definedness of *acc* in Section 4.1 and of x in case 2 of the proof of (15) in Section 5.)

WF-finiteInvis. No thread has an infinite execution sequence containing only invisible transitions. Formally, $(\forall i : u_i^\omega = 0)$.

WF-initExcl. For each protected variable x, the exclusive access predicates for x are initially disjoint, *i.e.*, $I \Rightarrow \text{disjoint}(e^x)$, where $\text{disjoint}(e^x) = \neg(\exists i, j : i \neq j \wedge e_i^x \wedge e_j^x)$.

WF-endExcl. A thread cannot take away another thread's exclusive access to a variable. Formally, for an exclusive access predicate e_i^x and $j \neq i$, transitions of thread j cannot falsify e_i^x.

4.1 Mutual-Exclusion Synchronization Discipline

The synchronization discipline requires that, for every variable $x \in V_{prot}$, (*i*) a transition of thread i executed from a state s may access x only if $s \models e_i^x$, and (*ii*) $\text{disjoint}(e^x)$ holds in every reachable state.

Let $acc(s_1, t, s_2)$ denote the set of variables accessed by execution of transition t from state s_1 to s_2. The set of accessed variables may depend on which branches of conditionals are taken. The ending state s_2 is included as an argument to *acc* because t may be non-deterministic. WF-acc ensures that *acc* is well-defined. Since guards do not contain protected variables, $acc(s_1, t, s_2) = \emptyset$ if t is disabled in s_1 (otherwise, $acc(s_1, t, s_2)$ would be the set of protected variables in t's guard).

We augment the system with a predicate q that holds iff the synchronization discipline has been violated. Formally, q is the least predicate that satisfies

$$\begin{aligned}&\forall i : \forall x \in V_{prot} : \forall t \in T_i : \forall \langle s_1, s_2 \rangle \in [\![t_i]\!] : s_2 \models q \iff \\ &\quad ((x \in acc(s_1, t, s_2) \wedge s_1 \not\models e_i^x) \vee s_2 \not\models \text{disjoint}(e^x) \vee s_1 \models q).\end{aligned} \tag{26}$$

The third disjunct in (26) implies that q is monotonic, *i.e.*, it can be truthified but not falsified.

Maintaining q involves accesses to q and accesses to variables that occur in exclusive access predicates. These accesses are ignored when determining $acc(s_1, t, s_2)$.

5 Proof That the Reduction Theorem Applies to the Mutual-Exclusion Synchronization Discipline

We prove in [SC02] that well-formed systems satisfy the hypotheses (11)–(18) of the reduction theorem. Most of the proofs are straightforward. Here we consider only the most interesting one.

Proof of (15). Let t_i be an invisible transition of thread i, and let t_j be a visible transition t_j of thread j, and let s_1, s_2, and s_3 be states such that $\langle s_1, s_2\rangle \in t_j$ and $\langle s_2, s_3\rangle \in t_i$. Let $t_i = g_i \to c_i$ and $t_j = g_j \to c_j$. t_j does not enable t_i, because c_j and g_i access disjoint sets of variables (because t_i is invisible and hence does not access unprotected variables, and protected variables do not appear in guards). t_i does not disable t_j, for analogous reasons. Thus, there exist states s_2' and s_3' such that $\langle s_1, s_2'\rangle \in t_i$ and $\langle s_2', s_3'\rangle \in t_j$. Transitions may be non-deterministic, so s_2' and s_3' are not uniquely determined by these conditions. It suffices to show that s_2' and s_3' can be chosen so that one of the following conditions (which correspond to the summands in (15)) holds: (*i*) $s_2' \models q$, (*ii*) $s_3' = s_3$ (*i.e.*, c_i left-commutes with c_j), or (*iii*) $s_3' \models q$. Let $A = acc(s_1, t_j, s_2) \cap acc(s_1, t_i, s_2')$.

case 1: $A = \emptyset$. This implies that

$$acc(s_1, t_j, s_2) = acc(s_2', t_j, s_3') \ \wedge \ acc(s_2, t_i, s_3) = acc(s_1, t_i, s_2'), \tag{27}$$

because the same branches of conditionals will be executed from either source state. This and $A = \emptyset$ imply that $(\forall x \in acc(s_2, t_i, s_3) : s_1(x) = s_2(x))$ and $(\forall x \in acc(s_1, t_j, s_2) : s_1(x) = s_2'(x))$. Thus, by resolving non-determinism (if any) in the transitions in the same way when executing t_i followed by t_j as when executing t_j followed by t_i to reach s_3, we obtain $s_3'(v) = s_3(v)$ for all variables $v \in V \setminus \{q\}$. We must exclude q here because acc does not reflect accesses used to update q, as stated in Section 4.1.

case 1.1: $s_3 \models \bar{q}$. If $s_3' \models \bar{q}$, then $s_3' = s_3$, *i.e.*, condition (*ii*) holds. If $s_3' \models q$, then condition (*iii*) holds.

case 1.2: $s_3 \models q$. We show that $s_2' \models q$ or $s_3' \models q$.

case 1.2.1: $s_1 \models q$. This and monotonicity of q imply $s_3' \models q$.

case 1.2.2: $s_1 \models \bar{q}$. This and $s_3 \models q$ imply that the synchronization discipline is violated either by execution of t_j from s_1 or by execution of t_i from s_2. The violation corresponds to the first or second disjunct in (26) being true (the third disjunct just makes q monotonic). Thus, there are 2×2 cases to consider.

case 1.2.2.1: $(\exists x \in V_{prot} : x \in acc(s_1, t_j, s_2) \wedge s_1 \not\models e_j^x)$. (27) implies $x \in acc(s_2', t_j, s_3')$. t_i is invisible, so it cannot truthify e_j^x, so $s_2' \not\models e_j^x$. Thus, the definition of q implies $s_3' \models q$.

case 1.2.2.2: $(\exists x \in V_{prot} : x \in acc(s_2, t_i, s_3) \wedge s_2 \not\models e_i^x)$. (27) implies $x \in acc(s_1, t_i, s_2')$. WF-endExcl implies t_j did not falsify e_i^x, so $s_1 \not\models e_i^x$. Thus, the definition of q implies $s_2' \models q$.

case 1.2.2.3: $(\exists x \in V_{prot} : s_2 \not\models \text{disjoint}(e^x))$. t_i is invisible, so it cannot falsify any exclusive access predicate, so $s_3 \not\models \text{disjoint}(e^x)$. s_3 and s_3' have the same values for all variables except q, so $s_3' \not\models \text{disjoint}(e^x)$. Thus, the definition of q implies $s_3' \models q$.

case 1.2.2.4: $(\exists x \in V_{prot} : s_3 \not\models \text{disjoint}(e^x))$. s_3 and s_3' have the same values for all variables except q, so $s_3' \not\models \text{disjoint}(e^x)$. Thus, the definition of q implies $s_3' \models q$.

case 2: $A \neq \emptyset$. Let x be the variable in A first accessed by execution of t_j from s_1 to s_2.

case 2.1: $s_1 \models e_j^x$. By definition of A, $x \in acc(s_1, t_i, s_2')$.

case 2.1.1: $s_1 \models \text{disjoint}(e^x)$. The hypotheses of cases 2.1 and 2.1.1, together with $i \neq j$, imply $s_1 \not\models e_i^x$. This and $x \in acc(s_1, t_i, s_2')$ imply $s_2' \models q$.

case 2.1.2: $s_1 \not\models \text{disjoint}(e^x)$. This and the definition of q imply $s_1 \models q$. This and monotonicity of q imply $s_2' \models q$.

case 2.2: $s_1 \not\models e_j^x$. The definitions of A and x imply that $x \in acc(s_2', t_j, s_3')$, because the first access to x by t_j precedes execution of conditionals in t_j whose conditions could be affected by execution of t_i from s_1. t_i is invisible, so it cannot truthify e_j^x, so $s_2' \not\models e_j^x$. Thus, the definition of q implies $s_3' \models q$.

6 Examples

This section contains examples of systems for which the current reduction is effective (*i.e.*, it reduces the number of reachable states) and the reduction in [Sto02] is not effective. In general, our method is effective whenever some variables can be classified as protected. These examples are based mainly on descriptions in [SBN$^+$97] of code in real systems.

Semaphores. A user thread sends a request to a device driver thread, asking the device driver to store data in a buffer b, and then waits for the result by invoking *sem*.down(), where *sem* is a semaphore, initialized to zero. The device driver thread receives the request, waits for the device to supply the data, stores the data in b, and then calls *sem*.up(). The buffer b can be classified as protected. For example, e^b_{user} holds when the program counter of the user thread points to a statement after the call to *sem*.down(), and e^b_{driver} holds when the program counter of the device driver thread points to a statement before the call to *sem*.up(). The semaphore ensures disjointness of e^b_{user} and e^b_{driver}.

Memory Re-use. Some systems re-use objects (or structures) by placing them on a free list when they are not in use. These objects may be protected by different locks each time they are re-used, violating the locking discipline of [Sto02]. For example, consider a file system in which blocks in a file are protected by the lock associated with (the i-node of) that file, and blocks on the free list are protected by the lock associated with the free list. A block may be in a different file, and hence protected by a different lock, each time it is re-used. Let m_F denote the lock associated with the free list. Let m_f denote the lock associated with file f. The exclusive access predicate e_i^b for a block b might be

$$(\text{onFreeList}(b) \wedge m_F.owner = i) \vee (\exists \text{ file } f : \text{allocatedTo}(b, f) \wedge m_f.owner = i)$$

Master-Worker Paradigm. In the master-worker paradigm, a master thread assigns tasks to worker threads. Typically, each task is represented by an object created by the master thread and passed to a worker thread. The master thread does not access a task object after passing it to a worker. Task objects can be classified as protected. Suppose each worker thread w has a field w.task that refers to the worker's task. For a task object x, the exclusive access predicate e^x_{master} holds before x has been passed to a worker thread, and e^x_w holds when $w.\text{task} = x$.

7 Comparison to Traditional Partial-Order Methods

This section demonstrates that our method has advantages over traditional partial-order methods even for some simple systems for which precise static analysis of transition dependencies is feasible. Consider a system with two threads that use monitors m_0 and m_1 as locks and use an integer variable y to implement a barrier. Let uppercase letters denote control points. Let *guard* $\rightarrow$ *stmt* denote a transition that blocks when *guard* is false and can execute *stmt* when *guard* is true. For $i \in \{0, 1\}$, the code for thread i is

$$\begin{array}{l} {}^{A}m_0.\text{acquire}();\ {}^{B}x_0 := i;\ {}^{C}m_0.\text{release}();\ {}^{D}m_1.\text{acquire}();\ {}^{E}x_1 := i; \\ {}^{F}m_1.\text{release}();\ {}^{G}y++;\ {}^{H}y = 2 \rightarrow \text{skip};\ {}^{I}x_i = i\ {}^{J} \end{array} \tag{28}$$

In the initial state, $x_j = j$ and $y = 0$, and both threads are at control point A. x_j is a protected variable, with exclusive access predicate $e_i^{x_j} = (m_j.owner = i) \vee (y = 2 \wedge i = j)$. y is not protected.

This system has 106 reachable states. With the reduction in this paper, transitions that update x_0 or x_1 are invisible; other transitions are visible. The reachable states of the reduced system are the reachable states of the original system in which every thread is ready to perform a visible transition or is at its final control point. There are 62 such states.

Traditional partial-order methods based on persistent sets [God96] (or ample sets [CGP99]) can also significantly reduce the number of explored states but do not achieve the same benefits as our reduction. For concreteness, we compare our method to selective search using the conditional stubborn set algorithm (CSSA) [God96]. We always resolve non-determinism in CSSA in a way that yields a minimum-size persistent set. CSSA is parameterized by dependency relations on operations. For acquire and release, we use the might-be-the-first-to-interfere-with relation in [Sto02, Fig. 3]. For accesses to y, we use the minimal might-be-the-first-to-interfere-with relation, based on the dependency relation on operations in which an increment to y is dependent with the condition $y = 2$ only in states in which the increment changes the truth value of the condition.

The selective search (using CSSA) explores 77 states. To illustrate why it explores more than the 62 states explored by our method, consider the reachable state s in which thread 0 is at control point D and thread 1 is at control point B. With the reduction in this paper, the transitions that update x_0 or x_1 are invisible, so the system passes through this invisible state by executing the enabled transition of thread 1; the enabled transition of thread 0 is not executed in s. In contrast, the selective search explores both enabled transitions in s, as explained in detail in [SC02].

This example can be generalized to show our method outperforming the selective search by an arbitrary amount: simply insert additional transitions that access x_0 before the transition m_0.release() in thread 0.

The selective search exploits some independence that our method does not, in particular, independence of release with acquire and release, and independence of acquire with acquire in some states. One way to obtain the benefits of both methods is to apply selective search to the reduced system. This works for systems for which sufficiently precise static analysis of dependencies between transitions is feasible (*cf.* Section 1). Another approach is to extend our method, *e.g.*, to incorporate the specialized treatment of monitor operations in [Sto02] that allows release to be classified as invisible.

8 How to Use the Reduction

The intended methodology for using the reduction is as follows.

1. Guess the set V_{prot} of protected variables and the exclusive access predicates e_i^x. These guesses determine visibility of transitions and hence define a reduced system, in which the transition relation of thread i is N_i, defined in (4).

2. Augment the reduced system with a predicate q, as described in Section 4.1.

3. Check whether $\bar{q}$ holds in all reachable states of the reduced system. Check this using your favorite technique: model checking, theorem proving, hand waving, *etc.*

4. If so, then the reduction theorem implies that $\bar{q}$ holds in all reachable states of the original system, *i.e.*, the guesses in Step 1 are correct. Traditional reduction theorems can now be used to infer other properties of the original system from properties of the reduced system.

5. If not, then for some variable x in V_{prot}, the reduced system has a reachable state in which the mutual-exclusion synchronization discipline for x is violated. Revise the guess for e^x (using the path to the violation as a guide) or re-classify x as unprotected, and then return to Step 1.

9 How to Use the Reduction Automatically for Systems with Monitors

The methodology in Section 8 is automatic except that the user must guess V_{prot} and the exclusive access predicates. For systems that use monitors for synchronization, this step, too, can be automated, based on the observation that the exclusive access predicates typically have the form $e_i^x = eap_i^{x,m}$, where

$$eap_i^{x,m} = init_i^x \vee (i = m.owner \ \wedge \ \neg init^x) \quad (29)$$
$$init^x = (\exists i \in \Theta : init_i^x). \quad (30)$$

and where the *initialization predicate* $init_i^x$ holds while thread i is executing code that initializes x. Note that the lock protecting a variable does not need to be held while the variable is being initialized.

Initialization predicates for variables in systems that correspond to Java programs can be guessed automatically: the initialization predicate holds when the thread's program counter is in the appropriate class initializer (for static fields) or the appropriate constructor invocation (for instance fields).

To use (29), we need to identify, for each variable x in V_{prot}, a monitor m that protects x. This can be done automatically by running a variant of the lockset algorithm [SBN+97] during state-space exploration of the reduced system.

10 Experimental Results

We implemented the similar reduction of [Sto02] in Java PathFinder (JPF) [BHPV00] and measured the benefit of the reduction for several programs with monitor-based synchronization. HaltException and Clean [BHPV00, Figure 1] are small "synchronization skeletons" supplied by the developers of JPF. Xtango-DP and Xtango-QS are animations of a dining philosophers algorithm and quicksort, respectively, from http://www.mcs.drexel.edu/˜shartley/; we replaced java.awt methods with methods having empty bodies, due to limitations of JPF. The lockset algorithm was used in all experiments. With negligible manual effort (to write a few lines of config files), the reduction decreases memory usage by a factor of 1.4MB/0.77MB $\approx$ 1.8 for HaltException, 4.3MB/2.2MB $\approx$ 2.0 for Clean, 609MB/236MB $\approx$ 2.6 for Xtango-DP, and 344MB/101MB $\approx$ 3.4 for Xtango-QS, compared to model checking with JPF'S default granularity, which executes each line of source code atomically. In a real JVM, bytecode instructions execute atomically. Our reduction preserves that semantics. JPF's source-line granularity does not: it can miss errors. Compared to bytecode granularity, our reduction decreases memory usage by a factor of 13.9MB/0.77MB $\approx$ 18 for HaltException and at least 1800MB/101MB $\approx$ 18 for Xtango-QS ("at least" reflects an out-of-memory exception).

Acknowledgements. We thank Shaz Qadeer for telling us about exclusive access predicates, Liqiang Wang for doing the experiments with JPF, and Patrice Godefroid for comments about partial-order methods.

References

[BR01] C. Boyapati and M. C. Rinard. A parameterized type system for race-free Java programs. In *Proc. 16th ACM Conference on Object-Oriented Programming, Systems, Languages and Applications (OOPSLA)*, volume 36(11) of *SIGPLAN Notices*, pages 56–69. ACM Press, November 2001.

[BHPV00] G. Brat, K. Havelund, S. Park, and W. Visser. Model checking programs. In *IEEE Int'l. Conference on Automated Software Engineering (ASE)*, pages 3–12, September 2000.

[CGP99] Edmund M. Clarke, Jr., Orna Grumberg, and Doron A. Peled. *Model Checking.* MIT Press, 1999.

[CL98] E. Cohen and L. Lamport. Reduction in TLA. In *Proc. 9th Int'l. Conference on Concurrency Theory (CONCUR)*, volume 1466 of *Lecture Notes in Computer Science*, pages 317–331. Springer-Verlag, 1998.

[Coh00] E. Cohen. Separation and reduction. In *Proc. 5th Int'l. Conference on Mathematics of Program Construction*, volume 1837 of *Lecture Notes in Computer Science*. Springer-Verlag, 2000.

[FF01] Cormac Flanagan and Stephen Freund. Detecting race conditions in large programs. In *Workshop on Program Analysis for Software Tools and Engineering (PASTE)*, pages 90–96. ACM Press, June 2001.

[FQS02] Cormac Flanagan, Shaz Qadeer, and Sanjit Seshia. A modular checker for multithreaded programs. In *Proc. 14th Int'l. Conference on Computer-Aided Verification (CAV)*, volume 2404 of *Lecture Notes in Computer Science*, pages 180–194. Springer-Verlag, 2002.

[God96] Patrice Godefroid. *Partial-Order Methods for the Verification of Concurrent Systems*, volume 1032 of *Lecture Notes in Computer Science*. Springer-Verlag, 1996.

[God97] Patrice Godefroid. Model checking for programming languages using VeriSoft. In *Proc. 24th ACM Symposium on Principles of Programming Languages (POPL)*, pages 174–186. ACM Press, 1997.

[Hol97] Gerard J. Holzmann. The Spin model checker. *IEEE Transactions on Software Engineering*, 23(5):279–295, May 1997.

[Koz94] D. Kozen. A completeness theorem for Kleene algebras and the algebra of regular events. *Information and Computation*, 110(2):366–390, 1994.

[Lip75] R. J. Lipton. Reduction: A method of proving properties of parallel programs. *Communications of the ACM*, 18(12):717–721, 1975.

[SBN+97] S. Savage, M. Burrows, G. Nelson, P. Sobalvarro, and T. E. Anderson. Eraser: A dynamic data race detector for multi-threaded programs. *ACM Transactions on Computer Systems*, 15(4):391–411, November 1997.

[SC02] S. D. Stoller and E. Cohen. Optimistic synchronization-based state-space reduction. Technical Report DAR-02-8, SUNY at Stony Brook, Computer Science Dept., August 2002. Available at www.cs.sunysb.edu/~stoller/optimistic.html.

[Sto02] S. D. Stoller. Model-checking multi-threaded distributed Java programs. *International Journal on Software Tools for Technology Transfer*, to appear.

[Val97] Antti Valmari. Stubborn set methods for process algebras. In D. Peled, V. R. Pratt, and G. J. Holzmann, editors, *Proc. Workshop on Partial Order Methods in Verification*, volume 29 of *DIMACS Series*, pages 213–231. American Mathematical Society, 1997.

[WR99] J. Whaley and M. C. Rinard. Compositional pointer and escape analysis for Java programs. In *Proc. ACM Conf. on Object-Oriented Systems, Languages and Applications (OOPSLA)*, pages 187–206. ACM Press, October 1999.

Checking Properties of Heap-Manipulating Procedures with a Constraint Solver

Mandana Vaziri and Daniel Jackson

Laboratory for Computer Science
Massachusetts Institute of Technology
Cambridge, Massachusetts, USA
{vaziri,dnj}@lcs.mit.edu

Abstract. A method for finding bugs in object-oriented code is presented. It is capable of checking complex user-defined structural properties – that is, of the configuration of objects on the heap – and generates counterexample traces with no false alarms. It requires no annotation beyond the specification to be checked, and is fully automatic.
The method relies on a three-step translation: from code to a formula in a first-order relational logic, then to a propositional formula, and finally to conjunctive normal form. An off-the-shelf SAT solver is then used to find a solution that constitutes a counterexample.
This underlying scheme, presented previously, does not scale readily. In this paper, we show how a suite of optimizations results in much improved scalability. The optimizations are based on a special treatment of relations that are known to be functional, and target all steps. The effect of the optimizations is demonstrated by application to the analysis of a red-black tree implementation.

1 Introduction

In previous work [13], we developed a scheme for finding bugs in Java code using a SAT solver. The code, along with a declarative specification, is translated first into a first-order relational formula, and from there into a propositional formula whose satisfying assignments correspond to counterexamples – traces that violate the specification.

This approach is inherently intractable, so it is essential to eliminate any unnecessary causes of complexity. One such cause that we have been aware of since the start is an uneconomical representation of fields. A field of a class is mathematically a function, since it maps an object to at most one other object, and its possible values can be encoded with a bit string of length $log(n)$ for each domain value, corresponding to the integer index of the field's value, drawn from n possible values. But our translation scheme, which was designed for a more general modelling language [11], encodes a function as a relation, with n^2 bits, one for each combination of domain and range values.

Unfortunately, it is not obvious how to exploit the tighter encoding of functions, since it is not well suited to applying the relational operators, especially

H. Garavel and J. Hatcliff (Eds.): TACAS 2003, LNCS 2619, pp. 505–520, 2003.

the image operator, which appears frequently, due to the translation of set and get operations on fields. Introducing an additional representation of each function in the standard form worsens performance, since the tighter encoding is now an addition, rather than a replacement.

This paper shows how to make effective use of the tighter encoding of functions. It exploits the fact that most of the relational formulas arising from an object-oriented program take a stylized form. A transformation of this form into another relational formula with additional relational variables is given, which can be translated into CNF, using some specialized logical simplifications, without any additional boolean variables.

Section 2 gives an overview of the basic approach, which we have described previously [13]. Section 3 explains the generic scheme for translating relational formulas into propositional formulas on which our previous work relied [11]. The new content of the paper is presented in Section 4, and evaluated experimentally in Section 5. The paper closes with related work (Section 6) and conclusions (Section 7).

2 Encoding Object-Oriented Code in Alloy

2.1 Overview and Illustration

Our analysis [13] gives a bounded interpretation to a fragment of Java code, by unwinding loops some number of times and by limiting the number of heap cells of each type. Procedure calls are handled by inlining; there is currently no treatment of recursion. The Java code is translated into Alloy [12], a modelling language based on first-order logic. User-defined properties are also expressed in Alloy, which allows succinct declarative expressions of complex structural properties. For example, the fact that a list is acyclic can be expressed using the transitive closure operator, and that red-black trees have the same number of black nodes on each path is expressible with set cardinalities. Given an Alloy model for the program, the Alloy Analyzer [11] is then used, together with a user-provided bound on the number of heap cells, to check properties, and to find counterexamples when they do not hold.

Our method differs from other verification approaches in that it targets properties of the heap. It considers all the possible initial configurations within finite bounds. If there is a property violation, it will determine the initial configuration responsible for it, as part of the counterexample trace. The analysis typically accounts for billions of cases, which would not be feasible with testing alone. The SAT solver – the Alloy Analyzer's core engine – works in a goal-oriented fashion. Since it tries to satisfy a boolean formula, it does not go through all the executions in turn, and may effectively search multiple executions at once. Our approach also does not perform approximations beyond considering a finite instance of the code. This means that there are no false error reports.

Consider the `swapTail` procedure (Figure 1), which purportedly takes two linked lists and swaps their tails. We use our analysis to check whether the

Code

```
class ListElem {
 int val;
 ListElem next;
}
class List {
 ListElem first;
 static void swapTail(List l, List m){
  if (l.first != null
           && m.first != null) {
   ListElem temp = l.first.next;
   l.first.next = m.first.next;
   m.first.next = temp;
  }
 }}
```

Property

```
fun Acyclic(x: List) {
 all e: x.first.*next |
          e !in e.^next
}
assert A {
 all l, m: List |
  Acyclic(l) && Acyclic(m)
  && swapTail(l,m) => Acyclic'(m)
}
check A for 2 List, 2 ListElem, 1 iteration
```

Counterexample

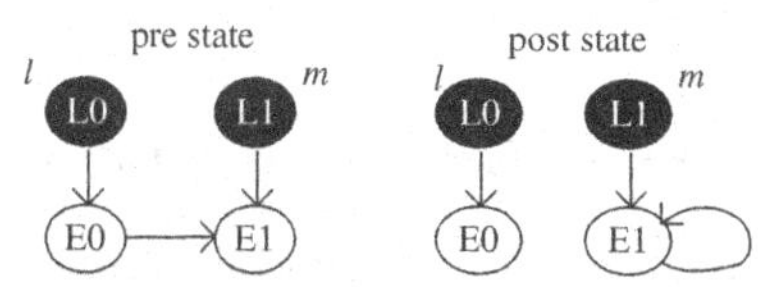

Computation Graph

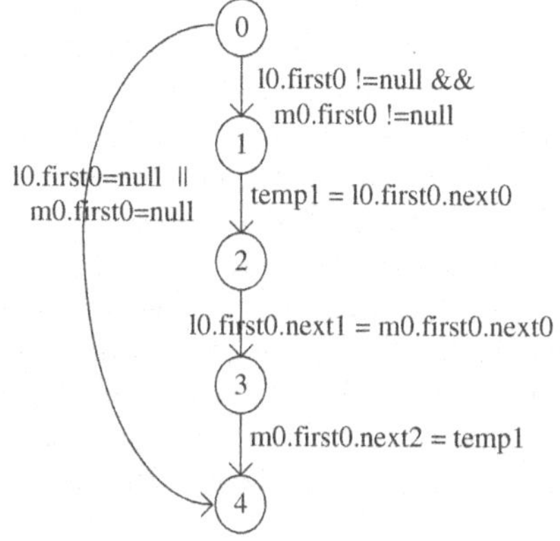

Free Variables

first_0 : List $\rightarrow!$ ListElem
$\text{next}_0, \text{next}_1, \text{next}_2$: ListElem $\rightarrow!$ ListElem
l_0, m_0 : List
temp_0, temp_1 : ListElem
E_{01}, E_{12}, E_{23}, E_{34}, E_{04}: Bool

Control Flow

$E_{01} \mid\mid E_{04}$
$E_{01} \Rightarrow E_{12}$
$E_{12} \Rightarrow E_{23}$
$E_{23} \Rightarrow E_{34}$

Data Flow

$E_{01} \Rightarrow \text{l}_0.\text{first}_0 \neq \text{null} \ \&\& \ \text{m}_0.\text{first}_0 \neq \text{null}$
$E_{04} \Rightarrow \text{l}_0.\text{first}_0 = \text{null} \mid\mid \text{m}_0.\text{first}_0 = \text{null}$
$E_{12} \Rightarrow \text{temp}_1 = \text{l}_0.\text{first}_0.\text{next}_0$
$E_{23} \Rightarrow \text{l}_0.\text{first}_0.\text{next}_1 = \text{m}_0.\text{first}_0.\text{next}_0 \ \&\&$
$\text{all o:ListElem-l}_0.\text{first}_0 \mid \text{o.next}_1 = \text{o.next}_0$
$E_{34} \Rightarrow \text{m}_0.\text{first}_0.\text{next}_2 = \text{temp}_1 \ \&\&$
$\text{all o:ListElem-m}_0.\text{first}_0 \mid \text{o.next}_2 = \text{o.next}_1$

Additional Frame Condition

$E_{04} \Rightarrow \text{next}_2 = \text{next}_0 \ \&\& \ \text{temp}_1 = \text{temp}_0$

Fig. 1. An Example of a Procedure and its Analysis

`swapTail` procedure preserves the property that its inputs are acyclic. We write the Alloy specification shown in Figure 1. The assertion `A` states that: for all `Lists` `l` and `m`, if they are both acyclic in the initial state, and `swapTail(l,m)` is called, then `m` is acyclic in the post state, which is indicated by the prime sign on the last appearance of the function `Acyclic`.

The auxiliary function `Acyclic(x: List)` defines the constraint that a list is acyclic, by stating that for all `ListElems` `e` reachable from `x.first`, where `x.first` is included, `e` is not reachable from itself.

The command that follows (`check A`) instructs the tool to use 2 heap cells per type and 1 iteration. The analysis produces a counterexample shown partially in Figure 1. Black circles represent heap cells of type `List`, and white ones are of type `ListElem`. Arrows represent fields. In the pre-state, list `m` is a list of one element, and `l` of two, and they share an element. In the post-state, `m` is a list with an element whose next field points to itself, and is therefore cyclic, violating the assertion.

2.2 Extracting a Computation Graph

We translate a Java procedure into an Alloy formula whose models correspond to executions. It is composed of two subformulas, encoding the control and data flow of the procedure.

We start with the procedure's control flow graph (CFG), with nodes representing its control points, and edges labeled with either Java statements or control predicates. We unroll the loops in the CFG up to a number of iterations (selected by the user), and inline procedure calls, to obtain a *computation graph*. For example, one unrolling of `a; while(p) s; b` gives the graph one would obtain as the standard CFG of `a; if(p) s; assert !p; b`.

We rename variable and field names, in such a way that no path has two assignments to the same variable or sets the same field name, but parallel paths may share names (just as in single static assignment [3], but without ϕ functions). Renaming is done by providing an index for each variable at each node in the computation graph. In what follows we use $name(v,i)$ to denote the name of variable v at node i.

Figure 1 shows the computation graph corresponding to the `swapTail` procedure. The edge between nodes (0) and (4) is traversed when the condition of the if statement is false.

2.3 Encoding the State, Control, and Data Flow

Variables in the Alloy formula are used to encode the state at the various control points of the procedure. We model a field of type t appearing in class c with a total function from c to t. Each type has a special atom representing null. Local variables and formal parameters are modelled as scalars, which are represented by singleton sets in Alloy.

In addition, the variables of the Alloy formula include a boolean variable[1] E_{ij} for each edge from node i to j in the computation graph. These are used to encode the control and data flow, and indicate whether an edge is traversed during an execution. The free variables for `swapTail` are shown in Figure 1, where a declaration of the form $f : A \rightarrow ! B$ says that f is a relation from A to

[1] Alloy does not have built-in booleans, but these can be easily encoded with sets.

B, restrained to be a total function from A to B, and $a : A$ declares a to be a scalar of type A.

The control flow is encoded with a formula that captures when an edge is traversed. For each node i, let $in(i)$ be the set of nodes having an outgoing edge to i, and $out(i)$ the set of nodes having an incoming edge from i. For each node i, we produce $\vee\{E_{ji} | j \in in(i)\} \Rightarrow \vee\{E_{ik} | k \in out(i)\}$, and the formula encoding the control flow is the conjunction of these formulas. These mean that if some node's incoming edge is traversed then some of its outgoing edges are also traversed. Infeasible paths are ruled out because some of the edges are labeled with control predicates, and these appear in the formula that encodes the data flow presented below. Note that if more than one outgoing edge is traversed, the constraint solver may generate an instance corresponding to more than one execution. But all these executions are feasible. It is a question of tool design which one is presented to the user. In the case of `swapTail`, the formula encoding control flow is shown in Figure 1.

We encode the data flow for each edge with a formula that indicates how variables are related before and after the execution of the statement corresponding to that edge. For each edge e from node i to j, we produce a formula: $E_{ij} \Rightarrow t$, where t is the translation of the Java statement corresponding to e into first-order logic. The formula that encodes the data flow is then the conjunction of these formulas. This means that whenever e is traversed, the effect of the Java statement encoded by t is observed. The translation rules for Java statements are given in our earlier paper [13]. In the case of `swapTail`, the formula encoding data flow is shown in Figure 1.

In Alloy, the expression $a.r$, where a is a set and r is a relation, denotes the relational image of a under r. So $\texttt{l}_0\texttt{.first}_0$ denotes the image of $\texttt{l}_0$ under function $\texttt{first}_0$. The formula

$$\texttt{all o: ListElem - l}_0\texttt{.first}_0 \mid \texttt{o.next}_1 = \texttt{o.next}_0$$

is a *frame condition*. It means that for all `ListElems` other than $\texttt{l}_0\texttt{.first}_0$, the next relation remains the same. Alloy is a declarative language in which variables that are left unconstrained can take on any value. Frame conditions are then needed to say that certain variables remain the same when an update happens.

Finally, we conjoin a set of additional frame conditions. When an edge connects nodes i and j that assign a different index to a field or variable v, but v is not modified by the statement associated with the edge, we produce the frame condition: $E_{ij} \Rightarrow name(v,j) = name(v,i)$. In the case of `swapTail`, the additional frame condition (shown in Figure 1) says that whenever E_{04} is traversed, the `next` relation and the `temp` variable remain the same.

3 Translation to Propositional Logic

In Alloy, every type consists of a set of atoms. The values of variables are relations, which are sets of tuples of atoms; and sets are treated as degenerate relations, consisting of a set of unary tuples. The user provides to our analysis a bound n on the number of heap cells for each class, and this is used to set *scopes* for the Alloy Analyzer, i.e. the number of atoms of each type. The analyzer uses the scope to translate an Alloy formula to propositional logic. It allocates a matrix of n^2 boolean variables to each binary relation r:

$$\begin{array}{c} r_{11} \cdots r_{1n} \\ \cdots\;\cdots\;\cdots \\ r_{n1} \cdots r_{nn} \end{array}$$

where r_{ij} is true if and only if r maps atom i of its domain to atom j of its range. After having allocated boolean variables to all relations in the formula, the analyzer then proceeds to combine these matrices into matrices of boolean formulas. For example, given a set a, represented as a degenerate relation, the relational image $a.f$ of a under relation f, gets the matrix:

$$\begin{array}{c} (a_1 \wedge f_{11}) \vee \cdots \vee (a_n \wedge f_{n1}) \\ \cdots \\ (a_1 \wedge f_{1n}) \vee \cdots \vee (a_n \wedge f_{nn}) \end{array}$$

which is the result of matrix multiplication, and states that atom i is an element of $a.f$ if and only if there is some atom j in a such that f maps j to i. Other Alloy expressions are translated into matrices of boolean formulas in a similar way [11].

To translate formulas, the analyzer combines these matrices into a single propositional formula. For example, the formula $f = g$, where f and g are binary relations, becomes:

$$(f_{11} \Leftrightarrow g_{11}) \wedge \cdots \wedge (f_{1n} \Leftrightarrow g_{1n}) \wedge \cdots \wedge (f_{n1} \Leftrightarrow g_{n1}) \wedge \cdots \wedge (f_{nn} \Leftrightarrow g_{nn}).$$

which states that variables f and g denote the same set of tuples: tuple (i, j) is in f if and only if it is in g.

Given a propositional formula, the analyzer then proceeds to transform it into conjunctive normal form (CNF) by renaming all subformulas with fresh propositional variables, and conjoining appropriate definitions for these variables to the whole formula [15]. This avoids the exponential blow-up in the size of the formula when it is translated into CNF using distributivity laws, but does increase the number of variables. An off-the-shelf SAT solver takes the CNF produced and attempts to find a model. In our case, a satisfying assignment corresponds to a counterexample, which is then output to the user in an appropriate fashion.

4 Exploiting Properties of Functions

A field declared in a class is modelled as a relation, but it always maps its object to exactly one other object (or to null). Mathematically, this is a function. By exploiting this fact, we can optimize different steps of the analysis presented in the previous section, with the goal of reducing the number of variables and clauses produced in the final CNF, since this will improve the SAT solver's performance.

The main optimization is a representation for functions that requires fewer boolean variables than the representation for general relations. However, this does not reduce the number of variables in the CNF, because the step that translates propositional formulas to CNF adds intermediate variables, and counteracts the benefit of the compact function representation. To obtain a real benefit we need two other kinds of optimizations: first a systematic introduction of variables in the first-order formula, and second a series of logical simplifications in the propositional formula. In the next sections, we describe how these optimizations work together to reduce the number of clauses and variables in the CNF.

4.1 Function Representation

A relation f that is a total function maps each atom in its domain to exactly one atom in its range. By representing this atom as an integer in binary form, the encoding of f requires only $\lfloor log(n) \rfloor + 1$ rather than n boolean variables in each row. From this tighter encoding:

$$\begin{array}{c} f_{11} \cdots f_{1l} \\ \cdots \cdots \cdots \\ f_{n1} \cdots f_{nl} \end{array}$$

we can extract the standard, $n \times n$ representation:

$$\begin{array}{ccc} \neg f_{11} \wedge \cdots \wedge \neg f_{1l} & \neg f_{11} \wedge \cdots \wedge \neg f_{1(l-1)} \wedge f_{1l} & \cdots \\ \cdots & \cdots & \cdots \\ \neg f_{n1} \wedge \cdots \wedge \neg f_{nl} & \neg f_{n1} \wedge \cdots \wedge \neg f_{n(l-1)} \wedge f_{nl} & \cdots \end{array}$$

where the formula at row i and column j is true if and only if row i in the compact representation of f represents integer j. Note that since $\lfloor log(n) \rfloor + 1$ bits can represent more than n values, we must add a side condition that constrains each row of the compact representation in such way that it represents an integer less than n.

If we incorporate this optimization in the Alloy Analyzer, this actually results in an *increase* in the number of variables in the final CNF. This is because the step that transforms propositional logic to CNF counteracts the gain of the compact representation, by renaming all the formulas in the converted matrix with propositional variables. So the resulting CNF has all the variables that it would have had without the compact representation, in addition to all the ones the representation introduces.

4.2 Introducing Alloy Variables

To avoid this problem, we first rename all subexpressions that are scalars, i.e. singleton sets, in the first-order formula. Most subformulas that appear in the translation of a fragment of Java code have the form:

$$v.f_1.\cdots.f_{k_1} = u.g_1.\cdots.g_{k_2},$$

where v and u are scalars, and $f_1, \cdots, f_{k_1}$, and $g_1, \cdots, g_{k_2}$ are functions, encoding fields. We rename subexpressions of the form $a.f$ by introducing an Alloy variable b, and conjoin definitions of the form $b = a.f$ with the whole formula. Variable b is a scalar since a is a scalar and f is a function. We obtain:

$$v_1 = v.f_1 \wedge \cdots \wedge v_{k_1-1} = v_{k_1-2}.f_{k_1-1} \wedge u_1 = u.g_1 \wedge \cdots \wedge u_{k_2} = u_{k_2-1}.g_{k_2} \wedge v_{k_1-1}.f_{k_1} = u_{k_2}.$$

The next section describes logical simplifications that allow a formula of the form $a.f = b$ to be translated compactly to CNF without adding any additional propositional variables. The CNF's for these formulas are then conjoined by taking the union of their clauses. Introducing an Alloy variable for the subexpression $a.f$ results in $\lfloor log(n) \rfloor + 1$ additional boolean variables. If this subexpression were translated to CNF without the introduction of Alloy variables and logical simplifications, it would result in at least n^2 additional boolean variables, since all the elements of the product (an $n \times n$ matrix) would be renamed.

4.3 Logical Simplifications

We now describe the logical simplifications that allow us to translate $a.f = b$ compactly to CNF, without introducing any additional propositional variables. They take advantage of the fact that a scalar is represented by a collection of propositional formulas having the property that exactly one of them is true. Informally, the first two simplifications help because they push disjunctions down in the formula's syntax tree. Disjunctions are a source of blow-up when transforming to CNF, and their effect is lessened if they are further away from the root.

Logical Simplification 1 Consider the formula:

$$(A_1 \wedge B_1) \vee \cdots \vee (A_n \wedge B_n) \tag{1}$$

where A_i and B_i $(1 \leq i \leq n)$ are boolean formulas. If exactly one of the A formulas is true, then it can be easily seen that (1) is logically equivalent to:

$$(\neg A_1 \vee B_1) \wedge \cdots \wedge (\neg A_n \vee B_n) \tag{2}$$

Logical Simplification 2 Consider the formula:

$$((A_1 \wedge B_1) \vee \cdots \vee (A_n \wedge B_n)) \Leftrightarrow C \tag{3}$$

where A_i and B_i $(1 \leq i \leq n)$ are boolean formulas. If exactly one of the A formulas is true, then it can be easily seen that (3) is logically equivalent to:

$$(A_1 \wedge (B_1 \Leftrightarrow C)) \vee \cdots \vee (A_n \wedge (B_n \Leftrightarrow C)) \tag{4}$$

Our final simplification is specific to the representation of integers, and relies on the fact that integers can be compared bit by bit.

Definitions. A *literal* is either a propositional variable, or the negation of one. Given a literal a, let $var(a)$ denote the propositional variable corresponding to a, and $phase(a)$ be $+$ $(-)$ if a is $var(a)$ $(\neg var(a))$.

Logical Simplification 3. Let A_i $(1 \leq i \leq n)$ be a collection of formulas of the form $a_1^i \wedge \cdots \wedge a_l^i$, such that for all i, j, and for all k $(1 \leq k \leq l)$, $var(a_k^i) = var(a_k^j)$, and let B_i be a similar collection. Consider the formula:

$$A_1 \Leftrightarrow B_1 \wedge \cdots \wedge A_n \Leftrightarrow B_n \tag{5}$$

If exactly one of the A_i is true, and similarly for the B_i, and for all i and k, $phase(a_k^i) = phase(b_k^i)$, then it can be seen that (5) is logically equivalent to:

$$var(a_1^1) \Leftrightarrow var(b_1^1) \wedge \cdots \wedge var(a_l^1) \Leftrightarrow var(b_l^1) \tag{6}$$

4.4 Using the Optimizations

Let us now compute the number of clauses and variables obtained in the CNF for $v.f_1.\cdots.f_{k_1} = u.g_1.\cdots.g_{k_2}$ using our optimizations, to compare them to the case with no optimizations.

We have seen that $v.f_1.\cdots.f_{k_1} = u.g_1.\cdots.g_{k_2}$ can be transformed into a conjunction of $k_1 + k_2$ formulas of the form $a.f = b$. Let k denote $k_1 + k_2$. Since conjunction of CNF can be obtained simply by taking union of clause sets, we can avoid variable introduction and obtain a formula of size $k\alpha$, if $a.f = b$ can be represented with α clauses.

In what follows, we compute α, but first we introduce some notation. Consider translating the formula $a.f = b$ to CNF. The variable a is a scalar and its compact representation requires l boolean variables: $a_1 \cdots a_l$, where l denotes $\lfloor log(n) \rfloor + 1$, and n is the scope. Function f has a compact representation having nl boolean variables: $f_{11} \cdots f_{1l} \cdots f_{n1} \cdots f_{nl}$.

Converting the compact representation of a to the standard one results in a vector of n elements. We use A_i to denote the formula on row i of this vector, and similarly B_i for b. Function f's compact representation results in an $n \times n$ matrix, and we use F_{ij} to denote the formula at row i, column j.
The formula $a.f = b$ is the conjunction of the following n formulas:

$$\begin{gathered}(A_1 \wedge F_{11} \vee \cdots \vee A_n \wedge F_{n1}) \Leftrightarrow B_1 \\ \wedge \cdots \wedge \\ (A_1 \wedge F_{1n} \vee \cdots \vee A_n \wedge F_{nn}) \Leftrightarrow B_n\end{gathered}$$

Exactly one of the A_i is true, so we can apply Logical Simplification 2:

$$\begin{gathered}A_1 \wedge (F_{11} \Leftrightarrow B_1) \vee \cdots \vee A_n \wedge (F_{n1} \Leftrightarrow B_1) \\ \wedge \cdots \wedge \\ A_1 \wedge (F_{1n} \Leftrightarrow B_n) \vee \cdots \vee A_n \wedge (F_{nn} \Leftrightarrow B_n)\end{gathered}$$

We can then apply Logical Simplification 1:

$$(\neg A_1 \vee (F_{11} \Leftrightarrow B_1)) \wedge \cdots \wedge \neg(A_n \vee (F_{n1} \Leftrightarrow B_1))$$
$$\wedge \cdots \wedge$$
$$(\neg A_1 \vee (F_{1n} \Leftrightarrow B_n)) \wedge \cdots \wedge (\neg A_n \vee (F_{nn} \Leftrightarrow B_n))$$

After moving terms around and factoring, we obtain:

$$\neg A_1 \vee ((F_{11} \Leftrightarrow B_1) \wedge \cdots \wedge (F_{1n} \Leftrightarrow B_n))$$
$$\cdots$$
$$\neg A_n \vee ((F_{n1} \Leftrightarrow B_1) \wedge \cdots \wedge (F_{nn} \Leftrightarrow B_n))$$

Note that for all i, the formulas $F_{i1}, \cdots, F_{in}$ and $B_1, \cdots, B_n$ satisfy the conditions of Logical Simplification 3. So we apply it to obtain:

$$(\neg A_1 \vee (f_{11} \Leftrightarrow b_1) \wedge \cdots \wedge (f_{1l} \Leftrightarrow b_l))$$
$$\cdots$$
$$(\neg A_n \vee (f_{n1} \Leftrightarrow b_1) \wedge \cdots \wedge (f_{nl} \Leftrightarrow b_l))$$

Therefore, formula $a.f = b$ results in $2nl$ clauses, and no additional intermediate variables. The formula $v.f_1.\cdots.f_{k_1} = u.g_1.\cdots.g_m$ results in $2nlk$ clauses, and since we added k variables to break it down, it has lk intermediate boolean variables.

Consider translating $v.f_1.\cdots.f_{k_1} = u.g_1.\cdots.g_{k_2}$ to CNF, without using optimizations. Each subexpression of the form $a.f$ results in a vector of n formulas, that are disjunctions of n conjunctions. For each of these formulas, we introduce n propositional variables to rename the conjunctions, requiring 3 clauses each for their definitions. We also introduce 1 variable to rename the whole formula, and its definition requires $n+1$ clauses. So the subexpression $a.f$ requires $n(n+1)$ additional variables, and $n(4n+1)$ clauses. Therefore there are $n(4n+1)k$ clauses and $n(n+1)k$ variables after the translation of each side of the equality. The equality itself adds $2n^2$ clauses. We obtain the numbers summarized in the following table.

	Clauses	Intermediate Variables
Non-Optimized	$(4k+2)n^2 + kn$	$kn^2 + kn$
Optimized	$2kn\lfloor log(n) \rfloor + k$	$k\lfloor log(n) \rfloor + k$

5 Example

We illustrate our optimizations on an implementation of insertion in red-black trees [5] (Figure 2). The code contains two classes `RBNode` and `RBTree`, and procedure `RBInsert`, which performs insertion into a red-black tree. This code is a close transcription of pseudocode presented in a popular algorithms book [5].

We are interested in checking that the red-black invariants are preserved: i.e. that all red nodes must have black children (`Inv1`), and that all paths leading

Code

```
class RBNode {
  boolean isRed; int key;
  RBNode right; RBNode left;
  RBNode parent;
  public RBNode(int i){
    isRed = false; key = i;
  }
}
class RBTree {
  RBNode root;
  void TreeInsert(RBNode z){
    RBNode k = null;
    RBNode x = this.root;
    while (x != null){
      k = x;
      if (z.key < x.key) x = x.left;
      else x = x.right;}
    z.parent = k;
    if (k == null) this.root = z;
    else if (z.key < k.key) k.left = z;
    else k.right = z;
 }
 static void LeftRotate(RBTree t, RBNode z){
   RBNode y = z.right;
   z.right = y.left;
   if (y.left != null) y.left.parent = z;
   y.parent = z.parent;
   if (z.parent == null) t.root = y;
   else if (z == z.parent.left)
       z.parent.left = y;
   else z.parent.right = y;
   y.left = z;
   z.parent = y;
 }
static void RBInsert(RBTree t, int i){
  RBNode h = new RBNode(i);
  t.TreeInsert(h);
  h.isRed = true;
  while (h != t.root &&
           h.parent.isRed == true){
    if (h.parent == h.parent.parent.left){
      RBNode y = h.parent.parent.right;
      if (y != null && y.isRed == true){
        h.parent.isRed = false;
        y.isRed = false;
        h.parent.parent.isRed = true;
        h = h.parent.parent;
      } else {
        if (h == h.parent.right) {
          h = h.parent;
          LeftRotate(t, h); }
        //h.parent.isRed = false; //bug seeded
        h.parent.parent.isRed = true;
        RightRotate(t, h.parent.parent);
      }
    } else { //same as above with
             // left and right inverted
    }
    t.root.isRed = false;
  }
 }
}
```

Specification

```
fun Inv1(t: RBTree) {
 all r: t.root.*(left + right) |
  r.isRed = true => {
  r.right != null => r.right.isRed = false
  r.left != null => r.left.isRed = false
}}
fun Inv2(t: RBTree){
 all r1, r2: t.root.*(left + right) {
  HasAtMostOneChild(r1)
      && HasAtMostOneChild(r2) =>
 #{r:RBNode|r in r1.*parent && no r.isRed}
  =
 #{r:RBNode|r in r2.*parent && no r.isRed}
}}
fun HasAtMostOneChild(r: RBNode){
 r.left = null || r.right = null
}
assert A { all t: RBTree, i: int |
 RBInsert(t,i) && Tree(t) =>
  Inv1(t) => Inv1'(t)
}
assert B { all t: RBTree, i: int |
 RBInsert(t,i) && Tree(t) =>
  Inv2(t) => Inv2'(t)
}
assert C { all t: RBTree, i: int |
 RBInsert(t,i) && Tree(t) =>
    Inv1(t) && Inv2(t) => Inv1'(t)
}
check C for 5 RBTree,5 RBNode,5 iteration
```

Counterexample

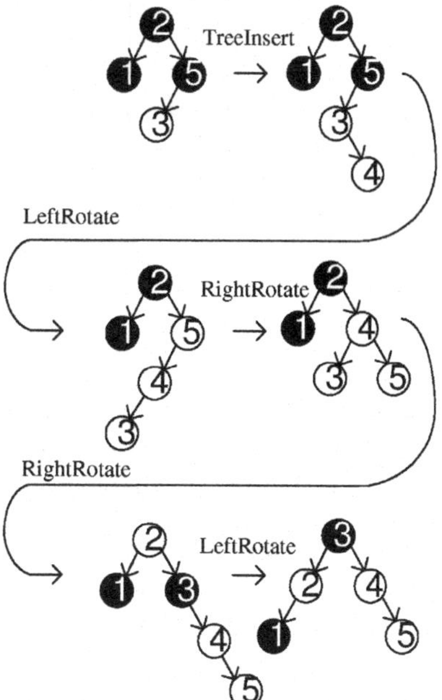

Fig. 2. Insertion into a Red-Black Tree and its Analysis

assertion	scope	# iter	counter?	time opt	clauses opt	vars opt	time	clauses	vars
A	2	2	no	0	6827	2218	0	15343	7638
	3	3	no	0	14443	4201	0	40042	18727
	4	4	no	3	35642	7887	20	82678	36316
	4	10	no	4	79496	15033	82	188452	81148
	4	20	no	13	152586	26943	–	–	–
	5	5	no	22	58056	13384	232	153259	64575
	5	10	no	43	102281	19854	506	283780	117344
	5	20	no	25	190731	32794	–	–	–
	6	6	no	159	85160	19659	–	–	–
	6	10	no	198	126700	25247	–	–	–
	6	20	no	514	230550	39217	–	–	–
B	2	2	no	0	7066	2310	0	15545	7694
	3	3	no	0	16300	4816	0	41827	19281
	4	4	yes	7	40950	9559	15	87654	37766
	4	10	yes	25	84804	16705	87	193404	82574
	4	20	yes	109	157894	28615	–	–	–
	5	5	yes	12	87369	22109	52	182058	72853
	5	10	yes	44	131594	28579	–	–	–
	5	20	yes	144	220044	41519	–	–	–
	6	6	yes	22	148548	38027	103	318908	121400
	6	10	yes	49	190088	43615	–	–	–
	6	20	yes	132	293938	57585	–	–	–
	7	7	yes	141	240865	62127	–	–	–
	7	10	yes	189	276652	66627	–	–	–
C	2	2	no	0	6867	2242	0	15537	7726
bug seeded	3	3	no	0	15165	4471	0	41172	19162
	4	4	no	2	37886	8679	18	85840	37450
	4	10	no	12	81302	15753	82	192286	82630
	4	20	no	62	153662	27543	–	–	–
	5	5	yes	18	75141	18608	65	172059	70344
	5	10	yes	43	118921	25013	140	303460	123573
	5	20	yes	100	206481	37823	–	–	–
	6	6	yes	77	124936	31383	202	298686	116224
	6	10	yes	82	166056	36915	–	–	–
	7	7	yes	93	199567	50690	–	–	–
	7	10	yes	239	234991	55145	–	–	–
	8	8	yes	272	349823	82336	–	–	–
	8	10	yes	641	386261	86216	–	–	–

Fig. 3. Results

to a node with at most one child have the same number of black nodes (`Inv2`). These invariants maintain a roughly balanced tree.

Figure 2 shows these invariants in Alloy. The function `Inv1` says that for all `RBNodes` `r` that are reachable from the root of `t` by following zero or more `left` or `right` fields (`t.root.*(left+right)`), have the property that if `r` is red, then both its children are black. The second property says that for all `RBNodes` `r1` and `r2` reachable from the root, if they both have at most one child[2] (indicated by the calls to function `HasAtMostOneChild`), then the cardinality of the set consisting of all black nodes on the path from `r1` to the root is equal to the cardinality of the corresponding set for `r2`. The expression `#e` denotes the cardinality of `e`, that is the number of tuples in it.

[2] In the original algorithm [5], trees have null leafs that are considered to be black. We do not have these; this is why we need the `HasAtMostOneChild` function.

The properties are followed by a series of assertions to be checked. For example, assertion `A` says that for all `RBTrees` `t` and all integers `i`, if the procedure `RBInsert(t,i)` is called and `t` is a well-formed tree (indicated by `Tree(t)`), then the `Inv1` property is preserved. A primed version of a function indicates the application of the corresponding property in the post-state, in this case the final state of `RBInsert(t,i)`, whereas an unprimed version indicates its application the initial state.

We checked these assertions using a prototype implementation for our analysis, which translates Java code directly to CNF using the optimizations, uses Alloy to translate the specifications to CNF, and conjoins the two. The results are shown in Figure 3. Times are in seconds. All experiments were run on a 1.1GHz PentiumIII with 640MB of memory, using the BerkMin SAT solver [8]. Some experiments were done after injecting a bug by removing one line in the code (indicated in Figure 2 by the comment `bug seeded`). In Figure 3, dashes indicate either that the experiment took more than 10 minutes or that there was a shortage of memory. The non-optimized experiments are done by translating a subset of Java code to Alloy and uses the Alloy Analyzer equipped with BerkMin as well.

Some of these experiments result in a counterexample. For instance, the counterexample corresponding to assertion `C` with a bug seeded, for scope of 5 and 5 iterations, is shown in Figure 2. The numbers on each node indicate the keys, and red nodes are shown in white. The counterexamples goes through 5 iterations to violate assertion 3.

The results show that the translation without optimization can obtain all the counterexamples very rapidly. This was expected; a fundamental assumption of our work, which we refer to as the *small scope hypothesis*, is that most bugs can be demonstrated with small counterexamples. The results also show that the analysis scales better with the optimizations. An empirical study [1] demonstrates that a scope of 6 is enough to obtain full statement and branch coverage for a variety of benchmarks. Our optimizations allow checking all assertions with a scope of 6, and as high as scope of 8 in some cases.

We can also increase the number of iterations to 20 and get an outcome within a minute or two in most cases. For `RBInsert`, 20 iterations for each loop correspond to 1540 lines of code. A state-of-the-art SAT solver can handle formulas with up to about 300,000 clauses. These results suggest that a code fragment of 1500 lines might be encodable within these limits. Of course, the tractability of the subsequent analysis is another matter. And in this case, since it is clear that fewer iterations suffice, the solver timings should be taken with a grain of salt.

6 Related Work

For a bounded instance of a program, our analysis explores *all* the possible inputs and executions, typically accounting for billions of cases. Unlike testing, it can also produce an initial configuration of the heap which leads to a property violation. It differs from finite state verification tools, such as model checking, in that it is modular: procedures may be checked in isolation without requiring a driver. It differs from shape analysis in that it produces sound counterexamples and no false alarms. It also requires no intermediate code annotations, or user-provided abstractions.

Finite State Verification. FeaVer [10] is a verification tool for C source code, based on the model checker Spin [9]. It extracts a model of a program automatically using a look-up table of abstractions provided by the user. The model is then verified with Spin, which outputs a counterexample when a property is violated. FeaVer has been used successfully to uncover hundreds of bugs in Lucent's PathStar call processing system.

Bandera [4] is a tool that allows analyzing Java source code with different verification tools. It extracts a finite state model of code using slicing and user-provided data abstraction. The result of the extraction is a model that may be mapped into several model checkers (SMV, Spin) and theorem provers (PVS). Unlike Feaver and Bandera, our analysis does not support user-provided abstraction.

The Java PathFinder [17] is an environment for checking Java bytecode, that integrates model checking, program analysis, and testing. It allows user-provided abstractions of the program, and uses the Bandera tool for slicing. Java PathFinder requires an initialization of the heap that fixes it to a particular configuration. Thus it is impossible to have the tool automatically find an initial configuration that breaks an assertion, as it can be done in our analysis.

The SLAM [2] tool is designed to check if a program obeys API usage rules. It does not require user annotations, and is fully automatic. It abstracts a program into a *boolean program* that is a conservative approximation. The boolean program is then subjected to reachability analysis to see if an error state is attainable. If this is not the case, then there is a guarantee that the original program cannot reach the error state. If an error state is reachable, then it is analyzed automatically to see if it is part of a feasible execution, in which case a counterexample is output to the user. If no feasible execution leads to the error state, then appropriate predicates are added to the abstraction, again automatically. The process then starts over with this refined abstract program. SLAM targets temporal safety properties, and not structural properties.

Shape Analysis. Shape analysis algorithms [16] can identify invariants for programs that manipulate heap-allocated storage. They represent the heap as *shape graphs*, conservative abstractions that capture properties at different points in the program. The parametric shape analysis (PSA) [16] method uses a 3-valued logic to represent shape graphs, and is a framework that can be instantiated with different *instrumentation predicates* that retain more refined information about concrete heaps, and can help to identify different classes of properties. Unlike our method, PSA can prove properties without bounds, but it may issue false alarms. In contrast to our property-independent translation, PSA requires instrumentation predicates that tailor the analysis for the discovery of particular properties. Recent work [14] presents space-efficient encodings of boolean formulas that represent shape graphs. Its goals not its methods are similar to ours.

Theorem Proving. The Extended Static Checker [6] uses a specialized theorem prover to check code against user-specified specifications. Structural properties such as those handled in our analysis are not expressible. Experience has shown that ESC requires many intermediate code annotations, making it less practical. An extension of ESC, the VeriFun tool [7], uses predicate abstraction, decision procedures, and automated successive refinement. It requires no user annotation beyond the property to be checked. It differs with our analysis in that it cannot readily handle the kinds of structural properties we consider here.

7 Conclusions

We presented a suite of optimizations that results in much improved scalability for our analysis of object-oriented code, which targets structural properties of the heap, requires no user-annotation, and outputs no false alarms. Our optimizations are a suite of simple but judiciously chosen logical simplifications, that are not incremental, i.e. their *composition* results in an improvement in scalability.

A conventional way to scale an analysis such as this is to require user-provided specifications for all procedures. The ability to handle longer code sequences allows a longer procedure to be considered, and for smaller procedures, it allows specifications to be omitted. The scalability of this analysis is therefore crucial to allow checking code fragments in which specifications are written at a coarser, more economical, granularity.

Our experimental results use a prototype tool that translates a subset of Java directly to CNF using the optimizations, while the non-optimized tool translated to Alloy, and therefore benefitted from the Alloy Analyzer's internal simplifications. As part of future work, we plan to incorporate our optimizations in the Alloy Analyzer, so that we can benefit from its simplifications as well. We also plan to run more experiments on different code bases, to further investigate the effect of our optimizations.

Acknowledgements. This work has greatly benefited from discussions with Manu Sridharan and Ilya Shlyakhter, and comments from anonymous reviewers. It was funded in part by ITR grant #0086154 from the National Science Foundation, by a grant from NASA, and by an endowment from Doug and Pat Ross. The first author thanks Joan Wheelis for her unbounded support, and dedicates this paper to the memory of her grandfather, Reza Safavi Golpayegani.

References

1. A. Andoni, D. Daniliuc, S. Khurshid, and D. Marinov. "Evaluating the Small Scope Hypothesis", MIT Laboratory for Computer Science, September 2002. Unpublished manuscript.
2. T. Ball, S. K. Rajamani. "The SLAM Project: Debugging System Software via Static Analysis", *Proc. POPL 2002*, January 2002.
3. D. R. Chase, M. Wegman and F. Zadeck. "Analysis of Pointers and Structures", *Proc. Conf. on Programming Language Design and Implementation*, 1990.
4. J. C. Corbett, M. B. Dwyer, J. Hatcliff, S. Laubach, C. S. Pasareanu, Robby, H. Zheng. "Bandera: Extracting Finite-State Models from Java Source Code", *Proc. International Conference on Software Engineering*, June 2000.
5. T. H. Cormen, C. E. Leiserson, R. L. Rivest. "Introduction to Algorithms", MIT Press, 1990.
6. D. Detlefs, K. R. Leino, G. Nelson, and J. Saxe. "Extended Static Checking". Technical Report 159, Compaq Systems Research Center, 1998.
7. Cormac Flanagan. Personal communication.
8. E. Goldberg and Y. Novikov. "BerkMin: A fast and robust SAT-solver", *In Design, Automation, and Test in Europe*, March 2002.
9. G.J. Holzmann. "The Model Checker Spin", *IEEE Trans. on Software Engineering*, Vol. 23, 5, May 1997.
10. G. J. Holzmann and M. H. Smith. "Automating Software Feature Verification", *Bell Labs Technical Journal*, Vol. 5, 2, April-June 2000.
11. Daniel Jackson. "Automating First-Order Relational Logic", *Proc. ACM SIGSOFT Conf. Foundations of Software Engineering*, San Diego, November 2000.
12. D. Jackson, I. Shlyakhter and M. Sridharan. "A Micromodularity Mechanism", *Proc. ACM SIGSOFT Conf. Foundations of Software Engineering*, 2001.
13. D. Jackson and M. Vaziri. "Finding Bugs with a Constraint Solver", *Proc. International Conference on Software Testing and Analysis*, August 2000.
14. R. Manevich, G. Ramalingam, J. Field, D. Goyal, M. Sagiv. "Compactly Representing First-Order Structures for Static Analysis", *In Proc. SAS 2002*, 2002.
15. D. A. Plaisted and S. Greenbaum. "A Structure-Preserving Clause Form Translation", *Journal of Symbolic Computation*, 2:293–304, 1986.
16. M. Sagiv, T. Reps, and R. Wilhelm. "Parametric shape analysis via 3-valued logic", *In ACM Transactions on Programming Languages and Systems*, 24(3), 217–298, 2002.
17. W. Visser, K. Havelund, G. Brat and S. Park. "Model Checking Programs", *International Conference on Automated Software Engineering*, September 2000.

An Online Proof-Producing Decision Procedure for Mixed-Integer Linear Arithmetic*

Sergey Berezin, Vijay Ganesh, and David L. Dill

Stanford University
{berezin,vganesh,dill}@stanford.edu

Abstract. Efficient decision procedures for arithmetic play a very important role in formal verification. In practical examples, however, arithmetic constraints are often mixed with constraints from other theories like the theory of arrays, Boolean satisfiability (SAT), bit-vectors, etc. Therefore, decision procedures for arithmetic are especially useful in combination with other decision procedures. The framework for such a combination is implemented at Stanford in the tool called Cooperating Validity Checker (CVC) [SBD02].
This work augments CVC with a decision procedure for the theory of mixed integer linear arithmetic based on the Omega-test [Pug91] extended to be *online* and *proof producing*. These extensions are the most important and challenging part of the work, and are necessary to make the combination efficient in practice.

1 Introduction

Formal verification methods benefit greatly from efficient automatic decision procedures. There has been ample research in developing efficient decision procedures for various satisfiability problems like *Boolean satisfiability* (SAT [MMZ+01,MSS99]), *bit-vectors* [Möl98], *linear integer and real arithmetic*, etc.

In practical examples, constraints from different theories are often mixed together. For example, it is not uncommon to see a constraint like the following:

$$2 * y + x > z \wedge f(x) \neq z \rightarrow A[2 * y + x] > 0,$$

which belongs to the combined theory of arithmetic, arrays, and uninterpreted functions. Consequently, there is a need for a decision procedure for the combination of theories.

Several combination methods like Nelson-Oppen [NO79], Shostak [Sho84], and their variants [RS01,BDS02a] have been developed. All these methods impose certain requirements on the individual decision procedures in order to achieve a sound, complete, and efficient combination. Satisfying these requirements greatly improves the usability of the individual decision procedures.

One of the tools that combine decision procedures is the *Cooperating Validity Checker* (CVC [SBD02]) developed at Stanford. It is based on the framework of cooperating decision procedures developed by Barrett [BDS02a] which, in turn, is based on

* This research was supported by GSRC contract SA3276JB, NSF grant CCR-9806889-002, and NSF ITR grant CCR-0121403. The content of this paper does not necessarily reflect the position or the policy of any of the funding agencies or the Government, and no official endorsement should be inferred.

H. Garavel and J. Hatcliff (Eds.): TACAS 2003, LNCS 2619, pp. 521–536, 2003.

Nelson-Oppen [NO79] and Shostak [Sho84] frameworks. Each decision procedure in the framework is responsible for solving the satisfiability problem for only one particular theory and does not interact directly with the other theories.

The current implementation involves decision procedures for the theory of uninterpreted functions, the theory of arrays [SBDL01], the theory of datatypes, and the theory of linear arithmetic over integers and reals, which is the subject of this paper. Additionally, Boolean combinations of constraints are handled on the top level by the SAT solver [BDS02b] based on Chaff [MMZ+01]. Thus, CVC as a whole serves as a decision procedure for the quantifier-free first-order theory of equality with arrays, recursive datatypes, and linear arithmetic [BDS00].

As with all combination methods, CVC imposes certain requirements on the individual decision procedures. In particular, each decision procedure must be *online* and *proof producing*. Online means that a new constraint can be added to the set of existing constraints at any time, and the algorithm must be able to take it into account with only incremental amount of work. When the set of constraints is determined to be unsatisfiable, the algorithm must also produce a proof of this fact.

Additionally, the theory of linear arithmetic is extended with the predicate $\mathsf{int}(t)$, which evaluates to true on a real-valued arithmetic term t, when t evaluates to an integer. The decision procedure must be able to handle constraints of the form $\mathsf{int}(t)$ and $\neg\mathsf{int}(t)$ in addition to the usual linear arithmetic constraints.

The reasons for the above requirements can be better understood from the architecture of CVC. At a very high level, CVC can be viewed as a SAT solver [DP60] which solves the satisfiability problem of the Boolean skeleton of the first-order formulas. Each time the SAT solver makes a decision, a new constraint is submitted to the appropriate decision procedure. Since decisions are dynamic, decision procedures must be able to receive a new constraint and process it efficiently (the *online* requirement).

Modern SAT solvers [SS96,MSS99,MMZ+01] use *conflict clauses* and *intelligent backtracking* to enhance performance. Backtracking implies that the solver may retract some constraints dynamically, hence, the decision procedure must support this operation. From an implementation point of view, this means that all the internal data structures in the decision procedure must be backtrackable.

To construct a conflict clause, one needs to identify those decisions made by the SAT solver which lead to a contradiction. CVC identifies such decisions by extracting them from the proof that the decision procedure constructs when it derives a contradiction. This explains the need for proof production in the decision procedures in CVC. As a bonus, the proofs can be checked by an external proof checker [Stu02] to increase the confidence in the results produced by CVC.

In addition to CVC, a few other tools combine online and proof producing decision procedures. Perhaps, the most similar to CVC is the Touchstone tool [NL00] developed at Berkeley. In particular, it has a simplex-based arithmetic desicion procedure, but only for real arithmetic.

This paper describes a decision procedure for mixed-integer linear arithmetic designed to meet the above requirements, and thus, fit the CVC framework. The decision procedure is based on an existing algorithm called *Omega-test* [Pug91], which is extended to be online, proof producing, and handle the $\mathsf{int}()$ predicate. Additionally, this implementation supports arbitrary precision arithmetic based on the GMP library [GMP]. The arbitrary precision arithmetic is crucial for solving sizable systems of mixed-integer constraints using Fourier-Motzkin approach, since variable elimination may produce large coefficients even if the coefficients in the original input are relatively small.

The choice of Omega-test over other algorithms for solving mixed-integer linear arithmetic problems (simplex, interior point method [BT97], earlier versions of Fourier-Motzkin elimination [Wil76], etc.) is driven by its simplicity and practical efficiency for a large class of verification problems. In particular, proof production is relatively easy to implement for the Omega-test.

The rest of the paper is organized as follows. Sections 2 and 3 review the original Fourier-Motzkin elimination method for real variables and its extension to integers (Omega-test), respectively. Both versions are then redesigned to make the algorithm online as described in sections 4 and 5. Section 4 also gives a brief overview of CVC. Proof production is described in section 6, and we conclude in section 7.

2 Fourier-Motzkin Elimination for Inequalities over Real Variables

The problem. Given a system of linear inequality constraints over real-valued variables of the form

$$\sum_{i=1}^{n} a_i x_i + c < 0,$$

where a_i's and c are rational constants, determine if this system is satisfiable. We only consider strict inequalities, since $\alpha \leq 0$ can be handled similarly to $\alpha < 0$. For simplicity, we assume that $\alpha \leq 0$ can be expanded into $\alpha < 0 \vee \alpha = 0$ and solved for each case in the disjunction. Here and in the rest of the paper, linear arithmetic terms are often denoted as α, β, γ, or t, possibly with subscripts. In this section, we do not consider equalities, since any equality can be solved for some variable and instantiated into the other constraints, thus obtaining an equivalent system without the equality.

Terminology. For the sake of terminological clarity, we say that a variable is ***eliminated*** if an equality constraint is solved for this variable and the result is substituted in the remaining constraints. When the Fourier-Motzkin reasoning on inequalities is applied to a variable, we say that such a variable is ***projected***.

Throughout the paper we assume that all the constants and coefficients are *rational*. Although we often refer to variables as real-valued, it is well-known that, under the above conditions, the system of linear constraints is satisfiable in reals if and only if it is satisfiable in rationals.

Intuitively, Fourier-Motzkin elimination procedure [DE73] iteratively projects one variable x by rewriting the system of inequalities into a new system without x which has a solution if and only if the original system has a solution (i.e. the two systems are *equisatisfiable*). This process repeats until no variables are left, at which point all of the constraints become inequalities over numerical constants and can be directly checked for satisfiability.

More formally, the projection procedure is the following. First, pick a variable present in at least one inequality, say x_n. All the inequalities containing this variable are then rewritten in the form $\beta < x_n$ or $x_n < \alpha$, depending on the sign of the coefficient a_n, where x_n does not occur in α or β. This creates three types of constraints: those with x on the right, with x on the left, and those without x:

$$\begin{cases} \beta_1 < x_n \\ \quad\vdots \\ \beta_{k_1} < x_n \end{cases} \qquad \begin{cases} x_n < \alpha_1 \\ \quad\vdots \\ x_n < \alpha_{k_2} \end{cases} \qquad \begin{cases} \gamma_1 < 0 \\ \quad\vdots \\ \gamma_{k_3} < 0. \end{cases} \tag{1}$$

If this system of constraints has a solution, then x_n must satisfy

$$\max(\beta_1, \ldots, \beta_{k_1}) < x_n < \min(\alpha_1, \ldots, \alpha_{k_2}).$$

Since real numbers are dense, such x_n exists if and only if the following constraint holds:

$$\max(\beta_1, \ldots, \beta_{k_1}) < \min(\alpha_1, \ldots, \alpha_{k_2}).$$

This constraint can be equivalently rewritten as

$$\beta_i < \alpha_j \quad \text{for all } i = 1 \ldots k_1,\ j = 1 \ldots k_2, \tag{2}$$

which is again a system of linear inequalities. We call them the *shadow constraints*, because they define an $n-1$-dimensional shadow of the n-dimensional shape defined by the original constraints (1). The shadow constraints (2) combined together with $\gamma_l < 0$ comprise a new system of constraints which is equisatisfiable with (1), but does not contain the variable x_n. This process can now be repeated for x_{n-1}, and so on, until all the variables are projected.

Observe that for a system of m constraints each elimination step may produce a new system with up to $(m/2)^2$ constraints. Therefore, eliminating n variables may, in the worst case, create a system of $4 \cdot (m/4)^{2^n}$ constraints. Thus, the decision procedure for linear inequalities based on Fourier-Motzkin even in the case of real variables has a doubly exponential worst case complexity in the number of variables.

3 Extension of Fourier-Motzkin Elimination to Integer Variables (Omega-Test)

Our version of the extension is largely based on the Omega approach [Pug91] with a few differences. First, we consider the system of *mixed integer linear constraints* which, in addition to linear equalities and (strict) inequalities may also contain $\mathsf{int}(t)$ or $\neg\mathsf{int}(t)$ for any linear term t, meaning that the linear term t is restricted to only integer (respectively, fractional) values.

If the term t is not a variable, the constraint $\mathsf{int}(t)$ is satisfiable iff $\mathsf{int}(z) \wedge z = t$ is satisfiable, where z is a new variable. Furthermore, $\neg\mathsf{int}(t)$ is satisfiable for any term t iff $\mathsf{int}(y) \wedge y < t < y+1$ is satisfiable for a new variable y. Hence, any system of mixed integer linear constraints may be converted to an equisatisfiable system of constraints with only equalities, inequalities, and predicates of the form $\mathsf{int}(x)$, where x is a variable.

3.1 Elimination of Equalities

As in the case of reals, all the equalities are eliminated first. If an equality contains a variable x that is not an integer, then we solve the equality for this variable and eliminate x from the system. Since this is the most efficient way of reducing the dimensionality of the problem, all such equalities are eliminated first.

Now suppose that an equality contains only integer variables:

$$\sum_{i=1}^{n} a_i x_i + c = 0. \tag{3}$$

Here we use the same variable elimination algorithm as in the Omega-test [Pug91]. If x is the only variable in (3), then there is only one value of x which can satisfy this equality constraint, namely $x = -(c/a)$. If this value is integral, we substitute it for x, and otherwise the system is unsatisfiable.

If there is more than one variable in (3), the equality is normalized such that all the coefficients a_i and the free constant c are relatively prime integers. It can always be done when the coefficients are rational numbers. If, after the normalization, there is a variable x_k whose coefficient is $|a_k| = 1$, then we simply solve for x_k and eliminate it from the rest of the system. Otherwise pick a variable x_k whose coefficient a_k is the smallest by the absolute value and define $m = |a_k| + 1$. Define also a modulus operation with the range $\left[-\frac{m}{2}, \frac{m}{2}\right)$ as follows:

$$a \,\mathbf{mod}\, m = a - m \left\lfloor \frac{a}{m} + \frac{1}{2} \right\rfloor .$$

The important properties of $\mathbf{mod}$ are that $a_k \,\mathbf{mod}\, m = -\text{sign}(a_k)$, and that it distributes over addition and multiplication, where $\text{sign}(x)$ is -1, 0, or 1 when $x < 0$, $x = 0$ and $x > 0$ respectively.

The next step is to choose a new variable σ and introduce two new constraints into the system:

$$\mathsf{int}(\sigma) \quad \text{and} \quad \sum_{i=1}^{n} (a_i \,\mathbf{mod}\, m) x_i + (c \,\mathbf{mod}\, m) = m\sigma. \tag{4}$$

The second constraint is derivable from (3) by applying $\cdot \,\mathbf{mod}\, m$ on both sides of (3) and propagating $\mathbf{mod}$ over addition and multiplication to the coefficients. Hence, the system remains equisatisfiable with the original.

Since $a_k \,\mathbf{mod}\, m = -\text{sign}(a_k)$, the equation (4) can be solved for x_k and x_k is eliminated from the system:

$$x_k = -\text{sign}(a_k) m\sigma + \sum_{i \in [1..n]-\{k\}} \text{sign}(a_k)(a_i \,\mathbf{mod}\, m) x_i + \text{sign}(a_k)(c \,\mathbf{mod}\, m). \tag{5}$$

Substituting the result into the original equation (3) and using the facts $|a_k| = m - 1$ and $a - (a \,\mathbf{mod}\, m) = m \left\lfloor \frac{a}{m} + \frac{1}{2} \right\rfloor$ (from the definition of m and $\mathbf{mod}$) we obtain:

$$-|a_k|\sigma + \sum_{i \in [1..n]-\{k\}} a'_i x_i + c' = 0, \tag{6}$$

where $a'_i = \lfloor \frac{a_i}{m} + \frac{1}{2} \rfloor + (a_i \bmod m)$ and $c' = \lfloor \frac{c}{m} + \frac{1}{2} \rfloor + (c \bmod m)$. The new system (which is the original system with x_k eliminated using (5), and (3) rewritten as (6)) contains the same number of variables as the original one. Moreover, the new coefficients a' in (6) are guaranteed to decrease by absolute value compared to (3), namely $|a'_i| \le \frac{2}{3}|a_i|$, except for the coefficient of σ which remains as large as that of x_k. This ensures that repeating the process above will eventually result in equality (6) having some variable with a coefficient 1 or -1. That variable can then be eliminated, reducing the overall dimensionality.

3.2 Projecting Variables from Inequalities

After eliminating all of the equalities, we are left with the system of (strict) inequalities over real and integer variables. Similar to the equality case, all the remaining real variables are projected first with the standard Fourier-Motzkin elimination procedure, resulting in a system of inequalities with only integer variables.

At this point, all the inequalities are normalized to make the coefficients be relatively prime integers, and a variable x_n is chosen for projection. Since x_n has an additional integral constraint, we cannot simply divide the inequality by the coefficient a_n unless it is 1 or -1, and in general, the system of inequalities is rewritten in the equivalent form, very much like in (1), only the coefficients of x_n are preserved:

$$\begin{cases} \beta_1 < b_n^1 x_n \\ \quad \vdots \\ \beta_{k_1} < b_n^{k_1} x_n \end{cases} \qquad \begin{cases} a_n^1 x_n < \alpha_1 \\ \quad \vdots \\ a_n^{k_2} x_n < \alpha_{k_2} \end{cases} \qquad \begin{cases} \gamma_1 < 0 \\ \quad \vdots \\ \gamma_{k_3} < 0, \end{cases} \tag{7}$$

where the coefficients a_i^j and b_i^j are positive integers. Similar to the original Fourier-Motzkin construction, for each pair of inequalities $\beta < bx_n$ and $ax_n < \alpha$, which is equivalent to

$$a\beta < abx_n < b\alpha, \tag{8}$$

the *real shadow constraint* is constructed:

$$a\beta < b\alpha. \tag{9}$$

However, the real shadow is a necessary but not a sufficient condition for the satisfiability of (8), since there might not be an integer value abx_n between $a\beta$ and $b\alpha$, even if there is a real one. In addition to the real shadow, at least one point $ab \cdot i$ must exist between $a\beta$ and $b\alpha$ for some integer i. A sufficient (but not necessary) condition is to demand that the gap between $a\beta$ and $b\alpha$ be at least $ab + 1$ wide:

$$\mathbf{D} \equiv b\alpha - a\beta > ab. \tag{10}$$

This constraint is called the *dark shadow constraint* (the object is "thick enough" to contain an integer point, and therefore casts a darker shadow; the term *dark shadow* is from [Pug91]). The dark shadow constraint is sufficient, but not necessary for an integer solution of x_n to exist. Therefore, if equation (10) makes the system unsatisfiable, we have to look for an integer solution outside of $\mathbf{D}$, i.e. in the *gray shadow*: $b\alpha \leq a\beta + ab$. Following the construction in the Omega-test [Pug91], $b\alpha$ on the right-hand side of (8) is replaced by the larger $a\beta + ab$, and dividing the result by a yields the following:

$$\beta < bx_n < \beta + b.$$

This means that if there is an integer solution to x_n, it must satisfy $bx_n = \beta + i$ for some $0 < i < b$, since β contains only integer variables with integer coefficients. We then try each such i in succession until a solution is found. In other words, the *gray shadow constraint* is:

$$\mathbf{G} \equiv \bigvee_{i=1}^{b-1} bx_n = \beta + i.$$

This is, obviously, the most expensive step of the algorithm, since it involves a lot of backtracking, but according to [Pug91], the dark shadow constraint almost always suffices in practice, and the gray shadow is often empty. Therefore, as a practical heuristic, the dark shadow constraint $\mathbf{D}$ is always tried first, and only if it fails, then a solution is searched for in the gray shadow $\mathbf{G}$.

4 Online Version of Fourier-Motzkin for Reals

In CVC, decision procedures are most effective when they are *online*, that is, the constraints are not given all at once but are fed to the decision procedure one at a time, and for each constraint the algorithm performs some relatively small amount of work to take that constraint into account and derive new constraints that follow from it.

In order to understand the reasons for being online and to clarify the important interface features that the decision procedure relies on, we give a brief introduction to the CVC framework. The goal of the following subsection is to provide just enough information about the interface and underlying structure of the CVC framework to understand the requirements for the online version of the decision procedure for mixed integer linear arithmetic. Therefore, some of the features are greatly simplified or omitted. For more details on CVC framework the reader is referred to [BDS00,BDS02b,BDS02a].

4.1 Brief Introduction to CVC Framework

At a very high level, CVC can be viewed as a SAT solver for the Boolean skeleton of the quantifier-free first-order formulas (figure 1). The SAT solver treats the atomic constraints from different theories as Boolean variables. It solves the satisfiability problem by *splitting cases* on each variable; that is, picking a variable, assigning it values `true` and `false` (making a *decision*), and solving the rest of the formula for each case recursively. If it finds a *satisfying assignment* to the variables, then the original formula is satisfiable. When a particular set of decisions results in a contradiction, the SAT solver backtracks and tries a different decision. If in all branches it derives a contradiction, then the formula is unsatisfiable.

Since the Boolean variables represent constraints from various theories, each time the SAT solver makes a decision, a new constraint is produced, which is simplified and dispatched to the appropriate decision procedure. When a decision procedure receives a constraint, it derives new constraints from the current and previously seen constraints, and asserts them back to the SAT solver. If a contradiction is detected, then the decision procedure asserts false as a new constraint. Note, that the new constraints may contain arbitrary Boolean combinations of atomic formulas, but the decision procedure always receives atomic constraints (equalities and theory-specific predicates over terms). In other words, the decision procedure can assume it always solves the satisfiability problem for a *conjunction of atomic constraints*. However, it is allowed to infer Boolean combinations of new constraints from the input set of constraints.

These decisions are dynamic, which requires decision procedures to be able to receive a new constraint and process it efficiently, deriving a contradiction as soon as possible to cut off the search early. This explains the *online* requirement. In some cases, however, a simplified constraint may be returned directly to the SAT solver without going through a decision procedure.

When the SAT solver backtracks, some of the constraints are effectively removed. Therefore, if a decision procedure stores some information about previously received constraints, it must be able to roll back to the appropriate state when the SAT solver backtracks. In other words, all the data structures which persist across calls to the decision procedure must be *backtrackable*. Below, in the description of the algorithm, we always assume that such backtracking mechanism is properly implemented and is completely transparent to the decision procedure.

To boost the efficiency of the SAT solver, the *intelligent backtracking* technique is utilized along with *conflict clauses* [MSS99]. To construct a conflict clause, one needs to identify a (preferably small) set of decisions made by the SAT solver that lead to the contradiction. One way of identifying such decisions is to extract them from the *proof* that the decision procedure constructs when it derives false. This explains the need for proof production in CVC decision procedures. As a bonus, the proofs can be checked by an external proof checker [Stu02] to increase the confidence in the results produced by CVC.

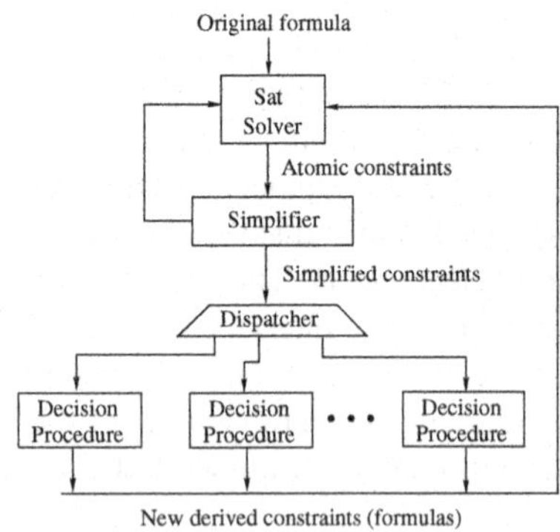

Fig. 1. Flow of constraints in CVC

Note, that intelligent backtracking requires only the set of assumptions (from the SAT solver decisions) used in the proof, and does not depend on the specific proof rules. This set can be computed by simply traversing the proof tree to the leaves and collecting the assumptions.

4.2 Online Fourier-Motzkin Elimination for Reals

In this and the subsequent sections the term *decision procedure* will refer to the decision procedure component from figure 1. In particular, we can always assume that the constraints dispatched to the decision procedure are *atomic* (no Boolean connectives) and *simplified*. The simplification step consists of theory-specific rewrites such as normalization of arithmetic constraints and elimination of equalities, so that only normalized inequality constraints reach the decision procedure.

Hence, the description of the algorithm consists of two parts: the simplifier, which is a set of equivalent transformations, and the decision procedure itself. The latter is presented as a function that takes a simplified atomic constraint and returns (possibly a Boolean combination of) new constraints back to the framework.

In the algorithm below, we assume a total ordering $\lessdot$ on all variables which defines the order in which the variables are projected from inequalities. In particular, x is said to be the *maximal* variable from a set of variables when it is the highest in this set w.r.t. $\lessdot$. In this section, we only consider equalities and inequalities over real-valued variables. Handling the constraints with $\mathsf{int}(t)$ predicate and integer variables will be described later in section 5.

Simplification step. Each equality constraint $t_1 = t_2$ is first rewritten as $t_1 - t_2 = 0$ and simplified by grouping like terms. If the resulting equality contains no variables (meaning $t_1 - t_2$ simplifies to a numerical constant), then it is checked for satisfiability, and the result is reported directly to the top-level SAT solver. Otherwise, it is rewritten in the form $x = \alpha$ for some variable x, and then x is replaced by α everywhere in the system, completely eliminating the variable x.

Similarly, an inequality $t_1 < t_2$ is rewritten as $t_1 - t_2 < 0$ and simplified. If the left-hand side simplifies to a constant, the inequality is evaluated to true or false and submitted back to the solver. Otherwise, it is rewritten as $\beta < x$ or $x < \alpha$ for the maximum variable x in $t_1 - t_2$ w.r.t. $\lessdot$, and forwarded to the decision procedure.

Decision procedure. Due to the simplification step above, the decision procedure receives only inequalities of the form $\beta < x$ or $x < \alpha$, where x is the maximal variable in α and β w.r.t. $\lessdot$. We say that the variable x in such inequalities is *isolated*.

The decision procedure maintains a backtrackable database $\mathrm{DB}_<$ of inequalities indexed by the isolated variable. Whenever a new inequality $x < \alpha$ arrives, this database is searched for the opposite inequalities $\beta < x$ and for each such inequality the new shadow constraint $\beta < \alpha$ is constructed and asserted back to the framework. The received constraint $x < \alpha$ is then added to the database. The inequalities of the form $\beta < x$ are handled similarly.

The newly generated constraint $\beta < \alpha$ is eventually simplified and submitted back to the decision procedure with a smaller variable (w.r.t. $\lessdot$) isolated, and this process repeats until no variables remain in the constraint.

The ordering $\lessdot$ on the variables guarantees that all the intermediate constraints that would be constructed by the offline version of the procedure are eventually constructed and processed by this online version, provided both algorithms project variables according to the same ordering. Assuming that the original offline version of Fourier-Motzkin elimination is complete and terminating implies that the online procedure is also complete and terminating. We formulate the completeness part of this statement more precisely as a lemma.

Lemma 1. ***(Local Completeness.)*** *Let* $\mathbf{C} = \{C_1, \ldots, C_k\}$ *be a set of linear arithmetic inequalities over real-valued variables* $x_1, \ldots, x_n$*, and* $\lessdot$ *be a total ordering on the variables. Let* $\mathcal{C}$ *be the set of constraints constructed by the offline algorithm while solving the original set of constraints* $\mathbf{C}$*. Then any constraint* $C \in \mathcal{C}$ *is also constructed by the online algorithm, regardless of the order in which the original constraints from* $\mathbf{C}$ *are submitted to the online algorithm.*

For the proof the reader is referred to the technical report version of this paper [BGD02].

5 Online Fourier-Motzkin Elimination for Mixed Integer Constraints

The online version of the decision procedure for integers cannot have such a direct correspondence to the offline version, since the order of the projection of variables depends on the integrality constraints, $\mathsf{int}(x)$ and $\neg\mathsf{int}(x)$, and the variable may become known to be integer only after it has already been projected or eliminated. A naive solution would be to backtrack and redo the projection and elimination steps. This could be a very costly operation.

Fortunately, there is a simple and elegant solution to this problem. Whenever a constraint $\mathsf{int}(x)$ arrives, a new constraint $x - \sigma = 0$ is added to the system, where σ is a new integer variable, and the fact $\mathsf{int}(\sigma)$ is recorded into a local database $\mathrm{DB}_{\mathrm{int}}$ indexed by σ. The resulting system is equisatisfiable with the original one (which includes $\mathsf{int}(x)$), but the variable x remains real-valued in the new system. Therefore, the projections and eliminations of x do not have to be redone. At the same time, the integrality of x is enforced by the integrality of σ.

In addition, for any integer constraint $\mathsf{int}(t)$ in $\mathrm{DB}_{\mathrm{int}}$, whenever the term t is rewritten to t' (because of some variable elimination), and t' simplifies to a constant term c, one must check that c is indeed an integer and assert unsatisfiability if it is not.

Just like the algorithm for only real variables, the online algorithm for deciding mixed-integer linear constraints consists of two parts: simplification and decision procedure.

Simplification step. This version of the simplifier performs the same transformations as the one for real variables (section 4.2). An equality constraint is first rewritten as $\gamma = 0$ and γ is checked for being a constant. If it is, the constraint is immediately checked for satisfiability and the result is returned directly to the SAT solver. Otherwise, if γ contains real-valued variables, then one such variable x is isolated and eliminated. If only integer variables remain in γ, then the iterative equality elimination algorithm is performed, as described in section 3.1. At the end of this process the equality $\gamma = 0$ is rewritten into an equisatisfiable system of equations

$$\begin{cases} x_1 = \beta_1 \\ \vdots \quad \vdots \\ x_k = \beta_k, \end{cases}$$

where each equation $x_i = \beta_i$ corresponds to the equation (5) in section 3.1 from each iteration of the algorithm. All the variables x_i are then eliminated by replacing them with their right-hand sides. Thus, equations are handled in the simplification step and never submitted to the actual decision procedure.

Inequalities are also transformed and simplified into $\gamma < 0$, then evaluated if γ is a constant. If γ contains variables, the inequality is rewritten to the form $\beta < ax$ or $ax < \alpha$ for some positive integer coefficient a, where the variable x is the maximal w.r.t. $\lessdot$. The new inequality is then forwarded to the decision procedure. Similar to the offline version of the algorithm, it is important to project real variables first. Therefore, we define $\lessdot$ such that real-valued variables are always higher in the ordering than the integer ones.

In the constraints of the form $\mathsf{int}(t)$ and $\neg\mathsf{int}(t)$ only the term t is simplified by combining like terms, and otherwise these constraints are passed to the decision procedure unmodified.

5.1 The Decision Procedure

First, observe that, due to the simplification step, only inequalities of the form $\beta < bx$ and $ax < \alpha$ and integer constraints $\mathsf{int}(t)$ and $\neg\mathsf{int}(t)$ are submitted to the decision procedure. Notice that inequality constraints always have the maximal variable isolated w.r.t. $\lessdot$. These inequalities are stored in the local database $\mathrm{DB}_<$. Additionally, whenever a term t in any constraint $\mathsf{int}(t) \in \mathrm{DB}_{\mathrm{int}}$ is rewritten to t' by the simplifier, $\mathsf{int}(t)$ is automatically replaced by $\mathsf{int}(t')$ in $\mathrm{DB}_{\mathrm{int}}$. Both local databases are also backtrackable.

The decision procedure receives a constraint C from the simplifier and returns, or *asserts*, new constraints back to the framework. We describe it as a case-by-case analysis of the constraint C.

1. $C \equiv \mathsf{int}(t)$:
   a) If t is a constant, then evaluate $\mathsf{int}(t)$, assert the result to the framework, and return. If t is not a constant, go to step 1b.
   b) If $t \notin \mathrm{DB}_{\mathrm{int}}$, then create a new integer variable z, add t and z into $\mathrm{DB}_{\mathrm{int}}$, assert the new facts:
   $$\mathsf{int}(z) \quad \text{and} \quad t - z = 0.$$
   Otherwise, if t $\in \mathrm{DB}_{\mathrm{int}}$, then ignore C and return.
2. $C \equiv \neg\mathsf{int}(t)$:
   Introduce a new integer variable z, add z to $\mathrm{DB}_{\mathrm{int}}$ and assert the new constraints:
   $$\mathsf{int}(z) \quad \text{and} \quad z < t < z + 1.$$
3. $C \equiv a \cdot x < \alpha$ (or $C \equiv \beta < b \cdot x$):
   a) Find all inequalities of the form $\beta < b \cdot x$ (respectively, $a \cdot x < \alpha$) in the database $\mathrm{DB}_<$, and for each such inequality perform the following steps:
      i. Generate and assert the real shadow constraint $R \equiv a \cdot \beta < b \cdot \alpha$.
      ii. If $x \in \mathrm{DB}_{\mathrm{int}}$ (in which case all the variables in α and β must also be in $\mathrm{DB}_{\mathrm{int}}$), then generate the integrality constraint $\mathbf{D} \vee \mathbf{G}$ (dark and gray shadows), where $\mathbf{D}$ and $\mathbf{G}$ are defined as in section 3.2:
      $$\mathbf{D} \equiv b \cdot \alpha - a \cdot \beta > ab \quad \text{and} \quad \mathbf{G} = \bigvee_{i=1}^{b-1} b \cdot x = \beta + i.$$

Table 1. Experimental comparisons of CVC vs. Omega on suites of randomly generated examples. CVC is generally slower than Omega approximately by a factor of 10.

#experiments in each suite	#formulas / #vars in each experiment	CVC completed*	Omega completed*	avg. slow-down factor
5996	1-4/1-5	5990 (99.9%)	5568 (93.0%)	13.4
395	1-10/1-20	393 (99.5%)	322 (81.5%)	192
65	10-50/10-50	63 (96.9%)	8 (12.3%)	7.8

*An experiment is completed if the tool terminates with the correct answer within 10 minutes.

Following the heuristic of Pugh [Pug91], the top-level SAT solver should first search for a solution in **D** before trying **G**.

b) Add the received constraint C to $\text{DB}_{<}$ and return.

It is not hard to see that each step of the algorithm above corresponds very closely to the similar steps in the offline version of the algorithm. The soundness and completeness of the procedure follow from the fact that the set of constraints asserted by the decision procedure at each step is always equisatisfiable with the given constraint C. The details of the formal proof (including termination) are in the technical report [BGD02].

The experiments summarized in table 1 indicate that most of the time the overhead of the CVC framework and arbitrary precision arithmetic slow down the algorithm only by a constant factor. Since this implementation is not yet tuned for efficiency, there are a few exceptional cases when CVC performs much worse than Omega, which explains the large slow-down factor in the second line of table 1. Specifically, in a few exceptionally slow examples in the second suite (the slowest takes less than 6 seconds) the slowdown is due to the large CVC framework overhead (over 90%), and lack of optimizations. In any case, this is a very reasonable price to pay for having the arithmetic decision procedure combined with other theories of CVC, since in many practical applications the arithmetic problems are very small and are not the bottleneck of the verification. Additionally, the resulting implementation proves to be much more stable than the original Omega-test, and produces proofs.

6 Proof Production

When the algorithm in section 5 reports that the system of constraints is unsatisfiable, it produces a proof of this fact which can be verified independently by an external proof checker. This increases our confidence in the soundness of the implementation.

Additionally, the proof production mechanism allows CVC framework to extract logical dependencies that drive the backtracking mechanism of the built-in SAT solver (see section 4.1). The details are out of the scope of this paper, but intuitively, if the proof of unsatisfiability depends only on a small subset of decisions made by the SAT solver, then the SAT solver memorizes this combination of decisions and avoids it in the future. This can dramatically reduce the size of the decision tree.

Due to the page limit, only a few proof rules are presented in this version of the paper. For the complete description of the proof system the reader is referred to the technical report [BGD02].

6.1 Natural Deduction

The proofs are represented as derivations in natural deduction extended with arithmetic and with specialized derived or admissible rules. The algorithm maintains the invariant that every constraint appearing in the algorithm has an associated proof with it. Since the online decision procedure is presented as a set of relatively simple transformations, it is natural to provide a specialized proof rule for each such transformation. These specialized rules can then be proven sound externally, either by manual inspection or with the help of automated theorem provers.

Definitions. An *inference rule*, or a *proof rule*, in general, is of the form

$$\frac{P_1 \quad \cdots \quad P_n \quad S_1 \quad \cdots \quad S_m}{C} \text{rule name}$$

where formulas P_i are the *premisses* (they are assumed to have proofs), S_i are side conditions (the rule is applicable only if all S_i are true), and the formula C is the *conclusion* of the rule. The semantics of a proof rule is that if all P_i are valid, then C is also valid, provided that all the side conditions S_j are true. In CVC, however, the dual semantics is used, i.e. whenever C is unsatisfiable, the system of constraints $\{P_1, \ldots, P_n\}$ is also unsatisfiable, provided that all side conditions S_j hold.

Recall, that our algorithm consists of two parts: the simplifier, which performs equivalent transformations, and the decision procedure, which derives new constraints out of existing ones. The rules for the equivalent transformations in the simplifier have a special form:

$$\frac{S_1 \quad \cdots \quad S_m}{t_1 \equiv t_2}$$

where t_1 and t_2 are arithmetic terms or constraints and S_i are side conditions (there are no premisses). The rules for the decision procedure steps normally have premisses, which are the constraints submitted to the decision procedure.

6.2 Proof Rules for Equivalent Transformations

Normalization. The simplifier step normalizes the constraints by making all coefficients relatively prime integers, which is done by multiplying a constraint by a constant. The corresponding proof rules state that multiplying an (in)equality by a (positive) number preserves the constraint. Below, only the rule for inequality is shown.

$$\frac{b \in \mathcal{R}, \; b > 0}{\sum_{i=1}^{n} a_i \cdot x + c < 0 \quad \equiv \quad b \cdot (\sum_{i=1}^{n} a_i \cdot x + c) < 0} \text{norm}_<$$

Variable elimination for equalities. Given an (in)equality, pick a variable to isolate and transform the constraint in such a way that the variable with some positive coefficient is solely on one side, and the rest of the term is on the other. For equalities, the isolated variable must always be on the left-hand side. For inequalities, it depends on the sign of the coefficient: if it is positive, the variable stays on the left-hand side, and all the other terms are moved to the right-hand side; otherwise the variable is isolated on the right-hand side. We only show one proof rule for equality and positive coefficient below. The other 3 rules (one for equality and negative coefficient, and the two cases for inequalities) are similar.

$$\frac{a_i > 0}{c + \sum_{j=1}^{n} a_j \cdot x_j = 0 \equiv a_i \cdot x_i = -\left(c + \sum_{j \in [1 \ldots n]-\{i\}} a_j \cdot x_j\right)} \mathrm{VI}_{=}^{+}$$

The next rule is for solving a constraint for the isolated variable x:

$$\frac{a \neq 0}{a \cdot x = \alpha \quad \equiv \quad x = \alpha / a} \text{Eq Elim.}$$

If the variable x is real-valued, then it can be eliminated from the system and replaced by α/a. The rules for integer variable elimination are more complex, but similar in spirit, and are omitted from this version of the paper.

6.3 Proof Rules for Inequalities

The proof rules in this section derive new constraints from already existing ones. These types of rules correspond to the actual Fourier-Motzkin projection of variables from inequalities.

Real shadow. Deriving the real shadow from two opposing constraints makes a simple and obvious proof rule:

$$\frac{\beta < b \cdot x \quad a \cdot x < \alpha}{a \cdot \beta < b \cdot \alpha} \text{Real Shadow.}$$

The rules for introducing dark and gray shadows follow the style of the Real Shadow rule. In its simplified form, the rule can be given as follows:

$$\frac{\beta < b \cdot x \quad a \cdot x < \alpha \quad \mathsf{int}(x)}{\mathbf{D} \vee \mathbf{G}} \text{Int Shadows,}$$

where α and β contain only integer variables, and $\mathbf{D}$ and $\mathbf{G}$ formulas are defined as in the algorithm in section 5.1.

The complete set of rules is described in the full version of this paper [BGD02]. These rules can be thought of as a practical axiomatization of linear arithmetic, where every step in the decision procedure has a corresponding proof rule justifying that step.

7 Conclusion

This paper presents the theory and some implementation detail of an *online* and *proof producing* decision procedure for a theory of mixed-integer linear arithmetic extended with the int() predicate. Additionally, the decision procedure supports arbitrary precision arithmetic.

A decision procedure is much more useful to the research community when it can be combined with other decision procedures. Therefore, designing a stand-alone decision procedure is only the very first step in the design process. The next and more difficult task is to enhance the algorithm with additional properties which enable it to communicate with other decision procedures. Namely, the decision procedure must be *online* and *proof producing*, and must support *backtracking*.

In our experience, conceptually the most difficult is the online property. Just adapting the original Omega-test to an online algorithm required significant efforts (before any implementation!). Proof production is the next difficult problem in the design process. It could have easily been the hardest one if CVC did not already have a thoroughly worked-out methodology for adding proof production to existing decision procedures. Nevertheless, the implementation and especially debugging of proof production still presents a challenge. Finally, backtracking is relatively easy to design and implement in the context of CVC, since the framework provides all the necessary data structures.

Since our algorithm is largely based on Omega-test, its performance is comparable with that of the original implementation of Omega-test. The overhead of the CVC framework and the additional requirements on the decision procedure slow it down by about a factor of 10. This is a very reasonable price to pay for having an arithmetic decision procedure be combined with other powerful decision procedures of CVC.

This reimplementation adds arbitrary precision arithmetic, and generally is much more stable than the Omega library code. The arbitrary precision arithmetic is crucial for solving sizable systems of mixed-integer constraints using Fourier-Motzkin approach, since repeatedly generating shadow constraints produces large coefficients even if the coefficients in the original input are relatively small.

Acknowledgements. The authors would like to thank the principal developers of CVC Aaron Stump and Clark Barrett for many insightful discussions about the theory and implementation of this decision procedure.

References

[BDS00] C. Barrett, D. Dill, and A. Stump. A Framework for Cooperating Decision Procedures. In David McAllester, editor, *17th International Conference on Computer Aided Deduction*, volume 1831 of *LNAI*, pages 79–97. Springer-Verlag, 2000.

[BDS02a] C. Barrett, D. Dill, and A. Stump. A Generalization of Shostak's Method for Combining Decision Procedures. In *4th International Workshop on Frontiers of Combining Systems (FroCos)*, 2002.

[BDS02b] C. Barrett, D. Dill, and A. Stump. Checking Satisfiability of First-Order Formulas by Incremental Translation to SAT. In *14th International Conference on Computer-Aided Verification*, 2002.

[BGD02] Sergey Berezin, Vijay Ganesh, and David L. Dill. Online proof-producing decision procedure for mixed-integer linear arithmetic. Unpublished manuscript. URL: `http://www.cs.cmu.edu/~berez/publications.html`, 2002.

[BT97] Dimitris Bertsimas and John N. Tsitsiklis. *Introduction to Linear Optimization.* Athena Scientific, Belmont, Massachusetts, 1997.

[DE73] George B. Dantzig and B. Curtis Eaves. Fourier-Motzkin elimination and its dual. *Journal of Combinatorial Theory (A)*, 14:288–297, 1973.

[DP60] Martin Davis and Hilary Putnam. A computing procedure for quantification theory. *Journal of the ACM*, 7(3):201–215, July 1960.

[GMP] GMP library for arbitrary precision arithmetic. URL: `http://swox.com/gmp`.

[MMZ+01] M. Moskewicz, C. Madigan, Y. Zhaod, L. Zhang, and S. Malik. Chaff: Engineering an Efficient SAT Solver. In *39th Design Automation Conference*, 2001.

[Möl98] M. Oliver Möller. Solving bit-vector equations – a decision procedure for hardware verification, 1998. Diploma Thesis, available at `http://www.informatik.uni-ulm.de/ki/Bitvector/`.

[MSS99] J. Marques-Silva and K. Sakallah. GRASP: A Search Algorithm for Propositional Satisfiability. *IEEE Transactions on Computers*, 48(5):506–521, 1999.

[NL00] George C. Necula and Peter Lee. Proof generation in the Touchstone theorem prover. In David McAllester, editor, *17th International Conference on Computer-Aided Deduction*, volume 1831 of *Lecture Notes in Artificial Intelligence*. Springer-Verlag, June 2000. Pittsburgh, Pennsylvania.

[NO79] G. Nelson and D. Oppen. Simplification by cooperating decision procedures. *ACM Transactions on Programming Languages and Systems*, 1(2):245–57, 1979.

[Pug91] William Pugh. The omega test: a fast and practical integer programming algorithm for dependence analysis. In *Supercomputing*, pages 4–13, 1991.

[RS01] H. Ruess and N. Shankar. Deconstructing Shostak. In *16th IEEE Symposium on Logic in Computer Science*, 2001.

[SBD02] A. Stump, C. Barrett, and D. Dill. CVC: a Cooperating Validity Checker. In *14th International Conference on Computer-Aided Verification*, 2002.

[SBDL01] A. Stump, C. Barrett, D. Dill, and J. Levitt. A Decision Procedure for an Extensional Theory of Arrays. In *16th IEEE Symposium on Logic in Computer Science*, pages 29–37. IEEE Computer Society, 2001.

[Sho84] R. Shostak. Deciding combinations of theories. *Journal of the Association for Computing Machinery*, 31(1):1–12, 1984.

[SS96] J. P. M. Silva and K. A. Sakallah. GRASP – A new search algorithm for satisfiability. In *Proceedings of the ACM/IEEE International Conference on Computer-Aided Design*, pages 220–227, 11 1996.

[Stu02] A. Stump. *Checking Validities and Proofs with CVC and flea.* PhD thesis, Stanford University, 2002. In preparation: check http://verify.stanford.edu/~ stump/ for a draft.

[Wil76] H. P. Williams. Fourier-Motzkin elimination extension to integer programming problems. *Journal of Combinatorial Theory (A)*, 21:118–123, 1976.

Strategies for Combining Decision Procedures*

Sylvain Conchon[1] and Sava Krstić[2]

[1] École des Mines de Nantes
[2] OGI School of Science & Engineering at Oregon Health & Sciences University

Abstract. Implementing efficient algorithms for combining decision procedures has been a challenge and their correctness precarious. In this paper we describe an inference system that has the classical Nelson-Oppen procedure at its core and includes several optimizations: variable abstraction with sharing, canonization of terms at the theory level, and Shostak's streamlined generation of new equalities for theories with solvers. The transitions of our system are fine-grained enough to model most of the mechanisms currently used in designing combination procedures. In particular, with a simple language of regular expressions we are able to describe several combination algorithms as strategies for our inference system, from the basic Nelson-Oppen to the very highly optimized one recently given by Shankar and Rueß. Presenting the basic system at a high level of generality and nondeterminism allows transparent correctness proofs that can be extended in a modular fashion whenever a new feature is introduced in the system. Similarly, the correctness proof of any new strategy requires only minimal additional proof effort.

1 Introduction

Efficient decision procedures exist for many first-order theories commonly occurring in modeling practice. Linear arithmetic, the pure theory of equality, and theories associated with algebraic datatypes are some examples. Since the interesting properties are often expressed by formulas involving symbols from more than one theory, what one really needs is the integration of these "little engines of proof" into a single efficient tool [12]. Several such systems have been designed [5,15] and used in a variety of applications: general purpose theorem provers, static analysis, extended type checking, hardware verification, etc.

The promise of combination provers is great, but their actual use is still limited and their design is in the state of active research and experimentation. The basic design principles have been set down in the landmark papers of Nelson and Oppen [8] and Shostak [14]. Nelson and Oppen described and proved a general combination algorithm, and Shostak offered an apparently more efficient algorithm, but of restricted scope. What exactly the scope of Shostak's method is has remained unclear for a long time, and it took twenty years to obtain the first correct versions of his algorithm [13,3,6].

* The research reported in this paper was supported by the NSF Grant CCR-9703218. It was performed while S. Conchon was with OGI School of Science & Engineering.

H. Garavel and J. Hatcliff (Eds.): TACAS 2003, LNCS 2619, pp. 537–552, 2003.

On the other hand, correctness of the Nelson and Oppen framework has not been a concern; a pleasing high-level proof is given by Tinelli and Harandi [16]. Correctness becomes a concern, however, as soon as we attempt to describe this framework at a lower level that explicates important implementation features, or to incorporate Shostak's algorithm into it.

Our goal in this paper is to describe the Nelson-Oppen framework at a level that is high enough to enjoy a simple correctness proof (based on the theorem of Tinelli and Harandi), and low enough to incorporate crucial optimizations, like variable abstraction with sharing, theory state normalization, and deduction by lookup.

Our system is described in Section 3 by a set of transformation rules which can be applied in arbitrary order. The generality and nondeterminism expose only the essential parts of the system and allow for simple correctness proofs. They also give us great flexibility to restrict the system further without needing to reprove most of the necessary correctness facts. We demonstrate this in Section 4, by expressing several interesting strategies with a simple language of regular expressions and proving their correctness with only a little extra effort.

We believe we have described the essence of Shostak's method by the rules we present in Section 5. The rules capture the inference pattern that is possible for the so-called *Shostak theories* and that allows these theories to "cooperate" in the Nelson-Oppen framework more efficiently than by using a generic search-and-backtrack mechanism. With these rules added to our inference system, it becomes possible to express complex algorithms, and we show in Section 6 a regular expression that (as a strategy) quite accurately describes the recent algorithm of Shankar and Rueß. The algorithm combines decision procedures of several Shostak theories and is the most detailed algorithm of this kind whose correctness has been proved [13].

2 Notations and Conventions

This section contains the notation and conventions used throughout the paper.

Given a first-order signature Σ and a fixed countable set X of variables, we will denote by $T_\Sigma(X)$ the set of terms constructed over Σ and X. We will use the symbols a, b to denote terms and x, y, z to denote variables. Viewing terms as trees, subterms within a given term a are identified by their positions. Given a position π, a_π denotes the subterm of a at position π, and $a[\pi \mapsto b]$ the term obtained by the *replacement* of a_π by the term b.

For simplicity we will consider only signatures without predicate symbols. *Literals* are thus equations $a \approx b$ between terms over Σ, and disequations $\neg(a \approx b)$ that will be written as $a \not\approx b$. *Formulas* over Σ are built from literals using the standard logical connectives. Sets of formulas are viewed as conjunctions of their elements.

We will write $a \bowtie b$ for a general literal (equation or disequation). If a and b are variables, we say that this literal is *simple*. Sets of simple equations are called *queries* and sets of disjunctions of simple equations are *answers*.

As usual, we say that a formula Φ over Σ is *satisfiable* (resp. *valid*) if it holds for some (resp. all) Σ-models and variable assignments. A *theory* is a satisfiable set of closed formulas over some signature Σ. If $\mathcal{T}$ and Φ are, respectively, a theory and a formula over Σ, we say that Φ is $\mathcal{T}$*-satisfiable* if $\mathcal{T} \cup \{\Phi\}$ is satisfiable. The entailment notation $\mathcal{T}, \Gamma \models \Phi$ means that the implication $\Gamma \longrightarrow \Phi$ holds in all models of $\mathcal{T}$ and for all variable assignments. A *decision procedure* for a theory $\mathcal{T}$ is an algorithm that decides for a given quantifier-free formula Φ whether $\mathcal{T} \models \Phi$ or not. As is well known, having a decision procedure for a theory amounts to having an algorithm that checks satisfiability of sets of literals.

A theory $\mathcal{T}$ is *stably-infinite* if every quantifier-free formula satisfiable in some model of $\mathcal{T}$ is also satisfiable in an infinite model of $\mathcal{T}$. All theories in this paper will be stably-infinite by assumption.

Two theories $\mathcal{T}_1$ and $\mathcal{T}_2$ are *disjoint* if they are defined over two disjoint signatures Σ_1 and Σ_2. We will use the notation $\mathcal{T}_1 + \mathcal{T}_2$ for the union of disjoint theories. Terms over $\Sigma_1 + \Sigma_2$ are usually called *mixed*; a mixed term is a *pure* i-term if its symbols are all in Σ_i.

3 The Equality Propagation Procedure

We present in this section an abstract version of the equality propagation procedure of Nelson and Oppen [8]. It combines decision procedures of disjoint stably-infinite theories into a single decision procedure for the union theory.

3.1 Abstract Combination Procedure

Let $\mathcal{T}_0, \dots, \mathcal{T}_n$ be disjoint stably-infinite theories and $\mathcal{T} = \mathcal{T}_0 + \cdots + \mathcal{T}_n$ the combined theory. In the following, we will use the term *satisfiable* to mean $\mathcal{T}$-satisfiable.

We define the operation of our abstract procedure by a set of inference rules, shown in Figure 1. The rules describe the evolution of the state of the procedure, represented as a *configuration* $\langle V \mathbin{[\!]} \Delta \mathbin{[\!]} \Gamma \mathbin{[\!]} \Phi_0, \dots, \Phi_n \rangle$, where Γ is a set of literals over $\mathcal{T}$, Δ is a set of disjunctions of simple literals, each Φ_i is a set of equations of the form $x \approx a$ where a is an i-term, and V is a set of variables containing those occurring in Γ and Δ. (The set V is redundant, but convenient for bookkeeping purposes.) We also use the symbol $\bot$ as a configuration, and call a configuration *proper* if it is not $\bot$. The aim of our inference system is to determine satisfiability of configurations, formally defined as follows.

Definition 1 (Satisfiability). *A configuration* $\langle V \mathbin{[\!]} \Delta \mathbin{[\!]} \Gamma \mathbin{[\!]} \Phi_0, \dots, \Phi_n \rangle$ *is* satisfiable *if the formula* $\Gamma \wedge \Phi_0 \wedge \cdots \wedge \Phi_n \wedge \Delta$ *is satisfiable. The configuration* $\bot$ *is not satisfiable.*

We say that a configuration $\mathcal{C}$ *reduces* to a configuration $\mathcal{C}'$, written $\mathcal{C} \Rightarrow \mathcal{C}'$, if $\mathcal{C}$ can be transformed into $\mathcal{C}'$ by applying one of the inference rules. Configurations that allow no reductions will be called *irreducible*.

Satisfiability of any set Γ of literals over $\mathcal{T}$ is clearly equivalent to the satisfiability of the corresponding *initial configuration* $\mathcal{C}_\Gamma = \langle V \parallel \emptyset \parallel \Gamma \parallel \emptyset \rangle$, where V is the set of variables in Γ. With this interpretation of Γ as a configuration, and in view of the following theorem, our inference system is indeed a nondeterministic decision procedure for $\mathcal{T}$.

$$\textbf{(Ab)stract}_i \quad \frac{\langle V \parallel \Delta \parallel \Gamma \uplus \{a \bowtie b\} \parallel \ldots, \Phi_i, \ldots \rangle}{\langle V \cup \{z\} \parallel \Delta \parallel \Gamma \cup \{a[\pi \mapsto z] \bowtie b\} \parallel \ldots, \Phi_i \cup \{z \approx a_\pi\}, \ldots \rangle}$$

if $a_\pi \in T_{\Sigma_i}(X);\ a_\pi \notin X;\ z \notin V$

$$\textbf{(Ar)range} \quad \frac{\langle V \parallel \Delta \parallel \Gamma \uplus \{x \bowtie y\} \parallel \Phi_0, \ldots, \Phi_n \rangle}{\langle V \parallel \Delta \cup \{x \bowtie y\} \parallel \Gamma \parallel \Phi_0, \ldots, \Phi_n \rangle}$$

$$\textbf{(De)duct}_i \quad \frac{\langle V \parallel \Delta \parallel \Gamma \parallel \Phi_0, \ldots, \Phi_n \rangle}{\langle V \parallel \Delta \cup \delta \parallel \Gamma \parallel \Phi_0, \ldots, \Phi_n \rangle}$$

if $\mathcal{T}_i, \Phi_i \models \Lambda \longrightarrow \delta;\ \Lambda \subseteq \Delta$ is a query; δ is an answer; $\Delta \not\models \delta$

$$\textbf{(Co)ntradict}_i \quad \frac{\langle V \parallel \Delta \parallel \Gamma \parallel \Phi_0, \ldots, \Phi_n \rangle}{\bot}$$

if $\Phi_i \wedge \Delta$ is not satisfiable

$$\textbf{(Br)anch} \quad \frac{\langle V \parallel \Delta \uplus \{x_1 \approx y_1 \vee \cdots \vee x_k \approx y_k\} \parallel \Gamma \parallel \Phi_1, \ldots, \Phi_n \rangle}{\langle V \parallel \Delta \cup \{x_i \approx y_i\} \parallel \Gamma \parallel \Phi_1, \ldots, \Phi_n \rangle}$$

if $\Delta \not\models x_i \approx y_i;\ 1 \le i \le k$

Fig. 1. Inference system for combining decision procedures

Theorem 1 (Correctness). *A set of formulas Γ is satisfiable if and only if there exists a proper irreducible configuration $\mathcal{C}$ such that $\mathcal{C}_\Gamma \Rightarrow^* \mathcal{C}$.*

We will turn to the proof of Theorem 1 after a brief discussion of the rules. For convenience we treat literals as syntactically symmetric in these rules, so that $a \bowtie b$ also matches $b \bowtie a$. The rules **Abstract**$_i$ $(0 \le i \le n)$ are used to *purify* the literals of Γ. If a_π is a pure i-subterm of a, then **Abstract**$_i$ replaces a_π in a with a new variable z, at the same time adding the equation $z \approx a_\pi$ to the set Φ_i. The rule **Arrange** just transfers simple literals from Γ to Δ. The rules **Contradict**$_i$, **Deduct**$_i$ and **Branch** perform *equality propagation* by moving to Δ new (disjunctions of) simple equations that are valid in some theory $\mathcal{T}_i$.

Given a query part Λ of Δ and an answer set δ entailed by Λ and Φ_i, the rule **Deduct**$_i$ adds δ to Δ if δ is not already entailed by Δ. The rule **Contradict**$_i$ produces the configuration $\bot$ as soon as the state Φ_i becomes incompatible with Δ. Finally, the rule **Branch** performs a case split by choosing an equation from a disjunction of simple equations contained in Δ.

Example 1. The following table shows the reduction of an unsatisfiable initial configuration to $\bot$. It also uses the rule **Share**$_i$ defined later in this section. The theory $\mathcal{T}_1$ is the theory of linear arithmetic and $\mathcal{T}_0$ is the theory of one uninterpreted unary symbol f.

V	Δ	Γ	Φ_0	Φ_1	Rule
x	$\emptyset$	$f(x) \approx x$ $f(2x - f(x)) \not\approx x$	$\emptyset$	$\emptyset$	
x, y	$\emptyset$	$y \approx x$ $f(2x - f(x)) \not\approx x$	$y \approx f(x)$	$\emptyset$	**Ab**$_0$
x, y	$y \approx x$	$f(2x - f(x)) \not\approx x$	$y \approx f(x)$	$\emptyset$	**Ar**
x, y	$y \approx x$	$f(2x - y) \not\approx x$	$y \approx f(x)$	$\emptyset$	**Sh**$_0$
x, y, z	$y \approx x$	$f(z) \not\approx x$	$y \approx f(x)$	$z \approx 2x - y$	**Ab**$_1$
x, y, z, u	$y \approx x$	$u \not\approx x$	$y \approx f(x), u \approx f(z)$	$z \approx 2x - y$	**Ab**$_0$
x, y, z, u	$y \approx x, u \not\approx x$	$\emptyset$	$y \approx f(x), u \approx f(z)$	$z \approx 2x - y$	**Ar**
x, y, z, u	$y \approx x$ $u \not\approx x, z \approx x$	$\emptyset$	$y \approx f(x), u \approx f(z)$	$z \approx 2x - y$	**De**$_1$
		$\bot$			**Co**$_0$

Remark 1. The inference system in Figure 1 leads naturally to a modularly designed combined prover of Nelson-Oppen style depicted in Figure 2. The prover consists of a core module and a set of theory modules. The behavior of the core module is specified using the rules in Figure 1. The rules suggest a natural set of interface functions for theory modules. Correctness of the prover follows from the fact that its behavior can be simulated by the inference system.

3.2 Proof of Theorem 1

The theorem follows from the following four lemmas. We give the proof only of the most important one. Complete proofs are given in the technical report [4].

Lemma 1 (Termination). *The relation $\Rightarrow$ is terminating.*

Lemma 2. *Every proper irreducible configuration is satisfiable.*

Proof. Let $\langle V \,[\!]\, \Delta \,[\!]\, \Gamma \,[\!]\, \Phi_0, \ldots, \Phi_n \rangle$ be a proper irreducible configuration. Since the rules **Abstract**$_i$ and **Arrange** cannot be applied, Γ must be empty. Since **Contradict**$_i$ does not apply, $\Phi_i \wedge \Delta$ is $\mathcal{T}_i$-satisfiable for every i. If Δ is an

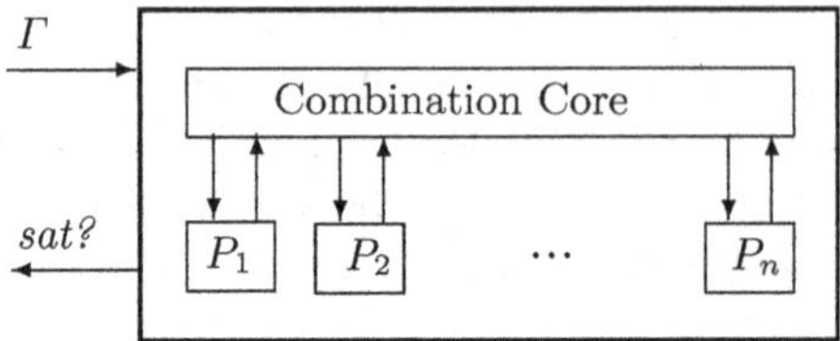

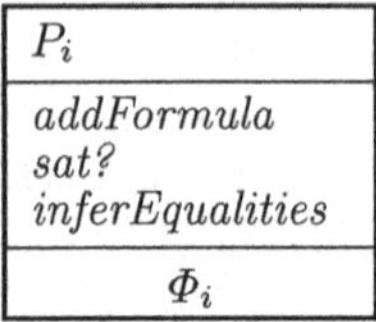

Fig. 2. Rudimentary architecture of a Nelson-Oppen prover based on the inference system in Figure 1. The interface function *addFormula* is needed to implement the rule **Abstract**$_i$; it adds a new pure formula to the state Φ_i of the theory module P_i. Implementation of the rule **Contradict**$_i$ requires the function *sat?* that reports whether P_i's state is inconsistent. Finally, for **Deduct**$_i$ we need the function *inferEqualities* that computes a new disjunction of equalities that can be inferred from Δ and Φ_i.

arrangement[1], then the theorem of Tinelli and Harandi [16] implies that $\Phi_0 \wedge \cdots \wedge \Phi_n \wedge \Delta$ is satisfiable, finishing the proof. If Δ is not an arrangement, we will show that that exists an arrangement Δ' such that $\Delta' \models \Delta$ and such that $\Phi_i \wedge \Delta'$ is $\mathcal{T}_i$-satisfiable. The proof will again follow from the theorem of Tinelli and Harandi.

Take Δ' to be a maximal satisfiable extension $\Delta \cup \{x_1 \not\approx y_1, \ldots, x_k \not\approx y_k\}$ of Δ with disequations that are not entailed by Δ. If for some $x, y \in V$, neither $x \approx y$ nor $x \not\approx y$ is entailed by Δ', then $\Delta' \cup \{x \not\approx y\}$ is a satisfiable extension of Δ', contradicting the maximality assumption about Δ'. Thus, Δ' is an arrangement.

It remains to prove satisfiability of $\Phi_i \wedge \Delta'$. Assuming the contrary, we have that $\Phi_i \wedge \Delta \wedge x_1 \not\approx y_1 \wedge \cdots \wedge x_k \not\approx y_k$ is not $\mathcal{T}_i$-satisfiable. In other words, we have $\mathcal{T}_i, \Phi_i \models \Delta \longrightarrow \delta$ where δ is the answer formula $x_1 \approx y_1 \vee \cdots \vee x_k \approx y_k$. Since the **Branch** rule cannot be applied, Δ must be a set of equations and disequations. Thus, Δ is equivalent to a formula of the form $\Lambda \wedge \neg\delta'$, where Λ is a query and δ' is an answer or false. Thus, we have $\mathcal{T}_i, \Phi_i \models \Lambda \longrightarrow \delta \vee \delta'$. Since the rule **Deduct**$_i$ cannot be applied, we conclude that $\Delta \models \delta \vee \delta'$ and then (since Δ implies $\neg\delta'$) that $\Delta \models \delta$. This contradicts the assumed satisfiability of Δ'.

Lemma 3 (Equisatisfiability). *If $C \Rightarrow C'$ is a non-branching reduction, then C and C' are equisatisfiable.*

Lemma 4 (Branching). *Suppose $C \Rightarrow C'$ is a branching reduction. Then:*

(a) if C' is satisfiable, then C is satisfiable;
(b) if C is satisfiable, then there exists a branching reduction $C \Rightarrow C''$ such that C'' is satisfiable.

Proof of Theorem 1. It suffices to prove that a configuration C is satisfiable if and only if there exists a proper irreducible C' such that $C \Rightarrow^* C'$. If C is irreducible,

[1] Δ is an *arrangement* if for every $x, y \in V$ either $x \approx y$ or $x \not\approx y$ is implied by Δ.

the claim is true by Lemma 2. For non-irreducible $\mathcal{C}$, we have by Lemmas 3 and 4 that $\mathcal{C}$ is satisfiable if and only if there exists a satisfiable $\mathcal{C}'$ such that $\mathcal{C} \Rightarrow \mathcal{C}'$. The proof follows by wellfounded induction over the terminating relation $\Rightarrow$.

3.3 Optimized Variable Abstraction

The rules **Share**$_i$ describe a space-efficient variable abstraction mechanism which allows us to replace a subterm a_π of a term a by an existing variable z which is known by one of the theories to be equal to a_π.

$$\textbf{(Sh)are}_i \quad \frac{\langle V \;[\!]\; \Delta \;[\!]\; \Gamma \uplus \{a \bowtie b\} \;[\!]\; \Phi_0, \ldots, \Phi_n\rangle}{\langle V \;[\!]\; \Delta \;[\!]\; \Gamma \cup \{a[\pi \mapsto z] \bowtie b\} \;[\!]\; \Phi_0, \ldots, \Phi_n\rangle}$$

if $a_\pi \in T_{\Sigma_i}(X)$; $a_\pi \notin X$; $\mathcal{T}_i, \Phi_i \models \Lambda \longrightarrow z \approx a_\pi$; $\Lambda \subseteq \Delta$ is a query

It is not difficult to show that Theorem 1 and the four lemmas needed for its proof all remain valid when the system in Figure 1 is extended by adding the rules **Share**$_i$.

3.4 Deduction in the Case of Convex Theories

A theory $\mathcal{T}$ is called *convex* if for every set Λ of literals the truth of a judgment of the form $\mathcal{T} \models \Lambda \longrightarrow a_1 \approx b_1 \vee \cdots \vee a_k \approx b_k$ implies $\mathcal{T} \models \Lambda \longrightarrow a_i \approx b_i$ for some i. This property allows us to simplify the system of Figure 1 by strengthening the side condition of **Deduct**$_i$ with an additional requirement that the answer formula δ be a single equation. Let us call this modified rule **DeductConvex**$_i$. The following theorem states that the system will remain correct after this change; the proof of Theorem 1 applies almost verbatim and only Lemma 2 requires a (straightforward) modification.

Theorem 2. *The correctness result expressed in Theorem 1 remains valid if for every convex theory $\mathcal{T}_i$ we replace the rule* **Deduct**$_i$ *in the inference system in Figure 1 with the rule* **DeductConvex**$_i$.

Corollary 1. *If all theories $\mathcal{T}_0, \ldots, \mathcal{T}_n$ are convex, then Theorem 1 remains valid when all the rules* **Deduct**$_i$ *are replaced with* **DeductConvex**$_i$ *and the rule* **Branch** *is excluded from the system.*

4 Strategies

Strategies introduce determinism in our inference system by constraining the shape of reduction chains. A variety of strategies can be described by using the simple language given in Figure 3. It is the language of regular expressions over the set of basic actions (rules of our inference system), extended with the operator $\oplus$. The figure also gives the semantics of the language: the concatenation

$(\cdot)$, and choice $(+)$ operators have their standard meaning, the star $(*)$ is for exhaustive application, and $\oplus$ denotes a left-associative choice that gives preference to its left argument. Clearly, every strategy e is sound in the sense that $\mathcal{C} \Rightarrow_e \mathcal{C}'$ implies $\mathcal{C} \Rightarrow^* \mathcal{C}'$.

$$a ::= \mathbf{Ab}_i \mid \mathbf{Ar} \mid \mathbf{Sh}_i \mid \mathbf{De}_i \mid \mathbf{Co} \mid \mathbf{Br}$$
$$e ::= a \mid e + e \mid e^* \mid e \cdot e \mid e \oplus e$$

$$\frac{\mathcal{C} \Rightarrow \mathcal{C}' \quad \text{by applying the rule } a}{\mathcal{C} \Rightarrow_a \mathcal{C}'}$$

$$\frac{\mathcal{C} \Rightarrow_e \mathcal{C}' \qquad \mathcal{C}' \Rightarrow_{e'} \mathcal{C}''}{\mathcal{C} \Rightarrow_{e \cdot e'} \mathcal{C}''} \qquad \frac{\mathcal{C}_0 \Rightarrow_e \cdots \Rightarrow_e \mathcal{C}_n \not\Rightarrow_e \qquad 0 \leq n}{\mathcal{C}_0 \Rightarrow_{e^*} \mathcal{C}_n}$$

$$\frac{\mathcal{C} \Rightarrow_e \mathcal{C}'}{\mathcal{C} \Rightarrow_{e+e'} \mathcal{C}'} \qquad \frac{\mathcal{C} \Rightarrow_{e'} \mathcal{C}'}{\mathcal{C} \Rightarrow_{e+e'} \mathcal{C}'} \qquad \frac{\mathcal{C} \Rightarrow_e \mathcal{C}'}{\mathcal{C} \Rightarrow_{e \oplus e'} \mathcal{C}'} \qquad \frac{\mathcal{C} \not\Rightarrow_e \qquad \mathcal{C} \Rightarrow_{e'} \mathcal{C}'}{\mathcal{C} \Rightarrow_{e \oplus e'} \mathcal{C}'}$$

Fig. 3. Syntax and semantics of a simple language for strategies.

For most of this section we will assume that all theories $\mathcal{T}_i$ are convex. Then, if a strategy e satisfies the condition

(S-1) *For every $\mathcal{C}$, there exists $\mathcal{C}'$ such that $\mathcal{C} \Rightarrow_e \mathcal{C}'$, and all such $\mathcal{C}'$ are irreducible.*

then e implements a decision procedure for the union theory $\mathcal{T}$. Indeed, for a given input Γ, we just need to find $\mathcal{C}'$ such that $\mathcal{C}_\Gamma \Rightarrow_e \mathcal{C}'$ and check whether $\mathcal{C}' = \bot$.

We will show several examples of strategies satisfying the property (S-1). Then we will see how to incorporate branching in the case when there are non-convex theories in the system.

4.1 The Basic Strategy

The following expression describes the original Nelson-Oppen algorithm for the disjoint union of convex theories.

$$\mathbf{Ab}^* \cdot \mathbf{Ar}^* \cdot (\mathbf{Co} \oplus \mathbf{De})^* \tag{1}$$

The action **Ab** is an abbreviation for $\mathbf{Ab}_0 + \cdots + \mathbf{Ab}_n$ and similarly **De** is the sum of all $\mathbf{De}_i$ (which are now $\mathbf{DeductConvex}_i$). The effect of $\mathbf{Ab}^*$ is "purification" of Γ; it reduces Γ to a set of simple literals. The action $\mathbf{Ar}^*$ then moves all these literals to Δ. Thus, $\mathbf{Ab}^* \cdot \mathbf{Ar}^*$ describes a strategy for the variable abstraction part of the algorithm.

The remaining expression $(\mathbf{Co} \oplus \mathbf{De})^*$ describes the equality propagation mechanism of the algorithm: repeated application of the rules $\mathbf{Contradict}_i$ or $\mathbf{DeductConvex}_i$ until the $\bot$ configuration is reached, or no more equations between variables can be deduced.

When applied to an arbitrary configuration $\mathcal{C}$, the strategy $\mathbf{Ab}^* \cdot \mathbf{Ar}^*$ produces configurations with empty Δ-part that are all equisatisfiable with $\mathcal{C}$. If $\mathcal{C}'$ is any of these configurations, and if it can be reduced in the original system, then every step in any reduction chain of $\mathcal{C}'$ must be by one of the rules $\mathbf{Contradict}_i$ or $\mathbf{DeductConvex}_i$. Thus, the strategy $(\mathbf{Co} \oplus \mathbf{De})^*$ when applied to $\mathcal{C}'$ produces irreducible configurations. This proves that the strategy (1) satisfies the property (S-1).

4.2 An Incremental Strategy

The following expression describes an incremental version of the strategy (1) which processes one literal of Γ at a time.

$$\left((\mathbf{Va}^1 + \cdots + \mathbf{Va}^m) \cdot (\mathbf{Co} \oplus \mathbf{De})^*\right)^* \tag{2}$$

Here we use $\mathbf{Va}^j$ as an abbreviation for the strategy $\mathbf{Ab}^* \cdot \mathbf{Ar}$ applied only to the jth literal of Γ. (A precise definition would require primitive actions $\mathbf{Ab}_i^j$ and $\mathbf{Ar}^j$.) The main idea of the strategy is that processing a new literal begins only after it has been checked that the contradiction cannot be reached from the literals that have already been processed.

When applied to a configuration $\mathcal{C} = \langle V \,[\!]\, \Delta \,[\!]\, \Gamma \,[\!]\, \Phi_0, \ldots, \Phi_n \rangle$, the strategy $\mathbf{Va}^1 + \cdots + \mathbf{Va}^m$ fails only if Γ is empty; otherwise, it produces configurations of the form $\langle V' \,[\!]\, \Delta' \,[\!]\, \Gamma' \,[\!]\, \Phi'_0, \ldots, \Phi'_n \rangle$, where Γ' is obtained by removing one literal from Γ. The outer closure operator in (2) guarantees that when the strategy (2) is applied to $\mathcal{C}$, the result will be a configuration equisatisfiable to $\mathcal{C}$ that is either $\bot$ or of the form $\mathcal{C}' = \langle V \,[\!]\, \Delta \,[\!]\, \emptyset \,[\!]\, \Phi_0, \ldots, \Phi_n \rangle$. Similarly as in the case of the strategy (1), we can see that $\mathcal{C}'$ is actually irreducible, proving that (2) satisfies (S-1).

4.3 Strategies with Sharing

The variable abstraction part of the previous strategies can be optimized against proliferation of new variables by an aggressive use of the rules $\mathbf{Share}_i$. Introducing sharing into the basic strategy gives

$$(\mathbf{Sh} \oplus \mathbf{Ab})^* \cdot \mathbf{Ar}^* \cdot (\mathbf{Co} \oplus \mathbf{De})^* \tag{3}$$

Similarly, the incremental strategy (2) can be optimized by replacing the action $\mathbf{Va}^j$ in it with the appropriate form of $(\mathbf{Sh} \oplus \mathbf{Ab})^* \cdot \mathbf{Ar}$. Checking the property (S-1) for these strategies proceeds as in the case of strategies (1) and (2), with minimal changes.

4.4 Branching Strategies

If some of the component theories $\mathcal{T}_i$ are not convex, then the corresponding rules **Deduct**$_i$ must be used in place of the simpler **DeductConvex**$_i$. The answer sets δ can now contain disjunctions and case splitting may be necessary to check the satisfiability of a configuration. A strategy that implements a decision procedure now must satisfy the following additional condition.

(S-2) *If $\mathcal{C}$ is satisfiable, then there exists a satisfiable $\mathcal{C}'$ such that $\mathcal{C} \Rightarrow_e \mathcal{C}'$.*

Since branching is expensive, the obvious approach is to use it only when everything else fails. This gives us strategies

$$(\mathbf{NO} \oplus \mathbf{Br})^* \tag{4}$$

where **NO** denotes any of the above strategies (1), (2) and (3) with **De**$_i$ denoting **DeductConvex**$_i$ or **Deduct**$_i$, depending on whether $\mathcal{T}_i$ is convex or not. We know that **NO** will reduce any configuration into one to which no rule applies, except possibly **Branch**. It follows that the strategy (4) produces only irreducible configurations. It is easy to check, using Lemma 4 that this strategy also satisfies (S-2).

5 Shostak Optimization

A modular design of a decision procedure for the combined theory $\mathcal{T} = \mathcal{T}_0 + \cdots + \mathcal{T}_n$ can be derived from the inference system given in Section 3. In Remark 1 and Figure 2 we sketched such a design. Note that the strategies of the previous section are possible ways of programming the control core module. The requirements for the theory modules can be seen from Figure 1: the rule **Abstract**$_i$ needs support for addition of a new formula to the state Φ_i of the theory module; **Contradict**$_i$ needs a decision procedure for $\mathcal{T}_i$; and **Deduct**$_i$ needs generation of answers from input queries. In principle, a theory module can implement this last task on top of its decision procedure: with a given input query Λ, it can search for an answer δ such that $\Lambda \wedge \neg\delta$ is unsatisfiable.

Now, for some theories there exist more efficient algorithms for computing answers to given queries. A prime example is the *free theory* over a signature consisting of uninterpreted functions, where the *congruence closure algorithm* [9,1] can process the input query and change its state appropriately so that new equations between variables can be directly seen from it. Shostak made an important discovery that a similar inference pattern is possible for many other theories [14]. Roughly speaking, the theory module maintains a union-find data structure on a set of terms so that the answer equation $x \approx y$ is deduced by checking that $\mathsf{find}(x) = \mathsf{find}(y)$ is true. To make such "trivial deduction" possible, the theory module must have some powerful mechanism for processing input queries. We describe it abstractly below by the concept of "state normalization" which essentially means bringing a set of equations (the original state together with the query equations) to some kind of normal form from which the maximum information about equalities between variables can be directly drawn.

To formalize the pattern, we need to make several assumptions. The first is that $\mathcal{T}_i$ is a convex theory with a *canonizer.* A canonizer is a function that for every term a returns a unique representative $\mathsf{canon}_i(a)$ in the equivalence class of the relation $\mathcal{T}_i \models a \approx b$.[2] A $\mathcal{T}_i$-term a is in *canonical form* when $\mathsf{canon}_i(a) = a$.

We will also assume that there is a function that picks a representative from each class of the equivalence relation on V defined by $\Delta \models x \approx y$. The representative of x will simply be denoted $\Delta(x)$. Extending this notation to terms, we will also write $\Delta(a)$ for the term in which every variable x is replaced by its representative $\Delta(x)$.

The following rule **TDeduct**$_i$ is a trivial special case of **Deduct**$_i$, where the answer $x \approx y$ is found by a simple lookup into the state. Similarly, **TShare**$_i$ is a special case of **Share**$_i$ that finds the required shared variable by inspecting the state.

$$\textbf{(TDe)duct}_i \qquad \frac{\langle V \,[\!]\, \Delta \,[\!]\, \Gamma \,[\!]\, \dots, \Phi_i \cup \{x \approx a, y \approx a\}, \dots\rangle}{\langle V \,[\!]\, \Delta \cup \{x \approx y\} \,[\!]\, \Gamma \,[\!]\, \dots, \Phi_i \cup \{x \approx a, y \approx a\}, \dots\rangle}$$

if $\Delta(x) \neq \Delta(y)$

$$\textbf{(TSh)are}_i \qquad \frac{\langle V \,[\!]\, \Delta \,[\!]\, \Gamma \uplus \{a \bowtie b\} \,[\!]\, \dots, \Phi_i \cup \{z \approx c\}, \dots\rangle}{\langle V \,[\!]\, \Delta \,[\!]\, \Gamma \cup \{a[\pi \mapsto z] \bowtie b\} \,[\!]\, \dots, \Phi_i \cup \{z \approx c\}, \dots\rangle}$$

if $a_\pi \in T_{\Sigma_i}(X)$; $a_\pi \notin X$; $\mathsf{canon}_i(\Delta(a_\pi)) = c$

The concept of state normalization requires a *normalization function* $\mathcal{N}_i$. If Φ_i' is the state obtained by adding equations of Δ to Φ_i, the idea is that $\mathcal{N}_i(\Phi_i, \Delta)$ denotes the first intermediate result in the (possibly multi-step) normalization process from Φ_i' to its normal form.

$$\textbf{(Nor)m}_i \qquad \frac{\langle V \,[\!]\, \Delta \,[\!]\, \Gamma \,[\!]\, \dots, \Phi_i, \dots\rangle}{\langle V \,[\!]\, \Delta \,[\!]\, \Gamma \,[\!]\, \dots, \mathcal{N}_i(\Phi_i, \Delta), \dots\rangle}$$

if $\mathcal{N}_i(\Phi_i, \Delta) \neq \Phi_i$

In order to make the Shostak inference pattern possible, the normalization function has to satisfy the following conditions.

Termination: There exists k such that $\mathcal{N}_i^k(\Phi_i, \Delta) = \mathcal{N}_i^{k+1}(\Phi_i, \Delta)$;

Equisatisfiability: $\mathcal{T}_i \models \Phi_i \wedge \Delta \longleftrightarrow \mathcal{N}_i(\Phi_i, \Delta) \wedge \Delta$;

Completeness: If $\mathcal{T}_i, \Phi_i, \Delta \models x \approx y$ and $\Delta(x) \neq \Delta(y)$, then there exist k and a such that $\mathcal{N}_i^k(\Phi_i, \Delta)$ contains equations $x \approx a$ and $y \approx a$.

[2] Some proofs require that canonizers satisfy additional conditions. It is safe to assume that: (1) $\mathsf{canon}_i(a)$ contains only variables that occur in a; (2) all subterms of a term in canonical form are canonical too; cf. [13].

Lemma 5. *If the above three conditions are satisfied, then Theorem 2 remains valid when the rule* $\mathbf{DeductConvex}_i$ *is replaced by* $\mathbf{Norm}_i$ *and* $\mathbf{TDeduct}_i$.

It can also be proved that $\mathbf{Norm}_i$ and $\mathbf{TShare}_i$ together have equal optimizing effect as $\mathbf{Share}_i$. A necessary condition for this is that the normalization produces equations in which the right-hand side is in canonical form and contains only representative variables.

Presently, concrete examples of normalization are known only for the free theories and for Shostak theories. Before describing them, we give two rules that bring canonization of terms and substitution of variables with their representatives into our system. These rules simplify the state Φ_i at the term level and are the reasonable first step for any state normalization function.

$$\textbf{(Su)bst}_i \quad \frac{\langle V \mathrel{[\!]} \Delta \mathrel{[\!]} \Gamma \mathrel{[\!]} \dots, \Phi_i \uplus \{x \approx a\}, \dots\rangle}{\langle V \mathrel{[\!]} \Delta \mathrel{[\!]} \Gamma \mathrel{[\!]} \dots, \Phi_i \cup \{x \approx \Delta(a)\}, \dots\rangle}$$

if $a \neq \Delta(a)$ for some i

$$\textbf{(Ca)nonize}_i \quad \frac{\langle V \mathrel{[\!]} \Delta \mathrel{[\!]} \Gamma \mathrel{[\!]} \dots, \Phi_i \uplus \{x \approx a\}, \dots\rangle}{\langle V \mathrel{[\!]} \Delta \mathrel{[\!]} \Gamma \mathrel{[\!]} \dots, \Phi_i \cup \{x \approx \mathsf{canon}_i(a)\}, \dots\rangle}$$

if $a \neq \mathsf{canon}_i(a)$

5.1 Free Theories

To define the state normalization function for a free theory $\mathcal{T}_i$, we need to assume that every variable in V occurs as the left-hand side in at least one equation of Φ_i, and that all equations of Φ_i are of the form $x \approx y$ or $x \approx f(y_1, \dots, y_k)$, where x and y_i are variables in V. (That is, the right-hand sides can contain at most one occurrence of functional symbols.) The normalization function $\mathcal{N}_i$ just picks one of the equations and replaces the variables on its right-hand side with their Δ-representatives. In other words, in this case we have $\mathbf{Norm}_i = \mathbf{Su}_i$.

Proving that the assumptions of Lemma 5 hold for this normalization function amounts to proving correctness of the congruence closure algorithm.

5.2 Shostak Theories

Some theories admit solutions to equations. A *solver* for a theory $\mathcal{T}$ is an algorithm solve that takes a $\mathcal{T}$-equation $u \approx v$ as input, and if this equation is $\mathcal{T}$-satisfiable, solve returns its general solution in the form of an equisatisfiable set of equations

$$x_1 \approx t_1, \dots, x_k \approx t_k,$$

where the variables $x_1, \dots x_k$ are those occurring in $u \approx v$ and none of them occurs in the terms t_i. (For more details about solvers, see [13,3,6].)

By definition, a *Shostak theory* is a convex theory with a canonizer and a solver. If $\mathcal{T}_i$ is a Shostak theory, we assume that every variable occurs at most once as a left-hand side in the equations of Φ_i, and if it does have such an occurrence, then it does not occur in any right-hand side. That is, viewed as a substitution, Φ_i is idempotent.

The normalization for a Shostak theory can now be defined by

$$\mathbf{Norm}_i = \mathbf{Ca}_i \oplus \mathbf{So}_i \oplus \mathbf{Su}_i$$

where the crucial new rule $\mathbf{Solve}_i$ is as follows.

$$(\mathbf{So})\mathbf{lve}_i \qquad \frac{\langle V \parallel \Delta \parallel \Gamma \parallel \ldots, \Phi_i \cup \{x \approx a, y \approx b\}, \ldots\rangle}{\langle V \parallel \Delta \parallel \Gamma \parallel \ldots, (\Phi_i \cup \{x \approx a, y \approx b\} \cup \mathsf{solve}(a = b))^2, \ldots\rangle}$$

if $\Delta(x) = \Delta(y)$; $a \neq b$; $a \approx b$ is $\mathcal{T}_i$-satisfiable

To explain the rule, we note first that the variables on the left-hand sides in the set $\mathsf{solve}(a = b)$ are those of a and b, and so no variable occurs twice as a left-hand side in $\Psi = \Phi_i \cup \{x \approx a, y \approx b\} \cup \mathsf{solve}(a = b)$. Thus, Ψ defines a substitution. It is not idempotent since the variables of a and b occur also in right-hand sides of Ψ. However, the composition $\Psi^2 = \Psi \circ \Psi$ is easily seen to be idempotent, and regarded as a set of equations, it is equisatisfiable with Ψ. Thus, Ψ^2 has all the properties required for the state.

Proving that the state normalization of Shostak theories satisfies the conditions of Lemma 5 requires an effort commensurable with proving correctness of the "single theory Shostak algorithm" (Algorithm S1 of [3]). As a consequence we obtain that for a Shostak theory $\mathcal{T}_i$ the set of rules $\mathbf{Subst}_i$, $\mathbf{Canonize}_i$, $\mathbf{Solve}_i$, $\mathbf{TDeduct}_i$ and $\mathbf{TShare}_i$ can replace $\mathbf{DeductConvex}_i$ and $\mathbf{Share}_i$ in our system.

6 The Shankar-Rueß Algorithm

A highly efficient algorithm to combine decision procedures of a free theory and several Shostak theories has recently been given and proved correct by Shankar and Rueß [13]. We show now that their algorithm can be with reasonable precision described as a strategy in the language of Section 4 extended with actions corresponding to the rules introduced in Section 5. As in [13], we assume that the free theory is $\mathcal{T}_0$, and that $\mathcal{T}_1, \ldots, \mathcal{T}_n$ are Shostak theories. The strategy is given by the expression

$$\left(\mathbf{abstraction} \cdot (\mathbf{Co} \oplus \mathbf{merge} \oplus \mathbf{infer} \oplus \mathbf{normalize})^*\right)^* \qquad (5)$$

where

$$\begin{aligned}
\mathbf{abstraction} &= (\mathbf{Va}^1 \oplus \cdots \oplus \mathbf{Va}^m) \cdot \mathbf{Su}_0^* \\
\mathbf{merge} &= (\mathbf{So}_1 \cdot \mathbf{Ca}_1^*) + \cdots + (\mathbf{So}_n \cdot \mathbf{Ca}_n^*) \\
\mathbf{infer} &= (\mathbf{TDe}_0 + \cdots + \mathbf{TDe}_n) \cdot \mathbf{Su}_0^* \\
\mathbf{normalize} &= (\mathbf{Su}_1 + \cdots + \mathbf{Su}_n) \cdot (\mathbf{Su}_1^* \cdots \mathbf{Su}_n^*)
\end{aligned}$$

Here **Va** denotes the strategy $(\mathbf{TSh} \oplus \mathbf{ASC})^* \cdot \mathbf{Ar}$, where **TSh** is the sum of all $\mathbf{TSh}_i$ and **ASC** is the sum of all $\mathbf{Ab}_i \cdot \mathbf{Su}_i^* \cdot \mathbf{Ca}_i^*$. As before, superscirpts indicate application to a particular literal of Γ.

The algorithm starts by executing an efficient *incremental* variable abstraction; hence the superscripts in **abstraction** and the outer star operator in (5). **abstraction** generates new equations only when the rules $\mathbf{TShare}_i$ fail to find shared variables. It also maintains the sets Φ_i in normal form by applying $\mathbf{Subst}_i$ and $\mathbf{Canonize}_i$ exhaustively. After this step comes the equality propagation mechanism. It immediately examines all theory states attempting to find a contradiction in one. If this fails, every Φ_i is satisfiable, and then the state normalization is initiated by **merge** which solves one equation $x \approx y$ in some Shostak theory state Φ_i when the variables x and y are equal in Δ but not yet in Φ_i. **merge** finishes by restoring the normal form of Φ_i with exhaustive application of $\mathbf{Canonize}_i$. ($\mathbf{Subst}_i$ is unnecessary here, since the right-hand side variables of Φ_i are all representatives.) When the state is in normal form and if x and y are equal in some Φ_i but not in Δ, **infer** propagates the new equality $x \approx y$ to Δ and normalizes the set Φ_0 by applying $\mathbf{Subst}_0$ exhaustively. Finally, **normalize** substitutes the variables in the Shostak theory states Φ_i by their new representatives which may have been added to Δ by **infer**.

7 Conclusion and Related Work

We have presented results of our initial study of design of correct algorithms for combining decision procedures. Having in mind a modular implementation with theory modules as black boxes and a programmable control core module, we formalized the entire system as an inference system that is convenient to reason about and to refine. Our system is of Nelson-Oppen type, but we have shown that the congruence closure algorithm and the Shostak algorithm can be incorporated into it with additional rules so that overall correctness is preserved. We have given a simple strategy language capable of expressing complex combination algorithms. Proving correctness of a concrete algorithm written as a strategy is reduced to proving one or two simple properties of the strategy; the rest follows from the correctness of the whole system.

The Nelson-Oppen method has been widely adopted as the basis for combination algorithms [12]. Its bare bones versions are described and proved correct by Ringeissen [10] and by Tinelli and Harandi [16]. We work at the level of abstraction that is close to these works, but our system is extended with implementation-related details.

A series of recent papers is devoted to proofs of correctness of various versions of the Shostak algorithm. Rueß and Shankar [11] and Ganzinger [6] consider the algorithm for combining a free theory with one Shostak theory. In Barrett, Dill and Stump [3], the algorithm is for the combination of a Shostak theory with any convex theory. Finally, Shankar and Rueß [13] settle the case of a free theory combined with an arbitrary number of Shostak theories. (The same case is considered in the preliminary draft [7].) We have borrowed from all these sources.

In particular, the idea to model the whole system by state-transformation rules is already in [6] and in [1,17], which also uses regular expressions to express various strategies for the same system. Our system allows arbitrary combinations of stably-infinite theories and so is significantly more general. Moreover, this generality does not come at the price of ignoring important details, as demonstrated by modeling the Shankar-Rueß algorithm as a strategy for our system.

We leave for future work a description of a modular implementation of our system, with precise interfaces for theory modules. The intention is to establish correctness of such an implementation by simulating it in our abstract system. A similar project has been carried out very recently by Barrett [2]. He verified a combination procedure described as a modular system with an impressive list of implementation features; his system includes non-convex theories, but allows only one Shostak theory. We believe our approach will lead to shorter and more general proofs.

We also believe our work will contribute to the understanding of the scope of the Shostak algorithm. We hypothesize that in a modular implementation there is no advantage in allowing the core module to have access to Shostak module primitives (canonizer and solver); the same efficiency can be achieved with a plain Nelson-Oppen core that communicates with Shostak theory modules through generic theory module interfaces, while canonizer and solver are used only to implement those interfaces. If this is correct, the Shostak algorithm would largely be a single theory affair; cf. [3]. We expect to gain some insights by comparing the complexity (number of reductions needed for a given initial configuration) of the Rueß-Shankar strategy against our best strategy that uses Shostak theories in a generic way.

Acknowledgments. We thank John Matthews and Andrew Tolmach for valuable discussions, comments, and corrections.

References

1. L. Bachmair, A. Tiwari, and L. Vigneron. Abstract congruence closure. *Journal of Automated Reasoning*, 2002. To appear.
2. C. Barrett. *Checking Validity of Quantifier-free formulas in Combinations of First-Order Theories.* PhD thesis, Stanford University, 2002.
3. C. W. Barrett, D. L. Dill, and A. Stump. A generalization of Shostak's method for combining decision procedures. In *Frontiers of Combining Systems (FROCOS)*, volume 2309 of *Lecture Notes in Artificial Intelligence*, pages 132–147. Springer-Verlag, 2002.
4. S. Conchon and S. Krstic. Strategies for combining decision procedures. Technical Report CSE-03-001, OHSU, 2003.
5. J.-C. Filliâtre, S. Owre, H. Rueß, and N. Shankar. ICS: Integrated Canonization and Solving (Tool presentation). In G. Berry, H. Comon, and A. Finkel, editors, *Proceedings of CAV'2001*, volume 2102 of *Lecture Notes in Computer Science*, pages 246–249. Springer-Verlag, 2001.

6. H. Ganzinger. Shostak light. In A. Voronkov, editor, *Automated Deduction – CADE-18*, volume 2392 of *Lecture Notes in Artificial Intelligence*, pages 332–347. Springer-Verlag, 2002.
7. D. Kapur. A rewrite rule based framework for combining decision procedures. In *Frontiers of Combining Systems (FROCOS)*, volume 2309 of *Lecture Notes in Artificial Intelligence*, pages 87–103. Springer-Verlag, 2002.
8. G. Nelson and D. C. Oppen. Simplification by cooperating decision procedures. *ACM Transactions on Programming Languages and Systems*, 1(2):245–257, 1979.
9. G. Nelson and D. C. Oppen. Fast decision procedures based on congruence closure. *JACM*, 27(2):356–364, 1980.
10. Ch. Ringeissen. Cooperation of Decision Procedures for the Satisfiability Problem. In F. Baader and K. U. Schulz, editors, *Frontiers of Combining Systems: Proceedings of the 1st International Workshop*, Applied Logic, pages 121–140. Kluwer Academic Publishers, 1996.
11. H. Rueß and N. Shankar. Deconstructing Shostak. In *Proceedings of the 16th Annual IEEE Symposium on Logic in Computer Science (LICS-01)*, pages 19–28. IEEE Computer Society, 2001.
12. N. Shankar. Little engines of proof. In L.-H. Eriksson and P. Lindsay, editors, *FME 2002: Formal Methods – Getting IT Right*, pages 1–20, Copenhagen, 2002. Springer-Verlag.
13. N. Shankar and H. Rueß. Combining Shostak theories. In S. Tison, editor, *Rewriting Techniques and Applications (RTA)*, volume 2378 of *Lecture Notes in Computer Science*, pages 1–19. Springer-Verlag, 2002.
14. R. E. Shostak. Deciding combinations of theories. *Journal of the ACM*, 31(1):1–12, 1984.
15. A. Stump, C. Barrett, and D. Dill. CVC: a Cooperating Validity Checker. In *14th International Conference on Computer-Aided Verification*, 2002.
16. C. Tinelli and M. T. Harandi. A new correctness proof of the Nelson–Oppen combination procedure. In F. Baader and K. U. Schulz, editors, *Frontiers of Combining Systems: Proceedings of the 1st International Workshop*, Applied Logic, pages 103–120. Kluwer Academic Publishers, 1996.
17. A. Tiwari. *Decision Procedures in Automated Deduction.* PhD thesis, University of Stony Brook, 2000.

Generalized Symbolic Execution for Model Checking and Testing

Sarfraz Khurshid[1], Corina S. Păsăreanu[2], and Willem Visser[3]

[1] MIT Laboratory for Computer Science, Cambridge, MA 02139, USA
khurshid@lcs.mit.edu
[2] Kestrel Technology LLC and [3] RIACS/USRA,
NASA Ames Research Center, Moffett Field, CA 94035, USA
{pcorina,wvisser}@email.arc.nasa.gov

Abstract. Modern software systems, which often are concurrent and manipulate complex data structures must be extremely reliable. We present a novel framework based on symbolic execution, for automated checking of such systems. We provide a two-fold generalization of traditional symbolic execution based approaches. First, we define a source to source translation to instrument a program, which enables standard model checkers to perform symbolic execution of the program. Second, we give a novel symbolic execution algorithm that handles dynamically allocated structures (e.g., lists and trees), method preconditions (e.g., acyclicity), data (e.g., integers and strings) and concurrency. The program instrumentation enables a model checker to automatically explore different program heap configurations and manipulate logical formulae on program data (using a decision procedure). We illustrate two applications of our framework: checking correctness of multi-threaded programs that take inputs from unbounded domains with complex structure and generation of non-isomorphic test inputs that satisfy a testing criterion. Our implementation for Java uses the Java PathFinder model checker.

1 Introduction

Modern software systems, which often are concurrent and manipulate complex dynamically allocated data structures (e.g., linked lists or binary trees), must be extremely reliable and correct. Two commonly used techniques for checking correctness of such systems are testing and model checking. Testing is widely used but usually involves manual test input generation. Furthermore, testing is not good at finding errors related to concurrent behavior. Model checking, on the other hand, is automatic and particularly good at analyzing (concurrent) reactive systems. A drawback of model checking is that it suffers from the state-space explosion problem and typically requires a closed system, i.e., a system together with its environment, and a bound on input sizes [9,19,6,4].

We present a novel framework based on *symbolic execution* [14], which automates test case generation, allows model checking concurrent programs that take inputs from unbounded domains with complex structure, and helps combat state-space explosion. Symbolic execution is a well known program analysis

H. Garavel and J. Hatcliff (Eds.): TACAS 2003, LNCS 2619, pp. 553–568, 2003.

technique, which represents values of program variables with *symbolic values* instead of concrete (initialized) data and manipulates expressions involving symbolic values. Symbolic execution traditionally arose in the context of checking sequential programs with a fixed number of integer variables. Several recent approaches [5, 3, 7] extend the traditional notion of symbolic execution to perform various program analyses; these approaches, however, require dedicated tools to perform the analyses and do not handle concurrent systems with complex inputs.

We provide a two-fold generalization of traditional symbolic execution. First, we define a source to source translation to instrument a program, which enables symbolic execution of the program to be performed using a standard model checker (for the underlying language) without having to build a dedicated tool. The instrumented program can be symbolically executed by any model checker that supports nondeterministic choice. The model checker checks the program by automatically exploring different program heap configurations and manipulating logical formulae on program data values (using a decision procedure).

Second, we give a novel symbolic execution algorithm that handles dynamically allocated structures (e.g., lists and trees), method preconditions (e.g., acyclicity of lists), data (e.g., integers and strings) and concurrency. To symbolically execute a method, the algorithm uses *lazy initialization*, i.e., it initializes the components of the method inputs on an "as-needed" basis, without requiring a priori bound on input sizes. We use method preconditions to initialize fields only with valid values and method postconditions as test oracles to check method's correctness; this builds on our previous work on the Korat framework [2] for specification-based testing. We also support partial correctness properties given as assertions in the program and temporal specifications.

The main contributions of our work are:

- Providing a two-fold generalization of symbolic execution: one, to enable a standard model checker to perform symbolic execution; two, to give a symbolic execution algorithm that handles advanced programming constructs;
- Performing symbolic execution of code during explicit state model checking
  - to address the state space explosion problem: we check the behavior of code using symbolic values that represent data from very large domains instead of enumerating and checking for a small set of concrete values;
  - to achieve modularity: checking programs with uninitialized variables allows checking of a compilation unit in isolation;
  - to check strong correctness properties of concurrent programs that take inputs from unbounded domains with complex structure;
  - to exploit the model checker's built-in capabilities, such as different search strategies (e.g., heuristic search), checking of temporal properties, and partial order and symmetry reductions;
- Automating non-isomorphic test input generation to satisfy a testing criterion for programs with complex inputs and preconditions;
- A series of examples and a prototype implementation in Java, that uses Java PathFinder [19] for model checking, Omega library [16] as a decision procedure, and Korat for program instrumentation; our approach extends to other languages, model checkers, and decision procedures.

```
class Node {
  int elem;
  Node next;

  Node swapNode() {
   if(next!=null)
    if(elem-next.elem>0){
      Node t = next;
      next = t.next;
      t.next = this;
      return t;
    }
   return this;
  }
}
```

Input list	+	Constraint	=>	Returned list
?		none	=>	?
E0 next		none	=>	E0 next
E0 next E1 next		(E0 <= E1)	=>	E0 next E1 next
E0 next E1		(E0 > E1)	=>	E1 next E0
E0 next E1 next		(E0 > E1)	=>	E1 next E0 next
E0 next E1 next		(E0 > E1)	=>	E1 next E0 next
E0 next E1 next ? next		(E0 > E1)	=>	E1 next E0 next ? next

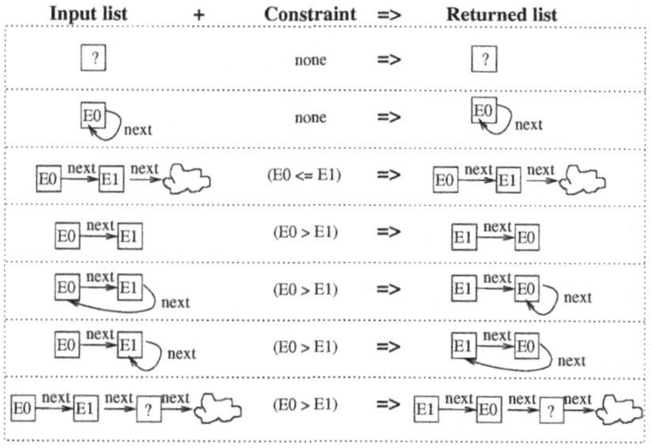

Fig. 1. Code to sort the first two nodes of a list (left) and an analysis of this code using our symbolic execution based approach (right)

Section 2 shows an example analysis in our framework. Section 3 describes traditional symbolic execution. Section 4 gives our algorithm for generalized symbolic execution. Section 5 describes our framework and Section 6 describes our implementation and instrumentation. Section 7 illustrates two applications of our implementation. We give related work in Section 8 and conclude in Section 9.

2 Example

This section presents an example to illustrate our approach. We check a method that destructively updates its input structure. The Java code in Figure 1 declares a class `Node` that implements singly-linked lists. The fields `elem` and `next` represent, respectively, the node's integer value and a reference to the next node. The method `swapNode` destructively updates its input list (referenced by the implicit parameter `this`) to sort its first two nodes and returns the resulting list.

We analyze `swapNode` using our prototype implementation (Section 6) and check that there are no unhandled runtime exceptions during any execution of `swapNode`. The analysis automatically verifies that this property holds.

The analysis checks seven symbolic executions of `swapNode` (Figure 1). These executions together represent all possible actual executions of `swapNode`. For each symbolic execution, the analysis produces an input structure, a constraint on the integer values in the input and the output structure. Thus for each row, any actual input list that has the given structure and has integer values that satisfy the given constraint, would result in the given output list. For an execution, the value "?" for an `elem` field indicates that the field is not accessed and the "cloud" indicates that the `next` field is not accessed.

Each input structure represents an isomorphism partition of the input space, e.g., the last row in the table shows an input that represents all (cyclic or acyclic)

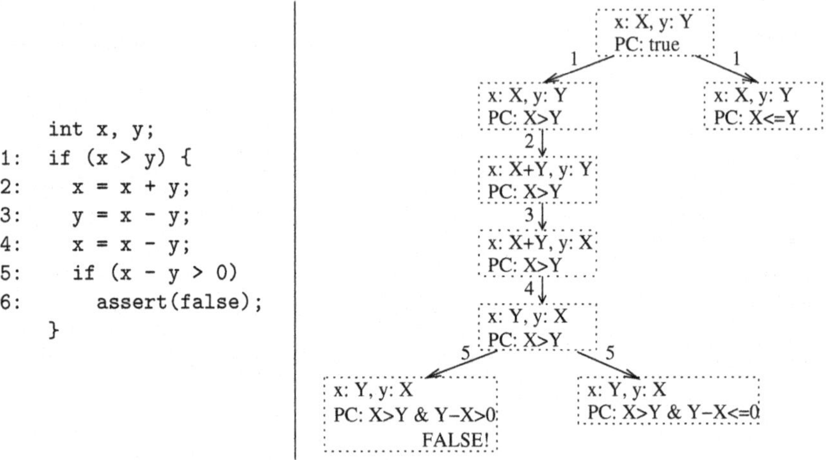

Fig. 2. Code that swaps two integers and the corresponding symbolic execution tree, where transitions are labeled with program control points

lists with at least three nodes such that the first element is greater than the second element; the list returned has the first two elements swapped.

If we comment out the check for `null` on line (1) in `swapNode`, the analysis reports that for the top most input in Figure 1, the method raises an unhandled `NullPointerException`. All other input/output pairs stay the same. The analysis, therefore, refutes the method's correctness by providing a counterexample.

The analysis supports method preconditions. For example, if we add to `swapNode` a precondition that the input list should be acyclic, the analysis does not consider the three executions (Figure 1), where the input has a cycle. The input structures and constraints can be used for test input generation.

3 Background: Symbolic Execution

The main idea behind symbolic execution [14] is to use *symbolic values*, instead of actual data, as input values, and to represent the values of program variables as symbolic expressions. As a result, the output values computed by a program are expressed as a function of the input symbolic values.

The *state* of a symbolically executed program includes the (symbolic) values of program variables, a *path condition* (PC) and a program counter. The path condition is a (quantifier-free) boolean formula over the symbolic inputs; it accumulates constraints which the inputs must satisfy in order for an execution to follow the particular associated path. The program counter defines the next statement to be executed. A *symbolic execution tree* characterizes the execution paths followed during the symbolic execution of a program. The nodes represent program states and the arcs represent transitions between states.

Consider the code fragment in Figure 2, which swaps the values of integer variables `x` and `y`, when `x` is greater than `y`. Figure 2 also shows the corresponding symbolic execution tree. Initially, `PC` is *true* and `x` and `y` have symbolic values `X` and `Y`, respectively. At each branch point, `PC` is updated with assumptions about the inputs, in order to choose between alternative paths. For example, after the execution of the first statement, both **`then`** and **`else`** alternatives of the **`if`** statement are possible, and `PC` is updated accordingly. If the path condition becomes *false*, i.e., there is no set of inputs that satisfy it, this means that the symbolic state is not reachable, and symbolic execution does not continue for that path. For example, statement `(6)` is unreachable.

4 Algorithm

This section describes our algorithm for generalizing traditional symbolic execution to support advanced constructs of modern programming languages, such as Java and C++. We focus here on sequential programs. Section 5 presents the treatment of multithreaded programs.

4.1 Lazy Initialization

The heart of our framework is a novel algorithm for symbolically executing a method that takes as inputs complex data structures with unbounded data. A key feature of the algorithm is that it starts execution of the method on inputs with *uninitialized* fields and uses *lazy initialization* to assign values to these fields, i.e., it initializes fields when they are first accessed during the method's symbolic execution. This allows symbolic execution of methods without requiring an a priori bound on the number of input objects.

We explain how the algorithm symbolically executes a method with one input object, i.e., the implicit input **`this`**. Methods with multiple parameters are treated similarly [2]. To execute a method `m` in class `C`, the algorithm first creates a new object `o` of class `C` with uninitialized fields. Next, the algorithm invokes `o.m()` and the execution proceeds following Java semantics for operations on reference fields and following traditional symbolic execution for operations on primitive fields, with the exception of the special treatment of accesses to uninitialized fields (Figure 3).

- When the execution accesses an uninitialized reference field, the algorithm nondeterministically initializes the field to the value **`null`**, to a reference to a new object with uninitialized fields, or to a reference of an object created during a prior field initialization; this systematically treats aliasing. When the execution accesses an uninitialized primitive (or string) field, the algorithm first initializes the field to a new symbolic value of the appropriate type and then the execution proceeds. Method preconditions are used to ensure that fields are initialized to values permitted by the precondition: when a reference field is initialized, the algorithm checks that the precondition does not fail for the structure and the path condition that currently constrain `o`;

```
if ( f is uninitialized ) {
   if ( f is reference field of type T ) {
      nondeterministically initialize f to
         1. null
         2. a new object of class T (with uninitialized field values)
         3. an object created during a prior initialization of a field of type T
      if ( method precondition is violated )
         backtrack();
   }
   if ( f is primitive (or string) field )
      initialize f to a new symbolic value of appropriate type
}
```

Fig. 3. Lazy initialization

– If the execution evaluates a branching condition on primitive fields, the algorithm nondeterministically adds the condition or its negation to the corresponding path condition and checks the path condition's satisfiability using a decision procedure. If the path condition becomes infeasible, the current execution terminates (i.e., the algorithm backtracks), otherwise the execution proceeds. This systematically updates path conditions on primitive fields.

Input generation. To generate inputs that meet a given testing criterion, the algorithm symbolically executes the paths specified by the criterion. For every path, it generates an input structure and a path condition on the primitive input values, which together define a set of inputs that execute the path. To handle programs that perform destructive updates, the algorithm builds mappings between objects with uninitialized fields and objects that are created when those fields are initialized; these mappings are used to construct input structures.

Isomorph breaking and structure generation. A nice consequence of lazy initialization of input fields is that for sequential programs, the algorithm only executes program paths on non-isomorphic[4] inputs. This can be used for systematic generation of inputs that have complex structural constraints by symbolically executing a predicate that checks the structural constraints, as in [2].

4.2 Illustration

We illustrate the algorithm using our running example from Figure 1. The symbolic execution tree in Figure 4 illustrates some of the paths that the algorithm explores while symbolically executing `swapNode`. Each node of the execution tree denotes a *state*, which consists of the state of the heap (including the symbolic values of the `elem` fields) and the path condition accumulated along the branch (path) in the tree. A transition of the execution tree connects two tree nodes

[4] This definition of isomorphism views structures as edge(node)-labeled graphs.

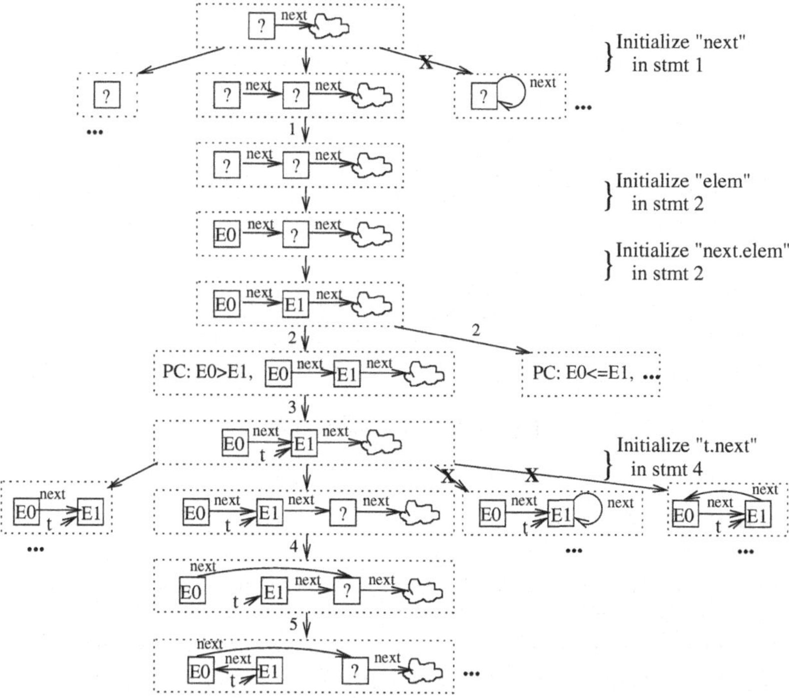

Fig. 4. Symbolic execution tree (excerpts), using notation described in Section 2

and corresponds to either execution of a statement of `swapNode` or to a lazy initialization step. Branching in the tree corresponds to a nondeterministic choice that is introduced to handle aliasing or build a path condition.

The algorithm creates a new node object and invokes `swapNode` on the object. Line (1) accesses the uninitialized `next` field and causes it to be initialized. The algorithm explores three possibilities: either the field is `null` or the field points to a new symbolic object or the field points to a previously created object of the same type (with the only option being itself). Intuitively, this means that, at this point in the execution, we make three different assumptions about the configuration of the input list, according to different aliasing possibilities. Another initialization happens during execution of statement (4), which results in four possibilities, as there are two `Node` objects at that point in the execution.

When a condition involving primitive fields is symbolically executed, e.g., statement (2), the execution tree has a branch corresponding to each possible outcome of the condition's evaluation. Evaluation of a condition involving reference fields does not cause branching unless uninitialized fields are accessed.

If `swapNode` has the precondition that its input should be acyclic, the algorithm does not explore the transitions marked with an "X". The input list corresponding to the output list pointed to by `t` in the bottom most tree node is shown on the bottom row of Figure 1.

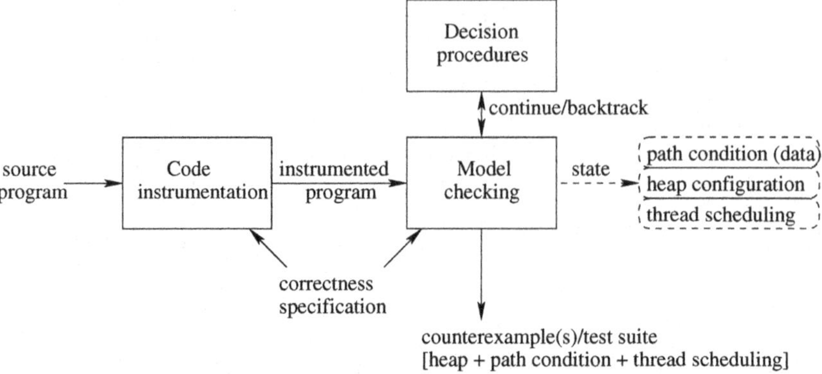

Fig. 5. General methodology

5 Framework

This section describes our symbolic execution based framework for checking correctness of software systems. Figure 5 illustrates our basic framework. To enable a model checker to perform symbolic execution (following the algorithm from Section 4), we instrument the original program by doing a source to source translation that adds nondeterminism and support for manipulating formulae that represent path conditions. The instrumentation allows any model checker that supports backtracking and nondeterministic choice to perform symbolic execution. Essentially, the model checker explores the symbolic execution tree of the program. Code instrumentation uses a correctness specification to add precondition checking (which is performed during field initialization) and post-condition checking (which is performed when an execution completes) to the original program. We describe some details of the instrumentation our prototype implementation performs in Section 6.

The model checker checks the instrumented program using its usual state space exploration techniques. A *state* includes a heap configuration, a path condition on primitive fields, and thread scheduling. Whenever a path condition is updated, it is checked for satisfiability using an appropriate decision procedure, such as the Omega library [16] for linear integer constraints. If the path condition is unsatisfiable, the model checker backtracks.

Correctness specifications can be given as preconditions and postconditions, assertions or more general *safety* properties. Safety properties can be written in the logical formalism recognized by the model checker or they can be specified with code instrumentation, as in [1]. The framework can be used for correctness checking and test input generation. While checking correctness, the model checker reports counterexample(s) that violate a correctness criterion. While generating test inputs, the model checker generates paths that are witnesses to a testing criterion encoded in the specification. Testing criteria can be encoded as correctness specifications as in [13,8]. For every reported path, the model checker also reports the input heap configuration, the path condition for the primitive input fields thread scheduling, which can be used to reproduce the error.

Multi-threaded and non-deterministic systems. Our framework allows a standard model checker to perform symbolic execution. We use the model checker also to systematically analyze thread interleavings and other forms of nondeterminism that might be present in the code. Our framework also exploits the model checker's built-in ability to combat state space explosion, e.g., by using partial order and symmetry reductions.

Loops, recursion, method invocations. We exploit the model checker's search abilities to handle arbitrary program control flow. We do not require the model checker to perform state matching, since state matching is, in general, undecidable when states represent path conditions on unbounded data. Note also that performing (forward) symbolic execution on programs with loops can explore infinite execution trees. Therefore, for systematic state space exploration we use depth first search with iterative deepening (Section 7.1) or breadth first search (Section 7.2); our framework also supports heuristic based search [10]. Our framework can be used for finding counterexamples to safety properties; it can prove correctness for programs that have finite execution trees and have decidable data constraints.

6 Implementation

We have implemented our approach in Java to check Java programs. For code instrumentation, we build on the Korat tool [2]. We use Java PathFinder(JPF) [19] for model checking the instrumented programs. As a decision procedure, we use a Java implementation of the Omega library [16], that manipulates sets of linear constraints over integer variables. This section outlines the instrumentation, briefly describes JPF, and presents a critique of our approach.

6.1 Instrumentation

Conceptually, the instrumentation proceeds in two steps. First, the integer fields and operations are instrumented. The declared type of integer fields of input objects is changed to `Expression`, which is a library class we provide to support manipulation of symbolic integer expressions. A type analysis is used to determine which integer variables have their declared types changed to `Expression`. Operations involving these variables are replaced with method calls that implement "equivalent" operations that manipulate objects of type `Expression`. We have not yet automated the type analysis, but we could use for this the abstraction component of the Bandera toolset [6] that performs the same kind of analysis, but with a different purpose[5].

Second, the field accesses are instrumented. Field reads are replaced by `get` methods that return a value based on whether the field is initialized or not

[5] Bandera performs a source to source translation to instrument a program, to reduce the cardinality of data sets associated with program variables.

```
class Node {
  Expression elem;
  Node next;
  boolean _next_is_initialized;
  boolean _elem_is_initialized;
  ...
  Node swapNode() {
   if(_get_next() != null)
    if(Expression._pc._update_GT(
          _get_elem()._minus(
             _get_next()._get_elem()),
          new IntegerConstant(0)) {
     Node t = _get_next();
     _set_next(t._get_next());
     t._set_next(this);
     return t;
    }
   return this; } }
```

```
class Expression { ...
 static PathCondition _pc;
 Expression _minus(Expression e){
   ...} }

class PathCondition { ...
 Constraints c;
 boolean _update_GT(Expression e1,
                    Expression e2){
  boolean result = choose_boolean();
  if (result)
      c.add_constraint_GT(e1,e2);
  else
      c.add_constraint_LE(e1,e2);
  if (!c.is_satisfiable())
      backtrack();
  return result;
  } }
```

Fig. 6. Instrumented code (left) and library classes (right)

(get methods implement the lazy initialization, as described in Section 4). Field updates are replaced by set methods which update the field's value. The get and set methods for a field also set a flag to indicate that the field is initialized.

As an illustration of the instrumentation, consider the code from Figure 1. Figure 6 gives part of the resulting code after instrumentation and the library classes that we provide. The static field Expression._pc stores the (numeric) path condition. Method _update_GT makes a nondeterministic choice (i.e., a call to choose_boolean) to add to the path condition the constraint or the negation of the constraint its invocation expresses and returns the corresponding boolean. Method is_satisfiable uses the Omega library to check if the path condition is infeasible (in which case, JPF will backtrack). Method _minus constructs a new Expression that represents the difference between its input parameters. IntegerConstant is a subclass of Expression and wraps concrete integer values. To keep track of uninitialized input fields we add a boolean field in the class declaration for each field in the original declaration, e.g., _next_is_initialized and _elem_is_initialized, which are set to true by get (set) methods.

To store the input objects that are created as a result of a lazy initialization, we use a variable of class java.util.Vector, for each class that is instrumented. The get methods use the elements in this vector to systematically initialize input reference fields. Our implementation also provides the library class StringExpression to symbolically manipulate strings.

6.2 Java PathFinder

Our current prototype uses the Java PathFinder model checker (JPF), an explicit-state model checker for Java programs that is built on top of a custom-made Java Virtual Machine (JVM). Since it is built on a JVM, it can handle all of the language features of Java, but in addition it also treats nondeterministic choice expressed in annotations of the program being analyzed. These features for adding nondeterminism are used to implement the updating of path conditions and the initialization of fields. JPF supports program annotations to cause the search to backtrack when a certain condition evaluates to true—this is used to stop the analysis of infeasible paths (when path conditions are found to be unsatisfiable). Lastly, JPF supports various heuristics [10], including ones based on increasing testing-related coverage (e.g., statement, branch and condition coverage), that can be used to guide the model checker's search.

6.3 Discussion

We use preconditions in initializing fields. In particular, a field is not initialized to a value that violates the precondition. Notice that we evaluate a precondition on a structure that still may have some uninitialized fields, therefore we require the precondition to be *conservative*, i.e., return `false` only if the initialized fields of the structure violate a constraint in the precondition. A conservative precondition or simply undecidability of path conditions may lead our analysis to explore infeasible program paths.

We have not provided here a treatment of arrays. Following [2], we could systematically initialize array length when an array field is first accessed, and then treat each array component as a field. We would like to extend our analysis to treat array length as a symbolic integer. Our algorithm handles subclassing: in step 3 in Figure 3 consider all objects created during a prior initialization of a field of type `T` or of a type `S`, where `S` is a subclass of `T`.

7 Applications

This section shows two applications of our framework: correctness checking of a distributed algorithm and test input generation for flight software.

7.1 Checking Multithreaded Programs with Inputs

We illustrate an application of our symbolic execution framework on an example that (incorrectly) implements a distributed algorithm for sorting linked lists with integers in ascending order[6]. To sort an input list, the algorithm spawns a number of threads proportional to the number of nodes in the list. Each thread is assigned two adjacent list nodes and allowed a maximum number of swaps it can perform on elements in these nodes. This example illustrates our symbolic execution technique in the context of concurrency, structured data (linked lists), integer values as well as method preconditions and partial correctness criteria.

[6] We can correctly sort a list using this algorithm by controlling the thread scheduler.

```
class List {
  Node header;

  //@ precondition: acyclic();
  void distributedSort() {
    if (header == null) return;
    if (header.next == null) return;
    int i = 0;
    Node t = header;
    while (t.next != null) {
      new Swapper(t, ++i).start();
      t = t.next;
    }
  }
  ...
}

class Swapper extends java.lang.Thread {
  //can swap current.elem,current.next.elem
  Node current;
  int maxSwaps;

  Swapper(Node m, int n) {
    current = m; maxSwaps = n;
  }
  public void run() {
    int swapCount = 0;
    for (int i = 0; i < maxSwaps; i++)
      if (current.swapElem()) swapCount++;
    //@ assert: if (swapCount == maxSwaps)
    //@            current.inOrder();
  }
}
```

```
class List { ...
  boolean acyclic() {
    Set visited = new HashSet();
    Node current = header;
    while (current != null) {
      if (!visited.add(current))
        return false;
      current = current.next;
    }
    return true;
  }
}

class Node {
  int elem;
  Node next;

  synchronized boolean swapElem(){
    synchronized (next) {
      if (elem > next.elem) {
        // actual swap
        int t = elem;
        elem = next.elem;
        next.elem = t;
        return true;
      } }
    return false; // do nothing
  }
  synchronized boolean inOrder(){
    synchronized (next) {
      if (elem > next.elem) return false;
      return true;
    } } }
```

Fig. 7. A distributed sorting method for singly linked lists

The Java code in Figure 7 declares a singly linked list and defines a method for sorting lists. The method `distributedSort` takes an input list and spawns several threads to sort the list. For each adjacent pair of nodes in the list, `distributedSort` spawns a new thread that is responsible for swapping elements in these nodes. This method has a precondition that its input list should be acyclic, as specified by the `precondition` clause.

The `swapElem` method returns `true` or `false` based on whether the invocation actually swapped out of order elements or whether it was simply a no-op. Note that `swapElem` is different from `swapNode` in Figure 1, that performs destructive updating of the input list. We use synchronization to ensure that each list element is only accessed by one thread at a time. The `assert` clause declares a partial correctness property, which states that if a thread performs the allowed maximum number of actual swaps, then the element in node `current` is in order.

We used our implementation to symbolically execute `distributedSort` on acyclic lists and analyze the method's correctness. The analysis took 11 seconds (on a 2.2 GHz Pentium with 2GB of memory) and it produced a counterexample:

```
input list: [X] -> [Y] -> [Z] such that X > Y > Z
Thread-1: swaps X and Y
Thread-2: swaps X and Z
resulting list: [Y] -> [Z] -> [X]; Y and Z out of order
```

The input list consists of three symbolic integers `X`, `Y`, and `Z` such that `X > Y > Z`. `Thread-1` is allowed one swap and `Thread-2` is allowed two swaps. `Thread-1` performs its swap before `Thread-2` performs any swap. Now `Thread-2` performs a swap. The resulting list after these two swaps is `[Y] -> [Z] -> [X]` with `Y > Z`. Since `Thread-1` is not allowed any more swaps, it is not possible to bring `Y` and `Z` in order. Thus, the input list together with this thread scheduling give a counterexample to the specified correctness property. Note that to analyze `distributedSort` we did not a priori bound the size of the list (and therefore the number of threads to spawn).

7.2 Test Input Generation

We applied our framework to derive test inputs for code coverage, specifically condition coverage, of an Altitude Switch used in flight control software (1800 lines of Java code) [11]. The switch receives as input a sequence of time-stamped messages indicating the current altitude of an aircraft as well as an indication of whether this reading is considered accurate or not (represented by strings). The input sequence of messages was implemented as a linked list with undefined length. The program was instrumented to print out the input sequence as well as the integer and string constraints, whenever a new condition, i.e. one that was not covered before, was executed. This application presents a program that has as input a data structure and manipulates both integer and string constraints.

We used breadth-first search during model checking to generate test inputs that cover all the conditions within 22 minutes of running time (on a 2.2 GHz Pentium with 2GB of memory). In contrast, we also used traditional model checking with JPF, where we fixed the input sequence to have 3 messages and the range of altitude values to be picked nondeterministically from 0 to 20000 feet—the model checking did not finish, and as a consequence did not generate test inputs, for about a third of the conditions before memory was exhausted.

8 Related Work

In previous work we developed Korat [2], a constraint solver for imperative predicates. Korat implements a novel search algorithm and performs a source to source translation to instrument a Java program and systematically handle aliasing and subclassing. Korat provides efficient generation of non-isomorphic inputs and was used to generate complex structures from preconditions for exhaustive black-box testing within a given input bound. The work we present here additionally provides input generation for white-box testing, supports symbolic manipulation of data values using a decision procedure, does not require bounds on input sizes, supports checking of multi-threaded programs and adapts Korat's instrumentation to enable any model checker to perform symbolic execution.

King [14] developed EFFIGY, a system for symbolic execution of programs with a fixed number of integer variables. EFFIGY supported various program analyses (e.g., test case generation) and is one of the earliest systems of its kind.

PREfix is a bug finding tool [3] based essentially on symbolic execution. PREfix has been used very successfully on large scale commercial applications. PREfix analyzes programs written in C/C++ and aims to detect defects in dynamic memory management. It does not check rich properties, such as invariants on data structures. PREfix may miss errors and it may report false alarms.

Several projects aim at developing static analyses for verifying program properties. The Extended Static Checker (ESC) [7] uses a theorem prover to verify partial correctness of classes annotated with JML specifications. ESC has been used to verify absence of such errors as null pointer dereferences, array bounds violations, and division by zero. However, tools like ESC cannot verify properties of complex linked data structures.

There are some recent research projects that attempt to address this issue. The Three-Valued-Logic Analyzer (TVLA) [17] is the first static analysis system to verify that the list structure is preserved in programs that perform list reversals via destructive updating of the input list. TVLA performs fixed point computations on shape graphs, which represent heap cells by shape nodes and sets of indistinguishable runtime locations by summary nodes. The lazy initialization of input fields in our framework is related to *materialization* of summary nodes in TVLA. We would like to explore this connection further.

The pointer assertion logic engine (PALE) [15] can verify a large class of data structures that can be represented by a spanning tree backbone, with possibly additional pointers that do not add extra information. These data structures include doubly linked lists, trees with parent pointers, and threaded trees. Shape analyses, such as TVLA and PALE, typically do not verify properties of programs that perform operations on primitive data values.

The Alloy constraint analyzer has been used for analyzing bounded segments of computation sequences manipulating linked structures by translating them into first order logic [18]. This approach requires a bound also on the input sizes and does not treat primitive data symbolically.

There has been a lot of recent interest in applying model checking to software. Java PathFinder [19] and VeriSoft [9] operate directly on a Java, respectively C program. Other projects, such as Bandera [6], translate Java programs into the input language of SPIN [12] and NuSMV [4]. They are whole program analysis (i.e., cannot analyze a procedure in isolation). Our source to source translation enables these tools to perform symbolic execution, and hence enables them to analyze systems with complex inputs and to analyze procedures in isolation.

The SLAM tool [1] focuses on checking sequential C code with static data, using well-engineered predicate abstraction and abstraction refinement tools. It does not handle dynamically allocated data structures. Symbolic execution is used to map abstract counterexamples on concrete executions and to refine the abstraction, by adding new predicates discovered during symbolic execution.

The Composite Symbolic Library [20] uses symbolic forward fixed point operations to compute the reachable states of a program. It uses widening to help termination but can analyze programs that manipulate lists with only a fixed number of integer fields and is a whole-program analysis.

9 Conclusion

We presented a novel framework based on symbolic execution, for automated checking of concurrent software systems that manipulate complex data structures. We provided a two-fold generalization of traditional symbolic execution based approaches. First, we defined a source to source translation to instrument a program, which enables standard model checkers to perform symbolic execution of the program. Second, we gave a novel symbolic execution algorithm that handles dynamically allocated structures, method preconditions, primitive data and concurrency. We illustrated two applications of our framework: checking correctness of multi-threaded programs that take inputs from unbounded domains with complex structure and generation of non-isomorphic test inputs that satisfy a testing criterion. Although we illustrated our framework in the context of Java programs, JPF, and the Omega library, our framework can be instantiated with other languages, model checkers and decision procedures.

In the future, we plan to investigate the application of widening and other abstraction techniques in the context of our framework. We also plan to integrate different (semi) decision procedures and constraint solvers that will allow us to handle floats and non-linear constraints. We believe performing symbolic execution during model checking is a powerful approach to analyze software. How well it scales to real applications remains to be seen.

Acknowledgements. The authors would like to thank Doron Peled for useful discussions and Viktor Kuncak, Darko Marinov, Zhendong Su, and the anonymous referees for useful comments. The work of the first author was done partly while visiting NASA Ames Research Center under the NASA Ames/RIACS Summer Student Research Program and was also funded in part by NSF ITR grant #0086154.

References

1. T. Ball, R. Majumdar, T. Millstein, and S. Rajamani. Automatic predicate abstraction of C programs. In *Proc. 2001 ACM SIGPLAN Conference on Programming Language Design and Implementation (PLDI)*, volume 36–5 of *ACM SIGPLAN Notices*, pages 203–213. ACM Press, June 2001.
2. C. Boyapati, S. Khurshid, and D. Marinov. Korat: Automated testing based on Java predicates. In *Proc. International Symposium on Software Testing and Analysis (ISSTA)*, July 2002.
3. W. R. Bush, J. D. Pincus, and D. J. Sielaff. A static analyzer for finding dynamic programming errors. *Software: Practice and Experience*, 30(7):775–802, 2000.
4. A. Cimatti, E. M. Clarke, F. Giunchiglia, and M. Roveri. NuSMV: A new symbolic model checker. *International Journal on Software Tools for Technology Transfer*, 2(4):410–425, 2000.
5. A. Coen-Porisini, G. Denaro, C. Ghezzi, and M. Pezze. Using symbolic execution for verifying safety-critical systems. In *Proc. 8th European Software Engineering Conference held jointly with 9th ACM SIGSOFT International Symposium on Foundations of Software Engineering*, pages 142–151. ACM Press, 2001.

6. J. Corbett, M. Dwyer, J. Hatcliff, S. Laubach, C. Păsăreanu, Robby, and H. Zheng. Bandera : Extracting finite-state models from Java source code. In C. Ghezzi, M. Jazayeri, and A. Wolf, editors, *Proc. 22nd International Conference on Software Engineering (ICSE)*, pages 439–448. ACM, 2000.
7. D. L. Detlefs, K. R. M. Leino, G. Nelson, and J. B. Saxe. Extended static checking. Research Report 159, Compaq Systems Research Center, 1998.
8. A. Gargantini and C. Heitmeyer. Using model checking to generate tests from requirements specifications. In *Proc. 7th European Engineering Conference held jointly with the 7th ACM SIGSOFT International Symposium on Foundations of Software Engineering*, pages 146–162. Springer-Verlag, 1999.
9. P. Godefroid. Model checking for programming languages using VeriSoft. In *Proc. 24th Annual ACM Symposium on the Principles of Programming Languages (POPL)*, pages 174–186, Paris, France, Jan. 1997.
10. A. Groce and W. Visser. Model checking java programs using structural heuristics. In *Proc. International Symposium on Software Testing and Analysis (ISSTA)*. ACM Press, July 2002.
11. M. P. E. Heimdahl, Y. Choi, and M. Whalen. Deviation analysis through model checking. In *Proc. 17th IEEE International Conference on Automated Software Engineering (ASE)*, 2002.
12. G. Holzmann. The model checker SPIN. *IEEE Transactions on Software Engineering*, 23(5):279–294, May 1997.
13. H. Hong, I. Lee, O. Sokolsky, and H. Ural. A temporal logic based theory of test coverage and generation. In *Proc. 8th International Conference on Tools and Algorithms for Construction and Analysis of Systems (TACAS)*, Apr. 2002.
14. J. C. King. Symbolic execution and program testing. *Communications of the ACM*, 19(7):385–394, 1976.
15. A. Moeller and M. I. Schwartzbach. The pointer assertion logic engine. In *Proc. SIGPLAN Conference on Programming Languages Design and Implementation (PLDI)*, Snowbird, UT, June 2001.
16. W. Pugh. A Practical Algorithm for Exact Array Dependence Analysis. *Communications of the ACM*, 35(8):102–114, 1992.
17. M. Sagiv, T. Reps, and R. Wilhelm. Solving shape-analysis problems in languages with destructive updating. *ACM Transactions on Programming Languages and Systems*, Jan. 1998.
18. M. Vaziri and D. Jackson. Checking properties of heap-manipulating procedures with a constraint solver. In *Proc. 9th International Conference on Tools and Algorithms for Construction and Analysis of Systems (TACAS)*, Poland, Apr. 2003.
19. W. Visser, K. Havelund, G. Brat, and S. Park. Model checking programs. In *Proc. 15th IEEE International Conference on Automated Software Engineering (ASE)*, Grenoble, France, 2000.
20. T. Yavuz-Kahveci and T. Bultan. Automated verification of concurrent linked lists with counters. In G. P. M. Hermenegildo, editor, *Proc. 9th International Static Analysis Symposium (SAS)*, volume 2477 of *Lecture Notes in Computer Science*. Springer-Verlag, 2002.

Code-Based Test Generation for Validation of Functional Processor Descriptions

Fabrice Baray[1,2], Philippe Codognet[2], Daniel Diaz[3], and Henri Michel[1]

[1] ST-Microelectronics, Central R&D, France
{Fabrice.Baray,Henri.Michel}@st.com
[2] University of Paris 6, LIP6, France
Philippe.Codognet@lip6.fr
[3] University of Paris 1, France
Daniel.Diaz@univ-paris1.fr

Abstract. Microprocessor design deals with many types of specifications: from functional models (SystemC or proprietary languages) to hardware description languages such as VHDL or Verilog. Functional descriptions are key to the development of new processors or System On Chips at STMicroelectronics.
In this paper we address the problem of automatic generation of high quality test-suites for microprocessor functional models validation. We present the design and implementation of a software tool based on constraint solving techniques which analyzes the control flow of the initial description in order to generate tests for each path. The test vectors are computed with a dedicated constraint solver designed to handle specific constraints related to typical constructs found in microprocessor descriptions. Results are illustrated with a case study.

Keywords: Code-based test generation, functional hardware verification, constraint solving techniques

1 Introduction

Current design methodology for microprocessors or complete *System On Chip* depends on the availability of a *simulation model*. Such a model is used for the following purposes:

1. early development of a compiler or more generally a full *software tool chain*. The development of software can thus proceed in parallel with the development of hardware.
2. early development of embedded software.
3. Using codesign, it is possible with such simulation models to benchmark and prototype complete platforms made of blocks which may not exist on silicon yet.
4. Hardware Verification: the simulation model serves as a *golden reference*, for a microprocessor or platform.

Being so crucial, the quality of a simulation model may affect drastically the timing of a design project.

H. Garavel and J. Hatcliff (Eds.): TACAS 2003, LNCS 2619, pp. 569–584, 2003.

1.1 Classification of Simulation Models

Simulation models are software programs which make the best effort to represent correctly the behavior of a hardware block. Ideally they should perform the right computations and produce accurate results, and optionally they should produce the right results at the right instants of time. Accordingly, we distinguish between:

- bit-true models: the computed results may be compared bit per bit with what produces the hardware
- cycle-accurate models: the results (change of output signals) are produced at exactly the same pace as the hardware.

Note that a simulation model which is not bit true may still be of some use to conduct benchmarking and performance estimation.

A second distinction is between the style of models, it can be an *hardware model* written in an high level hardware description language such as Verilog or VHDL, in this case the model will be used as input to synthesis tools to finally produce a network of transistors which constitutes the chip. Even with *high level* description languages such models bear some structural similarity with the hardware, and as a consequence are complex and slow. A different kind of models are *software models* which may have very little internal structural similarity with the hardware, but provide a good estimate (if not perfect) of the hardware behavior. Software models should be easier to write, and much faster to run (2 to 3 orders of magnitude is a common requirement).

In this paper we will concentrate on bit-accurate software simulation models and refer to them as *functional models* or equivalently (in the context of microprocessors) to ISS *Instruction Set Simulators.*

They represent the view of the machine that the programmer has when writing software. A software developer does not have to know details dealing with the pipeline, branch prediction, existence of multi execution units and other micro architectural aspects in order to write functionally correct software, even in assembly language. This view of the machine is in terms of architectural state (contents of registers, memories), the execution of an instruction causes a change from a stable architectural state to a new stable architectural state. In this view there is no notion of parallel execution or instructions whose execution may involve several cycles.

1.2 Use of a Simulation Model for Hardware Verification

Though formal verification methods are standard for microprocessor verification, the complete verification flow for a complex microprocessor still includes pseudo-random generation of very large test-suites (see for example [3] for the full picture of a complete verification flow).

The principle of verification using pseudo-random generation is to make sure that small sequences of assembler code exhibit the same behavior on the HDL model (typically VHDL or Verilog) and on the functional simulator.

In this method small sequences of assembler code are produced, with random (but directed) generators. A typical tool for this task is the Genesys tool ([2], [14]), another typical alternative is the Specman tool from Verisity Inc. The aim of these sequences is to test the VHDL model, and thus exercise all complex micro architectural (pipeline, branch prediction ...) mentioned above. Obviously, this method just includes a comparison between the HDL model and the reference simulator. If both the HDL model and the ISS exhibit the same bug, nothing more can be said on the matter. What is important though is to be sure that the test vectors, completely encompass all the possible behaviors of the reference simulator.

1.3 Differences between Bugs in ISS and in HDL Models

Experience in the verification of recent microprocessors or DSP design projects seems to indicate that the curves of rate of new bugs discovery always exhibit the same shape (see figure 1).

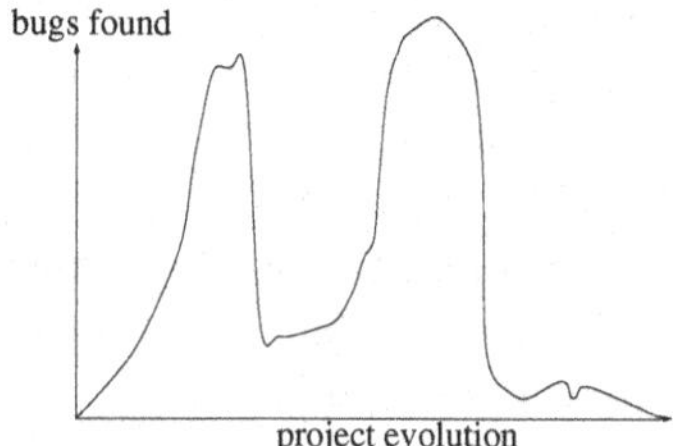

Fig. 1. Rate of new bugs discovery over project life

The rate of bugs discovery increases to a first peak, which corresponds to the time where

- the test generation machinery is in place
- the Hardware designers have implemented most instructions: the processor may not run many programs, but at least it can run simple programs.
- The architecture is mastered by both the hardware designers and the developers of the ISS model

Then, the rate of bug discoveries decreases. All complex microarchitecture mechanisms may not be implemented, for example the verification engineers are explicitly requested not to generate fragments of assembler with 2 consecutive *load* instructions because the memory control unit is far from mature. In this phase, many tests may be explicitly disabled from the test-suite because there is no point of hitting too much blocks where there are already many bugs to fix.

The second peak corresponds to the moment where all complex hardware models are in place and the verification engineers are requested to stress the hardware model as much as possible. At this point the bugs become more and more subtle ([10], and the time to solve a bug is much larger, debugging typically involves analyzing complex *waveforms* of signals : a very painful process.

It is a particularly annoying experience at this moment of the project to find out that discrepancy of behaviors between the Hardware model and the reference simulator are due to bugs in the (much less complex) functional model. Unfortunately it is not uncommon to find bugs in the ISS late in the design project.

The justification of the work presented in this paper is to make sure that the ISS reaches complete maturity in the first phase of the project (before the first peak in the bugs curve). At this moment it is crucial to have a test suite which has stressed the ISS in all possible ways (even if it has not stressed the Hardware model in all possible ways).

The automatically generated ISS test-suite is intended for the following uses:

- manual inspection of the results for compliance with the architecture manual
- comparison with an early version of the VHDL model (without all the complex mechanisms)
- comparison with an already existing ISS

In the remainder of this paper, section 2 introduces the semantic aspects addressed in our input language and the test generation methodology. Section 3 gives some key points on the input language analysis and the constraint problem generation. Section 4 describes the constraint solving general domain and why a new constraint solver was developed to solve our specific problem of test vector generation. Finally, we will mention one case study on a ST micro-controller with quantitative and comparative results.

2 Context

2.1 Input Language

Many languages exist to describe microprocessors architecture. They are used for either educational purposes [13], reference documentation of an instruction set (the Sparc Reference manual for example [18]), or they are real languages for which a compiler exists to convert the architectural description into an executable ISS. Many companies have used proprietary languages to develop microprocessors, (AMD RTL language for example [15]). STMicroelectronics also is using a language (*idl*) to derive several flavors of an ISS as part of the *flexsim* technology. Today SystemC avoids the need of a special compiler, all useful specific constructs useful to write a simulator being implemented as C++ classes.

In order to propose an open approach and avoid syntactic details from particular languages, we define in this section a small language called x which focuses only on key abstract semantic aspects. Note that this language is in fact the *functional* subset of SystemC, we can compile x source with a C++ compiler and the SystemC libraries.

An x description defines registers, memory and functions to represent execution of a functional cycle of the microprocessor. By functional cycle we mean the behavior to execute one instruction without taking into account hardware clock cycles. This cycle consists in fetching the instruction bytes from the memory, decoding the instruction and executing the effective operational part with the operand values. The x language, syntactically based on C, introduces the minimal structures to represent this kind of program, that is roughly : integer types, scalar and array variables, if-then-else and switch constructs and function definitions. The following table details the terminal symbols of the x grammar.

Terminal symbol	**Meaning**
K, V, T, F	constant, variable, type and function
uop, *bop*	unary and binary operator

Types T are integral types (either *signed* or *unsigned*). Since this is a language to model the behavior of processors, an integral type explicitly specifies the number of bits used to represent it. Signed entities are represented with a 2's complement encoding, other alternative integer encoding disappeared long ago among processors and it is highly unlikely that future processors adopt a different encoding for integers. For compatibility reasons with C++ we adopt a template notation, *signed int* $< 5 >$ for a signed integer type on 5 bits for example.

The language has support for unidimensional arrays. Elements in an array all have the same type. Elements are indexed with an integer starting at 0. The size s of an array is specified at declaration, the valid range of array indices being then $0..s-1$.

We implemented a subset of all operators of the C language, with the following restriction: all operators which are described as *implementation-defined* in C language reference [11] are either absent from our language or their semantics is more precise than in C. In particular ++ −− (post or pre increment or decrement) are absent because the semantics of expressions which contain multi side-effects is *implementation-defined*. Similarly calls to the same function in the same expression, and arguments evalation are done from left to right.

Unary operators *uop* are composed of logical not !, bitwise not ~ and arithmetic negation −. Binary operators *bop* are composed of classical arithmetic operators ($+ \ - \ * \ /$), classical bitwise operators (& | ^ >> <<), bit concatenation of two operands (*concat*), bit extraction (*extract*) and classical relational, equality and logical operators ($== \ \neq \ > \ \geq \ < \ \leq$ && ||).

Non terminal symbol	**Meaning**
D_v, D_f	variable and function definitions
E, S, P	expressions, statements and program

The abstract grammar is defined by the following rules ([...] is an optional construction) :

$D_v := T_0\ V_0, \ldots, V_n$ *variable definition*
$D_f := T\ F(T_0\ V_0, \ldots, T_n\ V_n)\ \{\ D_v^0; \ldots; D_v^m\ ;\ S_0 \ldots S_l\ \}$ *function definition*

$E := K$	*constant value*
$\mid V$	*variable access*
$\mid (E_1)$	
$\mid E_1 \; bop \; E_2$	*binary operator*
$\mid uop(E_1)$	*unary operator*
$\mid (T) \; E_1$	*casting operator*
$\mid F(E_0, \ldots, E_n)$	*function call*
$S := \{ \; [D_v^0; \ldots; D_v^n \; ; \; S_0; \ldots; S_m] \; \}$	*nested block*
$\mid V \; = \; E$	*assignment*
$\mid V \; := \; E$	*delayed assignment*
$\mid if \, (E) \; S_1 \; [else \; S_2]$	*selection statements*
$\mid switch \; (E)$	
$\quad case \; K_1 \; : \; [\ldots \; case \; K_o] \; : \; S_1^1 \; \ldots \; S_1^k$	
$\quad \ldots$	
$\quad case \; K_i \; : \; [\ldots \; case \; K_m] \; : \; S_n^1 \; \ldots \; S_n^k$	
$\quad default \; : \; S_{n+1} \; \ldots \; S_{n+1}^k$	
$\mid return \; (E)$	*return of function*
$P := D_v^0; \ldots; D_v^n; D_f^0 \; \ldots D_f^p \; \{ \; S_0; \ldots; S_m \; \}$	*global program*

In addition, the following restrictions apply : no nested function definitions, no recursive function call and functions need to be defined before being used.

It is worth noticing the existence of a delayed assignment which performs the assignment of a new value at the end of the execution cycle. This typical hardware functionality is mainly used to simplify the description which normally uses temporary variables to store intermediate results before assignment to registers and memory at the end of the cycle.

2.2 Test Generation Methodology

In a program P, the global variable definitions denotes the input values of the description. A test vector can be viewed as a couple $< v, P(v) >$, where v contains the input values for each global variable definition, and $P(v)$ contains the expected output values. In fact, the processor description is mainly composed of the decoding statements, leading to many *switch* instructions on the *codeop*. Therefore, this *branch specificity* naturally induces a *path coverage* criterion. *Path coverage* criterion is the closest quantitative approximation of the quality of the tests in this context. Therefore, the test generation strategy is decomposed into two phases :

1. the first one generates from the code as many *constraint stores* as paths in the description, this step will be explained in Section 3 ;
2. the second one analyzes the store to generate values for the test vector corresponding to this path, this step will be detailed in Section 4.

3 Constraint Store Generation

The method for generating constraints from a description in the x language is depicted on Figure 2, which illustrates the development tool called **STTVC** (ST Test Vectors Constructor).

We want to create a *code explorer* : a program which computes the test vectors according to the error types we want to detect in the ISS functional model. This is done by translating the hardware description in x into a C program, which is then linked to the STCS solver library. This translations is a purely static analysis, dealing mainly with type analysis.

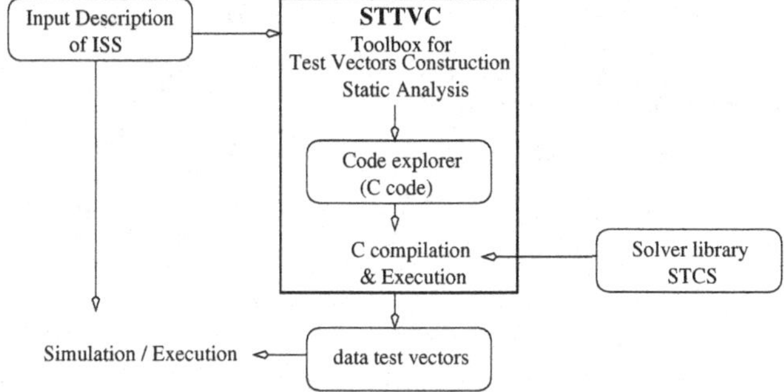

Fig. 2. Tool architecture

Let us now present through examples the path analysis induced by the path coverage criterion and then detail the generation of constraints associated to expressions, bit manipulations and array management.

3.1 Paths Analysis

Consider the two following fragments of code:

```
uint<8> X,Y,Z;

void cycle() {
  if (X==5) {             // first
    if (Y==5) {           // second
    }
  }
  if (Z>4 && Z<10) {     // third
  }
}
```

(a)

```
uint<8> X,Y,Z;

uint<8> f() {
  if (Z<10) return ..;
  return ..;
}

void cycle() {
  if (Z>4 && f()!=0) ;
}
```

(b)

Fig. 3. Code examples

Test vectors have to be found to distinguish between each path in this code. A path can be completely defined by giving a truth value for each conditional statement. For instance, a unique path is defined by considering, in the fragment (a), the first boolean expression being true, the second false and the third true.

Such a program can be represented by a control flow graph (CFG). A CFG is a directed graph where each node represents a statement and the arcs (eventually labeled with conditions on variables) represent the computational flow, together with a starting and an ending node. All function calls are inlined, creating a single CFG for the main function (in other words, the code is flattened). The CFGs of fragments (a) and (b) are shown in Figure 4.

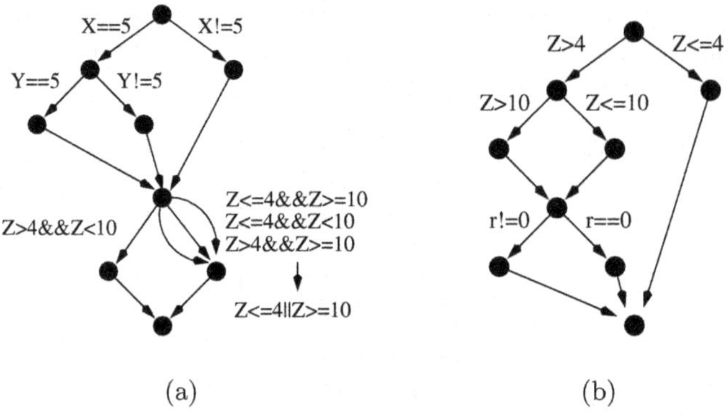

Fig. 4. Control Flow Graph

Exploring all paths of the code comes down to compute all paths in the graph from the starting node to the ending node. When a conditional expression uses a boolean operator (*and*, *or*) one has to generate one path for each combination of truth values for the involved sub-expressions. Therefore for a condition with n conjunctions, 2^n arcs join in the graph the *if* node and the nodes corresponding to the *then* and *else* statements. Simple optimizations can avoid spurious paths like in example (b) of figures 3 and 4 where the function call *f* is only evaluated when $Z > 4$.

From an implementation point of view, all truth values associated to conditional expressions can be grouped into a single boolean vector, called the *control flow vector* (CFV for short). Exploring all paths thus consists in generating all possible values for the CFV. Now, in order to generate the correct constraints, we simply have to rewrite the initial code by replacing all conditional expressions by a (boolean) test on the corresponding element of CFV and add the associated constraint to the current store.

Exploring all paths thus consists in enumerating all CFV exhaustively. An interesting optimization to avoid exploring useless paths is as follows : whenever the conditions on the labels of two arcs in a beginning of a path are inconsistent, all paths with this prefix can be discarded.

3.2 Variables, Expressions, and Assignments

The global and uninitialized variables of the program (like X, Y or Z in the previous example) are considered input variables. Solving the accumulated constraints on these variables provides a set of possible input values for each path.

All conditional expressions in the x code implicitly assume these constraints on the variables. Complex expressions are decomposed into primitive operations (see section 4) with temporary variables for the intermediate results.

Each temporary variable created for a binary operator has its own type which depends on the types of the operands. For instance, the addition of two 8-bit unsigned numbers gives an unsigned variable on 9 bits ; the extraction of 4 bits from a variable gives an unsigned variable on 4 bits. Details of the typing rules are strongly dependent from the input language semantics.

As observed, only conditional statements give rise to constraints, not assignment statements. An assignment should rather influence the following statements, as classically resolved by transforming code into a Static Single Assignment form (SSA) [6] – a process also called *spatial incarnation* [17]. For instance, an assignment $X{=}5$ cannot simply constrain X to be equal to 5 because it would prevent any further assignment of X to different values. Instead, all future uses of X should thereafter reference a new variable bound to the constant 5. Delayed assignments (executed at the end of a cycle execution) are also possible in the x language and in our translation method these delayed assignments do not generate constraints either.

Furthermore, notice that boolean expressions used in assignments do not generate constraints directly. The statement $B{=}(X{<}Y)$ does not imply that X is less than Y, but only that the value of B depends on the value of the condition. These kinds of constraints are classically called *reified constraints.*

3.3 Array Constraints

In [9,17], array manipulations are performed using equivalent constructions of SSA form. The key idea is to generate, for each assignment of an array element, a set of *element* constraints of the underlying Constraint Logic Programming language. A single assignment inside an array of size n thus introduces $2n-1$ *element* constraints (2 constraints for $n-1$ indices which are not assigned plus 1 for the assigned one). In the functional description of the ST processor that will be detailed later, memory is represented as an array which is addressed with 24 bits index registers. An address register of size v implies a 2^v memory size, the approach of [9] would lead therefore to a huge number of *element* constraints (proportional to number of write access $\times$ 2^v). This is unsolvable in practice. We have therefore developed another approach that is introduced by the following simple example :

```
uint<8> mem[256]
uint<8> X,Y;
void cycle() {
  if (mem[X]==5) { ... } // X index named X1
  mem[Y]=2;
  if (mem[X]==5) { ... } // X index named X2
}
```

The first idea consists in introducing directly in the solver an array type with two new constraints for read and write access to its elements (*tabRead* and *tabWrite*). These constraints are responsible for maintaining the consistency of the array values by enforcing the following rules. These two rules are equivalent, but the solver implementation takes into account the two propagations : from the indices relationship to the value relationship and vice versa.

$$\begin{aligned} i = j \quad &\Rightarrow T[i] = T[j] \\ T[i] \neq T[j] &\Rightarrow i \neq j \end{aligned}$$

For instance, if Y is equal to X, the second access to $mem[X]$ (identified by $X2$ below) should give the value 2. Two *tabRead* and one *tabWrite* constraints have to be added to the store but they are order-dependent as the order of accesses in the initial code must be guaranteed. This violates the classical constraint programming paradigm where constraint solving is order-independent. Moreover, static dependency analysis between variables is very limited in this approach because indices are only known dynamically.

Another strategy to handle array manipulations can be defined by dealing with this problem in two different steps. Since the complexity of array manipulations directly depends on the equality or inequality of indices, the first step can be to fix relationships between indices, and then push in a second step constraints enforcing such relationships.

For instance, among the three array accesses in the previous example, some may be *aliases* (refer to the same memory location, because the indices are the same). The number of possible relationships between n indices corresponds to the number of partitions of an n-set, which is the nth *Bell number* b_n [1].

example of relations		
(X_1, Y)	(X_1, X_2)	(Y, X_2)
$=$	$=$	$=$
$=$	$\neq$	$\neq$
$\neq$	$=$	$\neq$
$\neq$	$\neq$	$=$
$\neq$	$\neq$	$\neq$

formula of Bell numbers

$$b_0 = 1$$

$$b_{n+1} = \sum_{k=0}^{n} C_k^n b_k \text{ where } n \geq 0$$

$$C_k^n = \frac{n!}{k!(n-k)!} \text{ (binomial coeffs)}$$

The exponential complexity of the Bell numbers does not seem to be a problem considering that only a correct combination for indices is searched for. An *alias coverage* criterion could be defined to estimate the coverage of the different choices of indices relationship. This new coverage criterion makes sense to verify self reference to memory such as *mem[mem[i]] where mem[i]=i*. This second approach for array manipulation has the following advantages:

- variable independence can be analyzed in order to split the constraint store into independent groups of variables ;
- further graph analysis can be performed to deduce heuristics for variable ordering to solve the constraints with improved performances.

The main drawback of this solution is the fact that the choice of relationships between indices can be inconsistent with other constraints in the store. For instance, it is not possible to choose $Y = X_2$ and to generate a test for the path satisfying the second test. We rely on the backtracking mechanism of the constraint solver to recover from such failures. Moreover in many cases inconsistent choices are avoided with a symbolic solver.

4 Constraint Solving

Constraint Programming has proved to be very successful for Problem Solving and Combinatorial Optimization applications by combining the declarativity of a high-level language with the efficiency of specialized algorithms for constraint solving, borrowing sometimes techniques from Operational Research and Numerical Analysis, see [16] for a general survey and [12] for a complete description of the paradigm of Constraint Logic Programming on which this work has been based. We will first introduce the basic notions of classical constraint solving and then detail the specific constraint solver that has been developed, and its specific features.

4.1 Classical Constraint Solvers

A constraint is a logical relationship among several unknowns (or variables), each one taking a value in a given domain of possible values. A constraint thus restricts the possible values that variables can take. A *constraint satisfaction problem* (CSP for short) is defined as a triple $< \mathcal{X}, \mathcal{D}, \mathcal{C} >$, where $\mathcal{X}$ is a set of variables, $\mathcal{D}$ is a set of domains, that is, a finite set of possible values (one for each variable), and $\mathcal{C}$ a set of constraints restricting the values that the variables can simultaneously take. As in classical CSPs, we consider in this study finite domains for the variables (integers or naturals) and a solver based on arc-consistency techniques, in the spirit of [5]. Such a solver keeps internal representation of variable domains in order to handle all kind of constraints. For instance, the domain of an unsigned variable X, constrained by X *less than* a constant C can be exactly defined by an interval representation $[0 \ldots C]$. However for much more constrained variables, the interval representation is only an approximation of its effective domain.

Solving constraints consists in first reducing the variable domains through local propagation techniques and then finding values for each constrained variable in a *labeling* phase, that is, iteratively *grounding* variables (fixing a value for variables) and propagating its effect on other variable domains (by applying again the same arc-consistency techniques). The labeling phase can be improved by using heuristics concerning the order in which variables are considered and the order in which values are considered in the variable domains.

4.2 Specific Constraint Solver

The first idea to solve our test generation problem was to use the existing solver GNU Prolog [4], like in [8]. However such an approach has several drawbacks because the constraints we are dealing with include some peculiar operations derived from the hardware description language:

- defining typed variables with fixed bit size can be solved by simple domain reduction. But the casting operation between them can result in some loss of information on domain values. For instance, let Y and Z be unsigned variables on 8 bit which are constrained to be strictly greater than 0, and X be an unsigned 9-bit variable. The constraint $X = Y + Z$ reduces the domain of X to be greater than or equal to 2. But if an 8-bit unsigned variable T is equal to the casting of X, its value can be 0 or 1 due to the loss of the 9th bit of X. Moreover, another problem of the GNU Prolog solver is that it handles only natural but not integer (signed) variables;
- constraints on bit manipulation have to be handled specifically : bits extraction on variables such as $X = Y[5:3]$, (equating X to the slice composed of bits 3 to 5 of Y), and concatenation of variables such as $X = (Y : Z)$ (equating X to the concatenation of Y and Z). [8] proposes to consider variables as bit vectors and constraints on variable bits as several independent constraints on individual bits. This solution however cannot be combined with arithmetic constraints on the same variable and thus prevents possible domain reductions.
- array manipulations in the microprocessor description can simply be considered by adding to the solver a list of variables; but the number of created variables would become too large if the array represents memory

Due to these reasons, and to improve efficiency in the constraint solving process, one of the main contributions of this work concerns the development of a dedicated constraint solver, named STCS. STCS was mainly developed with the experience of GNU Prolog, but also introduces new specific constraints : *logical and* (X_Eq_Y_and_Z), *logical shift* (X_Eq_Y_slr_C), *bit concatenation* (X_Eq_Y-_concat_Z) and *bit extraction* (X_Eq_Y_extract_C) (X, Y, Z being variables, C a constant).

The solver implements these specific constraints with two internal representations of the domain of each variable : a simple interval representation for the arithmetic constraints (*min_value, max_value* values) and a *bit* representation in order to handle efficiently the *bit* based constraints. This bit representation maintains the information of known bits in the bit-vector. In the solver, the propagation is decomposed into bit propagation and interval propagation and coherence between the two representations is maintained by enforcing the following rules :

- at each interval modification, the bit representation is checked for modification (propagation of most significant bits, 1 for *min_value* and 0 for *max_value*, into the bit representation ;
- at each bit modification, a new *min_value, max_value* interval is computed according to the known bits.

Moreover, this new solver was developed as a general library, and is not limited to solve microprocessor test generation problems; it can be reused in other domains or other applications.

5 Case Study: STM7 Micro-Controller

In order to evaluate the performances and applicability of this innovative test generation method and the STTVC tool presented in the previous sections, we used a case study on a commercial ST microprocessor. The STM7 is a micro-controller with 6 internal registers, 23 main addressing modes and 45 main instructions, its description in x includes about 3000 lines of code. Combining the addressing modes with the instruction set gives about 700 various instructions.

Starting from an x functional description (issued from the IDL ST description), test vectors are generated with the STTVC tool described earlier and are simulated with three platforms : x, IDL and VHDL. The VHDL simulator is not able to simulate only a single cycle of the description and to directly input and output values for registers. Then, for that platform, the test vectors must be encapsulated into an assembler program which initializes the registers, let the processor reach a stable state by appending NOP instruction to the test and saves the context after each test cycle. For each simulation, the main result is composed of the set of test vectors which don't give the same results on all platforms. This summarizes the differences between the different models of the same micro-controller. On the other hand, efficiency results in terms of percentage of coverage and simulation time can be computed.

5.1 Evaluating the Number of Paths

The number of possible paths for the specification can be statically evaluated on the control flow graph. Each sequence of test statements introduces a multiplicative relationship between number of "before paths" and "after paths". Each nesting of test statements introduces an additive relationship and, for switch statements, m multiple cases with the same statements containing n paths (*case* without *break* in C) induce globally mn paths.

On the STM7 case study, the description defines 21 functions. The total number of potential paths is about 143 millions, which is a relatively frightening number. The *cut* in the path search space must be very efficient to handle such a description. In fact, the number of evaluated paths by STTVC tool, after constraint store consistency analysis and reduction of the search space, is 18457 which is a good result. This drastic reduction can be explained by analyzing the microprocessor description as follows: although each function has a great number of internal paths and can be called many times, each call activates only a small number of these paths.

In order to validate our *cut* implementation, STTVC was run without *cut* optimization during more than 2 days on the same example; we generated exactly the same test vectors.

5.2 Tests Generation

Table 1 presents statistics about the execution of STTVC on a SUN Ultra-SPARC-II 450 MHz processor with enough memory (only about 5Mo of memory used). The main point is that all impractical paths of the description are detected without labeling the variables (detecting an impractical path by labeling could be very time consuming).

This good result is mainly due to the detection by the domain inconsistency of impractical paths, but the symbolic solver also has an important impact. The role of the symbolic task is the same as the domain inconsistency (to avoid impractical paths) but the inconsistency relationship between variables which is handled symbolically is not detected by the basic domain propagation algorithm.

Array fails indicates the number of choices of relations (equalities, inequalities) among couples of indices which are not consistent with other constraints, but not deduced before the labeling. This stresses one drawback of this solution for handling arrays.

Table 1. Paths statistics

Checked paths	18457
Impractical paths detected by domain inconsistency	16299
Impractical paths detected by symbolic solver	236
Impractical paths detected by labeling	0
Array fails	56
Test vectors generated	1922
Global CPU Time	1 hour 05 minutes

In terms of generation time, the results vary a lot. Ninety percent of tests are trivial for the solver and can be computed in a time less than one second. For a small, but non predictable, number of paths, the constraint solver takes a lot of time to label variables to find a correct solution (the worst test case takes 13 minutes to compute). This result is not surprising. Due to the NP completeness of the constraint solving problem some constraint stores are more complex to solve.

5.3 Tests Execution

Given our generated test-suite with 1922 test vectors, the next step consists in executing the tests for acquiring error detection and coverage percentages in order to compare with coverage calculated with the simulation of classical manually written assembler test-suite.

In terms of cycle number, the STM7 assembler test suite is ten times bigger than our test vectors simulation with 18941 cycles and takes more time to execute, compared with only 1922 cycles for our solution; this is a very encouraging result. This important difference in simulation time has to be taken into account for all the coverage criteria analyzed below.

Table 2 compares the assembler test-suite and the STTVC test vectors simulation in terms of statement coverage. The covered statements are decomposed into two classes : NBB for normal basic blocks (649 max) and IBB for implicit basic blocks (48 max) which correspond to the *else* part of an *if* statement without *else* or to the *default* part of a *switch* statement without *default*.

Table 2. Statement coverage results

test type	covered	percentage
STTVC NBB	644	99.2%
ASM NBB	642	98.9%
STTVC IBB	35	72.9%
ASM IBB	0	0%

With this criterion, the results are quite similar. For the assembler test-suite the IBB blocks are not covered because it is based on classical micro-controller utilization. We can suppose that the 22 percent of IBB not covered by STTVC tests generation correspond to effectively "non reachable" IBB.

For results on the path coverage criterion, the assembler test-suite is simulated on the model with an annotation in order to dump the path description. By construction, the STTVC tests must cover all paths of the code description. First of all , we can observe that the ASM simulation doesn't give any path not generated by STTVC. Without any external tool to verify our implementation, this gives confidence in STTVC correctness. Furthermore, as could be expected, the assembler test suite covers only 72 percent of the test paths generated by STTVC.

6 Conclusion and Perspectives

We have presented a code-based test generation method for the validation of functional microprocessor description. It is based on the idea of solving constraint stores, each one representing a path in the control flow of the processor cycle. Due to the domain specific aspects, the solver contains dedicated primitive constraints to handle efficiently the bit manipulation operations of hardware descriptions.

Performances of this approach have been measured on a real case study, the STM7 microprocessor, in order to evaluate the quality of the test generation. A comparison with a classical assembler test suite shows the good results of our method in terms of both simulation cycles and path coverage percentage. Current and future research could concern the development of

- an enhanced propagation mechanism between numerical calculus and bit manipulation in order to avoid useless labeling ;
- a general framework for the symbolic solver in order to have a better detection of unpracticable paths ;
- tests generation for a better coverage criterion for the detection of human errors in the functional model, by using mutation aspects [7] ;
- a comparison between our constraint solver with bit oriented constraint and SAT techniques.

Acknowledgment. We thank Emanuele Baggetta for the development of a graphical interface to STTVC, and Jean-Claude Bauer who lead the STM7 ISS development effort.

References

1. www-gap.dcs.st-and.ac.uk/~history/Miscellaneous/StirlingBell/bell.html.
2. Aharon Aharon, Dave Goodman, Moshe Levinger, Yossi Lichtenstein, Yossi Malka, Charlotte Metzger, Moshe Molcho, and Gil Shurek. Test program generation for functional verification of powerpc processors in IBM. In *Design Automation Conference*, pages 279–285, 1995.
3. Françoise Casaubieilh, Anthony McIsaac, Mike Benjamin, Mike Bartley, François Pogodalla, Frédéric Rocheteau, Mohamed Belhadj, Jeremy Eggleton, Gérard Mas, Geoff Barrett, and Christian Berthet. Functional verification methodology of chameleon processor. In *Design Automation Conference, DAC'96*, pages 421–426, Las Vegas, Nevada, USA, 1996.
4. P. Codognet and D. Diaz. The gnu prolog system and its implementation. *Journal of Functional and Logic Programming*, 6, Oct 2001.
5. Philippe Codognet and Daniel Diaz. Compiling Constraints in clp(FD). *Journal of Logic Programming*, 27(3), June 1996.
6. R. Cytron, J. Ferrante, B.K. Rosen, Mark N. Wegman, and F. Kenneth Zadeck. Efficiently computing static single assignment form and the control dependence graph. *Transactions on Programming Languages and Systems*, 4:451–490, Oct 1991.
7. Richard A. DeMillo, Richard J. Lipton, and Frederick G. Sayward. Hints on test data selection: Help for the practicing programmer. *IEEE Computer*, pages 34–41, April 1978.
8. Fabrizio Ferrandi, Michele Rendine, and Donatella Sciuto. Functional Verification for SystemC Descriptions Using Constraint Solving. In Carlos Delgado Kloos and Jose da Franca, editors, *Design Automation and Test in Europe (DATE'02)*, pages 744–751, Paris, France, 4-8 March 2002.
9. Arnaud Gotlieb. *Génération automatique de cas de test structurel avec la programmation logique par contraintes.* PhD thesis, Université de Nice-Sophia Antipolis, 2000.
10. Richard C. Ho, C. Han Yang, Mark A. Horowitz, and David L. Dill. Architecture validation for processors. In *ISCA*, pages 404–413, 1995.
11. ISO/IEC 9899. *Programming languages – C*, first edition, 1990.
12. Joxan Jaffar and Michael J. Maher. Constraint logic programming: A survey. *The Journal of Logic Programming*, 19 & 20:503–582, 1994.
13. D. A. Patterson and J. L. Henessy. *Computer Architecture: A Quantitative Approach.* Morgan Kaufmann, 1990.
14. Shai Rubin, Moshe Levinger, Randal Pratt, and william Moore. Fast construction of test-program generators for digital signal processors. In *ICASPP'99 Conference Proceedings*, 1999.
15. David M. Russinoff and Arthur Flatau. Rtl: A verrified floating-point multiplier. In M. Kaufmann, P. Manolios, and J S. Moore, editors, *Computer Aided Reasoning: ACL2 Case Studies*, pages 199–200. Kluwer Academic Press, 2000.
16. P. van Hentenryck et al. V. Saraswat. Constraint programming. *ACM Computing Surveys*, 28, Dec 1996.
17. R. Vemuri and R. Kalyanaraman. Generation of design verification tests from behavioral vhdl programs using path enumeration and constraint programming. *Very Large Scale Integration (VLSI) Systems, IEEE Transactions on*, 3:201–214, 1995.
18. David L. Weaver and Tom Germond. *The SPARC architecture manual (version 9).* Prentice-Hall PTR, Upper Saddle River, NJ 07458, USA, 1994.

Large State Space Visualization*

Jan Friso Groote and Frank van Ham

Department of Computer Science, Technische Universiteit Eindhoven,
P.O.Box 513, 5600 MB Eindhoven, The Netherlands
{jfg,fvham}@win.tue.nl

Abstract. Insight in the global structure of a state space is of great help in the analysis of the underlying process. We present a tool to visualize the structure of very large state spaces. It uses a clustering method to obtain a simplified representation, which is used as a backbone for the display of the entire state space. With this tool we are able to answer questions about the global structure of a state space that cannot easily be answered by conventional methods. We show this by presenting a number of visualizations of real-world protocols.

1 Introduction

In the last decade, advances in computer hard- and software have made it possible to effectively analyze the behavior of complex software systems by means of state transition systems. Techniques based on explicit state enumeration can now deal with systems consisting of billions of states and have reached a scale at which they become sufficiently effective to assist in the design and testing of real world software systems. However, they also confront us with state transition graphs of enormous dimensions, of which the internal structure is generally a mystery. The most common approach to obtain insight in the structure of large state spaces is by abstracting from actions and/or state information, and by reducing the state space modulo a suitable equivalence. Although this approach maintains the behavioral aspect of state spaces, it destroys their structure. Typical questions that cannot be answered by using such techniques are:

- How many states are in each phase of a protocol?
- How many independent parts does the state space have, i.e. parts without a path between them? This question might be relevant to determine the effectiveness of different testing approaches.
- Are there hot-spots, i.e. groups of states that are visited relatively often when randomly traversing the state space? Are there parts of the state space that have extremely low probability to be visited?

In this paper we present a number of applications of a tool that can effectively display state transition systems consisting of millions of states and clarify their

* This work is a condensed version of [4] and was supported by the Netherlands Organisation for Scientific Research (NWO) under grant 612.000.101.

H. Garavel and J. Hatcliff (Eds.): TACAS 2003, LNCS 2619, pp. 585–590, 2003.

structure in this way. Essentially, the scalability of the technique is limited by the capacities of the graphics hardware. With the fast development of graphics hardware, our visualization technique will soon be suitable for even larger state spaces. Besides being scalable, this technique is also computationally inexpensive and very predictable, so local changes in structure do usually not lead to global changes in visualization. A prototype version of our tool is freely available for download from [6].

The basic idea underlying the visualization technique is to use a simplified representation in the form of a tree as a backbone for the entire structure. First the state space is layered using the distance of each node to the root. Then, the tree structure is obtained by clustering sets of states in each layer, such that for each set a unique path to the root is obtained. Each set of states is subsequently modeled using a disk shape in a three dimensional space. Finally, all disks are connected in a manner resembling cone trees [8], forming the shapes such as the ones in figures 1, 2 and 3. For a detailed description of the entire layout algorithm we refer to [5]. Note that visual cues such as interactive motion, colors, lighting and transparency all add strongly to the three dimensional perception of the shapes. The black-and-white still pictures in this print are by no means comparable to the onscreen images.

After visualizing the state space as a 3D-object we can use coloring to stress particular aspects of the state space. Typically, coloring can be induced by intrinsic properties such as the value of the transition label or state vector, or derived properties, such as the probability to visit a state during a random walk. The next sections discuss some interesting observations that can be made when applying this tool to a number of real-world examples.

2 The Alternating Bit and PAR Protocols

The Alternating Bit Protocol (ABP) is a communication protocol concerned with data transmission over an unreliable channel [1]. In this section we present visualizations of the ABP and one of its variations, the Positive Acknowledgement with Retransmission (PAR) Protocol that were modelled in [7]. Fig. 1 shows different visualizations of models of both protocols using two different data elements in the transmission. Individual states are depicted as spheres, with the initial state at the top, transitions between states are depicted as lines.

All visualizations depicted in Fig. 1 show a high degree of symmetry in the vertical axis, since the behavior for both data elements is identical. Note that the left visualization consists of more states than the middle one, even though they both describe the exact same protocol. This is due to the fact that the software used to extract the state space from its formal description suffers from state duplication. This is especially obvious in the bottom part of the left visualization, which duplicates itself. This can be remedied by applying a strong bisimulation reduction to the left state space, which gives us the middle state space. This visualization clearly displays regularities in the alternating bit protocol. The behavior in the top half is identical to the behavior in the bottom part, with the distinguishing factor being the control bit sent with the data. The four protrusions on both sides of the visualization represent errors in the transmission of the datum (1st and 3rd from the top) or errors in the acknowledgement of a transmission (2nd and 4th from the top).

The PAR protocol resembles the ABP, but differs in the way errors are handled. Where ABP assumes non-lossy channels, PAR does not. To cope with this additional problem a timer is integrated in the protocol, which generates a time-out on loss or corruption of a message. This explains why the 1st and 3rd protrusions are much smaller, as PAR deals with errors in transmission more efficiently than ABP: On loss or corruption a timeout is delivered directly to the sender, which can then immediately resend. The ABP has to use the acknowledgement channel to communicate this.

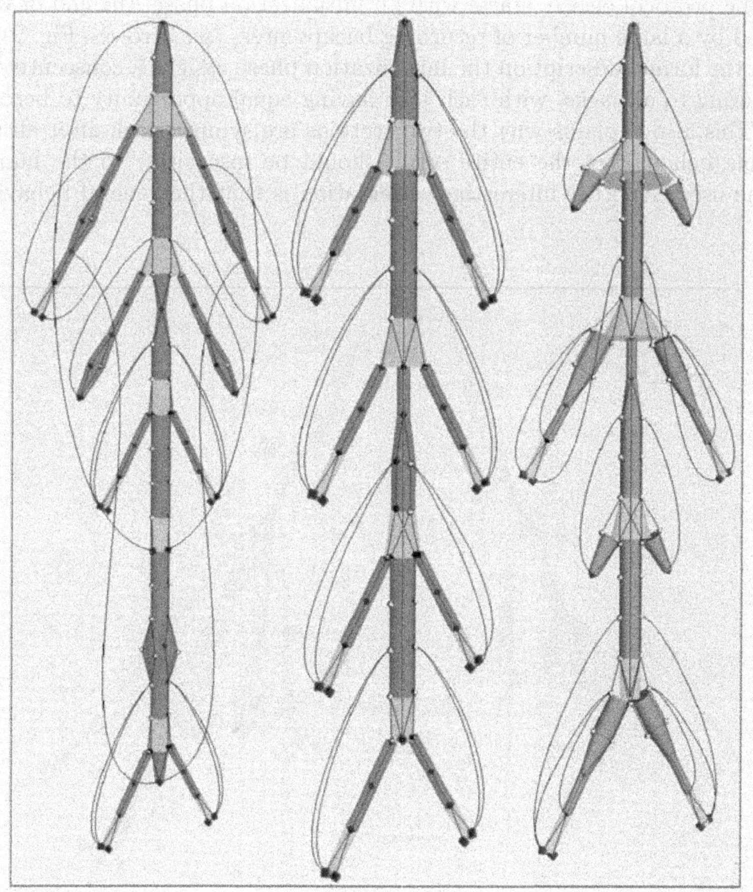

Fig. 1. Communication Protocols: ABP (*left*), ABP reduced modulo strong bisimulation (*middle*) and PAR reduced modulo strong bisimulation (*right*)

3 A Modular Jack System

This section deals with the communication protocol for a modular jack system. The protocol regulates the communication between an expandable set of industrial jack platforms, allowing the entire set of jacks to be operated from the controls of any one jack. All jacks are communicating via a ring-shaped shared bus. The protocol was formally modeled and analyzed in [3] and the exact formulation of the protocol that we visualize is distributed with the μCRL toolset [2]. Fig. 2 shows the visualization of the protocol when it has to synchronize two separate jack platforms. One of the immediate features is the existence of two separate but symmetric legs. Although this feature is very apparent from the picture, the researchers involved only realized this when observing the picture. Generally, the protocol for k jacks has k independent legs.

Another feature that is hard to extract using conventional analysis is the fact that the protocol clearly starts with an initialization phase, the end of which is marked by a large number of returning backpointers (see arrows - Fig. 2). Looking at the formal description the initialization phase assigns a consecutive global numbering to all jacks, with each jack having equal opportunity to become the first. This also explains why the two sections are symmetrical, after all the observable behavior of the entire setup should be insensitive to the numbering scheme used. Another interesting observation is that the general behavior of a

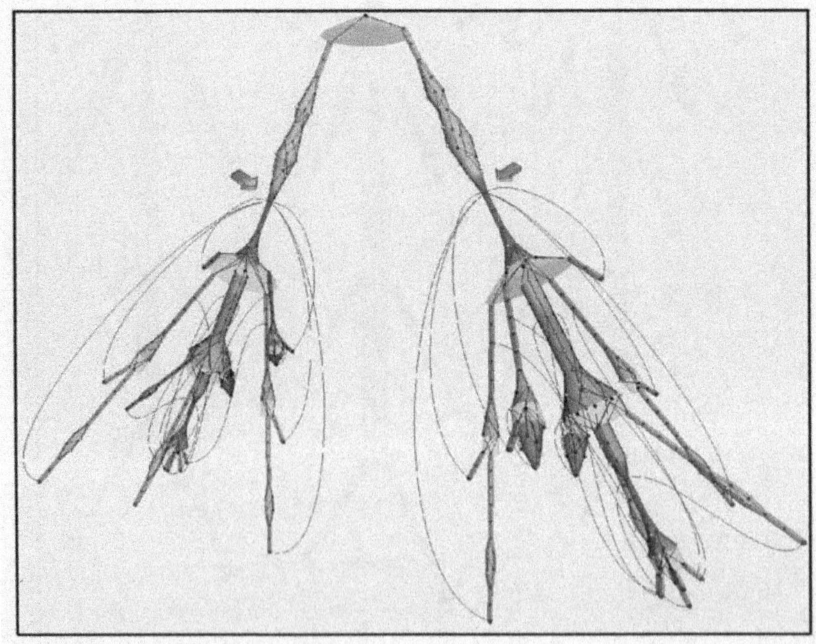

Fig. 2. Modular jack communication protocol for 2 jacks

system of two platforms is visually very similar to the behavior of a system of three platforms, consisting of approximately 3,000 states (Fig. 3). Notice the three identical sections and how different subsections of the graph visually correspond to sections of the two-platform graph. The fact that similar graphs give similar pictures is a major advantage of this method, allowing the application of insight gained in simplified versions of behavior to more complex behaviors. This visualization also shows a bug in the protocol: the small encircled section that splits off during the initialization phase of the protocol has no returning edges, which means that states at the end of this appendix are deadlock states. This was not the case in the two-jack version. Although these features can also easily be spotted by conventional analysis (actually, in this case they have been, see [3]), a picture in which you can actually point out the bug is a great asset. An additional feature is the ability to perform stochastic analysis on different

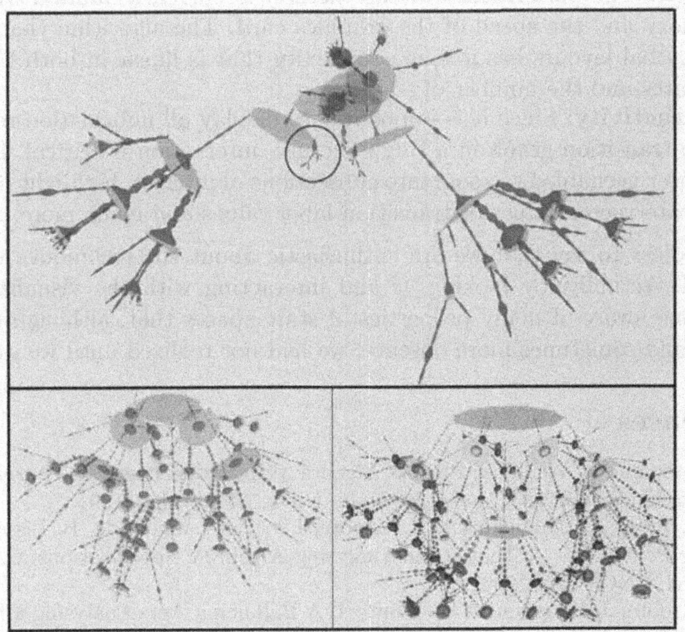

Fig. 3. Protocols for a setup of 3 jacks (2,860 states), 5 jacks (70,926) states and 7 jacks (1,025,844 states) respectively. Backpointers are hidden

automata. Assuming each transition has an equal probability of occurring, we can determine which states in the process have a relatively high probability of being visited by simulating a random walk. We can then visualize this information by coloring clusters based on these probabilities as is done in Fig 2. In this case high probability (darker) sections are located directly behind incoming backpointers and in areas with a large number of short cycles. These types of pictures are even more useful if measured real-world probability data is used to distinct between states that are in parts of the automaton that deal with, for example, error handling and states that are part of the main body of the process.

4 Conclusions

We presented a visualization tool to gain more understanding of large finite state spaces. Its main advantages over existing contemporary visualization tools are:

- **High scalability:** by not displaying each individual state and transition we can effectively visualize a number of nodes that is at least two orders of magnitude larger than the best conventional techniques.
- **Predictability:** In contrast to some other popular graph layout approaches (such as force directed methods) this method is highly predictable. As a consequence, similar input graphs also lead to similar looking visualizations.
- **Speed:** The performance of the method is currently limited by available memory and the speed of the graphics card. The algorithm that generates the global layouts has a time complexity that is linear in both the number of states and the number of edges.
- **Interactivity:** Since it is impossible to display all information related to a state transition graph in a single picture, interaction is critical. In our tool the user is enabled to zoom into subsections of interest, highlight parts based on state vector values or transition label values and much more.

It is needless to say that we are enthusiastic about the techniques we offer in this tool. Actually, by looking at and interacting with the visualization tool we became aware of many properties of state spaces that, although sometimes obvious and sometimes more obscure, we had not realized until we saw them.

References

1. J. Baeten and P. Weijland: Process Algebra. Cambridge Tracts in Theoretical Computer Science, Vol. 18. Cambridge Univ. Press, Cambridge, 1991.
2. S.C.C. Blom, W.J. Fokkink, J.F. Groote, I.A. van Langevelde, B. Lisser and J.C. van de Pol. μCRL: A Toolset for Analysing Algebraic Specifications. CAV '01, pp. 250–254, LNCS 2102, 2001.
3. J.F. Groote, J. Pang and A.G. Wouters. A Balancing Act: Analysing a Distributed Lift System. Technical Report, Dept. of Software Eng., CWI, Amsterdam.
4. J.F. Groote and F. van Ham. State Space Visualization. Technical Report #0214, Dept. of Mathematics and Computer Science, Technische Univ. Eindhoven, 2002.
5. F. van Ham, H. van de Wetering and J.J. van Wijk. Visualization of State Transition Graphs, Proc. IEEE Conf. on Information Visualization '01, pp 59–66, 2001.
6. F. van Ham. Interactive Visualization of State Transition Systems. Project website at *http://www.win.tue.nl/~fvham/fsm/*.
7. S. Mauw and G.J. Veltink (eds). Algebraic Specifications of Communication Protocols. Cambridge Tracts in Theoretical Computer Science, Vol. 36. Cambridge Univ. Press, Cambridge, 1993.
8. G.G. Robertson, J.D. Mackinlay and S.K. Card. Cone Trees: Animated 3D Visualizations of Hierarchical Information. CHI '91 Conf. Proc., pp 189–194, 1991.

Automatic Test Generation with AGATHA

Céline Bigot, Alain Faivre, Jean-Pierre Gallois, Arnault Lapitre,
David Lugato, Jean-Yves Pierron, and Nicolas Rapin

CEA/LIST/DTSI/SLA, CEA Saclay – Bat. 451
91191 Gif sur Yvette Cedex, France
{celine.bigot,alain.faivre,jean-pierre.gallois,
arnault.lapitre,david.lugato,jean-yves.pierron,
nicolas.rapin}@cea.fr

Abstract. This tool demonstration paper describes the AGATHA toolset, developed at CEA/LIST. It is an automated test generator for specifications of communicating concurrent units described using an EIOLTS (Extended Input Output Labeled Transition System) formalism which can be extracted, for example, from UML specification.

1 Introduction

Formal methods allow system analysis and test generation from specifications. This provides an early feedback on a system's behaviour. The economic goal of this specification analysis step is considerable, as it simultaneously reduces cost and time of validation, while increasing system reliability. But these formal techniques are generally quite complex in their use: that is why such techniques have not, at this time, penetrated the industrial domain. One way to decrease this complexity is to provide tools in which the use of those techniques are automated.

This tool demonstration paper describes the AGATHA toolset, developed at CEA/LIST. This toolset is an automated test generator from specifications of communicating concurrent units described using an EIOLTS formalism (Extended Input Output Labeled Transition System). At the present time, AGATHA deals with specifications written in the following languages : UML (the Unified Modeling Language) [1], SDL (Specification and Description Language) [2,3], STATEMATE language [4], ESTELLE [5]. For each of these languages there is a corresponding translator, in the toolset, that transforms the original specification into the EIOLTS language used by AGATHA. Figure 1 shows the main windows of the AGATHA toolset.

The presentation tool will focus on UML specification respecting modelling rules and some UML specializations. These specialization are attached or dedicated to the European project AIT-WOODES [6].

H. Garavel and J. Hatcliff (Eds.): TACAS 2003, LNCS 2619, pp. 591–596, 2003.

2 The AGATHA Kernel

There exist several ways to validate systems specifications. A first one consists in theorem proving and model checking. These kinds of techniques have proved successful for the validation of critical parts of systems. But two major drawbacks to these techniques remain:

1. the combinatorial explosion due to variable domains for the model checking,
2. a need for high-level skills from the developer –who must be aware of formal methods fundamentals– for theorem proving.

Automatic test generation is another way to tackle the problem of systems validation.

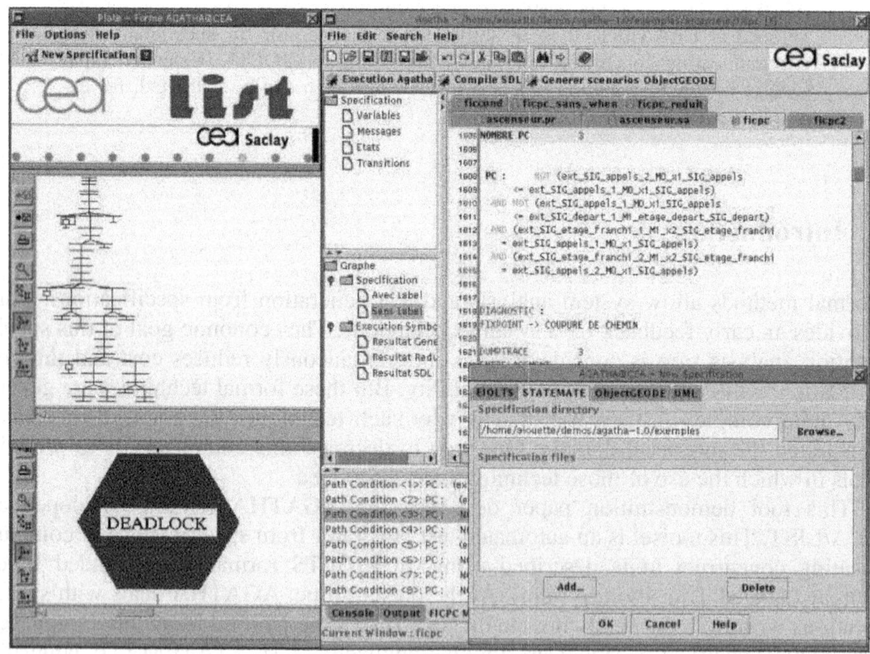

Fig. 1. Main windows of the AGATHA toolset.

The solution adopted in AGATHA is to provide an exhaustive symbolic path coverage. In the future, this criterion will help to use AGATHA for verification. If we want to demonstrate the truthfulness of a property on a specification, because of the exhaustivity obtained with AGATHA, we just have to demonstrate it on the obtained paths.

The following subsections are an overview of the different formal techniques used in AGATHA in order to reach this exhaustive symbolic path coverage.

Main principle: symbolic execution. The major drawback of numeric techniques is the combinatorial explosion due to variable domains. These domains can be huge, sometimes even infinite. AGATHA uses "symbolic execution" as defined by [7], [8], [9]. Symbolic calculus allows the handling of such domains because computing all the behaviours is not equivalent to trying all the possible values for inputs. Instead of giving values for inputs, they keep their status of symbol all along the execution.

So each behaviour no longer depends on the result of a calculus being completely performed, but on an expression representing constraints on the variables being denoted by the symbols of entries. Each transition fired from a point of the execution adds a new constraint on the variables. At any point of the execution, the entire constraint is called "path condition".

A symbolic state may represent an infinite set of numeric states. The execution tree resulting of the AGATHA computation is a finite tree of symbolic states. The construction of the execution tree is subordinated to reduction procedures in order to eliminate as many redundant paths as possible with different tactics.

A n-tuple of a symbolic node denotes a list of actual control nodes for each of the n concurrent modules. Different heuristics to compute comparison procedures for each symbolic node are also used (inclusion and equality procedures).

Moreover, we currently work on automating several abstraction techniques to reduce complexity and to terminate calculus in any case in order to obtain an exhaustive execution graph.

Simplification procedures. The deeper a point of execution, the bigger the expression representing its path condition. Symbolic expressions of variables may also rapidly grow. That is why a simplification procedure must be applied "on the fly" in order to shorten expressions and detect useless paths.

As of today we use a simplifier based on rewriting techniques. The rewriting engine is Brute [10] that is a part of the CafeOBJ toolset. The rewriting rules file of AGATHA is actually composed of more than three hundred rules. These rules allow both to maintain symbolic expressions within a reasonable size range, and to obtain normal forms for the expressions, easing the comparison between expressions needed in algorithms such as comparison procedures.

We also use a polyhedric tool, Omega [11], in order to compute the inclusion and equality procedures. Using this tool we are able to compare variables domains of two symbolic nodes.

Composition. The symbolic execution process is performed on one module, but the global application is generally composed of many, so they have to be merged.

There are two possible ways to merge modules. The first solution is to use the composition introduced by Milner [12]. The global module is made out of the transitions of its components, except those that are synchronized by a rendezvous. This is due to the fact that we only have communication with rendezvous in the EIOLTS input language of AGATHA. Each rendezvous is replaced by an equivalent transition obtained by eliminating the exchanged parameter. The other solution is to compute the symbolic execution on each module first and then merge the results to obtain the global application behaviour. The major benefit of this latter approach is the parallelization of the calculus: execution trees for each module can be computed separately.

At the moment, only the first solution is implemented in AGATHA. The second option will be integrated soon.

Constraints solvers. Once the execution tree is computed, the whole behaviour of the system is exhibited. Livelocks and deadlocks are visible. We use the DaVinci [13] graphical interface to represent the execution tree. A constraints solver, the Presburger tool Omega, may then be used to get the appropriate values for symbolic variables satisfying path conditions. Then it generates numerical test input sequences. We elect to generate one numeric test for each symbolic test which represents an equivalence class of numeric tests. So the constraints solver computes only one solution for each path condition.

Figure 2 shows the overall architecture of the AGATHA toolset

Fig. 2. Architecture of the AGATHA toolset.

3 Transcription of UML Models into EIOLTS

We connect the AGATHA toolset to the environment of the AIT-WOODDES project that offers a method for designing UML specification, an automatic code generator and validation tools. We implement the translation algorithms in the Objecteering 5 UML modeling tool [14]. In this context we generate tests for UML models designed with the ACCORD methodology [15]. The accepted UML models are designed with class diagrams. Each class should have one or more statechart diagram that represents its dynamic behaviour. Collaboration diagrams are used to model interactions between instances of classes. The results provided by AGATHA will be turned into UML sequence diagrams.

The translation from UML to EIOLTS is a two-step process illustrated in Figure 3. First, the UML specification is checked against consistency rules to verify that the translation modules will be able to translate the specification to EIOLTS; this module also transforms the UML model into an equivalent UML model, only using a restricted set of UML's elements. Secondly, another module translates this restricted UML into an EIOLTS file. The subset of UML that is used is designed to achieve the same level of simplicity in the description of the state machines than the EIOLTS input language of AGATHA.

The generated EIOLTS file is processed by the kernel of AGATHA. Finally, a module analyses the resulting file, translates these results in sequence diagrams and bring these charts back into the Objecteering CASE tool.

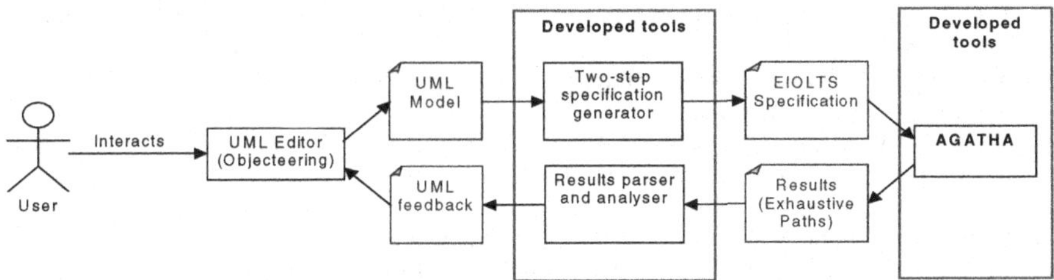

Fig. 3. Translation from UML to EIOLTS.

4 Conclusion

In this tool demonstration paper we have described the AGATHA toolset allowing software developers to validate UML specifications. This toolset may be completely transparent for the user and definitely user-oriented.

Some improvements are foreseen: enriching AGATHA with theorem proving in order to prove properties about the system or connecting an existing model checker to AGATHA. For very large or complex systems AGATHA will also embed new automatic simplification procedures, not working on generated expressions, but on the model itself, and based on abstraction principles. Finally a selection of relevant tests will be performed, along with an estimate of their covering, with respect to criteria or test purposes defined by the user.

References

1. Rumbaugh, I. Jacobson, G. Booch, The Unified Modelling Language Reference Manual, Reading, MA: Addison-Wesley, 1998.
2. Union Internationale des TELECOMMUNICATION, Langage de programmation – Langage de description et de spécification du CCITT – Norme SDL, Recommandation UIT T Z.100, 03/93.

3. D. Lugato, Nicolas Rapin, J.-P. Gallois, Verification and tests generation for SDL industrial specifications with the AGATHA toolset, Proceeding of Workshop on Real-Time Tools, CONCUR'01.
4. D. Harel, Statecharts: a Visual Formalism for Complex Systems, Science of Computer Programming, vol. 8, pp. 231–274, 1987.
5. ISO, *Information processing system, system interconnection, a formal description based on an extended state transition model*, Geneva, 1997.
6. AIT-WOODDES Project N IST-1999-10069, http://wooddes.intranet.gr/.
7. L. A. Clarke. A system to generate test data and symbolically execute programs, IEEE Transactions on software Engineering, vol. SE-2, n°3, September 1976, pp 215–222.
8. J.C. Huang. An approach to program testing, ACM computing surveys.7(3): 113-128, September 1975.
9. J. C. King. Symbolic execution and program testing, Communication of the ACM,19(7). July 1976.
10. M. Ishisone, T. Sawada, Brute: brute force rewriting engine, GAIST, January 2001, http://www.theta.theta.ro/cafeobj.
11. W. Kelly, V. Maslov, W. Pugh, E. Rosser, T. Shpeisman, D. Wonnacott, The Omega Library version 1.1.0, University of Maryland, November 1996, http://www.cs.umd.edu/projects/omega.
12. R. Milner. Communication and concurrency, Prentice Hall International, 1989.
13. M. Worner, M. Frohlich, DaVinci Tool version 2.1, Bremen University, July 98, http://www.informatik.uni-bremen.de/davinci.
14. Objecteering Tool version 5, Softeam Paris, 2001, http://www.softeam.fr.
15. S. Gérard, N. S. Voros, C. Koulamas, Efficient system modeling of complex real-time industry; networks using the ACCORD/UML methodology, DIPES 2000.

LTSA-MSC: Tool Support for Behaviour Model Elaboration Using Implied Scenarios

Sebastian Uchitel, Robert Chatley, Jeff Kramer, and Jeff Magee

Department of Computing, Imperial College
{su2|rbc|jk|jnm}@doc.ic.ac.uk

Abstract. We present a tool that supports the elaboration of behaviour models and scenario-based specification by providing scenario editing, behaviour model synthesis, and model checking for implied scenarios.

1 Introduction

The design of concurrent systems is a complex task prone to subtle errors. Behaviour modelling has proved to be successful in helping uncover flaws at design time; however, it has not had a widespread impact on practitioners because model construction remains a difficult task and because the benefits of behaviour analysis appear at the end of the model construction effort. In contrast, scenario-based specifications have a wide acceptance in industry and are well suited for developing first approximations of intended behaviour; however, they are still maturing with respect to rigorous semantics and analysis tools. This paper presents a tool for supporting a process for elaborating system models and specifications that exploits the potential benefits of behaviour modelling and scenario-based specifications yet ameliorates their shortcomings.

From a novice user's perspective, the tool allows creating message sequence chart (MSC) specifications [1], obtaining feedback on scenarios that are missing, and adding them as positive or negative scenarios. The theory behind the feedback is that of implied scenarios [5, 6]. They signal aspects of the MSC specification that need further elaboration due to the concurrent nature of the specified system and the partial nature of the specification. From an advanced user's perspective, the tool also allows accessing the behaviour models that are synthesised for implied scenario detection. These models are the basis for reasoning on system design. Behaviour models can be viewed, edited, analysed and animated using the tool.

2 The Elaboration Process

Scenario notations such as MSCs (see Figure 1) describe two distinct aspects of a system. Firstly, they depict a series of examples of what constitutes acceptable system behaviour. These examples consist of sequences of messages – called traces – that system components are expected to send each other. Secondly, scenario notations

H. Garavel and J. Hatcliff (Eds.): TACAS 2003, LNCS 2619, pp. 597–601, 2003.

outline the high-level architecture of the system. Scenarios depict with vertical arrows, or instances, which system components are involved in providing the intended system behaviour. They also describe component interfaces because they illustrate which messages are being sent and received by each component. By architecture we mean the system components and their interfaces.

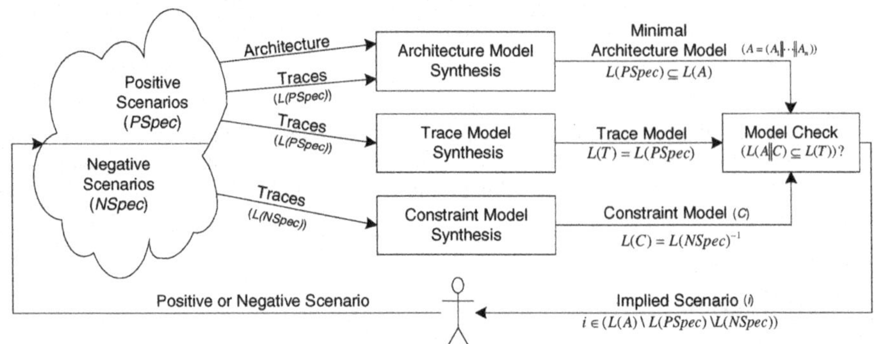

Fig. 1. An overview of the elaboration process

Implied scenarios indicate gaps in a scenario-based specification that are the result of specifying the behaviour of a system from a global perspective yet expecting it to be provided by independent entities with a local system view. If the architecture does not provide components with a rich enough local view of what is happening at a system level, they may not be able to enforce the intended system behaviour. Effectively, what may occur is that each component may, from its local perspective, believe that it is behaving correctly, yet from a system perspective the behaviour may not be what is intended. These additional system traces resulting from the inadequate local view of components are called implied scenarios.

The process (depicted in Figure 1) starts with a MSC specification comprised of two parts [6]: a positive part (*PSpec*) that describes the intended system behaviour and a negative part (*NSpec*) that describes undesired behaviour. The positive part of the MSC specification is defined in terms of basic and high-level MSCs [1]. The negative part is using an adapted version of basic MSCs [6]. The semantics of the MSC language determines a set of traces for each part: *L*(*PSpec*) and *L*(*NSpec*). Note that we interpret messages as synchronous hand-shaking communication, and also adopt weak sequential composition for the semantics of high-level MSCs.

From the MSC specification we synthesise three different behaviour models in the form of labelled transition systems (LTS) where transitions are labelled with the messages that components send each other. Using the positive system traces, *L*(*PSpec*), and architectural information, the architecture model synthesis builds the architecture model (*A*) as the parallel composition of components models $A_1,\ldots,A_n$ where the alphabet of A_i coincides with the interface of component *i*. Thus, we have $A=(A_1\|\ldots\|A_n)$ where $\|$ is the LTS parallel composition operator, and *L*(*PSpec*) is a subset of *tr*(*A*) where *L*(*A*) is the set of maximal traces exhibited by LTS A. In addition *A* can be proven to be the minimal model (with respect to trace inclusion) that complies with the MSC architecture and that includes all the specified traces (*L*(*PSpec*)). Thus, maximal traces in *L*(*A*)*L*(*PSpec*) are implied scenarios. The second behaviour model we build is the trace model (*T*). This model is built from the set of positive system traces (*L*(*PSpec*)), ignoring the specified architecture, such that *L*(*T*)=*L*(*PSpec*) (assuming *L*(*PSpec*) is a regular language). The third behaviour model we build is the constraint model (*C*). This is built from the set of negative system traces (*L*(*NSpec*)) so that it captures the complement of the traces the system should not exhibit: $L(C)=L(NSpec)^{-1}$.

We are interested in maximal traces that are exhibited by the architecture model (*A*), have not been specified in the positive part of the MSC specification (*L*(*PSpec*)) and have not already been explicitly prohibited in the negative part of the MSC specification (*L*(*NSpec*)). Thus, we are interested in the following set of traces: $(L(A)\backslash L(NSpec))\backslash L(PSpec)$. These traces can be detected by model-checking $L(T)\subseteq L(A\|C)$. If the inclusion does not hold, an implied scenario is generated as a counter-example. Note that for non-regular positive MSC specifications [3], $L(T)\subseteq L(PSpec)$ holds rather than $L(T)=L(PSpec)$. However, implied scenarios can still be detected with the same inclusion test.

According to whether users consider the implied scenario intended or undesired system behaviour, the positive or negative part of the scenario specification is updated. By repeating the process it is possible to iteratively elaborate scenario-based specifications and behaviour models

In principle, the elaboration process based cannot be guaranteed to converge to a state where there are no more implied scenarios to be validated. This is reasonable as, on each acceptance of an implied scenario, stakeholders could keep on introducing new functionality in the form of traces that the underlying architecture model could not perform, including the addition of new message labels or even components. However, supposing that at some point all the positive behaviour of the system has been captured, it may be possible to converge to a stable specification by rejecting the rest of the implied scenarios. To support convergence we have introduced an expressive negative scenario notation [6], which in our experience, assuming *L*(*PSpec*) is regular, suffices to make the elaboration process converge. However, this remains an open question that we intend to investigate in future work.

As mentioned earlier, four artefacts are produced as a result of the incremental elaboration process. The *first* is a MSC specification that has been evolved from its original form to cover further aspects of the concurrent nature of the system being described, including possible functional aspects. The *second* is the architecture model, which preserves the system architecture and provides the specified positive behaviour; however, it may exhibit additional unspecified behaviour. The *third* is the trace model, which captures precisely the traces specified as positive behaviour. The *fourth* is the constraint model, which captures the properties that the architecture model should comply with if it is to avoid the negative scenarios and provide only the specified system behaviour.

The architecture model provides the basis for modelling and reasoning about system design. In fact it is the model that needs to be further developed through architectural and design decisions as designers towards implementation. The constraint model aids the design process as it models the properties that the architecture model must satisfy.

An important observation regarding the convergence of the elaboration process is that even if the iterative process is cut off before converging, it still allows the

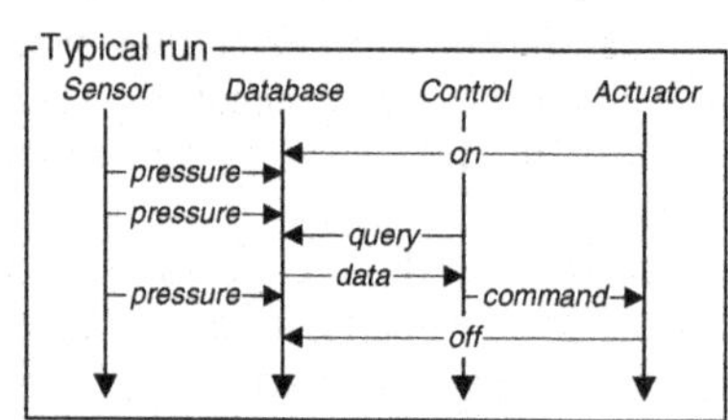

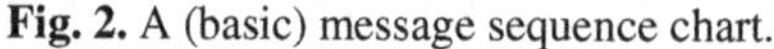

Fig. 2. A (basic) message sequence chart.

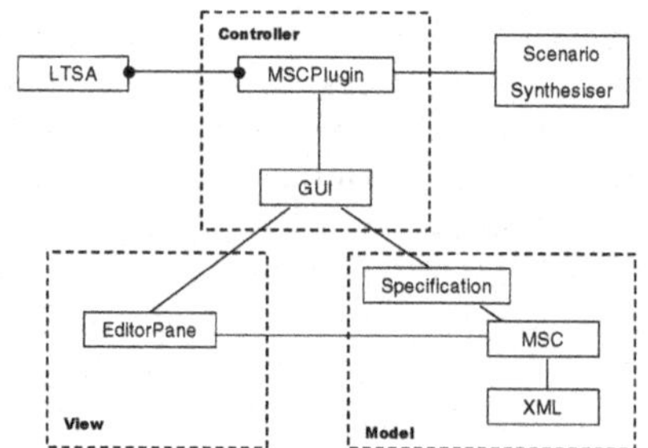

Fig. 3. Architecture of the MSC editor plug-in.

elaboration of the initial MSC specification into a more complete system description, and produces three behaviour models that help developers reason about the design of the system.

3 The Tool Implementation

The tool was implemented in Java as an extension of the Labelled Transition System Analyser (LTSA) [2]. LTSA uses the FSP process calculus [2] to specify behaviour models. From the FSP description, the tool generates a LTS model. The user can animate the LTS by stepping through the sequences of actions it models, and model-check the LTS for various properties, including deadlock freedom, safety and progress properties. The MSC extension builds on this introducing a graphical editor for MSCs and by generating an FSP specification from a scenario description. FSP code is generated for the architecture, trace and constraint models described previously. LTSA model checking capabilities (safety and deadlock freedom checks) are then used to detect implied scenarios.

The architecture of LTSA was adapted so that extra modules can easily be plugged in and out without having to recompile the code for the core system. All of the code associated with a plug-in module is archived into a jar file and is dynamically loaded by the core LTSA using techniques based on reflection. The core code then interrogates the plug-ins to find out whether they require extra graphical components (for instance menus, toolbars, display panels etc) to be added to user interface.

The basic architecture of the MSC editor plug-in is shown in Figure 3. Circles on the line connecting LTSA and the MSC plug-in denote the loose coupling that exists between them. The architecture is based on the familiar Model-View-Controller pattern. The underlying representation of the model is an XML tree. This allows us to easily load and save the data to a file. Other parts of the tool access and manipulate the model through objects representing the Specification, BMSCs, HMSCs, Instances etc, rather than exposing the underlying XML.

The view component generates and displays message sequence charts that can be edited. The view requests data from the model and rebuilds its display every time that it is notified that the model has changed. The GUI controller listens for events caused by user interaction and sends updates to the model when the user edits one of the diagrams. Then the view is informed and it rebuilds the display based on the updated model. The controller will pass the model (Specification) to the ScenarioSynthesiser that generates the textual FSP description of the scenario model. The core of LTSA is then called to check the model. From the information that LTSA returns, the plug-in can build a message sequence chart describing any implied scenario that may be present in the model, and pass it to the GUI to display to the user. LTSA also generates a state model that can be displayed as a set of state transition diagrams.

4 Conclusions and Future Work

The LTSA-MSC tool [4] has been used successfully on a number of medium-sized case studies. It has proven to support the elaboration of scenario-based specifications and behaviour models in a practical and cost-effective manner. As part of the STATUS project we are taking a scenario-based approach to modelling and simulating software systems with a view to assessing them for usability early in the design process. We hope in the future to extend the tool with a graphical front end that can mock up the proposed user interface for the system.

Acknowledgements. This work has been partially supported by Status ESPIRIT project (IST-2001-32298) and the Aedus EPSRC platform grant GR/R95715/01

References

[1] ITU, *Message Sequence Charts*, International Telecommunications Union. Telecommunication Standardisation Sector, Recommendation Z.120, 1996.

[2] J. Magee and J. Kramer, *Concurrency: State Models and Java Programs*. New York: John Wiley & Sons Ltd., 1999.

[3] R. Morin, *On Regular Message Sequence Chart Languages and Relationships to Mazurkiewicz Trace Theory* in International Conference on the Foundations of Software Science and Computation Structure (FOSSACS'01), Genova, 2001.

[4] S. Uchitel, *LTSA-MSC Tool*. Department of Computing, Imperial College, 2001.

[5] S. Uchitel, J. Kramer, and J. Magee, *Detecting Implied Scenarios in Message Sequence Chart Specifications* in Joint 8th European Software Engineering Conference (ESEC'01) and 9th ACM SIGSOFT Symposium on the Foundations of Software Engineering (FSE'01), Vienna, 2001.

[6] S. Uchitel, J. Kramer, and J. Magee, *Negative Scenarios for Implied Scenario Elicitation* in 10th ACM SIGSOFT Symposium on the Foundations of Software Engineering (FSE'02), Charleston, 2002.

Author Index